THE
STRUGGLE
FOR
DEMOCRACY

THE
STRUGGLE
FOR
DEMOCRACY

Edward S. Greenberg
UNIVERSITY OF COLORADO

Benjamin I. Page
NORTHWESTERN UNIVERSITY

HarperCollinsCollegePublishers

Executive Editor: Lauren Silverman
Development Editor: Arthur Pomponio
Project Editor: Melonie Parnes
Design Supervisor: Lucy Krikorian
Text Design: Robin Hoffmann
Cover Design: Kay Petronio
Cover Photo: Photoworld / FPG International
Photo Reseacher: Leslie Coopersmith
Production Manager: Willie Lane
Compositor: Waldman Graphics, Inc.
Printer and Binder: R. R. Donnelley & Sons Company
Cover Printer: The Lehigh Press, Inc.

THE STRUGGLE FOR DEMOCRACY

Library of Congress Cataloging-in-Publication Data

Greenberg, Edward S.
  The struggle for democracy / Edward S. Greenberg, Benjamin
I. Page.
      p. cm.
  Includes indexes.
  ISBN 0-06-042478-8 (Student edition)
  ISBN 0-06-501157-0 (Instructor's edition)
  1. United States—Politics and government. 2. Democracy—
United States. I. Page, Benjamin I. II. Title.
JK274.G69 1992
321.8'042'0973—dc20   92-11456
                                                       CIP

94 95   9 8 7 6 5 4

 This book is printed on recycled paper as part of our ongoing efforts to address environmental concerns.

BRIEF
CONTENTS

DETAILED CONTENTS

Politics   143

What Government Does   565

Chapter 16   Foreign Policy and National Defense   566

FEATURES

POLITICS AND FILM

RESOURCE FEATURES

PREFACE

Two major concerns animated the writing of this textbook. First, we were impressed by the yearning for freedom and democracy that is sweeping the world. We thought it would be timely, in light of recent events, to reexamine the health and vitality of freedom and democracy in the United States, the original home of liberal democracy and the inspiration for much that has transpired in the world. Second, we were surprised by the extent to which new analytical approaches to American politics, prevalent at the graduate level and in the professional journals, have failed to make an appearance in introductory textbooks. This is unfortunate, because several of these new approaches make it easier to understand what is going on in American politics, and are, therefore, important for students to know.

Our experience in teaching the introductory course in American government and politics is that students are confused by the sheer avalanche of details and unsure how to evaluate what they learn about the political process. Our goal in this textbook is to provide a simple framework to organize the details and a standard by which to judge the progress and prospects of the American political experiment. The framework shows how governmental institutions and actors, political institutions and processes (like elections, parties, public opinion, interest groups, and social movements), and deep structural elements (like the constitutional rules, the economy, the culture, the characteristics of the American population, and the place of the United States in the world system) interact to determine what government does. This emphasis on the importance of underlying structures and how they shape politics and government is unique among introductory texts. Democracy—understood as a form of governance characterized by popular sovereignty, political equality, and liberty—is the standard we use to evaluate the American system. The provision of a coherent standard against which to measure the progress of our institutions, based on the most cherished of American values, is also unique among the leading introductory textbooks in government and politics.

The dramatic thread that holds the discussion together is the "struggle for democracy." We believe the United States is a far more democratic place than it was, and that the main cause of this happy development has been the determination of the American people to struggle for popular sovereignty, equality, and liberty. We believe, moreover, that the United States is less democratic than it might be and that further progress will depend on the continuing struggle for democracy. This "struggle" theme weaves throughout the discussion and is the subject of a special boxed feature that appears in each chapter.

COVERAGE

We have included all of the usual topics covered in the introductory course: the Founding, the Constitution, federalism, and political development; public opinion, voting and elections, political parties, interest groups, the mass media; Congress, the presidency, the executive branch/bureaucracy, and the courts; state and local government; and policy outputs, including civil rights and liberties, social welfare, economic policy, and foreign and military policy. We have tried to make this material fresh, however, by organizing it within an innovative yet simple framework, and by raising important issues in democratic theory. Each standard topic is treated analytically in relationship to a multitude of governmental, political, and structural factors, and normatively in terms of its relationship to democracy.

Our approach allows us not only to talk about the traditional topics in a fresh way but to pay attention to topics that are not well covered in other texts. There is, for instance, much greater attention paid to *structural* factors and their impact: the free enterprise system; the nature of U.S. society and its population; the political culture; and the international economic, political, and military systems. There is, moreover, a greater emphasis on the presentation of *historical* materials, since the intellectual themes that animate the text require such attention, especially to American political history as the history of the struggle for democracy. There is, finally, much attention paid to *comparative* materials, since the authors believe that better understanding, especially of structural factors, can only occur if students are drawn out of parochial perspectives. Comparative materials are highlighted in the body of the text by a small globe in the margin.

Though we hold definite views about democracy and its desirability, we are aware that many of the issues addressed in the book are not settled and that some scholars and citizens may well disagree with us. Hence the text gives ample space to views that do not agree with our own.

The text depends on empirical evidence of many kinds, from the latest quantitative studies in the social sciences to qualitative historical studies and journalistic accounts. Where controversy or uncertainty exists, we acknowledge it frankly. Although students need to know which facts and explanations are settled and known, they also need to know when information or explanation remains unsettled and open to debate. In this way we hope to introduce students to the idea that social science is an ongoing enterprise in which many questions are not yet answered. We do not leave students rudderless, however; the text framework allows students to raise their own questions and to incorporate new information and explanations as they encounter them.

FEATURES

We have incorporated a number of features that are intended to make learning more interesting and effective.

The following features are found in each chapter:

- *The Struggle for Democracy* is a boxed feature that highlights political struggles throughout our history to enhance popular sovereignty, political equality, and liberty. Examples range from Thomas Paine's 1776 publication of *Common Sense* to the present-day struggle of women for increased representation and power in governmental institutions.

- *In this chapter* lists major topics to be discussed.

- An *opening story* highlights the major themes of the chapter by describing an important event or development that continues to affect contemporary American politics, such as the Vietnam War, Watergate, the Reagan revolution, the savings and loan crisis, and the war with Iraq.

- Bold terms are keyed to a *glossary* that appears at the end of the text.

- *Comparative* materials are highlighted in the margin by a globe that helps bring them to students' attention.

- A chapter *Summary* helps students review important chapter materials.

- *To Ponder* is a list of questions with no easy answers designed to stimulate class discussion.

- A list of annotated *Suggestions for Further Reading* helps students delve deeper into subjects that are of interest to them.

The following appear frequently, though not in every chapter:

- *Doing Politics* boxes highlight how people at all levels in the political system go about the business (and play) of politics.

- *Film and Politics* boxes look at how Hollywood has portrayed various aspects of American politics. This feature is unique in introductory textbooks, and reflects the importance we attribute to popular culture in shaping American political life.

- *Resource* boxes provide additional information, often of a technical nature.

We also provide several appendixes, to which students may frequently refer:

- "Film and American Politics," an annotated list of over 100 films (available at local video stores) that address issues raised in the text.

- An acronym index

- The Declaration of Independence

- The Constitution

- *The Federalist Papers*, Nos. 10, 51, and 78.

- A list of the Presidents of the United States and Congresses
- A glossary of technical terms

SUPPLEMENTS

HarperCollins has assembled an impressive array of text supplements to aid instructors in teaching and students in learning. Many of the supplements are directly tied to the theme "the struggle for democracy," thereby helping students see connections between what they read in the text, hear and see in the class, and research and write about in their assignments.

FOR THE INSTRUCTOR

Teaching Portfolio

This extensive instructor's resource includes the *Instructor's Manual, Struggle for Democracy Lecture Series, Guide for Interpreting the Media,* and *Multimedia Handbook.* The general editor of the kit is John Winkle of the University of Mississippi. All of these resources are inserted into a portfolio, enabling instructors to take out and use whatever part of the kit is relevant to the day's lecture. The resources are all tied closely to the text.

INSTRUCTOR'S MANUAL   Written by Neal Tannahill of Houston Community College and Robert E. Hogan of Rice University, this 200-page resource will help instructors prepare stimulating lectures, classroom activities, and assignments. The features of the manual include class outlines and summaries; a broad range of teaching suggestions; ideas for student research; and suggestions for discussions that complement the themes in the text. For each text chapter, the *Instructor's Manual* helps instructors integrate all of the supplements available from HarperCollins.

THE STRUGGLE FOR DEMOCRACY LECTURE SERIES   To help you to incorporate the expertise of others into your lectures, we have asked specialists in various areas of political science to produce lectures appropriate for 50-minute classes. Each lecture in the series complements or elaborates upon the themes and discussions in *The Struggle for Democracy.* The subjects of the lectures include "Women and Politics" by Pippa Norris of Harvard University; "The Environment and Politics" by Michael Kraft of the University of Wisconsin—Green Bay; "Urban Politics" by Ester Fuchs of Barnard College; "Latinos and Politics" by Rodney Hero of the University of Colorado; "National Health Care" by Ted Marmor of Yale University; "Constitutionalism" by Lief Carter of the University of Georgia; "Bill of Rights" by John Winkle of the University of Mississippi; "Congress" by David Cannon of the University of Wisconsin—Madison; "Public Policy" by Peter Eisinger of the University of Wisconsin—Madison; "Federalism" by David Walker of the University of Connecticut; and "Blacks and Politics" by Diane Pinderhughes of the University of Illinois.

GUIDE FOR INTERPRETING THE MEDIA   This guide, written by David Paletz of Duke University, helps students interpret the viewpoints and biases of American media: newspapers, periodicals, radio and television news programs, and individual columnists. It begins with a chapter that shows how media influences politics and the way we interpret political events and issues. A series of active learning exercises help students examine events and issues from the viewpoint of different media. These exercises, tied to the themes in the text, include discussion questions. Finally, the guide includes an annotated listing of the various media and their biases.

MULTIMEDIA HANDBOOK   This brief manual will help you bring media presentations of important political events, like the civil rights movement, into your classroom. It lists and describes all of the videos, films, laser disks, transparencies and software that HarperCollins provides to text adopters. The handbook also includes discussion questions, and shows how you might use the media to complement the themes and discussions in *The Struggle for Democracy*. Finally, it offers an annotated listing of over 70 films and videos available through Indiana University.

Test Bank

Over 2500 test questions have been developed by Ken Kollman of Northwestern University. Many of the questions are expressly designed to reinforce and test students' knowledge of the *concepts* and *themes* presented in the text. All answers are keyed by page reference to the corresponding discussions in the test. Questions are given in several formats, including multiple choice, short answer, true/false, and essay. The questions are available both in paper and electronic formats, the latter of which are for use with IBM and Macintosh microcomputers.

Testing Software

TESTMASTER   In addition to the traditional printed format, the complete Test Bank is also available free of charge on *Testmaster*, HarperCollins's computer test-generating system. Flexible and easy to use, *Testmaster* may be obtained for use both with the IBM-PC and most compatibles, and the Macintosh.

GRADES   Grade-keeping and classroom-management software, free to instructors, maintains data sets for up to 200 students. It is suitable for use with the IBM-PC and most compatibles.

Data Resource Package

Prepared by Neal Tate of University of North Texas, the *Data Resource Package* is a compilation of data on the economy, public opinion, elections, income, and political conditions. Presented in both printed and electronic form, over 40 tables of data, as well as graphical representations of that data, can be manipulated with multiple variables.

Transparency Resource Package

The 80 full-color transparencies included in this package reinforce the information and themes presented in *The Struggle for Democracy*. These maps, timelines, and graphs (the latter taken from the *Data Resource Package*) include a narrative description and lecture notes that will help stimulate classroom discussions. The transparencies have been assembled by Stephen Van Beek of San Jose State.

Multimedia

LASER DISC *American Government: Issues and Images* is a two-sided videodisc developed in consultation with American Government professors and a multimedia courseware developer. Also available on video tape, the program contains 46 motion picture excerpts from network news, newsreel collections, cable archives, and state historical societies. The videodisc has been specifically designed for classroom use, and includes pedagogically focused clips from campaign commercials, convention debates, and both historic and recent footage of domestic and foreign policy issues. With the press of a single button the disc can instantly display the moment of political or government history that will best illustrate the points in your lecture.

HARPERCOLLINS'S MEDIA PROGRAM HarperCollins has made available a wide selection of films and videos for instructors to integrate into their course material.

Instructors may choose from many excellent programs. *The Power Game*, Hedrick Smith's popular four-part PBS documentary on the elected (and unelected) government in Washington, and *Eyes on the Prize*, the award-winning six-part series on the civil rights movement, are both available through Harper-Collins's media policy. Also available is *The Thirty-Second President*, Bill Moyers's examination of the office in the age of soundbites, from his PBS series *A Walk Through the Twentieth Century*. *The Challenge of the Presidency*, a one-hour videotape, combines David Frost's thoughtful interviews of former presidents Reagan, Carter, Ford, and Nixon. Adopters of *The Struggle for Democracy* may also receive a unique *Newsreel Video*, a selection of authentic newsreel footage that captures the key American political events of the past six decades.

FOR THE STUDENT

Study Guide

The *Study Guide*, written by Mary L. Carns of Stephen F. Austin State University, reinforces text discussions to help students improve their understanding of American government and politics. Written in a straightforward way, the guide includes an introduction, chapter summaries, key concepts, crossword puzzles which test students' knowledge of key terms, suggested paper topics, and research questions and resources. Sample tests, including a mix of conceptual and factual questions, will help students evaluate their understanding of each chapter.

Practicing Political Science

Neal Tannahill of Houston Community College has prepared a student supplement that incorporates a series of learning skills and development projects with critical thinking exercises. Topics include "Using Graphs to Present and Analyze Data," "Separating Fact from Opinion," "Using Library Resources," and "Studying the Constitution."

Thinking About the Environment

Written by Joseph Karlesky of Franklin and Marshall College, this supplemental text on environmental policy provides an awareness test and four case studies which motivate students to think about questions and issues raised in this policy area.

American Government Computer Simulations

Created by Intentional Educations, *Democracy in Action: American Government Simulations* teaches students the inner workings of government by challenging them to make real-life political decisions. It focuses on topics of key importance, including the judiciary; interest groups; Congress; federalism; public policy; presidential elections; urban politics; and politics, elections, and redistricting. In each simulation, students assume a different role (e.g., Supreme Court justice, state budget director, PAC leader, member of Congress, and so forth), as they face the same problems and questions as these political figures. The simulations are divided into three parts: a short introduction detailing important background information; a glossary defining key terms; and the simulation itself, the section in which the students take on the roles and learn the outcomes of their decisions. With color screens and graphics and simple directions, each simulation in *Democracy in Action* also has a number of variations, so the exercises can be used more than once. The simulations may be obtained for use both with the IBM-PC and most compatibles and with the Macintosh. There are a total of eight different simulations currently available.

Supershell Student Tutorial Software

Prepared by Robert E. Hogan of Rice University and Neal Tannahill of Houston Community College, this computerized student tutorial guide is designed to help students retain the key concepts and ideas they have read. This versatile drill-and-practice software contains multiple-choice, true-false, and short answer questions for each chapter in the text that provide students with immediate feedback. Questions are referenced to the pages in the text where relevant information is presented. Students may print out narrative chapter outlines or consult an easy-to-use tutorial guide. In addition, a flash card program is included to drill students on the terms in the text's glossary. The *Supershell Student Tutorial Software* is provided free of charge to instructors.

Harper Data Analysis Package

William Parle of Oklahoma State University has prepared a student data analysis package for the IBM-PC which performs several basic statistical functions, including cross tabulations. Free to instructors, the package comes with a "real world" data set, a complete "Help" menu and "Help" files, a data dictionary, a set of screen instructions, and a *User's Manual*.

ACKNOWLEDGMENTS

Writing and producing an introductory textbook is an incredibly complex, cooperative enterprise in which many people besides the authors play key roles. We would like to take the opportunity to thank them, one and all. We start with the many wonderful people at HarperCollins College Publishers. We owe a special debt to Lauren Silverman, our executive editor, whose guidance, attention, affection, and intelligence guided us from the beginning to the end of the project. Every author team should be blessed with such an editor at least once in its career. We started as business associates; we finished as friends. Special thanks also go to Marianne Russell and Susan Katz who believed in and supported this book from the beginning. Three development editors—John Haber, Dan McMillan, and Arthur Pomponio—helped us keep our argument straight and our eye on the prize. Arthur was especially helpful in pulling together all the pieces of the project at the end. Project editor Melonie Parnes guided the translation of our word-processed pages into a four-color, hard-bound book. Lucy Krikorian coordinated the book design and artwork, the stunning results of which you will see in the pages of this book.

There are many colleagues we want to thank. Ken Kollman, a graduate student at Northwestern, and Vicki Ash, a graduate student at the University of Colorado, were both wonderful research assistants whose help we couldn't have done without. Ken also played an important role in the development of ancillary materials. Thad Tecza and Doug Costain, both of the University of Colorado, provided materials and offered comments on several chapters. William Haltom of the University of Puget Sound wrote the first draft of the chapter on civil rights and liberties.

HarperCollins enlisted the advice of many political scientists on various aspects of this project. Their advice was invaluable, and the final version of the text is far different (and no doubt better) than it would have been without their help.

The following political scientists advised HarperCollins on the original prospectus:

Ross Baker, Rutgers University

Bill Bianco, Duke University

Seth Hirshorn, University of
    Michigan

William Kelly, Auburn University

Mike Munger, University of Texas

Eric Uslaner, University of Maryland

Charles Walcott, University of
    Minnesota

The following political scientists read and commented on one or more chapters:

Gordon Alexandre, Glendale
    Community College

Evelyn Brodkin, University of
    Chicago

Joseph S. Brown, Baylor
    University

Mary Carns, Stephen F. Austin
    University

Jim Carter, Sam Houston State
    University

David Cingranelli, State University
    of New York at Binghamton

Euel Elliott, University of Texas

Robert S. Erikson, University of
    Houston

Thomas Ferguson, University of
    Massachusetts, Boston

M. Lauren Ficaro, Chapman
    University

Doris A. Graber, The University of
    Illinois

Bruce E. Gronbeck, University of
    Iowa

Russell L. Hanson, Indiana
    University

Gary C. Jacobson, University of
    California at San Diego

Richard Lehne, Rutgers University

Dean E. Mann, University of California

Michael W. McCann, University of Washington

Carroll R. McKibbin, California Polytechnic State University

Neil Milner, University of Hawaii

Kristen R. Monroe, Princeton University

Laurel A. Myer, Sinclair Community College

Mark P. Petracca, University of California

Russell D. Renka, Southeast Missouri State University

Leroy N. Rieselbach, Indiana University

David W. Romero, University of California

Francis E. Rourke, Johns Hopkins University

Donald L. Scruggs, Stephens College

Daniel Wirls, University of California

Eugene R. Wittkopf, Louisiana State University

The following political scientists participated in focus groups for the text and supplements, or reviewed the supplements:

Ryan Barrilleaux, University of Miami

Stephen Bennett, University of Cincinnati

James Bromeland, Winona State University

Gregory Casey, University of Missouri

Paul Chardoul, Grand Rapids Community College

Allan J. Cigler, University of Kansas

Landon Curry, University of Texas

Christine Day, University of New Orleans

John Geer, Arizona State University

John Green, University of Akron

Roberta Herzberg, Indiana University

Ronald J. Hrebenar, University of Utah

David Hunt, Triton College

William Jacoby, University of South Carolina

Fred Kramer, University of Massachusetts

Joel Lieske, Cleveland State

Louise Mayo, County College of Morris

Albert Nelson, University of Wisconsin—La Crosse

David Nice, Washington State

Toby Paone, St. Charles County Community College

Curtis G. Reithel, University of Wisconsin—La Crosse

Sue Tolleson Rinehart, Texas Tech University

Phyllis F. Rippey, Western Illinois University

David C. Saffell, Ohio Northern University

John M. Shebb, University of Tennessee

David A. Smeltzer, Portland State University

C. Neal Tate, University of North Texas

Robert Thomas, University of Houston

Elliot Vittes, University of Central Florida

Charles Walcott, University of Minnesota

Nelson Wikstrom, Virginia Commonwealth University

The following political scientists were kind enough to read and comment on the entire manuscript:

Gordon Alexandre, Glendale Community College

Jim Carter, Sam Houston State University

Mary Carns, Stephen F. Austin State
   University
Gregory L. Goodwin, Bakersfield
   College
Fred A. Kramer, University of
   Massachusetts
Andrew Milnor, State University of
   New York at Binghamton

Albert J. Nelson, University of
   Wisconsin
Toby Paone, St. Charles County
   Community College
John M. Scheb, University of
   Tennessee

EDWARD S. GREENBERG
BENJAMIN I. PAGE

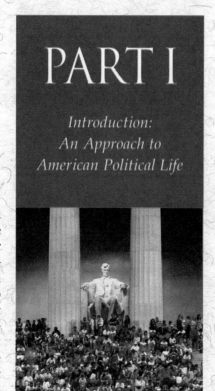

PART I

*Introduction:
An Approach to
American Political Life*

In Part I, we explain the overall plan of the book, describe the main themes that will recur throughout its pages, and suggest why the topics that will be explored are important to know. While acknowledging that American politics and government can be confusing, we show how one can make sense of the way politics and government work, and make judgments about them using widely shared American values. The material in this part of the book, that is to say, shows how American politics and government can be *understood* and *evaluated*. It does this in two ways. First, it presents a simple framework for understanding why and how political events happen, focusing on how political and governmental institutions and processes work, how they are related to each other, and how they are, in turn, shaped by things like the economy, the social structure, cultural ideas, and our nation's place in the world. Second, it defines democracy as a form of political community where popular sovereignty, political equality, and liberty exist, it tells why it is important that a society be democratic, and it shows how democracy can be used as a standard to evaluate the progress and prospects of American political life.

This part also introduces the central dramatic thread that ties the book together: *the struggle for democracy*. It tells how the book will go about making the point that American political life has always involved a struggle among individuals, groups, classes, and institutions over the meaning, extent, and practice of democracy, and that the struggle continues in our own day. It also introduces the idea that while democracy has made a great deal of progress over the years in the United States, it remains only imperfectly realized and threatened by new problems that only vigilant and active citizens can meet.

1

Understanding and Evaluating American Politics

UNTIL JUSTICE ROLLS DOWN LIKE WATERS
AND RIGHTEOUSNESS LIKE A MIGHTY STREAM

MARTIN LUTHER KING JR

THE STRUGGLE FOR DEMOCRACY

Why should there not be a patient confidence in the ultimate justice of the people? Is there any better, or equal, hope in the world? (Abraham Lincoln, First Inaugural Address)

We live in an age of democratic upsurge. People the world over, often at great risk to themselves, have been demanding the right to govern themselves, free from the guiding hands of kings, religious autocrats, military dictators, or party bosses. Who among us has not been moved and inspired by the recent struggles for democracy in South Africa, Eastern Europe, the former Soviet Union, and Latin America?

Most Americans are heartened but not surprised at this worldwide struggle for democracy, for we recognize the right of people to rule themselves as a fundamental human right, as an essential part of what it means to be a human being. The prospect of living in a political system where the people are ruled, instead of ruling, seems not only unappealing but also contrary to our most fundamental sense of right and wrong.

We in the United States are participants in this worldwide drama. We are participants because American political ideas and institutions often have provided inspiration for democratic movements around the world. But we are also participants in the sense that the struggle for democracy continues in our own political life, for democracy has yet to be fully realized even in America. The struggle for democracy is a major feature of our history and a defining characteristic of our politics. The struggle to protect, enrich, and expand democracy in the United States is the central theme of this book.

In this opening chapter, we describe a way to understand how American politics works and a way to think more clearly about the nature of democracy. Armed with these two sets of tools, we will, in the remainder of the book, proceed to analyze the workings of American politics and to compare American political reality to the democratic ideal. What to do with the results of this exploration is entirely up to you in your role as a citizen of the United States.

TO UNDERSTAND AND TO EVALUATE

The pages of newspapers and magazines, as well as our television screens and our radios, are filled with news about government decisions, political maneuvering and conflict, social and economic developments, and U.S. relations with other nations. However, because this avalanche of information comes to us in unconnected bits and pieces, jumbled and out of context, making sense of it is no easy task. In fact, for many Americans, our political life seems hopelessly confused and confusing.

It need not be so. We will show how it is possible to make sense of this diverse information, for things are not as disconnected and random as they seem. There are regular tendencies and patterns in our political life; we just have to know where to look for them. There are, moreover, ways to evaluate what we observe in terms of our most cherished values. Knowing where to look for these treasures, however, requires a map. The purpose of this book is to provide you with just such a map. While there is plenty of detailed information in this text, our principal concern is to provide a map to help you *understand* and *evaluate* our political life.

We will do two things in this chapter to help you understand and evaluate. First, we will describe a framework for comprehending *why* political events occur, in terms of how political and governmental institutions and processes work, how they are related to each other, and how they are, in turn, shaped by things like the economy, the social structure, cultural ideas, and our nation's place in the world system. Second, we will define *democracy* and argue that the *democratic ideal* should be used as a standard for evaluating the quality of our political life.

In order to give life and concreteness to this discussion, we will begin with some real events, people, and institutions: those involved in the passage of the federal legislation of the 1960s that forced an end to the legal segregation of black people in the South. After we tell this story in broad outline, we will briefly describe our analytical framework and show how it can be used to increase your understanding of the civil rights story in particular and American politics in general. The story will also introduce you to the dramatic thread that runs through each chapter of this text: the struggle for democracy.

THE COLLAPSE OF JIM CROW

The Civil War ended slavery in the United States, but it did not end racial discrimination. After a brief period of black emancipation, a rigid system of racial separation and subordination known as "**Jim Crow**" was put into place throughout most of the South by the beginning of the twentieth century. It was still firmly entrenched 50 years later. Racial discrimination was not, of course, a strictly southern affair; many northerners were just as prejudiced, only more hypocritical about it. The formalization of discrimination under an elaborate umbrella of laws separating the races was, however, largely confined to the South.

Jim Crow extended racial separation in the South to nearly every sphere of life, including separate drinking fountains.

Black Americans were elated in 1954 when the U.S. Supreme Court announced its landmark *Brown v. Board of Education* decision, declaring segregation in public schools to be unconstitutional. "We conclude," wrote Chief Justice Earl Warren for a unanimous court, "that in the field of public education the doctrine of 'separate but equal' has no place. Separate educational facilities are inherently unequal." Many people expected that this decision would not only end segregation in the public schools but also undermine the entire structure of segregation under which blacks in the South had for many years been economically subordinated, excluded from politics, and left unprotected against violence and intimidation.

Those who thought the *Brown* decision would immediately overturn the racial order in the South were to be disappointed. In most of the South throughout the remainder of the 1950s and into the early 1960s, schools and public facilities remained segregated, violence and intimidation were directed against blacks who spoke out, and blacks continued to be denied the right to sit on juries, to hold public office, or even to vote. (This story is told, though not entirely accurately, in the film, *Mississippi Burning*. See the box.) The examples that follow will illuminate the situation.

- Dr. Benjamin Fine, education editor of the *New York Times*, describes high school student Elizabeth Eckford's attempt to attend her first day of school at Little Rock's previously all-white Central High School in September 23, 1957:

  I was standing in front of the school that day. Suddenly there was a shout—"they're here! The niggers are coming." I saw a sweet little girl who looked about fifteen, walking alone. She tried several times to pass through the guards. The last time she tried, they put their bayonets in front of her. When they did this, she became panicky. For a moment she just stood there trembling. Then she seemed to calm down and started walking toward the bus stop with the mob baying at her heels like a pack of hounds. The women were shouting, "Get her!

Elizabeth Eckford braves a mob while trying to integrate Little Rock's Central High School in 1957.

POLITICS
AND
FILM

*What's Wrong
with This
Picture?*

Gene Hackman and Willem DaFoe portray FBI agents who battle the KKK in Mississippi in the early 1960s.

During the summer of 1964, three civil rights workers involved in a campaign to help black citizens register to vote (in a project known as Mississippi Freedom Summer) disappeared after being arrested for a minor driving violation in Philadelphia, Mississippi. The bodies of the three young people (one black, and two white) were later

found buried in an earthen dam by FBI agents. The perpetrators turned out to be local Klansmen and their allies in the Philadelphia sheriff's office. Director Alan Parker's *Mississippi Burning* is a powerful fictionalized account of the investigation that brought the murderers to justice. The film is wrenchingly graphic, showing as no other film has, the terror under which blacks lived in the deep South during this period. Lynching, beatings, and church burnings are portrayed in moving detail.

Willem DaFoe and Gene Hackman play two FBI agents sent to Philadelphia to investigate the disappearances. The DaFoe character, who comes to the FBI by way of Harvard Law School and the Justice Department, plays by the book and makes no progress in cracking the case. The Hackman character, a native Mississippian and former small town sheriff, is familiar with towns like Philadelphia, and his contacts with the townspeople help him slowly uncover the conspiracy. When the investigation reaches a dead end because of DaFoe's earnest but ineffectual methods, and the violence against blacks reaches a fever pitch, Hackman decides to use

Lynch her!'' The men were yelling, ''Go home, you bastard of a black bitch!'' She finally made it to the bus stop and sat down on the bench. I sat down beside her and said, ''I'm a reporter from the *New York Times*, may I have your name?'' She just sat there, her head down. Tears were streaming down her cheeks from under her sunglasses. . . .[1]

Though the Supreme Court ruled that desegregation of public schools must proceed ''with all deliberate speed,'' it would be some time yet before children like Elizabeth Eckford would see much change. As late as 1964—ten years after *Brown*—fewer than *1 percent* of all black children in the states of Alabama, Arkansas, Georgia, Mississippi, and South Carolina were attending school with white children.

• The U.S. Civil Rights Commission had this to say on voting in Mississippi:

In Walthall County in 1961 a voter registration worker accompanying Negro applicants for registration was struck by the registrar with the butt of a gun.

his own brutal methods. The Klan is fought using Klan methods. Justice is achieved by vigilante means.

In addition to the call for vigilante justice as the only way to get results, a common theme in Hollywood films (note, especially, the extensive series of films by Charles Bronson), there are several additional troubling aspects of *Mississippi Burning*. First, the film seriously misrepresents the role of African-Americans in their own liberation. Parker shows blacks only as helpless victims, sheeplike and unprepared for what befalls them, turning to white outsiders (like the FBI) for help and protection. Nowhere to be seen on the screen are the courageous efforts to transform Mississippi by blacks themselves. The activists of the Southern Christian Leadership Conference, the Congress on Racial Equality, and the Student NonViolent Coordinating Committee (which conceived of and ran the Mississippi Freedom Summer project) are absent. So too are the many ordinary Mississippi black citizens who were brave enough to join rallies, protests, and demonstrations.

Second, Parker seriously misrepre-

sents the role of the FBI. While it is true that the Bureau broke the case, it must be pointed out that the FBI was no friend of the civil rights movement during the long tenure of J. Edgar Hoover. Indeed, Hoover was actively hostile to the movement and its leadership. He believed that the movement was communist at its core and spent much of his time trying to discredit it and its leaders. His vendetta against Martin Luther King, Jr., is well known and the Bureau's unwillingness to protect civil rights workers throughout the South is almost legendary. The Bureau was particularly remiss in protecting the Freedom Riders and activists trying to register voters in Mississippi. Parker's error in showing a black FBI agent in his film is particularly glaring for the Bureau was lily-white at the time. Hoover was literally pushed into the Philadelphia investigation by public pressure and only began to integrate the Bureau when he could no longer hold out. To turn the tragedy of Chaney, Goodman, and Schwerner (the three disappeared civil rights workers) into a celebration of the FBI may strike some people as odd, indeed.

Later that day he was arrested and charged with breach of the peace. . . . In Rankin County in 1963 the sheriff, armed with a blackjack, and several deputy sheriffs assaulted and beat several Negroes waiting in the registrar's office. In Holmes County in 1963 two firebombs were thrown into the house of Hartman Turnbow, a local Negro farmer and a leader in the registration effort, a few weeks after he and others had attempted to register. . . . In Mississippi . . . several Negro leaders who had urged their people to vote were murdered, one of them on the courthouse lawn in Brookhaven in the summer of 1955.[2]

Despite the *Brown* decision, segregation remained firmly in place throughout the early 1960s. Jim Crow laws and social customs kept the races apart in almost every area of life, including hotels, places of entertainment, recreation, and transportation. "Colored Only" and "Whites Only" signs on park benches, rest rooms, lunch counters, and buses were a normal part of the southern landscape in those years.

While Elizabeth Eckford and her friends attended segregated schools, played in segregated playgrounds, rode in segregated buses, swam in segregated pools, and ate at segregated lunch counters, their parents found themselves barred from good jobs, unable to secure business loans, blocked from living in neighborhoods with decent housing, denied access to good hospitals and doctors, and denied the right to vote in most communities. In 1960, only 5.2 percent of the eligible black population was registered to vote in Mississippi; only 15.2 percent were registered in Alabama; 15.7 percent in South Carolina; 23.8 percent in Virginia; and 29.3 percent in Georgia.[3] Without the vote, blacks went largely without the protection and services usually provided by elected officials. In 1957, there were virtually no black elected officials in the South, and fewer than 100 in the entire nation. Black people were essentially deprived of the rights of citizenship and excluded from the democratic political process.

The Legislative Triumphs of 1964 and 1965

This situation changed only after a long struggle, when the U.S. Congress and the president enacted two key laws in 1964 and 1965 that declared Jim Crow illegal and took steps to end it.

On July 2, 1964, roughly ten years after *Brown*, President Lyndon Johnson signed the Civil Rights Act of 1964 into law. The Act banned racial discrimination in public accommodations (hotels, restaurants, terminals, movie theaters, etc.). It gave the attorney general additional powers to protect citizens against discrimination in voting, education, and employment, and it cut off federal funds to segregated institutions and programs. Finally, it allowed the federal government to sue states that continued to maintain segregated schools.

Only eight months later, in a dramatic appearance before a joint session of Congress, President Johnson introduced a sweeping bill designed to put the force of the federal government behind black citizens' right to vote in the former states

President Johnson signs the historic Civil Rights Act of 1964 surrounded by leaders of civil rights organizations, congressional leaders, and key members of his administration.

of the Confederacy. He told members of Congress and a national television audience that further delay in guaranteeing the right to vote to black Americans would be intolerable: "Their cause must be our cause, too," he told his listeners. "Because it is not just Negroes, but really it is all of us who must overcome the crippling legacy of bigotry and injustice. And we shall overcome." The Voting Rights Act sailed through Congress and was signed into law by President Johnson on August 6, 1965, in the same room in which Lincoln had signed the Emancipation Proclamation. The most important features of the law were the suspension of **literacy tests** and the assignment of federal voting registrars (to take over from local ones) in those states and counties where fewer than half the eligible population had voted in the 1964 election.

The civil rights legislation of 1964 and 1965 was to have a profound impact on American life. After years of delay and resistance, the legal foundations of a segregated society were finally swept away. The desegregation of southern public schools finally made significant headway. "Whites Only" and "Colored Only" signs came down throughout the South. Finding blacks and whites together in movie houses, restaurants, and public transportation became so common that it eventually lost its novelty. The use of terror against the black population largely ceased.

Black voter registration and voting turnout increased dramatically. As early as 1966, the percentage of eligible voters registered had increased to 27.8 in Mississippi, 48.9 in Alabama, 46.7 in Virginia, 48.0 in South Carolina, and 43.2 in Georgia.[4] The number of black elected officials increased by leaps and bounds all over the deep South, reaching nearly 1,500 by 1970.[5] This tangible increase in black political power changed how state and local governments treated their black constituents. The struggle for democracy made a difference.

The great increase in numbers of black voters also led vote-seeking white politicians, many of whom had built careers on a platform of "white supremacy," to change their approach toward black citizens. Senator Strom Thurmond of South Carolina, the standard-bearer for the prosegregation Dixiecrats in the 1948 presidential election, eventually sent his children to integrated public schools. James Eastland of Mississippi, for many years a formidable roadblock to civil rights bills as chair of the Senate Judiciary Committee, is reported to have approached the NAACP for help in mobilizing black support for his last campaign for office.[6] George Wallace, whose stand in "the schoolhouse door" to block desegregation at the University of Alabama brought him national notoriety, won his last election by forging a political alliance with black political organizations.

One should not exaggerate the extent of improvement in the lives of black Americans following the passage of the 1964 and 1965 civil rights bills. These laws did little to alter the more informal and impersonal forms of housing, education, and job segregation in the North. They did little to improve the economic well-being of black Americans or the squalid conditions in northern central cities, where many of them lived. Nor did they prevent the "backlash" against further civil rights measures that continues to affect American politics today. They left unresolved the difficult question of whether and how the lingering effects of past slavery and discrimination could be erased; most white Americans opposed—and continue to oppose—the idea of affirmative action or quotas. Having said this, however, one must still conclude that the changes in the South between 1957 (the year Elizabeth Eckford braved the mob at Central High School) and the late 1960s was truly extraordinary and a milestone in America's struggle for democracy.

The civil rights movement has had little positive impact on the economic
well-being of inner-city African-Americans. The 1992 Los Angeles riots
were a vivid reminder of how serious a problem this has become. Here a
shop owner in south-central Los Angeles watches as his store burns
down.

A FRAMEWORK FOR UNDERSTANDING AMERICAN POLITICS

How did this legislative revolution happen? How was it possible that landmark
civil rights bills were produced by a federal government that as late as the mid-
1950s was relatively uninterested in the "Negro problem"? In short, *why* were
these laws passed? What were the causes?

It is a complex story, with multiple causes. We cannot give all the details
here (some will be added in later chapters). What we will do, instead, is provide
some *general* ideas about how to answer "why" questions about politics, that is,
some general ideas about the causes of political events. These ideas, which amount
to a conceptual scheme or analytical framework, refer to the workings of the
American political system in general and will be used to answer "why" questions
throughout the book. After briefly describing the framework, we will show how
it applies to the specific case of the civil rights acts.

The information in this text is organized around a relatively simple analytical
framework that is designed to help us understand why things happen the way
they do in politics. Our framework combines elements from several different kinds
of political theories.[7] It suggests, for one thing, that the many diverse individuals,
organizations, processes, and institutions involved in American politics can be
grouped into a limited number of types; that is, we will speak of "political parties," "interest groups," "Congress," "the presidency," "the economic system,"
and other categories of political *actors* or *influences*—people, groups, and institutions that have their own special ways of working and that interact with each
other to influence what the government does. The first step in understanding why
something happened in politics is to identify which political actors and influences

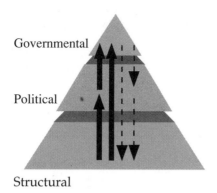

Governmental

Political

Structural

Figure 1.1
Understanding why
political events happen

were involved, what they did, and why. Separate chapters of this book are devoted to explaining how the various types of political actors and influences work.

Moreover, our framework indicates that these political actors tend to interact with each other in somewhat different ways, depending upon which *level* of the political system they belong to. This is shown in Figure 1.1. We distinguish among three different levels. First, and most obvious, is the *governmental* level, which includes all public officials and official institutions (Congress, the presidency, the executive branch, and the Supreme Court) that have formal, legal responsibilities in making policy. Second is the *political* level, which includes public opinion, political parties, interest groups, elections, the mass media, and social movements. These political actors and processes do not consist of public officials but are actively involved in transmitting individual and group interests, preferences, and demands to government officials and in affecting the policies that the government pursues. In one sense, of course, everything discussed in this book is "political," but we reserve the term "political level" to refer to individuals and institutions that are directly involved in politics without holding formal government office. Third is the *structural* level, which includes deeper, more fundamental and enduring factors that influence government: the nature of the U.S. economy, the population, the constitutional rules of the game, the political culture, and the place of the United States in the international system.

You need not worry about remembering exactly which actors and influences belong to which of the three analytical levels. That will become obvious, because the chapters of the book devoted to particular actors are organized into three main sections: the first deals with the structural level, the second with the political, and the third with the governmental. Nor do you need to worry about exactly how the people and institutions at the different levels interact with each other. That will become clear as we go along.

You will soon see how this framework can help answer "why" questions about politics. You will see, for example, that it is seldom a sufficient explanation of a political event to say that "President Johnson did it," or "President Bush wanted it." What the president wants and does can be very important, but we also need to ask *why* he wanted it and why he was able to get it. That will usually require a look at other *governmental* institutions (why did Congress go along? Why did the executive branch follow the president's instructions? Why didn't the Supreme Court interfere?). It will also require a consideration of *political* institutions and processes: was the president responding to demands from public opinion or from organized interest groups? Why was a president who wanted this policy elected in the first place? Often, a full explanation will require consideration of *structural* factors: did the state of the U.S. economy make this policy necessary? Did international trade or the world balance of power make a difference? How about the age, health, and occupational patterns of the American population?

To put this a little more abstractly, we believe that American political life must be understood as an *integrated whole*; that what goes on in government can only be comprehended within a larger context defined by all three levels of analysis. Actions by public officials are not simply the product of the personal desires of such officials (though these are important), but also of the influences and pressures brought to bear by other *governmental* institutions and by individuals, groups, and classes at work in the *political* sphere. The political sphere, in turn, can often be understood only when we see how it is shaped by its larger *structural* context, including such things as the economy and the political culture.

Applying the Framework to the Civil Rights Case

Let's see how we can use this analytical framework to illuminate the reasons why the landmark Civil Rights Acts of 1964 and 1965 were passed. We will first focus on the activities of *governmental* officials, such as presidents, senators, and members of the House of Representatives, and the institutions of which they were a part. Much like a motion picture camera pulling back and widening its lens to take a broader picture, we will then talk about the ways in which *political* influences impinged upon and shaped the behavior of public officials as they pondered the civil rights issue. Pulling our imaginary camera back even further and opening our lens to its widest angle, we will then talk about *structural* developments that impinged upon and shaped both politics and government. The analysis of the Civil Rights Acts in terms of the interaction of government, politics, and structure will illustrate the way of looking at American politics that will be used throughout this book. It will also provide a first glimpse of how various political institutions work, about which you will learn much more later.

GOVERNMENTAL INFLUENCES   The main governmental actors pushing for these civil rights laws were Presidents Kennedy and Johnson, supported by strong majorities in Congress; opposing them were the organizational arrangement of Congress, which makes it easy for minorities to block or delay any legislation, and particular features of Congress, which at that time gave extra power to white southern congressmen.

On June 11, 1963, President John F. Kennedy addressed the nation on the issue of the civil rights of black Americans, calling for sweeping legislation to end legal segregation and officially sanctioned discrimination. He had been slow to embrace the civil rights issue, but on this evening he spoke passionately.

> This Nation was founded on the principle that all men are created equal, and that the rights of every man are diminished when the rights of one man are threatened.... It ought to be possible for American consumers of any color to receive equal service in places of public accommodation, such as hotels and restaurants and theaters and retail stores, without being forced to resort to demonstrations in the street, and it ought to be possible for American citizens of any color to register and to vote in a free election without interference or fear of reprisal.

President Kennedy delivers his historic civil rights speech from the Oval Office of the White House.

Congress is not easily pushed into action, however, because of the way it is organized and conducts its business (you will learn much more about this in Chapter 11, "Congress"). It was especially difficult to move Congress on the subject of civil rights in the early 1960s because of the power wielded in both the House and the Senate by white southerners who had served there a long time and had chaired powerful committees. Two of them stood directly in the path of a sweeping civil rights bill: Judge Howard Smith of Virginia, Chairman of the House Rules Committee, and James Eastland of Mississippi, Chairman of the Senate Judiciary Committee, both of whom had buried (by not acting upon) civil rights measures in the past.

In the Senate, proponents of civil rights legislation also had to contend with the rules allowing for extended debate. Unless a two-thirds majority of the Senate voted to cut off discussion, a determined minority could **filibuster**, that is, talk a bill to death and not allow it to come to the floor for a vote. On several occasions in the past, the threat of filibuster by southern senators had blocked civil rights legislation.

President Kennedy soon discovered that his widely admired speech and his intensive efforts to win the support of the leaders of business, labor, religion, and communications were having little effect in moving his bill forward. By November 12, the *New York Times* was talking of a "pervasive attitude of discouragement" and a "feeling of helplessness" among civil rights advocates.

Then, later in November 1963, President Kennedy was assassinated. When Vice-President Lyndon Johnson assumed the office of president, he transformed the national grief over the assassination into popular support for several Kennedy-initiated legislative programs, including civil rights, and used his legislative skills to enact them into law.

Johnson came to the presidency with 23 years of experience in Congress and with substantial Democratic party majorities in the House of Representatives and in the Senate. Prior to assuming the vice-presidency in 1961, he had been generally recognized as a master of the legislative process. Johnson brought all his legendary skills to bear in the service of the civil rights bill. He called in political debts owed to him in Congress. As a Texan, he was able to court powerful southern legislative leaders like Richard Russell of Georgia. He listened seriously to the concerns of the Republican leader of the Senate, Everett Dirksen of Illinois, and compromised certain provisions of the bill to make him more comfortable with the legislation. (Northern small businesses were excluded from certain antidiscrimination provisions, for example; once the bill was aimed exclusively at the South, Dirksen and most northern Republicans came aboard.) Johnson encouraged business, labor, churches, and civil rights groups to lobby Congress. He used presidential appearances to build public support for civil rights legislation.

After these efforts, bipartisan majorities in both Houses of Congress supported the civil rights bill. Even this did not ensure passage, however. Judge Smith in the House and Senator Eastland and the filibuster in the Senate still stood in the legislative path.

Much to everyone's surprise, Judge Smith suddenly agreed to report a strong civil rights bill to the floor. Whether he did so because he sensed the possibility of being outvoted on his own Rules Committee (which had added several liberal members in 1963) or because of the persuasive powers of Lyndon Johnson cannot be known. Whatever the cause, the crumbling of this bastion allowed for speedy and decisive action. The House of Representatives approved the Civil Rights Act of 1964 by a vote of 290–130.

In the Senate, passage of the bill was not assured, because of the twin threats of Eastland's Judiciary Committee and a southern filibuster. The first threat was eliminated when civil rights forces convinced their Senate colleagues to bypass the Judiciary Committee and to bring the bill directly to the floor for action. The second threat was defeated by a bipartisan coalition of Republicans and nonsouthern Democrats molded together by Democratic Senator Hubert Humphrey and Republican Senate leader Everett Dirksen, under the attentive eye of Lyndon Johnson. The Senate voted its approval for the measure on June 10, 1964, by a margin of 73–27, after enduring a filibuster by southern senators that lasted 83 days. **Cloture**, or the vote to close debate, had never before been invoked for a civil rights bill in the history of the Senate. Senator Dirksen, explaining his support for the Senate's unprecedented action, observed that "this is an idea whose time has come. It will not be stayed. It will not be denied."

After the events of 1964, the Voting Rights Act of 1965 was passed almost as an afterthought. President Johnson's landslide reelection victory in November 1964 over Republican Senator Barry Goldwater (who had opposed the Civil Rights Act) brought with it much larger—overwhelmingly large—Democratic majorities in both the House and the Senate, which quickly and easily enacted the new law.

POLITICAL INFLUENCES   Public officials and political leaders do not simply act as they wish. More often than not, they are influenced in their behavior by people and organizations outside of government who make their desires known to them. There is no denying that public officials and government institutions played a central role in the formulation of the civil rights acts, but the story cannot end here, for we must take into account the political pressures pushing public officials to action and the political processes that put those officials into office.

Let's again pull back the camera and broaden our view to take into account the *political* level. Presidents Kennedy and Johnson, and congressional leaders like Senators Humphrey and Dirksen, did not act in a vacuum. We have already hinted at certain political factors, including the shift of the national Democratic party to

THE STRUGGLE FOR DEMOCRACY

The Young Thurgood Marshall

Thurgood Marshall became one of the nation's most prominent civil rights attorneys, representing Linda Brown and other plaintiffs in *Brown v. Board of Education*, and a distinguished member of the U.S. Supreme Court. In the following selection, historian William Chafe tells the story of Marshall's early days as a civil rights lawyer in the South, when he repeatedly risked his life in the struggle for democracy.

During the 1940s Marshall traveled throughout the South, organizing teachers to fight for equal pay, mobilizing parents to insist on equal bus transportation, and enlisting lawyers to risk their practices by standing up for equality. He lived with the people, rarely spending more than a dollar for a meal, never more than two dollars for a room. Wherever he went he built alliances, showing the people he worked with that here was someone they could "travel the river" with. "Everybody loved Thurgood," one NAACP staff officer said, "[he] had the common touch." While previous NAACP leaders had spoken down to the people, another black observed, "Thurgood Marshall was of the people. He knew how to get through to them. Out in Texas or Oklahoma or down the street here in Washington at the Baptist Church, he would make these rousing speeches that would have them all jumping out of their seats."

Marshall's own courage in the face of constant danger became legendary, inspiring others to follow his example. In Tennessee, in the aftermath of the Columbia riot, his car was stopped three times by police harassing him, trying to scare him away. But Marshall never wavered. As Herbert Hill of the NAACP observed, "he was a very courageous figure. He would travel to the court houses of the South, and folks would come from miles, some of them on muleback or horseback, to see 'the nigger lawyer' who stood up in white men's courtrooms." More to the point, when he got to those courtrooms he often won, demonstrating to local residents that a black man could stand up in the face of white intimidation and prevail.

From William H. Chafe, *The Unfinished Journey* (New York: Oxford University Press, 1986), p. 149.

support civil rights, the shift in political power to the Democrats after Kennedy's assassination, and the anti-Goldwater landslide of 1964. Even more fundamentally, by 1963 and 1964, the country was in turmoil, with pressure building to do something substantial about civil rights.

The Civil Rights Movement Most important in bringing pressure to bear was the civil rights movement. In the late 1950s and early 1960s, this movement, whose seeds had been planted many years earlier by the activities of such organizations as the NAACP (see the box on Thurgood Marshall), the Congress of Racial Equality (CORE), and the National Urban League, brought large numbers of black Americans—as well as some sympathetic whites—into the streets of southern cities, towns, and hamlets to protest segregation and second-class citizenship. Their main weapon was nonviolent civil disobedience.

In 1957, a black woman named Rosa Parks was arrested for refusing to give up her seat on a city bus to a white, as required by a city ordinance, and sparked a successful protest and boycott movement among Montgomery, Alabama, blacks that lasted 381 days and brought its leader, the Reverend Martin Luther King, Jr., to national attention. In 1960, four black students from North Carolina A&T sat down at the "whites only" lunch counter of the Greensboro Woolworth's store and demanded service. Their bravery and dignity in the face of mob intimidation sparked a nationwide lunch-counter student sit-in movement to end segregation. In 1961, integrated "freedom riders" (including a number of college students from the North) rode Greyhound buses throughout the deep South to press for government action against segregated transportation. The mob violence that greeted them sparked sympathetic demonstrations throughout the nation. By 1963, mass demonstrations against segregation were common throughout the South—there were close to 1,500 during the year, with almost 20,000 civil rights demonstrators arrested[8] and no sign that demonstrations were about to diminish.

Matters reached an emotional peak in the spring of 1963 in Birmingham, Alabama, where Sheriff "Bull" Connor used cattle prods, fire hoses, and police dogs against school children who were demonstrating for an end to segregation in the city's downtown stores. In August, over a quarter of a million people gathered at the Lincoln Memorial in Washington, D.C., to demand the passage of civil rights legislation. It was here that Martin Luther King, Jr., delivered his "I Have a Dream" speech that so moved the nation.

The civil rights movement had two main effects. First, the turmoil it caused forced government officials in the Kennedy and Johnson administrations to act, fearing blame for a failure to keep order. Second, the movement helped reinforce

Martin Luther King waves to an enthusiastic crowd after delivering his historic and moving "I Have a Dream" speech at the Lincoln Memorial.

Question: Do you think white students and [black] students should go to the same schools or separate schools?

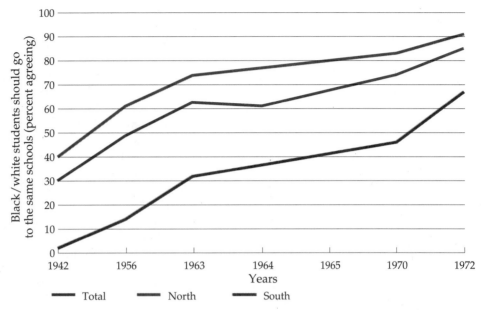

Figure 1.2 White public opinion on school integration, 1942–1972

Source: Tom W. Smith and Paul S. Sheatsley, "American Attitudes Toward Race Relations," Public Opinion Quarterly, Vol. 7, No. 5, October/November 1984.

and strengthen procivil rights pressure that was building among other political-level actors.

Other Pressures Political leaders were also feeling pressure from public opinion, which had slowly and gradually become far more favorable to black equality. The change between the early 1940s and the early 1960s was enormous: the majority of white Americans had once favored segregation of schools, housing, and public accommodations, but now a substantial majority favored integration in all these areas (see Figure 1.2). The change was especially marked among southern whites. As we will see, public opinion plays a central part in democratic politics.

Other political-level factors were also important. The mass media, especially the national television networks, publicized the civil rights struggle in a sympathetic fashion and highlighted incidents of violent resistance in the South. Most labor unions and many business corporations (seeking tranquil work places and enhanced economic development) came to side publicly with the aspirations of black Americans to end segregation. Religious and civic groups across the nation strongly supported the civil rights cause by 1963, as did the most prestigious and influential charitable foundations, such as Ford and Rockefeller. Such influential southern moderates as Governor Terry Sanford of North Carolina and journalists Ralph McGill and Hodding Carter also embraced the cause of full citizenship rights for blacks.

STRUCTURAL INFLUENCES*   But voters, interest groups, political parties, and mass movements—like public officials—do not act in a vacuum. While their choices and actions matter a great deal, they, like those in government, are not free to do exactly as they please. And what they please is not random or uncaused. The choices made by these various individuals and groups are very strongly influenced by the unending changes that go on in society. More often than not, we will find that the underlying causes of a particular governmental decision or policy can be traced to developments in society and the economy, the international system, and the set of ingrained ideas that we call the *political culture.*

Let's once again pull back the camera so that the structural level comes into view. The passage of the Civil Rights Act can only be understood in the context of important structural changes in American life. Take the impact of economic change. During the first half of the twentieth century, the United States became an urban and industrialized nation, especially outside the South. To serve its vast need for labor, American industry actively sought large influxes of people to work in its mills and factories, including black Americans from the South. Blacks were not only pulled from the South by the lure of industrial jobs in the North but also were pushed by deteriorating southern economic conditions as small farms gave way to larger, more mechanized farms requiring fewer laborers. This helped spur one of the greatest population movements in recent history. At the beginning of the twentieth century, most American blacks lived in the South; most worked on farms. By the late 1950s, almost half of all blacks in the United States lived outside the South, a majority worked in industrial occupations, and most lived in cities.

This change had important consequences. Urban industrial jobs for black people and the concentration of blacks in northern cities provided the resources and audiences for black entrepreneurs, politicians, artists, and civic and charitable organizations. Cultural and civic life thrived. These successes impressed white observers, who began to discard old racist theories that blacks were genetically inferior and to apply the powerful cultural ideas of democracy and equal opportunity. Public opinion began to oppose discrimination and segregation. Moreover, blacks had equal citizenship rights in the North. They began to register, to vote, and to exert political power. Since blacks were concentrated in states with large numbers of electoral votes, presidents as well as members of Congress began to pay attention. Some labor unions, with increasing numbers of black members, slowly came to include issues important to blacks on their legislative agendas.

The emergence of the United States as a world power during and after World War II also helped prepare the ground for the civil rights acts. Combat service by black Americans in World War II and in Korea increased respect for blacks among other Americans. It also spurred blacks' impatience with their treatment as second-class citizens. Furthermore, American political leaders found racial segregation to be increasingly inconvenient, embarrassing, and counterproductive in its Cold War struggle with the Soviet Union, since much of the competition between the two superpowers took place among dark-skinned peoples of the Third World.

Thus, structural changes fed into the political-level shifts in public opinion, interest groups, and political parties, and to the rise of the civil rights movement, all of which, in turn, moved government officials to action. See Figure 1.3.

---

*This section draws upon Richard P. Young, "Societal Change and the Evolution of American Race Relations" (Ph.D. dissertation, Stanford University, 1979).

One mark of the strides African-Americans have made in some areas of American life since the 1960s is the rise of General Colin Powell to the position of Chairman of the Joint Chiefs of Staff. As chairman, he supervised military planning and operations for Desert Shield and Desert Storm in the Persian Gulf.

Future Uses of the Analytical Framework

Now that we have used our analytical framework to analyze the passage of the civil rights acts, you can begin to see how it can be used to answer "why" questions *in general*, and how it will be used in the remainder of this book.

It should begin to be clear, for example, that the governmental, political, and structural levels of analysis must be considered together if we are to understand what goes on in American political life. Actions by public officials and institutions can only be understood if they are seen in relationship to such political influences as the actions of interest groups, social movements, and voters. These, in turn, can only be understood if they are seen in relationship to such structural factors as the economy, the culture, and the international system.

It should also be clear that there is seldom, if ever, a single cause that explains a government decision or policy. Instead, decisions and policies generally have *multiple causes*. Because this is the case, the analysis of policy making can start with any relevant actor, at any analytical level, as long as the effects of other actors at other levels are eventually brought into the picture.

To say that decisions and policies have multiple causes is *not* to say that all causes are equal, however. At many points in this book, we will attempt to judge which factors are more fundamental and which are less important. (This is often difficult, since the study of politics is not a laboratory science; scholars frequently disagree. We will note when this is so, and we will point out alternative methods for judging causes.) While all sorts of factors must be given their due, sometimes political-level factors, such as voters and interest groups are the most important in affecting what government does. At other times, the calculations and self-interest of individual public officials are more important.

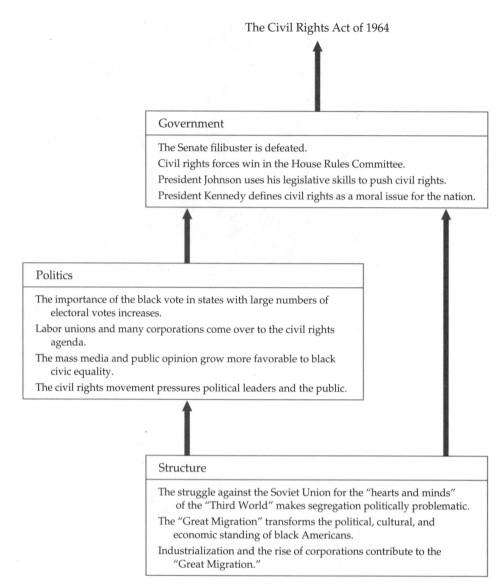

The Civil Rights Act of 1964

Government

The Senate filibuster is defeated.
Civil rights forces win in the House Rules Committee.
President Johnson uses his legislative skills to push civil rights.
President Kennedy defines civil rights as a moral issue for the nation.

Politics

The importance of the black vote in states with large numbers of
  electoral votes increases.
Labor unions and many corporations come over to the civil rights
  agenda.
The mass media and public opinion grow more favorable to black
  civic equality.
The civil rights movement pressures political leaders and the public.

Structure

The struggle against the Soviet Union for the "hearts and minds"
  of the "Third World" makes segregation politically problematic.
The "Great Migration" transforms the political, cultural, and
  economic standing of black Americans.
Industrialization and the rise of corporations contribute to the
  "Great Migration."

Figure 1.3 Why the 1964 Civil Rights Act happened (read from the bottom)

Often, however, we shall find that the most powerful explanations are located at the structural level—that the lines of influence flow from the structural, to the political, to the governmental level. This is so because it is structural factors, related to the economy, the culture, the population, and so forth, that largely shape the definition of the political agenda, determine the distribution of resources and power in society, and influence the wants and the perceptions of political actors. Without dramatic changes in the economy, black migration, changing cultural perceptions among and about black people, and America's new and important role in the world, for instance, the Civil Rights Acts of 1964 and 1965 would simply never have occurred.

Having provided these analytical tools for understanding American politics, we can now move on to a quite different topic: how to *evaluate* our political life.

DEMOCRACY AS A STANDARD FOR EVALUATING POLITICAL LIFE

As citizens we want to be able not only to understand American political life but also to make some judgments about it, perhaps with an eye to improving things. In order to *evaluate*, however, we need a measuring rod, a standard against which to compare reality. There are many standards that might be used for this purpose. Some standards ask how "good" or "bad" government policies are in terms of our own self-interest: do they help me or hurt me? Other standards ask whether government policies are fair or unfair compared to our own moral beliefs about equality, community, freedom, or justice. Still others focus on whether government policies help or hurt the environment, economic growth, world peace, or American national interests.

Though each of these standards can be used to evaluate what government does (and each will be mentioned at various points in this book), none is suitable as a *general standard*, because each is based on particular personal values about which people strongly disagree. What is needed is a standard based on widely shared values—a standard that seems reasonable, even self-evident, to most people. In our view, the standard that best fits the bill is the ideal of *democracy*.

As political scientists, we try to understand how our political system works, analyzing the *processes* by which government decisions are made. Our standard of evaluation, it follows, should be related to the question of how well or how badly the political process itself works, in terms of the values and preferences of all citizens, and not simply whether or not the resulting policies serve particular

I know of no safe depository of the ultimate powers of society but the people themselves. (Thomas Jefferson)

The people!—the people is a great beast. (Alexander Hamilton)

values that some people favor. We want to be able to make judgments about the political process and, if we find problems, to offer ideas about how to improve it, using criteria most people can support, even if they continue to disagree about particular policies. We believe that most Americans agree that the best way to fashion public policy, the best way to take account of all citizens' preferences, is the democratic way.

In this book, therefore, we will frequently ask: "How democratic is the American political system?" "Which features contribute to, or detract from, democracy?" "How could the system be made more democratic?" In the remainder of this chapter, we will define *democracy*, describe some of its merits, answer some objections to it, and show how the democratic ideal can be used to evaluate American political life.

The Root Meaning of Democracy

Many of our ideas about democracy originated with the ancient Greeks. The Greek roots of the word *democracy* are *demos*, meaning "the people," and *kratein* meaning "to rule." The fundamental meaning of *democracy*, then, is "rule by the people" or, to put it another way, self-government by the *many*, as opposed to the *few* or the *one*. This is similar to Lincoln's definition in his Gettysburg Address: "government of the people, by the people, and for the people."

Most Western philosophers (and rulers) before the eighteenth century were not friendly to the idea of rule by the many. Down through the ages, most political thinkers believed that governing is a difficult art, requiring the greatest sophistication, intelligence, character, and training. It is not something to be left to ordinary people. Most preferred rule by a select *few* (whether an aristocracy, theocracy, or meritocracy) or rule by an enlightened *one* (whether philosopher king, divinely appointed monarch, or military chieftain). In practice, most governments were quite undemocratic.

The idea that ordinary people might rule themselves represents an important departure from such beliefs. The seeds of this idea were first planted in the fifth century B.C. in certain Greek city-states, including Athens and Sparta, where political systems appeared in which "a substantial number of free, adult males were entitled as citizens to participate freely in governing."[9] The idea was further nurtured during the second and third centuries B.C. in republican Rome, where all male citizens elected the consuls, the chief magistrates of the city. The Venetian Republic that dominated the Adriatic region in the fifteenth and early sixteenth centuries served as another example that societies could be self-governing, stable, and prosperous. Proponents of the democratic idea would have these important examples to refer to as they increasingly built the case for democracy, beginning in the eighteenth century.

At the heart of democratic theory is faith in the capacity of ordinary human beings to govern themselves wisely. As the philosopher John Dewey put it,

> The foundation of democracy is faith in the capacities of human nature; faith in human intelligence and in the power of pooled and cooperative experience. It is not belief that these things are complete but that if given a show they will grow and be able to generate progressively the knowledge and wisdom needed to guide collective action.[10]

Also crucial to the concept of democracy is the idea that it is the purpose of a government to serve *all* of its people and that, ultimately, none but the people themselves can be relied upon to know and to act in accord with their own values and interests. Power in any other hands can lead to tyranny.

Direct Versus Representative Democracy

To the ancient Greeks, democracy meant rule by the people exercised *directly* in open assemblies. They believed that democracy implied face-to-face participation by the people in community decision making. For them, the very meaning of the term "citizen" was inseparable from this idea of continuous involvement in the public life of the community. To be a passive observer was to be a noncitizen. To the Greeks, moreover, to be a citizen was the essence of humanness. People were fully human only to the extent that they were part of, and involved in, the life of human community and to the extent that they interacted with other human beings in the public arena.

This idea that democracy means people actively and directly ruling themselves, without intermediaries, representatives, or leaders, has appealed to some more recent thinkers as well, including Thomas Jefferson:

> . . . I would say, purely and simply, [democracy] means a government by citizens in mass, acting directly and personally . . .; and that every other government is more or less republican [i.e., democratic], in proportion as it has in its composition more or less of this ingredient of the direct action of the citizens.[11]

Direct participatory democracy requires, however, that citizens be able regularly to meet together to debate and to decide the issues of the day. Such a thing was possible in fifth century Athens, which was small enough to allow all citizens to gather together in one place. In Athens, moreover, citizens had time to meet and to deliberate, because much of the productive work of society was done by slaves. In the present-day Israeli kibbutz, adult membership is rarely above 350, a number that is easily accommodated in the community's dining hall. Work on kibbutz farms and factories, moreover, is cooperative and shared, as are the jobs of child rearing, meal preparation, laundry, and the like, so that significant time is generated for community activities, including self-government. These cases suggest that direct democracy is possible in small communities with significant leisure time.

As appealing as this form of democracy might be, however, it does not seem possible in societies like the United States, which are large and populous, and where people lack the time necessary for continuous involvement in public meetings.[12] Although Thomas Jefferson advocated "direct action of the citizens" as the ideal form of democracy, he lamented that "such a government is evidently restrained to very narrow limits of space and population."[13] He recognized, as we must, that democracy in large societies must necessarily involve the **representative** principle. Millions of citizens cannot meet in open assembly. By "representative," we mean a system in which the people select others, called "representatives," to act in their place. Though indirect, representative democracy seems to be the only form of democracy possible in large-scale societies, political commentators like Benjamin Barber and Robert Dahl, among others, have argued that the

In the New England town meeting, citizens of local communities gather together to discuss, argue, and decide public issues. This exercise in direct, participatory democracy is facilitated by the small size of the town meeting.

participatory aspects of direct democracy are worth preserving as an ideal and that certain domains of everyday life, like the work place, could be enriched by more direct democratic practices.[14] It is worth pointing out, moreover, that direct democracy can and does flourish in some local communities today. The New England town meeting is the best example.

Fundamental Principles of Representative Democracy

In a large society such as the United States, *democracy* means rule by the people, exercised indirectly through elected representatives. Still, this definition is not sufficiently precise to use as a standard to judge the American political process. We need a more precise measuring rod, which can be provided in terms of three fundamental, interrelated attributes of democracy: *popular sovereignty*, *political equality*, and *political liberty*. A society in which all three flourish, we argue, is a healthy democratic society. A society in which any of the three is absent or impaired falls short of the democratic ideal. Let us see what each of them means.

POPULAR SOVEREIGNTY *Popular sovereignty* means, essentially, that government does what the people want. The ultimate source of all public authority in a democracy is the people. The sovereign people may choose to delegate some of their authority to representatives and officials, but they can reclaim it at any time. If ultimate authority resides, not in the hands of the *many*, but in the hands of the *few* (as in an aristocratic order) or of the *one* (whether a benevolent king or a ruthless dictator), then democracy does not exist.

How can we recognize popular sovereignty when we see it? Four observable conditions are especially important: (1) government policies reflect the popular will; (2) people participate in the political process; (3) high-quality information and debate are available; and (4) the majority rules.

Government Policies Reflect the Popular Will One sign of popular sovereignty is a close correspondence between what government does and what the people want it to do. It is hard to imagine a situation in which the people rule but government officials make policy contrary to the people's wishes.

This raises the issue, however, of the short run versus the long run. Does the democratic ideal require that government always do exactly what the people want, right away, responding to every whim and passing fancy of the people? This question has troubled many democratic theorists, and most have answered that democracy is best served when public officials and representatives respond to what might be called the "deliberative will" of the people: the will of the people arrived at after a period of reflection and discussion with others. We might, then, want to speak of policies reflecting the popular will "in the long run." As we will see in Chapter 5, "Public Opinion," however, this issue is not really as worrisome as it seems, because the American public is not, in fact, subject to whims or delusions; its collective policy preferences tend to be stable, coherent, and sensible.

People Participate in the Political Process   How do we know what the popular will is, and what makes the people's representatives respect it? Widespread participation in politics is a sign and a guarantee that the popular will is both expressed and enforced. Without widespread participation (at least widespread formation of political opinions and expression of those opinions in surveys, public discussion, or by other means), the nature of the popular will can only be guessed at. And without participation, nothing guarantees that officials will respond to the popular will. Widespread popular participation—at least in voting and elections—is necessary in order to ensure that responsive representatives are chosen and that they have continuous incentives to pay attention to the people.

Moreover, popular participation is essential, because the deliberative will of the people can only emerge from a process of reflection and discussion with others. If we interpret democracy as a kind of dialogue among the people and between the people and their leaders, democracy becomes more vital and alive as more and more people join the conversation.[15] Because participation makes for more interested, rational, aware, and public-spirited citizens, it contributes to the formation and the expression of a richer, more rational, and more deliberative popular will.[16]

Because participation is so central to popular sovereignty, we can say that the less political participation there is in a society, the weaker is the democracy. This is particularly true if a society systematically denies some group of citizens the opportunity to participate in politics, as was the case in the Jim Crow South, which largely excluded black people prior to the civil rights movement and the landmark legislation of 1964 and 1965.

High-Quality Information and Debate Are Available   The formation of an authentic popular will requires not only participation by ordinary citizens but also the availability of accurate political information, insightful interpretations, and vigorous debate. These are largely the responsibility of government officials, opposition parties, opinion leaders, and the mass media. If false or biased information is provided, if policies are not challenged and debated, or if misleading interpretations about the political world (or none at all) are offered, then the people cannot form opinions in accord with their values and interests, and popular sovereignty cannot be said to exist.

The Majority Rules   What, exactly, do we mean by the "popular will," or the will of "the people"? How, in other words, can the opinions and preferences of many individual citizens be combined into a single popular will, to reach a single, binding decision? Since unanimity is unlikely (and insistence on unanimous agreement

Some political scientists are concerned that in the age of the "sound bite," complex issues are reduced to mere slogans.

for policy changes would enshrine the status quo), this requires a voting-type *decision rule*. If the actions of government are to respond to all citizens, with each citizen counted equally, the only decision rule that makes sense is majority rule.[17] The only alternative to majority rule is minority rule, which would unacceptably elevate the *few* over the *many*.

In practical terms, what this means is that the popular will, formed in the best circumstances after careful deliberation, is discovered by ascertaining the positions on public issues of the majority of citizens.

The intimate connection between democracy and majority rule has long been noted. Aristotle put it in the following terms in his *Politics*: ". . . but as the people are in the majority, and what they vote is law, it follows that such a state must be a democracy." Abraham Lincoln agreed:

> . . . A majority, held in restraint by constitutional checks, and limitations, . . . is the only true sovereign of a free people. Whoever rejects it, does, of necessity, fly to anarchy or to despotism. Unanimity is impossible; the rule of a minority, as a permanent arrangement, is wholly inadmissible; so that, rejecting the majority principle, anarchy, or despotism in some form, is all that is left.[18]

Many claims have been made for the superiority of majority rule.[19] First, majority rule is the only decision rule that recognizes the intrinsic worth and equality of human beings; any other decision rule puts a minority of one sort or another at the head of the queue and weights the preferences of some people more heavily than others. It is, then, the only popular sovereignty decision rule that is consistent with political equality (discussed below).[20] Second, majority rule maximizes the number of people involved in decision making. This enhances participation, which is important to popular sovereignty. Third, majority rule may be more likely to reach correct decisions, because it relies on "pooled judgments"—

judgments that take into account a broader range of information, opinions, and expertise than any other decision rule. Finally, because more people are involved in making decisions under majority rule arrangements, policies that result from such a process are more likely to be accepted by the people than decisions made in other ways.

POLITICAL EQUALITY   The second fundamental principle of democracy, following popular sovereignty and closely intertwined with it, is political equality.

Imagine, if you will, a society in which one person could cast 100 votes in an election, another 50 votes, and still another 25 votes, while many unlucky folks had only 1 vote each—or none at all. We would surely find such an arrangement a curious one, especially if that society described itself as a democracy. We would react in this way because equality of citizenship has always been central to the democratic ideal. Democracy is a way of making decisions in which each person has one and only one voice. It means that people deliberate about their common problems and concerns as equals. Any other arrangement would violate our belief in the intrinsic worth of the individual and would fail to ensure that government pay equal attention to the values and interests of all citizens.

Popular sovereignty cannot work on any other basis than political equality. Without it, we would have no way in which to accurately gauge or to enforce the popular will.

Most people know this intuitively. Our sense of what is proper is offended, for instance, when some class of people is denied the right to vote in a society that boasts the outer trappings of democracy. The denials of citizenship rights to blacks in present-day South Africa or in the American South before passage of the Voting Rights Act of 1965 are two examples. We count it a victory for democracy when previously excluded groups are enfranchised.

Does democracy require *material* equality, that is, equality of income and wealth? Figures as diverse as Aristotle, Rousseau, and Jefferson all thought so, based on the belief that great inequalities in wealth inevitably turn into political inequality. Political scientist Robert Dahl describes the problem in the following way:

> Economic resources are to some extent convertible into political resources. If citizens are unequal in economic resources, so are they likely to be unequal in political resources; and political equality will be impossible to achieve. In the extreme case, a minority of rich will possess so much greater political resources than other citizens that they will control the state, dominate the majority of citizens, and empty the democratic process of all content.[21]

In later chapters, we will see a number of specific ways in which money and other resources can be used to gain unequal political influence, through campaign contributions, lobbying, and the like.

The ideal society for the practice of democracy, according to both Aristotle and Jefferson, is one with a large middle class built on a wide dispersion of private property, without an arrogant and overbearing wealthy class, and without a discontented and dangerous poverty-stricken class. Concerning this point, Jefferson once suggested that while "an equal division of property is impractical . . . legislators cannot invent too many devices for subdividing property."[22] We leave it to you to judge the reasonableness of such a seemingly radical view, and to determine how much income and wealth inequality is acceptable in a democracy.

POLITICAL LIBERTY   Our third basic element of democracy is political liberty. Political liberty refers to certain basic freedoms that are essential to the formation and expression of the popular will and to its translation into policy. These essential liberties include the freedoms of speech, of conscience, of the press, and of assembly and association, which are embodied in the First Amendment to the U.S. Constitution.

Without these liberties (and a few more, including freedom from arbitrary arrest and the right to run for public office), the other fundamental principles of democracy could not stand. Popular sovereignty cannot be guaranteed if people are prevented from participating in politics or if opposition to the government is crushed. Popular sovereignty cannot prevail if the voice of the people is silenced, if citizens are not free to argue and debate, and to form and express their political opinions. Political equality is violated if some people but not others can speak out.

For most people in the United States or abroad, democracy and liberty are inseparable. The concept of "self-government" implies not only the right to vote and to run for public office but also the right to speak one's mind, to petition the government, and to join with others in political parties, interest groups, or social movements. The democratic uprising that swept through Eastern Europe during the early 1990s, to take an example, generated demands not only for elected governments but also for an environment of political freedom that would make such elections meaningful.

Since popular sovereignty rests on the formation and the transmission of the popular will, it requires political liberty. For informed popular preferences to be transmitted to government, means must exist by which new opinions can be formed as conditions, needs, and tastes in society change. To form such opinions, people must enjoy an unrestricted opportunity to argue, deliberate, persuade, propose, and decide without fear. Without the freedom and opportunity to do these things, old ideas would become rigid and incipient ideas would die stillborn. Without political freedom, people would be unable to persuade others to change their minds, and society would be unable to learn and adapt. Political liberty is a necessary condition of popular sovereignty in a representative democracy. It is required if people are to govern themselves.[23]

Over the years, a number of political philosophers and practitioners have viewed liberty as *threatened* by democracy, rather than as essential to it. We will have more to say about this later, when we consider several possible objections to democracy. But it is our position that self-government and political liberty are inseparable, in the sense that the former is impossible without the latter. It follows that a majority cannot deprive an individual or a minority of its political liberty without violating democracy itself.

Possible Objections to Democracy and Majority Rule

Having described some of the virtues of majority rule democracy, we must acknowledge that it is not perfect. There is no guarantee, for instance, that democracy will always lead to good decisions. A majority, like a minority, can be unwise; it can be cruel and uncaring; it can get carried away by fads and fashions; and it can be misled by unscrupulous or incompetent leaders.

Democratic theorist Robert Dahl points out, however, that no convincing evidence can be produced to show that any other form of decision making is devoid of the same problems or consistently leads to better and wiser decisions.[24] The historical record on the results of rule by aristocrats, kings, princes, civil servants, or experts is not encouraging. Given its many other virtues, we would probably do best to stick with majority rule, despite its faults.

More serious, perhaps, than the absence of guarantees that a majority will make good decisions are a number of objections to majority rule that focus on its possible threat to minorities and to liberties, the purported incompetence of the people, and the problem of intense preferences. Let's look at each.

DOES "MAJORITY TYRANNY" THREATEN LIBERTY? James Madison and other founders of the American republic feared that majority rule would undermine freedom and would threaten the "inalienable rights" of the individual. They translated this fear into a constitutional plan that tried to moderate the influence of the majority with such features as indirect elections, the separation of powers, and checks and balances (see Chapter 2 for a full discussion of these issues).

The fears of the Founders were not without foundation. The popular "passions" (as they put it) have sometimes stifled the freedoms of groups and individuals who have dared to be different. Until quite recently, for instance, a majority of Americans were unwilling to allow atheists or Communists the same rights of free speech as they allowed others. Conscientious objectors were harshly treated during World Wars I and II. College and professional athletes who felt uncomfortable about wearing American flags on their uniforms during the Persian Gulf War found it wise to keep their views to themselves after a Seton Hall basketball player was driven off his team by hostile fans for refusing to go along with the swelling patriotic mood of the time.

Nevertheless, without discounting the importance of examples of majority tyranny during our history, there is simply no substantial evidence that the *many* consistently threaten liberty more than the *few* or the *one*; or, to put it another way, the majority does not seem to be a special or unique threat to liberty. Violations of freedom, unfortunately, have many sources and seem as likely to come from minorities (especially from powerful individuals and groups or from government officials) as from the majority.

In three periods of our own history, liberty was especially endangered. In the late 1790s, criticism of public officials was made a crime under the Alien and Sedition Acts. After World War I, a "Red Scare" swept the nation, highlighted by the infamous antiradical, antiimmigrant, and antiunion raids of Attorney General Palmer. In the late 1940s and early 1950s, another "Red Scare," conventionally known as "McCarthyism," was unleashed. The first two assaults on liberty were initiated by high government officials who acted without any discernible sign of majority pressure to do so. The third, while eventually supported by the majority, at least for a short time, may have been initiated by conservative political elites in an effort to discredit and to roll back the liberal New Deal.[25]

Liberty is essential to self-government, and threats to liberty, whatever their origin, must be guarded against by those who love democracy. We must remain concerned about research findings that show lower support for civil liberties among the mass public than among elites.[26] We must continue to worry about occasional outbreaks of intolerance for, and ill treatment of, dissenters by the majority. But we must firmly reject the view that majority rule inevitably or uniquely threatens liberty. The two, in our view, are inseparable.

Senator Joseph McCarthy of Wisconsin issues a warning about the "red tide" of communism sweeping the nation. McCarthy uncovered few communists, but managed to wreck the lives of many innocent people, and helped create an atmosphere that threatened liberty in the United States for many years.

ARE THE PEOPLE IRRATIONAL AND INCOMPETENT?   Political scientists and others have spent decades studying the attitudes and behavior of citizens in the United States, and some of the findings are not encouraging. For the most part, the evidence shows that individual Americans do not care a great deal about politics and are rather poorly informed, unstable in their views, and not much interested in participating in the political process. These findings have led some observers to assert that citizens are ill-equipped for the responsibility of self-governance and that public opinion (i.e., the will of the majority) should not be the ultimate determinant of what government does.[27]

In Chapter 5, "Public Opinion," we will see, however, that this evidence about individuals often has been misinterpreted and that the American public as a *collective* body is more informed, sophisticated, and stable in its views than it is generally given credit for.

DO DEMOCRACY AND MAJORITY RULE THREATEN MINORITIES?   One of the most familiar objections to majority rule is the purported threat that majorities pose to the rights of minorities. The worry is that unbridled majority rule leaves no room for the claims of minorities. This worry has solid historical foundations, for majorities, both here and elsewhere, have trampled on the rights of minorities with depressing frequency. Majority opinion in the United States, for instance, probably once held that "the only good Indian is a dead Indian." Majorities long held that black Americans were inferior to whites and undeserving of full citizenship rights. Asian, Eastern European, and Latin American immigrants to our shores have all been subjected to periods of intolerance on the part of majorities.

Even acknowledging these grievous examples, however, it may be that the threat of majority tyranny is exaggerated. As Robert Dahl points out, there is no evidence to support the belief that minority rights are better protected under alternative forms of political decision making, whether rule by the few or by the one.[28]

Moreover, it is not clear that a minority can ever feel entirely secure unless it has full power of decision over all matters that directly or indirectly affect it. In extreme cases this may require (and justify) formation of a separate, independent country. But within a single nation like the United States, any broad minority power would raise the specter of minority tyranny, which is certainly not preferable to majority rule.

In any case, democracy, as we have defined it, itself requires the protection of crucial minority rights. Recall that majority rule is only one of the defining conditions of popular sovereignty and that popular sovereignty is only one of the three basic attributes of democracy, the others being *political equality* and *political liberty*. The position of minorities is protected in a fully developed democracy, in our view, by the requirements for equal citizenship (the right to vote, to hold public office, to be protected against violence, and to enjoy the equal protection of the law) and access to the full range of civil liberties (speech, press, conscience, and association). To the extent that a majority violates the rights of minorities— to that exact extent—does society fall short of the democratic ideal.

DOES MAJORITY RULE IGNORE INTENSE PREFERENCES?   A final objection to majority rule is that a political system in which each citizen has an equal voice may override the preferences of those citizens who feel most strongly. Those who care the most may know the most about a subject and would presumably benefit the most from a favorable decision. Why not give them an extra voice in decision making? Some "pluralist" scholars have suggested that organized political groups reflect intense preferences and that making decisions by competition and negotiation among organized groups, rather than by simple majority rule, takes intensity into account better.[29]

This line of argument, however, ignores the fact that majority rule itself takes account of the intensity of preferences. For one thing, those in a democracy who feel strongly about something are free to use their time and energy to persuade others. Any superior wisdom can be offered in the marketplace of ideas, where it has a good chance of prevailing. For another thing, people who feel especially

In a democracy, the intensely felt views of minorities can often change the views of the majority. AIDS activists such as these have helped make this important health issue a part of public debate.

strongly about one issue can bargain and compromise with those who care more about some other issue, giving up what matters little to them for the sake of what matters a lot. Majority rule does not merely involve counting heads on each single issue; it also involves assessing the popular will on whole packages of issues considered together. In judging among different packages of policies, each citizen takes special account of those parts of each package that she or he feels most strongly about. Thus, in majority rule choices among packages of policies, individuals' intensity of preferences among *issues* is taken into account.

What majority rule does not do is to count the wishes of some *people* more heavily than those of others on all issues taken as a whole. This, we believe, is quite appropriate. There is no way of knowing whether some people have more intense overall political feelings than others; any effort to judge such a thing by peoples' actions risks encouraging behavior that should be discouraged (throwing bricks through windows, for example, in order to demonstrate "intensity") and risks mistaking differences in resources—money, education, organizational skills, or free time—for differences in how intensely people feel. Even if we could somehow tell that some people have more intense political views than others, it would not necessarily be good to take that into account. To give some people a greater political voice than others, for any reason, violates political equality and is incompatible with democracy as we understand it.

That is one problem with "pluralistic" notions of democracy, which settle for something other than majority rule. They legitimize unequal advantages for people who have the most money, skills, and organizational power. (As we will see in Chapter 7, "Interest Groups," not everyone is equally represented by political organizations.) Moreover, conceptions of democracy that fall short of majority rule tend to lose their usefulness as ideal standards, because they can be used to rationalize almost anything as "democratic." If a standard can be met by practically any reality, it provides little critical leverage and little inspiration for improvement. Our strict standard of majoritarian democracy, which insists upon political equality, makes it easy to assess whether or not particular aspects of American politics fall short of the ideal and should be improved.

Democracy as an Evaluative Standard

After this discussion, it should be easy to see how and why the democratic ideal can be used as a measuring rod to evaluate American politics. It is important to remember, of course, that democracy is not the only available measuring rod. Each of us has a set of values or cherished goals by which we can also judge government policies: efficiency, community, national strength, law and order, equality, and more. The advantage of using democracy as the main evaluative standard in this book derives from its peculiar relevance for judging the adequacy of the political *process* and from its exalted position among the values held by most Americans.

We have learned that the fundamental attributes of democracy are popular sovereignty, political equality, and political liberty. Each suggests a set of questions that we will use throughout this book to evaluate American political life.

POPULAR SOVEREIGNTY   Does government, in the long run at least, do what citizens want it to do? Does government policy reflect deliberative public opinion? (See Chapter 5, "Public Opinion.") Are citizens involved in the processes by which public policy is fashioned? (See Chapter 9, "Voting and Elections.") Are political institutions, such as political parties, elections, interest groups, and social movements, effective in transmitting citizens' preferences in an accurate and unbiased manner to political leaders? (See Chapters 7, 8, 9, and 10 on those institutions.) What is the quality of the dialogue by which citizen preferences on public issues are formed? Do the media and political leaders provide accurate and complete information? (See Chapter 6, "The Mass Media.")

POLITICAL EQUALITY Do some individuals and groups have persistent and substantial advantages over other individuals and groups in the political process? Or is the political game open to all on a relatively equal basis?

POLITICAL LIBERTY Are citizens' rights and liberties universally available, protected, and used? (See Chapter 19, "Rights and Liberties.") Are people free to vote? Can they speak freely and freely form groups to petition their government? Do public authorities, private groups, or the majority threaten liberty?

The questions we have raised will help us assess where we are and where we are going as a democracy. We do not believe that popular sovereignty, political equality, and political liberty are attainable in perfect form. They are, rather, ideals to which our nation can aspire and standards against which we can measure reality. They can help us identify where democracy may be in jeopardy or where it is becoming more vigorous.

SUMMARY

The purpose of the chapter has been to provide you with some analytical and evaluative tools to better understand and evaluate American politics.

To *analyze* is to make sense of the confusing details of everyday events and to see *why* things happen the way they do. To analyze properly, it is important to have a simplified framework or conceptual scheme of the way the world works, in order to help sort the endless facts into coherent patterns. The framework presented in this book visualizes the world of American politics as a set of interrelated *actors* and *influences*—institutions, groups, and individuals—that operate on three interconnected levels: the *structural*, the *political*, and the *governmental*. This framework was used to help account for the passage of the Civil Rights Acts of 1964 and 1965 and for the collapse of legally enforced racial segregation, showing how actions at the governmental level (the actions of institutions and public officials, such as presidents and members of Congress) were shaped by political-level actors (social movements, public opinion, and interest groups) and how the actions of both governmental and political actors were in turn shaped by developments at the structural level (in the U.S. economy, population, and culture, and in the international system). This way of looking at American political life as an ordered, interconnected whole will be used throughout the remainder of the book.

In order to *evaluate*, it is essential that we have some standard by which to compare how our political system is functioning with how we think it *ought* to function. We suggested in this chapter that democracy, understood as popular sovereignty, political equality, and political liberty, provides an excellent standard for this purpose. While there are other ways in which we can evaluate our political life (for we value other things besides democracy), it remains true that democracy holds a very special place in our pantheon of values and is particularly relevant to judging political processes. For this reason, democracy will serve as the main standard of evaluation to be used throughout this book.

To Ponder

1. Are democratic societies more stable in the long run than other forms of government? Are they more just? Are they more efficient? Why?

2. Is democratic decision making with widespread popular participation a luxury we cannot afford in the nuclear age?

3. Are there ways to incorporate some aspects of direct, participatory democracy into American society? Would this be a good thing? Why?

4. Where do individual rights and freedoms come from? How can we tell the difference between a fundamental "right" and a simple want or desire?

Suggested Readings

Alford, Robert, and Roger Friedland. *Powers of Theory*. Cambridge, MA: Cambridge University Press, 1985.
> A detailed survey of the leading models and theoretical approaches to the understanding of society, economy, and state.

Barber, Benjamin. *Strong Democracy*: Participatory Democracy for a New Age. Berkeley: University of California Press, 1984.
> The case for direct, participatory democracy by a leading contemporary political theorist.

Dahl, Robert A. *A Preface to Democratic Theory*. Chicago: University of Chicago Press, 1956.
> The classic statement of the "pluralist" conception of democracy, criticizing pure majority rule.

————. *Democracy and Its Critics*. New Haven, CT: Yale Unversity Press, 1989.
> A sweeping defense of democracy against its critics by one of the most brilliant political theorists of our time.

Held, David. *Models of Democracy*. Stanford, CA: Stanford University Press, 1987.
> A highly accessible review of many possible meanings of democracy.

Spitz, Elaine. *Majority Rule*. Chatham, NJ: Chatham House, 1984.
> A provocative and richly detailed defense of majority rule democracy.

Notes

1. Daisy Bates, *The Long Shadow of Little Rock* (New York: David McKay, 1962), pp. 69–70.
2. "Voting in Mississippi: A Report of the U.S. Civil Rights Commission," Washington, D.C., 1965.
3. "Negro Registration in the South Has Increased Dramatically," *New York Times* (May 15, 1966), p. 1.
4. *Ibid.*
5. Harold Stanley and Richard Niemi, *Vital Statistics in American Politics* (Washington, D.C.: Congressional Quarterly Press, 1990), p. 365.
6. Richard Polenberg, *One Nation Divisible: Class, Race, and Ethnicity in the United States Since 1938* (New York: Penguin, 1980), p. 180.
7. See Robert Alford and Roger Friedland, *Powers of Theory* (Cambridge, MA: Cambridge University Press, 1985); Martin Carnoy, *The State and Political Theory* (Princeton, NJ: Princeton University Press, 1984).
8. William Brink and Louis Harris, *The Negro Revolution in America* (New York: Simon & Schuster, 1964), p. 46.
9. Robert A. Dahl, *Democracy and Its Critics* (New Haven, CT: Yale University Press, 1989), p. 13.

10. John Dewey, *The Public and Its Problems* (New York: Holt, 1927), p. 211.

11. From "To John Taylor," May 28, 1816, John Dewey, ed., *The Living Thoughts of Thomas Jefferson* (New York: Longmans, Green, and Co., 1940).

12. See Robert A. Dahl, *After the Revolution: Authority in the Good Society* (New Haven, CT: Yale University Press, 1970). Jane Mansbridge, *Beyond Adversary Democracy* (New York: Basic Books, 1980) emphasizes the relevance not only of size but also of the homogeneity or heterogeneity of interests within a polity.

13. From "To John Taylor."

14. See Benjamin Barber, *Strong Democracy: Participatory Democracy for a New Age* (Berkeley: University of California Press, 1984); Peter Bachrach, *The Theory of Democratic Elitism* (Boston: Little, Brown, 1967); Robert A. Dahl, *A Preface to Economic Democracy* (Berkeley: Unversity of California Press, 1985); C. B. MacPherson, *Democratic Theory: Essays in Retrieval* (Oxford: Clarendon, 1973); and Carole Pateman, *Participation and Democratic Theory* (London: Cambridge University Press, 1970).

15. Barber, *Strong Democracy*; Joshua Cohen, "Deliberation and Democratic Legitimacy," in Alan Hamlin and Phillip Pettit, eds., *The Good Polity* (London: Blackwell, 1989); and Mansbridge, *Beyond Adversary Democracy.*

16. Gabriel Almond and Sidney Verba, *The Civic Culture* (Boston: Little, Brown, 1965); Max Eldin, "Political Efficacy at Work: The Connection Between More Autonomous Forms of Workplace Organization and a More Participatory Politics," *American Political Science Review*, Vol. 75 (1981); Edward S. Greenberg, *Workplace Democracy* (Ithaca, NY: Cornell University Press, 1986); Ronald M. Mason, *Participation and Workplace Democracy* (Carbondale: Southern Illinois Unversity Press, 1965); and Carole Pateman, *Participation and Democratic Theory.*

17. Kenneth Arrow, *Social Choice and Individual Values* (New York: Wiley, 1951) shows that neither majority rule nor any other decision rule satisfying certain attractive conditions can be guaranteed to produce a single definite outcome under all circumstances. We cannot be sure how often it will actually do so. But Kenneth May, "A Set of Independent, Necessary, and Sufficient Conditions for Simple Majority Decision," *Econometrica*, Vol. 20 (1952), pp. 680–684, shows that *only* majority rule can guarantee popular sovereignty, political equality, and neutrality among policy alternatives. See also Douglas W. Rae, "Decision Rules and Individual Values in Constitutional Choice," *American Political Science Review*, Vol. 63 (1969), pp. 40–53; and Phillip D. Straffin, Jr., "Majority Rule and General Decision Rules," *Theory and Decision*, Vol. 8 (1977), pp. 351–360.

18. From the first Inaugural Address.

19. Dahl, *Democracy and Its Critics*, ch. 10.

20. See May, "A Set of Independent, Necessary, and Sufficient Conditions."

21. Dahl, *Preface to Economic Democracy*, p. 68.

22. Quoted in Richard Schlatter, *Private Property: The History of an Idea* (New Brunswick, NJ: Rutgers University Press, 1951), p. 196.

23. Robert Dahl, "On Removing Certain Impediments to Democracy in the United States," *Political Science Quarterly*, Vol. 92, no. 1 (Spring 1977), p. 14; Elaine Spitz, *Majority Rule*, (Chatham, NJ: Chatham House, 1984), p. 83; Dahl, *Democracy and Its Critics*, p. 170.

24. Dahl, *Democracy and Its Critics*, p. 156.

25. David Caute, *The Great Fear* (New York: Simon & Schuster, 1978); Victor Navasky, *Naming Names* (New York: Viking, 1980); Michael Rogin, *The Intellectuals and McCarthy* (Cambridge: MIT Press, 1967).

26. See Bernard Berelson, Paul F. Lazarsfeld, and William McPhee, *Voting* (Chicago: University of Chicago Press, 1954); V. O. Key, *Public Opinion and American Democracy* (New York: Knopf, 1961); and Herbert McClosky and Alida Brill, *Dimensions of Tolerance* (New York: Russell Sage, 1983). But see, in rebuttal, James L. Gibson, "Political Intolerance and Political Repression During the McCarthy Red Scare," *American Political Science Review*, Vol. 82 (1988), pp. 511–529.

27. Walter Lippmann, *The Phantom Public* (New York: Macmillan, 1925).

28. Dahl, *Democracy and Its Critics*, p. 161.

29. David Truman, *The Governmental Process* (New York: Knopf, 1951); Robert Dahl, *Who Governs* (New Haven, CT: Yale University Press, 1961).

PART II

Structure

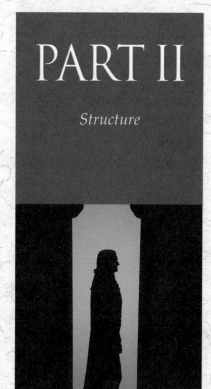

The chapters in Part II focus on structural influences on American politics. Structural influences are enduring features of American society that play a substantial role in determining what issues become important, how political power is distributed in the population, what perceptions guide the behavior of citizens and public officials, and how political and governmental institutions operate. We made the point in Part I that what government does can only be understood within the structural context within which government institutions operate. This section is about that structural context.

The constitutional rules-of-the-game are a particularly important part of the structural context of American political life. These rules, how they were first formulated and how they have changed over the years, is the subject matter of two chapters in this part. Chapter 2 tells the story of the Constitution, why a constitutional convention was convened in Philadelphia in the summer of 1787, what the Founders intended to accomplish at the convention, and how specific provisions of the document have shaped our political life since the founding. The main focus is on provisions like the separation of powers, checks and balances, and federalism, that were designed to encourage popular consent and to discourage tyranny, particularly the tyranny of the majority. Chapter 3 looks at federalism in considerable detail and examines how it has changed over the years. Both chapters explore the relationship of the constitutional rules and the practice of democracy in the United States.

The basic characteristics of society also influence how political and governmental institutions and processes work. To understand politics and government, we first need to know what kinds of individuals, groups, and classes populate the United States, and why they have certain beliefs, concerns, and interests. We also need to know why some have the resources to gain a hearing from public officials while others do not; why citizens and officials worry about certain problems and not others; and why some government programs seem appropriate but not others. Chapter 4 examines these issues, looking in detail at the American economy, the American population, the political culture, and our place in the world. Together, the chapters in this part of the book serve to show the structural underpinnings of American political life and set the stage for all the chapters that follow.

2

*The Making
of the
Constitution*

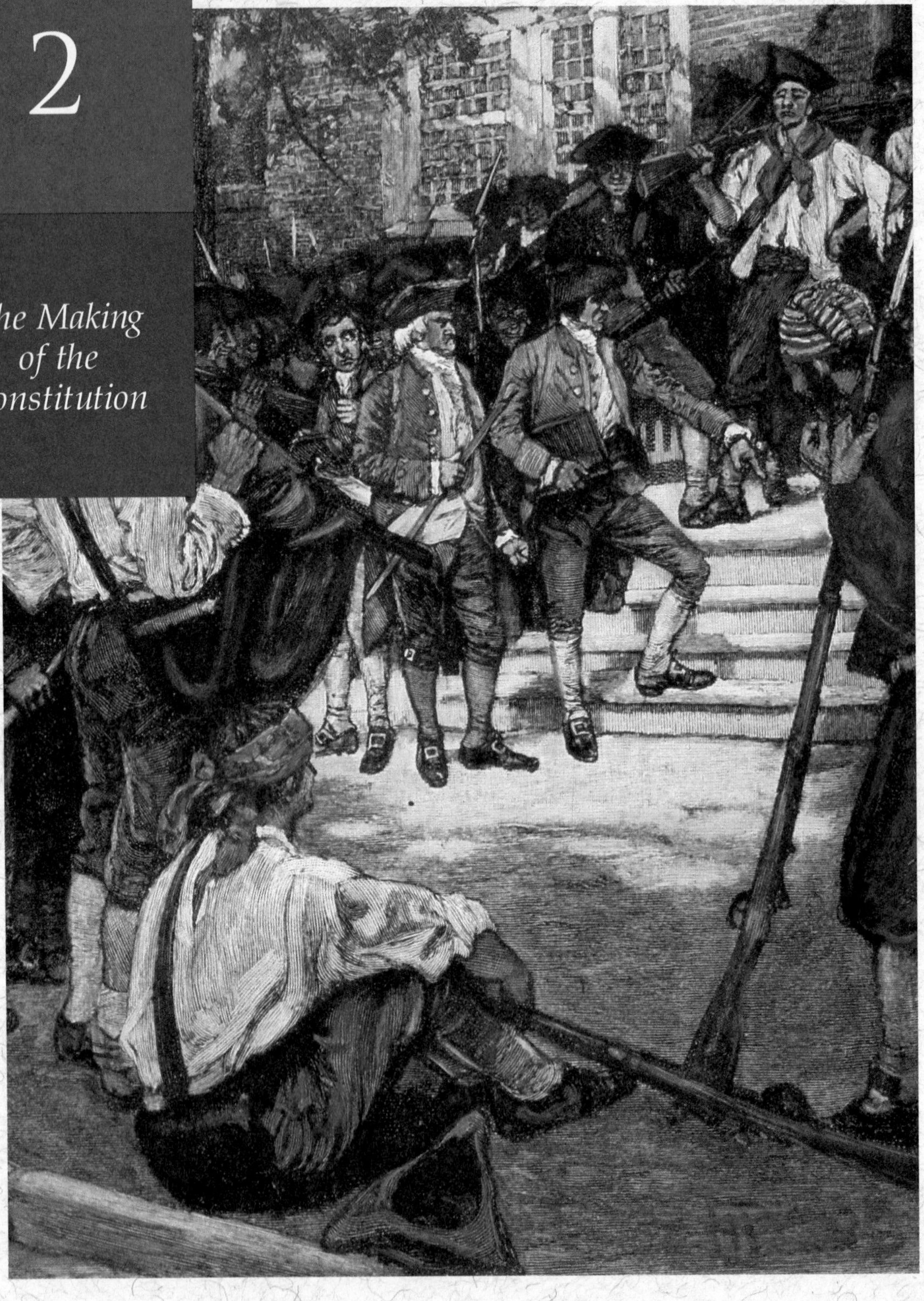

SHAYS'S REBELLION

Artemas Ward, commander of the American forces at Bunker Hill and a Revolutionary War hero, could not convince the crowd of several hundred armed farmers to allow him to enter the courthouse. He spoke to the farmers for almost two hours, alternately pleading and threatening, but to no avail. His demands that the armed guards be removed from the doors were met with jeers and chants of "adjourn without delay." Though most admired him as a military leader, they were determined that he not hold court that day in September 1786, for his purpose as a state judge was to preside over farm foreclosure proceedings. He left Worcester in a fury, unable to convince the militia to come to his assistance, and carried word of the rebellion to Boston.[1] Other judges trying to hold court in western Massachusetts in the summer and fall of 1786 had no better luck.

The farmers of western Massachusetts were probably not a rebellious lot by nature, but desperate times pushed many of them to desperate actions. All over the new nation, the end of the Revolutionary War brought economic readjustment, the collapse of prices for agricultural products, and widespread economic distress and poverty among farmers. Poor farmers sought relief from their troubles from state governments, and, for the most part, political leaders responded. Several states lent money (in the form of script, or paper money) to farmers to pay their taxes and debts. Other states passed **"stay" laws**, postponing tax and mortgage payments.

In Massachusetts, however, the state legislature, dominated by financial and merchant interests located primarily in Boston, blocked all relief measures for poor farmers. Worse yet, the legislature and the governor decided that all state debts were to be paid off in full in order to establish the creditworthiness of the state. The state's debt, accumulated to pay the costs of the Revolutionary War, was primarily owed to a handful of the wealthiest citizens of the state who had bought up outstanding notes for pennies on the dollar. To make good on this debt, the legislature levied heavy taxes that fell disproportionately on farmers, especially those in the western part of the state. When taxes could not be paid, which was distressingly common, monies could only be raised by the state through foreclosure proceedings: the public sale of farmers' lands, buildings, and livestock. Tax foreclosures and jailing for debt (under draconian prison conditions, in Northampton, the cells in the debtors prison were not even 4 feet high; in Worcester, the cells were 4 feet by 11 feet and were without light, heat, or ventilation[2]) became quite frequent in Massachusetts during this period. It was in response to these conditions that many western Massachusetts farmers took up arms to prevent courts from sitting.

By September 1786, Governor James Bowdoin had seen enough. He issued a proclamation against unlawful assembly and called out the militia to enforce it. Six hundred soldiers were sent to Springfield to ensure that the state supreme court could meet and issue the expected indictments against the leaders of the insurrection. They were met there by five or six hundred armed farmers led by a former Revolutionary War officer, Captain Daniel Shays. After a long standoff, the militia withdrew, leaving the rebels in charge and the court unable to meet.

These events only hardened the resolve of the governor to break the rebellion. Realizing that the local militia were sympathetic to the plight of their neighbors, the governor organized a special armed force recruited entirely from the counties in and around Boston. This force proved too much for the hastily organized and ill-equipped force under Daniel Shays. By the spring of 1787, the Boston militia had defeated the rebels in two pitched battles—one at Springfield and the other at Petersham—and Shays's Rebellion (as it was soon called) was at an end.

Though the insurrection was put down rather handily, most of the nation's leading citizens were alarmed by the apparent inability of the government of the Confederation to maintain public order. Shays's Rebellion realized their worst fears about the dangers of majority rule and the "popular passions" unchecked by a strong government. George Washington worried: "If government cannot check these disorders, what security has a man . . . ?"[3] It was in this climate of crisis that a call was issued for a constitutional convention to meet in Philadelphia in order to correct the flaws in our first constitution. Rather than amend the Articles of Confederation, however, the men who met in Philadelphia in the summer of 1787 wrote an entirely new constitution.

This chapter is about the founding of the United States and the formulation of the constitutional rules-of-the-game that structure American politics today. Significant attention is also paid to conflicts over the meaning of *democracy* and *liberty* in the new nation. We will see that the struggle for democracy has been a feature of political life in the United States from the very beginning.

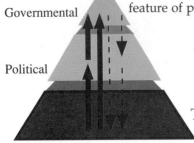

Governmental

Political

Structural

THE AMERICAN REVOLUTION AND THE DECLARATION OF INDEPENDENCE

Initially, the American Revolution was waged more to preserve an existing way of life than to create something new. The colonists wanted to preserve the English constitution and their rights as English subjects.[4] These traditional rights of life, liberty, and property were threatened by British policies on trade and taxation. Revolutions rarely stay on the track planned by their leaders, however. Our own revolution fits this pattern. Though it was sparked by a concern for liberty— understood as the preservation of traditional rights against the intrusions of government—it also stimulated the development of sentiments for popular sovereignty. The tension between these two principles would animate much of American politics for years to come.

The Declaration of Independence

By the time the Second Continental Congress began its session on May 10, 1775, the battles of Lexington and Concord already had been fought. Within a few days of the opening of the session, news of the victory of the Green Mountain boys at Fort Ticonderoga had reached the delegates. In this atmosphere, the Congress set about organizing an army and a navy, sent diplomats to plead the case of the colonies and to seek assistance in the various European capitals, asserted control over Indian affairs on the frontier, and appointed George Washington commander-in-chief of the armed forces. At first, they did not have independence in mind.

Pushed by the logic of armed conflict, the desire to maintain the rights of Englishmen in an empire that seemed uninterested in allowing their enjoyment, the attempt to maintain linkages of affection to a monarch who was loath to return his affection, and the urgings of Thomas Paine (see box), the colonists concluded by the spring of 1776 that separation and independence were inescapable. This sentiment for independence took its first official form when South Carolina adopted its own constitution and declared itself free from British control. The legislature of Virginia followed suit, its delegates boldly proclaiming that "the United Colonies are, and of right ought to be, free and independent States." Spurred by the examples of these two states, the Continental Congress appointed a special committee in early June to draft a declaration of independence.

The committee selected Thomas Jefferson of Virginia to draft the document. With only minor revisions by John Adams and Benjamin Franklin, Jefferson's draft was brought to the floor of the Congress on July 2 and adopted on July 4 without dissent (New York abstained). The declaration was then handwritten on parchment and signed by the delegates on August 2. It is this version that is on display today at the National Archives in Washington, D.C.

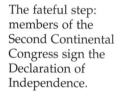

The fateful step: members of the Second Continental Congress sign the Declaration of Independence.

THE STRUGGLE FOR DEMOCRACY

★

Thomas Paine and Common Sense

A remarkable pamphlet by the radical firebrand Thomas Paine helped break the last fragile ties of colonial loyalty to, and affection for, Great Britain. *Common Sense*, published on January 9, 1776 in Philadelphia, was soon reprinted and distributed everywhere in the colonies. Efforts to suppress its sale by British officials failed everywhere. It is, without a doubt, the most successful and widely read political pamphlet in history; conservative estimates put its readership at about 1 million persons, roughly one-half of the adult free population of the colonies. Contemporaries attest to its impact. George Washington observed that "*Common Sense* is working a powerful change in the minds of men" and stopped offering toasts to the king at formal occasions. Reports of converts to the cause of independence and against the institution of monarchy were widespread. One Connecticut man wrote admiringly to Paine that "you have declared the sentiments of millions. . . . We were blind, but on reading these enlightening words the scales have fallen from our eyes."

The appeal of *Common Sense* was twofold. First, Paine brought together fragments of arguments for independence and against the institution of monarchy (and for self-government) that had been circulating since the outbreak of hostilities but that had not yet been spoken aloud clearly, coherently, and forthrightly. Second, and perhaps more important, Paine made these arguments in a direct, down-to-earth language that appealed to the common person rather than to the highly educated person in the colonies and assured a wide readership. An entirely self-educated man, Paine announced, "As it is my design to make those that can scarcely read understood, I shall therefore avoid every literary adornment and put it in language as plain as the alphabet."

Here is some of what he wrote:

On the Institution of Monarchy

(On the accession of William the Conqueror to the throne of England)

A French bastard landing with an armed banditti and establishing himself King of England against the consent of the natives, is in plain terms a very paltry rascally original. . . . The plain truth is that the antiquity of the English monarchy will not bear looking into.

THE POLITICAL THEORY OF THE DECLARATION OF INDEPENDENCE   The ideas in the Declaration of Independence reflected the political culture of that era and remain very much a part of the American political culture today. The principal influence on Jefferson's creation were the writings of the English philosopher John Locke, especially his widely read work *The Second Treatise on Government*. The common ideas in *The Second Treatise* and Jefferson's Declaration are so familiar to us today that we might easily miss their revolutionary import for most of the world when they were first written. In the late eighteenth century, most societies in the world were ruled by "divine right" kings, or hereditary aristocracies, subject to little or no control by their subjects. Locke and Jefferson posed the seemingly outrageous argument that legitimate government could only be established by the

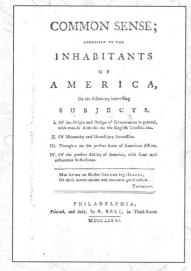

COMMON SENSE;

ADDRESSED TO THE

INHABITANTS

OF

AMERICA,

On the following interesting

SUBJECTS.

I. Of the Origin and Design of Government in general, with concise Remarks on the English Constitution.

II. Of Monarchy and Hereditary Succession.

III. Thoughts on the present State of American Affairs.

IV. Of the present Ability of America, with some miscellaneous Reflections.

Man knows no Master save creating Heaven,
Or those whom choice and common good ordain.
THOMSON.

PHILADELPHIA;
Printed, and Sold, by R. BELL, in Third-Street.
MDCCLXXVI.

(On hereditary rule)

Of more worth is one honest man to society, and in the sight of God, than all the crowned ruffians that ever lived.

One of the strongest natural proofs of the folly of hereditary rights in kings is that nature disproves it, otherwise she would not so frequently turn it into ridicule, by giving mankind *an ass for a lion.*

On the Absurdity of Subordination to Britain

[England] is not the parent country of America because this new world hath been the asylum for the persecuted lovers of civil and religious liberty from every part of Europe.

There is something absurd in supposing a continent to be perpetually governed by an island.

. . . Ye that oppose independence now, ye know not what ye do: ye are opening a door to external tyranny.

I challenge the warmest advocate for conciliation to show a single advantage this continent can reap by being connected with Great Britain . . . no nation in a state of foreign dependence can ever achieve material eminence [or political greatness].

Paine's radical views on the monarchy, the French Revolution, poverty, and religion kept him in hot water with officials in the United States, England, and France, where he lived off and on for the last three decades of his life.

Source: Common Sense; Eric Foner, *Tom Paine and Revolutionary America* (New York: Oxford University Press, 1976), pp. 76–79; and Page Smith, *A New Age Now Begins: A People's History of the American Revolution* (New York: McGraw-Hill, 1976), pp. 679-683.

people and governed with their consent. These ideas sparked a very responsive chord among peoples everywhere when they were first presented, and they remain extremely popular all over the world today, more than 200 years later. The argument is as follows.

- Human beings possess rights that cannot be legitimately given away or taken from them:

  We hold these truths to be self-evident, that all men are created equal, that they are endowed by their Creator with certain unalienable Rights, that among these are Life, Liberty, and the Pursuit of Happiness.

- People create government to protect these rights:

   That to secure these rights, Governments are instituted among Men, deriving their just powers from the consent of the governed.

- If government fails to protect rights or itself becomes a threat to rights, people can withdraw their consent from the government and create a new one of their own choosing:

   That whenever any Form of Government becomes destructive of these ends, it is the Right of the People to alter or to abolish it, and to institute new Government, laying its foundation on such principles, and organizing its powers in such form, as to them shall seem most likely to effect their Safety and Happiness.

The Declaration of Independence left much unsettled, however. After the clause on slavery was removed from the section on grievances at the insistence of the southern colonies, for instance, the issue was not addressed again, leaving the status of this institution strangely uncertain in a new nation founded on the principle that "all men are created equal." Also left for later action was the question of whether the colonies were declaring for independence as a single new nation or as 13 separate nations.

The Political Theory and Practice of the Revolutionary Era

The Continental Congress took a practical step toward independence by passing a resolution advising each colony to adopt a new government free from royal control. The resolution suggested that "the exercise of every kind of authority under the . . . Crown should be totally suppressed" and that "all the powers of government [be placed] under the authority of the people of the colonies."[5] Spurred by the outbreak of hostilities, the upsurge in sentiment for independence, and the Declaration itself, revolutionary conventions in 11 of the 13 colonies created new governments by the end of the war in 1783.

Interestingly, each state began with a *written* constitution. The English constitution was then, and remains today, an unwritten one. The colonists believed that written constitutions better embody the compact reached between free people to form a government, a view first expressed in the signing of the Mayflower Compact by the Massachusetts Bay colonists in 1620. Written constitutions that spell out the organization of government and the rights to be guaranteed by government, it was believed, were the best safeguard against misunderstandings and transgressions, much like a contract in the business world. Written constitutions, by specifying the forms of representative government, by strictly limiting its powers, and by organizing a system of law that made clear the rules for governors and the governed alike, were thought to be the best protection for liberty.

The provisions in these new constitutions tell us a great deal about the political ideas that prevailed during this period.

- *Bills of Rights.* Most of the state constitutions, following Virginia's lead in June 1776, included bills of rights: a listing of those rights that could not be violated by government, even one based on popular consent.

- *Restrictions on the powers of the executive.* It was widely believed that all rulers are tempted by the attractions of power and are prone to tyranny. As one delegate to the Delaware constitutional convention put it, "the executive power is ever restless, ambitious, and ever grasping at increase of power."[6] What was wanted was a manager or an administrator rather than a ruler—one who would execute the policies of the legislative body and one who was without independent power. The states took various steps to put this sentiment into action: election of the executive by the legislature; limitations on terms of office (in nine states, the term was for a single year; in seven, limits were placed on the number of times the governor could be reelected); limitations on the power to make appointments; denial of veto power over legislative action; restrictions on the governor's role in the budget process; and more.

- *Legislative supremacy.* The new state constitutions sought to make the legislature supreme and to protect it from the intrusions of the executive. Most of the state constitutions gave a broad range of powers to the legislative branch, including many that traditionally had been the prerogative of the executive in Britain: for example, declaring war and peace, granting pardons, and conducting foreign policy.

- *Frequent elections.* The new state constitutions were also notable for requiring frequent elections. Apparently agreeing with John Locke that even an elected legislature can become tyrannical if its members remain in office too long without need to place themselves before the judgment of the people, most of the states required annual elections for their lower Houses and short legislative sessions.

- *Limited suffrage.* While the new state constitutions were far more democratic than anything else then existing in the world, the retention of property qualifications for voting and office holding made these constitutions less democratic than we expect today. Large numbers of white males (roughly 30 to 40 percent)[7] were excluded from political life in the states because they did not own the requisite amount of land (25 settled acres or 500 unsettled acres in Virginia, for instance), could not afford to pay the poll tax, or did not pay the minimum level of property tax. Women were also excluded from voting and office holding, as were slaves, and most "free blacks" (blacks who were not slaves). The terms "the people" and "popular consent," then, implied a much narrower conception of "people" and "popular" than we hold today.

THE ARTICLES OF CONFEDERATION: THE FIRST CONSTITUTION

The Founders almost certainly did not envision the creation of a single, unified nation as the goal of the Revolution. At most, the members of the Continental Congress and political leaders in the states envisioned a loose **confederation** between the states, with each state retaining most of its powers and independence. This should not be surprising. The prevailing view of the time was that a government based on popular consent and committed to the protection of individual rights was only possible in small, homogeneous republics where government was close to the people and where fundamental conflicts of interest among the people did not exist. Given the great variation among the colonies in terms of ways of life and economic interests, and given the great geographical expanse of the colonies, a single unified republic seemed out of the question.

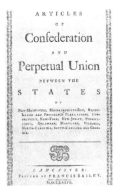

The Articles of Confederation was the first constitution of the United States. It formed a loose confederation of largely independent states, with very little power in the central government.

Provisions of the Articles

In light of these sentiments, it's hardly surprising that our first constitution created a nation that was not a nation at all, but rather a loose confederation of states. A draft of this first constitution, known as the Articles of Confederation, was introduced in the Continental Congress only a week after the adoption of the Declaration of Independence on July 4, 1776. Its principal author was John Dickinson of Pennsylvania. Congress was apparently in no rush to act, taking over a year to adopt Dickinson's handiwork. The Articles were not approved by the states (unanimity of all the states was required for adoption) until 1781, for the states were loath to give up very many of their independent powers, even to this new confederation, which the Articles referred to as a "league of friendship."

The Articles created in law what had existed in practice from the time of the Declaration of Independence: a loose confederation of independent states, with little power in the central government, where most of the decisions about the issues of the day took place in the state legislatures (see Figure 2.1). Like the member states of the United Nations today, each state jealously guarded and exercised its independence during the war, while the Continental Congress tried to coordinate their efforts. As historian Gordon Wood describes it,

Figure 2.1 The Articles of Confederation

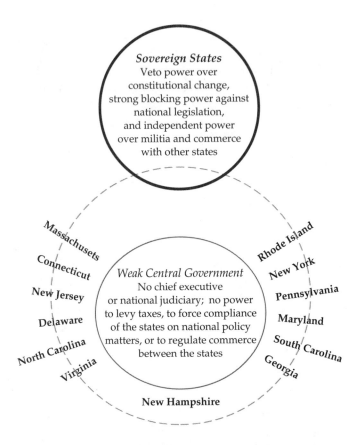

the states not only jealously guarded their independence and sovereignty by repeated assertions and declarations, but in fact assumed the powers of a sovereign state ... making war, providing for armies, laying embargoes, even in some cases carrying on separate diplomatic correspondence and negotiations abroad.[8]

If the objective was to preserve the independence of the separate states, then the provisions of the Articles accomplished their objective. While there was a central government of sorts—there was a Congress, for instance—it had little to do and had virtually no power. It could make war or peace, but it had no power to levy taxes (even customs duties) to pursue either goal. It could not regulate commerce between the states or deny states the right to collect customs duties. It had no independent chief executive to ensure that the laws passed by Congress were enforced, nor a national judiciary to adjudicate disputes between the states. Legislating in the few areas of responsibility assigned to the central government—to establish a postal service, to set uniform standards of weights and measures, and to manage affairs with the Indians—was almost impossible in light of the rule that all congressional legislation had to be approved by 9 of the 13 states. Finally, any defects in the new constitution were difficult to remedy in light of the provision that amendment of the Articles required the unanimous approval of the states.

Unsolved Problems

The Articles did what their authors wanted them to do: preserve the power, independence, and sovereignty of the states, and ensure that the central government did not encroach on the liberty of the people. Unfortunately, there were also many problems that the confederation was ill-equipped to handle.

There was, in the first place, the problem of the debt. The central government relied upon the states to comply voluntarily with its annual tax assessment (based on the value of property in each of the states). The states were not eager to cooperate, many paying less than 10 percent of what was owed. As a result, the bonds and notes of the confederate government—which, for the most part, were for debts incurred during the war—became almost worthless (giving rise to the saying "not worth a Continental"), and the government's ability to increase its borrowing was stymied.

There was also the government's inability to defend American interests in foreign affairs. Without a chief executive, with veto power in the hands of the states, and devoid of a standing military, the confederation lacked the capacity to reach binding agreements with other nations or to deal with a wide range of problems that originated outside the borders of the new nation. These problems included the continuing presence of British troops in western lands ceded to the new nation by the Treaty of Paris that ended the Revolutionary War, violent clashes with the Indians on the western frontier, and piracy on the high seas.

Finally, the government was unable to prevent the outbreak of commercial warfare between the states. Being virtually independent states, with the power to levy customs duties, many states became intense commercial rivals of their neighbors and sought to gain every advantage that they could against the products of other states. New York and New Jersey, for instance, imposed high tariffs on goods that crossed their borders from other states. Such a state of affairs worked against the development of stable regional and national markets, considerably slowed the rate of economic growth, and threatened financial chaos.

THE CALLING OF THE CONSTITUTIONAL CONVENTION

It is now conventional wisdom among historians that it was the failures of the Articles of Confederation just described that led most of the leading citizens of the confederation to believe that a new constitution was desperately needed for the fledgling nation. What is left out of many accounts of the convening of the Constitutional Convention in Philadelphia, however, is the story of the growing concern felt by many of the most influential men in the confederation about the democratizing and egalitarian tendencies set loose by the Revolution.

The initial objectives of the American war for independence were freedom of trade and protection of traditional English liberties. War and revolution always demand popular participation and sacrifice, however. People must be willing to pay taxes and to volunteer for the fighting; they must be willing to risk their lives and property. In order to get them to do so, revolutionary leaders tend to describe their struggle in universal terms, applicable to all. In the American Revolution, as in all revolutions, appeals to the people for the defense of freedom and for the spread of the blessings of liberty were often translated by the people to mean their right to better access to the means of government and to the means of livelihood.[9] Almost certainly, the common people were convinced that success would bring substantial improvements in their lives.[10]

This fever for popular participation and greater equality is not what most of the leaders of the American Revolution had in mind. As historian Richard Hofstadter puts it, "as the revolution took away the restraining hand of the British government, old colonial grievances of farmers, debtors, and squatters against merchants, investors, and large landholders had flared up anew; the lower orders took advantage of new democratic constitutions in several states, and the possessing classes were frightened."[11]

Republicanism

The Founders were republicans. (Small "r" republicanism refers here to a theory of government and not to a political party, such as the modern-day Republican party). **Republicanism** is a theory of how nontyrannical governments might be constituted; of how people might organize their political institutions to protect their liberties from the intrusions of kings (the *one*), nobles and aristocrats (the *few*), and even the majority of the people (the *many*). It is a doctrine that believes that governments must be based on *popular consent* (thus rejecting the claims of hereditary rulers), *limited* in its powers (thus protecting liberty), and *inoculated against* the sometimes rash judgments of *the majority* (thus preventing majority tyranny). These objectives may be best attained, in the republican view, by election of representatives by an electorate, based on a restricted suffrage, and by the prevention of the concentration of governmental powers—executive, legislative, and judicial—in a single governing body.

While republicanism was far more democratic than other important political doctrines and practices in the late eighteenth century, it was less democratic than

---

Table 2.1

Comparing Eighteenth Century Republicanism and the Democratic Ideal

Republicanism	Democracy
1. Government based on popular consent	1. Government based on popular consent
2. Indirect rule by the people (representation)	2. Direct or indirect rule by the people, or both
3. The *people* narrowly defined (by education, property holding, social standing)	3. The *people* broadly defined
4. Elected representatives act as "trustees" (act on their own to discover the public good)	4. Elected representatives act as "delegates" (instructed by the people; accurately reflect their wishes)
5. Barriers to majority rule	5. Encouragement of majority rule
6. Government strictly limited in function	6. Government does what the people want it to do
7. Government safeguards rights and liberties, with a special emphasis on property rights	7. Government safeguards rights and liberties, with no special emphasis on property rights

---

we would find acceptable today because of the limitations on the participation of the people that it advocated (see Table 2.1). According to republican doctrine, for instance, the right to vote is restricted to only a part of the adult population, not necessarily a majority. Republican doctrine taught that those eligible for election to office ought to be from that body of men most fit by birth, education, and standing in the community to exercise judgment and wisdom in public affairs. Moreover, representatives were to exercise independent judgment once in office, taking into account the needs and interests of the entire community rather than the simple opinions of the people. This view is captured in the remarks of Jeremy Belknap, one of the delegates to the convention: "Let it stand as a principle that government originates from the people; but let the people be taught . . . that they are not able to govern themselves."[12]

To most of the framers, republicanism and democracy were not identical. The difference is captured in the following observation of one prominent advocate of a new constitution, Fisher Ames:

> A republic is that structure of an elective government, in which the administration necessarily prescribe to themselves the general good as the object of all their measures; a democracy is that, in which the present popular passions, independent of the public good, become a guide to the rulers. In the first, the reason and interests of society govern; in the second, their prejudices and passions.[13]

Republicanism, then, represents a step on the road to democracy, with its belief in popular consent and indirect election of public officials, yet it retained enough aristocratic or elitist features to keep it well short of the democratic ideal. While republicans believed in popular consent, for instance, they envisioned a political order in which a natural elite rules in the general interest. James Madison complained in *The Federalist, No. 62*, for instance, that democratic tendencies in the states were allowing government "to fall into the Hands of those whose ability or situation in Life does not entitle them to it."

Democratizing Tendencies

> [Democracies] have ever been spectacles of turbulence and contention; have ever been found incompatible with personal security or the rights of property; and have in general been as short in their lives as they have been violent in their deaths. (Madison, *The Federalist*, No. 10)

The belief that democracy was on the rise was not unfounded. The Revolution, as we have already suggested, was launched in the name of independence, republicanism, and free trade, but over time it began to take on a more democratic character as it increasingly engaged the common people. In the mid-1780s, for instance, conventions became increasingly popular as a way to bypass legislatures. Many Americans apparently came to believe that elected state legislatures were becoming bastions of privilege that had to be placed under more direct popular control. They established numerous state and county conventions to monitor and control closely the actions of state legislators. These conventions issued specific instructions to representatives on how they were to vote on the issues before them. Both conventions and direct instructions, of course, struck directly at the heart of the republican conception of the legislature as a deliberative body shielded from popular opinion.[14]

The constitution that the state of Pennsylvania adopted in 1776 was also an affront to republican principles. Benjamin Rush, a signatory to the Declaration of Independence, described it as "too much upon the democratic order."[15] This constitution replaced the property qualification to vote with a very small tax (thus allowing many more people to vote), created a single-house legislative body whose members were to be elected in annual elections, mandated that legislative deliberations be open to the public, required that proposed legislation be widely publicized and only voted upon after a general election had been held (making the canvassing of public opinion easier), and eliminated the office of governor in favor of an elected executive committee.

To many advocates of democracy, including Tom Paine, the Pennsylvania constitution was the most perfect instrument of popular sovereignty. To others, like future president John Adams, it worked against every principle of good government, for good government, in their view, required governance by the qualified, deliberation, immunization from special interests and popular opinion, and the means to execute laws once they were adopted.[16] To James Madison, the Pennsylvania case was a perfect example of the possibility of popular tyranny exercised through the legislative branch of government. Because we are generally more favorable today about democracy than were the framers, we are likely to see their worries as somewhat exaggerated and overwrought. Nevertheless, we must note the seriousness of their concerns.

The Threat to Property Rights

One of the central axioms of the republican doctrine, perfectly captured in John Locke's *Second Treatise on Government*, is that in a good society, people should be protected in the enjoyment of their property. They should be free, that is to say, to accumulate, use, or exchange property as they wish, no matter how much they possess compared to others. Developments toward the end of the 1770s and the beginning of the 1780s seemed to some to put this right in jeopardy. There was, in the first place, a growing popular mood of hostility toward privilege of any kind, whether of social standing, education, or wealth. Writers increasingly derided aristocratic airs, expressed their preference for unlettered, plain-speaking leaders, and pointed out how wealth undermined the equality of rights.[17] There was, in the second place, a trend toward legislative protection of debtors and the consequent undermining of the financial position of debt holders. Examples include the issuance of cheap paper money (which debt holders were forced to accept in payment of debts) by states like Rhode Island and North Carolina and enactment of "stay-acts" in several states, which forbade foreclosures for nonpayment of debts. Popular opinion, while strongly in favor of property rights (after all, most of the debtors in question were owners of small farms), also sympathized with farmers who were hard pressed to pay their debts with increasingly tight money and believed—with some reason—that many creditors had accumulated notes speculatively or unfairly and were not entitled to full repayment. There was, third and finally, Shays's Rebellion, described in some detail in the opening pages of this chapter.

THE CONSTITUTIONAL CONVENTION

By 1787, most of America's economic, social, and political leaders were convinced that the new nation and the experiment in self-government were in great danger of failing. First, the central government under the Articles of Confederation could not protect or advance the national interest in the world, pay its debts, guarantee domestic tranquility, or establish a unified national economy. Second, democratic and leveling tendencies were threatening to undermine the republican principles of the new nation. These concerns helped convince the states to select 73 delegates to attend the Constitutional Convention in Philadelphia (only 55 actually showed up for its deliberations). The goal was to create a new government capable of providing stability and energy.

Who Were the Founders?

The convention officially convened on May 25, 1787, with George Washington presiding. It met in secret for a period of almost four months in the terrible heat of the Philadelphia summer. By the end of their deliberations on September 17, the delegates had hammered out a constitutional framework for the nation that has served as the foundation for the rules-of-the-game for American government and politics to the present day.

Who were these delegates? For one thing, they were not common folk. There were no ordinary laborers, skilled craftspeople, small farmers, women, or racial minorities in attendance. For the most part, the delegates were wealthy men: holders of government bonds, real estate investors, successful merchants, bankers, law-

The original
Constitution is
preserved and on
public display at
the National
Archives in
Washington, D.C.

yers, and owners of large plantations worked by slaves. They were, for the most
part, very well educated for their time, far better than the average American, and
solidly steeped in the classics. The journal of the convention debates kept by James
Madison of Virginia shows that the delegates were conversant with the great
works of Western philosophy and political science, and quoted Aristotle, Plato,
Locke, Montesquieu, and scores of other thinkers with great facility and frequency.
They were also a surprisingly young group, averaging barely more than 40 years
of age. Finally, they were a group with very broad experience in American politics,
almost all of them having been active in the Revolution and in the postwar state
governments. More than half of them had served in Congress.

The Debate over the Intentions of the Framers

Ever since the publication in 1913 of historian Charles Beard's provocative book
An Economic Interpretation of the Constitution,[18] debate has raged among scholars
about the motives and intentions of the framers. Beard boldly claimed that the
framers were engaged in a conspiracy to protect their immediate and personal
economic interests. Those who controlled the convention and the ratification process after the convention, he suggested, were owners of public securities interested
in a government that could pay its debts, merchants interested in protections of
commerce, and land speculators interested in the protection of property rights.

Beard has his defenders and detractors.[19] It is generally agreed that Beard
overemphasized the degree to which the framers were driven by the immediate
need to "line their own pockets," failed to give credit to other more noble motivations, and even got many of his facts wrong. A simple "class analysis" is not
supportable. On the other hand, Beard was probably close to the mark in suggesting that broad economic and social-class motives were at work in shaping the
actions of the framers.[20] This is not to suggest that they were not motivated by
such concerns as the national interest, economic stability, or the preservation of
liberty. It is to suggest, however, that the ways in which they understood the

national interest, economic stability, and the preservation of liberty were fully compatible with their own positions of economic and social eminence.

It is fair to say that the Constitutional Convention was the work of American notables deeply concerned about the instability and the economic chaos of the Confederation and about the threat of a rising democracy to the kind of society in which they held a favored position. As one historian has put the issue, "what was at stake for [the framers] was more than speculative windfalls in securities; it was the question of what kind of society would emerge from the revolution when the dust had settled. . . ."[21] To argue that economic motives did not exist because political and ideological issues were at stake, as some do,[22] will not do. Clearly, a complex mixture of motives, ranging from the economic to the philosophical, was at play among the delegates.[23]

Consensus and Conflict at the Convention

The delegates to the convention agreed with one another on many fundamental points. There was a consensus, for instance, on the need to scrap the Articles of Confederation and substitute a new constitution in its place. In deciding to do this, in one of its first official acts, the delegates went far beyond their instructions from Congress.

The delegates also agreed on the need for a substantially strengthened national government to protect American interests in the world, to provide for domestic tranquility, and to regulate interstate commerce. Such a government could only come about by weakening the power and sovereignty of the states. Nationalists like Alexander Hamilton had long argued this position. By the time of the convention, even traditional decentralists like James Madison had changed their minds. As Madison put it, some way must be found "which will at once support a due supremacy of the national authority, and leave in force the local authorities so far as they can be subordinately useful."[24]

But the delegates also believed that a strong national government is potentially tyrannical and therefore should not be allowed to fall into the hands of any particular interest or set of interests, whether a small group of aristocrats or, most important, the majority. Their most important task became that of finding a formula for instituting republican government—one based on popular consent but one whose deliberations and decisions would not be directly or unduly swayed by public opinion. As Benjamin Franklin put it, "We have been guarding against an evil that old states are most liable to, excess of power in the rulers, but our present danger seems to be defect of obedience in the subjects."[25]

Instituting republican government, however, would be no easy task, in the view of many of the framers, because a virtuous people, the raw material for republican government, did not seem to exist in America. The task of the framers was to arrange governmental institutions in such a way that it would preserve the essentials of republicanism in a society composed of an "immoderate and unvirtuous" people; to find, as James Madison put it, "a republican remedy for the diseases most incident to republican government."[26]

Despite this general consensus, the delegates disagreed on a sufficient number of details to take up 115 days of sometimes heated debate. The most important debates involved the conflict between large and small states over the issue of representation in the national government, the status of slavery, and the selection of the president.

"Remember, gentlemen, we aren't here just to draft a constitution.
We're here to draft the best damned constitution in the world."
Drawing by P. Steiner; © 1982 The New Yorker Magazine, Inc.

THE GREAT COMPROMISE   By far the most intense of the debates concerned the
so-called **Virginia Plan** for the organization of a new national government, drafted
by James Madison. The Virginians had met in advance of the convention and had
prepared a set of proposals designed to create a strong central government controlled, in the main, by the wealthiest and most populous states: Virginia, Massachusetts, and Pennsylvania. In the Virginia Plan, a national legislature with
power to appoint the executive and the judiciary and to veto all state laws would
have seats apportioned to the states on the basis of population. The smaller states,
alarmed by what they believed to be a naked power grab by the larger states,
countered with a set of proposals drafted by William Patterson of New Jersey
(thereafter known as the **New Jersey Plan**), whose central feature was a single-
house legislature in which each state had but a single vote, regardless of population size. The New Jersey Plan envisioned a slightly more powerful national
government but one that was to be organized on representational lines not unlike
the Articles of Confederation, in which each of the states remained sovereign. The
Virginia Plan, on the other hand, with its strong national government run by a
popularly elected legislature, called for a fundamentally different sort of national
union—one where national sovereignty was superior to state sovereignty.

Debate on this issue was so intense that no decision could be reached on the
floor of the convention. This is hardly surprising, because it concerned the very
nature of the new nation. As a way out of this impasse, the convention appointed
a committee to hammer out a compromise. The Committee of Eleven met over
the Fourth of July holidays while the convention was adjourned. It presented its
report, sometimes called the Great Compromise, and sometimes called the Connecticut Compromise (because it was drafted by Roger Sherman of that state) on
July 5, 1787. Its key feature was a two-house national legislature in which each
state's representation in the lower house was to be based on size of population
(thus favoring the large states), while representation in the upper house was to
be equal for each of the states (thus favoring the small states). Though the vote
on July 16 to adopt this compromise was an extremely close one—five in favor,

four against, and two abstaining—it managed to break the logjam at the convention and to cool some of the tempers that were threatening to bring the proceedings down.

SLAVERY   The delegates were also forced to grapple with the issue of slavery in a nation that had just fought a revolution in support of the proposition that "all men are created equal." While there was great distaste for the institution of slavery among many non-Southern delegates, and some attempt to outlaw its practice, the delegates ultimately recognized that the southern states (where close to one-half of the total population of the Confederation lived) would never agree to a provision outlawing the institution. Its adoption, therefore, would jeopardize the entire effort to create a new national union. Southern bargaining power was so substantial, in fact, that the delegates adopted three provisions that explicitly recognized the legal standing of slavery (without mentioning it by name). First, it counted three-fifth's of a state's slave population in the calculation of how many representatives a state was entitled to in the House of Representatives (Art. I, Sec. 2, para. 3). Second, it forbade enactments against the slave trade until the year 1808 (Art. I, Sec. 9). Third, it required nonslave states to return runaway slaves to their owners in slave states (Art. IV, Sec. 2, para. 3).

The delegates postponed the hard decision on slavery in the interest of forming the new union. It would take a terrible and brutal civil war to settle the issue. George Mason of Virginia had a foreboding of such an outcome when he observed about slavery that ". . . providence punishes national sins by national calamities."[27]

THE PRESIDENCY   The Virginia Plan called for a single executive, while the New Jersey Plan called for a plural executive. In the spirit of cooperation that pervaded the convention after the Great Compromise on representation, the delegates quickly settled on the idea of a single executive. They could not agree, however, on how this executive should be elected. Both sides rejected the idea of the direct election of the chief executive, of course, because this would be "too much upon the democratic order," but they locked horns on the Virginia Plan's method of selection by the vote of state legislatures. The compromise that was eventually struck involved provision for the election of an **electoral college**, based on the total number of representatives from each of the states in Congress. Should the electoral college fail to give a majority to any person, which most framers assumed would turn out to be the norm, they agreed that the selection of a president would become the responsibility of the House of Representatives. (See Art. II, Sec. 1, paras. 2 and 3.) As we will see, the system of presidential election did not work out as they expected and became far more democratic over the course of our history.

What the Framers Wrought

In order to understand American politics today, it is extremely important to know and to understand the Constitution of the United States. To be sure, the document has been amended from time to time and some important things have changed: in particular, democratic control of government and the scope of federal government authority have both greatly increased. But the major outlines of our present-day government are expressed in, and substantially determined by, the

RESOURCE
FEATURE

*Reading the
Constitution*

Members of the convention sign their names to the Constitution on September 17, 1787. The Constitution did not become the law of the land, however, until the ninth state, New Hampshire, ratified it nine months later.

The Constitution of the United States deserves a slow and careful reading. Every word counts. Each word or phrase tells something important about how American government works. If you keep in mind how the document is organized—as outlined below—it will help you understand the structure of the Constitution as a whole and will make it much easier to find specific provisions when you look them up.

The Constitution begins with a Preamble, which declares that "(w)e the people" (not just the separate states) establish the Constitution and lists its purposes.

Article I concerns the legislative branch. It provides for a House of

Constitution that was written in Philadelphia. The U.S. Constitution, in fact, can be considered one of the major structural factors that has influenced the evolution of American government and continues to shape politics today. Advice on how to read the Constitution is offered in "Resource Feature."

We urge students to reread the Constitution carefully at this point and to return to its provisions each time we reach chapters discussing specific institutions, such as Congress, the presidency, the judiciary, and state and local governments. The full text of the document is given in Appendix III; it should be consulted frequently.

Here we will give a brief overview of what kind of government was created by the new Constitution. We emphasize four main features.

THE FRAMERS CREATED A FEDERAL SYSTEM WITH A RELATIVELY STRONG CENTRAL GOVERNMENT   The Articles of Confederation envisioned a nation structured as a loose union of politically independent units (like nations in the United Nations today), with little power in the hands of the central government. The Constitution fashioned a federal system, in which some powers are left to the states, some powers are shared by the component units and the central government, and some

Representatives, elected by the people and apportioned according to population; and then a Senate, with equal representation for each state. After discussing various congressional roles and procedures (Secs. 4–7), it goes on in Sec. 8 to enumerate the specific powers of Congress, concluding with the "necessary and proper" clause. It then limits Congress's powers (Sec. 9) and those of the states (Sec. 10).

Article II deals with the executive branch. It vests the executive power in a single president of the United States. After describing the complex electoral college scheme for indirectly electing presidents (changed, in effect, by the development of a party system) and dealing with the qualifications, removal, compensation, and the oath of office, it describes presidential powers and duties (Secs. 2 and 3) and provides for impeachment.

Article III concerns the judicial branch. It vests the judicial power in a Supreme Court, letting Congress establish other courts if desired. It provides for a limited original jurisdiction and (subject to congressional regulation) for broader appellate jurisdiction (i.e., jurisdiction to review lower court decisions). It specifies a right to jury trials and then (Sec. 3) defines treason, ruling out certain punishments for it.

Article IV deals with interstate relations, requiring that full faith and credit be given other states' acts and that fugitives (slaves) be delivered up. Sec. 3 provides for admission of new states and the regulation of U.S. territories. Sec. 4 guarantees a republican form of government to the states.

Article V provides for two ways of proposing constitutional amendments and for two ways of ratifying them; it forbids amendments changing equal state suffrage in the Senate or (before 1808) prohibiting the slave trade or changing the apportionment of taxes.

Article VI assumes the debts of the Confederation; makes the Constitution, laws, and treaties of the United States the supreme law of the land; and requires an oath of U.S. and state officials.

Article VII provides that the Constitution will be established when ratified by nine state conventions.

powers are granted to the central government alone. As Madison puts it in *Federalist* No. 46, the state and national governments "are but different agents and trustees of the people, constituted with different powers."

The powers in the Constitution, however, tilt toward the center[28] (see Figure 2.2). This recasting of the union from a loose confederation to a more centralized federal system is boldly stated in Article VI, Section 2, commonly called the "supremacy clause":

> This Constitution and the Laws of the United States which shall be made in Pursuance thereof; and all Treaties made, or which shall be made, under the Authority of the United States, shall be the supreme Law of the Land; and the Judges in every State shall be bound thereby, any Thing in the Constitution or Laws of any State to the Contrary notwithstanding.

The framers also signaled a move away from the confederation by deemphasizing the states as the main actors in the creation of the Constitution. They did so by beginning the Preamble with the famous words, "We the People of the United States . . ." rather than with the words "We the states. . . ."

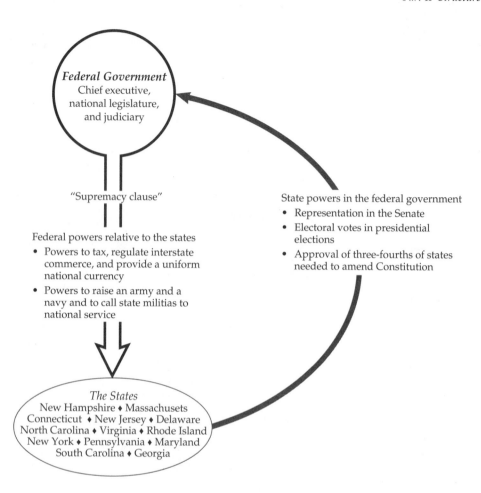

Figure 2.2 The centralized federalism of the Constitution

Federal Government
Chief executive, national legislature, and judiciary

"Supremacy clause"

Federal powers relative to the states
- Powers to tax, regulate interstate commerce, and provide a uniform national currency
- Powers to raise an army and a navy and to call state militias to national service

State powers in the federal government
- Representation in the Senate
- Electoral votes in presidential elections
- Approval of three-fourths of states needed to amend Constitution

The States
New Hampshire ♦ Massachusets
Connecticut ♦ New Jersey ♦ Delaware
North Carolina ♦ Virginia ♦ Rhode Island
New York ♦ Pennsylvania ♦ Maryland
South Carolina ♦ Georgia

Finally, centralized power was enhanced by exclusively assigning important powers and responsibilities to the national government: to regulate commerce; to provide a uniform currency; to provide uniform laws on bankruptcy; to raise and support an army and a navy; to declare war; to collect taxes and customs; to provide for the common defense of the United States; and more (for these provisions, see Art. I, Sec. 8). Especially important for later constitutional history is the last of the clauses in Section 8, which states that Congress has the power to "make all laws which shall be necessary and proper" for carrying out its specific powers and responsibilities. We shall see later how this **elastic clause** became one of the foundations for the growth of the federal government in the twentieth century.

The framers did not render the states powerless, however, as you will see in the next chapter. In our systems, states remain important actors.

THE FRAMERS CREATED A REPUBLICAN SYSTEM OF GOVERNMENT   Recall that republican doctrine advocates a form of government that, while based on popular consent and some popular participation, limits office holding and the right to vote, places obstacles in the path of majoritarian democracy, and limits the purposes and powers of the government. All of these principles are expressed in the U.S. Constitution.

Limited Government   The basic purpose of the U.S. Constitution, like any written constitution, is to define the purposes and powers of the government. Such a definition of purposes and powers automatically places a boundary between what is permissible and what is impermissible. By listing the specific powers (as in Art. I, Sec. 8) of the national government, and specifically denying others to the national government (as in Art. I, Sec. 9 and in the first ten **amendments** to the Constitution, known as the Bill of Rights), the Constitution carefully limited what government may legitimately do.

To further ensure that the federal government would not exceed its limits, the framers subdivided and parceled out central government sovereignty to separate and competing institutions. These constitutional features, called *separation of powers* and *checks and balances*, are discussed later in this section.

Limits on Majoritarian Democracy   Being sorely afraid of the "levelling tendencies" and potential for tyranny they thought inherent in unbridled democracy, the framers created a Constitution in which the people rule only indirectly, barriers are placed in the path of majorities, and deliberation is prized over conformity to the popular will (see Figure 2.3). As political philosopher Robert Dahl puts it,

> . . . the framers gave much narrower scope to the principles of consent and political equality. . . . They created a government that would demand obedience to its laws from a majority of adults—women, non-whites, and some white males—who were excluded from active participation in making those laws, whether directly or through their elected representatives. . . . In order to achieve their goal of preserving a set of inalienable rights superior to the majority principle . . . the framers deliberately created a framework of government that was carefully designed to impede and even prevent the operation of majority rule.[29]

Of the three branches of government, only part of one was made directly accountable to the people: the House of Representatives (Art. I, Sec. 2, para. 1). The president and members of the Senate were to be elected indirectly, with judges appointed by the president and confirmed by the Senate. The "unbridled passions of the people" (as the framers tended to put the matter) were made difficult to express through the electoral process, moreover, by provisions that representatives, senators, and presidents be elected for different terms of office, from different constituencies, and (often) at different times. (See the electoral provisions of

Figure 2.3 Mechanisms in the Constitution that limit the role of the majority

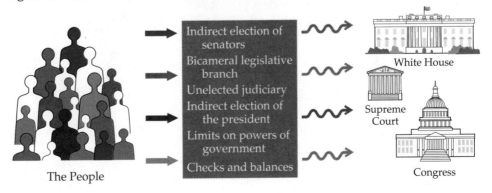

The People

Indirect election of senators

Bicameral legislative branch

Unelected judiciary

Indirect election of the president

Limits on powers of government

Checks and balances

White House

Supreme Court

Congress

The French philosopher Montesquieu formulated many of the ideas about mixed and balanced government that influenced the framers.

Arts. I, II, and III.) These noncongruencies in the electoral mechanisms were intended to ensure that the popular will, at least in the short run, was unlikely to overwhelm those who governed.

Finally, the framers rejected the advice of radical democrats like Thomas Paine, Samuel Adams, and Thomas Jefferson to allow amendment of the Constitution by simple majority and made the amendment process exceedingly cumbersome and difficult. By these provisions, the framers designed a system in which the popular will, while given some play (more than existed anywhere in the world at the time), is largely deflected and slowed, allowing somewhat insulated political leaders to deliberate at their pleasure.

Balanced Government   American revolutionaries were at first most worried about the power of the executive and of judges, and counterposed legislative supremacy as a solution to these twin evils. The men who were involved in drafting the Constitution, however, while remaining leery of executive and judicial power, had come to fear unchecked legislative power during the Articles of Confederation period. The way out of this impasse, they determined, was the ancient notion of mixed or balanced government, popularized in their own day by the French philosopher Montesquieu. The central idea of balanced government is that concentrated power of any kind is dangerous and that the solution is to divide power and place it into different hands; that is, the judiciary, the legislative, and the executive powers, must not be combined (as in parliamentary systems, for instance, where executive and legislative powers come together in legislative control of the prime minister) but, rather, parceled out into separate institutions.

Although the Constitution clearly empowers only the Congress to declare war, in recent decades, presidents have launched military operations like this one in Panama, without first securing congressional assent.

To further ensure that power could not be exercised in a tyrannical fashion, the framers believed that the legislative, executive, and judicial powers must be made to check one another. The principle was described nicely by Thomas Jefferson: "... the powers of government should be so divided and balanced among several bodies of magistracy, as that no one could transcend their legal limits, without being effectually checked and constrained by the others."[30]

The Constitution effectively puts these ideas into practice. Article I (on the legislative power), Article II (on the executive power), and Article III (on the judicial power) designate separate spheres of responsibility and enumerate specific powers attached to these responsibilities. We call this the **separation of powers**. Additionally, the framers formulated a series of provisions requiring that each branch play a role in the activities of the others so that, as Madison later explained, "ambition ... be made to counteract ambition."[31] We call these provisions **checks and balances**. Let us take a few examples of checks and balances. Congress cannot legislate on its own, but requires presidential approval (unless two-thirds of both houses vote to override the president's veto) and judicial support. Presidents are bound by laws passed by Congress (they must "take care that the laws be faithfully executed," Art. II, Sec. 3), are constrained by legislatively mandated budgets, and are constrained by judicial interpretations of statute and constitutional law. The judicial branch may pass on the legality of congressional and presidential action but is itself dependent on the former for defining its jurisdiction, formal organization, and budget (see Art. III, Secs. 1 and 2), and on the latter for enforcing its decisions. Each branch has power, but none is able to exercise all of its powers on its own. Each branch, that is to say, has a check on the power of the others (see Figure 2.4).

Figure 2.4 How the Constitution arranges for each branch to be checked by the other two

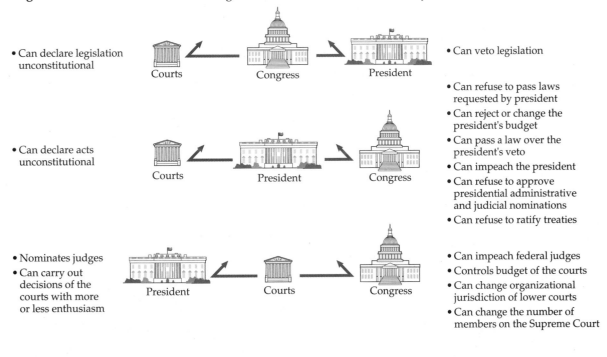

• Can declare legislation unconstitutional

Courts   Congress   President

• Can veto legislation

• Can declare acts unconstitutional

Courts   President   Congress

• Can refuse to pass laws requested by president
• Can reject or change the president's budget
• Can pass a law over the president's veto
• Can impeach the president
• Can refuse to approve presidential administrative and judicial nominations
• Can refuse to ratify treaties

• Nominates judges
• Can carry out decisions of the courts with more or less enthusiasm

President   Courts   Congress

• Can impeach federal judges
• Controls budget of the courts
• Can change organizational jurisdiction of lower courts
• Can change the number of members on the Supreme Court

THE FRAMERS PROTECTED PROPERTY RIGHTS AND CREATED THE CONDITIONS FOR A NATIONAL ECONOMY   Recall that the framers were particularly worried about the possibility that a system "too much upon the democratic order" might eventually threaten private property. Recall that in the Lockean philosophical universe, which largely defined the thinking of the framers, the right to accumulate, use, and transfer property was one of the fundamental, inalienable rights that governments were instituted among men to defend.

Property rights are protected in several places in the Constitution. Article I, Section 10 forbids the states from impairing the obligation of contracts, coining money, or making anything but gold and silver coin a tender in payment of debts; that is, the states could no longer help debtors by inflating money or forgiving debts, or otherwise infringing on the property of creditors, as had happened in such places as Rhode Island under the Articles of Confederation. Article IV, Section 1 further guarantees contracts by establishing that states must give "full faith and credit" to the public acts, records, and judicial proceedings of every other state, which meant that one could no longer escape legal and financial obligations in one state by moving to another (which was possible under the Articles). In addition, the United States assumed as valid against itself, that is, guaranteed to pay in full, all debts contracted under the Articles of Confederation (Art. VI, Sec. 1). Article IV, Section 2, paragraph 3 even protected private property in slaves by requiring states to deliver escaped slaves back to their owners.

The framers helped create the conditions for a national economy in other ways. Article I, Section 8 grants Congress the power to regulate commerce with foreign nations and among the states (ending the chaos of individual states' regulations); to coin money and regulate its value (thus establishing a uniform national currency); to establish uniform laws of bankruptcy; and to protect the financial fruits of invention by establishing patent and copyright laws. At the same time, Article I, Sections 9 and 10 broke down barriers to trade by forbidding states from imposing taxes or duties on other states' exports, or entering into foreign treaties, or coining money, or laying any imposts or duties on imports or exports.

RATIFICATION

Having agreed to the specific provisions of the constitutional document by September 8, 1787, the delegates remanded it to a committee on style (whose members were William Samuel Johnson, Alexander Hamilton, James Madison, Rufus King, and Gouverneur Morris) to polish its final language. The committee completed its work on September 12 and submitted it to the convention for final approval. That approval came on September 17, with the agreement of each of the 12 states represented at the convention (Rhode Island refused to send delegates). Only 3 of the 42 delegates did not sign. The convention adjourned after formally notifying Congress of the completion of its work.

One of the truly remarkable things about this story is how the delegates to the convention proposed that the new constitution be ratified. Recall that Congress had instructed the convention to propose alterations to the Articles of Confederation. Recall also that amendment of the Articles of Confederation required the unanimous consent of the 13 states. To follow such a course would have meant instant rejection of the new constitution, because Rhode Island surely would have voted against it, and there is reason to believe that one or two additional states would have opposed it as well. Acting boldly, the framers simply stated that ratification would be based on guidelines specified in Article VII of the unratified document they had just written, namely approval by 9 states meeting in special constitutional conventions. Congress agreed to this procedure, voting on September 28 to transmit the constitution to the states for their consideration.

The **Federalists** did a better job of making their case than the **Anti-Federalists** (those who opposed the constitution). Their intellectual advantages were nowhere more obvious than in the 85 articles written in defense of the constitution for New York newspapers, under the name "Publius," by Alexander Hamilton (who wrote the most), James Madison (who wrote the best), and John Jay (who wrote only three). Collected later and published as *The Federalist Papers*, these articles strongly influenced the debate over ratification and remain the most impressive commentaries ever written about the U.S. Constitution (see numbers 10 and 51 by Madison in the Appendix).

The struggle over ratification mainly pitted the wealthy and urban interests against the less wealthy and rural interests. It also pitted advocates of small scale, decentralized republican government against advocates of a more centralized system.[32] Opposition to the constitution also came from those who were concerned about the absence of a bill of rights. Though the Federalists (those who supported the constitution) firmly believed that a bill of rights was unnecessary because of the protection of rights in state constitutions and the many safeguards against tyranny in the federal constitution, they promised to add it during the first session of Congress. They kept their promise. The First Congress passed a bill of rights in the form of the first ten amendments to the Constitution (Table 2.2). The amendments were ratified by the required 11 states by December 15, 1791.

Table 2.2
The Bill of Rights[a]

Amendment I	Freedom of religion, speech, press, and assembly
Amendment II	The right to bear arms
Amendment III	Prohibition against quartering of troops in private homes
Amendment IV	Prohibition against unreasonable searches and seizures
Amendment V	Rights guaranteed to the accused: requirement for grand jury indictment; protections against double jeopardy, self-incrimination; guarantee of due process
Amendment VI	Right to a speedy and public trial before an impartial jury, to cross-examine witnesses, and to have counsel
Amendment VII	Right to a trial by jury in civil suits
Amendment VIII	Prohibition against excessive bail and fines, and cruel and unusual punishment
Amendment IX	Rights not listed in Constitution retained by the people
Amendment X	States retain those powers not denied to them by the Constitution or delegated to the national government

[a]See Appendix for a full enumeration.

Patrick Henry was among the nation's most passionate anti-Federalists because he believed that the new Constitution threatened people's liberty.

Ratification of the constitution was a very close call. Most of the small states quickly approved, attracted by the formula of equal representation in the Senate. Federalists organized a victory in Pennsylvania before the Anti-Federalists realized what had happened. After that, the ratification struggle was very hard. Rhode Island voted no. North Carolina abstained because of the absence of a bill of rights and did not vote its approval until 1790. In the largest and most important states, the vote was exceedingly close. Massachusetts approved by a vote of 187–168; Virginia by 89–79; and New York by 30–27. The struggle was especially intense in Virginia, where prominent, articulate, and influential men were involved on both sides of the question. The Federalists could call on George Washington, James Madison, John Marshall, and Edmund Randolph. The Anti-Federalists could counter with George Mason, Richard Henry Lee, and Patrick Henry. Patrick Henry was particularly passionate, as always, in his views, saying the constitution "squints towards monarchy." Though New Hampshire technically put the constitution over the top, being the ninth state to vote approval, proponents did not rest easily until approval was narrowly voted by Virginia and New York.

Despite the passions that were released during the debate over the refashioning of the nation's fundamental law, Americans very quickly accepted the new order and eventually came to venerate the Constitution. It is not entirely clear why this happened. Perhaps it was simple weariness from the long effort to win independence and to create a new nation. Perhaps it was because George Washington was elected the nation's first president under the new Constitution, lending great legitimacy to the new venture. Perhaps it was because most of the prominent political figures involved in the struggle for independence and in the ratification fight, and even those in the Anti-Federalist camp, quickly came over to the Federalist side.

THE PLACE OF THE CONSTITUTION IN AMERICAN POLITICS

The Rules of the Game

The Constitution that the framers created is the basic rule book for the game of American politics. Constitutional rules apportion power and responsibility between governmental branches, define the fundamental nature of the relationships between governmental institutions, specify how individuals are to be selected for office, and tell how the rules themselves may be changed. Every aspiring politician who wants to attain office, every citizen who wants to influence what government does, and every group that wants to advance its interests in the political arena must know the rules and must shape their strategic behavior in order to use the rules to best advantage. Because the Constitution has this character, we understand it to be a fundamental structural factor influencing all of American political life.

Liberty and the Growth of Democracy

The framers believed that liberty and popular sovereignty were contradictory. Because they especially valued liberty, they tried in a variety of ways to control the play of popular democracy in American political life, using constitutional mechanisms.

We believe that they did not fully appreciate the extent to which liberty, popular sovereignty, and political equality are compatible. We made the case in Chapter 1 that most people today include political liberty as a basic attribute of democracy itself; they believe—quite correctly in our view—that democracy is only possible where popular sovereignty, political equality, and political liberty coexist. The framers' contribution to the advance of democracy is, then, ambiguous, for, while they tried to control popular sovereignty and political equality, they made an important contribution by strengthening and protecting political liberty.

However, their efforts to contain democracy were not entirely successful. Popular democracy proved to be an idea of such power that our political life has become considerably more democratic than the framers imagined or wanted. This democratization of American politics, as well as the ongoing historical "struggle for democracy" that caused it, will be recounted at various places in this book. This should remind us that constitutional rules, like all rules, can and do change over time.

SUMMARY

This chapter reviews the complex history of the founding of the American republic. It focuses on the debate among the American people about the proper form of government and the values that ought to animate and to shape the behavior of such a government. It reviews the debate between proponents of liberty, order, popular consent, and democracy, and it shows how that debate played itself out in the formulation of our two constitutions: the Articles of Confederation and the U.S. Constitution.

The first constitution joining the American states was the Articles of Confederation. Under its terms, the states were organized into a loose confederation, in which states retained full sovereignty and the central government had little power. Because of a wide range of defects in the Articles of Confederation and fears among many American leaders that democratic and egalitarian tendencies were beginning to spin out of control, a gathering was called to meet in Philadelphia to amend the Articles of Confederation. The delegates chose, instead, to formulate an entirely new constitution, whose most important characteristics were federalism, a strengthened national government, balanced government, characterized by the separation of powers and checks and balances, and indirect and limited democracy.

The Constitution was ratified in an extremely close vote of the states after a hard-fought struggle between the Federalists and Anti-Federalists. Despite the "close shave," the Constitution became very popular among the American people within only a few years of the ratification fight. The Constitution became far more democratic over the years than was originally intended by the framers.

To Ponder

1. What would America look like today had the close vote on ratification of the Constitution gone the other way? What if we continued to live under the terms of our first constitution, the Articles of Confederation?

2. Do you find republican government (not the political party) more or less appealing than democratic government (again, not the political party)? Which seems more appealing to you? Why?

3. What do you imagine America would be like today had it remained a British colony? Think about Canada and Australia to help in working out an answer.

Suggested Readings

Beard, Charles A. *An Economic History of the Constitution*. New York: Macmillan, 1913.
> The classic and controversial work by the progressive historian that sparked decades of debate among historians about the motivations of the Founders.

Brown, Robert. *Charles Beard and the Constitution*. Princeton, NJ: Princeton University Press, 1956.
> The most influential refutation of the Beardian thesis on the motivations of the Founders.

The Federalist. Clinton Rossiter (ed.). New York: New American Library, 1961.
> Classic commentaries on the Constitution and its key provisions, written by Alexander Hamilton, John Jay, and James Madison.

Hanson, Russell L. *The Democratic Imagination in America*. Princeton, NJ: Princeton University Press, 1985.
> A book about the changing meaning over the years of the word *democracy* in American history.

McDonald, Forrest. *We the People: The Economic Origins of the Constitution*. Chicago: University of Chicago Press, 1958.
> A ringing refutation of the Beardian thesis.

Main, Jackson Turner. *The Anti-Federalists*. Chapel Hill, NC: University of North Carolina Press, 1961.
> The ratification struggle seen from the point of view of its opponents.

Storing, Herbert J. *What the Anti-Federalists Were For*. Chicago: University of Chicago Press, 1981.
> The most complete collection available on the published views of the Anti-Federalists. Includes convincing commentary by Storing.

Wills, Gary. *Explaining America: The Federalist*. New York: Doubleday, 1981.
> A fresh look at the writing of the Constitution by one of America's most provocative intellectuals.

————. *Inventing America: Jefferson's Declaration of Independence*. New York: Random House, 1978.
> A different and controversial look at the intellectual origins of the American experiment.

Wood, Gordon. *The Creation of the American Republic*. New York: Norton, 1972.
> The most exhaustive and respected source on America's changing ideas during the period 1776–1787 or from the start of the American Revolution to the writing of the Constitution.

Notes

1. This story is from Page Smith, *A People's History of the Young Republic: The Shaping of America, Vol. 3* (New York: McGraw-Hill, 1980), p. 25.
2. Smith, *Shaping of America*, p. 13.
3. Quoted in Jackson Turner Main, *The Anti-Federalists* (Chapel Hill, NC: University of North Carolina Press, 1961), p. 62.
4. Gordon S. Wood, *The Creation of the American Republic* (New York: Norton, 1972), p. 12.
5. Quoted in Wood, *Creation of the American Republic*, p. 132.

6. Quoted in Wood, *Creation of the American Republic*, p. 135.

7. James A. Morone, *The Democratic Wish* (New York: Basic Books, 1990), p. 36.

8. Wood, *Creation of the American Republic*, pp. 356–357.

9. See Hanna Arendt, *On Revolution* (New York: Viking, 1965).

10. Smith, *Shaping of America*, pp. 8–9.

11. Richard Hofstadter, *The American Political Tradition* (New York: Vintage Books, 1948), p. 4.

12. Quoted in Main, *Anti-Federalists*, p. 163.

13. Fisher Ames to John Rutledge, quoted in Russell L. Hanson, *The Democratic Imagination in America* (Princeton, NJ: Princeton University Press, 1985), p. 86.

14. Wood, *Creation of the American Republic*, pp. 311–318.

15. Wood, *Creation of the American Republic*, Chap. 8.

16. Samuel Elliot Morison, *The Oxford History of the American People* (New York: Oxford University Press, 1965), p. 274.

17. See Wood, *Creation of the American Republic*, p. 400.

18. Charles Beard, *An Economic History of the Constitution* (New York: Macmillan, 1913).

19. For criticism of Beard, see Robert Brown, *Charles Beard and the Constitution* (Princeton, NJ: Princeton University Press, 1956); Leonard Levy, *Constitutional Opinions* (New York: Oxford University Press, 1986); Forrest McDonald, *We the People: The Economic Origins of the Constitution* (Chicago: University of Chicago Press, 1958); and Gordon Wood, *The Convention and the Constitution* (New York: St. Martin's, 1965).

20. Hofstader, *American Political Tradition*; Morone, *Democratic Wish*, p. 60.

21. Staughton Lynd, *Class Conflict, Slavery, and the United States Constitution* (Indianapolis: Bobbs-Merrill, 1967), p. 70.

22. John P. Roche, ''The Founding Fathers: A Reform Caucus in Action,'' *American Political Science Review* (December 1961), pp. 799–816.

23. Robert A. McGuire and Robert L. Ohsfeldt, ''An Economic Model of Voting Behavior over Specific Issues at the Constitutional Convention of 1787,'' *Journal of Economic History* Vol. 66 (March 1986), pp. 79–111, show that voting patterns at the Convention were broadly consistent with our interpretation of the Founders' motives. While certain choices concerning a stronger or weaker national government were affected by delegates' personal characteristics (e.g., service in the Revolutionary War, ownership of slaves or of public securities, English ancestry), even more important were their states' economic interests and ideology (e.g., slave holding, net public debt, coastal or inland status, size of population).

24. Wood, *Creation of the American Republic*, p. 473.

25. Benjamin Franklin, quoted in Wood, *Creation of the American Republic*, p. 432.

26. *The Federalist*, ed. by Clinton Rossiter (New York: New American Library, 1961), Nos. 10 and 39.

27. Max Farrand, *The Records of the Federal Convention of 1787* (New Haven, CT: Yale University Press, 1937).

28. ''The Invention of Centralized Federalism,'' in William Riker, ed., *The Development of Centralized Federalism* (Boston: Kluwer Academic Publishers, 1987).

29. Robert A. Dahl, ''On Removing the Impediments to Democracy in the United States,'' *Political Science Quarterly*, Vol. 92, No. 1 (Spring 1977), p. 5.

30. Thomas Jefferson, *Notes on the State of Virginia*, ed. by Thomas Perkins Abernathy (New York: Harper & Row, 1964), p. 120.

31. *The Federalist*, No. 51.

32. See Main, *The Anti-Federalists*; Wood, *Creation of the American Republic*; Smith, *Shaping of America*, p. 99; and Herbert Storing, *What the Anti-Federalists Were For* (Chicago: University of Chicago Press, 1981), p. 71.

3

Federalism

FEDERALISM IN ACTION: AUTOMOBILE FUEL EFFICIENCY AND CLEAN AIR

In the autumn of 1990, the states of California and New York beat the U.S. national government to the punch in making cars more fuel efficient and in cutting air pollution. The way they did so illustrates how our federal system works.

There were many reasons to worry about energy and pollution at that moment. The United States was then engaged in a tense confrontation with Saddam Hussein's Iraq over the August 2 Iraqi invasion of Kuwait. Troops had been sent to the Persian Gulf area. The embargo against Iraqi and Kuwaiti oil, together with fears of war, had caused the world price of crude oil to more than double, from $18 per barrel to about $40. That price jump severely jolted the U.S. economy, which was already sliding into a recession, and highlighted the United States's increasing dependency on oil from the unstable Middle East. Moreover, our vast consumption of gasoline for automobiles was polluting the air and contributing to global warming.

In Congress, a majority of U.S. senators favored a bill requiring that new automobiles get about 40 miles per gallon by the year 2001—up from the current requirement of 27.5 miles per gallon—so that they would burn less energy and produce less exhaust. But the automobile industry mounted a massive lobbying campaign against the bill as "horrendously expensive." The Bush administration's secretaries of Transportation and Energy opposed it, as did senators from states that produce cars (Michigan) or oil (Texas). Representative John Dingell from Detroit, a staunch backer of the automobile industry and the United Auto Workers, and head of the Energy and Commerce Committee in the House of Representatives, threatened to bury the bill there even if it made it through the Senate.[1]

On September 25, the bill was killed when backers fell 3 votes short of the 60 (out of 100) needed to cut off Senate debate and to force a final vote. The bill's chief sponsor, Senator Richard Bryan of Nevada (a state with widely scattered towns, where fuel efficiency counts), lamented this setback for "a real energy conservation policy." A Sierra Club official declared: "Today the gas guzzler won and they're popping the champagne corks in Saddam Hussein's palace."

In our federal system, however, policy is not only made in Washington; the individual states have a role as well. Within two days after defeat of the Senate bill, the important political action shifted to New York and California. New York, which had failed to meet national air quality standards, adopted California's strict antipollution rules for cars and trucks for the 1993 model year. More important, California developed even stricter air quality standards that would affect the whole United States.[2]

California, with 22 million vehicles on its roads, suffered from the worst smog in the country and had long pioneered efforts to control air pollution. The federal Clean Air Act of 1970 allowed states to set higher standards for themselves than the federal government required for the nation as a whole, and California had repeatedly done so, provoking other states like New York to follow suit. Unable to ignore the huge California market, automobile manufacturers and oil companies had to develop new technologies that were then used around the country.

On September 28, 1990, the California Air Resources Board adopted far-reaching new rules designed to reduce the average vehicle's hydrocarbon emissions by 75 percent between 1994 and 2003. Beginning in 1994, increasing proportions of new cars would have to meet stricter standards, emitting no more than one-half (and then no more than one-third) of the hydrocarbons allowed in 1993. Moreover, beginning in 1998, some new cars sold in California (10 percent by 2003) would have to have *zero* emissions, giving manufacturers incentives to build and to sell electric cars. Oil companies were required to sell cleaner-burning gasoline by 1992 and to make available still cleaner-burning fuels like methanol and natural gas.

A General Motors official declared that the new rules "will change the very nature of passenger cars and trucks." An executive officer of the California Air Resources Board agreed that the rules "will redefine what we consider an environmentally acceptable car for the next two decades."

About one month later, spurred on by California's action, a conference committee of the U.S. House and Senate finally reached agreement on the landmark Clean Air Act of 1990, designed to halt production of chemicals that destroy the ozone layer, to require urban areas to reduce smog, to cut industrial emissions of sulfur dioxide and nitrogen oxide that cause acid rain, and to control various toxic air pollutants. This national legislation also imposed some new limits on motor vehicles, requiring that tailpipe emissions of hydrocarbons and nitrogen oxides be reduced, that pollution control equipment last longer, that cleaner, experimental gasoline be offered for sale, and that manufacturers build an experimental fleet of even cleaner cars for sale in southern California. However, Representative Dingell had succeeded in watering down and delaying many of the automobile-related provisions, so the result was not nearly so strict as the California rules. New York City's Environmental Protection Commissioner declared: "New York City's worst air problem is caused by automobiles and the bottom line of the Clean Air Act is: automobiles, one; clean air, nothing." "(I)t should be implemented half a decade sooner," said a lobbyist for the Sierra Club.[3]

The 1990 Clean Air Act continued to allow individual states to impose stricter standards, like the California ones. New York officials indicated that they would probably do so. Other states like Massachusetts did, too. But New Yorkers pointed out that they could not solve their air quality problems alone if states such as Pennsylvania and Maryland failed to follow suit, since the prevailing winds brought as much as half of New York's smog from areas south of the state.

This story, like many others we could have told, shows that state and local governments, as well as the national government, make policies that have important effects on people's lives. This division of power between the national government and the states is what we call *federalism*. States with different interests and different circumstances (e.g., California, Michigan, Texas, and Nevada, with respect to automobiles) sometimes move in different directions. In some cases, states like California innovate, ahead of the national government, and come up with policies that are eventually adopted by other states or by the nation as a whole.

Furthermore, the story illustrates the complex nature of federalism. It was the national Clean Air Act of 1970, after all, that explicitly allowed California to enact its own stricter air standards. The authority of national, state, and local governments differs from one subject to another. Sometimes the national government "preempts" an area of policymaking, totally taking it over; at other times, matters are left entirely to the states and localities; and often authority overlaps, with complex combinations of policy made at the national, state, and local levels.

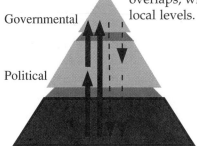

Governmental

Political

Structural

FEDERALISM—AN AMERICAN INVENTION

The United States is full of governments. We have not only a "federal" government in Washington, D.C., (which, in order to avoid confusion, we will refer to in this chapter as the *national* or central government) but also governments in each of 50 states and in each of thousands of smaller governmental units, such as counties (about 3,080 of them), cities, towns and townships, school districts, and special districts that deal with such matters as parks and sanitation. According to one estimate, there are a total of about 82,000 local governments in the United States, even without counting school districts[4] (see Figure 3.1).

All of these governments are organized and related to each other in a particular way. The small governments—counties, cities, towns, and special districts—are legal creatures of state governments. They can be created, changed, or abolished by state laws, at the states' convenience. But state governments themselves have much more independence. Together with the national government in Washington, D.C., they form what is known as a *federal* system. The existence of a federal system may be the most important single fact about American politics; it affects practically everything else.

What Is Federalism?

Federalism can be defined as a system in which significant government powers are divided between the central government and smaller governmental units. Neither one completely controls the other; each has some room for independent action. A federal system can be contrasted with a confederation, on the one hand, or a unitary government, on the other. In a confederation (like the present-day United Nations or our government under the Articles of Confederation during and just after the Revolutionary War), the constituent units or states get together for certain common purposes but retain ultimate authority and can veto major

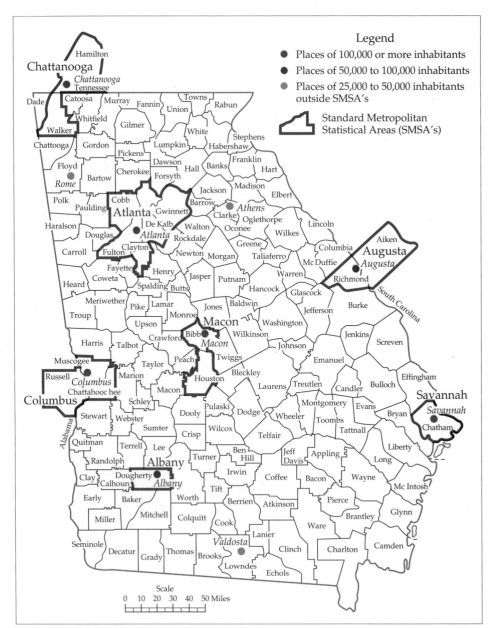

Figure 3.1 Multiple governments in the federal system

Source: U.S. Bureau of the Census, 1970.

actions. In a **unitary system** (which characterizes most governments in the world today), the central government has all the power and can change its constituent units or tell them what to do. These three different types of governmental systems are contrasted in Figure 3.2.

Some of the elements of federalism go back in history at least as far as the Union of Utrecht in the Netherlands in 1579, but federalism as it exists today is largely an American invention.[5] It emerged from the particular way in which our states declared independence from Britain—becoming, in effect, separate nations—and then joined together as a single country. Federalism is not a common way of organizing governments around the world. At the beginning of the 1990s, according to their formal structure, 140 of the 159 member countries in the United Nations (88 percent of them) had unitary rather than federal governments. In the years since the founding of the United States, however, a number of important countries—mostly large and diverse ones—have also established federal systems, often modeling them on the U.S. system.

Scholars argue about which foreign countries "really" have federal governments. Federalism is a matter of degree. The 19 countries with formally federalist constitutions vary: German "Laender" and Mexican states do not have exactly the same independent powers as American states do. Among the many unitary countries some (like the United Kingdom and Italy) have subunits with a certain amount of autonomy, while others (like France and Japan) are more completely dominated by the central government. There are no neat boundaries; scholars have suggested that there is a continuum from "unitary," to "formally federal," "quasi-federal," "federal," and "confederal" polities.[6] Moreover, countries change their systems—or even disintegrate —from time to time, especially when ethnic minorities demand self-rule. Federalism in the Soviet Union used to be mostly fictitious, but it turned very real in 1991 as the Soviet republics declared their independence. Yugoslavia also fell apart. Separatist pressures have buffeted Canada and India. Still, we can observe patterns in the types of countries that have had federal systems.

Figure 3.2 Types of political systems

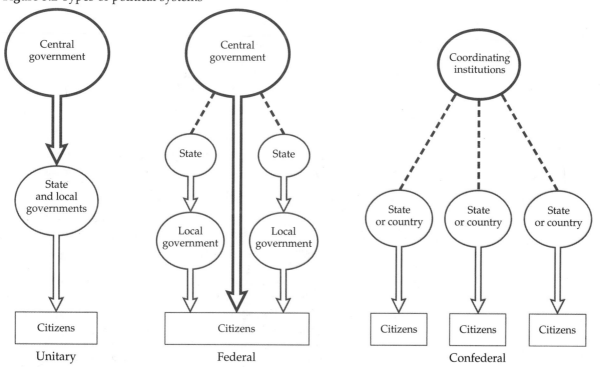

Why Federalism?

American federalism is best understood as a result of the historical process by which the original colonies became independent states and formed a confederation and then a nation. But we can gain further insight into *why* the United States adopted and has continued a federal system if we look at what other countries with similar systems have in common (see Table 3.1). Most federal systems around the world are found in countries that are geographically large and have regions that differ in terms of economic activity, religion, ethnicity, and language. In Germany, for example, the conservative Catholics of the south have traditionally been different from the liberal Protestants of the north and east. In Canada, the farmers of the central plains are not much like the fishermen of Nova Scotia, and the French-speaking (and primarily Catholic) residents of Quebec differ markedly from the English-speaking Protestants of the rest of the country. German, French, and Italian are dominant languages in different parts of Switzerland. India consists of many dramatically different ethnic and religious groups, living far apart in different climates and speaking different languages.

The United States, too, is rather large and diverse, though certainly less diverse than India or the former Soviet Union. From the early days of the Republic, the slave-holding and agriculture-oriented South was quite distinct from the merchant Northeast, and some important differences persist today. Illinois is not Louisiana; the farmers of Iowa differ from defense and electronics workers in California. In the *Federalist Papers*, the Founders argued that this size and diversity made federalism especially appropriate for the new United States.

U.S. Federalism—Pro and Con

Federalism is one of the key *structural* characteristics of American government, affecting many aspects of politics. For example, federalism tends to prevent the emergence of fully unified or disciplined political parties. It limits what the Congress and the president can do, by reserving some powers to the states. It allows for a patchwork of different policies to be pursued in different states and in different regions. Federalism also may have important effects on how well democracy works, as we will explore in the following paragraphs.

Over the years, from the framing of the U.S. Constitution to the present day, people have offered a number of strong arguments for and against federalism. Let us consider some of these arguments.

PRO: DIVERSITY OF NEEDS   The oldest and most important argument in favor of federalism is that, in a large and diverse country, needs and wants and conditions differ from one place to another. Why not let different states enact different public policies to meet their own needs? This might enhance popular sovereignty and majority rule democracy, in the sense that distinct majorities in different states could do what they want instead of being subordinated to a single national majority.

At the Constitutional Convention, Luther Martin took this argument so far as to oppose the new republic itself: "The different states, composing an extensive federal empire, widely distant one from the other, may have interests so totally distinct, that the one part might be greatly benefited by what would be destructive to the other."[7] Alexander Hamilton, a strong advocate of union, felt obliged in

Table 3.1
Selected Federal and Unitary Countries

Name	Land Area (sq. miles)	Population	Major Languages	Major Religions (at least 1% of population)	Comments
I. Federal					
Canada	3,849,672	26,620,500	English, French	Roman Catholic, Protestant, Eastern Orthodox, Jewish	Regionally diverse economy
Germany	137,820	78,934,300	German	Roman Catholic, Protestant, Muslim	Regionally diverse economy and religious cleavages
India	1,222,559	685,184,692	Hindi, Teluga, Bengali, Marathi, Tamil, Urdu, English, nine others	Hindu, Muslim, Christian, Sikh	Extremely diverse ethnically, religiously, and economically
Mexico	756,066	81,484,551	Spanish	Roman Catholic, Protestant	Regionally diverse economy
Nigeria	356,669	119,812,200	English, Hausa, Yoruba, Ibo	Muslim, Protestant, Roman Catholic, Indigenous, Traditional	Major regional cleavages
Switzerland	15,943	6,619,973	German, French, Italian	Roman Catholic, Protestant	Regional and linguistic cleavages
USSR (until 1991)	8,649,800	286,731,000	Russian, Ukranian, Belorussian, Polish, Turkish, Uralian, Caucasian, 12 more	Orthodox Christian, Muslim, Protestant, Roman Catholic	Extremely diverse ethnically, religiously, and economically
USA	3,679,192	249,632,692	English, Spanish	Protestant, Roman Catholic, Jewish, Muslim	Regionally diverse economy
II. Unitary					
France	210,026	56,555,700	French	Roman Catholic, Protestant, Muslim	Relatively homogeneous
Denmark	16,638	5,129,779	Danish	Lutheran	Relatively homogeneous
Hungary	35,920	10,450,000	Hungarian	Roman Catholic, Protestant	Relatively homogeneous
Japan	145,883	123,255,000	Japanese	Shinto, Buddhist, Christian	Relatively homogeneous

1787 to declare that the idea that the national government might become stronger than state governments was "shocking to common sense."[8]

CON: LACK OF NATIONAL STANDARDS   On the other hand, the "needs" that different states pursue may not be worthy ones. William Riker points out that, historically, one of the main effects of federalism was to let white majorities in the southern states enslave and then discriminate against black people, without interference from the North.[9] In attempting to block the registration of a black student at the University of Alabama in 1963, Governor George C. Wallace spoke of the "right of state authority in the operation of the public schools, colleges, and universities"; he refused to submit to "illegal usurpation of power" by the central government. Isn't it often better to insist on national standards that apply everywhere?

PRO: CLOSENESS TO THE PEOPLE   It is sometimes claimed that state and local governments are closer to ordinary citizens, who have a better chance to know their officials, to be aware of what they are doing, to contact them, and to hold them responsible for problems. Thus, President Ronald Reagan, in his 1982 State of the Union address, declared "[My New Federalism] will be designed and administered closer to the grassroots and the people it serves . . . the programs will be more responsive to both the people they are meant to help and the people who pay for them."[10]

CON: LOW VISIBILITY AND LACK OF POPULAR CONTROL   However, geographical closeness may not be very important. In fact, more Americans are actually better informed about the *national* government than they are about state and local governments. The national government gets much more media attention. Also, more people vote in presidential elections—50–55 percent of those eligible—than in state or local elections (often only 30–40 percent). When more people know what the government is doing and when more people vote, they are better able to insist that the government do what they want. For that reason, responsiveness to ordinary citizens is probably greater in national government, and democratic control probably works better. Thus, the government in Washington, D.C., may actually be "closer" to most citizens than their nearby state capital is.

PRO: INNOVATION AND EXPERIMENTATION   When states have independent power, they can try out new ideas. Individual states can be "laboratories." If the experiments work, others can adopt their ideas. Various states have led the way in such matters as allowing women and 18-year-olds to vote before the nation as a whole did, just as California pioneered in fighting air pollution (recall our opening story), New York led in dealing with water pollution, and various states in the 1980s explored ways of ensuring that women would be paid equally for doing jobs of "comparable worth." Early research by political scientist Jack Walker showed that certain states, especially New York, California, and Massachusetts, often took the lead in policy innovation.[11]

Likewise, when the national government is controlled by one political party, federalism allows states with majorities favoring a different party to compensate by enacting different policies. In the late 1970s, for example, while the relatively liberal Carter administration was in power in Washington, D.C., a tax revolt began with Proposition 13 in California. In the 1980s, as the Reagan administration cut back on many domestic social programs, a number of states took up the slack by expanding their own programs. This aspect of diversity in policymaking is related to the Founders' contention that "tyranny" is less likely when government's power is dispersed. Multiple governments reduce the risks from bad policy or blockage of the popular will; if things go wrong at one governmental level, they may go right at another.

CON: LACK OF UNIFORMITY IN RULES AND PROGRAMS   Diversity and experimentation in policies, however, are not always good. Divergent regulations can cause confusion or inefficiency that spills over from one state to another. If New Jersey imposed severe restrictions on the size and weight of trucks traveling on its highways, New York might be severely affected. If cities around the country set different limits on noise at airports, airplane manufacturers and airlines would be unsure of what sorts of planes to build and use. (In 1990, Congress set uniform airplane noise standards for the whole country.)

Certain kinds of government policy simply don't work very well, or don't work at all, without uniform national rules. When factories in the Midwest spew into the air oxides of nitrogen and sulfur that fall as acid rain in the Northeast, northeastern states can do nothing about it. Midwestern states may refuse to pay what it would cost to help the northeasterners. Only national action can solve the problem. Similarly, it is very difficult for cities or local communities to do much about poverty or other social problems. If they raise taxes to pay for social programs, businesses and the wealthy may move out of town and the poor may move in, leaving the city impoverished.[12] During the 1970s and 1980s, many factories moved from the Frost Belt to the Sun Belt, partly in search of low taxes and a good "business climate," where wages were low and organized labor was kept at bay by "right-to-work" laws. An ad in the *New York Times* proclaimed, "When the old corporate tax bite eats away profits, CUT OUT FOR TEXAS."[13]

Thus, innovation by local governments can be undercut by competition among communities for wealth and resources. Only a national government can deal with many aspects of taxes and spending that affect people across state boundaries or that induce competition among states.

As the arguments about federalism indicate, a lot is at stake. It is not likely, however, that Americans will ever have a chance to vote "yes" or "no" on the federal system itself. What we can decide is *how much* federalism we will have and how much power over various policies will go to the states as compared to the national government. In the early 1990s, for example, many states were backing a constitutional amendment to increase their powers. In making decisions about matters of this sort, it is useful to bear in mind the arguments we have just outlined.

It is also important to bear in mind that the national government often has a different political constituency from states and that the nature of the difference changes from one time to another. Arguments about federalism do not just concern abstract institutional arrangements; they affect who wins and who loses valuable benefits. People's opinions about federalism often depend upon their ideologies and upon who happens to control the national government at the moment. During the 1960s and 1970s, for example, liberals, minorities, and city dwellers tended to have much more faith in the national government, where liberal Democrats were powerful, than they did in the states. In the 1980s, when Republican administrations dominated Washington, D.C., some of these same liberal groups turned to the states, where they then had more influence.

THE CONSTITUTION AND SHARED POWERS

We have called federalism a *structural* fact about American government because it is enshrined in the U.S. Constitution. Federalism is deeply established and would be extremely difficult to abolish, even if most Americans wanted to be rid of it. The Constitution embodies federalism in two main ways. First, power is expressly shared with, and reserved to, the states. Second, the national government itself partly functions through state-based institutions.

The Constitution makes clear that state governments have independent powers. The "Supremacy Clause" in Article VI, Section 1 declares that the Constitution, laws, and treaties of the United States shall be the "supreme law of the land," but Article I, Section 8 enumerates what kinds of laws Congress has the power to pass, and the Tenth Amendment declares that the powers not delegated to the United States by the Constitution, nor prohibited by it to the states, are *"reserved to the states* (emphasis added) respectively, or to the people." (This provision is unique to the United States; other federal systems, like Germany's, reserve to the *national* government all functions not explicitly given to the states.) That is, the Constitution specifically lists what the national government can do: lay taxes, regulate commerce, establish post offices, declare war, and the like, plus make laws "necessary and proper" for carrying out those powers; it then provides that all other legitimate government functions can be performed by the states, except for a few things, such as coining money or conducting foreign policy, which are excluded by Article I, Section 10.

Moreover, the Constitution's provisions about the formation of the national government recognize a special position for the states. The Constitution declared in Article VII that it was "done in Convention" "by the unanimous consent of the *states* (emphasis added) present" and provided that it would go into effect, not when a majority of all Americans voted for it, but when the conventions of nine *states* (emphasis added) ratified it. Article V provides that the Constitution can be amended only when the legislatures or conventions in three-quarters of the states ratify an amendment. Article V, Section 3, paragraph 1 makes clear that no states can be combined or divided into new states without the consent of the state legislatures concerned.

The Constitution also provides special roles for the states in the workings of the new national government itself: in deciding who could vote for members of the U.S. House of Representatives (Art. I, Sec. 2); in giving each state two senators, who cannot be taken away, even by Constitutional amendment (Art. V), and who, until 1913, were chosen by the state legislatures rather than by the voters (Art. I, Sec. 3); and in the complicated system for choosing a president (Art. II, Sec. 2).

In addition, Article IV of the Constitution sets forth a few provisions regulating relations among the states, including the requirements that each state give "full faith and credit" to the public acts, records, and judicial proceedings of every other state, and that citizens in each state are entitled to all the "privileges and immunities" of citizens in the several states. Also, fugitives from justice have to be delivered up to a state demanding them back. The Constitutional provisions underlying the federal system are summarized in Table 3.2.

We suggest that you look back at the Constitution in the Appendix to remind yourself where these provisions appear and exactly what they say. As you reread the Constitution, you will see that the Founders clearly intended to establish a

Trying to amend the Constitution: These protesters back the Equal Rights Amendment for women, which did not quite win ratification in the necessary three-quarters of the states.

Table 3.2
Constitutional Underpinnings of Federalism

1. Supremacy of the national government in its own sphere
   Supremacy Clause (Art. VI)
2. Limitations on national government powers and reservation of powers to the states
   Enumerated national powers (Art. I, Sec. 8)
   Limits on national powers (Art. I, Sec. 9; Art. IV, Sec. 3; Eleventh Amendment)
   Bill of Rights (Amendments 1–10)
   Reservation Clause (Tenth Amendment)
3. Limitations on state powers
   Original restrictions (Art. I, Sec. 10)
   Civil War amendments (Amendments 13–15)
4. State role in national government
   Ratification of Constitution (Art. VII)
   Amendment of Constitution (Art. V)
   Apportionment and election of representatives (Art. I, Sec. 2 and Sec. 4)
   Two senators from each state (Art I, Sec. 3)
   No deprivation of state suffrage in Senate (Art. V)
   Choice of senators (Art. I, Sec. 3; however, see Seventeenth Amendment)
   Election of president (Art. II, Sec. 1; however, see Twelfth Amendment)
5. Regulation of relations among states
   Full faith and credit (Art. IV, Sec. 1)
   Privileges and immunities (Art. IV, Sec. 2)

federal system, with powers divided between the states and the national government. At the same time, however, you will see that the exact division of powers is left rather vague. The working out of the exact nature of state and national government powers has been a major subject of struggle and conflict in American history—struggle that has taken place in the courts and legislatures, but also in a civil war.

STRUGGLE OVER THE WORKING OF FEDERALISM

It took a long time after the adoption of the Constitution for the present federal system to emerge. There were ebbs and flows in the relative power of the states and federal government. Bit by bit, however, through a series of stages and milestone events, the national government gained ground. This partly reflected the trends of increased industrialization and economic growth, and increasing foreign policy involvement, discussed in the next chapter. But the particular milestones in the evolution of federalism also resulted from bitter and divisive struggles over a series of issues, especially slavery, race, and regional economic interests. There were several threats or attempts by states to "nullify" national government laws, and the bloody and destructive Civil War was fought over the question of whether southern states had the right to secede from the Union.

During the late 1790s, for example, during the administration of John Adams, Thomas Jefferson's Republicans deeply resented the Alien and Sedition Acts, which the Federalists used to restrict political dissent. The Virginia and Kentucky Resolutions (secretly authored by Jefferson) declared that states did not have to obey unconstitutional national laws and indicated that the states could decide what was unconstitutional. In that case, the more agrarian, democratic, and liberal South was opposing a national government run by the more merchant-oriented, conservative Federalists of the Northeast. About a decade later, the merchants of New England turned things around by strongly opposing Republican President Monroe's War of 1812 against Britain, which interfered with their trade; at the Hartford Convention, they (like Jefferson previously) declared that unconstitutional actions by the national government, namely the embargo on trade with Britain, could be declared null and void by the states. Neither effort at nullification prevailed, however. Nor did the later effort by John C. Calhoun and other southern agriculturalists to declare the "tariff of abominations," the high 1833 tariff (which raised the prices of imports and hurt their agricultural exports), to be null and void.

These early struggles demonstrate three things: (1) the exact shape of federalism matters. It can affect things like wars, civil liberties, and trade, which have an impact on many people's lives. (2) Important conflicts have been waged over these issues. (3) Peoples' positions on matters of high "principle," such as the proper nature of federalism, have had a way of shifting, depending on the immediate issues at stake. The advocates of "states' rights" have sometimes been northerners, sometimes southerners; sometimes Republicans, sometimes Federalists (sometimes liberals, sometimes conservatives), depending upon exactly who would gain or lose.

The ultimate shape of federalism in the United States, however, was strongly affected by the Supreme Court and by events surrounding the Civil War.

Supreme Court Review Over the States

One crucial question about federalism in the early years of the United States concerned who, if anyone, would enforce the Supremacy Clause. Who would make sure that the U.S. laws and Constitution were actually the "supreme law of the land," controlling state laws? The answer turned out to be that the U.S. Supreme Court would do it, but this answer emerged only gradually and haltingly as the Court established its power within the federal system.

In *Chisholm v. Georgia* (1793), for example, the Supreme Court heard a suit by two citizens of South Carolina against the state of Georgia over a debt. After Georgia refused to appear, the Court ordered payment of the money to the Carolinians. But what one scholar calls a "gale of opposition" from states' rights advocates led to the adoption of the Eleventh Amendment to the Constitution, taking away any U.S. judicial power over suits commenced against a state.[14]

Only after the strong-willed but more subtle John Marshall became chief justice in 1801 and established the Supreme Court's authority to declare national laws unconstitutional in *Marbury v. Madison* (1803) (see Chapter 14, "The Courts"), did the Supreme Court return to the question of power over the states. In *Fletcher v. Peck* (1810), it finally acted to hold a state law unconstitutional under the U.S. Constitution. In 1795, the state of Georgia had sold a huge tract of land, including most of what is now Mississippi and Alabama, at bargain prices, because many members of the legislature were bribed to do so. Amidst scandal and public outrage, a new legislature voted to rescind the sale, but meanwhile millions of acres had been resold to more or less innocent third parties. After a complicated series of events, the Supreme Court ruled that the third-party titles to the land were valid, because the rescinding act violated the U.S. Constitution. Exactly what provision of the Constitution (if any) was violated was left murky. However, what is remembered about *Fletcher v. Peck* is not that the Supreme Court, in order to protect property rights, let land speculators get away with fleecing the people of Georgia, but, rather, that the Court for the first time clearly exercised the power to hold state laws unconstitutional. As in *Marbury v. Madison*, Chief Justice Marshall cleverly avoided explicit discussion of the Court's power. He simply took it for granted and used it.[15]

Soon, in *Martin v. Hunter's Lessee* (1816), the Supreme Court solidified its position in relation to the states by explicitly upholding as constitutional Section 25 of the Judiciary Act of 1789, which allowed the Court to use a "writ of error" to review (and overturn) state court decisions that denied a claim made under the Constitution or laws or treaties of the United States. In language important to the interpretation of federalism, Justice Story declared that the Constitution was the creation of "the people of the United States," not of the individual states, and that the people could and did decide to modify state sovereignty.[16]

The Triumph of National Power

The struggles over federalism in the nineteenth and twentieth centuries resulted in gradual increases in the power of the national government and the placing of certain new limits on the states. Sometimes the U.S. Supreme Court led the way. Undoubtedly, the most important example is Chief Justice Marshall's decision in the case of *McCulloch v. Maryland* (1821).

Federalism often involves a struggle over resources. Here governors urge the national government to give more money to the cities.

The state of Maryland imposed a tax on notes issued by the Bank of the United States, which had been incorporated by Congress in 1816. The U.S. government argued that such a tax on a federal entity was invalid. Maryland replied that incorporation of the bank was unconstitutional, exceeding Congress's powers, and, in any case, states could tax whatever they wanted within their own borders. But in *McCulloch*, Chief Justice Marshall upheld the constitutionality of the bank's incorporation and its immunity from taxation, and made a major statement justifying extensive national authority. He declared that the Constitution emanated from the sovereign people. The people made their national government supreme over all rivals within the sphere of its powers, and those powers must be construed generously if they are to be sufficient for the "various crises" of the age to come. Congress had power to incorporate the bank under the clause of Article I, Section 8, authorizing Congress to make all laws "necessary and proper" for carrying into execution its named powers. Moreover, Maryland's tax was invalid, because "the power to tax involves the power to destroy," which would defeat the national government's supremacy within its sphere. Justice Marshall's broad reading of the "necessary and proper" clause laid the foundation for steady expansion of what the national government could do in the years ahead. He made clear that states would not be allowed to interfere.[17]

At times during the nineteenth century, the Supreme Court limited state government actions based on the Constitution itself (the "contract clause," for example), without any legislation from Congress. At times it also ruled that provisions of the U.S. Constitution (e.g., the "commerce clause") may actually *exclude* states from acting in certain areas where they might interfere with federal legislation. This doctrine of "preemption" remains with us still. When the national government has acted on a certain subject, the states cannot do so.

Soon the issue of slavery in the western territories came to dominate disputes about the nature of federalism. As new, nonslave states were settled and sought to join the Union, white southerners feared that their political power in Washington, D.C., (especially in the Senate)—and therefore their ability to protect their own slave system—was slipping away. The Missouri Compromise of 1820 established an equal number of slave and free states, and banned slavery in the territories above a line running westward to the Rockies from Missouri's southern

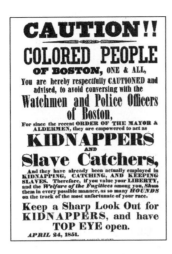

The Fugitive Slave Act of 1850 outraged many northerners. This poster by Boston abolitionists warns escaped slaves that they might be captured and sent back to the south.

border. But the acquisition of vast new territories in the Southwest through the Mexican War reopened the question as to whether new states would be slave or free. The Compromise of 1850 admitted California as a free state and temporarily balanced matters (in white southerners' eyes) by enacting the Fugitive Slave Act, which compelled private citizens in the North to help return runaway slaves, but many northerners bitterly resented that act. The decision in 1854 to organize Kansas and Nebraska as territories and let them decide for themselves whether to become slave or free states (even though they were above the Missouri Compromise line and therefore supposed to be free) led to violence between pro- and anti-slavery forces in "bleeding Kansas."

In 1860, the northern and southern wings of the Democratic party split apart, and Republican Abraham Lincoln was elected president. South Carolina seceded from the Union, soon followed by the other six states of the deep South, which created the Confederate States of America. President Lincoln decided to relieve the besieged U.S. garrison at Fort Sumter, South Carolina, and the Civil War began.

CRUCIAL EFFECTS OF THE CIVIL WAR   The northern victory in the Civil War was a crucial event for American federalism. For one thing, it decisively established that the Union was indissoluble; states could not withdraw or secede. For another, it resulted in constitutional changes that subordinated the states to certain new kinds of national standards, enforced by the central government. In particular, the Fourteenth Amendment (1868) declared that *no state* (emphasis added) shall "deprive any person of life, liberty, or property, without due process of law; nor deny to any person within its jurisdiction the equal protection of the laws." The "due process" clause eventually became the vehicle by which the Supreme Court ruled that the civil liberties of the Bill of Rights (which in the original Constitution were protected only against the national government) were also protected against the states. And the "equal protection" clause eventually was made the foundation for protecting the rights of blacks, women, and other categories of people against discrimination by state or local governments. (These matters are discussed in Chapter 19, "Rights and Liberties.")

Still another effect of the Civil War was to set precedents for an enormous expansion of the federal government's power, especially in wartime. President Lincoln exerted extraordinary emergency powers, spending government money without congressional authorization, suspending the writ of habeas corpus in war zones, and freeing slaves in occupied southern territories by the Emancipation Proclamation. The huge military and industrial effort of waging the war established patterns for future government action of many sorts.

NATIONAL GOVERNMENT EXPANSION   Since the Civil War, the activities of the national government have expanded greatly, eventually reaching the present-day situation, in which they touch on almost every aspect of daily life and are thoroughly entangled with state government activities. During the late nineteenth century, the national government was increasingly active in administering western lands, subsidizing economic development (granting railroads enormous tracts of land along their transcontinental lines), helping farmers, and beginning to regulate business, particularly through the Interstate Commerce Act of 1887 and the Sherman Antitrust Act of 1890.

These activities gave the national government increasing weight in relation to the states, which was greatly accentuated by Woodrow Wilson's "New Freedom" programs of 1913–1914, and especially by Franklin Roosevelt's New Deal of the 1930s and Lyndon Johnson's Great Society measures of the 1960s. The New Deal created many new, national regulatory agencies to supervise various aspects of business, including communications (the Federal Communications Commission, or FCC), airlines (CAB), financial markets (SEC), and utilities (FPC), and labor-management relations (NLRB). (These and other acronyms are spelled out in Appendix II.) The New Deal brought national government spending in areas like welfare and relief that had previously been reserved almost entirely to the states, and the Great Society increased this tendency. But wars were crucial: the federal government did not spend as much as the states and localities until two years of World War I (temporarily) and then World War II. Ever since World War II, the federal government has *spent* nearly twice as much per year as the states and localities put together, though, increasingly, the states—and especially local governments—have had many more civilian *employees*[18] (see Figure 3.3).

For a time, the U.S. Supreme Court resisted the growth in national government power; it struck down a national Child Labor Law as unconstitutional in 1918 and in the 1930s declared unconstitutional such important New Deal measures as the National Recovery Act and the Agricultural Adjustment Act. For the most part, however, the Supreme Court has been a nationalizing force. It has interpreted the Constitution more and more broadly, to permit ever-expanding national government authority. After 1937, warding off President Roosevelt's court-packing plan, the Court approved the essential elements of the New Deal, including the Social Security Act and the National Labor Relations Act. Since that time, the Court has approved virtually every piece of national legislation that has come before it.

An important example is the Civil Rights Act of 1964, which rests on a very broad interpretation of the commerce clause. In the 1964 Act, the national government asserted a power to forbid discrimination at lunch counters and other public accommodations on the grounds that they are engaged in interstate commerce: they serve food imported from out of state. State economies are so closely tied to each other that, by this standard, practically every economic transaction everywhere affects interstate commerce and is subject to national legislative power.

Today, too, federalism is very different from what it was in the 1790s or early 1800s. One major difference is that the national government is dominant in many

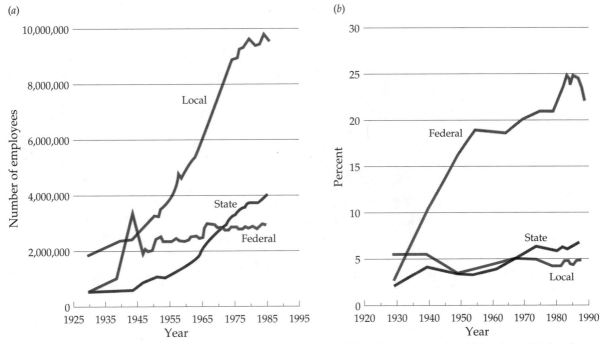

Figure 3.3 The size of federal, state, and local government. (*a*) Number of federal, state, and local government employees. (*b*) Government spending as a percentage of GNP.

Source: Harold Stanley and Richard G. Niemi, Vital Statistics on American Politics, *2nd ed. (Washington, D.C.: Congressional Quarterly, 1990), pp. 292, 308.*

policy areas; it calls the shots for the states. Another is that state and national government powers and activities have become deeply intertwined and entangled with each other. An old, simple-minded metaphor for federalism is of a "layer cake": a system in which state and national powers are neatly divided like layers of pastry. If we stay with the bakery image, a much more accurate metaphor is now that of a "marble cake," in which elements of national and state influence swirl around each other, without any clear boundaries.[19]

Contemporary disputes and conflicts over federalism are much milder than they once were: no more civil war; no more nullification; not even state governors "standing in the schoolhouse door" to prevent desegregation. As we will see in the next section, now arguments about federalism are more likely to concern the amount and type of national grants to the states and restrictions that the national government imposes on the states.

NATIONAL GRANTS-IN-AID TO THE STATES

The aptness of the "marble cake" metaphor is especially evident in programs in which the national government grants money for use by the states, within programs largely shaped or regulated by the national government. Grants-in-aid of this sort involve a complicated mixture of national and local government activity and control.

President Johnson
visits sites of the
Job Corps, part of
his Great Society.

The Growth of Grants-in-Aid

National government grants began, in a sense, at least as early as the 1787 North-west Ordinance, which organized the territory of the Midwest north of the Ohio River and east of the Mississippi River. It granted land for government seats, schools, and colleges in the territory, and imposed various regulations, such as forbidding the importation of any new slaves. The national government was not very active in the early nineteenth century, but it did provide some land grants to the states to help build roads, canals, railroads, and the like, and gave the states modest cash grants for the maintenance of state militias. In 1862, the Morrill Act gave the states U.S. public lands to establish and support agricultural colleges.

Some small cash grant programs were begun around 1900 for agriculture, vocational education, and matching funds to build highways. At the beginning of the twentieth century, annual national grants to the states totaled only some $6 million; they grew to about $100 million in the early 1920s (the bulk going for highways) and nearly $300 million toward the end of the 1930s.[20] But by far the biggest growth occurred during the 1950s, 1960s, and 1970s, under both Republican and Democratic administrations, as a result of Dwight Eisenhower's interstate highway program and Lyndon Johnson's Great Society. The annual amount of national grants-in-aid reached $91.5 *billion* by 1980: close to $500 for each person in the country. Between 1960 and 1975, the total amount of annual grants doubled every five or six years. In terms of constant 1980 dollars (i.e., adjusting for inflation), the amount grew a bit more slowly but still tripled from $7.9 billion in 1950 to more than $20 billion in the early 1960s, and then quadrupled again to $91.5 billion, its peak, in 1980[21] (see Figure 3.4).

The key reason for this increase in national grant money to the states was that Congress sought to deal with many nationwide problems—especially interstate highways, poverty, crime, and pollution—by setting policy at the national level and by providing money from national tax revenues, while having state and local officials carry the policies out. The argument in favor of doing this had three parts.

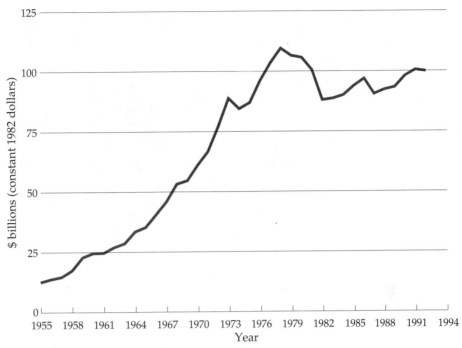

Figure 3.4 The growth of federal grants-in-aid

Source: Advisory Commission on Intergovernmental Relations, Significant Features of Fiscal Federalism *(Washington, D.C.: 1990), Vol II, p. 42.*

First, the states could not or would not do many of these things on their own. They would not spend their own money, either because much of the benefit would go to people in other places (Milwaukee, Wisconsin, for example, did not want to pay for a cleanup of Lake Michigan, which would benefit Chicago, Illinois) or because such spending would put them at a competitive disadvantage in terms of attracting business investment and high-income citizens. As we have seen, antipoverty measures and other redistributive programs are hard to enact locally, because a state or a city that helps the poor may drive its industrial base away with high taxes, while its benefit programs attract more and more poor people to move in from elsewhere. In terms of our framework, this is a *structural* reason for the growth of national government involvement.

Second, national government tax revenues seemed abundant in the 1960s, when these programs were begun (at least until the Vietnam War began to devour resources), and the money came mostly from the federal income tax, which at that time was rather progressive; that is, people with high incomes paid a higher percentage of what they earned than people with low incomes. This seemed an especially appropriate source of money to combat poverty.

Third, and finally, many of these programs involved complicated goods and services that had to be provided at the local level—not like Social Security pension checks, which can be sent in the mail from Washington, D.C., but new kinds of job training, new classes in the schools (compensatory education, preprimary preparation, special education), new medical programs and institutions (clinics or

National "Head Start" grants-in-aid for local preschool programs are among the most popular and enduring legacies of the Great Society.

health maintenance organizations for the poor, reimbursement programs for local doctors and hospitals), new plants for sewage treatment, and the like. Local officials on the scene seemed to be the appropriate people to carry out these programs.

CATEGORICAL GRANTS   Many of the new programs were established through **categorical grants**, which gave the states money but clearly specified the category of activity for which the money had to be spent and often defined rather precisely how the program had to work. This was true, for example, of the Elementary and Secondary Education Act of 1965, the Medicaid program of 1965, and the Clean Air Act of 1970. In a few cases, like the Community Action program under the Equal Opportunity Act of 1964 (the "War on Poverty"), the national government actually bypassed state and local governments altogether, giving money directly to community organizations for antipoverty activities.

As the new programs were developed and enacted, there was much talk about the "marble cake" metaphor and a new system of "cooperative" federalism.[22] Soon, however, conflicts between the national and state governments emerged. In some cases, the national rules and guidelines were vague, and state and local governments used the money for purposes that were different from what Congress intended. This is not surprising, since the point was to get states and localities to do things they would not otherwise have done. So national government agencies tended to tighten up their rules. But when rules and procedures were strict, state and local governments complained about "red tape" and objected that they were being forced to do things that they did not want to do. And when state and local governments were bypassed, there was a great outcry. The Community Action program, for example, designed to fund local organizations and to empower poor people, was abolished when it aroused vehement objections from mayors and others whose authority was threatened.[23]

Some of the objections came from people who disagreed with the program's goals. For example, a number of state and local officials simply did not want to spend a lot of money—national or local—on antipoverty programs. In part, this was a partisan matter; Republican officials in some of the states tended to oppose redistributive programs enacted by the Democratic Congress and the president in Washington, D.C. They were happy to get national government money but wanted to use it for different purposes. They worked to get the programs altered or abolished.

BLOCK GRANTS AND REVENUE SHARING   Thus, the Republican Nixon and Ford administrations from 1969 through 1976 tended to loosen national control, moving more toward **block grants**, which gave money for more general purposes and with fewer rules than did categorical grant programs. There was also a trend toward **general revenue sharing**, with no federal controls at all. Already in the 1960s, five block grant programs had been established, for such purposes as community development, law enforcement assistance, and employment training and assistance. President Nixon spoke of a "New Federalism" and pushed to increase these kinds of grants, with few strings attached, which often provided money for general purposes under an automatic "formula" related to the number of needy residents, the total size of the population, the average income level, or other statistical characteristics of each state or locality.

The use of such formulas has changed the politics of national grants. Many disputes have focused on adjusting the formulas to benefit one state or region rather than another. Cities and states from the Frost Belt, for example, fought some bitter battles with those from the Sun Belt in the late 1970s over exactly how formulas would be set. The use of formulas also means that statistical counts by the census affect how much money states and localities get, so census counts themselves become subjects of political conflict. In 1990, Illinois, New York, and Chicago sued the Commerce Department over alleged undercounts of their populations (especially the urban poor); the city of Detroit desperately tried to show that its declining population still exceeded the important 1 million mark.

Block grants and revenue sharing fell out of favor, however, in the late 1970s. From 1972 to 1986, some $85 billion were spent on general revenue sharing from the national government to state and local governments. But this program did not grow very fast, and an increasing number of strings were attached to the money. General revenue sharing was ended in 1987. Indeed block grants and general

When 1990 census takers failed to count some of the urban poor and homeless, cities got less money in national grants.

revenue sharing programs together did not grow as fast as categorical programs (only 11 percent between 1975 and 1978, compared with 56 percent for categorical grants). They reached their peak in 1978 at 27 percent of total grants but then declined to 18 percent in 1986.

The problem was that the strongest backers of the grant programs, namely Democrats in Congress, groups of beneficiaries like the elderly, the poor, black people, and environmentalists, and service providers like teachers, social workers, and health care professionals, all tended to distrust state and local governments. They knew that local governments often had different goals; they feared that special interests at the local level would divert money away from its original targets, so they insisted that the national government keep tight regulations on what local governments could do with grant money.

Thus, the Democrats in Congress defeated most of President Reagan's 1981 effort to promote still another "new federalism" by consolidating 57 programs into a few block grants; so many restrictions were imposed that the nine new block grants resembled categorical grants. At the same time, money for any sort of federal grants was beginning to dry up.

The Slowdown in Federal Money: Structural, Political, and Governmental Factors

By the beginning of the 1980s, the flow of federal money to the states had begun to slow down. The reasons included certain *structural* factors—the general decline in the U.S. economy at the end of the 1970s and increasing pressure on national tax revenues—together with major *political* and *governmental* changes: increased interest group pressure to cut domestic spending, and the arrival of the new Reagan administration, which was committed to such cuts.

As we have indicated, block grants and revenue sharing lost support among liberals in Congress, because much of the money went for purposes other than what they had in mind: many of the dollars they wanted to use to rebuild poor inner-city neighborhoods in Detroit and New York, for example, were spent instead on beautifying downtown shopping areas in places like Twin Falls, Idaho. Some law enforcement assistance money went to heavy weaponry for police (antiriot guns and armored cars). Automatic funding formulas spread cash widely, not only to poor areas, but also to affluent suburbs; not only to the declining Frost Belt, but also to the growing Sun Belt, which further reduced the enthusiasm of northern liberals for general grants. At the same time, many conservatives were objecting to the more closely targeted and regulated categorical grant programs. They complained about red tape and said that the federal bureaucracy was not responsive to local needs and local ways of doing things.

THE EFFECTIVENESS OF GRANTS   Reinforcing these objections, a number of scholars and journalists wrote books about the failures of "implementation." They implied that relationships between state and national governments were so complicated and that so many different, uncoordinated agencies were involved—with rigid rules and doubtful competence—that there was simply no hope of attaining the objectives of national legislation. An especially influential book about the failure of a minority assistance program administered by the Economic Development Administration in Oakland, California, convinced many people that such federal programs were doomed to failure.[24]

Later research has indicated that this discouraging conclusion was overstated. True, some complexity is inherent in a federal system, and fairly specific rules seem to be necessary to ensure that national purposes are carried out. Also, it is difficult to be sure exactly how effective a particular program is without doing an elaborate social experiment, which would be very expensive and might raise ethical questions if a "control group" were deprived of benefits. Still, there is reason to believe that many federal grants-in-aid, especially categorical grants, have had good effects and have been administered efficiently and effectively.

One study of health, housing, and education programs in several locations expressed surprise at finding a high level of "cooperation, competence, energy, and seriousness" among national, state, and local administrators. Some implementation problems had emerged at the beginning, but, once programs were well under way, most were effective, largely because they developed a corps of highly professional administrators who were committed to the programs' purposes. Several were redistributive programs that the states would not have undertaken on their own. For such programs to succeed, they had to be insulated from local politics.[25]

A CONSERVATIVE TURN IN POLITICS   Complaints from scholars and politicians about inefficiency played a part in slowing the flow of federal dollars to the states during the end of the 1970s, but more important in eliminating funds were certain *structural* factors. After the oil crisis and price rises of 1973–1974, which doubled the price of crude oil, the American economy sank into a period of "stagflation"—simultaneous inflation (rising prices) and stagnation (low growth, high unemployment). At the same time, international economic competition was getting rough. Japanese electronic goods and automobiles took over more and more of the U.S. market; U.S. firms had a harder and harder time selling their products abroad. Things got even worse after the second oil price shock of 1979. For the next three or four years, the United States suffered through its worst recession since World War II, with inflation rising to a rate of 13.5 percent in 1980, unemployment soaring to 9.6 percent, and the stock and bond markets falling.[26]

With these structural forces at work, the response at the *political* level was a very conservative one. Most business firms fought to reduce their costs by eliminating expensive government regulations, lowering wages, and cutting their taxes. As we will see in Chapter 8, "Political Parties," even some multinational, capital intensive firms that had traditionally supported the Democrats were no longer willing to pay taxes for domestic social programs. Instead, they wanted to cut taxes and to shift spending to the military, where a buildup could help protect markets and investments in the Third World. Practically all segments of American business began investing money in think tanks, publications, and political action committees to promote these conservative causes and to assist conservative (mostly Republican) political candidates.[27]

Together with discontent about stagflation and foreign policy failures under the Carter administration, the outpouring of conservative money helped in 1980 to elect as president Ronald Reagan, who was committed to cut domestic spending, cut taxes, and increase military spending. Thus, *governmental* influences changed.

When the Reagan administration took office in 1981, with much strengthened Republican representation and with weakened and apprehensive Democrats in Congress, it did exactly what it said it would do. Reagan's dramatic 1981 success in cutting taxes is described in Chapter 12 on the Presidency. Another major shift in policy was that federal grants-in-aid to the states were cut back. It was not just that they no longer grew so quickly; they actually declined, in terms of purchasing power and as a proportion of the Gross National Product. By 1984, states and localities were getting only about one-quarter of their revenues from the federal government rather than their accustomed one-third.[28] (Glance back at Figure 3.4.)

During the rest of the 1980s, grants-in-aid stabilized and then rose somewhat, but state populations and state needs were growing, too. The national government's contribution, as a proportion of the nation's economy, did not return to the 1980 peak of 3.4 percent of GNP; the 1991 figure was only 2.2 percent.[29] No wonder that during the 1990s many state governments were in crisis.

NATIONAL VERSUS LOCAL CONTROL

Federal money, though less abundant than it once was, is still a major source of revenue for states. In response, **intergovernmental lobbies** by state and local governments, often with permanent offices in Washington, D.C., actively try to influence national policy. In the 1990 conflict over the national budget, for example, when a "summit" agreement was worked out by the Bush administration and

"Sorry, but all my power's been turned back to the states."

Drawing by Lorenz; The New Yorker Magazine, Inc.

Opposition to federal court-ordered busing for school integration formed
one element in a conservative turn in U. S. politics at the end of the
1970s. The photograph shows a demonstration in Charleston, South
Carolina, against federal court-ordered busing.

congressional leaders, state governors and legislators immediately objected. An
analyst for the National Conference of State Legislatures said that various provisions would cost states about $7 billion over five years, while proposed increases
in federal taxes on tobacco, gasoline, and alcohol would (by decreasing consumption and displacing state taxes) cut state tax revenues by about $7.6 billion over
the same period.[30]

Many contemporary aspects of federalism involve not money, but *control*.
The national government exerts strong control over many state-administered pro-
grams, using a variety of different means, particularly **mandates** and **conditions**.
The way federalism works today reflects the historical developments just outlined.

Forms of Federal Regulation

MANDATES   The government in Washington, D.C., often imposes a mandate, or
demand, that the states carry out certain policies even when little or no national
government aid is involved. This is especially true of regulations involving civil
rights and the environment. Most civil rights policies flow from the Equal Protection Clause of the Fourteenth Amendment to the U.S. Constitution, which explicitly restricts state action, and from national legislation, which attempts to impose
uniform national standards. Most environmental regulations also come from the
national government, since problems of dirty air, polluted water, and acid rain
cross state boundaries. Many civil rights and environmental regulations are enforced by the federal courts, which interpret and carry out requirements of the
U.S. Constitution and federal legislation.

Since the 1954 Supreme Court decision in *Brown v. Board of Education*, for
example, which held that school segregation violates the U.S. Constitution, the
federal (i.e., national) courts have required that many local school districts admit

black children to previously all-white schools. They have required local governments to redraw attendance boundaries so that schools will not stay segregated due to segregated housing patterns. And, in some cases, where local officials have resisted—in Boston, for example—the courts have appointed special federal "masters" with authority to administer the schools themselves.

Federal courts also have forced local fire departments not to discriminate against black people in their hiring decisions; have insisted on scattered (rather than concentrated and segregated) locations for public housing; and have ordered communities to end police brutality against blacks. Courts have mandated extensive reform of overcrowded state prisons, most notably in Texas, though the Supreme Court—as it moved in a more conservative direction—severely restricted these and other kinds of suits. National laws and regulations like the Clean Air Act of 1990 have required that state governments set up envionmental protection agencies and enforce federal standards that limit the kinds and amounts of pollutants that can be discharged.

CONDITIONS ON AID   As we have already seen, many categorical grant-in-aid programs require that states spend the money only in certain restricted ways. Increasingly, even general block grants have carried conditions. This is still the most important way in which the national government controls state government actions. In theory, these conditions are "voluntary," because states could say no to the aid, but, in practice, there is no clear line between incentives and coercion. Since states cannot generally afford to give up federal money, they have to accept the conditions.

Some of the most important provisions of the 1964 Civil Rights Act, for example, are those which declare that no federal aid of any kind can be used in ways that discriminate against people on grounds of race, gender, religion, or national origin. Thus, the enormous program of national aid for elementary and secondary education, which began in 1965, became an irresistible lever for forcing schools to desegregate. Likewise, the national money that goes to universities to help with teaching and research would be cut off if universities discriminated in admissions or hiring.

As these examples suggest, some conditions on grants-in-aid "cross over" to affect matters not directly related to the main purpose of the grant. The national government uses its money to get leverage over many diverse matters. During the energy crisis of the 1970s, all states were required to impose a 55 mile-per-hour speed limit or lose a portion of their highway assistance funds. All states did so. Similarly, in 1984, all states were required to set a minimum drinking age of 21 or have their highway aid cut by 15 percent.

Often the national government "preempts" state government action concerning some policy area—that is, it sets up laws and standards that override any state rules—but it relies on state enforcement of the national standards. Examples include clean air standards, occupational health and safety rules, and environmental restrictions on surface mining.

State Innovation and Burdens on the States

During the 1980s and early 1990s, when the national government was slowing down its spending on domestic programs and its grants to the states, a number of state governments moved to take up the slack. Many states, for example, increased their Medicaid programs to help the poor with medical expenses; by 1989, the states were paying 44 percent of all Medicaid costs, and the national government 56 percent. One enthusiast commented: "Look at the states. The Great Society has just begun."

As we have seen, California and New York innovated certain environmental matters, moving ahead of the more cautious Reagan and Bush administrations. Some states also took the lead in requiring that women be paid according to the "comparable worth" of their jobs. After the Supreme Court's 1989 *Webster* decision, which gave the states more leeway to regulate abortion, several states liberalized their abortion laws or turned back efforts to make them more restrictive.

New programs, however, require new taxes, especially when national government grants-in-aid are harder to get. Many states raised sales taxes and excise taxes on gasoline, cigarettes, alcohol, and the like, all of which hit low- and middle-income people particularly hard. These taxes hurt. State governments face painful choices, either to raise taxes or to cut popular programs, neither of which is likely to please the voters. Annual budget crises and huge deficits have become routine.

By the beginning of the 1990s, therefore, state politics had become hazardous to the health of incumbents. Voters were angry and tended to throw state governors out of office, often after their first terms. In 1990, when nearly all of the incumbent senators and representatives running for office were reelected, the party in power lost 14 of the 36 gubernatorial elections. Incumbent governors were defeated in Florida, Kansas, Michigan, Minnesota, Nebraska, and Rhode Island, and party control of the governorship switched in eight other states, including Texas and Ohio. In Connecticut, third-party candidate Lowell Weicker defeated both the Republican and the Democratic hopefuls. In Massachusetts, Democratic candidate John Silber narrowly lost after campaigning *against* the unpopular policies of Democratic Governor (and former presidential candidate) Michael Dukakis.[31]

DEMOCRACY AND FEDERALISM

We have dealt with federalism in this early section of the book because federalism is a crucial *structural* factor that affects many different aspects of politics, from the nature of the party system, to the way in which public policy is organized, to the way in which the president is chosen. It is a crucial part of the rules of the game, which we will encounter again and again.

The federal system has many consequences. One, certainly, is a high degree of *complexity* in policymaking and policy implementation. The involvement of many different state, local, and national agencies in the same policy areas means that there is room for confusion and inefficiency

Federalism does permit *diversity* of responses to diverse situations, and it allows for *experimentation* and for trying out policies different from those of the particular party that is running things in Washington, D.C. At the same time, it entails substantial *inequality* of certain kinds that we may think inappropriate. The individual states, for example, each set their own levels of benefits under the Aid to Families with Dependent Children (AFDC) welfare program, which is partly paid for by the national government. Benefits vary widely from state to state: in one year, Mississippi paid only $91 per month, while Vermont paid $400. Unemployment insurance benefits vary from only one-fifth of former wages to

THE STRUGGLE FOR DEMOCRACY

Letting 18- to 20-Year-Olds Vote

On June 19, 1968, students at University of the Pacific in Stockton, California, began a national campaign to lower the voting age from 21 to 18. They called their drive "LUV" (Let Us Vote) and claimed to have the support of such diverse groups as the American Legion, the Junior Chamber of Commerce, and the American Federation of Labor and Congress of Industrial Organizations (AFL-CIO).[a] For the next few years, they represented what had become a new voice in American politics—the young.

In 1971, the Twenty-Sixth Amendment to the U.S. Constitution proclaimed the right of 18- to 20-year-olds to vote in all federal, state, and local elections, overriding contrary state laws and expanding the electorate by about 11 million people. How this came about illustrates the struggle for more democracy in the United States, as well as the difficulties of managing a federal system.

At the *structural* level, international events—namely the Vietnam War—and changing demographics were very important causes of the new amendment. That thousands of young men were

mature enough to fight and die for their country provided an overwhelming moral argument in favor of letting them vote. Getting young people to "work within the system," rather than protesting outside it, provided a strong practical argument. Moreover, evidence that young people were better educated than their elders (more of them were completing high school and going on to college) undermined the old argument that ignorant youth were incapable of making intelligent political decisions.

At the *political* level, student groups like LUV and public-interest lobbies like Common Cause put their efforts into the amendment. Democrats saw the registration of millions of young voters as an opportunity to move the electorate in their own liberal direction. When surveys showed young people to be little different in political affiliations from anyone else, however, and when it became clear that radical student protestors were a small minority, Republicans jumped on the bandwagon and supported the amendment as well.

At the *governmental* level, the Twenty-Sixth

close to one-half. Some people feel that such benefits should be more nearly equal across the country. Similarly, for many years, federalism permitted slavery and then official "Jim Crow" segregation in the South. Today, local control of law enforcement, together with the Supreme Court's reliance upon "community standards" to define "obscenity," means that a rap group's performances or records may be declared illegal and punished in one town but may be perfectly legal in another. Some observers argue that free speech, freedom from racial discrimination, and access to minimum welfare benefits should follow nationwide standards.

Eighteen-year-olds register to vote. Their right to do so in all states was established in 1971 by the Twenty-Sixth Amendment to the U.S. Constitution.

Amendment cured a new problem of American federalism: dual systems of voter registration. Beginning in 1970, by congressional legislation, national elections for Congress and the presidency had included 18- to 20-year-old participants, but many state and local elections did not. The Supreme Court had upheld the right of states to set voting ages for their own elections. The result was a mess. Different groups of voters had to be registered separately for the two kinds of elections, even when both were held at the same time and in the same place.

After Congress overwhelmingly voted for the amendment in March 1971, it took only two months and seven days—the shortest time ever for a constitutional amendment to be ratified—for it to be approved by the required 38 states. (One 64-year-old state representative in Alabama, trying to filibuster, declared, "I'm physically unable to stand here any longer.") After Ohio became the thirty-eighth and decisive state to ratify the amendment, President Nixon said: "Some 11 million young men and women who have participated in the life of our nation through their work, their studies, and their sacrifices for its defense now are to be fully included in the electoral process of our country. I urge them to honor this right by exercising it, by registering and voting in each election."[b]

[a]"Collegians Open Voting-Age Drive," *New York Times* (December 20, 1968), p. 51.
[b]"States Ratify Full 18-Year-Old Vote," *New York Times* (July 1, 1971), p. 1.

As we have mentioned, certain kinds of policies are inherently difficult or impossible to carry out at the state or local levels. If we want redistributive programs, for example, which transfer resources from the rich to the poor, or if we want to protect the environment across city and county and state lines, it is necessary either to abandon federalism or to tilt it toward predominant national government power. Voting rights for 18-year-olds provides a similar example (see "Struggle for Democracy").

In terms of our theme concerning *democracy*, it is not easy to judge whether federalism is a help or a hindrance. On the one hand, retaining some political

The First Amendment to the U.S. Constitution protects free speech
against interference by state or local governments. The controversial rap
group 2 Live Crew encountered hostile police in many communities
where it performed.

power in the states does promote democracy by permitting state governments to
counterbalance actions by the national government that may be unpopular. It also
promotes democracy by allowing people in each community to do what their own
majorities prefer, rather than all having to conform to a single national majority.
Obviously, if local communities are very different from each other, separate and
divergent local majorities may include more people, in total, than could be brought
together in a single national majority.

On the other hand, federalism can interfere with democracy, since democratic processes may not work as well at the state level as they do at the national
level. In state politics, popular participation tends to be lower; politics tends to be
less visible; interest groups may have an easier time getting their way. The well
organized and the affluent may have extra influence. Political equality, a crucial
aspect of democracy, may be impaired. (We will pursue this theme further in
Chapter 15, "State and Local Government.") The national government, and especially popular presidents, seem better able to mobilize the public, make politics
visible, and ensure that government responds to what ordinary citizens want. To
the extent that this is true, a federal system that gives power over some important
political decisions to the states may dilute democratic control.

SUMMARY

Federalism, a system in which political powers are divided between the state and
national governments, is a key structural aspect of American politics. Federalism
is unusual in the world today; it is most frequent among large, diverse countries.

Arguments in favor of federalism have to do with diversity of needs, closeness to the people, experimentation and innovation. Arguments against federalism involve national standards, popular control, and needs for uniformity.

The Constitution specifies the powers of the national government and reserves all others (except a few that are specifically forbidden) to the states. The Constitution also provides special roles for the states in adopting and amending the Constitution and in choosing national officials. The precise balance of federalism has evolved over time, with the national government gaining ground as a result of Supreme Court decisions, the Civil War, expanding national domestic programs, and two world wars. Now the national government spends about twice as much money as the state and local governments put together, though the latter have many more civilian employees.

Contemporary federalism involves complex, "marble cake" relations among the national and state governments, in which federal grants-in-aid play an important part. Grants for many purposes grew rapidly in the 1950s, 1960s, and 1970s. Then, under the Reagan and Bush administrations, the flow of money slowed down, but it remains important. The national government also influences or controls many state policies through mandates (especially involving civil rights and the environment) and conditions on aid. As federal aid slowed down, the states innovated and tried to take up the slack, but they are under great financial pressure. Federalism has mixed implications for democracy.

To Ponder

1. Are state governments more democratic than the national government?

2. Should there be national standards for protection of the environment, or should those be left to the states?

3. Is the Constitution a contract among sovereign states, or does it establish a national, sovereign government?

4. Why do some countries with federal systems tend to break up and others do not?

Suggested Readings

Grodzins, Morton. *The American System: A New View of Government in The United States.* Daniel J. Eleazar (ed.). Chicago: Rand McNally, 1966.
> Describes and approves of a complex intermingling of national, state, and local government functions.

Henig, Jeffrey. *Public Policy and Federalism.* New York: St. Martin's, 1985.
> Shows how public policy is made in the federal system.

Peterson, Paul E., Barry G. Rabe, and Kenneth Wong. *When Federalism Works.* Washington, D.C.: Brookings, 1986.
> Analyzes the workings of several national programs that are implemented at the state and local level.

Riker, William H., *Federalism: Origin, Operation, Significance.* Boston: Little, Brown, 1964.
> A classic discussion of what federalism is and its effects.

Notes

1. Richard L. Berke, "Bill to Raise Cars' Fuel Efficiency Dies with Senate Vote on Debate," *New York Times* (September 26, 1990), p. A10.

2. Richard W. Stevenson, "California to Get Tougher Air Rules," *New York Times* (September 27, 1990), pp. A1, A13; Jorge Casuso, "California Sets New Air-Quality Standards," *Chicago Tribune* (September 29, 1990), pp. 1, 6.

3. Keith Schneider, "Lawmakers Reach an Accord on Reduction of Air Pollution," *New York Times* (October 23, 1990), pp. A1, A12; Allan R. Gold, "Critics Say Cars Got Break on Clean Air," *New York Times* (October 30, 1990), p. A14.

4. Robert Lorch, *State and Local Politics* (Englewood Cliffs, NJ: Prentice-Hall, 1986), pp. 221, 227.

5. J. C. Boogman and G. N. van de Ploat, eds., *Federalism* (The Hague: Martinus Nijhoff, 1980), p. 95; Geoffrey Sawyer, *Modern Federalism* (Australia: Pitman Publishing, 1976), p. 1.

6. Gabriel Almond and G. Bingham Powell, Jr., *Comparative Politics: System, Process, and Policy* (Boston: Little, Brown, 1978), p. 234.

7. Luther Martin, quoted in Zagarri, *The Politics of Size* (Ithaca, NY: Cornell University Press, 1987), p. 89.

8. Mike Edelhart and James Tinen, *America the Quotable* (New York: Facts on File, 1983), p. 57.

9. William H. Riker, *Federalism: Origin, Operation, Significance* (Boston: Little, Brown, 1964), ch. 6.

10. Quoted in Robert Jay Dilger, ed., *American Intergovernmental Relations Today* (Englewood Cliffs, NJ: Prentice-Hall, 1986), p. 188.

11. Jack Walker, "The Diffusion of Innovations Among the American States," *American Political Science Review*, Vol. 63 (1969), p. 883.

12. Paul E. Peterson, *City Limits* (Chicago: University of Chicago Press, 1981).

13. Jeffrey Henig, *Public Policy and Federalism* (New York: St. Martin's, 1985), p. 155.

14. Robert G. McCloskey, *The American Supreme Court* (Chicago: University of Chicago Press, 1960), pp. 30–36. In 1821, in *Cohens v. Virginia*, the Court declared that it could hear legal *appeals* by citizens against a state; it could just not hear a suit that a citizen had "commenced."

15. McCloskey, *American Supreme Court*, pp. 49–53.

16. McCloskey, *American Supreme Court*, pp. 60–63.

17. McCloskey, *American Supreme Court*, pp. 66–68.

18. Advisory Commission on Intergovernmental Relations, *Significant Features of Fiscal Federalism* (Washington, D.C., 1990), Vol. II, pp. 33, 39, 67; *Historical Statistics of the United States, Colonial Times to 1970*, pp. 1114–1115, 1130, 1132; Harold Stanley and Richard G. Niemi, *Vital Statistics on American Politics*, 2nd ed. (Washington, D.C.: CQ Press, 1990), pp. 292, 308.

19. Morton Grodzins, *The American System: A New View of Government in the United States*, ed. by Daniel J. Eleazar (Chicago: Rand McNally, 1966).

20. David B. Walker, *Towards a Functioning Federalism* (Cambridge, MA: Winthrop, 1981), pp. 60–63; U.S. Bureau of the Census, *Statistical History of the U.S.* (Stamford, CT: Fairfield, 1963), pp. 484–516.

21. Paul E. Peterson, Barry G. Rabe, and Kenneth Wong, *When Federalism Works* (Washington, D.C.: Brookings, 1986), p. 2.

22. Grodzins, *American System*.

23. Daniel Patrick Moynihan, *Maximum Feasible Misunderstanding* (New York: Free Press, 1970).

24. Jeffrey L. Pressman and Aaron Wildavsky, *Implementation*, 3rd ed. (Berkeley, University of California Press, 1984). See also Martha Derthick, *New Towns in Town: Why a Federal Program Failed* (Washington D.C.: Brookings, 1977), and Eugene Bardach, *The Implementation Game*, 4th ed. (Cambridge, MA: MIT Press, 1982).

25. Peterson, Rabe, and Wong, *When Federalism Works*, pp. xii, 7.

26. *Statistical Abstract*, 1989, pp. 395, 463.

27. Thomas Ferguson and Joel Rogers, *Right Turn: The Decline of the Democrats and the Future of American Politics* (New York: Farrar, Straus & Giroux, 1986); Thomas Byrne Edsall, *The New Politics of Inequality* (New York: Norton, 1984).

28. Peterson, Rabe, and Wong, *When Federalism Works*, p. 2.

29. Stanley and Niemi, *Vital Statistics on American Politics*, p. 299.

30. Michael deCourcy Hinds, "Governors Say Budget Plan Shifts More Burdens to States," *New York Times* (October 5, 1990), pp. A1, A25.

31. *New York Times* (November 8, 1990), pp. A1, A14.

4

Structure: The Development of the United States

DATSUN STORMS AMERICA[1]

They named the new car Datsun rather than Nissan, its name in Japan, so that the company would not be embarrassed if its attempt to sell cars in the United States failed. Nissan officials had reason to worry. The first car they tried to sell here in 1961 was, in the words of Nissan's west coast manager, Yutaka Katayama, "simply awful." It was boxy and utilitarian, without any attention to style. It was almost impossible to start in cold weather, and its brakes were weak. Most important, it was underpowered compared not only to large American cars but also to small imports like the VW "bug." Just enough Americans bought Datsuns, however, given their low price and reliability, that Nissan managed to hang on during the 1960s.

The breakthrough came in 1970 with the introduction of the Datsun 510. The new model included most of the changes recommended by Katayama. It was, according to all of the automotive magazines, an inexpensive, surprisingly powerful, stylish, exquisitely engineered car—and fun to drive. It was also reliable, easy to maintain, and fuel efficient. It was far better than anything else available on the import market and without any competition at all from American automobile makers. Nissan sold 100,000 in its first year and began to overtake Volkswagen as the top-selling small import car.

Detroit was slow to respond to the challenge of small imports. In the 1950s and 1960s, after all, the American automobile industry was at the height of its power and profitability. The Big Three—General Motors, Ford, and Chrysler—were selling 10 to 11 million large, heavy, gas-guzzling cars per year, most of which were loaded with expensive options that drove up the profit margin on each unit. Engineering quality received less attention than it had in the past, but sales figures seemed to prove to executives that Americans didn't care about such things very much. Declining dealership service also didn't seem to cut into sales, so automobile executives paid little attention to this end of the business.

It's not as if they weren't warned about what was coming. Charley Maxwell, an extremely knowledgeable and well-respected oil industry analyst, was sent by his Wall Street firm to talk to the Big Three automobile executives in June 1973 about his pessimistic findings on future oil prices. He told them that the era of cheap energy was coming to an end and that they might want to rethink their commitment to big cars. He was told on more than one occasion that his fears were groundless, that Americans would not buy little cars, and that "little cars make little profits."

At about the same time, David Davis was reporting on the new European front-wheel drive cars to GM executives. A former editor of *Car and Driver* magazine, working on special assignment for General Motors, Davis reported that GM's European competitors were building better engineered, more fuel efficient, and far more reliable cars. Front-wheel drive cars, by eliminating the drive shaft that ran under the car, were lighter (enhancing fuel efficiency) and roomier than comparable American models. Davis recommended not only that GM think about producing small, front-wheel drive cars but also that it shift to front-wheel drive throughout its product line. GM thanked him for his report and filed it away. Innovation on such a scale was simply too expensive and risky, he was told. Besides, Americans were still buying GM products in numbers that suggested consumer satisfaction. Why change?

The two oil price shocks—one in 1973 and the other in 1979—turned the automotive world on its head. When the price of a gallon of gasoline increased fivefold, consumer interest in cars that got 12 miles per gallon waned. When the price of new cars escalated, spurred by the inflation of the 1970s, consumer interest in expensive, high-maintenance cars waned as well. Japanese and European automakers were there to fill the gap. Detroit's response was pathetically weak. Starting very late in the front-wheel, small-car sweepstakes game, countering initially with the ill-fated Maverick, Pinto, and Vega, the Big Three lost shares of the American market that it has never been able to regain. By 1991, imports accounted for nearly 40 percent of the U.S. car market, with the Japanese accounting for roughly three out of four imports.[2] In that same year, the Big Three reported record losses ($4.7 billion in the first two quarters of 1991), and talk was widespread about the possible collapse of at least one of the American giants. The Brookings Institution reported in 1991, moreover, that its studies showed substantially higher consumer confidence in Japanese automobiles than in American ones, with many consumers saying that they would not even think of test-driving an American car.

Changes in the standing of the U.S. car industry has had wide-ranging effects. Most immediately affected were the Big Three's stockholders and employees, with the former suffering loss of stock value and many of the latter losing their jobs. The decline of the automobile industry was also bad news for the many companies that supplied parts (windshields, bumpers, radios, spark plugs, hoses, plastic moldings, and more) to the Big Three. These developments, in turn, spelled economic disaster for communities that depended on the economic health of the Big Three and their suppliers. During the economic boom years of the 1980s, cities like Detroit, Toledo, and Gary experienced dramatic increases in unemployment, business failures, and the size of their welfare roles.

Many workers from the so-called rust belt region of the nation decided that enough was enough, and they moved themselves and their families to the Sun Belt states to look for work. Places like Detroit, which had grown and prospered because of the rise of the automobile industry had come full circle. Such cities had once been magnets, attracting rural and southern migrants— black and white. Now there was little to keep workers there.

The decline of the Big Three is part of a larger story that has had, and will continue to have, many ramifications: the general decline of the United States as the world's leading manufacturer. What happened in the automobile industry also happened in steel, ship building, consumer economics, and microchips. Some worry that it may soon happen in computers and biotechnology. This fundamental manufacturing transformation has, in turn, adversely affected the U.S. balance of trade position and has contributed to our relative decline in world financial markets. Economic change on this scale, of course, has affected the American standard of living, the migration patterns, the occupational choices of the population, and the health of local communities. Not surprisingly, as we shall soon see, this transformation, and what to do about it, have become important issues in American politics.

This story points to several of the many structural factors that shape American politics and what government does. It highlights the fact that many developments that occur in the economy and in society, well away from the White House, the halls of Congress, and the chambers of the Supreme Court, affect the quality of our lives, the kinds of problems we have to grapple with, the issues that eventually become part of the American political agenda, and the distribution of political power.

Constitutions similar to our own exist in other countries where politics and government are very different. This suggests that the constitutional rules of the game are not the only factors affecting political life. Also important is the nature of society. The basic characteristics of a society influence how political and government institutions and processes work in practice.

The constitutional rules of the game and the basic characteristics of society are what we call *structural* factors affecting politics. As we suggested in Chapter 1, structural factors provide the context or environment within which politics and governing take place. If we want to understand politics and governing, we first need to know what kinds of individuals, groups, and classes populate the United States, and why they have certain preferences, concerns, and interests; why some have the resources to gain a hearing from public officials while others do not; why citizens and officials worry about certain problems and not others; and why some government policies seem appropriate but not others. This chapter concerns such matters and how they reflect the underlying structures of our society: the characteristics of the *American people, the economy*, and the *political culture*, as well as the U.S. *position in the world*. In conjunction with Chapters 2 and 3, our examination of the structural underpinnings of American political life is completed with this chapter and sets the stage for all that follows.

Governmental

Political

Structural

THE AMERICAN PEOPLE

The "typical" American today is very different from the "typical" American of 1950 or 1940, let alone 1790. Where we live, how we work, our racial and ethnic composition, and our average age and standard of living—all have changed substantially. Each change has influenced our political life.

Population Change[3]

POPULATION GROWTH Between the 1790 and 1990 censuses, our population increased from about 3.9 million (not counting Native Americans) to approximately 250 million. Steady growth began almost immediately after the founding of the Republic, fueled by high birth rates and successive waves of immigration (see Figure 4.1). Immigration was especially significant between 1840 and 1860, and between 1881 and 1910. Immigration has also increased significantly over the past two decades. (See Figure 4.2.)

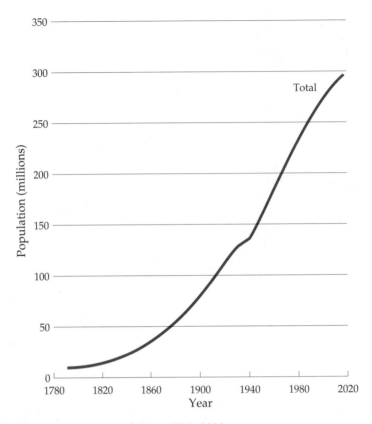

Figure 4.1 U.S. population, 1790–2020

Source: U.S. Bureau of the Census, Statistical Abstract of the U.S., 1987 (Washington, D.C.: U.S. Government Printing Office, 1986), pp. 8, 15.

DIVERSIFICATION   Ours is an ethnically, religiously, and racially diverse society. The white European Protestants, black slaves, and Native Americans who made up the bulk of the U.S. population when the first census was taken in 1790 were joined by Catholic immigrants from Germany and Ireland in the 1840s and 1850s. In the 1870s, large numbers of Chinese migrated to America, drawn by jobs in railroad construction. Around the turn of the century, most immigration was from eastern, central, and southern Europe, with its diverse ethnic, language, and religious groups. Today, most immigration is from Asia and Latin America (see Figure 4.3). This most recent immigration, like all the previous ones, has both added to the rich language, cultural, and religious diversity of our nation and created significant political and social tensions.

The arrival of immigrants who are very different from the native majority has sometimes sparked anti-immigration agitation. **Nativist** reactions to Catholic migrants were common throughout the nineteenth century. Anti-Chinese agitation swept the western states in the 1870s and 1880s. Alarm at the arrival of waves of immigrants from eastern, southern, and central Europe in the early part of this century led Congress virtually to close the doors of the United States in 1921 and to keep them closed until the 1950s. The present Spanish-speaking immigration has led to legislation in several states designating English as the official language

(*a*)

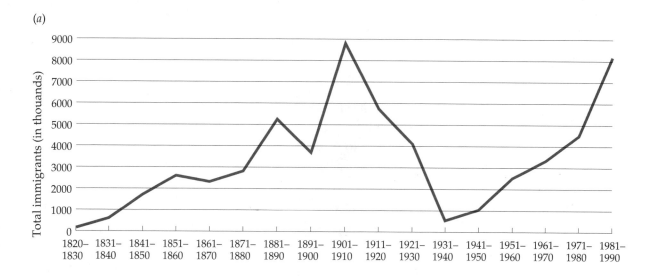

(*b*)

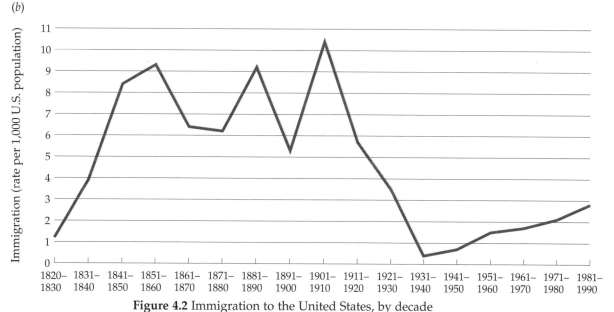

Figure 4.2 Immigration to the United States, by decade

Source: Statistical Abstracts of the United States, 1991 *(Washington, D.C.: U.S. Census Bureau, 1991), Table 5.*

and to various attempts to restrict and slow the pace of entry of newcomers. Fear that social services and social welfare systems are straining under the weight of recent immigrants compelled Congress to pass a new immigration law in 1990 that favors those with higher education and technical and scientific skills.

Ethnic, racial, and religious diversity seems to be an important factor explaining the relatively low level of class consciousness and unionization in the United States. Diversity multiplies interests and makes it difficult for people from different backgrounds to organize parties and unions along class lines. The gulf

A GROWING DIVERSITY

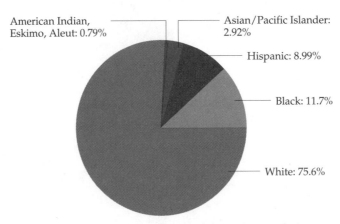

American Indian, Eskimo, Aleut: 0.79%

Asian/Pacific Islander: 2.92%

Hispanic: 8.99%

Black: 11.7%

White: 75.6%

Figure 4.3 The racial composition of the U.S. population

Source: Washington Post, *September 23, 1991, p. 7, based on data from the Bureau of the Census.*

between blacks and whites has been especially significant. Countries where politics divide along class lines, such as Sweden, Norway, Denmark, The Netherlands, and Austria, have relatively homogeneous populations.

FROM URBANIZATION TO SUBURBANIZATION While we began as a country made up of rural and small-town people, we very rapidly became an urban people. By 1910, there were 50 cities that had populations of more than 100,000, including 3 with more than 1 million (New York, Philadelphia, and Chicago). The process of urbanization, caused mainly by the industrialization of the nation—the rise of large manufacturing firms required many industrial workers, while the mechanization of farming meant that fewer agricultural workers were needed—continued unabated until the mid-1940s. After World War II, a massive federal and state

One outcome of the increased immigration from Latin America and Asia has been the diversification of the racial composition of many occupations.

Moving-in day in the suburbs. Unprecedented levels of government spending on highways and mortgage loan guarantees helped fuel the explosive growth of the American suburbs after World War II.

road building program and government-guaranteed home loans for veterans (the G.I. bill) started the process by which the United States became an overwhelmingly suburban nation (see Figure 4.4).

This shift in location of the population from rural areas to cities, and from cities to suburbs, has important ramifications. The continued drain from rural areas has sapped the vitality of small-town life in many parts of the country and

Figure 4.4 Population shift: from rural, to urban, to suburban

Source: New York Times, *September 11, 1990, based on data from the Census Bureau.*

	Cities	Suburbs	Rural areas
1950	32.9%	23.2%	43.9%
1960	32.3%	30.6%	37.0%
1970	31.4%	37.2%	31.4%
1980	30.0%	44.8%	25.2%
1988	31.3%	45.7%	22.9%

has diminished the power of the rural voice in state and national politics. Central cities, for their part, burdened with populations of the poor and less well-to-do and a shrinking tax base, find it increasingly difficult to provide the level and quality of public services considered the norm only a few years ago. Heavily dependent on the assistance of the federal government, moreover, central-city populations have become even more consistently Democratic in their voting preferences than in the past. The distant suburbs, relatively prosperous and self-sufficient, populated with middle-class and working-class homeowners, on the other hand, gradually have become a bastion of more conservative politics and one of the principal centers of the revival of the Republican party.

THE RISE OF THE SUN BELT   The U.S. population has steadily moved west and south. In 1790, the census found the center of population to be 23 miles east of Baltimore; by 1990, it had shifted to central Missouri.

The acceleration of the movement of the population west and south since World War II seems to have several causes, all of which are related, in one way or another, to the changing location of employment. Heavy manufacturing, traditionally located in the East and upper Midwest, has suffered serious setbacks (see the opening story on Nissan), and people looking for work have had to go elsewhere. Many companies, moreover, have shifted their activities to the non-

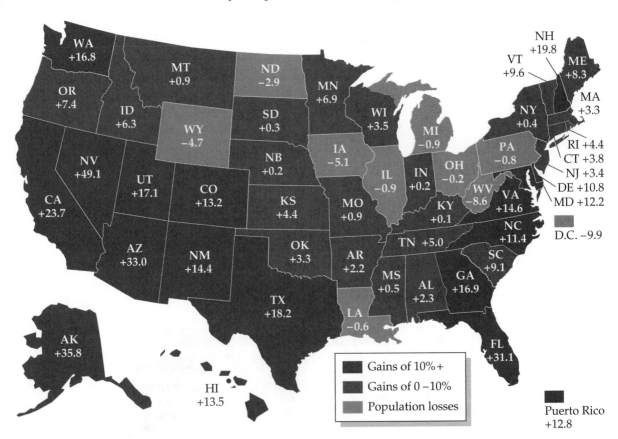

Figure 4.5 Population change in the states, 1980–1990

Note: Data are preliminary and subject to change.

Source: U.S. Bureau of the Census.

union and low-tax Sun Belt states. Finally, there has been a heavy flow of federal government defense dollars and associated jobs to the South, Southwest, and West.

This population movement has many political consequences, of course, not least of which is a shift in political power between the states. Following each census from 1950 to 1990, states in the East and the upper Midwest lost congressional seats and presidential electoral votes, while states in the West and the South gained at their expense. Figure 4.5 shows the extent of change during the 1980s. Because the Sun Belt states are generally more conservative than the other states, this has further weakened the Democratic party.

Work and Occupation

At the time of the first census in 1790, almost three-quarters of all Americans were engaged in agriculture. Most of the rest of the population were engaged in retail trade, transportation, and skilled trades closely connected to agriculture. About 80 percent of the working, male, nonslave population were self-employed, owners of small farms, stores, wagons and horses, and workshops.[4]

The American occupational structure was radically transformed by the **Industrial Revolution**, which brought large mass production industries, characterized by the assembly line, semiskilled labor, and the weekly paycheck. By 1910, the proportion of the labor force in agriculture dropped to only 32 percent, and those working for others for wages and salaries swelled to over 69 percent.[5] By 1940, the "typical" American was a blue-collar worker (40 percent of all working people) though white-collar workers were rapidly catching up (24 percent).

In 1950, the United States became the first nation in the world in which white-collar workers (clerical, technical, professional, managerial, services, and sales) were in the majority. The decline of certain manufacturing industries, the disappearance of the small family farm, and the rapid rise of the high technology and information sector, have accelerated the shift of employment from factory and farm to the office. Today, the "typical" American worker is no longer a blue-collar

In his typically comic yet penetrating way, Charlie Chaplin shows that the Industrial Revolution often made workers feel that they were simply extensions of their machines.

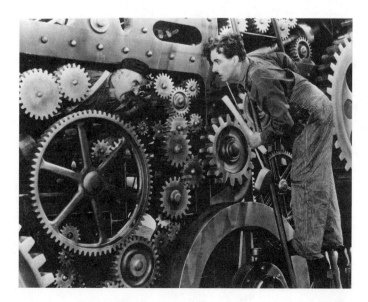

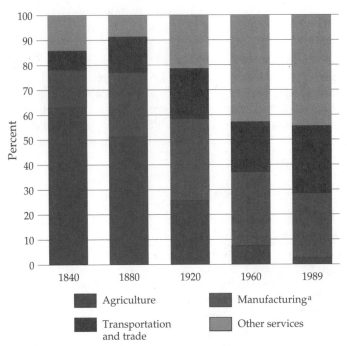

Figure 4.6 Changes in U.S. occupational structure

*a*Includes manufacturing, mining, and construction.

Source: Department of Commerce and Department of Labor. Economic Report of the President, February 1991, p. 114.

person working in a large factory or a farmer plowing his own field, but an office worker plying his or her skills in a large public or private bureaucracy. The Office of Technological Assessment reported in 1988 that 44 percent of the American work force was engaged in creating, processing, and transmitting information. Figure 4.6 shows how the American occupational structure has changed over the years.

Many political implications flow from this change in the American occupational structure. Occupational change creates new winners and losers, and tilts the balance of political power. It also changes the kinds of demands placed on government. Displaced workers, for instance, are likely to insist on expanded welfare benefits, job retraining programs, and policies to encourage economic development.

The shift from manufacturing to service occupations also affects the fortunes of labor unions, which, in turn, affects the balance between the political parties. As heavy industry has become less important in the American economy, the proportion of Americans who belong to labor unions has declined sharply, from approximately 33 percent in the early 1950s to less than 18 percent today. Since unions always have been a mainstay of the Democratic party and a strong voice for liberal social policy, this decline in union strength has diminished the support for the Democratic party in national elections and for a liberal policy agenda in the nation.

Women increasingly work in white collar and professional occupations, a development that has had important political consequences.

The expansion of service, clerical, technical, and other kinds of white-collar jobs has coincided, moreover, with a substantial expansion in the number of female workers. The participation of women in the paid work force (counting both full-time and part-time work) has passed 75 percent and is rapidly approaching the participation rate for men. In fact, fully 60 percent of all new jobs in the 1980s went to women, mostly in the white-collar and service sectors. This massive entry by women into working life outside of the home has had, and will probably continue to have, enormous political consequences. For one thing, paid work has improved women's income (though women still earn only about three-quarters of what men earn) and has increased their self-confidence. These have no doubt contributed to the formation of the women's movement. Because even women with young children are working outside the home in unprecedented numbers, moreover, we are likely to see strong pressures for government-funded child care and early education, and for the extension of the school day.

The Aging of the American Population

One of the most significant trends in the United States and in other industrialized countries is the aging of the population. In 1800, the median age (i.e., the age with one-half of the population above it and one-half below it) was just under 16. Today it is 33. By 2030, it is likely to be 38. Needless to say, the proportion that is elderly (over 65) continues to expand at a healthy clip. Over 10 percent of Americans (about 28 million) are elderly today. By 2030, it is likely to be 20 percent. The very old—those over 85—are becoming an especially significant part of the elderly population (see Figure 4.7).

An aging population has significant political implications. The issue of Social Security and how it is to be financed is likely to remain an important part of the political agenda for the foreseeable future, for instance. Because the elderly require more medical care than the young, moreover, the questions of the appropriate role of government in the provision of medical care also will become an increasingly important part of our national debate. A large elderly population, which is

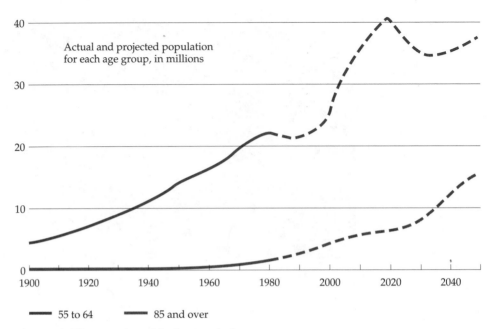

Actual and projected population
for each age group, in millions

—— 55 to 64   —— 85 and over

Figure 4.7 The growing elderly population

Source: New York Times, *November 13, 1989, based on data from the Census Bureau.*

characterized by a relatively high voting turnout in elections at all levels, is likely to press political decision makers to transfer public expenditures from programs that serve the young to those that serve the old. How younger working taxpayers will react to the increased burdens that they will be asked to carry will be an interesting story to keep our eye on in the future.

The Standard of Living

The United States enjoys one of the highest standards of living in the world. Blessed with rich farmland, abundant natural resources, cheap energy, numerous navigable rivers, a talented and energetic people, a wide ocean preventing interference from abroad, and a relatively open economy, Americans have enjoyed a high standard of living almost from the nation's birth. Economic growth and improvement in the standard of living were particularly impressive during the post-Civil War industrial revolution and the period after World War II.[6] By the mid-1960s, the United States was, by far, the world's richest nation (see Figure 4.8).

RECENT REVERSES   Until just a few years ago, most Americans were confident that economic growth and improvement in living standards would continue indefinitely. A 1969 report of the U.S. Department of Health, Education, and Welfare reflected this outlook: "The most obvious fact about American income is that it is the highest in the world and rising rapidly. In terms of gross national product per capita—or any other measure of the average availability of goods and services—the United States far outranks its nearest competitors."[7]

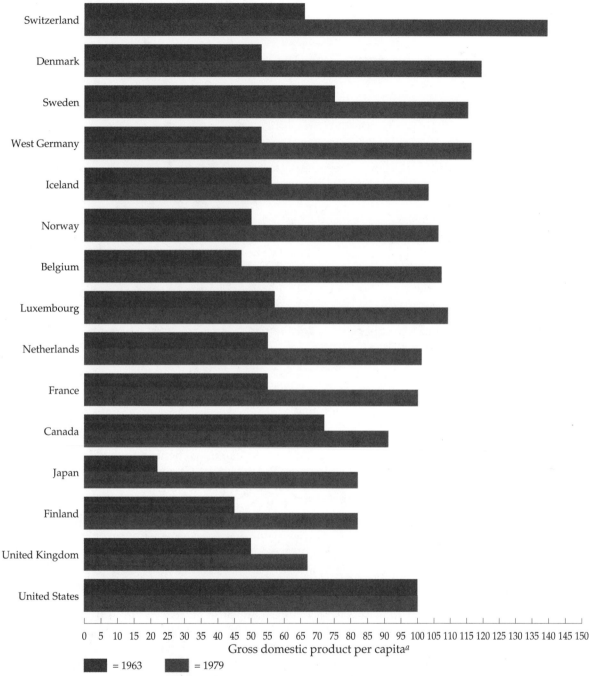

Figure 4.8 The United States in the world economy, 1963 and 1979

[a]The gross domestic product per capita for each nation is determined as a percentage of U.S. gross domestic product per capita (100%).

Source: OECD national accounts. For 1979 figures, see September 1980, "Main Economic Indicators," p. 169 for GNP, p. 170 for population

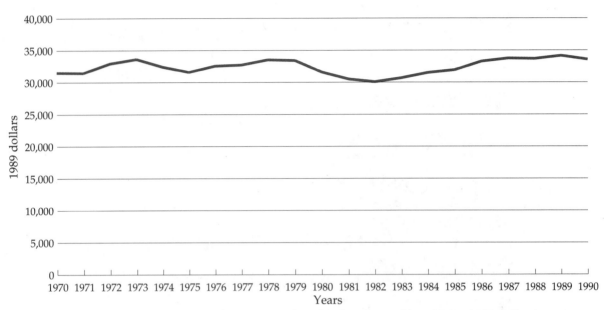

Figure 4.9 Trends in U.S. median family income (in constant, 1989 dollars)

Source: Economic Report of the President, 1991 (Washington, D.C.: U.S. Government Printing Office) and the U.S. Census Bureau.

Nothing lasts forever. Shortly after HEW wrote so confidently, the standard of living began to stagnate. By the late 1970s, the United States had slipped to tenth in the world in GDP per capita rankings, behind Switzerland, Denmark, Luxembourg, The Netherlands, Iceland, West Germany, Belgium, Norway, and Sweden (see Figure 4.8). Median family income stagnated for most of the 1970s and 1980s. It wasn't until 1987 that the 1973 level was surpassed (see Figure 4.9).[8] The tendency toward stagnation in living standards is politically important, because the American people have come to expect steady improvement in how well they live. Unease and discontent find expression in many areas of politics, including rising hostility toward taxes, new immigrants, and welfare recipients.

INEQUALITY   Inequality in income and wealth among Americans has been high for a long time and is becoming more pronounced. Figure 4.10 shows the proportion of total national income received by each fifth of the population ("quintiles") over the past several decades. Several things are apparent. First, the top fifth of all families received at least eight times more income than the bottom fifth throughout the postwar era. Second, income inequality became much more pronounced during the 1980s. The Congressional Budget Office reports that the top 1 percent of families captured 60 percent of all the gain in national income during the decade. Table 4.1 shows how income inequality changed for the top and bottom 20 percent of families.

Income inequality is also high in the United States when compared to other Western democratic nations. The bottom 20 percent of families take roughly 6.5

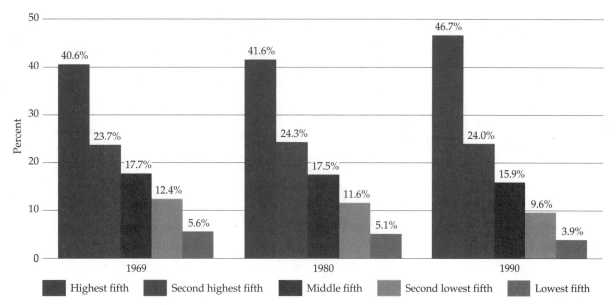

Figure 4.10 Income distribution in the United States (1969–1990) (percentage of income received by each fifth of the population)

Source: Current Population Reports, Series P-60, U.S. Bureau of the Census.

percent of total income in most of the Western European nations, for instance, as compared to 4.3 percent in the United States.[9] Figure 4.11 shows how countries compare when the average household income of the top 20 percent is divided by the income of the bottom 20 percent (the higher the number, the more inequality exists). The United States is notable for outranking most nations on this measure.

Wealth is even more unequally distributed among Americans than income. According to the Office of Management and Budget, the lowest 20 percent of asset owners in 1973 controlled only 0.2 percent of total national wealth—houses, stock, bank accounts, and the like—while the top 20 percent controlled 76 percent. *Forbes*

Table 4.1
Change in U.S. Average Family Income, 1979–1987, Adjusted for Family Size, Government Benefits, Taxes, and Inflation

	Lowest Fifth of Families	Highest Fifth of Families
All families	−9.2%	18.7%
Families with children	−13.8	18.7
Family head under age 35	−23.3	12.2
Family head over age 65	22.8	19.9

Source: U.S. House of Representatives Ways and Means Committee.

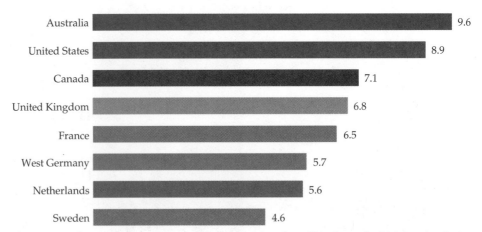

Australia	9.6
United States	8.9
Canada	7.1
United Kingdom	6.8
France	6.5
West Germany	5.7
Netherlands	5.6
Sweden	4.6

Figure 4.11 Comparing income inequality (ratio of median household income of top and bottom 20 percent)

Source: World Bank, World Development Report *(New York: Oxford University Press, 1990).*

Magazine reported in 1984 that the nation's richest 482 families and individuals owned about 40 percent of all nonresidential private assets, totaling about $2,200 billion.[10] Like income, wealth inequality also increased during the 1980s.[11]

POVERTY   No discussion of inequality can skip over the subject of poverty. It is an undeniable fact that a sizeable number of Americans are poor and that progress in reducing its incidence has slowed considerably. In 1955, almost 25 percent of Americans fell below the federal government's official **poverty line**. By 1973, the figure had fallen to 11.6 percent, whittled down by the civil rights movement, a rapidly expanding economy, and the antipoverty programs of the federal government. Beginning in the late 1970s, however, the percentage of Americans classified as poor began to inch upward. It receded a bit in the mid-1980s and started to rise again in the early 1990s (see Figure 4.12).

The proportion of American families living in poverty and suffering homelessness has increased significantly since 1980.

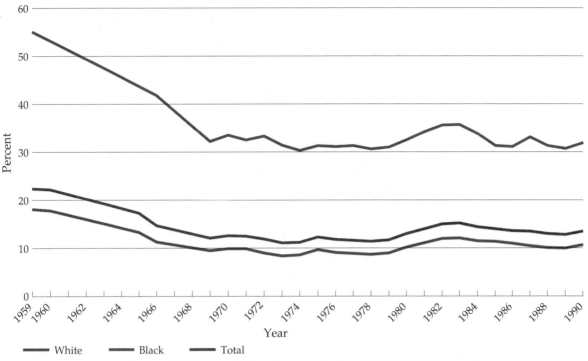

Figure 4.12 Persons below the poverty level, 1959–1990 (percent)

Source: U.S. Bureau of the Census, Current Population Reports, "Money Income and Poverty Status in the United States," Series P-60.

The distribution of poverty is not random but concentrated among racial minorities, female-headed households, and children. About one in three black Americans live in poverty, as do three in ten Hispanics, one in three in female-headed households, and one in five children. One recent report claims that 5.5 million children under the age of 12 go hungry every day in the United States.[12]

There is also considerably more poverty in the United States than in other Western democratic nations, as shown in Figure 4.13. Most experts attribute the difference to the much smaller role of social welfare in the government of the United States (see Chapter 18 for details).

What do we make of inequality and poverty in the United States? Your response is probably affected by your personal values, your judgment about the reasons why some people are rich and some are poor (luck? effort? reward?), and your assessment of the possibilities for alleviating inequality and poverty at reasonable cost. What is impossible to ignore, however, is the fact that material inequality and poverty have important implications for American politics. For one thing, inequalities in living standards help determine the nature of social problems in the United States that eventually demand the attention of government. Crime, drug use, and family disintegration are tied to economic distress. A society with significant levels of inequality and widespread poverty must pay attention to the discontents and disruptions that are its natural consequence. Policing and social welfare programs are two of several possible policy responses.

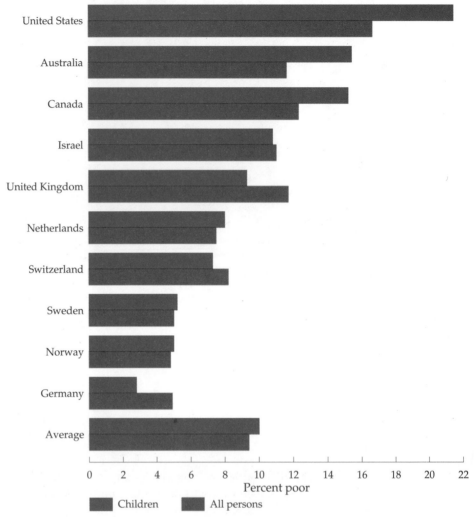

Figure 4.13 Comparative poverty rates, 1987

Source: The 1991 Green Book, Committee on Ways and Means, U.S. House of Representatives, 1991. Based on testimony of Timothy Smeading before the Joint Economic Committee of Congress, May 11, 1989 (using LIS Database). Because of different databases, figures differ slightly from official government ones.

Inequality is also important for how democracy works. Extensive *material inequality*, as we suggested in Chapter 1, may undermine the possibilities for *political equality*, one of the foundations of democracy. Those with access to financial resources can use such resources to enhance their political voice and their ease of access to public officials. Those with less, vote less often than others. Those without money are unlikely to make contributions to political campaigns or political action committees, or form interest groups. Those worried about putting food on the table are unlikely to be able to buy television time or advertising space to address the issues that concern them. That is why Thomas Jefferson feared that democracy couldn't survive in a highly unequal society.

THE AMERICAN ECONOMY

Virtually everything we have discussed so far in this chapter is shaped by the American economy. The growth, diversification, and geographical dispersion of the American population, for instance, can be traced to economic changes. Occupations, standards of living, and inequality of income and wealth are closely connected to the operations of our economic institutions. Even important elements of the American political culture, as we shall soon see, are associated with our economy and how it works. It is not unreasonable to suggest, in fact, that virtually everything that goes on in American political life is, in one way or another, affected by the operations of our economic system.

The kind of economic system that we have in the United States is called **capitalism**, though the terms "market economy" or "free enterprise" are often used instead. A *capitalist economy* is defined by two characteristics: private ownership and the existence of markets to coordinate economic activity.

Capitalism does not exist anywhere in a pure form. Most capitalist nations in Europe have considerable government ownership of such basic industries as railroads, airlines, electrical power, and television. Even in the United States, there is considerable government involvement in economic coordination and planning (see Chapter 17 for details).

How Our Economic System Has Changed over the Years

While the United States has had a capitalist economy for a long time, it has changed considerably over the years. Up until the Civil War (excepting the slave South), American capitalism was defined by numerous, small, and competitive enterprises, first tied to agriculture and then increasingly to industry. After the Civil War, and partly as a result of it, the economy became increasingly industrialized and concentrated in giant enterprises.[13] The Civil War helped spur the Industrial Revolution: factories and shipyards were built, technological breakthroughs occurred, thousands of miles of rail lines were laid, and fortunes were made (useful for further investment) on government contracts for war materials. It also temporarily eliminated the South as a significant political power in Washington, D.C., and allowed the North to enact government policies favorable to the development of free enterprise: the Homestead Act of 1863 (opening the West to the family farm); a very high protective tariff to protect new industries; and subsidies for railroad construction. By the turn of the century, only 35 years after Lee's surrender at the Appomattox Court House, the United States was the world's leading industrial power, accounting for almost 24 percent of the world's total manufacturing output.[14]

Industrial enterprises grew to unprecedented size in the late nineteenth and early twentieth centuries. Workers were gathered together into work places that were of enormous size, requiring coordination by an army of managerial personnel. Markets were no longer local and regional but national and even international in scope.[15] Partly, this change in scale was related to technology: the steam engine, electrical power, the conveyer belt, and the like, provided the means for gathering together thousands of working people for purposes of industrial production. Partly, this change in scale was tied to cost: most of the new technologies—steel making being a case in point—required unheard of levels of investment. Large enterprises were also encouraged by changes in the laws of incorporation, which

Revolutions in technology, corporate law, and industrial organization
made giant enterprises, like this Jones and Laughlin steel complex
outside of Pittsburgh, Pennsylvania, common features of the American
landscape in the early twentieth century.

allowed competing corporations to merge into single, giant enterprises. A wave
of mergers between 1896 and 1904 fashioned a corporate-dominated economy so
familiar to us today.[16]

THE GOLDEN AGE OF THE AMERICAN CORPORATION   The steady growth in the
size of corporations, their consolidation into ever larger units, and their increasing
importance in the economy continued virtually unabated (with a brief but painful
pause during the Great Depression) until the early 1970s. By 1973, the *Forbes* 500
largest corporations accounted for 42 percent of total U.S. assets and over 35 percent of total U.S. revenues. In that same year, the *Fortune Magazine* 200 largest
industrial corporations accounted for 62 percent of total industrial assets, 65 percent of industrial sales, and 63 percent of total profits.[17] Many economists and
politicians worried that their sheer size and domination of markets were making
the economy less competitive than it ought to be. Many commentators also worried that this much concentrated economic power can be, and often is, translated
into political power (see Chapter 7).

After World War II, the largest American corporations became overwhelmingly **multinational** in character. While remaining American owned and controlled, their activities became worldwide in scope. This multinationalization had
started over a half-century before, as American oil companies scoured the world
for petroleum reserves and markets, but, in the postwar period, others joined the
game. Their success was unquestionable. As late as 1975, 11 of the largest 15
corporations in the world were American; as recently as 1981, 40 percent of the
world's total foreign direct investment was still accounted for by the United
States.[18] Multinationalization inevitably affected U.S. foreign policy. With worldwide economic interests at stake, American political leaders had no choice but to
be attentive to developments and events in the far corners of the world.

The largest American corporations are also multinational corporations in the sense that they produce and market their products all over the world.

TRANSFORMATION AND UNCERTAINTY   A transformation of the American economy is now underway. This transformation, and the problems and opportunities it produces, will affect American politics.

Business consolidation accelerated during the 1980s, fueled by developments in the international economic environment and by the Reagan administration's "hands-off" stance toward corporate mergers. At this writing, the concentration at the top of the American economy—the percentage of all economic activity and assets accounted for by the largest companies—is at its highest level in our history. This may further reduce competition in the economy, perhaps leading to calls for antitrust action, and may enhance the political power of the corporate community.

American corporations are also becoming more closely intertwined with corporations from other countries, either through outright purchase of stock or through joint ventures, such as the one between General Motors and Toyota. This blurs the distinction between American, Japanese, British, and German companies. It is not yet clear whether this will help or hurt the American people. What is clear, however, is that in a transnational, integrated global economy, the destiny of any single nation, no matter how powerful, is not entirely in its own hands but is affected by the decisions of people, organizations, and governments in other nations. Potentially, this development places many economic enterprises out of the reach of the instruments of American democracy.

Finally, the United States is undergoing a *relative* decline from its lofty position as the world's preeminent economic power.[19] This relative decline is most evident in basic manufacturing. In steel, for instance, the United States accounted for almost one-half of world output in 1950; today, it accounts for less than 15 percent. American automakers supplied almost one-half of the world's cars as recently as 1960; today, it provides less than 20 percent (see the opening story on

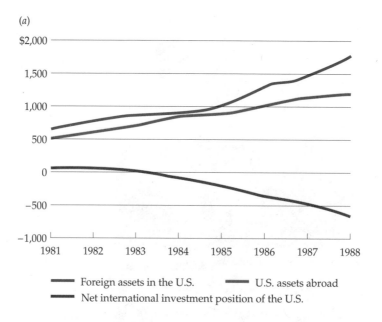

Foreign assets in the U.S.   U.S. assets abroad
Net international investment position of the U.S.

(b)

	1965–1980 Exports	Imports	1980–1987 Exports	Imports	1981–1988 Average trade balance
Japan	11.4%	4.9%	5.8%	3.6%	$52 billion
United States	6.4%	5.5%	−0.5%	9.7%	−$97 billion

Figure 4.14 Changes in the U.S. economic position in the world. (*a*) International investments in billions of current dollars. (*b*) Black ink to red—average rate of growth in trade.

Source: New York Times, *March 4, 1990, based on data from the Department of Commerce* (a) *and World Bank; OECD* (b).

Nissan). Our seemingly unassailable lead in "high-tech" specialty manufacturing has dwindled as well. The U.S. share of electronics production fell dramatically in the 1980s, for instance, as did the U.S. lead in computer chip technology. The United States is also losing shares in robotics, aerospace, and machine tools, and is now running a deficit with Japan and Europe in patents for new inventions and technologies. This new situation has raised "protectionist" sentiment and attempts in Congress to protect American industry from foreign competition (see Figure 4.14).

The United States, moreover, is no longer the preeminent power in world finance. The United States became the leading creditor nation in the world after World War I, and dominated international finance for many years. By 1987, however, it had become the leading debtor nation in the world. United States banking institutions, for a long time the largest and most influential in the world, are now ranked as a group well below banks of the new financial colossus, Japan. By 1988, only one of the top 15 banks in the world was American owned. In 1987, the Tokyo Stock Exchange's share of world equity capital passed that of the New York Stock Exchange.

The relative decline of the United States in the world economy matters in many ways. As we lose shares of world trade and borrow more (usually from abroad) to cover our trade and financial deficits, several consequences may follow: the standard of living stagnates or declines as workers' wages are pressured, American companies become vulnerable to takeovers, decisions that will affect the overall health of the American economy are increasingly made by foreign central banks and companies, and the status of the United States as a world superpower gradually erodes (we will discuss this in the next section). Most of these problems eventually become part of the American political agenda; they become grist for the mill of presidents, Congress, and voters, affecting public policies that range from federal taxes to education, social welfare, national defense, and business regulation, to mention only a few of the most obvious.

THE UNITED STATES IN THE WORLD SYSTEM

The Basis of the Rise to World Power

Historian Paul Kennedy, in his widely acclaimed book *The Rise and Fall of the Great Powers*, suggests that the military and diplomatic power of a nation tends to be based on its relative economic standing in the world. An examination of the history of the "Great Powers," over a period of 500 years, led him to the following conclusion:

> ... the historical record suggests that there is a very clear connection in the long run between an individual Great Power's economic rise and fall and its growth and decline as an important military power.... This ... is hardly surprising, since it flows from two related facts. The first is that economic resources are necessary to support a large-scale military establishment. The second is that, so far as the international system is concerned, both wealth and power are always relative ... [what matters, that is to say, is not how much wealth a nation has but how much it has compared to its rivals].[20]

If Kennedy is correct, the rise of the United States as a world political and military power in this century is entirely expected, given the growth to dominance of its economy.

America's Rise to Superpower Status

Until the late nineteenth century, the attention of the United States was focused mainly inward, on the task of filling in the continent (see Figure 4.15). It is a story of vast population movements, economic development, the rise of cities, and the construction of transportation and communications linkages that in the end spanned the continent. Territory was, in part, bought from others. President Jefferson doubled the size of the United States when he purchased the vast Louisiana Territory from Napoleon in 1803. Florida was acquired from Spain in 1819. A small parcel of land was bought from Mexico in 1853, known as the Gadsden Purchase. Oregon (which included the present state of Washington) was added to U.S. boundaries after a settlement with Great Britain in 1846. Alaska was purchased from Russia in 1867.

Conquest also played a role. The movement west required the removal of Native American populations from the lines of advance. Military pressure on Mex-

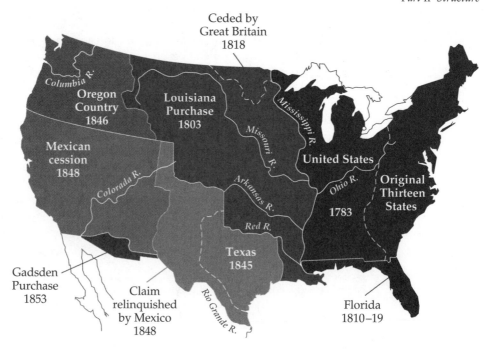

Figure 4.15 Territorial additions to the United States to 1853

Source: Jonathan Hughes, American Economic History *(Glenview, IL: Scott, Foresman, 1987).*

ico played a role in Texas's bid for independence and admission into the Union in 1845. The Mexican War in 1848 led to the addition of vast territories in what is now California and the American Southwest.

It was war with Spain in 1898 that first launched the United States onto the superpower stage. With its easy victory, the United States gained the former Spanish colonies of Cuba and the Philippines. Both were occupied by U.S. military forces and turned into U.S. protectorates.

It was World War I that confirmed this new status. America's great industrial strength worked to tip the balance in that terrible struggle. Her industrial capacity alone was two-and-one-half times greater than that of Germany and the Axis powers. She produced one-half the world's food exports and could easily transport it to her allies, because she was the world leader in shipbuilding. Fast becoming the world's banker, the United States was able to finance allied purchases of munitions and arms. Finally, though it came late in the war, the ability of the United States to pour 300,000 fresh troops per month into France in the last year of the war proved to be decisive.[21]

American involvement in the war and its membership in the club of great powers did not lead immediately, however, to world diplomatic and military leadership. To be sure, the war further entrenched the position of the United States as the world's leading industrial, trading, and financial power. Nevertheless, after the disillusionment of the war fought "to end all wars," the United States turned inward, taken over by strong isolationist sentiments among both elites and the people.

The United States as a Superpower

World War II propelled the United States into the leadership position that its economic position in the world had portended since 1900. The wars stimulated a massive expansion of the entire industrial infrastructure of the economy. Factories were built to turn out uniforms, arms, tanks, airplanes, and warships; transportation systems were upgraded to ship war materials; new forms of business-government cooperation were invented to coordinate the war effort. While this improvement of the economic infrastructure was proceeding, the financial and production infrastructures of our prewar economic and diplomatic rivals—Britain, France, Japan, and Germany—were devastated by the war. By the end of the war, the United States was responsible for one-half of the total manufacturing, shipping, and exporting of the entire world.[22]

World War II also solidified the position of the United States as the leading creditor nation in the world. By the end of the war, the United States held two-thirds of the gold reserves of the world in its vaults, and the American dollar became the principal **reserve currency** in world trade.

The United States emerged from the war with a large military establishment and military superiority in most areas where it counted. There was also a new belief among both the population and the nation's leaders that "isolationism" was dangerous and contrary to long-term national interests.

Within a decade of the end of World War II, given full development of all of these trends, the United States stood as the unchallenged economic, political, and military power among the Western nations. For the first time, the United States was willing and able to exercise leadership on the world level. It was the United States that pulled the major capitalist nations together for the first time in their history into a political and economic alliance; provided funds for the rebuilding of Europe and for development projects in the Third World; led the movement toward the liberalization of trade by the lowering of tariff barriers; provided a stable dollar to serve as the basis of the international monetary system; and organized and largely paid for the joint military defenses of them all. Is it any wonder, then, that *Life* magazine editor Henry Luce was moved to label the period the "American Century"?

The "fly in the ointment," of course, was the Soviet Union. Although badly crippled by the war (it is said that 20 million of its citizens died in the conflict), the Soviet Union entered the postwar era with the world's largest land army, superpower ambitions of its own, and a strong desire to keep the nations on its periphery in eastern and southern Europe in hands it considered friendly. In the ensuing Cold War between them, which began in the late 1940s and lasted for four decades, the two superpowers came to face each other as leaders of conflicting political, economic, and ideological alliances; became engaged in a nuclear arms race; and fought surrogate wars with each other in various locations in the Third World, from the Belgian Congo, to Central America, to Afghanistan. (We will have more to say about the Cold War in Chapter 16.)

America's superpower status had many implications, in addition to the obvious transformations in U.S. foreign policy. For one thing, superpower status required a large military establishment and tilted government spending priorities toward national defense. For another thing, it enhanced the role of the president in policymaking and diminished that of Congress, as we shall see in Chapter 12,

"The President: Tribune of the People?" Finally, superpower status and the struggle with the Soviet Union contributed to a climate of opinion favoring secrecy in the name of "national security," with unfortunate implications for the practice of democracy.

A Multipower-centered World?

The 1980s and the 1990s saw startling changes in the world political, military, and economic systems. Communism collapsed in Eastern Europe. The Soviet Union ceased to exist.

The disappearance of Soviet power would seem to indicate the emergence of the United States as the world's single greatest power. The Persian Gulf War perhaps confirms such a development, at least in the military arena. However, the relative economic decline of the United States continues in the face of the fantastic economic performance of Europe, Japan, and several Pacific Rim nations, including South Korea, Hong Kong, Taiwan, and Singapore. If historian Paul Kennedy is correct, this should eventually translate into relative military and diplomatic decline as well. This remains to be seen.[23] It is worth noting, in this regard, that the United States is finding it increasingly difficult to lead Europe (especially Germany) and Japan on economic, trade, and military matters.

The bipolar world of the post-World War II years has given way to a world with multiple centers of power—a pluralistic world with the United States as the most powerful nation.[24] Whether a safer and more humane world order emerges from this transformation remains to be seen. What is clear is that this new world order will offer many challenges and opportunities for American politics and governance. Issues like U.S. policy on national and ethnic aspirations in Eastern Europe, foreign aid to the fragments of the former Soviet Union, alternative uses for the so-called peace dividend, and the improvement of American economic competitiveness will demand attention from American leaders and citizens.

One sign of the collapse of the U.S.–U.S.S.R. bipolar world order was the withdrawal of tanks of the former Soviet Union from Germany in 1991.

THE AMERICAN POLITICAL CULTURE

The kinds of choices Americans make in meeting these challenges and opportunities will depend a great deal on the fundamental beliefs of Americans about human nature, society, economic relations, and the role of government. Public policy tends to reflect our ideas and beliefs as a people. These fundamental beliefs that have political consequences make up the American *political culture*. The general outlines of the American political culture are discussed in this section. Many of the details on how these beliefs are expressed in everyday politics can be found in Chapter 5, "Public Opinion."

There is a great deal of evidence that most Americans share a political culture. To be sure, we are a vast, polyglot mixture of races, religions, ethnicities, occupations, and life-styles. Nevertheless, one of the things that has always struck observers of the American scene is the degree to which a broad consensus seems to exist on many of the fundamental beliefs that shape our political life. We focus here, not on transitory ideas about particular issues that are in the headlines at the moment, but on what might be called *foundation beliefs*—beliefs that shape how people classify, think about, and resolve particular issues that arise in the headlines or in their local communities.

Classical Liberalism

The foundation of our political culture is *classical liberalism*.[25] The ideas, values, and assumptions of classical liberalism pervade every nook and cranny of our society and leave their mark on virtually every social, economic, and political decision that we make individually or collectively. America, in the words of historian Louis Hartz, is "a liberal civilization."[26]

The term "liberalism" may cause some confusion, because we associate it today with a political tendency, found mainly in the Democratic party, that favors an expanded role for government in society and greater controls on business. Such an understanding misses the broader significance of liberalism in American life. It's important to recognize that both modern liberals (from President Franklin D. Roosevelt to the Reverend Jesse Jackson and Senator Ted Kennedy) *and* modern conservatives (from Senator Robert A. Taft to Presidents Ronald Reagan and George Bush) are part of the same *classical liberal* tradition; they are two tendencies within a single tradition.

COMPETITIVE INDIVIDUALISM   At the heart of classical liberalism is the belief that people are by nature self-interested and competitive. Americans have long believed that an individual's fate is, and should be, tied to his or her own efforts. Those with talent, grit, and the willingness to work hard are more likely than not to end up on top; those without at least some of these qualities are more likely than not to wind up on the bottom of the heap. The broad popularity of what has been called "individualism" has been around since the very earliest days of the nation, drawing comment in 1845 from that perceptive observer of American life, Alexis de Tocqueville:

> They owe nothing to any man, they expect nothing from any man; they acquire the habit of always considering themselves as standing alone, and they are apt to imagine that their whole destiny is in their own hands.[27]

Individualism also means that people are naturally competitive, always striving to better themselves in relation to others. Their aim is not only to "keep up with the Joneses," but to pass them by. An abundance of popular nonfiction literature in America always has conveyed this theme, ranging from the Horatio Alger books of the turn of the century to the many guidebooks on "getting rich" of today.

The belief in competitive individualism affects the way we think about many politically relevant issues, including inequality. The evidence suggests that Americans overwhelmingly endorse the idea of "equality of opportunity" (the idea that people ought to have an equal shot in the competitive game of life) but overwhelmingly reject the idea that people should have equal rewards. Not surprisingly, Americans tend to look favorably on government programs that try to equalize opportunity—Head Start, education programs of various kinds, school lunch programs, and the like—but are generally against programs that limit wealth and income (because this would deny people the fruits of their hard work) or that redistribute wealth and income to the poor. Since, it is assumed, people get different rewards based on their own efforts, belief in equality of opportunity is perfectly consistent with highly unequal outcomes; that is, Americans find inequality of income and wealth acceptable, so long as it is the outcome of a process in which individuals compete with each other on an equal basis.[28] This contrasts with Sweden, where citizens generally believe that equality of condition is an important value and support government policies to redistribute income.[29]

The strong sense of individualism that is so central to the American political culture is not found in most other modern capitalist nations. In Japan, for instance, commitment to the work team, to the company, and to the community is more highly regarded than commitment to personal advancement. In Sweden, people are less likely to talk about their individual rights and more about their social obligations.[30]

PRIVATE PROPERTY   Another important component of classical liberalism is the idea that human beings have a natural right to accumulate, enjoy, and transfer private property as they please. It is mainly to seventeenth-century philosopher

In Japan, commitment to the work team and the company are more important cultural values than they are in the United States.

John Locke that we owe most of our present ideas on the subject, though the American experience with widespread property ownership has fortified this belief. Locke argued that, while God gave the earth and its resources in common to human beings, He also gave human beings a set of abilities like industry (the willingness to work hard) and creativity, which they have a right and an obligation to use. When they use these abilities, people turn common property into private property. By mixing their labor with the naturally occurring abundance of the earth (the land, forests, rivers, and so on), people are justified in taking the product of that effort for their own as private property. Because people are different in their abilities and willingness to work, this process always will result in inequality. Inevitably, some will end up with more property than others.

LIMITED GOVERNMENT   The Founders believed that the main purpose of having a government is to protect rights, particularly property rights. When government does more, it almost invariably interferes with basic rights. If it does so, people have a right to dissolve their government and to form a new one. Our own Declaration of Independence expresses this sentiment in words that are very familiar to Americans.

 This belief is not universally shared. In such countries as Japan, Sweden, Germany, and France, where government always has been powerful and has played an important role in directing society and the economy, limited government has little attraction.

THE FREE MARKET   Classical liberals, following Adam Smith, believe that, if the market were left alone to operate in its natural fashion, it would coordinate the multitude of complex exchanges and interactions that make up the economy in a nearly perfect fashion, following the laws of supply and demand. The market, in turn, works best if people are free to pursue their own interests. Since the market is efficient and effective if left alone, government should not interfere with its operations. Though few Americans today accept this "pure" free market ideal, most Americans today, as in the past, believe that the private sector (responding to markets) is usually more effective and efficient than the public sector.

Given the esteem in which individualism, private property, and the market are held, as well as the success of the American economy, it is entirely understandable that Americans tend to hold the business system in very high regard. While few would go as far as President Calvin Coolidge, who proclaimed that "the business of America is business," many observers have noted the strong commitment of Americans to its own way of conducting its economic life.

One indicator of the general high regard in which the economic system is held by Americans is the almost complete lack of support for movements in favor of alternatives to it. Socialism and communism, for instance, while occasionally enjoying moments of popularity with particular groups in the population, have never had either long-term or widespread support among Americans. In many European countries, by way of contrast, socialism has been popular for many years, and communism has attracted many others.

The classical liberal tradition influences many aspects of public policy in the United States. Eminent economist John Kenneth Galbraith once decried the fact that ours is a society in which great private wealth exists side by side with public squalor. By that he meant that Americans favor private consumption over public provision, and private over public initiatives.[31] In other developed capitalist nations, citizens and political leaders believe that extensive and high-quality public services in mass transit, health care, housing, and education are part and parcel of the good society (see Chapters 17 and 18).

Citizenship and the Nature of the Political Order

Certain beliefs about what kind of political order is most appropriate and what role citizens should play shape the actual behavior of citizens and political decision makers on a daily basis.

DEMOCRACY   At the time of its founding, democracy was not highly regarded in the United States. During our history, however, the practice of democracy has been enriched and expanded, and the term "democracy" has become an honored one.[32]

Democracy first became widely popular at the time of the presidency of Andrew Jackson (from 1829 to 1837), spurred by his celebration of the "common man" (see the feature on Walt Whitman). The prestige of the word *democracy* was further improved by Abraham Lincoln's praise of majoritarian democracy. The Populist movement during the latter part of the nineteenth century championed the peoples' right to regulate and to control what it considered irresponsible economic power. The Progressive movement during the early part of the twentieth century advocated the direct election of senators, the **direct primary** for nominating candidates, and the right of the people to recall their elected representatives and to legislate through the **referendum**. By the end of the Progressive movement, it was no longer permissible in public life in the United States to disparage democracy openly as a principle of government.

This regard for the principle of democracy is one of the bedrocks of the American belief system today. This is not to say that people always behave in a democratic fashion (after all, blacks were denied the vote and other citizenship rights in many parts of the nation until the 1960s); it is to say that most Americans believe in democracy as a general principle and take seriously claims that their behavior is not consistent with it.

FREEDOM AND LIBERTY   Foreign visitors always have been fascinated by the American obsession with "rights." Academic studies confirm how central the idea of freedom is to peoples' conception of themselves as Americans. There is even reason to believe that freedom (also called "liberty") is at the very top of the list of American beliefs and that it is more strongly honored here as an idea than elsewhere.[33] From the very beginning, what attracted most people to the United States was the promise of freedom in the New World. Many came for other reasons, to be sure: a great many came for strictly economic reasons; some came as convict labor; some came in chains as slaves. The majority of those who came to these shores, however, seem to have done so in order to taste of the freedom to speak and think as they chose, to worship as they pleased, to read what they might, and to assemble and petition the government if they had a mind to do so.

Like many things, however, to believe in something is not necessarily to act in a way that is consistent with that belief. There have been many intrusions on basic rights during our history. Later chapters address this issue more closely.

THE STRUGGLE FOR DEMOCRACY

★

Walt Whitman: Poet of Democracy

The democratic process requires a political culture that respects ordinary people and believes in their ability to govern themselves. Walt Whitman was one of the giants of American letters who helped fashion the transformation of the American political culture from its aristocratic roots. Whitman was a printer and a crusading newspaper editor, best known, then and now, as a poet whose celebration of the common people earned him the title "the poet of democracy."

Whitman was a physically imposing man. He was a rugged outdoorsman who did not fit easily into literary circles. His poetry contributed to his reputation as a firm individualist. Instead of writing in the conventional poetic diction, he used the speech of common Americans.

During the Civil War, Whitman chronicled the experience of soldiers, citizens, and even President Lincoln in his poetry. When his brother was wounded, he went to Washington, D.C., to see him and stayed on to do all he could to help in the hospitals. His personal contact with wounded soldiers deeply affected him and reaffirmed his democratic sentiments.

Whitman's celebration of the dignity of common people and the character of their everyday lives is captured in these selections from his most famous work, *Leaves of Grass* (1855):

(15) The pure contralto sings in the organloft,
The carpenter dresses his plant . . . the tongue of
  his foreplane whistles its wild ascending lisp,
The married and unmarried children ride home to
  their thanksgiving dinner,
The pilot seizes the king-pin, he heaves down
  with a strong arm,
The mate stands braced in the whaleboat, lance
  and harpoon are ready,

The duck-shooter walks by silent and
  cautious
    stretches,
The deacons are ordained with
  crossed hands at the altar,
The spinning-girl retreats and
  advances to the hum of the big
  wheel,
The farmer stops by the bars of a
  Sunday and looks at the oats and
  rye, . . .
The machinist rolls up his sleeves . . . the
  policeman travels his beat . . . the gatekeeper
  marks who pass,
The young fellow drives the express-wagon. . . . I
  love him though I do not know him;

(24) Whoever degrades another degrades me . . .
  and
    whatever is done or said returns at last to me,
And whatever, I do or say I also return.
I speak the password primeval. . . . I give the sign
  of
    democracy;
By God! I will accept nothing which all cannot
  have their counterpart of on the same terms.

POLITICS AND FILM

The Common Man (and Woman) Takes on the Big Guys

The populist strain in the American political culture is commonly featured in Hollywood films. Hollywood always has found it hard to resist stories of the common person's struggle against the economically and politically powerful, given the appeal of this theme at the box office.

Frank Capra's classic films of the 1930s and 1940s are the most well known of this genre.

In Capra's most admired movies, members of the snootier classes were greedy or black-hearted swine. In Capra's America good, upright, innocent Mr. Deeds, Mr. Smith, John Doe, and George Bailey were all at the mercy of vile capitalists, lawyers, and politicians who infested society. . . . In *Mr. Deeds Goes to Town*, in *Mr. Smith Goes to Washington*, in *Meet John Doe*, and in *It's a Wonderful Life*, the nastiness of society's pillars is drawn in harsh caricature strokes. . . .ᵃ

In Capra's films, the common man always overcomes the odds; the powerful are vanquished, and the values of hard work, simplicity, honesty, and self-reliance are rewarded. Victories don't come so easily in today's films for those who take on the big shots. Francis Ford Coppola's *Tucker* chronicles the story of automobile visionary Preston Tucker (played by Jeff Bridges), who dared to take on the Big Three automobile companies in the late 1940s with a revolutionary car that combined advanced safety features, sleek design, and high performance.

True to the values of entrepreneurship and the "can do" attitude, Tucker begins to build the car in his barn with the help of his family and skilled automobile workers who share his dream. Though Tucker eventually manufactures 51 Tucker Torpedoes (many of which are used in the film), his enterprise collapses in the face of a conspiracy between the large automobile corporations in Detroit and their political allies in Washington, D.C. The happy ending of the Capra films is absent, perhaps reflecting director Coppola's own bitter experience of trying to create an independent and visionary film studio (Zoetrope Studios) in the mist of the Hollywood giants.

In *Silkwood*, the villain is the powerful Kerr-McGee Corporation, whose energy-based empire (oil and nuclear power) not only dominated the regional economy but also wielded imposing influence in Washington, D.C. (in the form of Senator Kerr of Oklahoma). Meryl Streep plays Karen Silkwood, a worker in the Kerr-McGee Cimarron nuclear power plant who is radicalized by the corporation's lax attention to worker safety. Fighting the apathy and eventual hostility of her fellow workers, who are worried about losing their jobs, and the threats of company officials, Silkwood takes her crusade to union officials (who are sympathetic but powerless) and thinks about going

POPULISM   There always has been a strong "populist" strain in the American political culture. The term "populism" refers to the hostility of the common person to power and the powerful. While public policy is not often driven by populist sentiments (for the powerful, by definition, exercise considerable political influence), it has always been part of the American belief system and has sometimes been expressed in visible ways in American politics (as well as in our films; see "Politics and Film").

public with her damning information. For her trouble, she is purposely contaminated by plutonium, though it is never clear whether the culprit is a fellow worker or the company. Just like the real Karen Silkwood, the heroine dies in a car crash on her way to meet a *New York Times* reporter with her story and supporting evidence. The film implies, with its menacing headlights glaring through the rear window of Silkwood's car, that she was murdered—a view held to this day by many unionists, feminists, and friends of Silkwood. Again, the Hollywood film has come a long way from the innocent optimism of Frank Capra.

Capra is partially revived in *Wall Street*, director Oliver Stone's indictment of the Reagan "go-go" 1980s. The targets in the film are, as the title suggests, Wall Street (a familiar target of American populism), where people seem to make money through shrewd financial manipulations without benefit of making anything useful, and its most visible manifestation, Gordon Gekko (loosely modeled on convicted inside trader, Ivan Boesky). The protagonist, Bud Fox (played by Charlie Sheen), is an ambitious son of a working-class father, who has fallen in with Gekko, attracted by the glamour and riches of his life, and who has forgotten the fundamental values of his airplane mechanic father (played by Martin Sheen).

Bud sees the light, however, when Gekko's machinations threaten to destroy the company that his father works for and the jobs that his father and his friends depend upon. He then cooperates with the authorities, in return for a reduced prison sentence, to bring Gekko down. Bud only returns to his fundamental values and is reunited with his family, however, through a circuitous and morally ambiguous route that would never have occurred in Capra's films.

[a]L. Russell Baker, "Capra Beats the Game," *New York Times*, September 9, 1991.

One of the most common targets of populist sentiment has been concentrated economic power and those who exercise it. Andrew Jackson mobilized it in his fight against the Bank of the United States in the 1830s. The Populist and Progressive movements directed their political and legislative efforts against the new corporations of their day, especially the banks and the railroads. Corporations were the target of popular hostility during the dark days of the Great Depression and also in the 1970s, when consumer groups made the lives of some corporate

Table 4.2
Religious Affiliation

	Belong to Churches or Religious Organizations	Do Unpaid Voluntary Work for Churches or Religious Organizations
	%	%
United States	57	23
Northern Ireland	51	14
Netherlands	35	9
Republic of Ireland	31	8
Great Britain	22	7
Spain	15	10
West Germany	13	7
Norway	10	6
Belgium	9	5
Sweden	9	5
Finland	9	4
Italy	7	5
France	4	3
Denmark	4	2

Source: Social Surveys, The Gallup organization, 1981.

executives extremely uncomfortable. Contemporary public opinion polls are almost unanimous in finding strong popular support for free enterprise existing side by side with negative feelings about corporations and corporate leaders.

Piety

The United States is, by any measure, a strikingly religious society. In the 1980 election, all three candidates—Jimmy Carter, John Anderson, and Ronald Reagan—claimed to be "born again." Polls conducted over the past two decades show that around 40 percent of the American people claim to have had a personal experience with the Lord. The American people are clearly more religious than people in any other western society (see Tables 4.2–4.4).

The level of piety in the United States, in fact, approaches the level of piety found in the non-Western and less economically developed parts of the world. In the parlance of the social sciences, the United States is an "outlier," in the sense that it does not fit the normal pattern: the more developed a society becomes (in terms of industrialization, education, caloric intake, etc.), the more secular it tends to become. Most studies show that piety is highest in the least developed nations of Asia, Africa, and Latin America; piety is least pronounced and society is the most secular in the Scandinavian countries, Germany, and Japan. The United States is the exception.[34]

Piety affects politics. While churches and religious believers often have found themselves on the liberal side of the political divide—note their substantial

Table 4.3
"Which, if any, of the following do you believe in?"

	God			Heaven			Hell		
	Yes	No	Don't Know	Yes	No	Don't Know	Yes	No	Don't Know
	%	%	%	%	%	%	%	%	%
United States	95	2	3	84	11	5	67	26	7
Republic of Ireland	95	3	2	83	10	7	54	35	10
Northern Ireland	91	3	5	81	10	9	65	21	14
Spain	87	8	6	50	38	12	34	52	14
Italy	84	10	6	41	44	15	31	52	17
Belgium	77	12	10	33	45	22	18	60	23
Great Britain	76	6	9	57	32	11	27	63	11
West Germany	72	16	12	31	54	15	14	73	13
Norway	72	22	7	48	42	11	22	68	11
Netherlands	65	25	10	39	47	14	15	71	14
France	62	29	9	27	65	9	15	77	8
Denmark	58	27	15	17	67	16	8	81	12
Sweden	52	35	14	26	59	14	10	80	10

Source: Social Surveys, The Gallup Organization, 1981.

Table 4.4
"Do you find that you get comfort and strength from religion or not?"

	Yes	No	Don't Know
	%	%	%
United States	79	17	4
Republic of Ireland	79	17	5
Northern Ireland	70	22	7
Italy	63	30	7
Spain	57	34	9
Belgium	47	32	20
Great Britain	46	49	5
West Germany	44	39	14
Netherlands	43	44	13
Norway	40	38	22
France	37	57	6
Denmark	29	60	11
Sweden	27	63	10

Source: Social Surveys, The Gallup Organization, 1981.

More people are church-goers in the United States than in any other western industrial nation.

involvement in the abolitionist, civil rights, and anti-Vietnam War movements—the overall effect of religion on politics probably has been conservative. This is another reason why socialist and social democratic parties have had little success in America. One may see evidence for this conclusion in the many official and semiofficial statements against communism, Marxism, and socialism that have been pronounced by most of the established churches, whether Catholic or Protestant. One may also see it in the fact that the highest levels of piety are found in the United States among nonwhites, people with the least amount of education, and those at the lower end of the income scale—precisely the population groups that are the strongest supporters of leftist political parties in Europe. One may also see it in the fact that polls show that the most religious among the American population are also the most politically conservative.

STRUCTURAL INFLUENCES ON AMERICAN POLITICS

We have now examined structural factors that influence American politics. These influences are summarized in Figure 4.16. In Chapters 2 and 3, we dealt with the fundamental rules of the game; in this present chapter, we considered the nature of the American population, economy, political culture, and place in the world. Our position has been that each influences important aspects of politics and government in the United States. We would also suggest that these structural factors are interrelated; each helps define the others in important ways. The kind of constitutional rules we have are, to a substantial degree, shaped by beliefs about the nature of the individual, society, and government that make up our political culture. The political culture, in turn, with its ideas celebrating the market, competitive individualism, and private property, is perfectly attuned to a free enterprise economy. The way in which the economy operates and develops has a lot to do with the life of the American people (where people live, what kind of work they do, etc.) and the nation's place in the world. The characteristics of the American population trigger their own effects—their level of education and skill has a lot to do with American economic performance, for instance.

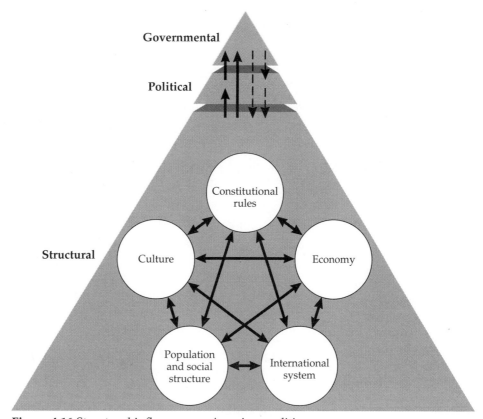

Figure 4.16 Structural influences on American politics

One of the recurring themes that will appear throughout this book is the substantial growth in the size, reach, and responsibilities of the federal government. Much of this growth, we will see, is because of changes in the structural factors described in this chapter.

SUMMARY

How politics and government work in practice is shaped by such structural factors as the nature of the population, the economy, the nation's place in the world, and the political culture. This chapter looks at the development and interaction of each of these four structural factors and how each influences important aspects of politics and government.

The most important changes in the American population are its growth; diversification along ethnic, religious, and racial grounds; relocation from rural to urban and suburban areas and to the Sun Belt; and its gradual aging. The population is also marked by the existence of substantial inequalities in income and wealth, and a surprisingly high level of poverty. These factors affect the agenda of American politics and the distribution of political power.

The American economy is a capitalist or free enterprise economy. It has changed from a highly competitive, small enterprise form to a highly concentrated, corporate-dominated, multinational one. The relative decline of the U.S. position in the world economic system has had important reverberations in American politics.

The United State's emergence as a superpower in the twentieth century changed the content of foreign policy, the balance of power between the president and Congress, the size of the federal government, and the priorities of the government's budget. The collapse of communism in Eastern Europe and the Persian Gulf War affirmed the position of the United States as the world's most important military power, but relative economic decline has forced the United States to share power in the political and economic arenas with western Europe and Japan. This new situation is filled with uncertainties that will affect U.S. foreign and domestic policy.

The foundation of the American political culture is classical liberalism, with its beliefs in individualism, limited government, private property, and the market. Beliefs about democracy, liberty, and the primacy of the common people also help define the political culture, as does a strong pietistic streak. The political culture shapes American ideas about what the good society looks like, the appropriate role for government, and the possibilities for self-government.

To Ponder

1. Is it likely that the current wave of immigrant groups will be incorporated into American society in the same way that previous immigrant groups were incorporated? Why, or why not?

2. Is political democracy possible where great inequalities in income and wealth exist? Would efforts to change these inequalities endanger freedom?

3. Will present occupational trends make the American people more or less able to act as citizens of a democracy?

4. What are the likely political consequences if the American standard of living fails to grow or declines in the years ahead?

5. Will the "internationalization" of the economy lead to more or less government regulation of business?

6. How will the end of the Cold War and the breakup of the Soviet Union alter what government does?

Suggested Readings

Bellah, Robert N., et al. *Habits of the Heart.* Berkeley: University of California Press, 1985.
   A convincing description of competitive individualism and its effects.

Chafe, William H. *The Unfinished Journey.* New York: Oxford University Press, 1986.
   A very compelling history of postwar America, with special attention to how structural transformations have shaped American political life.

Friedman, Milton. *Capitalism and Freedom.* Chicago: University of Chicago Press, 1962.
   The classic defense of free market capitalism.

Gilpin, Robert. *The Political Economy of International Relations.* Princeton, NJ: Princeton University Press, 1987.
   A survey of the world economy and the place of the United States in it.

Hanson, Russell. *The Democratic Imagination in America*. Princeton, NJ: Princeton University Press, 1985.

> A history of the democratic idea in America; stresses its changing character.

Hughes, Jonathan. *American Economic History*. Glenview, IL: Scott Foresman, 1987.

> An economic history of the United States, with special attention to the nature of the population, technology, business practices, and the international setting.

Kennedy, Paul. *The Rise and Fall of the Great Powers*. Princeton, NJ: Princeton University Press, 1987.

> An influential treatment of the relationship between economic and military power, with special attention to the recent relative decline of the United States.

Levy, Frank. *Dollars and Dreams*. New York: Russell Sage, 1987.

> A balanced presentation of the best contemporary information on the distribution of wealth and income in the United States.

McClosky, Herbert and John Zaller. *The American Ethos*. Cambridge, MA: Harvard University Press, 1981.

> A compelling look at the essentials of the American political culture.

Wills, Gary. *Under God: Religion and American Politics*. New York: Simon & Schuster, 1991.

> The best recent interpretation of the centrality of religion in American political life.

Notes

1. David Halberstam, *The Reckoning* (New York: William Morrow, 1986).

2. Kevin L. Kearns, "GM, Ford, Chrysler: Helpless Giants," *Washington Post* (reprinted in the *Boulder Daily Camera*, June 23, 1991), p. B1.

3. Much of the information in this section is from *Oxford Analytica: America in Perspective* (Boston: Houghton Mifflin, 1986).

4. Michael Reich, "The Proletarianization of the Workforce," in Richard Edwards, et al., eds., *The Capitalist System* (Englewood Cliffs, NJ: Prentice-Hall, 1966), p. 125.

5. These two figures are from Stanley Lebergott, "The American Labor Force," in Davis, et al., *American Economic Growth* (New York: HarperCollins, 1972), p. 187; Reich, "The Proletarianization," p. 124.

6. Louis M. Hacker, *The Course of American Economic Growth and Development* (New York: Wiley, 1970), p. 24.

7. Quoted in *Oxford Analytica*, p. 57.

8. Kevin Phillips, *The Politics of Rich and Poor* (New York: Random House, 1990), ch. 1.

9. *Business Week* (September 1989), p. 14.

10. Phillips, *The Politics of Rich and Poor*, ch. 1.

11. The statistics in this section are from diverse government sources and are reported in Phillips, *The Politics of Rich and Poor*, ch. 1.

12. Robert Pear, "5.5 Million Children in U.S. Are Hungry," *New York Times* (March 15, 1991), p. 18.

13. For this story, see Edward S. Greenberg, *Capitalism and the American Political Ideal* (Armonk, NY: M.E. Sharpe, 1985), ch. 4.

14. Paul Kennedy, *The Rise and Fall of the Great Powers* (New York: Random House, 1987), ch. 5.

15. On these characteristics in all industrial capitalist systems in this period, see Robert Heilbroner, *The Nature and Logic of Capitalism* (New York: Norton, 1986), p. 160.

16. On this history, see Thomas C. Cochran and William Miller, *The Age of Enterprise* (New York: HarperCollins, 1961); Greenberg, *The American Political Ideal*; Louis M. Hacker, *American Economic Growth and Development*; and Robert Wiebe, *The Search for Order* (New York: Hill and Wang, 1967).

17. "Conglomerate Mergers," *Report of the Committee on Small Business*, U.S. House of Representatives (October 2, 1980), p. 52.

18. U.S. Department of Commerce, *International Direct Investment* (Washington, D.C.: U.S. Government Printing Office, 1984), p.1.

19. The following statistics are from Phillips, *The Politics of Rich and Poor*, ch. 5.

20. Kennedy, *The Rise and Fall*, p. xxiii.

21. See Kennedy, *The Rise and Fall*, pp. 271–274.

22. Kennedy, *The Rise and Fall*, p. 358.

23. For a counterargument to Kennedy, see Joseph S. Nye, *Bound to Lead: The Changing Nature of American Power* (New York: Basic Books, 1990).

24. *Ibid.*

25. Everett C. Ladd, Jr., "Traditional Values Regnant," *Public Opinion* Vol. 1, No. 1 (March/April 1978), p. 45.

26. Louis Hartz, *The Liberal Tradition in America* (New York: Harcourt, Brace Jovanovich, 1955), p. 2.

27. Alexis de Tocqueville, *Democracy in America*, Vol. 2 (New York: Langley Press, 1845), p. 107.

28. For evidence sustaining this conclusion, see Jennifer Hochschild, *What's Fair? American Beliefs About Distributive Justice* (Cambridge, MA: Harvard University Press, 1981); Herbert McClosky and John Zaller, *The American Ethos: Public Attitudes Toward Capitalism and Democracy* (Cambridge, MA: Harvard University Press, 1984); and Sidney Verba and Gary R. Orren, *Equality in America* (Cambridge, MA: Harvard University Press, 1985).

29. Verba and Orren, *Equality in America*, p. 255.

30. M. Donald Hancock, *Sweden: The Politics of Post-Industrial Change* (Hinsdale, IL: Dryden Press, 1972); and Kay Schlozmand and Sidney Verba, *Insult to Injury* (Cambridge, MA: Harvard University Press, 1979).

31. McClosky and Zaller, *The American Ethos*, pp. 270–271.

32. For the history of the meaning of the term "democracy," see Russell Hanson, *The Democratic Imagination in America* (Princeton, NJ: Princeton University Press, 1985).

33. McClosky and Zaller, *The American Ethos*, p. 18.

34. For a brilliant exposition of this point and its meaning, see Walter Dean Burnham, "The 1980 Earthquake," in Thomas Ferguson and Joel Rogers, eds., *The Hidden Election* (New York: Pantheon, 1981). Also see Gary Wills, *Under God: Religion and American Politics* (New York: Simon & Schuster, 1991).

PART III

Politics

In Part II we discussed a number of fundamental *structural* factors that affect how American politics works: the Constitution, our federal system, the nature of our population and society, the economy, and the international system. Throughout the remainder of the book we will see that these factors have pervasive effects on political processes, governmental institutions, and public policies.

Now we turn to the political level of analysis, discussing in separate chapters public opinion, the mass media, organized interest groups, social movements, and elections. These people and institutions are affected in many ways by the structural factors already discussed. They, in turn, strongly affect the governmental institutions that will be the subject of the next section of the book. They are not formally part of government, but they directly influence what sorts of people are chosen to be government officials—who is elected president and who goes to Congress, for example. They also affect what these officials do when they are in office and what sorts of public policies result.

We will see that each of the political-level institutions has its own special characteristics and its own particular ways of working. We will also see that these institutions interact with each other in complicated ways, often competing to influence the government. Some of them make more positive contributions to democracy than others do.

Public opinion, for example, (Chapter 5) turns out to be a more serious and more sensible influence on government than many observers used to think. This is fortunate, since the preferences of ordinary citizens can be considered the bedrock of democracy. The mass media (Chapter 6) are essential for providing information that the public needs, but the quality of this information may be diminished by certain kinds of biases, sometimes resulting in manipulation of public opinion. Organized interest groups (Chapter 7), especially business corporations, appear to have a substantial impact on government, sometimes producing policies different from what ordinary citizens would want. Political parties (Chapter 8) can play a crucial part in mobilizing the public and communicating its wishes to government, but weakness and decentralization impair their ability to do so. Moreover, parties tend to reflect the wishes of organized interests and activists as well as the general public.

Elections (Chapter 9) are supposed to be the key mechanism by which democracy works and the public makes its voice heard. But elections also facilitate influence by organized interests and party activists. Under certain unusual conditions social movements (Chapter 10) can push aside politics as usual and profoundly affect government—particularly when they succeed in convincing the general public that their cause is just.

The following six chapters, then, discuss how political-level institutions work, how they affect policy making, and what part they play in helping or hindering democracy.

5

Public Opinion

THE VIETNAM WAR AND THE PUBLIC

On August 2, 1964, the U.S. Department of Defense announced that the U.S. destroyer *Maddox*, while on "routine patrol" in international waters in the Gulf of Tonkin near Vietnam, had undergone an "unprovoked attack" by three North Vietnamese PT boats, which had launched torpedoes and fired 37-millimeter guns. Two days later, the Defense Department reported a "second deliberate attack" on the *Maddox* and its companion destroyer, the *C. Turner Joy*. At 11:37 P.M. that night, on nationwide television, President Lyndon Johnson referred to "open aggression on the high seas" and declared that the renewed hostile actions required that he use military force in reply. Air attacks were launched against four North Vietnamese PT boat bases and an oil storage depot.[1]

Years later, the "Pentagon Papers" (a formerly secret Defense Department study) and other sources revealed that the American people had been deceived. The *Maddox* had not been on an innocent cruise: sailing past South Vietnamese gunboats which—with U.S. planning and support—had just raided a North Vietnamese island, it had steamed near the coastline, deliberately provoking North Vietnamese radar defenses. The second "attack" apparently never occurred; it was imagined by an inexperienced sonar man in dark and stormy seas. At the time, however, only a few skeptics raised questions. On August 7, by a vote of 88–2, the Senate passed the Tonkin Resolution, which approved the president's taking "all necessary measures," including the use of armed force, to repel any armed attack and to assist any ally in the region. A legal basis for full U.S. involvement in the Vietnam War was established.

For more than a decade, the United States had been giving large-scale military aid to the French colonialists and then the South Vietnamese government in order to fight nationalists and communists in Vietnam. More than 23,000 U.S. military "advisers" were there by the end of 1964, occasionally engaging in combat. But the American public knew and cared little about the guerilla war. Few knew exactly where Vietnam was. A "permissive consensus" existed; people were willing to go along when their leaders told them that action was essential in order to resist communist aggression. In May 1964, among the only 37 percent of Americans who offered any opinion, three times as many wanted to maintain the present policy or get tougher (12 percent) as wanted to get out of Vietnam (4 percent).[2]

After the Tonkin incident, people paid more attention. Public support for the war increased. When asked in August what should be done next in Vietnam, 48 percent said to keep troops there, get tougher, or take definite military action; only 14 percent said negotiate or get out. Through the fall of 1964, more people wanted to step up the war than wanted to pull out, with many endorsing the current policy. In 1965, after the United States began the heavy "Rolling Thunder" bombing of North Vietnam (ostensibly in retaliation for guerilla raids on U.S. bases in South Vietnam) and after large numbers of U.S. troops were landed and gradually engaged in combat in the South, the permissive consensus continued. Month after month, pollsters found that only small minorities wanted to withdraw from Vietnam; as many or more wanted to escalate further, and the center of gravity favored continuing the current policy.

As the war continued, however, the number of U.S. troops in Vietnam rose rapidly: from 184,300 at the end of 1965 to 385,300 in 1966, 485,600 in 1967, and 536,100 at the end of 1968. American casualties increased, with 1,369 killed in 1965, 5,008 in 1966, 9,377 in 1967, and 14,589 in 1968, plus many more wounded (92,817 in 1968) and a few captured or missing.[3] Television news began to display weekly casualty counts in the hundreds, with pictures of dead American soldiers going home in body bags. The war became expensive, as politicians put it, in "American blood and treasure." Senate hearings aired antiwar testimony. Peace marches and demonstrations, although resented by much of the public, nonetheless accentuated the unpleasantness of the war.

By October and December 1967, with heavy battles fought at Con Thien and Dak To, about as many people (45 percent yes, to 46 percent no) agreed as disagreed with the proposition that the United States "made a mistake" sending its troops to fight in Vietnam. A large majority said they favored "Vietnamization": bringing U.S. troops home as South Vietnamese replaced them.

Then catastrophe struck: at the end of January 1968, during the Tet holidays, the National Liberation Front (NLF) and the North Vietnamese army launched massive coordinated attacks throughout South Vietnam, including an assault on the U.S. embassy in Saigon. The American public was shocked by televised scenes of urban destruction and bloody corpses, of U.S. soldiers destroying Ben Tre village "in order to save it," of marines bogged down in the rubble of the ancient city Hue, and of a 77-day siege of Khe Sanh. Although the NLF suffered heavy losses (which were not well covered by the U.S. press at the time), the unmistakable lesson of Tet was that victory, if feasible at all, was going to be very costly.

The initial public reaction was to fight back. The proportion of Americans describing themselves as "hawks" who wanted to step up the military effort (rather than "doves" who wanted to reduce it) rose from 52 percent in December 1967, to 61 percent in early February 1968. But, then, criticism of the war by politicians, newspaper editorials, television commentators like Walter Cronkite, and others mushroomed. President Johnson—staggered by a surprisingly strong vote for antiwar candidate Eugene McCarthy in the New Hampshire primary—announced that he would limit the bombing of North Vietnam, seek a negotiated settlement, and withdraw as a candidate for reelection. In March 1968, only 41 percent of Americans described themselves as "hawks," a very sharp drop from the 61 percent of early February (see Figure 5.1).

By January 1969, when the new Nixon administration took office, a substantial majority of the public favored monthly reductions in the number of U.S. soldiers in Vietnam: 57 percent approved the idea, and only 28 percent disapproved. In June, Nixon announced the withdrawal of 25,000 troops, followed by announcements of 35,000 more in September, another 50,000 in December, and (in April 1970) 150,000 to come during the following year. Large majorities of the public approved the withdrawals. Most wanted to continue them, even if the South Vietnamese government collapsed. There can be little doubt that public opinion influenced Johnson's and Nixon's deescalation of the war.

This did not mean that a majority of Americans wanted to get out of Vietnam immediately; most disliked the idea of a communist victory. But

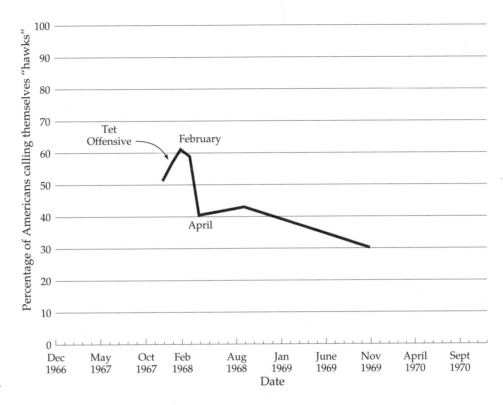

Figure 5.1 The Vietnam War: "Hawks" versus "Doves"

Source: Gallup Surveys.

antiwar marches and demonstrations continued, and, during 1970 and 1971, many people wanted a faster pace of withdrawal. Gradually, U.S. troops came out; in January 1973, after the intensive Christmas bombing of North Vietnam, a peace agreement was finally signed. Two years later, the North Vietnamese army took control of Saigon and unified Vietnam.

The Vietnam story illustrates several important points about public opinion: how government officials can sometimes lead or manipulate opinion (as with the fabricated Gulf of Tonkin incident), especially when it concerns obscure matters in faraway lands; how events and circumstances, as well as reports in the mass media, affect opinion; and how public opinion, even on foreign policy matters, can have a strong impact on policymaking. In this chapter, we will explore the nature, sources, and effects of public opinion, and its relation to ideas about democracy.

Governmental

Political

Structural

DEMOCRATIC THEORY AND PUBLIC OPINION

Public opinion can be defined as the *political attitudes and beliefs expressed by ordinary citizens.* If democracy is, as Abraham Lincoln put it, "government of the people, by the people, and for the people," then clearly public opinion—especially the collective policy preferences of ordinary citizens—plays a crucial part in democratic government. In a perfect democracy, based on popular sovereignty and majority rule, the government would do exactly what its citizens wanted.

One important test of how well democracy is working, then, is how closely government policy corresponds to the expressed wishes of its citizens. To what extent does the government respond to public opinion, as opposed, say, to the wants of organized interest groups? This is a key factor in judging how well democracy works in the United States and how various political institutions and processes contribute to or detract from democracy.

Curiously, though, many leading thinkers, including some who say that they believe in democracy, have expressed grave doubts about the wisdom of the public—doubts about the quality and stability of public opinion, and even about whether it exists. James Madison, Alexander Hamilton, and other Founders of our national government worried about "passions" of the public and "fluctuations," "violent movements," or "temporary errors and delusions" of opinion. They designed the Constitution specifically to put checks on the public through such devices as an appointed judiciary and only *indirect* election of senators and the president.[4]

The French observer, Alexis de Tocqueville, expressed concern about dangers of the "tyranny of the majority." Walter Lippmann, an early student of public opinion, declared that most people do not know what goes on in the world; they have only "stereotypes" or "pictures in their heads." Lippman approvingly quoted Sir Robert Peel's reference to "that great compound of folly, weakness, prejudice, wrong feeling, right feeling, obstinacy and newspaper paragraphs which is called public opinion."[5]

Modern survey researchers have not been much kinder. The first voting studies, carried out during the 1940s and 1950s, turned up what was considered appalling evidence of public ignorance, lack of interest in politics, and reliance on group or party loyalties rather than judgments about the issues of the day. Repeated surveys of the same people found that their responses seemed to change randomly from one interview to another. Philip Converse, a leading student of political behavior, coined the term "nonattitudes": on many issues of public policy, many or most Americans seemed to have no real views at all but simply offered "doorstep opinions" to satisfy interviewers.[6]

What should we make of this? If ordinary citizens are poorly informed and capricious in their views or if they have no real opinions at all, it hardly seems desirable, or even possible, that public opinion could determine what governments do. Both the feasibility and the attractiveness of democracy seem to be thrown into doubt. When we examine just what sorts of opinions ordinary Americans have, however, and how those opinions are formed and changed, we will see that these fears and indictments of public opinion are very much exaggerated.

WHAT PEOPLE KNOW ABOUT POLITICS

Years ago, those who wanted to find out anything about public opinion had to guess, using such clues as what their own friends and neighbors thought, or what newspaper editorials and "letters to the editor" said, or what sorts of speeches won cheers at political rallies. But those methods were defective, because newspaper editors, letter writers, personal acquaintances, and rally audiences are not necessarily representative of the whole public. Different sorts of people in different parts of the country may think quite differently. It was easy to be wrong in guessing what the average American thought.

Now all that has changed because of an ingenious invention. An opinion poll or **survey**, based on personal (or, increasingly, telephone) interviews with a rather small number of randomly chosen Americans—usually about 1,000 or 1,500 of them—can reveal with remarkable accuracy what all 260,000,000 or so of us are doing and thinking. The secret of success is to make sure that the **sample** of people interviewed is representative of the whole population—that the proportions of people in the sample who are young, old, female, college educated, black, rural, Catholic, southerners, westerners, and so forth, are all about the same as the proportions in the U.S. population as a whole. This representativeness is achieved best when the sample being interviewed is chosen *randomly* (by chance) from the population, with each individual having an equal chance of being chosen. Statisticians can then use probability theory to tell us how close the survey's results are likely to be to what the whole population would say if given the same survey. Most surveys try for a 95 percent chance of being accurate within 3 or 4 percentage points.[7] (See the accompanying "Resource Feature" box about the development of polls.)

The many hundreds of polls and surveys of the last five or six decades have provided a great deal of information about public opinion. One thing they have shown is that the early surveys were right: most ordinary Americans do *not* know or care a lot about politics.

Nearly everyone knows some basic facts, such as the name of the capital of the United States and the length of the president's term of office. But only about two-thirds of adults know which party has the most members in the House of Representatives. Only about one-half know that there are two U.S. senators from their state, and fewer can name their congressperson. (In the 1980s, 62 percent gave the wrong name for their congressperson or said they did not know.[8]) And only about 30 percent know that the term of a U.S. House member is two years.[9]

People have particular trouble with technical terms, abbreviations, and geography. In the 1960s, only 38 percent knew that Russia was not a member of NATO (the North Atlantic Treaty Organization) an alliance directed against the Soviet Union. In the 1970s, only 23 percent knew that the United States and the Soviet Union were the nations involved in the important "SALT" (Strategic Arms Limitation Talks). Many are fuzzy about where such places as Nicaragua, Iran, and Lithuania are, and who is running things there.

The things that most Americans don't know may not be so vital however. If citizens are aware that there is a military alliance of Western countries, for example, or that arms control talks have gone on between the United States and the Soviet Union, is it crucial that they recognize the acronyms "NATO" or "SALT"? How important is it for people to know that the term of office for U.S. House of Representatives members is two years, so long as they are aware of the opportunity to vote each time it comes along? Perhaps most people know as much as they need to know in order to be good citizens.

In any case, the lack of knowledge does not just represent stupidity or laziness. There are good reasons for it. Most people are busy with their jobs and families. They don't have much time or energy left for politics. Unless following politics happens to give them pleasure, there is little reason for them to invest much effort in it. "Rational choice" scholars remind us that a single citizen has only a miniscule chance of determining the outcome of an election in which thou-

RESOURCE FEATURE

The Development of Polls

Modern methods of polling first won prominence in 1936, when George Gallup, Elmo Roper, and Archibald Crossley used sophisticated sampling and interviewing techniques to ask Americans how they were going to vote in the 1936 presidential election. For many previous elections, the *Literary Digest*, a weekly magazine, had conducted national "straw votes" by sending ballots to people listed in telephone and car ownership directories. Those lists were quite unrepresentative of the population in the 1930s, because many people did not own telephones or cars; many lower-income citizens were left out of the straw vote. In previous elections, the *Literary Digest* had been lucky, because low-income people had voted about the same as everyone else, so the straw poll came out about right. In 1936, however, poor people voted overwhelmingly for President Franklin D. Roosevelt and his New Deal, while wealthier people tended to vote against them. The *Literary Digest* predicted that the Republican challenger, Alf Landon, would defeat Roosevelt. But Gallup, Roper, and Crossley, with their more representative samples, all predicted victory for Roosevelt. When Roosevelt won by a landslide, scientific polling methods became the standard and straw votes fell out of favor.

Pollsters have not entirely escaped trouble since then. In 1948, early polls showed Republican Thomas E. Dewey so far ahead of President Harry Truman that nearly everyone became certain of a Dewey victory; several newspapers even printed early editions declaring Dewey elected. But the polling had stopped too soon and missed a last-minute Truman surge; Truman won by a narrow margin. Since then, polls generally have kept asking questions right up to election day and have warned that results hold only for the time of a poll, not necessarily for the

The polls stopped asking questions too early in the 1948 election campaign and missed the last-minute surge by which President Harry Truman defeated his Republican challenger, Thomas Dewey. Here Truman makes fun of the *Chicago Tribune*.

future. Even so, in the 1980 election, the pollsters failed to predict correctly that "undecided" voters would tilt heavily toward challenger Ronald Reagan; most polls showed him neck and neck with Jimmy Carter, even though Reagan proceeded to trounce Carter, with 51 percent of the national vote to 41 percent for Carter, and with 489 electoral votes to Carter's 49.

Polls generally carry a warning about the margin of error in their results. Because of the nature of sampling, even highly rigorous surveys, such as the National Election Studies at the University of Michigan, can be off by several percentage points. Furthermore, the exact wording of poll questions makes a big difference and has to be watched carefully. Still, in recent decades, their record of accuracy has been quite impressive. Gallup's election predictions have averaged only 1.4 percentage points off the actual results, for example. Polls and surveys are also usually quite accurate in telling what policies Americans prefer and what values they hold.

sands or millions vote; from a purely selfish point of view, it is not worth a lot of trouble to decide how to vote. The real surprise may be that people know as much as they do.

We do not mean to minimize the consequences of the public's lack of certain kinds of knowledge. It has some extremely important implications. As we will see in Chapter 7, for example, "low-visibility" politics, outside the public's awareness, sometimes produces policies contrary to what an informed public would want. Nor do we mean to encourage complacency, fatalism, or public ignorance; efforts to alert and to educate the public, and to arouse people to be good citizens, can be very valuable. But low levels of information are a reality that must be taken into account. It is unrealistic to expect that the public possesses detailed knowledge about a wide range of political matters.

By the same token, we should not expect the average American to have an elaborately worked out **ideology**, or system of interlocking attitudes and beliefs. You yourself may be a consistent liberal or conservative (or populist, socialist, libertarian, or something else), with many opinions that hang together in a coherent structure. But surveys show that most people's attitudes are only loosely connected to each other. Most people have opinions that vary from one issue to another—some conservative and some liberal. In-depth interviews indicate that these are often linked by underlying themes and values, but not in the neat ways that the leading ideologies would dictate.[10]

For the same reasons, we should not be surprised that people's expressed opinions on issues tend to be unstable. Many Americans give different answers when a survey question is repeated four years or two years or even a few weeks after their first response. Scholars have disagreed about what these unstable responses mean. (Do people have no definite opinions, or do the survey interviews simply fail to measure them?[11]) But, very likely, people's uncertainty and lack of information plays a part.

None of this, however, means that public opinion, as a whole, is unreal or unstable or irrelevant. The collective whole is greater than its individual parts.

An interviewer for an NBC "exit poll" at work near Raleigh, North Carolina.

Even if there is some randomness in individuals' expressions of political opinions (i.e., even if individuals tend to think one thing but sometimes say something else because of what comes to mind or what they have recently heard), for example, the responses of thousands or millions of people tend to average out the randomness and reveal a very stable *collective* public opinion. Americans' collective policy preferences are actually very stable over time; that is, the percentage of Americans that favors a particular policy usually stays about the same, unless circumstances change in important ways. Year after year, for instance, very high and steady majorities of the public have said that they want to spend more on education and on protecting the environment. Other examples of opinion stability will be mentioned later in this chapter.

Moreover, even if most people have only a limited set of basic values and form many of their opinions by deferring to those they trust (party leaders, television commentators, or the like) rather than by compiling their own mass of information, the resulting public opinion need not be ignorant or unwise, because trusted leaders may themselves take account of the best available information. Some recent research has indicated that Americans' collective policy preferences react rather sensibly to events, changing circumstances, and new information, so that we can speak of a "rational public."[12]

Not all scholars are convinced that public opinion acts rationally, but the evidence is clear, at least, that the American public as a whole has real opinions, not just "nonattitudes," and that the Founders' fears of capriciousness and fluctuations in public opinion are no longer justified, if they ever were.

POLITICAL ATTITUDES

Basic Values and Beliefs

More fundamental than opinions about specific policies are Americans' basic beliefs and values. Often there is a high degree of *consensus* (agreement) about such matters. This is especially true of certain values involving freedom, democracy, capitalism, and equal opportunity.

FREEDOM   Scholars have written that "(n)o value in the American ethos is more revered than freedom. The rights of individuals to speak, write, assemble and worship freely, to engage in occupations and pastimes of their own choosing, and to be secure from arbitrary restraints on their conduct are central to the nation's democratic tradition."[13]

A number of surveys over the years have documented this enthusiasm for liberty, at least in the abstract. Eighty-nine percent of Americans, for example, agreed that they believed in "free speech for all no matter what their views might be." Large majorities have said that freedom to worship as one pleases "applies to all religious groups, regardless of how extreme their beliefs are."[14]

This high regard for liberty in the abstract often falls apart, however, when it comes to specific cases of extreme or threatening minorities. Many people, especially in the 1950s, have opposed allowing Communists or Nazis—or even Socialists or atheists—to hold meetings, to teach school, or to have their books in public libraries.[15] Large majorities have favored the saying of prayers in the public schools, even though the Supreme Court long ago ruled that that would violate the Constitution. And most Americans favor censoring obscene books. (See Figure

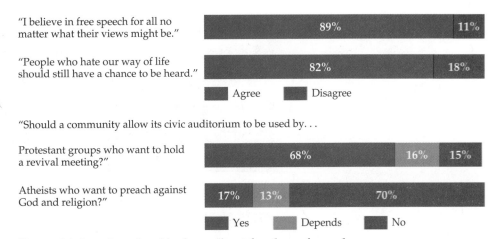

Figure 5.2 Americans' ambivalence about freedom of speech

Source: Herbert McClosky and John Zaller, The American Ethos: Public Attitudes Toward Capitalism and Democracy *(Cambridge, MA: Harvard University Press, 1984), pp. 25, 37.*

5.2: the majority supports free expression but opposes letting atheists speak in a civic auditorium.) Thus, many Americans are willing to sacrifice certain people's liberty for the sake of morality and order, though they do not want government interfering with their own speech or beliefs.

ECONOMIC LIBERTY   The public is generally enthusiastic about *economic* liberty. Private ownership of property, for example, is strongly supported: 84 percent have said that it is "necessary for economic progress," and 87 percent have said that it is "as important to a good society as freedom." There is overwhelming rejection of communism or socialism. Americans so obviously believe in freedom to choose their jobs, to spend their money as they wish, and to own whatever they can afford to buy, that surveys do not even bother to ask about it.

CAPITALISM   The word *capitalism* is not particularly popular in the United States, but the substance of it—free markets and private ownership of the means of production—has strong support. Surveys have found that large majorities agree that "the free enterprise system (is) necessary for free government" (80 percent) and that, on the whole, our economic system is "just and wise" (77 percent). Most say that the private enterprise system is "generally a fair and efficient system," that it "gives everyone a fair chance," and that freedom depends upon it. Most Americans say that they believe in the idea of working hard. They think it is fair to tie economic rewards to work and that it is necessary to do so in order to get people to work.[16]

EQUALITY   Americans favor equality of opportunity, but they are not much interested in equality of result. There is not much public support for substantial redistribution of wealth or income, especially as compared with the attitudes of citizens in other advanced industrial countries. In one survey, only 13 percent of Americans said that reducing income inequality was an "essential" government responsibility, compared to 25 percent of Britons and 29 percent of West Germans.

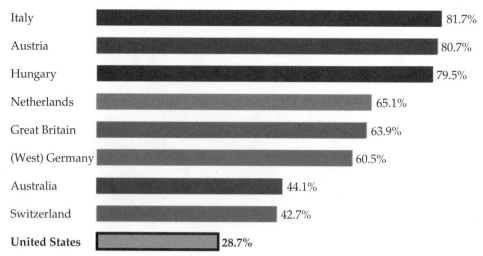

Figure 5.3 Support in various countries for reducing income inequality

Source: Data from Inter-university Consortium for Political and Social Research, 1987.

Only 34 percent of Americans, compared to 55 percent of Britons and 60 percent of West Germans, said the same about guaranteeing jobs.[17] (For related data see Figure 5.3.) Most Americans tend to think that people generally should be left to get ahead on their own, so long as they have a fair start.

This does not mean that people want unrestrained private enterprise, however. For one thing, there is overwhelming sentiment in favor of **equality of opportunity**. Most Americans think that everyone should have an equal chance to do well and that government should help make sure that they can. In one survey, *98 percent* agreed that "(e)veryone in America should have equal opportunities to get ahead," and 98 percent also agreed that "(c)hildren should have equal education opportunities." Moreover, most Americans believe in some sort of **safety net** for those who fall behind in the competitive race and cannot help themselves. For decades, most Americans have favored a whole series of government social welfare programs, such as aid with education, medical care, and jobs, that depart from a pure free enterprise system. "Big business" is unpopular, too. Most of the public favors various kinds of government regulation of business, in the public interest, especially for protection of the environment.

The ideas of equal opportunity, regulation, and safety nets can come into conflict with the ideas of economic liberty and capitalism. How, for example, can the poor be helped without taxing people with higher incomes, and thereby perhaps limiting *their* liberty? How can the children of the poor get opportunities that are equal to those for children of the rich, without redistributing income or restricting the freedom of the rich to spend money on their children? On the other hand, how free can people be if they are desperately poor?

Some Americans (those who call themselves **conservatives**) tend to put more emphasis on economic liberty and freedom from government interference. Others (known as **liberals**) stress equality of opportunity and the need for government regulation and safety nets. This is one of the main sources of political disagreement in America; it makes up a big part of the difference between the ideologies of liberalism and conservatism.

Most Americans revere the flag and oppose the liberty of others to burn it, as these Minnesota anarchists did in a Washington, D.C., demonstration.

Confusingly, however, the terms "liberalism" and "conservatism" are also used to refer to positions on such social issues as abortion, pornography, crime, and political dissent. Those who favor free choices are often said to be liberals, while those preferring government enforcement of order and traditional values are called conservatives. And, on foreign policy issues, "hawks" favoring use of U.S. military force abroad are sometimes called conservatives and "doves" are sometimes called liberals. Opinions on these various matters do not necessarily have much to do with each other. Many people are liberal in some ways but conservative in others. Moreover, the definitions of *liberal* and *conservative* seem to vary at different moments in American history.

DEMOCRACY The American public strongly believes in democracy—popular sovereignty, political equality, majority rule, and political liberty. According to one survey in the 1950s, 95 percent agreed that "(e)very citizen should have an equal chance to influence government policy."[18] Overwhelming majorities of Americans say that public officials should be chosen by majority vote (95 percent), that everyone is entitled to the same legal rights and protections no matter what their political beliefs are (93 percent), and that people in the minority should be free to try to win majority support for their opinions (89 percent).[19]

Support for majority rule and popular control of government is rock solid, as is evident in the strong public opposition to any arrangements that are thought to dilute democracy, even the electoral college (which can elect presidents with only a minority of the nationwide vote), or proposals for longer presidential terms (which would tend to insulate presidents from control by the voters). In 1980, for example, 67 percent approved of getting rid of the electoral college, and, in 1986, 70 percent opposed a six-year presidential term.[20]

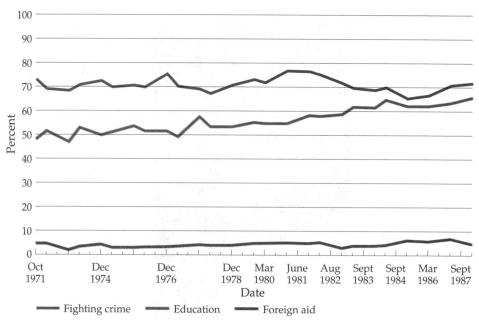

Figure 5.4 Public support for spending more on various programs

Source: Data from Roper and NORC surveys.

Policy Preferences

We can learn a lot about Americans' policy preferences from graphs that show what percentages of the public have favored various government policies at different times. Besides showing what sorts of policies have been popular or unpopular, these graphs indicate how *stable* collective public opinion generally is and how sharply the public distinguishes among different policies.

Figure 5.4, for example, shows that large and rather stable majorities of Americans (60 percent or 70 percent in recent years) have thought that we are spending "too little," rather than too much or about the right amount, on fighting crime and on education. These are very popular programs. The public has given similarly high and stable support to Social Security, environmental programs, and government help with medical expenses. This was true even while the Reagan administration was cutting such programs. Most Americans want more of them, not less.

By contrast, very few people—only about 5 percent—have thought too little was being spent on foreign aid; many more think "too much" is being spent. Foreign aid, except for disaster relief, is generally unpopular. Large majorities oppose military aid or arms sales abroad. The space program wins only a little more support. Defense spending has had public approval during wars and crises, but in recent years—especially after the end of the Cold War—many more people have wanted to cut than to increase military spending. Most Americans would prefer to shift financial resources from the military to domestic problems.

Similarly, Figure 5.5 shows how the public has distinguished clearly among different circumstances when deciding whether or not it approves of allowing

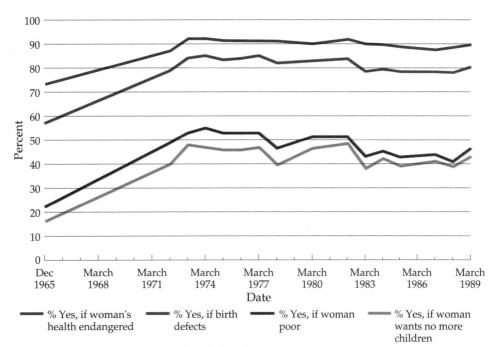

Figure 5.5 Public approval for legal abortion

Source: Data from NORC surveys.

legal abortions. During most of the 1980s and into the 1990s, about 90 percent of Americans approved of abortion if a woman's health were endangered. About 80 percent would permit abortion in cases of serious birth defects. But only about 50 percent or less approved of abortion if a woman were poor or simply wanted no more children.

This same graph indicates how approval of abortion under each of the different circumstances rose markedly between 1965 and the early 1970s. Since no surveys were conducted for several years in between, we cannot tell exactly when public opinion changed or how smoothly it did so, but nearly all of the change occurred *before* the Supreme Court's *Roe v. Wade* decision in January 1973, declaring that the Constitution protects a woman's right to have an abortion. Changing public attitudes may have affected the Court's decision; they did not result from it.

Other surveys have revealed very strong liberalizing trends, over many years, concerning civil rights and civil liberties. Beginning in the 1940s or 1950s, and continuing through the 1980s and 1990s, more and more Americans have favored having black and white children go to the same schools; integrating work, housing, public accommodations; and letting various dissenting groups (Communists, Socialists, atheists, and others) teach school, speak in public, and have their books in libraries. These trends are discussed further in Chapter 19, ''Rights and Liberties.''

In the realm of foreign policy, public opinion sometimes changes suddenly, as we saw in the case of ''hawks'' and ''doves'' after the Tet offensive during the

Vietnam War. Major international events make a difference. But often foreign policy opinions, too, are quite stable. Since World War II, for example, two-thirds or more of those giving an opinion have generally said that the United States should take an "active part" in world affairs. The exact percentage favoring an active role has varied somewhat, rising to a peak of about 83 percent in 1965, near the onset of the Vietnam War, dropping to about 62 percent after the failure of that war, and recovering a bit in later years. But it has remained consistently high, not fluctuating much with alleged public "moods."[21] As we have seen, however, general support for internationalism does not imply support for foreign aid, and the public has been wary about the use of troops abroad.

An interesting historical example of opinion change involves the public's attitudes about whether or not Communist China should be admitted to the United Nations. In the early 1950s, when U.S. and Chinese troops had been shooting at each other in Korea, very large majorities of Americans (80 or 90 percent) opposed admission. Gradually, over a 20-year period, that opposition decreased. By the time President Nixon was opening friendly relations with China (a decision that may have been influenced by this liberalizing public opinion), a majority of Americans actually favored admission of China to the UN—and China was, in fact, admitted.

Party Loyalties

Besides holding the basic values and the specific policy preferences we have discussed, most Americans also feel loyalty to a political party. When survey researchers ask people whether, generally speaking, they consider themselves Republicans, Democrats, independents, or what, most Americans pick one of the two major parties. Even if they start out saying "independent," usually they admit that they "lean" toward one party or another. That sense of belonging to a party is called **party identification**.

Most people begin to identify with a party when they are rather young (usually adopting the same party as their parents), and most tend to stick with it through the rest of their lives. They use the party label to help organize their thinking about politics: to guide them in voting, in judging new policy proposals, and so on. People who consider themselves Democrats are much more likely than Republicans to vote for Democratic candidates and to approve of Democratic presidents; they tend to belong to different social and economic groups; and they are somewhat more likely to favor policies associated with the Democratic party.

Since the highly popular New Deal of the 1930s, more Americans have identified themselves as Democrats than as Republicans. The Democrats have been the majority party. But the big Democratic advantage of the 1950s and 1960s declined substantially, beginning in the 1970s, until the parties were almost even. In the fall of 1964, at a Democratic party peak, 52 percent of those surveyed said that they considered themselves Democrats, and only 25 percent said that they considered themselves Republicans, but in 1984 the figure was just 37 percent Democrats and 27 percent Republicans. After that the Democrats recovered a bit. You can see these trends in Figure 5.6, which omits independents. The party balance has important effects on who rules in Washington, D.C., and especially on which party controls Congress, though there have been several Republican presidents, even while more Americans considered themselves Democrats.

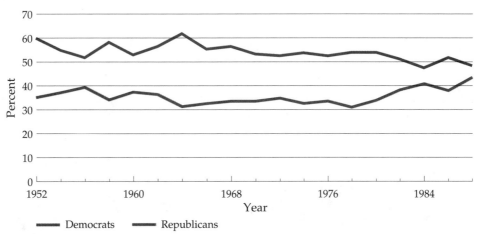

Figure 5.6 Trends in party identification

Source: Data from National Election studies, University of Michigan, gathered in the autumn of election years.

PARTY DECLINE   There also has been a decline in the proportion of people who identify with either one of the two parties, and a rise in the number of independents, from about 23 percent to about 35 percent of the population. While the reasons for this decline are not completely clear, they seem to have to do with the disappointments of the Vietnam War, urban unrest, Watergate, and the economic hard times of the 1970s, plus a growing sense that differences between the parties are no longer as clear or as important.[22] We will discuss this further in Chapter 8, "Political Parties."

Evaluations of Government's Performance

Another important aspect of public opinion involves citizens' judgments of how the government is doing. In particular, pollsters regularly ask people whether they approve or disapprove of "President _____'s handling of his job." The percentage of people who say that they approve—the president's "approval rating"—is taken as a crucial indicator of *presidential popularity*. Trends in presidential popularity are often displayed in a sort of rising and falling "fever chart"; they tend to fluctuate more than party loyalties or policy preferences.

George Bush for instance, maintained a fairly steady, high popularity rating of around 65 percent during his first two years in office; then the Persian Gulf War boosted it to a record 89 percent in March 1991, after which it steadily declined rather sharply in response to economic recession, falling below 40 percent in April 1992.

We will see in Chapter 12, "The Presidency" that a president's popularity has very important consequences. It is a good predictor of whether or not he will win reelection and whether his party will win or lose congressional seats. It affects how much influence he has in Congress and how effectively he can persuade the public to agree with his policy stands. A president who is very popular with the public can be a political powerhouse; an unpopular president is in serious trouble.

President George Bush and General Norman Schwartzkopf exult at a
victory parade after the war with Iraq. The war gave a strong boost to
Bush's popularity. Soon, however, Bush's popularity fell steeply, as
people turned their attention to the U. S. economy, which had become
mired in recession.

The public's evaluations of presidents' handling of their jobs depend on how
well things are actually going. The state of the economy is especially important:
when the country is prosperous, the president tends to be popular; when there is
high inflation or unemployment, the president's popularity falls. International
crises can lead the public to "rally 'round the flag" and to support the president
(providing that leaders of both parties are doing so), but that only lasts a little
while, unless the crisis works out well. If bad news keeps coming, people begin
to disapprove of the president's performance.[23] The American public's general
confidence or trust in government institutions also tends to react according to how
particular institutions, or the government generally, are performing. During the
Watergate scandal in 1974, for example, fully 42 percent of the public said that
they had "hardly any confidence at all" in the people running the executive
branch, up from just 18 percent the year before. But confidence in the Supreme
Court, which ordered President Nixon to turn over his incriminating tapes, rose.[24]

Similarly, citizens' sense of **political efficacy**—their feelings about whether
government pays any attention to ordinary people, whether voting does any good,
and so forth—has varied somewhat, depending on how things are going. The
proportion of Americans who felt highly "efficacious" (i.e., able to influence the
political system) fell during the troubled 1970s but rose again during the more
prosperous and successful 1980s, only to drop in the early 1990s.

It is widely believed that high feelings of confidence and efficacy are essential
to satisfactory government. If most people feel disillusioned or impotent, democracy can hardly be said to be working well. On the other hand, it would be no
improvement for people to live in a dream world of trust when their government
was doing badly.

SOURCES OF POLITICAL BELIEFS

Where do all of these political attitudes and opinions come from? Political learning, sometimes called **political socialization**, begins when people are very young.
Their families and schools play key parts as agents of socialization. However,

people continue to form and to change their political attitudes and beliefs throughout their lives, as they are exposed to new experiences and political events.

Family

Most children get their first ideas about politics from their parents and siblings.
Very early, perhaps by the age of 5 or 6, they learn that they are Americans, living
in a great country that is "free." They begin to hear about the existence of a
government headed by a distant but powerful president, who is often seen as
paternal and benevolent.

Before long, by about the second or third grade, children begin to learn that
"we" (our family) are Republicans or Democrats, just as "we" are Baptists or Jews
or Catholics. At first, this idea doesn't have much content; there are simply two
parties, like two sports teams, and we root for ours against the opposition. But
gradually children learn that the parties stand for somewhat different things.
"We" believe that government should do some things and not do others.

Most children—though certainly not all—adopt their parents' party identification and keep it the rest of their life. One leading study, based on interviews
with high school students and their parents, found that 59 percent of the young
people identified with the same party as their parents.[25]

It was once thought that this represented a blind "habit"—that people mind-
lessly carried on their parents' party tradition, even if it made no sense in their
own lives. But there is reason to believe that people inherit more than a party
label from their parents; it goes along with ethnicity, religion, and a set of values,
beliefs, and practices that form part of a person's identity. Moreover, people's life
circumstances—their levels of education, types of occupation, places of residence,
and so on—often resemble those of their parents, so that a party affiliation that
makes sense for the parents may make sense for them, too. Finally, it has become
clear that when peoples' circumstances change, they *do* often change party loyalty;
it is not a rigid habit.

Young children learn which party "we" favor from parents and friends.

Drawing by Lorenz; The New Yorker Magazine, Inc.

"My grandson, needless to say. is also pro-Reagan."

Schools encourage patriotism.

Schools

When children go to school, they are exposed both to classroom teaching and to interaction with other students. In class they salute the American flag and talk about "liberty and justice for all." The president and the U.S. government become more familiar. The idea of democracy gets introduced, often through voting for class officers and (in election years) straw votes for presidential candidates. Ideas of order and authority are conveyed by the system of classroom discipline.

From their peers, students learn a bit more about "us" and "them"— Republicans and Democrats. By going home and asking their parents why their friends belong to a different party, they stimulate political discussion and learn more about what the parties stand for. A few policy issues come up: environmental concerns, for example, fit well with young children's interest in plants and animals, and are often emphasized in class and on the playground.

In later grades and in high school, the political lessons become more explicit. Social studies, history, and civics classes deal with the structure of the U.S. government, often explicitly arguing the virtues of liberty, democracy, and equal opportunity. Slightly different lessons are taught in different communities: middle- and upper-middle-class children, for example, may get more encouragement than working-class children to get out and make the system work for them. Compared with white children, black children are less likely to say that the government is "very helpful," but black high school students seem to respond more to civics instruction.[26] All are taught the duty to vote. A few get involved in protests and demonstrations.

Of course, political learning does not stop in high school; college and experiences throughout life make a difference, too. But, by the time they reach their twenties, most Americans have a reasonably well-formed set of basic values, a sense of belonging to a political party, some policy preferences, and some evaluations of government performance. In 1991, for example, fully 88 percent of college freshmen surveyed said that the government was not doing enough to control pollution.[27]

Students at the
City University of
New York protest
budget cuts.

Workplace and Home

When young adults go to work for the first time, economic realities suddenly become more pressing; government policies about taxes, unemployment insurance, and pensions begin to have a personal impact. Some people adjust their party loyalties, even their world views and ideologies. Liberal idealists may begin to worry more about economic efficiency, keeping taxes low, and "meeting a payroll." Conservative enthusiasts of free enterprise, finding themselves at the mercy of market forces, may begin to hanker for some government protection. Working-class and poor people generally develop more sympathy for the underdog than do those who are making a lot of money. The unemployed become less enthusiastic about the American dream.[28]

There are also indications that the organization of the work place makes a difference. Assembly line workers, used to taking orders, tend not to participate actively in politics unless a strong labor union mobilizes them—as fewer and fewer do. Workers in cooperatively owned and operated businesses, like the plywood plants of the Northwest, tend to participate more and to undertake collective action.[29] Small businesspeople, on their own against a sometimes hostile world, learn to push government to get what they want. Corporate executives take for granted that politicians will pay attention when they call.

As people establish homes and families, they begin to worry about property taxes, schools for their children, protection against crime, and efficient garbage collection. They tend to get more involved in politics.

Political Events

What happens in the political world often changes people's attitudes and beliefs. This is especially true for the young, who tend to solidify their policy preferences and party loyalties in response to the historical moment at which they come of age. But it is true of adults, too. People change their evaluations of presidents quickly when surprisingly good or bad things happen. They also adjust their policy preferences to new circumstances, as in the case of Vietnam, the admission of China to the UN, and other issues that we have mentioned. Party loyalties, once thought to be virtually immune to change, now are known to adjust to the parties' performances in war and peace and to their management of the economy.[30]

Of course, political events do not always speak for themselves; often they become known to the public only through the mass media, which may bring particular biases or points of view to bear. As we will discuss further in Chapter 6, "The Mass Media," the mass media report experts', commentators', and political leaders' interpretations of what is going on, with significant effects on public opinion. Public debate and discussion, even by protestors and holders of minority views, can play a critical part in helping the public to change its opinions; hence the importance of protecting rights of free speech, the subject of the feature "Struggle for Democracy."

Economic and Social Structure

The various agents of socialization or sources of political learning affect different people in different ways. They lead to some group differences, which we describe later. But, more important, millions of Americans tend to learn many of the *same* ideas and attitudes, based on a common history and shared experiences, and based on particular characteristics of the American economy, American culture, and American society. These characteristics, which we have referred to as *structural*, have profound effects on American public opinion and make it different from public opinion in other countries.

Americans' deep commitment to democracy, for example, undoubtedly stems from 200 years of a generally successful experience with democratic institutions. It has been supported by social conditions that help make democracy work—economic affluence (for most people) and high levels of education.

Similarly, the public's enthusiasm for political and economic liberty, and the people's embrace of private property and a free enterprise system, have a lot to do with the existence of a capitalist economy in the United States and with its success at producing abundant goods. The particular vision of equal opportunity found in the United States, too, has roots in American history, particularly the successful absorption of diverse immigrant groups—largely through their own efforts and struggles.

The economic and social structures that have shaped Americans' basic values of democracy, liberty, equality, and the like, have also affected many of our policy preferences, such as the reluctance to have government interfere with the economy and (at the same time) the desire for social welfare policies to soften the impact of the market. Similarly, the shape of the international system—the U.S. position as a superpower, or the friendly or unfriendly acts of other nations—affects what kinds of foreign policy the public favors.

Structural changes bring about changes in policy preferences. International economic competition in the 1970s, for example, and the hard economic times that followed, resulted in less public support for spending on certain domestic programs. Perceptions of a Soviet military buildup during those same years increased the public's desire to spend more on the military, whereas the decline and final collapse of Communist strength in the 1980s and the 1990s led people to favor arms control and cuts in military spending. At the end of 1990, for example, after five years of Gorbachev's conciliatory behavior as leader of the Soviet Union, far more Americans favored U.S.–Soviet trade (19 percent more), exchange of scientists, arms control agreements, and other cooperative measures than had done so in 1982.[31]

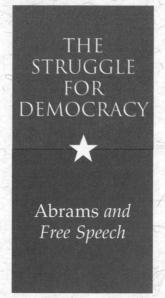

THE STRUGGLE FOR DEMOCRACY

★

Abrams *and* Free Speech

In August 1918, five Russian-born immigrants in New York City printed and distributed 5,000 leaflets that attacked the "hypocrisy" of the "coward" President Wilson for sending U.S. troops to intervene in the Russian Revolution. They denounced capitalism as the "enemy of the workers of the world," asserted that ammunition factories were producing bullets, bayonets, and cannon "to murder not only the Germans, but also your dearest, best, who are in Russia and are fighting for freedom," and called for a general strike.

The five were tried, convicted, and sentenced to 20 years in prison, under the Espionage Act of 1918, for conspiring, while the United States was at war with Germany, to publish "disloyal, scurrilous and abusive language about the form of Government of the United States" and language intended to encourage resistance to the war and curtailment of war production. They appealed their conviction on the grounds that the First Amendment to the Constitution protects freedom of speech and the press. The Supreme Court turned them down.

The five immigrants went to jail, but what is remembered from *Abrams et al. v. United States* is the eloquent defense of free speech in Justice Oliver Wendell Holmes's dissenting opinion, which subsequently has become part of our constitutional tradition. Holmes, while expressing no agreement with the "creed of ignorance and immaturity" in the leaflets, denied that the defendants had actually attacked the U.S. form of government or specifically intended to cripple prosecution of the war. Even if they had, no harm was done; no more than nominal punishment should be inflicted. Holmes declared that "we should be eternally vigilant against attempts to check the expression of opinions that we loathe and believe to be fraught with death, unless they so imminently threaten immediate interference

with the lawful and pressing purposes of the law that an immediate check is required to save the country." Persecution for the expression of ideas, he acknowledged, is tempting. "But when men have realized that time has upset many fighting faiths, they may come to believe that . . . the ultimate good desired is better reached by free trade in ideas—that the best test of truth is the power of the thought to get itself accepted in the competition of the market. . . ."

Our present constitutional protections for free speech, which have advanced a great deal since the time of *Abrams*, are discussed in Chapter 19, "Rights and Liberties."

Source: Abrams et al. v. United States, 250 U.S. 616.

Supreme Court Justice Oliver Wendell Holmes, Jr.

When we think about public opinion as a source of influence on policymaking, then, it is important to remember that public opinion is itself affected by structural factors. This is one of the ways in which the economic and social structure of the United States, and the shape of the international system, affect government policy.

HOW PEOPLE DIFFER

In describing American public opinion as a collective whole, we do not want to ignore important distinctions among different sorts of people in different circumstances. Black people and white people; Catholics, Jews, and Protestants; southerners and northeasterners; poor people and rich people; women and men—all tend to differ in their political attitudes.

Race and Ethnicity

Among the biggest differences are those between white and black Americans. Blacks, who remained loyal to the Republican party (the party of Lincoln) long after the Civil War, became Democrats in large proportions with the New Deal of the 1930s and have remained so ever since.[32] Today, blacks are the most solidly Democratic of any group in the population. During the 1983–1990 period, 67 percent called themselves Democrats and only 6 percent called themselves Republicans.[33]

Black Americans also have tended to be much more liberal than whites on economic issues, especially those involving aid to minorities or help with jobs, housing, medical care, education, and so on, as indicated in Figure 5.7. This reflects blacks' economically disadvantaged position in American society and the still real effects of slavery and discrimination. Overall, in 1988, twice as many blacks located their political views on the "liberal" side of a 7-point scale (48 percent) as on the conservative side (24 percent), whereas whites were about equally split (25 percent liberal, 27 percent conservative).[34] On some social issues, however, blacks tend to be rather conservative, reflecting strong religious values.

Other ethnic groups are not so distinctive in their opinions as blacks. Irish-Americans and people of Italian, Polish, and other Southern or Eastern European ancestry, for example, became strong Democrats as part of the New Deal coalition. But, as they achieved success economically, their economic liberalism faded and their social conservatism prevailed. By the 1980s, these groups were not much different from average Americans.

"The government in Washington should do everything
possible to improve the standard of living of all poor Americans"

| Blacks | Strongly agree: 42.5% |

| Whites | Strongly agree: 16.3% |

Figure 5.7 Attitudes of black and white Americans about government help for the poor

Source: General Social Survey Cumulative data set, 1972–1990.

Hispanics—people of Spanish-speaking background—represent the fastest-growing ethnic group in America, numbering about 21 million, or 8 percent of the population, in 1990. But they really constitute several quite different groups. Cuban Americans, many of whom are refugees from the Castro regime, tend to be conservative Republicans, strongly anti-Communist, and skeptical of government social welfare programs. People of Mexican or Puerto Rican ancestry, on the other hand, are mostly Democrats, quite liberal on economic matters, though rather traditional on social questions, reflecting their predominant Roman Catholicism.

Hispanics are one of the least politically active groups in the United States. Despite efforts by such groups as the Southwest Voter Education Project, the government's Current Population Survey found that only about 29 percent of eligible Hispanics voted in the 1988 presidential election, compared with 59 percent of non-Hispanic whites and 52 percent of blacks.[35] Low incomes, suspicion of the authorities, and lack of facility with the English language discourage participation. The Hispanic community's low participation rate and its internal divisions make it a sleeping giant in American politics, capable of great influence—especially in such key states as Texas, California, and Florida—but not yet making its weight felt fully.

Religion

Ethnic differences are often interwoven with differences in religious faith and values, which have their own special importance. Roman Catholics, who constitute about 27 percent of the U.S. population,[36] were heavily Democratic after the New Deal but now resemble other Americans in their party affiliations. Catholics' economic liberalism has faded somewhat with rises in their incomes, but it remains substantial. Catholics have tended to be especially concerned with family issues and to espouse morality (e.g., antipornography laws) and law and order, though this has been exaggerated. Despite the antiabortion teachings of the Catholic church, for example, Catholic citizens support birth control and the right to have abortions in about the same proportions as do other Americans.

American Jews (only about 2 percent of the U.S. population) began to join the Democratic party in the 1920s and did so overwhelmingly in the 1930s, in response to Franklin D. Roosevelt's New Deal social policies and his foreign policy

First communion at a Catholic church in Tarzana, California. Catholics tend to be economically liberal and socially conservative.

of resisting Hitler. Most Jews have stayed with the party; next to blacks, they remain the most Democratic group in the United States—50 percent Democrat and only 18 percent Republican in 1988.[37]

Jews are exceptionally liberal on such social issues as civil liberties and abortion. They also tend to be staunch supporters of civil rights, despite tensions with blacks over such matters as Jewish shopkeepers in black ghettoes, U.S. policy toward Israel and the Palestinians, and anti-Semitic remarks by some black leaders. Rising incomes have somewhat undercut Jews' economic liberalism, but they remain substantially more supportive of social welfare policies than other groups.

The 4 million or so members of the Church of Jesus Christ of Latter Day Saints, or Mormons,[38] are distinguished by being the most staunchly conservative and most solidly Republican of any major religious denomination. A 1989–1990 survey found that Mormons were 51 percent Republican and only 22 percent Democrat, whereas Presbyterians were 44 percent Republican (28 percent Democrat), Episcopalians 41 percent Republican, and Lutherans more evenly divided: 37 percent Republican, 26 percent Democrat.[39]

The large Protestant majority of Americans, of course, does not differ much from the U.S. average in most respects. But Protestants come in many varieties, from the relatively high-income (socially liberal, economically conservative) Episcopalians and Presbyterians to the generally liberal Universalist-Unitarians and middle-class northern Baptists, to the lower-income and quite conservative (though often Democratic) Southern Baptists and evangelicals of various denominations.

In the early 1980s, evangelical Christians played an important part in the "new right" segment of Ronald Reagan's conservative coalition, pushing hard for their positions against abortion, against pornography, for law and order, and for their version of family values. Many were disappointed by their failure to achieve their goals, some of which were not widely supported by the population as a whole. They became less active politically in the early 1990s, though they remain a potentially significant force.

Region

It is still true that "the South is different." True, regional differences have been reduced due to years of migration by southern blacks to northern cities, the movement of industrial plants and northern whites to the Sun Belt, and economic growth catching up with that of the North. But the large black population and the primarily agricultural economy of the South have put their stamp on southern politics to the present day.

Even now, white southerners tend to be somewhat less enthusiastic about civil rights than northerners; only people from the Mountain West are nearly as conservative on racial issues.[40] Southerners also tend to be conservative on social issues, such as school prayer, crime, women's rights, and abortion, and supportive of military spending and a strong foreign policy (though fairly liberal on economic issues, such as job guarantees and health insurance). These distinctive policy preferences gradually have undercut southern whites' traditionally strong identification with the Democratic party, especially since the 1960s and 1970s, when the national Democrats became identified with liberal social policies and antiwar foreign policy. Figure 5.8 shows differences in party loyalties among regional and other social groups.

The skyline of New York City, where political attitudes on such issues as the environment differ from those of people living in the Sawtooth Mountains in Stanley, Idaho.

Northeasterners tend to be the most different from southerners, with midwesterners, appropriately, in the middle. Pacific Coast residents resemble northeasterners in many respects, but people from the mountain states tend to be quite conservative; between the 1950s and the 1980s, they moved strongly against job guarantees and health insurance, for example.[41] The mountain states' traditions of game hunting in wide-open spaces have led them, like southerners, to cherish

Figure 5.8 Party loyalties among different social groups

Source: Cumulative data from General Social Surveys, 1983–1990.

	Democrats	Independents	Republicans
Whites	33.9%	33.2%	31.7%
Blacks	67.0%	26.1%	5.9
Rich	28.8%	30.0%	40.8%
Middle income	38.0%	31.4%	29.6%
Poor	45.2%	31.8%	22.2%
Grade school education	48.2%	31.3%	19.6%
High school	37.3%	33.1%	28.4%
College	31.6%	32.0%	35.0%
Under 30 years old	30.2%	39.4%	29.4%
Over 30	41.5%	30.3%	27.1%
East	37.2%	35.1%	26.4%
Midwest	36.8%	33.8%	28.3%
South	44.0%	30.6%	24.4%
West	34.1%	30.7%	33.8%
Male	35.1%	35.6%	28.2%
Female	41.6%	29.9%	27.2%
City residence	49.5%	30.0%	19.0%
Suburb	32.2%	34.4%	32.4%
Small town	38.5%	32.9%	27.4%
Rural	37.6%	30.1%	31.2%

Would allow an open homosexual to speak in their community.

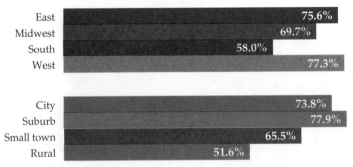

Figure 5.9 Tolerance for homosexuality by region and type of community

Source: Cumulative data from General Social Surveys, 1972–1990.

the right to bear firearms and to resist gun controls. As Figure 5.9, on permitting homosexuals to speak in communities, indicates, there are substantial regional differences on social issues.

City and Country

Whatever region they live in, urban, rural, and suburban residents tend to differ from each other in understandable ways. City dwellers are especially conscious of poverty, unemployment, and urban problems; many of them want the federal government to help. Suburbanites, who are more comfortably off, are somewhat less eager to fight poverty and are more resistant to high taxes, though they tend to be highly concerned about the environment and to be socially liberal, strongly favoring free choice in matters of sex, religion, and life-style.

Country dwellers tend, on the average, to be conservative, both economically and socially (see Figure 5.9); to favor military strength; and to support law and order and conventional morality, while opposing stringent gun controls.

Social Class

Compared with much of the world, the United States has had rather little political conflict among people of different *incomes* or *occupational* groupings; in fact, rather few Americans think of themselves as members of a "class" at all. The label of "working class," which in Europe has been a badge of pride for members of powerful organized labor movements and social democratic parties, is mostly rejected by Americans; nearly everyone considers herself or himself to be "middle class."

Still, since the time of the New Deal, substantially more low-income people— poor people, as well as blue-collar workers and union members—have identified themselves as Democrats rather than as Republicans. The opposite is true at the top of the income and occupational scales. More business executives, doctors, lawyers, and other highly paid people identify themselves as Republicans. In 1988, 47 percent of those with incomes under $15,000 thought of themselves as Democrats, but only 24 percent of those with incomes over $75,000 did so.[42] This is one of the most enduring differences between the Republican and Democratic parties.

Lower-income people also have some distinctive policy preferences. Not sur-

Strongly agree that the government should improve the standard of living
of all poor Americans.

Income level

Figure 5.10 Income levels and attitudes toward government help for the poor

Source: Cumulative data from General Social Surveys, 1986–1990.

prisingly, they tend to favor much more government help with jobs, education,
housing, medical care, and the like, whereas the highest-income people, who
would presumably pay more and benefit less from such programs, tend to oppose
them (see Figure 5.10). To complicate matters, however, some groups of high-
income people—especially highly educated professionals—tend to be very liberal
on social issues involving sexual behavior, abortion rights, free speech, and civil
rights. They also tend to be especially eager for government action to protect the
environment. Once again, no simple "liberal-conservative" distinction can accurately sum up all differences in opinions.

Educational Level

The level of formal education that people reach is related to their income level,
because education helps people earn more and also because the wealthy can put
their children through more and better schooling. But education has some distinct
political effects of its own.

As we will see in Chapter 9, "Voting and Elections," education is the strongest single predictor of participation in politics. College-educated people are much
more likely to vote, to talk about politics, to go to meetings, to sign petitions, and
to write letters than are people who have attained only elementary or high school
educations. The highly educated know more about politics. They know what they
want and how to go about getting it. Those with more schooling also have some
distinctive policy preferences. As we have indicated, they are especially protective
of civil rights, civil liberties, and individual freedom—for homosexuals, atheists,
protestors and dissenters, and others (see Figure 5.11). Education may contribute
to tolerance by exposing people to diverse ideas or by training them in elite-backed
norms of tolerance.

Schooling completed

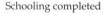

Figure 5.11 Tolerance for atheists by level of education

Source: Cumulative data from General Social Surveys, 1972–1990.

The most highly educated people tend to be the most tuned in to news and commentary in the media, and tend to change their opinions somewhat more quickly than others do. This is unusual; most of the groups that we have discussed, even those with rather distinctive policy preferences, tend to change opinion together, in the same directions, and at about the same times.[43]

Gender

Women and men are not so different, politically, as one might expect. They belong to the Republican and Democratic parties in nearly the same proportions (women being slightly more Democratic) and differ only moderately on certain kinds of issues.

Of course, women were prevented from participating in politics for a large part of our history; they only got the vote by constitutional amendment in 1920. Not all of them immediately took advantage of this new opportunity. For many years, women voted and participated at lower rates than men—about 10 or 15 percent lower in the elections of the 1950s, for example—and, only after the women's movement gained force during the 1970s, did substantial numbers of female candidates begin to run for high offices. Though an office-holding gap remains, the participation gap has now virtually disappeared.[44]

Women do differ somewhat from men in certain policy preferences. Women tend to be more opposed to violence, whether by criminals or by the state. More of them oppose capital punishment and the use of military force abroad. More favor arms control and peace agreements. Women also tend to be somewhat more supportive of protective policies that care for the weak and the helpless.[45]

Contrary to common impression, women have not been particularly more supportive than men of women's rights or abortion. This is another case, like that of Catholic Americans and the Catholic church, in which the opinions of ordinary members of social groups are not necessarily the same as those of organizations that claim to represent them. Women do differ among themselves, however; professionals and others working outside the home are much more liberal on these issues than are homemakers.

Age

The young and old differ on certain matters that touch their particular interests (e.g., the draft in wartime or the drinking age), but the chief difference is that young people are more attuned to the particular times in which they are growing up. Those who were young during the 1960s were especially quick to favor civil

Agree that the government is spending "too little" on the environment.

Under 30 years old	73.3%
Over 30 years old	55.0%

Figure 5.12 Support for spending more on environmental programs, by age

Source: Cumulative data from General Social Surveys, 1972–1990.

rights for blacks, for example. During the 1980s and 1990s, young people have been especially concerned about environmental issues (see Figure 5.12). Often social change occurs by *generational replacement*: old ideas die off with old people.

The opinions of Americans in various social, economic, and geographical groupings differ in interesting ways, which often affect the shape of political struggles. But these opinions are generally most important when they are combined, constituting the collective opinion of the entire American public. Now we can return to *collective* public opinion in the nation as a whole, and how it relates to democratic politics.

PUBLIC OPINION AND POLICY

We have argued that one crucial test of how well democracy is working is how closely a government's policies correspond to the expressed wishes of its citizens. How close, then, is the relationship in the United States between what the citizens want and what the government does?

Effects of Public Opinion on Policy

Our opening story about the Vietnam War suggested that, at least under some circumstances, public opinion does affect policymaking. Other evidence indicates that it very often does so, though not always.

One striking example of government responsiveness to the public involves the federal budget for 1991. In the fall of 1990, after months of secret "summit" negotiations and hardball pressure, the Bush administration and leading congressional Democrats announced agreement on a comprehensive plan to reduce the budget deficit by $500 billion over five years, mainly by increasing taxes on gasoline and heating oil, aviation, alcohol, and cigarettes, and by raising certain Social Security and Medicare taxes. It quickly became clear, however, that the new burdens fell mostly on low-income people, who already had lost out in previous tax changes. Many of these measures were very unpopular. According to one poll, 87 percent of Americans declared that they would be "willing" to raise taxes on people with incomes over $100,000 in order to reduce the deficit; 85 percent were willing to raise alcohol taxes, and 58 percent were willing to cut defense spending. But only small minorities accepted certain key elements of the summit plan: only 36 percent were willing to raise the tax on gasoline, only 27 percent were willing for the government to provide fewer services "even in health and education," and only 17 percent were willing to raise Medicare charges. The public expressed anger at Congress, and President Bush's popularity dropped sharply.[46]

Congress heard the public outcry. Representatives from both parties abandoned the plan. After intense bargaining they agreed on a new budget that would cut the deficit just as much but would shift the burden more to higher-income people, by raising the top income tax rate from 28 percent to 31 percent, raising Medicare taxes on those with high incomes ($50,000–$125,000), and increasing the gasoline tax by only 5 cents per gallon instead of 10 cents.[47]

Usually public opinion influences policymaking in less dramatic ways, without the sort of conflict that was played out in 1990. Looking at many different policy issues—foreign and domestic—one scholar found that U.S. government policy corresponded with what opinion surveys said the public wanted about two-

Table 5.1
Government Responsiveness to Large, Stable Changes in Public Opinion

	Direction of Policy Changes					
	Congruent		*Noncongruent*		*Total*	
Opinion Change	%	N	%	N	%	N
Large (10%+) and stable	87	(53)	13	(8)	54	(61)
Small and/or fluctuating	63	(33)	37	(19)	46	(52)
	76	(86)	24	(27)	100	(113)

Yule's Q = 0.58.

Source: Benjamin I. Page and Robert Y. Shapiro, "Effects of Public Opinion on Policy," *American Political Science Review* Vol. 77 (March 1983), p. 181.

thirds of the time. The same two-thirds correspondence appeared when other scholars investigated how a number of *changes* in public opinion related to changes in federal, state, and local policy. In fact, in cases in which public opinion changed by a substantial and an enduring amount and the issue was prominent, government policy moved in the same direction *87 percent* of the time within a year or so afterwards[48] (see Table 5.1).

According to still another study, the policies enacted in particular *states* correspond rather closely to the opinions of the states' citizens; that is, states with mostly liberal citizens tend to have mostly liberal policies, whereas states with mostly conservative citizens have mostly conservative policies. Using sophisticated research methods, this study largely ruled out the possibility that policy differences cause the opinion differences (i.e., that citizens go along with whatever their government is doing), rather than vice versa. Public opinion seems to be a significant influence upon government policy. Changes in opinion really do bring about changes in policy.[49]

This evidence does not completely settle the matter. For one thing, even if public opinion is a "proximate" influence on policy (i.e., even if opinion "stands next" to policymaking and directly affects it), we still need to know what factors affect public opinion itself. If public opinion can be manufactured by the media or easily *manipulated* by interest groups or political leaders (as in the Tonkin Gulf example), then it would not make much sense to talk about democratic policymaking. It would be the media and elites and leaders that really controlled policy, with public opinion simply acting as a transmission belt.

We have already mentioned reasons for being skeptical of the idea that public opinion can be pushed around at will. Usually personal experiences, objective events, and structural realities, rather than politicians' rhetoric, have the most to do with the shape of public opinion. Of course, the exceptions, like the Tonkin Gulf incident, stand out; they may be most common in foreign affairs, where the government sometimes can control what information is made available. We need to discuss opinion manipulation further in later chapters. For now, however, the main point is that public opinion is a substantial and important proximate influence on policymaking.

SUMMARY

Public opinion consists of the political attitudes and beliefs expressed by ordinary citizens; it can be measured rather accurately through polls and surveys. The democratic ideals of popular sovereignty and majority rule imply that government policy should respond to the wishes of its citizens. An important test of how well democracy is working, therefore, is how closely government policy corresponds to public opinion.

Most people do not know a lot of facts about politics; they are more concerned with everyday life and do not have well-worked-out ideologies or highly stable policy preferences. Contrary to the fears of the Founders and others, however, the *collective* public opinion of Americans is quite real and stable, and takes account of available information.

Americans mostly put a high value on freedom, economic liberty, capitalism, equality of opportunity (but not equality of result), and democracy. Liberals and conservatives tend to disagree about how much emphasis should be placed on economic liberty, as opposed to equality of opportunity and safety nets for the unfortunate. In recent years, large majorities of Americans have favored substantial government action to fight crime; to help with education, Medical Care, and Social Security; and to clean up the environment. Most people have been skeptical of foreign aid, and many have wished to cut spending on defense and the space program. Support for civil rights, civil liberties, and the right to have an abortion has increased. Most people identify with a political party, and most evaluate the performance of presidents based on how things are going.

People learn their political attitudes and beliefs from their families, peers, schools, and workplaces; they also respond to political events and public debate. Economic and social structures of the United States strongly affect public opinion.

Opinions and party loyalties differ according to race, religion, region, urban or rural residence, social class, education level, gender, and age. Blacks, Jews, and low-income people tend to be particularly liberal and Democratic; white Protestants and the wealthy tend to be conservative and Republican.

Public opinion has substantial effects upon what the federal, state, and local governments do. However, the government's responsiveness to public opinion is not perfect.

To Ponder

1. Is it desirable for a government to do exactly what its citizens want? What are the alternatives?

2. Can the public be trusted to take account of the best available information about public policies? How can it do so?

3. Can public opinion be manipulated?

4. Do group differences in opinions raise any major problems for American politics?

Suggested Readings

Erikson, Robert S., Norman R. Luttbeg, and Kent L. Tedin. *American Public Opinion: Its Origins, Content, and Impact*, 4th ed. New York: Macmillan, 1991.

A comprehensive textbook, with abundant data and citations.

Hochschild, Jennifer L. *What's Fair? American Beliefs About Distributive Justice.* Cambridge, MA: Harvard University Press, 1981.
     Explores public opinion through in-depth interviews with a small number of people.

McClosky, Herbert, and John Zaller. *The American Ethos: Public Attitudes toward Capitalism and Democracy.* Cambridge, MA: Harvard University Press, 1984.
     A major study of some of Americans' most important beliefs and values.

Page, Benjamin I., and Robert Y. Shapiro. *The Rational Public: Fifty Years of Trends in Americans' Policy Preferences.* Chicago: University of Chicago Press, 1992.
     Extensive description of opinion trends and argument that the public is rational.

Sussman, Barry. *What Americans Really Think and Why Our Politicians Pay No Attention.* New York: Pantheon, 1988.
     A brief and lively account of public opinion, by a leading journalistic analyst of polls.

Notes

1. Joseph C. Goulden, *Truth Is the First Casualty: The Gulf of Tonkin Affair—Illusion and Reality* (Chicago: Rand McNally, 1969).

2. John E. Mueller, *War, Presidents and Public Opinion.* (New York: Wiley, 1973), p. 81.

3. U.S. Department of Defense, OASD (Comptroller), *Selected Manpower Statistics.* (Washington, D.C.: Government Publications, June 1976) pp. 59, 60.

4. Alexander Hamilton, James Madison, and John Jay, *The Federalist Papers,* ed. by Clinton Rossiter (New York: New American Library, 1961 [1787–88]). See Benjamin I. Page and Robert Y. Shapiro, *The Rational Public: Fifty Years of Trends in Americans' Policy Preferences* (Chicago: University of Chicago Press, 1992), chaps. 1, 2.

5. Walter Lippmann, *Public Opinion* (New York: Macmillan, 1922), p. 127.

6. Philip E. Converse, "The Nature of Belief Systems in Mass Publics," in David Apter, ed., *Ideology and Discontent* (New York: Free Press, 1964), pp. 206–261.

7. Robert S. Erikson, Norman R. Luttbeg, and Kent L. Tedin, *American Public Opinion: Its Origins, Content, and Impact,* 4th ed. (New York: Macmillan, 1991) tells more about the techniques and the statistics of polling.

8. Calculated from General Social Survey, 1983–1987.

9. Page and Shapiro, *Rational Public.*

10. Robert E. Lane, *Political Ideology: Why the American Common Man Believes What He Does* (New York: Free Press, 1962); Jennifer L. Hochschild, *What's Fair? American Beliefs About Distributive Justice* (Cambridge, MA: Harvard University Press, 1981).

11. Converse, "Nature of Belief Systems"; Christopher H. Achen, "Mass Political Attitudes and the Survey Response," *American Political Science Review,* Vol. 69 (1975), pp. 1218–1231.

12. Page and Shapiro, *Rational Public.*

13. Herbert McClosky and John Zaller, *The American Ethos: Public Attitudes toward Capitalism and Democracy* (Cambridge, MA: Harvard University Press, 1984).

14. McClosky and Zaller, *American Ethos,* pp. 32, 37.

15. Samuel Stouffer, *Communism, Conformity, and Civil Liberties* (New York: Doubleday, 1955); but also see James A. Davis, "Communism, Conformity, Cohorts, and Categories: American Tolerance in 1954 and 1972–73," *American Journal of Sociology,* Vol. 81 (November 1975), pp. 491–513.

16. McClosky and Zaller, *American Ethos,* pp. 108, 133, 135, 140.

17. Russell Dalton, *Citizen Politics in Western Democracies* (Chatham, NJ: Chatham House, 1988), p. 100.

18. James W. Prothro and Charles M. Grigg, "Fundamental Principles of Democracy: Bases of Agreement and Disagreement," *Journal of Politics,* Vol. 22 (1960), pp. 276–294.

19. Robert S. Erikson, Norman R. Luttbeg, and Kent L. Tedin, *American Public Opinion: Its Origins, Content, and Impact,* 3rd ed. (New York: Macmillan, 1988), p. 103.

20. George Gallup, Jr., *The Gallup Poll* (Wilmington, DE: Scholarly Resources, 1980), p. 258; 1986, p. 217.

21. William Caspary, "The 'Mood Theory': A Study of Public Opinion and Foreign Policy," *American Political Science Review*, Vol. 64 (1970), pp. 536–547.

22. Walter Dean Burnham, "Dealignment," MacKuen, Erikson and Stimson, "Macropartisanship," *American Political Science Review*.

23. Samuel Kernell, "Explaining Presidential Popularity," *American Political Science Review*, Vol. 72 (June 1978), pp. 506–522; Richard A. Brody, *Assessing the President: The Media, Elite Opinion, and Public Support* (Stanford, CA: Stanford University Press, 1991).

24. Richard G. Niemi et al., *Trends in Public Opinion: A Compendium of Survey Data*, (Westport, CT: Greenwood Press, 1989), p. 97.

25. Calculated from M. Kent Jennings and Richard Niemi, *The Political Character of Adolescence* (Princeton, NJ: Princeton University Press), p. 41.

26. Edward S. Greenberg, "Black Children and the Political System," *Public Opinion Quarterly*, Vol. 34 (1970), pp. 333–345; Jennings and Niemi, *Political Character*, pp. 205–206.

27. *New York Times*, January 29, 1991, p. A18.

28. Kay Lehman Schlozman and Sidney Verba, *Insult to Injury* (Cambridge, MA: Harvard University Press, 1979), p. 141.

29. Edward S. Greenberg, *Workplace Democracy: The Political Effects of Participation* (Ithaca, NY: Cornell University Press, 1986).

30. Morris P. Fiorina, *Retrospective Voting in American National Elections* (New Haven, CT: Yale University Press, 1981).

31. John E. Reilly, ed., *American Public Opinion and U.S. Foreign Policy 1991* (Chicago: Chicago Council on Foreign Relations, 1991), p. 20.

32. John R. Petrocik, *Party Coalitions: Realignments and the Decline of the New Deal Party System* (Chicago: University of Chicago Press, 1981), p. 38.

33. Calculated from pooled General Social Survey data. See also "Opinion Roundup: Party Support," *Public Opinion* (September/October 1988), p. 34.

34. Niemi et al., *Trends*, pp. 19–20.

35. U.S. Department of Commerce, *Current Population Reports: Voting and Registration in the Election of November, 1988* (Washington, D.C.: U.S. Government Printing Office, 1989), p. 4.

36. "Religion in America," *The Gallup Report* (April 1987), p. 20. (*New York Times*, April 10, 1991, p. A1 says 26 percent.)

37. *New York Times*, April 10, 1991, p. A11 says Jews were 43 percent Democrat, 22 percent Republican in 1989–1990.

38. Constant H. Jacquet, Jr., ed. *Yearbook of American and Canadian Churches* (Nashville, TN: Abingdon Press, 1989).

39. *New York Times*, April 10, 1991, p. A11.

40. Peter F. Galderisi, et al., eds., *The Politics of Realignment* (Boulder, CO: Westview Press, 1987), pp. 91–97.

41. Galderisi et al., *Realignment*, pp. 94–95.

42. "Opinion Roundup: Party Support," p. 34.

43. Page and Shapiro, *Rational Public*, chap. 7.

44. M. Margaret Conway, *Political Participation in the United States* (Washington, D.C.: Congressional Quarterly, 1985), p. 27.

45. Robert Y. Shapiro and Harpreet Mahajan, "Gender Differences in Policy Preferences: A Summary of Trends from the 1960s to the 1980s," *Public Opinion Quarterly*, Vol. 50 (1986), pp. 42–61.

46. *New York Times*, October 9, 1990, p. A11.

47. *New York Times*, October 25, 1990, p. A1.

48. Alan D. Monroe, "Consistency Between Public Preferences and National Policy Decisions," *American Politics Quarterly*, Vol. 7 (January 1979), pp. 3-19; Benjamin I. Page and Robert Y. Shapiro, "Effects of Public Opinion on Policy," *American Political Science Review*, Vol. 77 (March 1983), pp. 175–190.

49. Gerald C. Wright, Jr., Robert S. Erikson, and John P. McIver, "Public Opinion and Policy Liberalism in the American States," *American Journal of Political Science*, Vol. 31 (November 1987), pp. 980–1001.

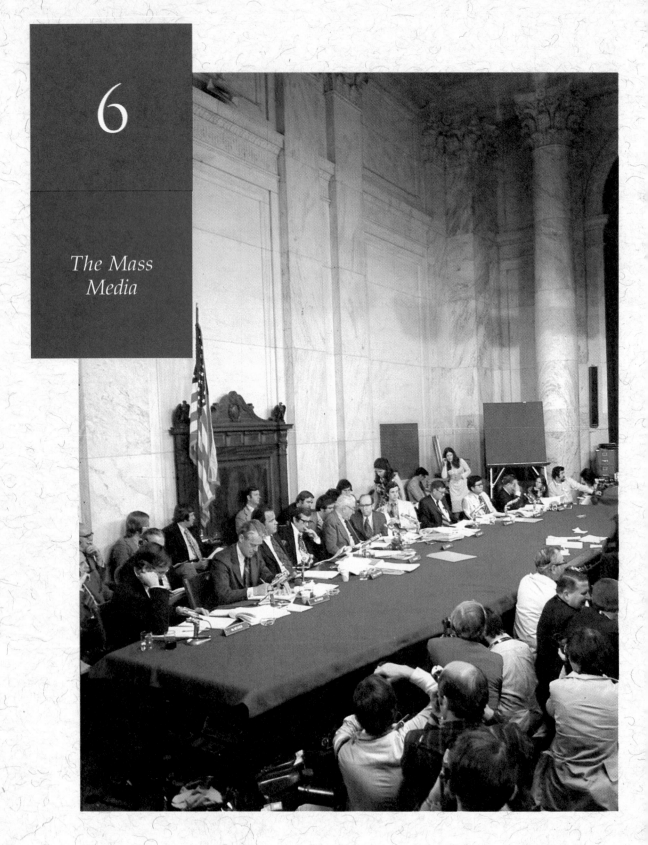

6

*The Mass
Media*

COVERING THE WATERGATE SCANDAL

A ringing telephone woke 29-year-old *Washington Post* reporter Bob Woodward on Saturday morning, June 17, 1972. Could he come into the office? Five men had been arrested for burglary at the headquarters of the Democratic National Committee in the opulent Watergate apartment office complex; they were carrying photographic equipment and electronic gear.[1]

At the *Post*'s newsroom, Woodward learned the details that had been phoned in by a veteran police reporter. The five men arrested at 2.30 A.M. had been wearing business suits and surgical gloves. They had been carrying a walkie-talkie, 40 rolls of film, cameras, lock picks, pen-size tear gas guns, bugging devices for telephones and rooms, and many sequentially numbered $100 bills.

The Yale-educated Woodward, who during his nine months with the paper had been writing stories about unsanitary restaurants and small-time police corruption, also learned that hard-driving college dropout Carl Bernstein (only 28 years old but with 12 years of newspaper experience) was working on the same story. The initially uneasy collaboration between Woodward and Bernstein was to produce one of the most remarkable stories in the history of American journalism.

At the preliminary hearing in court that afternoon, Woodward heard accused burglar James McCord describe his profession as "security consultant," recently retired from government: "CIA," he whispered to the judge. Meanwhile, Bernstein learned from Miami contacts that the four other accused burglars had anti-Castro histories and possible CIA connections; one was rumored to be recruiting militant Cubans to demonstrate at the upcoming Democratic national convention. The *Post* ran a front-page story on Sunday on the plot to bug the Democrats, offering no explanation of motives.

The *Post* editors assigned Bernstein and Woodward to follow up the story. The Associated Press wire service revealed that McCord was security coordinator for the Committee to Reelect the President (CREEP), the chief Republican campaign organization for 1972. John Mitchell, President Nixon's campaign manager and former attorney general, denied that the burglars were acting for the campaign. A police source told the *Post*, however, that the burglars' address books and papers referred to E. Howard Hunt, "W. House" or "W.H." With a few phone calls, Woodward was able to establish that Hunt was a consultant working for Charles W. Colson, special counsel to the president of the United States and widely known as Nixon's "hatchet man." "White House Consultant Linked to Bugging Suspects," Woodward's story was headlined.

Presidential Press Secretary Ronald Ziegler described the incident as a "third-rate burglary attempt," not worthy of further White House comment; President Nixon flatly said that "(t)he White House has had no involvement whatever. . . ." But *Newsday* and the *New York Times* established that the CREEP office of G. Gordon Liddy, a former White House aide, had received many phone calls from one of the burglars. The *Times* reported that $100,000 in that burglar's bank account had come from a Mexico City lawyer. Bernstein traced $25,000 of the money to the head of Nixon's 1968 Midwest campaign, who told Woodward that it consisted of contributions to CREEP that he had personally turned over to Maurice Stans, finance chairman of CREEP.

Throughout the summer and fall of 1972, the "Woodstein" pair pursued leads with scores (eventually hundreds) of sources, most of whom insisted on anonymity, including a bookkeeper for CREEP, the treasurer of the committee, FBI agents, and the mysterious "Deep Throat," an administration insider whom Woodward says that he often met after midnight in an underground parking garage. Slowly and painstakingly, they put together pieces of an amazing story.

The Watergate break-in turned out to be just the tip of the iceberg. CREEP had kept hundreds of thousands of dollars in a secret fund, controlled by top White House and campaign officials, and had used them to run a massive campaign of espionage, sabotage, and dirty tricks against Democratic candidates. They had forged a letter that drove Democratic front-runner Edmund Muskie to distraction; they had provided the psychiatric records that caused Thomas Eagleton to resign as vice-presidential nominee; they had disrupted schedules and had harassed candidates' families. After months of front-page *Post* stories zeroing in on the secret fund, illegal campaign contributions, and dirty tricks, the October 10 "Woodstein" story put the picture together: "FBI Finds Nixon Aides Sabotaged Democrats." Over the next few days, the *Post*, *Time* magazine, and the *New York Times* reported several direct links to the White House, including some through Chief of Staff H. R. Haldeman.

But the country wasn't convinced. The White House cried "hearsay," "innuendo," partisan politics: this was a last, desperate preelection effort by the failing McGovern campaign and by what Senator Robert Dole called its "partner-in-mudslinging," the *Post*. At the end of August, after his renomination, President Nixon blandly referred to "technical violations . . . on both sides" and claimed that White House counsel John Dean had investigated and reported that no one "presently employed" in the administration had been involved in this "very bizarre incident." The grand jury indicted only Hunt, Liddy, and the five burglars. And the *Post*'s credibility was hurt by a minor factual error about the Haldeman link.

Despite substantial coverage of Watergate by leading newspapers and the television networks, and fairly high public awareness, it did not become much of an issue in the 1972 presidential election.[2] Nixon overwhelmingly defeated McGovern, by 62 percent to 38 percent of the popular vote. Only later revelations led to the series of trials, congressional investigations, and impeachment hearings that eventually drove Richard Nixon from office and convicted a number of his aides of crimes.

But Bernstein's and Woodward's tenacious investigative reporting (propelled by "Deep Throat" and other sources) uncovered many of the key facts and set those events in motion. In May 1973, the *Post* won the Pulitzer Prize for distinguished public service in journalism. Some observers complained that the *Post* had unfairly hounded the Nixon administration, but most concluded that it had served democracy well by digging out important facts for the American people.

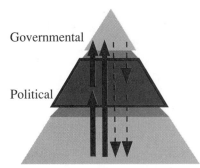

Governmental

Political

Structural

THE MASS MEDIA AND POLITICS

Journalist and scholar Walter Lippman once declared that "[a] free press is not a privilege, but an organic necessity in a great society. Without criticism and reliable and intelligent reporting, the government cannot govern."[3]

The central idea of democracy is that ordinary citizens should control what their government does. However, citizens cannot hope to control officials, to choose candidates, to speak intelligently with others about public affairs, or even to make up their minds about what policies they favor, unless they have good information about politics. Most of that information must come through the mass media. How well democracy works, then, depends partly on how good a job the mass media are doing.

One possible role for the media in democracy is that of *watchdog* over government. The idea is that the press—acting more vigorously and independently than the pet in the cartoon—should dig up facts and warn the public when officials are doing something wrong.

The First Amendment to the Constitution ("Congress shall make no law . . . abridging freedom of . . . the press") helps ensure that the media can expose officials' wrongdoing without fear of censorship or prosecution. This is a treasured American right that is not available in many other countries. Censorship is usually very tight under authoritarian regimes. Even in a democratic country, such as Great Britain, strict secrecy laws limit what the press can say. In 1984, for example, British civil servant Sarah Tisdall was fired and sent to jail for six months for telling the *Guardian* that the then defense minister, Michael Heseltine, planned to give a purposefully misleading statement to the House of Commons.[4] In many

PUBLIC WATCHDOG

countries, including France, Israel, and Sweden, the government owns and operates major television channels, and makes sure that programs are not too critical.[5]

In the United States, freedom of the press is not perfect; in 1989, for example, Columbian journalist Patricia Lara was jailed and deported from the United States because she appeared on an Immigration and Naturalization Service list of about 40,000 people suspected of "subversive Communist or terrorist activities."[6] Still, the press generally fares much worse elsewhere. The United States is widely regarded as having the most free press in the world.

As the Watergate story indicates, the press in the United States sometimes does carry out a watchdog role. But how common is it? We will see that, even without formal censorship or government ownership of the media, various factors, including the way in which the mass media are organized and the routines of news gathering, limit the extent to which the media are willing or able to be critical of government policies.

Many Americans saw the *Post*'s pursuit of the Watergate story as a great achievement of investigative journalism. Polls showed that public confidence in the media rose significantly after the Watergate affair, and many young men and women were inspired to go to journalism schools and to take up careers as reporters. But some people complained that the *Post* was pursuing a partisan vendetta against the Nixon administration; the handling of Watergate was just the most blatant example of an antiestablishment bias. Is the press *too* critical, too quick to blow scandals out of proportion and to destroy political leaders' careers?

A second role for the mass media in a democracy is to make clear what *electoral choices* the public has: what the political parties stand for and how the candidates shape up in terms of their personal character, their knowledge and experience, and their positions on the issues. Here and in Chapter 9, "Voting and Elections," we will see that the media do not always convey such information effectively.

A third role for the mass media is to present a diverse, full, and enlightening set of *ideas about public policy*: how well current policies are working, what alter-

Gary Hart was the leading Democratic candidate for president in 1987, but his campaign collapsed after the media publicized evidence of an extramarital affair which Hart had denied.

native policies might be tried, and what effects they would have. How much information do the U.S. media actually convey? How diverse and how accurate is that information? Are there any systematic biases: is the press too liberal, for example, or too conservative? Are some voices heard and not others? If so, what does this imply about political equality?

Beyond these three roles, the mass media play other important parts in the political system. The media may act as a vehicle for the government, political parties, and interest groups to speak to citizens, educating or persuading, or perhaps manipulating, their opinions. The media may also serve as a channel of communication among political and governmental institutions, helping Congress, the president, and members of the executive branch to figure out what the others are doing. Finally, the media—mostly owned by large corporations—may themselves be political actors, with their own goals and interests, influencing political leaders and public opinion. Thus, the mass media serve as a critical link among political and governmental institutions, but they also act as political institutions in their own right.

In this chapter, we explore how the media function as a political institution and how they interact with other political actors and with governmental institutions. We begin with *structural* factors, the historical developments that have made the media what they are today. Next, we discuss how they are organized and how they work, going on to deal with possible biases in what the media broadcast and print, the effects of the media on politics, and issues of government regulation.

STRUCTURE: THE DEVELOPMENT
OF JOURNALISM IN AMERICA

At the time of the American Revolution, communication was difficult. It ordinarily took several days for news to travel from Boston to New York by horseback. A few local newspapers existed in the big cities, but they were expensive to print and expensive to buy; their small circulations were mostly limited to affluent merchants and tradesmen who needed to know shipping schedules and the prices of goods. Before the 1830s, the other main newspapers were organs of the Federalist, Republican, or Democratic political parties, which argued issues in a fiercely partisan fashion.[7] Many newspapers continued to be partisan in later years as well. (During Abraham Lincoln's presidency, rather confusingly, the *St. Louis Democrat* was biased toward Republican causes, and the *St. Louis Republican* favored the Democrats.)[8] Such limited media could not carry out the watchdog role very successfully or convey full information about electoral choices or public policy.

Newspapers

Modern newspapers have been made possible by technological developments and a tremendous growth and modernization of American society. During the nineteenth century, newspapers acquired machinery for large-scale printing, a sizable audience of readers, and a dependable network for gathering news. Key technological breakthroughs included the invention in 1814 of the "cylinder" press, powered by steam, which supplied ink from a revolving drum; the replacement of hand-manufactured type with a machine for typecasting (1822); a machine for

The first "penny paper" was the New York *Sun*, established in 1833. Despite its dull format and small headlines, the *Sun* gained popularity with human interest stories like the one reported in this edition about a pistol-packing Irish police captain.

large-scale papermaking (1830); and the rotary press (1847). Meanwhile, the population grew and public education spread, creating a large, literate audience. Improvements in home lighting made nighttime reading easier.

In 1833, the first "penny paper," the *New York Sun*, was founded. It and its successors, especially James Gordon Bennett's *New York Herald*, reached mass audiences of ordinary working people by means of low prices and local human interest stories, written in a breezy and often sensational style that is still with us today. Bennett pioneered society news, exposés of upper-class scandals, and spectacular coverage of bizarre murder trials, along with modern financial news.

Then the invention of the telegraph revolutionized news gathering and transmission. The first "wire" story was sent from Washington, D.C., to Baltimore in 1844. In 1848, six New York papers formed the Associated Press, a cooperative that pooled news and distributed it almost instantly among many cities. This made it possible to reach hundreds of thousands, or even millions of people, with fast-breaking national news, in a fashion that we now take for granted.

Sensational treatment of the news mushroomed at the end of the nineteenth century. Joseph Pulitzer of the New York *World* (1883) and William Randolph Hearst, the strong-willed publisher of the New York *Journal* (1885)—upon whose career the film *Citizen Kane* is based—combined sensationalism and political crusades, creating "yellow journalism" (named after Pulitzer's "Yellow Kid" cartoon), with full-color illustrations and comics, and oversized headlines. Hearst's crusades included, in 1898, stirring up war fever against Spain over Spanish control of Cuba, a key step in the emergence of the United States as a world power. Hearst's headlines proclaimed that the Spanish had blown up the U.S. battleship *Maine* in a Cuban harbor, though Spanish involvement was never proven and most historians believe the explosion was an accident. "You furnish the pictures and I'll furnish the war," cabled Hearst to artist Frederick Remington in Cuba. Today's tabloids may not have started any wars, but their technological workings and their journalistic techniques are much like those of Hearst's papers.

The growth of telegraphed national news and large-circulation newspapers also led to a new sort of news: bland, "objective" news stories that relied heavily on interviews and that scrupulously attributed all opinions to named sources. Such stories could be sent all over the country and used by many different kinds of newspapers without offending readers from diverse audiences. The Associated

William Randolph Hearst's *New York Journal* stirred up war fever in 1898
with unsubstantiated charges that the Spanish had blown up the U. S.
battleship *Maine* in Cuba.

Press employed its own reporters and sent their stories to hundreds of papers.
The International News Service, Scripps-Howard Service, and other "wire
services" soon did the same. Today, the Associated Press (AP) stands as the
preeminent source of national and international news for most newspapers and
as a major source for television networks. Many small papers simply print AP
stories intact.

The development of wire services meant that political news could be spread
much more quickly, to much bigger audiences, and in a much more nationally
uniform way than ever before. This trend was accentuated by the development of
large "chains" of newspapers, owned by the same company and with uniform
editorial policies. Thus, the changing *structural* factors of industrialization and
technology changed the shape of political communication and the shape of politics. The increasing objectivity and widening circulation of the media had obvious
advantages for democracy, but also some disadvantages, which we will discuss.

"Objective" news came to be exemplified by the *New York Times*, which
Adolph S. Ochs began to revitalize in 1896. The *Times*, claiming to publish "All
The News That's Fit to Print" and aspiring to be America's "newspaper of record,"
specialized in thoroughness rather than liveliness or cleverness. Its deadpan re-
cording of the ruminations of authoritative sources sometimes outrages critics
who think that the *Times* is too passive in the face of officials' lies (a whole periodical is now devoted to "The Lies of Our *Times*"), but it remains the preeminent
U.S. journal for reporting on international affairs, and it is rivaled only by the
Washington Post for extent of domestic political reporting.

Magazines and Electronic Media

The Italian inventor Guglielmo Marconi put together the first practical radio in
1895; commercial radio stations with broad audiences were established in the
United States during the 1920s. Soon stations all over the country were organized
into networks that shared news and other programs. By 1938, the three radio
networks had 97 percent of the nighttime broadcasting power of all U.S. radio

In 1991, millions of Americans stayed glued to their television sets for reports on the Persian Gulf war with Iraq.

stations.[9] In the depths of the Great Depression of the 1930s, millions of Americans could hear the reassuring voice of President Roosevelt giving "fireside chats." Later, millions could hear the latest news about the battles with Japan and Nazi Germany in World War II, which they could also see in dramatic movie newsreels and in the glossy pictures of the new *Life* magazine (started in 1936), which offered a grab bag of photos of movie stars, nature, art, and daily life, as well as royalty.

Magazines grew. Old journals of opinion, like *The Nation* and the *Atlantic Monthly*, continued to be published. Beginning in the 1920s, Henry Luce's *Time*, the weekly newsmagazine, brought analysis and interpretation of the week's news, written in a quick and colorful style, to hundreds of thousands and then millions of readers; it was later joined by *Newsweek* and *U.S. News & World Report*. Large-circulation magazines, like the *Saturday Evening Post*, *Life*, and especially *Readers' Digest*, gained circulations in the millions; *Readers' Digest* reached more than 9 million people in the United States and 6 million people overseas in 1950, and it continued to hold a circulation of 16 million in the late 1980s.[10] (The pictorially oriented *Life* and *Saturday Evening Post*, however, were killed in the 1960s by competition from television.) Countless specialized journals appeared, providing information and entertainment of diverse sorts. By the 1970s and 1980s, national editions of several newspapers, like the *New York Times*, the *Wall Street Journal*, and *USA Today* became, in effect, daily newsmagazines for a national audience.

The television revolution transformed American media yet again. Television was invented just before World War II; it was developed commercially in the late 1940s and invaded American households on a large scale in the 1950s. In 1950, only 12 percent of American households owned a television set, but by 1960 87 percent did (see Figure 6.1 for the growing number of households). Scores and then hundreds of television stations were established around the country. Most of the main VHF (Very High Frequency) channels were affiliated with one of the three major networks—ABC, CBS, and NBC—which provided the bulk of prime-time programming. The networks also produced and distributed national news programs, which in 1963 were expanded from 15 minutes to 30 minutes of early

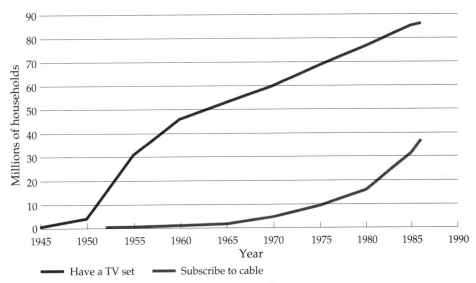

Figure 6.1 The rise of television

Source: Jerry L. Salvaggio and Jennings Bryant, eds., Media Use in the Information Age *(Hillsdale, NJ: Lawrence Erlbaum Associates, 1989), pp. 290–293.*

evening time, and which became *the* major source of news for most Americans. Since then, polls regularly have shown that most people name television as their most important source of news, and most say that they trust television a great deal.

Now practically all American families (98 percent of them) have at least one television set. Most have more than one, with remote tuning to get dozens of UHF (Ultra High Frequency) channels—an innovation of the 1970s—along with the 12 VHF channels. Nearly two-thirds of U.S. families now have cable service,[11] which gives them a wide range of channels that often include CNN (Cable News Network), broadcasting political news 24 hours a day, and C-Span, the ultimate fare for political junkies, serving up live coverage of Congress and other political institutions for the truly dedicated (see "Resource Feature"). Typically, between 8 and 9 P.M., approximately 95–100 million Americans are watching television.[12] Practically every American can, in his or her own living room, see and hear the president of the United States and keep track of events in Eastern Europe, China, South Africa, Iraq, or any other place of interest around the world.

Radio, once thought dead, has been reborn, especially for commuters, joggers, and people who work at home. Besides music, AM and FM stations offer frequent news bulletins and lengthy call-in talk shows, in which all manner of political opinions, including the cranky and the outrageous, are voiced. PBS (Public Broadcasting System) stations provide extended news analysis and commentary, some of which is quite insightful.

Personal computers in many homes create possibilities of ordering special information from a host of services or even of talking back to politicians—registering opinions by wire. Information technology is changing quickly. There is talk of "custom feeds" of television news for local mixing; of two-way video communication; and of instant electronic referendum voting.

Since 1979, cable television viewers have been able to treat themselves to unedited speeches, congressional proceedings, dedications, and other political events on C-Span. The network broadcasts nearly 5,000 hours of political programming a year, including 2,000 hours of live broadcasts. The CEO of C-Span commented: "There's probably 10% of our audience out there that watches 20-plus hours a month. For those people, it's obviously made a huge difference in their lives, huge. I mean it's their life."

Source: "C-Span: Documenting a Decade of Public Affairs," *Broadcasting*, April 3, 1989, pp. 62–69.

People with their own video recorders now can become do-it-yourself electronic journalists, passing on videotapes of hot news stories to television news shows. In 1991, for example, a bystander on an apartment balcony recorded Los Angeles police officers beating and kicking black motorist Rodney King (which gave him nine skull fractures, a shattered eye socket and cheekbone, a broken leg, a concussion, injuries to both knees, and nerve damage that partially paralyzed his face) after his arrest for speeding; broadcasts of the videotape created a nationwide furor about police brutality and calls for reform of the L.A. police force.[13]

We see, then, that transformations of the mass media in the United States have been shaped by structural developments in the U.S. economy and society. The most important structural changes have involved population expansion and dispersion, technological innovation, and (as we will see later) new forms of corporate business organization. The result is a vast and pervasive mass media industry, which itself is part of our economic structure and which has enormous effects on politics. This has made it possible (though not inevitable) for citizens to get the kinds of information they need in order for democracy to work properly.

HOW THE MEDIA WORK

Organization of the Mass Media

In the United States, the media are privately owned, usually very large businesses. Television stations keep their exact revenue figures secret, but it is estimated that in 1990 the total gross revenues for the entire Los Angeles television market were $867.7 million and for the whole New York City market were $970.5 million, that is, close to $1 *billion* each.[14] All together, the television stations and networks, newspapers, and magazines bring in many billions of dollars a year.

Some television stations and newspapers—especially the smaller ones—are owned locally by families or by groups of investors. Many of the biggest stations and papers, however, and the television networks, are owned by large media corporations, which, in turn, are often subsidiaries of enormous conglomerates. General Electric bought RCA, and its subsidiary NBC, in 1986 (see Figure 6.2). Gulf + Western has a strong position in book publishing and films. The Japanese firm, Sony, bought CBS television (for $2 billion) and Columbia Pictures in 1987. Rupert Murdoch's Newscorp owns companies with newspapers, magazines, television, motion pictures, and book publishers, including HarperCollins, the publisher of this book.

The concentration of ownership has been increasing. In 1981, 46 corporations controlled most of the activity (i.e., more than half the circulation and revenues) of daily newspapers, magazines, television, books, and motion pictures. By 1986, the 46 had shrunk to 29. Fifteen companies, headed by Gannett (*USA Today* and 92 other dailies), Knight-Ridder, and Newhouse, dominated the newspaper business. In fact, by 1985, the ten largest chains accounted for nearly half the total

Figure 6.2 Corporate ownership of mass media

Source: Doris Graber, Mass Media and American Politics, *3rd ed. (Washington, D.C.: Congressional Quarterly, 1989), p. 43.*

Law professor Anita Hill's televised charges of sexual harassment
threatened the confirmation of Supreme Court Justice Clarence
Thomas in 1991.

daily newspaper circulation (63 million copies) in the United States. Six corporations, led by Time-Warner (with 40 percent of all magazine revenues), controlled most magazine publishing. The owners of the three television networks (General Electric-NBC, Sony-CBS, and Capital Cities/ABC), dominated television. Ten corporations received more than half of the $10 billion in book publishing revenues in 1985. And four firms (Warner Communications, Gulf + Western, Universal-MCA, and Coca-Cola—at that time owner of Columbia Pictures) got more than half the gross box office revenues from movies.[15]

The owners of these media firms and conglomerates are mostly wealthy and conservative; they are certainly not very critical of the American free enterprise system, within which they have done so well. As we will see, this may affect the ideological content of what the media broadcast.

There has been a strong tendency for newspapers to merge. In the vast majority of towns and cities with any paper at all (in 98 percent of them, as of 1986) there is now only one newspaper.[16] In some cities, two newspapers appear, but they are owned by the same people and share printing and other facilities, such as the San Francisco *Chronicle* and the *Examiner*. At the beginning of the 1990s, this was true of 22 cities, including San Francisco, Seattle, Detroit, and Cincinnati.[17]

Moreover, most newspapers and television stations, whoever owns them, depend largely on the same sources for news. The Associated Press wire service is now subscribed to by almost all major newspapers in the country. The AP supplies most of the main national and international news stories—even those that are rewritten to carry a local reporter's by-line. Most of what appears on network television news, too, is inspired by the AP wire. Television news departments keep film crews in only a few cities and seldom do their own investigative reporting. The story that you hear and the politician's face that you see on television are usually heard and seen by millions of other Americans at the same time.

Along with this centralization and unification of the mass media, however, there is also quite a lot of diversity, for those who make the effort to seek it out.

People who are especially interested in politics can find special publications that look at the world in a way that they find compatible or interesting, whether it is *The Nation* (liberal), *National Review* (conservative), *Commentary* (neoconservative), *Mother Jones* (irreverent), *The New York Review of Books* (intellectual and critical), *The New Yorker* (lofty), *Rolling Stone, Spy,* or dozens of others with small circulations.

Media corporations, like other corporations, are in business primarily to make a profit. This fact has important consequences. It means, for example, that the major media must appeal to large audiences and get many people to buy their publications or the products that they advertise. If most people are mainly interested in entertainment and want their news short, snappy, and sensational, that is what they will get, on network television news and in *USA Today.* Those who want more hard news are invited to try the *New York Times, Washington Post, Congressional Quarterly,* or a journal of opinion.

Clearly, most Americans do not want a lot of meaty political news. Just before a U.S.-Soviet summit meeting, in 1987, when NBC broadcast a prime-time, hour-long interview with Mikhail Gorbachev, only 15 percent of the national audience tuned in. More preferred "Kate and Allie," "Frank's Place," or "The World's Greatest Stuntman." In noncrisis periods, foreign affairs stories average only about 11 percent of all stories in American newspapers and about 16 percent of the stories on national newscasts.[18] At the beginning of 1991, television was saturated with coverage of the Middle East—the U.S. air and ground war against Iraq, Scud missiles hitting Israel and Saudi Arabia, the plight of Kurdish refugees—but, by the summer of 1991, the networks had returned to routine entertainment.

The profit motive also means that the biggest mass media tend to appeal to the lowest common denominator, avoiding controversial material that might seem "extreme," too liberal, too conservative, or otherwise offensive to substantial groups of viewers. Examples are legion. In the 1980s, General Motors canceled sponsorship of an Easter program on the life of Jesus because evangelical groups objected. Advertisers withdrew from a CBS documentary on gun control and from a series of interviews with ex-President Nixon. A number of public television stations refused to air a program on Palestinian grievances because of strong objections by Jewish groups.[19] Despite some outstanding "specials," most viewers of the mass media are not exposed to a lot of controversial ideas.

 The power of the audience to determine what appears in newspapers and on television might be seen as a force for democracy, enabling as many people as possible to see and hear what they want, while those who do not share average tastes can look for specialized media outlets. But there are at least three possible problems with this analysis. First, some argue that it would be better to provide more political information, even if people were not eager for it, in order to help society as a whole, by ensuring that citizens form reasonable political opinions and make sound decisions. This argument is often invoked in countries with government-owned media (see Figure 6.3). Second, consumer sovereignty over the media is not really the same as one-person, one-vote, majority rule democracy. The print media are less concerned with average citizens than with those who will buy the most from advertisers—a more affluent, middle- to upper-middle-class group. When the media respond to protests, it is usually to those who are noisiest and best organized. Third, and perhaps most important, advertisers and media owners are not actually forced to maximize the size of their audiences or advertising revenues on every program; they can give up some immediate income for

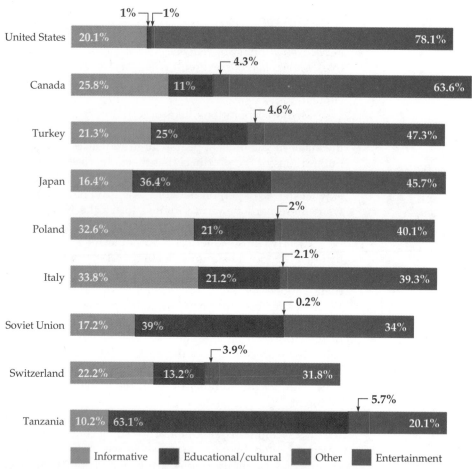

Figure 6.3 What's on TV: the United States compared with other countries

U.S. figures based on author's calculation from Harry Castleman and Walter J. Podrazik, The TV Schedule Book *(New York: McGraw-Hill, 1984), pp. 278–279. Refers only to the three major networks and only to national programming, based on Winter 1983. All other figures from* UNESCO Statistical Yearbook *(Paris: UNESCO, 1990), pp. 10–26 to 10–33.*

the sake of other aspects of profit making or for causes in which they strongly believe. Advertisers can, for example, pressure the media not to expose environmentally damaging activities by their own companies. Newspapers can ignore policy proposals that they think are too expensive. Television stations can go easy on politicians who regulate them.

In 1990, for example, NBC's "Today" show planned a program on consumer boycotts but was distressed to learn that the most visible and effective current boycott was directed against General Electric (GE), NBC's owner, because of GE's production and promotion of nuclear weapons. "Today" repeatedly postponed the show, telling a participant that it wanted a boycott that was "small," "local," and "sexy"; it finally featured a table full of boycotted products from Phillip Morris, Hormel, and Nike, conspicuously omitting any lightbulbs or other GE products.[20]

News Making

The kind of news that the media present is affected by the organization and technology of news gathering and news production. It makes a difference where reporters are, what sources they talk to, and what sorts of video pictures are available.

WHERE THE NEWS COMES FROM   For national news, most reporters are located in Washington, D.C., site of the main federal government institutions, or in New York City, the biggest city and the center of media operations. This means that national news has a strong Washington–New York orientation. When big events happen elsewhere, reporters may be flown in, if there is time, or the work of local newspaper or television reporters may be transmitted to other parts of the country by wire services and the television networks.

The television networks and most newspapers cannot afford to station reporters in many cities outside Washington, D.C., and New York City. The networks usually just add Chicago, Los Angeles, Miami, and Houston or Dallas. Often significant stories from outside the main media centers simply do not make it into the national news. A study of the late 1980s, for example, found that 39 percent of all network coverage of state news was devoted to just four states: New York, California, Texas, and Florida.[21]

Newspapers print mostly wire service reports of news from elsewhere around the country. The television networks' assignment editors also rely on the wire services to decide what stories to cover; during one month that was studied, NBC got the idea for 70 percent of its domestic film stories from the wire services.[22]

Since it takes a long time (about six hours) to shoot pictures, transport them back to the studio, and process and edit them, most television news stories are assigned to predictable events—news conferences and the like—long before they happen, usually in one of the cities with a permanent television crew. For such spontaneous news as riots, accidents, and battles, special video camera crews can

During the Persian Gulf war, television networks were saturated with war footage released by the U. S. Defense Department as well as live CNN coverage of destruction in Baghdad and Jerusalem.

Near Baghdad, Iraq

be rushed to the location, but usually they arrive after the main events occur and have to rely on "reaction" interviews. If action pictures are obtained, they usually do not get to the studio until well after the event has happened (during the Vietnam War, most film came days late), and are edited into a generic story line so that it won't seem dated. Only a few exceptionally important, ongoing crises, like the Iraq war, are covered with live action footage sent by satellite.

Very few newspapers other than the *New York Times* can afford to station reporters abroad. Even the *Times* and the networks and wire services cannot cover most nations of the world on a regular basis. They keep reporters in the few countries that are of greatest interest to Americans—those that have big effects on American interests or enjoy close economic or cultural ties with the United States, such as Russia, Great Britain, Germany, Israel, Japan, and China. For other countries, they depend on "stringers" (local journalists who file occasional reports), or, in case of a few crises or other big events, they send in news teams on a temporary basis, like the armies of reporters who swarmed to Saudi Arabia during the Persian Gulf War.

Year in and year out, therefore, most media attention is devoted to limited areas of the world. A study of the late 1970s, for example, found that Western European countries were mentioned in 30 percent of international stories on network news, the Middle East in 30 percent, and Eastern Europe and the USSR in 19 percent; however, Latin America, Sub-Saharan Africa, and East Asia were each mentioned in fewer than 15 percent of the stories, and Canada and South Asia barely appeared at all. Coverage of Southeast Asia and the Pacific dropped from 34 percent to 9 percent after the Vietnam War ended.[23]

Beyond a few favorite nations, foreign news tends to be episodic. An unfamiliar country, such as Romania, Bangladesh, or Iraq suddenly jumps into the headlines with a spectacular story of a coup, a famine, or an invasion, which comes as a surprise to most people because they have not been prepared by background reports. For a few days or weeks, the story dominates the evening news, with intensive coverage through pictures, interviews, and commentaries. Then, if nothing new and exciting happens, the story grows "stale" and disappears from the media. Most viewers are left with a little more understanding of the country than they began with. This makes it difficult to form judgments about U.S. foreign policy.

OFFICIAL SOURCES   A newspaper reporter's work is usually organized around a particular "beat," which he or she checks every day for new stories. Most political beats center on some official government institution that regularly produces news, such as a local police station or city council, the White House, Congress, the Pentagon, an American embassy abroad, or a country's Foreign Ministry. Television news teams (except for White House reporters) are more apt to jump from one story to another, but they still mostly focus on official sources.

In fact, much of the news is created or originated by officials, not by reporters. Investigative reporting of the sort that Bernstein and Woodward did on Watergate is rare, because it is so time consuming and expensive. Most reporters get most of their stories quickly and efficiently from press conferences and the press releases that officials write, along with comments solicited from other officials.

One pioneering study found that government officials, domestic or foreign, were the sources of nearly three-quarters of all news in the *New York Times* and the *Washington Post*. Moreover, the vast majority—70–90 percent—of all news stories were drawn from situations over which the news makers had substantial control, such as press conferences (24.5 percent), interviews (24.7 percent), press releases (17.5 percent), and official proceedings (13 percent).[24] An exhaustive study of "CBS Evening News," "NBC Nightly News," *Newsweek*, and *Time*, found much the same thing. Most stories concerned "knowns" (famous people, especially officials) and their conflicts, decisions, and personnel changes; most stories came from official sources.[25] The same was true of wire service reports and local newspapers.

Reporters and officials work with each other every day and need each other. Reporters want stories; they have to cultivate access to people who can provide stories with quotes or anonymous "leaks." Officials want favorable publicity and want to avoid or counteract unfavorable publicity. Thus, a comfortable relationship tends to develop. Even when reporters put on a show of aggressive questioning at White House press conferences, for example, they usually work hard to stay on good terms with officials and to avoid fundamental challenges to their positions. This may be one reason that the local reporters Woodward and Bernstein made more progress on the Watergate story than the large White House press corps did. White House reporters eventually began to suspect that the president's press secretary and even the president himself were lying, but they were slow to confront them. Remember that Woodward and Bernstein themselves mostly relied on officials; they were fortunate to find middle-level officials who were estranged or guilt-ridden and would talk against the president. Interesting news often comes from angry or disenchanted officials.

The heavy reliance on official sources means that government officials may often be able to control, to a large extent, what journalists report and how they report it. The Reagan administration was particularly successful at agreeing on a "story of the day" and at having many officials feed that story to reporters, with a unified interpretation.[26]

PRESSURE   Occasionally, high officials resort to direct pressure or intimidation to affect how news is reported. In 1983, for example, a young *New York Times* reporter in El Salvador, named Ray Bonner, having traveled widely around the country, upset U.S. Ambassador Deane Hinton by filing stories that indicated that the antigovernment rebels there had substantial popular support, while the U.S.-backed government had engaged in terrorism, torture, and massacre of its own people. After the *Times*' executive editor flew to El Salvador and met with the ambassador, Bonner was replaced with a reporter who paid more attention to the embassy's daily press briefings about Communist threats to the "democratic" government of El Salvador.[27]

Pressure also can come from media owners and advertisers. The Cincinnati *Enquirer* virtually ignored the colossal scandal involving Charles Keating's Lincoln Savings & Loan company and fired a zealous editor who wanted to pursue it; the chairman of the *Enquirer* (and of the Associated Press) was Bill Keating, Charles's brother.[28] The Anchorage, Alaska, *Times*, which was purchased by Veco International, a company hired by Exxon to work on the enormous Exxon *Valdez*'s oil spill, illustrated stories of the cleanup with before-and-after pictures provided by, but not attributed to, Exxon.[29]

Advertisers, media owners, and high government officials mainly exert influence over media coverage quietly and inconspicuously, however, through the editors and producers who are hired and fired by media owners. Newspaper and magazine editors and television producers are the people who assign reporters to stories, review and edit their work, and decide what to print or put on the air. They exert control over journalists, not just by assigning, accepting or rejecting, and altering their stories, but also by administering praise, criticism, promotions, and advice. Successful reporters quickly learn what sorts of stories please their bosses and what sorts of stories don't, so that direct pressure is usually unnecessary.

Decisions about what kinds of news to print or to televise are largely explained in terms of professional judgments about what is "newsworthy." Exactly what makes a story newsworthy is difficult to spell out, but experienced editors make quick and confident judgments of what their audiences (and their employers) want. If they were consistently wrong, they would probably not remain editors for very long.

In practice, newsworthiness seems to depend upon such factors as novelty (man bites dog, not dog bites man); drama and human interest; relevance to the lives of Americans; high stakes (e.g., physical violence or conflict); and comprehensibility. Some trivial topics are judged newsworthy: during President Bush's first year in office, Millie, the Bush family dog, was mentioned in more television stories than were three Cabinet secretaries.[30] As the term "story" implies, news works best when it can be "framed" as a familiar kind of narrative: an exposé of greed or corruption, conflict between politicians, or a foreign affairs crisis. On television, of course, dramatic or startling film footage helps make a story gripping.

OBJECTIVITY   Political news does not make much sense without *interpretation* of what it means and whether it is good or bad. Under the informal rules of "objective" journalism, however, explicit interpretations by journalists are avoided, except for "commentary" or "editorials" that are labeled as such. Most interpretations are left implicit (making them hard to detect or argue with) or are given by "experts" who are interviewed for comments.

Experts are selected partly for reasons of convenience and audience appeal: scholars who live close to New York City or Washington, D.C., who like to speak in public, and who are good at coming up with colorful quotations on a variety of subjects are phoned again and again. They often show up on television to comment on the news of the day and even on issues that are far from their special expertise. At one time, the "king of quotes" was Norman Ornstein of the American Enterprise Institute, who in a single year was quoted more than 300 times by major print news organizations and at least as often by smaller newspapers.[31]

The experts and commentators featured in the media are often ex-officials and are usually in harmony with the political currents of the day; that is, they tend to reflect a fairly narrow spectrum of opinion close to that of the party in power in Washington, D.C., especially the party of the president. During the 1980s and early 1990s, for example, the experts most frequently quoted on television were a handful of former Reagan or Bush administration officials and others associated with conservative think tanks, such as the American Enterprise Institute and the Center for Strategic and International Studies. Experts from such liberal research organizations as the Institute for Policy Studies or the Institute for Defense Analysis barely appeared at all.[32] During the war with Iraq, of 878 "experts" quoted on network television news, only 1 was a national leader of a peace group.[33]

Anti-establishment journalist I. F. Stone in his office. Stone's *Weekly* gained much attention for its criticism of the Vietnam war. Most news in the U. S. media, however, comes from official sources.

During other administrations, different kinds of experts were favored, for example, the antipoverty warriors of the Johnson administration. But radical independent thinkers like Noam Chomsky or I. F. Stone, whose *Weekly* became influential for a time during the Vietnam War, have rarely penetrated the mainstream media at all.

Research centers and think tanks, such as the Hoover Institution, the Heritage Foundation, the Brookings Institution, and others, which publish policy-oriented books and articles and get good media exposure for their experts, are an important source of ideas and analyses that eventually work their way through the media to affect public opinion. These think tanks popularize and apply academic scholars' theories and findings to policy problems. They also serve as a channel through which corporations and large donors may affect the course of public opinion and public policy, since their funding comes heavily from corporate sources, which may influence what the foundations study and how they study it.

Is the News Biased?

Few subjects arouse more conflict and disagreement than the question of whether the mass media in the United States are biased in a liberal or a conservative direction. For years, a number of journalists and scholars have maintained that the media tend to be a proestablishment, conservative force, reflecting their corporate ownership and their dependence on official sources for news. During the 1970s and 1980s, conservative critics counterattacked, arguing that liberal media elites regularly published and broadcast antiestablishment, antiauthority news with a liberal bias.[34]

Surveys of reporters and journalists suggest that they tend to be somewhat more liberal than the average American—though by no means radical—on certain issues, including the environment, arms control, civil rights and liberties, abortion, and womens' rights.[35] This is especially true of those employed by the most elite media organizations: the *New York Times*, the *Washington Post*, CBS news, PBS, and the like. It is possible that reporters' liberalism has been reflected in the treatment of stories about such issues as nuclear energy, the greenhouse effect, and toxic waste.

Reporters' personal values probably affect what appears in the media, though there is little or no systematic evidence about the extent to which they actually do. Journalists' commitment to the idea of objectivity helps them resist temptation, as does critical scrutiny and rewriting by editors. And, in any case, the liberalism of journalists may be offset by conservatism among media owners and publishers.

The owners and top managers of most media corporations tend to be very conservative. The shareholders and executives in billion-dollar-a-year corporations are not very interested in undermining capitalism or, for that matter, in increasing their taxes or labor costs, or in offending their advertisers. These owners and managers ultimately decide which reporters, newscasters, and editors to hire or fire, to promote or discourage. Journalists who want to get ahead have to come to terms with the policies of those who own and run media businesses.

One sign of conservatism in the media is provided by newspapers' endorsements of presidential candidates, which are mostly decided upon by the owners and publishers of those newspapers. In every presidential election since 1964, more newspapers—usually many more—have backed the Republican than the Democratic candidate. In 1988, for example, one week before the election, 195 dailies had endorsed George Bush, whereas only 51 had endorsed Michael Dukakis.[36]

One reason that observers keep arguing about the question of bias is that it is not easy to define it exactly or to measure it. Some scholars simply have counted how many references to some political figure or policy (e.g., presidential candidate Richard Nixon or the Vietnam War) seemed to be positive or negative.[37] However, negative coverage may reflect objectively bad news, like Vietnam War casualties or the Watergate revelations, rather than bias, or the media may just be quoting what leading news sources are saying, whether the sources are right or wrong.

The idea of "bias" implies a deviation from some perfect representation of objective reality. Yet there is lots of room for argument about which aspects of reality are worth reporting (surely not all of it—not ordinary people eating and sleeping), what the facts are, and what is true and what is false. Is the truth whatever our best experts say it is? If so, who gets to decide who are the best experts?

DOMINANT POINTS OF VIEW   Even if we cannot be sure whether or not the media are biased, it is easy to identify certain tendencies in media coverage, certain beliefs that are assumed, and certain values and points of view that are emphasized while others seldom appear. Most news about foreign affairs, for example, takes a definitely American, patriotic, or *ethnocentric*, point of view. It focuses on things that interest and concern ordinary Americans, and tends to put the United States in a good light and its opponents in a bad light. Throughout the year 1980, for example, U.S. newspapers and television devoted enormous coverage to the fate of 49 American diplomats held hostage in the U.S. embassy in Teheran, Iran. Over the years, however, the slaughter of millions of people in Indonesia, Nigeria, East Timor, Cambodia, and other places have received much less attention—to say nothing of the day-to-day suffering of poor and oppressed people around the world, which goes on all the time and does not usually seem "newsworthy."

Ethnocentrism, together with a heavy reliance on U.S. government news sources, means that most foreign news coverage fits well with U.S. foreign policy.

In portraying dissenters (such as this peace protester), the media tend to emphasize the unusual, the violent, or the bizarre.

Studies show that, historically, the media have tended to go easy on such right-wing dictators as the Shah of Iran, Marcos of the Philippines, and Somoza of Nicaragua, as long as they are firm allies of the United States, even when they have been very unpopular with their own people.[38] On the other hand, the media tend to go along with the U.S. government in assuming the worst about official "enemies." During the Cold War, for example, the media publicized unsubstantiated accusations that the Soviet Union had tried to kill Pope John Paul II in 1982, had used germ warfare in Cambodia, and had deliberately shot down a Korean airliner in 1983.[39]

The broadcast charges of a "deliberate, unprovoked" Soviet attack on KAL 007 contrasts with the media's willingness in 1987 to believe that the United States' shooting down of an Iranian airliner was accidental.[40] The press's glorification of Lech Walesa, the labor leader who fought the Communist regime in Poland during the 1980s, contrasts with the muted treatment of reformist Catholic Archbishop Romero, harassed and ultimately assassinated by associates of the U.S.-backed regime in El Salvador.[41] Similarly, the U.S. media printed strong condemnations of Iraq's 1990 invasion of Kuwait, which produced few Kuwaiti casualties, but virtually ignored during the 1980s Iraq's aggressive war against Iran, involving chemical warfare and millions of dead and wounded. The difference is this: the U.S. government strongly opposed Iraq in 1990 but had quietly backed it against Iran earlier.

In foreign policy crisis situations, the reliance on official news sources means that the media sometimes propagate government statements that are false or misleading, as in the case of the Korean airliner or the announcement of unprovoked attacks on U.S. destroyers in the Gulf of Tonkin at the beginning of the Vietnam War. (Recall the Vietnam story in Chapter 5.) Secret information about such matters as the power of potential adversaries also can be controlled by the government. The widely publicized "missile gap" that led to a big arms buildup during the Kennedy years and the "window of vulnerability" that preceded the Reagan defense budget increases both turned out to be unfounded.[42] It is still unclear whether officials knew at the time that they were misleading the public.

The media are generally kind to incumbent presidents—at least popular presidents. Other officials and candidates are more vulnerable to scandal. The media gave much attention to allegations of womanizing and excessive drinking directed at Senator John Tower during his confirmation hearings to become Secretary of Defense.

Another tendency of the media is to run stories generally approving of our American-style capitalist economic system and disapproving of variants or alternative systems, like European social democracies. Individual corporations are criticized for errors and misdeeds, but the economic system itself is rarely challenged. This is hardly surprising, since most Americans like the U.S. system, but it discourages consideration of alternatives. Dissenters and demonstrators tend to be portrayed as "deviants," and only their tactics (especially violent tactics), not their ideas, tend to get media attention.[43] Even organized labor in the United States, unlike most other advanced industrial countries, has tended to get a bad press, with emphasis on corruption or strike disruptions rather than on the substance of labor's grievances.[44]

Incumbent politicians receive plenty of negative publicity when they are weakened and unpopular or when there is evidence of scandal in their personal or financial lives, which makes for dramatic human interest stories. The media made much of White House Chief of Staff John Sununu's "frequent flying" at the taxpayers' expense. But incumbents are essential news sources; in day-to-day coverage, most incumbents are treated with considerable respect and deference. Press coverage of the president tends to be especially favorable, while that of Congress has been more negative.[45] For the same reason, the views of the incumbent political party in Washington, D.C., especially the party of the president, tend to receive a lot of attention: the officials, experts, and commentators quoted in the media tend to come mostly from whichever party is in power.

To say that the media have these tendencies—whether we choose to call them "biases" or not—is to say that the media are influenced by the major structural and political forces in the United States. The position of the United States in the international system and the nature of the U.S. economic and social systems deeply affect every individual and institution in the country, including the media. The political forces that are dominant in the country at a given time also tend to dominate the media. This puts limits on how well the press can perform a watchdog function.

At the same time, most communications scholars agree that media coverage of political news has certain distinctive features that follow from specific characteristics of the mass media themselves, including the prevailing technology and organization of news gathering, corporate ownership, and the free enterprise need to appeal to mass audiences. These structural characteristics of the media mean that news, especially on television, tends to be *episodic, fragmented, personalized,* and *dramatic*, rather than sustained, analytical, or dispassionate.[46] As a result, the media provide less useful or enlightening political information to citizens than they might. The public's capacity to form intelligent opinions is weakened. Popular sovereignty and democracy suffer.

EFFECTS OF THE MEDIA ON POLITICS

The old idea that the mass media have only "minimal effects" on politics and don't really matter much is now discredited. The contents of the media do make a difference; they impact on public opinion and on policymaking in a number of different ways.

Several studies, for example, have demonstrated *agenda-setting* effects. The topics that get the most coverage in the media are the same ones that most people say are the "most important problems" facing the country. This correlation does not result just from the media printing what people are most interested in; it is a real effect of what appears in the media. In controlled experiments, people who are shown doctored television news broadcasts emphasizing a particular problem mention that problem as being important more often than people who see regular broadcasts.[47]

Of course, media managers don't arbitrarily decide what news to emphasize; their decisions reflect what is happening in the world and what American audiences care about. If there is a war or an economic depression, the media report lots of news about it. But some research has indicated that trends in what the media cover sometimes diverge from actual trends in problems (publicity about crime, for example, may reflect editors' fears or a few dramatic incidents, rather than a rising crime rate). When the two diverge, it seems to be the media's emphasis rather than real trends that affects public opinion.[48] Examples include periodic surges and declines of stories about the AIDS epidemic or about the drug problem.

Experiments also indicate that the media's **framing** or interpretation of stories affects how people think about political problems. Whether citizens ascribe poverty to laziness of the poor or to the nature of the economy, for example, depends partly on what kinds of stories (about poor individuals or about economic trends) the media run.[49]

What appears in the media also affects people's *policy preferences*. One study found that changes in collective public opinion (i.e., changes in the percentages of the public that favored various policies) could be predicted rather accurately by what sorts of stories were on the network television news between one opinion survey and the next. News from experts, commentators, and popular presidents had especially strong effects, while news attributed to interest groups had no impact or even a negative effect.[50]

By affecting what people think is important, how they understand problems, and what policies they want, media broadcasts and publications indirectly affect what government does, because the government responds to public opinion. In addition, the media affect who is elected to office; as we will see in Chapter 9, "Voting and Elections," media stories about the character of presidential and other candidates have enormous effects on fund raising and on citizens' judgments of who would make a good leader.

In addition, what appears in the media has a direct effect on policymaking. Policymakers learn about the world and about each other's activities from the media. Investigative journalism that exposes problems often leads state, local, and federal officials to act, whether or not the story is big enough to gain public attention or to change public opinion. A before-and-after study of an NBC news story on the "Home Health Hustle," for example, found a wave of effects among the public and policymakers.[51] Sometimes journalists and politicians actively work together: the journalists expose problems that the politicians want to solve, and then the politicians' statements, hearings, and bills prolong the story for journalists to continue reporting.

CENSORSHIP AND GOVERNMENT REGULATION

The government has less legal control over the media in the United States than in most other countries. In fact, the U.S. Constitution offers strong protections of freedom of the press. But the government does enforce various technical and substantive regulations on the electronic media.

Early in American history, the government sometimes interfered with the press in a heavy-handed way. Under the Alien and Sedition Acts of 1798, for example, several anti-Federalist newspaper editors were jailed for criticizing John Adams's administration. Subsequently, censorship often has been imposed in wartime. During the Civil War, the War Department required newspapers to clear all telegraphed information with the department; when that failed, they harassed reporters. During World War I, the Post Office Department refused to deliver 44 newspapers and magazines through the mail because of alleged pro-German or pro-Socialist content. And, as we saw in the last chapter, the distribution of anti-war leaflets could bring jail sentences. In World War II, the Office of Censorship

Coverage of the Persian Gulf war, even more than previous wars, was carefully controlled and censored by the U. S. military.

monitored all news entering and leaving the country, but it focused mainly on news about casualties and troop and ship movements rather than on political matters.[52]

Constitutional Protection

At least since several Supreme Court cases of the 1920s and 1930s, the press has enjoyed a great deal of constitutional protection. The First Amendment provision that Congress shall make no law "abridging freedom of speech, or of the press" has been upheld by the Supreme Court to prevent federal censorship of newspapers or magazines. Only under the most pressing circumstances of danger to national security can the government engage in "prior restraint" and prevent publication of material to which it objects.

On June 30, 1971, for example, the Supreme Court denied a request by the Nixon administration to restrain the *New York Times* and the *Washington Post* from publishing excerpts from the "Pentagon Papers," a secret Defense Department history of the U.S. involvement in Vietnam. The Court declared that "(t)he Government 'thus carries a heavy burden of showing justification for the enforcement of such a restraint.' . . . The Government had not met that burden."[53] Justice Hugo Black's stirring concurring opinion has become an important statement on freedom of the press (see "The Struggle for Democracy").

In a sense, however, the "Pentagon Papers" case was an easy one, because it concerned the right to publish a two-year-old history and analysis of past government actions, not information about current military or foreign policy actions that could jeopardize American lives. During wartime (including undeclared wars), the government has asserted broad powers to control what reporters can see and what they can print. During the war with Iraq, for example, the U.S. military imposed an elaborate system of control and censorship, requiring reporters to work only in escorted "pools," limiting their access to U.S. troops, and censoring their stories. The media—though they later protested—went along with this system at the time, and large majorities of the public approved of it.

Besides the constitutional limits on censorship, newspapers and magazines are also protected against most kinds of punishment after they have printed something. Punishable obscenity, for example, has been narrowly defined, and the Constitution has been interpreted as preventing libel laws from being used against publications that print truthful material or that comment upon public figures, as long as they take reasonable care not to spread damaging falsehoods. The Fourteenth Amendment now protects freedom of the press against action by state or local governments in the same way that the First Amendment constrains the federal government. (See Chapter 19, "Rights and Liberties.")

Although the government has many informal ways of influencing the press, then, there is little formal regulation of newspapers or magazines in the United States.

Electronic Media

The electronic media, however—radio and television—are more susceptible to direct government regulation, though such regulation is now very limited.

The federal government has broad powers to regulate use of the airwaves, which are considered to be public property. Ever since the passage of the Radio

THE
STRUGGLE
FOR
DEMOCRACY

★

*The Pentagon
Papers and
Freedom of
the Press*

In 1967, when the Vietnam War was going badly for the United States, Secretary of Defense Robert MacNamara commissioned a top-secret historical study to see exactly what had gone wrong. The Pentagon researchers spent 18 months and compiled 47 volumes of material on U.S. involvement in Southeast Asia. Their final report, submitted in January 1969, was a devastating account of misrepresentations, falsehoods, civilian bungling, military blunders, and deception by American officials.[a]

Two years later, in March 1971, Daniel Ellsberg (one of the Pentagon researchers) provided a copy of the report to the *New York Times*. The *Times* then spent three months agonizing over whether or not to publish it, with editors saying yes but business and legal people saying no. Finally, on June 13, 1971, the *Times* published six solid pages of excerpts from the report (which came to be known as the "Pentagon Papers") and promised nine more installments.

Outraged at what he considered a breach of national security, President Nixon had Attorney General Mitchell ask the *Times* to cease publication; when they refused, the government obtained a restraining order in Federal District Court and stopped the *Times* from publishing anything beyond the third installment. This was the first time since the Alien and Sedition Acts of 1798 that the American government had tried in advance to prevent a newspaper from publishing news or commentary.

But the *Washington Post*, after a brief internal struggle, took up where the *Times* had left off. When the attorney general went back to court and stopped the *Post*, 19 other newspapers in rapid succession continued publication. Furthermore, the newspapers that were stopped appealed their restraining orders to the Circuit Court of Appeal and finally to the Supreme Court.

On June 30, the U.S. Supreme Court ruled, by a vote of 6–3, in favor of the newspapers. The justices wrote nine separate opinions; two of the six that favored the newspapers did so on narrow grounds. The concurring opinion by Justice Hugo Black made the most eloquent case for absolute First Amendment protection of freedom of the press. Black wrote the following:

Paramount among the responsibilities of a free press is the duty to prevent any part of the Government from deceiving the people and sending them off to distant lands to die of foreign fever and foreign shot and shell. . . . The *New York Times* and the *Washington Post* and other newspapers should be commended for serving the purpose that the Founding Fathers saw so clearly. In revealing the workings of government that led to the Vietnam War, the newspapers nobly did precisely that which the founders hoped and trusted they would do."

---

[a]James Aronson, *The Press and the Cold War*, new and expanded ed. (New York: Monthly Review, 1990) pp. 292–295.

Act of 1927 and the Communications Act of 1934, which established the Federal Communications Commission (FCC), the government has licensed radio and television stations and has required them to observe a number of rules as a condition for obtaining licenses.[54] This is an example of how what we call *governmental* institutions (in this case, a regulatory agency in the executive branch) can affect institutions that we call *political* (the media and public opinion).

FCC rules specify the frequencies on which stations can broadcast and the amount of power that they can use, in order to prevent interference among broadcasters of the sort that had brought chaos to radio during the 1920s. Government regulations divide the VHF (Very High Frequency) television band into 12 channels and allocate them in such a way that most major cities have three VHF stations—the main reason for the emergence of three major networks.

For a long time, federal rules prohibited networks or anyone else from owning more than 5 VHF stations around the country. This was expanded to 12 stations in 1989 and entirely deregulated by 1990.[55] FCC rules also insisted on local control of programming, giving local affiliate stations considerable influence over the networks through "clearance" of national programs.

The FCC was mandated by Congress to regulate the airwaves for the "public interest, convenience, or necessity." This vague phrase has been interpreted to include "the development of an informed public opinion through the public dissemination of news and ideas concerning the vital public issues of the day," with ideas coming from "diverse and antagonistic sources," and with an emphasis on service to the local community. In practice, it has mainly meant FCC pressure (backed up by the threat of not renewing stations' licenses) to provide a certain number of hours of news and "public service" broadcasting. Thus, government regulation created an artificial demand for news programming, before it became profitable, and contributed to the rise of network news and its expansion from 15 to 30 minutes in 1963, as well as the development of documentaries and specials. As one network executive observed, "news, for most stations, is the price of the license."[56] In that way, government regulation contributed to informed public opinion and to democracy.

For many years, the **"fairness doctrine"** of 1949 required that licensees present contrasting viewpoints on any controversial issue of public importance that was discussed. This led to efforts at "balance"—presenting "two sides" on any issue that was mentioned—and sometimes to avoidance of controversial issues, though it was left mostly up to broadcasters to decide what was important or controversial and what constituted a fair reply and a fair amount of time to give it.

Fairness is not easy to define; which of the unlimited number of possible opinions deserve a hearing? The FCC itself long ago made clear that it did not intend to make time available to "Communist viewpoints," and both of the "two sides" have generally been quite mainstream. As the Reagan-appointed FCC moved in a conservative direction during the 1980s and criticized the "fairness doctrine," the Democratic-dominated Congress attempted to enact the doctrine into law in 1987, but President Reagan vetoed the bill. The FCC subsequently abolished the doctrine, ruling that it was unconstitutional.[57]

Similarly, the **"equal time" provision** of the 1934 Communications Act required that, *except* for news programs, stations that granted (or sold) air time to any one candidate for public office had to grant (or sell) other candidates equal time. This threatened to cause great expense for the media when minor party

Election year debates, like this one in 1988 between presidential candidates George Bush and Michael Dukakis, have become a regular feature on television.

candidates insisted on their share of air time or when opponents wanted to reply to political speeches by incumbent presidents in election years; it led to some curtailment of political programming. "Equal time" provisions were suspended in 1960 to allow televised debates between candidates John F. Kennedy and Richard Nixon, and, in 1976 and 1980, the FCC permitted the staging of the Ford-Carter and Carter-Reagan debates as "public meetings," sponsored by the League of Women Voters, to get around the provision. Then, in 1983, the FCC declared that radio and television broadcasters were free to stage debates at all political levels among candidates of their own choosing.[58]

In short, government regulation of the media does not presently amount to much. In recent years, many proposals have been made to regulate media treatment of political campaigns in order to avoid or to reduce the impact of brief, negative television advertisements. Ideas include outlawing short ads; requiring longer, issue-oriented discussions; or using public funds to pay for substantial blocks of air time that would be devoted to discussion of issues.

THE MASS MEDIA AND DEMOCRACY

Mass media are essential to the workings of democracy in a large modern nation. Without media, ordinary citizens would have little hope of learning what was happening abroad; they could not begin to think about what sorts of policies the United States should pursue in foreign affairs. Nor, without media, could most Americans learn what their government was doing domestically or what sorts of candidates were running for office. Hundreds of millions of Americans spread out over 4 million square miles of territory could not possibly communicate effectively by means of face-to-face contact or word of mouth.

Thus, the spread of mass media in the United States, and the penetration of newspapers, radio, and television into millions of homes, has undoubtedly helped democracy. It has made it much easier for ordinary citizens to form policy pref-

RESOURCE FEATURE

≈

How to be an Alert Media Consumer

Noam Chomsky, a famous linguist and one of the sharpest critics of the U.S. mass media, once wrote that he was mystified about why his teeth were wearing down, until his wife pointed out that he ground them in rage every time he read the *New York Times.*[a] But Chomsky and other careful observers manage to ferret out useful bits of information from the media, even when they think news stories are parroting the official line. If you yourself want to form your own judgment about the news media and get the most you can from them, here are some guidelines.

1. *Go beyond network television news.* Compare its coverage of issues with the coverage on television documentaries and in newspapers and magazines. Do news programs leave important things out? What? Why?

2. *Expand the points of view to which you are exposed.* Take a look at opinion magazines with which you generally disagree, and question your own beliefs. Which viewpoints are presented in the mainstream media, and which are not?

3. *Analyze news stories.* Watch out for stereotypes and simple plot lines. What concrete facts and evidence are offered? What are the news sources? Whose interests might the story serve? Whose viewpoint is left out?

4. *Read between the lines.* Watch for hints that the reporter does not really believe what a news source is saying. Watch for contradictions. Watch for stray facts that don't fit the story line, and try to make sense of them.

5. *Challenge what you read or see.* Ask what is assumed to be true simply because "everybody" believes it; are you sure it is correct? What has been left out? How would a person from another country—or from another planet—interpret the story?

[a]Noam Chomsky, "All the News That Fits: Noam Chomsky on the *New York Times,*" *Utne Reader* (February/March 1986), pp. 50–55.

erences, to judge the actions of government, and to figure out who they want to govern them. Mass media allow the "scope of conflict" to be broadened, so that citizens, rather than just political leaders or special-interest groups, can know what is going on and have a voice in politics.

At the same time, many advocates of democracy are highly critical of the media. We have seen that there are some grounds for criticism. Scholars who would like the media to be highly informative, analytical, and critical, are appalled at the personalized, episodic, dramatic, and fragmented character of most news stories, which do not provide sustained and coherent explanations of what is going on.[59]

Others worry about ideological biases from a leftist media elite or from a corporate-owned and fundamentally conservative media industry. Some criticize the media's nationalistic and ethnocentric tendencies to support official U.S. foreign policy at the cost of ignoring or misunderstanding important things that are happening in the world, or of passing along deliberate untruths. If the media systematically present one-sided or false pictures of politics, then people may form mistaken policy preferences, and government responsiveness to those preferences cannot be considered as constituting democracy.

We have pointed out some examples of media coverage that may mislead citizens, but we also have mentioned the great difficulty of defining or measuring "bias" systematically and the strong differences of opinion on this subject. Students should form their own judgments by reading and watching the media with a keen critical eye, alert to possible omissions or distortions. Some suggestions about how to do this are offered in the "Resource Feature" on page 207.

Aside from questions of bias, if the mass media fail to present informative, analytical, sophisticated coverage of political issues, doesn't that constitute a major flaw in democracy? A shortage of information certainly would seem to make it difficult for people to form intelligent judgments. On the other hand, some observers argue that people do not need a lot of detailed information; they just need to know what the issues are and what is advocated by the leaders or groups that they trust, who share their values.[60] Perhaps skimpy treatment of the news is enough, as long as it is not terribly biased and as long as diverse elite interpretations are offered. If so, the crucial question is whether political competition is working and whether contending political parties and groups are expressing diverse views in the media. If you believe that extensive public deliberation and discussion are essential to democracy, however, then such a minimal standard for the media will not suffice.

SUMMARY

There is disagreement about how well the media act as public watchdogs and how well they provide information about public policy and electoral choices.

The nature of the mass media in the United States largely has been determined by structural factors: technological developments (the invention of printing presses, wire services, radio, television, computers, and satellites), the growth of the American population and economy, and the development of a privately owned, corporation-dominated media industry.

The profit motive leads the major media to appeal to large audiences by limiting the quantity and depth of political news, by appealing to patriotism and other mainstream political values, and by emphasizing dramatic stories with visual impact and human interest. Media owners and advertisers sometimes shape the news to help (or to avoid hurting) their own businesses, or to express values supportive of free enterprise and the existing social system.

News making is organized around New York City, Washington, D.C., and a handful of major cities in the United States and abroad. Most foreign countries are ignored unless there are transient crises or other big stories to communicate. Most news comes from government officials, who cultivate friendly relations with the press and provide accessible press conferences and handouts, as well as sometimes pressure the media.

Observers disagree sharply about whether the media are biased in a liberal or a conservative direction. The liberal tendency of reporters probably tends to be balanced or reversed by conservative owners and by the editors that owners appoint. The U.S. media tend to reflect ethnocentrism; support for U.S. foreign policy; support for American-style capitalism; and generally favorable treatment of politicians in power, except for the publicizing of personal scandals and of criticizing officials who have lost popularity.

Media stories have substantial effects on the public's perceptions of problems, its interpretations of events, its evaluations of political candidates, and its policy preferences.

The media are protected from many kinds of government interference by the First Amendment to the Constitution. But censorship occurs during wars and crises; officials have indirect ways of influencing the news; and the electronic media are subject to direct regulations. Formal regulations of content, however, like the "fairness doctrine" and "equal time" provisions, have lapsed. Possible regulation of negative campaign ads and other matters are under discussion.

The media provide citizens with political information that is essential to the working of democracy. At the same time, however, many observers criticize the media for not being sufficiently informative or analytical. Others worry about possible liberal or conservative biases, or about tendencies to support official policy. Students are advised to scrutinize the media carefully and skeptically, to make use of the available information, and to form their own judgments.

To Ponder

1. Is the news biased? If so, how? Is objectivity possible?

2. Do the media present enough enlightening political information and analysis?

3. In what ways, if any, would you want television news to be different? How could such a change be brought about? Would people watch such improved news?

4. What are the advantages and disadvantages of government-operated news media, as opposed to free enterprise journalism?

Suggested Readings

Bagdikian, Ben. *The Media Monopoly*, 2nd ed. Boston: Beacon Press, 1987.
 Analyzes the corporate structure of the media and its consequences.

Bennett, W. Lance. *News: Politics of Illusion*, 2nd. ed. New York: Longman, 1988.
 A critique of the news as trivial and uninformative.

Bernstein, Carl, and Bob Woodward. *All the President's Men*. New York: Simon & Schuster, 1974.
 Tells how the *Washington Post* reporters pursued the Watergate story.

Entman, Robert M. *Democracy Without Citizens: Media and the Decay of American Politics*. New York: Oxford University Press, 1989.
 Discusses biases, effects of the media, and how to improve journalism.

Gans, Herbert J. *Deciding What's News*. New York: Random House, 1979.
 A thorough, inside look at several major news organizations.

Graber, Doris. *Mass Media and American Politics*, 3rd ed. Washington, D.C.: *Congressional Quarterly*, 1989.
 A basic textbook on the subject.

Herman, Edward S., and Noam Chomsky. *Manufacturing Consent: The Political Economy of the Mass Media*. New York: Pantheon, 1988.
 Offers evidence for a "propaganda model" of news as serving U.S. foreign policy.

Lichter, S. Robert, Stanley Rothman, and L. S. Lichter. *The Media Elite*. Bethesda, MD: Adler and Adler, 1986.
 A critique of journalists as liberal and antiauthority.

Parenti, Michael. *Inventing Reality: The Politics of the Mass Media*. New York: St. Martin's, 1986.
 A critique of the media as conservative servants of the economic and political system.

Notes

1. Carl Bernstein and Bob Woodward, *All the President's Men* (New York: Simon & Schuster, 1974) tells the reporters' own story of their pursuit of the Watergate story. Len Colodny and Robert Getler, *Silent Coup* (New York: St. Martin's, 1991), discusses Woodward's background in Naval Intelligence and his past connections with Alexander Haig (who may have been Deep Throat) and other military men apparently disillusioned with Nixon.

2. Gladys Engel Lang and Jurt Lang, *The Battle for Public Opinion: The President, the Press, and the Polls During Watergate* (New York: Columbia University Press, 1983), ch. 3 and p. 51.

3. Walter Lippman, Address in London, May 27, 1965.

4. *New York Times*, March 24, 1984, p. A5.

5. Doris Graber, *Mass Media and American Politics*, 3rd ed. (Washington, D.C.: *Congressional Quarterly*, 1989), p. 36.

6. Nicols Fox, "Seige of the First Amendment," in *Washington Journalism Review* (December 1990), p. 44.

7. Bernard Roshco, *Newsmaking* (Chicago: University of Chicago Press, 1975), ch. 3, gives a good, brief history of the daily press in America.

8. James Keogh, *President Nixon and the Press* (Ramsey, NJ: Funk & Wagnalls, 1972), p. 17.

9. Edward Jay Epstein, *News from Nowhere: Television and the News* (New York: Vantage, 1973), p. 51.

10. *The World Almanac 1991* (New York: Scripps-Howard), p. 312.

11. *The World Almanac 1991*, p. 318.

12. Graber, *Mass Media*, p. 4.

13. "Videotape of Beating by Officers Puts Full Glare on Brutality Issue," *New York Times*, March 18, 1991, p. A1.

14. Telephone conversation with Paul Kagan and Associates, Inc., Carmel, California, summer 1990.

15. Ben Bagdikian, *The Media Monopoly*, 2nd ed. (Boston: Beacon Press, 1987), pp. 20–26; Graber, *Mass Media*, p. 45.

16. Bagdikian, *Media Monopoly*, p. 74.

17. *Enclyclopedia Britannica*, Book of the Year, 1989, p. 285.

18. Graber, *Mass Media*, p. 328.

19. Graber, *Mass Media*, p. 57.

20. Todd Putnam, "The GE Boycott: A Story NBC Wouldn't Buy," *Extra!* (January/February 1991), pp. 4–5.

21. Graber, *Mass Media*, p. 90.

22. Epstein, *News from Nowhere*, p. 142.

23. James F. Larson, "International Affairs Coverage on U.S. Evening Network News, 1972–1979," in William C. Adams, ed., *Television Coverage of International Affairs* (Norwood, NJ: Ablex, 1982), p. 37.

24. Leon V. Sigal, *Reporters and Officials: The Organization and Politics of News Reporting* (Lexington, MA: D. C. Heath, 1973), p. 124.

25. Herbert J. Gans, *Deciding What's News: A Study of CBS Evening News, NBC Nightly News, Newsweek, and Time* (New York: Random House, 1979), pp. 9, 10, 16, and ch. 4.

26. Mark Hertsgaard, *On Bended Knee* (New York: Farrar, Straus, & Giroux, 1988), p. 5.

27. Michael Massing, "About-Face on El Salvador," *Columbia Journalism Review* (November/December 1983), pp. 42–49.

28. *Washington Monthly*, May 1990, p. 57.

29. *Washington Monthly*, July/August 1990, p. 48.

30. *Washington Monthly*, February 1990, p. 44.

31. Steven Waldman, "The King of Quotes: Why the Press Is Addicted to Norman Ornstein," *Washington Monthly* (December 1986), p. 34.

32. Marc Cooper and Lawrence C. Soley, "All the Right Sources," *Mother Jones* (February/March 1990), pp. 20–27, 45–48.

33. *Extra!* Vol. 4, No. 3 (May 1991), p. 5.

34. Peter Braestrup, *Big Story: How the American Press and Television Reported and Interpreted the Crisis of Tet 1968 in Vietnam and Washington,* 2 vols. (Boulder, CO: Westview Press, 1976).

35. William Schneider and I. A. Lewis, "Views on the News," *Public Opinion,* Vol. 8 (August/September 1985), p. 7; Karlyn Keene et al., "Monitoring Media Attitudes," *The American Enterprise* (July/August 1990), p. 95; S. Robert Lichter, Stanley Rothman, and L. S. Lichter, *The Media Elite* (Bethesda, MD: Adler and Adler, 1986).

36. *Editorials on File,* Vol. 19, No. 21 (November 1–15, 1988), p. 1272.

37. Edith Efron, *The News Twisters* (Los Angeles: Nash, 1971).

38. William A. Dorman and Mansour Farhang, *The U.S. Press and Iran: Foreign Policy and the Journalism of Deference* (Berkeley, CA: University of California Press, 1987); Raymond Bonner, *Waltzing with a Dictator: The Marcoses and the Making of American Policy* (New York: Times Books, 1987).

39. Edward S. Herman and Noam Chomsky, *Manufacturing Consent: The Political Economy of the Mass Media* (New York: Pantheon, 1988).

40. Robert Entman, "Hegemonic Socialization, Information Processing, and Presidential News Management: Framing the KAL and Iran Air Incidents," paper delivered at the 1990 annual meeting of the American Political Science Association, San Francisco; Seymour Hersh, *The Target Is Destroyed: What Really Happened to Flight 007 and What America Knew About It* (New York: Random House, 1986).

41. Hertsgaard, *On Bended Knee,* p. 71.

42. Fred Kaplan, *The Wizards of Armageddon* (New York: Simon & Schuster, 1983); Tom Gervasi, *The Myth of Soviet Military Supremacy* (New York: HarperCollins, 1986).

43. Todd Gitlin, *The Whole World Is Watching* (Berkeley, CA: University of California Press, 1980).

44. Michael Parenti, *Inventing Reality: The Politics of the Mass Media* (New York: St. Martin's, 1986).

45. Graber, *Mass Media,* pp. 237, 263.

46. W. Lance Bennett, *News: Politics of Illusion,* 2nd ed. (New York: Longman, 1988).

47. Shanto Iyengar and Donald R. Kinder, *News That Matters* (Chicago: University of Chicago Press, 1987).

48. G. Ray Funkhauser, "The Issues of the Sixties: An Exploratory Study in the Dynamics of Public Opinion," *Public Opinion Quarterly,* Vol. 37 (Spring 1973), pp. 62–75.

49. Shanto Iyengar, *Is Anyone Responsible? How Television News Frames Political Issues* (Chicago: University of Chicago Press, 1991).

50. Benjamin I. Page, Robert Y. Shapiro, and Glenn R. Dempsey, "What Moves Public Opinion?," *American Political Science Review,* Vol. 81 (1987), pp. 23–43.

51. Fay Lomax Cook, et al. "Media and Agenda Setting: Effects on the Public, Interest Group Leaders, Policy Makers, and Policy," *Public Opinion Quarterly,* Vol. 47 (Spring 1983), pp. 16–35.

52. Jean Folkerts and Dwight C. Teeter, *Voices of a Nation: A History of the Media in the U.S.* (New York: Macmillan, 1989), pp. 214, 348–349, 456–457.

53. *New York Times Co. v. United States,* 403 U.S. 713 (1971).

54. Epstein, *News from Nowhere,* ch. 2.

55. Bagdikian, *Media Monopoly,* p. 15.

56. Epstein, *News from Nowhere,* pp. 48, 60.

57. Graber, *Mass Media,* p. 119; see also pp. 114–199.

58. Graber, *Mass Media,* p. 115.

59. Bennett, *News.*

60. Benjamin I. Page and Robert Y. Shapiro, *The Rational Public: Fifty Years of Trends in Americans' Policy Preferences* (Chicago: University of Chicago Press, 1991).

7

*Interest Groups
and
Corporations
in American
Politics*

INTEREST GROUPS AND THE SAVINGS AND LOAN CRISIS

Most experts believe that the federal bailout of the failed savings and loan industry will cost American taxpayers more than $500 billion. This bailout, by far the largest in American history, will cost every man, woman, and child more than $2,000. It will also make it difficult to pay for urgent health, education, and environmental needs in the years ahead. Though the disaster had many authors, principal among them were interest groups representing business in general and the savings and loan industry in particular.

The banking, securities, and savings and loan industries had been closely regulated by the federal government since the 1930s, when some of the more reckless practices of the financial community helped bring on the Great Depression. During the 1970s, however, the financial community and a wide range of conservative and business interest groups pressed political leaders to loosen the government's regulatory hand, arguing that regulation was imposing an unnecessary burden on American enterprises, interfering with the efficiencies of the market, and making American products noncompetitive in world markets. This massive lobbying effort helped change the regulatory climate in the nation's capitol during the Carter administration. The election in 1980 of Ronald Reagan, who ran on a platform pledging to "get government off of the backs of the American people," further encouraged the deregulation sentiment.

Nowhere was deregulation to have greater impact than on the savings and loan industry in which conservative investment strategies based on home mortgage loans had long been mandated by law. Under intense lobbying pressure from individual savings and loan associations in congressional districts and the U.S. League of Savings Institutions (the industry trade association acknowledged as "among the most effective and influential in Washington"[1]), Congress gradually deregulated the industry. Congress listened, because the savings and loan industry contributed a lot of money to members of Congress ($1.78 million during the 1988 elections), particularly to key members of the House and Senate banking committees. Congress obliged by removing limits on the interest rates that savings and loan institutions (S&Ls) could pay on their deposits, and by allowing them to lend money on commercial ventures in addition to home mortgages. Congress also increased the federal guarantee on deposits in the S&Ls from $40,000 to $100,000.

President Ronald Reagan, whose campaign also was heavily supported by the industry, added to the deregulatory climate by appointing a close friend of the savings and loan industry to head the Federal Home Loan Bank Board (or the FHLBB), the principal federal regulatory agency in this field. The Board eased regulations on how the "thrifts" could be run, who could run them, and how they could invest their money.

213

These legislative and administrative changes allowed "thrifts" to move into riskier commercial and real estate loans, to decrease their accounting and reporting requirements, and to reduce the level of reserves required to back loans. This substantial decrease in federal oversight of the savings and loans institutions, and the higher federal deposit insurance limits (the provision to double deposit insurance was written by the chief lobbyist of the U.S. League of Savings Institutions) made the "thrifts" virtually risk-free for investors and served to attract them in droves. As Anthony Lewis put it in the *New York Times*, "soon financial cowboys were taking over many of the institutions and lending money on very risky ventures. . . ."

The "high-roller" S&Ls were particularly active in Texas, and, when the economy of that state hit the skids in the mid-1980s, they were dragged down with it. Risky loans and speculative practices can pay off, especially when the economy is rapidly expanding. But such practices invite disaster when the economy stagnates or declines, and real estate values go down instead of up, as they did in Texas. Firms like Empire Savings and Loan were left out on a limb. Once a small conservative "thrift," it had begun to grow at an astonishing rate during the early 1980s, doubling in size every few months. Investigators later learned that its growth was based on "land flips" (repeatedly buying and selling the same piece of property with other thrifts, pocketing large fees for each transaction) and massive loans to real estate development companies that were building thousands of apartments and condominiums during a time when vacancy rates were at record high levels. Vernon Savings and Loan was not only involved in similar risky business activities (in the end, 96 percent of its loans proved to be in default) but also paid for its owner's yacht, airplanes, a California beach home, club memberships, and $100 per day for flowers. Empire and Vernon were not atypical; their practices were common throughout the state. When a majority of their risky loans proved to be noncollectible, many went into receivership, with the insurance bill for lost depositors' accounts landing squarely in the lap of the federal government and the taxpayers.

In those few instances when the FHLBB took action against particularly egregious behavior, influential members of Congress of both parties sometimes intervened to protect the company. Speaker of the House Jim Wright pressured the Bank Board to stop "hounding" Texas thrifts and delayed legislation that would have tightened regulation. Also noteworthy was the case of Lincoln Savings and Loan of California and its flamboyant president, Charles Keating. The company appeared to be in serious trouble in 1987, and the FHLBB was anxious to shut it down before things got worse. Five U.S. senators met with the head of the FHLBB and with bank examiners involved in the case in April to plead the case of Lincoln and to prevent a federal takeover. It was later revealed that the owner of Lincoln Savings and Loan had contributed $1.3 million to the campaigns of these five senators, including contributions totaling $897,000 to Senator Alan Cranston (D) of California. Federal action was delayed for two more years. When asked whether these contributions had influenced the senators, Keating said, "I want to say in the most forceful way that I can, I certainly hope so."[2] When Lincoln collapsed in 1989, the bailout bill came to $2.5 billion.

This story highlights the important role played by interest groups in American politics, the subject of this chapter. The chapter also looks at the political activities of business corporations and the debate about how much influence they wield. Our goal is to understand better the relationship between interest groups and democracy. We want to know whether popular sovereignty, political equality, and political liberty are enriched or diminished by the activities of interest groups. To answer these queries, however, we must first understand how structural, political, and governmental factors shape interest groups and what they do.

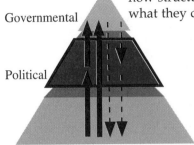

Governmental

Political

Structural

WHAT ARE INTEREST GROUPS?

Interest groups are private organizations that try to shape public policy. They are made up of individuals or other organizations that share an interest that they are trying to protect or advance with the help of government. To do this, interest groups try to influence the behavior of political decision makers, such as presidents, members of Congress, executive branch officials, or judges. These efforts are often perceived by decision makers as constituting pressure on them, so interest groups are often called **pressure groups**. The term "**lobbies**" is also commonly used, as in references to the "dairy lobby" or the "gun lobby." This term comes from a long history of interest groups' representatives collaring members of Congress in the lobbies, cloakrooms, and hallways of the Capitol building. Interest groups today, however, do far more than lobby in the traditional meaning of the term.

WHAT ROLE FOR INTEREST GROUPS IN A DEMOCRATIC SOCIETY?

The Evils of Faction

Interest groups have not had a good press. They are usually regarded as narrowly self-interested, out for themselves, and without regard for the public good. The dangers to good government from special interest groups is a familiar theme in American politics.

The theme appears in *The Federalist* No. 10, in which James Madison defines *factions* (his term for interest groups) in the following manner: ". . . a number of citizens, whether amounting to a majority or a minority of the whole, who are united and actuated by some common impulse of passion, or of interest, adverse to the rights of other citizens or to the permanent and aggregate interests of the community."[3]

Though Madison worried about factions, he believed that they were inevitable in a free society, in which people have diverse interests based on economic circumstance, property ownership, occupation, and region. "The causes of faction," he pointed out, "are sown in the nature of man."[4] To try to eliminate them would require tyranny. The remedy would be "worse than the disease."[5] The only alternative, he believed, was to organize constitutional government in a way that would moderate the bad effects of factions and to have a society that would be so

In the late nineteenth century, most Americans thought of the Senate as the captive of the "trusts" and other special interests. Here is the popular Keppler cartoon "Bosses of the Senate" on that subject.

large that no single faction could dominate public life. Factions could neither be eliminated nor made to serve the public good; their bad effects could only be controlled. This is hardly a ringing endorsement.

The theme of selfish special interests has recurred throughout American history. President Andrew Jackson attacked the Bank of the United States and its supporters as a selfish special-interest group during the presidential campaign of 1832. During the Progressive Era at the turn of the century, journalists like Ida Tarbell, Lincoln Steffens, Upton Sinclair, and Frank Norris (known collectively as the **muckrakers**) made the theme of the unholy alliance of the **trusts** (the Sugar Trusts, the Oil Trust, the Bank Trust, and so on), lobbyists (the Railroad Lobby, the Steel Lobby, and more), and corrupt public officials a centerpiece of political life.

In our own day, Ralph Nader and other consumer advocates have revived the theme of selfish interests as one of the central ideas in their successful effort to increase the regulatory role of government. Democratic presidential candidate Walter Mondale learned to his regret during the 1984 campaign that a string of endorsements from such organizations as the AFL-CIO and the American Federation of Teachers could all too easily allow his Republican opponents to label him the "special-interest" candidate.

Groups as Instruments of Democracy

For many political scientists, however, interest groups do not hurt democracy and the public interest but are an important instrument to attain both. The argument of **pluralist** political scientists is shown in Figure 7.1 and is as follows:[6]

- Free elections, while essential to a democracy, do not adequately communicate the wants and interests of the people to political leaders. At most, elections allow voters to decide who shall hold public office. Elections do not readily communicate what the people want in terms of policy. This is better communicated to political leaders on a day-to-day basis by the many groups and organizations to which people belong.

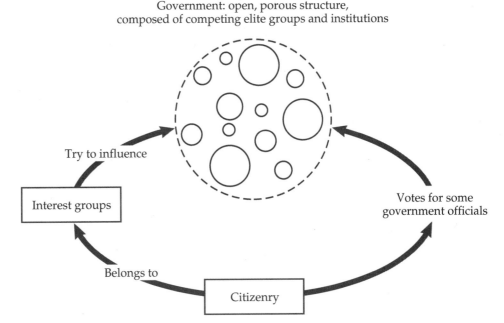

Figure 7.1 The pluralist view of how American politics work

Source: Edward S. Greenberg, The American Political System, *5th ed. (Glenview, IL: Scott, Foresman, 1989).*

- The interest group system is democratic, because people in the United States are free to join or to organize groups that reflect their interests. While inequalities give certain groups of people an advantage over others in forming groups, groups are so easy to form that perfectly ordinary American citizens are able to create them without too much difficulty.

- The interest group system is democratic, because American government is open to the influence of groups once they are formed. Because of federalism, checks and balances, and the separation of powers, government power in the United States is broadly dispersed, making governmental institutions remarkably porous and open to the entreaties of the many and diverse groups that exist in society. The ease of group formation and the accessibility of government means that any and all interests in society can have their views taken into account by some political decision maker.

Pluralists see interest groups, not as a problem, but as an additional tool of democratic representation, similar to other democratic instruments, such as public opinion and elections.

INTEREST GROUP FORMATION: STRUCTURAL, POLITICAL, AND GOVERNMENTAL INFLUENCES

Nobody knows exactly how many interest groups exist in the United States. Experts agree, however, that the number has increased dramatically since 1968. Much of the increase is accounted for by the creation of new kinds of organizations: "public-interest" or citizen groups organized around some cause or idea, rather than an economic or occupational interest. These include environmental, consumer, civil rights, and women's organizations, as well as ideological organizations like the Committee on the Present Danger (a conservative foreign policy organization) and CISPES (an organization opposed to U.S. intervention in Central America). However, while the proliferation of "public-interest" groups has garnered most of the attention, business, producer, and occupational groups still dominate by their sheer numbers: one study done during the Reagan years showed that corporations made up 52 percent of all organizations having Washington, D.C., representatives, that trade and other business associations accounted for another 20 percent, and that professional associations accounted for an additional 8 percent.[7]

Structural factors account for most of what the interest group system looks like. Interest groups seem to flourish when there are many interests, where the political culture supports the pursuit of private interests, where the rules make it easy to organize such interests, and where government is sufficiently active that its policies have consequences for private parties.

Diverse Interests

The United States, as we learned in Chapter 4, is a diverse and complex society. We are a nation of many races, religions, and ethnic groups distributed across a vast continent. Work and occupations have become more complex as agricultural and craft pursuits have been augmented by factory, office, and laboratory occupations. The economy has changed from one of small competitive firms, substantial income, and wealth equality to one characterized by national and global corporations, and substantial distances between the rich and the poor. Technological and scientific developments have produced a host of new products, problems, ways of life, and occupations. These trends have contributed to diversification and complexity, and an inevitable multiplication of interests.

The Political Culture

The United States is a place that honors the pursuit of private, particular, and narrow interests. In classical liberalism (see Chapter 4), the pursuit of self-interest is not only permitted but also celebrated as the basis of the good and prosperous society. To be sure, classical liberalism deplores an activist government. But, as Adam Smith pointed out in his classic work on market capitalism, *The Wealth of Nations*, people are by nature self-interested and will take advantage of whatever opportunities present themselves. If opportunities present themselves in the form of getting government to do something that might be helpful, then so be it.

The Rules of the Game

The rules of the political game in the United States encourage the formation of interest groups. The First Amendment to the Constitution, for instance, guarantees citizens the right to speak freely, to assemble, and to petition the government, all of which are essential to the ability of citizens to form organizations for the advancement of their interests before government. Moreover, the government is organized in such a way that decision makers are relatively accessible to interest groups. Because of federalism, checks and balances, and the separation of powers, there is no dominant center of decision making as there is in such unitary states as Great Britain and France. Instead, important decisions are made by many officials, on many matters, in many jurisdictions. Consequently, there are many more places where interest group pressure can be effective. Finally, there are no strong centralized political parties in the United States that might serve to overcome the decentralized, fragmented quality of the policymaking process in the United States, as there are in the European democracies. The upshot is easy group access.

The Growth in Government

Government does far more today than it did during the early years of the Republic. As government takes on more responsibilities, it quite naturally comes to have a greater impact on virtually all aspects of economic, social, and personal life. People, groups, and organizations are increasingly affected by the actions of government, so the decisions made by presidents, members of Congress, bureaucrats, and judges have increased relevance. It would be surprising, indeed, if, in response, people, groups, and organizations did not try harder to influence the decisions made by public officials.

Disturbances

The formation of interest groups is possible in the United States because of the freedom of citizens to express themselves and to form organizations, by the fragmented and decentralized organization of government that makes political decision makers accessible, and by a political culture that celebrates the pursuit of self-interest. These *enabling* conditions explain why interest groups are possible at all.

The number of interest groups increases as society becomes more complex and diverse (thus proliferating interests) and as government assumes a greater role in society, thereby affecting the lives of more and more Americans. These *encouraging* conditions help explain why there has been a steady increase in the number and kinds of interest groups since World War II.

These *enabling* and *encouraging* conditions, however, don't tell us enough about how and why interest groups form. The proliferation of interests does not seem to lead to the formation of groups unless these interests are threatened in some way, usually by economic and social change.

This is known as the "disturbance" theory of interest group formation.[8] Examples consistent with this theory are common. Thus, farmers formed the Grange in the late nineteenth century when their way of life was threatened by banking and railroad practices.[9] The successes of the consumer movement and the environmental protection movements during the late 1960s and the early 1970s played an important role in the creation of hundreds of political action committees (PACs) by corporations that felt threatened.[10]

Incentives

Some social scientists argue that people do not form groups when their common interests are threatened unless the group can give back some selective benefit to them.[11] A *selective benefit* is a benefit that is available to members but not to non-

Discontent among American farmers in the late nineteenth century led to the formation of protest organizations and, eventually, the Populist party. This is a rendering of a meeting of the Grange where farmers are expressing their discontent.

members. If someone can get the benefit without joining the group, then joining makes no sense. He or she would be a **free-rider** (along for the ride without contributing). This tends to come into play when a group is interested in some *collective good*, a governmental program that will assist all members of some category whether they belong to a formal organization or not. All wheat farmers, for instance, benefit from programs of governmental price supports for wheat and need not join the National Wheat Growers Association to get the benefit. To the extent that people do join, Olson argues, it is because the association has benefits that are available only to its members, like discounted life and health insurance programs for members of the Wheat Growers Association.

This theory of how groups form emphasizes how difficult and unlikely it is that they are formed at all. It cannot account, therefore, for the great proliferation of interest groups since the end of the World War II and the upsurge in group formation during the 1960s and 1970s, especially of the "public-interest" and ideological variety.[12] The proliferation of such groups suggests that groups form, not only around material and selective incentives, but also around *purposive* (ideological, issue-oriented) and *solidaristic* (the sense of being part of something that one values) incentives as well. People join groups, for instance, because they believe in a particular cause (like nuclear disarmament, civil rights, prayer in the public schools, or an end to abortion) or because they enjoy the companionship or social life afforded by belonging to a group.

THE DIVERSITY OF INTEREST GROUPS

There are two ways of categorizing interest groups: by organizational form or by type of interest represented.

By Organizational Form

Interest groups come in a variety of forms. Let's look at the most common ones.

THE SINGLE ENTERPRISE AS INTEREST GROUP   It is increasingly common for a single company—usually but not always a very large corporation—to maintain a Washington, D.C., office in order to keep an eye on administrative, legislative, and judicial actions that might affect the company and to convey the company point of view at important points in the policymaking process. In the past, single enterprises hired Washington, D.C., lawyers or "consultants" to carry out these tasks. Today, it is common for major corporations to have their own Washington, D.C., office. The expansion has been spectacular. During the 1970s, the number of Washington, D.C., offices of corporations increased by more than 500 percent, and the size of the average office of each of them experienced a similar expansion.[13]

THE INDIVIDUAL MEMBERSHIP ORGANIZATION   At the opposite end of the spectrum are interest groups that depend on large numbers of members as the basis of their influence. Members of Congress and the White House are often impressed with the views of groups that can claim thousands of members who are likely to go to the polls at election time. Their voice is even more likely to be heard if the membership is made up of people willing and able to make financial contributions to individual candidates or to the association's political action committee. Large-membership organizations with substantial resources, like the American Medical Association, the American Bar Association, the National Rifle Association, and the National Board of Realtors, can usually gain a hearing for their views in Washington, D.C.

THE ORGANIZATION OF ORGANIZATIONS   Some interest groups are made up of other organizations. Because they are usually comprised of organizations from all parts of the country, represent important economic interests, and affect the be-

Once a sleepy street, K Street in Washington, D.C., is now the headquarters location of many of the nation's interest groups.

havior of many potential voters, these so-called peak associations can be very influential in the Washington, D.C., pressure system. Familiar organizations of organizations include the U.S. Chamber of Commerce (made up of local chambers of commerce), the AFL-CIO (made up of a majority of the nation's labor unions), and the Business Roundtable (made up of the chief executive officers of the nation's largest corporations). Trade associations, made up of business firms in a single industry (like the National Association of Homebuilders and the American Bankers Association), are also active and influential in all aspects of the Washington, D.C., political scene and in most state capitals.

THE STAFF ORGANIZATION AS INTEREST GROUP Many "public-interest" or citizens groups with offices in Washington, D.C., are small-scale organizations run by a professional staff, with a very small membership base, financed by a few wealthy contributors interested in a cause or by grants from private foundations. One study found that almost one-third of all public-interest groups had no membership whatsoever, that over one-half had no way for members to affect the decisions of the interest group (for those that had membership), and that more than two-thirds had no local chapters.[14] Some of the more familiar associations in this category include the American Conservative Union, the Center for Auto Safety, the Liberty Lobby, and Zero Population Growth.

By Type of Interest Represented

Another way to think about interest groups is in terms of the type of interest they represent. The most common distinction made is between economic and noneconomic groups. The former has some economic stake that it wishes to protect or to advance by means of government action. The latter is motivated by a desire to see a set of ideas form the basis of public policy (liberal or conservative ideology, for instance), to advance a general cause, such as civil rights or environmental protection, or to bring a single issue to the attention of policymakers (gun control, an end to abortion, and so on).

ECONOMIC INTEREST GROUPS *Producer groups* represent enterprises that produce some good or service. In this group, we would include business and agriculture. Because of the vast resources at their disposal and because of their strategic role in the health of the economy, these groups wield enormous power in Washington, D.C. Agriculture has more than held its own over the years through such organizations as the American Farm Bureau Federation and scores of commodity groups—the American Dairy Association and the American Wheat Growers Association are good examples. Business seems to have enhanced its influence in recent years considerably.

Professional groups represent the interests of professionals, such as doctors, lawyers, and dentists. Because of their importance in local communities and because of their ability to make substantial campaign contributions, such organizations are very influential in the policymaking process on matters close to their professional expertise and concerns.

Though *labor unions* are sometimes involved in what might be called "public-interest" type activities (advancing a liberal ideology and supporting civil rights legislation, let's say), their main role in the United States has been to protect the jobs of their members and to gain maximum wage and benefit levels for them.

President Reagan sent a message to organized labor when he fired striking air traffic controllers early in his first administration.

Unlike labor unions in most of the rest of the world, which are as much political and ideological organizations as economic ones, American labor unions are conventionally described as "bread and butter" unions. Their lobbying activities in Washington, D.C., tend to revolve around legislation, judicial interpretations, and administrative rulings that affect their ability to protect the jobs of their members and to maintain or increase the size of union membership rolls.

Most observers of the Washington, D.C., scene are convinced that the political power of labor unions in Washington, D.C., has eroded in a rather dramatic fashion over the past several decades.[15] The best evidence for this view is the string of legislative defeats suffered by organized labor during the late 1970s, even as a Democratic president sat in the White House (Carter) and large Democratic party majorities prevailed in both houses of Congress. In 1978, organized labor failed in its efforts to reform the nation's labor laws, to create a consumer protection agency, and to gain a strong federal commitment to full employment (the Humphrey-Hawkins bill). The retreat of organized labor in Washington, D.C., was given impetus by the strongly probusiness Reagan administration during the 1980s, which broke the strike of the air traffic controllers' union (PATCO), supported the use of the bankruptcy laws by corporations to get out of union contracts, and filled the National Labor Relations Board (NLRB) with people who were unsympathetic to organized labor.

The declining influence of labor unions may be a matter of declining membership. Labor union membership always has been low in the United States compared with other Western nations, and it has been declining at a brisk pace in recent years (see Figures 7.2 and 7.3).

The place of labor unions in American society has also been undermined by the emphasis on rugged individualism in the American culture and various unsavory practices (not always accurately attributed to them). The ambiguity Americans feel toward labor unions is reflected in Hollywood's treatment of unions (see "Politics and Film").

Americans have always been uncertain about labor unions. Most recognize that unions have done much to protect workers against exploitation and injustice in the work place, yet many also worry that unions have become powerful and often corrupt special-interest groups, out only for themselves. Not surprisingly, this uncertainty is reflected in films about labor unions.

The brilliant independent filmmaker John Sayles makes the case for unions in *Matewan*. His film focuses on the beginning of the long labor wars in the West Virginia coal fields in the town of Matewan in 1920. Sayles paints a grim picture of the lives of miners and their families; life in Matewan, like life in the other coal field towns, is short, nasty, and virtually devoid of hope. Finally pushed to revolt by their misery, the miners go on strike, only to face the company's use of strikebreakers, who are first immigrant Italians and then blacks. The company is determined to undermine the miners' resolve and to foment interethnic and interracial strife that will leave them disunited and weak (such tactics were commonly used during this period). Joe Kenehan, the labor union organizer, played by Chris Cooper, tries to keep the miners unified, brings blacks and Italians into the union, and slowly shapes a successful resistance to the coal company. Realizing that the miners are on the verge of winning, the company brings hired "goons" to Matewan to break the strike. The film ends with a deadly gun battle in the streets of the town, a preview of the violence that was to hit West Virginia in subsequent years. The film paints its heroes and villains in unambiguous black and white. *Matewan* is saved from being a cinematic version of a 1930s-style, Socialist realism mural by a very strong

cast and the evocative cinematography of Academy Award winner Haskell Wexler.

Martin Ritt's *Norma Rae* is a celebration of the promise of labor unions to workers who are at the very bottom of the heap. Sally Field plays the title role in this film about one woman's successful effort to organize southern textile workers. Ritt shows us why workers need unions by dramatizing the dangerous and unhealthy conditions in the mill and the living conditions of those who must live on low wages. Norma Rae, a mother and a widow who has finally had it with the company and her living conditions, joins forces with a union organizer and begins to fight back. Sally Field plays Norma Rae as a resilient, spunky, wisecracking, and courageous woman who manages to bring her fellow workers, at first afraid or apathetic, over to the union side. The film is given its magic by Field's engaging performance (for which she won an Academy Award), especially her touching relationship with the union organizer, who is from a world that is entirely different from her own. The movie hit the theaters just as real textile workers began their nationwide boycott campaign against J. P. Stevens. The union won in the movie and in the J. P. Stevens campaign.

Director Paul Schrader shows us the dark side of organized labor in his grim film on the automobile industry, *Blue Collar*. Richard Pryor, Harvey Keitel, and Yaphet Kotto play three buddies who work in an automobile plant and who concoct a scheme to steal money from their union local. They are driven to this desperate act by the almost hopeless quality of their lives, which Schrader shows in graphic detail: the noise and repetitive boredom of their assembly line jobs, the financial

trap that each of them is in, and the empty quality of their lives off the job. These three small-time operators only find $600 in the union treasury but discover a notebook that documents union officials' involvement in loan-sharking operations. This is the jackpot that they've been looking for, a ticket to escape their dead-end jobs, for they intend to use the notebook to blackmail the culprits. The attempt is doomed from the start, however, for the union is much stronger than they are. In the end, the three friends are destroyed: one is killed on the job and the other two are turned against each other by the skillful manipulations of union leaders who use race as their tool. The picture of the union painted by Schrader is unrelentingly negative. It is both uncaring and corrupt, and, when need be, evil.

In *F.I.S.T.*, director Norman Jewison tells the tale of a union that begins in the 1930s as a protector of exploited workers and as an expression of their aspirations but that becomes increasingly corrupt as it becomes more powerful. The transformation of the union is shown in the transformation of Johnny Kovak, played by Sylvester Stallone (who also cowrote the screenplay), who helps build the union as an idealistic reformer and ends as an out-of-touch labor potentate, protected by his alliance with organized crime, and prone to use violence to get his way. The union portrayed in the film is the Federation of Interstate Truckers (F.I.S.T.). The similarities to the notorious Teamsters Union and their former president, Jimmy Hoffa, are obvious. At the end of the film, Stallone testifies before a Senate committee, much as Hoffa and other Teamster leaders did before the McClellan committee. The message of the film is not only that power corrupts but also that labor unions are no better at protecting and caring for their members than are the giant corporations for whom they work.

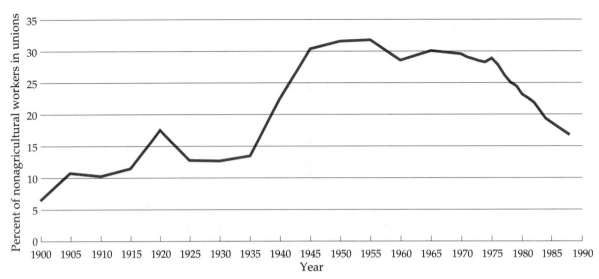

Figure 7.2 Union membership has been declining in the United States since the 1950s

Source: Leo Troy and Neil Sheflin, U.S. Union Sourcebook (West Orange, NJ: Industrial Relations Data and Information Services, 1985), A-1, A-2, 3-10; and Statistical Abstracts of the United States, 1990, Table 689.

NONECONOMIC GROUPS   Public-interest or citizens' groups try to get government to do things that will benefit the general public—as they define it, of course— rather than the direct material interests of their own members.[16] They tend to be motivated by ideological concerns or a cause.

Public-interest groups of one kind or another always have been around, but the great upsurge in their numbers and influence has taken place since 1960, and especially since 1968.[17] According to one study, about one-half of all such groups have been formed since 1968.[18]

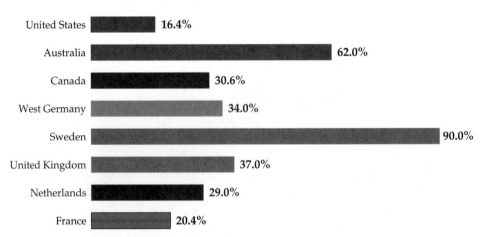

Figure 7.3 Union membership is low in the United States compared to other democratic countries (organized labor as a percentage of total labor force, 1989)

Source: Central Intelligence Agency, World Fact Book (Washington, D.C.: CIA, 1990).

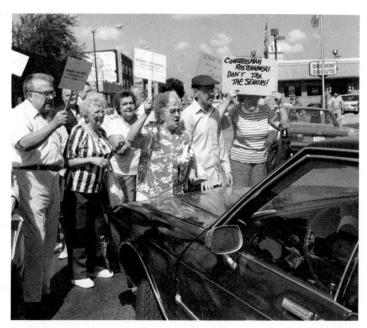

Senior citizen interest groups showed their power by mobilizing members to oppose increased taxes to cover the costs of catastrophic health care. Here seniors express their views to Ways and Means chair Dan Rostenkowski of Illinois.

Many public-interest groups were spawned by social movements (see Chapter 10). The consumer movement, whose most influential figure was (and is) Ralph Nader, formed scores of organizations to monitor automobile, airline, and product safety; to force the agricultural industry to make foods more wholesome; to push for regulation of children's television; and much more. These organizations include the Center for Auto Safety, the Project on Corporate Responsibility, Congress Watch, the Tax Reform Research Group, the Health Research Group, and Public Interest Research groups in each of the states. The environmental movement spurred the growth of existing organizations, such as the National Wildlife Federation, and the founding of more aggressive new ones, such as the Friends of the Earth, the Environmental Defense Fund, and the Natural Resources Defense Council. The women's movement led to the creation of the National Organization for Women and the National Abortion Rights League. The conservative upsurge during the 1970s and 1980s led to the creation of such organizations as the National Conservative Political Action Committee, the Students for a Better America, the Moral Majority, and the Mountain States Legal Foundation.

Public-interest groups generally do not use material incentives to convince people to work for them or to contribute to their activities. Such organizations depend primarily on *solidaristic* and *purposive* incentives; they depend, that is, on people's satisfaction in working with others to accomplish some end in which they believe. Their ability to maintain themselves as organizations over the long haul seems to depend on a mix of dedicated people who are willing to work in the interests of some cause or ideology, for generally long hours and with little compensation.[19]

... With billions of dollars of tax breaks on the line, major corporations, trade associations, and pressure groups hired the biggest names in Washington to protect themselves. The result was perverse: The populist tax bill [of 1986], an all-out attack on the special interests that swarmed over the nation's capital, was producing a huge windfall for the lobbyists who represented those interests. Some wags began to refer to the bill as the "Lobbyists' Relief Act of 1986." Fred Wertheimer, president of the citizen's lobby Common Cause, quipped, "It's not clear yet what the tax-reform fight is going to mean for the average taxpayer, but Washington special-interest lobbyists have just landed in hog heaven."

Many of the lobbyists were former members of Congress and former aides, whose stock-in-trade was their expertise in the system and their access to old colleagues and bosses. The lucrative allure of tax reform caused ever more of these people to join the lobbyists' ranks. Congressional and administration officials were transformed, almost overnight, from being the people sought out for tax favors to the people who were doing the seeking. They traded power for money. Two of [House Ways and Means Committee Chairman Daniel] Rostenkowski's former top aides—John Salmon and James Healey—were included among their ranks; both had left the Hill after many years to earn the big bucks of lobbying. Salmon represented a liquor company and one of the nation's largest tax-shelter syndicators; Healey worked for Allied Signal, Exxon, Johnson & Johnson, Chrysler-Mitsubishi, Union Pacific, Bethlehem Steel, and the investment banking house Salomon Brothers. Buck Chapoton, the former Treasury tax official, also used his expertise to secure a highly paid lobbying position for commercial banks. Roderick DeArment, formerly [Senator Robert] Dole's staff director on the Finance Committee, lobbied for a group of chief executive officers who favored reductions in corporate tax rates, as well as that for the Solar Energy Industries Association and for a trade association of cellular-telephone companies.

Tax lobbyists were a virtual who's who of the once-powerful in Washington. There were mini-alumni associations that comprised lobbyists who had once worked in the Senate for Russell

WHAT INTEREST GROUPS DO

Interest groups exist for a very simple purpose, though how they go about achieving it is not so simple. Their task is to convey the views and to defend the interests of some sector of society to public officials. The purview of interest groups, then, is as wide as the reach of government officials; their activity, that is to say, is aimed at wherever decisions are made in the government, whether in the legislative, executive, or judicial branch of the federal government, or in the states and the cities of the nation.

There are two basic types of interest group activity. The first, called here the *inside game*, involves the *direct* interaction of the interest group representative and government officials. It is the kind of interest group activity that has been around the longest and is the most familiar. There are no signs that this style of lobbying has lost any of its vigor, despite its age. The second, called here the *outside game*,

Long, Bob Dole, or Lloyd Bentsen of Texas. Their world was a kind of inbred village, in which everybody knew everybody else, and in which information swirled like gossip. It was a tightly knit network of tax insiders and former insiders. Everyone talked the same language and sought the same facts. "All of us have just come off the Hill. We worked with the people we lobby. They're our friends," explained lobbyist Denise Bode, a former aide to Senator David Boren, Democrat of Oklahoma.

There was plenty of work for everyone: U.S. Steel hired Kip O'Neill, the son of House Speaker Tip O'Neill; Senator Dole's daughter worked as a lobbyist for the real estate sales firm Century 21. Companies were tripping over each other to get their points across. The law firm of Patton Boggs & Blow, which was run by Tommy Boggs, the son of late House Majority Leader Hale Boggs, housed two hostile, corporate consolidations: the Coalition to Reduce High Effective Tax Rates, which favored reform's goal of abolishing tax breaks to pay for lower rates, and the Basic Industries Coalition, which favored retaining corporate tax breaks, even if it meant higher rates. . . .

The involvement of lobbyists extended beyond the sterile halls of congressional office buildings. Washington was a virtual money machine, and lobbyists provided much of the fuel. Fundraisers of one kind or another were held almost every night of the week, and lobbyists would stuff checks in their pockets and jump from one to another. It was as if there were a nightly sale, and the members of Congress were the merchandise. Evenings were filled with so much drinking and eating at fundraiser cocktail parties that several of the biggest lobbyists in town had to put themselves on "controlled fasts" under the care of a diet doctor during the tax-reform effort. J. D. Williams, Tommy Boggs, James Free of Charls E. Walker Associates, Robert Barrie of General Electric, and Geoffrey Peterson of the Distilled Spirits Council all decided that they did not have to be the fattest corporate lobbyists in town to be the most successful.

Source: From Jeffrey H. Birnbaum and Alan S. Murray, *Showdown at Gucci Gulch* (New York: Vintage Books, 1988), pp. 177–178.

involves interest group efforts to mobilize public opinion, voters, and important contributors in order to bring pressure on elected officials. It is an *indirect* form of influence and is becoming increasingly common.

The Inside Game

The term "lobbying" conjures up visions of a cigar-chomping representative of some powerful interest, with his arm around the shoulder of an important senator or representative, advising him on how he ought to vote on some obscure provision of the tax code, as an envelope, fat with currency, is slipped into his suit pocket. Or it conjures up images of favors given, all-expenses-paid vacations at exotic spots, substantial honoraria paid for brief appearances at association headquarters, and other unsavory exchanges verging on bribery.

The images both reveal and confuse. These things surely occurred in the past; some of them (especially payment of honoraria) go on today; some of them will surely go on in the future. In the main, however, the images do not help us fully understand the intricacies of the inside game. This game does not always involve money or favors; more broadly, it is the politics of insiders. It is the politics of the "old-boy" network. It is the politics of "one-on-one" persuasion, in which the skilled lobbyist tries to persuade a strategically placed decision maker to understand and to sympathize with the point of view of the interest group. Access is critical if one is to be successful at this game, as is an intimate understanding of the game itself: its rules, the key players, and the flow of the action.

Many of the most successful lobbyists are recruited from the ranks of retired members of the House, the Senate, and high-level bureaucratic officials, as the box on the Tax Reform Act of 1986 shows. Promise of lucrative employment for their skills is what keeps so many of them around Washington, D.C., after their tenure of office is over. Few return to where they came from. The very best of them have been in and out of one office or another in one administration or another for many years, know the Washington, D.C., scene like a wine connoisseur knows wine, and are compensated very well for their services. What works at key moments in the policy process may be a phone call to the right person, an important piece of intelligence picked up during a lunch conversation, or an introduction made at a diplomatic reception. It is something not done very easily by an outsider.

Most observers of the Washington, D.C., scene seem to agree that the inside game is most effective when the issues are narrow and technical, do not command much media attention or public passion, and do not stir up counteractivity by other interest groups. This is not to say that interest groups play a role only on unimportant matters. Great benefit can come to an interest group from a small change in a single provision of the tax code or in a slight change in the wording or timing of an administrative ruling. In the massive tax legislation of 1981, for instance, the American Bankers Association was instrumental in the creation of tax breaks for IRAs (Individual Retirement Accounts); the U.S. League of Savings and Loans played a similar role in gaining special treatment for All Saver accounts; and the Electronics Industry Association was at the center of the action on the 10 percent research and development write-off.

LOBBYING CONGRESS   The essence of the inside game in Congress is the cultivation of personal relationships with those who matter, whether they be Senate and House leaders, other influential and well-placed legislators, chairpersons of important committees or subcommittees, or key members of the professional staffs. Relations with subcommittee members and staff are particularly important in the intricate and intimate lobbying game.

The heart of the legislative process in Congress is not the floor debate, but the workings of the specialized committees and subcommittees of the House and Senate. The skilled lobbyist spends his or her time cultivating relationships with the key members of such committees and with their professional staffs, and transmitting information that is useful to members and staff. In the view of the lobbying fraternity, nothing is more important than the ability to establish personal contacts with the staff. Members of Congress are busy; they sit on several committees and subcommittees, they must attend to their districts, they must worry about reelection. On many issues, they have neither the time nor interest in developing a detailed expertise. The committee and subcommittee staffs, therefore, take on an enormous importance, and the rational lobbyist does well to focus attention there

Until he ran afoul of the "conflict of interest" laws, Michael Deaver used his reputation as confidant of Ronald and Nancy Reagan to become one of the nation's most powerful lobbyists.

and to be as helpful as possible. As one lobbyist put it, "if you have a staff member on your side, it might be a hell of a lot better than talking to the member."[20]

Making contact is as complicated and as varied as human communication itself. Contact is eased considerably if the interest group has made a significant financial contribution to the campaign, as Charles Keating of Lincoln Savings and Loan did, described in this chapter's opening story. A relationship can be cemented across a desk in a legislative office or in the hallway at the water fountain. It can take place over lunch in one of Washington, D.C.'s many fashionable restaurants. It can take place on an interest-group-sponsored vacation to some nice location. It can take place at the headquarters of an interest group, where the legislator has been given an honorarium to chat with its members.

Nothing beats the personal contact: the passing of a useful piece of information; the presentation of research results; the conveying of the point of view of interests that are important back home in the district; the helping to craft detailed legislation; the drafting of speeches. The good lobbyist cultivates such contacts and shows how he or she can be helpful. It is essential if one is to be listened to; it is essential if one is going to have one's calls put through or returned.

Interest group representatives also spend time offering testimony at public committee or subcommittee hearings. While the hearing is probably less important in shaping legislation than the direct communications made prior to, or even after, the formal public hearings, the testimony may play a role in mobilizing public opinion behind or against a bill, showing members of the interest group or the CEO of the corporation that the lobbyist is doing his or her job, or allowing a legislator to take a position that may not be to the initial liking of his or her district or state. Hearings are often used to bring some issue to the public's attention. They can be devices by which a legislator uses friendly interest groups to build public support for something that he or she wants to do; they can be a device by which interest groups convince legislators to allow them to make a case to the public.

LOBBYING THE EXECUTIVE BRANCH   Career civil servants and upper-level appointees in the executive branch have a great deal of discretionary authority because Congress, when it legislates, tends to formulate broad policies, leaving it to bureaucratic agencies to fill in the details. The Environmental Protection Agency (EPA), for instance, is charged with setting standards with regard to particular air and waterborne pollutants.

Given the broad powers they carry, it behooves most interest groups to establish stable and friendly relationships with those agencies of the executive branch that are most relevant to their interests. Pharmaceutical companies, for instance, stay in touch with the relevant people at the FDA. Real estate interests and developers need to stay in contact with the Department of Housing and Urban Development (HUD) (James Watt, the former Secretary of the Interior in the first Reagan administration, is reported to have been paid $250,000 by a client for a single phone call to a well-placed official in HUD).

As with lobbying Congress, the key to success in the lobbying game with the executive branch is personal contact and long-term relationships. Once established, interest group representatives can convey technical information, present the results of their research, help public official deflect criticism, and show how what the group wants is compatible with good public policy and the political needs of the official. In a pinch, and as a last resort, they can give the implication that there will be future opposition and adverse publicity for noncooperation, or a job or lucrative consulting contract after retirement from public service for cooperation. Threats are not to be issued lightly, however, for they damage long-term relationships. Implied understandings about postcareer service benefits are, unfortunately, much more common.

The payoffs from attentiveness to the bureaucracy can be considerable. The tobacco industry was able to convince the EPA in 1990, for instance, to "blackball" scientists with strong antismoking views as candidates for a scientific advisory panel on the potential dangers of secondary cigarette smoke.[21]

LOBBYING THE COURTS   Interest groups also lobby the courts but not in the same way in which they lobby Congress and agencies in the executive branch. A group

Interest groups sometimes believe that behind-the-scenes lobbying is not sufficient to convey their views to political leaders. Here members of women's organizations demonstrate against the nomination of Robert Bork to the Supreme Court.

may find that neither Congress nor the White House is favorably disposed to its interests, and that the courts can serve as an alternative route to the transformation of public policy. The NAACP realized that the improvement of the lot of black people was very low on the agenda of presidents and members of Congress during the 1930s, 1940s, and 1950s, and turned to the courts for satisfaction. The effort paid off in the *Brown v. Board of Education* (1954) decision, which ruled that "separate but equal" education was unconstitutional.

Going to court is a secondary strategy for most groups, because they must have **standing**; the group must be a party to the case, able to demonstrate a direct injury. Going to court, moreover, is very expensive and beyond the means of many groups. The Women's Equity Action League once lost a case when, faced with an appeal on a suit which it had initially won, it had to drop the suit because it could not afford the $40,000 trial transcript fee.[22] The litigation game remains, then, an instrument of the largest and richest of the interest groups and the private corporations that can afford to play.

When interest groups get involved in court actions there are a number of things they do. For one thing, they can file *amicus curiae* (or friends of the court) briefs in cases involving other parties. In this kind of brief, a person or an organization that is not party to the suit may file an argument in support of one side or the other in hopes of swaying the views of the judge or judges. Major controversies before the Supreme Court on issues like abortion, free speech, or civil rights attract scores of *amicus curiae* briefs on both sides.

Interest groups sometimes also get involved in the process of appointment and approval of federal judges. Particularly controversial appointments, like that of Louis Brandeis in 1916 (who corporate interests considered to be too liberal) and of Robert Bork in 1987 (who many women's and civil rights interests considered to be too conservative), stimulated a wide range of interest groups to get involved in everything from letter-writing campaigns, to the presentation of testimony before the Senate Judiciary Committee, to television advertising.

The Outside Game

A member of Congress, the head of an agency in the executive branch, or a special assistant to the president is more likely to listen to a lobbyist if he or she is convinced that a great many politically active people stand behind the lobbyist. The outside game is a form of interest group activity in which such support is identified, created, mobilized, and brought to bear on policymakers in government.

MOBILIZING MEMBERSHIP   When a bill that is relevant to the interest group comes before Congress or a ruling on a regulation comes before an agency in the executive branch, the efforts of the group's lobbyist are greatly enhanced if decision makers know that the folks back home care about the decision. Interest groups with a large membership base will try to persuade its members to send letters and to make phone calls to the appropriate officials. This sort of effort is particularly important in persuading members of the House and Senate, who are always worried about the next election, especially if the interest group membership base is concentrated in his or her congressional district or state.

Interest group leaders generally do not wait for their members to react spontaneously, but use direct mailings to sound the alarm to their members. Mailings define the threat to the members, suggest a way to respond to the threat, and supply the addresses and phone numbers of the people in Washington, D.C., to contact. Members are grouped by congressional district and state and are given the addresses of their own representatives or senators, especially if they chair the most relevant committees or subcommittees. Often, groups include a preprinted postcard or letter for the member to sign and mail to the relevant officials.

ORGANIZING THE DISTRICT   Members of Congress are most attuned to those in their state or district who can affect their reelection prospects. The smart interest group, therefore, will not only convince its own members in the state and district to put pressure on the senator or House representative but also will make every effort to be in touch with the most important campaign contributors and opinion leaders there. When the Public Securities Association (which represents major banks and Wall Street investment houses) wanted to save the tax exemption for "tax-free" municipal bonds in the 1986 Tax Reform bill, it hired a firm to organize politically influential people and groups in the districts of key members of the House Ways and Means Committee (which is responsible for writing tax bills legislation). Realizing that "tax-free" municipal bonds are the main way in which various governments borrow to pay for things from stadiums, to hospitals, to sewage treatment plants, to university buildings, and business and industrial parks, the firm concentrated on building a coalition of local government officials, small-business owners, newspaper publishers, construction firms, labor unions, and other interested parties to bring pressure on Ways and Means Committee members.

SHAPING OPINION   "Educating" the public on issues that are important to the interest group is one of the central features of new-style lobbying. The idea is to shape public and elite opinion in such a way that government officials will be favorably disposed to the views of the interest group. This attempt to shape public and elite opinion comes in many different forms.

Mobilizing public opinion and the voters are important strategies of interest groups playing the "outside game."

Publication of Research Results　Almost every interest organization has a research staff or access to professionals who will do research for it. When the organization believes that it has research results that will bolster its position, it usually calls a press conference to present a summary and mails the research report to influential people in government, the media, and education. The Tobacco Institute regularly reports on the alleged failure of scientists to establish a direct linkage between smoking and cancer. The Citizens for Tax Justice publishes an annual list of major corporations that pay little or no federal tax.

Advertising　Interest groups often conduct national and regional advertising campaigns to impress their views on government policy. Sometimes this takes the form of pressing a position on a particular issue, such as the National Abortion Rights League's advertising against the nomination of Robert Bork to the Supreme Court or Northrop's touting the B-2 Stealth bomber when the future of its funding was in doubt in 1989. Sometimes it will be "image" advertising, in which some industry (like the chemical industry, through the efforts of the Chemical Manufacturers Association) conveys its positive contribution to American life.[23] Sometimes it will take the form of "advocacy" advertising, in which an interest group, usually a corporation or set of corporations, conveys its position on a broad ideological and policy agenda. The most visible participant in these activities during the 1970s and 1980s was Mobil Oil, with its celebrations of the business system and warnings about the dangers of big government appearing on the pages of the nation's newsmagazines and the "Op-Ed" page of the *New York Times*.

Maintaining Working Relations with the Media　The smart and well-heeled interest group will regularly prepare materials that are of use to radio, television, newspapers, and magazines. Many produce opinion pieces, magazine articles, television and radio "bites," and even television documentaries. Many interest group media campaigns involve "staged" events to be covered as news. The environmentalist group Greenpeace puts the news media on full alert, for instance, when it conducts a disruption of a whaling operation or a nuclear weapons test.

Targeted Mailings   Given computerized mailing lists, it has become quite easy to identify target groups to receive mailings on particular issues. Groups pushing for cuts in the capital gains tax rate, for instance, may direct their mail communication to holders of the American Express card or to ZIP code addresses identified as upper-income neighborhoods. People for the American Way, a group opposed to censorship and the rise of the radical right, focuses its mailings on readers of the *New Republic*, the *Nation*, or the *New York Times*, members of the American Civil Liberties Union, and residents of high-education neighborhoods. Antiabortion groups target members of Catholic and fundamentalist Protestant churches for its communications.

INVOLVEMENT IN ELECTION CAMPAIGNS   Interest groups are key players in American electoral politics. The range of their activities is rather wide.

The Interest Group Scorecard   Many interest groups rate members of Congress on their support for the interest group position on a selection of key votes in the House and Senate. This practice is most common among public interest and ideological groups, though labor unions and business organizations are involved as well. These ratings are distributed to members of the interest group and other interested parties in hopes that it will influence their voting behavior in upcoming elections. See Table 7.1 for an example.

Shaping Party Platforms   Many interest groups try to shape the Republican and Democratic party platforms. This will usually work only if the group has had a friendly, long-term relationship with key sectors of the party or some candidate, is ideologically close to the party, or has made substantial contributions to party candidates in the past. Thus, organized labor is an important force in writing the Democratic platform; business organizations play an important role in writing the Republican platform.

Pitching-in During the Campaign   Interest groups encourage their members to get involved in the electoral campaigns of candidates who are favorable toward their interests. Groups often assist campaigns in more tangible ways: allowing use of their telephone banks, mailing lists, xerox machines, computers, and the like. Some interest groups help with fund-raising events or ask its members to make financial contributions.

Endorsements   A few interest groups, mostly of the public-interest or citizens group variety, will endorse particular candidates for public office. The strategy can backfire and is somewhat risky, for to endorse a losing candidate is to risk losing access to the winner. Nevertheless, it is fairly common now for labor unions, environmental organizations, religious groups, and ideological groups to make such endorsements.

Table 7.1
Ratings of Members of Congress by Organizations, 101st Congress,
House of Representatives

	ADA	AFL–CIO	CCUS	ACU
The Most Liberal				
Dellums (D—CA)	100	100	20	0
Edwards (D—CA)	100	100	20	0
Waxman (D—CA)	100	100	30	4
Gejdenson (D—CT)	100	100	30	0
Morrison (D—CT)	100	100	30	4
Lewis (D—GA)	100	100	40	4
Hayes (D—IL)	100	100	30	0
Markey (D—MA)	100	100	40	0
Studds (D—MA)	100	100	40	0
Wolpe (D—MI)	100	100	40	4
Owens (D—NY)	100	100	20	4
Coyne (D—PA)	100	100	10	4
Unsoeld (D—WA)	100	100	40	4
The Most Conservative				
Herger (R—CA)	10	25	100	100
Ros-Lehtinen (R—FL)	0	40	100	100
Hiler (R—IN)	0	0	100	100
Miller (R—OH)	0	17	100	100
Ritter (R—PA)	10	17	100	100
Hansen (R—UT)	0	8	100	100

Key: ADA— Americans for Democratic Action.
        AFL-CIO— American Federation of Labor–Congress of Industrial Organizations.
        CCUS— Chamber of Commerce of the United States.
        ACU— American Conservative Union.

Source: Congressional Quarterly 1989 Almanac (Washington, D.C.: Congressional Quarterly Press, 1989),
pp. 70B–71B.

Political Action Committees (PACs)   The most important development in American
electoral politics over the course of the past two decades has been the rise of
political action committees (PACs) as an important part of financing electoral campaigns. We will say more about PACs in the next section.

THE INTEREST GROUP SYSTEM AND DEMOCRACY

The political scientist E. E. Schattsneider once observed that the flaw in the pluralist (or interest group) heaven is "that the heavenly chorus sings with a strong
upper class accent."[24] If this is true, then the norm of political equality is violated
by the interest group system, and democracy is less fully developed than it might
be. In this section, we look at possible inequalities and evaluate their effects.

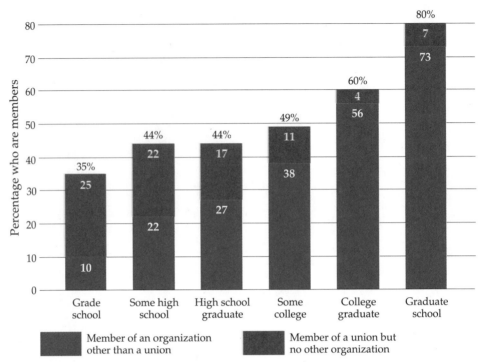

Figure 7.4 Organizational membership by level of education

Source: From Kay Schlozman and John Tierney, Organized Interests and American Democracy *(New York: HarperCollins, 1986), p. 62. Based on data from the 1976 Metropolitan Work Force Survey.*

Representational Inequalities

We look first at who interest groups represent.

MEMBERSHIP BIAS   It is an old cliché that Americans are joiners. Americans gravitate, it is said, to service and fraternal clubs (Kiwanas, Lions, Optimists, JCs), civic organizations (League of Women Voters), sports organizations (Little League, Pop Warner Football, YMCA Basketball), public-interest groups (proabortion, antiabortion, environment, gun control), labor unions, veteran's organization, charitable groups (the Red Cross, the local symphony orchestra support group), professional associations (the American Bar Association, the American Political Science Association), and more. The cliché, like all clichés, is only partially accurate, for only 40 percent of the population join an organization other than a labor union; only 52 percent join any organization at all. More important, the tendency to join an organization is not randomly distributed among the American people. Those who are the best educated (see Figure 7.4), have the highest incomes, and have the most prestigious occupations join more than others.[25]

SECTORAL BIAS   Significant inequalities also exist in terms of the *sectors* of American society that are represented in the interest group system. For the most part, the interest group game in Washington, D.C., is dominated in sheer number and weight of activity by corporations, business trade associations, and professional associations. To be sure, these three do not entirely monopolize the game (see Table 7.2). Other sectors play a role: labor unions, citizen's groups and civil rights organizations, groups advancing the interests of women and the elderly, and even groups that are advocates for the poor. Nevertheless, the disproportionalities are striking: business, trade, and professional associations account for over two-thirds of all associations that have a lobbying presence in Washington, D.C. The representational advantage of business and the professions is increasing. Furthermore, there is evidence that business and professional groups last longer than others. Public-interest groups tend to come and go.[26]

Resource Inequalities

Business corporations and the professions (doctors, lawyers, dentists, accountants, and so on) are the most economically well-off sectors of American society. It is hardly surprising that interest groups representing them enjoy a substantial resource advantage over others. Interest groups representing business and the professions can afford to spend far more than other groups to hire professional lobbying firms, form their own Washington, D.C., "liaison" office, place advertising in the media, conduct targeted mailings, mobilize their members to contact government officials, and to do all of the other activities of old- and new-style lobbying. Not many Americans can fly high-government officials to important meetings in their own planes, as corporations do routinely. Not many other groups can match the routine lobbying presence of large corporations. When the Senate was considering the Telecommunications Equipment Competition Act in

Table 7.2
Organizations Having Washington Representation

	All Organizations Having Washington Representation
Corporations	45.7%
Trade and other business associations	17.9
Foreign commerce and corporations	6.5
Professional associations	6.9
Unions	1.7
Citizens' groups	4.1
Civil rights groups/Minority organizations	1.3
Social welfare and the poor	.6
New Entrants (elderly, women, handicapped)	1.1
Governmental units—U.S.	4.2
Other foreign	2.0
Other unknown	8.2
	100.2%
	(N = 6601)

Sources: Based on information taken from Arthur C. Close, ed., *Washington Representatives— 1981*, 5th ed. (Washington, DC: Columbia Books, 1981); and Denise S. Akey, ed., *The Encyclopedia of Associations*, 16th ed. (Detroit, MI: Gale Research Company, 1981). From Kay Lehman Schlozman and John T. Tierney, *Organized Interests and American Democracy* (New York: Harper & Row, 1986), p. 67.

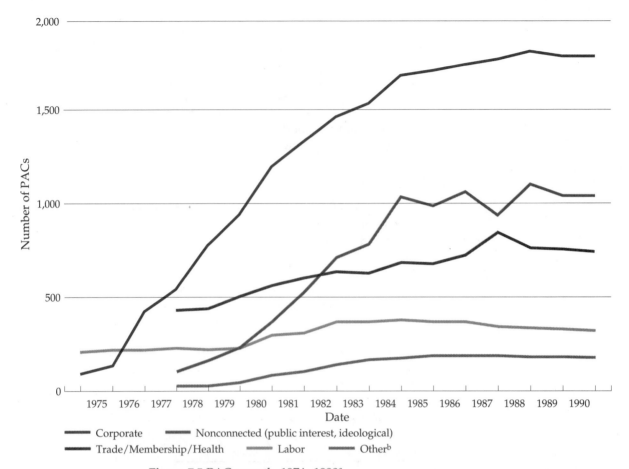

Figure 7.5 PAC growth, 1974–1990[a]

[a]For the years 1974 through 1976, numbers are not available for nonconnected PACs, Trade/ Membership Health PACs, and PACs in the "other" category.

[b]"Other" category includes PACs formed by corporations without capital stock and PACs formed by incorporated cooperatives.

Source: Federal Election Commission, 1991 Annual Report.

1991, for instance, the seven regional phone companies had 15 lobbyists at work on an around-the-clock basis. Consumer groups could field but a single lobbyist.

Interest groups representing business and the professions are also the major players in PAC fund raising and spending, as shown in Figures 7.5 and 7.6. During the 1990 elections, PACs representing business and the professions accounted for roughly 60 percent of all PACs and PAC contributions to congressional candidates.

PACs representing the least privileged sectors of American society are notable for their absence. As Republican Senator Robert Dole of Kansas once put it, "there aren't any Poor PACs or Food Stamp PACs or Nutrition PACs or Medicare PACs."[27] The way the PAC campaign contribution system works makes a difference in what Congress does.[28]

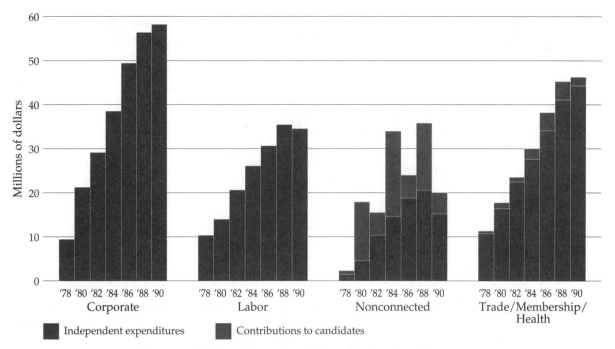

Figure 7.6 PAC support of candidates by election cycle[a]

[a]Chart does not include activity by PACs of cooperatives and corporations without capital stock.

Source: Federal Election Commission, 1991 Annual Report.

Access Inequality

Inequalities of representation and resources are accentuated by the ability of some groups to form relatively stable alliances with important government institutions and decision makers. While scholars have not developed precise measures for this phenomenon or reached a consensus on its exact form and extent, they have identified several basic types in this alliance system.

CAPTURE   Because regulatory agencies and industries being regulated must coexist over the long haul, must come to depend on each other for technical information, and are prone to trade top personnel over the years, there is a tendency for regulatory agencies to become allies, protectors, and advocates of the industries that they regulate. Most often cited is the case of the Interstate Commerce Commission (ICC), which was created to regulate the railroad industry in the late nineteenth century but which, over time, came to be a creature of the railroad industry.[29] Some scholars have rejected this "life cycle" theory of "capture" in favor of one that argues that regulatory agencies are intended, from their very inception, to protect particular industries.[30] While "capture" theories are no longer as popular among political scientists as they once were, they still sensitize us to the potential problems posed by the alliance of private and public power for democracy.

CLIENTELISM AND INTEREST GROUP LIBERALISM   "Capture" theories refer to regulatory agencies and regulated industries. Two other approaches argue that private–public alliances are much more widespread than suggested by "capture" advocates. "Clientelism" identifies many situations in which private interests are protected and promoted by patrons throughout the federal bureaucracy, with most of these private interests being businesses: bankers and the Treasury Department; agricultural organizations and the Department of Agriculture; ranchers and the Department of the Interior; organized labor and the Department of Labor; and so on.[31] The theory of "interest group liberalism" focuses on the process by which Congress allows private organizations to formulate many of the details of policies that directly affect them.[32] Again, most involve business. Thus, shippers are allowed to help determine rate structures; doctors, to help shape the details of the Medicare program; the Rivers and Harbors Congress (a private trade association), to work with the Corps of Engineers', and the National Petroleum Council, to help set Department of the Interior's oil policy. With the deregulation of several industries, including banking, transportation, and communication, there may well be less "clientelism" and "interest group liberalism" than in the past, but it is difficult to say for sure. Scholars have not yet reached an agreement on the matter.

IRON TRIANGLES AND SUBGOVERNMENTS   Another popular way to describe the alliance of private and public power in Washington, D.C., is in terms of "iron triangles" or "subgovernments." In this three-way arrangement (see Figure 7.7), an alliance is formed between a private-interest group (usually, but not always, a business corporation), a bureaucratic agency, and some committee or subcommittee of Congress. Among journalists, the most commonly cited "iron triangle" is the alliance among the Pentagon, defense contractors, and the armed services committees of Congress. The alliance among the Department of Agriculture, agricultural commodity organizations, and the agricultural committees of Congress has also received a great deal of attention.

"Iron triangles" are more common in the United States, where central government power is fragmented and where the legislative branch plays an important

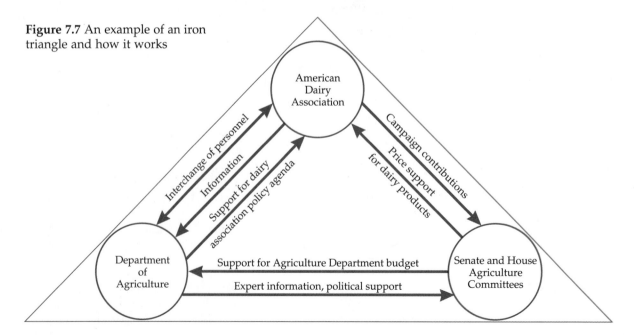

Figure 7.7 An example of an iron triangle and how it works

role in policymaking, than in countries with parliamentary systems. In Great Britain, the cabinet, the prime minister, and the ministries are the principal policymakers, and the government and parties are highly centralized. Ordinary members of the House of Commons (called "backbenchers") play almost no policy role, and the committees of the House are unimportant. As a consequence, interest groups in Great Britain concentrate their attention on the parties, cabinet ministers, and the permanent civil service. In most continental European countries, interest groups tend to be organized into large peak associations, representing business, labor, and agriculture, which are regularly consulted by the ministries involved in planning. Again, relationships with parliamentary committees by narrow interest groups are uncommon. Hence, "iron triangles" are not formed.

Clearly, there is no consensus among scholars about all of this. Talk of capture, clientelism, and subgovernments is common in the political science discipline; no good way of measuring the incidence of each is yet available. Some even suggest that these forms are becoming less important and that the private-interest and public-power alliances are not as closed to outsiders as in the past.[33] But no matter how this debate is settled among scholars, it remains the case that each of these models of the policy process in Washington, D.C., is characterized by the existence of privileged access for some, the frequent exclusion of majorities of the public, and the violation of the principle of political equality.

The Special Place of Business Corporations

We have already seen many of the advantages that business corporations enjoy over others in the policy process in Washington, D.C. The largest corporations are way ahead of all of their competitors in terms of the number of interest organizations that represent them, the number of lobbyists that they employ, the level of resources available to them and expended for political purposes, their ease of access to government officials, and their ability to shape public perceptions and opinions.

It is an old saw in political science, however, that resources do not necessarily translate into real political influence. An interest group may have enormous resource advantages over other interest groups, for instance, but may use its resources ineffectively. Or, an interest group with great resources may find itself opposed by other interest groups that together might be able to mobilize impressive resources of their own. A powerful interest group may also find that an elected politician is not cooperative because the voters in his or her district are of a different mind than the interest group. Given this imperfect correspondence between resources and influence, what can reasonably be said about the scale of business and corporate power in Washington, D.C.?

One must start with the observation that business does not always get its way in Washington, D.C. There are many issues of great importance on which business in general, or one corporation in particular, loses in the give and take of politics. There are times when business finds itself squared off against powerful coalitions of other interest groups (labor, consumer, and environmentalist groups, let us say). There are many occasions—perhaps most of the time, in fact—when business interest groups find themselves divided or even at odds with one other. The trucking, railroad, and airline industries, for instance, may have a common stance on labor unions but have important conflicts of interest about federal transportation policy.

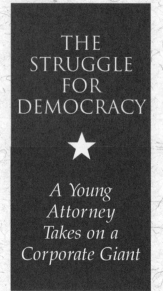

THE
STRUGGLE
FOR
DEMOCRACY

★

*A Young
Attorney
Takes on a
Corporate Giant*

Ralph Nader has become the nation's most prominent and influential consumer advocate. In the following story, Pulitzer Prize winning journalist David Halberstam tells how he first came to public prominence.

Ralph Nader was thirty-two years old in 1966 when he took on General Motors. He was a solitary, distant, wary person who confided in no one and whose closest friends were amazed at how little they knew about him. A complete loner, without an institutional base such as a university appointment or an office in government, he was the most unlikely of young men to challenge a giant industry. Yet his timing was perfect. The auto industry was ripe for criticism, and many Americans, without knowing it, were ready for a citizen's challenge to an entity that for them had come to symbolize an increasingly haunting aspect of American life—bigness and power without apparent accountability. . . .

He made contact with some of the new muckrakers who were beginning to assemble in Washington, and did some more writing. In 1964, for the grand sum of $2000, he signed a contract with a publisher named Richard Grossman to write a book on auto safety. Grossman had been looking for a writer to delve into the subject. A year later Nader published *Unsafe at Any Speed*, an unsparing critique of Detroit's lack of concern for safety and its preoccupation with styling and profit. At first it appeared that the book would disappear with few traces. But it was extremely critical of the Corvair, GM's latest compact, and its publication happened to coincide with a large number of suits filed against GM based on Corvair accidents.

If Nader was looking for a larger constituency, then GM soon helped him find it. At the time that Nader was readying his book there were 103 Corvair lawsuits pending against GM. Already skittish about these suits, GM officials became even more nervous with the appearance of the book by this new troublemaker. They were suspicious: He was so passionate about the issue, and yet he did not hold a job. Whom, they wondered, did he really work for? What was he after? Was he in some way connected to these law-

It must also be said that many Americans see no conflict between corporate and business political power and the health and well-being of American society. It is widely believed that what is good for business is good for America; to some extent this is true. For this reason, many Americans do not begrudge business its significant political influence.

Politicians, journalists, and scholars remain undecided about the actual extent of corporate political power. There is a wide range of assessments.

Business as Powerless   Business leaders and the business press often complain that business is without power in Washington, D.C. It is difficult to know whether such a claim is genuinely believed or whether it is meant strictly for public consumption, but it can hardly be sustained, given the comparative advantage that

Nader, wary in the best of times, soon sensed he was being followed. Then friends of his phoned to report that private eyes seemed to be tracking him. He began to receive odd phone calls which, he was sure, were designed to discover whether or not he was at home. Then there were provocative approaches from young women. Two particularly inept investigators managed to follow the wrong man, a reporter for the *Washington Post* named Bryce Nelson. That put the *Post* onto the story. In time General Motors was obliged to admit that it had placed Nader under investigation. At the same time Senator Abraham Ribicoff of Connecticut was about to hold hearings on auto safety. Nader and Jim Roche of GM—the one voluntarily and the other involuntarily—became the stars of the show. GM found itself publicly apologizing to Nader, the man it had set out to discredit, and eventually settled with him out of court for $425,000 for invasion of privacy. It was an incident that reflected the worst of a giant institution and the best of a solitary American citizen.

suits? Failing to understand Nader's motivation, sensing that he was in some unacceptable way different, GM inevitably concentrated on his personal life—sending out investigators to find something to discredit him. The investigation was unbelievably shabby and crude and provided an insight into the reaction of a mighty institution challenged in a way which it did not understand. . . .

Source: From David Halberstam, *The Reckoning* (New York: William Morrow, 1986), pp. 490, 494–496.

business enjoys over other groups in terms of resources, access, legitimacy, and organizational presence. This view of business as helpless victim is generally articulated during times when some restrictions have been placed on corporate behavior. Examples include the period of the New Deal in the 1930s and the consumer and environmental reform period in the early 1970s. The story of Ralph Nader's conflict with General Motors, an important factor in the rise of the consumer movement, is described in "The Struggle for Democracy."

Business as an Interest Group Just Like Any Other Interest Group Many scholars working in the pluralist tradition believe that the corporation is no more or less important than any other interest group. Even if it were occasionally admitted that corporations and business interest groups have access to more resources than other groups, it is argued that the activities of other interest groups make it difficult, if not impossible, for corporations to play a dominant role in the policymaking process.

Business Corporations as the Dominant Players in the Policymaking Game   Political scientist and economist Charles Lindblom argues that corporations wield such disproportionate power in American politics that they undermine democracy. He closes his widely read book, *Politics and Markets*, with the following observation: "The large private corporation fits oddly into democratic theory. Indeed, it does not fit."[34]

What he discovered was that government officials tend to defer to the needs of the corporations in the long run because of the central role that corporations play in the economic health and well-being of the United States. Because of their vital role in the economy, officials tend to interpret business corporations, not as "special interests," but as the voice of the national or general interest, and listen more attentively to their demands and entreaties than they do to other sectors of American society. In this sense, corporations enjoy a "privileged position" in American politics.

The Waxing and Waning of Corporate Power   Alternatively, it may be that corporate political power is not a constant but waxes and wanes over time.[35] Corporate political power has been dominant over that of all other groups at certain times, such as the 1920s and the late 1970s and early 1980s. It has been comparatively weak relative to other groups at other times, such as the early 1970s, when the power of corporations was matched by that of the consumer and environmental movements.

Corporate power seems to reach its apex under certain conditions.[36] During *bad economic times*, for instance, Americans are more interested in getting the economy going again than in undertaking reforms that cut into corporate profits. Politicians in bad times are more solicitous of corporate interests. In good economic times, like the late 1960s, politicians are less worried about corporate profits drying up if tax monies are used for social purposes.

Corporations are most powerful, moreover, when they can build coalitions. Most of the time, corporations are in competition with one another; they do not form a unified political bloc capable of moving government to action on their behalf. On those few occasions when corporations feel that their collective interests are at stake, however, they are capable of coming together to form powerful political coalitions. "When business is both mobilized and unified, its political power can be formidable."[37] During the mid-1970s, corporations felt that they were under assault, and they responded by building broad political coalitions that proved to be irresistible. These became the foundation of the movement for deregulation and an important part of the conservatizing of American politics that led to the election of Ronald Reagan in 1980.

Taken to an extreme, this approach implies that corporations can see their influence wax to dominance or wane to near powerlessness, but such an interpretation is neither persuasive nor necessary. Perhaps the best way to think about corporations in American politics is to see their power waxing and waning within a generally privileged position; that is, corporations enjoy substantial built-in advantages over competing groups as a matter of course. Within this generally "privileged position," however, corporate power may be more powerful at certain

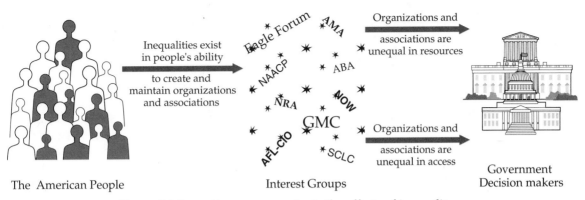

Figure 7.8 Interest groups accentuate the effects of inequality

times and less powerful at other times. Waxing and waning goes on, to be sure, but only within the boundaries of a game in which corporations enjoy advantages over other groups. When corporations feel that their collective interests are at stake—when labor unions are particularly aggressive or when government's regulatory burden is perceived to be too heavy—*and* when they are able to come together in a united front, they are simply unbeatable.[38] This cannot be said for any other segment of American society.

CURING THE MISCHIEF OF FACTIONS?

James Madison was thinking mainly about the tyranny of "majority factions" when he referred to the "mischief of factions." The politics of faction, we have learned, however, is usually not the province of majorities, but of narrow, particularistic, and privileged interests. This is problematic in two respects. First, it undermines political equality, which is so vital for a functioning democracy (see Figure 7.8). Second, it makes it difficult for the United States to formulate broad and coherent national policies. Policy tends to be, instead, a glued-together patchwork of agreements made between narrow factions, each with its own ends in mind.

Here, then, is a dilemma. We are saddled with a politics of faction that significantly undermines political equality and the likelihood of making coherent national policy, yet the right of the people to form groups for the purpose of petitioning the government is one of our most fundamental and cherished rights. Can we alleviate some of the most pressing "mischiefs of faction" without diminishing our freedom?

Americans have been worried about the politics of faction for a long time, and more than a few efforts have been made to solve some of the most glaring problems. *Disclosure* has been the principal tool of regulation. The Public Utilities Act of 1935 required that lobbyists for that industry register with Congress. Registration requirements were added for lobbyists for the shipping and maritime industries under the Merchant Marine Act of 1938. In 1946, Congress imposed a requirement that all lobbyists working in Congress be registered (the Federal Regulation of Lobbying Act). It is generally acknowledged that this legislation has not been very effective. It is not only indifferently enforced, but it also does not deal with lobbying before other branches of government or with the diverse forms of "outside" lobbying.

Reformers also have tried to *regulate* some of the most troublesome abuses of the politics of faction. Sections of the Ethics in Government Act (1978), for instance, try to regulate abuses of the so-called revolving door, in which former government officials become lobbyists for those interests with which they formerly dealt in their official capacity. The Act forbids ex-officials from lobbying their former agency for a year, or from lobbying at all (with no time limit) on any issue in which the official was substantially involved. It remains to be seen whether the Act will be effectively enforced.

Another major effort to alleviate some of the mischiefs of faction involves the attempt to control some of the campaign practices of PACs. The evidence seems to suggest that PAC money in campaigns is becoming more rather than less important in American politics and that it is becoming increasingly dominated by narrow segments of American society.

While disclosure of lobbying activity and the regulation of some of the worst abuses of the interest group system are to be applauded, many worry that these reforms do not get to the heart of the main problems. These problems, as already outlined, are related to the narrowness and the particularism of interest group politics and its undermining of both political equality and policy coherence.

Recognizing this, some political scientists have suggested that we focus our efforts on strengthening institutions of majoritarian democracy. The key institution of majoritarian democracy, at least in theory (as we shall see in the next chapter), is the political party. Parties can, as political scientist Walter Dean Burnham puts it, ". . . generate countervailing collective power on behalf of the many individually powerless against the relatively few who are individually—or organizationally—powerful."[39] Others believe that the narrowness of interest group politics might be tempered by strengthening the presidency, our only nationally elected office.[40] Still others have proposed that the fragmentation of Congress, a trend that substantially contributes to the interest group "feeding frenzy," be reversed and that formal and informal congressional leadership positions be strengthened.

Efforts to reform the interest group system in the service of majoritarian democracy may be frustrated in the end by the inescapable fact that highly unequal resources eventually will find their way into our political life. Those with the most resources and interests to protect will usually find a way to influence government officials in ways and to an extent beyond the capacities of most other Americans. It is for this reason that Thomas Jefferson and Abraham Lincoln worried about the possibilities of democracy in a society marked by great inequalities in wealth and income. Whether there is a way to decrease inequalities without seriously eroding our liberties remains to be seen, though the experience of other capitalist democracies in Western Europe suggests that such a thing may be possible.

SUMMARY

Americans always have been ambivalent about the place of interest groups in a democratic society, seeing them as special interests that undermine the public good and make the pursuit of the public interest extremely difficult. A newer tradition, pluralism, sees them as an important addition to the representative process in a democracy.

A number of constitutional provisions, such as the right to petition the government, federalism, and checks and balances, as well as a number of cultural features of American society, have provided a supportive setting for the development of interest groups. The growth and diversification of American society, and the expansion of the role of government, have contributed to the proliferation of interests and the number of groups that represent those interests.

Interest groups come in a wide variety of forms, ranging from the small organization in Washington, D.C., to "peak associations" made up of other organizations. Interest groups also can be differentiated by the kinds of interests that are represented. The most important economic interests include business, agriculture, labor, and the professions. Noneconomic groups, usually called "public interest" or "citizens' groups," try to advance some issue or ideological interest that is not connected to the direct material benefit of their own members. There has been a significant expansion in the number of such groups since 1968.

Interest groups attempt to influence the shape of public policy in a number of ways. In the inside game, interest group representatives are in direct contact with officials in the government and try to build influence on the basis of personal relationships. In the outside game, interest groups attempt to apply indirect pressure on officials by mobilizing other groups, the members of one's own group, public opinion, elite opinion, and the electorate to support their positions on policy matters.

The interest group system in its present form makes political equality less likely and thus helps to diminish democracy in the United States. The special place of the large corporations seems especially problematic.

To Ponder

1. Are there ways to reform the interest group system that would both enhance democracy and protect our freedom?

2. Is there reason to worry, as James Madison did, about the tyranny of a majority faction?

3. Is the decline of labor union power inevitable? Is it a good thing?

4. Is business too powerful in American life, or is the business point of view too often ignored?

5. Are there too many interest groups?

6. Why are most citizen's groups on the liberal end of the political spectrum? Is such a thing inevitable or accidental?

Suggested Readings

Berry, Jeffrey M. *The Interest Group Society.* Glenview, IL: Scott, Foresman/Little, Brown, 1989.
   A comprehensive textbook, reporting the latest research on the nature of the interest group system.

Dahl, Robert A. *A Preface to Democratic Theory.* Chicago: University of Chicago Press, 1956.
   The leading theoretical statement of the pluralist position and the democratic role of the interest group.

Ferguson, Thomas, and Joel Rogers. *Right Turn: The Decline of the Democrats and the Future of American Politics.* New York: Hill and Wang, 1986.

> A lively and controversial account of the role of corporations in the Reagan revolution.

Lindblom, Charles. *Politics and Markets.* New York: Basic Books, 1977.

> A controversial and widely commented-upon book, in which one of the leading pluralist theorists concludes that the modern corporation is incompatible with democracy.

Olson, Mancur. *The Logic of Collective Action.* Cambridge, MA: Harvard University Press, 1965.

> A "rational-choice" argument on the place of material and selective benefits in the formation and maintenance of groups, and the difficulty of forming groups based on values and ideology.

Schlozman, Kay Lehman, and John T. Tierney. *Organized Interests and American Democracy.* New York: HarperCollins, 1986.

> An important textbook that also includes the results of the authors' own research on the Washington, D.C., pressure community.

Vogel, David. *Fluctuating Fortunes: The Political Power of Business in America.* New York: Basic Books, 1989.

> A look at the political power of large corporations during the 1970s and 1980s; useful for its wealth of information, even if the author may sometimes underestimate the extent of business political power.

Notes

1. Michael M. Thomas, "The Greatest American Shambles," *The New York Review of Books,* January 31, 1991, p. 31.
2. Steven Walden and Rich Thomas, "How Did It Happen?" *Newsweek,* May 21, 1990, p. 28.
3. *The Federalist* (New York: New American Library, 1961).
4. *The Federalist,* p. 79.
5. *The Federalist,* p. 78.
6. Arthur F. Bentley, *The Process of Government* (Chicago: University of Chicago Press, 1908); David Truman, *The Governmental Process* (New York: Knopf, 1951); V. O. Key, *Politics, Parties, and Pressure Groups* (New York: Thomas Y. Crowell, 1952); Robert Dahl, *A Preface to Democratic Theory* (Chicago: University of Chicago Press, 1956); and Robert Dahl, *Who Governs?* (New Haven, CT: Yale University Press, 1961).
7. Kay Lehman Schlozman and John T. Tierney, *Organized Interests and American Democracy* (New York: HarperCollins, 1986), pp. 77–78.
8. Truman, *Governmental Process.*
9. Truman, *Governmental Process,* p. 88.
10. David Vogel, *Fluctuating Fortunes: The Political Power of Business in America* (New York: Basic Books, 1989), ch. 8.
11. Mancur Olson, *The Logic of Collective Action* (Cambridge, MA: Harvard University Press, 1965).
12. For a summary of critiques of Olson, see Brian Barry and Russell Hardin, eds., *Rational Man and Irrational Society?* (Newbury Park, CA: Sage Publications, 1982); and Terry Moe, *The Organization of Interests* (Chicago: University of Chicago Press, 1980).
13. Vogel, *Fluctuating Fortunes,* p. 197.
14. Jeffrey M. Berry, *Lobbying for the People* (Princeton: Princeton University Press, 1977).
15. Thomas Edsall, *The New Politics of Inequality* (New York: Norton, 1984); Michael Goldfield, *The Decline of Organized Labor in the United States* (Chicago: University of Chicago Press, 1987); Edward S. Greenberg, *Capitalism and the American Political Ideal* (Armonk, NY: M. E. Sharpe, 1985); and Vogel, *Fluctuating Fortunes.*
16. Berry, *Lobbying for the People,* p. 7.

17. Berry, *Lobbying for the People*; David Broder, *Changing the Guard* (New York: Simon & Schuster, 1980); Hugh Heclo, "Issue Networks and the Executive Establishment," in Anthony King, ed., *The New American Political System* (Washington, D.C.: the American Enterprise Institute, 1978); Schlozman and Tierney, *Organized Interests*; Jack L. Walker, "The Origins and Maintenance of Interest Groups in America," *The American Political Science Review*, Vol. 77, No. 2 (June 1983), pp. 390–406; and G. K. Wilson, *Interest Groups in the United States* (New York: Oxford University Press, 1981).

18. Berry, *Lobbying for the People*, p. 289.

19. Walder, "The Origins and Maintenance"; Vogel, *Fluctuating Fortunes*.

20. Jeffrey M. Berry, *The Interest Group Society* (Glenview, IL: Scott, Foresman/Little, Brown, 1989), p. 141.

21. "Tobacco Group Lobbies EPA on Study Panel," *The New York Times National Edition*, October 22, 1990, p. A11.

22. Karen O'Connor, *Women's Organizations' Use of the Courts* (Lexington, MA: Lexington Books, 1980), p. 118.

23. Schlozman and Tierney, *Organized Interests*, p. 175.

24. E. E. Schattsneider, *The Semisovereign People* (New York: Holt, 1960), p. 35.

25. Schlozman and Tierny, *Organized Interests*, pp. 60–64.

26. Schlozman and Tierney, *Organized Interests*, pp. 77, 79.

27. "Money Talks, Congress Listens," *Boston Globe*, December 12, 1982, p. A24.

28. Dennis Quinn, "Business Political Power: The Case of Taxation," *The American Political Science Review*, Vol. 85, No. 3 (September 1991), pp. 851–874.

29. Marver Bernstein, *Regulating Business by Independent Commission* (Princeton, NJ: Princeton University Press, 1955).

30. George J. Stigler, "The Theory of Economic Regulation," *Bell Journal of Economics and Management Science* Vol. 2 (1971); Gabriel Kolko, *The Triumph of Conservatism* (New York: Free Press, 1963).

31. Grant McConnell, *Private Power and American Democracy* (New York: Knopf, 1967).

32. Theodore Lowi, *The End of Liberalism* (New York: Norton, 1969).

33. Hugh Heclo, "Issue Networks."

34. Charles Lindblom, *Politics and Markets* (New York: Basic Books, 1977), p. 356. For criticisms of Dahl and Lindblom from the Left, see John Manley, "Neo-Pluralism: A Class Analysis of Pluralism I and Pluralism II," *The American Political Science Review*, Vol. 77 (June 1983), pp. 368–383. For criticisms from the Right, see Irving Kristol, *Two Cheers for Capitalism* (New York: Basic Books, 1977) and James Q. Wilson, "Democracy and the Corporation," in Robert Sessen, ed., *Does Big Business Rule America?* (Washington, D.C.: Ethics and Public Policy Center, 1987).

35. Vogel, *Fluctuating Fortunes*.

36. *Ibid.*

37. Vogel, *Fluctuating Fortunes*, p. 291.

38. *Ibid.*

39. Walter Dean Burnham, *Critical Elections and the Mainsprings of American Politics* (New York: Norton, 1970), p. 133.

40. John E. Chubb and Paul E. Peterson, "American Political Institutions and the Problem of Governance," in Chubb and Peterson, eds., *Can the Government Govern?* (Washington, DC: Brookings Institution, 1989).

8

Political Parties

ROOSEVELT'S ELECTORAL VICTORY AND LEGISLATIVE DEFEAT

The *Literary Digest* went from a respected journal of opinion to the nation's laughingstock almost overnight. It had confidently informed its readers several weeks before the 1936 election that Republican challenger Alf Landon of Kansas would handily defeat the incumbent president, Franklin D. Roosevelt. Confidence in the *Digest*'s accuracy was high, given its track record in previous elections. Most newspapers endorsed Landon, and many of them predicted victory for their favored candidate.

Roosevelt won every state in the union except Maine and Vermont, 423 out of 431 electoral votes, and 60.8 percent of the popular vote. In the congressional races, the Democrats padded their already substantial advantage in both Houses. The Seventy-fifth Congress, convening in early 1937, would have 75 Democrats and 17 Republicans in the Senate, and 334 Democrats and only 89 Republicans in the House of Representatives. The scale of the Democratic victory in state houses and governorships across the nation was almost as great. The reputation of the *Literary Digest* never recovered from its embarrassing prediction, and it soon went out of business.

These Democratic party successes reflected a fundamental shift in the country. Democrats replaced Republicans as the dominant party in American politics. This process of party **realignment** began in the late 1920s, accelerated during Roosevelt's electoral defeat of President Herbert Hoover in 1932, and reached full fruition in the 1936 landslide victory. The 1936 election, by joining together the South, northern urban areas, white ethnics, blacks, organized labor, Jews, and Catholics, solidified the so-called **New Deal coalition** that was to dominate American politics for the next three decades.

The 1936 election was one of those rare campaigns in which the issues were fairly clear-cut and the choices between the parties and the presidential candidates were unambiguous. The election was a referendum on the **New Deal**, Roosevelt's program to end the Great Depression and to alleviate the distress and misery caused by it. The Democrats' campaign asked the American people to endorse or to reject a new conception of the role of government: an activist role, in which government would assume broad new economic and social responsibilities. The Republican party position was that the free market economy should be left to work its way out of temporary problems and that relief for the poor and the unemployed should be left mainly to the states and private charity.

The 1936 campaign was a heated one, because great issues were at stake. The Hearst newspapers charged that Roosevelt was surrounded by a "Communist entourage." Business publications talked of Roosevelt as a power-mad dictator, a fomenter of class conflict, and a traitor to his class. Republican National Chairman John Hamilton warned that the new Social Security Act would force

253

all Americans to wear metal identity dog tags. Republican vice-presidential candidate Frank Knox warned that "we are not in a political campaign. We are in a campaign to save America . . . from fanatics, theorists and experimenters . . . seeking to impose a new and alien kind of government."[1]

Roosevelt eventually responded in kind. In a speech in New York City on the eve of the election, Roosevelt claimed that his campaign and that of the Democratic party was against the forces of "selfishness and greed" that were trying to saddle the country with the doctrine that "Government is best which is most indifferent to mankind." He "welcomed the hatred" of such forces, he said, and warned that, in his second administration, they would meet their master.[2] He intended to bring this about, he promised, by defending and expanding the New Deal.

Roosevelt was unable to deliver on his promises. Despite his personal landslide victory and the dominance of the Democratic party, the president failed in his efforts to extend the New Deal. His most visible defeat came with his proposal to expand the size of the Supreme Court. Frustrated by court decisions that had invalidated important pieces of New Deal legislation, Roosevelt proposed that the president be allowed to appoint a new justice for each sitting justice who had reached the age of 70 (up to a total of six). His aim was to create a majority on the Court favorable to the New Deal. The president lost badly on the issue. He was abandoned by many members of his own Democratic party in Congress and around the country. Appeals to party loyalty, liberal use of patronage and government contracts, and reminders of past political debts and obligations were to no avail.

His defeat on the court-packing issue was but the first in a string of defeats. His bill to regulate child labor was watered down to such an extent that it hardly resembled what he had proposed. His effort to reorganize the federal bureaucracy and to create two new cabinet departments went down in a resounding defeat. His farm bill met a similar fate. In each and every one of these defeats, it was key members of his own party that stood in the way of success. He became very bitter toward party leaders, legislators, and activists who had abandoned him. He complained to one confidant that "it's a terrible thing to look over your shoulder when you are trying to lead—and to find no one there."[3]

This story tells us a great deal about American political parties and how they are different from political parties in other democratic countries. In most parliamentary systems (like Great Britain, Germany, or Sweden), a political party that enjoys a large majority (like the Democrats did after the 1936 election) would have no trouble passing legislation to which its leadership was committed. In such systems, members of political parties tend to vote as a unified block in parliament, usually guided by the wishes of the prime minister, the cabinet, or party central committees, or all of these. American political parties are different. They do not act in a unified fashion. Elected and appointed officials carrying the party label are as likely as not to go their own way, to ignore the appeals of party leaders, and to strike their own deals. This chapter will discuss why this is so and what implications this has for the workings of democracy in the United States. We will see that such structural factors as constitutional rules, culture, and the economy are important in determining what kind of parties we have.

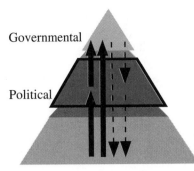

Governmental

Political

Structural

POLITICAL PARTIES AND THEIR ROLE IN A DEMOCRACY

Political parties are organizations that try to gain control over government by electing officials to public office who carry the party label. In representative democracies, parties are the principal organizations that recruit candidates for public office, run such candidates against the candidates of other political parties in competitive elections, and try to organize and coordinate the activities of government officials under party banners.

The Founders were generally critical of parties, even the rudimentary and ill-formed parties of their own day. In his farewell address to the nation in 1796, President George Washington warned his fellow citizens "in the most solemn manner against the baneful effects of the spirit of party." Benjamin Franklin once observed that "ignorance leads Men into a Party, and Shame keeps them from getting out again." John Adams was the gloomiest of the lot: ". . . the division of the Republic into two great parties . . . is to be feared as the greatest political evil under our Constitution."[4]

The Progressives believed that political parties were undemocratic and corrupt instruments of the "bosses," and created devices like the **direct primary** (in which voters rather than party leaders nominate candidates) and the **nonpartisan election** (without party labels) to break their hold. In our own day, public opinion polls show that a majority of Americans are highly skeptical about politicians and political parties, and remain uncertain about the relationship between parties and democracy.[5]

Many Americans, however, agree with political scientist E. E. Schattschneider that "modern democracy is unthinkable save in terms of the parties."[6] The reason is that parties are essential for majority rule:

> . . . the parties are the special form of political organization adapted to the mobilization of majorities. How else can the majority get organized? If democracy means anything at all it means that the majority has the right to organize for the purpose of taking over the government.[7]

Let's see how parties and majority rule are related.

Parties Can Help Form Majorities

To win elections, parties must first mobilize and activate their natural supporters: those who share their core goals and values. These natural supporters must be persuaded that the party stands for things they favor and is worth voting for, giving money to, campaigning for, and working actively for. Parties' mobilizing activities can contribute to democracy by educating people about politics, showing them how to pursue their interests and values, and getting them involved in political life.

To win an election, parties must also move beyond their core supporters and attract a broad range of voters. Elections create an incentive to incorporate as many voters as possible, with a majority being the optimal goal.

In order to increase their electoral appeal, moreover, parties usually try to put together broad group coalitions. Parties in the United States recruit candidates for public office from many ethnic and racial groups, for instance. Language in party platforms tries to placate and attract various interest groups. Party officeholders try to make decisions that take into account the preferences of a wide range of groups. This process contributes to the formation of majorities where none may have existed before.

Parties Can Make Majority Preferences Effective

The task of making informed choices about candidates and public policies is so complicated and so time consuming that a conscientious citizen, without help, might be unable to do anything else but pay attention to public affairs. It is not unusual for American voters to face a score or more of offices to fill in national, state, and local elections, along with a dozen or more ballot issues. Political parties can greatly simplify matters for the voter. The party can serve as ". . . a useful cue for voters, particularly the least informed and interested, who can use party as a shortcut or substitute for interpreting issues and events they may little comprehend."[8] Idealized notions about fully informed citizens may not be very practical. For most people, it is rational and sensible not to spend much time on politics. Party cues can be very helpful.

Competition between political parties can also increase public awareness of, and interest in, candidates and issues. Party competition, by "expanding the scope of conflict,"[9] attracts attention and gets people involved. By contrast, much interest group activity is conducted behind closed doors, out of the public eye. Parties can make politics more open and thus more democratic.

Democracy would not be served if majorities were unable to translate their wishes into governmental action. Political parties can be the glue that holds to-

Political parties generally try to broaden their appeal by running candidates from a wide range of ethnic, racial, and religious groups.

gether the various and sundry offices in the government, giving unity and direction to the actions of officeholders. This potential contribution of parties is especially important in the United States, where the constitutional design of government fragments and decentralizes power.

Finally, parties can help make officeholders more accountable. When things go wrong or promises are not kept, it is important in a democracy for citizens to know who is responsible. Where there are many offices and branches of government, however, it is hard to pinpoint responsibility. Officials tend to blame others. Citizens find it difficult to unravel the details. Political parties can simplify this difficult task by allowing for collective responsibility. Citizens can pass judgment on the governing ability of a party as a whole and decide whether to retain the incumbent party or throw it out of office.

We suggest here that parties *can be* an important tool of majority rule. Whether our own political parties play such a role is the question that we explore in the remainder of this chapter. We begin by describing the most important characteristics of the American party system.

THE TWO-PARTY SYSTEM

While our political party system shares certain characteristics with other political party systems around the world, it is quite unique in some essential ways.

Two-Party Dominance

The United States comes closer to having a "pure" two-party system than any other nation in the world. Most nations have either one-party systems or multiparty systems. Most Western democracies have multiparty systems (see Table 8.1). In the United States, however, two parties have dominated the political scene since 1836, and the Democrats and the Republicans have controlled the presidency and Congress since 1858. Minor or third parties have rarely polled a significant percentage of the popular vote in either presidential or congressional elections (more will be said about third parties later).

Competition on the national level between the two dominant parties has been remarkably close since the end of the Civil War. There were 31 presidential elections between 1868 and 1988, and the difference in popular vote between the candidates of the two major parties exceeded 20 percentage points only 5 times. Less than 10 percentage points separated them 19 times. In most presidential elections, a swing of only 5–10 percentage points in the popular vote would have changed the final results (see Figure 8.1). Party competition for Congress has been even closer. There has not been a single congressional election since 1932 in which party differences in the popular vote exceeded 20 percentage points. Less than 10 percentage points have separated the two major parties in most elections.

While the United States is a two-party system at the national level, it has always been a different story at the regional, state, and local levels. From the end of the Civil War to the 1960s, for instance, the deep South was solidly Democratic, devoid of serious party competition. Until recent times, the Plains States and New England were solidly Republican. Urban areas today are disproportionately Democratic; most suburbs are strongly Republican. There are some local communities, moreover, where elections are held on a nonpartisan basis, as are elections to the state legislature in Nebraska.

Table 8.1
Party Systems in Other Democratic Nations

Nation	Parties with Seats in Parliament in 1990	Nation	Parties with Seats in Parliament in 1990
Australia	Australian Labor Liberal National	Japan	Liberal Democratic Japan Socialist Clean Government Communist Democratic Socialist
Canada	Progressive Conservative Liberal New Democratic	Germany	Christian Democratic Union Christian Social Union Social Democratic Free Democratic Green
France	Socialist Rally for the Republic Union for French Democracy Centrists Communist	Spain	Socialist Workers Popular Convergence and Unity Social Democratic Center
Italy	Christian Democratic Communist Socialist Social Democratic Italian Social Movement Radicals Green Liberal	Sweden	Social Democratic Moderate Liberal Center Communist Green
		United Kingdom	Conservative Labour Social Democratic

Source: Central Intelligence Agency, *World Fact Book* (Washington, D.C.: CIA, 1990).

Figure 8.1 Winning margins in presidential elections since 1868

Source: Authors' calculations, based on Congressional Quarterly's Guide to U.S. Elections *(Washington, D.C.: CQ Press, 1988).*

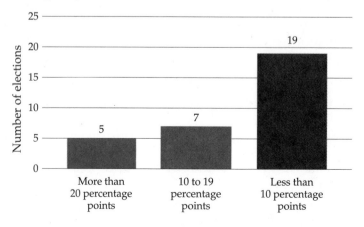

A History of the Two-Party System

Although the United States has had a two-party system for most of its history, it would be a mistake to assume that this system has been static. The party system has, in fact, changed a great deal, both mirroring and playing a central role in the dynamic and sometimes chaotic story of the development of the United States, as described in Chapter 4.

THE FIRST PARTY SYSTEM: FEDERALISTS VERSUS DEMOCRATIC REPUBLICANS Although the Founders were hostile to parties in theory, they created them almost immediately. The first was formed in the 1790s by George Washington's energetic Secretary of the Treasury, Alexander Hamilton. In a successful effort to push through the administration's ambitious legislative program, Hamilton persuaded sympathetic members of Congress to form a loosely organized party that eventually took the name "Federalist."

Thomas Jefferson, James Madison, and others formed a party in Congress to oppose the Hamilton program of protective tariffs, a national bank, and federal assumption of revolutionary war debts, which they believed hurt the economic interests of many groups in American society.[10] They called their faction Republican, though the Federalists tried to discredit them by calling them Democratic Republicans (the term *democratic* was a term of derision, not praise, in those days).

The Federalists and Democratic Republicans also were divided sharply on foreign policy. The Federalists, being close to New England and New York merchant and banking interests, favored a policy of trade and good relations with Great Britain, despite Great Britain's policy of preying on American shipping in the Atlantic. The split between the two parties was widened by their bitter debate over the stance to be taken on the new revolutionary government in France, with Jefferson and the Democratic Republicans favorable to it, and the Federalists hostile (though officially neutral).

In full control of the federal government after the election of their candidate John Adams as president in 1796, the Federalists passed the notorious Alien and Sedition Acts to repress dissent and opposition to Federalist policies. The Acts were aimed mainly against Jefferson's party. Ten Republican editors and printers were imprisoned and fined. Rather than be intimidated, the Republican party used the Alien and Sedition Acts to rally opposition to the Federalists and won a decisive victory in the election of 1800. Jefferson's victory was but the prelude to a string of spectacular successes by Democratic Republican presidential candidates.

The Federalists became tainted by their sympathies with Great Britain in an anti-British era (note the War of 1812), by their attempt to take New England out of the Union during the war, and by their inability to transform themselves from a party of the wealthy in an age when democracy was becoming more popular. They very quickly disappeared. By 1816, the first two-party system had evolved into a one-party or no-party system, generally known (because of the absence of party competition) as the "Era of Good Feelings."

THE SECOND PARTY SYSTEM: DEMOCRATS VERSUS WHIGS The nonparty system that prevailed during the 1820s "Era of Good Feelings" gave way in the 1830s to a strong two-party system. The Democrats (formerly the Democratic Republicans) and the Whigs were parties of a very different sort from those in the first party system. Instead of being loosely organized groups of local dignitaries and public officials, the parties that emerged in the 1830s were well-organized parties, with

The second party system was characterized by well-organized parties, skilled in the use of methods (like this parade) to mobilize the "common man" to participate in electoral politics.

sharply contrasting programs tied to a highly partisan electorate. The change was caused by a significant democratization of American life. By the 1820s and 1830s, legal barriers to voting by adult white males had disappeared. In addition, most states had passed laws requiring the direct popular election of presidential electors, taking the process out of the hands of state legislatures. With the expansion of the franchise and the popular election of presidents, it became clear that power in American politics would go to those organizations that were able to reach, organize, and mobilize millions of voters. In these changed circumstances, loosely organized parties of local dignitaries would no longer do.

The democratization of the electorate did not lead, however, to political contests of the sort that pitches the weak against the strong, the poor against the rich, or the people against elites. Differences between the Democrats and the Whigs were more often than not based on disagreements among various business and economic interests. The Whigs favored a protective tariff, a national bank, and a federal program of internal improvements (roads, canals, etc.); the Democrats, under the leadership of Andrew Jackson, opposed all three. While the Jacksonian struggle against the Bank of the United States was couched in "populist" terms (the common people versus the wealthy), the Democrats and antinational Bank forces were financed by state banks across the country that would greatly benefit from the defeat of an important economic rival.[11]

Neither national party was able to withstand the drift of the country toward civil war. The northern and southern wings of each party mirrored the split in the nation. The Whig party simply disintegrated and disappeared. Several of its fragments came together with "free soilers" (who opposed the expansion of slavery into the western territories) and antislavery Democrats to form a new Republican party—the ancestor of present-day Republicans—which ran its first presidential candidate, John Fremont, in the election of 1856. The Democrats survived but could not agree on a candidate to run against Republican Abraham Lincoln in 1860, so each wing of the party nominated its own candidate.

FROM THE CIVIL WAR TO 1896: REPUBLICANS AND DEMOCRATS IN BALANCE   Once the southern states had reentered the union after **Reconstruction**, the Republicans and Democrats found themselves roughly balanced in national politics. Between

1876 and 1896, the Democrats managed to control the presidency for 8 of 20 years, the Senate for 6 years, and the House of Representatives for 14 years. Each party had a strong regional flavor. The Democratic party was primarily a white southern party, though Catholics and many workers in northern urban areas supported it as well. The GOP (another name for the Republican party, meaning "Grand Old Party") became a party of business, the middle class, and newly enfranchised blacks.

THE PARTY SYSTEM OF 1896: THIRTY-SIX YEARS OF REPUBLICAN DOMINANCE   Underneath the apparent calm of a balanced two-party system, however, a storm was brewing. The late nineteenth century was a time of very rapid transformation of the American economy and society, with massive disruptions in the fabric of everyday life, as we saw in Chapter 4. Farmers and industrial workers were especially hard hit, and they responded with social protest movements (see Chapter 10). Workers turned to the strike weapon, while farmers responded by forming third parties. The Greenback party, whose platform called for an inflated currency (to pay off loans with cheaper dollars), won over 300,000 votes in the 1880 presidential election. The People's party, more commonly known as the Populist party, garnered over 1 million votes in the 1892 presidential election, or 8.5 percent of the total. It won four states in the electoral college, running on the slogan "wealth belongs to him who creates it." During the 1890s, Populist party candidates also won governorships in eight states and control of at least as many state legislatures. Most significantly, the party proved to be popular, not only with farmers in the West and the South, but also with unions and workers in industrial cities all over the nation. It also managed to create an alliance of black and white small farmers in many of the states of the deep South, posing a threat to the area's traditional leadership.

In 1896, the Populist party joined with the Democratic party to nominate a single candidate for the presidency, the charismatic orator William Jennings

Strikes were quite common in the late nineteenth century, with government usually intervening on the side of management. Here federal marshalls try to control people striking against the Pullman Coach Company.

Bryan, who urged "free coinage of silver" to help debtors with cheaper currency (which also pleased silver mining companies).

The threat of a radical agrarian party, joining blacks and whites, and farmers and unionists, proved to be too much for many Americans and contributed to one of the most bitter electoral campaigns in U.S. history. Conservative Democrats deserted their party to join the Republicans. Businesses warned each other and their workers in no uncertain terms about the dangers of a Populist-Democratic victory. Newly formed business organizations, such as the National Association of Manufacturers, spread the alarm about a possible Democratic victory. In the South, efforts to intimidate potential black voters increased dramatically.[12] Mark Hanna, the "boss" of the GOP and president of the Hanna Steel Company, raised the enormous sum (for that era) of $3.3 million to back McKinley's run for the presidency.[13]

The Republicans won handily and dominated American politics until the Great Depression and the election of 1932. Between 1896 and 1932, the Republicans won control of both houses of Congress in 15 out of 18 elections, and of the presidency in 7 out of 9. But this is not the only reason that the election of 1896 is considered to be so important. First, after 1896, the voting participation rates of the American people dropped sharply and never fully recovered (more on this in the next chapter).[14] Second, the states of the deep South, using both law and intimidation, removed blacks from the electorate. This eliminated the Republican party as a factor in southern politics and firmly established a one-party Democratic system that would last for more than one-half century.

THE NEW DEAL PARTY SYSTEM: DEMOCRATIC PARTY DOMINANCE   In the opening pages of this chapter, we told part of the story of the 1932–1936 realignment from Republican to Democratic dominance. The Great Depression, the New Deal, and the leadership of President Franklin D. Roosevelt fundamentally changed the conception of the proper role of the federal government, the groups aligned with each of the two parties, and the relative balance of power in the country between Democrats and Republicans.

Election returns make clear the fundamental shift in party dominance. During the 40 years from 1932 through 1972, the Democrats won 7 out of 11 presidential elections, enjoyed control of the Senate and the House of Representatives for all but 4 years, and prevailed in a substantial majority of governorships and state legislatures across the nation.

The Democrats also enjoyed a large lead over the Republicans in party identification among the electorate (as the newly developed opinion polls and surveys showed) and were supported by a broad coalition of groups. By the middle of the 1930s, workers, Catholics, Jews, unionists, small and medium-sized farmers, people in urban areas, white ethnics, southerners, and blacks were firmly in the Democratic party camp. Most would remain there until the 1960s or longer. Several scholars have suggested, moreover, that some large multinational corporations and major investment banks were an integral part of the coalition as well, supplying personnel, ideas, and campaign money throughout the period.[15]

A POST-NEW-DEAL PARTY SYSTEM?   After the stunning Reagan victories in 1980 and 1984, many people thought that the United States might be in the midst of another major realignment and transition to a new party system, dominated by the Republican party. It is now clear, however, that such a change never occurred. To be sure, the New Deal party system deteriorated, and the New Deal coalition slowly came unglued—the defection of the white South is particularly noteworthy in this respect—but what took its place is not yet clear. The party system in the 1980s was not like the traditional ones, in which one party controlled the government, led in party identification among the electorate, dominated the states, and defined the public agenda.

First, while Republicans held the presidency from 1980 to 1992, Democrats retained a virtual stranglehold on Congress.[16] For another thing, Republicans failed to make much headway in cutting into strong majorities in state legislatures and governorships. Furthermore, Republicans were unable to win a majority to identify with their party.

Finally, there was no wholesale substitution of one policy agenda for another, as in past realignment periods. Despite the "Reagan Revolution," public opinion polls continued to report strong majorities in favor of a government role in the management of the economy, the alleviation of poverty, and provision of Social Security, environmental protection, product safety, and civil rights guarantees. While the so-called social issues (abortion, child care, drug use, etc.) became more prominent, this did not mean wholesale rejection of the dominant issues of the New Deal party system and their replacement by an alternative issue agenda. Indeed, opinion on many social issues became increasingly liberal.[17]

What all of this added up to is unclear. The term *realignment* seems too strong, though it might fit some day if Republicans were to gain strong majorities at all levels in the political system. Many political observers have suggested the term **dealignment** as a way to capture both the ambiguity of the change that is going on and the decreasing tendency of Americans to care about parties at all.[18]

Explaining Realignment

In the history of the two-party system in the United States, we see five relatively stable periods, each stretching over 30 or 40 years, linked to one another by much shorter periods (sometimes including only a single election, as in 1896, and sometimes spanning several elections, as in 1932 and 1936) of transformation, or realignment. Figure 8.2 shows this history in graphic form. *Realignment* means that a new party system has taken the place of the old. The new party system differs from the old in a variety of ways, even when the names of the party stay the same (as has occurred in all realignments since the Civil War). Party systems tend to differ from one another on the issues that get attention, the party loyalties of voters, the group foundations of the parties, and the policies of the federal government.[19]

Realignments seem to be triggered by the transformation of structural factors. They occur when the old party system is unable to accommodate or solve problems that develop during rapid social, economic, and cultural change. Thus, the rise of the Jacksonian party is associated with the dynamic growth of free enterprise, the expansion of the size of the population, and pressures from the common people for some role in political life. The Jacksonian system gave way to a new party system under the great pressures of North-South conflict that led to civil war. The transition to the system of 1896 is associated with rapid industrialization, the rise of large corporations, and the threat posed by radical worker and

Figure 8.2 Party systems and realignment

farmer movements. The New Deal party system grew out of the crisis of the Great Depression and favorable public reactions to government efforts to deal with the economic collapse.

Scholars disagree about how realignment takes place. Most political scientists believe that it involves the movement of blocs of voters from one party to another and the entrance of new voters. The idea here is that citizens feel unhappy about the course of affairs in the nation and express themselves either by switching their party allegiance (as blacks did around 1936, when they switched from the Republican to the Democratic party) or by voting in higher proportions than in the past (as many blue-collar workers did in 1932 and 1936, and as fundamentalist Christians did in 1980).

Other political scientists believe that change first occurs among powerful economic elite groups. Thomas Ferguson and Joel Rogers suggest that realignment is best explained by shifts in the behavior of "major investors," especially business groups.[20] The New Deal party system, they argue, was less a product of shifts among voters than it was the formation of a new coalition of business interests who wanted free trade and were willing to back social reforms in exchange. They locate the end of the New Deal party system in the abandonment of New Deal policies by business interests when the pressures of international economic competition made them oppose spending tax money on social programs. Ferguson and Rogers believe that voters eventually follow the lead of major investors, who define the issues, pose the alternatives, and fund parties and candidates. Changes in partisan identification and voting behavior in the electorate is not the cause of realignment, but an effect, according to this interpretation. Of course, it is possible that realignments may start at either the mass or elite levels, or both at once. The evidence does not yet allow us to choose.

Why a Two-Party System?

Most Western democracies have multiparty systems. Why are we so different from other countries? There are several possible answers.

ELECTORAL RULES   Most other democratic nations elect their representatives on the basis of **proportional representation** (PR).[21] Each party, in such an electoral system, is represented in the legislative branch of government in rough proportion to its percentage of the popular vote in an election. In a perfect PR system, a party receiving 40 percent of the vote would receive 40 seats in a 100-seat legislative body; a party receiving 22 percent of the vote would receive 22 seats; and so on.

Fourth Party System		Fifth Party System	Dealignment
Democrats v. Republicans (Republican dominance)	Realignment	Democrats v. Republicans (Democratic dominance)	(No dominant party; divided government)

1932 1936   1980

In such a system, even small parties would have a reason to maintain their separate identities, for no matter how narrow their appeal, they would win seats as long as they could win a proportion of the popular vote. Voters with strong views on an issue or with strong ideological outlooks could vote for a party that closely represented their views. A vote for a small party would not be wasted, for it would ultimately be translated into legislative seats and perhaps a place in the governing coalition. Israel and the Netherlands come closest to having a pure PR system, organized on a national basis; most other Western European nations have departures of varying significance from the pure form. Most, for instance, vote on slates of party candidates within multimember electoral districts, apportioning seats in each district according to each party's percentage of the vote.

Elections in the United States are organized on a *plurality, "winner-take-all," single-member-district* basis. Each electoral district in the United States, whether it is an urban ward, a county, a congressional district, or a state, generally elects only one person to a given office and does so on the basis of whoever wins the *most* votes (not necessarily a majority). This arrangement creates a powerful incentive for parties to coalesce and for voters to concentrate their attention on big parties. Let's see why.

From the vantage point of party organizations, this type of election discourages minor-party efforts, because failure to win a plurality leaves such a party with no representation at all. Leaders of such parties are tempted to merge with a major party. By the same token, a disaffected faction or group within a party is unlikely to leave the party and go out on its own in an electoral system like ours, because the probability of gaining legislative seats is very low.

From the voter's point of view, a single-member, "winner-take-all" election means that a vote for a minor party is wasted. Those who vote for a minor party may feel good, but voters have few illusions that such votes will translate into representation and are not inclined to do so.

The effect of the American form of election is accentuated by the fact that the main prize in our political system—the presidency— is elected in a single gigantic district: the nation.[22] In parliamentary systems, the executive power is lodged in a cabinet, led by a prime minister, in which many parties may be represented. It is not uncommon in parliamentary systems for the prime minister to come from one of the lesser parties (Italian Prime Minister Giovanni Spadolini came from a party with only 3 percent of the parliamentary seats). In such systems, parties have an incentive to maintain their separate identities. In the United States, only one party candidate can win a plurality of the electoral votes in the contest for the presidency. Minor parties are really not in the game for the main prize.

Table 8.2
Legal Obstacles to Third Parties

Selected Requirements to Gain a Place on the Ballot

State	Requirement (Selected)[a]
California	Signatures of 10 percent of voters in gubernatorial election (76,714 in 1990)
Florida	181,421 signatures (1990), 10 cents per signature "validating" fee
Louisiana	5 percent of state voters must register in name of new party
Nevada	10 percent of registered voters must register in name of new party; signatures of 10 percent of the total vote for U.S. House of Representatives
Texas	Convention participants and petition signers must total 1 percent of gubernatorial vote

[a] Democratic presidential candidates required only 25,500 signatures to run in every primary and caucus in the nation in 1988.

Source: Edward Feigenbaum and James Palmer, *Ballot Access* (Washington, D.C.: Federal Election Commission, 1988).

RESTRICTIONS ON MINOR PARTIES Once a party system is in place, the dominant parties often establish rules that make it difficult for other parties to get on the ballot. This is true in the United States, where a number of very formidable legal obstacles exist for gaining access to the ballot. While some of these restrictions have been eased because of successful court challenges by recent minor party presidential candidates, the path to the ballot remains a difficult one in many states (see Table 8.2). Ross Perot, however, was able to gain the ballot in 50 states.

The way in which the federal government partially funds presidential campaigns has made the situation of third parties even more difficult. Major-party candidates automatically qualify for federal funding once they are nominated. Minor-party candidates must attract a minimum percentage of the votes in the general election to be eligible for public funding. They are, furthermore, not reimbursed until after the election. Moreover, federal funding is given to the Democrats and Republicans to run their conventions; minor parties receive none.

Finally, the television networks are no longer obliged to give equal time to parties other than the Republicans and the Democrats. Congress took special action to suspend the Federal Communications Commission's "equal time" and "fairness doctrine" requirements to allow televised debates between presidential aspirants within each of the major parties, and between the major party nominees in the general election campaign.[23] Perot joined the debates in 1992, however, after he was invited in by Clinton and Bush.

POPULAR ATTITUDES The attitudes of the American people are also an important factor in maintaining a two-party system. Once a party system is in place, it comes to seem natural—the only possible kind of party system. This attitude is passed on to children by families, schools, and the media. Children learn that there are only Democrats and Republicans and that their family is one or the other.

As we saw in Chapter 4, moreover, the political culture does not provide fertile ground for a broad range of ideologically distinctive parties. The broad consensus on classical liberalism—individualism, private property, limited government, and the market—allows little space for parties outside of the consensus.

THE ABSENCE OF A STRONG LABOR MOVEMENT   The relative weakness of the American labor movement has been noted in several places in this book. The organized labor movement was instrumental in the creation of Socialist and Labor political parties in the Western European countries that challenged traditional liberal (free enterprise, small government) and traditional conservative (monarchist, Catholic, and aristocratic) parties. The British Labour party, for instance, was created by trade union officials and Socialists in 1906. The deeply divided French labor movement helped form both the Socialist party and the Communist party. Strong Socialist and Labor parties in Europe did not replace traditional Liberal and Conservative parties but spurred them on to more spirited organizing and electioneering of their own. The result has been the creation of a basic three-party system in many European countries—Conservative, Liberal, and Labor or Socialist—with a number of small satellite parties (encouraged by PR electoral systems) clustered about them. The United States lacks both the traditional conservative party groupings that grew out of feudalism and a strong labor movement. This is not necessarily a problem; it simply helps us to understand why a broad range of parties does not exist in America.

Minor Parties in the Two-Party System

Minor parties have played a less important role in the United States than in virtually any other democratic nation. In our entire history, only a single minor party (the Republican) has managed to replace one of the major parties. In our entire history, moreover (not counting the Republicans), only five minor parties have been able to win even 10 percent of the popular vote in a presidential election, and only seven have managed to win a single state in a presidential election. In 1992, Ross Perot garnered 19 percent of the vote under the "United We Stand" party label.

TYPES OF MINOR PARTIES   Protest parties sometimes arise as part of a protest movement. The American party, popularly known as the "Know Nothing" party—because it started as a secret society, the existence of which the members would not acknowledge—wanted to restrict immigration to the United States and thrived on antiforeigner sentiment during the late 1840s. The People's or Populist party grew out of the western and southern farm protest movement against monopolistic practices in the railroad and banking industries. George Wallace, famous for standing in the schoolhouse door to prevent the integration of the University of Alabama when he was governor, formed the American Independence party to oppose federal activism in civil rights.

We also have had several ideological parties over the years. These include the Socialist party, the Socialist Labor party, the Socialist Workers party, and the Communist party. None of these parties has had a significant electoral impact, except the Socialist party under Eugene Debs, which won 6 percent of the popular vote in 1912. The Libertarian party, committed in its words to the "complete pri-

Eugene Debs, candidate of the Socialist party, polled 6 percent of the vote in the 1912 presidential election.

vatization" of society and the virtual elimination of government, has had the most substantial recent showing of minor parties, particularly in Alaska and the western states outside of California. Ross Perot, running against "the mess in Washington," gained significant attention in 1992.

Single-issue parties are barely distinguishable from interest groups, though they do run their own candidates for public office. They include the venerable Prohibition party that has been around since 1869, the Vegetarian party, and the Right to Life party (antiabortion). The Women's party was active from 1913 to 1920 and played a role in obtaining the right of women to vote. The Free Soil party, which opposed the spread of slavery into the western states from 1848 to 1852, became one of the founding elements of the Republican party.

Splinter parties form when a faction within one of the major political parties bolts to run its own candidate for president. The Progressive or "Bull Moose" party under former President Teddy Roosevelt, broke with the Republican party in 1912 over the GOP's renomination of the less popular President William Howard Taft and its hostility to progressive legislation. (This split enabled Democrat Woodrow Wilson to win.) In the 1948 election, the Dixiecrats broke with the Democratic party because of the Democratic party's support for federal civil rights legislation and ran Senator Strom Thurmond (then a Democrat) for president. In that same election, the Progressives ran former Vice-President Henry Wallace in response to what it considered the Democratic party's abandonment of the New Deal and growing hostility to our wartime ally, the Soviet Union.

THE ROLE OF MINOR PARTIES   It is not entirely clear what role minor parties play in American politics.[24] Sometimes minor parties articulate new ideas that are eventually taken over by one or both major parties. The Free Soil party advocated policies on the admission of new states that became part of the Republican party agenda in 1856. The Socialist party under Norman Thomas advocated public works projects as a way to battle unemployment during the Great Depression, an idea that became part of the Democratic New Deal legislative package.

Sometimes minor parties allow those with grievances to express themselves in a way that is not possible within the major parties. More cynical observers suggest that this allows unhappy groups to "blow off steam" without seriously disturbing the normal political process or threatening those holding public office. Less cynical observers believe that this expression of discontent with the major parties and the threat that major-party voters will defect keeps the major parties responsive and responsible.[25]

Because minor parties, by definition, are unlikely to win national elections, they are usually not as cautious as the major parties. They tend to be loud, unambiguous about policies, and ideologically committed. As such, they probably expand the scope of conflict in American politics, increase interest and attention among at least some segments of the public, and bring a few more Americans into the political process.

THE PARTIES AS ORGANIZATIONS

> I don't belong to an organized political party. I'm a Democrat.—Will Rogers.[26]

 American parties don't look much like parties in other democratic countries. In most democratic countries parties are fairly well-structured organizations, led by party professionals, and committed to a set of policies and principles (and, sometimes, to an ideology). They also tend to have clearly defined membership requirements, centralized control over party nominations and electoral financing, and discipline over party members holding political office. None of this is true for our own major parties. We look at each in this section.

The Weak and Insubstantial Nature of Our Parties[27]

The classic boss-led political machines of American folklore—so long identified with names like Tammany Hall, "Boss Tweed" of New York, Richard Daley of Chicago, Harry Byrd of Virginia, and Huey Long of Louisiana—have disappeared from the cities and states where they once existed, mainly the result of reforms that ended party control over government contracts and jobs (see Chapter 15, "State and Local Government," for details on the urban machine). Political machines have never existed at the national level. There has never been a "boss" of any of our major political parties. There have been leaders with clout, reputation, and vision, to be sure, but never a "boss" that could issue commands and be reasonably certain that such commands would be obeyed. Even popular, charismatic, and skillful presidents, including George Washington, Abraham Lincoln, Woodrow Wilson, Franklin D. Roosevelt, Harry Truman, John F. Kennedy, and Ronald Reagan, have had nearly as much trouble controlling the many diverse and independent groups and individuals within their own parties as they have had dealing with the opposition. Recall that Franklin D. Roosevelt could not get his way with the Democratic party, even after his decisive electoral victory in 1936.

The vagueness of party membership is a good indicator of the insubstantial nature of our parties. Think about what it means to be a Republican or a Democrat in the United States. Americans do not join parties in the sense of paying dues and receiving a membership card. To Americans, being a member of a party may mean voting most of the time for the candidate of a party or choosing to become a candidate for one of them. Or it may mean voting in a party primary. Or it may mean contributing money to, or otherwise helping in, a local, state, or national campaign of one of the party candidates. Or it may just mean that one generally prefers one party to another most of the time. These are loose criteria for membership, to say the least—looser than for virtually any other organization that one might imagine.

THE FORMAL ORGANIZATION OF THE PARTIES   The Republican and Democratic parties, it is often said, are not organizations in the usual sense of the term, but loose collections of local and state parties, candidates and officeholders, and associated interest groups that get together every four years to nominate a presidential candidate. There is more to the national parties than this stereotype suggests, but not much.

Unlike a corporation, a bureaucratic agency, a military unit, or even political parties in most other countries, the presumptive leaders of the major American political parties cannot issue orders that get passed along a chain of command to those at the bottom. Each level of the party is relatively independent and acts in concert with the others—on occasion—not on the basis of orders, but on the basis of common interests, sentiment, and the desire to win elections. There are few resources or devices within either of the two parties to compel one level of the party organization to do the bidding of another. Most important, the national party is unable to control its most vital activity—the nomination of candidates running under its party label—or the flow of money that funds electoral campaigns, or the behavior of its officeholders.

This is not to suggest that the parties are entirely devoid of tools to encourage coordination and cooperation between its various levels. The *national party conventions* are the governing bodies of the parties (see Chapter 9 for more on the conventions). Convention delegates meet every four years, not only to nominate presidential and vice-presidential candidates, but also to settle on a party **platform** and to revise party rules. (These events are often contentious, as the box on the Mississippi Freedom Democratic party shows.)

Though the national convention is the formal governing body of each of the parties, it cannot dictate to party candidates and party organizations at other levels of jurisdiction. The presidential nominee need not adhere to either the letter or the spirit of the party platform, for instance, though most nominees stay fairly close to the platform most of the time (usually because the winning candidate's supporters control the platform writing committee). State and local party organizations may nominate whomever they choose to run for public office and may or may not support key planks in the party platform. The all-white Mississippi delegation to the 1964 Democratic convention even refused to endorse Lyndon Johnson, the Democratic presidential candidate.

The Democrats and Republicans each have a *national committee*,[28] whose purpose is to conduct the business of the party during the four years between national conventions. While the national committees have little power, they provide valuable services for local and state parties, and for party candidates at all levels.

The national committees are made up of elected committeemen and committeewomen from each of the states (usually apportioned on the basis of state population and party strength in the last election), an increasingly sizeable staff, and a chairperson. The national committees rarely meet. The real business of the committee is run by the party chairperson, assisted by the committee staff. Paul

Jesse Jackson and his "Rainbow Coalition" movement tried for many years to force the Democratic party to pay more attention to the needs of minorities and the poor.

Kirk, the Democratic party chairman during the Reagan years of the early 1980s, was particularly known for his appeals to moderate and conservative Democrats and for his successful emulation of Republican techniques of raising money (quite a bit of it, to the party's later dismay, from savings and loan institutions). His successor in 1989, Ronald Brown, was the first black chairman of a party; he attempted to reconcile Jesse Jackson supporters with the main body of the party.

The chairperson exercises little power when a president from his or her party is in office. When the opposition controls the presidency, the party chairperson exercises more influence in party affairs, though the extent of that power should not be exaggerated.

Almost as old as the national party committees, but entirely independent of them, are the *congressional campaign committees* that help members of Congress campaign for reelection. They help raise money, provide media services (like making short videotapes of the members of Congress for local television news shows), do research, and whatever else party members in Congress deem appropriate. These committees are controlled by party members in Congress, not the party chairperson, the national committees, or even the president.

Each of the parties has a wide range of *affiliated groups* that circle the parties, like planets circle around the sun. Each party has its own organizations for women (the National Federation of Republican Women; the National Federation of Democratic Women) and young people (the Young Republicans, the Young Democrats). Each has closely affiliated research groups: the Heritage Foundation for the Republicans, and the Brookings Institution for the Democrats. Each has organized policy and ideological reform groups, such as the Democratic Leadership Conference (to try to move the party to a more "centrist-moderate" position), Jesse Jackson's liberal Rainbow Coalition, and Senator Jesse Helms ultraconservative Congressional Club. Each of these affiliated groups is mostly free to go its own way; the national parties have limited power to shape their actions.

THE STRUGGLE FOR DEMOCRACY

★

Fannie Lou Hamer and the Mississippi Freedom Democratic Party

Fanny Lou Hamer's story electrified the nation and threatened to ruin Lyndon Johnson's party. Hamer, a 40-year-old black sharecropper from Mississippi, testifying before the Credentials Committee of the Democratic Party Convention and a national television audience, described what had happened to her when she tried to register to vote.

They beat me and they beat me with a long, flat blackjack. I screamed to God in my mind. My dress worked itself up. I tried to pull it down. They beat my arms until I had no feeling in them.

The 1964 Democratic Party convention in Atlantic City was meant to be a celebration of President Lyndon Johnson and a launching pad for the fall presidential campaign against Republican Barry Goldwater. The idea was to downplay intraparty conflicts, convey a message of unity and purpose to the country, and focus on defeating the Republicans. The Mississippi Freedom Democratic party's (MFDP) appeal to the Credentials Committee to be seated in place of the state's official Democratic

party delegation in the racially charged atmosphere of 1964 threatened to throw a wrench into the convention party.

The Mississippi Freedom Democratic party was created by black and white Mississippians in 1963 as a vehicle to encourage black political participation in the most segregated state in the Union. Only 5 percent of blacks in the state were registered to vote. Efforts by blacks to register were typically met with firings, threats, mortgage foreclosures, and violence (see Chapter 1). Hamer and the others who had founded the MFDP thought that they had a good chance to be seated at the convention. The regular Mississippi Democratic party remained lily-white (precinct and county party meetings were closed to blacks) at a time when the national party had embraced the civil rights cause, and it openly supported the Republican candidate Barry Goldwater. The insurgents believed that a new party organization, open to all Mississippians and committed to supporting the Democratic party nominee and platform in Atlantic City, could not fail to win the fight to be seated as

The Primacy of Candidates

In Germany, individual candidates for the Bundestag (the equivalent of Congress) are less important than the political parties.[29] Candidates are nominated by local party committees, dominated by party regulars. Party lists for the general election are drawn up by state (Länder) party organizations, which are also dominated by party regulars. Independent candidates cannot force themselves on the party through primaries or caucuses open to the public, as in the United States, because such extraparty devices do not exist. Money for conducting electoral campaigns, moreover, is mostly raised and spent by the party organizations, not individual candidates (there is also much free television and radio time provided to the par-

the official delegation. Many Mississippians, black and white, put their reputations, fortunes, and lives on the line to change the political climate of their state. Eventually, over 80,000 citizens of the state participated in MFDP delegate selection meetings—far more than participated in the affairs of the regular party.

Lyndon Johnson would have none of it. He was angry that the credentials fight was detracting from his renomination, and he feared that replacing the official delegation would lead to the wholesale defection of the South in the November elections. He rejected a compromise offer by several leading Democrats to seat both delegations. All he was willing to deliver were two at-large seats to the MFDP and a pledge that no segregated delegations would be seated at future Democratic conventions. The pledge was made official party policy and eventually made American politics more democratic by lowering racial barriers to participation in party affairs in all of the states. It was a bitter pill to swallow, however, for those who had risked so much to be there and who had expected so much. Hamer and the other MFDP delegates left Atlantic City in anger and disgust.

Sources: William H. Chafe, *The Unfinished Journey* (New York: Oxford University Press, 1986), pp. 311–314; Godfrey Hodgson, *America in Our Time* (New York: Vintage, 1978), pp. 213–215; and Taylor Branch, *Parting the Waters: America in the King Years,* 1954–63 (New York: Simon & Schuster, 1988), pp. 819–820)

ties and substantial government money to help run campaigns and other party affairs). The state and federal party organizations also run virtually every aspect of the Bundestag campaign. Finally, the campaign is waged between parties and their alternative programs, not between individual candidates, and the electorate tends to make its choices based on feelings about the parties rather than the candidates.

American politics is "candidate centered." The weakness of our parties as organizations is most apparent in their inability to select and to channel the activities of those who run for public office under the party banner (see the box on advance work for party candidates).

DOING POLITICS

Advance Work for Party Candidates

The following profiles Jack Weeks and some of his colleagues who worked on presidential nominating campaigns in 1988:

... Advance people are a subculture within a subculture. They are political trailblazers, moving one step ahead of the candidate to scout out the lay of the land, so they often wind up in the same bars at the same time. A few of the other advance people—John Toohey and Steve Rabinowitz with Illinois Senator Paul Simon, Dennis Walto with former Colorado Senator Gary Hart—were Week's subordinates in 1984, when he worked with Hart.

This year, despite occasional sniping between Senator Albert Gore, Jr.'s and Dick Gephardt's campaign managers, it has been a relatively friendly competition among Democrats. In the bar, the political enemies fraternized easily, touting their candidates with what often seemed to be tongues in cheeks. A Simon advance man was talking with his fiancée, who does advance for Richard Gephardt. (But party lines

aren't often crossed: When Tom Synhorst, Republican Senator Robert J. Dole's Iowa campaign manager, wandered into the Savery, people wondered audibly if he was lost.) ...

For true political gypsies, advance work supplies the political drug in its purest form. There's no room for self-doubt, no time for indecision. An advance man comes into a town cold and knows that in four days the world is going to drop out of the sky in a fleet of Lear jets and he had better have something to show it. He's got to recruit volunteers, get a site, pull together a crowd and ensure there is a place from which reporters can file their stories, which become the advance man's trophies. "The ultimate is a piece on the national news or in the *New York Times*," says Barry Wyatt, head of advance for Richard Gephardt. "It's not uncommon to find advance people, after they've been on the road for a couple of months, with a satchel full of clippings."

Perhaps the most important part of

In most European countries, people vote for parties rather than for individual candidates, as this German ballot shows.

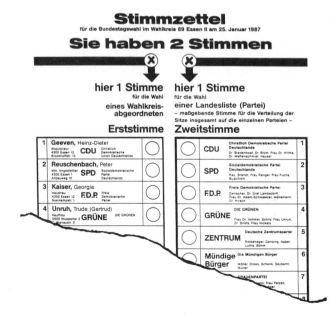

an advance man's job is to orchestrate the symbolism, to make sure the picture the press gets is the picture a campaign wants it to get.

Jack F. Kemp's people, for example, are always looking for a football the former professional quarterback can throw—a *local* football, preferably, not one of the several pigskins they carry with them. When the Buffalo, N.Y., Congressman was campaigning in Minnesota recently, Peter Sterling, 22, his deputy regional political director, found the football in a sporting goods store at a mall a couple of days before Kemp was to arrive. Sterling pressed a clerk into service as a wide receiver, mapped out his pass route and told the press the play. All that was left was for Kemp to arrive and throw. Cameras rolled and, as planned, it made the local news.

Life on the road never really loses its appeal, but as gypsies get older, the real world tends to intrude. On a wall at Jack Weeks's house in Boston is a large map of the United States. His sons John, who is 3, and Christopher, 7, keep track of his progress across the country with colored pins. Weeks calls them twice a day when he's on the road, but he knows that there is no substitute for being home. "You don't have a personal life on the road," he said. "You have conversations, that's all you have."

Beginners tend to think advance is glamorous. "You're in Las Vegas one week, Texas the next, then you're somewhere else, you're all over the country," said Weeks. "The press is around, you get to see the candidate every three or four days.

"But think of it," he continued. "You're not really seeing the country. I mean, I look at the ceiling in the hotel, what kind of ceiling do I have? Then the event happens, and you're gone, you're somewhere else doing the same thing all over again."

Source: From John Homans, "The Lure of the Political Road," *New York Times Magazine* (March 13, 1988), p. 17.

In most parliamentary systems, as in Germany, candidates are pretty much beholden to the party. Parties select candidates, are responsible for most of a candidate's campaign financing, and strongly influence their behavior once in office. Here the opposite is true; candidates are primary, and the parties are secondary, in the sense that party activities are shaped by the electoral needs of their candidates. Candidates have independent sources of campaign financing, their own campaign organizations, and their own campaign themes and priorities.

Once in office, though they may be influenced by a degree of party loyalty, candidates are largely free to go their own way, influenced by calculations of how to win the next election. If candidates in office refuse to toe the "party line," as vague as that line usually is, the party can do little about it. President Franklin D. Roosevelt could not even get his Vice-President John Garner to support many of his New Deal programs. During the fight over FDR's court-packing scheme, Garner showed his displeasure by staying home in Texas.

Our parties seem to be becoming even more "candidate centered." In the past, party candidates were usually nominated in district, state, and national conventions, where party regulars played a major role. They are now almost exclusively nominated in primaries or "grass roots" caucuses, where the party organizations are almost invisible. Nomination comes to those who are best able to raise money, to gain access to the media, and to form their own electoral organizations. Nominations are increasingly slipping out of the grasp of party regulars and officials. Nominees are so independent that they sometimes oppose party leaders and reject traditional party policies. Republicans were embarrassed when David Duke, former Grand Wizard of the Ku Klux Klan, was elected to the Louisiana State Legislature in 1988 under the Republican banner and ran for the governorship as a Republican in 1990, despite the opposition of Louisiana and national Republican officials.

Party Goals

Obviously, parties want to win elections. But for what purpose? That's not as easy to answer as it may seem, given the fragmentation and complexity of the party organizations. Each component tends to have its own goals.

Party activists, the people who do the most important organizational work of the parties—those who work for candidates, raise money for the party, hold party offices, serve as delegates to party conventions—can be divided into two main subgroups, with somewhat different goals.[30] *Party professionals* are the traditional party workers whose first commitment is to the party itself. They tend to be pragmatic, oriented to winning elections. Issues and ideology are less important to them than finding candidates who can appeal to as many voters as possible. *Party amateurs* are party people who tend to be motivated by ideological or issue concerns. To them, the party is an instrument for advancing an ideological agenda (usually liberalism in the Democratic party and conservatism in the Republican party) or a particular issue, such as civil rights or abortion. Party amateurs, while interested in finding a winning candidate, often want candidates to conform to their ideological or issue agenda.

Party officeholders first and foremost want to retain their positions or gain higher office, and they mold most of their behavior with an eye on the next elec-

Ron Brown, chair of the Democratic National Committee during the early 1990s, greets party contributors.

tion. Even officeholders who came to office on ideological or issue-oriented grounds tend to moderate their positions in order to ensure reelection.

Party voters are not so easy to pigeonhole. They are a diverse lot, only loosely connected to the party organization. Some want ideological and issue purity from the party. Others seek party victory, even if it only means the lesser of two evils wins.

Financial contributors are also diverse in their goals. Many are interested in ideological and policy issues. Many are attracted to a particular candidate and want to help. Others give out of loyalty to the party. The biggest corporate and PAC contributors, it is probably safe to say, are trying either to guarantee access to officeholders or to encourage or discourage the enactment of policies relevant to their interests. Ferguson and Rogers suggest that it is just such large contributors or investors who define the general orientation of our parties. It is one of the reasons why, they suggest, our political parties are loath to challenge corporate interests.[31]

The Ideological Ambiguity of the Parties

Since the Republican and Democratic parties are both broad coalitions, seeking to attract as many individuals and groups as possible in order to prevail in winner-take-all, single-member-district elections, there are strong pressures on them to be ideologically ambiguous. Commitment to a set of coherent ideas may drive away people who disagree. As one student of the parties has put it, "the natural outcome of a campaign strategy designed to attract all groups (and to repel none) is that the party's ideology is not easily brought into sharp focus."[32]

 ARE THERE IDEOLOGICAL DIFFERENCES BETWEEN THE PARTIES?   Ideology may be understood as an organized set of beliefs about the fundamental nature of the good society and the role government ought to play in achieving it. In other Western democracies, it is common for the major parties to be aligned quite closely with an ideology, in the sense that their activists, members, and officeholders identify with it, campaign with themes based on its ideas, and are guided in their actions in government by it. In other Western democracies, Socialist and Labor parties often contest elections against Liberal and Conservative or Catholic parties, with Marxist, Christian Socialist, Monarchist, Neo-Fascist, Separatist, and other parties entering into the contest as well.

Ideological contests are not the norm in U.S. elections. By and large, Democrats and Republicans believe in the same ideological fundamentals (though they do differ, as we shall see, on policy). The two parties are both committed to the Constitution and the Bill of Rights. Both believe that free enterprise is the best of all economic systems. Both believe in individualism. Both celebrate the flag and the nation. It may be most accurate to say that our parties are ideological—people in them believe in a coherent set of ideas about the nature of the good society, economy, and polity—but that they are not ideologically opposed to one other. Historian Daniel Boorstein has put it as follows:

> The disagreement among American political parties . . . has been over the practical question of how to secure the agreed objective, while conciliating different interests, rather than over ultimate values or over what interest is paramount.[33]

Table 8.3
Convention Delegates and the Public on the Issues

	Democratic Delegates	The Public			Republican Delegates
		Democratic Voters	Total Adults	Republican Voters	
Political philosophy					
Describe own political views as conservative	5%	22%	30%	43%	60
Describe own political views as liberal	39	25	20	12	1
Size of government					
Prefer smaller government providing fewer services	16	33	43	59	87
Prefer bigger government providing more services	58	58	44	30	3
Domestic policy					
Favor increased federal spending on education programs	90	76	71	67	41
Favor increased federal spending on day care and after-school care for children	87	56	52	44	36

Delegates' views are based on telephone interviews with 739 delegates to the Republican National Convention, conducted July 22–Aug. 4, and with 1,059 delegates to the Democratic National Convention, conducted June 20–July 12. Views of total adults and each party's registered voters are based on telephone interviews conducted as part of New York Times/CBS News Polls in August, July, May, or March, 1988.

Does the absence of ideological opposition between the two parties mean, as American independent candidate George Wallace put it in 1968, that "there's not a dime's worth of difference" between Democrats and Republicans? Are they as much alike as Tweedledee and Tweedledum?

No. The evidence indicates that the differences between Democrats and Republicans are real and important. There is much to disagree about over the details of public policy, even if there is agreement on fundamental values and objectives. It is possible to agree on the need for a strong national defense, for instance, yet to disagree about how much money to spend on which particular weapons systems. It is possible to agree on the efficiency and productivity of free enterprise, yet vigorously to disagree about the proper role for government in protecting and managing it.

	Table 8.3 *(continued)*				
	Convention Delegates and the Public on the Issues				
		The Public			
	Democratic Delegates	*Democratic Voters*	*Total Adults*	*Republican Voters*	*Republican Delegates*
Say abortion should be legal, as it is now	72	43	40	39	29
Say government is paying too little attention to the needs of blacks	68	45	34	19	14
Foreign and military issues					
Favor keeping spending on military and defense programs at least at current level	32	59	68	73	84
Are more worried about Communist takeover in Central America than about U.S. involvement in a war there	12	25	37	55	80
Support use of military to stop inflow of drugs	54	61	61	63	67

IN WHAT SENSE ARE THE PARTIES DIFFERENT?   The Democratic and Republican parties differ in a number of ways. They differ, for instance, in the *perceptions of the electorate.* According to studies reported by the Center for Political Studies of the University of Michigan, over 60 percent of the American people report that they see the parties as different on a whole range of issues. Most see the Democrats as the more liberal party (in the sense of favoring "an active federal government, helping citizens with jobs, education, medical care, and the like"[34]) and the Republicans as the more conservative people (opposing this government activism). The parties also differ in terms of *who supports them.* Americans who classify themselves as liberals overwhelmingly support Democratic candidates; self-described conservatives overwhelmingly support Republicans. This is not surprising.

Our parties also tend to write different *political platforms.* Scholars have carefully examined Republican and Democratic party platforms from 1944 through 1980 and have discovered some persistent differences between the platforms of the two parties in terms of *rhetoric* (Republicans tend to talk more about opportunity and freedom), *issues* (Democrats worry more about poverty and social welfare), *public policies* advocated, and *pledges* made.[35] It is important to note, however, that Republican and Democratic platforms tend to overlap more than they diverge.

Party activists of one party are quite different in their views than party activists and voters in the other party. Republican national convention delegates are usually more conservative than Republican voters. Democratic national convention delegates are more liberal than Democratic voters (see Table 8.3). The same is true for those who take part in primaries and grass roots caucuses when compared to the average voter.

Finally, the parties differ in the *voting behavior* of their elected representatives. Republican members of Congress tend to vote differently than Democrats, with the former considerably more conservative on domestic issues. More will be said about this in Chapter 11, "Congress." This translates into public policy. Republicans and Democrats produce different policies on taxes, corporate regulation, and welfare when they are in power.[36]

ARE THE PARTIES BECOMING MORE IDEOLOGICAL?   Many people believe that the parties—especially the Republican party—are becoming more ideological.[37] It would be hard to miss the fact that the Republican party did become more consistently conservative after the mid-1970s. Largely gone from the party are so-called liberal Republicans from the Northeast (like the Rockefellers, Saltonstalls, and Weickers). Their place has been taken by fundamentalist Christians, prolife activists, antitax advocates, and former Democrats of a conservative or "neoconservative" stripe, such as U.N. Ambassador Jean Kirkpatrick in the Reagan administration and Senator Phil Graham of Texas. There is also evidence that the business community swung very heavily toward the Republicans during this period and pushed a strongly conservative agenda.[38]

While the Democratic party remains the favored locus of groups on the "left" in American politics, such as Jesse Jackson's Rainbow Coalition, it is also the party of conservative southerners such as Sam Nunn of Georgia, and antispending **"neoliberals"** such as Senator Bill Bradley of New Jersey. Bill Clinton imposed a middle-of-the-road philosophy on the party during his 1992 presidential campaign. Ideological diversity, and thus ideological ambiguity as a party, remains the watchword for Democrats.

Commentator Patrick J. Buchanan entered the 1992 Republican presidential nomination race to force George Bush to support conservative Republican principles.

The Parties in Government

Fearful of the tyrannical possibilities of a vigorous government, the framers designed a system of government in which power is so fragmented and competitive that effectiveness is unlikely. One of the roles that political parties can play is to overcome this "deadlock" by persuading officials in the different branches of government to cooperate with one another on the basis of party loyalty.[39] The constitutionally designed conflict between president and Congress might be bridged when a single party controls both branches, for instance.

The problem of governing presented by fragmented and separated powers in the United States is almost unique among the Western democracies. In parliamentary systems like those of Great Britain, Germany, and Japan, there is no separation of powers between the branches of the national government. The executive and the legislative branches are combined; the prime minister is the leader of the majority party in Parliament and is elected by and from that body. Members of the Cabinet, the heads of the executive of government, are themselves members of Parliament.

We will learn in considerable detail what parties do in government in later chapters on Congress (Chapter 11), the president (Chapter 12), the executive branch (Chapter 13), and the courts (Chapter 14). In general, we will see that the parties only partially improve the coherence and responsiveness of our government. The parties seem to be the best thing we have for making government work in a cohesive and responsive fashion, but they do not consistently do the job very well. Being organizationally weak and ideologically ambiguous, unable to command the complete loyalty and attention of their adherents or to influence strongly their behavior, parties are tremendously handicapped in playing this important role.

Though parties are rarely able to overcome the "deadlock" of American politics, they sometimes do. There have been brief periods in our history when the ties of party between presidents, members of Congress, and the heads of the executive branch agencies have been strong, resembling something like party government in Great Britain. These few occasions (between 1933 and 1936 when Franklin D. Roosevelt fashioned the first New Deal, in 1965 and 1966 when Lyndon Johnson created the Great Society, and in 1981 and 1982 when Ronald Reagan led a tax and budget revolution) are notable for their infrequent occurrence.

THE PROBLEM OF DIVIDED GOVERNMENT   For much of the past three decades, Republicans controlled the presidency, while the Democrats controlled Congress (see Figure 8.3), giving rise to the problem of divided government. The election of Bill Clinton in 1992 has eased worries somewhat about this potential problem. Divided party control, when it occurs, exaggerates the problems caused by the constitutional separation of powers. At best, it leads to governmental paralysis, stalemate, and delay.[40] At worst, divided party control of government can bring open warfare between the two branches—what two political scientists have called "institutional combat."[41]

"Institutional combat" involves efforts by one branch of government to diminish another and build its own autonomous power to govern. During the 1980s, the Democratic-dominated Congress denied approval to presidential nominees at a greater rate than in the past (e.g., Reagan's Supreme Court nominee, Robert Bork, and Bush's Defense Secretary nominee, John Tower), tied the hands of Re-

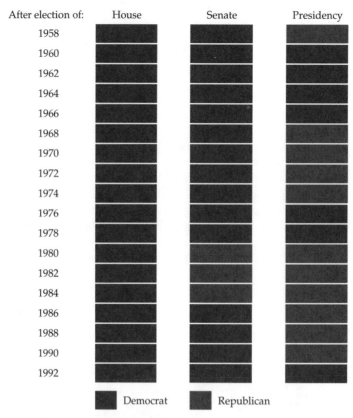

Figure 8.3 Party control of Congress and the Presidency

publican presidents by writing highly detailed legislation, and investigated executive branch wrongdoing in as public a fashion as possible (as in the Iran-Contra and HUD scandals). For their part, Republican presidents questioned the patriotism of the Democratic Congress, leaked unflattering FBI and Justice Department confidential information where it might be useful, and cooperated with Republican members of Congress to push highly publicized ethics investigations against the Democratic congressional leadership (Speaker Jim Wright and Whip Tony Coelho, both of whom resigned).

Parties in the Electorate

Parties are not only organizations and officeholders; they are also images in the minds of voters and potential voters, mental cues that affect the behavior of the electorate. This aspect of the parties was discussed in Chapter 5 and will be considered in greater detail in the next chapter. For now, we simply reiterate the point that partisanship is declining among the American electorate.[42]

Americans are less prone to identify with one of the two main parties than they were in the past. They are also more likely than in the past to vote for candidates of different parties (see Figure 8.4), behavior that leads to divided government. There also has been a measurable decline in the regard and respect in

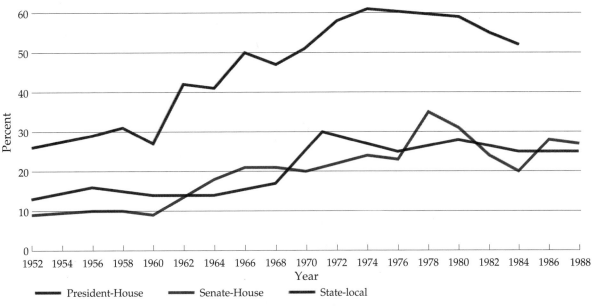

Figure 8.4 Split-ticket voting, 1952–1988

Source: Calculated by the editors from National Election Studies data. Harold W. Stanley and Richard G. Niemi, Vital Statistics on American Politics *(Washington, D.C.: CQ Press, 1990).*

which the parties are held. It is not so much that the American people are hostile toward the parties but that they are no longer confident that parties can help make the government responsive and responsible to the people.

If parties were not important to the practices of democracy, none of this would be cause for concern. Given their potential centrality to popular sovereignty, however, the decline of partisanship is important.

PARTY DECLINE AND REFORM

Though a few scholars are not convinced that the parties are in decline,[43] the evidence presented so far would seem to indicate otherwise. We have seen a noticeable decline in party identification, popular regard for parties, and willingness to vote a straight-party ticket, each indicating that parties are no longer as central as they once were in tying people's everyday concerns to their choices in the political system. We have also seen that parties are steadily losing their control over what have long been understood to be central party functions: nominating candidates and organizing campaigns. Parties must share the former with individual candidates and voters, and the latter with candidate electoral organizations, pollsters, direct mail companies, and campaign consulting firms.

One leading textbook on American political parties paints a disturbing picture of what the relative decline of the parties might mean in the long run:

> What seems likely . . . is a politics of greater fluidity and instability, carried on by a wider range of political organizations. . . . The erosion of the one, stable, long-run loyalty in American politics will contribute to a politics more often

dominated by the short-term influences of the charismatic candidate or the very salient issue. In its volatility, its lack of continuity, and its lack of predictability, the new electoral politics may increasingly resemble that of the one-party factional and personal politics in the American South in the 1930s and 1940s.[44]

The decline of parties probably will also lead to an increase in the influence of interest groups. This may, in turn, contribute to two additional problems. First, to the degree that national policy is the outcome of interest group demands without the aggregative influence of political parties, it will lack coherence. Second, since the interest group system is particularly well suited to those with substantial resources, the decline of parties will probably push the worst-off members of society even further outside the policymaking process. If this should develop, political equality will be eroded further.

Political parties are the closest thing we have to an institution capable of fashioning policy coherence out of interest group politics, while at the same time bringing broad elements of the public into the political arena. The relative decline of political parties ought to be of concern, then, to those Americans who care about coherence and rationality in our public life, and about its democratic character.

If political parties are important to the practice of democracy but are declining in their effectiveness, what might be done about it? Can the parties be revitalized as democratic instruments? There is no settled answer. Politicians, journalists, and scholars disagree.

The View That Parties Should Not Be Substantially Reformed

Not everyone believes that the parties should be strengthened, even if such a thing were possible. Those in the Madisonian tradition, who fear the tyrannical possibilities of an active and dynamic government, for instance, do not want substantial changes in the parties. Our protections as a free people are based, in their view, on the constitutional prevention of the dominance of a majority faction; we do not want a party system that empowers the majority. Madisonians also worry that parties in the European style—organized and ideologically coherent—would raise the stakes of politics, making it too important who wins and who loses, thereby accentuating divisions along lines of race, religion, ethnicity, class, and economic interest. Better, they say, to keep our present party system, with all its incoherence and diffuseness, because it preserves consensus and stability, mutes conflict, and brings about healing and accommodation.[45]

The Responsible-Party Model

The most elaborate and extensive set of proposals for reform of the parties is that which calls for responsible-party government in the United States.[46] Proponents of the responsible-party model want a party system that looks a great deal like the parliamentary party systems of Western Europe, where parties stand for clearly defined programs, compete against other parties with distinctive stands, put their programs into effect once in office by controlling party officeholders, and face the voters based on their performance in office.

Such a party system, its many adherents contend, would make elections more meaningful, by making choices clear and important, and would therefore increase interest and participation among the public. It would also make leaders more responsible and responsive, because the American people would know which party to blame for failure and which to praise for success. The American people would know which party had lived up to its promises and which ones had not.

The responsible-party model has never gotten very far in the United States. It is a matter mostly for scholarly debate. It has not had much resonance among the American people or support from practicing politicians. This is hardly surprising, for virtually every aspect of our society works against it. Particularly important are structural factors.

Our constitutional rules, as indicated at several points in this chapter, virtually assure that we will have parties of a fragmented and decentralized sort. Most important in this regard are federalism, the separation of powers, and single-member-district, winner-take-all elections.

American political culture has long been antiparty in sentiment, hostile to the concentration of political power so essential to the responsible-party model, and more prone to vote for the best man or woman than for the best party. Our commitment to individualism, moreover, makes the notion of party discipline highly distasteful to many Americans.

One of the most fundamental reasons that European parties are the way they are is because labor in the European countries has been well organized and politically active. Labor in these countries has been instrumental in the formation of Labor, Socialist, and Communist parties; sectors of society who have been worried about the possible victory of such parties have formed Liberal (i.e., free market), Conservative, and Christian parties to oppose them. Labor, as we learned in Chapter 7, is neither well organized nor politically active in our own country, so one impetus to the creation of strong parties has never existed.

Nor is there any indication that the public is interested in a fundamental change in the party system toward more powerful and responsible parties. If anything, public opinion seems to favor a move away from the primacy of parties.

Even if creating responsible parties were possible, proponents are vague about leadership in these strengthened parties and the mechanisms by which party ideologies and platforms are fashioned. If parties are to present clear policy and ideological positions, what assurances are there that such positions will have been democratically decided or will reflect what the people want? Without internal democracy in such parties, the voters might still be left with a choice of the "lesser of two evils." Unrepresentative elites are as likely as not to run the show, with obvious consequences for popular sovereignty and political equality.

More Modest Proposals

Though parties of the sort that are described in the responsible-party model are both unlikely to appear and problematic in several respects, the present decline of the parties must be reversed if they are to play a role in making popular sovereignty a reality. For many scholars, and increasingly for practicing politicians, the costs of a weak party system are becoming evident. It may well be that America's difficulties in the world economy, at least partially attributable to the drift and indecisiveness of the federal government, rooted in weak parties, will create strong popular and elite demands for a program of party strengthening.

Many reform proposals seem politically achievable. These include calls for changes in federal and state laws that would deemphasize primaries, increase public funding for party activities, provide free radio and television time to the parties, and remove spending limits on parties in electoral campaigns. Each is quite common already in the European democracies. Other possible reforms look to changes within the parties themselves: more party institutional advertising, enhanced fund raising and other campaign services, regular policy forums, and increases in the number of unpledged delegates at national conventions.[47]

It is at least conceivable that reforms like these might stop the decline of parties and enhance their role in American politics and governing. Such changes might represent a net gain in the ability of the American people to participate in politics and to keep their representatives responsible and responsive. This would represent an increase in popular sovereignty and political equality, especially if wider involvement in party affairs were somehow encouraged. This would be no small achievement.

SUMMARY

The American party system is unique among the Western democracies in several respects. First, ours is a relatively pure two-party system and has been so since the 1830s. Second, our two-party system is made up of parties that are fragmented and decentralized, with very little power to be found in the national party organizations over individual candidates, officeholders, or state and local party organizations. They are also ideologically ambiguous and diffuse.

Though made up of the same two parties for well over a century, the two-party system has not been stagnant. It has undergone a series of realignments, spurred by structural changes in society and the economy, in which the relative power of parties has shifted, as have voting alignments among the public, dominant political coalitions, and public policy.

Political parties have always been associated with democracy. Because of the fragmented and decentralized nature of our parties, however, American parties have had a difficult time fulfilling their democratic promise. In elections, they convey highly ambiguous cues to voters. In government, they play but a small role in providing institutional cohesion and are unable, except on rare occasions, to overcome the constitutional separation of powers.

Recognizing that parties are inescapably linked to the practice of democracy, many scholars and practitioners have advocated a variety of reforms to strengthen them. The most elaborate reform package is the responsible-party model. There is very little prospect for such a wholesale change in the party system. More modest reforms, however, that would give parties a greater role in candidate selection, control of campaigns, and the actions of partisan officeholders are not out of the question and seem essential if the decline of the parties is to be halted.

To Ponder

1. Are parties really necessary for a democracy? Are there other institutions that could take over for parties and do just as well?

2. Should American parties be more ideologically coherent? What would such parties do to the kind of politics that we practice in the United States? Would the consequences be beneficial or not?

3. Imagine, if you will, politics without parties. What would politics in a society without parties look like?

4. Would strong parties be a threat to liberty?

Suggested Readings

Burnham, Walter Dean. *Critical Elections and the Mainsprings of American Politics.* New York: Norton, 1970.
> The classic analysis of the realignment process in the American party system.

Key, Jr., V. O. *Southern Politics.* New York: Knopf, 1949.
> Though dated, a penetrating and entertaining look at politics in a region devoid of real parties, and a model, perhaps, of what politics might look like in the United States if so-called dealignment continues.

Polsby, Nelson. *Consequences of Party Reform.* New York: Oxford University Press, 1983.
> A discussion of how changing the rules has consequences for the parties—some intended and many unintended.

Ranney, Austin. *Curing the Mischiefs of Faction.* Berkeley, CA: University of California Press, 1974.
> The history of dissatisfaction with our political parties, the many efforts to reform them, and the consequences of reform.

Reiter, Howard L. *Parties and Elections in Corporate America.* New York: St. Martin's, 1987.
> An unconventional look at parties that places them within the context of corporate capitalism.

Sabato, Larry J. *The Party's Just Begun.* Glenview, IL: Scott, Foresman, 1988.
> An analysis of what's wrong with American parties and a reform agenda for fixing them.

Sorauf, Frank J., and Paul Allen Beck. *Party Politics in America.* Glenview, IL: Scott, Foresman, 1988.
> An updated version of the leading textbook on political parties.

Sundquist, James L. *Dynamics of the Party System.* Washington, D.C.: Brookings Institution, 1983.
> A history of the party system and its transformations, rich in detail and theoretically sophisticated.

Notes

1. Page Smith, *Redeeming the Time: Vol. 8 of the People's History of the United States* (New York: McGraw-Hill, 1987), p. 669.

2. Smith, *Redeeming the Time,* p. 243.

3. James MacGregor Burns, *Roosevelt: The Lion and the Fox* (New York: Harcourt, Brace, 1956), p. 319.

4. All of the above cited in Charles Henning, *The Wit and Wisdom of Politics* (Golden, CO: Fulcrum, 1989), p. 168.

5. Frank J. Sorauf and Paul Allen Beck, *Party Politics in America* (Glenview, IL: Scott, Foresman, 1988), p. 5.

6. E. E. Schattschneider, *Party Government* (New York: Holt, Rinehart and Winston, 1942), p. 208.

7. E. E. Schattschneider, *Party Government,* p. 208.

8. Larry J. Sabato, *The Party's Just Begun* (Glenview, IL: Scott Foresman, 1988), p. 8.

9. E. E. Schattschneider, *The Semi-Sovereign People* (New York: Holt, Rinehart and Winston, 1960).

10. Thomas Ferguson, "Party Realignment and American Industrial Structure: The Investment Theory of Political Parties in Historical Perspective," in Paul Zarembka, et al. (eds.), *Research in Political Economy, Vol. 6* (Greenwich, CT: JAI Press, 1983), pp. 31–35.

11. Ferguson, "Party Realignment," pp. 35–41; Howard L. Reiter, *Parties and Elections in Corporate America* (New York: St. Martin's, 1987), pp. 79–83.

12. C. Vann Woodward, *The Strange Career of Jim Crow* (New York: Oxford University Press, 1966).

13. Herbert Alexander, *Financing Politics* (Washington, D.C.: *Congressional Quarterly*, 1980), p. 5.

14. Walter Dean Burnham, *Critical Elections and the Mainsprings of American Politics* (New York: Norton, 1970).

15. Ferguson, "Party Realignment"; Edward S. Greenberg, *Capitalism and the American Political Ideal* (Armonk, NY: M. E. Sharpe, 1985).

16. Benjamin Ginsberg and Martin Shefter, *Politics By Other Means: The Declining Significance of Elections in America* (New York: Basic Books, 1990).

17. Thomas Ferguson and Joel Rogers, *Right Turn: The Decline of the Democrats and the Future of American Politics* (New York: Hill & Wang, 1986), ch. 1.

18. Helmut Norpoth and Jerrold Rusk, "Partisan Dealignment in the American Electorate," *American Political Science Review* Vol. 76 (September 1982). See Sabato, *The Party's Just Begun*, and James A. Sundquist, *Dynamics of the Party System* (Washington, D.C.: Brookings Institution, 1983).

19. On realignment, see Burnham, *Critical Elections*; William Nisbet Chambers and Walter Dean Burnham, eds., *The American Party Systems* (New York: Oxford University Press, 1967); Jerome Clubb, et al., *Partisan Realignment* (Newbury Park, CA: Sage Publications, 1980); V. O. Key, Jr., "A Theory of Critical Elections," *Journal of Politics*, Vol. 17 (1955), pp. 3–18; and Sundquist, *Dynamics of the Party System*.

20. Ferguson and Rogers, *Right Turn*.

21. The classic statement on the impact of electoral rules is found in Maurice Duverger, *Political Parties* (New York: Wiley, 1954).

22. Sorauf and Beck, *Party Politics in America*, p. 44.

23. Nelson W. Polsby, *The Consequences of Party Reform* (New York: Oxford University Press, 1983), p. 83.

24. Steven J. Rosenstone, et al., *Third Parties in America* (Princeton, NJ: Princeton University Press, 1984).

25. Rosenstone, et al., *Third Parties in America*, p. 222.

26. Quoted in Sorauf and Beck, *Party Politics in America*, p. 101.

27. Sorauf and Beck, *Party Politics in America*, p. 70.

28. On the national committees, see Cornelius P. Cotter and Bernard Hennessy, *Politics Without Power: The National Party Committees* (New York: Atherton, 1964).

29. Colin Campbell, et al., *Politics and Government in Europe Today* (Orlando, FL: Harcourt Brace Jovanovich, 1990), pp. 304–310.

30. Ranney, *Curing the Mischiefs of Faction* (Berkeley, CA: University of California Press, 1974); James Q. Wilson, *The Amateur Democrat* (Chicago: University of Chicago Press, 1962).

31. Ferguson and Rogers, *Right Turn*.

32. William J. Keefe, *Parties, Politics, and Public Policy in America*, (Washington, DC: CQ Press, 1991), p. 65.

33. Quoted in Henning, *Wit and Wisdom of Politics*, p. 171.

34. Benjamin I. Page, *Choices and Echoes in Presidential Elections* (Chicago: University of Chicago Press, 1978), p. 63.

35. Alan D. Monroe, "American Party Platforms and Public Opinion," *American Journal of Political Science*, Vol. 27 (February 1983), p. 35; Gerald Pomper, *Elections in America* (New York: Longman, 1980), p. 169.

36. Douglas Hibbs, *The American Political Economy* (Cambridge, MA: Harvard University Press, 1987); Dennis P. Quinn and Robert Shapiro, "Business Political Power: The Case of Taxation," *The American Political Science Review*, Vol. 85 (September 1991), pp. 851–874.

37. Polsby, *Consequences of Party Reform*, pp. 85–88.

38. Thomas Byrne Edsall, *The New Politics of Inequality* (New York: Norton, 1984); David Vogel, *Fluctuating Fortunes* (New York: Basic Books, 1989).

39. James MacGregor Burns, *Deadlock of Democracy* (Englewood Cliffs, NJ: Prentice-Hall, 1967).

40. Hedrick Smith, *The Power Game* (New York: Random House, 1988), p. 652.

41. Ginsberg and Shefter, *Politics By Other Means*.

42. The evidence for these points is reviewed in Sabato, *The Party's Just Begun*, ch. 4.

43. Xandra Kayden and Eddie Mahe, Jr., *The Party Goes On: The Persistence of the Two-Party System in the United States* (New York: Basic Books, 1985); Gerald M. Pomper, *Party Renewal in America* (New York: Praeger, 1981); Sabato, *The Party's Just Begun*.

44. Sorauf and Beck, *Party Politics in America*, p. 493.

45. Herbert Agar, *The Price of Union* (Boston: Houghton Mifflin, 1950); Pendleton Herring, *The Politics of Democracy* (New York: Norton, 1940); and Ranney, *Curing the Mischiefs of Factions*.

46. E. E. Schattschneider, *Party Government*, (New York: Rinehart, 1942); and Burns, *Deadlock of Democracy*.

47. Sabato, *The Party's Just Begun*, ch. 6 and 7.

9

Voting and
Elections

THE 1992 ELECTION

Bill Clinton's 1992 election victory—with 43 percent of the popular vote to 38 percent for George Bush and 19 percent for independent Ross Perot, and with 370 electoral votes for Clinton, 168 for Bush, and none for Perot (see Figure 9.1)—followed several familiar patterns. The Republicans did best in the South and the Democrats did best in the Northeast. As usual, most Democrats voted for the Democratic candidate and most Republicans voted for the Republican. Most blacks, Jews, union members, and poor people voted for Democrat Clinton, while most upper income people, white males, Protestants, and, especially, evangelical Christians voted for Republican Bush. (See the table on page 295.) As usual, high income people turned out to vote at higher rates than low income people or Hispanics.

Still, it was a remarkable election. Turnout was up to 55 percent of voting-age adults, low compared with other countries but the highest U.S. figure since 1972. Perot's was the strongest third candidate vote since 1912. The Democrats overturned 12 years of Republican presidential dominance, even raising more money than the GOP. The mass media played surprising new roles, and candidates' fortunes zoomed up and down like roller coasters.

In the spring of 1991, after defeating Iraq in Operation Desert Storm, President Bush enjoyed unprecedented popularity: Some 90 percent of Americans said they approved of the way he was handling his job. Nearly everyone assumed that Bush would easily win reelection. Many prominent Democrats decided not to run. Senators Jay Rockefeller (West Virginia), Al Gore (Tennessee), Sam Nunn (Georgia), and Lloyd Bentsen (Texas), and Representative Richard Gephart (Missouri) quietly bowed out early. Jesse Jackson, who had electrified minorities and liberals in 1984 and 1988, decided to sit this one out. Mario Cuomo, Governor of New York and the favorite of many Democrats, agonized for some time, but eventually opted out, too. Thus some key decisions about who would *not* be the next president were made long before the campaigning and voting began.

The Democratic candidates who decided to run seemed even less likely to win than those who had sought the Democratic nomination in 1988, the snidely nicknamed "seven dwarfs." First there was Paul Tsongas, a serious but stiff-mannered former governor of Massachusetts, recently recovered from cancer treatment. Tsongas began a lonely campaign in neighboring New Hampshire before anyone else. As concerns about economic troubles grew, the "pro-business Democrat" Tsongas's "Call to Economic Arms," advocating economic growth incentives, deficit cutting, and higher taxes, gathered some popular support.

Then there was Senator Tom Harkin (Iowa), who won a following among labor union members and liberal intellectuals, but sounded too harsh to some voters and too liberal to others. Senator Bob Kerrey of Nebraska boasted telegenic looks and a Vietnam war record, but seemed unable to put together a clear message or raise campaign money. Governor Douglas Wilder of Virginia, a black fiscal conservative, withdrew in a bitter feud with Senator Charles Robb of his own state.

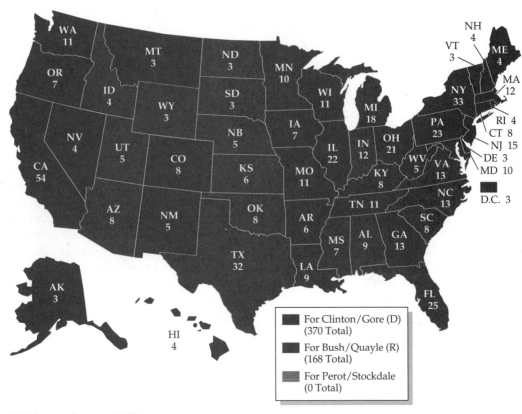

Figure 9.1 Electoral votes, 1992

Source: "The Vote for President," New York Times, *November 5, 1992, B2.*

And there was Jerry Brown, former governor of California, who condemned the power of money in politics and swore to take back America for the people. Brown excited a band of young volunteers and stimulated many small contributions through his "800" telephone number.

Somewhere in this pack was Clinton of Arkansas, whom his peers had voted the best governor in the country. Clinton had positioned himself as a "moderate" Democrat, close to the American mainstream on social issues (patriotism, capital punishment, abortion rights), very respectful of economic incentives and private enterprise, but advocating a fairly activist domestic role for the federal government. Clinton assembled a high-energy team of campaign advisors, including poll-taker and chief strategist Stanley Greenberg and "ragin' Cajun" attack artist James Carville. He raised a great deal of money (helped particularly by the Goldman Sachs investment firm) and won powerful media support. Soon *New York Times* columns began calling bright, youthful, former Rhodes-scholar Clinton the leading Democrat—though none of them were thought to have much of a chance against Bush.

Several odd things happened on the way to the election. President Bush's enormous popularity began to slide, from nearly 90 percent in March 1991, to 70 percent in June, 60 percent in October, 50 percent in December, and just 40 percent in February, 1992, as Americans focused on the painful economic recession, with a 7.5 percent unemployment rate, four years of stagnant incomes, and fears of permanent job losses. The incumbent president, admired for his foreign affairs skills, was widely blamed for errors or inaction at home. Suddenly the Democrat nomination seemed worth something. Even Bush's own renomination by the Republicans was challenged by belligerently conservative columnist Pat Buchanan. Candidates campaigning in New Hampshire found closed factories, boarded-up storefronts, and angry voters.

Clinton's road to the Democratic nomination was bumpy. Just as he was advocating "investment" in the economy, health care, education and the like, and overtaking favorite son Tsongas in the New Hampshire polls, Clinton was slammed by a supermarket tabloid story in which nightclub singer Gennifer Flowers claimed that she had had a long extramarital affair with the governor. Clinton's denials, and his joint appearance with his wife Hillary on "60 Minutes," where they acknowledged past marital troubles, did not prevent a sharp drop in popular standing. Still reeling from the charge of infidelity—while similar rumors about Bush got little attention—Clinton was hit by accusations that he had maneuvered in 1969 to avoid being drafted for the Vietnam war. Many pronounced Clinton's candidacy dead. He seemed lucky to salvage a respectable 26 percent of the New Hampshire vote to Tsongas's 34 percent, while Buchanan amassed a shocking 40 percent protest vote against Bush.

As other Democrats dropped out of the race, however, Clinton kept on ticking. He won many Southern votes in Georgia, South Carolina, and the "Super Tuesday" states. He attacked Tsongas hard in Florida as a threat to Social Security benefits, and in Illinois and Michigan for advocating tax increases on the middle class. Tsongas, short of charisma or money to combat Clinton's more populist appeals, faded fast. Clinton's only remaining Democratic opponent, Jerry Brown, battered Clinton badly in New York but lost. Clinton then won in Pennsylvania and clinched the nomination in California on June 2.

As Clinton staggered toward the Democratic nomination, a new nightmare threatened: H. Ross Perot, the feisty electronics billionaire from Texas, announced on "Larry King Live" that he might run for president if volunteers put him on the ballot in every state. Perot frequented TV talk shows, pungently describing U.S. economic troubles and promising to "look under the hood" and fix things up. Perot's popularity soared. Early summer polls showed him actually leading in a three-way race, before a barrage of media reports tagged him with autocratic and paranoid tendencies and a history of lucrative government contracts.

Then came the Democratic convention in July, where an uplifting film "reintroduced" Governor Clinton, showing his humble origins, his handshake

H. Ross Perot won 19 percent of the popular vote in 1992, the most for any third candidate since 1912.

with John F. Kennedy, warm family life with Hillary and Chelsea, and accomplishments in Arkansas. Millions of TV viewers watched the harmonious Democrats—in all their racial, ethnic, and sexual diversity—condemn the Republicans' "failed" economic policies, call for change, and enthusiastically nominate Clinton and Al Gore. To top it off, Perot announced that he was quitting the race. Clinton and Gore launched a bus tour of middle America and zoomed upward in the polls, to a 20-point lead over Bush and luckless Dan Quayle.

The Republican convention, highlighting the party's right wing ("We are engaged in a religious war . . ." thundered Buchanan) and "family values" that seemed to exclude single parents, gays, and working women, did not regain much ground for Bush. The president and his surrogates tried a succession of themes: bashing Hillary Clinton, touting foreign policy successes, attacking Clinton on taxes and "trust." But nothing seemed to work. Clinton-Gore, charging that Bush had no economic plan for the future, held on to a 12 to 15 percent poll lead through September. There was talk of a landslide.

But early in October the race was transformed once again. Perot jumped back in and spent more than $60 million of his own money on unprecedented half-hour TV slots (e.g., "Plain Talk about Jobs, Debt and the Washington Mess"). In the three, three-way debates, he hit hard at the "giant sucking sound" of jobs going to Mexico and the pre-invasion buildup of Saddam Hussein. Perot zipped back up to 22 percent support. In the final two weeks of the campaign, Bush went into "attack mode," hitting Clinton for "leading anti-American demonstrations on foreign soil" in 1969 (even, perhaps, consorting with the KGB in Moscow), for "waffling" and evading, for secret tax plans. Al Gore was "Mr. Ozone"; both were "bozos." Clinton's lead narrowed to single digits.

In the end, however, it was a classic case of electoral punishment. With the economy still weak, Clinton hung on to win.

The 1992 elections did not much change the party balance in Congress. The Democrats' 269:166 control of the House of Representatives dropped just a bit, and in the Senate they kept their solid 57 to 43 majority. Still, the new Congress was dramatically different, with many new members, many more women and minorities, and lots of fresh ideas.

House incumbents had a hard time, with voters' resentment of legislative gridlock and overdrafts at the House bank, together with redistricting. Fifty-three incumbents quit early; another 19 (a record number) lost in the primaries, and 38 more lost their seats in the November election. This meant a total of 110 new faces in the House. The "Year of the Woman" actually came to pass. The Senate's meager total of two women jumped to six, with Carol Moseley Braun (Illinois) becoming the first black woman senator in U.S. history. In the House, the number of women nearly doubled from 28 to 47. Minorities also did well: Native American Ben Nighthorse Campbell (Colorado) joined Braun in the Senate, and in the House new districts produced 13 new black and 7 new Hispanic members, for totals of 38 and 17.*

Divided party government was over, at least for a while. A new Democratic Congress was in place to cooperate with a new, activist Democratic president.

---

*"The Elections," *New York Times*, November 5, 1992, Section B.

How Groups Voted, 1992			
Group	% for Clinton	% for Bush	% for Perot
Men	41	38	21
Women	46	37	17
Whites	39	41	20
Blacks	82	11	7
Hispanics	62	25	14
Asians	29	55	16
Married	40	40	20
Unmarried	49	33	18
18–29 years old	44	34	22
30–44 years old	42	38	20
45–59 years old	41	40	19
60 and older	50	38	12
Not high school graduate	55	28	15
High school graduate	43	36	20
College graduate	40	41	19
Post graduate education	49	36	15
White Protestant	33	46	21
Catholic	44	36	20
Jewish	78	12	10
White born-again Christian	23	61	15
Family income under $15,000	59	23	18
$30,000–49,000	41	38	21
$75,000 and over	36	48	16
Family financial situation better today	24	62	14
same today	41	41	18
worse today	61	14	25
Republicans	10	73	17
Independents	38	32	30
Democrats	77	10	13
Liberals	68	14	18
Moderates	48	31	21
Conservatives	18	65	17
Employed	42	38	20
Full-time student	50	35	15
Unemployed	56	24	20
Homemaker	36	45	19
Retired	51	36	13
Total vote	43	38	19

Source: Exit poll of 15,490 voters conducted by Voter Research and Surveys, reported in *New York Times* November 5, 1992, p. B9. From THE NEW YORK TIMES, November 5, 1992, p. B9. Copyright © 1992 by The New York Times Company. Reprinted by permission.

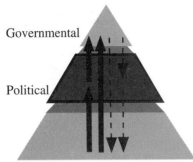

Governmental

Political

Structural

ELECTIONS AND DEMOCRACY

Elections are fundamental to democratic politics. They are supposed to be the chief means by which citizens control what their government does; that is, they are the principal means by which popular sovereignty and majority rule are supposed to work. Millions of people around the world have protested, demonstrated, and even fought for the right to hold free elections. Many important struggles for democracy in the United States have involved conflicts over the right to vote.

But can elections actually ensure that governments will do what their people want? If so, how? In a small, participatory democracy like a town meeting, the answer is easy: people simply vote directly on what to do. A new road gets built, or the town library gets expanded, if and only if a majority of citizens votes to do it. In a large, complicated society like the entire United States, however, it is not generally feasible to have everyone vote directly on policies. That would take too much time and energy, and citizens could not become experts on everything. As we indicated in Chapter 1, the best that can be done is *representative* democracy, in which we choose representatives (e.g., members of Congress, a president, state legislators, governors) to do the policymaking.

Once we settle for representative democracy, however, it is not so obvious how we can control our representatives. How can we make certain that public officials will be responsive to us, that they will work for what we the people want rather than pursue their own ends or respond to special interests?

Twenty thousand women march down New York's Fifth Avenue for the right to vote, which was not won in most states until 1920.

Democratic theorists have suggested several different ways in which two-party elections of representatives (the sort of elections that are usual in the United States) could or should lead to democratic control of government. We will briefly discuss three of these ways, indicating how they might bring about democratic results and why they might or might not work in practice.[1] Each of these three ways requires that political parties be more unified than the ones we now have if elections are to serve as democratic instruments. The rest of this chapter is concerned with what actually goes on in American elections and whether or not elections actually bring about democratic control.

Responsible-Party Government

The theory of **responsible-party** government is based on the old, commonsense idea of elections providing a *"real choice"*: political parties stand for different policies, the voters choose between them, and the winning party carries out its mandate. More precisely, the responsible-party theory assumes that each of the two parties is cohesive and unified; that each takes a clear policy position that differs significantly from the other party's position; that citizens accurately perceive these positions and vote on the basis of them; and that the winning party, when it takes office, does exactly what it said it would do. If all these conditions are met, then obviously the party with the more popular policy positions will win and enact its program. Government will do what the voters want—or at least more nearly so than if the other party had won. Moreover, in the course of defending their platforms, the parties may help educate citizens about public policy and mobilize them to take part in politics.[2]

Even if an election were to work exactly as the responsible-party theory dictates, however, a serious problem arises: this would not actually guarantee that the winning party would take policy positions that pleased the voters! It can only guarantee that the winner's stand is less *un*popular than the loser's, which may not make it particularly popular at all. To put it in terms of our earlier discussion of democracy, a responsible-party system does not guarantee either popular sovereignty or political equality for ordinary citizens. Under the terms of the theory, crucial decisions about what the parties will stand for and what choices they will present to the voters are made by someone other than ordinary citizens: party leaders, for example, or interest groups.

Moreover, the conditions under which responsible-party theories are supposed to work are not met, and are not ever likely to be met, in the United States. As we have seen, the Republican and Democratic parties are *not* very unified or cohesive, for reasons deeply rooted in our Constitution and our political structure. The parties do *not* always take clear stands, but are sometimes deliberately ambiguous. Nor do the parties necessarily take stands that are distinctly different from each other. Sometimes, avoiding unpopular or "extreme" positions, both parties say very nearly the same things. Furthermore, voters do not vote solely on the issues, and parties do not always keep their promises.

Clearly, the responsible-party theory does not describe exactly what happens in American elections. One question we will want to consider is whether it comes close enough to the truth to describe at least a part of reality. We will see that it does. Another question is whether responsible-party ideas provide useful standards for judging what goes wrong with elections and how they might be improved. To some extent, they may, particularly with respect to the clarity of stands on issues and the mobilization of voters.

Electoral Competition

A very different, and much less obvious, sort of democratic control is suggested by theories of **electoral competition**. Here again (as in the responsible-party theory), the idea is that two political parties each take clear, unified stands on the issues of the day, that citizens vote on the basis of the issues, and that the winning party does what it promises to do. But electoral-competition theories have no expectation or desire that the parties' stands will be sharply different from each other. Instead, the whole point is that both parties should compete for votes by taking the *most popular positions* that they can. Both parties are therefore likely to end up standing for the *same* policies: those favored by the most voters. Then, according to the theory, it does not matter which party wins; the winner enacts the platform that the voters want. Democracy is assured by the "hidden hand" of competition. According to this economics-style way of thinking, selfish, vote-seeking parties do what the voters want, in just the same way that selfish, money-seeking business firms are forced to produce what consumers want.[3]

Electoral competition theories postulate that both parties, competing for votes, tend to take policy stands near the midpoint of public opinion. If citizens' preferences are organized along a single dimension, such as the liberal-conservative continuum shown in Figure 9.2, and if various other assumptions are met, then these theories say that both parties will take positions exactly at the *median* of public opinion, that is, at the point where exactly one-half the voters are more liberal and one-half the voters are more conservative. (If a party took a position away from the median, the other party could easily win more votes by taking a position closer to the median.) This would be the ideal democratic outcome, because, by the logic of this figure, a majority of citizens would prefer policies at the median point over policies anywhere else on the continuum. There exists no more popular outcome.

Electoral-competition theories do not promise that the parties will educate or mobilize voters, as responsible-party theories do. But they have the advantage of depending only upon selfish (vote-seeking) motives among politicians. Most important, they suggest how popular sovereignty and a perfectly democratic outcome—rather than just the lesser of two evils—might result from elections.

Again, however, the conditions assumed by electoral-competition theories are not likely to correspond exactly to what happens in the real world. Electoral competition ensures democratic control only *if* parties are unified and take clear stands, for purely and directly vote-seeking reasons; it can break down if parties

Figure 9.2 Electoral competition

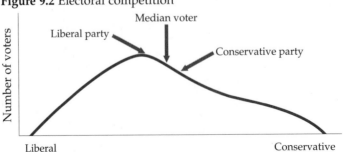

are fragmented or ambiguous, care about policies, or seek contributors' dollars rather than citizens' votes. For democratic control to be perfect, everyone has to vote; voters have to consider nothing other than the issues (not being distracted by candidates' personalities or images, for example) and must know where the parties stand. And the parties have to keep their promises. None of these things is likely to happen.

Again, the question is whether these conditions are *close enough* to the truth so that electoral-competition theories can tell us something about real elections. We will see that they do; electoral competition provides one of the main reasons that government policy is significantly influenced by public opinion. Moreover, by looking at how actual elections deviate from the theoretical ideal (e.g., how money and campaign contributions sometimes push parties away from popular policies), we can see specific ways in which American elections might be improved as instruments of democracy.

Electoral Reward and Punishment

A third process by which elections might bring about democratic control of government is suggested by theories of **electoral reward and punishment**, or "retrospective voting." Here the idea is that unified parties compete for votes, not by taking specific stands on the issues, but by emphasizing their competence and their sharing of the public's goals, and by trying their best to advance those goals when they take office. Voters don't bother to form preferences about complex issues and don't necessarily trust parties' promises; in each election, they simply make *retrospective* (backward-looking) *judgments* about how well incumbent officials have done in the past, rewarding success with reelection and punishing failure by throwing the incumbents out. The result is that politicians who want to stay in office have strong incentives to bring about peace and prosperity, and to solve problems that the American people want solved. Politicians' ambitions force them to anticipate what the public wants and to accomplish it.[4] This reward-and-punishment version of democratic control requires very little of voters—no elaborate policy preferences, no study of campaign platforms—just judgments of how well or how badly things have been going. Also, like electoral-competition theories, this version relies on politicians' selfishness rather than their altruism. It allows time for deliberation, and it lets leaders try out experimental or temporarily unpopular policies, as long as the results work out well and please the public in time for the next election. On the other hand, reward and punishment may be a rather blunt instrument: getting rid of bad political leaders only after (not before) disasters happen, without guaranteeing that the next group of leaders will be any better. Moreover, the reward-and-punishment version focuses only on the most crucial issues and may leave room for unpopular policies on issues that are less visible. It may also encourage politicians to produce deceptively happy results that fade after election day.

Each of the three theories only partly explains what happens in American elections. None of them—alone or together—works well enough to guarantee perfectly democratic outcomes from U.S. elections.

One flaw common to all of them is that these processes can bring about government responsiveness to all citizens only if *all* citizens have the right to vote and only if all citizens exercise that right. However, millions of Americans cannot or do not go to the polls. Their voices are not clearly heard; political equality is not achieved. Even after two centuries of struggle to expand the right to vote, nonparticipation remains a major problem for American democracy.

Another problem besetting all three theories is that money, organizational resources, and activism—not just citizens' policy preferences and votes—influence the stands that parties take and the outcomes of elections, as we saw in Chapter 8, "Political Parties." This means that money givers, activists, and the leaders of organized groups have more influence than ordinary citizens do; again political equality is not realized.

Still another problem (a rather subtle one) is that citizens' policy preferences and goals may themselves be manipulated, so that government responsiveness to them does not necessarily ensure authentic democracy.

POLITICAL PARTICIPATION

Political participation refers to political activity by individual citizens. It includes *"unconventional"* participation, in demonstrations, boycotts, and the like, of the sort that will be discussed in Chapter 10, "Social Movements," and also *"conventional"* participation: writing letters, contacting officials, going to meetings, working on campaigns, and giving money. The most basic form of modern political participation, however, the one that plays the most central part in theories of democratic control through elections, is the act of voting.

The Expansion of the Franchise

As we saw in Chapter 2, in the early years of the United States, the **franchise** (the right to vote) was quite restricted. Most people could not vote at all. Slaves, Native Americans, and—in most places—women were excluded altogether. In most states, people without property were not allowed to vote, and, in some states, people with the wrong religion were excluded. Moreover, most branches of the federal government were insulated from the citizenry. People could vote for their state legislators and members of the House of Representatives, but senators were selected by the state legislatures for long, staggered terms in office, and the president was chosen by an elaborate, indirect system involving state legislatures, electors, and the House of Representatives. The Supreme Court (protected by lifetime tenure) and top executive branch officials were appointed by the president and were confirmed by the Senate. Democratic control of government was severely limited.

Furthermore, it was not always easy to get to the polls. The first election (1788–1789) was an especially messy affair. Voting days were different everywhere, with House elections held on December 22 in Connecticut, on January 7–10 in Maryland, and anywhere from February 11 to April 27 in New Jersey. Voters had to go to their county seats, which in Virginia sometimes meant traveling nearly 50 miles over mountains and watercourses. Upon arrival, the polls might be open or they might not, depending on the sheriff's humor. The whole process was so restricted, difficult, and confusing that only 11 percent of the Americans eligible to vote, or about *1 American in 40*, actually voted in the first presidential election. A modern human rights monitoring group would not have been pleased.[5]

One of the most important developments in the political history of the United States, and an essential part of the struggle for democracy, has been the expansion of the right to vote. The extension of the franchise has been a lengthy process, lasting 200 years. It has not been smooth or simple; surges of democratization have sometimes been followed by setbacks, and victories have been achieved only through vigorous political struggle by people in all walks of life.

The first barriers to fall were those concerning property and religion. So strong were the democratic currents in the years leading up to the election of Andrew Jackson, that by 1829 property and religious requirements had been dropped in all states except North Carolina and Virginia. (Virginia finally went along in 1852.) That left universal white male **suffrage**, or ability to vote, firmly in place in the United States. The idea was so well established by the 1830s that de Tocqueville reported that opponents of suffrage "hide their heads."[6] European countries did not attain universal white male suffrage until the late nineteenth and early twentieth centuries.

Expanding the suffrage to include blacks and women was much more difficult and painful. Ironically, universal white male suffrage was often accompanied by withdrawal of voting rights from black freedmen, even though new "free" states had been admitted to the union before the Civil War.[7] It took the bloody Civil War to free the slaves, and the Fifteenth Amendment to the U.S. Constitution (1870) to formally extend the right to vote to all blacks, North and South. Even so, blacks were effectively disenfranchised in the South by the end of the nineteenth century and mostly remained so until the civil rights movement and the Voting Rights Act of 1965.

Democracy was further expanded when women won the right to vote with the Nineteenth Amendment to the Constitution (1920), after a long political battle. (See "The Struggle for Democracy" on women winning the right to vote.) Residents of the District of Columbia were allowed to vote for president (though not Congress) after 1961, and 18–20-year-olds gained the franchise in 1971.

The result of these changes at the state and national levels was an enormous increase in the proportion of Americans who were *legally eligible* to vote: from about 23 percent of the adult population in 1788–1789, to nearly 100 percent—practically all citizens except felons and people in mental institutions—by the beginning of the 1970s.

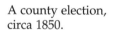

A county election, circa 1850.

THE STRUGGLE FOR DEMOCRACY

★

Women Win the Right to Vote

The struggle for women's suffrage was long and difficult. What began as a radical idea at the famous Seneca Falls Convention in 1848 became law in 1920, through the efforts of a powerful social movement.

Women's suffrage organizations were formed soon after the Civil War. For more than two decades, though, womens' organizations, primarily the radical National Woman Suffrage Association (NWSA) and the more conservative American Woman Suffrage Association (AWSA), feuded over how to pressure male politicians. Women like Susan B. Anthony (with the NWSA) and Lucy Stone (with the AWSA) were divided by temperament and ideology. Anthony favored dramatic action to expose men's hypocrisy. At an 1876 centennial celebration of the United States in Philadelphia, Anthony and several other women marched onto the platform, where the emperor of Brazil and other dignitaries sat, and handed over a declaration of women's rights. They then marched off the platform and read aloud the declaration. Stone favored quieter methods of persuasion.

Then, in 1890, the two main organizations joined together to form the National American Woman Suffrage Association (NAWSA). They dropped such controversial demands as divorce reform and legalized prostitution in favor of one order of business: women's suffrage. The movement was now focused, mostly united, and growing more powerful every year. One major boost was the endorsement of women's suffrage by the Women's Christian Temperance Union (WCTU), a vigorous organization whose primary goal was the abolition of the liquor trade. The NAWSA and the WCTU joined other women's groups to form an umbrella group, the General Federation of Women's Club (GFWC), which boasted 2 million members by 1910.

During the first two decades of the twentieth century, women's groups worked state by state, senator by senator, pressuring male politicians to support women's suffrage. After two prominent senators from New England were defeated in 1918 primarily because of the efforts of suffragists and prohibitionists, the political clout of the women's groups reached an all-time high. By spring 1919, Congress passed the Nineteenth Amendment, and the necessary 36 states ratified it the following year. By uniting around a common cause, women's organizations gained for women the right to vote.

Source: Nancy E. McGlen and Karen O'Connor, *Women's Rights: The Struggle for Equality in the Nineteenth and Twentieth Centuries* (New York: Praeger, 1983), ch. 3.

DIRECT ELECTIONS   Another trend has involved more and more direct election of government officials, overcoming their old insulation from the public. The development of a two-party system made a big difference. By the time of the Jefferson–Adams election of 1800, most state legislatures allowed popular voting for presidential electors. That and the practice of electors "pledging" to vote for a particular presidential candidate, together with the rise of two political parties to focus choices, meant that the voters could choose their president more or less directly. The later innovations of nominating presidential candidates in national conventions (by 1840) and of electing convention delegates directly in primaries (with upsurges after 1900 and in the 1970s) probably also increased democratic control of government, though we will see that each of these methods has anti-democratic features of its own.

Popular election of U.S. senators did not come until 1913, with the Seventeenth Amendment to the Constitution. Since 1913, all members of the Senate have been subject to direct choice by the voters, just as members of the House of Representatives have been from the country's beginnings.

Taken together, the expansion of the franchise and the development of direct, two-party elections have represented major successes in the struggle for democracy. But victory is not yet complete.

The Vanishing Electorate

During the first century or so of American history, not only did more and more people gain the right to vote, but also higher and higher proportions of eligible voters actually "turned out" on election day and voted. It is not easy to be sure of the exact **turnout** percentages because of data inaccuracies and voting fraud, but, in presidential elections, the roughly 11 percent of eligible voters who turned out in 1788–1789 jumped to about 31 percent in 1800 (when Thomas Jefferson was elected) and to about 57 percent in 1828 (Andrew Jackson's first victory). By 1840, the figure had reached *80 percent*, and it stayed at about that level until 1896.[8]

The disturbing fact, however, is that today far fewer people participate in politics in the United States than did so during most of the nineteenth century. Since 1912, only about 55–65 percent of eligible Americans have voted in presidential elections and still fewer in other elections—40–50 percent in "off-year" (nonpresidential year) congressional elections and as few as 10–20 percent in minor local elections. In recent years, the turnout rate has dropped to the low end of those ranges. It was only 36 percent in 1986 and 37 percent in 1990; in those years little more than *one-third* of eligible Americans participated in electing congressional representatives; hence the talk about a "vanishing electorate." (Take a look at Figure 9.3.)

The United States' voting turnout rate is exceptionally low compared with other modern industrialized countries, where 80 percent rates are common (see Figure 9.4). Most observers consider this a serious problem for democracy in America, particularly since (as we will see) those who vote tend to be different from those who do not. Nonvoters do not get an equal voice in political choices. Political equality, one of the key elements of democracy, is violated.

CAUSES OF LOW TURNOUT   Why do so few Americans participate in elections? Scholars disagree, but several factors seem definitely to be at work: compulsory registration, lack of attractive choices, changes in eligibility rules, alienation of the public about politics, and lack of mobilization of voters by the parties.

Registration   In the United States, only those who take the initiative and get registered before an election are permitted to vote in it. Sometimes registration is made difficult, with limited locations, limited office hours, and requirements to register long before the election. This is especially hard on people who move from one community to another. In 1988, about 35 percent of the nonvoters, but only 16 percent of voters, said that they had moved in the past two years.[9]

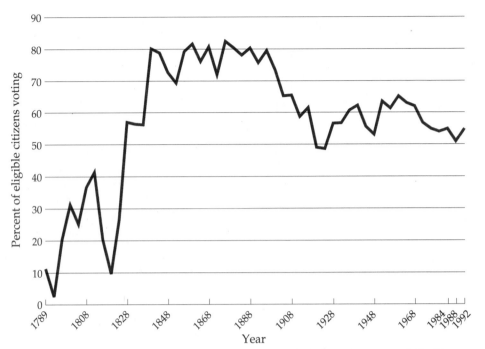

Figure 9.3 The rise and fall of turnout in presidential elections (percent of eligible voting age population voting)

Source: Walter Dean Burnham, "The Turnout Problem," in A. James Reichley, ed., Elections American Style *(Washington, D.C.: Brookings Institution, 1987), p. 113–114, and authors' research.*

In most European countries with high turnout rates, the government, rather than individual citizens, is responsible for deciding who is listed as eligible to vote. In fact, in some countries, such as Belgium and Luxembourg, citizens are *required* to vote and may have to pay a fine if they don't. In Italy, voting is not compulsory, but an individual's failure to vote is publicized. Moreover, in most countries, election days are holidays; unlike Americans, Europeans do not have to vote very early or late in the day or get special permission to leave their jobs in order to go to the polls.

Political equality and popular sovereignty in the United States could certainly be increased if voting were made easier. Possible ways of doing so include the national use of "postcard" registration, same-day registration, an extended voting period, such as the two-and-a-half weeks tried in Texas, or the broadened right of absentee voting granted in California.

Lack of Attractive Choices Many scholars believe that the nature of the political parties and the choices that they offer also affect turnout. As Figure 9.4 indicates, countries with proportional representation and multiparty systems—that is, with diverse parties from which to choose—have averaged an 83 percent turnout rate, whereas single-district, plurality vote countries (which usually have just two parties) have had a voter turnout rate that is closer to 70 percent. Also, unlike most European countries, the United States does not have a workers' party to mobilize

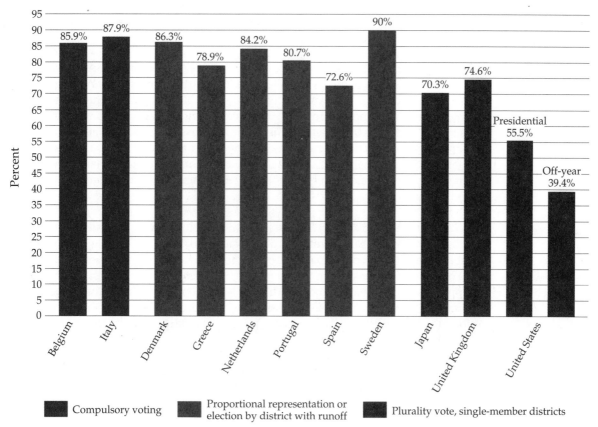

Figure 9.4 Voting turnout in different countries

Source: Walter Dean Burnham, "The Turnout Problem," in A. James Reichley, ed., Elections American Style *(Washington, D.C.: Brookings Institution, 1987), p. 107.*

blue-collar workers and poor people. Walter Dean Burnham argues that the crushing defeat of the Populists and radical Democrats in 1896 led to a conservative realignment that excluded many citizens and discouraged people from voting for years afterwards.[10] Shortly thereafter, such progressive "reforms" as registration requirements also reduced participation and cut into the political strength of immigrants in the big cities—perhaps deliberately.[11] According to this point of view, some groups and organized interests in society are happy with low turnout, especially among lower-income citizens, and try to discourage broader participation.

Changes in Eligibility Rules   Changes in eligibility rules also have affected turnout rates. As Figure 9.3 makes clear, turnout as a proportion of eligible voters dropped sharply just after women were enfranchised in 1920, because at first women were less likely to vote than men. (That difference gradually disappeared and is now gone. In fact, in 1988, 58 percent of women but only 56 percent of men reported voting.) Similarly, turnout percentages dropped a bit after 18-year-olds won the vote in 1971, because young people do not participate as much; they are less firmly established in local communities. But the enfranchisement of young voters, which reduced turnout, has been partly balanced by rising educational levels (since people with more education are more likely to vote) and by somewhat easier registration requirements.

Alienation The alienation and apathy about politics that many Americans felt after the 1960s as a result of the Vietnam War, urban unrest, the Watergate and Iran-Contra scandals, and various economic troubles probably contributed to recent declines in turnout.[12] In 1988, 59 percent of nonvoters said that government "is run by a few big interests looking out for themselves" and 67 percent said that people in government "waste a lot of money paid in taxes."[13] Just about as many voters said the same things, casting some doubt upon the idea that alienation is a major cause of abstention from voting, yet certainly abstention cannot be attributed to contentment or satisfaction, either.

Lack of Voter Mobilization by Parties A related factor may be the failure of parties in the 1980s and 1990s to register poor black and Hispanic people. Both the Republican and Democratic parties sometimes showed little eagerness to increase the number of voters among the poor, possibly because of worries that they would support Jesse Jackson or other candidates who were more liberal than most party officials.[14] Also, during the Reagan and Bush administrations, neither party clearly stood for the kinds of active domestic programs that the public continues to favor (see Chapter 5).

 CAMPAIGN PARTICIPATION Despite the low voter turnout levels in the United States, however, Americans are actually more likely than people in other countries to participate actively in campaigns. In a typical U.S. presidential election, like that of 1984, some 12 percent give money, 8 percent attend meetings, 9 percent wear a button, and fully 32 percent say that they try to persuade someone to vote their way.[15] Much the same thing is true of contacting officials and writing letters, which some 25 percent of Americans say they have done in the past year, according to recent surveys.[16] Exactly why Americans vote less but campaign more than citizens elsewhere is something of a mystery.

Student volunteers work on Bill Clinton's 1992 New Hampshire primary campaign.

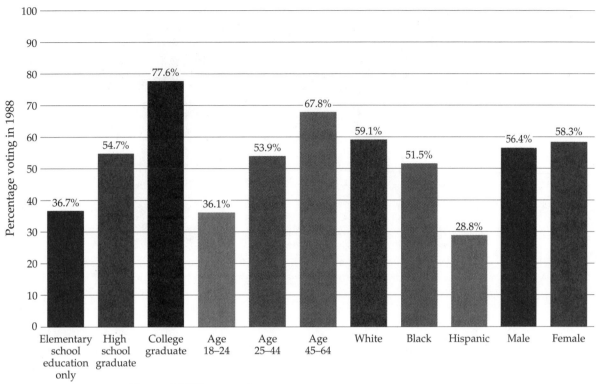

Figure 9.5 Who votes[a]

[a]The figures given are for the 1988 presidential election.

Source: U.S. Bureau of the Census, reported in World Almanac *(New York: Scripps-Howard, 1990), p. 339.*

Who Votes?

For the most part, politically active people are those with higher than average incomes and formal education. These people are also more likely to vote.[17] This difference has important effects on the working of democracy, because it undermines political equality; some kinds of people have more representation and more influence than others.

There is a "class bias" in both political participation and voting. In 1988, for example, 78 percent of adults with four or more years of college reported that they voted, but only 55 percent of high school and fewer than 42 percent of those who did not graduate from high school did so. The very young are unlikely to vote: only 33 percent of 18- to 20-year-olds did so in 1988, compared with 73 percent of 65- to 74-year-olds. The unemployed (39 percent) and Hispanics (29 percent) also have especially low turnout rates.[18] (See Figure 9.5.)

In the past, fewer black people voted than whites, but now the proportions are much more nearly equal (59 percent of whites and 52 percent of blacks voted in 1988)[19]; the remaining differences result from blacks' lower average levels of income and education. Blacks are at least equally likely to vote, and sometimes more so, than whites of similar background.

Careful statistical analyses indicate that the crucial factor in voter turnout is *level of formal education.* Other things being equal, college-educated people are

Hispanics have the potential to become an important force in American politics, but their low registration and voting rates have limited their influence.

much more likely to vote than are the grade-school or high school educated.[20] There are several possible reasons for this: people with more education learn more about politics, are less troubled by registration requirements, and are more self-confident about their ability to affect political life.

DOES IT MATTER WHO VOTES?   How much difference do participation biases make? Some observers have argued that it doesn't matter if many people don't vote, because their preferences aren't much different from those who do; the results would be about the same if everyone voted. In 1988, for example, even though nonvoters were disproportionately young, had low incomes, and had less than a college education, 50 percent of them said that they preferred George Bush for president; only 34 percent favored Democrat Michael Dukakis. Their votes would apparently have changed nothing.[21] Other observers say that low voter turnout is a positive benefit (as supposedly less educated people are easily swayed), increasing the stability of the system and discouraging demagoguery.[22]

However, we should not be too quick to accept these arguments, which have something in common with the nineteenth-century view that husbands were well suited to protect the interests of their nonvoting wives. Present-day nonvoters are definitely different from voters. Even if their expressed preferences about politics do not look very distinctive, their objective circumstances differ. Hispanics, the young, and people of low income would presumably benefit from particular kinds of government policies that are of less interest to other citizens (e.g., certain domestic social welfare programs). A political system that included and mobilized these people vigorously—perhaps through strong labor unions or a sympathetic political party—might well produce different policies more along the lines of European social welfare systems.[23] Of course, we cannot be sure that they would, but one sign of what a difference participation can make is the great change that took place when black Americans won effective voting rights. The number of black elected officials in the United States rose sharply, from 1,472 in 1970 to 3,503 in 1975, 5,014 in 1985, and 7,225 in 1989,[24] and nonblack politicians and officials paid much more attention to black constituents.

In any case, broader participation in U.S. elections would increase popular sovereignty and political equality, and thus would contribute to democracy. The limited size of the American electorate means that the struggle for democracy has not fully succeeded.

CAMPAIGNING FOR OFFICE

The ideas we discussed about how elections might ensure democratic policymaking all depend in various ways upon what sorts of choices are presented to the voters: whether candidates take clear policy stands, whether they differ from each other, whether they stand for what the average voter wants, and so forth. In evaluating the role of elections in democracy, therefore, we need to examine the nature of the choices.

Running for a Presidential Nomination

WHO HAS A CHANCE?   The major party candidates for president of the United States are chosen well before the November election, and often they are effectively chosen even before the parties hold nominating conventions. They are drawn from a rather small pool of potential candidates. Despite what mothers tell their children, not every American has a significant chance of becoming president.

For any given election, in fact, only a handful of candidates are serious possibilities. So far in American history, these virtually always have been middle-aged or elderly white men (though women can be expected to join the group soon), with strong educational backgrounds, fairly high incomes, and substantial experience as public figures—usually as government officials (especially senators or governors) or military heroes. Movie stars, business executives, and others who would be president almost always have to perform lesser government service before they are seriously considered for the presidency. Ronald Reagan, for example, most of whose career was spent acting in motion pictures and on television, served as governor of California before being elected president.

In recent years, the presidency has been practically monopolized by governors (who have demonstrated executive ability), vice-presidents (who have had a close look at how it's done), and U.S. senators (who have been exposed to a wide range of U.S. foreign and domestic policies). Since 1936, 39 percent of all presidential nominees have been governors, 33 percent vice-presidents, and 17 percent senators.[25] The vice-presidency is clearly the best single stepping-stone. Since 1900, 5 of the 16 presidents have succeeded from the vice-presidency to the presidency, and two others—Nixon and Bush—have been former vice-presidents elected in their own right.

Serious candidates for president almost invariably represent mainstream American values and policy preferences. Seldom does an "extreme" candidate get very far. Serious candidates almost always are acceptable to the business community and have enthusiastic support from at least some sectors of industry or finance. Acceptability to average voters and to businesspeople and financial backers is brought about both by the parties' desires to nominate winners and by the filtering process involved in gaining previous offices. Those who win elections to Congress and governorships and therefore emerge as presidential candidates have already demonstrated popular appeal to voters (as electoral-competition theories suggest), and also have demonstrated an ability to raise money for campaigns and to motivate party activists.

POLITICS
AND
FILM

*Campaigns
on Film*

Election campaigns are highly entertaining dramas. They dominate television news and draw extensive newspaper and television network coverage. It is somewhat surprising, therefore, that election campaigns have not drawn much attention from Hollywood. There are a few exceptions, however, worth looking at.

The Last Hurrah is John Ford's portrayal of the decline of old-style politics and the birth of a new style, and a statement about what has been lost in the transition. Spencer Tracy plays Frank Skeffington, mayor and machine boss of an unnamed, small eastern city, who is running for reelection. The machine (see the discussion of the urban machine in Chapter 15, "State and Local Government") is a benevolent and largely beneficial political organization (though it does suffer from petty corruption) that has enabled the Irish and other ethnic minorities to displace the wealthy Yankees from political power, and to gain needed services from government. The Yankees are not about to give up power, however. They tap a mediocre but photogenic candidate to run against Skeffington and put their money behind him,

focusing on the relatively new medium of television (the film was made in 1958). They are inept in the use of television at first but slowly gain skill in its use. Skeffington campaigns like he always has: hearing complaints from constituents; attending wakes; speaking at union meetings, church gatherings, and civic events; and granting small favors. Much to his surprise, he loses the election. His campaign strategy of personal contact is no match for the new media-style campaign. He promises his followers that he will run for the governorship, but Ford leaves the viewer with the impression that politicians like Skeffington will be as extinct as dinosaurs in the coming media age.

The media campaign has arrived with a vengeance in the Michael Ritchie, Robert Redford film *The Candidate*. Redford plays an idealistic and reluctant candidate for the Senate in California (modeled, apparently, on a real candidate and senator, John Tunney), who agrees to be a candidate only on the condition that he be allowed to run on the issues and talk seriously with the electorate about them. His campaign soon turns into a disaster: he is unable

GETTING STARTED   A senator or a governor who wants to run for the presidency usually begins at least two or three years before the election by testing the waters, asking friends and financial backers if they will support a run, and observing how people react to the "Great Mentioner." A friendly journalist may write that Senator Blathers "has been mentioned" as a smart, attractive, strong candidate; Blathers waits to see whether anyone agrees. The precandidate may commission a national poll to check for name recognition and a positive image. He may put together an informal organization to round up private endorsements, commitments, and financial contributions, perhaps setting up private PACs to gather money. He may meet a few voters and try out a speech (usually very quiet, but crucial). (For the Hollywood view of campaigning, see the box above.)

If all goes well at this early stage, the presidential aspirant becomes more serious, assembling a group of close advisors, formulating strategy, raising large amounts of money, and putting together organizations ("Draft Blathers" or "Citi-

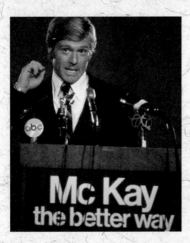

as "... nothing less than the best movie yet done about politics in coaxial America," Ritchie and Redford seem to suggest that the juggernaut of modern campaigns inevitably overwhelms even the best candidates.

In *Power*, director Sidney Lumet focuses on the professionals who run modern campaigns. Richard Gere plays a consultant who creates the sound bites, advertising, and staged television spots that dominate political campaigns. Gere is a hired gun; it matters little to him who the candidate happens to be. He is willing and able to package anyone who wants to buy his services. In a frankly unbelievable development, Gere runs across a candidate who turns even his stomach, which causes him to see the error of his ways. He goes over to the other candidate and advises him to talk seriously to the people about the issues, and to eschew most of the tricks of the modern campaign trade. Surprisingly and unconvincingly, in a wink perhaps at Frank Capra-style optimism, his new candidate wins the election. Nevertheless, Lumet still manages to show us a very good inside look at the machinery of campaigning in America.

to gain media attention against the incumbent, the issues become lost in superficial news coverage, and he falls further and further behind in the polls. Enter Peter Boyle, playing a hard-nosed, professional campaign consultant, who fashions a modern campaign based on the sound bite, advertising, and staged television events. In the end, the change in strategy works, and Redford wins the election in a close race. In the process, however, the man that began the campaign is swallowed up whole by the process and is unrecognizable in the end. In this film, which *Los Angeles Times* critic Charles Champlin described

zens for Blathers" committees) in key states. One major decision is how to pitch the campaign: as an "outsider" getting rid of the mess in Washington, D.C., like Jimmy Carter in 1976 and Ronald Reagan in 1980? As the most competent and most centrist standard-bearer for the party, like Michael Dukakis in 1988? As the voice for a particular program, such as helping the deprived, like Jesse Jackson in 1984 and 1988? Another major decision involves which state primaries and caucuses to enter. Each entry takes a lot of money, energy, and organization, and any loss is embarrassing, but to win the nomination it is generally necessary to put together a string of primary victories.

PRIMARIES AND CAUCUSES Party nominees for president are chosen every four years at national party **conventions**, made up of state delegations from around the country. Since the 1970s, most of the delegates to the conventions—currently about 67 percent of the Democratic delegates and 55 percent of the Republican delegates—are chosen in state **primary elections**, with direct voting by rank-and-file party members.[26] (Some primaries are "open" to all voters; others are "closed," that is, reserved for those who register with the party.) The popularly elected delegates are supplemented by "superdelegates," usually congresspeople and local officials, who become convention delegates by appointment. Relatively few states now use **caucus** systems, in which active party members and officials choose delegates to state conventions, where, in turn, the national convention delegates are chosen.

The "smoke-filled rooms" and deal making among party leaders that once characterized national conventions (it took ten ballots for the Republicans to nominate Warren Harding in 1920, for example) are mostly a thing of the past. Now the trick is to win delegates in primaries and caucuses and among party officials.[27]

Momentum   It is especially important for a candidate to establish "**momentum**" by winning early primaries and caucuses. Early winners get press attention, financial contributions, and better standings in the polls, as voters and contributors decide they are "viable" candidates and must have some merit if people in other states have supported them. All these factors—attention from the media, money, and increased popular support—help the candidates who win early contests to go on and win more and more contests.[28]

At the beginning of each presidential election year, therefore, a number of candidates descend upon the sites of the early contests: the Iowa caucuses, the New Hampshire primary, and the "Super Tuesday" Southern primaries, which were bunched together to enhance regional clout. The candidates make speeches, meet with potential supporters and money givers, and press the flesh at farmhouses, malls, and factory gates. Representatives of the national press follow along, capturing each gaffe or coup, filming sound bites for television news, and making their own judgments about who is "viable" and who has "character." Campaign workers go door to door, talking up their candidates, passing out literature, and getting people to the polls. Expensive paid advertisements blanket the television and radio airwaves. Winners in the primaries and caucuses move on to the next; others drop out.

Arkansas Governor Bill Clinton campaigns in Harlem before the 1992 primaries.

How to Win   Four main factors affect candidates' success in gathering delegates.

1. General *attractiveness of the candidate*, especially the personal image conveyed by television, but also the candidate's stands on issues and his or her connections with the good or bad times that the country is enjoying.

2. *"Viability,"* as judged by the media and as reflected in the polls. Our plurality voting system, under which the candidate with the most votes wins, however badly the vote is split, makes citizens especially reluctant to vote for someone who has no chance.

3. *Organizational strength*, particularly the number of hard-working activists who will pack the caucuses or get voters to the polls.

4. *Money* to pay for the television ads, organizing, and travel that a campaign requires.

Money can help make candidates look more attractive, win votes, seem more viable, and build strong organizations; lack of money can destroy a campaign entirely.

In recent years, most successful presidential nominees have won primary after primary, gathering in the supporters of losing candidates who bowed out, and have gone on to the convention with a substantial plurality of delegates. Michael Dukakis, for example, entered the 1988 Democratic convention with about 2,876 delegates (70 percent of the total) committed to him; Jesse Jackson, Dukakis's nearest competitor, had only 1,218 delegates.[29]

THE CONVENTION   When there is a foreordained front-runner, the national convention—usually held in July or August in a major city, such as New York or Houston—generally becomes a coronation ceremony, in which prepledged delegates ratify the selection of the leading candidate, accept a ticket-balancing choice for the vice-presidency, and put on a colorful show for the media and the country. Speeches and videos explain why "our" party, with vision, experience, and heart, is far better than "theirs." Enthusiasm and unity are staged for the national television audience; it is a disaster if serious conflicts break out or the timing goes wrong. (Convention wrangling pushed McGovern's acceptance speech, which was supposed to be the climax of the convention, way past prime time, so that it was televised at 3 A.M. Eastern Standard Time.)

The Republican and Democratic convention delegates tend to be different from each other, reflecting the nature of their party coalitions. Delegates to both are predominately white and financially well off, but the Democrats typically have many more black, Hispanic, female, and working-class delegates. In 1988, for example, 52 percent of the Democratic delegates were women, compared with 37 percent of the Republican delegates; 39 percent of the Democratic delegates had family incomes under $50,000, compared with 23 percent of the Republican delegates; and 21 percent of the Democratic delegates were black, compared with only 3 percent of the Republican delegates.[30] Democratic delegates sometimes also seem to be rowdier and more excited about politics. In addition, convention delegates of the two parties tend to differ substantially on certain political issues, with Democratic delegates tending to be much more liberal, Republican delegates much more conservative, and the average American citizen somewhere in the

Violent confrontations between police and demonstrators opposed to the Vietnam war at the 1968 Democratic convention in Chicago hurt the chances of nominee Hubert Humphrey. The 1984 Republican presidential convention in Dallas, which resembled a coronation ceremony, boosted President Reagan's re-election campaign.

middle. In 1988, for example, 90 percent of Democratic delegates favored increased federal spending on education, as did 71 percent of American adults, but only 41 percent of Republican delegates favored it. Similar differences showed up on day care, abortion, government attention to blacks, military spending, and U.S. policy on Central America.[31] (See Figure 9.6.)

Only occasionally nowadays is there a real contest at the national convention, in which delegates may have to decide between their "professional" minds and their "purist" hearts: whether to nominate a likely winner or one who stands for ideas that they hold dear (as when the Republicans renominated President Ford rather than their favorite, Ronald Reagan, in 1976). The evidence from polls indicates, in fact, that, in virtually all recent conventions, the party nominee has been the candidate who was most popular with rank-and-file party identifiers in the nation as a whole. Still, the big differences between the delegates of the two parties tend to push the nominees and the positions of the parties apart, as in responsible-party rather than electoral-competition theories.

NOMINATION POLITICS AND DEMOCRACY What does all this have to do with democratic control of government? Several things. For one, the nomination process is fairly good at coming up with candidates who are personally attractive to voters and who take stands with wide popular appeal, as *electoral-competition* theories seek. For another, as the sharp differences between Republican and Democratic convention delegates indicate, Republican and Democratic nominees tend to differ in certain systematic ways, in accordance with *responsible-party* theories. Party platforms, too—the parties' official statements of their stands on issues—tend to include appeals to average voters but also distinctive appeals to each party's constituencies.

The crucial role of party activists and money givers in selecting candidates means that nominees and their policy stands are partly chosen to appeal to party

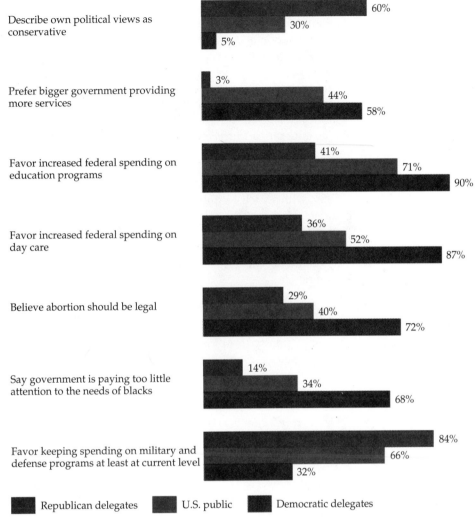

Figure 9.6 Convention delegates versus the public

Source: New York Times, *August 14, 1988, p. A32.*

elites and financial contributors, rather than to ordinary voters. Thus, neither party's nominee may stand exactly for what ordinary citizens want, preventing a perfectly democratic outcome.

Campaigning for the White House

We have been focusing on how outsiders and political challengers try to win party nominations. Things are different for incumbent presidents, such as George Bush in 1992, Ronald Reagan in 1984, Jimmy Carter in 1980, and Richard Nixon in 1972, or for "heir apparent" vice-presidents, such as Bush in 1988 or Nixon in 1960. These candidates must also enter and win primaries, but they have the machinery of government working for them and—if times are reasonably good—a unified party behind them. They campaign on the job, taking credit for policy successes while discounting failures. Sometimes they can plead the press of business and conduct a "Rose Garden" campaign without leaving the White House. Winning nomination is usually easy.

Incumbents and challengers alike, having won a party nomination, must face the autumn campaign, which traditionally begins at the beginning of September, on Labor Day. Now the candidates set up a campaign organization in each state, sending aides to coordinate their own backers and local party leaders. Intense money raising continues, and a new round of public financing kicks in. Candidates plan itineraries to make three or four speeches in different media markets each day, concentrating on big states but also touching the whole country.

The media blitz begins, with many brief (15- or 30-second) "spot" commercials on television, including "attack" ads, like the famous Willie Horton spot in 1988, with which Republicans raised racial fears and portrayed Democratic candidate Michael Dukakis as soft on crime. Political consultants use voter focus groups to identify "hot button" emotional appeals. Negative advertising has been heavily criticized as simplistic and misleading, and it sometimes causes a sympathetic backlash, but more often it is effective and difficult to control or counteract.

Another element of strategy, especially for Democrats, is to get potential supporters registered and to the polls. For years, organized labor has energized registration and turnout campaigns. Senator Alan Cranston (D–CA) organized several "nonpartisan" voter registration groups, gathering funds from various big money sources, including $850,000 from savings and loan executive Charles H. Keating and hundreds of thousands of dollars from Gallo Winery, the Trial Lawyers association, and the Teamsters, Sheet Metal Workers, and Hotel Employees unions.[32] As we have noted, however, during the 1980s and early 1990s, many Democratic officials seemed to lose their enthusiasm for mobilizing minority and low-income voters.

As the Watergate case (described in Chapter 6) indicates, campaign strategies sometimes also have included "dirty tricks," designed to sabotage the opponent's campaign, upset schedules, plant rumors, and the like. We will see that strategies

A Republican group in 1988 used the case of Willie Horton, a convicted murderer who was furloughed from a Massachusetts prison and then committed a rape, to imply that Democratic candidate (and Massachusetts governor) Michael Dukakis was soft on crime.

have even included arranging—or sabotaging—world events that reflect well or badly on the incumbent.

INFORMING VOTERS   What kinds of information do voters get in campaigns?

Issues   Some of it concerns issues. In accord with electoral-competition theories, both the Republican and Democratic candidates usually try to appeal to the average voter by taking similar, popular stands on policy, especially foreign policy. In 1968, for example, Richard Nixon took positions close to the midpoint of public opinion on most (90 percent) of the issues studied, and Hubert Humphrey did so quite often as well (65 percent).[33] George Bush and Michael Dukakis both hewed close to the center in 1988. On the other hand, as responsible-party theories suggest, Republican and Democratic candidates usually do differ systematically from each other on certain issues, such as medical care, federal aid to education, social welfare, civil rights, the environment, and abortion. On these issues, the Democratic candidate tends to take a more liberal stand than the Republican, just as Democratic party identifiers, activists, money givers, and convention delegates tend to be more liberal than their Republican counterparts. This varies, however; Dukakis, though labeled a "liberal" in 1988, expressed little excitement about traditional Democratic programs.

Presidential candidates usually do not say a great deal about specific issues; they tend to be vague and *ambiguous*, in order to avoid offending voters who disagree. No one could object to George Bush's 1988 promises to be an "education president" and an "environmental president"; what did he mean? For the same reason, candidates emphasize *symbolic* matters that appeal to virtually everyone, like Bush's invocation of the American flag and the pledge of allegiance in 1988.

Past Performance   Often candidates talk about past performance and future goals. The "Out" party blames the "In" party for wars, recessions, and other calamities. Nixon in 1968 spoke of "sirens in the night" due to crime and urban riots; Reagan in 1980 bemoaned the high "misery index" of inflation and unemployment. The "In" party brags about how it has brought peace and prosperity, and it paints a warm picture of a glorious future, without saying exactly how it will come about.

Incumbent presidents, of course, can *act* in ways that accurately or inaccurately suggest successful performance. They can try to schedule recessions for off years, pumping up the economy in time for reelection (as in 1972 and 1984), or they can make dramatic foreign policy moves just before election day. The opposition sometimes fights back. It has been charged (though not proven) that, when President Carter tried to negotiate the release of U.S. hostages from Iran before the election in 1980, the Reagan campaign, fearing an "October surprise," secretly met with the Iranians and urged delay until after the election.[34] But the incumbent president usually has more power to act, and any opposition meddling with U.S. foreign policy raises legal questions.

Personal Characteristics   Most of all, however, voters get a chance to learn about the real or alleged personal characteristics of the candidates. Even when the candidates are talking about something else, they can give an impression of either competence or incompetence. Jimmy Carter, for example, emphasized his expertise as a "nuclear engineer." Gerald Ford was haunted by films of stumbling on airplane ramps. Candidates come across as warm or cold. Dwight D. Eisenhower's

Dwight Eisenhower, popularly known as "Ike," was one of the most popular American politicians of the twentieth century.

radiant grin appeared everywhere in 1952 and 1956 (as did Reagan's in 1984), but Richard Nixon was perceived as cold and aloof in 1968, despite clever efforts at selling his personality. Candidates also can seem strong or weak. George Bush overcame the so-called wimp factor in 1988 with his tough talk about crime and the flag, but Michael Dukakis's missteps—looking silly riding in a tank, failing to express outrage at a reporter's hypothetical question about a rape of his wife—made him look weak to many voters.

The sparse and ambiguous treatment of policy issues in campaigns, and the emphasis on past performance and personal competence, fit better with ideas about electoral reward and punishment than they do with responsible parties or issue-oriented electoral competition. But candidate personalities have a tricky relation to democratic control of government. Obviously, it is useful for voters to pick presidents who possess competence, warmth, and strength, and citizens may be more skillful at judging people than at figuring out complicated policy issues. On the other hand, perhaps voters can be fooled by dirty tricks or slick advertising that sells presidential candidates' personalities[35] and tears down the opponents. Moreover, the focus on personal imagery may distract attention from policy stands. If candidates who favor unpopular policies are elected on the basis of attractive personal images, democratic control of policymaking is weakened. By the purchase of advertising and the hiring of smart consultants, money may, in effect, overcome the popular will.

Money and Elections

THE COST OF PRESIDENTIAL CAMPAIGNS   Presidential campaigns cost enormous amounts of money. In 1988, for example, George Bush's prenomination campaign reported direct spending of $30.64 million, and Dukakis's, $28.16 million. In ad-

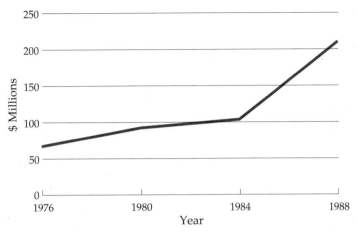

Figure 9.7 Rising costs of campaigns for presidential nominations

Source: New York Times, *August 27, 1989, p. A23.*

dition, state and national parties spent at least $8.3 million, and that is probably only a fraction of the total; substantial amounts of campaign spending, especially "soft money" for local parties, go unreported.[36] Looking at *all* the campaigns in 1988, not just the presidential one, the total amount of money spent just on political advertising was $227 million—up 48 percent from 1984.[37]

The trend in campaign costs over the years has moved steadily and rapidly upward. In 1984, for example, when the presidential candidates ran 166 minutes of national television ads in the last ten days of the election, candidates spent a total of $154 million on spot advertising: *100 times* the amount spent in 1952.[38] Reported direct spending for nomination campaigns in 1976 was only $66.9 million for all presidential candidates, but it jumped up to $92.3 million in 1980, $103.6 million in 1984, and $210.7 million in 1988[39] (see Figure 9.7).

There is actually room for argument about whether we should think of this as a lot of money or a little money. The $210.7 million in direct spending on all presidential candidates in 1988, for example, translates to less than $1 for each person in the country. And the figures above are not adjusted for inflation. But the growth in campaign spending is real; it has far outstripped inflation or increases in the price of advertising.[40] Furthermore, the amounts involved, most of which come from private sources, are large enough to be daunting to prospective candidates and to raise questions about whether money buys political influence.

WHERE DOES THE MONEY COME FROM? Since 1971, substantial amounts of money have come from the federal treasury, paid by the taxpayers—some $46 million for the general election in 1988. Taxpayers can check off a box on their tax form and thereby authorize a $1 contribution from public funds (not their own taxes), and the government "matches" small contributions to candidates. Public financing, though not popular with the citizenry, has the advantage of eliminating any question of bribery or buying of favors.

However, public money accounted for only about 31 percent of campaign spending in 1988. The rest had to come from contributions by individuals and by PACs (political action committees), set up by businesses, labor unions, and special-

RESOURCE FEATURE

What Is Allowed in Campaign Finance

The rules concerning campaign money change from time to time; here is how things stood in 1990.

- *Individuals'* contributions were limited to $1,000 directly to any one candidate in one election cycle and to $5,000 to any one PAC per year. But "independent" expenditures on behalf of a candidate or a party were unlimited, and people could contribute to as many different PACs as they wanted. Total contributions to all candidates, PACs, and party committees were limited to $25,000 per year.

- *PACs* were limited to a $5,000 contribution per candidate per election, and a given PAC could receive no more than $5,000 from any one person. But there was no limit on the number of PACs that an interest group could form or to which an individual could contribute—a big loophole.

- *Parties* were limited, through a complicated formula, in their contributions to, or on behalf of, candidates. But "party-building" activities at the state and local levels had no limits. Money spent in this way is called "soft money."

- *Candidates* had to report to the Federal Election Commission (FEC) any contributions over $500. Candidates who received public funding, which all had done, had to report all expenditures and contributions, and their expenditures were subject to limits tied to inflation. Presidential candidates could receive federal matching funds for any contribution up to $250, providing an incentive to ask lots of people for small sums.

Source: Frank Sorauf, *Money in American Elections* (Glenview, IL: Scott, Foresman, 1988).

interest groups. The same 1974 and later "reforms" that required candidates to report the source of their funds and that prohibited any individual from contributing more than $1,000 directly to a candidate also left some enormous loopholes. PACs were legalized (even for business and unions, which were formerly prohibited from making political contributions) and now are allowed to contribute up to $5,000 per candidate; furthermore, people are permitted to contribute $5,000 to each of as many PACs as they want. Individuals and PACS can also spend unlimited amounts of money in support of any candidate, as long as the spending is "independent" of the candidate. The "fat cats" are back; anyone who wants to invest a lot of money in politics can figure out a way to do it. (See the "Resource Feature.")

Much of the money comes from individuals and organizations that want something from government: tax benefits, regulatory relief, military contracts, or something else. For example, Common Cause found that the 249 people who provided $100,000 each (a total of almost $25 million) to the Republican party for 1988 as part of "Team 100" included Eastern Airlines Chairman Frank Lorenzo, who early in 1989 received a favorable decision from the president not to mediate Eastern's labor strike. Team 100 also included Ronald Perelman, William Belzberg, Henry Kravis, George Roberts, T. Boone Pickens, Meshulam Riklis, and other prominent figures involved in takeovers and leveraged buyouts, which generally require government approval. It included corporate raider Paul Bilzerian, real estate developer Donald Trump, and savings and loan executive Charles H. Keating, Jr., all of whom had legal problems with the government. Oil companies and their executives gave at least $1.7 million to Team 100. Several of them, including Occidental, were interested in opening up offshore drilling in California and Florida or opening the Arctic National Wildlife Refuge for drilling. Atlantic Richfield had been assessed for unpaid windfall profits taxes; Petrofina and Occidental both received favorable settlements of government fines for oil price overcharging. Other members of Team 100 included executives of such agribusinesses as Archer Daniels Midland Corp., a big producer of soybean products, corn sweeteners, and ethanol, all of which rely heavily on federal subsidies.[41]

DOES MONEY TALK?   It is widely believed, though difficult to prove, that money givers often get something from their contributions. The point is not that politicians take outright bribes (a practice that is probably much rarer than it once was), but rather that cozy relationships develop between politicians and major money givers. Contributors gain access—a friendly hearing—to those whom they have helped to win office. Contributors' money increases the chances of victory for like-minded politicians who hold the "right" policy views and can be counted on to do the right thing without any need for pressure.

What is clear is that money givers are different from average citizens. They have special interests of their own. The top-spending PACs in the early part of the 1990 electoral cycle, for example, did not equally represent all ordinary consumers or taxpayers. They represented the trade unions of certain kinds of well-organized workers, such as teamsters, automobile workers, mail carriers, teachers, machinists, and communications workers, and also such groups as doctors, realtors, Jesse Helms's conservative political club, state and local government employees, AT&T, trial lawyers, and the National Rifle Association.[42] Many kinds of people were left out.

The result is political inequality. Those who are well organized or have a lot of money and are willing to spend it on politics have a better chance of influencing policy than ordinary citizens do. Thus, elections provide one way in which the interest groups described in Chapter 7 can turn their economic power into political power, overcoming the legal equality embodied in the idea of "one person, one vote." Business interests, which provided 65 percent of the $160 million in PAC contributions to congressional candidates in 1988,[43] have a particular advantage that touches both parties. This is a major problem for the working of democracy in the United States. Over the years, many reforms have been considered—especially substituting public money for private—but those who benefit from the system (namely interest groups and incumbent politicians) are adept at resisting changes in the law and at getting around any changes that occur.

ELECTION OUTCOMES

After the parties and candidates have presented their choices, the voters decide. Presidential elections are held on the first Tuesday after the first Monday in November of each year that is divisible by four; "off-year" congressional elections come on the other even-numbered years. Exactly how people make their voting decisions affects how well or how poorly elections contribute to democratic control of government.

How Voters Decide

It is not easy to find out why people vote the way they do. When asked directly, citizens often give uninformative or unreliable answers, such as, "I vote for the best person, no matter what party." Therefore, scholars perform statistical analyses of survey data to uncover voting patterns. They check what sorts of people (with what party affiliations, what opinions about issues, and what perceptions of candidates' personal qualities) tend to vote for one candidate rather than another. Even with the help of sophisticated methods, it is hard to be sure what causes people to behave in different ways, but there is general agreement that feelings about the *parties, candidates*, and *issues* all have substantial effects.

SOCIAL CHARACTERISTICS AND PARTY LOYALTIES   People's socioeconomic status, religion, and ethnic backgrounds are significantly related to how they vote. Since the 1930s, for example, black people, Jews, and lower-income citizens have tended heavily to vote for Democrats, while white Anglo-Saxon Protestants and the wealthy have voted mostly for Republicans. In 1988, 86 percent of blacks, but only 40 percent of whites, voted for Dukakis against Bush. Sixty-two percent of people with family incomes under $12,500, but only 32 percent of those with incomes over $100,000, voted for Dukakis. Sixty-four percent of Jews but only 18 percent of white fundamentalist or evangelical Christians[44] voted for Dukakis (see Figure 9.8). Similar patterns show up in congressional elections. In 1990, only 39 percent of those with incomes over $100,000 (compared with about 52 percent of citizens nationwide) voted for Democratic congressional candidates. But 78 percent of black voters cast ballots for the Democrats, as did 74 percent of Jews and 66 percent of those with family incomes under $15,000.[45]

To some extent, these social patterns work through long-term attachments to, or "identification" with, the political parties. As we saw in previous chapters, most Americans say that they consider themselves Republicans or Democrats. Party loyalties vary among different groups of the population, often because of past or present differences between the parties on policy issues. The relationship between party loyalties and certain policy preferences—especially those related to New Deal social welfare issues—means that party-line voting can accomplish some of the same things that issue voting is supposed to do in responsible-party theories. Party cues help people vote for candidates who are close to them on the issues.

Party loyalties are good predictors of how people vote. Those who say that they consider themselves Republicans tend to vote for Republican candidates in one election after another, and those who consider themselves Democrats vote for Democratic candidates. This is especially true in congressional elections and in state and local races, where most voters know little more about candidates than their party labels. In 1990, for example, 80 percent of people who considered themselves Democrats voted for Democratic candidates for the House of Representatives, and 78 percent of Republicans voted for Republicans.[46] But it is also true of presidential elections. In every election from 1952 through 1988, 90 percent or more of "strong" Republicans voted for the Republican candidate. In all those elections, except for 1972, when many abandoned McGovern, 84 percent or more of "strong" Democrats voted for the Democratic candidate.[47]

Because party loyalties are so important, some scholars speak of a "**normal vote**": a proportion of the votes that each party would win if only party and

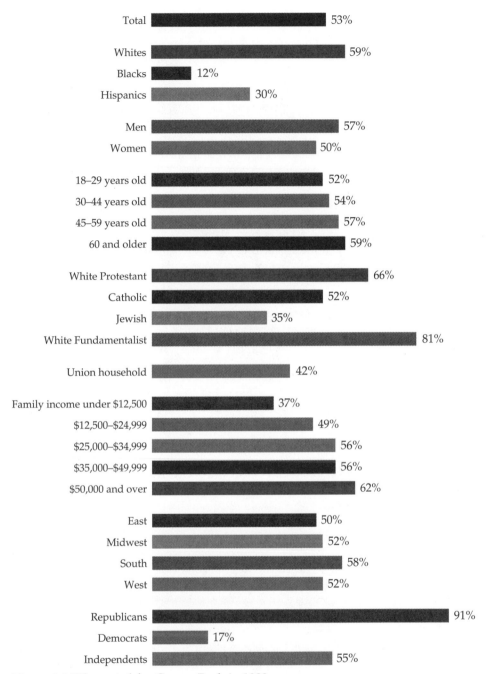

Figure 9.8 Who voted for George Bush in 1988

Source: CBS/NYT survey reported in the New York Times, *November 10, 1988, p. A6.*

nothing else affected voting decisions. Since party loyalties are rather stable over time (changing in large numbers only during "realignment" periods, such as those of 1896 or 1932), the normal vote stays about the same from one election to another. If nothing else were going on, the majority party, which ever since 1932 has been the Democratic Party, would win every election. In fact, this has been very nearly true of congressional elections; the Democrats have won majorities in the U.S. House of Representatives and the Senate in almost every election since the 1930s.

But the results of recent presidential elections indicate that something else has been going on. In fact, of the ten presidential elections between 1952 and 1988, the Democrats won only three, or 30 percent! This is hardly an imposing winning streak for the majority party. Most recent presidential elections have been *"deviating"* elections, in which the minority party has won. (See the list of election outcomes in the Appendix.)

We know part of the reason for this: party loyalties have been weakening. Even though strong party identifiers have continued to vote for their party, there have been fewer strong party identifiers since about 1968; increasing numbers of people consider themselves independents and just "lean" toward a party.[48] Moreover, while the number of whites in the South who consider themselves Democrats declined sharply (from 80 percent in 1952 to only 37 percent in 1984)[49] because of civil rights, defense, and other issues, some continued for a while to call themselves Democrats but voted for Republican presidential candidates.

CANDIDATES   Another reason why presidential-election outcomes have not simply reflected the party balance and why the Democrats have lost so often, is that voters pay a lot of attention to their perceptions of the personal characteristics of candidates. They vote heavily for candidates who have experience, appear strong and decisive, and seem to display personal warmth. The Republican candidate in 1952 and 1956, Dwight D. Eisenhower, had a tremendous advantage in this respect over his Democratic opponent, Adlai Stevenson; so did the Republican Richard Nixon over George McGovern in 1972, and the Republicans Ronald Reagan over Walter Mondale in 1984 and George Bush over Michael Dukakis in 1988. Only in 1964 did the Democratic candidate (Lyndon Johnson) appeal to voters substantially more than the Republican candidate (Barry Goldwater). In elections between 1952 and 1972, the contrast between Republican and Democratic candidates typically gained the Republicans 4 or 5 percentage points—just enough to overcome the Democrats' advantage in the normal vote.

ISSUES   Voters also pay attention to issues, even beyond the party-cleavage issues that are reflected in party loyalties. Sometimes this means choosing between different *policy proposals* about the future, such as Goldwater's promises to cut back the welfare state, or McGovern's pledges to redistribute income and to help the poor. (This sort of issue voting may have increased since the tame years prior to 1964.[50]) More often, however, issue voting has meant *retrospective* voting, making judgments about the past, especially on major questions about war or peace and the state of the economy. The voters tend to reward the incumbent party for what they see as good times and to punish it for what they see as bad times.

Foreign policy can be important. Bitter disillusionment over the Korean War hurt the Democrats in 1952, just as Lyndon Johnson's Vietnam War lost the Democrats votes in 1968, and unhappiness about the Iranian hostages and the Soviet intervention in Afghanistan hurt Jimmy Carter and the Democrats in 1980. Re-

The year-long ordeal of hostages taken from the U.S. embassy in Teheran, Iran, together with economic troubles at home, contributed to the defeat of President Jimmy Carter in 1980.

publican candidates Eisenhower, Nixon, and Reagan could claim to be tough and successful peacemakers. During nearly all of the last 40 years, in fact, Republican candidates have been seen as better at providing foreign policy strength and at keeping us out of war. George Bush enjoyed this advantage in 1988 and held on to some of it in 1992, after the victory over Iraq.

The economy matters, as well. After severe economic downturns, Americans tend to vote the incumbent party out of office, as they did to the Republicans during the Great Depression in 1932. For many years, the Democrats were seen as the party of prosperity, but, after the combined onslaught of inflation and recession during the 1970s, Democrat Jimmy Carter was punished at the polls in 1980, and the parties were viewed as more nearly equal in this respect.

One way to see the regular, systematic effects of electoral reward and punishment is to look at the number of votes for congresspersons that the incumbent party wins in off-year elections, when there are no presidential candidates with unique personalities to complicate voting choices. Changes in the economy one year before an off-year election—particularly percentage changes in real per capita income—are strong predictors of how well the incumbent party will do. When Americans' incomes go up, they are much more likely to vote for the incumbent party than when their incomes go down.[51]

Do Elections Matter?

When we ask whether or not elections "make a difference," we are likely to look for dramatic cases in which big issues were at stake between the two parties and the election ushered in a new era of policymaking and party realignment: the Republican wins of 1860 (leading to the Civil War and the end of slavery) and 1896 (defeating agrarian radicals and consolidating the forces of industrialization), or the Democratic victory of 1932, which inaugurated the New Deal and many of our contemporary social welfare programs. The 1980 Reagan victory, too, had major policy effects, though it did not bring a large-scale realignment of party loyalties.

Such decisive elections are rare, however; it does not usually make such a dramatic difference whether the Republicans or the Democrats win. Still, whether or not the final choice is critical, elections do matter, in several different ways that bear upon questions of democratic control.

In terms of the responsible-party governmental theory, for example, the fact that Republicans tend to be more conservative than Democrats on a number of economic and social issues provides voters with a measure of democratic control by enabling them to detect differences and make choices. With the theory of electoral punishment, the control voters exercise is expressed by either reelecting successful incumbents or throwing failures out of office. Finally, as electoral competition theories point out, elections force parties to compete by nominating centrist candidates and by taking similar issue stands that are close to what most Americans want. This, in fact, may be the chief way in which citizens' policy preferences affect what their government does.

Clearly, U.S. elections help make the public's voice heard, but they do not bring about perfect democracy. Two key reasons for this are the limited and biased participation of citizens, and the crucial role of money and activists in affecting election outcomes, both of which impair political equality by giving some sorts of people more political influence than others. The nature of our political parties, of course, has a great deal to do with both of these reasons (see Chapter 8).

In later chapters, we will see how these features of elections carry through the political process to allow various people and organizations, other than the general public—especially interest groups, corporations, and elite party coalitions—to exert influence on policymaking. Elections serve as a major conduit by which many people and institutions at the *political* level, who don't hold office, influence *governmental* officials and institutions that make policy.

SUMMARY

Elections are the most important means by which citizens can exert democratic control over their government. Voters can choose *responsible parties* to carry out their distinctive programs. *Electoral competition* forces vote-seeking parties and candidates to appeal to the center of public opinion. *Electoral reward and punishment* gives officials incentives to carry out policies that will win public approval. However, none of these processes guarantees a perfectly democratic outcome.

Political participation can be conventional (voting, helping in campaigns, contacting officials) or unconventional (protesting or demonstrating). The right to vote, originally quite limited, was expanded in various historical surges to include nearly all adults and to apply to most major offices. Turnout has declined, however, and in recent years only about half the eligible voters have cast ballots for president. Candidates for president start by testing the waters, raising money, and forming campaign organizations; in a series of state primaries and caucuses, they seek delegates to the national nominating conventions, which generally choose clear front-runners or incumbent presidents. Democratic convention delegates tend to be more liberal, black, Hispanic, female, and working-class than Republican delegates. In the autumn campaign, candidates jet from city to city, addressing rallies and organizing media blitzes. Candidates are generally vague about issues: they build personal images and emphasize past performance.

About one-third of the cost of presidential campaigns is paid from public funds; the rest from individuals and PACs, many of which seek self-benefiting policies. Contributions probably subvert democracy by leading to a degree of political inequality.

Voters' decisions depend heavily upon party loyalties, the personal characteristics of the candidates, and issues, especially the state of the economy and of U.S. foreign policy. After recessions and unsuccessful wars, the incumbent party generally loses. Elections "matter," not only when there is a clear choice, but also when electoral reward or punishment occurs, or when electoral competition forces both parties to take similar, popular stands.

To Ponder

1. What should elections be like in order to ensure democratic control? How close does the United States come to that ideal?

2. Why do relatively few Americans vote but relatively many engage in campaign activities?

3. How would *you* organize a campaign for the presidency?

4. Why has the majority party lost so many presidential elections?

5. How, if at all, would you reform the electoral system?

Suggested Readings

Blumenthal, Sidney. *Pledging Allegiance: The Last Campaign of the Cold War.* New York: HarperCollins, 1990.
    A scathing account of the 1988 presidential campaign as cynical, negative, and vacuous.

Burnham, Walter Dean. *Critical Elections and the Mainsprings of American Politics.* New York: Norton, 1970.
    The classic discussion of realigning elections and historical patterns in U.S. voting behavior.

Ferguson, Thomas, and Joel Rogers. *Right Turn: The Decline of the Democrats and the Future of American Politics.* New York: Farrar, Straus & Giroux, 1986.
    A provocative and fast-moving account of major investors in the electoral process.

Fiorina, Morris. *Retrospective Voting in American National Elections.* Cambridge, MA: Harvard University Press, 1981.
    A sophisticated statistical analysis of voting on the basis of party loyalty and past- and future-oriented issue concerns.

Nie, Norman, Sidney Verba, and John R. Petrocik. *The Changing American Voter*, enlgd ed. Cambridge, MA: Harvard University Press, 1979.
    A study of how citizens' issue orientations and ideological thinking may have increased.

Polsby, Nelson, and Aaron Wildavsky. *Presidential Elections*, 7th ed. New York: Free Press, 1988.
    A thorough textbook on the nomination process, campaigning, and voting.

Wolfinger, Raymond E., and Steven J. Rosenstone. *Who Votes?* New Haven, CT: Yale University Press, 1980.
    Shows how personal characteristics and registration laws affect whether or not people go to the polls.

Notes

1. For further discussion, see Benjamin I. Page, *Choices and Echoes in Presidential Elections: Rational Man and Electoral Democracy* (Chicago: University of Chicago Press, 1978), ch. 2.

2. See Austin Ranney, *The Doctrine of Responsible Party Government: Its Origins and Present State* (Urbana, IL: University of Illinois, 1962); E. E. Schattschneider, *Party Government* (New York: Holt, Rinehart and Winston, 1942).

3. See Anthony Downs, *An Economic Theory of Democracy* (New York: HarperCollins, 1957); Otto Davis, Melvin Hinich, and Peter Ordershook, "An Expository Development of a Mathematical Model of the Electoral Process," *American Political Science Review*, Vol. 64 (June 1970), pp. 426–448; James M. Enelow and Melvin J. Hinich, *The Spatial Theory of Voting: An Introduction* (New York: Cambridge University Press, 1984); Peter C. Ordeshook, *Game Theory and Political Theory: An Introduction* (New York: Cambridge University Press, 1986).

4. See V. O. Key, Jr., *Public Opinion and American Democracy* (New York: Knopf, 1961); Morris P. Fiorina, *Retrospective Voting in American National Elections* (Cambridge, MA: Harvard University Press, 1981).

5. Neil Spitzer, "The First Election," *The Atlantic* Vol. 262, No. 5 (November 1988), pp. 18–20.

6. Chilton Williamson, *American Suffrage* (Princeton, NJ: Princeton University Press, 1960), pp. 223, 241, 260. More precisely, there was universal suffrage for white male *taxpayers*.

7. See John Hope Franklin, *From Slavery to Freedom* (New York: Knopf, 1967); Leon Litwack, *North of Slavery* (Chicago: University of Chicago Press, 1961).

8. Walter Dean Burnham, "The Turnout Problem," in James Reichley, ed., *Elections American Style* (Washington, D.C.: Brookings Institution, 1987), pp. 113–114.

9. *New York Times*, November 21, 1988, p. B16.

10. Walter Dean Burnham, *Critical Elections and the Mainsprings of American Politics* (New York: Norton, 1970).

11. Walter Dean Burnham, "The System of 1896," in Paul Kleppner, et al., *The Evolution of American Electoral Systems* (Westport, CT: Greenwood Press, 1981), p. 148.

12. Paul R. Abramson and John H. Aldrich, "The Decline of Electoral Participation in America," *American Political Science Review*, Vol. 76 (September 1982), pp. 502–521.

13. *New York Times*, November 21, 1988, p. B16.

14. Walter Dean Burnham, "The Class Gap," *The New Republic*, Vol. 198 (May 9, 1988), pp. 30–34.

15. Russell Dalton, *Citizen Politics in Western Democracies* (Chatham, NJ: Chatham House, 1988), p. 42.

16. Authors' calculation from 1984–1990 General Social Survey (GSS).

17. Sidney Verba and Norman H. Nie, *Participation in America* (New York: HarperCollins, 1972).

18. U.S. Bureau of the Census, *Current Population Survey*, November 1988; reported in *1990 Almanac* (Boston: Houghton Mifflin), p. 42.

19. Census figures in *1990 Almanac*, p. 42.

20. Raymond E. Wolfinger and Steven J. Rosenstone, *Who Votes?* (New Haven, CT: Yale University Press, 1980).

21. E. J. Dionne, "If Nonvoters Had Voted: Same Winner, but Bigger," *New York Times*, November 21, 1988, p. B16.

22. Bernard R. Berelson, Paul F. Lazarsfeld, and William N. McPhee, *Voting* (Chicago: University of Chicago Press, 1954).

23. See John Stephens, *The Transition from Capitalism to Socialism* (London: Macmillan, 1979).

24. Joint Center for Political Studies, Washington, D.C., *Black Elected Officials: A National Roster*, reported in *1990 Almanac* (Boston: Houghton Mifflin), p. 46.

25. Harold Stanley and Richard Niemi, *Vital Statistics on American Politics* (Washington, D.C.: *Congressional Quarterly*, 1988), p. 213; updated to include the 1988 election.

26. Stanley and Niemi, *Vital Statistics*, pp. 53–55.

27. Nelson Polsby and Aaron Wildavsky, *Presidential Elections*, 7th ed. (New York: Free Press, 1988).

28. Larry Bartels, *Presidential Primaries and the Dynamics of Public Choice* (Princeton, NJ: Princeton University Press, 1988); John Aldrich, *Before the Convention* (Chicago: University of Chicago Press, 1980).

29. *New York Times*, July 21, 1988, p. A21.

30. *New York Times*, August 14, 1988, p. A32.

31. *New York Times*, August 14, 1988, p. A32.

32. *Washington Post* National Weekly Edition, August 14–20, 1989; *New York Times*, December 6, 1989, p. A17.

33. Page, *Choices and Echoes*, p. 39.

34. Gary Sick, "The Election Story of the Decade," *New York Times*, April 15, 1991, p. A15.

35. Joe McGinniss, *The Selling of the President, 1968* (New York: Pocket Books, 1970).

36. *New York Times*, August 27, 1989, p. A23; *New York Times*, December 6, 1989, reports that party national committees amassed about $50 million in unregulated funds in 1988 and that state parties in just nine states spent $28.5 million.

37. *New York Times*, February 17, 1989, p. D15.

38. Sig Mickelson, *Whistle Stop to Sound Bite* (New York: Praeger, 1989), p. 155.

39. *New York Times*, August 27, 1989, p. A23.

40. Frank Sorauf, *Money in American Elections* (Glenview, IL: Scott, Foresman, 1988), p. 343.

41. Jean Cobb and Jeffrey Denny, "The Fat-Cat Club: Membership Has Its Privileges," *Washington Post* National Weekly Edition, April 2–8, 1990, p. 25.

42. *New York Times*, August 31, 1990, p. A10.

43. *New York Times*, September 16, 1990, p. A18.

44. *New York Times*, November 10, 1988, p. B6.

45. *New York Times*, November 8, 1990, p. A19.

46. *New York Times*, November 8, 1990, p. A19.

47. Herbert B. Asher, *Presidential Elections and American Politics: Voters, Candidates, and Campaigns Since 1952*, 4th ed. (Chicago: Dorsey, 1988), pp. 88, 89.

48. Asher, *Presidential Elections*, p. 43.

49. Asher, *Presidential Elections*, p. 42.

50. Norman H. Nie, Sidney Verba, and John R. Petrocik, *The Changing American Voter*, enlgd ed. (Cambridge, MA: Harvard University Press, 1979).

51. Gerald H. Kramer, "Short-term Fluctuations in U.S. Voting Behavior, 1896–1964," *American Political Science Review*, Vol. 65 (March 1971), pp. 131–143; Edward R. Tufte, *Political Control of the Economy* (Princeton, NJ: Princeton University Press, 1978).

10

*Social
Movements*

THE WOMEN'S MOVEMENT MAKES A DIFFERENCE

"Women's Bodies Are Not Federal Property." So read one of the many signs of the roughly 2,500 demonstrators gathered in front of President George Bush's oceanside home in Kennebunkport, Maine. The demonstration was the first of many across the country on "Mobilization Day for Abortion Rights" (November 11, 1989). Their purpose was to voice support for a woman's right to have an abortion, to protest against administration abortion policies, and to express anger over the Supreme Court's just announced *Webster* decision.

The largest demonstration—about 300,000 people, according to police estimates—took place in Washington, D.C., at the Lincoln Memorial. The speakers at the Washington gathering blasted Bush administration antiabortion policies, warned the Supreme Court to halt its drift against abortion rights, celebrated recent electoral victories of prochoice candidates, and pledged to continue the struggle for abortion rights in each of the states.

Speaker after speaker, ranging from leaders of women's organizations to politicians eager to get on the prochoice train before it left the station, echoed these themes. Several promised that abortion would be the issue of the 1990s and that political leaders would do well to get on the right side of the issue. David Dinkins, the newly elected prochoice mayor of New York City, told the crowd that "the people spoke and people were heard, and the people said 'We believe in choice, we believe in liberty, and we will never be denied.' " The most militant note was struck by NOW (National Organization for Women) president Molly Yard: "And so we say to you, Mr. President, we say no. We will not obey your dictates nor those of the Reagan Court."[1] Some expressed their concerns in a more dramatic fashion. Sit-ins at public buildings, disruptions of traffic, and symbolic protests were common elsewhere in Washington, D.C.

The modern Women's movement (also known as the Feminist or Women's Liberation movement) burst on the political scene in the late 1960s. Establishing a woman's right to an abortion was among its most important objectives, because movement activists believed that a woman's right to control her own body was fundamental to nearly every aspect of women's progress. This objective seemed to have been reached when the Supreme Court ruled in *Roe v. Wade* (1973) that a woman's right to an abortion (in the first two trimesters of pregnancy) was constitutionally protected.

With the right to abortion seemingly won by *Roe*, the Women's movement turned its attention to other matters. This allowed the initiative on abortion to shift to its Prolife opponents. The Prolife movement eventually became an important part of the conservative and Republican resurgence that resulted in the election of Ronald Reagan. The movement helped shape public policy during the Reagan-Bush years, and abortion became an important **litmus test** for judicial appointments.

The Supreme Court reshaped the political landscape when it announced its decision in the case of *Webster v. Reproductive Health Services, Inc*, on July 3, 1989. The decision upheld the right of the state of Missouri (and, by implication, the other states) to restrict severely the right of women to terminate their pregnancies. Because *Webster* seemed to threaten the fundamental gains that prochoice forces had won in the *Roe* decision, it galvanized the Women's movement and refocused attention on the abortion issue. *Webster* triggered demonstrations in scores of cities and communities. It sparked women's groups to redouble their lobbying efforts in Congress and state legislatures where prolife forces had had a virtual free hand for years. Voting registration increased perceptibly among prochoice women in the months after *Webster,* as did contributions to and membership in women's organizations like NOW and NARAL (the National Abortion Rights Action League). More women than ever told pollsters that the abortion issue was now the main political issue for them and that it would affect how they voted in coming elections. This was especially true of women under the age of 45. One young woman who participated in her first political demonstration after *Webster* explained her action in the following way: "This is really the first issue that's moved me to be politically active. It's something I feel is so fundamentally a personal decision. I'm going to get as active as I can be."[2]

The effects of the revitalized Women's movement were felt in the political arena in very short order. Almost immediately after the *Webster* decision, Governor Robert Martinez of Florida, long an outspoken foe of abortion, called the Florida legislature into special session to consider legislation designed to restrict abortions in that state. He was confident of passage, as were most observers of Florida politics. Much to the surprise of the experts, each of his bills suffered a crushing defeat as legislators, pushed by demonstrations, shifts in public opinion, and lobbying efforts by a broad range of women's groups, rushed to distance themselves from the governor.

The changed political landscape represented by events in Florida was also mirrored in electoral victories by prochoice candidates in the 1990 gubernatorial races in New Jersey and Virginia, with women voters representing an important component of the winning margin in both states. Dinkins's victory in the New York City mayoral race was also attributed to his prochoice position. Congress signaled its understanding of the new political equation by passing a bill, later vetoed by President Bush, that would allow the federal government to pay for abortions for poor women whose pregnancies resulted from rape or incest. Leading Republicans began to speak of the party as a tent big enough to cover prochoice advocates as well as the prolife advocates who had dominated the party during the Reagan years. Public opinion polls showing that only a small minority of Americans favor an outright ban on abortions (a majority, however, favor some restrictions on abortions) no doubt contributed to this rethinking.

It remains to be seen how the abortion issue will eventually play out in American politics. The Court has decided in two major cases, *Webster* and *Planned Parenthood v. Casey* (1992), that states are allowed to restrict abortions in ways that do not impose "undue burdens" on women, so the action on abortion will take place in state legislatures, in Congress, and in elections at all levels of jurisdiction. Public policy on abortion will depend a great deal on the relative influence and staying power of the prochoice and prolife movements in these arenas. What is clear, however, is that the contemporary Women's movement and the Prolife movement have had an enormous impact on the agenda of the American political system and will surely continue to do so for a very long time to come.

The Prolife movement has had an important impact on American politics. Here, a member of Operation Rescue, a prolife organization, protests for the rights of the "unborn."

This chapter is about social movements. Social movements receive less attention by political scientists than elections, parties, and interest groups, but they are no less important. Many social movements in addition to the Women's and Prolife movements have influenced what government does. Such movements often use unconventional and disruptive tactics. They sometimes provide a way for those without a voice in American politics to be heard and to be taken seriously. They often protect and sustain fundamental rights and encourage public awareness and participation in public affairs. Participation in movement activity is also risky. For all of these reasons, social movements are an integral part of the story of the struggle for democracy.

Governmental

Political

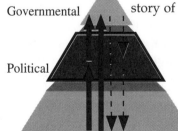

Structural

WHAT ARE SOCIAL MOVEMENTS?

Many social movements have left their mark on American political life and have shaped what government does in the United States. A list of the most important ones appears in Table 10.1. Common to all of them is the following: each has tried to achieve social change, acting outside the normal channels of government and politics, using what sociologists call *collective action* (acting in concert with others, rather than as isolated individuals).[3] Several elements of this definition deserve more comment.

Table 10.1
The Most Important American Social Movements

Name	Description
Abolitionist	Active in the northern states during the three decades preceding the Civil War; committed to the abolition of slavery in all of the states and territories.
Populist	A political movement of disaffected farmers in the South and the West in the 1880s and 1890s that sought public control over railroads, banks, and grain elevators, and the provision of cheap money.
Labor	The effort by working people, stretching from the post–Civil War period to the present, to protect jobs, to ensure decent wages and benefits, and to guarantee a healthy work environment. The effort to form labor unions to meet these goals was particularly prominent during the 1880s, 1890s, and 1930s.
Women's Suffrage	Active in the late nineteenth and early twentieth centuries, this movement used disruptive tactics, education, and lobbying tactics to win voting rights for women.
Civil Rights	The goal of this movement was to win civil and political rights for black Americans; it was especially effective during the 1960s in using disruptive tactics such as sit-ins, nonviolent civil disobedience, and mass demonstrations to gain concessions from political leaders.

Generally, social movements are the political instruments of excluded groups or political outsiders. Movements often help those who are outside the mainstream to gain a hearing from the public and political decision makers. Insiders don't need social movements; they can rely, instead, on interest groups, PACs, lobbyists, campaign contributions, and the like.

Social movements are mass, grass roots phenomena. Since outsiders and excluded groups are generally without the financial and political resources of insiders, they must take advantage of what they have: numbers, energy, and commitment. In order to gain the attention of the public and decision makers, moreover, social movements often use unconventional and even disruptive tactics like demonstrations and sit-ins. Officials and citizens almost always complain that social movements are ill-mannered and uncivilized, and that the members don't behave themselves. People in social movements are likely to answer that that is precisely the point.

People would not take on the considerable risks involved in joining others in a social movement unless they felt a strong shared sense of grievance against the status quo and a desire to bring about social change. Social movements tend

Table 10.1 (*continued*)
The Most Important American Social Movements

Name	Description
Anti-Vietnam War	A movement during the late 1960s and early 1970s, directed against the continued involvement of the United States in the Vietnam War.
Women's Liberation or Feminist	The contemporary expression of the Women's movement; having already won the right to vote, many women became active in the struggle to gain equality in all aspects of American life during the 1970s and 1980s.
Anti-Nuclear	A movement, sporadically active during the 1970s and 1980s, that wanted to end the nuclear arms race (e.g., "The Freeze" campaign) and the construction of nuclear power plants.
Environmental	Came to prominence in the 1970s and continues to be influential; its goals range from control of pollution to protection of wilderness areas.
Religious Fundamentalist	The latest of several periodic upsurges of religious fundamentalism to take political form during our history; became an important part of the conservative resurgence of the 1970s and 1980s, the electoral victories of Ronald Reagan and George Bush, and the fight against abortion.

New social problems often generate new social movements. Here a group marches to demand government action to combat the AIDS epidemic.

to happen when a significant number of people come to define their own troubles and problems not in personal terms but in more general, social terms (the belief that there is a common cause for all of their troubles), and when they believe that the government can be moved to action on their behalf. This is a rare combination. It is why social movements are so difficult to organize and to sustain.

SOCIAL MOVEMENTS AND DEMOCRACY

At first glance, social movements do not seem to fit very well in a democracy. First, social movements usually start out as *minority* phenomena, whereas democracy requires majority rule. Second, social movements often use disruptive tactics when it seems that many channels already exist—voting, petitioning and writing to policymakers, writing letters to the editor, and more—for people to express their grievances. In this section, we talk about how social movements *can* (and often do) help make American politics more democratic.

Social Movements Can Increase the Level of Popular Involvement and Interest in Politics

In one sense, this is simply true by definition: social movements are the instruments of outsiders. Thus the Civil Rights movement encouraged the involvement of black Americans in the South who had long been barred from the political life of their communities. The Women's Suffrage movement encouraged the involvement of women who had long been excluded from voting. The Fundamentalist movement spurred the political involvement of previously politically apathetic evangelicals.

Social movements also encourage popular participation by dramatizing and bringing a range of issues to public attention that have been ignored or dealt with behind closed doors. This is because their unconventional and often disruptive actions make them highly visible. They offer irresistible fare for the television camera. Social movements "broaden the scope of conflict"[4] and make politics the province of the many rather than the few. Social movements can stimulate the degree of *popular involvement* that is essential to a democracy.

Social Movements Often Allow Those Without Substantial Resources to Enter the Game of Politics

Most social movements are made up of people who do not have access to the money, time, contacts, or organizational resources that fuel normal politics. It is one of the main reasons why they are outsiders. While some movements do not fit this picture—people involved in the Abolitionist, Women's, and Environmentalist movements, for instance, were mainly from the more economically privileged parts of the American population[5]—most have served as a vehicle for less well-off Americans. The collective-action aspects of social movements and the disruptive tactics associated with such mass mobilizations can serve as a substitute for missing political resources. Social movements can help those unable to create a permanent lobbying organization in Washington, D.C., to form a PAC, to circulate a newsletter, to make a sizable contribution to a candidate, or to buy time on television or radio in order to express their views on the issues. As such, they can help increase *political equality*.

Social Movements Can Convince the Majority
That New Policies Are Needed

Social movements are the province of minorities. In a democracy, minorities can rightly have their way only if they can convince enough of their fellow citizens that what they want is reasonable. Before the 1930s, for instance, only a minority of Americans was convinced that labor unions were a good idea. The Great Depression and a vigorous and militant Labor movement changed the opinion climate in the nation, and created the basis for new government collective-bargaining policies. Issues like gender-based job discrimination and pay inequity were not important to the general public until they were brought center stage by the Women's movement. The anti-Vietnam War movements began with only a few, like Mary Beth Tinker (see "The Struggle for Democracy"), but eventually won over the majority.

Sometimes it takes the energy of a social movement to overcome the anti-majoritarian aspects of our constitutional system and get anything done at all. As political scientist Theodore Lowi has described the issue,

> . . . our political system is almost perfectly designed to maintain an existing state of affairs. . . . Our system is so designed that only a determined and undoubted majority could make it move. This is why our history is replete with social movements. It takes that kind of energy to get anything like a majority. . . . Change comes neither from the genius of the system nor from the liberality or wisdom of its supporters and of the organized groups. It comes from new groups or nascent groups—social movements—when the situation is most dramatic.[6]

It is important to note that many of the social reforms of which most Americans are most proud—the right of women to vote, citizenship rights for blacks, Social Security, collective bargaining, and environmental protection—were less the result of "normal" politics than of social movements started by minorities.

Not all social movements, of course, are able to convince the majority to see things their way. The Socialist movement, active and enjoying some success around the turn of the century, for instance, never managed to enlist the majority's approval. The Fundamentalist movement during the 1970s was unable to force a change in policies regarding prayer in the public schools.[7]

THE RISE OF SOCIAL MOVEMENTS

A certain combination of factors, mainly structural in nature, is apparently necessary for a social movement to develop.

Social Distress

Those who are safe, prosperous, and unthreatened have no need of social movements. Those whose lives are made difficult and unsafe, or whose way of life is threatened by economic and social change, on the other hand, often find that social movements are an attractive instrument to call attention to their plights and to press for changes in the status quo.[8]

Social distress caused by economic and social change helped to create the conditions for the rise of most of the major social movements in American history. The Populist movement, for instance, occurred after western and southern farmers

THE
STRUGGLE
FOR
DEMOCRACY

★

*Mary Beth
Tinker Protests
the War*

In 1965, the war in Vietnam was just escalating, and widespread opposition to it had not yet appeared. Taking an open antiwar stand against prevailing opinion was not easy at that time, and few took the risk. One who did was a 13-year-old eighth grader in Des Moines, Iowa, named Mary Beth Tinker, who felt strongly that the war was wrong. To express her feelings, she chose to wear a black armband to school. As she described it:

. . . I went to school and I wore the armband all morning. The kids were kind of talking, but it was all friendly, nothing hostile. Then I got to my algebra class, right after lunch, and sat down. The teacher came in, and everybody was kind of whispering; they didn't know what was going to happen. Then this guy came to the door of the class and he said, Mary Tinker, you're wanted out here in the hall. Then they called me down to the principal's office.

Mary was suspended from school by the principal, a decision that was eventually upheld by the school board. She and her parents insisted that

Mary had the right to wear an armband so long as it did not disrupt classes or bother her classmates, but school officials were adamant. Mary held her ground, even in the face of several attempts to intimidate her.

People threw red paint at our house, and we got lots of calls. We got all kinds of threats to our family, even death threats. They even threatened my little brothers and sisters, which was really sick. People called our house on Christmas Eve and said the house would be blown up by morning. There was a radio talk-show host . . . who started in on our family, the Tinker family. . . . One night he said that if anyone wanted to use a shotgun on my father he would pay court costs if anything happened.

Mary's rights to wear an armband to protest the war in Vietnam was eventually upheld by the Supreme Court. By the time the Court ruled on the case, many other Americans had joined her in opposition to the government's Vietnam policy.

Source: Peter Irons, *The Courage of Their Convictions* (New York: Free Press, 1988), pp. 231–253.

suffered great economic reverses during the latter part of the nineteenth century. The Labor movement during the 1930s was spurred by the virtual collapse of the industrial sector of the American economy, historically unprecedented levels of unemployment, and widespread destitution. The context for the rise of the Civil Rights movements was widespread economic distress among black Americans and the denial of basic citizenship rights and protections in the South. The rise of the Fundamentalist movement seems to have been associated with the perceived threat to religious and family values by the general secularization of American life and the popularity of alternative life-styles (the drug-based counterculture and the gay movement, in particular). For many women, distress caused by discrim-

Many Americans with strong religious beliefs have become politically active in recent years because of their anxiety about the secularization of American life.

inatory hiring, blocked career advancement, and unequal pay at a time when they were entering the job market in increasing numbers during the 1960s and 1970s made the option of a movement an attractive one.[9]

Resources for Mobilization

Social strain and distress are almost always present in society. Social movements will only occur, it seems, when the aggrieved group has the resources (including skilled leaders) to organize.[10] The Populist movement, to take one case, was built on a previously existing set of social networks and organizations, particularly the National Grange. The Labor movement could depend on some existing unions, talented labor organizers, a vigorous labor press, and attention to labor problems by the mass media. The Women's movement's assets included a sizable population of educated and skilled women, a lively women's press, and a broad network of "consciousness raising" activities.[11] The Fundamentalist movement could build on a base of skilled clergy (like Jerry Falwell), an expanding fundamentalist church membership, religious television and radio networks, and highly developed fund-raising technologies.[12]

For its part, the Civil Rights movement could count on black-owned newspapers and radio stations, organizationally skilled clergy, an expanding pool of college-educated youth, and blocs of black voters located in electorally important states. The existence of experienced, tested, and effective organizations like the Congress of Racial Equality (CORE), the Urban League, and the National Association for the Advancement of Colored People (NAACP) was invaluable.

Supportive Environment

The rise of social movements requires more than the existence of resources for mobilization among aggrieved groups. The times must also be right, in the sense that a degree of support and tolerance must exist for the movement among the public and society's leaders.[13] The Populist upsurge took place, for instance, in a context in which many Americans other than farmers were also concerned about the power of the new corporations. Fundamentalists organized when many other Americans had also come to be concerned about changes in social values and practices, and when the Republican party was looking for a way to detach traditional Democratic voters from their party. The Labor movement's upsurge during the 1930s coincided with the electoral needs of the Democratic party[14] and a growing sense among some corporate leaders that collective bargaining was essential to economic growth and stability.[15] The Women's movement surged at a time when public opinion was becoming much more favorable toward women's equality. By the early 1970s, for instance, few Americans believed it was acceptable to pay women less than men for the same job, a quite commonly accepted notion in the 1930s and 1940s.[16]

We see the same thing at work with regard to the Civil Rights movement. It made its demands at a time when overt racism among the public was in decline outside the South and when national leaders were becoming increasingly concerned about the effects of the southern caste system on American foreign policy and the economy. Sympathy for black demands by political leaders was further encouraged by the rising electoral power of black Americans in the large states outside the South. Support by an increasing number of religious leaders for black aspirations also helped.

Sense of Efficacy

Some scholars believe that those who are on the outside looking in must come to believe that action on their part will make a difference if they are to develop a movement. People who are in aggrieved groups must feel *efficacious*; they must believe that their actions will have an impact on decision makers. Without this, grievances might explode into brief demonstrations or riots, but they would not support a long-term movement effort requiring time, commitment, and risk.

It may well be that the highly decentralized and fragmented character of our political system helps to sustain a sense of efficacy, since movements can often find places in the system where they can be heard by officials. Fundamentalist social movements have had little impact on educational curricula in unitary systems like Great Britain, for instance, where educational policy is made in London, so few try to do anything about it. Here, fundamentalists know they can gain the ear of local school boards and state officials in regions where religious belief is strong.[17]

Catalyst

Social movements seem to require some precipitating event or events that set them in motion. One can identify several catalysts for the Civil Rights movement, but none was more compelling than Rosa Parks and the Montgomery bus boycott. As the story is told, Rosa Parks boarded a city bus in Montgomery, Alabama, on a cold fall day in 1955 to go home after work. She sat in the "colored" section, as

Rosa Parks refused to give up her seat on a city bus to a white person, as the law required, and helped spark the Montgomery bus boycott and the civil rights movement.

she was obliged to do under the law. After several stops, the "white" section became filled with passengers. Mrs. Parks was asked to give up her seat so that a white could be seated, which she was also obliged to do under the law. She refused. We will probably never know whether her refusal was because her feet hurt or (more likely) because she, like so many other black Americans, was simply tired of being treated like a second-class citizen a full year after the *Brown* decision had been announced (see "The Struggle for Democracy" in Chapter 1 for a discussion of the *Brown* decision).

Her arrest helped to set off a movement. Of her act, black writer and activist Eldridge Cleaver later observed, "Somewhere in the universe a gear in the machinery shifted."[18] It shifted for many other people in Montgomery, at least, for her arrest sparked a remarkable boycott of the city buses that lasted for 381 days. For over a year, 42,000 black men, women, and children walked and car pooled to jobs and schools rather than continue in the old ways. By the time the Supreme Court ruled that Montgomery buses must be integrated, the local black community had demonstrated its capacity to conduct mass actions in the face of terror and intimidation.

A number of catalytic events set the Women's movement into motion. There was the publication of Betty Friedan's *The Feminine Mystique*, which spoke to women's discontent ("a problem that has no name," as she put it) in a way that no one else had done before. The example of the Civil Rights movement showed many women that outsiders could gain a hearing in American politics if they were willing to use collective-action tactics. There was also the failure of the federal government to enforce Title VII of the 1964 Civil Rights Act, which guaranteed women protections in the area of equal employment. Finally, younger women active in the Civil Rights and Anti-Vietnam War movements discovered that they were not well treated, despite the prevailing egalitarian rhetoric, and concluded that women's problems could only be addressed if women took their own political initiative.

DOING POLITICS

Alice McGoff's First Demonstration

Alice McGoff didn't think of herself as a political person, but Judge Arthur Garrity's court order mandating busing of black children to Charlestown High School as part of a program to integrate the Boston schools made her angry. The judge's order, she believed, would destroy the close-knit Irish neighborhood in which Charlestown High played an important role. In his prize-winning book Common Ground, *J. Anthony Lukas tells of Alice McGoff's first demonstration.*

Alice hauled herself out of bed, put on her Thomas Collar, and joined the women who were already gathering in Hayes Square. Word had spread quickly through the town, and by 10:30 about four hundred mothers—many wearing shorts and sandals on this steamy Indian summer day—began lining up in the middle of Bunker Hill Street. Some cradled infants in their arms, others pushed strollers or held young children by the hand. On the sidewalks, knots of teenagers and adult males— among them Danny McGoff—had gathered to watch. When some of the men tried to join the march, Pat Russell—wearing her "Mother Power" T-shirt—borrowed an electric bullhorn from the police. "No men or boys in this march today," she bellowed. "This is a woman's march. We don't want any of you guys in it." . . .

Pat gave the women their marching orders. "We are going to pray in silence," she told them. "We are going to pray for our children; we are going to pray for our families; we are going to pray for our town. If Martin Luther King could do it, so can the women of Charlestown." Then they set off up the street, led by a three-year-old girl carrying an American flag. . . .

As they advanced on Monument Square, the women encountered a phalanx of police drawn up across High Street at the corner of Cordis Street, still a block and a half from the high school. A formidable force confronted them there. . . .

. . . Ten feet short of the first policemen, the women stopped. Pat Russell stepped forward and told Superintendent Lawrence Carpenter of the MDC police that she had Captain MacDonald's permission to continue, but Carpenter told her that if she went past that point she and her followers would be arrested. Then he ordered them to disperse.

Indignantly, Pat refused. "We have permission to march and offer our prayers to God. That's what we're going to do."

"Beyond this point, you'll be within a hundred yards of the high school. We'll have to arrest you." . . .

For nearly an hour, as the mothers prayed and the police twirled their batons, the negotiators huddled in the street beneath the Bunker Hill monu-

WHAT DO SOCIAL MOVEMENTS DO?

Social movements use collective-action, nonconventional tactics at some moments in their histories to make their points. Such tactics depend on the dramatic gesture and are often disruptive (see "Doing Politics," on Alice McGoff's first demonstration). The Women's Suffrage movement used the mass demonstration and the hunger strike to great effect. The Labor movement invented the sit-down strike and plant takeover as its most effective weapons in the 1930s. The Anti-Vietnam

ment trying to resolve their impasse, but they were caught in a stalemate which offered neither side an attractive option. . . .

Now Superintendent Jordan took the bullhorn. "Ladies," he warned, "you will not be permitted to march past this point. You have fifteen minutes to walk to the Training Field or you will be subject to arrest."

The remaining mothers seemed determined. Grimly, those still accompanied by children shunted them to husbands, relatives, or friends on the sidewalk. . . .

The minutes ticked by. A few mothers, mindful of the analogy which Pat Russell had drawn with Martin Luther King's marches, struck up "We Shall Overcome," but the song trailed off after a few seconds. Nobody seemed to know the words. Just then Pat Russell shouted, "Okay, girls, this is it. We're going through. Heads down. Hard and heavy. But keep your hands at your sides. If they touch a woman, they won't be able to hold this town—and they know it."

Alice struggled to her feet. From her position in the second row of marchers, she could look across the ten feet of pavement directly into the gray eyes of an MDC sergeant who glared grimly back at her.

. . . the women moved forward in a tight platoon, many still chanting "Hail Marys" and "Our Fathers" under their breath. Some were already weeping. Others had their eyes closed, with purses, shopping bags, or pillows over their faces to ward off the expected blows. . . .

Abruptly, the Tactical Patrol Force waded into the bobbing sea of women. Quickly, the mothers were herded into two groups, one shoved down the steep hill of Cordis Street, the other pushed back along High Street. Alice had advanced barely four yards when the force of the TPF charge sent her reeling down Cordis Street. . . .

Here and there, the TPF—whose job was to intimidate—used more force than was necessary. Women screamed and stumbled. Some fell against cars or sprawled on the street. A few husbands and sons tried to help their women, but the TPF would brook no male interference. One youth was heaved against an automobile. Several men were arrested.

In five minutes the skirmish was over. . . .

On Cordis Street, Alice leaned against a tree, tired but exhilarated. She felt as if she'd just fought the American Revolution. They'd gone up against the toughest cops in the city and survived. . . .

Source: From J. Anthony Lukas, *Common Ground: A Turbulent Decade in the Life of Three American Families* (New York: Vintage Books, 1986), pp. 271–276.

War movement added guerrilla theater and politicized rock concerts to its normal complement of tools such as mass demonstrations.

The most effective tool of the Civil Rights movement was nonviolent civil disobedience. A particularly dramatic and effective use of this tactic took place in Greensboro, North Carolina. Four black students from North Carolina A&T sat down at a "whites only" lunch counter on February 1, 1960, and politely asked to be served. When requested to leave, they refused. They stayed put and remained calm even as a mob of young white men screamed at them, covered them

Police brutality against peaceful demonstrators in Birmingham, Alabama, many of them young children, shocked people across the nation and generated sympathy for the demands of African Americans.

with ketchup and mustard, and threatened to lynch them. Each day more students from the college joined them. By the end of the week, over 1,000 black students had joined the sit-in at Woolworth's to demand an end to segregation. This was like a match that ignited the South. Within two months, similar sit-ins had taken place in nearly 60 cities across nine states; almost 4,000 young people had tasted a night in jail for their actions. Their bravery galvanized other blacks across the nation and generated sympathy among many whites. The student sit-in movement also spawned a new and more impatient civil rights organization, the Student Nonviolent Coordinating Committee (SNCC).

Another particularly effective use of nonviolent civil disobedience was organized in Birmingham, Alabama, by the spiritual leader of the Civil Rights movement, Dr. Martin Luther King, Jr., who led a massive series of nonviolent demonstrations to demand the integration of public accommodations and schools. Nonviolent demonstrators, most of whom were schoolchildren, were assaulted by snarling police dogs, electric cattle prods, and high-pressure fire hoses that sent demonstrators sprawling. Police Commissioner Eugene "Bull" Connor filled his jails to overflowing with hundreds of young marchers who resisted only passively, alternately praying and singing civil rights songs, including "We Shall Overcome." The quiet bravery of the demonstrators and the palpable sense among public officials and private-sector leaders in the nation that matters were quickly spinning out of control finally moved President Kennedy on June 11, 1963, to introduce his historic civil rights bill for congressional consideration.

Social movements are rarely unified on issues of strategy and tactics, however. Social movements are generally made up of a core of activists, a wider circle of people from the aggrieved group who are occasionally active (other farmers, women, blacks, fundamentalists, workers, and the like), and a larger audience made up of the general population and political leaders. To be successful, social movements must be able to play to all three audiences. They must maintain the

WE SHALL OVERCOME

We shall overcome, we shall overcome,
We shall overcome someday.
Oh, deep in my heart, I do believe,
We shall overcome someday.

We are not afraid, we are not afraid,
We are not afraid today.
Oh, deep in my heart, I do believe,
We shall overcome someday.

The truth will make us free, the truth will
  make us free,
The truth will make us free someday.
Oh, deep in my heart, I do believe,
We shall overcome someday.

We'll walk hand in hand, we'll walk
  hand in hand,
We'll walk hand in hand someday.
Oh, deep in my heart, I do believe,
We shall overcome someday.

The Lord will see us through, the Lord
  will see us through,
The Lord will see us through someday.
Oh, deep in my heart, I do believe,
We shall overcome someday.

. . .

We shall live in peace, we shall live
  in peace,
We shall live in peace some day.
Oh, deep in my heart I do believe,
We shall overcome some day.

The whole wide world around, the whole
  wide world around,
The whole wide world around some day.
Oh, deep in my heart I do believe
We shall overcome some day.

enthusiasm of activists, attract more activists and support from the aggrieved group, gain sympathy from the general public, and force a positive response from public officials.

The problem is that satisfying one may work against satisfying others. Activists in social movements tend to be attracted by expressions of strong principle and defiant and courageous actions. Both work against the probability of winning the sympathy of the public and the compliance of public officials. This often leads to a division of labor within social movements in which one branch engages in militant actions, while another is more moderate in its actions and more accommodating with the powers that be. It is also one of the reasons that social movements have a tendency to splinter into factions. In the Civil Rights movement, the Student Nonviolent Coordinating Committee took the militant path and had virtually nothing to do after a time with the moderates of the NAACP and the Southern Christian Leadership Conference. In the Labor movement during the 1930s, the American Federation of Labor resisted the militant tactics of the CIO (Congress of Industrial Organizations) almost as much as employers did. In the Women's movement in the 1970s, radical and socialist feminists would have virtually nothing to do with the moderates of NOW.

Social movements often aim for the dramatic gesture to bring attention to their concerns. Here a demonstrator protests vividly against the Persian Gulf War.

THE DECLINE OF SOCIAL MOVEMENTS

Social movements are very difficult to maintain. The historical record shows that they either disappear after a time or become transformed into interest groups. Let's look at both processes.

Success can undermine a social movement as surely as failure. Unless it can find other issues around which to organize, a social movement will find that achieving its central goal destroys its very reason for being. The Abolitionist movement became irrelevant with the passage of the Thirteenth Amendment ending slavery. The Women's Suffrage movement disappeared after passage of the Nineteenth Amendment granting women the right to vote. Passage of major civil rights bills in 1964 and 1965 that met the main goals of the Civil Rights movement (an end to official segregation in the South and guarantees of full citizen rights for all black Americans) caused significant declines in grass roots activity among the black population and in the political influence civil rights organizations had with national political leaders.

Social movements, as we have seen, also tend to fragment into warring factions. Because social movements try to address different audiences—activists, the general public, and political decision makers—they tend to generate internal division over the most appropriate tactics and strategies. These divisions can become quite heated in light of the fact that movements attract people who feel passionately about some problem, have risked a great deal to get involved, and are attempting to change an entrenched status quo. In such a context, it is difficult to keep disputes at a low temperature. The Populists split over the place of blacks in the movement. Students for a Democratic Society (SDS), the main organization of the antiwar movement of the late 1960s, split over the use of violence as a tactic after the destructive rampage of its "weatherman" faction along Chicago's posh "million dollar mile." The Women's movement was split by the often acrimonious divisions among mainstream feminists, radical feminists, and socialist feminists.[19]

The Civil Rights movement was fragmented by the radicalization of portions of the black community and the rise of "black power" as the reigning ideology among many blacks, especially the young. Frustrated by the lack of progress on many fronts, and taking pride in black identity, many blacks in the movement rejected the gradualist and integrationist orientation for a radical and separatist one. The commitment to nonviolence, while retained by the Reverend King's SCLC and the NAACP, was renounced by SNCC, the Black Muslims and their popular spokesman Malcolm X, and the new Black Panther Party for Self-Defense. The movement never recovered from this split.

Social movements also decline when popular support for their goals begins to erode. This can happen under a variety of circumstances: the public may perceive that enough has been done already to meet the grievances of the members of the movement or that the movement has gone too far, asking too much of other Americans. Or, the public may simply get bored and move on to other issues. All of these factors were in play as the Civil Rights movement became decreasingly relevant to political decision makers after the 1960s.

Activists may simply become weary of the struggle. Because social movements ask so much of their adherents in terms of time, financial sacrifice, and risk (of injury, job loss, jail, etc.), and because they depend on nonmaterial inducements to encourage participation (ideology, an attractive goal, a sense of solidarity, etc.), it is difficult to sustain high levels of active involvement for very long.

Successful social movements almost always will spark a reaction from groups that oppose their gains. These reaction groups are often more powerful than the protest movement itself. The Civil Rights movement, for instance, sparked an antifederal government backlash among white southerners during the 1970s and 1980s that contributed to the success of politicians like George Wallace, the formation of the New Right,[20] and contributed to the election of Ronald Reagan. The Women's movement sparked a powerful backlash among some fundamentalist religious groups and among many women committed to traditional female roles within the family. The latter was exemplified by Phyllis Schlafly's Eagle Forum, which led the fight against the ERA. The successes of the Environmental movement during the 1970s energized a powerful, well-funded, and well-organized counteroffensive by America's leading corporations and business organizations.[21]

Successful social movements in the United States eventually become organized, bureaucratic interest groups.[22] The grass roots labor insurgency of the 1930s, for instance, eventually gave rise to large bureaucratic labor unions. The grass roots Women's movement eventually gave rise to organizations like the National Organization for Women (NOW). Such bureaucratic organizations tend to be conservative and cautious; social movements tend to be radical, dramatic, and disruptive. The former are concerned with fund raising and access to the powerful. The latter want to mobilize the grass roots. This being so, the transition from social movement to interest group tends to dampen and tame the wild and unpredictable energies of the grass roots, and decreases the pressure on the powerful.[23]

A successful social movement like the civil rights movement sometimes generates a countermovement opposed to its main goals and aspirations.

THE IMPACT OF SOCIAL MOVEMENTS

Social movements have had a significant impact on American politics and on what government does. Not all social movements are equally successful, however. What makes some more successful than others seems to be the proximity of the movement's goals to American values (see Chapter 4), its capacity to win public attention and support, and its ability to affect the political fortunes of elected leaders.

Social Movements with Little Impact

When a social movement has few followers and activists, little support among the general public, and is unable to disrupt everyday life significantly or to affect the electoral prospects of politicians, it will not have much of an impact. The antibomb Peace movement during the 1950s failed to affect public policy. This was also true of the Poor People's movement led by the Reverend Ralph Albernathy during the late 1960s. The anti-Gulf War movement didn't make much of an impression in 1991.

A social movement is less likely to have an impact on policy, moreover, when it stimulates the formation of a powerful countermovement. The rational politician may find it prudent to take no action at all when he or she has difficulty calculating the relative weight of the two sides in a dispute between movements. This seems to be what happened to the proposed Equal Rights Amendment to the Constitution, which failed to receive the approval of the necessary three-fourths of the states after anti-ERA forces rallied to block action during the 1970s.

Social Movements That Have Been Repressed

Social movements committed to radical changes in society and the economy tend to threaten widely shared values and the interests of powerful individuals, groups, and institutions. As a result, they rarely gain widespread popular support and almost always gain the hostility of national leaders. Such movements very often face repression of one kind or another.[24] The Labor movement in the late nineteenth and early twentieth centuries, for instance, was hindered by court injunctions, laws against the formation of labor unions, violence by employer-hired armed gangs, and strike-breaking actions by the National Guard and U.S. armed forces. In 1877, 60,000 National Guardsman were mobilized in ten states to break the first national railroad strike. The strike against Carnegie Steel in 1892 in Homestead, Pennsylvania, brought the mobilization of 10,000 militiamen, the arrest of 16 strike leaders on conspiracy charges, and the indictment of 27 labor leaders for treason. The Pullman strike of 1894 was abruptly ended by federal troops and the arrest and indictment of union leaders.

Other troublesome social movements have stimulated similar responses. Thus, the radical branch of the student antiwar movement was crippled during the late 1960s and early 1970s by widespread infiltration by the Federal Bureau of Investigation (FBI) and other federal, state, and local police agencies; by the use of **agents provocateurs**, arrests for minor infractions; and by the frequent use of conspiracy trials. The "black power" wing of the Civil Rights movement had all of these tactics used against it, as well as several highly visible instances of official violence, including the notorious shooting of Black Panther leader Fred Hampton in Chicago during a police raid. The FBI and local police "red squads" in southern California encouraged violent conflicts between black nationalist organizations and the Black Panthers in the late 1960s.[25]

Social Movements That Have Partially Achieved Their Goals

Some social movements have enough power and public support to generate a favorable response from public officials but not enough to force them to go very far. That is to say, government may respond in a partial or half-hearted way. Franklin D. Roosevelt responded to the social movements pressing for strong antipoverty measures during The Great Depression by proposing passage of the Social Security Act, which fell far short of movement expectations.[26] The Wagner Labor Relations Act, passed in 1935 in response to a vibrant Labor movement, allowed **collective bargaining** but ignored many of its other demands (including union participation in management). The Prolife movement discovered that President Reagan was willing to use movement rhetoric and to appoint sympathetic judges but was unwilling to submit antiabortion legislation to Congress.

Social Movements That Have Achieved Their Main Goals

Those social movements that have many supporters, wide public sympathy, do not challenge the basics of the economic and social order, and wield some clout in the electoral arena are likely to achieve a substantial number of their goals. The Women's Suffrage movement, which was able to push through the Nineteenth Amendment, is a good example.

So, too, is the Civil Rights movement, which forced action on the Civil Rights Act of 1964 and the Voting Rights Act of 1965. These enactments helped sound the death knoll of the "separate but equal" doctrine enunciated in the infamous *Plessy* decision (1897), engineered the collapse of "Jim Crow" arrangements in the South, and made the guarantee of full citizenship rights for black Americans a reality. The Voting Rights Act was particularly important in transforming the politics of the South. Black registration and voting turnout increased dramatically all over the region during the late 1960s and 1970s. Black elected officials filled legislative seats, city council seats, the mayor's office in large and small cities, jury boxes, and sheriff's offices. Between 1970 and 1989, the number of black elected officials increased five-fold, from 1,472 to over 7,000 (see Figure 10.1). In 1989, voters in Virginia elected the first black governor in the nation, Douglas Wilder, a man who had once worked his way through college as a waiter in a segregated private club.[27]

White elected officials, tacking with the new winds of change, soon began to court the black vote. George Wallace, he who had first become famous by standing in the schoolhouse door to prevent the integration of the University of

Figure 10.1 African-American elected officials

Source: "Black Elected Officials: A National Roster," (Washington, D.C.: Joint Center for Political Studies, 1990).

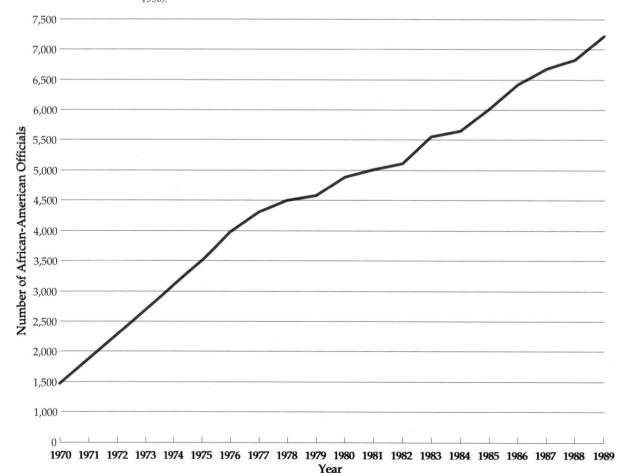

Increased importance of the African-American electorate in the South after passage of the 1965 Voting Rights Act dramatically altered the behavior of Southern politicians. Governor George Wallace first gained national attention when he stood in "the school house door" to block the integration of the University of Alabama. In his last gubernational campaign, he actively courted the African-American vote.

Alabama and he who had once kicked off a political campaign with the slogan "Segregation Today, Segregation Tomorrow, Segregation Forever," actively pursued the black vote in his last run for public office.

Legislation and constitutional amendments are not the only indicators that a social movement has made a major impact on politics and policy, however. Other measures of success include increased respect for members of the movement, changes in fundamental underlying values, increased representation in decision-making bodies, and the like. The Women's movement has had this kind of success. Though the Equal Rights Amendment failed to be approved (its main goal), women's issues came to the forefront during these years and, to a very substantial degree, the demands of the movement for equal treatment and respect made great headway in many areas of American life.[28] ("Politics and Film" on *Thelma and Louise* shows an example of how the movement affected Hollywood.)

A Caveat on the Success of Social Movements

No social movement can be entirely successful. Though some partially or fully achieved their initial goals, few have been able to alter the fundamental structural conditions that caused distress and gave rise to grievances in the first place. This is apparent when we look at the Civil Rights movement.

Despite the important gains of civil rights laws, the movement has not enjoyed much success in changing forms of racial discrimination based on practices rather than law. Housing segregation remains very much a part of the American landscape, for instance. One recent study reports that black Americans find it more difficult than any other racial or ethnic group to buy suburban homes, and traces

POLITICS AND FILM

Thelma and Louise Create a Flap

Thelma and Louise and the Women's movement are inexorably linked. It is hard to imagine, in the first place, that this "buddy-road-outlaw" movie, with women as the central protagonists, could have been made before the modern Women's movement or that a paying audience would have flocked to it, as it has. Hollywood has traditionally preferred its women subordinate, objects of men's designs and desires, or bimbos, or victims. Thelma and Louise don't fit the mold; these lively "good old girls" depend on their own devices, take their own pleasures, and make their own way as women in a man's world, even if the outcome for them is tragic.

Susan Sarandon and Geena Davis star as a waitress and a housewife whose weekend away from it all turns into a tragicomedy. Their troubles begin when Louise (Sarandon) shoots the man who is sexually assaulting Thelma (Davis) in the parking lot of a roadside honkeytonk. They flee the scene, thinking the police will not believe their story, given the absence of witnesses and physical evidence of assault, as well as Thelma's flirtatious behavior in the bar. Their escape turns into a mad adventure that carries them across state lines, into several intended and unintended skirmishes with the law, and encounters with several despicable men who they regularly best. Like many films of this genre—including, most especially, *Butch Cassidy and the Sundance Kid*—we come to care for these rogues, knowing full well that the end does not bode well for them. The only difference, and it's an extraordinary difference, is that these rogues are women.

The reaction to the film in some quarters was unusually hostile. John Leo complained in *U.S. News and World Report* of the film's "explicit fascist theme." Richard Johnson wrote of the film's "pathetic stereotypes of testosterone-crazed behavior" in the *New York Daily News*. Sheila Benson of the *Los Angeles Times* complained about the film's "awful contempt for men." Liz Smith, writing in *Newsday*, declared that "they are terrible role models." Defenders of the film point out that violence on the screen is not exactly a rare occurence in the modern cinema—note the general mayhem of any number of films ranging from *Rambo*, to *Robocop*, to the Freddy Kruger series—and that complaints about a single, provoked (attempted rape) killing seem somehow unfair. Nor could it be simple lawbreaking that is at issue, for lawbreaking by genial rogues is another staple of American film. It's hard to escape the conclusion that what is bothersome is that the transgressions were committed by women. It may well be that the complaints about the film were triggered by a general discomfiture with the Women's movement and the changes in sex roles and relationships it has wrought.

Despite the controversy, *Thelma and Louise* was a surprise box office success, suggesting that many Americans, men and women, are now prepared to see women on the screen in a different light. We are likely to see more films in the future that treat women as shapers of their own lives and place them in unfamiliar roles.

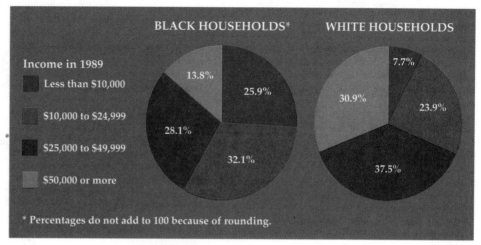

Figure 10.2 Fewer black households in the middle class

Source: New York Times, *November 26, 1990, p. A11.*

this outcome to the practices of real estate agents and lending institutions.[29] A recent National Research Council report shows that blacks are significantly behind whites, moreover, in their access to quality health care and education. The report concluded that integration of blacks into a "color blind society is unlikely in any foreseeable future."[30]

It must also be pointed out that the Civil Rights movement has had very little impact on the economic situation of the black population. While a significant black middle class has emerged over the past several decades because of better opportunities in both the private and public sectors, the general economic situation of blacks has never come close to catching up to the majority population (see Figure 10.2). In recent years, it has actually declined.[31] In terms of ownership of assets, the disparity between blacks and whites is even more pronounced. On average, black households own only about *one-tenth* the assets that whites hold (see Figure 10.3).[32]

The results of the economic disparity between black and white Americans, as well as that between middle-class and lower-class blacks, is seen most dramatically in the desperate situation of black residents of urban ghettos like South Central Los Angeles. A deadly combination of poverty, violence, and declining social services actually has produced a substantial decline in the life expectancy among this group in recent years.[33]

SOCIAL MOVEMENTS IN AMERICAN POLITICS

Though no social movement is ever entirely successful, it remains the case that movements represent an important gain for democracy in the United States. Without them, our politics would be dominated by a form of electoral politics in which the less advantaged play a smaller role than other Americans, and an interest-group system that heavily overrepresents the interests of business and upper-income people. Social movements are one of the most effective means by which

Percentages of households owning each item in 1984, the most recent figures available.

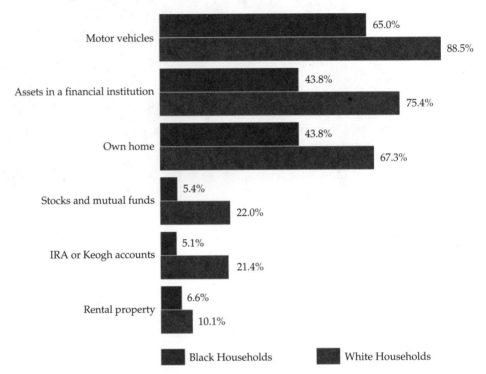

Figure 10.3 The racial gap in household assets

Source: New York Times, *November 26, 1990, p. A11, based on data from the U.S. Census Bureau.*

outsiders enter the game of American politics and make the playing field a little more level. While they tend to be noisy, impolite, and disruptive, they make our political process more democratic than it might otherwise be.

SUMMARY

Social movements dramatically emphasize the point that the *struggle for democracy* is a recurring feature of our political life. They are mainly the instruments of political outsiders who want to gain a hearing in American politics. Social movements contribute to democracy by increasing the visability of important issues, by encouraging wider participation in public affairs, and (sometimes) by providing the energy to overcome the many antimajoritarian features of our constitutional system.

Social movements try to bring about social change through collective action. Their rise is tied to the availability of organizational and leadership resources among a group of people who have a strong sense of grievance and a supportive political environment. Their decline is associated with a number of things, including goal attainment, factional splits, exhaustion, and replacement by interest groups.

Social movements have had an important impact on our political life and in determining what our government does. Some of our most important legislative landmarks can be attributed to them. However, social movements do not always get what they want. They seem to be most successful when their goals are consistent with the central values of society, have wide popular support, and fit the needs of political leaders.

To Ponder

1. Would we need social movements if our democracy worked better?

2. Do social movements do more harm than good because of their disruptive tactics and the conflict they encourage?

3. Must social movements become interest groups?

4. Is American politics so dominated by interest groups that social movements are the only hope for preserving democracy?

5. What have social movements accomplished in American history? Would such accomplishments have happened anyway, without social movements?

Suggested Readings

Branch, Taylor: *Parting the Waters: America in the King Years, 1954–1963*. New York: Simon & Schuster, 1988.
> A detailed and compelling description of the civil rights movement, with a particular focus on Martin Luther King, Jr. Winner of the National Book Award and the Pulitzer Prize.

Brecher, Jeremy. *Strike!* Boston: South End Press, 1972.
> A dramatic account of the history of the grass roots Labor movement from 1877.

Bruce, Steve. *The Rise and Fall of the New Christian Right.* New York: Clarendon Press, 1990.
> The most complete analysis of the Fundamentalist movement and its impact on American politics.

Chafe, William. *The Unfinished Journey.* New York: Oxford University Press, 1986.
> A justly celebrated history of America since the end of World War II, with a particular focus on the Civil Rights and Women's movements.

Deckard, Barbara Sinclair. *The Women's Movement.* New York: HarperCollins, 1983.
> An exhaustive treatment of the Women's movement, why it happened, and the issues yet to be resolved.

Klein, Ethel. *Gender Politics.* Cambridge, MA: Harvard University Press, 1984.
> An analytically sophisticated and empirically detailed examination of the emergence of the Women's movement and feminist politics.

Phillips, Kevin P. *Post-Conservative America.* New York: Random House, 1982.
> A compelling account of the rise of the New Right and the coming of Reaganism.

Mansbridge, Jane J. *Why We Lost the ERA.* Chicago: University of Chicago Press, 1986.
> Mansbridge argues that the strong ideological inducements necessary to retain the involvement of movement activists worked against the attempt by the Women's movement to push through the Equal Rights Amendment.

Miller, James. *Democracy Is in the Streets.* New York: Simon & Schuster, 1987.
> A sophisticated account of the student antiwar movement and its roots in a particular strand of participatory democratic theory.

Piven, Francis Fox, and Richard A. Cloward. *Poor People's Movements.* New York: Vintage, 1979. A controversial treatment of poor people's movements which argues that they are successful only as long as and to the extent that they remain grass roots insurgencies.

Notes

1. Quotes are from Robin Toner, "Abortion Rights Rallies: Capital to Coast," *New York Times*, November 12, 1989, p. A10.

2. Dan Balz, "Getting Ready for the Next Round," *Washington Post Weekly Edition*, July 31–August 6, 1989, p. 15.

3. Joyce Gelb, *Feminism and Politics: A Comparative Perspective* (Berkeley: University of California Press, 1989), pp. 14, 30. Also see Doug McAdams, *Political Process and the Development of Black Insurgency* (Chicago: University of Chicago Press, 1982), p. 37.

4. E. E. Schattschneider, *The Semi-Sovereign People* (New York: Holt, Rinehart and Winston, 1960), p. 142.

5. Richard Polenberg, *One Nation Divisible* (New York: Penguin, 1980), p. 268.

6. Theodore J. Lowi, *The Politics of Disorder* (New York: Basic Books, 1971), p. 54.

7. Steve Bruce, *The Rise and Fall of the New Christian Right* (New York: Clarendon Press, 1990).

8. Neal J. Smelser, *Theory of Collective Behavior* (New York: Free Press, 1962).

9. Barbara Sinclair Deckard, *The Women's Movement* (New York: HarperCollins, 1983); Ethel Klein, *Gender Politics: From Consciousness to Mass Politics* (Cambridge, MA: Harvard University Press, 1984), ch. 2.

10. John D. McCarthy and Mayer N. Zald, "Resource Mobilization and Social Movements: A Partial Theory," *American Journal of Sociology*, Vol. 82, No. 6, pp. 1212–1241.

11. Jo Freeman, *The Politics of Women's Liberation* (New York: David McKay, 1975).

12. Bruce, *Rise and Fall of the New Christian Right*, ch. 2.

13. Peter K. Eisenger, "The Condition of Protest Behavior in American Cities," *American Political Science Review*, Vol. 67 (1973), pp. 11–28.

14. Francis Fox Piven and Richard A. Cloward, *Poor People's Movements* (New York: Vintage, 1979), ch. 3.

15. Edward S. Greenberg, *Capitalism and the American Political Ideal* (Armonk, NY: M. E. Sharpe, 1985), ch. 6.

16. Klein, *Gender Politics*, pp. 90, 91.

17. Bruce, *Rise and Fall of the New Christian Right*, pp. 70–71.

18. Quoted in William H. Chafe, *The Unfinished Journey* (New York: Oxford University Press, 1986), p. 162.

19. Freeman, *Politics of Women's Liberation*; Susan M. Hartmann, *From Margin to Mainstream: American Women and Politics Since 1960* (Philadelphia: Temple University Press, 1989), ch. 3; Jane Mansbridge, *Why We Lost the ERA* (Chicago: University of Chicago Press, 1986).

20. For a compelling analysis of the rise of the New Right, see Kevin P. Phillips, *Post-Conservative America* (New York: Random House, 1982).

21. For this story, see Thomas Byrne Edsall, *The New Politics of Inequality* (New York: Norton, 1984); Greenberg, *Capitalism and the American Political Ideal.*

22. Gelb, *Feminism and Politics.*

23. Piven and Cloward, *Poor People's Movements.*

24. On repression see David Caute, *The Great Fear* (New York: Simon & Schuster, 1978); Robert Justin Goldstein, *Political Repression in Modern America* (Cambridge, MA: Schenkman, 1978); Alan Wolfe, *The Seamy Side of Democracy* (New York: David McKay, 1978).

25. See Cathy Perkus, ed., *Cointelpro: The FBI's Secret War on Political Freedom* (New York: Monad Press, 1975).

26. Greenberg, *Capitalism and the American Political Ideal.*

27. From the Joint Center for Political Studies, reported in Susan Anderson, "Eyes on the Prizes Not the People," *The Nation*, October 16, 1989, p. 422.

28. Chafe, *Unfinished Journey*; Deckard, *The Women's Movement*; Freeman, *Politics of Women's Liberation*; Klein, *Gender Politics*.

29. Constance Hays, "Study Says Blacks, More than Other Groups, Face Segregation," *New York Times*, March 14, 1989, p. A1.

30. Julie Johnson, "Blacks Found Lagging Despite Gains," *New York Times*, July 28, 1989, p. A5.

31. Jeremiah Cotton, "Opening the Gap: The Decline in Black Economic Indicators in the 1980s," *Social Science Quarterly*, Vol. 70, No. 4 (December 1988), pp. 803–819.

32. *Household Wealth and Asset Ownership* (Washington, DC: U.S. Bureau of the Census, 1984).

33. Philip Hilts, "Life Expectancy for Blacks in U.S. Shows Sharp Decline," *New York Times* (November 29, 1990), p. 11.

PART IV

*Government
and Governing*

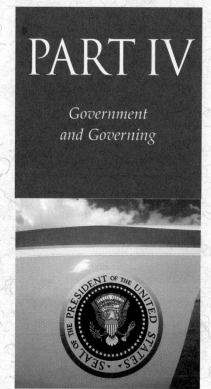

The chapters in Part IV examine how federal government institutions operate and how and why public officials, both elected and nonelected, behave as they do while in office. Part IV includes chapters on the presidency, Congress, the executive branch, the Supreme Court, and state and local government.

The chapters in this part assume that government institutions and public officials can only be understood in their structural and political contexts, points already made in Parts I, II, and III of this book. Their behavior and operations make sense, that is to say, only when we understand how structural factors (like the constitutional rules, the economy, the political culture, the nature of the population, and the United States's place in the world) make their mark, and how the preferences of individuals, groups, and classes are transmitted to government institutions and public officials by political level institutions (like elections, parties, interest groups, public opinion, and social movements). The chapter on Congress, for instance, tells how the constitutional rules have shaped the way the institution is organized and operates, how economic and population change have helped determine the congressional agenda, how members of

Congress attend to and respond to pressures arising from political level institutions like elections and public opinion, and how Congress is affected by the operations of other governmental level institutions like the president and the Court. This holistic approach to understanding government institutions and public officials is evident, as well, in the chapters on the presidency, the Court, the executive branch, and state and local government.

Democracy is the evaluative thread that runs through each chapter. We ask about the degree to which federal government institutions and public officials advance or retard the practice of democracy in the United States. We ask whether popular sovereignty, political equality, and liberty are enhanced or diminished by the way the presidency, Congress, the executive branch, the Supreme Court, and state and local government operate. We conclude that democratic practices have gradually improved over the years at the governmental level, but that significant barriers to the full realization of democracy still exist. Each chapter examines the nature of these barriers and evaluates some of the reforms that have been proposed to make government more democratic.

11

Congress

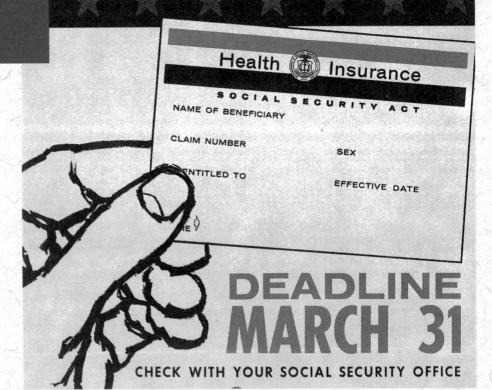

ENACTING MEDICARE

"If people were dying right and left for lack of medical care you'd read about it in the papers."[1] So said Republican House Minority Leader Charles Halleck of Indiana when asked in 1959 about the need for a federal medical insurance program for the elderly. Witnesses appearing before the House subcommittee on aging of the Labor and Public Welfare Committee told a different story:

> I live with my wife and my income is $1,500 a year. Well, we are old people and we don't require much. . . . We don't eat much so we get by in a manner. But I want to ask you . . . what do we do if something happens and we need medical care on $1,500 a year? . . . (a retired working man)
>
> How many times have I heard them say, "We have savings, we took care of our money and we were getting along all right, but because Paw had that stroke and went to the hospital for 6 weeks, or months, had to have that operation . . . that took nearly all we had saved and now we don't know how we will manage." (a retired electrical worker)

When Representative Halleck made his observation, only about one in three Americans were protected by private health insurance plans; fewer than one in five elderly Americans were covered. Many faced the cruel choice of doing without medical care or risking financial disaster. By contrast, virtually every Western European nation provided medical insurance or medical care for its citizens.

The idea of universal medical insurance kicked around for a long time in the United States but made little headway before the 1960s. The authors of the Social Security Act in 1935 wanted to include medical insurance, but President Roosevelt rejected the idea. President Truman asked Congress to consider universal medical insurance after his election in 1948. His bill was defeated by the combined opposition of the Republican party, the southern conservatives of his own party, and the American Medical Association (AMA), which denounced "socialized medicine" in the most expensive and extensive lobbying campaign to date in U.S. history.

Advocates of a federal medical insurance program began to gain ground during the 1950s when they shifted their agenda from insurance coverage for everyone to insurance coverage for the elderly. The problems of the elderly—extensive poverty, poor nutrition, and lack of access to medical care—were beginning to gain the attention of the media, university researchers, the public, and many politicians, particularly members of Congress. This was, in part, a result of the rapid growth in the size of the elderly population (see Chapter 4) and, in part, the result of lobbying by newly created interest groups (like the National Council of Senior Citizens).

A bill providing medical insurance for those receiving Social Security was introduced in Congress in 1957 by Democratic Representative Aime Forand of Rhode Island. Polls showed that a substantial majority favored the Forand bill. Labor unions and senior citizen organizations lobbied hard for the bill and generated a flood of mail to congressional offices. Liberal Democratic members of Congress eagerly responded and pressed for passage. The Democratic Advisory Council endorsed the bill. Senator Jack Kennedy, already thinking ahead to his run for the presidency in 1960, made the bill one of the pillars of his ten-point "bill of rights for our elderly citizens" in 1958. Once again, however, the formidable combination of the Republican party, southern Democrats, and the AMA (now joined by the American Dental Association, the American Hospital Association, and the American Nursing Association) doomed the bill.

Prospects for elderly medical insurance (now called Medicare) seemed much better during the early 1960s. A strong advocate, John F. Kennedy, was now president. The 1962 congressional elections sent additional Democratic Medicare advocates to Congress. Public opinion polls, meanwhile, showed that two out of three Americans supported Medicare legislation.

In 1964, Medicare legislation was defeated once again. Though the southern Democratic-Republican alliance (called the **conservative coalition**) was weakened by the 1960 and 1962 elections, it still commanded slim majorities on key committees that controlled the flow of legislation in Congress. The AMA once again gave generous campaign contributions to wavering representatives and senators on key committees.

After the historic 1964 election, the public finally had its way. Democrat Lyndon Johnson, who made Medicare a central theme of his campaign, won 61 percent of the popular vote and 90 percent of the electoral vote. Democrats won a sweeping victory in the House, adding 38 to their majority, and made a gain of two seats in the Senate. Though it proved to be impossible to remove recalcitrant conservative Democratic chairmen from their positions, additional liberal Democrats were added to the committees, tipping the balance of power. Wilbur Mills, chairman of the powerful Ways and Means Committee, and one of the shrewdest legislators in Congress, could read the new calculus: a popular president who advocated medical insurance for the elderly; an overwhelmingly liberal Congress; unprecedented popular support for Medicare in the polls; and the prospect of losing control of his own committee. Much to the surprise of the AMA, Mills not only supported the Medicare bill but also extended its scope to include physicians and drug fees. With victory in the House Ways and Means Committee, which had been the main roadblock in the past, proponents of Medicare pushed it through to final victory in the House (by a vote of 320–115) and in the Senate (by a vote of 68–21). The Republican leadership opposed it to the end—party spokesman John Byrnes said, "I still believe the majority is in error and I think the country will come to regret having pursued this course"[2]—but it no longer had the votes to block what the people wanted.

With former President Harry Truman at his side, Lyndon Johnson signed the Medicare bill. "No longer," he said, "will older Americans be denied the healing miracle of modern medicine. No longer will illness crush and destroy the savings that they have so carefully put away over a lifetime so that they might enjoy dignity in their later years."[3] Medicare has since become one of the most popular and effective federal programs.

This story points out, at a time when there is a great deal of grumbling about the ineffectiveness of Congress, that it is sometimes capable of responding to the wishes of the people and of fashioning effective and coherent national policies. It also shows, however, how many barriers exist to this kind of action, particularly the peculiarities of congressional organization and procedures, and the substantial influence of interest groups. In this chapter, we examine the factors that affect the ability of Congress to be both effective and responsive to the American people. We pay particular attention to the effects of public opinion, interest groups, political parties, the rules and organizational structures of Congress, and the electoral calculations of representatives and senators. We will also see that such structural factors as constitutional rules and economic and social change influence Congress and what it does.

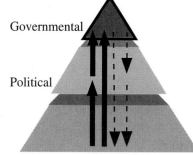

Governmental

Political

Structural

THE STRUCTURAL FOUNDATIONS OF THE MODERN CONGRESS

Constitutional Design

As we saw in Chapter 2, the framers were ambivalent about democracy. They fashioned a constitutional system designed to prevent tyranny (whether by a king or by the majority) and to protect a substantial realm of personal freedom. However, they also placed many roadblocks in the way of popular sovereignty (particularly majority rule) and political equality. We can see this ambivalence at work in their design of the legislative branch of government. These constitutional rules of the game significantly affect what Congress is like today.

The framers wanted the legislative branch to be the center of policymaking for the federal government. In Article I, Section I of the Constitution, they gave Congress the power to make the laws: "All legislative power herein granted shall be vested in a Congress of the United States. . . ."

The framers divided the legislative branch into two houses, or chambers. This followed the precedents of the British Parliament, which was organized into the House of Commons and the House of Lords, as well as the colonial legislatures in America. It was also consistent with the republican idea that laws should be made without haste, after patient deliberation. Single-house legislative bodies, they believed, would be prone to rash action.

As we learned in Chapter 2, the most heated and lengthy debates during the entire Constitutional Convention concerned the forms of representation in Congress. The "Great Compromise" apportioned the House of Representatives on the basis of population and the Senate on the basis of equal representation of the states. This arrangement significantly enhanced the power of states with small populations.

Terms for members of the House of Representatives were set at two years. Terms for members of the Senate, on the other hand, were set at six years, with

THE STRUGGLE FOR DEMOCRACY

The Direct Election of Senators

It's not exactly clear what the framers had in mind when they handed the job of electing members of the U.S. Senate to the state legislatures. By the end of the nineteenth century, the process of selection, besides being out of step with the strong democratic sentiments of the time, had become riddled with corruption and inefficiency.

For one thing, outright bribery of state legislators by prospective senatorial candidates had become widespread. To be successful at bribery required, of course, access to funds that allowed one to outspend rivals. This, in turn, required that prospective senators be personally wealthy—thus, the popular designation of the Senate in the late nineteenth century as the "millionares' club"—or tied to powerful economic interests. One notorious case was that of William Lorimer of Illinois, who was elected to the Senate in 1909, despite widely publicized evidence that he was being paid

by several large corporations (yet had no apparent duties) and had paid off key Illinois legislators to secure his election.

For another thing, party competition in the states made it difficult for state legislatures to agree easily on a selection. Things became especially difficult when one party controlled the state House of Representatives and the other party controlled the state Senate, or when party competition was close and each took turns in power. In the first type of situation, deadlocks would develop that would deprive states of representation in the Senate. Several states were without one of their senators for over two years during the 1890s. In 1895, the Delaware legislature took 217 ballots over a period of three months without being able to make a decision. In the second type of situation, winning parties in the legislature would quickly throw out senators of the other party, sub-

only one-third of the seats up for election at each election cycle. By this arrangement, the framers hoped to prevent the takeover of Congress by transitory popular majorities.

The Constitution called for the election of senators, not by the people, but by state legislatures. Again, the objective seems to have been to insulate one house of Congress from popular pressures and to make it a seat of deliberation and reflection. As James Madison put it, "the use of the Senate is to consist in its proceeding with more coolness . . . and with more wisdom than the popular branch."[4] Election of senators by state legislatures could not survive the democratizing tendencies in the country, however. The Seventeenth Amendment, passed in 1913, gave the people the power to elect senators directly. See the story of this successful struggle for democracy above.

When the Founders thought about governing, they thought primarily about Congress. In defining the powers and responsibilities of Congress, they were

stituting their own people as quickly as possible. Sometimes, the U.S. Senate would refuse to seat these new people, further confusing the situation and diminishing the representation of the state in Washington, D.C.

The call for the direct election of senators was first made by labor and farmers' groups in the last third of the nineteenth century, mainly on the grounds of democracy and the need to separate the U.S. Senate from the "grip of the plutocrats." Progressive reformers added their own voices, mainly on the grounds of efficiency and good government. By the turn of the century, as far as we are able to tell, given the absence of polling, most Americans favored the direct election of senators. Both parties endorsed the idea. The House of Representatives passed resolutions in favor of a constitutional amendment changing the Senate selection process in every Congress after 1900. But the constitutional proposal, not surprisingly, died in the Senate each time.

Frustrated in the Senate, reformers did an end run, concentrating on the states. Their main reforms were enactments mandating popular referendums on potential Senate candidates and compelling state legislatures to follow the lead of the voters in these referendums when electing senators. By 1912, 29 states had instituted these electoral reforms, effectively placing the selection of senators into the hands of the people in a majority of states. The method was proved in 1910 in the state of Nevada when a Democratic-controlled state legislature elected Republican George Nixon to the Senate because he had won a popular referendum over his Democratic rival.

The U.S. Senate, seeing the proverbial handwriting on the wall, finally gave in and approved a proposal for a constitutional amendment for the direct election of senators in 1912. The requisite number of states approved the Seventeenth Amendment in 1913.

Source: Bob Dole, *Historical Almanac of the United States Senate* (Washington, D.C.: U.S. Government Printing Office, 1989), pp. 180–184; J. W. Peltason, *Understanding the Constitution* (New York: Holt, Rinehart and Winston, 1988), p. 254.

largely defining the powers and responsibilities of the national government itself.[5] Article I, Section 8 lists the specific powers and responsibilities of Congress. Among the most significant of these **enumerated powers** are the power to tax and spend; to borrow; to regulate commerce between the states and with foreign countries; to raise, support, and maintain an army and a navy; to provide for a uniform system of weights and measures; to provide a monetary system; to set up federal courts; to establish post offices and post roads; to declare war; and to make rules for the conduct of government. There is also a provision—known as the elastic clause—that has allowed Congress to legislate in areas not mentioned in the Constitution or imagined by the framers: Congress shall have power "to make all laws which shall be necessary and proper for carrying into execution" all of its other powers. In addition to the grants of power to Congress as a whole, the Constitution also defines particular responsibilities for the House of Representatives and for the Senate. These are summarized in Table 11.1.

Table 11.1

Constitutional Differences Between the House and the Senate

Senate	House of Representatives
Six-year term	Two-year term
Two senators per state	Number based on population size (minimum of one per state)
100 members	435 members (total determined by Congress)
Minimum age: 30 years	Minimum age: 25 years
One-third up for election at each election cycle	Entire membership up for election at each election cycle
Power of advice and consent for judicial and upper-level executive branch appointments	Originates revenue bills
Power of advice and consent over treaties	
Power to try for impeachment	Power to bring impeachment charges

The framers wanted to create an energetic government with a strong legislative branch, but, fearing tyranny, they also specifically wanted to limit congressional power. Article I, Section 9 prohibits **bills of attainder**, **ex post facto** laws, the granting of titles of nobility, and the suspension of the right of **habeas corpus**. Other prohibitions are in the Bill of Rights. Note that the First Amendment, perhaps the most important constitutional proviso protecting political liberty, begins with the words "Congress shall make no law. . . ."

The framers created separate legislative, executive, and judicial branches and gave each of them some role to play in the activities of the others so that "ambition might check ambition" and protect against tyranny (see *Federalist*, No. 51 in the Appendix). The constitutional rules of the game specify that Congress must share its legislative power, for instance, with both the president, who must sign congressional bills before they can become law, and the Supreme Court, which can rule on the constitutionality of legislation. Congress shares in the executive power by virtue of its responsibilities for approving or disapproving presidential nominees and treaties, making the federal budget, and legislating the organization of the executive branch. These are but a few examples from a rich set of interdependencies that Congress shares with the other two branches.

The Historical Development of Congress[6]

These constitutional rules remain important in shaping how Congress is organized and how it operates, but so are other structural, political, and governmental factors. Particularly important for understanding how Congress has changed during the course of American history are the structural changes described in Chapter 4.

THE FIRST CONGRESS   The First Congress convened on March 4, 1789, in the Federal Hall in New York City—the temporary seat of government. It operated with-

Federal Hall in New York City was the location of the first session of the U.S. Congress.

out standing committees. Because both House and Senate were small bodies, neither needed strong leadership to manage its business. Each house considered bills, meeting as a "committee of the whole," in which all members participated. Once the general outlines of a bill were agreed to, it was sent either to a specially formed ad hoc committee of the House or the Senate, or to an officer in the executive branch to fashion the details in advance of the final floor vote.[7] Members made up the rules as they went along. The issues that they dealt with were important, but the flow of business was manageable, because the federal government did not play a very large role in American life. Though they were skilled and experienced politicians, few members saw service in Congress as a lifelong career. Most expected to return to private life or to politics in their home states. This was to change over the years as the United States grew from a small agricultural and trading nation on the periphery of the world system to an urban, industrialized superpower.

INCREASE IN SIZE   The most obvious change has been the growth in the size of Congress. Because the Senate is made up of two senators from each state, it naturally grows as the number of states in the nation increases. The Senate in the First Congress had 26 members, representing the 13 states; the Senate in our own day has 100 members, representing 50 states.

Membership in the House of Representatives is apportioned to each state on the basis of its population size. Rapid population increase in the nineteenth century brought the number of representatives in the House from 65 in 1788 to 435 in 1912. Because House members believed that they had reached the limit of a functioning legislative body, they froze the upper limit at 435, where it has remained. Because the American population continued to grow after 1912, while the size of the House remained fixed, the average population size of each congressional district has increased rather dramatically, from a little over 200,000 in 1912 to almost 600,000 today (see Figure 11.1). This makes it more difficult for a House member to meet more than a small percentage of his or her constituents on a face-to-face basis.

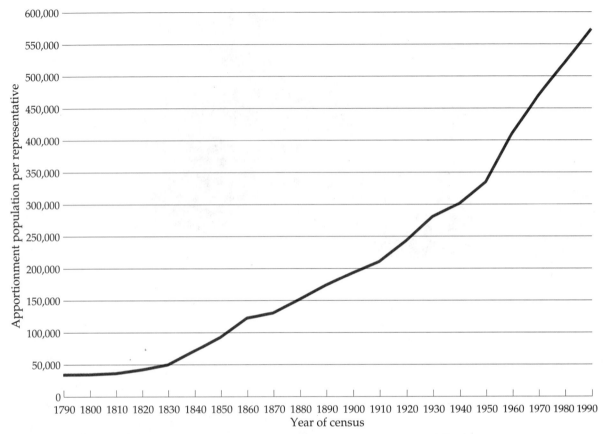

Figure 11.1 Growth in the average size of congressional districts

Source: Roger H. Davidson and Walter J. Oleszek, Congress and Its Members, *3rd ed. (Washington, D.C.: CQ Press, 1990), p. 26.*

INCREASE IN THE VOLUME OF CONGRESSIONAL BUSINESS   The federal government plays a larger role in American life now than the framers envisioned because of structural changes in America. Urbanization, population growth, industrialization, new forms of business organization, and our emergence as a superpower have generated a wide range of problems and opportunities that seem to require a vigorous and interventionist government. As government has taken on more responsibilities, the sheer volume of business of Congress has expanded accordingly.

One way to see this is to look at the change in the number of bills introduced during each session of Congress. In the First Congress, 144 bills were introduced; 16,184 were introduced in the One Hundred and First (1990–1991) Congress. Congress also has substantially expanded the size of the staff it uses to conduct its expanding legislative business (see Figure 11.2).

INSTITUTIONALIZATION   As Congress grew in size and considered ever more complex issues, it became more "institutionalized"[8]; that is, it became more *structured, organized, regularized,* and *rule-bound.* Formal ways of doing things replaced

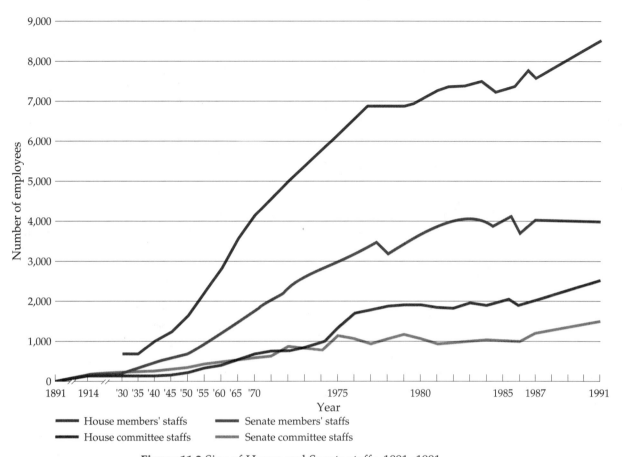

Figure 11.2 Size of House and Senate staffs, 1891–1991

Source: Norman J. Ornstein, Thomas E. Mann, and Michael J. Malbin, Vital Statistics on Congress,
*1989–1990 (Washington, D.C.: Congressional Quarterly, 1990), p. 130; and the Clerk of the U.S. House of
Representatives and the General Accounting Office for 1991.*

many informal arrangements. Legislative business today is done mainly in specialized committees and subcommittees by subject-matter specialists and professional staff. Much of the coordination is accomplished by elaborate rules of procedure (particularly in the larger House of Representatives), well-understood
precedents, and widely accepted norms of behavior. This is very different from
the First Congress.

Congress also has become more "professionalized," in the sense that its
members increasingly think of their jobs as careers. Until the late nineteenth century, members of Congress came and went frequently. From the late nineteenth
century to the present, however, there has been a steady trend toward lower membership turnover and much longer average terms in office. We will explore the
implications of this development for democracy later.

DECLINE IN POLICY LEADERSHIP Another historical trend has been a shift in the
center of national policymaking leadership, from Congress, where the Founders

expected it to reside, to the president. Both Congress and the American people expect the president to take the lead in foreign policy and military affairs, for instance, and to make most of the tough decisions, as in the Persian Gulf War and its aftermath. Congress plays a more significant role in domestic policymaking, but here too, presidents have significantly expanded their role, assuming responsibility for fashioning a legislative program for the nation.

Most of the changes in the balance of power between the two branches can be traced to structural changes. When the United States became a world superpower, for instance, the president became more powerful because of his constitutional responsibilities for diplomacy and the conduct of war. As the economy of the United States became dominated by extremely large corporations, the government's role in economic management became more vital and Congress gradually deferred to the president's ability to steer the economy with a single hand.

The shift in power to the executive branch in the U.S. government, though substantial, is not nearly as far along as in other democratic countries, like Britain and France. In England, important bills are written in the ministries, approved by the cabinet, and debated in the House of Commons. Members are allowed only 12 days during a session to introduce bills (always minor ones) and 10 days to make motions. Party discipline ensures that members of Parliament rarely will amend legislation and that the fate of legislation is never in doubt. In France, the National Assembly is constitutionally prohibited from legislating in certain areas (like regulation) that are left to the executive branch. The government (the prime minister and the Cabinet) controls the legislative process, having the power to substitute its bills for those of legislators, to restrict amendments, and to limit debate.

In the United States, Congress remains a formidable and independent branch, less powerful than in the past, but still able to go head to head with the president on most issues. When faced with evidence of decline relative to the president, moreover, Congress occasionally has been able to reform and renew itself.[9]

REPRESENTATION AND DEMOCRACY

Ours is a representative democracy in which the members of the House and the Senate serve as our legislative representatives in Washington, D.C. We want to ask in this section whether members carry out this representative responsibility in a way that can be considered democratic. To answer this, we need to look at the many aspects of representation.

Styles of Representation

In a letter to his constituents written in 1774, English parliamentarian and philosopher Edmund Burke described two principal styles of representation. As a *delegate*, the representative tries to mirror perfectly the views of his or her constituents. As a *trustee*, the representative acts independently, trusting to his or her own best judgment of the issues. Burke preferred the trustee approach:

> Your representative owes you, not his industry only, but his judgment; and he betrays you, instead of serving you, if he sacrifices it to your opinion.[10]

Abraham Lincoln thought otherwise:

> While acting as [your] representative, I shall be governed by [your] will, on all subjects upon which I have the means of knowing what [your] will is. . . ."[11]

The choice between these two styles of representation for members of Congress is based probably less on personal tastes than on judgments about the relative safety of their seats. Representatives and senators without real electoral competition can better afford to choose the "trustee" style. Senators with six-year terms have more leeway than representatives to assume the "trustee" style.

Who Are the Members of Congress?

One way to represent is to be similar to that which is being represented. If we want a political system in which the views of women are taken into account, for instance, we might want a significant number of women in Congress. From this perspective, a perfectly representative legislative body would have characteristics similar to the characteristics of the general population in terms of race, sex, ethnicity, occupation, religion, age, and the like. In this sense, the U.S. Congress is highly *unrepresentative*, though important gains were made in 1992.

GENDER AND RACE   Congress has long been a bastion of white males[12] and remains so today. Figure 11.3 compares the characteristics of the members of the

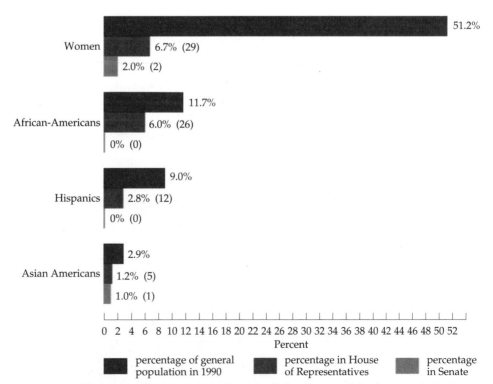

Figure 11.3 Women and minorities in the 102nd Congress and in the population*ᵃ*

*ᵃ*Numbers in parentheses indicate the total number of individuals.

Sources: Congressional Quarterly, *November 10, 1990, pp. 3835–3837, and the Bureau of the Census.*

In 1916, Republican Jeanette Rankin of Montana became the first woman elected to Congress. Though other women subsequently were elected to Congress, they remain seriously under-represented.

One Hundred Second Congress with the characteristics of the general population in 1990. Both women and racial minorities are significantly underrepresented, especially in the Senate. Black representation reached its peak during the post-Civil War Reconstruction period, when blacks played an important political role in several southern states. They disappeared from Congress for many years after the reimposition of white supremacy in the South at the end of the nineteenth century. Though a handful of black representatives from northern cities served during the first half of the twentieth century—Oscar DePriest from Chicago's predominantly black South Side and Adam Clayton Powell from New York's Harlem, for instance—no significant numbers of black legislators entered Congress until the late 1960s. Their numbers are still well below what one might expect, given the proportion of blacks in the American population.

The first woman to sit in Congress was Jeannette Rankin of Montana, who was elected in 1916. The number of women has slowly increased, reaching a total of 47 in the House and 6 in the Senate in the One Hundred Third Congress. This is the highest ever. Proportionally, however, female representation is still only about one-half the average for legislative bodies around the world.[13] Moreover, women are not in the leadership in either chamber. The improvement in political participation and self-confidence among women caused by the Women's movement may increase the number of female lawmakers in the future, though progress has been painfully slow.

SOCIAL CLASS　Members of Congress are far better educated than the remainder of the population. They tend to come from very high-income families and enjoy incomes that are substantially above average. About one-half are lawyers. Most of the rest have backgrounds in business (including farming) or the professions. Notable for their absence are lawmakers from blue-collar families or from traditional blue-collar jobs, whether skilled, semiskilled, or unskilled.

Does it matter that Congress is unrepresentative demographically of the American people? Some political scientists and close observers of Congress think not. They suggest that the need to face the electorate forces lawmakers to be attentive to all significant groups in their constituencies. A representative from a farm district listens to farm constituents, even if that representative is not a farmer. A representative from a district in which significant numbers of steelworkers live is going to worry about the health of the steel industry, whatever the representative's own occupational background might be.

Nevertheless, many who are not well represented—women, blacks and other racial minorities, and the poor—believe that their interests would get a much better hearing if their numbers were substantially increased in Congress. Would federal legislation to protect the civil rights of blacks have been delayed for over 100 years after Lincoln's Emancipation Proclamation if blacks had been among the nation's lawmakers? The demographic disparity between the American population and the makeup of Congress suggests some violation of the norm of political equality, an important element of democracy.

The Electoral Connection

The election is the principal instrument in a democracy for linking citizens to those in government. Let's see how congressional elections affect the quality of representation in the United States.

ELECTORAL DISTRICTS   Each state is entitled to two senators. This gives extraordinary power in the legislative process to small states. Alaska, for instance, has exactly the same number of senators as California, although it has but one-fiftieth of California's population. This arrangement can substantially distort popular sentiment and, thus, diminish democracy. Republicans took control of the Senate after the 1980 election by winning 22 of 34 Senate elections, even though they won less than a majority of Senate votes cast nationwide. This was possible because most of their victories were in the smaller states.[14]

Representation in the House of Representatives is according to population. **Reapportionment** of House seats between the states occurs every ten years after the national census (see Figure 11.4 for the most recent changes). As population shifts within and between states, the boundaries of existing congressional districts must be redrawn. In the past, this was left entirely to state legislatures. Very often, the result was congressional districts of vastly different population size—in New York in the 1930s, some congressional districts were ten times larger than others—and a significantly overrepresented rural population. The Supreme Court ruled in *Wesberry v. Sanders* (1964), however, that the principle of one-person-one-vote applies to congressional districts. Today, all congressional districts are roughly equal in size of population.

While congressional districts must be approximately the same size in terms of population, state legislatures are still relatively free to draw district lines where they choose. The party that controls the state legislature usually tries to draw district lines in a way that will help them win elections. The resulting districts are often strange indeed. Rather than compact and coherent districts, neighborhoods, towns, and counties can be strung together in odd-looking ways in order to take full partisan advantage of the redistricting process. When taken to the extreme, such a process is called **gerrymandering** after Governor Elbridge Gerry of Massachusetts, who signed a bill in 1811 that created a district that looked like a salamander. It made wonderful raw material for editorial cartoonists.

Changes in number of House seats after 1992

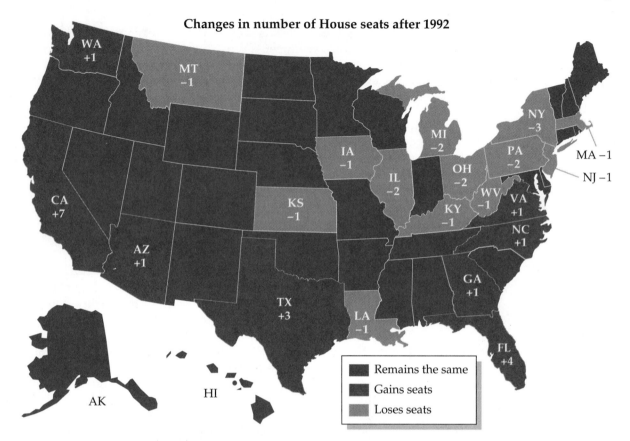

Figure 11.4 States gaining and losing Congressional seats as a result of the 1990 census

Source: The Christian Science Monitor, *September 26, 1991, p. 1.*

The Supreme Court has tried to prevent the most flagrant abuses, especially when some identifiable group of voters (like racial minorities) is disadvantaged, but it is a practice that is difficult to regulate. Parties in power will always try to draw district lines to their own advantage, though the courts may begin to intervene here as well.

"Gerry-Mander," the title of Elkanah Tinsdale's 1812 cartoon of a Massachusetts district drawn to ensure the election of a Republican candidate, became a new word in the American political vocabulary.

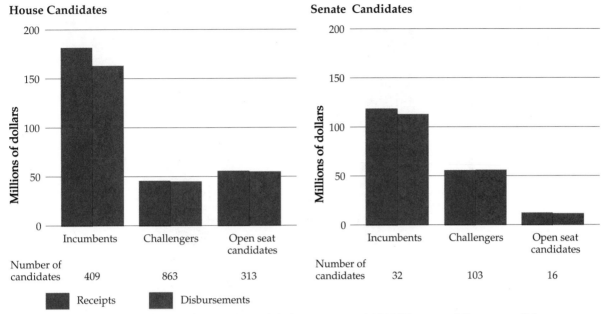

Figure 11.5 Receipts and disbursements of 1990 House and Senate candidates

Source: Federal Election Commission, Annual Report 1991.

MONEY AND CONGRESSIONAL ELECTIONS   Running for the House or the Senate is a very expensive proposition, and it keeps getting more expensive. In the 1990 elections, candidates for the House of Representatives spent a total of $265 million—$609,000 each. Senate candidates spent a grand total of $180 million—$5.5 million each. Incumbents spent the most, by far, in races for both houses (see Figure 11.5). The grand totals are but averages; they hide some of the most frenzied spending, most often in closely contested Senate races. In his Senate race against Harvey Gantt in 1990, for instance, Jesse Helms spent $13.4 million.

There is nothing particularly surprising about these increases. Inflation has played a part. So has the ever greater reliance on expensive campaign technologies: mass and targeted mailings; polling; focus groups; television, radio, and print advertising; phone banks, and the like. So, too, has the decline of party loyalty in the electorate, which compels each candidate to try to reach each and every potential voter.

Spending matters. Though the candidate who spends the most money does not always win, the amount of money spent is related to the *probability* of winning. This is especially true for challengers and for those elections in which an incumbent is not involved.[15] Because money matters, candidates spend a great deal of time and effort in making sure that they have enough. It would not be far off the mark to suggest that candidates are obsessed with fund raising.

It is virtually all that challengers do at the beginning of their campaign. Life for them is an endless round of fund-raising letters, phone call appeals to PACs and wealthy individuals, social gatherings, dinners, benefits, and the like. The ability to raise a sufficient amount of money, in fact, becomes an indicator to other politicians and the media whether the candidate should be taken seriously.

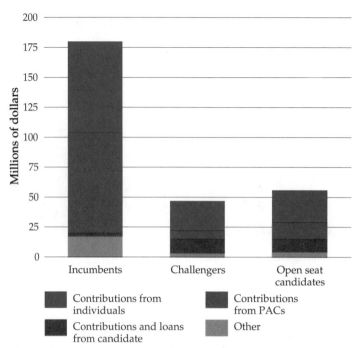

Figure 11.6 House candidates' source of receipts, 1990

Source: Federal election commission, Annual Report 1991.

The dollars that support congressional campaigns come from four main sources: individuals, parties, the candidates, and PACs (see Figure 11.6). The largest portion comes from individual contributors—about 55 percent in recent elections. Not surprisingly, individual contributors, especially those giving the maximum allowed of $1,000 per campaign to several candidates, are significantly more affluent than the average citizen.

About one-third of the money for congressional campaigns comes from PACs, with most going to incumbents. It is the fastest growing part of the campaign financing system. PACs can contribute up to $5,000 per candidate per election, and there is no limit to what they can spend overall. The National Rifle Association, for instance, contributed over $1 million to 292 House candidates in the 1986 election. PACs are also free to spend without limit on general issue campaigns that are often thinly veiled efforts to help a particular candidate or party. National Conservative Political Action Committee (NICPAC), a conservative ideological PAC, to take one example, was, for all intents and purposes, a part of the 1980 and 1984 Republican national campaign.

Many people believe that the increased role of PACs in congressional campaigns increases the influence of interest groups in general and business interests in particular. Corporate, trade and professional groups together account for over 60 percent of all PAC expenditures in congressional races (see the more detailed discussion in Chapter 7). Since a substantial portion of "nonconnected" PACs are ideologically conservative and probusiness groups, the figures on business influence are probably underestimated. Some commentators have traced Democratic congressional support for traditional Republican economic positions in the 1980s to the party's aggressive courting of business PACs by the Democratic Congressional Campaign Committee under former Representative Tony Coelho of California. In explaining why he had voted for President Bush's capital gains tax cut proposal, one Democratic representative put the matter rather directly: "It's as simple as he who pays the piper plays the tune. . . . I get elected by voters, I get financed by contributors. Voters don't care about this [capital gains], contributors do."[16]

The remainder of the money comes from two sources: candidates' contributions out of their own pockets (challengers or candidates for open seats) and the parties, which contribute less than 2 percent of the total. Party contributions are in the form of a $5,000 payment per campaign to each candidate and coordinated spending—outlays for such services as polling, ads, and time on television and radio that is not counted as candidate spending. This has been as high as $800,000 for some Senate candidates in recent elections. The Republicans have been far more successful in the collection and use of such monies.

There are no legal limits on what individuals, groups, and corporations may give to the parties for general education, registration, and "get-out-the-vote" campaigns. Nor are there limits on how much of this so-called **soft money** parties can spend, even though such spending obviously benefits individual candidates. Republicans have been particularly good at raising and spending soft money in recent elections.

THE INCUMBENCY FACTOR   Given the high turnover of House members after the 1992 national elections, it is something of an exaggeration to claim, as several congressional scholars do, that ". . . it is nearly impossible to topple a House incumbent, short of a major scandal or misstep."[17] It is true, nevertheless, that incumbents win at higher rates than in the past and that the number of competitive districts across the nation has declined.[18] In elections stretching from 1950 to 1988, over 90 percent of House incumbents ran for reelection, and over 90 percent were successful (Figure 11.7).

In the Senate, lower but still impressive rates of success for incumbents have prevailed. The somewhat more competitive nature of Senate elections may be traced to the transformation of the South from a one-party, Democratic stronghold (where incumbents have almost never lost) to a more competitive two-party system. Outside the South, incumbent success in the Senate is close to that in the House. The same should become true of the South in the future as the transformation plays itself out over the next decade or so.

Things may now be changing, however. Voter discontent with Congress during the 1990 elections resulted in a significant decline in the average incumbent's margin of victory. In 1986 and 1988, incumbents won about 68 percent of the vote, on average; in 1990, the margin fell to 63.5 percent.[19] In 1992, an unusually large number of voluntary retirements and electoral defeats occurred because of redistricting and public anger over "check bouncing" in the House of Representatives. Concern about the incumbency effect also has sparked a "term limitation movement" in many states.

WHY INCUMBENTS HAVE AN ADVANTAGE   Incumbents generally have several advantages over their potential rivals. For one thing, incumbents easily attract contributions. PACs and interest groups want access to key decision makers in

Figure 11.7 Incumbent reelection rates, 1946–1992.

Source: Congressional Quarterly, *November 10, 1990, p. 3797 and authors' research.*

the House and the Senate. They look at campaign contributions as an "investment," a way to guarantee that their phone calls will be answered, that they will be allowed to make their case, and that their interests will be taken into account.[20] To contribute to a challenger is to jeopardize access if the challenger loses; it is probably why incumbents get $9 for every $1 challengers get (see Table 11.2).

The flow of money to incumbents is particularly heavy for those who sit on key committees or hold important leadership posts. During consideration of the 1986 tax reform bill, PACs gave one-third of their total $66.8 million in contributions to members of the two tax-writing committees of Congress.

Incumbents not only have more money but also spend more. In the 1990 congressional elections, Senate incumbents outspent challengers by a 2:1 margin; House incumbents outspent their challengers by a 3.5:1 margin. Moreover, incumbents control the congressional machinery, which they use to help their reelection chances.[21] Already well known, members of Congress have many ways to advertise their accomplishments and to keep their names before the public.[22] The **franking privilege** allows members of Congress to mail newsletters, legislative updates, surveys, and other self-promoting literature free of charge. The resulting volume of mail is simply staggering. About four million pieces of free mail goes out to constituents *every single day* while Congress is in session.[23] The House and the Senate also provide travel budgets for lawmakers so that they can make periodic visits back to their state or district. Because members believe that time spent in their district helps their electoral chances—a belief supported by a great deal of research[24]—they spend an increasing amount of time back home. Some manage to spend three or four days per week in their district or state, meeting constituents, giving speeches, raising money, and so on. The congressional leadership helps by scheduling important legislative business for the Tuesday–Thursday period.

Discontent with Congress has helped fuel a sometimes bitter national campaign to limit the number of terms that may be served by senators and representatives. Many believe, as does the cartoonist David Horsey, that such measures are anti-democratic.

Incumbents use their offices to "service the district." One way in which they do this is through **casework**: helping constituents solve red-tape problems with the federal bureaucracy, whether it be speeding up the arrival of a late Social Security check or expediting the issuance of a grazing permit on public land.[25] Generous budgets to staff offices in the constituency help representatives and senators do casework. Another way in which they "service the district" is to provide **pork**: federal dollars in the form of contracts, facilities, and subsidies. In his first three years as chairman of the Appropriations Committee, Senator Robert Byrd of West Virginia managed to steer $750 million in federal contracts and grants to his state, along with 3,000 federal jobs. Challengers can promise to deliver more pork, but incumbents can point to tangible accomplishments.

It may also be that incumbents are stronger candidates than challengers. It's probably why they were successful in the first place. Knowing this, the opposition party often runs into difficulty fielding viable challengers.

Finally, incumbency may be explained by a factor that is not often mentioned: members of Congress may be doing a relatively good job of representing their constituents who choose to reelect them. Research shows that the link between public opinion in the constituency and the voting behavior of members of Congress is quite substantial. Members vote in conformity with majority opinion in their districts about two-thirds of the time.[26] As a whole, Congress produces laws that are consistent with national public opinion at about the same rate.[27]

Though the "incumbency factor" is more important than in the past and receives a great deal of attention from scholars, journalists, and the public, it is important not to exaggerate its extent. Because there are voluntary retirements, as well as some electoral defeats, about 20 percent of House members are replaced at each election cycle. Over three election cycles (six years), three-fifths of House members are replaced. This represents a significant turnover of membership

---

Table 11.2
Top Senate PAC Recipients, 1989–1990

In the past two years, political action committees have contributed $21.6 million to the campaign committees of incumbent senators.

These 15 senators have received the most PAC support during that time. The chart below shows their committee assignments, the PAC contributions each received, and the special interest groups that contributed the most to each.

Senator	PAC Total	Biggest Special Interest Contributors	
John D. Rockefeller IV (D-W.Va.)	$886,142	Energy	$ 67,700
Committees: Energy and Natural Resources;		Insurance	60,850
Commerce, Science and Transportation; Finance;		Hospitals	57,250
Veterans Affairs			
Phil Gramm (R-Tex.)	879,547	Energy	139,980
Committees: Appropriations; Banking, Housing		Finance	109,950
and Urban Affairs; Budget		Real Estate/Construction	60,625
Paul Simon (D-Ill.)	877,297	Pro-Israel	122,651
Committees: Budget; Foreign Relations;		Transportation Unions	61,742
Judiciary; Labor and Human Resources		Construction Unions	50,455
Carl M. Levin (D-Mich.)	836,397	Pro-Israel	130,800
Committees: Armed Services; Governmental		Transportation Unions	72,000
Affairs; Small Business		Construction Unions	50,325
J. James Exon (D-Neb.)	792,538	Transportation Industry	102,702
Committees: Commerce, Science and		Insurance	74,500
Transportation; Armed Services; Budget		Communications	70,873
Max Baucus (D-Mont.)	791,338	Finance	81,000
Committees: Finance; Agriculture, Nutrition and		Insurance	57,100
Forestry; Environment and Public Works; Small		Pro-Israel	48,000
Business			
Rudy Boschwitz (R-Minn.)	790,535	Pro-Israel	77,329
Committees: Foreign Relations; Agriculture,		Food	71,965
Nutrition and Forestry; Budget; Small Business		Insurance	50,925

---

within a relatively short period of time. The percentage is even higher after reapportionment, like in the 1992 election. Nor are incumbents safe in the face of public outrage like that generated by the House "check bouncing" scandal. Incumbency is important, but it does not shield Congress from the tides of public opinion, as some suggest.

HOW DEMOCRATIC? Representatives and senators pay a great deal of attention to the interests and the preferences of people in their districts and states. Because they are worried about getting reelected, they try to see as many people as they can during their frequent visits, and they pay attention to their mail and the public opinion polls. To a considerable degree, moreover, they vote and pass laws in accordance with public opinion.

It is also the case, however, that, in a substantial number of cases, they do *not* follow public opinion. On many issues out of public view, moreover, the public

Senator	PAC Total	Biggest Special Interest Contributors	
Howell T. Heflin (D-Ala.)	766,686	Energy	86,500
Committees: Energy and Natural Resources;		Pro-Israel	83,850
Agriculture, Nutrition and Forestry; Judiciary		Insurance	59,248
Tom Harkin (D-Iowa)	762,627	Pro-Israel	116,050
Committees: Agriculture, Nutrition and Forestry;		Insurance	49,170
Appropriations; Labor and Human Resources;		Transportation Unions	49,140
Small Business			
J. Bennett Johnston (D-La.)	740,789	Energy	236,500
Committees: Energy and Natural Resources		Aerospace/Defense	71,000
(Chair); Appropriations; Budget		Transportation	42,000
Daniel R. Coats (R-Ind.)	679,556	Insurance	71,675
Committees: Armed Services; Labor and Human		Aerospace/Defense	58,375
Resources		Communications	57,791
Bill Bradley (D-N.J.)	645,804	Finance	76,975
Committees: Finance; Energy and Natural		Insurance	52,700
Resources		Energy	45,500
Mitch McConnell (R-Ky.)	632,168	Energy	89,813
Committees: Energy and Natural Resources;		Pro-Israel	80,600
Foreign Relations; Agriculture, Nutrition and		Food	61,647
Forestry; Rules and Administration			
John W. Warner (R-Va.)	605,282	Energy	78,750
Committees: Armed Services; Environment and		Aerospace/Defense	76,732
Public Works		Transportation	38,000
Albert Gore Jr. (D-Tenn.)	577,994	Insurance	55,376
Committees: Armed Services; Rules; Commerce,		Communications	43,699
Science and Transportation		Construction Unions	38,743

Table 11.2 (continued)
Top Senate PAC Recipients, 1989–1990

Source: Washington Post computer analysis of 1989-1990 PAC contribution data collected through March 31 by the Federal Election Commission. Special interest groupings are based on a classification system initially developed by Common Cause and provided to The Post. *Washington Post National Weekly Edition,* June 25–July 1, 1990, p. 14.

may have no opinions. It is in these areas where one can see the influence of money and interest groups at work. The lobbying community, we have learned, overwhelmingly represents business and the professions. Moreover, legislators who are almost entirely on their own in organizing and financing their reelection campaigns are tempting targets for interest groups and PACs. To the degree that these influences distort popular sovereignty and undermine political equality, democracy is impaired.

HOW CONGRESS WORKS

Though Congress has lost some of its policymaking role to the president over the years, it remains a vital center of power in our national government. It has not become a place, as legislative bodies have become in many parliamentary systems,

The Senate must approve senior presidential administrative appointments. Here Robert Gates testifies before the Senate Intelligence Committee in 1991 as part of the confirmation process for his appointment as Director of the Central Intelligence Agency.

 where policy is debated and where the executive's bills are rubber-stamped. In Britain, roughly 97 percent of the government's (the Cabinet) bills are approved by the House of Commons.[28] By all accounts, Congress remains the most powerful legislative body among the Western democratic nations. It has power; it must be attended to by other political actors; it plays an important part in making policy. It has the main responsibility for *making laws* and *raising revenues* to run the government. The Senate must *approve appointments* to the Supreme Court and senior positions in the executive branch, as well as *treaties* with other nations. Congress also exercises *oversight* functions, reviewing the performance of executive branch agencies to ensure that laws are being properly administered and that power is not being abused. In this section, we turn our attention to the way in which Congress is organized and functions as a working legislative body. We first want to know how issues come to congressional attention, that is, how items become a part of the legislative agenda.

Where the Congressional Agenda Comes From

Congress is embedded in a rich structural, political, and governmental environment that influences what it pays attenton to. The other branches of government are a constant influence on the congressional agenda, for instance. Federal courts may rule on the constitutionality of laws passed by Congress, and, if such laws are overturned, they spark a legislative reaction. After the Supreme Court ruled that states were free to restrict abortions in the *Webster* case (1989), Congress reacted by expanding public funding of abortions in Washington, D.C.

The president and the executive branch are also important in shaping the legislative agenda. Many of the bills that are introduced into the House and the Senate by lawmakers are actually drafted in places like the Department of Agriculture and the Commerce Department and come to Congress after being cleared by the Office of Management and Budget. Much of what Congress does by way of lawmaking is in response to the legislative program of the president, usually presented in conjunction with his annual State of the Union, Economic, and Budget messages. Congress must also monitor how the president and the federal bureaucracy administer the laws, and the Senate is responsible for approving or disapproving federal court and executive branch leadership appointments, as well as treaties sent over to the Hill by the president.

The congressional agenda is also shaped by the many groups and individuals that comprise its political environment. Because of their important role in electoral financing, interest groups play a particularly important role in defining the issues before the House and the Senate. Lawmakers must balance the needs and demands of interest groups against those of the voters, the constituents, and the public. The media are also a continuous player in shaping what issues are attended to in the legislative branch. Social movements, at times, impose their own needs.

At a more fundamental level, it is structural change that mobilizes political and governmental institutions, groups, and individuals. Economic dislocations, for instance, may trigger demands for congressional action from voters, interest groups, and other government officials. Population change, including immigration and aging, adds a range of new issues to the congressional menu, as do changes in the U.S. economic and military position in the world.

Congressional Committees

Most of the work of Congress takes place in its many committees and subcommittees. This is relatively unique among the democratic nations whose legislative bodies lack strong committees with real power. In the British House of Commons, for instance, committees cannot offer amendments that alter the substance or general principles of bills. Even allowable amendments, involving implementation only, are unlikely to be offered, given party and Cabinet control over Members of Parliament (MPs). In France, committees of the National Assembly cannot substitute their own bills for those of the government. No such restrictions apply for the U.S. Congress.

WHY COMMITTEES? Committees serve several useful purposes. They allow Congress to process rationally the huge flow of business that comes before it. The committees serve as screening devices, allowing only a small percentage of bills to take up the time of the parent legislative bodies.

Committees are also islands of specialization, whose members and staff develop the expertise to handle complex issues and to meet executive branch experts on equal terms. The Ways and Means Committee of the House can go toe-to-toe with the Treasury Department; the House and Senate Armed Services Committees can generate expertise equal to that of the Department of Defense. It is one of the reasons Congress remains a vital lawmaking body.

Committees are also useful to members of Congress who use their committee positions to generate benefits for their districts or states. The rational legislator, in fact, usually tries to get a committee assignment that will allow for an efficient servicing of his or her constituency. This is important, we have seen, for reelection.

WHAT KINDS OF COMMITTEES?   There are several kinds of committees, each of which serves a special function in the legislative process (see Table 11.3).

A **standing committee** is a relatively permanent committee, specified in the House and Senate rules. In most cases, standing committees are the first stop for House and Senate bills. The size of committees and their subject matter jurisdictions were set in the Legislative Reorganization Act of 1946 and have been slightly altered several times since. The ratio of Democrats to Republicans on committees is set for each house through a process of negotiation between majority and minority party leaders. The majority party naturally enjoys a majority on each of the committees and controls the chair, and it usually demands an extra-heavy majority on the most important committees, such as Appropriations, Budget, Rules, and Ways and Means. Not surprisingly, the decision about the ratio of Democrats and Republicans on committees is a point of considerable contention between the two parties.

The avalanche of legislative business cannot be managed and given the necessary specialized attention in the full House and Senate standing committees. For most bills, hearings, negotiations, and markup take place in **subcommittees**. It is in the subcommittees, moreover, where most oversight takes place. The number of subcommittees has multiplied rapidly since the early 1970s when the Democratic party (which controlled the House) decided to parcel out committee powers and responsibilities to over 150 subcommittees. These reforms strengthened the subcommittees by granting each of them a budget and a professional staff, free from the control of the chair of the standing committee, as well as a fixed jurisdiction. Subcommittee chairs were also given additional authority over the conduct of subcommittee business, budget, and staff.

This has substantially decentralized power in the House, giving rise to what some congressional scholars call "subcommittee government." While the proliferation of subcommittees has a good legislative rationale—managing the flow of business and bringing specialized knowledge to bear—it mainly provides members of the majority party with an important base from which to advertise themselves and serve their district.[29]

Select committees are temporary committees created to conduct studies or investigations. They have no power to report bills. They exist because there are sometimes matters that standing committees and subcommittees cannot handle or do not wish to handle. Often the issues before select committees are highly visible and gain a great deal of public attention for their members. The Iran-Contra hearings, for instance, were conducted by special select committees in both the House and the Senate. This was also true of the congressional committees investigating the Watergate scandal and the assassination of President Kennedy.

Joint committees, with members from both houses, are organized to facilitate the flow of legislation. The Joint Budget Committee, for instance, helps to speed up the normally slow legislative process for considering the annual federal budget.

While it is probably an exaggeration to call **conference committees** the "third house of Congress," as some political observers do, there is no denying their central role in the march of bills through the legislative labyrinth. Although they are supposed to "split the difference" between versions of bills coming out of the House and the Senate, conference committees sometimes will add, subtract, or amend provisions that are of great consequence. The bill that a conference committee reports must be voted up or down without changes by each house.

Table 11.3
Standing Committees of Congress

(Classification of committee type is that of the Democratic party, the majority party in both houses of the 102nd Congress.)

Senate	House

Major (No senator can serve on more than two committees)
   Agriculture, Nutrition and Forestry
   Appropriations
   Armed Services
   Banking, Housing and Urban Affairs
   Budget
   Commerce, Science and
     Transportation
   Energy and Natural Resources
   Environment and Public Works
   Finance
   Foreign Relations
   Government Affairs
   Judiciary
   Labor and Human Resources
	Exclusive (A representative cannot sit on any other committee except the Budget Committee.)
	   Appropriations
	   Rules
	   Ways and Means
	
	Major (A representative may serve on only one of the following committees.)
	   Agriculture
	   Armed Services
	   Banking, Finance and Urban Affairs
	   Education and Labor
	   Energy and Commerce
	   Foreign Affairs
	   Judiciary
	   Public Works and Transportation

Minor (No senator can serve on more than one committee.)
   Aging
   Budget
   Intelligence
   Rules and Administration
   Small Business
   Veterans' Affairs
	Nonmajor (A representative may serve on two committees if he or she has no major committee assignment.)
	   Budget
	   District of Columbia
	   Government Operations
	   House Administration
	   Interior and Insular Affairs
	   Merchant Marine and Fisheries
	   Post Office and Civil Service
	   Science, Space and Technology
	   Small Business
	   Standards of Official Conduct
	   Veterans' Affairs

Select
   Children, Youth and Families
   Hunger
   Narcotics Abuse and Control
	Select Committees
	   Aging
	   Children, Youth and Families
	   Hunger
	   Intelligence
	   Narcotics Abuse and Control

Lieutenant Colonel Oliver North is sworn in before giving testimony to
the Senate Select Committee investigating the Iran-Contra scandal.

GETTING ON COMMITTEES   Because committees are so central to the legislative
process, getting on the right one is important for reelection and for achieving the
policy goals of members of Congress. Committee assignments are largely determined by the political parties, members' seniority, and members' preferences.
Each party in each chamber goes about the assignment process in a slightly different way. House Democrats use their Steering and Policy Committee, chaired
by the Speaker, to make assignments. House Republicans use a Committee on
Committees, on which strong Republican states are most heavily represented. In
the Senate, both parties use small steering committees made up of party veterans
and leaders to make assignments. For Republicans, the key player in the appointment of this committee is the chairperson of the Republican Conference (all Republican senators); for Democrats, the key player is the Majority Floor Leader.

   Committee assignments are mainly a problem for newcomers to Congress
and for members who are trying to change their committee assignments. Most
lawmakers get settled into a committee, become specialists in the area of that
committee's jurisdiction, and gradually move up the committee hierarchy as they
accumulate years of service.

   The principle of seniority generally prevails in the appointment of committee
and subcommittee chairs. For most of this century prior to the 1970s, appointment
by seniority was an unbreakable rule. The most senior committee member of the
majority party automatically became chair of the committee; the most senior member of the minority party automatically became the ranking minority member.
Both Republicans and Democrats in the House instituted the secret ballot among
party members for the election of chairs after 1974, however, and now seniority
is occasionally ignored. This is rare, however. Removal of powerful chairs, such
as Wright Patman from the House Banking Committee in 1975, is not the norm.

   New members of the House and the Senate submit their preferred committee
assignments to the relevant party organizations. For the most part, they try to get

an assignment to a committee that will help them get reelected. Chances are slim that they will be assigned to one of the elite power committees, given their lack of seniority—the Senate Finance and House Ways and Means committees, let us say, or the Appropriations committees—so most members of Congress try for an assignment that will help them service their district: Agriculture if from a farming constituency; Interior if from a mining or an oil constituency; Armed Services or Defense if from a district or a state that has important military posts or defense contractors; and so on.[30] For the most part, they get their way if there are openings.

COMMITTEE CHAIRS Not so long ago, chairs of committees were the absolute masters of all that they surveyed. From 1910, when substantial power was stripped from the Speaker of the House and distributed to committee chairs, until the early 1970s, when the Democrats reined in the autocratic chairs they had created, those who headed congressional committees were their unchallenged masters. Committee chairs could assign staff, control the budget, create or abolish subcommittees at will, control the agenda, schedule meetings, and report (or refuse to report) bills to the floor.

Over the last two decades, power has migrated in both houses from the chair to the subcommittees, on the one hand, and to the party and house leadership (as we shall see later) on the other. Decisions that were entirely the province of the chair in the past are now entirely in other hands or are shared with others.

This is not to suggest that committee chairs are unimportant. Indeed, chairs remain the most influential and active members of committees. Committee chairs today cannot command obedience, but they are at the center of all of the lines of communication, retain the power to schedule meetings and control the agenda, and are usually the most senior and experienced member of their committee, to whom some deference is owed.[31]

Political Parties in Congress

The electoral needs of lawmakers and the organization of Congress along committee and subcommittee lines radically fragments and decentralizes the institution. At times, the institution threatens to fly apart, with each member of Congress going his or her own way. How is it that Congress is able to operate at all? What forces help to pull these fragments together so that concerted and rational action on the nation's business is sometimes possible? The answer may be found in a number of institutions that help foster cooperation and coordination. The most important of these are the political parties, congressional leadership, and ideology, though none entirely solve the problem of fragmentation.

Political parties have a strong presence in Congress. Members come to Washington, D.C., as elected candidates of a political party. At the opening of each session, they organize their legislative business along political party lines. At the opening of each new Congress, each party caucus or conference meets to select party committees and officers. The majority party in the House selects the Speaker of the House, while the majority party in the Senate selects the president pro tempore and the Majority Leader. The majority party in each house also selects committee and subcommittee chairs, and decides the party ratios on them. Technically, the majority party only nominates and introduces motions to the full House and Senate to effect all of the above, but it always wins on a straight party line vote.

THE PARTY COMPOSITION OF CONGRESS   The Democratic party has dominated the modern Congress (see Figure 11.8). It has been the majority party in the House of Representatives for all but four years since 1932. In the Senate, the Republicans have managed to be in the majority for only ten years since 1932. Democratic domination of House elections has remained solid, despite the GOP landslides in the 1980 (Reagan), 1984 (Reagan), and 1988 (Bush) presidential elections. The party division in the Senate is much closer, and it would not overly shock political

Figure 11.8 The party division in Congress, 1932–1994. (*a*) Democratic strength in the House of Representatives. (*b*) Democratic strength in the Senate.

Source: National Journal, *November 10, 1990, p. 2715 and authors' research.*

(*a*)

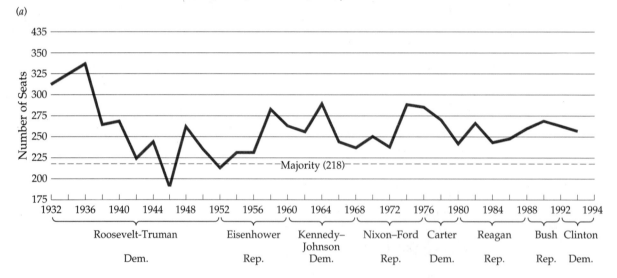

(*b*)

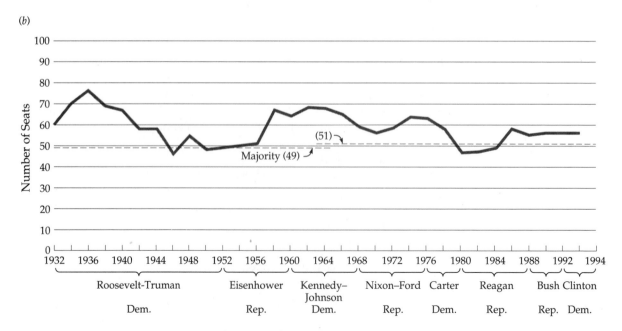

professionals if the Republicans were to recapture that body. Because of the great advantages enjoyed by incumbents, however, the probability of continued Democratic congressional dominance remains very high.[32]

PARTY VOTING   The political parties provide some glue for melding together the decentralized fragments of Congress and for lending some coherence to the legislative process. Party labels are important cues for members of Congress as they decide how to vote on issues before the committees and on the floor of the House and the Senate. We know this from a long tradition of research on party divisions in roll call voting. This research tells us that party affiliation is the best predictor of the voting behavior of members of Congress. If you believe, as we do, that parties are the most important instrument in a democracy for assuring that the preferences of the people guide the behavior of their leaders, then this is good news indeed.

Figure 11.9 shows how often a majority of Democrats opposed a majority of Republicans in recent Congresses. We see that party cohesion is fairly substantial in both chambers.

While the parties serve as the main bonding agents in Congress, one shouldn't read more into this than is warranted. The glue of the parties is very weak, indeed. Although party label remains the best predictor that we have of the voting behavior of members of Congress, the party is not nearly as important as it is in parliamentary systems like that of Great Britain. There, not just simple majorities, but at least 90 percent of the members of one party oppose at least 90 percent of the members of the main opposition party on virtually every major vote.[33] In the German Bundestag, party line votes have averaged close to 98 per-

Figure 11.9 Partisan roll calls in Congress[a]

[a]Percentage of recorded votes in which a majority of Democrats opposed a majority of Republicans.

Source: Congressional Quarterly Weekly Report *(December 28, 1991) p. 3789.*

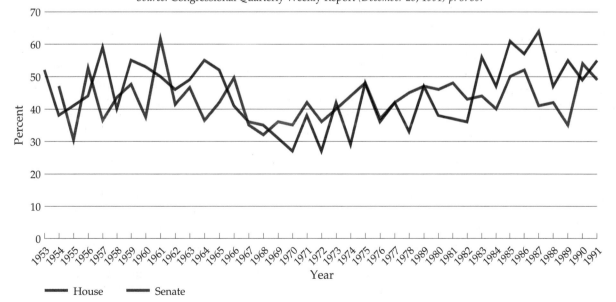

cent in recent years. On major issues like the budget, typically 100 percent of one party opposes 100 percent of the other party (or parties) in both Great Britain and Germany.

It's not entirely clear whether party voting differences are caused directly by party affiliation or indirectly by the character of constituencies. Some scholars have found strong independent party effects. Others argue that the tendency of people in the same party to vote together is a reflection of the fact that Democratic lawmakers come from districts and states that are similar to each other and that Republican lawmakers come from ones that are different from those of Democrats. Republicans generally come from higher-income districts than Democrats. Democratic districts, in turn, tend to have more union members and racial minorities in them. The strongest tie, in this line of argument, is between the member of Congress and the constituency and not between the member and the party.[34]

Differences in party voting also may be attributed to ideological differences between the two parties. Democrats tend to fall on the liberal side of the ideological spectrum, whereas Republicans tend to fall on the conservative side.[35] This seems to be the case, not because the parties can compel compliance and discipline, but because people who see the world in liberal terms tend to drift toward the Democratic party, while those who see the world in conservative terms find their way to the Republican party.

The importance of ideology in Congress is shown by the existence of cross-party ideological coalitions. They go in both liberal and conservative directions. Moderate Republicans from the Northeast, popularly known as the "Gypsy Moths," are nearly as likely to vote with their Democratic colleagues as with their copartisans. Southern Democratic conservatives are more likely to vote with Republicans than with their own party on major issues. The support of those "Boll Weevil" Democrats was an important reason the Reagan legislative program enjoyed such success in 1981 and 1982.[36] Judge Clarence Thomas won confirmation to the Supreme Court because nine Democratic senators broke with their party colleagues.

PARTY DISCIPLINE   American parties are weak organizations, virtually without resources to impose discipline on their legislative representatives. Members of Congress are essentially independent operators who mount their own campaigns. Their reelection prospects depend on their own ability to service their district and to maintain good relationships with their constituency. They do not depend on the party.

Our parties, moreover, have no power to compel compliance with party positions or to discipline recalcitrant members who stray from the party line, assuming that a party line can be discerned. Party caucuses have no authority to strip lawmakers of their party label, no matter how egregious their behavior. At most, they can sometimes remove a renegade party member from an important committee. The Democrats did this to Representative Phil Gramm of Texas in 1983, removing him from his post on the Budget Committee after he led the fight for the Reagan budget proposal against his own party.

Congressional Leadership[37]

The political parties also work through the leadership structure of Congress, since the leaders of the majority political party are, at the same time, the leaders of the House and the Senate.

Speaker of the House Thomas Foley of Washington and Senate Majority Leader George Mitchell of Maine were treated by the press, the public, and other public officials as the principal spokespersons of the Democratic-dominated Congress during the Republican presidency of George Bush.

LEADERSHIP IN THE HOUSE   The leader in the House of Representatives is the Speaker of the House. The position is recognized in the Constitution and stands in the line of succession to the presidency, right after the vice-president. The Speaker is treated by his colleagues, the president, and the media as the spokesperson for the House in general and the majority party in Congress in particular. Because of divided party control of the presidency and Congress in recent years—a Republican president and a Democratic House—the Speaker receives the kind of attention usually given to the leader of the opposition in parliamentary systems. Speakers like "Tip" O'Neill of Massachusetts, Jim Wright of Texas, and Thomas Foley of Washington have been among the most visible and recognizable congressional figures of their day.

Until 1910, the Speaker exercised great power over the House legislative process. The basis of his power was his right to appoint committees and their chairs, and his position as chair of the Rules Committee. The revolt of the rank and file against Speaker "Uncle Joe" Cannon in 1910 resulted in the Speaker's removal from the Rules Committee and the elimination of his power to appoint committees and their chairs.

From 1910 until the early 1970s, the weakened Speaker competed with a handful of powerful committee chairmen for leadership of the House. A few Speakers, such as Sam Rayburn of Texas, were able to lead by sheer dint of their personality and interpersonal skills, but power tilted toward the chairs most of the time.

The Democratic Caucus staged a revolt against the committee system after 1974 and restored some of the powers of the Speaker. Responsibility for committee appointments was transferred from the Ways and Means Committee to the Committee on Committees, chaired by the Speaker; a new Steering and Policy Committee, chaired by the Speaker, was created; and the power to appoint all Democratic members of the powerful Rules Committee was given to him.[38] Adding these to their other powers—referral of bills to committee, control of the House agenda, appointment of select committees, and direction of floor debate—gave such Speakers as "Tip" O'Neill considerable leadership resources.

The Democratic Caucus, when it is the majority—which is virtually all of the time now—also selects a *Majority Floor Leader* to help the Speaker plan strategy and manage the legislative business of the House. Neither House nor party rules spell out the responsibilities of this office. The nature of the job depends very much on what the Speaker wants and the incumbent's talents and energy. In recent years, the Majority Floor Leader position has been a way station on the road to the Speakership; Jim Wright and Tom Foley both held the job. The Speaker is also assisted by *party whips*, who act as liaisons between the leaders and the rank and file. They count heads on important bills, explain leadership positions, try to persuade, gather legislative intelligence, and ensure that the faithful get to the floor to cast their votes.

The minority party—now almost always the Republicans—elects a *Minority Floor Leader*. The Minority Floor Leader is the chief spokesperson and legislative strategist for the opposition. He not only tries to keep his forces together but also seeks out members of the majority party who might be won over against the House leadership on key issues. Minority Leader styles differ greatly. Robert Michel of Illinois tried to cooperate with the Democratic party majority, believing that it was the only way to win approval for portions of the GOP agenda. This style was heartily rejected by a vocal GOP minority led by *minority whip* Newt Gingrich of Georgia, whose style was to attack and to expose the shortcomings of the Democrats as part of an overall strategy to gradually win a Republican majority in elections for the House.

LEADERSHIP IN THE SENATE   Leadership in the Senate is less visible. Those with the formal leadership titles exercise little influence. The presiding officer of the Senate is the vice-president of the United States, but he is rarely in evidence and has no power other than the right to vote to break a tie, should one occur on the Senate floor. The majority party elects a *president pro tempore* (always the member with the most seniority) to preside in the absence of the vice-president. That job is such an unrewarding chore that even the president pro tempore rarely acts as the presiding officer.

The Senate *Majority Leader* is as close as one comes to a leader in this body, but the powers of the office pale before those of the Speaker of the House. He has some influence in committee assignments, assignment of office space, and control of access to the floor of the Senate. He is also important in the scheduling of the business of the Senate. The degree of actual influence is based less on formal powers, however, than on skills of personal persuasion, the respect enjoyed from colleagues, visibility in the media as majority party spokesperson, and the role as the center of many of the various communications networks.

The power of the position is thus personal and not institutional; it cannot be passed on to the next leader. Some leaders have failed to use the office to gain mastery of the legislative process (Mike Mansfield), some have been moderately successful (Robert Byrd), while only a few have developed the office to the limits of its potential (Robert Taft and Lyndon Johnson). The majority party in the Senate remains a body of independent, relatively equal members tied together very loosely by the thin threads of party loyalty, ideology, and their mutual concern for the next election. It is not an environment conducive to decisive leadership.

The Senate *Minority Leader* exercises even less power than the Majority Leader. A skilled politician can use the position, however, to articulate the minority legislative program, rally the troops for partisan battle when necessary, and force concessions from the majority. Robert Dole of Kansas was extremely effective, as was Everett Dirksen of Illinois in the early 1960s.

Members of the Congressional Black Caucus pose on the steps of the Capitol. The Black Caucus has become an important factor in the legislative process in recent years.

Caucuses

Another instrument by which lawmakers attempt to fashion coherence in a legislative environment that favors decentralization and fragmentation is the caucus. A caucus is a group formed by lawmakers who share a particular set of policy interests that are not otherwise recognized in the formal organization of the House or the Senate. These informal organizations are not recognized in congressional rules, nor do they receive appropriations to run their affairs. Nevertheless, they are both numerous—over 100 of them in the One Hundred and First Congress—and important in the legislation process.[39] They serve as a basis for the formation of political coalitions that cross the boundaries between committees, parties, and even chambers.

Rules and Norms

Like all organizations, Congress is guided by both formal rules and informal norms of behavior. Rules specify precisely how things should be done and what is not allowed. Norms are generally accepted expectations about how people ought to behave and how business ought to proceed. Some norms of behavior are common to both houses of Congress. Senators and representatives are expected to act with courtesy and civility toward one other, even if they detest one another; thus the informal prohibition against the use of names and the elaborate references to the "honorable gentleman from Wisconsin" or the "senior senator" from California. Some observers believe that civility has declined in recent years. The nastiness surrounding the Bork and Thomas Supreme Court nomination fights in the Senate are good examples of this mood change. Senators and representatives are also expected to become specialists in some area or areas of policy and to defer to the judgment of specialists on most bills. This mutual deference is known as **reciprocity**. Lawmakers are also expected to be willing to compromise, strike deals, and "horse-trade." Finally, they are all expected to respect the reelection motivations of their colleagues and to be willing to make certain accommodations in the legislative schedule for such purposes.

Because of its large size, legislative life in the House of Representatives is much more rule-bound than in the Senate; it tends to be more organized and hierarchical (see Table 11.4 on the differences between the two chambers). Leaders in the House have more power, procedures are more structured, and the members have a harder time making their mark. The Senate tends to be a more open and fluid place, and it lodges less power in its leaders than does the House. Each senator is more of an independent operator than his or her House colleagues. The Senate is a much more relaxed place that accommodates mavericks and tolerates the foibles of its members. Because there are fewer of them, and because they have larger constituencies and longer terms, senators have more visibility and prestige. We can see this in the frequency with which senators become presidential aspirants—something that is quite uncommon for representatives.

Table 11.4
Differences Between the House and Senate: Rules and Norms

Senate	House
Informal, open, nonhierarchical	Rule-bound, hierarchical
Leaders have few formal powers	Leaders have many formal powers
Members may serve on two or more major committees	Members restricted to one major committee
Less specialized	More specialized
Nonrestricted floor debate	Restricted floor debate
Unlimited amendments possible	Limited amendments
Amendments need not be germane	Amendments must be germane
Unlimited time for debate unless shortened by unanimous consent or halted by invocation of cloture	Limited time for debate
More prestige	Less prestige

Differences between the House and the Senate are especially apparent in floor debate. Bills are scheduled for floor debate in the Senate, for instance, not by a powerful Rules Committee, but by **unanimous consent**, meaning that business can be blocked by a single dissenter. Unlike the House, where debate on a bill is strictly regulated as to amendments and time limit, the Senate's tradition allows for unlimited numbers of amendments and unlimited debate. Senators in the minority have used this tolerance of unlimited amendments and debate to good effect. Democratic Senator Howard Metzenbaum (Ohio) and former Republican Senator Lowell Weicker (Connecticut) were acknowledged masters of the "endless amendments" ploy to block legislation. Senators also can try to talk a bill to death through a filibuster. Senators have been known to talk for hour upon hour, often working in shifts. The only requirement is that they say something; they cannot hold the floor without speaking. During a filibuster, senators have read from novels or have quoted verse, have told stories about their children, and have quoted long lists of sports statistics. The purpose is to force the majority to give up the fight and to move on to other business. The record for a single senator belongs to Strom Thurmond of South Carolina, who held the floor for over 24 hours during the debate over the 1957 Civil Rights bill.

When a very strong majority favors a bill or when a bill that has great national import and visibility is before the body, the Senate can close debate by invoking cloture. Cloture requires support by three-fifths of those present and voting. It is very rarely tried; it very rarely succeeds. The most famous case of the invocation of cloture was in 1964, when the Civil Rights bill was brought to a vote after a lengthy filibuster by southern senators was broken.

Congressional Staff

Most of the media attention during deliberations on the Tax Reform Act of 1986 went to lawmakers like Dan Rostenkowski and high executive branch officials like Secretary of the Treasury James Baker. Most of the drafting of the final legislative package was done, however, by David Brockman, chief of staff of the Joint Committee on Taxation. There is nothing unusual in this. The size and influence of the congressional staff—what some Washington, D.C., observers call the "shadow government"—has grown enormously over the past quarter century. About 20,000 people (more than three times the number of only 25 years ago) now work directly for members of Congress, the vast network of committees and subcommittees, and specialized institutions within Congress. The reasons for this growth are tied to the interests of each member of Congress and to the needs of the institution as a whole. For members, staff help them keep in touch with, and service, the constituency, and do their jobs as legislators. For the institution, staff helps Congress keep up with the expertise of the executive branch.

In the House, each representative has about 18 staff members, while, in the Senate, each senator has about 32, though there is great variation, given that budget for staff is based on state population size. Each member may use the staff as he or she wishes. In general, about one-half of staff time is devoted to constituency service and reelection, and about one-half to legislative activities.[40] This is remarkably different from Great Britain, where members of Parliament share secretaries and offices.

Congress enhances its expertise by creating and staffing a range of specialized agencies that serve Congress as a whole: the Congressional Budget Office,

DOING
POLITICS

*A Senate Aide
Makes a
Difference*

Senate aide Mark Bisnow recounts some of his Capitol Hill experiences in the following selection.

The hour hand edged toward midnight on the clock above, but Senator John Danforth had settled at my desk on the second floor of the Capitol, propped up his feet, and asked if I had any interesting memos he could read. Danforth was an impressively intellectual legislator, but his unusual request at this late hour, I knew, had less to do with an inquisitive mind than with sheer political horse sense. All evening I (as an aide to Senate Republican Leader Bob Dole) had been cloistered in negotiations on the 1987 trade bill with Danforth's aide, Sue Schwab—a young, knowledgeable, and above all savvy adviser who had brought her boss to my office at just the right moment. Our discussion had foundered on a key word, and Danforth, one of the Senate's most influential players on trade issues, firmly urged us to find a middle ground. No doubt Sue expected that his hovering presence would quickly bring me around.

She was almost right. Senator Danforth himself did not participate in our continuing talks—he knew that

Sue was better versed in the details and had utmost confidence in her judgment—but with tactical adroitness he wandered into the adjoining conference room regularly to see how we were doing and to remind us that he was waiting. Meanwhile Senator Dole, who as party leader juggled many simultaneous obligations, had departed the office to other activities, delegating me to reach a compromise in his behalf. Under normal circumstances it might have been hard to resist Danforth's entreaties; he was, after all, a United States senator, and not least a friendly and important member of my boss's party. But earlier in the day I had recommended to Dole what I thought our position ought to be, and he had, in his clear if laconic way, nodded and told me to "work it out." Now I felt an obligation to protect his interests.

Fortunately I was not left holding the fort alone: I had invited an ex-Dole aide and one-time Reagan trade adviser, Claud Gingrich, to stop by and lend a second opinion; and current Reagan trade officials Alan Holmer and Judy Bello had agreed to station themselves in the Senate Reception Room, a hundred yards away, to supply needed detail, for which purpose I shuttled

the Library of Congress, the Office of Technology Assessment, and the Government Accounting Office. When an important piece of legislation comes before Congress—let's say the president's budget—lawmakers need not depend on the data and studies provided by the executive branch—in this case, the Treasury, the Council on Economic Advisors, and the Office of Management and Budget—but can call on its own Joint Budget Committee and the Congressional Budget Office staff for an independent assessment.

Some scholars, journalists, and lawmakers worry about the growing influence of staff. Senator Patrick Leahy of Vermont once complained of staff: "Senators, I fear, are becoming annoying constitutional impediments to the staff.... Someday we may just allow the staff to vote and skip the middleman."[41] Overwhelmed by conflicting commitments, so the argument goes, lawmakers have allowed unelected personal, committee, and institutional staff to draft legislation, to negotiate on legislative details, to guide questioning at hearings, to deal with

through darkened corridors once or twice during the evening. Sheila Burke, Dole's hardworking chief-of-staff, remained on the scene, as she often did, late into the night, and aides from other offices continually passed through. The Leader's suite functioned as a nerve center for the Senate, and in these gilded and high-ceilinged rooms, crystal chandeliers gazing over our work, it was easy indeed to feel powerful. Claud, Alan, and Judy agreed strongly with the position I had staked out, and Sheila offered her traditional encouragement. Ultimately I persuaded myself that our position was no less than critical to U.S. trade policy—and that Senator Danforth's presence, if anything, signified his eagerness for a result, giving us the upper hand if we could simply hold out.

Suddenly Dole phoned in for a status report. Sheila took the call, explaining that we were stalled on one word and describing Danforth's exasperation. It happened that the word was pivotal; we were drafting what would be enacted as the "Super 301" provision of the trade law, requiring retaliation against foreign markets hostile to American exports, and the language we chose would determine how many specific countries and practices an administration would be mandated to target. But the idea that one word could divide as admittedly sounded trivial, and Dole, who deservedly possessed a reputation as the Senate's most effective legislator, instructed us to give Danforth what he wanted. To Dole it was not worth the fight that I had supposed: he calculated that in return for a concession Danforth would give us something on another occasion when it mattered more. The negotiation was quickly adjourned.

Moments like this captured the delight and frustration of an aide. I have helped draft a major initiative—most of which would survive the intervention of my boss, become law, and have real impact. And yet I had latitude only as he gave it to me. I gladly accepted the arrangement. No one had elected me; it was exciting enough to operate in the shadow of public figures and satisfying enough to be able to invest public policy with as much of my own viewpoint as I did.

Source: From Mark Bisnow, *In the Shadow of the Dome: Chronicles of a Capitol Hill Aide* (New York: William Morrow, 1990), pp. 15–17.

interest groups, and to strike deals with executive branch officials. Many worry that the proliferation of staff intermediaries makes real deliberation between lawmakers less likely.[42] Others, less worried, respond that staff merely do what lawmakers want them to do and that the range of discretion practiced by staff is exaggerated (see "Doing Politics" above). None has job tenure; none are members of the Civil Service; and all can be fired if they don't stick pretty close to the needs and the interests of the individual member of Congress or of Congress as an institution.

Legislative Responsibilities: How a Bill Becomes a Law

We can put much of what we have learned to work by seeing how a bill works its way through the legislative labyrinth to become a law. The path by which a bill becomes a law is so strewn with obstacles that few survive. Only about 6 percent of all bills introduced into the One Hundred and First Congress were enacted. To make law is exceedingly difficult; to block bills from becoming laws is a relatively easy matter. At each step along the way (see Figure 11.10), a "no" decision can stop the passage of a bill in its tracks. As one account puts it,

> A United States Congressman [and Senator] has two principal functions: to make laws and to keep laws from being made. The first of these he and his colleagues perform only with sweat, patience, and a remarkable skill in the handling of creaking machinery; but the second they perform daily, with ease and infinite variety.[43]

INTRODUCTION OF THE BILL   A bill can only be introduced by a member of Congress. In reality, bills are often written in the executive branch or by interest groups. The initial draft of the bill that became the Tax Reform Act of 1986, for instance, was fashioned in the Treasury Department by a committee headed by then Secretary James Baker. With the exception of tax bills (which must originate in the House), a bill may be introduced in either the House or the Senate. In the House, a member does so by putting it into the **hopper** (a box watched over by one of the House clerks). In the Senate, a member must announce a bill to the body after being recognized by the presiding officer.

The lawmaker who introduces the bill is its *sponsor* (see Table 11.5). Shrewd lawmakers try to build support by signing on as many cosponsors as possible; it's even better for the bill if cosponsors cross party and ideological lines.

COMMITTEE ACTION   The presiding officer in the Senate and the Speaker in the House refer the bill to the appropriate standing committee. About 80 percent of the time, the rules are pretty clear about which committee is the appropriate one. Revenue bills go automatically to the Ways and Means Committee in the House and to the Finance Committee in the Senate. In the other cases, leaders can exercise some discretion or even send a bill to more than one committee. The more non-automatic referrals there are, of course, the more power there is in the hands of House and Senate leaders. Bills they like can go to friendly committees; bills they don't like can go to unfriendly ones. The 1964 Civil Rights bill, for instance, was routed to the sympathetic Commerce Committee rather than to the hostile Judiciary Committee, which was chaired by arch-segregationist James Eastland of Mississippi.

Committee chairs will normally pass the bill on to the appropriate subcommittee for hearings. Many bills die at this stage, when either the subcommittee or the full committee declines to consider it further.

If the bill makes it this far, the subcommittee will generally hold **hearings** on it, taking testimony from those for and against it. Subcommittee staff not only help prepare representatives and senators for the questioning but also often take part in the questioning themselves. The subcommittee may then forward the bill as rewritten by the staff and subcommittee members, or it can decide to allow the bill to go no further.

Rewriting the bill is called the **markup**. This is usually a very intense period of bargaining and deal making, with an eye toward fashioning a bill that will

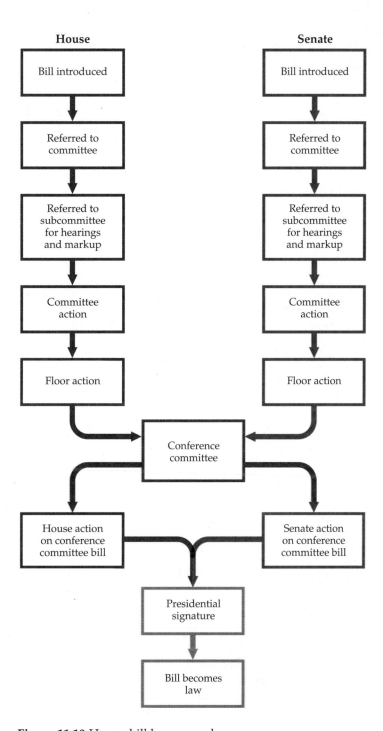

Figure 11.10 How a bill becomes a law

Note: Most, but not all bills, follow this pattern. A bill can be derailed at any stop in the above passage. A subcommittee or a committee can refuse to report a bill; a bill may be defeated on the floor of each chamber; a conference committee may fail to reach agreement on a compromise; the conference bill may be defeated in either chamber; and the president may veto the bill.

Table 11.5
Types of Legislation

Bill: Most legislative proposals before Congress are in a bill form. They are designated H.R. (House of Representatives) or S. (Senate) according to where they originate, followed by a number assigned in the order in which they were introduced, from the beginning of each two-year congressional term. *Public bills* deal with general questions, and become public laws if approved by Congress and signed by the president. *Private bills* deal with individual matters, such as claims against the government, immigration and naturalization cases, and land titles. They become private laws if approved and signed.

Joint Resolution: A joint resolution, designated H. J. Res. or S. J. Res., requires the approval of both houses and the president's signature, just as a bill does, and has the force of law. There is no significant difference between a bill and a joint resolution. The latter generally deals with limited matters, such as a single appropriation for a specific purpose. Joint resolutions also are urged to propose constitutional amendments, which do not require presidential signatures, but become a part of the Constitution when three-fourths of the states have ratified them.

Concurrent Resolution: A concurrent resolution, designated H. Con. Res. or S. Con. Res., must be passed by both houses but does not require the president's signature and does not have the force of law. Concurrent resolutions generally are used to make or amend rules applicable to both houses or to express their joint sentiment. A concurrent resolution, for example, is used to fix the time for adjournment of a Congress and to express Congress's annual budgeting plan. It might also be used to convey the congratulations of Congress to another country on the anniversary of its independence.

Resolution: A simple resolution, designated H. Res. or S. Res., deals with matters entirely within the prerogatives of one house. It requires neither passage by the other chamber nor approval by the president and does not have the force of law. Most resolutions deal with the rules of one house. They also are used to express the sentiments of a single house, to extend condolences to the family of a deceased member, or to give "advice" on foreign policy or other executive business.

Source: Roger H. Davidson and Walter J. Oleszek, *Congress and Its Members* (Washington, D.C.: Congressional Quarterly Press, 1990), p. 312.

muster majority support in the full committee and the floor of the House and the Senate, and gain the support of the president. The staff plays a central role in the markup. Lawmakers and staff are usually in contact with relevant interest groups and executive branch policymakers, as well.

The subcommittee reports its action to the full committee. The committee chair, in consultation with other important members of his or her committee, may choose to hold its own hearings and markup sessions, may decide to kill the bill outright, or may simply accept the action of the subcommittee. On most bills, if the subcommittee has done its job well and has consulted with the most important players on the full committee—especially the chair—the committee will simply rubber-stamp the bill and move it along for floor action.

FLOOR ACTION   If a bill is favorably reported from committee, congressional leaders schedule it for floor debate. In the House, a bill ordinarily first must go to the Rules Committee for a rule under whose terms a bill will be considered. A rule will specify things like the amount of time for debate and the number (if any) of amendments allowed. The Rules Committee may choose not to issue a rule at all or to drag its feet, as it did with civil rights bills until the mid-1960s. Or it can grant a "closed rule," allowing only an up-or-down vote without amendments, as it generally does with tax bills. Floor debate in the Senate, where rules do not limit debate, is much more freewheeling.

After floor debate, the entire membership of the chamber votes on the bill, either as reported by the committee or (more often) after amendments have been added. If the bill receives a favorable vote, it then goes through the same obstacle course in the other house or awaits action by the other house if the bill was introduced there at the same time.

CONFERENCE COMMITTEE   Even if the bill makes it through both houses, its journey is not yet over. Bills passed by the House and the Senate are almost always different from one another, sometimes in minor ways and sometimes in quite substantial ways. Before going to the president, conflicting versions of a bill must be rewritten so that a single bill gains the approval of both houses of Congress. This compromise bill is fashioned in a conference committee made up of members from both the House and the Senate. It must be voted up or down on the floors of the House and the Senate; no amendments or further changes are allowed. If, and only if, both houses approve it, the bill is forwarded to the president for his consideration.

PRESIDENTIAL ACTION   The president plays an important constitutional role in turning a bill into a law; it is why he or his assistants and advisors are usually consulted throughout the legislative process. If the president approves the bill, he signs it and it becomes law. If he is not particularly favorable but does not want to block the bill, it becomes law after ten days if he takes no action. He can also **veto** the bill and return it to Congress. A bill can still become law by a two-thirds vote of each house, which would override the president's action. A president can also kill a bill at the end of a congressional session if he takes no action and Congress adjourns before ten days pass. This is known as a **pocket veto**.

Oversight

Oversight is another important responsibility of Congress. Oversight involves keeping an eye on how the executive branch carries out the provisions of the laws that Congress has passed, and on possible abuses of power by its officials, including the president. Oversight is primarily the province of the committees and subcommittees of Congress, and it is among Congress's most visible and dramatic actions. In recent years, public attention has been especially drawn to committee investigations of the Iran-Contra affair, the scandals at the Department of Housing and Urban Development, the savings and loan bailout debacle, and criminal activity at BCCI (The Bank of Commerce and Credit, International).

Senator Alan Cranston of California defends his acceptance of campaign contributions from Charles Keating of the failed Lincoln Savings and Loan Association before the Senate Ethics Committee in 1991. His Senate colleagues voted to reprimand him for his actions.

Hearings are an important part of the oversight process. Testimony is taken from agency officials, outside experts, and such congressional investigatory institutions as the Government Accounting Office (GAO) and the Office of Technology Assessment. The hearings are not simply information-gathering exercises, however. As often as not, they are designed to send signals from committee members to the relevant part of the bureaucracy. Hearings that focus on the overly aggressive efforts of IRS agents to collect taxes, for instance, are a clear signal to IRS officials that they had better rein in their agents before the next round of hearings on the budget. Hearings that focus on abuses in the awarding of defense contracts, to take another familiar example, are designed to force more stringent contracting behavior by the Pentagon.

Congress spends an increasing amount of its time on oversight. Given the scale of federal government activities, however, it can only pay attention to a small tip of the iceberg that is the executive branch. If it can't do it all, how does it decide where to direct its attention? For the most part, it responds to the complaints and the entreaties of constituents and interest groups.[44] This ensures not only that important problems will be attended to, but also that the representatives and senators who are involved can claim credit and stockpile goodwill (and contributions) for the next election cycle. One problem with this "firealarm" model of oversight, however, is the favored attention it gives to the concerns of organized interest groups.

CONGRESSIONAL ETHICS

To many Americans, the phrase "congressional ethics" is an oxymoron, that is, a contradiction in terms. While most Americans would probably not go as far as Mark Twain, who once described Congress as the only "distinctively native American criminal class . . . ,"[45] it is widely believed that things are not as they should be in Congress with regard to ethical behavior. While there is no evidence that members of Congress are any less honest than any other group of professionals—being in the public eye and under constant press scrutiny, in fact, probably keeps the number of lawbreakers among them comparatively low—the number of recent, highly publicized cases has not helped their collective reputation. Jim Wright was forced to quit the Speakership in 1989, for instance, after the House Ethics Committee supported charges of fund-raising improprieties brought against him by Representative Newt Gingrich of Georgia. Majority Whip Tony Coelho was forced out of office in the same year on charges of conflict of interest. "Abscam," an FBI "sting" operation in the early 1980s, netted six representatives who had agreed to accept bribes from agents posing as wealthy Arabs pushing for special legislative treatment.

Other Americans worry about what seem to be undue and excessive privileges paid for by taxpayers: discounted meals, haircuts, medical care, and electronic goods; protection against parking tickets and bounced checks; and periodic "junkets" to exotic locations, purportedly on legislative business. Still others believe that the main ethical problem of Congress is the close relationship members enjoy with interest groups and their dependence on those who give them large contributions.[46]

The growing public outcry over these developments has forced Congress to create codes of ethics for its members and to establish ethics committees in both houses in order to oversee them. The codes of ethics concentrate primarily on disclosure of personal finances, restrictions on the amount of outside income that a member can earn, and regulation of the personal use of taxpayer-provided services, such as the frank and staff. Most observers and many lawmakers do not believe, however, that these reforms have gone very far in restricting practices that undermine public confidence in the ethical conduct of members of Congress. Many Americans have responded by supporting the national movement to limit the terms of members of Congress and by voting against incumbents with increasing frequency.

CONGRESS, PUBLIC POLICY, AND DEMOCRACY

Democracy

Now that we know more about what representatives and senators do and how Congress operates, we can turn our attention to the central theme of this text: how our political institutions contribute to, or detract from, democracy.

One of the main dramas of congressional life is the struggle between majority public opinion and interest groups as the engine of the legislative process. Each and every member of Congress, we have seen, face both kinds of pressure from their constituencies. The evidence that we have presented suggests that, when the public is aware of issues and expresses its opinion, Congress is quite responsive to it. There are many examples. Medicare legislation, as described in this chapter's opening story, closely followed popular sentiment. When Ronald Reagan tried to scale back Social Security and the federal role in environmental protection, he was unable to do so, despite his enormous personal popularity. Members of Congress knew from their constituents and from public opinion polls that strong national majorities opposed him.

This connection between majority opinion and congressional behavior operates through a number of mechanisms, reviewed in this and earlier chapters, including public opinion polls, mail from constituents, electoral competition, and the party system. The connection between the majority and congressional behavior is especially clear during "realignment" periods, described in Chapter 8, "Political Parties." A realignment brings a new wave of lawmakers into Congress. Riding the crest of a critical election and supported by a new consensus in public opinion, the new legislative majority refashions the congressional machinery—particularly its committee system—and takes public policies in new directions. The period after 1896, for instance, saw a shift in policy toward support for industrialization and the large corporation. The period after 1932 saw the federal government take on responsibility for management of the economy and the alleviation of some forms of social distress.[47]

While Congress responds to popular preferences to an impressive degree, it is far from perfect in doing so. There is not only the one-in-three times (on average) when it acts contrary to public opinion but also the many occasions when it must grapple with issues about which the public is either unaware or has no opinion. It is here that interest groups become especially important. It seems that, when the issues before Congress are technical and obscure, and public attention is low, Congress is responsive to narrow, particularistic, and privileged interests. At such times, lawmakers parcel out government benefits to the well organized in their districts and states. This is significantly related to the prominent role played by interest groups, large contributors, and PACs. While it is hard to prove the existence of *quid pro quos*—trading campaign contributions for legislative favors—the suspicion of such arrangements is widespread among citizens and professional Congress watchers alike. At the least, lawmakers hear frequently from the organized. The general public may not know the details of a congressionally mandated action in the Interior Department, for instance, but one can be sure that mining and oil interests will be in touch. Interest groups, of course, "sing with a strong upper-class accent"; they seriously overrepresent the privileged. This poses serious problems for the principle of political equality. Since the few are heard at the expense of the many, moreover, popular sovereignty is not well served in this aspect of congressional functioning.

The relationship between Congress and democracy, then, is a complicated one. The suggestion just made is that Congress is frequently, but not always, an effective instrument of democracy. The principles of popular sovereignty and political equality are especially at risk when Congress responds to organized and privileged groups rather than to the public. To the degree that this is a problem, however, the blame should probably not be on the shoulders of Congress but on a party system that does not work as well as it might as a democratic instrument. When the party and electoral systems accurately transmit popular preferences to Congress, legislators respond.

Congress as Policymaker

A frequently heard criticism of Congress is that it is so parochial and fragmented that it cannot fashion coherent national policy.[48] The argument goes like this. First, Congress is filled with members who are judged by the voters on the basis of their individual attributes and service to the district and to interest groups, not on the basis of the performance of Congress as a whole. One result is that lawmakers worry more about themselves than the standing and effectiveness of their institution or its collective, national, policymaking responsibilities.[49]

Second, because lawmakers are responsive to organized interests, serve the constituency as their first order of business, and try to avoid difficult decisions that might put their reelection at risk (or so it is claimed), Congress cannot easily tackle the nation's most difficult problems or think about solutions in general terms. Congress would rather practice "distributive" politics, in which benefits are parceled out to a wide range of constituency and interest group claimants. While this conforms to the self-interested electoral calculations of the individual member, it is, according to many, the basis for the overall ineffectiveness and decline of Congress as an institution relative to the presidency. Increasingly, it is suggested, both the American people and public officials look to the president for leadership on crucial national issues.

It is hard to assess the validity of these criticisms. The evidence is mixed. We have seen that Congress has, at times, fashioned broad and coherent national policies in response to tangible problems and strong majority opinions. We have also seen that Congress retains a far greater policymaking role than legislative bodies in parliamentary systems. Nevertheless, it is inescapable that Congress seems to function best as a policymaker when the president is able to provide strong leadership. Although Congress is able to lead on individual pieces of legislation, both Congress and the American people now expect the president to take the lead in fashioning broad legislative programs for the country.[50]

SUMMARY

The framers of the Constitution wanted to fashion a legislative branch that was both energetic and limited. They granted Congress legislative power, gave it an existence independent of the executive branch, and enumerated an impressive range of powers. They also gave the other branches powers to check legislative excesses, created a bicameral body, and strictly denied certain powers to Congress.

Structural change has shaped Congress, influencing it to increase in size, expand the volume and complexity of its business, and become more institutionalized and professional.

Congress is a representative institution. Its members are constantly balancing the preferences of the people in their constituencies and important interest groups and contributors. Because elections are the most important mechanism for representation and because they are the way in which members attain office, elections dominate the time and energy of lawmakers and shape how Congress organizes itself and goes about its business.

To conduct its business, Congress depends on an elaborate set of norms and rules, a web of committees and subcommittees, political parties, legislative leaders, and an extensive staff. Several of these instruments encourage fragmentation, decentralization, and occasional gridlock but also the development of the specialized expertise that allows Congress to meet the executive branch on equal terms. Others help members coordinate and expedite legislative business.

Congress is highly responsive to majority opinion when the issues are visible to the American people and when the people have formed clear preferences about them. Much of the time, however, Congress responds mainly to interest groups and those who make large contributions, putting the principles of popular sovereignty and political equality at risk. A stronger party system would probably make Congress a more consistent instrument of democracy.

To Ponder

1. Has the preservation of Congress as a strong, independent policymaking voice in our national affairs helped or hindered the country? Would things be better if the president had more power?

2. Would a parliamentary system be more efficient and effective than the kind of legislative branch we now have? Would a parliamentary system be more democratic?

3. Would strengthening our political parties help or hinder the ability of Congress to carry out its responsibilities?

4. Are representatives and senators more or less honest than other professionals, like doctors, lawyers, and accountants?

5. Has the influx of money into congressional elections helped or hurt democracy? If the latter, how might the collection and use of campaign funds be better controlled?

Suggested Readings

Birnbaum, Jeffrey H., and Alan S. Murray. *Showdown at Gucci Gulch: Lawmakers, Lobbyists, and the Unlikely Triumph of Tax Reform*. New York: Vintage Books, 1988.
> A wonderfully revealing and entertaining account of the passage of the 1986 Tax Reform Act; filled with memorable characters and the details of legislative life.

Caro, Robert. *The Years of Lyndon Johnson*. New York: Knopf, 1982.
> This classic and award-winning biography of Lyndon Baines Johnson of Texas reveals more about how Congress worked in the "old days" than virtually any academic treatise.

Davidson, Roger H., and Walter J. Oleszek. *Congress and Its Members*, 3rd ed. Washington, D.C.: Congressional Quarterly Press, 1990.
> A detailed summary of the prevailing scholarly and journalistic literature on the U.S. Congress.

Dodd, Lawrence C., and Bruce I. Oppenheimer. *Congress Reconsidered*, 4th ed. Washington, D.C.: Congressional Quarterly Press, 1989.
> Original articles summarizing research on virtually every aspect of Congress by leading congressional scholars.

Fenno, Richard F., Jr. *Home Style: House Members in Their Districts*. Boston: Little, Brown, 1978.
> A modern classic that examines what members do in their districts and why they do it.

Fiorina, Morris P. *Congress: Keystone of the Washington Establishment*, 2nd ed. New Haven, CT: Yale University Press, 1989.
> A very influential book that worries about how the individualistic rational calculations of members of Congress may hurt collective responsibility and institutional effectiveness.

Mayhew, David R. *Congress: the Electoral Connection.* New Haven, CT: Yale University Press, 1974.
>   This study argues that the primacy of electoral calculations for members of Congress shapes the organization and operation of Congress.

Smith, Hedrick. *The Power Game: How Washington Works.* New York: Random House, 1988.
>   A highly entertaining look at how policy is made in Washington, D.C., by a very perceptive journalist.

Vogler, David J., and Sidney R. Waldman. *Congress and Democracy.* Washington, D.C.: Congressional Quarterly Press, 1985.
>   An attempt to grapple with the complicated question of the relationship between Congress and democracy; the authors conclude that Congress's failure to meet democratic standards hurts its legitimacy with the American people.

Notes

1. Quoted in James L. Sundquist, *Politics and Policy* (Washington, D.C.: Brookings Institution, 1968), p. 303. Most of the remainder of this story is from ch. 7 of Sundquist's book.
2. *Congressional Record*, Vol. III (July 17, 1965), p. 17739.
3. *Public Papers on the Presidents*, 1965, p. 813.
4. Charles Warren, *The Supreme Court in U.S. History* (Boston: Little, Brown, 1919), p. 195.
5. Roger H. Davidson and Walter J. Oleszek, *Congress and Its Members* (Washington, D.C.: Congressional Quarterly Press, 1990), p. 18.
6. For a review of the literature on the history of Congress, see David W. Brady and Elaine K. Swift, "Out of the Past: Theoretical and Methodological Contributions of Congressional History," *P.S.: Political Science and Politics* (March 1991), pp. 61–64.
7. Nelson Polsby, "The Institutionalization of the U.S. House of Representatives," *The American Political Science Review*, Vol. 62, No. 2 (March 1968), p. 151.
8. Polsby, "The Institutionalization of the House of Representatives," pp. 144–168.
9. Lawrence C. Dodd, "Congress and the Quest for Power," in Lawrence C. Dodd and Bruce Oppenheimer, eds., *Congress Reconsidered*, 4th ed. (Washington, D.C.: Congressional Quarterly Press, 1989).
10. Quoted in Charles Henning, *The Wit and Wisdom of Politics* (Golden, CO: Fulcrum, 1989), p. 235.
11. Abraham Lincoln, Announcement in the *Sagamo Journal*, New Salem, Illinois, June 13, 1836.
12. Davidson and Oleszek, *Congress and Its Members*, p. 119.
13. Janet Clark, "Getting There: Women in Public Office." *Annals*, Vol. 515 (May 1991), p. 63.
14. Gary C. Jacobson, *The Politics of Congressional Elections*, 2nd ed. (Boston: Little, Brown, 1987), p. 16.
15. Jacobson, *Politics of Congressional Elections*, p. 49.
16. Tom Kenworthy, "The Color of Money," *Washington Post Weekly Edition*, November 6–12, 1989, p. 13.
17. Davidson and Oleszek, *Congress and Its Members*, p. 59.
18. David R. Mayhew, "Congressional Elections: The Case of the Vanishing Marginals," *Polity*, Vol. 6 (1974), pp. 298–301.
19. "Elections in 1990," *Congressional Quarterly Weekly Report* (November 10, 1990), p. 3800.
20. Richard Hall and Frank W. Wayman, "Buying Time: Moneyed Interests and the Mobilization of Bias in Congressional Committees," *American Political Science Review* (September 1990), Vol. 84, No. 3, pp. 797–820.
21. David R. Mayhew, *Congress: The Electoral Connection* (New Haven, CT: Yale University Press, 1974).
22. Howard L. Reiter, *Parties and Elections in America* (New York: St. Martin's, 1987), p. 197.

23. Hedrick Smith, *The Power Game: How Washington Works* (New York: Random House, 1988), p. 146.

24. Malcolm Jewell, "Legislators and Their Districts," *Legislative Studies Quarterly*, Vol. 13, No. 3 (August 1988), pp. 403–412.

25. Bruce Cain, John Ferejohn, and Morris Fiorina, *The Personal Vote: Constituency Service and Electoral Independence* (Cambridge, MA: Harvard University Press, 1987); and Glenn Parker, *Homeward Bound: Explaining Change in Congressional Behavior* (Pittsburgh: University of Pittsburgh Press, 1986).

26. R. S. Erikson, "Constituency Opinion and Congressional Behavior," *American Journal of Political Science*, Vol. 22 (1978), pp. 511–535; Robert S. Erikson and Gerald C. Wright, "Voters, Candidates, and Issues in Congressional Elections," in Lawrence C. Dodd and Bruce I. Oppenheimer, eds., *Congress Reconsidered*, 4th ed. (Washington, D.C.: Congressional Quarterly Press, 1989), pp. 91–116.

27. Alan Monroe, "Consistency Between Public Preferences and National Policy Decisions," *American Politics Quarterly*, Vol. 7 (1979), pp. 3–19; Benjamin I. Page and Robert Y. Shapiro, "Effects of Public Opinion on Policy," *American Political Science Review*, Vol. 77 (1983), pp. 175–190.

28. Richard Rose, "Politics in England," in Gabriel A. Almond and G. Bingham Powell, Jr., eds., *Comparative Politics Today* (Glenview, IL: Scott, Foresman/Little, Brown, 1988), p. 162.

29. Morris P. Fiorina, *Congress: Keystone of the Washington Establishment*, 2nd ed. (New Haven, CT: Yale University Press, 1989); Mayhew, *Congress: the Electoral Connection*.

30. David A. Rhode and Kenneth A. Shepsle, "Democratic Committee Assignments in the House of Representatives: Strategic Aspects of a Social Choice Process," in Matthew D. McCubbins and Terry Sullivan, eds., *Congress: Structure and Policy.* (New York: Cambridge University Press, 1987).

31. Richard L. Hall, "Committee Decision Making in the Postreform Congress," in Laurence C. Dodd and Bruce I. Oppenheimer, eds., *Congress Reconsidered*, 4th ed. (Washington, D.C.: Congressional Quarterly Press, 1989).

32. Fiorina, *Congress*, p. 134.

33. Frank J. Sorauf and Paul Allen Beck, *Political Parties in America* (Glenview, IL: Scott, Foresman/Little, Brown, 1988), p. 410.

34. Davidson and Olezsek, *Congress and Its Members*, p. 347.

35. Robert S. Erikson and Gerald C. Wright, "Voters, Candidates, and Issues in Congressional Elections," in Laurence C. Dodd and Bruce I. Oppenheimer, eds., *Congress Reconsidered*, 4th ed. (Washington, D.C.: Congressional Quarterly Press, 1989).

36. Jacob O. Stampen and John R. Davis, "Multi-Issue Coalitions in the Congress," paper presented at the Supercomputing Conference, Orlando, Florida, November 1988.

37. See John J. Kornacki, ed., *Leading Congress: New Styles, New Strategies* (Washington, D.C.: Congressional Quarterly Press, 1990).

38. Lawrence C. Dodd and Bruce I. Oppenheimer, "Consolidating Power in the House: The Rise of a New Oligarchy," in Laurence C. Dodd and Bruce I. Oppenheimer, eds., *Congress Reconsidered* (Washington, D.C.: Congressional Quarterly Press, 1989).

39. Susan Webb Hammond, "Congressional Caucuses in the Policy Process," in Lawrence C. Dodd and Bruce I. Oppenheimer, eds., *Congress Reconsidered* (Washington, D.C.: Congressional Quarterly Press, 1989).

40. Fiorina, *Congress*, pp. 118–121; Michael Malbin, *Unelected Representatives* (New York: Basic Books, 1980).

41. Jeffrey H. Birnbaum and Alan S. Murray, *Showdown at Gucci Gulch: Lawmakers, Lobbyists, and the Unlikely Triumph of Tax Reform* (New York: Vintage Books, 1988), p. 217.

42. Fiorina, *Congress*, pp. 120–121.

43. Robert Bendiner, *Obstacle Course on Capitol Hill* (New York: McGraw-Hill, 1964), p. 15.

44. Matthew D. McCubbins and John Schwartz, "Congressional Oversight Overlooked: Police Patrols and Fire Alarms," in Matthew D. McCubbins and Terry Sullivan, eds., *Congress: Structure and Policy* (Cambridge, MA: Cambridge University Press, 1987).

45. Henning, *Wit and Wisdom of Politics*, p. 38.

46. Philip M. Stern, *The Best Congress Money Can Buy* (New York: Pantheon, 1988).

47. David W. Brady, *Critical Elections and Congressional Policymaking* (Stanford, CA: Stanford University Press, 1988).

48. Fiorina, *Congress*; Mayhew, *Congress: the Electoral Connection*; Jacobson, *Politics of Congressional Elections*.

49. Morris P. Fiorina, ''The Decline of Collective Responsibility'' *Daedalus*, Vol. 109, No. 3 (Summer 1980); Cain, Ferejohn, and Fiorina, *The Personal Vote*.

50. Sundquist, *Politics and Policy*, pp. 425–429.

12

The President: Tribune of the People?

THE REAGAN REVOLUTION

When Ronald Reagan took office as president of the United States in January 1981, he buoyantly interpreted his landslide victory in the November elections as a mandate to pursue sweeping changes in government policy. In his Inaugural Address, Reagan promised a "new American revolution." He would "get government off the backs of the people" by cutting back regulations; he would fight "fraud, waste, and abuse" and would put America's fiscal house in order by cutting spending on domestic programs; he would spur economic growth by sharply cutting taxes; and he would "rebuild" America's armed strength by sharply increasing military spending.

The Reagan Legislative Program: Once in office, Reagan made his tax and budget proposals a top priority. On February 18, 1981, he announced his "Program for Economic Recovery." He asked Congress for action on the largest tax cut in American history ($750 billion over six years), targeted primarily at upper-income groups and corporations; the steepest rise in defense spending in peacetime American history (20 percent per year); and major reductions in domestic social programs, eliminating some of them entirely, like job training and public-service employment.

The Response: The Reagan program was breathtaking in scope, and radical in its implications for the role of government in American life. Democrats in Congress were alarmed. Even some of Reagan's strongest backers among conservative Republicans expressed skepticism. How would the numbers add up: how could taxes be cut, the defense budget be increased, and Social Security be left alone without piling up huge deficits? The Democrats' opposition seemed formidable. They still controlled a large majority of seats (243 out of 435) in the House of Representatives, which would have to agree to any laws that would change taxes or appropriations. The slim new Republican majority in the Senate couldn't do anything by itself. Many observers thought that nothing much would come of Reagan's proposals: they would be buried in committees, or compromised, and business would go on as usual.

The Reagan Offensive: President Reagan thought otherwise. He brought all his personal skills and energy, and every resource of the presidency, to bear upon the task of passing his program. From the start, he cultivated friendly relations with congressmen of both parties, even his arch foe Thomas P. ("Tip") O'Neill (Speaker of the House of Representatives), with whom he joked and told Irish stories. In stark contrast to the aloof Jimmy Carter, Reagan invited Democratic congresspersons to the White House for informal chats or breakfast gatherings. He would also give some members presidential cuff links or arrange for them to use the presidential box at the Kennedy Center for the Performing Arts.

Reagan offered more than personal charm. He also proved to be a skilled and shrewd deal maker in the frenetic trading for votes: sugar price supports to win over members of Congress from Louisiana; funding increases for Amtrak

411

and Conrail and energy subsidies to the poor to keep moderate Republican legislators from the Northeast (the so-called gypsy moths) behind the tax and budget package; natural gas deregulation and a slowdown in conversion to coal for congressmen from the oil-producing states, Oklahoma and Texas. Nor, in passing out carrots, did Reagan neglect the stick: Democrats from conservative areas in the South, where a majority of voters had supported Reagan, found the White House turning up the heat in their own districts, mobilizing wealthy conservative groups like the National Conservative Political Action Committee, the Moral Majority, and business political action committees; sending Vice-President Bush and Congressman Jack Kemp to stir up pressure; and getting major campaign contributors to urge cooperation with Reagan.[1]

Reagan also worked to build up his popularity with the general public, aiming to go over the head of Congress and to create public pressure to pass his program. Like most new presidents, Reagan began with a fairly high level of popular approval. He was able to sustain and increase it in the early months because of his genial and winning public personality, the emotional patriotism that swelled among the American people on the return of U.S. hostages from Iran in January, and the successful launching of the space shuttle Columbia.

In April, Reagan turned his survival of an assassination attempt into a public relations triumph, displaying courage and humor. (On awakening from surgery, he is reported to have said to his wife Nancy, "Honey, I forgot to duck.") While still recovering, Reagan made a dramatic televised appearance before Congress to plead for his program. As Dan Rostenkowski, leader of the Democrats on the tax issue, put it: "(T)he President can gear up his army with just one television appearance. That's fighting the Army, Navy, Marines and Air Force."[2]

Reagan's popularity was so high by the time he left the hospital, especially in the districts of southern conservative Democratic members of Congress (known as the "boll weevils"), that the Democratic liberal majority and the Democratic House leadership were virtually helpless to stop the tide. The question on the tax and appropriations bills had become a simple one: "Are you with Ronald Reagan or against him?"[3]

Success: With the question posed this way, Ronald Reagan could not lose. Although polls showed continuing public support for most domestic social programs, the politicans were awed by the scale of Reagan's electoral victory and by the height of his popularity. Speaker "Tip" O'Neill said that he received "more letters than I had seen in my entire career . . . asking me to give the president's program a chance."[4]

The administration's budget sailed through the Senate by a vote of 72–20, with hardly a change. Budget aide David Stockman later gloated: "The politicians had flinched. They had rubber-stamped the Reagan Revolution."[5] Though Republicans were in the minority in the House of Representatives, Reagan also got his way there at every critical juncture.

Promising "no compromise," Reagan turned up the pressure, telling the San Antonio Jaycee Convention that it was time to "restore economic sanity" and finish the job. Hoarse and tired after that speech, he nonetheless telephoned final appeals to 16 wavering House members, apologizing for the late calls, answering questions, noting problems, staying low key and persuasive. (O'Neill lamented, "The members adored it when he called . . . they can go back to their districts and say, 'I was talking to the President the other day.' "[6]) The next day Reagan won the budget "reconciliation" vote, shattering the Democrats' unity by winning a batch of "boll weevil" votes from the South, and got most of what he wanted in domestic budget cuts and the defense buildup.

The president also worked tirelessly for his tax cut bill. In order to win the votes of Democratic "boll weevils" who were worried about deficits, he agreed to reduce the tax cut from 30 percent to 25 percent and to give it a later starting date. He countered talk of the bill as a giveaway to the rich by insisting that it would spark economic growth and help all Americans. He countered worries about a deficit with the "supply side" gospel that growth would increase tax receipts. The demoralized Democrats engaged in a bidding war, promising even deeper tax cuts for oil and gas and other industries. Much to their surprise, Reagan happily embraced these cuts, too, and the administration's Economic Recovery Tax Act was passed on July 29, 1981.

Effects: the Reagan Revolution would prove to have profound effects, not all of them happy. During most of the 1980s, for example, the economy as a whole grew rapidly, but wealthy people got most of the gains, while the middle class and the poor made little or no progress.[7] For years, the tax cuts limited the availability of new money for domestic programs. (Stockman eventually admitted that this was one purpose of the tax cuts.[8]) U.S. military power grew enormously—and at great cost—at the same time that the Communist threat was collapsing of its own weight. There were huge budget deficits, averaging $165 billion per year (compared with an average of $28 billion for the previous 30 years); the Reagan deficits *tripled* the total national debt built up since the nation's founding and continued to haunt the country on into the 1990s. These matters will be discussed in detail in later chapters. But whatever the long-term problems, in the short run the Reagan Revolution was a huge political success.

Reagan and the Modern Presidency: Very few politicians, journalists, or political scientists anticipated Reagan's success. Observers were astounded. The conventional wisdom of the 1970s had been that the presidency was "imperiled" and that strong presidential leadership was unlikely, if not impossible.

If we take things at face value, it appears that Ronald Reagan was a heroic figure, able single-handedly to shake America from its lethargy and to reinvigorate the presidential office. We shall see in this chapter, however, that presidential will, determination, and personality represent only part of the story. No matter what the leadership qualities of a president are, he always plays on a field determined by the constitutional design and evolution of the office, a particular *governmental* and *political* environment, and a larger context of economic, social, cultural, and international *structure*. Moreover, what sort of president we have, and what he wants and tries to accomplish, is itself influenced by political and structural factors.

Reagan's Political Context: The times were ripe for Ronald Reagan's brand of leadership. During the 1970s, the nation had experienced dramatic drops in its international economic and military standing, in confidence in its fundamental institutions, and in corporate profits and people's standards of living. Polls showed that people were ready, even desperate, for change. Media, business, and academic elites began calling for a reorientation of public policy. Conservative political action committees, think tanks, and interest groups, fueled by massive corporate funding, mounted a campaign for a conservative policy renewal in Washington, D.C. Congress, itself under pressure from financial contributors and unsure of how to escape the downward spiral, looked for presidential leadership and ultimately responded when Reagan provided it. The Reagan Revolution, from this viewpoint, involved much more than Ronald Reagan; to understand it requires that we understand not just the personality, style, and effectiveness of Reagan as president but also the governmental, political, and structural contexts within which he operated.

The decisions and choices made by the person who sits in the Oval Office, his skills and personality and character, profoundly affect the nature of our political life. But individual presidents should not be considered free agents who can do as they wish. After presidents take the oath of office, they enter into an "institution" that is stable and permanent. The presidency is not entirely plastic, ready to be molded into whatever shape a president desires. It is strongly shaped by individuals and groups from the governmental and political spheres, by rules and traditions, and by the structural sphere (the economy, culture, population, and the international system).

In this chapter, we focus on the interplay among individual presidents, the office of the presidency, and the spheres of government, politics, and structure. We shall show how the presidency has changed over the years. Most important, we shall raise questions about the implications of the modern presidency for the practice and enjoyment of democracy, asking whether presidents tend to embody the wishes of the citizenry or to thwart them.

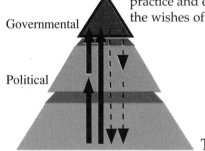

Governmental

Political

Structural

THE EXPANDING PRESIDENCY

Modest Beginnings

The increase in presidential responsibilities, burdens, power, and impact in a little over 200 years is obvious if we compare the presidencies of George Bush and George Washington—200 years apart.

In 1990, George Bush presided over a federal budget involving $1,252 *billion* in annual expenditures and a federal establishment with approximately 2.8 million civilian employees. He made decisions concerning laws, regulations, and spending that touched every aspect of the society and the economy. He was commander in chief of the armed forces, with some 2 million men and women in uniform; 909 military bases at home and 395 scattered throughout the non-Communist world; and perhaps 20,000 deliverable nuclear warheads, enough to obliterate every medium-sized or large city in the world many times over. Bush's United States in 1990 had a population of about 250 million diverse people, living in cities, suburbs, and countryside, and working in offices, factories, shops, and fields; a gross national product of $5,463 billion, or nearly $22,000 for each person in the country; and a land area of some 3.6 million square miles, stretching from Alaska to Florida and from Hawaii to Maine.

President George Washington reviews his troops before sending them to Pennsylvania to quell the "Whiskey Rebellion" of economically pressed farmers. Washington raised a larger force for this purpose than he had led against Cornwallis at Yorktown.

By contrast, when George Washington took office as the first president, he had a total budget (from 1789 through 1791) of just $4,269,000 and only a handful of federal employees. Even by 1801 there were still only about 300 federal office-holders in the capital. Washington's cabinet consisted of just five officials: the secretaries of state, war, and the treasury, a postmaster general, and an attorney general who acted as his personal attorney rather than as head of a full-fledged Justice Department. The entire Department of State consisted of just one secretary, one chief clerk, six minor clerks, and one messenger.

In 1790, even though the United States had just won its war for independence from England, only about 700 Americans were in uniform, and they had no way to project force around the world. Federal government functions were few. In fact, the new president had to work hard to get across the idea that he was as important as the governor of Massachusetts; when George Washington toured New England, only his skill and obstinacy got Governor Hancock to call on him, rather than vice versa. The entire United States consisted of only the 13 original eastern and south-eastern states, with only 891,364 square miles of land area; the population was only about 4 million persons, most of whom were living on small farms.

The Founders' Conception of the Office of President

The Founders certainly had in mind a presidency more like Washington's than Bush's. As we discussed in Chapter 2, Article II of the Constitution provided for a single executive that would be strong compared with the Congress-dominated Articles of Confederation, but the Constitution's sparse language barely hinted at the range of things that twentieth-century presidents would do. The Constitution made the president "commander in chief" of the armed forces, for example, with-out any suggestion that there would be a vast standing army that presidents could commit to conflicts abroad without declarations of war. It empowered presidents to appoint and to "require the opinion in writing" of executive department heads, without indicating that a vast federal bureaucracy would evolve. The Constitution provided that presidents could from time to time "recommend . . . measures" to Congress, without specifying that they would propose legislative programs dominating the legislative agenda. Still, the vague language of the Constitution proved flexible enough to encompass the great expansion of the presidency. (Students should reread Article II of the Constitution, in Appendix III.)

The Dormant Presidency

In Chapter 4, we described some of the great structural changes in the economy, society, and territory of the United States that led to an enormous expansion in the federal government. Certain presidents played important parts in these trends, and the office of the presidency changed, along with the country. (Look again at the Appendix, in which all past presidents are listed. If you do not already know the names and dates of the most prominent presidents, you should learn them.)

From the time of George Washington's inauguration at Federal Hall in New York City—when the future site of the capital in Washington, D.C., was still undeveloped swampland—for the 100 years until the end of the nineteenth century, the presidency, for the most part, conformed to the designs and the intentions of the Founders. The presidency did not, by and large, dominate the political life of the nation. Policymaking at the federal level tended to be located in Congress. Presidents saw their responsibility as primarily involving the execution of policies decided by Congress. Congress was a fully coequal branch of government, or perhaps more than equal; its members felt in no way inferior to, or subordinate to, the president.

Why does the early presidency seem so puny in comparison with the contemporary presidency? Surely it is not because early presidents were less intelligent, vigorous, or ambitious; some were and some weren't. A far more satisfying answer is that the nation did not often require a very strong presidency prior to the twentieth century, particularly in the key area of foreign policy and military leadership. As Alexander Hamilton put it in *The Federalist Papers*, "of all the cases of concerns of government, the direction of war most peculiarly demands those qualities which distinguish the exercise of power by a single head."[9] Only in the twentieth century did the United States become a world power, involved in military, diplomatic, and economic activities around the globe. With that development came a simultaneous increase in the power and responsibility of the president.

It was not until the late nineteenth century, moreover, that the economy of the United States was transformed from a simple, free market economy of farmers and relatively small firms, requiring little government supervision, to a corporate-dominated economy, with units so large that their every action had social consequences. The great increase in the public consequences of private business actions eventually led to a demand for more management by the government of the American economic system. As this role of government grew during the course of the twentieth century, so, too, did that of the president.

Though the presidency was largely dormant during the late eighteenth and most of the nineteenth centuries, events and the actions of several presidents during this period anticipated what was to happen to the office in our own time.

Precedents were set; expectations were formed; rules were changed. Several presidents and their actions stand out as particularly important in connection with the eventual development and expansion of the office.

The administration of **George Washington** set the stage in several important respects. Most significantly, Washington solidified the prestige of the presidency at a time when executive leadership was mistrusted. His administration also clearly affirmed the primacy of the president in foreign affairs (particularly in making peace with Great Britain and in dealing with revolutionary France). Further, Washington set a precedent for presidential involvement in fashioning a domestic legislative program, by promoting Treasury Secretary Hamilton's proposals for a uniform currency, a central bank, protective tariffs to protect American manufacturers, and transportation projects.

Though **Thomas Jefferson** was hostile to a vigorous central government before assuming office (he thought democracy worked better in small jurisdictions that were close to the people), his presidency is notable for his bold action in acquiring the Louisiana Purchase from France, which roughly doubled the size of the United States and opened the continent for Americans all the way to the Pacific Ocean. Again, we see here the seeds of increased foreign policy responsibilities for the president.

Andrew Jackson's presidency is especially notable for its effects on the place of the presidency in the affections of the American people. It was Jackson who helped transform the presidency into a popular institution, a place within the government where the needs and aspirations of the people might be met. Part of this had to do with his rough-hewn frontier style; part had to do with the manner of his election (he was elected with broader popular participation than ever before); and part had to do with his vigorous opposition to the Bank of the United States, which was seen by most of the population as a tool of the wealthy.

James Polk is often ignored in civics books' accounts of "great" presidents. But Polk was very important for the development of the presidency because of his energetic exercise of his powers as commander in chief of the armed forces. By moving U.S. troops into combat zones where Mexican and Republic of Texas forces were engaged, and knowing that U.S. troops would be fired upon, he effectively sparked a war with Mexico that resulted in the further territorial expan-

President Andrew Jackson was widely hailed as a hero for opposing the "monster" Bank of the United States.

President Lincoln and General McClellan at the Civil War battlefield of Antietam.

sion of the United States to include most of what is now the southwestern United States plus California.

The federal government and the duties of the president remained very small through the first half of the nineteenth century. Many early and mid-nineteenth century presidents, like Tyler, Taylor, Fillmore, Pierce, and Buchanan, had little to do and are little remembered.

Abraham Lincoln is probably the most important president of the nineteenth century in terms of the later development and expansion of the office. It was under Lincoln that we see the most dramatic exercise of the commander in chief's "war powers" before modern times. In order to win the Civil War and to preserve the Union, Lincoln invoked "emergency powers" based on his broad reading of the Constitution: he raised and spent money and deployed troops on his own, with Congress only acquiescing afterward. He temporarily suspended the right of habeas corpus and allowed civilians to be tried in military courts. He freed the slaves in the confederate states by issuing the Emancipation Proclamation. During the Civil War, government tax revenues escalated, expenditures increased to unprecedented levels, and the number of civilian federal employees exploded.

After the Civil War was over, the federal government and the presidency shrank once again. But then the government's domestic functions gradually grew toward the end of the nineteenth century as the country industrialized; presidents administered new programs in the Department of Agriculture (1861) and then the Department of Commerce and Labor (established in 1903, made separate in 1913), and the Pendleton Civil Service Act of 1883 laid the foundations for a modern administrative state (discussed further in Chapter 13, "The Executive Branch").

The Twentieth-Century Transformation

The growth of the presidency accelerated at the beginning of the twentieth century. When **Theodore Roosevelt** took office in 1901, he vigorously pushed the prerogatives and enhanced the powers of the office as no president had done since

Lincoln. He was happiest when he was moving the troops as commander in chief or serving as the nation's chief diplomat: he sent the "Great White Fleet" of navy steamships around the world to demonstrate American power; he intervened in small nations around the Caribbean to protect American economic and political interests; and he successfully mediated a dispute between Japan and Russia, for which he won the Nobel Peace Prize.

On the domestic front, Theodore Roosevelt pushed for the regulation of the new and frightening business corporations, especially by "busting" trusts, and he established many national parks. In "Teddy" Roosevelt we see the coming together of an energetic and ambitious political leader and a new set of structural factors in the United States, most especially, emergence as a world power and an industrialized economy.

Woodrow Wilson's presidency marked further important steps in the expansion of the federal government and the presidency. Wilson's "New Freedom" domestic program built upon the Progressive measures of Theodore Roosevelt, including further regulation of the economy by the Federal Reserve Board (1913) and the Federal Trade Commission (1914). Wilson was a great admirer of the British parliamentary system, in which the prime minister formulated the nation's legislative agenda. Wilson was able to do much the same sort of thing himself, because the climate was ripe for reform of American business.

Even more important were foreign affairs. The United States had already emerged on the world stage at the turn of the century, with the Spanish-American War and the Great White Fleet. Under Wilson, World War I brought an enormous increase in activity: a huge mobilization of military manpower (from 144,846 soldiers on active duty in 1911 to 2.8 million in 1918) and a large, new civilian bureaucracy to oversee production and distribution of food, fuel, and armaments by the U.S. "arsenal of democracy." Although these temporary agencies were dismantled at the end of the war, the federal government and the presidency never returned to their earlier modest scale.

It is **Franklin Roosevelt**, however, who presided over the most significant expansion of presidential functions and activities in American history. In a very real sense, the founding of the modern American presidency occurred during Roosevelt's administration, in response to the Great Depression and World War II. In 1931, there were some 600,000 federal employees; a decade later, the number topped 1,400,000. The depression had devastated the American economy: at the beginning of 1933, more than one-third (37.6 percent) of nonfarm workers were unemployed.[10] Many companies went bankrupt; countless farmers lost their land. In its first 100 days, the Roosevelt administration and the Democratic majority in Congress pushed into law a series of measures for economic relief that grew into vast programs of conservation and public works, farm credit, business loans, and relief payments to the destitute.

Besides these temporary antidepression measures, Roosevelt's New Deal also permanently established a number of independent regulatory commissions to regulate aspects of business (the stock market, telephones, utilities, airlines) and enacted programs like the Social Security Act to insure workers and their families against disability or retirement and the Wagner Act to help workers join unions and bargain collectively with their employers. Each of these measures required an administrative apparatus; each brought the president into more intimate involvement in the U.S. economy. By the end of the 1930s, a whole new structure was in place to coordinate the new agencies, and in 1939 the Executive Office of the President was established to help the president oversee the federal bureaucracy.

The biggest changes associated with Roosevelt's presidency, however, resulted from World War II. War with Germany and Japan was slow in coming, but, when it came, the government once again mobilized the entire population and the whole economy for the war effort.

In 1941, there were 1.8 million men and women on active military duty; by 1945, 12 million were in uniform. Most were demobilized at the end of the war, but the armed forces remained much larger than in the 1930s and were built up once again for the Cold War and the Korean War. The number of military personnel settled at a level of about 2.7 million in the late 1950s and stayed in that range for decades afterward, with only a small rise for the Vietnam War. The outcome of World War II established the United States as a military superpower, overshadowing formerly mighty enemies and allies, unrivaled by any other country but the Soviet Union. Since the time of Roosevelt, all U.S. presidents have administered a huge national security state with large standing armed forces, nuclear weapons, and bases all around the world.

Similarly, World War II brought unprecedented governmental involvement in the economy, with temporary "war agencies" regulating prices and rationing necessities, monitoring and stimulating industrial output, and helping to develop manpower for domestic production. These agencies were dismantled after the war, but they trained a large cadre of officials in an activist view of what the federal government could and should do, and they set precedents for presidential and governmental actions that continue to the present day. All presidents since Roosevelt have presided over a huge government apparatus that has been active in domestic, as well as foreign, policy.

Individual Presidents: How Important Are They?

We cannot be sure to what extent presidents themselves caused this great expansion of the scope of their office. Presidents Lincoln, Wilson, and Roosevelt, for example, not only reacted vigorously to situations but also helped to create those situations; each had something to do with the coming of the wars that were so crucial in adding to their activities and powers. Presumably, not every president would have made the Louisiana Purchase, as Jefferson did, or would have fought the Great Depression so actively and transformed the shape of the presidency so thoroughly, as Roosevelt did. Yet the great presidents were also the product of great times; they stepped into situations that had deep historical roots and dynamics of their own.

Lincoln found a nation in bitter conflict over the relative economic and political power of North and South, focused on the question of slavery in the western territories; war was a likely, if not inevitable, outcome. Wilson and Roosevelt each faced a world in which German expansion threatened the perceived economic and cultural interests of the United States, and in which U.S. industrial power permitted a response. The depression, resistant to Herbert Hoover's more traditional voluntaristic, free market remedies, fairly cried out for a new kind of presidential response. Thus, the great upsurges in presidential power and activity were, at least in part, results of forces at the *structural* level—results of developments in the economy, the culture, American society, and the international system.

PRESIDENTIAL PERSONALITY AND STYLE

Since the president is a single, very visible human being, the American presidency looks like a highly personal office. It seems to change drastically with the personality and style of the person who occupies that office. Indeed, political scientists have written of the "protean" presidency, alluding to the Greek god Proteus, who could change his shape at will,[11] to describe the transformative powers of a single president. As we suggested earlier, however, reality is more complicated than that. The presidency is not just an individual; it is an institution. It is shaped by many other forces both inside and outside government. The president is not an absolute monarch whose whims are law, and we don't get our presidents by chance, like hereditary kings. Nevertheless, the personalities and styles of presidents do make a difference and are worth our attention. We will take a quick look at each of the presidents who have held office since World War II, focusing on their political styles.

The Operating Styles of Recent Presidents

HARRY TRUMAN   Truman's style was feisty and combative, whether taking on Congress, the Republicans, the Soviets, or the press. (When the *Washington Post*'s music critic panned a piano performance by the president's daughter Margaret, Truman called him a "frustrated old man" and an "eight-ulcer man on a four-ulcer job."[12]) Truman won reelection in 1948 in a come-from-behind struggle, in which his "give 'em hell" style of attacking the Republican-controlled Congress apparently greatly pleased the average American. His bold decisions to challenge the Soviets in Europe and to send troops to Korea were admired by some but castigated by others.

DWIGHT EISENHOWER   Eisenhower was a commanding personality who radiated warmth, often displaying a wide grin. Eisenhower's overwhelming popularity was manifested in the polls and in two landslide electoral victories, in which countless Americans wore "I like Ike" buttons. Much like our first war-hero president, George Washington, Eisenhower's public persona was that of a father figure, above the political fray, presiding over the executive branch by means of a staff system. Recent scholars, however, have argued that Eisenhower exerted firm control through "hidden-hand" techniques.[13] Eisenhower enjoyed eight years of relative peace and prosperity; he called himself a "modern Republican," accepting much of the New Deal and Fair Deal social programs inherited from the Democrats Roosevelt and Truman but offering little further innovation.

JOHN KENNEDY   Kennedy was a glamorous president, handsome, young, energetic, stylish, and blessed with a winning sense of humor. (Once a high school boy asked President Kennedy how he had become a war hero. Kennedy replied, "It was absolutely involuntary. They sank my boat."[14]) Elected in 1960 as a Democrat who promised to "get America moving again" after the quiet Eisenhower years, Kennedy encountered a resistant conservative coalition of Republicans and southern Democrats in Congress. Domestically, he could do little more than lay out part of the agenda for what became Johnson's Great Society; in foreign affairs, he pursued anti-Communist activism. Years later, average Americans (though

---

Table 12.1
Presidential Greatness

In 1982, a sample of 953 professors of American
history rated the presidents as follows:

Great
 1. Lincoln
 2. F. Roosevelt
 3. Washington
 4. Jefferson

Near Great
 5. T. Roosevelt
 6. Wilson
 7. Jackson
 8. Truman

Above Average
 9. J. Adams
10. L. Johnson
11. Eisenhower
12. Polk
13. Kennedy
14. Madison
15. Monroe
16. J.Q. Adams
17. Cleveland

Average
18. McKinley
19. Taft
20. Van Buren
21. Hoover
22. Hayes
23. Arthur
24. Ford
25. Carter
26. B. Harrison

Below Average
27. Taylor
28. Tyler
29. Fillmore
30. Coolidge
31. Pierce

Failure
32. A. Johnson
33. Buchanan
34. Nixon
35. Grant
36. Harding

Source: Robert K. Murray and Tim H. Blessing, *Journal of
American History,* December 1983.

not so many historians) rated Kennedy as one of the "great" presidents (see
Table 12.1).

Kennedy was a president with enormous charm, charisma, and style; he was
a leader much admired at home and abroad. Yet, in terms of public policy, President Kennedy did not leave much of a mark. This suggests that, while the personal qualities of a president are important in determining the effectiveness
of leadership, the context and situation in which he finds himself may well be
decisive.

LYNDON JOHNSON Johnson, the former Senate Majority Leader and vice-president who assumed the presidency in 1963 when Kennedy was assassinated, was
spectacularly successful in enacting his Great Society domestic program but then
was battered by the Vietnam War and urban unrest. His style and approach to
the office, successful at certain times in his presidency, served him ill in the end.

At his best, Johnson seemed to be a giant of a man, physically large, bursting
with superhuman energy (he has "extra glands," his fellow Texan, Jack Valenti,
once remarked), working his will on Congress; his powerful personal presence

President Richard Nixon, shown visiting China, scored a number of foreign policy successes.

overawed those he could grasp in his hands. But Johnson's style worked better on the floor of the Senate than on the world stage or on television; there he appeared to be stiff and sober and even a purveyor of deception ("my granddaddy fought at the Alamo"). The press began to talk about a "credibility gap." When things went wrong in Vietnam, Johnson did not seek reelection.

RICHARD NIXON   Nixon was seen by many Americans as a cold, awkward, and perhaps ruthless personality but also as an experienced, shrewd, hard-driving professional, especially adept at foreign policy. Elected in 1968 after pledging to restore law and order at home and to bring peace to Vietnam, Nixon struggled with only limited success to appoint conservative Supreme Court justices, to cut domestic programs, and to centralize control of the federal bureaucracy; he acquiesced in the Democratic Congress's expansion of Social Security and Food Stamps. Nixon scored great successes, however, in opening relations with Communist China and in promoting détente with the Soviet Union. The Nixon style of secretiveness and distrust of those around him no doubt contributed to his behavior in trying to cover up the Watergate crimes and misdeeds (recall Chapter 6); his "hardball" style and image of trickiness left him few friends among other political leaders or the public when the Watergate affair unraveled, and he resigned in disgrace in 1974. While Nixon was a very effective president in some respects, this is another case in which presidential style and personality apparently mixed with a set of unexpected events to destroy a presidency.

GERALD FORD   Ford ascended from the vice-presidency when Nixon resigned and served as president only briefly, until he lost the 1976 election to Jimmy Carter. Ford was widely perceived as solid but unexciting, a former college football center unused to playing quarterback. The effect of Ford's honest and reassuring manner was undercut by public suspicions of a deal when he pardoned Nixon for any crimes committed in the Watergate affair. Ford's apparent propensity for stumbling and pratfalls caused him to become the butt of jokes about physical clumsiness. More important, he had the misfortune to occupy the presidency during a period of deep economic recession and rapid inflation, just after the first OPEC oil price rise of 1973–1974.

President Jimmy Carter won points from the public for his industriousness and informality, but was voted out of office after domestic and foreign policy troubles.

JIMMY CARTER   Carter ran for the presidency as an outsider, projecting an image of moral rectitude and criticizing the "Washington establishment." Carter's relaxed, open, and unassuming "down-home" style, and his deeply religious Southern Baptist values, initially reassured a nation troubled by Vietnam and Watergate.[15] His honeymoon did not last long, however. He alienated people and damaged his reputation with failed efforts to cut public works projects and to defend his advisor Bert Lance against charges of unethical behavior as a banker. Soon newsmagazines depicted a disorganized administration, "radiating chaos" and making enemies on Capitol Hill. Some Americans began to see Carter's awkward speaking style and his efforts at the common touch (wearing sweaters for televised White House talks, for example) as undignified, and his decision making as weak, anguished, or vacillating. His confession of responsibility for a "crisis of the American spirit" apparently provoked more embarrassment than support.

The Carter presidency was, therefore, already in a weakened state when it was hit by a deadly series of events: the second big OPEC oil price rise (in 1979), which helped plunge the United States deeper into economic "**stagflation**"; the introduction of Soviet troops into Afghanistan; and the taking of American hostages in Iran. An image of presidential ineffectuality spread. Carter's popularity in the opinion polls plummeted. Not surprisingly (and in accordance with the "electoral punishment" model discussed in Chapter 9), Carter was decisively repudiated in the 1980 election. He later, however, established a reputation as an outstanding ex-president, specializing in issues of human rights and international peace.

RONALD REAGAN   Like Carter, Reagan also was an "outsider" who attacked the government in Washington, D.C. But Reagan offered some sharp stylistic contrasts with his predecessor. While Carter was cool, Reagan radiated warmth; whereas Carter worried publicly about the nation's "malaise," Reagan conveyed bubbling optimism; Reagan, a long-time movie and TV actor, charmed the public with self-deprecating humor and roused public passions with dramatic appeals and emotion-laden anecdotes; and while Carter often seemed uncertain, Reagan nearly always knew what he wanted. Reagan also had the good fortune to serve as president at a time when the U.S. economy was ready to recover from the oil price shocks and when the Soviet Union was becoming weaker and more conciliatory. At the same time, whereas Carter may have immersed himself too deeply in minor details, Reagan presided rather loosely over the executive branch, leaving specifics to others. Reagan's fuzziness about facts was notorious. At one press conference, he mistakenly claimed that submarine-launched ballistic missiles could be recalled in flight.

GEORGE BUSH Bush, Reagan's vice-president and his successor as president in 1989, projected an image of a "kinder, gentler" president but also less forceful or charismatic. Visiting an elementary school in 1991, and encountering skepticism about whether he was really the president, Bush pulled out a green card and asked, "will you accept American Express?"[16]

Born to a wealthy and prominent family in Connecticut, Bush received a private education at Andover and Yale. He headed West, making his own mark in the rough-and-tumble Texas oil business, and then compiled a long vita in a series of appointive positions in the federal bureaucracy. At one time, Bush was dogged with a "wimp" or "lap dog" label but shed it by means of fierce 1988 campaign rhetoric, his invasion of Panama, and war against Iraq. With a somewhat awkward public manner, lacking Reagan's warmth, popular appeal, or skill at shaping domestic legislation, and facing even stronger Democratic majorities in Congress, Bush neither sought nor achieved much in the way of domestic policy. In the realm of foreign policy, where he felt most comfortable, Bush had the good luck to witness the complete collapse of communism in Eastern Europe and the Soviet Union.

These thumbnail sketches of recent presidents are intended to highlight variations in presidential style and personality. But they cannot take us very far toward understanding what kinds of personal differences are most important or how personalities interact with the institution of the presidency. A more systematic analysis is required. One such analysis—a controversial one—has been proposed by political scientist James David Barber.[17]

A Theory of Presidential Character

According to Barber, much depends upon the president's character, world view, and style. *Style* refers to the president's habitual way of dealing with his main political tasks; it is established in early adulthood with the person's "first independent political success." Herbert Hoover, for example, is said to have acquired his style of intense, self-sacrificing "homework" as a student at Stanford University, where he served diligently as manager of the student government.

A president's *world view*, in this scheme, refers to beliefs about social causality, human nature, and the central moral conflicts of the time. World views are acquired in adolescence and form the basis of political philosophies or ideologies: Hoover's belief, for example, that the federal government should not upset states' rights by direct involvement in relief programs during the depression or Franklin Roosevelt's contrary view that such involvement was altogether proper.

Most central to Barber's theory, though, is the concept of *character*: the president's enduring orientation toward life and toward himself, which is mainly formed in childhood. One crucial dimension of character involves whether a president is *active* or *passive*: full of energy, like the human cyclone Lyndon Johnson, or inactive, like the nap-taking Calvin Coolidge. Another key dimension concerns whether a person is *positive* or *negative*, whether he feels good or bad about life, about the job of the presidency, and about himself.

When these dimensions are combined, they suggest four fundamental types of character. Barber most admires the *active-positive* type; healthy, full of energy and enthusiasm for the job, a "doer." Barber places such presidents as Franklin Roosevelt and John Kennedy in this category, along with Jimmy Carter, Gerald Ford, and Harry Truman.

Active-negative personalities, on the other hand, are said to be dangerous. Their activity has a compulsive, aggressive quality, as if they were trying to compensate for something; it sometimes leads to rigid, inflexible behavior, with disastrous results. Woodrow Wilson, for example, may have suffered damaged self-esteem as a child because of his domineering father, a strict preacher and scholar who humiliated young "Tommy" Wilson in public and forced him to produce perfect translations from Greek and Latin. Wilson subsequently resented authority figures and resisted compromise, even to save his beloved League of Nations treaty.[18] Barber also includes as active-negative personalities Richard Nixon and Lyndon Johnson, both of whom—in the Watergate scandal and the Vietnam War—seemed stubbornly to pursue a course of action after it had disastrously failed.

According to Barber, a *passive-positive* personality like William Howard Taft, Warren Harding, or perhaps Ronald Reagan, deprived of love in childhood, seeks love and affection by being agreeable and cooperative rather than assertive. Passive-positive presidents don't usually accomplish much. A *passive-negative* personality, like Calvin Coolidge or perhaps Dwight Eisenhower, compensates for low self-esteem and a feeling of uselessness by doing dutiful service—doing little and enjoying it less, withdrawing from conflict by emphasizing vague principles and standing for rectitude.

ASSESSING THE BARBER THEORY   Barber's theory has provoked strong criticism. Some scholars argue that character comes in many more than four types. Some say that it is difficult or impossible to be sure how to pigeonhole individual presidents. Was Reagan, who reshaped American politics, really "passive"? Others suggest that ideology may be more important than character in determining how presidents approach their job. Maybe Barber confuses activist Democrats' personalities with their political philosophies. Still others suggest that presidents are less affected by their character than by events and circumstances; the situation may make the person, rather than vice versa. Perhaps it was the failure of the Vietnam War, rather than a character defect, that made Lyndon Johnson's outlook negative at the end of his presidency.[19]

Thus, many political scientists are skeptical of Barber's theory. Most of them would put less emphasis on character and more emphasis on a president's situation and surroundings, as we do in this book. Still, the theory is intriguing since it suggests that the "climate of expectations," the mood and desires of the citizens at a given moment in history, leads voters to choose a particular kind of president. Thus, the personal characteristics of presidents may be "intervening variables," which affect what happens but which themselves mostly reflect various political and structural factors.

Trends in the Modern Presidency: Beyond Personality and Style

The important but limited role of presidents' personal characteristics is clear from a look at enduring *trends* in the presidency—major changes that occurred, sometimes with the help of "great" presidents, but often happening regardless of who was president—and from certain kinds of *shifts* (particularly the changes in which a political party controls the government) that may bring forth different sorts of presidents at different times. In both cases, something more fundamental is going on than a simple change of personality in the White House.

Some of the most important changes in the "Protean presidency" have occurred over many years of American history, constituting such powerful, continuing trends that they seem to be historically inevitable or at least to represent fundamental historical forces far stronger than any particular political leaders. Two of these basic trends, from the time of the founding of the United States to the present day, are as follows.

1. *The tremendous increase in the power, responsibilities, burdens, and impact of the presidency*

2. *A significant increase in the closeness of the presidents to the general public,* as leaders and inspirers of ordinary citizens and as responders to, and democratic representatives of, the people.

These trends in the presidency are closely related to the structural trends in American political development that we discussed in Chapter 4: the great expansion in the size of the United States; the political, military, and economic interactions with the rest of the world; the rise of domestic governmental responsibilities; the revolution in mass communications; and the growth of democracy throughout the political system. Presidents have taken part in each of these trends, reflecting them, symbolizing them, and affecting them.

THE JOB OF THE PRESIDENT

Too Much to Do?

Since Franklin Roosevelt's day, the American presidency has involved powers and duties unimagined by the Founders that touch the daily lives of everyone in the United States and indeed everyone in the world. Political scientist Clinton Rossiter's writings have introduced generations of students to the many different "hats" that presidents wear.[20]

 1. CHIEF OF STATE   The president is the symbol of national authority and unity. In contrast to European parliamentary nations, like Great Britain and Norway, where the king or queen acts as chief of state while a prime minister serves as head of the government, the two functions are combined in the American presidency. It is the president, for instance, who performs the many ceremonial duties, from lighting the national Christmas tree to proclaiming National Dairy Month, that are done by members of the royal family in other nations. Jimmy Breslin, an irreverent New York reporter, once wrote, "the office of President is such a bastardized thing, half royalty and half democracy, that nobody knows whether to genuflect or spit."[21]

2. COMMANDER IN CHIEF   The Constitution clearly lodges command over American armed forces in the office of president. The development of so-called war powers has grown enormously over the years, to the point at which President Bush was able quickly to put more than 500,000 U.S. troops in the Persian Gulf area, poised to strike Iraq once Congress authorized the use of force.

3. CHIEF LEGISLATOR   While constitutional responsibility for the legislative agenda, at first glance, seems clearly lodged in Congress, over the years the initiative for public policy has shifted to the president and the executive branch. To a large extent, Congress now awaits and responds to presidential actions. The twentieth century is dotted with presidential labels on legislation: Wilson's New Freedom; Roosevelt's New Deal; Truman's Fair Deal; Kennedy's New Frontier; and Johnson's Great Society. While Ronald Reagan's program bore no such title, Reagan nevertheless pushed through major changes in 1981 and remained the dominant legislative force during much of the 1980s.

4. MANAGER OF THE ECONOMY   We now expect presidents to worry about and do something about the economy. The Great Depression convinced most Americans that the federal government has a role to play in fighting economic downturns, and the example of Franklin Roosevelt convinced most Americans that the main actor in this drama ought to be the president. The new role was recognized with the passage of the Employment Act of 1946, which mandated that the president report on the state of the economy and recommend actions to maintain employment and control inflation. The role is now so well established that even conservative presidents, like Ronald Reagan and George Bush, have felt compelled to encourage the involvement of the federal government in the prevention of bank failures, the stimulation of economic growth, and the promotion of American trade.

5. CHIEF DIPLOMAT   The Constitution, by specifying that the president ". . . shall have the power . . . to make Treaties" and to appoint and receive ambassadors, unambiguously lodges the main diplomatic responsibility of the United States in that office. It is in this role, perhaps, that American presidents are most visible: traveling abroad, meeting with foreign leaders, negotiating and signing treaties. President Bush's successful negotiations with the Soviet Union and his extraordinary efforts to assemble and hold together the multinational coalition against Iraq (making many personal telephone calls to foreign heads of state and pouring

U.S. President George Bush, acting as chief diplomat, met with Russian President-elect Boris Yeltsin at the White House in June 1991.

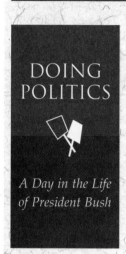

DOING POLITICS

A Day in the Life of President Bush

His working day on June 15, 1989, began for President George Bush at 7 A.M., with a phone call from German Chancellor Helmut Kohl reporting on Soviet President Mikhail Gorbachev's visit to Germany. Bush then took his Marine One helicopter to the Air Force One presidential plane, which flew to Georgia while he dictated letters, read briefings, studied the speech he would soon give, conferred on the Savings and Loan situation, and talked with Attorney General Thornburgh and Treasury Secretary Brady.

At the Federal Law Enforcement Training Facility in wet, green, rural Glynco, Ga., Bush laid a memorial wreath to slain graduates of the facility, talked with the center's staff, and delivered an outdoor speech (removing his jacket to address the crowd that had waited 2½ hours in the sweltering heat) that boosted the anticrime legislative proposals which would be sent to Congress that afternoon. Shaking hands and thanking everyone after the speech, Bush invited a group of U.S. ambassadors who were taking antiterrorist training to come to a John Denver concert at the White House on Sunday. At about the same time, his office was releasing a letter to Congress urging the passage of his Savings and Loan bailout legislation, which passed that evening.

Returning on the plane, Bush answered a reporter's questions on China,

the clean-air bill, health, aging and racism, emphasizing his concern about education and drugs. He told a funny, unprintable anecdote to Press Secretary Marlin Fitzwater. By early afternoon he was on the South Lawn of the White House, watching an arts performance by disabled children, including a rendition of "We Are the World" by a 14-year-old blind boy, a former beggar from the streets of Bangkok, who, Bush later said, made him feel choked up. At 2:45 P.M., Bush and his wife Barbara stood on stage with Kenny Rogers and Pearl Bailey, singing "Put a Little Love in Your Heart"; 15 minutes later he met with the National Security Council to discuss arms control.

That was not all. Bush still had a reception with the Republican National Committee and an evening Spectacular honoring the armed forces to prepare for. The note-taking reporter, who afterwards referred to Bush's "graceful informality" and "slightly distant elegance" and to the administration's "steady and cautious" character, described Bush's day as "not untypical." But of course no single day can be typical; the frenetic travel schedule apparently ruled out the 65-year-old president's usual jogging or "power walk."

Source: Roger Rosenblatt, "A Day in the Life of President Bush," *U.S. News & World Report*, June 26, 1989, pp. 26–27.

---

forth a torrent of persuasion, incentives, and threats) made the diplomatic function especially prominent in his presidency.

Several other "hats" could be mentioned: the president, for example, serves as head of his political party and as leader and representative of the general public—topics that we will discuss further.

Each of these presidential functions is demanding; together, they are overwhelming. The modern president is a busy person. Little wonder that Barber acknowledges that passive presidents "may be a vanishing breed."[22] The demands of the job are great. Consider, for example, one day in the hectic life of President George Bush, as summarized in "Doing Politics."

THE PRESIDENT'S STAFF AND CABINET

The White House Staff

Of course, presidents do not face their burdens alone; they have many advisors and helpers. The White House staff, for example, which is specially shaped to fit the particular needs of each president, includes a number of close advisors. One top advisor, usually designated **chief of staff**, tends to serve as the president's "right-hand man." For most of President Bush's first term, John Sununu (a conservative former governor of New Hampshire who had helped Bush win the crucial 1988 primary in that state), exercised a firm hand on virtually all aspects of domestic and foreign policy, from budget problems to the Persian Gulf War. Sununu took a particular interest in energy and environmental matters; twice he succeeded in thwarting the Environmental Protection Agency's initiatives on global warming and federal protection of wetlands.[23]

Different presidents have used their chiefs of staff in different ways. Franklin Roosevelt kept a tight rein on things himself, granting equal but limited power and access to several close advisors. Dwight Eisenhower, used to the hierarchical army staff system, gave overall responsibility to his chief of staff, Sherman Adams. Likewise, Richard Nixon relied heavily on his tough chief of staff, Bob Haldeman. In the Reagan White House, however, during the first administration, James Baker shared power with Assistant to the President Michael Deaver and Counsellor to the President Edwin Meese.

Chiefs of staff who abrasively give orders to cabinet members and other high officials tend to make enemies and are vulnerable to any hint of scandal. Sherman Adams was forced to resign after he had accepted gifts from a lobbyist; Haldeman was toppled by Watergate; after Sununu took heavy criticism for his "frequent flying" for private and political purposes at government expense, he departed from the administration and was replaced by Samuel Skinner.

Another important staff member in most presidencies is the **national security advisor**, who is also head of the president's national security staff, operating out of the White House basement. The national security advisor generally meets with the president every day in order to brief him on foreign policy matters and to advise him on foreign policy decisions. Some recent national security advisors, such as Henry Kissinger (under Nixon) and Zbigniew Brzezinski (under Carter), have been strong foreign policy voices who often clashed with the secretary of state (in Kissinger's case, this was eventually resolved by appointing him secretary of state himself) and with the director of the Central Intelligence Agency for the president's ear on foreign policy. Presidents Reagan and Bush, however, appointed such "team players" as "Bud" MacFarlane and John Poindexter (Reagan) and Brent Scowcroft (Bush), who closely reflected the president's wishes and coordinated matters with the various executive departments.

Most presidents also have a top domestic policy advisor, who coordinates plans for new domestic laws and regulations and spending, through this role is often subordinate to that of the chief of staff and is not usually very visible. Close political advisors, usually old comrades of the president from past campaigns, may be found in a number of different White House or other government posts (James Baker served as Bush's secretary of state, for example), or may have no official position at all. Prominent in every administration is the press secretary, who holds press conferences and briefs the media; this may or may not be the same person who is director of communications, the person who manages how the president and his activities are presented to the public. These positions, along with that of in-house pollster or public opinion surveyor, have become increasingly important as the president's connections with the public have grown closer.

Nearly all presidents have a legal counsel; a special assistant to act as liaison with Congress; another to deal with interest groups; another for political matters; and still another for intergovernmental relations—relations with state and local governments. However, the exact shape of the White House staff changes greatly from one presidency to another.

These staff members are president's left and right hands. They are the people he talks to every day; they are the ones who do their best to see that he gets his way. They and their deputies leave messages that "the White House wants . . ." all around Washington, where they are treated with deference, if not affection. Aides often jockey for position and bicker among themselves. In the second Reagan administration, Chief of Staff Donald Regan offended other staffers with his imperious manner and was eventually deposed—apparently with a push from the First Lady, Nancy Reagan.[24]

But one thing is certain: staff members have to speak accurately for the president. They must do what the president wants or what he *would* want if he knew the details. The ideal staffer knows exactly what the boss wants and does it, with or without being told; otherwise, he or she won't last long. This was one reason for the widespread skepticism that greeted the Tower Commission's conclusion in 1987 that President Reagan had been out of touch and unaware of the illegal diversion of money from the Iran arms sales to finance Contra rebels in Nicaragua. Of course it can be useful for a president to create the *impression* that staff members are acting on their own, particularly when they are doing something illegal or unpopular. One of Eisenhower's favorite "hidden-hand" techniques was to have Sherman Adams take the heat for tough decisions. Nixon did much the same thing with Bob Haldeman so that people would often criticize the "palace guard" rather than the president himself. Likewise, John Sununu served as President Bush's "bad cop," upsetting many members of Congress.[25]

White House Chief of Staff John Sununu after resigning in 1991.

The Executive Office of the President

One step removed from the White House staff, mostly housed in its own building nearby, is a set of organizations that form the Executive Office of the President (EOP). Most important of these is the **Office of Management and Budget (OMB)**. The OMB is in charge of the numbers. Acting on agency requests, it advises the president on how much the administration should propose to spend for each government program and where the money will come from. The OMB also exercises "legislative clearance"; that is, it examines the budgetary implications of any proposed legislation and sometimes kills proposals as too expensive or inconsistent with the president's philosophy or goals. The director of the OMB can be a major figure in the administration, as was the case with David Stockman, the chief architect of President Reagan's 1981 budget and tax proposals that were described at the beginning of this chapter. Richard Darman, President Bush's director of the OMB, had broad domestic responsibilities and frequently tangled with Congress over his budget-cutting proposals.

Another unit in the Executive Office of the President is the **Council of Economic Advisors (CEA)**, a small group of economists who advise the president on economic policy. Sometimes the head of the Council may exercise great influence because of his relationship to the president. Walter Heller played such a role during the Kennedy administration. At other times, the head of the Council may be almost invisible. Ronald Reagan did not warm to the "doomsayers" on the Council during his administration, so the Council was generally shunted aside. President Bush, however, revived the CEA under economist Michael Boskin.

The Executive Office of the President also includes the **National Security Council (NSC)**, a body of leading officials from the State and Defense Departments, the CIA, the military, and elsewhere to advise the president on foreign affairs; it has been particularly active in crisis situations and covert operations. The NSC's staff, charged with various analytical and coordinating tasks, is headed by the president's national security advisor. At times the NSC staff has gone beyond analysis actually to conduct operations (most famously in the Iran-Contra affair, when weapons were secretly sold to Iran in the hope of freeing U.S. hostages and some of the proceeds were illegally diverted to the Nicaraguan "Contra" rebels, under the direction of Lieutenant Colonel Oliver North).[26] The NSC staff was also important in planning and coordinating the Persian Gulf War.

In recent years, the Executive Office of the President also has included the Office of Science and Technology Policy; the Council on Environmental Quality; and the Office of United States Trade Representative. Again, however, the makeup of the EOP changes from one administration to another, depending upon which national problems seem most pressing and upon the preferences and operating styles of individual presidents. One recent arrangement is shown in Figure 12.1.

The Executive Office of the President has a measure of independence. Its employees cannot be considered personal arms of the president in the same way in which the White House staff is, and they do not meet with him as frequently, but they are generally loyal and responsive to the president and assist him to establish central authority over the wider bureaucracy of the executive branch. Much of that bureaucracy is more distant and more independent, sometimes responding to constituency pressures that conflict with the president's program. Federal agencies outside of the immediate reach of the president and his staff are

Figure 12.1 The executive office of the President[a]

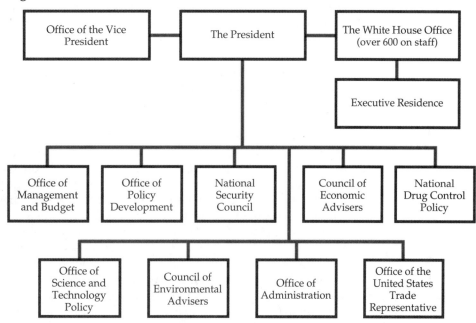

[a]Pictured is the organization of the Executive Office of the President at the beginning of the Bush administration in 1989.

Source: U.S. Government Manual, *1990–1991, p. 86; George C. Edwards III and Stephen J. Wayne,* Presidential Leadership, *2nd. ed. (New York: St. Martin's Press, 1990), p. 170.*

more likely to go their own way. We will have more to say about this phenomenon here and in Chapter 13, "The Executive Branch."

The Vice-Presidency

Vice-presidents find themselves in an awkward position, because their main job is to be available in case something happens to the president. They play what has been called "American roulette," hoping or fearing to take over the presidency if the president dies or otherwise leaves office—and many do. In the twentieth century, Theodore Roosevelt, Calvin Coolidge, Harry Truman, Lyndon Johnson, and Gerald Ford all became president in this way; they have constituted nearly one-third of the presidents we have had since 1900. These are not bad odds for such high-stakes roulette. Moreover, two others—Richard Nixon and George Bush—were elected to the presidency on their own after having served as vice-president. The two-term limit on presidents (imposed in 1951 by the Twenty-Second Amendment to the Constitution) makes such succession easier. All in all, the vice-presidency is the best available steppingstone for becoming president of the United States.

The vice-presidency itself, however, is not highly regarded. John Nance Garner, Franklin Roosevelt's first vice-president, once said in his earthy Texan way that the office was "not worth a pitcher of warm spit." When Harry Truman was informed that Franklin Roosevelt wanted him on the 1944 ticket as vice-president, Truman complained: "I don't want to be Vice-President. I bet I can go down the street and stop the first ten men I see and that they can't tell me the names of two of the last ten Vice-Presidents of the United States."[27]

Within administrations, vice-presidents mostly have tended to be fifth wheels, not personally or politically close to the president (since they are usually chosen to "balance the ticket") and not fully trusted (since they cannot be fired). The Constitution mentions nothing about what vice-presidents should do except preside over the Senate, a duty that is largely ceremonial, except for rare tie-breaking votes, and that usually is left to senators who act as "president pro tem." Anything else is up to the president. Vice-presidents often spend their time running minor errands of state, attending funerals of foreign leaders who are not important enough to demand presidential attention, or carrying out limited diplomatic missions. Dan Quayle's early tasks included helping American businesses sell goods abroad: AT&T telephone equipment in Indonesia, Boeing airliners to Japan and Bolivia, *Wall Street Journal* newspapers in Singapore.[28]

Many vice-presidents have been virtually frozen out of the policymaking process. President Eisenhower cruelly told the press that he might be able to cite something important that Vice-President Nixon had done if he had a week to think about it. Harry Truman was never told of the existence of the Manhattan Project to build the atomic bomb and felt "the moon, the stars, and all the planets had fallen on me" when he suddenly had to assume the presidency.[29] In a few cases, presidents have been seriously and publicly at odds with their vice-presidents.

In recent years, however, several presidents have realized that it is a favor to the country to give their potential successors some training before they take over the job. John Kennedy put Lyndon Johnson in charge of an interagency task force to oversee the space program; Jimmy Carter gave Walter Mondale a number of domestic policy assignments. Ronald Reagan made clear that he wanted George Bush to be loyal, quiet, and discrete, but he included Bush in major policy meetings and put him in charge of antidrug efforts. President Bush gradually gave Dan Quayle more to do, having him work on the space program, government deregulation efforts, and aspects of policy planning for the Gulf War.

In 1804, the Twelfth Amendment fixed the flaw in the original Constitution under which Aaron Burr, Thomas Jefferson's running mate in 1800, had tied Jefferson in electoral votes and had tried, in the House of Representatives, to grab the presidency for himself. Since then, vice-presidents have been elected specifically to that office on a party ticket with their president. But now there is another way to become vice-president. The Twenty-Fifth Amendment (ratified in 1967) provides for succession in case of the temporary or permanent inability of a president to discharge his office. It also states that, if the vice-presidency becomes vacant, the president can nominate a new vice-president, who would take office upon confirmation by both houses of Congress. This is how Gerald Ford became vice-president in 1973, when Spiro Agnew was forced to resign because of a scandal, and how Nelson Rockefeller became vice-president in 1974, when Ford replaced the resigned President Nixon (see Table 12.2).

Table 12.2
Presidential Succession and the Twenty-Fifth Amendment

Under the Twenty-Fifth Amendment to the U.S. Constitution, if the president is removed from office, dies, or resigns, the vice-president becomes president.

Whenever the office of vice-president is vacant, the president nominates a new vice-president, who takes office when he has been confirmed by majority vote of both houses of Congress.

If the president (*or* the vice-president and a majority of the cabinet) submits to Congress a written declaration that the president is unable to discharge the powers and duties of his office, the vice-president becomes acting president.

If the president later submits a written declaration that no inability exists, he resumes the powers and duties of his office, *unless* the vice-president, a majority of the cabinet, and a two-thirds vote in both houses of Congress declare that he is unable to do so.

The Cabinet

The President's cabinet is not mentioned in the Constitution. No legislation designates the composition of the cabinet, its duties, or its rules of operation. Nevertheless, all presidents since George Washington have had one. It was Washington who established the practice of meeting with his top executive officials as a group to discuss policy matters. Later presidents continued the practice, some meeting with the cabinet as often as twice a week—as James Polk and Andrew Johnson did—but others paying it less attention. Andrew Jackson, for example, depended much more on a "kitchen cabinet" of informal advisors than on one composed of the heads of the executive departments.

In recent times, the cabinet has consisted of the heads of the major executive departments, plus the vice-president, the director of the Central Intelligence

President George Bush at a cabinet meeting.

Agency, and whichever other officials the president deems appropriate. Often this has included the ambassador to the United Nations. The cabinet is a highly visible symbol of the executive branch of the United States government.

Rarely, if ever, though, have presidents actually relied upon the cabinet as a decision-making body. Presidents know that they alone will be held responsible for decisions and that they alone keep the power to make them. As Abraham Lincoln put it when he disagreed with the entire cabinet, "eight votes for and one against; the nays have it!"

Most recent presidents have only infrequently convened the cabinet and have rarely done serious business with it. Ronald Reagan held only a few cabinet meetings each year, and those meetings were so dull and unimportant that he was said to doze off from time to time during them. Bush was less apt to sleep but little more inclined than Reagan to take the cabinet seriously, using meetings mainly as photo opportunities.

WHY THE DECLINE OF THE CABINET ?   One reason for the decline of the cabinet is simply that government has grown large and specialized. Most department heads are experts in their own areas, with little to contribute on the broad range of government policies. It could be a waste of everyone's time to engage the secretary of Housing and Urban Development in discussions of military strategy or the secretary of state in deliberations about domestic agricultural programs.

Another reason is that cabinet members occupy an ambiguous position: they are advisors to the president but also represent their own constituencies, including permanent civil servants in their departments and organized interests served by their departments. They may have substantial political stature of their own, somewhat independent of (and even rival to) the president's. Richard Fenno tells the rather extreme story of Jesse Jones, Franklin Roosevelt's secretary of commerce, who used his close ties with businessmen and Congress to bring about policies that defied the president's wishes.[30]

Most presidents deliberately appoint some department heads with independent power bases to help get things done and to sell the president's program. Often, for example, the secretary of commerce has ties with business; the secretary of labor, with unions; and the secretary of agriculture, with farmers. This sometimes leads to tension between the president and department heads, and it makes the cabinet an awkward body for doing business.

Most presidents also try to include in the cabinet some people with whom they have close personal and political ties: former campaign managers, advisors, and so on. Thus, John Kennedy appointed his brother Robert attorney general. When criticized, Kennedy replied (tongue firmly in cheek): "I can't see that it's wrong to give him a little legal experience before he goes out to practice law."[31] Likewise, Richard Nixon appointed his campaign manager and former law partner John Mitchell to that same post, as did Ronald Reagan with Edwin Meese; George Bush named his long-time friend and advisor James Baker secretary of state. This gives the president a high-level advisor and close control over a department at the same time. Baker, for example, was extremely valuable to Bush in negotiating warmer U.S.-Soviet relations, in helping to assemble the worldwide coalition against Iraq after the invasion of Kuwait, and in arranging peace talks between Israel and its Arab neighbors.

Either way, however, as independent powers or as close presidential confidants, cabinet members acquire importance from their relationships with the president or with their own departments and constituencies, not from their membership in the cabinet as a collective body.

THE PRESIDENT AND THE BUREAUCRACY

Many people assume, without thinking about it much, that the president has firm control over the executive branch of government: he can simply order departments and agencies to do something, and they will do it. But Richard Neustadt, in his important book *Presidential Power*, showed that that is far from the whole truth.[32] Yes, presidents can issue orders, as Harry Truman did in 1951 when he fired General Douglas MacArthur as commander of U.S. forces in Korea for defying Truman's policies and for threatening to take the war into China; but such actions can be very costly. MacArthur arrived home a hero, welcomed by ticker-tape parades in New York City and allowed to address a joint session of Congress. Truman lost significant political support and never regained the momentum of his presidency. Such a drastic use of command power on such a major matter ordinarily makes sense only as a last resort, after all other methods have failed.

Moreover, in the day-to-day operation of government, direct command is seldom feasible. For one thing, too much is going on. Presidents cannot keep personal track of each one of the millions of government officials and employees. They can only issue general guidelines and pass them down the chain of subordinates, hoping that their wishes will be followed faithfully. But lower-level officials, protected by civil service from being fired, may have their own interests, their own institutional norms and practices, that lead them to do something different. It is said that President Kennedy was reminded of this rather painfully during the Cuban Missile Crisis of 1962, when Soviet Premier Khrushchev demanded that U.S. missiles be removed from Turkey in return for the removal of Soviet missiles from Cuba: Kennedy is said to have been surprised to learn that the missiles had not already been removed, for he had ordered it done a year earlier. Those who were responsible for carrying out this directive had not followed through.[33]

To a large extent, a president must *persuade* other executive branch officials to do things: he must bargain, compromise, and convince others that what he wants is in the country's best interest and in their own interest as well. Neustadt put it very strongly: "Presidential power is the power to persuade."[34] But, of course, presidents can do many other things as well: appoint top officials who share their goals; put White House observers in second-level department positions; reshuffle, reorganize, or even—with the consent of Congress—abolish agencies that are not responsive; influence agency budgets and programs through OMB review; and stimulate pressure on departments from Congress and the public.

Still, the president's ability to give orders and to gain bureaucratic acquiescence is limited. In terms of our analysis of what affects government policy, the federal bureaucracy is not merely a creature of the president but is itself subject to influences from the *political* level—especially from public opinion and organized interests, often working through Congress. Congress, after all, appropriates the money. This constrains what presidents can do and helps ensure that the executive branch will respond to broad forces in society rather than simply to the wishes of one leader. (See Chapter 13, "The Executive Branch.")

THE PRESIDENT AND CONGRESS: PERPETUAL TUG OF WAR

Structural Bases of Conflict in the Constitution

The President and Congress are often at odds. This is a *structural* fact of American politics, deliberately intended by the Founders when they wrote the Constitution: they created a system of checks and balances, setting "ambition to counter ambition." Since virtually all constitutional powers are shared, there is potential for conflict over virtually all aspects of government policy. (Glance back at Articles I and II, in Appendix III.)

Under the Constitution, presidents may propose legislation and can sign or veto bills passed by Congress, but both houses of Congress must pass any laws and can override presidential vetoes. Presidents can appoint ambassadors and high officials and make treaties with foreign countries, but the Senate must approve them. Presidents nominate federal judges, including those who would sit on the Supreme Court, but the Senate must approve the nominations. Presidents administer the executive branch, but Congress appropriates funds for it to operate, writes the legislation that defines what it is to do, and oversees its activities. Furthermore, presidents cannot always count on members of Congress—even their fellow partisans—to agree with them. As Oklahoma Republican Representative Mickey Edwards said in 1990 when he was upset by President Bush's reversal of his "no new taxes" pledge: "We admire the President, and we support the President, but we don't work for the President."[35]

The potential conflict written into the Constitution becomes real because the president and the Congress often disagree about national goals, especially when the president and members of Congress belong to different parties. Since the end of the 1960s, the voters have frequently elected Republican presidents, along with Congresses controlled by large majorities of Democrats. This is unheard of in the parliamentary systems of many countries, where the legislatures choose the chief executives. It can happen in the United States, because there are *separate elections* for the president and members of Congress. Moreover, the elections do not all come at the same time. In presidential election years, two-thirds of the senators do not have to run and are insulated from the political forces that affect the choice of a president. In nonpresidential "off" years, all members of the House and one-third of the senators face the voters, who sometimes elect a Congress with views quite different from those of the president chosen two years earlier. In 1986, for example, halfway through President Reagan's second term, the Democrats recaptured control of the Senate and caused Reagan great difficulty with Supreme Court appointments and other matters.

Another reason for conflict between the president and Congress is that the opinions they hear and the pressures they feel may have different sources. Some political scientists argue that presidents, with their high-visibility, relatively high-participation election campaigns, and their presence on television, tend to hear from and represent the general public rather than organized interest groups. Members of Congress, it is argued, are more open to the blandishments and appeals of organized interest groups, especially PACs, which contribute so handsomely to their campaigns. This is why lobbyists for organized interest groups are so in evidence in the corridors, hallways, offices, and committee rooms of Congress. On the other hand, some presidents—probably including Ronald Reagan—have represented ideological factions of their parties that do not stand as close as the average member of Congress to the wishes of ordinary citizens.

For all these reasons, our constitutional *structure* means that presidents are limited and affected in what they can do by another *governmental* institution—namely Congress—which, in turn, reflects various *political* forces.

And the Winner Is!

Not only do Congress and the president often disagree; one or the other tends to come out on top at different periods of time. The uneven expansion of the presidency throughout American history can be interpreted in terms of the shifting ascendancy of one branch or another. After the highly visible and successful presidencies of Washington and Jefferson, for example, Congress dominated an "era of good feelings"; after the lively Jackson presidency, the "Whig presidents" were mostly weak, and Congress, rather than the president, dealt with economic expansion and the slavery issue. After Lincoln's strong wartime presidency, there followed a long period of legislative ascendancy as Congress came to be the dominant federal voice in the reconstruction of the South after the Civil War and in the pro-business laissez-faire policies of the late nineteenth and early twentieth centuries. From this point of view, the presidencies of Theodore Roosevelt (1901–1909) and Woodrow Wilson (1913–1921) represent brief periods of presidential ascendance during a half-century of congressional domination. It is only with the Great Depression, the New Deal, World War II, and the powerful example of Franklin Roosevelt that the presidency gained the power and responsibility that it would never again relinquish.

President Franklin Roosevelt as the United States declared war against Japan in December, 1941. Roosevelt's waist-down paralysis from polio was seldom evident in photographs.

CYCLES OF CONGRESSIONAL RESURGENCE   This pattern suggests that presidents may tend to emerge as dominant during times of great national crisis (war or depression, for example), when Americans will unite under strong leadership; however, when the crisis is over, there is often a reaction against the strains of crisis management, a reduction in federal government activity, and a return to a more relaxed system of congressional government. It may be that the character and personality of the presidents we choose—and how much latitude we allow them once they are in office—reflect the different expectations the public maintains of these different situations.

Since World War II, with the immensely increased international role of the United States, all presidents have been active in foreign affairs; none have accepted subordination to Congress in the fashion of the nineteenth century or even the 1920s. Yet some indications remain of a cycle in presidential–congressional relations. After Lyndon Johnson's successes in enacting his Great Society programs of the 1960s, for example, and after his very assertive foreign policy moves in Vietnam and elsewhere, followed by the secretive and equally assertive Nixon administration, complaints were heard of an "imperial presidency."[36] Then Congress fought back.

During the 1970s, Congress cut off U.S. aid to South Vietnam and halted the bombing of Cambodia. Overriding a presidential veto, it passed the War Powers Resolution—an effort to control the future use of U.S. troops abroad. Congress restricted presidents' "impoundments" of congressionally appropriated money and tried to increase Congress's role in the budgetary process by setting up the Congressional Budget Office and a system of budget resolutions and reconciliations. Congress also reduced presidents' emergency powers, restricted executive agreements and arms sales abroad, and generally played a more active part in foreign policy. After investigating and publicizing assassination plots against foreign leaders, mind-altering drug experiments, and illegal spying on American citizens, it increased congressional oversight of CIA covert operations.

THE REAGAN PRESIDENTIAL RENEWAL   This period of congressional resurgence did not last long. After the crises and traumas of the late 1970s, President Reagan took office and reasserted presidential authority in all areas.

Reagan's 1981 tax and budget success, which we described at the beginning of this chapter, was one of the first and most dramatic signs of change. Suddenly Congress's hard-won tools for budgetary control were overcome by a presidential "blitzkrieg"; suddenly programs that had been popular for decades were in jeopardy; suddenly members of Congress were terrified of being chased out of office by a political giant.

Reagan went on to initiate or to continue a number of covert actions abroad, in Nicaragua, Afghanistan, Angola, and elsewhere. He used U.S. military force selectively, picking weak opponents like Grenada and Libya but withdrawing American Marines from Lebanon when 241 of them were killed in a suicide truck bomb attack.

For nearly eight years, President Reagan thoroughly dominated American politics. Yet signs of a new revival in Congress could be seen as early as 1982 and 1983, when some of the 1981 tax cuts were reversed and when pressure began to mount to slow the military buildup and to try harder to negotiate with the Soviets. By 1987, after the election of a Democratic majority in the Senate, Reagan was unable to prevail on many new initiatives; his nomination of the highly conservative Robert Bork to the Supreme Court, for example, was defeated.

George Bush and Congress   When George Bush took office in 1989, winning a narrow victory in the popular vote and facing an even stronger Democratic Congress than Reagan had, he continued to assert presidential authority in foreign affairs, most notably in building friendlier relations with the Soviet Union and in rolling back Iraq's attack on Kuwait. But Bush could succeed on the domestic front only by vetoes or deference to the congressional branch. Bush's 1990 budget negotiations led to an embarrassing revolt in his own party, and few of his limited legislative proposals got anywhere. The cycle of changes in presidential–congressional relations continued.

What Makes a President Successful with Congress?

A number of political scientists have studied presidents' successes and failures in getting measures that they favor enacted into law by Congress. They have suggested various reasons why some presidents at some times and on some issues do better than others.

PARTY CONTROL   The most important factor is a simple one: party control of Congress. When the same political party controls both the presidency and the Congress, presidents tend to get their way. When the opposite party controls Congress, presidents tend to be frustrated. The bigger a majority that the president's party has, the better presidents do[37] (see Figure 12.2). This does not necessarily mean that presidents actively whip their fellow partisans into line. As we

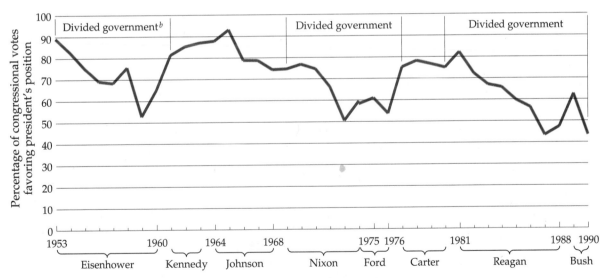

Figure 12.2 Presidential success in Congress[a]

[a]For each year from 1952 through 1990, this graph shows what percentage of the time the president's position won in both the House and the Senate.

[b]Divided government: Congress is wholly or partly controlled by opposite party from presidency. Occurs in 1954–1960, 1969–1976, and 1981–1990.

Sources: Harold Stanley and Richard Niemi, Vital Statistics on American Politics *(Washington, D.C.: Congressional Quarterly Press, 1990), pp. 248–249;* Congressional Quarterly Weekly Report, *October 13, 1990, p. 3387.*

have seen, the parties are rather weakly organized in Congress and do not often enforce discipline. But party members do tend to be like-minded; they tend to vote together because they share the same values, and, for the same reason, they tend to go along with a president of their own party. So, when Congress is full of members of the president's party, it tends to pass legislation that the president likes; when it is not, it doesn't pass legislation that the president likes. Republican Presidents Nixon, Reagan, and Bush eventually ran up against assertive Democratic Congresses.

POPULARITY   Presidents are also more successful when their own popularity is high and are less successful when it is low.[38] Some of this may result from members of Congress fearing that the president's electoral "coattails" will defeat them in the next election if they don't go along, but coattails have not been very strong in recent years. More important, the popularity of presidents seems to be taken as signaling the popularity of their programs, and members of Congress tend to go along with public opinion.

FOREIGN POLICY   Presidents tend to do better on foreign policy issues than on domestic ones. Political scientist Aaron Wildavsky has gone so far as to refer to "two presidencies," with the president much more dominant on foreign matters. His investigations found that, during the 1948–1964 period, 59 percent of presidents' proposals on foreign policy were passed but only 40 percent of presidents' proposals on domestic matters were passed.[39]

This difference may have decreased somewhat since the Vietnam War, but it remains significant. Congressional Democrats, at least, tend to defer to Republican presidents on foreign policy.[40] President Reagan generally got his way on foreign policy issues that mattered most to him. And the congressional vote in January 1991, authorizing President Bush to use force against Iraq, once again illustrated presidential primacy in foreign affairs. Even though a bare majority of the general public probably opposed use of force at that time, and many organized interest groups were against it, the president's argument that he needed the authority in order to pressure Saddam Hussein into concessions was enough to tip the balance and produce a 52–47 vote of approval in the Senate.

APPOINTMENTS   On certain, special kinds of issues, presidents nearly always get their way. The Senate, for example, confirms some 99 percent of the appointments of officials submitted by presidents. Battles over confirmation are uncommon, and presidential losses, such as the defeats of Nixon's Supreme Court nominees Clement F. Haynsworth and G. Harold Carswell, or Reagan's nominee Robert Bork, are even more rare; they generally happen only when a president is severely weakened and the Senate is controlled by the opposition. On the other hand, this does not mean that presidents are all-powerful on appointments; they take account of what Congress wants when they are deciding whom to appoint in the first place. "Senatorial courtesy," for example, allows the senior senator of the president's party to blackball potential nominees from his state.

VETOES   When the issue is a presidential veto of legislation, the president again is very likely to prevail. As Figure 12.3 shows, vetoes have not been cast often, except by certain "veto-happy" presidents, like Roosevelt, Truman, Ford, and (at an earlier time) Cleveland. But when vetoes have been cast, they have seldom

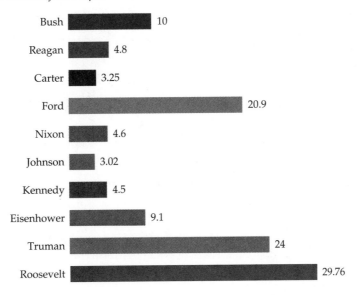

Figure 12.3 Presidential vetoes (average number per year)

Source: Calculated by the authors from Harold Stanley and Richard Niemi, Vital Statistics on American Politics *(Washington, D.C.: Congressional Quarterly Press, 1990), p. 252.*

been overridden—only 5 percent of the time for Truman and only 1½ percent for Roosevelt. The Democrats' moderate success in overriding Reagan's vetoes (12 percent of the time) was unusual and did not extend to President Bush. Bush, in his first three years in office, had a perfect record of sustaining vetoes on civil rights, the extension of unemployment benefits, and a number of other issues.

LEGISLATIVE SKILLS   Undoubtedly, the president's legislative skills make a difference too, at least on certain key bills. Lyndon Johnson's famous personal "treatment" and his wheeling and dealing surely picked up votes, as did Ronald Reagan's efforts on the 1981 tax and budget measures. Some presidents, like Johnson, Reagan, Kennedy and Ford, have paid a lot of attention to legislative relations, carefully organizing their liaison staffs, doing "head counts" of voting intentions, and passing out favors and compromises in order to win. Others, like Eisenhower, Nixon, and Carter, have been more detached and less skillful. Still, the effects of these differences in skill and effort do not show up clearly in statistical studies of legislative success. They may matter less than insiders think.

THE PRESIDENT AND THE PEOPLE: AN EVOLVING RELATIONSHIP

The complicated relationships that exist among the president, the executive branch as a whole, and Congress (all *governmental* units) have a lot to do with the different *political* forces that act upon them at different times—with the ways in which public opinion, the political parties, and organized interests affect what they do differently. Particularly important is the special relationship that exists between the president and the general public, which has evolved over many years.

Beginnings: A Distant Presidency

The Founders thought of the president as an elite leader, relatively distant from the people, interacting with Congress often but with the people only rarely. Most nineteenth-century presidents and presidential candidates believed and practiced this ideal. They seldom made speeches directly to the public, for example, averaging generally ten or fewer such speeches per year.[41]

In the earliest years of the American Republic, presidents were not even chosen directly by the voters. According to the original Constitutional scheme, the people only voted on state legislators and members of the House of Representatives. The state legislators then chose presidential electors, who were to exercise their independent judgment as an electoral college in nominating candidates for president; then, if (as expected) no candidate won a majority of electoral votes, the winner would be selected by state delegations in the House of Representatives. The Constitution thus envisioned a very indirect democracy in relationship to the presidency. The president, in the view of the Founders, was not to be a tribune of the people.

Getting Closer to the People

This system quickly evolved into a more democratic one, in which the people played a more direct part. Already by 1800, the two-party system had begun to develop, with parties nominating candidates and running them under party labels that provided voters with clearer choices; electors were pledged in advance to support their parties' candidates. The two-party system also made it easier for presidential candidates to win clear-cut victories in the electoral college and thereby took the House of Representatives out of the process. Early in the nineteenth century, state legislatures began to turn over the power to choose presidential electors to the people, by direct election. By 1832, the president system for electing presidents was mostly in place, with the winner in the electoral college nearly always the winner of a plurality of the popular vote.

As we saw in Chapter 9, "Voting and Elections," the numbers and kinds of people entitled to vote for president were broadened as well. Property and religious qualifications were dropped; slaves were freed and given the right to vote; women, Native Americans, and 18-year-olds won the franchise. By the early 1970s, the electorate eligible to choose presidents consisted of nearly all adults (except felons and the insane) who chose to participate. Additionally, the rise of direct primaries to nominate presidential candidates, during the Progressive period and especially in the 1970s, brought the general public into full-fledged participation in the choice of presidents.

GOING PUBLIC   By the beginning of the twentieth century, the presidency had begun to change markedly. Presidents began to speak directly to the public. Theodore Roosevelt, for example, embarked upon a series of speech-making tours in order to win passage of legislation to regulate the railroads. Woodrow Wilson went further, making appeals to the public a central part of his presidency and creating an entirely new constitutional theory advocating close connections between the president and the public. Wilson's very expansive conception of the leadership role of the president and its basis in the president's link to the people deserves emphasizing, because it has become part of the outlook of most contemporary presidents.

Wilson saw the desires of the public as the wellspring of democratic government: "... as is the majority, so ought the government to be."[42] He argued that presidents are unique because only they are chosen by the entire nation. Presidents, he argued, should help educate the citizens about government, should "interpret" their true will, and should faithfully respond to it. (See "The Struggle for Democracy," p. 446)

Wilson's theory of the presidency has been followed, more and more fully, in twentieth-century thought and practice. Harry Truman echoed Wilson in a 1959 lecture: "The president is the representative of the whole nation and he is the only lobbyist that all the 160 million people in this country have.[43] All presidents, especially since Franklin Roosevelt, now attempt to respond to public opinion; to one degree or another, all attempt to speak directly to the people about policy. The extent of change is striking. In the nineteenth century, for example, fewer than 1 percent of presidents' official statements and messages were oral; nearly all were written. Only about 7 percent were addressed to the people; the bulk went to Congress. In the twentieth century, by contrast, nearly one-half of official statements (42 percent) have been oral and nearly one-half (41 percent) have been addressed directly to the people.[44]

Contemporary Presidents More and more frequently, presidents "go public," using television to bypass the press in order to speak to the public directly about policy. They have held fewer news conferences with White House correspondents, dropping from Hoover's and Roosevelt's averages of six or seven per month to Carter's and Reagan's average of fewer than one per month. (Bush increased the number somewhat.) But, since Hoover's administration, all presidents have given an average of about ten major addresses to the national public per year, with a slight increase over time; there also has been a huge increase in minor addresses to special audiences, from Hoover's 10 per year to Eisenhower's 30, Kennedy's 50, and Carter's and Reagan's 50 per year.[45]

President Kennedy appeared on television more frequently than any president before or since, logging 30.4 hours of exposure in his first 19 months in office. Much of that time was devoted to live daytime press conferences, in which Kennedy established his reputation for style and wit. Richard Nixon pioneered prime-time television addresses, at which Ronald Reagan later excelled. Bush generally displayed less rhetorical polish but often spoke to large audiences, as with his address in January 1991 announcing the initiation of war against Iraq, which reached more television viewers than any previous program in history.

More and more often, presidents have travelled outside the White House, making public appearances (see Figure 12.4, p. 448). Often the settings convey a visual message: Nixon wearing a hard hat and waving to cheering construction workers in order to show his support for the "silent majority"; Carter strolling down Pennsylvania Avenue on inauguration day to demonstrate his common touch; Bush visiting a flag factory just after the 1988 election. Most spectacular is travel abroad, which displays the chief executive as "presidential," as head of state, and highlights his foreign policy achievements: Kennedy speaking at the Berlin Wall in 1963, for example; Nixon raising his glass in toast at the Great Hall of the People in Beijing in 1972; Reagan strolling through Red Square in Moscow with Mikhail Gorbachev in 1988; Bush in Moscow in the summer of 1991.

THE STRUGGLE FOR DEMOCRACY

★

Woodrow Wilson and Presidential Democracy

The struggle for democracy is sometimes carried out by officials as well as citizens, and it sometimes concerns the realm of ideas as well as practice. Thomas Woodrow Wilson was, in a sense, an accidental president: a Democrat in the midst of a Republican era, elected in 1912 only because William Howard Taft and the independent "Bull Moose" Theodore Roosevelt had split the Republican vote. Yet Wilson embodied the strongly Progressive sentiment of his time and played a crucial part in the democratization of the American presidency.

Even after citizens had won the right to vote directly for pledged presidential electors and after the franchise had been extended to all adult males, presidents remained rather remote from the public and from what the Founders had feared as the public's "passions." Presidential candidates conducted election campaigns coyly, not appealing directly for votes and refusing to say where they stood on the issues. Once in office, presidents dealt with Con-

gress and the executive branch but declined to discuss the merits of public policy with the ordinary citizenry.

Woodrow Wilson, scholar and politician, changed all that, both in theory and in practice. He argued that presidents are special because they, alone among government officers, are elected by a national electorate and can claim a national mandate. Presidents, therefore, should both lead and respond to the public, "interpreting" the true desires of the citizenry, winning public support for policies in accord with those desires, and providing energetic leadership; when necessary, they should overcome obstruction by Congress. In short, the president should give much greater weight to public opinion than the Founders had intended.

Wilson acted on his vision. He began to give many public speeches directly to the people, rather than written communiques to government agencies and Congress. He revived the practice, which Jefferson had abandoned, of delivering the State of

Leading Public Opinion

Especially since the rise of television, modern presidents have enhanced their power to shape public opinion, as Reagan did in mobilizing support for his tax and budget cuts in 1981, as Kennedy did when he dramatically called up the reserves during the Berlin crisis in 1961, and as Bush did in building support for the Persian Gulf war. Studies have found that, when a popular president takes a stand in favor of a particular policy, the public's support for that policy tends to rise. A determined president, delivering many speeches and messages over a period of several weeks or months, can expect to gain 5–10 percentage points in support for that policy in the polls.[46] This is not an enormous effect; presidents often have to compete with others who influence the public, and, if they are too

We now take it for granted that modern presidents follow Wilson's practice of "going public." But Wilson forged the crucial connection between the presidency and the people. He once declared of the president:

The nation as a whole has chosen him, and is conscious that it has no other political spokesman. His is the only national voice in affairs. Let him once win the confidence of the country, and no other single force can withstand him, no combination of forces will easily overpower him. . . . He is the representative of no constituency, but of the whole people. When he speaks in his true character, he speaks for no special interest. If he rightly interprets the national thought and boldly insists upon it, he is irresistible. . . .[a]

[a]*Woodrow Wilson, Constitutional Government in the United States,* quoted in James M. Burns, *Presidential Government* (Boston: Houghton Mifflin, 1965), p. 96.

Source: Jeffrey K. Tulis, *The Rhetorical Presidency* (Princeton, NJ: Princeton University Press, 1987).

the Union Address in person rather than in written form. And he declared in his first Address that the people were his true audience, not just Congress. Finally, he appealed directly to the public to pressure their senators into supporting the League of Nations treaty. Such use of public opinion had been rare among nineteenth-century presidents.

persistent, they tend to lose their audience. But it is enough to confirm Theodore Roosevelt's claim that the presidency is a "bully pulpit." And presidents undoubtedly have a much greater *indirect* impact, influencing what others say and helping to shape the Washington, D.C., agenda and the terms of public discourse.

IS THIS DEMOCRACY?   The power to lead the public also implies a power to manipulate public opinion, if a president is so inclined: to deceive or mislead the public so that it will approve of policies that it might oppose if it were fully informed. This may happen especially in foreign affairs, where presidents can most easily control information. Presidential candidate and then president, John F. Kennedy, for example, encouraged belief in an illusory "missile gap" with the Soviets; President Johnson purposely misstated the facts about the Gulf of Tonkin

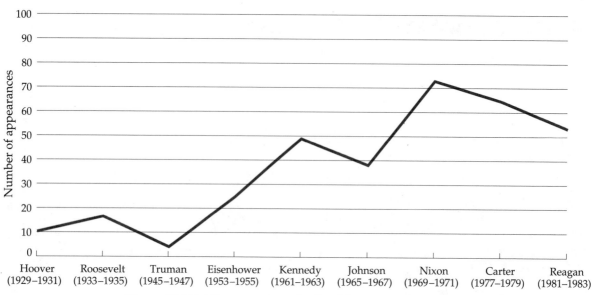

Figure 12.4 Public appearances by Presidents

Source: Samuel Kernell, Going Public *(Washington, D.C.: Congressional Quarterly Press, 1986), p. 94.*

incident at the beginning of the Vietnam War (see Chapter 5, "Public Opinion"); President Reagan engaged in a number of deceptions, misleading the public about the "deliberate" Soviet shooting down of a Korean airliner, the U.S. invasion of Grenada, the situation in Nicaragua, and various other matters. After the war with Iraq, questions arose over how accurately President Bush had explained the situation. Domestic matters are not completely free from manipulation of symbols, either; Bush's characterization of the Democrats' 1991 civil rights bill as a "quota bill" drew blood, even though the bill explicitly outlawed quotas.

Those who seek energetic presidential leadership must face the possibility that that leadership will go wrong and result in demagoguery or manipulation. This dilemma cannot be solved. Power to do good is power to do evil as well. But some safeguards can be found in the capacity of the public to judge character when it is choosing a president and the ability of other national leaders to counteract a deceitful president. Presidents Johnson and Nixon learned this bitter lesson: the former declined to run for a second term; the latter resigned. The most serious threats to democracy may come when leaders of both parties are united and no one challenges falsehood, as sometimes occurs in the case of nationalistic and apparently "patriotic" acts of foreign policy that the public might oppose if it were told the facts.

Responding to the Public

In any case, the relationship between presidents and the public is very much a two-way street. Besides leading the people, presidents definitely tend to respond to public opinion. This is true because presidents are elected, and a candidate (like Barry Goldwater in 1964) whose goals are very far out of line with what the public favors is not likely to be elected in the first place, as indicated by the electoral-competition theory of elections. Also, presidents who are in office want to be reelected or to win a favorable place in history, and they know that they are unlikely to do so if they defy public opinion on many major issues. Usually they try to anticipate what the public will want, as the electoral reward-and-punishment theory indicated.

QUIET INFLUENCE   For the most part, this influence of public opinion is so quiet as to be almost invisible. What presidents *want* to do closely resembles what the public wants—that is partly why they were elected in the first place—so there is often no conflict or struggle to observe. Only rarely does a modern president get badly out of touch with the public, so that the full power of public opinion is revealed. When the Reagan administration hinted at cuts in Social Security, for example, in 1981 and again in 1982, the storm of protest led to a very hasty retreat. Despite his great popularity, moreover, Reagan was unable openly to deliver substantial or continuous aid to the Nicaraguan Contras because Congress understood that about two-thirds of the public opposed the president on this issue.

More often, in day-to-day politics, it simply turns out that what the president does is largely in harmony with what the general public wants. Johnson's Great Society programs responded to strong public support for such programs as federal aid for education, medical care, and civil rights. When the public during the late 1960s and early 1970s wanted more "law and order," President Nixon made appointments of conservative judges to the Supreme Court and arranged for federal aid for local law enforcement. When public opinion moved (temporarily) toward favoring a buildup of defense during the late 1970s, Presidents Carter and Reagan followed suit. When polls showed public willingness to defend Saudi Arabia but hesitation about using troops to liberate Kuwait, President Bush went slowly (and waited until after the 1990 elections). Bush's policies were in harmony with the public's willingness to give trading privileges to China and the Soviet Union but its reluctance to extend financial aid to the Soviets.[47] As a general matter, when polls show that public opinion has changed, presidents have tended to shift policy in the same direction: this has been true about 84 percent of the time.[48]

LISTENING TO THE PUBLIC   There is plenty of evidence that presidents care about what the public is thinking. Presidents and their staff carefully read the available public opinion surveys and often conduct their own polls. Ronald Reagan, the "Great Communicator," was also a "Great Listener"; his chief pollster, Richard Wirthlin, developed the most thorough and intensive polling operation yet devised. Spending about $1.1 million per year from the Republican National Committee, Wirthlin carried out more than 500 surveys on a monthly schedule, asking questions of more than 500,000 Americans concerning such matters as the public's feelings about foreign countries, the popularity of American and world leaders, and the public's reactions to events like the bombing of Libya, summit meetings, terrorist hijackings, and the crash of the spacecraft *Challenger*, as well as various foreign and domestic policies. He had Americans' policy preferences computed by congressional district, so that President Reagan often knew more about what constituents wanted than their congressmen and congresswomen did. All this information helped the administration package and "sell" its programs. More important, from the point of view of democracy, it helped the president choose policies that the American public favored and adjust those that proved unpopular.[49] President Bush's people, though apparently less systematic than Reagan's, kept track of the opinion polls as well.

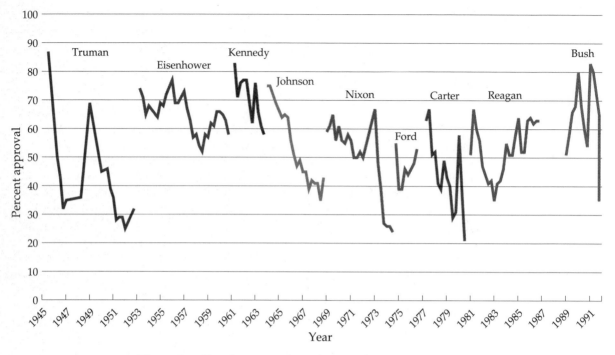

Figure 12.5 Trends in Presidential popularity

Source: Gallup surveys, reported in Harold Stanley and Richard Niemi, Vital Statistics on American Politics *(Washington, D.C.: Congressional Quarterly Press, 1900), p. 256; CBS/NYT surveys reported in the* New York Times, *November 26, 1991, p. A1.*

Presidential Popularity

The public's influence does not only proceed through its opinions about specific policies. Even more important, it works through **presidential popularity** or unpopularity. Since the 1930s, the Gallup organization has regularly asked Americans whether they "approve" or "disapprove" of President X's "handling" of his job. The percentage of people approving varies from month to month and year to year, and, as time passes, it forms a sort of "fever chart" of how the president is doing with the public (see Figure 12.5).

Presidents care a great deal about these numbers, because they have a lot to do with how much clout the president has in Congress, how his party will do in midterm elections, and how he himself will do in reelection or in the history books. Presidents try to figure out what causes their popularity to go up and down. They do everything they can to make it go up.

RISES AND FALLS IN PRESIDENTIAL POPULARITY   What does cause presidents' popularity to rise or fall? Historically, most presidents have begun their term of office with a fairly favorable rating—60 percent or more approving of how the president is handling the job. Most tended to lose popularity as time passed. But this does not represent some inexorable working of time, because not all presidents lose popularity. Eisenhower and Reagan actually gained popularity in their second terms. Those who lose popularity do so in response to bad news. Good news increases a president's popularity.

Good and Bad News   One of the most serious kinds of bad news involves *economic recessions*. When the economy goes sour, fewer Americans approve of the president's handling of his job. This happened to Reagan from late 1981 to early 1983, during the worst recession of the postwar period, when his popularity dropped from a high point of 68 percent to a low point of only 35 percent approving of his handling of the job. It began to happen to Bush in mid-1990 (before the invasion of Kuwait) as the economy faltered. Another important kind of bad news concerns an unsuccessful *war*, especially a limited war that drags on with high casualty rates, like the Korean War, which detracted from Truman's already low popularity in 1950 and 1951, or the Vietnam War, which badly eroded Johnson's popularity from 1965 to 1968. The Watergate scandal did much the same thing to Nixon in 1973 and 1974. On the other hand, of course, peace and prosperity tend to send presidents' popularity ratings upwards, as economic recovery did for Reagan. President Bush's approval rating soared to 89 percent upon the successful conclusion of the war with Iraq, before falling sharply in the recession.[50]

President Bush's popularity fell sharply during the 1991–1992 recession; his only hope for re-election was that the economy would recover in time.

Certain kinds of symbolic events, or crises in which Americans' patriotism is invoked and there is a *"rally 'round the flag,"* can produce at least a temporary surge in presidential popularity. Even Bush's immense gain in popularity from the war with Iraq was only temporary, as the messy aftereffects of the war became apparent and as the public turned its attention to domestic problems. Four months after the war, one poll found that general approval of Bush's handling of his job dropped from an astounding 88 percent to a still strong 75 percent. Approval of his handling of foreign policy fell from 83 percent to 68 percent, and only a meager 41 percent approved of his handling of the economy, with 48 percent disapproving.[51] It was downhill from there.

Presidents are aware, at least in general terms, of what helps or hurts them with the public; they know that they will win electoral rewards if things go well but will face electoral punishment if things go badly. They have strong incentives, therefore, to anticipate public reactions and to do things that will turn out to please the public.

Presidents as Tribunes

Taken together, the evidence indicates that there is considerable truth in the idea that presidents are "tribunes" of the people. Presidents are close to the public (closer, sometimes, than Congress is), both leading public opinion and responding to it. It is important not to take this idea too far, however. We have seen that presidents occasionally have misled the public and have manipulated public opinion. Sometimes, too, they ignore public opinion or defy it. In some cases, they respond, instead, to organized interest groups. In some cases, they respond to the activists and money givers in their own political parties, by carrying out the party's ideological agenda more fully than the public would like. Public opinion is not the only political factor affecting presidents.

THE PRESIDENCY, INTEREST GROUPS, AND POLITICAL PARTIES

The relationship of interest groups with presidents, like other aspects of interest group politics, forms a sort of dark continent. Much of what goes on is probably kept hidden from scholars and observers; for example, presidents' public calendars of appointments cannot be trusted to list all interest group leaders whom they meet. But we can be reasonably sure, from various hints and fragments of evidence, that organized groups exert important kinds of influence on presidential policy.

Interest group money and activity help presidential candidates win nomination and election, so that those who take office do not simply reflect the preferences of ordinary citizens; they tend to share, or at least sympathize, with the goals of their benefactors. At a minimum, presidents generally give special access to those who helped get them into office, such as the contributors to President Bush's campaign mentioned in Chapter 9, "Voting and Elections." Moreover, in some policy areas, it is impossible for the president to govern without the cooperation of organized groups; this is especially true of businesspeople and the heads of large corporations, who occupy a "privileged position" as spokespersons for what government must do if a free enterprise economy is to flourish.[52]

Precisely which interest groups have a greater influence on policy depends significantly upon which party controls the presidency, because many groups are more closely allied with one party than with the other. Since the 1930s, for example, organized labor has been closely tied to the Democratic party; since the 1960s, this has been true of civil rights organizations, womens' groups, and environmental organizations as well. In addition, the Democrats have received money and backing from certain multinationally oriented, capital-intensive firms and investment bankers, and from figures in construction, real estate, and the entertainment industry. The Republican party, on the other hand, has had much closer ties to most manufacturing firms, small businesses, and organizations of well-to-do professionals, such as doctors and lawyers.[53] Democratic presidents, therefore, spend more time with and pay more attention to groups that represent some sectors of the business community, labor, and minorities; Republican presidents are more attentive to those groups that represent industrial corporations.

Political Parties

Parties are clearly important. Republican presidents tend to do different things than Democratic presidents do. Changes in party control of the presidency produce significant changes in policy.

Despite the pressure put on American political parties to compete for votes by "moving to the center," as electoral-competition theories suggest, they also maintain some real differences, as the responsible-party model indicates. (See Chapter 9, "Voting and Elections.") The parties consist of activists and money givers with distinctive policy goals, and ordinary voters who differ, though less sharply, in the same sorts of ways. Without activists and money givers, a party could hardly exist. Yet many of these people invest in politics because they care about what the government does. They insist on nominating and electing presidents who substantially share their views and who will try to carry out party-backed programs once they are in office.

The result of party influence, as we have indicated, is that there are *cycles* of presidential action, depending upon which party holds office; Democratic presidents tend to fight unemployment, to favor civil rights and environmental measures, and to promote domestic social welfare programs; Republicans tend to worry about inflation, to cut domestic expenditures, and to take conservative stands on social issues, such as abortion. President Eisenhower's presidency, for example, was a rather conservative one; liberal programs formulated by congressional Democrats at the end of the Eisenhower years were enacted into policy under Democratic presidents Kennedy and Johnson, and the cycle started over under conservative Republican President Nixon.[54] President Carter represented only a weak manifestation of the Democratic phase of the cycle, since he was hampered by economic and foreign policy crises; the United States soon turned to the conservatism of Republican presidents Ronald Reagan and George Bush.

Such cycles may relate to the preferences of the general public in a curious way. At each election in the cycle, the program of the winning party tends to represent what the public wants—at least somewhat better than the other party does. There can be little doubt, for example, that in 1960 many Americans were ready for a change, eager to "get the country moving again," or that in 1980 many Americans wanted to whittle down certain domestic programs, cut their tax burden, and build up the military. The "climate of expectations" favors one party or the other, depending on the times. But party victories carry the seeds of their own destruction, because each party tends to go further in its favored direction than the public wants. Thus, Johnson's Great Society led to a desire for retrenchment; Reagan's attacks on domestic social programs and the massive military buildup led to a desire for peace, arms control, and renewal of domestic programs. Party influences upon the presidency probably tend to cause some "oversteering" in one direction and then another: some movement of policy opposed to what the public wants. In fact, since the presidency belongs to only one party at a time, it may tend to oversteer more and get more out of touch with the public than does the compromising, two-party Congress.

SOCIAL MOVEMENTS   Social movements occasionally provide yet another political-level influence on presidents, in at least two different ways. Sometimes mass demonstrations and protests cause disruption that is inconvenient or dangerous to ignore and lead presidents to take actions in order to defuse them. Sometimes mass movements produce changes in general public opinion that, in turn, affect presidents. Either way, presidents and other political leaders have to pay attention. As we have seen, this was true of the civil rights movement that led up to the major civil rights legislation of 1964 and 1965; it was also true of the antiwar movement that affected the decisions to deescalate the Vietnam War in 1968 and 1969.

The result of all of these factors is that the president is only partly a tribune of the people: he is also a partial servant of interest groups, political parties and party coalitions, the media, and mass movements.

STRUCTURE: THE ENDURING PRESIDENCY

Many of the influences upon presidents that we have discussed so far operate at the *political* level of analysis. Some (especially public opinion) provide substantial continuity from one president to the next; others (especially political parties) lead to zigzags or cycles. But all of them involve broad societal influences on what presidents do. The presidency is not really as personal as it might have seemed when we discussed individuals' styles and character at the beginning of this chapter. In modern times, at least, there have been no purely accidental presidents. Who presidents are, and what they stand for, is carefully screened by voters, political parties, the media, and interest groups. When they are in office, too, presidents must respond to those people and institutions.

Thus, we can speak of an "enduring" presidency—a presidency that does not merely fluctuate with the whims of whoever holds office but reflects the goals and preferences of the people, groups, and institutions that make up American society. Even major changes from one president to another—the partisan cycles, for example—usually reflect the nature of party coalitions in the country and changes in public opinion.

But the enduring presidency goes beyond that. Both continuities and changes in what presidents do tend to reflect influences at the *structural* level of analysis, basic features of society that influence: (1) the kinds of problems and issues that come to be part of the public agenda; (2) the ways in which people, groups, and parties think about these problems and issues and how they think presidents ought to deal with them; and (3) the distribution of political resources and power that helps determine which people and groups will get a hearing from the president. As we have emphasized throughout this book, a real understanding of American politics must take into account what goes on at the structural level, in the economy, in society, in the culture, and in the international system.

The International System

Thus, all U.S. presidents, from the end of World War II to the end of the Cold War, pursued a broadly similar set of foreign policies. While postwar presidents differed in their means, they fundamentally agreed on the ends: the containment of the influence of the Soviet Union; the solidification of the Western alliance; the encouragement of open economies in which American business might compete; and opposition to leftist or nationalist movements in the nations of the Third World. The reason for this continuity is that U.S. foreign policies reflect the basic features of the international system, the U.S. position in that system (including its immense resources and superpower status), and the nature of U.S. economic interests.

When the international system changes, presidential policy tends to change—whoever is president. Thus, when it became painfully evident by the 1970s that the United States had lost international economic competitiveness, measures were introduced by Presidents Carter and Reagan to reduce taxes, to lighten the burden of regulation, to subsidize high-technology industries, and to encourage exports. When the Soviet Union began to move in conciliatory directions and the Cold War ended, Presidents Reagan and Bush responded, despite their history of fierce anti-Communism.

The Economy

Similarly, all presidents, whether Democrat or Republican, must see that the economy remains healthy, with a proper balance between growth and inflation. A healthy economy is essential for a president's own popularity and his continuation in office, for the generation of tax receipts to fund government programs, and for the maintenance of social peace and stability. A healthy economy, in turn, requires that the main investors in the American economy—wealthy individuals, banks (both foreign and domestic), and corporations—continue to have confidence in the future. This has tended to bring a set of policies among presidents that favor such investors.

The presidency, then, like all the other institutions of our national government, reflects influences at the political level—interest groups, political parties, and especially public opinion. At the same time, in order to understand what presidents do, we need to understand what factors at the structural level affect both the political level and presidents themselves.

SUMMARY

The American presidency began small; only a few nineteenth-century presidents, such as Jefferson, Jackson, Polk, and Lincoln, made much of a mark. In the twentieth century, however, as a result of industrialization, two world wars, and the Great Depression, presidential powers and resources expanded greatly. The presidency largely attained its modern shape under Franklin Roosevelt.

Presidents have varied in personality and style. Personality and style have consequences that scholars have tried to analyze systematically; great leaders can make things happen. But the kinds of president we get are largely determined by such political-level factors as public opinion, interest groups, and political parties.

Moreover, despite the enormous resources and large staffs available to presidents, they are constrained in what they can do, especially concerning domestic policy. Presidents cannot always control their own executive branch. They engage in tugs-of-war with Congress, struggling to enact their programs with varying success, depending upon their own party's strength in the legislature, their own popularity, and the nature of the issue.

The presidency has become a far more democratic office than the Founders envisioned. Presidents listen to public opinion and respond to it, as well as lead (and sometimes manipulate) the public. But this does not make presidents pure tribunes of the people, because they are also influenced by interest groups, party activists, and money givers in ways that can diverge from what the public wants. Presidents are also affected by such structural factors as the nature of the American economic and social systems and the U.S. role in the international system and the world economy.

To Ponder

1. Do presidents shape great events, or do great events shape presidents?

2. Which is more frequent—presidential responsiveness to public opinion or presidential manipulation of public opinion?

3. How much difference does the character and personality of presidents make?

4. How could democratic control of the presidency be increased?

Suggested Readings

Barber, James David. *The Presidential Character: Predicting Performance in the White House*, 3rd ed. Englewood Cliffs, NJ: Prentice-Hall, 1985.
    A fascinating, though controversial, account of presidential personalities and their impact.

Cannon, Lou, *President Reagan: The Role of a Lifetime.* New York: Simon & Schuster, 1991.
    A close, critical look at Ronald Reagan and his presidency.

Neustadt, Richard E. *Presidential Power and the Modern Presidents: The Politics of Leadership from Roosevelt to Reagan.* New York: Free Press, 1990.
    The classic study of how presidents do or don't get their way, updated to include recent presidencies.

Tulis, Jeffrey K. *The Rhetorical Presidency.* Princeton, NJ: Princeton University Press, 1987.
     Tells how presidents have moved from the Founders' conception of a distant relationship
     with the public to the modern closeness.

Notes

1. Hedrick Smith, "The President as Coalition Builder: Reagan's First Year," in Thomas E. Cronin, ed., *Rethinking the Presidency* (Boston: Little, Brown, 1982), pp. 277–281.

2. Smith, "The President as Coalition Builder," p. 278.

3. David A. Stockman, *The Triumph of Politics: How the Reagan Revolution Failed* (New York: HarperCollins, 1986), p. 174.

4. Thomas P. O'Neill (with William Novak), *Man of the House: The Life and Memoirs of Speaker Tip O'Neill* (New York: Random House, 1987).

5. Stockman, *The Triumph of Politics*, p. 169.

6. O'Neill, *Man of the House*, pp. 341–342.

7. Kevin Phillips, *The Politics of Rich and Poor: Wealth and the American Electorate in the Reagan Aftermath* (New York: Random House, 1990).

8. Stockman, *The Triumph of Politics*.

9. *The Federalist Papers*, No. 74.

10. *Historical Statistics of the United States: Colonial Times to 1970* (U.S. Department of Commerce), Part I, p. 126.

11. Richard A. Watson and Norman C. Thomas, *The Politics of the Presidency*, 2nd ed. (Washington, D.C.: Congressional Quarterly Press, 1988), pp. 13–14.

12. Merle Miller, *Plain Speaking* (New York: Berkely, 1974), p. 88.

13. Fred I. Greenstein, *The Hidden-Hand Presidency: Eisenhower as Leader* (New York: Basic Books, 1982).

14. Paul F. Boller, Jr., *Presidential Anecdotes* (New York: Oxford University Press, 1981), pp. 299, 302.

15. Bruce Miroff, "The Presidency and the Public: Leadership as Spectacle," in Michael Nelson, *Presidency and the Political System*, 2nd ed. (Washington, D.C.: Congressional Quarterly Press, 1988), pp. 279–283.

16. Andrew Rosenthal, "Low Key Supplants Grandeur for Bush," *New York Times*, March 13, 1991, p. A10.

17. James David Barber, *The Presidential Character: Predicting Performance in the White House*, 3rd ed. (Englewood Cliffs, NJ: Prentice-Hall, 1985).

18. Alexander L. George and Juliette L. George, *Woodrow Wilson and Colonel House* (New York: John Day, 1956).

19. See Alexander George, "Assessing Presidential Character," *World Politics* (January 1974), pp. 234–282; Jeffrey Tulis, "On Presidential Character," in Jeffrey Tulis and Joseph M. Bessette, eds., *Presidency in the Constitutional Order* (Baton Rouge: Louisiana State University Press, 1981); Michael Nelson, "The Psychological Presidency," in Michael Nelson, ed., *The Presidency and the Political System*, 2nd ed. (Washington, D.C.: Congressional Quarterly Press, 1988), pp. 185–206.

20. Clinton Rossiter, *The American Presidency*, rev. ed. (New York: Harcourt, Brace and World, 1960).

21. Quoted in Laurence J. Peter, *Peter's Quotations* (New York: Morrow, 1977), p. 405.

22. Barber, *Presidential Character*, p. 124.

23. Philip Shabecoff, "Over E.P.A. Protest, White House Alters Wetland Agreement," *New York Times*, February 8, 1990, p. 1.

24. Donald Regan, *For the Record* (San Diego: Harcourt Brace Jovanovich, 1988); Kitty Kelley, *Nancy Reagan: The Unauthorized Biography* (New York: Simon & Schuster, 1991), focuses on petty scandal and personal flaws, slighting the First Lady's crucial role in protecting President Reagan and helping his self-presentation.

25. Dan Baly and Ann Devray, "Tiring of Hardball, Hill Ready to Bench Sununu," *Washington Post*, October 9, 1990, p. A1.

26. Theodore Draper, *A Very Thin Line: The Iran-Contra Affairs* (New York: Hill and Wang, 1991).

27. Jonathan Daniels, *The Man of Independence* (Philadelphia: Lippincott, 1950), p. 232.

28. Michel McQueen and Gerald F. Seib, "Has Quayle Learned Enough in Two Years? The Public Is Skeptical," *Wall Street Journal*, May 7, 1991, pp. A1, A22.

29. Samuel Gallu, *Give 'Em Hell Harry* (New York: Viking Press, 1975), p. 17.

30. Richard F. Fenno, Jr., *The President's Cabinet* (New York: Vintage, 1959), pp. 239–244.

31. Benjamin Bradlee, *Conversations with Kennedy* (New York: Norton, 1975), p. 38.

32. Richard E. Neustadt, *Presidential Power and the Modern Presidents: The Politics of Leadership from Roosevelt to Reagan* (New York: Macmillan, 1990).

33. Graham T. Allison, *Essence of Decision: Explaining the Cuban Missile Crisis* (Boston: Little, Brown, 1971).

34. Neustadt, *Presidential Power*, ch. 2.

35. *New York Times*, July 19, 1990, p. A2.

36. Arthur M. Schlesinger, Jr., *The Imperial Presidency* (Boston: Houghton Mifflin, 1973).

37. George C. Edwards, III, *Presidential Influence in Congress* (San Francisco: Freeman, 1980); Jon Bond and John Fleischer, *The President in the Legislative Arena* (Chicago: University of Chicago Press, 1990).

38. Edwards, *Presidential Influence*, pp. 90–100.

39. Aaron Wildavsky, "The Two Presidencies," in Aaron Wildavsky, ed., *Perspectives on the Presidency* (Boston: Little, Brown, 1975), pp. 448–461.

40. Steven Shull, *The Two Presidencies: A Quarter-Century Assessment* (Chicago: Nelson Hall, 1991); Bond and Fleischer, *The President in the Legislative Arena*.

41. Jeffrey K. Tulis, *The Rhetorical Presidency* (Princeton, NJ: Princeton University Press, 1987), Chs. 2–3, esp. p. 64.

42. Woodrow Wilson, *Leaders of Men*, ed. by T. H. Vail Motter (Princeton, NJ: Princeton University Press, 1952), p. 39; quoted in Tulis, *Rhetorical Presidency*, ch. 4, which analyzes Wilson's theory at length.

43. Harry S Truman, lecture, Columbia University, April 27, 1959.

44. Tulis, *Rhetorical Presidency*, pp. 138, 140.

45. Samuel Kernell, *Going Public: Strategies of Presidential Leadership* (Washington, D.C.: Congressional Quarterly Press, 1986), pp. 69, 86, and ch. 4.

46. Benjamin I. Page and Robert Y. Shapiro, "Presidents as Opinion Leaders: Some New Evidence," *Policy Studies Journal*, Vol. 12 (June 1984), pp. 649–661; Benjamin I. Page, Robert Y. Shapiro, and Glenn R. Dempsey, "What Moves Public Opinion," *American Political Science Review*, Vol. 81 (March 1987), pp. 23–43.

47. *New York Times*, June 11, 1991, p. A10.

48. Benjamin I. Page and Mark P. Petracca, *The American Presidency* (New York: McGraw-Hill, 1983), p. 122. See Benjamin I. Page and Robert Y. Shapiro, "Effects of Public Opinion on Policy," *American Political Science Review*, Vol. 77 (March 1983), pp. 175–190.

49. Jack J. Honomichl, "How Reagan Took America's Pulse," *Advertising Age*, January 23, 1989, pp. 1, 25, 32.

50. Studies of what affects presidential popularity include John E. Mueller, "Presidential Popularity from Truman to Johnson," *American Political Science Review*, Vol. 64 (March 1970), pp. 18–34; Richard A. Brody and Benjamin I. Page, "The Impact of Events on Presidential Popularity: The Johnson and Nixon Administrations," in Aaron Wildavsky, ed., *Perspectives on the Presidency* (Boston: Little, Brown, 1975), pp. 136–148; Samuel Kernell, "Explaining Presidential Popularity," *American Political Science Review*, Vol. 72 (June 1978), pp. 506–522.

51. *New York Times*, June 11, 1991, p. A10.

52. Charles E. Lindblom, *Politics and Markets* (New York: Basic Books, 1977).

53. Alexander Heard, *The Costs of Democracy* (Chapel Hill, NC: University of North Carolina Press, 1960); Thomas Ferguson and Joel Rogers, *Right Turn* (New York: Farrar, Straus & Giroux, 1986).

54. James Sundquist, *Politics and Policy: The Eisenhower, Kennedy, and Johnson Years* (Washington, D.C.: Brookings Institution, 1968).

13

The Executive Branch

THE EPA SURVIVES

William Ruckelshaus acknowledged the cheers of the large crowd at the Environmental Protection Agency (EPA) in Washington, D.C., with a wave of his hand and a broad smile. The newly appointed head of the EPA told the gathering that he wanted to restore the agency's credibility by returning it to its primary mission of protecting the nation's environment. His statement was welcomed with a collective sigh of relief from the agency's career personnel and environmental groups. Ruckelshaus's predecessor, Ann Gorsuch, a protégée of Interior Secretary James Watt (and a believer in the notion that government regulation of business is contrary to the American way of life), had tried to gut the EPA.

Watt set the terms of the new order immediately after the 1980 election when he announced that Interior Department personnel were to sever all contacts with representatives of environmental organizations. Watt and Gorsuch next purged visible environmental advocates from Interior Department and EPA scientific advisory bodies. EPA personnel were ordered to resign leadership positions in environmental organizations. While EPA ties to its traditional environmental constituencies were being severed, new lines of communication were being opened to business and industry. The watchword at the newly oriented EPA was "cooperation rather than confrontation" with the business community.

Gorsuch also signaled the new order at the EPA when she recommended that her agency's budget be cut by more than 20 percent. She eagerly made additional cuts when ordered to do so by Budget Director David Stockman. Deep staff cuts followed: hundreds were fired, and thousands resigned in disgust. Research, field investigations, and fines against polluters all declined. Gorsuch also announced a substantial loosening of air and water pollution standards.

Morale at the agency was low. The appointed political leadership looked at agency career personnel as the enemy; career people looked at Gorsuch and her people as violators of the EPA's mission. While the political appointees seemed to have the upper hand in the beginning, career staff struck back by leaking embarrassing documents to the press, environmental organizations, and friendly congressional committees. Particularly embarrassing were revelations about financial corruption, plans for the wholesale weakening of standards for air and water pollution and for toxic waste dumps, and mismanagement of the superfunds program (to clean up toxic sites).

Matters reached the political exploding point when House committees, controlled by the rival Democratic party, opened hearings on mismanagement and fraud at the EPA. When the president ordered Gorsuch to refuse to turn over relevant documents to Congress on the grounds of "executive privilege," suspicions were fueled that things were even worse than advertised at the EPA. Revelations that superfund head Rita Lavelle had delayed action to clean up toxic sites in California in order to hurt the senatorial bid of Democrat Jerry Brown fueled the flames.

Congress struck back by citing Gorsuch for "contempt of Congress," while the media, quick to sense blood, swooped down on the EPA for more news of misdeeds. Many career and professional employees were only too happy to help Congress and the press. Seeing his environmental policy in shambles, President Reagan ordered Gorsuch to ask Lavelle to resign, sent the FBI to gather documents to support possible prosecutions, and, when none of this quelled public and congressional criticism, forced Gorsuch to resign.

To repair the damage to his administration, President Reagan abandoned the Watt-Gorsuch approach at the EPA. His appointment of William Ruckelshaus served this purpose well. Ruckelshaus had been the first head of the EPA under Richard Nixon and was widely admired by EPA career and professional employees, as well as by environmental organizations. He was a skilled Washington insider who had held several important administrative posts in the past, and he was respected for his integrity and managerial skills.

Ruckelshaus moved quickly after his appointment sailed through the Senate. In a whirlwind series of meetings, he reassured environmental groups and agency civil servants that he was committed to the reestablishment of EPA's historic mission. He fulfilled his promises by firing all of Gorsuch's political appointees, stepping up the pace of EPA research and violations investigations, imposing increasingly stiff fines on polluters, and convincing the president to increase the staff and budget for his agency.

Ruckelshaus's appointment quieted much of the criticism of President Reagan's environmental policy. The cost to the president was high, however: he abandoned one of the central elements in his program to "get government off the backs" of the business community.

This story highlights many of the things that we will learn in this chapter. Most important, it demonstrates that the executive branch is not simply a bureaucratic extension of the president's will, operating at his beck and call. Political and governmental influences, such as interest groups, Congress, the media, and public opinion, shape the kind of bureaucracy we have. So do such structural factors as the Constitution, the economy, and the political culture. So do the backgrounds and training of the people who work in the government.

Ultimately, this chapter is about how our bureaucracy affects the health and vitality of democracy in the United States. As we look at this question, we will also try to dispel some of the prevailing myths about "**bureaucracy**."

Governmental

Political

Structural

CHARACTERIZING THE U.S. BUREAUCRACY: STRUCTURAL INFLUENCES

The American bureaucracy is different from bureaucracies in other democratic nations. Such structural influences as the American political culture and the constitutional rules of the game have a great deal to do with these differences.

A Hostile Political Culture

Americans do not trust government; nor do they think it can accomplish most tasks assigned to it. They believe, on the whole, that the private sector can usually do a better job.

This hostile environment influences the bureaucracy in several ways. For one thing, our public bureaucracy is surrounded by more statutory restrictions and is subject to more intense legislative oversight than bureaucracies in other democratic nations. Because civil servants have so little prestige, moreover, many of the most talented people in our society tend to stay away; they do not aspire to be civil servants. As strange as this may seem, the opposite is the case elsewhere. In France, Great Britain, and Germany, for instance, the higher civil service is filled by the best graduates of their country's elite universities and are accorded enormous prestige. Finally, the highest policymaking positions in the executive branch are closed to civil servants and are reserved for presidential political appointees. This is not true in other democracies.

Incoherent Organization

Our bureaucracy is an organizational hodgepodge. It does not take the standard pyramidal form, like bureaucracies elsewhere. There are few clear lines of control, responsibility, and accountability. Some bureaucratic units have no place at all in relationship to other agencies and departments. As one of the leading students of the federal bureaucracy once put it, "[other societies have] a more orderly and symmetrical, a more prudent, a more cohesive and more powerful bureaucracy . . . [whereas] we have a more internally competitive, a more experimental, a noisier and less coherent, a less powerful bureaucracy. . . ."[1] Our bureaucracy was built piece by piece over the years in a political system without a strong central government. Bureaucracies in other democratic nations often were created at a single point in time, by powerful political leaders, for example, Frederick the Great in Prussia and Napoleon in France.[2]

The proliferation of federal agencies can have confusing and comical results.
Drawing by Victor, © 1981. The New York Magazine, Inc.

"H.U.D. called the F.A.A. The F.A.A. called the S.E.C. The S.E.C. called G.S.A. G.S.A. called O.M.B. O.M.B. called Y-O-U."

Divided Control

Adding to the organizational incoherence of our federal bureaucracy is the fact that bureaucratic agencies have two bosses—the president and Congress—who are constantly vying for control. This derives from the separation of powers and checks and balances in our Constitution, which gives each branch a role in the principal activities and responsibilities of the other branches. No other democratic nation opts for this arrangement, preferring, instead, a parliamentary system in which legislative and executive power are combined in a parliamentary body, dominated by the cabinet and the prime minister. Bureaucrats in parliamentary systems have a single boss, a minister appointed by the prime minister.

Open and Porous

Because of incoherent organization, the lack of a chain of command with clear lines of authority and accountability, and divided control at the top, ours is an extremely open and porous bureaucracy. It is possible to get a hearing and a response from bureaucrats without necessarily starting at the top, as one would have to do in France, Japan, or Germany. In one sense, this is potentially a very democratic development, encouraging citizen participation in bureaucratic affairs. In practice, however, it provides a very fertile environment for interest groups. Iron triangles and other forms of privileged access abound, as related in Chapter 7.

TRANSFORMATION OF THE EXECUTIVE BRANCH: THE STRUCTURAL CONTEXT

Executive departments and officers are mentioned in the Constitution only in an indirect, offhand way. The Constitution neither specifies the number or kinds of departments to be established nor describes other executive agencies. The framers apparently wanted to leave these questions to the wisdom of Congress and the president.

We saw in the last chapter that the Executive Branch grew from very modest beginnings in President Washington's administration to a very large bureaucracy in our own day of about 2.8 million civilian employees working in 14 departments, a White House mini-bureaucracy, and literally hundreds of bureaus, agencies, commissions, services, and boards. Figure 13.1 depicts the overall organization of the federal government and suggests the extraordinarily wide range of its responsibilities.

A Brief Administrative History of the United States

The most immediate causes for the transformation of the role of the federal government and the scale of the bureaucracy are political-level pressures—public opinion, voters, parties, interest groups, and social movements—on government decision makers. The more fundamental causes are changes in such structural factors as the U.S. economy, its population, and the role of the United States in the world. We can see the interaction of these factors in the following brief history of the American bureaucracy.

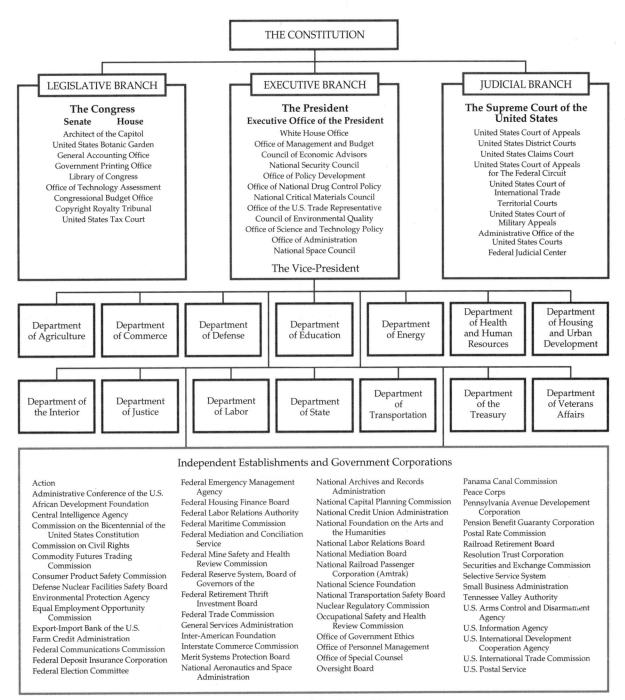

Figure 13.1 The government of the United States

Source: U.S. Government Organization Manual.

Until the Civil War, the federal government had few responsibilities and the administrative apparatus of the executive branch was relatively undeveloped. Alexis de Tocqueville, the perceptive French observer of the fledgling American democracy, could hardly find a government at all: "[in America], society governs itself for itself."[3]

The problems and opportunities created by rapid population growth, westward expansion, the Industrial Revolution, economic instability, and the emergence of the giant corporation in the last quarter of the nineteenth century gradually changed people's thinking about the appropriate responsibilities of government and the size of the bureaucracy.[4] The Interior Department, created in 1849, was given responsibilities for Indian Affairs, the conduct of the census, and regulation of public lands and mining. The Department of Justice was created in 1870 to handle the enormous and growing federal government's legal burden in the fields of civil and criminal law, antitrust, tax, and natural resources. The Department of Agriculture became a full-fledged cabinet department in 1889 in response to the economic crisis in the farm economy and the demands of farm groups. The Department of Labor was created in 1913 to try to ease some of the tensions and the conflicts that existed between labor and capital. The Commerce Department was created in the same year to foster technological development, standardization, and business cooperation.

The rise of the large corporations in the late nineteenth and early twentieth centuries, and the problems caused by them, also contributed to a rethinking of the role of the federal government. Monopoly practices in the railroad, manufacturing, oil, and banking industries triggered reform movements that resulted in new federal regulatory laws, of which the most important were the Interstate Commerce Act (1887) and the Sherman Antitrust Act (1890). Progressive reformers and farsighted business leaders who were worried about growing public hostility to big business helped convince Congress to pass such landmark legislation as the Federal Reserve Act (passed in 1914 to stabilize the banking industry), the Pure Food and Drug Act (1906), the Meat Inspection Act (passed in 1906 in response to the horrors reported in Upton Sinclair's *The Jungle*), and the Federal Trade Commission Act (1914).[5] Each piece of legislation was a response to a set of problems, each expanded the federal government's responsibilities, and each created a new executive branch agency to carry out the law.

It was the Great Depression that forever changed how Americans thought about government. President Franklin Roosevelt and Congress responded to economic collapse, widespread social distress, and serious threats of violence and social conflict with a range of new programs: work programs for the unemployed; poor relief; Social Security; regulation of banks and the securities industry; agricultural subsidy programs; collective bargaining; and programs to encourage business expansion. Needless to say, these initiatives caused an expansion in the size of the federal bureaucracy.

World War II, the long Cold War with the Soviet Union, and America's new role as a super power, also brought a substantial increase in the federal government's responsibilities and in the size of the executive branch. Some old-line departments, such as the State Department, grew substantially after World War II. The Department of Defense was created by merging the old Army and Navy Departments and adding an Air Force component. New administrative units like the Central Intelligence Agency, the National Security Agency, the National Security Council, the Agency for International Development, and the U.S. Arms

Control and Disarmament Agency were created to fill new needs and missions. The Atomic Energy Commission was created both to regulate and to encourage atomic power and weapons production. The Internal Revenue Service expanded its operations so that it could collect the revenues to pay for these new responsibilities. By 1950, a federal bureaucracy of substantial size and impact was firmly in place.[6]

During the 1960s and 1970s, successful social reform movements and important changes in public opinion convinced political leaders to take on new responsibilities in the areas of civil rights, urban affairs, environmental and consumer protection, and education. Important among these initiatives was the formation of the Department of Health, Education, and Welfare (now the Department of Health and Human Services *and* the Department of Education). Each expansion of responsibility, as in the past, brought an expansion in the size of the executive branch. Though the so-called Reagan Revolution slowed the growth in the federal government's responsibilities, it was unable to roll back most of the programs or agencies created since the Great Depression.

BUREAUCRACY

Bureaucracy has always been a dirty word in American politics, and it remains so today. The word implies red tape, inefficiency, and nonresponsiveness. Politicians are always promising to "clean up the bureaucratic mess in Washington." To social scientists, however, *bureaucracy* and *bureaucrat* are neutral terms that describe a type of social organization and the people who work in it. Bureaucracies are generally defined as *large organizations*, in which people with *specialized knowledge* are organized into a clearly defined *hierarchy* of bureaus or offices, each of which has a specified *mission*. There is a clear *chain of command*, in which each person has one and only one boss or supervisor, and a set of *formal rules* to guide behavior. Appointment and advancement, moreover, are based on *merit* rather than inheritance, power, or election. This description is, of course, a model or an "ideal type"; in the real world, there are many deviations.[7]

One advantage of a bureaucratic organization is its ability to organize large tasks.[8] Hierarchical organizations with clear chains of command are able to mobilize and to coordinate the efforts of thousands of people. Bureaucratic organization enabled the Defense Department to deploy over 500,000 troops and 11 million tons of weapons and equipment to the Saudi Arabian desert in a matter of months in preparation for the Persian Gulf War against Iraq.

Another advantage of bureaucracies is the concentration of specialized talent that is found in them. People enter bureaucratic organizations on the basis of merit. They either pass an examination to determine if they are qualified, or they bring to their jobs the kind of experience or training that the bureaucratic organization needs. Thus, the Public Health Service recruits doctors, nurses, and technicians. The National Weather Service wants the best meteorological scientists. People in bureaucratic organizations tend to remain in the same agencies or bureaus for years, moreover, honing their narrow specializations, getting very good at what they do. These specialists can be rapidly mobilized when a president or a congressional committee needs information that will enable them to make national policy. To combat AIDs, for instance, they can turn to the scientists and doctors at the National Center for Disease Control or the National Institutes of Health for help.

Bureacratic organizations have the capacity to perform large-scale tasks like the transport and deployment of hundreds of thousands of troops and tons of equipment and supplies to the Persian Gulf during the Gulf War.

Despite the complaints and jokes about bureaucracy, then, it has considerable advantages as a form of organization. This is not to say, of course, that bureaucracy is unproblematic; it is to say that the American rhetorical distaste for bureaucracy tends to hide some of its benefits.

HOW THE EXECUTIVE BRANCH IS ORGANIZED

The executive branch is made up of several different kinds of administrative units (see Table 13.1). *Departments* are headed by cabinet-level secretaries, appointed by the president and approved by the Senate. Departments are meant to carry out the most essential government functions. The first three, as we have seen, were War, State, and Treasury. The only debate surrounding the creation of these "core" departments concerned the power of removal: who could fire whom. Many in Congress believed that the method for removing department secretaries should be the same as appointment: presidential action, followed by the advice and consent of the Senate. James Madison's argument that this would cause administrative chaos and inefficiency won the day. The issue did not entirely die, however. Radical Republicans after the Civil War passed the Tenure of Office Act, requiring Senate approval of the president's removal of executive personnel as a way to maintain congressional control over the reconstruction of the southern states. When President Andrew Johnson refused to abide by its terms, he was impeached (but not convicted). The issue was finally settled by the Supreme Court in the case of *Meyers v. the United States* (1926), which ruled in favor of the president's sole power of removal.

Over the years, departments were added as the need arose or as powerful groups in society demanded it. Powerful interest groups were behind the creation of the Departments of Agriculture, Commerce, Labor, and Education, for instance.

Sometimes departments are formed as a way for a president and members of Congress to signal a new national commitment or to cement political alliances

Table 13.1
The Executive Departments

Department	1991 Budget Outlays (in billions of dollars)	Civilian Employees, 1991
Agriculture	$55.4	114,407
Commerce	2.8	61,631
Defense	288.2	1,022,097
Education	24.8	4,655
Energy	13.5	17,710
Health and Human Services	153.2[a]	123,202
Housing and Urban Development	23.5	13,366
Interior	6.1	72,835
Justice	8.7	84,146
Labor	5.7	17,473
State	4.3	24,903
Transportation	9.8	66,499
Treasury	277.9[b]	158,960
Veterans	30.4	248,841

[a] Excludes Social Security.

[b] Includes interest on the national debt.

Source: The Budget of the United States, Fiscal 1992.

with important constituencies. Lyndon Johnson persuaded Congress to create the Department of Housing and Urban Development in 1965 and the Department of Transportation in 1967 for these reasons. Jimmy Carter highlighted his concerns in the midst of the OPEC oil crisis by persuading Congress to create the Department of Energy. He supported the creation of the Department of Education to acknowledge the political backing of the National Education Association.

Subdivisions within cabinet departments are known as *bureaus* and *agencies*. In some departments, like HUD, these subdivisions are closely controlled by the department leadership, and the entire department works very much like the textbook hierarchical model. In others, where the bureaus or agencies have fashioned their own relationships with interest groups and powerful congressional committees, departments are little more than holding companies for powerful bureaucratic subunits.[9] This was true of HEW, where the Public Health Service and the Office of Education pretty much went their own way. During the long reign of J. Edgar Hoover, the FBI did virtually as it pleased, even though it was (and remains) a unit within the Justice Department.

Government corporations are agencies that operate in a market setting and are organized very much like a private company. They can sell stock, retain and reinvest earnings, and borrow money, for instance. They are usually created to perform some crucial economic activity that private investors are unwilling or unable to perform. Amtrak, for instance, was created to provide passenger rail service after the virtual collapse of the private customer rail industry. The U.S. Postal Service was transformed from an executive department to a government corporation in 1970 to increase efficiency. Recently, the Resolution Trust Corporation was created to coordinate the bailout of the S&L industry.

Independent regulatory commissions, such as the Securities and Exchange Commission or the Interstate Commerce Commission, are responsible for regulating those sectors of the economy where the free market does not work properly to protect the public interest. The commissions are "independent" in the sense that they stand outside the departmental structure and are protected against direct presidential or congressional control. Commissions are run by commissioners with long, overlapping terms, and many require a balance between Republicans and Democrats.

The remainder of the agencies, which do not fit into any of the departments and are not corporations or regulatory commissions, are simply referred to as *independent executive agencies.* These include such large and powerful agencies as the General Services Administration (in charge of all federal government buildings, equipment, and supplies) and such tiny agencies as the American Battlefield Monuments Commission.

WHAT DO BUREAUCRATS DO?

Executing the Law

The term *executive branch* suggests the branch of the federal government that executes or carries out the law. The framers assumed that Congress would be the principal national policymaker and that the president and those he appointed to administrative positions in the executive branch "shall take care that the laws be faithfully executed. . . ." (Article II, Section 2).

Executing the law is not so easy, however. It is not always clear what the law means. To be sure, Congress sometimes passes a law with clearly stated goals and procedures to guide the actions of the president and the bureaucrats in the executive branch. Often, however (all too often according to some critics[10]), Congress passes laws that are vague about goals and short on procedural guidelines. Congress may do so because its members believe that something should be done about a particular social problem but are short on ideas on how to solve it or its members may have definite ideas but disagree among themselves. The Office of Economic Opportunity was created in 1965 as part of Lyndon Johnson's War on Poverty, with a mandate to eliminate poverty, for example, but it received virtually no guidance about what time frame was contemplated or what specific things it ought to do. In 1989, President George Bush announced a "war on drugs" without providing details of an overall strategy or specific procedures for bureaucrats in the Drug Enforcement Administration and other agencies to follow. Vaguely written statutes and directives, then, leave a great deal of discretion to bureaucrats.

Rule Making

You may be surprised to learn that a great deal of law is made by bureaucrats. Congress often gives bureaucratic agencies the power to write specific rules. Because of the complexity of the problems that government must face, Congress tends to create agencies and to specify the job or mission that it wants done and then leaves it to the agency to use its expertise to do it. Congress created the Environmental Protection Agency (EPA), for instance, and gave it a mission—to help coordinate the cleanup of the nation's air and water—but it left to the EPA the power to set specific standards for communities and businesses to meet. The standards set by the EPA have the force of law unless they are rescinded by Congress or the courts. The Federal Drug Administration writes rules about the introduction of new drugs that researchers and pharmaceutical companies are obliged to follow. New and proposed rules are published daily in the *Federal Register*, a truly formidable document.

Some critics believe that Congress delegates entirely too much lawmaking to the executive branch,[11] but it's difficult to see what alternative it has. Congress can change the rules written by bureaucrats if they drift too far from congressional intent or constituent desires. When the Federal Trade Commission (FTC) tried to write rules about advertising on children's television that rankled advertisers and station owners, for instance, Congress rescinded the FTC action. Bureaucratic rule making is also carefully watched by presidents and (increasingly) by the courts.

Adjudicating

Congress has given some executive branch agencies the power to conduct quasi-judicial proceedings in which disputes are resolved. Much as in a court of law, the decisions of an administrative law judge, unless appealed to a higher panel, have the force of law. The National Labor Relations Board, for instance, adjudicates disputes between labor and management on matters concerning federal labor laws. Disputes may involve claims of unfair labor practices, for instance—firing a labor organizer falls under this category—or disagreements about whether proper procedures were followed in filing for a union certification election.

Bureaucrats exercise a great deal of discretion. They do not simply follow a set of orders from Congress or the President, but find many opportunities to exercise their own judgment. Because bureaucrats make important decisions that have consequences for many other people, groups, and organizations, we can say that they are policymakers. They are *unelected policymakers*, however, and this should immediately alert us to some potential problems with regard to the practice of democracy.

WHO ARE THE BUREAUCRATS?

Because bureaucrats exercise substantial discretion as policymakers, we want to know who they are. How representative are they of the American people? In a democracy, one would probably want to see a pretty close correspondence between the people and bureaucrats.

The Merit Services

There are three different personnel systems in the executive branch: the career civil service, separate merit service in specific agencies, and political appointees.

THE CAREER CIVIL SERVICE   From the election of Andrew Jackson in 1828 until the late nineteenth century, the executive branch was staffed through the "**spoils**" system. It was generally accepted that the "spoils of victory" belonged to the winning party. Winners were expected to clear out people who were loyal to the

This drawing depicts the assassination of President James Garfield by a disgruntled job-seeker.

previous administration and to replace them with their own people. Also known as **patronage**, this system of appointment occasioned no great alarm in the beginning because of the small and relatively unimportant role of the federal government in American society. The shortcomings of the War Department and other bureaucratic agencies during the Civil War convinced many people that reform of the federal personnel system was required. Rampant corruption and favoritism in the government service during the years after the Civil War gave an additional boost to the reform effort, as did the realization that the growing role of the federal government required more skilled personnel. The final catalyst for change was the assassination of President James Garfield by a person who (it is said) badly wanted a government job but could not get one.

The Civil Service Act of 1883, which also is known as the Pendleton Act, created a bipartisan Civil Service Commission to oversee a system of appointments to certain executive branch posts on the basis of merit. Competitive examinations were to be used to determine merit. In the beginning, the competitive civil service system included only about 10 percent of federal positions. Congress gradually has extended the reach of the career civil service; today it covers about 58 percent of all federal employees. In 1978, Congress abolished the Civil Service Commission and replaced it with two separate agencies: the Office of Personnel Management and the Merit Systems Protection Board. The former administers the civil service laws, advertises positions, writes examinations, and acts as a clearinghouse for agencies that are looking for workers. The latter settles disputes concerning employee rights and obligations, hears employee grievances, and orders corrective action.

MERIT SERVICE IN SPECIFIC AGENCIES   Many federal agencies require personnel with particular kinds of training and experience appropriate to their special missions. For such agencies, Congress has established separate merit systems that are administered by the agency itself. The Public Health Service, for instance, needs to recruit doctors and has its own system for doing so. The State Department has its own examinations and procedures for recruiting foreign service officers. NASA (National Aeronautics and Space Administration) recruits its own scientists and engineers without the help of the Office of Personnel Management. The FBI tests and selects its own agents. About 35 percent of all federal civilian employees fall under these agency-specific merit systems.

Who Are Civil Servants?

Civil servants (this term covers the career civil service and the agency merit services) are very much like other Americans. In strictly demographic terms, the civil service is filled with people who are very much like other Americans.[12] There is the same diversity of occupations. Educational levels, regional origins, average income, and age distribution almost exactly match that of the general population. Their political beliefs and opinions are similar to those of other Americans, though they tend to be somewhat more Democratic and *slightly* more liberal than the national average.[13] Women and minorities are very well represented (the latter are actually overrepresented).[14] In addition, the demographic representativeness of the bureaucracy is far greater in the United States than in virtually any other democratic nation.[15]

   A few anomalies ought to be mentioned, however. First, women and minorities are overrepresented in the very lowest civil service grades and are underrepresented in the highest grades. They also are far less evident in the special-agency merit systems (such as the Foreign Service and the FBI) and in the professional categories (scientists at National Institutes of Health; doctors in the Public Health Service). Second, the averages hide some distinct patterns in the agencies, which, because of their special missions, tend to draw a particular kind of person. The personnel of the Bureau of Land Management and the Bureau of Alcohol, Tobacco and Firearms are primarily males from rural and agricultural backgrounds, educated in state land-grant colleges. Women are better represented in the Department of Justice, where personnel tend to come from urban areas in the East and from elite colleges and universities.[16] Almost two-thirds of the work force in the Department of Health and Human Services is female, while only about one-fourth of those in the Post Office are. This suggests that the overall work force of the civil service closely corresponds to the overall American population, but particular departments and agencies may deviate quite substantially.

Women and minorities are overrepresented in lower-level jobs in the executive branch, like these workers processing tax returns for the Internal Revenue Service.

The representative character of the merit services here contrasts sharply with the situation in Great Britain and France. Those of aristocratic background have long dominated the upper levels of the civil service in the former; graduates of the elite "grand écoles," like the École National d'Administration, dominate in the latter.

Political Appointees

The highest policymaking positions in the federal bureaucracy (e.g., department secretaries, assistants to the president in the White House office, and leading officials in the Central Intelligence Agency) do not enter government service by way of competitive merit examinations but by presidential appointment. There are about 1,500 of these "Executive Schedule," schedule C, and Noncareer Executive appointments. These top patronage positions, in theory at least, allow the president to translate his electoral mandate into public policy by permitting him to put his people in place in key policymaking jobs. To be sure, presidents want to appoint experienced people who are familiar with the work of the department or agency to these posts, but policy and ideological agreement with the president and party loyalty are equally important. Most presidents use patronage not only to build support for their programs but also to firm up their political coalition by being sensitive to the needs of important party factions and interest groups.

Ronald Reagan differed greatly from other presidents in the degree to which he used ideology as a "litmus test" for high bureaucratic appointments.[17] His main instrument for making the bureaucracy conservative was the Presidential personnel office, which depended on advice from conservative organizations such as the Committee on the Present Danger, the Heritage Foundation, and the American Enterprise Institute.

Unlike the vast majority of federal government employees covered by civil service regulations, top political appointees are not at all representative of the American people. This is important for the practice of democracy, because it is these officials who exercise the most discretion and make the most important policy decisions. To be sure, background is not everything in the determination of the outlook and behavior of political appointees, but it cannot be discounted either.

One exhaustive study, covering the years 1897 to 1973, found that over 90 percent of all cabinet officials belonged to the social elite (listed in various social registers and either members of exclusive private clubs or graduates of exclusive prep schools) or the business elite (defined by membership on a corporate board or by partnership in a top corporate law firm). These public officials were almost exclusively members of high-status Protestant denominations, came from families in business or the professions, and were descended from northern European or English ancestors.[18]

One historian studied the composition of top foreign policymakers in the Departments of State, Defense, War, Treasury, and Commerce, the Central Intelligence Agency, and the Export-Import Bank, and concluded that "foreign policy decision-makers are in reality a highly mobile sector of the American corporate structure."[19] Between 1944 and 1960, almost 60 percent of all foreign policymaking posts were held by people who were on leave from corporate law firms, investment and banking houses, or industrial corporations. There is no reason to believe that this pattern has changed.

Political appointees do not last very long on the job, however. On average, they stay in office only 22 months, leading political scientist Hugh Heclo to call them "birds of passage."[20] They leave for many reasons. Most are accomplished people from the private sector who only see government service as a short-term commitment. Most make financial sacrifices in order to become top bureaucratic officials. Many don't find the notoriety appealing. Finally, many become frustrated at how difficult it is to change public policy and to see it implemented (see "Doing Politics").

THE FEDERAL BUREAUCRACY AND DEMOCRACY

In this section, we turn to the problem of the relationship between the bureaucracy and democracy. We use the definition of *democracy* set out in Chapter 1: a system of government characterized by popular sovereignty, political equality, and political liberty.

Popular Sovereignty

Popular sovereignty refers to the fit between what the people want and what the government does. It requires that the bureaucracy be accountable to the people. Strangely enough, the framers gave very little thought to the accountability of the executive branch, assuming, perhaps, that once policy was made by Congress or the president, implementation would follow automatically.[21]

It should be understood that maximizing democratic accountability in the bureaucracy may conflict with other things that we care about. Accountability assumes close control of bureaucratic behavior, either directly by the people or indirectly by the people through Congress and the president. It implies limitations on bureaucratic discretion. Decreasing the scope of discretion may have the effect, however, of reducing the efficiency and effectiveness of bureaucratic institutions, because it decreases the free play of bureaucratic expertise. It is a choice we must make as citizens.

PUBLIC OPINION   Scrutiny by the public is an important instrument of democratic control. Most Americans, however, have no opinions about bureaucratic agencies, as such. The public focuses mainly on the *content* of public policies rather than on the bureaucratic agencies or the bureaucrats who carry them out. Americans have opinions about Social Security—the level of benefits, eligibility, taxes, and so on— but do not concern themselves much with the Social Security Administration, per se. Most have opinions about our balance-of-trade problems with other nations but give little thought to the Export-Import Bank. In general, then, public opinion does not directly affect, let alone control, bureaucratic behavior.

There are exceptions, however. Some bureaucratic agencies, perhaps because of their size or their impact, or the media attention that they receive, are constantly in the public eye and occasion the development of opinions. Because taxes are a constant irritant for most people, Americans tend to have opinions—not very favorable, to be sure—about the Internal Revenue Service and its agents. Most of us have something to say about the Defense Department, especially when stories appear about $200 screwdrivers and weapons systems like the B-1 bomber that do not work as advertised.

DOING POLITICS

How Civil Servants Can Sabotage Political Appointees

Often sabotage is unrecognizable because of the virtually invisible ways civil servants can act in bad faith toward political executives. In addition to the bureaucracy's power of withholding needed information and services, there are other means. Like a long-married couple, bureaucrats and those in their networks can often communicate with a minimum of words: "If congressional staffs I trust call up and ask me, I might tell them. But I can also tell them I don't agree with the secretary by offering just technical information and not associating myself with the policy."

An official who does not want to risk direct dealings with Congress can encourage a private interest group to go to the agency's important appropriations and legislative committees, as one political executive discovered: "When we tried to downgrade the . . . bureau, its head was opposed, and he had a friend in a lobby group. After they got together rumblings started from the appropriations committee. I asked [the committee chairman] if he had a problem with this reorganization, and he said, "No, you have the problem because if you touch that bureau I'll cut your job out of the budget." . . .

Political appointees can sometimes encounter much more vigorous forms of sabotage. These range from minor needling to massive retaliation. Since information is a prime strategic resource in Washington, the passing of unauthorized messages outside channels often approaches an art form. There are routine leaks to build credit and keep channels open for when they might be needed, positive leaks to promote something, negative leaks to discredit a person or policy, and counterleaks. There is even the daring reverse leak, an unauthorized release of information apparently for one reason but actually accomplishing the opposite.

There is no lack of examples in every administration. A political executive may discover that an agency subordinate "has gone to Congress and actually written the rider to the legislation that nullified the changes we wanted." A saboteur confided that "no one ever found it was [a division chief] who prepared the list showing which lobbyist was to contact which senator with what kind of argument." Still another official reported he had "seen appointees kept waiting in the outer office while their subordinate bureau officials were in private meetings with the congressional staff members." But waiting lines lack finesse. The telephone can be used with more delicacy, particularly after office hours: "The night before the hearings [a bureaucrat] fed the questions to the committee staff and then the agency witnesses spent the next two days having to reveal the information or duck the questions and catch hell." A young staff civil servant described how his superior operated:

> I used to sit in [the bureau chief's] office after 6 P.M. when all the important business got done. He'd call up a senator and say, "Tom, you know this program that you and I got through a while back? Well, there's no crisis, but here are some things I'd like to talk to you about." He'd hang up and get on the phone to [a House committee chairman] and say, "I've been talking with Tom about this issue, and I'd like to bring you in on it." Hell, you'd find [the bureau chief] had bills almost drafted before anybody else in the executive branch had ever heard about them.

Source: Hugh Heclo, *A Government of Strangers* (Washington, D.C.: Brookings Institution, 1977).

The Federal Emergency Management Agency (FEMA) coordinates federal relief after national disasters. It was heavily criticized for its slow response to the 1989, Bay-area earthquake (pictured here) and hurricane Andrew in Florida in 1992.

A disaster or a string of disasters can focus public attention on an agency, as NASA discovered to its discomfort after defects developed in the Hubble telescope. Charges of "too little, too late" hounded the Federal Emergency Management Agency (FEMA) after hurricane Andrew in 1992. Lax regulation by the Federal Home Loan Bank Board helped bring on the S&L crisis.

A handful of agencies like the FBI are very adept at shaping public opinion in their favor. Under the shrewd leadership of longtime director J. Edgar Hoover, the FBI built a reputation as a great crime fighter through such public relations gimmicks as the "Ten Most Wanted List," encouragement of, and technical support for, favored radio and television programs, and well-publicized, staged arrests of easily apprehended bank robbers and kidnappers. More difficult problems, such as organized and white-collar crime, received a lower priority.

Public opinion is also sometimes conveyed to bureaucrats by social movements. Thus, the heightened public concern about environmental quality was vividly communicated to officials at the Environmental Protection Agency and the Interior Department by the Environmental movement. Women's health matters became more prominent in the research priorities of the National Institutes of Health after the Women's movement made them an issue.

For the most part, however, public opinion controls the federal bureaucracy only indirectly and intermittently. For popular sovereignty to be effective, it must usually work through elected officials like the president and the Congress who are themselves accountable to the people.

THE PRESIDENT AND THE FEDERAL BUREAUCRACY   The president, being the nation's chief executive, is the formal head of the executive branch. The president's leadership position is recognized in the Constitution's grant of executive power, its designation of the president as commander in chief of the armed forces, and its charge that he ensure that the laws be faithfully executed.[22] In reality, however,

The Pentagon, said to be the world's largest building, houses a part of the largest department in the federal government: Defense.

he has only limited abilities to control the executive branch as we saw in the last chapter. Virtually every modern president has been frustrated by the discovery that he cannot assume that bureaucrats will do what he wants them to do.[23]

Richard Nixon was so frustrated by his inability to move the federal bureaucracy that he came to think of it as an alien institution filled with his Democratic party enemies. His strategy was to intimidate bureaucrats or to bypass them. He created the notorious "plumbers" unit in the White House to act as his personal domestic surveillance and espionage unit. Revelation of its activities was one of the factors leading to his impeachment by the House of Representatives in the Watergate scandal. Ronald Reagan, also distrustful of the regular bureaucracy and frustrated by what he considered to be its unwillingness to support his foreign policy program, allowed Oliver North to use the National Security Council to sell arms to Iran and to funnel the money to the Contra rebels in Nicaragua.

Why are presidents so frustrated by the bureaucracy? If a president is the chief executive, why can't he simply issue orders? In fact, so much works against the president as leader of the executive branch that it is a wonder that he exercises any influence at all.

The sheer size and complexity of the executive branch is important in this equation. There is so much going on, in so many agencies, involving the activity of tens of thousands of people, that simply keeping abreast of what's going on is no easy task. Moreover, because of civil service regulations, presidents have no say about the tenure or salary of most bureaucrats. When presidents want something to happen, moreover, they are unlikely to get instantaneous acquiescence from bureaucrats who do not fear them as they would fear a private employer. Presidents also find that they are not the only ones trying to control the actions of bureaucrats; they must always share executive functions with Congress and sometimes with the courts. Finally, bureaucratic agencies are heavily insulated against presidential efforts to control them because of agency alliances with powerful interest groups.

Presidents are not entirely helpless, of course. They have a number of ways in which they can encourage bureaucratic compliance.[24] Occasionally, because of a crisis or a widely shared national commitment, decisive bureaucratic action is possible: Roosevelt's New Deal era, Lyndon Johnson's first years as president, Ronald Reagan's first administration, and World Wars I and II come to mind.

Even during ordinary times, however, the president is not helpless. First, although it is difficult to measure precisely, the president's prestige as our only nationally elected political leader makes his wishes hard to ignore. Teddy Roosevelt once called the presidency a "bully pulpit." What he meant was that it is the president and only the president who can speak for the nation, set the tone for the government, and call the American people to some great national purpose. A popular president, willing and able to play this role, is hard to resist. Bureaucrats are citizens and respond like other Americans to presidential leadership. When a president chooses to become directly involved on some bureaucratic matter—a phone call to a reluctant agency head, a comment about some bureaucratic shortcoming during a press conference—most bureaucrats respond.

The power of appointment is also an important tool of presidential leadership. Though he has only about 1,500 patronage appointments, they include the most important policymaking posts in the federal bureaucracy. If a president is very careful in filling these positions with people who support him and his program, he greatly increases his ability to have his way. Though the Senate must advise and consent to many of his choices, it rarely interferes, recognizing, perhaps, that a coherent administration requires that a president must have his own people in place. This is not always true, however, as the Senate's rejection of George Bush's first nominee for defense secretary, John Tower, suggests.

The president's power as chief budget officer of the federal government is also a formidable tool of administration. No agency of the federal bureaucracy, for instance, is allowed under the law to make its own budget request directly to Congress. The president's main budgetary instrument, the Office of Management and Budget (or OMB), also has the statutory authority to block proposed legislation coming from any executive branch agency if it deems it contrary to the president's budget or program. Bureaucrats concerned with the level of their agency's appropriation or its ability to affect legislation in its area of responsibility ignore the president at their own risk.

From the presidential point of view, the bureaucracy always seems on the verge of spinning out of control. In the years since World War II, a sizable bureaucracy has developed—the White House office and the Executive Office of the President, described in Chapter 12—to help the president stay on top of the far-flung executive branch. The aim is to reach the point where there is a reasonable probability that things will happen when the president says, "Do this! Do that"! The development of the legislative and budget coordination responsibilities of the OMB under recent presidents is the most important example.[25]

Even with these administrative tools, however, the president is limited in his ability to act as chief executive. Except for his control over the military, his ability to demand obedience from bureaucrats is not impressive. He must share influence with others. This is very different from parliamentary regimes, where the head of government exercises more direct and decisive control. A British prime minister, for instance, can appoint, transfer, or dismiss cabinet secretaries and ministers at will, reorganize the ministries, and alter personnel policies, including the duties and pay of civil servants.[26]

CONGRESS AND THE FEDERAL BUREAUCRACY   The president and Congress share control over the executive branch. Congressional tools of control, in fact, are at least as formidable as those of the president.[27] Congress legislates the mission of bureaucratic agencies and the details of their organization. When the Interstate Commerce Act was passed in 1887 to regulate the railroads, for instance, Congress created the Interstate Commerce Commission to carry out its provisions. When Congress legislated a public works program to put unemployed people to work during the Great Depression, it created the Works Progress Administration to run it.

Congress can also alter agency policy or behavior. For many years, it prevented the Federal Trade Commission from requiring health warnings on cigarette packages because of pressure from the tobacco industry. Responding to religious and conservative lobbies concerned with federal support for what they considered to be pornography, Congress rewrote the rules for funding grants for the National Endowment for the Arts in 1990.

Congress plays a principal role in determining the federal budget. In theory, Congress uses the budget process to assess the performance of each agency each year, closely scrutinizing its activities before determining its next appropriation. In fact, Congress has neither the time nor the resources to do such a thing, but it tends to give each department and agency some small increment over what it had in the previous year.[28] Of course, if a particular agency displeases Congress, its budget may be cut; if a new set of responsibilities is given to an agency, its budget is usually increased. Sometimes these agency budget actions are taken with the full concurrence of the president; often, they are not. Congress sometimes will lend a sympathetic ear and increase budgets for agencies that are not favored by the president. Congress consistently gave more money than President Reagan wanted to the EPA, the National Institutes of Health, and the National Science Foundation.

Oversight is the way in which Congress assures itself that the laws it has passed are carried out in a way that is satisfactory to it. Oversight activities are described in detail in Chapter 11. Hearings are the main instrument of oversight, used to convey congressional positions to bureaucrats.[29]

Senator Jesse Helms of North Carolina led the conservative assault on the National Endowment for the Arts for purportedly funding pornography, and forced his congressional colleagues to change some of the rules by which the NEA operates.

In oversight, as in most of its other dealings with the executive branch, Congress does not always speak with a single voice, however. Congress is a highly fragmented and decentralized institution, with power dispersed among scores of subcommittees. More often then not, the activities of a particular bureaucratic agency are the province of more than a single committee or subcommittee, and the probability of receiving mixed signals from them is very high. A skilled administrator can often play off these competing forces against each other and gain a degree of autonomy for his or her agency. Confusion about congressional intent is more common, however—a situation that does not enhance public accountability and control.

POPULAR SOVEREIGNTY RECONSIDERED   Popular sovereignty requires that government does what the people want it to do. What the people want is conveyed to the executive branch directly by public opinion and indirectly through Congress and the president. The materials that we have reviewed in these pages suggests that popular sovereignty is less vital than we might like it to be in a democracy.

Public opinion, we have seen, is only indirectly and intermittently effective in directly shaping bureaucratic behavior, primarily because few people have knowledge of, or interest in, most agencies in the federal bureaucracy. In the main, they like most agencies that they come in contact with but do not like the "bureaucracy" in general.[30] Neither one of these popular "wills" offers much guidance to bureaucrats who are trying to do their job.

The problem is that bureaucrats who want to do what the people want them to do do not get much guidance from the president or Congress. The messages are garbled and confused, filled with "noise," in the technical jargon. First, Con-

Figure 13.2 Popular control of the bureaucracy: imperfect sovereignty

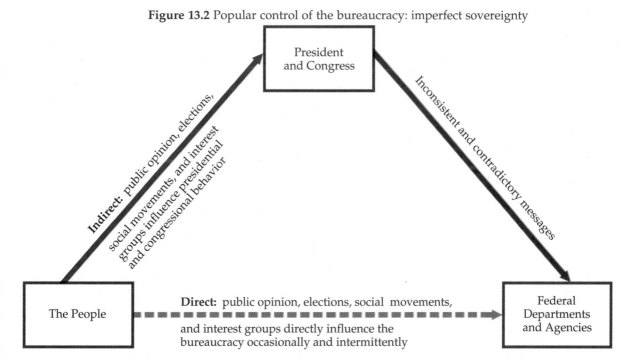

gress is internally divided, with different messages going out to the bureaucracy from its various committees and subcommittees. Second, the perpetual conflict between the president and Congress means that there is no center of authority in the national government.

Political Equality

In several respects, the bureaucracy meets the standard of political equality. There is no reason to believe that federal agencies treat classes of citizens unequally on a regular basis, for instance, though there are occasional incidents in which some—racial minorities and women, in particular—have been treated unfairly. We also know that the American people are fairly well represented, both in a demographic sense and in terms of their outlooks, among federal workers, except at the level of political appointees. In another important respect, however, the standard of political equality is not met, namely, in the overrepresentation of interest groups. We have seen throughout this text that the interest group system is the most significant source of inequality in American politics. It should come as no surprise to learn that this inequality is re-created in many of the actions of the federal bureaucracy.

As we saw in Chapter 7, the federal bureaucracy is permeated by networks of government interest group alliances. In most cases, the interests that are disproportionately represented are business interests. Business advisory councils are liberally sprinkled throughout the executive branch. Bureaucratic agencies often act as the supporters and protectors of these interest groups against other government bodies, other interests, and the public. Sometimes the symbiotic relationship becomes so pronounced that the private interest group comes to make its own public policies and regulations, with the federal agency serving to legitimate its actions. Thus, bankers closely advise the Treasury Department on rules and regulations pertinent to bank policy. Oil industry groups help the Interior Department set federal oil policy. Political scientist Grant McConnell once described this situation in the following way: "The existence of an array of narrow-interest-centered power structures within the open framework of American political life is no secret. It is not a hidden government, it is highly visible to anyone who spends time in Washington or who reads news beyond the headlines."[31]

It's no great mystery why interest groups are able to penetrate the federal bureaucracy and play an important role in its activities. One reason is the absence of central administrative direction. With no clear leadership at the top, each agency must fashion its own political alliances in order to protect itself. Agencies fashion their alliances where they can: with other executive branch agencies when there are common interests, with congressional committees and subcommittees, and with interest groups. When the Reagan administration wanted to cut the annual appropriation for the National Science Foundation in the early 1980s, for instance, its leaders mobilized friendly members of Congress and university and scientific associations in its defense.

Another reason that agencies welcome interest group alliances is to help in their skirmishes with other federal agencies. The Defense Department and NASA annually disagree about how much of the space program ought to be devoted to military projects. In their struggle before the White House staff, the OMB, and Congress, each throws allied interest groups—defense contractors, scientific organizations, patriotic groups, and so on—into the breach.

Political Liberty

It is difficult to reach a firm conclusion about the role of the federal bureaucracy in protecting and sustaining political liberty, because it is made up of so many agencies. For the most part, these agencies go about their business—delivering the mail, advising farmers, funding scientific research, collecting taxes, providing disaster relief, issuing statistical reports, issuing Social Security checks, and so on—without affecting political liberty one way or the other. Nevertheless, there are at least two things that worry many observers.

First, the combination of bureaucracy and contemporary computer technology gives the federal government enormous information-gathering capabilities. The Internal Revenue Service collects information about Americans, as do the Census Bureau, the Veterans Administration, and the Social Security Administration. The Post Office has been known to keep files on American citizens, as has the National Security Administration and the Federal Bureau of Investigation. Some observers believe that increasingly centralized and easily accessible files containing vast amounts of confidential information about individuals constitutes, in and of itself, a threat to liberty. In the hands of unscrupulous officials, such information might be used to intimidate those individuals.

Second, while federal agencies do not normally intrude on the liberty of Americans, enough of them have done so to cause concern among those who cherish freedom. During the post-World War I "red scare," the Immigration and Naturalization Service and the Justice Department harassed dissident organizations and individuals. During the early 1970s, the Law Enforcement Intelligence Unit of the Justice Department funded "red squads" in police departments all over the nation to spy on and disrupt legal political organizations opposed to United States policy in Vietnam. Antiwar organizations were also the targets of infiltration by the Central Intelligence Agency (which is forbidden by law to engage in activities within U.S. borders), mail openings by the Post Office, and international telephone intercepts by the National Security Agency. The Internal Reve-

Many civil libertarians believe that the collection and centralized storage of information on every citizen of the United States by the federal government represents a standing threat to freedom.

nue Service allowed itself to be used by presidents to harass their political opponents: Franklin Roosevelt and Richard Nixon were the most frequent users of this service.[32]

The agency that has most consistently violated the freedoms of the American people, however, is the Federal Bureau of Investigation during the long tenure of Director J. Edgar Hoover. During the McCarthy hysteria in the 1950s, Hoover set up a program for Americans to report the suspicious behavior of their neighbors to the FBI. For over two decades, the FBI was involved in "broad efforts to disrupt and investigate the National Lawyers Guild (a liberal, prolabor lawyers group) . . . although government officials decided as long ago as 1958 that they could not prove that the organization was subversive."[33] Under a program called *Cointelpro*, the bureau engaged in a campaign to harass and discredit civil rights leaders and to disrupt the legal activities of civil rights organizations. The vendetta against Martin Luther King, Jr., was particularly ugly. Apparently appalled by King's "I Have a Dream" speech at the Lincoln Memorial in 1963 (for it established him in Hoover's eyes as the "most dangerous and effective Negro leader in the country"), Hoover decided to "take him off his pedestal [and] reduce him completely in influence. . . ." To this end, the FBI taped King's phones, instituted continuous surveillance on his activities, leaked incriminating information about his private life to the press, mailed anonymous letters to King's wife, implying improprieties on the part of her husband, and directed threats at him, including a bizarre note in which it suggested he commit suicide.[34]

It may well be that the behavior of the FBI and other agencies damaging to civil liberties are the proverbial exceptions that prove the rule. There is no way to know for sure. These examples, suggest, however, that Americans cannot afford to be complacent about the state of their liberties. Their preservation is part of the continuing struggle for democracy.

THE FEDERAL BUREAUCRACY: COMMON CRITICISMS

Bureaucrats are often portrayed in popular culture as lazy paper shufflers or as indifferent, unresponsive, and inhumane clerks denying us the benefits or services to which we are entitled. Occupational-prestige polls always find civil servants near the bottom (close to politicians, we might add). Politicians feed on this popular culture when they "run against Washington," promising to pare the bureaucracy down to size and to get it off the backs of the American people.

Let's look at the most common criticisms of the federal bureaucracy and see if they have merit.

Criticism Number 1: The Federal Bureaucracy Is Always Expanding

Surprisingly, this complaint has no basis in fact. While the number of federal civilian employees expanded dramatically in the twentieth century, it has remained relatively stable since the mid-1960s, at roughly 2.8 million. Government does more and spends more money today than it did in 1950, but it does so with about the same number of employees.

Nor is it the case that all bureaucratic agencies grow without stopping. Even important ones can decrease in size. The Department of Defense and the State Department have gotten smaller since 1970.

Criticism Number 2: The Federal Bureaucracy Is Not Effective

By *effective*, we mean "able to carry out missions and reach goals." The record of the federal bureaucracy with respect to effectiveness is mixed. NASA landed a man on the moon in less than a decade, fulfilling President Kennedy's promise to the American people. But, by the same token NASA has suffered repeated problems in its shuttle program.

Recall that the framers did not want an effective government or bureaucracy, because they were worried first and foremost about tyranny. They created a system in which power would be fragmented. They were willing to trade effectiveness for inoculation against an overbearing and threatening government. Remember, also, that the federal bureaucracy was not designed as a rational machine with a clear chain of command, as in most democratic nations. It is, instead, an architectural hodgepodge, with parts added on as the political process demanded.

Finally, consider the phrase "compared to what?" While most of us are absolutely certain that the federal bureaucracy cannot be as effective in meeting its goals as private organizations, the evidence for such a belief is not overwhelming. Some studies on productivity, costs, and innovation show no public–private differences.[35] More research needs to be done on this issue, to be sure, but there are no grounds at the present time to accept the conventional wisdom.

Criticism Number 3: The Federal Bureaucracy Is Wasteful and Inefficient

Waste in government is such an enduring theme in American politics that it is difficult to imagine a political campaign without it. The issue, again, is more complex than it may seem.

In actuality, the opportunity for agencies to waste money is quite limited, since the bureaucracy has discretionary control over only about 5 percent of the total federal budget. Ninety-five percent is earmarked, or distributed to beneficiaries by formula, or are *entitlements* (these are discussed further in Chapter 18). Almost all of the federal budget goes toward paying the interest on the national debt, to direct payments to individuals (military pensions, Social Security, etc.), to direct transfers, to grants-in-aid to states and localities, and to contracted services.[36] In addition, the use of the small discretionary pot is closely monitored and encumbered with strict rules on its use. None of this suggests that there isn't waste or inefficient use of taxpayers' money in bureaucratic agencies. It is to say, however, that the charges are probably exaggerated. Of course, if what we mean by "waste of taxpayers' money" is spending on programs that we don't like (for some, it may be welfare; for others it may be a new strategic missile), then our complaint is not with the bureaucracy but with the policy-making branches of the federal government: the president and Congress.

Perhaps more important, there are certain things that we want government to do that are not efficient in strictly market terms (profit and loss) but are worth doing anyway: pollution control, first-class airports and harbors, national defense, and scientific research come to mind.

Where there is inefficiency and waste, of course, the president and Congress must insist that the bureaucracy do better. Many critics believe that the best place to start is in the Defense Department, where secrecy and the enormous size of its annual budget make accountability difficult and problems almost inevitable.

Criticism Number 4: The Bureaucracy Is Buried in Red Tape

Americans complain incessantly about bureaucratic rules, regulations, formal procedures, and forms. Our discontent is summarized by the term "red tape." We have all, at one time or another, felt stymied by rules and procedures, aggravated by delays, and frustrated by forms, and have cried out "red tape"! But how valid is the complaint?

Again, we run into the problem of measurement. How can we be sure that there is more red tape in the federal bureaucracy than there is in other large institutions? Surely, there are miles of red tape in places like universities and corporations. Red tape is probably in the eye of the beholder. What is a waste of time and an inconvenience to one person may represent good public policy to another. The charge of "red tape" is almost always hurled at agencies that are carrying out policies which we don't like. For example, following federal procedures for the disposal of dangerous chemicals may not be what chemical companies would want to do on their own, but Americans have shown that they want strong environmental protection laws.

There is some truth to the stereotypes about the federal bureaucracy. It is large; there are programs that do not work; there is waste and inefficiency; there is a great deal of red tape. We would suggest, however, that the stereotypes greatly exaggerate the extent of the problem, for our measuring instruments are very imprecise. Nor do we have reason to believe that the pathologies are unique to the federal bureaucracy. Finally, we must recognize that many of the pathologies, to the extent that they do exist, do not necessarily originate in the bureaucracy but are imposed by other governmental bodies and the provisions in the Constitution.

REFORMING THE FEDERAL BUREAUCRACY

How should we fix what's wrong with the federal bureaucracy? It depends on what you think is wrong (see Table 13.2).

Table 13.2
Major Commissions on Reform of the Federal Bureaucracy

Name	Chair	Year	Appointed by	To Make Recommendations About	Results
1. Brownlow Commission	Louis Brownlow	1936	Franklin Roosevelt	Nonresponsiveness to presidential leadership	Various recommendations to strengthen the power of the president over the bureaucracy. Several were legislated, including the creation of the Executive Office of the President.
2. Hoover Commission (first)	Herbert Hoover	1947–1949	Harry Truman	Proliferation of federal agencies and bureaucratic nonresponsiveness to presidential leadership	Main recommendations were to enhance the role of the president as chief executive and to reorganize departments into more coherent functional units. Many recommendations were legislated, including strengthening the Executive Office of the President and the Bureau of the Budget, creation of the Office of Personnel, and reorganization of several departments and agencies.
3. Hoover Commission (second)	Herbert Hoover	1953–1955	Dwight Eisenhower	Uncontrolled growth of the federal bureaucracy and unwarranted competition with private enterprise	Almost none of its recommendations to curtail nonessential government services was instituted.
4. Ash Council	Roy Ash	1971	Richard Nixon	Bureaucratic nonresponsiveness to presidential leadership	Transformation of the Bureau of the Budget into the more powerful Office of Management and Budget and creation of a Domestic Council to parallel the National Security Council.
5. Grace Commission	J. Peter Grace	1982	Ronald Reagan	Bureaucratic inefficiency and waste	Over 2,500 recommendations for privatization of government services, user fees for government services, and enhanced presidential management of the executive branch were made, but only a handful of minor enactments resulted.

Scaling the Bureaucracy Down to Size

People who worry about the size of government have proposed several changes, including hiring freezes, restrictions on the creation of new departments and bureaus, and even the elimination of bureaucratic units. Ronald Reagan wanted to abolish the Departments of Education and Energy. Congressional opposition prevented this from happening. The most popular reform idea during the Reagan years, still much talked about today, is **privatization**, the transfer of many government functions to the private sector. There is talk of turning postal services and prison systems over to private contractors.[37]

Making the Federal Bureaucracy More Effective

Many people believe that, for the federal bureaucracy to achieve its missions and goals, policymakers must first provide clear policy signals.[38] How such a thing could be done, short of fundamental changes in our political system, is not entirely clear. Others suggest much greater discretion for civil servants as they carry out their responsibilities. Usually connected to this is a proviso for improving the professional and technical skills of civil servants, either by improved training programs or by providing higher pay to attract more talented people. The Senior Executive Service was created in 1978 to do this, but it is not clear whether it has made a great deal of difference in the quality of senior civil servants.

Protecting Against Bureaucratic Abuses of Power

There are many who believe that a bureaucracy of the size and shape of our present one, while necessary in a modern society, is potentially dangerous. Closer control over the bureaucracy by elected political bodies and by clear legislative constraints has been the preferred solution. There are many legislative enactments that try to keep bureaucratic activity within narrow boundaries. The Legislative Reorganization Act of 1970 was partially designed to improve congressional subcommittee oversight capabilities. The Congressional Budget and Impoundment Control Act of 1974 was designed to enhance Congress's ability to shape the federal budget and to monitor agency use of federal monies. The Freedom of Information Act of 1966 was designed to enhance the ability of the press and private citizens to obtain information about bureaucratic policies and activities. The Ethics in Government Act of 1978 strengthened requirements for financial disclosure by officials and prohibitions against conflicts of interest.

Reformers have proposed two additional innovations. The first would require that each federal agency have an **ombudsman**, a Swedish term for an official whose job is to hear citizen complaints about bureaucratic action (or inaction) and to seek redress of grievances. Many local communities and universities now have such officials, but not much headway has been made at the federal level. The second would offer protection for **whistleblowers**, those bureaucrats who report abuses of power, corruption, financial mismanagement, or other official malfeasance. All too often, these courageous people, acting in the public interest, are fired or harassed on the job (see "The Struggle for Democracy"). The Merit Systems Protection Board is supposed to offer such protection, but most observers do not believe that it has been entirely effective.

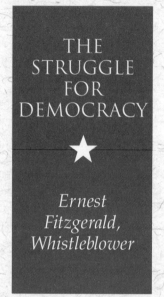

THE STRUGGLE FOR DEMOCRACY

★

Ernest Fitzgerald, Whistleblower

The American people can only control their government when they have accurate information about what is going on. The problem of obtaining timely and accurate information is particularly difficult in the bureaucracy, given its size, complexity, operations out of the public and media view, and the general unwillingness of agency leaders to report problems in the programs that they run. *Whistleblowers* is a word that has been coined for those people who work for the government who, at considerable risk to themselves, bypass their superiors and report government corruption, malfeasance, and program failures to the American people.

Perhaps the best-known whistleblower in recent times is Ernest Fitzgerald, who worked for the Pentagon as a civilian cost accountant. He was one of many civilian employees at the Department of Defense who had become alarmed at the waste, cost overruns, and nonperforming weapons systems that they saw all around them during the late 1960s and had become angry at efforts by the military brass and defense contractors to cover up matters. He came to national attention when he revealed the existence of a $2 billion cost overrun on the Lockheed C-5A military transport plane before Senator

William Proxmire's Joint Economic Committee in 1968 and 1969. Though celebrated by Congress and the media for his testimony, he was fired by direct order of President Richard Nixon in 1970. He was reinstated after a long and costly court battle in 1973, but he was given a lesser job with few responsibilities. He went to court again and won full reinstatement, but not until 1982. Unfortunately, given what he went through, potential whistleblowers may think twice about blowing the whistle on misconduct in the future. It is why many people believe that we need legislation to protect such individuals.

Increasing Popular Participation

Many people worry that federal bureaucrats go about their business without the public having much say in what they do. Without citizen input, it is argued, bureaucrats lose touch with the people whom they serve—a situation that leads to irrational policies and citizen alienation from the bureaucracy. Citizen participation in agency affairs has been pushed by some reformers as a solution.[39] The antipoverty program of Lyndon Johnson's Great Society required the "maximum feasible participation" of the poor in its design and implementation. President Bush's Housing secretary, Jack Kemp, introduced tenant councils to help administer federal housing programs at the neighborhood level.

Enhancing Democracy

There are, finally, proposals to enhance democracy in bureaucratic affairs. For the people to rule, popular sovereignty, political equality, and political liberty must flourish.

Popular sovereignty requires that the elected representatives of the people closely control the bureaucracy.[40] Popular sovereignty implies that administrative discretion be narrowed as much as possible and that clear directions and unambiguous policies be communicated from elected officials to bureaucratic agencies. How might such a thing be achieved?

Some have argued that the only public official who has an interest in seeing that the bureaucracy *as a whole* is well run and coherently organized is the president.[41] Accordingly, one suggestion for reform is to increase the powers of the president so that he can, in fact and not just in name, be the chief executive.[42]

Another way to enhance the ability of elected leaders to issue clear directives and coherent policies is to have them speak with a more unified voice. But this, we have seen, is unlikely to happen in our constitutional system of separation of powers and divided government. Short of a fundamental constitutional reform that would change the United States into a parliamentary democracy—which is not about to happen—the only instrument that is available for overcoming the separation of powers is political parties. Political party reform would seem to be at the very top of the agenda, then, for those who care about the state of popular sovereignty in the United States.

We have learned throughout this book that the interest group system is the most significant factor in American political life that works to undermine political equality. We have seen how interest groups have carved out privileged positions at various places in the federal bureaucracy, made all the worse by their alliances with assorted congressional committees and subcommittees. The most significant reform to enhance political equality would involve diminishing the power and influence of interest groups.

To the extent that bureaucratic intrusions on political liberty involve autonomous agencies following their own agenda—like the FBI under Hoover—enhancing the control of elected officials over them would represent important safeguards to liberty. To the extent that bureaucratic intrusions on political liberty involve actions carried out at the request of elected officials—like presidential use of the IRS against opponents and of the CIA to disrupt the activities of dissident groups—improving the degree of popular control over elected political officials would represent an additional safeguard. Such reforms would not, however, completely guarantee the protection of liberty from bureaucratic action. What remains to us in the face of violations of our rights is our constitutional tradition, our willingness to stand up for our rights and the rights of others, and, even granted their imperfections, the courts.

SUMMARY

The executive branch has grown in size and responsibility. Growth is a consequence of a transformation in the conception of the proper role of government on the part of the people and elites in response to structural changes in the economy and society. While "bureaucracy" is not a popular term in the American political tradition, we have created a sizable one. Partly, this is because bureaucratic organizations have certain strengths that make them attractive for accomplishing large-scale tasks.

Bureaucrats are involved in three major kinds of activities: executing the law, making rules, and adjudicating disputes. In each of these, they exercise a great deal of discretion. Because they are unelected policymakers, democratic theory demands that we be concerned about who the bureaucrats are. In the merit services, they are very much like other Americans in terms of background and attitudes. Political appointees, however, the most important bureaucratic decision makers, are very different from their fellow citizens. Democracy also requires that the federal bureaucracy be under popular control, that political equality be the context of bureaucratic behavior, and that the executive branch enhance, rather than endanger, freedom. The evidence on this is mixed. The executive branch is fairly responsive to the popular will, but popular control is undermined by incoherent organization and divided control between the president and Congress. Bureaucratic operations depart substantially from the norm of political equality because of the significant influence of interest groups. Political liberty has been occasionally threatened by such agencies as the FBI.

Bureaucratic pathologies, while real, are either exaggerated or the result of political forces outside the bureaucracy itself: the constitutional rules and the struggle between the president and Congress.

Proposals to reform the executive branch are related to what reformers believe is wrong with the federal bureaucracy. Those who want to make democracy more of a reality propose strengthening our political parties, giving more control over the bureaucracy to the president, and diminishing the role of interest groups.

To Ponder

1. What would we lose or gain if our bureaucracy worked more like the bureaucracies in other democratic nations?

2. Can you imagine other forms of organization besides bureaucracy that would be appropriate for conducting the government's business?

3. What should be the first responsibility for our civil servants—to follow the directives of elected officials or to respond to the needs of each person with whom they deal?

4. Should we have more or fewer political appointees in the executive branch?

5. What changes would you like to see in the federal bureaucracy? How are these changes related to your basic political values?

Suggested Readings

Burnham, David. *A Law Unto Itself: Power, Politics, and the IRS.* New York: Random House, 1989.
> A muckraking look at the IRS and how it affects the lives of Americans.

Chubb, John E. and Paul E. Peterson. *Can the Government Govern?* Washington, D.C.: Brookings Institution, 1989.
> A collection of original essays concerned with the declining effectiveness of government and what might be done about it.

Goodsell, Charles T. *The Case for Bureaucracy.* Chatham, NJ: Chatham House, 1983.
> A well-written polemic that gives the other side of the bureaucratic story.

Gruber, Judith E. *Controlling Bureaucracies: Dilemmas in Democratic Governance.* Berkeley, CA: The University of California Press, 1987.
>   An exploration of the practical and philosophical problems inherent in different ways of controlling the bureaucracy.

Heclo, Hugh. *A Government of Strangers.* Washington, D.C.: Brookings Institution, 1977.
>   A look at political appointees and how they attempt to gain control of the agencies that they head.

Skowronek, Stephen. *Building a New American State: The Expansion of National Administrative Capacities, 1877–1920.* New York: Cambridge University Press, 1982.
>   A careful historical analysis of the first budding of an expanded federal bureaucracy.

Stillman, Richard J., II. *The American Bureaucracy.* Chicago: Nelson-Hall, 1987.
>   A comprehensive textbook on the federal bureaucracy.

The Washington Monthly. Washington's leading journal of "bureaucracy bashing"; filled with outrageous, and sometimes illuminating, stories.

Notes

1. Wallace Sayre, "Bureaucracies: Some Contrasts in Systems," *Indian Journal of Public Administration,* Vol. 10, No. 2 (1964), p. 223.

2. Richard J. Stillman, II, *The American Bureaucracy* (Chicago: Nelson-Hall, 1987), p. 18.

3. Alexis de Tocqueville, *Democracy in America,* 2 vols. (New York: Vintage Books, 1945), Vol. I, p. 59.

4. Stephen Skowronek, *Building a New American State: The Expansion of National Administrative Capacities, 1877–1920* (New York: Cambridge University Press, 1982), pp. 19–46.

5. See Edward S. Greenberg, *Capitalism and the American Political Ideal* (Armonk, NY: M. E. Sharpe, 1985); Samuel P. Hays, *The Response to Industrialization* (Chicago: University of Chicago Press, 1957); Gabriel Kolko, *The Triumph of Conservatism* (Chicago: Quadrangle, 1967); Robert Wiebe, *The Search for Order: 1877–1920* (New York: Hill and Wang, 1967); and James Weinstein, *The Corporate Ideal in the Liberal State* (Boston: Beacon Press, 1968).

6. Matthew A. Crenson and Francis E. Rourke, "American Bureaucracy Since World War II," in Louis Galambos, ed., *The New American State* (Baltimore, MD: Johns Hopkins University Press, 1987).

7. Classic discussions of bureaucracy include Michel Crozier, *The Bureaucratic Phenomenon* (Chicago: University of Chicago Press, 1964); Anthony Downs, *Inside Bureaucracy* (Santa Monica, CA: Rand, 1964); Alvin W. Gouldner, *Patterns of Industrial Bureaucracy* (New York: Free Press, 1954); James G. March and Herbert Simon, *Organizations* (New York: Wiley, 1958); Robert Michels, *Political Parties* (New York: Free Press, 1962) (originally published in 1915); and most importantly, Max Weber, *Economy and Society,* (London: Owen, 1962), vol. 1.

8. Kenneth J. Meier, *Politics and the Bureaucracy: Policymaking in the Fourth Branch of Government* (Boston: Duxbury Press, 1979), p. 52.

9. Meier, *Politics and the Bureaucracy,* p. 23.

10. Theodore J. Lowi, *The End of Liberalism,* 2nd ed. (New York: Norton, 1979).

11. Lowi, *End of Liberalism.*

12. See Samuel Krislov and David H. Rosenbloom, *Representative Bureaucracy and the American Political System* (New York: Praeger, 1981).

13. Kenneth John Meier, "Representative Bureaucracy: An Empirical Analysis," *The American Political Science Review,* Vol. 69 (June 1975), p. 532.

14. See the review of evidence in Charles T. Goodsell, *The Case for Bureaucracy* (Chatham, NJ: Chatham House, 1983), pp. 86–88. Also see Stanley Rothman and S. Robert Lichter, "How Liberal Are Bureaucrats," *Regulation* (November-December 1983).

15. Meier, "Representative Bureaucracy," pp. 537–539.

16. Stillman, *American Bureaucracy,* p. 139.

17. Richard P. Nathan, *The Administrative Presidency* (New York: Wiley, 1983).

18. Beth Mintz, "The President's Cabinet, 1897–1973," *The Insurgent Sociologist*, Vol. 5, No. 3 (Spring 1975).

19. Gabriel Kolko, *The Roots of American Foreign Policy* (Boston: Beacon Press, 1969), p. 17.

20. Hugh Heclo, *A Government of Strangers* (Washington, D.C.: Brookings Institution, 1977), p. 103.

21. Judith E. Gruber, *Controlling Bureaucracies: Dilemmas in Democratic Governance* (Berkeley, CA: University of California Press, 1987), p. 7.

22. Robert Fried, *The Performance of American Democracy* (Boston: Little Brown, 1976); and Meier, *Politics and the Bureaucracy*, p. 145.

23. The classic observation of Richard Neustadt in his book *Presidential Power* (New York: Wiley, 1960).

24. Terry M. Moe, "Control and Feedback in Economic Regulation," *The American Political Science Review*, Vol. 79, 1985, pp. 1094–1116; and Richard W. Waterman, *Presidential Influence and the Administrative State* (Knoxville: University of Tennessee Press, 1989).

25. Francis E. Rourke, "Bureaucracy in the American Constitutional Order," *Political Science Quarterly*, Vol. 102, No. 2 (Summer 1987), pp. 217–232.

26. Colin Campbell, et al., *Politics and Government in Europe Today* (New York: Harcourt Brace Jovanovich, 1990), pp. 112–113.

27. Mathew D. McCubbins, "The Legislative Design of Regulatory Structure," *American Journal of Political Science*, Vol. 29, 1985, pp. 421–438.

28. Richard Fenno, *The Power of the Purse* (Boston: Little, Brown, 1966); and Aaron Wildavsky, *The Politics of the Budgetary Process* (Boston: Little, Brown, 1964).

29. John A. Ferejohn and Charles R. Shipan, "Congressional Influence on Administrative Agencies: A Case Study of Telecommunications Policy," in Lawrence C. Dodd and Bruce I. Oppenheimer, eds., *Congress Reconsidered*, 4th ed. (Washington, D.C.: Congressional Quarterly Press, 1989).

30. See the summary of polls in Goodsell, *Case for Bureaucracy*, ch. 2.

31. Grant McConnell, *Private Power and American Democracy* (New York: Knopf, 1967), p. 339.

32. David Burnham, *A Law Unto Itself: Power, Politics, and the IRS* (New York: Random House, 1989).

33. William Glaberson, "FBI Says It Disrupted Lawyers Guild," *New York Times* (October 13, 1989), p. A12.

34. Quotes are from *New York Times*, April 16, 1976, p. 1. On the campaign against King, see Taylor Branch, *Parting the Waters: America in the King Years* (New York: Simon & Schuster, 1988); Noam Chomsky, *Cointelpro* (New York: Monad Press, 1975); David Garrow, *The FBI and Martin Luther King* (New York: Norton, 1981); and Kenneth O'Reilly, *Racial Matters: The FBI's Secret File on Black America, 1960–1972* (New York: Free Press, 1989).

35. The evidence is reviewed in Goodsell, *The Case for Bureaucracy*, ch. 3.

36. Stillman, *American Bureaucracy*, p. 17.

37. See Emanuel S. Savas, *Privatization: The Key to Better Government* (Chatham, NJ: Chatham House, 1987); Sheila B. Kamerman and Alfred J. Kahn, eds., *Privatization and the Welfare State* (Princeton, NJ: Princeton University Press, 1989).

38. Lowi, *End of Liberalism*.

39. Milton Kotler, *Neighborhood Government* (Indianapolis, IN: Bobbs-Merrill, 1969); Marilyn Gittell, *Participants and Participation* (New York: Praeger, 1967).

40. Gruber, *Controlling Bureaucracies*, p. 194.

41. Terry M. Moe, "The Politics of Bureaucratic Structure," in John E. Chubb and Paul E. Peterson, *Can the Government Govern?* (Washington, D.C.: Brookings Institution, 1989), p. 280.

42. John E. Chubb and Paul E. Peterson, "American Political Institutions and the Problem of Governance," In John E. Chubb and Paul E. Peterson, *Can the Government Govern?* (Washington, D.C: Brookings Institution, 1989), p. 41; James Sundquist, *Constitutional Reform and Effective Government* (Washington, D.C.: Brookings Institution, 1986).

14

The Courts

THE COURT CHANGES COURSE

On January 22, 1973, the U.S. Supreme Court made abortion legal in the United States. Writing for a 7–2 majority in the case of *Roe v. Wade*, Justice Harry Blackmun argued that a state's interest in regulating abortion to protect the life of a fetus can only override a women's fundamental right to privacy when the fetus becomes *viable* (able to live on its own). The opinion also said that the fetus cannot be considered a person with rights under the Constitution. Finally, it rejected the state of Texas's claim that human life begins at conception, saying that "adopting one theory of life" by statute was constitutionally impermissible.

Sixteen years later, in the case of *Webster v. Reproductive Health Services*, the Supreme Court retreated from *Roe* and dramatically diminished a woman's right to have an abortion. Speaking for a 5–4 majority, Chief Justice William Rehnquist upheld a Missouri law that barred use of public monies and facilities to perform abortions and required physicians to test for fetal viability at 20 weeks. Most important, the language of the decision invited other states to legislate limits on abortions. Guam, Louisiana, Utah, and Pennsylvania did so in very short order.

The Constitution had not been amended in the years between *Roe* and *Webster*, yet the interpretation of the constitutional standing of privacy and the right of the states to regulate abortions had changed substantially. To understand this transformation in constitutional interpretation, it is important to appreciate the major transformations that occurred in American politics in the decade and a half following *Roe*. Most important was the rise of conservatism and the political fortunes of the Republican party, and the decline of liberalism and of the Democratic party. This transformation affected each of the branches of the federal government, including the Supreme Court.

The Roe decision was a product of its time. It was decided by a court that could sometimes muster a liberal majority—Justices William Douglas, William Brennan, and Thurgood Marshall formed the core; Justices Potter Stewart and Harry Blackmun often joined them; and Justice Lewis Powell only did so from time to time. Moreover, the decision was rendered at a time when the Women's movement was at the height of its political influence (see Chapter 10) and was espousing a program in which the right to unrestricted access to abortions was a major objective.

The Women's movement, confident that the right to an abortion had been established, turned its attention elsewhere. In doing so, it left the playing field open to groups opposed to abortion. Most important, *Roe* sparked the formation of the "Right to Life" movement that became an important part of a conservative Republican coalition that took shape in the years after *Roe*. One student of the Prolife movement has described the important place of the abortion issue in this political transformation:

> Abortion suddenly became the right issue, and what an issue it was. As the bottom-line demand of the women's movement, it was a quick and easy symbol for sexual permissiveness and feminism, and opposition to it signaled

an uneasiness about the whole feminist agenda. It was a Catholic issue, theoretically mobilizing those millions of voters. It was a moral issue, giving conservatives that human dimension they so often seemed to lack. It had a fanatic following who had already demonstrated their capacity to work tirelessly. It was the kind of issue that people could rally around."[1]

The conservative movement, with the antiabortion issue at its core, managed to break away significant numbers of Catholics and southern white Protestants from the New Deal coalition that had dominated American politics for so long and helped refashion the public agenda in the nation. It also contributed mightily to the election of Ronald Reagan and a Republican Senate in 1980, and to the reelection of Reagan in 1984.

Fortunately for conservatives and the prolife movement, a string of retirements from the Supreme Court gave President Reagan the opportunity to refashion the Court in his own conservative image. Though he lost in his attempt to appoint Robert Bork to the Court, Reagan gained Senate approval for the appointment of other conservatives: Sandra Day O'Connor, Antonin Scalia, and Anthony Kennedy. He also succeeded in elevating Justice William Rehnquist to the position of Chief Justice. Though Justices Blackmun, Brennan, and Marshall remained loyal to their position enunciated in *Roe*, the shift in the nation's politics and the appointive powers of a popular president contributed to the formation of a new and formidable Supreme Court conservative majority that was willing to backtrack on its earlier decision.

This story tells us many things about the Supreme Court that will be elaborated in this chapter. Like the president and the Congress, the Court makes decisions that have important consequences for the American people. Unlike the president and the Congress, it does not pass new laws but interprets the meaning of the law, especially the Constitution. In doing so, however, the Court cannot help but make law. In this sense, the Court is a national policymaker.

This story also shows that the Court is embedded in a rich governmental, political, and structural environment that shapes its behavior. The other branches of government impinge on its deliberations; political institutions like elections, interest groups, and social movements matter; and structural factors like economic and social change influence its agenda and decisions.

Finally, the story raises the issue of democracy, which is the central theme of this book. In this chapter, we consider the ambiguous relationship of the Court and democracy.

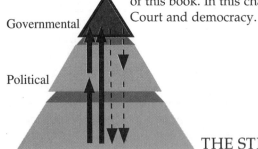

Governmental

Political

Structural

THE STRUCTURAL CONTEXT OF COURT BEHAVIOR

Constitutional Powers

"The judicial Power of the United States shall be vested in one supreme Court, and in such inferior Courts as the Congress may from time to time ordain and establish." (Art. II, Sec. 1)

We are under a Constitution, but the Constitution is what the judges say it is, and the judiciary is the safeguard of our liberty and our property under the Constitution. (Charles Evans Hughes, speech, 1907).[2]

The Constitution speaks only briefly about the judicial branch and doesn't provide much guidance about what it is supposed to do or how it is supposed to go about its job. It says little about its powers in relationship to the other two federal branches or about its responsibilities in the area of constitutional interpretation. Article III is considerably shorter than Articles I and II on Congress and the president. It creates a federal judicial branch; it says that judges shall serve life terms (good behavior); it specifies its jurisdiction; and it grants Congress the power to create additional federal courts as needed. Article III of the Constitution is virtually devoid of detail.

The most interesting silence in the Constitution is the omission of any explicit mention of **judicial review**, the power of the Court to declare state and federal laws and actions null and void when they conflict with the Constitution. Debate has raged for many years over the question of whether the framers intended that the Court should have this power.[3] The framers believed that the Constitution ought to prevail when other laws were in conflict with it. But did they expect the Court to be the main wielder of this power? Jefferson and Madison believed that Congress and the president were each capable of rendering their own judgments about the constitutionality of their actions. Alexander Hamilton, on the other hand, believed that the power of judicial review was inherent in the notion of the separation of powers and was essential to balanced government.

Hamilton's view was probably the prevailing one among the framers. They were firm believers, for instance, in the idea that there was a "higher law" to which governments and nations must conform. Their enthusiasm for written constitutions was based on their belief that governments must be limited in what they can do in the service of some higher or more fundamental law, such as that pertaining to individual rights. The attitudes of the time strongly supported the idea that judges, being free from popular pressures and conversant with the legal tradition, were best able to decide when statutory and administrative law were in conflict with fundamental law[4] (See Table 14.1 on the varieties of law). It still remains something of a mystery, however, why the framers said nothing explicitly about such an important power.

MARBURY V. MADISON   Chief Justice John Marshall boldly claimed the power of judicial review for the Supreme Court in the case of *Marbury v. Madison* in 1803.[5] The case began with a flurry of judicial appointments by President John Adams in the final days of his presidency, after his party's resounding defeat in the election of 1800. The apparent aim of these so-called midnight appointments was to establish the federal courts as an outpost of Federalist power (federal judges are appointed for life) in the midst of Jeffersonian control of the presidency and the Congress.

William Marbury was one of the "midnight appointments," but he was less lucky than his colleagues. Though his commission was signed and sealed, it had not been delivered to him before the new administration took office. Jefferson's Secretary of State James Madison refused to deliver the commission, sensing what the Federalists were up to. Marbury sued Madison, claiming that the secretary of state was obligated to deliver the commission, and asked the Supreme Court to

---

Table 14.1
The Varieties of Law

Law in the United States has four sources: a constitution, a legislature, an administrative agency, or a court.

Constitutional law is the most basic form of law in that it sets the rules of the game for the entire governing process and in that no other law or regulation may violate it. In our federal system, the U.S. Constitution is not only superior to all statutes and regulations made by the other branches of government but also is superior to state constitutions.

Statutes are the laws made by legislative bodies, including the Congress of the United States. They are usually more detailed than constitutional provisions.

Administrative rules and regulations are issued by officials of the executive branch when authorized to do so by Congress. When the Occupational Safety and Health Administration issues a regulation requiring shields on band saws in lumber mills, it is making administrative law.

Court-made law is fashioned in the course of deciding cases that come before the courts. The interpretations that courts make of all other kinds of law—constitutional, statute, and administrative—are binding on every person and institution that falls within the jurisdiction of a particular court. Supreme Court interpretations (known as opinions) of constitutional issues, such as the unacceptability of segregated education in *Brown v. Board of Education*, are the most far-reaching examples of this kind of lawmaking.

---

issue a **writ of mandamus**, a court order compelling an official to act, in order to force Madison to do so.

Marshall faced a quandary. If the Court decided in favor of Marbury, Madison would almost surely refuse to obey, opening the Court to ridicule. The fact that Marshall was a prominent Federalist political figure might even provoke the Jeffersonians to take more extreme measures against the Court. On the other hand, if the Court ruled in favor of Madison, it would suggest that an executive official could defy the clear provisions of the law without penalty.

Marshall's solution was worthy of Solomon. The Court ruled that William Marbury was entitled to his commission and that James Madison had broken the law in failing to deliver it. However, the Court could not compel Madison to comply with the law, because the provision of the Judiciary Act of 1789 that granted the Court the power to issue writs of mandamus in such cases as this was itself unconstitutional. The statute was unconstitutional because it sought to expand the **original jurisdiction** of the Supreme Court as defined in Article III, which could not be done except by constitutional amendment.

On the surface, the decision was an act of great modesty. It suggested that the Court could not force the action of an executive branch official. It suggested that Congress had erred in the Judiciary Act of 1789 by trying to give the Supreme Court too much power. Beneath the surface, however, was a less modest act: the claim that judicial review was the province of the judicial branch alone. In Marshall's words, "it is emphatically the province and duty of the judicial department to say what the law is."

Chief Justice John Marshall dominated the Supreme Court from 1801 to 1835 and wrote most of its early landmark opinions, including *Marbury v. Madison* (1803) affirming the Court's power of judicial review.

The Marshall Court and later Courts used this power with great restraint, perhaps recognizing that its regular use would invite retaliation by the other branches of government. Judicial review was not exercised for another 54 years after *Marbury* (1857) and has been used to declare acts of Congress unconstitutional only about 100 times since then. The Court has been much less reluctant to overrule the laws of the states and localities: it has done so over 1,000 times.

Judicial review does not exist in all democratic countries. In Great Britain, where there is no written constitution or bill of rights, the fundamental law is simply the body of laws passed by Parliament. No court can declare a parliamentary action null and void. In Switzerland, the high court can exercise judicial review over the actions of the cantons (like our states) but not those of the national assembly. France has only had limited judicial review since 1958. In Japan and Germany, on the other hand, post-World War II constitutions established strong powers of judicial review and courts have vigorously exercised these powers. Canada and Australia each have a long tradition of judicial review.

Judicial review raises questions about democracy. It involves the right of a body shielded from direct accountability to the people—federal judges are not elected and serve for life—to set aside the actions of government bodies whose members are directly elected. Some believe that this is the only way to protect the rights of minorities and to preserve the rules of the democratic process. Others believe that it has no place in a democratic society. We will come back to this issue later in this chapter.

Structural Change and Constitutional Interpretation

Scholars generally identify three periods in the history of constitutional law in the United States.[6] We will see how changes in constitutional law have been influenced by structural factors, particularly economic change.

PERIOD I: FROM MARSHALL TO THE CIVIL WAR   We saw in Chapter 4 how the United States experienced significant growth and change during the first 75 years of its existence. This was accompanied by changes in constitutional law. Chief Justice John Marshall, who presided over the Supreme Court from 1801 to 1835,

| Table 14.2 |
| The Court's Exercise of Judicial Review |

Years	Federal	State and Local
1789–1799	0	0
1800–1809	1	1
1810–1819	0	7
1820–1829	0	8
1830–1839	0	3
1840–1849	0	9
1850–1859	1	7
1860–1869	4	23
1870–1879	8	36
1880–1889	4	46
1890–1899	5	36
1900–1909	9	40
1910–1919	5	118
1920–1929	15	139
1930–1939	13	93
1940–1949	2	58
1950–1959	4	60
1960–1969	16	149
1970–1979	19	193
1980–1987	14	125
Total	120	1,151

Source: Lawrence Baum, *The Supreme Court*, 3d ed. (Washington, D.C.: Congressional Quarterly Press, 1989), pp. 177, 180.

was the key figure during this important period in our history. Marshall was a follower of the doctrines of Alexander Hamilton, who believed that American greatness depended on a strong national government, an alliance between government and business, in which industry was encouraged, and a national free market economy freed from the regulatory restraints of state and local governments. In a string of opinions that have shaped the fundamentals of American constitutional law, Marshall interpreted the Constitution to mean "maximum protection to property rights and maximum support for the idea of nationalism."[7]

Federal Supremacy and National Power The framers created a system of "centralized federalism." A number of decisions by the Marshall Court emphasized the "centralized" part of the formulation and significantly enhanced national power over the states. These cases are discussed in Chapter 3.

A National Economy *Gibbons v. Ogden (1824)* helped create the foundations of a national economy in which commerce could flow freely between the states. According to the Court, power over interstate commerce was entirely in the hands of the national government, and no state could interfere with it by imposing taxes or tariffs. Historian Charles Warren called the decision "the emancipation procla-

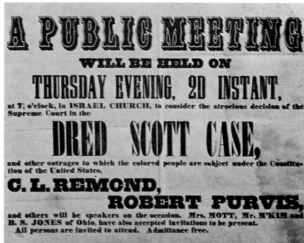

The Supreme Court's *Dred Scott v. Sandford* decision in 1857, which defined black slaves as nothing more nor less than property, generated widespread outrage and protests outside the South and helped bring on the Civil War.

mation of American commerce."[8] In *Dartmouth College v. Woodward* (1819), the Court ruled that a corporation was considered "a person under the law" and that, like any other citizen, the terms of its contract (in this case, to form and operate as a corporation) could not be impaired or changed by the state. The decision reassured business leaders that corporations would be largely free from state regulation.

Slavery The Court proved no more adept than the other branches of government in dealing with the issue of slavery. Chief Justice and southern sympathizer Roger Taney spoke for the majority in 1857 in one of the most disastrous cases ever rendered by the Court: *Dred Scott*. The case involved a slave who sued for his freedom on the grounds that his owner had taken him into a territory (Minnesota) where slavery was illegal under the terms of the Missouri Compromise. The Court declared the Missouri Compromise (which had helped to preserve a very fragile peace between the North and the South) unconstitutional and defined slaves as mere property, no different from any other form of property, without rights as individuals. The public outcry against this decision outside the South added another spark to the coming conflagration, the Civil War.

PERIOD II: GOVERNMENT AND ECONOMY The Civil War and the Industrial Revolution triggered the development of a mass production economy that was dominated by the business corporation. Determining the role to be played by government in such an economy was a central theme of late nineteenth- and early twentieth-century American political life. The courts were involved in this rethinking. At the beginning, the Supreme Court took the position that the corporation was to be protected against regulation by state and federal governments; by the end, it caved in to the expansion of government regulation and management of the economy during the crisis of the Great Depression.

The main bastion for protection of the corporation was the Fourteenth Amendment. This amendment was passed in the wake of the Civil War to guarantee the citizenship rights of freed slaves. In one of the great ironies of American history, this expansion of federal power over the states to protect rights—the operative phrase was from Section 1: "nor shall any state deprive any person of life, liberty, or property without due process of law"—was gradually translated by the Court to mean protection of corporations (which were "persons" under the law) and other forms of business from state regulation.

This reading of a particular brand of economic theory, laissez faire, into constitutional law made the Supreme Court the principal ally of business in the late nineteenth and early twentieth centuries. The Court overturned efforts by state and federal governments to provide welfare for the poor, to regulate manufacturing monopolies, to initiate an income tax, to regulate interstate railroad rates, to provide scholarships to students, to regulate wages, hours, and working conditions, and to protect consumers against unsafe or unhealthy products. The Court also supported the use of injunctions to halt strikes.

The business–Supreme Court alliance lasted until the Great Depression. The New Deal reflected a new national consensus about the need for a greatly expanded federal government with a new set of responsibilities: to manage the economy; to provide a safety net for the poor, the unemployed, and the elderly; to support collective-bargaining arrangements between labor and management; and to regulate business in the public interest. The Supreme Court, however, was opposed. Filled with justices born in the nineteenth century and committed to the unshakable link between the Constitution and laissez faire economic doctrine, the Court dealt a series of stunning reversals to the New Deal in 1935 and 1936. It overturned the Agricultural Adjustment Act, the National Industrial Recovery Act, the Bituminous Coal Act (which regulated wages and working conditions in the mining industry), and a New York minimum wage law. Waiting in the wings for Court scrutiny were the Wagner Labor Relations Act and the Social Security Act, and their prospects for survival did not look good.

In an extraordinary turn of events (already reviewed in Chapter 8, "Political Parties"), the Supreme Court reversed itself in 1937, finding the Social Security Act, the Labor Relations Act, and state minimum wage laws acceptable. It is not entirely clear why the so-called "switch-in-time-that-saved-nine" occurred, but surely Roosevelt's landslide election in 1936, the heightening of public hostility toward the Court, and Roosevelt's plan to "pack the Court" all played a role. Whatever the reason, the Court abandoned its effort to prevent the government from playing a central role in the management of the economy and the regulation of business, and came to defer to the political branches of government by the end of the 1930s. In doing so, it brought another constitutional era to a close.

PERIOD III: INDIVIDUAL RIGHTS AND LIBERTIES   Three fundamental issues of American constitutional law—the relationship of the states to the nation, the nature of private property and the national economy, and the role of government in the management of the economy—were essentially settled by the time World War II occurred. Since then, the Court has turned its attention to the relationship between the individual and government.[9]

Most of this story is told in Chapter 19, "Rights and Liberties," so not much will be said here. For now, it is sufficient to point out that the Court, especially during the tenure of Chief Justice Earl Warren, rendered a series of decisions that expanded protections for free expression and association, religious expression, fair trials, and civil rights for minorities. In another series of cases dealing with the apportionment of electoral districts, the Court declared for political equality, based on the principal of "one person, one vote." In many of its landmark decisions, the Court applied the Bill of Rights to the states. Though the Court's behavior was not blameless during and after the war, it made significant strides in expanding the realm of individual freedom.

Constitutional law and the Court do not stand still, however. Like all political institutions, both are responsive in the long run to changes in the world around them. In this light, it is not surprising that the highly conservative justices appointed by Presidents Reagan and Bush have moved the Court away from some of its earlier decisions on rights and liberties. Whether things have gone far enough in a new direction to constitute a new constitutional period remains to be seen. Chapter 19 will address this issue in more detail.

THE FEDERAL COURT SYSTEM: ORGANIZATION AND JURISDICTION

Ours is a federal court system. There is one system for the national government (the federal courts) and one in each of the states. Each state has its own system of courts adjudicating cases on the basis of its own constitution, statutes, and administrative rules. In total, the great bulk of laws, legal disputes, and court decisions (roughly 99 percent) are located in the states. The most important political and constitutional issues, however, eventually reach the federal courts. In this chapter, our focus is on the federal courts.

The existence of a dual court system—state courts and federal courts—has important consequences. For one thing, though they share a **common law** tradition, each of the states has created a slightly different body of legal precedents over the years, especially in the area of private law (having to do with businesses, contracts, families, and so on). For another thing, since the boundaries between state and federal law are less clear-cut in practice than in theory (e.g., states and the federal government each have laws concerning civil rights), litigants attempt to channel their cases to the kind of court where they think that they have the best chance of winning. Blacks who were trying to end school segregation in the South during the 1950s and 1960s took their complaints to the federal courts; school districts that were trying to protect segregated systems of education usually turned to their own state courts for protection.

The only court specifically mentioned in the Constitution's Article III is the Supreme Court. The framers left the task of establishing "such inferior courts as [it] may from time to time ordain and establish" to Congress. Beginning with the Judiciary Act of 1789, Congress has periodically reorganized the federal court system. The end result is a three-tiered pyramidical system (see Figure 14.1). At the bottom are 94 federal district courts, with at least one district in each state. In the middle are 13 courts of appeal. At the top of the pyramid is the Supreme Court. Congress also created a number of courts to adjudicate cases in highly specialized areas of concern, like taxes.

Article III does not offer many guidelines for the federal court system, but the few requirements that exist are very important. The Constitution requires, for instance, that federal judges serve "during good behavior," which, in practice, means for life. Since impeachment by Congress is the only way to remove federal judges, the decision about who will be a judge is a very important one. Article III

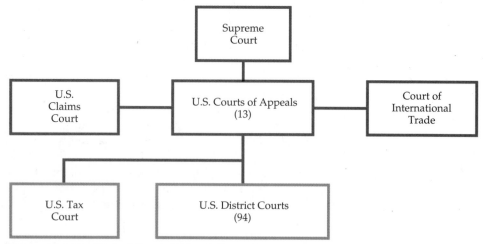

Figure 14.1 The United States Federal Court System

Source: Administrative Office of the U.S. Courts.

also says that Congress cannot reduce the salaries of judges once they are in office. This provision was designed to maintain the independence of the judiciary by protecting it from legislative intimidation.

Article III also specifies the jurisdiction of the federal courts. The federal courts hear cases in the following categories:

- The Constitution—disputes involving the First Amendment or the Commerce clause are examples.

- Federal statutes and treaties—include disputes involving ambassadors and other diplomats

- Admiralty and maritime issues

- Controversies in which the United States government is a party

- Disputes between the states

- Disputes between a state and a citizen of another state

- Disputes between a state (or citizen of a state) and foreign states or citizens

Federal District Courts

Most cases in the federal court system are first heard in one of the 94 district courts. District courts are courts of *original jurisdiction*; they do not hear appeals from other courts. They are also trial courts; some employ juries (either **grand juries** that bring indictments or **petit** (trial) **juries** that decide cases), and some are heard only by a judge.

Most of the business of the federal courts takes place at this level. Over 300,000 cases are filed annually. About 80 percent of these cases are civil cases, and about 20 percent are criminal cases. (Some very important cases are tried in the district courts. See the story of Judge John Sirica in "The Struggle for Democracy.") The former include everything from antitrust cases brought by the federal government to commercial and contract disputes between citizens (or businesses) of two or more states. The latter include violations of federal criminal laws, such as bank robbery, interstate drug trafficking, and kidnapping.

Most civil and criminal cases are concluded at this level, either through pre-trial settlement or a trial verdict. In a handful of cases, however, one of the parties to the case may feel that a mistake has been made in trial procedure or in the law that was brought to bear in the trial. Or, one of the parties may feel that a constitutional issue is at stake that was not taken into account at the trial stage or was wrongly interpreted. In such cases, one of the parties can appeal to a higher court.

U.S. Courts of Appeal

The United States is divided into twelve geographic jurisdictions (see map, Figure 14.2), called **circuits**, to hear appeals from the district courts. There is also a thirteenth, called the U.S. Court of Appeals for the Federal Circuit, located in Wash-

Figure 14.2 U.S. Federal Circuit Courts, made up of 13 Judicial Circuits and 94 U.S. District Courts

Note: The remaining two circuit courts, the D.C. Circuit and Federal Circuit, are located in Washington, D.C.

Source: Administrative Office of the U.S. Courts (January 1983).

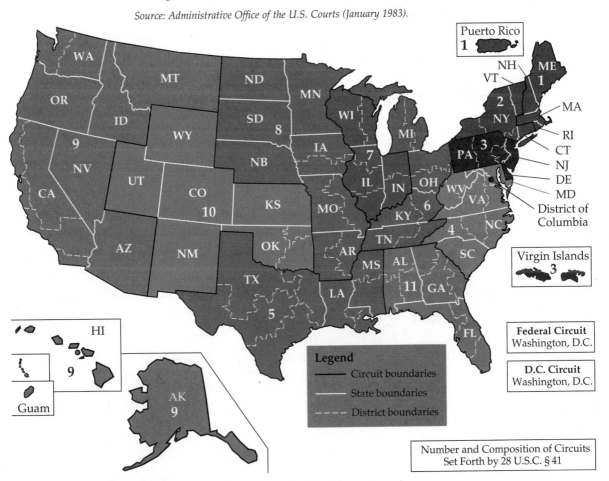

THE STRUGGLE FOR DEMOCRACY

District Judge John Sirica and the Watergate Case

Federal District Judge John Sirica was not popular with defense attorneys, prosecutors, or federal circuit court judges who often overturned his decisions on appeal. This former club fighter, sparring partner to welterweight champion Jack Britton, and crony of heavyweight champion Jack Dempsey, was as pugnacious in the courtroom as he was in the ring. What brought him the most trouble was his intense grilling of witnesses and attorneys when he thought that a line of questioning was inadvertently or purposefully skirting around the truth. Responding to his critics, he summed up his judicial philosophy in the following way: "I don't think we should sit up here like nincompoops. The function of a trial court is to search for the truth." He was especially incensed by the barely concealed lying of the defendants and the lack of zeal on the part of federal prosecutors in the trial of the Watergate burglars, over which he presided in 1973.

The defendants had been caught red-handed in an attempt to install telephone bugs and to steal confidential materials from the Democratic National Committee headquarters in the Watergate complex in Washington, D.C. The nation would later learn that the entire enterprise was part of a larger White House effort to use the power of government to attack any and all enemies of President Nixon. The burglars, however, were willing to take the fall for their higher-ups in return for sizable cash payments and promises of presidential clemency. They told federal prosecutors that the burglary was a rogue operation, run and financed by E. Gordon Liddy and James McCord, former CIA operatives now working on the Committee to Reelect the President (CREEP). The Cuban burglary team arrested at Watergate pleaded guilty. A jury found Liddy and McCord guilty as charged.

Sirica was not amused. Before passing sentence

ington, D.C., which hears cases on patents and government contracts. Almost 40,000 cases are filed annually in the federal appeals courts, though only about 5,000 reach the formal-hearing stage. Cases cannot originate in these courts but must come from other courts to them. Because they exist only to hear appeals, we refer to them as **appellate courts**. New factual evidence cannot be introduced before such courts; no witnesses are called or cross-examined. Lawyers for each side argue with each other and make their case for the judges not by the examination of witnesses or documents, but by the submission of **briefs** that set out the legal issues at stake. Judges usually convene as panels of three or more (extremely important cases may have up to seven members) to hear oral arguments from the lawyers on each side of the case and to cross-examine them on points of law.

Judge Sirica

James McCord had second thoughts about being a fall guy for his superiors; the money and promised executive clemency did not seem worth it to this church-going, family man. He wrote a letter to Judge Sirica that lifted the lid off the Watergate operation for all to see. In it, he revealed that high government officials had committed perjury, that pressure had been applied to witnesses to lie in court, and that officials in the White House were involved.

The letter was the opening wedge in a series of trials and congressional investigations that would reveal the immense conspiracy against the democratic process, of which Watergate was only the tip of the iceberg. It would never have happened had one federal district judge not been willing to stand firm.

on the defendants, he observed, "I am still not satisfied that all the pertinent facts that might be available have been produced before an American jury." True to his reputation, "Maximum John" Sirica threw the book at the convicted conspirators, in each case imposing the maximum jail time allowed by law.

Sources: Carl Bernstein and Bob Woodward, *All the President's Men* (New York: Warner, 1975), pp. 256–260, 304–306; J. Anthony Lukas, *Nightmare: The Underside of the Nixon Years* (New York: Viking, 1976), pp. 300–306.

Weeks or even months later, after considerable study, writing, and discussion among the judges, the panel issues a verdict. In important cases, the verdict is usually accompanied by an **opinion** that sets out the reasoning behind it.

Once appellate decisions are published, they become **precedents** that guide the decision of other judges. While judges do not slavishly follow precedent, they tend to move away from it only when necessary and only in very small steps. This doctrine of closely following precedent as the basis for legal reasoning is known as **stare decisis**.

The American and British judicial systems are both grounded in this tradition of deciding cases on the basis of precedents from previous cases. Most continental European countries, on the other hand, have judicial systems grounded in the Roman law tradition. This tradition emphasizes elaborate legal codes to cover most aspects of daily life, social intercourse, and business. Courts in Germany and France decide cases by comparing legal disputes to these codes rather than to previous decisions.

The Supreme Court

Congress determines how many judges sit on the Supreme Court. In the beginning, the Court had 6 members. The Federalists reduced the number to 5 in 1801 to prevent newly elected president Thomas Jefferson from filling a vacancy. In 1869, Congress set the number at its present 9 members (8 justices and a chief justice). It has remained this way ever since, weathering, as we have seen, the effort by Franklin Roosevelt to "pack" the Court by expanding its size to 15 with more politically congenial justices.

The Supreme Court is both a court of original jurisdiction and an appellate court. Disputes involving ambassadors and other diplomatic personnel, two or more states, the federal government and a state, or a state and a citizen from another state start in the Supreme Court rather than in some other court.

The Supreme Court serves as an appellate court for the federal appeals courts and for the highest courts of each of the states. Certain disputes *must* be accepted on appeal by the Supreme Court for consideration; namely, those in which a state or a federal law has been declared unconstitutional, or in which the highest state court has denied a claim of one of the parties that a state law violates federal law or the Constitution (see Figure 14.3).

Congress determines the appellate jurisdiction of the Court. In 1869, a Congress controlled by radical Republicans removed the Court's power to review cases falling under the Reconstruction program for the South.

As the highest appellate court in the federal court system, the decisions and opinions of the Supreme Court become the main precedents on federal and constitutional questions for courts at all other levels of jurisdiction. This is why Supreme Court decisions receive so much attention from other political actors, the media, and the public.

APPOINTMENT TO THE FEDERAL BENCH

Because federal judges are appointed for life and make important decisions, it matters in a democratic society who they are and how they get to the bench. If they are isolated from popular influence, then democracy is at risk. We will see that the courts are not divorced from or above the political process but are an integral part of the political interplay of American life. The voice of the people affects judges. Whether it is strong enough to sustain democracy is a subject that we will address throughout the remainder of this chapter.

Who Are They?

Appointees to the federal bench must be (by custom, not law) lawyers, but they need not have judicial experience. Almost one-half of all Supreme Court justices during this century have had no prior experience as judges. Among the ranks of the "inexperienced" are some of the most prominent and influential justices in

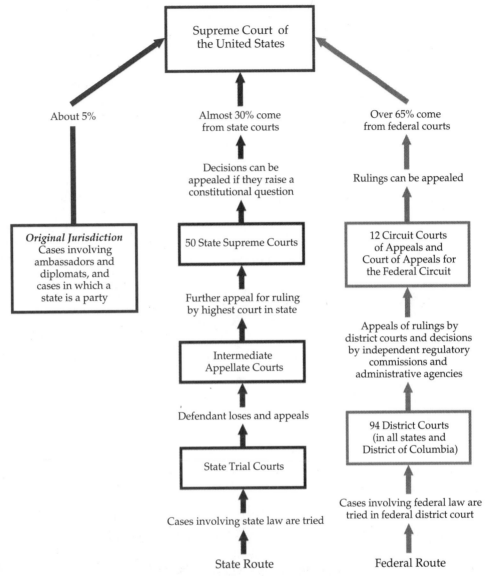

Figure 14.3 How cases get to the Supreme Court

Source: Adapted from David O'Brien, Storm Center *(New York: W.W. Norton, 1990).*

our history, including Louis Brandeis, Harlan Stone, Charles Evans Hughes, Felix Frankfurter, Earl Warren, and present Chief Justice William Rehnquist.[10] Because federal judges are lawyers, they tend to come from backgrounds that are more privileged than the American norm. What is harder to explain is why federal judges, and particularly Supreme Court judges, come from the most elite parts of the legal profession. For the most part, they are white, male, Protestants from upper-income or upper-middle-class backgrounds, who attended the most selective and expensive undergraduate and graduate institutions.[11] There have been only two black Justices (Thurgood Marshall and Clarence Thomas), a single woman (Sandra Day O'Connor), five Jews, and seven Catholics on the High Court during its entire history. The representativeness of judicial appointments at the circuit and district court levels is better, but still a long way from reflecting the composition of the legal profession, much less the American people as a whole. If you believe, as most observers of the courts do, that judges bring their personal outlooks to bear when they are deciding cases, then this significantly unrepresentative composition of the federal judiciary may be cause for concern.

The Appointment Process

Federal judges assume office after they have been nominated by the president and have been approved by the Senate. Presidents realize that judicial appointments are a way for them to shape the nation's business for many years after they leave office. Consequently, they pay attention to the judicial appointment process.

In some respects, all presidents approach the appointment process in the same way. After defining who he is interested in in general terms, the president delegates the task of identifying judicial candidates to one or more senior White House staff members and the attorney general. Lists of potential candidates are drawn up after wide consultation with influential senators (who must eventually approve the nominee), party luminaries, state and local bar associations, legal scholars, and leaders of important interest groups. The FBI conducts background checks of the leading candidates, and the American Bar Association is asked to evaluate them. The lists of candidates are almost always made up of lawyers who have been tied to, and actively involved in, national politics. Presidents tend to consider only those who have been active in their own party, for they are the most likely to share their policy and ideological commitments.[12] Some high Court nominees have even been close advisors to the president prior to their appointment: Felix Frankfurter to Roosevelt; Arthur Goldberg to Kennedy; Abe Fortas to Johnson; and Warren Burger to Nixon.

Presidents commonly nominate people for the Court who agree with them on ideological and policy grounds. Conservative justices William Rehnquist (left) and Clarence Thomas (right) were the picks of conservative presidents Reagan (who nominated Rehnquist to be Chief Justice) and Bush.

Presidents take many things into consideration besides merit. No president wants a nomination rejected by the Senate, so he and his advisors consult with key senators, especially those on the Judiciary Committee, before nominations are forwarded. Nominations for district court judgeships are subject to what is called **senatorial courtesy**: the right of the senior senator from the president's party in the state where the district court is located to approve the nominee. In the past, senatorial courtesy was so strong that the appointment process was reversed in practice: senators simply forwarded the name of the person whom they wanted nominated, and the White House concurred. Senatorial courtesy does not operate, however, for appointments to the circuit courts, whose jurisdictions span more than a single state, or to the Supreme Court, whose jurisdiction is the entire nation. Nevertheless, presidents must be extremely attentive to the views of key senators.

On occasion, despite presidential efforts to placate it, the Senate has refused to give its "advice and consent." Of the 143 nominees for the Supreme Court since the founding of the Republic, the Senate has refused to approve 28 of them, of which only 5 were in this century. There have also been several near-defeats; Bush's nominee Clarence Thomas was only confirmed by a margin of four votes. Rejection of nominees has usually happened when the president was weak or when the other party was in control of the Senate, especially when the president was trying to make **lame-duck** appointments. Several recent presidential defeats—Nixon's nominees Harold Carlswell and Clement Haynsworth, and Reagan's nominee Robert Bork—were the product of deep ideological differences between the president and the Senate majority.

Though presidents must be concerned about the merit of their candidates and their acceptability in the Senate, they also try by their appointments to make their mark on the future. Presidents go about this in different ways.

President John F. Kennedy, worried about the fate of his legislative program and foreign policy initiatives in a Congress that was dominated by powerful southern committee chairmen, nominated judges that would be acceptable to the South. Many of these prosegregation judges eventually frustrated Kennedy and

Robert Bork, President Reagan's nominee for the Court, was turned down by an historic margin after lengthy committee hearings and a bruising debate on the floor of the Senate. Many Americans and a majority of senators considered his views too extreme.

his brother, Attorney General Robert Kennedy, when the administration later pushed its civil rights agenda.

Jimmy Carter wanted to be remembered as the president who opened public service and the courts to women and minorities. Figure 14.4 shows that he appointed more women, blacks, and Hispanics to the federal bench than any recent president.

Other presidents have been most interested in nominating judges who shared their ideological and programmatic commitments. John Adams nominated John Marshall and a number of other judges to protect Federalist principles during

Figure 14.4 Female and minority judicial appointees (through 1990)

Sources: Sheldon Goldman of University of Massachusetts (Johnson, Nixon, Ford); Justice Department (Carter, Reagan, Bush); Congressional Quarterly, January 19, 1991.

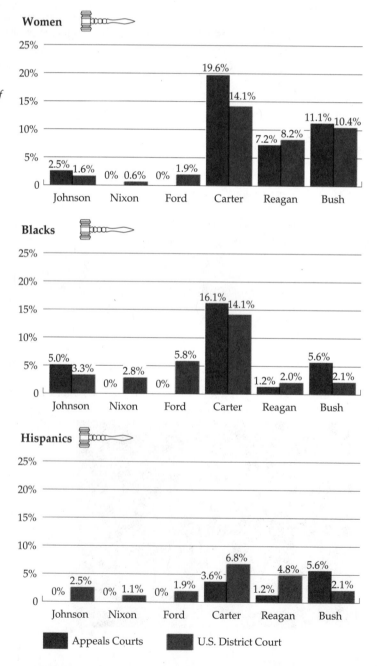

the ascendancy of the Jeffersonians. Franklin Roosevelt tried to fill the courts with judges who favored the New Deal. Ronald Reagan favored conservatives who were committed to rolling back affirmative action, abortion rights, protections for criminal defendants, and broad claims of standing in environmental cases. George Bush continued this conservative drift with his nominations, including that of David Souter and Clarence Thomas to the Supreme Court. As one judicial observer put it, "There is no area in which conservatives are more happy with George Bush than in judicial nominations."[13]

Nominating candidates for the federal bench in general and the Supreme Court in particular is hardly a scientific process. Presidents are often disappointed in how their nominees turn out. Felix Frankfurter became more conservative in his years on the Court, upsetting Franklin Roosevelt's expectations. Dwight Eisenhower was dumbfounded when his friend and nominee, Earl Warren, became the leader of a Court that transformed constitutional law with regard to civil rights and criminal procedure. Nixon was puzzled when Chief Justice Warren Burger voted with a unanimous Court to override the president's claim of executive privilege and forced him to give up the documents that would seal his fate in the Watergate affair. George Bush was surprised when his nominee, David Souter, refused to vote for the overturn of *Roe* in *Planned Parenthood v. Casey* (1992). Despite these dramatic examples, the past political and ideological positions of federal court nominees are a pretty good guide to their later behavior on the bench.[14]

THE SUPREME COURT IN ACTION

The Supreme Court meets from the first Monday in October (set by statute) until late June or early July, depending on the press of business. Let's see how it goes about deciding cases.

Norms of Operation

The Court is a tradition-bound institution defined by many rituals and long-standing norms. Brass spittoons still stand next to each justice's chair; quill pens and inkwells still grace the desks of competing counsel. Pages only gave up knickers in 1963; required formal wear (with tails) for lawyers was only recently abandoned. When the justices meet in public session to hear oral arguments or to announce decisions, they enter the courtroom in the same way: the chief justice is the first to emerge from behind the curtain that is draped behind the bench; the remainder enter in order of seniority.

More important than rituals are norms, unwritten but clearly understood ways of behaving. One norm is *secrecy*, which keeps the conflicts between justices out of the public eye and elevates the stature of the Court. Justices do not grant interviews very often. Reporters are not allowed to stalk the corridors for a story. Clerks are expected to keep all memos, draft opinions, and conversations with their justices confidential. Justices are not commonly seen on the frantic Washington, D.C., cocktail party circuit. When meeting in conference to argue and decide cases, the justices meet alone, without secretaries or clerks. While a breach of secrecy has occurred on occasion, allowing "insider" books like *The Brethren* to be published, they are the exceptions. As a result, we know less about the inner workings of the Court than about any other branch of government.

Oral argument and the announcement of decisions happen here in the main courtroom of the Supreme Court building.

Courtesy is another norm. Though justices may sometimes express their displeasure and distaste for each other in private, in public they treat each other with great formality and respect. The justices shake hands before court sessions and conferences. They refer to each other as "my brother" or my "dissenting brother." Differences of opinion are usually respected; justices are allowed every opportunity to make their case to their fellow justices.

Seniority is another important norm. Seniority determines the assignment of office space, the seating arrangements in open court (the most junior are at the ends), the order of speaking in conference (the chief justice, then the most senior, etc.), and the order of voting (the most junior goes first).

Finally, the justices are expected to stick very closely to *precedent* when they are reaching a decision. When the Court departs from precedent, it is essentially overruling its own past actions, exercising judicial review of itself. In most cases, departure from precedent comes in only very small steps over many years, for example, several decisions chipped away at the "separate but equal" doctrine of *Plessy v. Ferguson* before it was decisively reversed in *Brown v. Board of Education* (see Chapter 1). If there is a significant ideological turnover on the court, however, change can come more quickly. The Rehnquist Court has been particularly aggressive in overturning precedents on the civil rights, criminal justice, and abortion fronts.

Controlling the Agenda

The Court has a number of screening mechanisms to control its agenda and to focus its attention on cases that involve important federal or constitutional questions.

Several technical rules help keep down the numbers. Cases must be **real and adverse**, meaning that they must involve a real dispute between two parties. The Court will not provide "advisory" opinions to guide the other branches. Disputants in a case must have standing, meaning that they must have a real and direct interest in the issues that are raised. The Court sometimes changes the definition of *standing* to make access easier or more difficult. The Warren Court favored a broad definition of *standing*, inviting litigation. The Rehnquist court tightened the definition, making it harder for people suing in the name of some larger group of affected people—consumers, racial minorities, and so on—to bring cases. Cases must also be **ripe**, meaning that all other avenues of appeal have been exhausted and that injury has already taken place (it will not accept hypothetical or predicted injury cases). Appeals must also be filed within a specified time limit, paperwork must be proper and complete, and a filing fee of $200 must be paid. The fee can be waived if a petitioner is indigent and files an affidavit *in forma pauperis* (in the manner of a pauper). One of the most famous cases in American history, *Gideon v. Wainwright* (1963), which established the right to counsel in criminal cases, was submitted *in forma pauperis* on a few pieces of lined paper by a Florida State Penitentiary inmate named Clarence Earl Gideon.

The most powerful tool that the Court has for controlling its own agenda is the power to grant or not to grant a **writ of certiorari**. A grant of cert is a decision of the Court that an appellate case raises an important federal or constitutional issue that it is prepared to consider. Law clerks in the chief justice's office prepare a brief summary of each petition for the justices, along with a recommendation on whether or not to grant cert. The clerks, in consultation with the chief justice, prepare a "discuss list" of cases that they are recommending for cert. Under the **rule of four**, petitions are granted cert if at least four justices vote in favor. There are several reasons why a petition may not command four votes, even if the case involves important constitutional issues: it may involve a particularly controversial issue that the Court would like to avoid, or the Court may not yet have developed a solid majority and wishes to avoid a split decision. Few petitions survive all of these hurdles. Of the 5,000 or so cases that are filed in each session, the Court grants cert for only a little more than 200. For cases denied cert, the decision of the lower court stands.

Deciding how freely to grant "cert" is tricky business for the Court. Used too often, it threatens to inundate the Court with cases. Used too sparingly, it leaves in place the decisions of 12 different circuit courts on substantial federal and constitutional questions.

Deciding Cases

In about 25 percent of cases, the issues are so clear-cut and the justices are so united that a decision is rendered without hearing oral argument (called **per curiam** decisions). The remaining 150 or so cases are scheduled for oral argument. Lawyers on each side are alerted to the key issues that the justices wish to consider, and new briefs are invited. Briefs are also submitted on most important cases by other parties who may be interested in the disputes. These "friends of the court," or **amicus curiae**, briefs may be submitted by individuals, interest groups, or some agency of the federal government, including the Justice Department or even the president. These briefs are sometimes quite influential and shape important sections of the opinion of the court. Some cases bring an avalanche of such briefs. In the *Webster* case, 78 briefs were filed.

Each case is argued for one hour, with one-half hour given to each side in the dispute. Oral argument is not so much a presentation of arguments, however, as it is a give and take between the lawyers and the justices, and among the justices themselves. Some justices, like Antonin Scalia, are famous for their close grilling of lawyers. When the federal government is a party to the case, the solicitor general or one of his deputies presents the oral arguments.

"*Well, heck! If all you smart cookies agree, who am I to dissent?*"

Drawing by Handelsman, © 1972 The New Yorker Magazine, Inc.

After hearing oral arguments and reading the briefs in the case, the justices meet in conference to reach a decision. They meet on Wednesday afternoons to consider cases that were argued on Monday, and on Fridays to consider cases that were argued on Tuesdays and Wednesdays. The custom is for each justice to state his or her position on the case in turn, starting with the chief justice and moving through the ranks in order of seniority. Chief justices of great stature and intellect, like John Marshall and Charles Evans Hughes, have used the opportunity to speak first as a way of structuring the case and of swaying votes. Others, like Warren Burger, who did not command much respect from the other justices, were less able to shape the decision process. The statement of each justice makes it clear in most cases how the Court is divided on the issues, so votes are usually unnecessary. When matters are not so clear, voting takes place in reverse order of seniority, with the chief justice voting last.

Political scientists have tried to determine what factors are most important in predicting how justices will vote. One approach looks at the ideological predilections of the justices and manages to explain a great deal about voting behavior.[15] Another focuses on the diaries and personal papers of retired justices and shows that a great deal of negotiating and "horse-trading" goes on, with justices trading votes on different cases and joining opinions they do not like so that they can have a hand in modifying them.[16] Another approach tries to link voting behavior to social background, types of previous judicial experience, and the political environment of family upbringing.[17] None have been totally successful, primarily because much of what the Court does in conference is secret and can only be painfully and imperfectly reconstructed.[18] About all that one can say is that the justices tend to form relatively stable voting blocs that make Court decisions on a wide range of issues relatively predictable.

The vote in conference is not final. As Justice John Harlan once explained it, "the books on voting are never closed until the decision finally comes down."[19] The justices have an opportunity to change their vote in response to the opinion

	Table 14.3	
	Justices Who Have Dissented Most Often	
Justice		Dissents Per Term
W. Douglas, 1969–1974		38.5
J. Stevens, 1975–1988		21.2
T. Marshall, 1969–1988		15.4
J. Harlan, 1955–1971		15.1
W. Rehnquist, 1971–1988		13.8
W. Brennan, 1969–1988		13.0
F. Frankfurter, 1939–1962		10.9
P. Stewart, 1969–1981		10.8
H. Blackmun, 1971–1988		10.7
B. White, 1969–		10.6

Source: David M. O'Brien, *Storm Center: The Supreme Court in American Politics* (New York: Norton, 1990), p. 319.

supporting the majority decision. The opinion is a statement of the legal reasoning that supports the decision of the Court. There are three kinds of opinions. The **opinion of the Court** is the opinion of the majority. A **concurring opinion** is the opinion of a justice or justices who support the majority decision but have different legal reasons for doing so. A **dissenting** opinion presents the reasoning of the minority. Very often, dissenting opinions offer arguments that become the basis for future Court majorities. The rate of dissent is increasing. Eight of the top ten dissenters (in numbers of dissents) have been on the Court within the past two decades (see Table 14.3).

If he votes with the majority in conference, the chief justice assigns the opinion. He can assign it to any justice in the majority, often to himself. Some jurists and scholars believe that this power to assign is the most important role of the chief justice, and it is guarded jealously. Warren Burger was so anxious to play a role in opinion assignments that, much to the distress of his colleagues, he would often delay announcing his vote so that he could place himself with the majority.[20] Justice William Douglas angrily charged that Burger only voted with the majority in *Roe* so that he could assign the case to a justice who was closer to the minority view. Other chief justices, such as John Marshall and Charles Evans Hughes, liked to keep the most important cases for themselves, rather than assigning them to others. If the chief justice's opinion is with the minority, the opinion is assigned by the most senior member of the majority.

The justice assigned to write the opinion does not work in isolation. He or she is not only assisted by law clerks but also by other justices, who helpfully provide memoranda suggesting wording and reasoning. Most opinions go through numerous revisions, during which time a considerable amount of bargaining goes on. In this process, the Court acts like "nine independent law firms," drafting opinions and negotiating compromises either directly between the senior partners (the justices) or their associates (their clerks).

It is only when an opinion is completed that a final vote is taken in conference. Justices are free to change earlier votes: they can join the majority if they are now persuaded by its reasoning; or a concurring opinion can be so compelling that the majority may decide to replace the original majority opinion with it.

Key Personnel

THE CHIEF JUSTICE   The formal powers of the office of chief justice are not impressive. Whatever power a chief justice has is a mix of his own leadership abilities, the prestige of the office derived from the actions of past chief justices, such as Marshall, Hughes, and Warren, and a set of norms that make him "first among equals."

The chief justice also has certain administrative responsibilities. He is in charge of the management of the Supreme Court building and the personnel who work there, from guards and cooks to maintenance workers. He also serves as chair of the U.S. Judicial Conference, which coordinates many of the activities of the federal court system (budgets, procedures, and the like) and of the Federal Judicial Center, which does research and trains personnel for the administration of the federal courts. Former Chief Justice Warren Burger estimated that about one-third of his time was spent on these various administrative activities. (Table 14.4 lists all chief justices.)

THE SOLICITOR GENERAL   The solicitor general is appointed by the president to serve as the representative of the U.S. government before the Supreme Court. He and his staff decide which cases to appeal from the lower courts and which cases between private parties or the states to join on an amicus curiae basis. He and his staff prepare new briefs or revise briefs written by the Justice Department or other

Table 14.4
Chief Justices of the Supreme Court

Chief Justice	Appointing President	Dates of Service
Jay, John	Washington	1789–1795
Rutledge, John	Washington	1795–1795
Ellsworth, Oliver	Washington	1796–1800
Marshall, John	Adams, J.	1801–1835
Taney, Roger Brooke	Jackson	1836–1864
Chase, Salmon Portland	Lincoln	1864–1873
Waite, Morrison Remick	Grant	1874–1888
Fuller, Melville Weston	Cleveland	1888–1910
White, Edward Douglass	Taft	1910–1921
Taft, William Howard	Harding	1921–1930
Hughes, Charles Evans	Hoover	1930–1941
Stone, Harlan Fiske	Roosevelt, F.	1941–1946
Vinson, Frederick Moore	Truman	1946–1953
Warren, Earl	Eisenhower	1953–1969
Burger, Warren Earl	Nixon	1969–1986
Rehnquist, William Hubbs	Reagan	1986–

federal agencies on all of the relevant cases, and he serves as the government's representative in oral argument.

Although the office is hardly visible to the public, it is very important in the relationship between the judicial and executive branches of the federal government. The solicitor general screens cases from around the country and only submits those that he considers to be of the greatest constitutional moment. There is evidence that the Court pays close attention to what he submits when it is deciding whether or not to grant certiorari because, being the representative of the president, he signals what the administration considers to be most important.[21] Such a signal is hard to ignore.

LAW CLERKS   Supreme Court clerks are a very select group of young lawyers recruited from among recent graduates of the most prestigious law schools in the United States. Most of them go on to distinguished legal careers; many become law school professors; a few, like William Rehnquist, become Supreme Court justices. Their main role is to assist the justice to whom they are assigned in the preparation of cases. This involves a wide range of activities. The "Doing Politics" box tells what the work of Supreme Court clerks is like. Clerks prepare memoranda on cases being considered for certiorari, screen petitions for *in forma pauperis* filings, do legal research, and increasingly write initial drafts of opinions. Their particular duties or the time spent on each duty varies widely, because each justice decides how to use his or her clerks. Some justices are close to their clerks, treat them very much as colleagues, and give them important responsibilities in writing opinions and in negotiating revisions with the clerks of the other justices. Other justices like to keep their clerks on a shorter lead, giving them less independence. Because of the escalating work load of the Court, however, the trend over recent decades has been for clerks to assume more and more responsibility for drafting and revising opinions, though each justice has the final word.

Chief Justice William Rehnquist meets with his law clerks to discuss pending cases.

DOING
POLITICS

*The Life and
Times of
Supreme Court
Law Clerks*

A few outstanding law school graduates get to spend a year clerking for a Supreme Court justice. Two leading journalists, who interviewed many clerks, report on their work in the following selections:

The clerks loved their jobs. The way things worked in the Chief's chambers gave them tremendous influence. Warren told them how he wanted the cases to come out. But the legal research and the drafting of Court opinions—even those that had made Warren and his Court famous and infamous—were their domain. . . .

At about 11 o'clock White summoned his three clerks. He wanted them to do some research on the 125 death penalty cases on which cert petitions were pending. Did these other death penalty laws also provide the judge or juries with the option of imposing the death sentence? Or were some of them mandatory laws that automatically imposed the sentence for certain specified crimes. He also wanted more statistics on how often juries or judges imposed the death penalty when it was an option.

White's clerks left his office. They knew nothing more than what they had heard on the grapevine: that White had tentatively voted months before at conference to strike the laws. White had never told them. They had had Socratic dialogues with him, but he had never tipped his hand.

The clerks spent three frantic hours researching White's questions. The cert petitions did not indicate whether the laws in each case had provided for optional or automatic sentencing. So they had to look up each law. It was after lunch when they finished. . . .

Douglas's abuses of his clerks were legend. He "fired" his clerk in the 1968 term one day before the clerk's wedding. The clerk had planned to hold his wedding reception at the Court the next day, and he went ahead, fearing that Douglas would appear and evict everyone from the building. Douglas arrived and, for the first time in an entire term, was gracious. The "firing" was never mentioned again.

The following term, Douglas told one of his two clerks that he would be fired except for the fact that he was a nice boy and that he was so incompetent that he would not be able to get another job. "I can get better legal advice from drunks in the gutter," Douglas said. . . .

One of Stewart's clerks was given the memo to forward to the Chief and to the other chambers. Reading it over, the clerk thought his boss was being too conciliatory to the Chief. Burger's standing section was not good enough. The opinion was more important than the Chief's ego. Since Stewart had left for Earl Warren's funeral and was not likely to be back that day, the clerk took matters into his own hands and slipped the original and all copies of the memo into his desk drawer. He would raise the subject with Stewart the next day. He hoped Stewart would

THE SUPREME COURT AS A NATIONAL POLICYMAKER

People often say that the Court should not make policy but should only settle disputes. But, because the disputes it settles involve contentious public issues (like abortion rights and affirmative action) and fundamental questions about the meaning of our constitutional rules, the Court can't help but make public policy, even if it doesn't want to do so. We have already seen many examples in this

be glad the memo had not been sent. . . .

During his first term, Rehnquist worried some about what influence his clerks might have on his opinions. He had clerked at the Court after law school and had written a magazine article in 1957 alleging that most law clerks were generally "to the 'left' of either the nation or the Court." He described the bias as "extreme solicitude for the claims of Communists and other criminal defendants, expansion of federal power at the expense of State power, great sympathy toward any government regulation of business."

He mentioned the possibility of "unconscious slanting of material by clerks" when reviewing cert petitions. And though he had written that he didn't think clerks exercised too much influence in the actual drafting of opinions, he was careful when he got to the Court to write all the first drafts himself. Midway through his first full term, he realized that he had been wrong. The legal and moral interchanges that liberal clerks thrived on were good for the Justices and for the Court. Rehnquist grew to trust his clerks; they would not be so foolish as to try putting something over on him. And there was the question of efficiency. The clerks were helpful with first drafts. It saved him time, and helped focus his own thinking.

Rehnquist was known around the Court for his friendliness toward clerks. He learned their names, and found some of them as interesting as the Justices. He suggested letting the clerks into the Justices' dining room or setting up a lounge for both clerks and Justices. Those ideas got nowhere, but he did get a Ping-Pong table for the Court. . . .

One of Stewart's clerks took up the cause of a federal prisoner serving twenty years for bank robbery (*Fontaine v. U.S.*). The man alleged that his guilty pleas had been coerced through physical abuse while he was in the hospital suffering from a gunshot wound, heroin addiction and mental illness. The record gave some support to his claim that these factors had caused him to waive his rights for a lawyer and plead guilty. The Court was going to deny cert, until Stewart circulated a long dissent from denial of cert that his clerk had prepared. The conference later voted 8 to 1 to direct the district judge to grant the man a hearing, shaming some of the clerks in the other chambers for their failure to discover the possibility that the allegation of coercion might be valid. . . .

Douglas's three clerks were working day and night to answer his queries as fast as humanly possible. At least once they brought sleeping bags to the office and spent the night to meet a deadline.

Source: Selections from Bob Woodward and Scott Armstrong, *The Brethren: Inside the Supreme Court* (New York: Simon & Schuster, 1979), pp. 9, 124, 217, 240, 245, 269–270, 319, 356–357.

chapter of Court decisions that have shaped important aspects of our national policies. To be sure, there are certain restrictions on the Court's power to make policy; it must, for instance, wait for cases to reach it, and it must stay close to precedent. Being without enforcement powers, moreover, the Court must also worry about the problem of compliance (more on this later). Nevertheless, it makes decisions that are legally binding on other political actors and citizens on matters of public policy in the course of settling disputes.

It seems likely that the Court recognizes and cultivates its policymaking role. In the main, the Court does not see itself as a court of last resort, righting routine errors in the lower courts or settling minor private disputes. It sees itself, instead, as the "highest judicial tribunal for settling policy [and constitutional] conflicts"[22] and chooses its cases accordingly. The fact that decisions are not simply handed down but come with an opinion attached for the purpose of guiding the actions of other courts, litigants, and public officials is another demonstration that the Court recognizes its policymaking role.

The Debate over Judicial Activism

Has the Court become too vigorous in its policymaking role? Many people think so; others think not. That the Court is more active now than in the past (in the sense that it exercises more power in policymaking) is fairly obvious. Whether it is inappropriate or not depends on your view of the role of the judiciary in a democracy.

JUDICIAL REVIEW   We have already seen how the Court under John Marshall's leadership claimed the right of judicial review in the case of *Marbury v. Madison* (1803). The power was not exercised by the Court to any great extent until the late nineteenth century. The rate of judicial review has picked up during the twentieth century, however, with most of the Court's adverse attention being paid to the states. The trend suggests that the Court has become more willing in modern times to monitor the activities of other governmental entities (see Table 14.2). Conservatives were particularly unhappy about the liberal Warren Court's willingness to overturn state laws on racial segregation and criminal procedure. Now that conservatives enjoy a comfortable majority on the Court, their criticism of this aspect of judicial policymaking has diminished.

REVERSING PAST COURT DECISIONS   We have seen that adherence to precedent is one of the traditional norms that guides judicial decision making. The Warren, Burger, and Rehnquist Courts (particularly the last), however, have not been reluctant to overturn previous Court decisions. The most dramatic, of course, was the reversal of *Plessy* by *Brown*, though there have been many others, including the *Roe* to *Webster* change, and the rapid overturns of precedents involving the rights of criminal defendants. Critics claim that this creates instability and uncertainty on the meaning of the law, and an inappropriate assertion of power. Others claim that the Court must be able to fit the law with the times and changing circumstances.

TAKING ON "POLITICAL" MATTERS   Critics claim that the Court increasingly is taking on matters that are political and that are best left to the other branches of government. Examples most often cited are the Court's willingness to rule on the issue of malapportionment in *Baker v. Carr*, after many years of avoiding the issue as too political, and its tendency to become increasingly involved in the process of drawing electoral district boundaries in the states. Defenders of the Court argue that, when such basic constitutional rights as equality of citizenship are at peril, then the Court is obligated to protect such rights, no matter what other government bodies may choose to do.

REMEDIES The activity that has generated the most criticism in recent years derives from the Court's increased tendency to impose broad remedies. A **remedy** is what a court determines must be done to rectify a wrong. With the tremendous increase in the number of class action suits since the 1960s, the Court has shown a greater willingness to impose remedies that require other governmental bodies to take action. Some of the most controversial of these remedies include court orders requiring states to build more prison space and mandating that school districts bus students to achieve racial balance. Such remedies often require that governments spend public funds for things they do not necessarily want. Critics claim that the Court's legitimate role is to prevent government actions that threaten rights and liberties, not to compel it to take action to meet some policy goal.

Much of the debate about the role of the Court centers on the issue of "original intention." Advocates of "original intention" and its twin "strict construction," believe that the Court must be guided by the original intentions of the framers and the words found in the Constitution. They believe that the expansion of rights that had occurred since the mid-1960s—like the right to privacy that formed the basis of the *Roe v. Wade* decision and new rights for criminal defendants—are illegitimate, having no foundation in the framers' intentions or the text of the Constitution.

Proponents of "loose construction" believe that the intentions of the Founders are impossible to determine and unduly constricting. Jurists, in this view, must try to reconcile the fundamental principles of the Constitution with changing conditions in the United States.

There is no doubt that the modern Court is more activist than it was in the past and that most justices today hold a more expansive view of the role of the Court in forging national policy than their predecessors. Despite all of the debate about whether this is proper, the Court is likely to remain activist for a long time to come. First, belief in judicial activism, whether it is admitted or not, is shared by liberals and conservatives alike: "The ideologically conservative Burger and Rehnquist Courts . . . have been as activist as the liberal Warren Court. Their differences lie in the directions in which they have pushed constitutional law and politics."[23] Second, it is unlikely that the justices, once having tasted the fruit of political power, are likely to give it up easily and take a back seat to the president and Congress. Finally, important tools of judicial power, such as the rules that allow class action suits and broad remedies, remain in place, and there is no indication so far that the Rehnquist Court is about to set them aside.[24] Because the Court is likely to remain in an activist mode, it is also likely that the debate about judicial activism will not disappear from American politics.

THE COURTS AND DEMOCRACY: THE POLITICAL AND GOVERNMENTAL CONTEXT

Courts make public policy and will continue to do so. Fears of an "imperial judiciary," however, are somewhat exaggerated. Rather than a federal court system in which judges are free to make public policy on their own, ours is a system in which judges are constrained by the actions and preferences of many other polit-

ical and governmental actors, including, to some degree, the people. The degree
to which the people play a role in influencing the actions of the courts is, of course,
a key determinant of the quality of American democracy.

Governmental Influence on the Court

The Court must coexist with other governmental bodies that have their own powers, interests, constituencies, and visions of the public good. Recognizing this, the
Court usually tries to stay somewhere near the boundaries of what is acceptable
to other political actors. It does so for a number of reasons.

First, being without "purse or sword," the Court cannot force others to comply with its decisions. It can only hope that respect for the law and the Court will
be enough to cause government officials to do what it has mandated in a decision.
If the Court fails to gain voluntary compliance, it risks a serious erosion in its
influence, for it then appears weak and ineffectual.

The president, being the chief executive, is supposed to carry out court de-
crees. However, presidents who have opposed or have been lukewarm to particular decisions have been known to drag their feet. The *Brown* decision is a good
example. In a follow-up case to determine the timetable for desegregation (usually
referred to as *Brown II*), the Court used the phrase "with all deliberate speed."
President Eisenhower opposed the *Brown* decision and did little to encourage
compliance by southern states. Because the race question was not a central concern
for him in the first two years of his administration, President Kennedy did not
put very much pressure on recalcitrant states and school districts to desegregate.
As Justice Hugo Black finally complained in 1964, "there has been entirely too
much deliberation, and not enough speed."[25] It was not until the very last year
of the Johnson administration (1968) that the Justice Department brought its first
suits against school segregation in the North and the West.

Second, both the president and Congress have certain constitutional powers
that give them some degree of influence over the Court. In addition to the Court's
dependence on the president to carry out its decisions (when the parties to a
dispute do not do it voluntarily), the president influences the direction of the Court
by his power of appointment. He also can file suits through the Justice Department; try to move public opinion against the Court (as Richard Nixon tried to do);
and threaten to introduce legislation to alter Court organization or jurisdiction (as
Franklin Roosevelt did with his "court packing" proposal), or both.

Congress retains the power to change the size, organization, and jurisdiction
of the federal courts. The Jefferson-controlled Congress postponed a session of the
Supreme Court in 1802 so that the Court would not be able to hear a suit that
challenged their repeal of the Judiciary Act of 1801. It also "sent a message" to
the Court when it instituted impeachment proceedings against Justice Samuel
Chase, apparently for the sole crime of being a Federalist. During the Civil War,
Congress removed the Court's jurisdiction on habeas corpus cases so that civilians
could be tried in military courts. Congress can also bring pressure to bear by being
unsympathetic to pleas from the justices for pay increases or for a suitable budget
for clerks or office space. The Senate also plays a role in the appointment process,
we have learned, and can convey its views to the Court during the course of
confirmation hearings.

Political Influences on the Court

Interest groups, social movements, and the public not only indirectly influence the Court through the president and Congress but often directly do so. An important political tactic of interest groups and social movements is the **test case**. A test case is an action brought by a group that is designed to challenge the constitutionality of a law or an action by government. Groups wishing to force a court determination on an issue that is important to them, will try to find a person (called a plaintiff) on whose behalf they can bring a suit. When Thurgood Marshall was chief counsel for the NAACP in the 1950s, he spent a long time searching for the right plaintiff to bring a suit that would drive the last nail into the coffin of the *Plessy* "separate but equal" doctrine. He settled on a fifth-grade girl attending a segregated school in Topeka, Kansas, named Linda Brown. Several years later they were successful in *Brown v. Board of Education*.

Test cases also can be created by purposely breaking a law that an individual or group believes to be unconstitutional so that it can be tested in the courts. This was one of the pillars of the nonviolent civil rights movement in the South during the 1960s. It is a strategy that has been used at various times by antidraft groups, antitax protestors, and prolife groups, such as "operation rescue," which purposely breaks local ordinances and state laws to test their constitutionality in court.

Prolife groups have invented a variation on the test case—what might be called the *reverse test-case*. This may be defined as an effort to force a test case by the other side that is likely to fail. In the 1990s, prolife groups persuaded the legislatures of Guam (1990), Utah (1991), Pennsylvania (1991), and Louisiana

NAACP attorney Thurgood Marshall selected Linda Brown, a Topeka, Kansas elementary school student, to be the principal plaintiff in the historic case *Brown v. Board of Education* that successfully challenged school segregation.

(1991) to pass laws that severely restrict a woman's right to an abortion. Their hope was that these laws would be challenged by "prochoice" groups in the courts as unconstitutional and that just the right case would reach the Supreme Court to enable the new antiabortion majority to further weaken or even overturn the *Roe* decision. In 1992, though the Court upheld most provisions of the Pennsylvania law (*Planned Parenthood v. Casey*), it refused to overturn *Roe*, much to the chagrin and surprise of prolife groups.

Many test cases take the form of **class action suits**. These are suits brought by an individual, not only for himself or herself, but also for a class of people in a similar situation. A suit to prevent dumping of toxic wastes in public waterways, to use an example, is brought by an individual in the name of all people living in the area who are adversely affected by the resulting pollution. Class action suits were invited by the Warren Court's expansion of the definition of *standing* in the 1960s. The Rehnquist Court later narrowed the definition of *standing*.

Interest groups often get involved in suits, even when they are not party to the case, by filing amicus curiae briefs. Such briefs set out the group's position on the constitutional issues or talk about some of the most important consequences of deciding the case one way or the other. In a sense, this activity is a form of lobbying.

The Court does not usually stray very far from the opinions of elites and the public.[26] Disastrous decisions like *Dred Scott* seem to be the proverbial exceptions that prove the rule. Social and economic elites bring their influence to bear in a number of ways. As we learned in previous chapters, their influence is substantial in the media, the interest group system, party politics, and elections at all levels. It follows, then, that elites will play a substantial role in the thinking of presidents and members of Congress as they, in turn, deal with the Court. In addition to this powerful but indirect influence, the Court is also shaped by developments on issues and doctrine within the legal profession as these are expressed by bar associations, law journals, and law schools. Elites act even more directly on the Court when the interest groups and the associations that they run bring suits in the federal courts or file amicus curiae briefs in disputes that are of interest to them.

Public opinion influences the Court, but the extent of its effects are unclear. Some research shows that the Court conforms to public opinion about as much as the president and Congress do (about three-fifths of the time). Other research shows public support for Court action only about one-third of the time.[27] That public opinion is important should not be surprising. After all, justices read the same newspapers and watch the same news programs as other Washington, D.C., decision makers. They cannot help but be influenced by changes in the opinion climate of the nation. Surely the civil rights movement and the resultant change in public opinion on the issue of race had something to do with the vigorous civil rights program of the Court during the 1960s.

Antidemocratic Aspects of the Court

Democracy requires popular sovereignty. We have seen that popular preferences play a larger role in the actions of the Court than might appear to be the case at first glance. Court decisions are consistent with the opinions of the public in a substantial proportion of cases. However, the relationship is far from perfect. This would not have displeased the framers. As Alexander Hamilton put it in *Federalist*, No. 78, the Constitution established a judiciary that was to serve as "an excellent barrier [against public opinion] . . . and the encroachments of the representative body."

The Court's relationship to public opinion is problematic in democratic terms. Not only does it fail to conform to public opinion much of the time, but also it often lags, even when it eventually comes into line with public opinion. If we believe in the adage, "justice delayed is justice denied," then this is a significant problem. In the late nineteenth and early twentieth centuries, the Court blocked the introduction of highly popular government efforts to regulate big business. During the Great Depression, the Court's strong commitment to laissez-faire economics in the midst of a national economic emergency almost led to a constitutional crisis. Many commentators believe that the abortion decisions of the Rehnquist Court are significantly out of line with public opinion. In *Rust v. Sullivan* (1991), it upheld a Reagan administration ban on the mention of abortion at federally funded family planning clinics. The Gallup Poll reported that 66 percent of respondents disapproved of this policy.

The public shapes the Court indirectly through elected institutions like Congress and the president. However, two factors make the influence of the public less than it might be. First, as we saw in earlier chapters, Congress and the president are themselves far from perfect as democratic instruments of the people. Second, though the president and Congress constrain its behavior, the Court is able to go its own way to a considerable degree.[28] The Court is a fully coequal branch of the federal government, able to give and take on even terms with the other two branches.

The Court also frequently aligns itself with powerful economic groups in American society, shaping constitutional interpretation to protect their interests. As political scientists Mark Silverstein and Ben Ginsburg point out, ". . . Chief Justice John Marshall sought to establish the judiciary as a central, national political institution by championing the forces of capitalism in an era of expanding industrialism" during the first third of the nineteenth century. Later, the Court "found important constituent support among industrial capitalists seeking to stem the progressive tide of regulatory efforts."[29] The Court was also a strong ally of business in the desperate effort to hold off Roosevelt's New Deal.

Democracy also requires liberty and political equality. To many people, the protection of freedom and equality is the primary mission of the Court. Although the Court has played an important role in the protection and extension of civil liberties and citizenship rights, its actions over the long course of our history have not been entirely praiseworthy. By and large, the Court has generally gone along with government efforts to silence dissident voices and to keep minorities from enjoying the full protection of the law. For instance, it went along with local, state, and federal actions to punish dissident voices during the McCarthy era's hysteria during the 1950s.[30] It also approved the forced relocation and internment of Japanese Americans during World War II. While the Warren Court changed much of this, some argue that the Rehnquist Court may be returning to more traditional patterns.[31]

The Court supported the federal government's plan to put Americans of Japanese descent in internment camps during World War II. Here a grandfather waits with his grandchildren to be transported to one of the several camps located in the western United States.

Democracy and the Court Reconsidered

People disagree about what the role of the Court should be in a democracy. To the framers, who believed (unlike the authors of this text) that popular democracy and liberty are contradictory, the appropriate role for the Court is that of protector of liberty against public opinion and the elected branches. They had in mind a frankly antipopular sovereignty institution. Most Americans today think better of democracy than the framers did, so this openly antidemocratic conception of the Court's role is probably not as appealing as in the past. Americans no doubt want the Court to champion liberty but in a broader context that includes an appreciation for popular sovereignty and political equality.

From the point of view of the conception of democracy used throughout this book, the appropriate role for the Court is to encourage the play of popular sovereignty, political equality, and liberty in American politics. In the game of American politics, the role of the Court ought to be that of a referee ensuring that the rules of democracy are followed. The rules of the game of democracy involve assurances that the majority will prevail in the determination of public policy, that all members of society will be allowed to enter on an equal basis into the public dialogue about the public business, and that each individual will be allowed all of the rights of conscience and expression connected with human dignity. We have learned at various places in this book that the Court does not always live up to these standards, but that it must do so for the health of democracy goes without saying.

Finally, some scholars believe that the Court can play a role in enriching democracy by raising the most fundamental issues of our political life to public attention. Issues of individual freedom, equality, and the role of government are highlighted in virtually all of their decisions, and, to the degree that they stimulate public debate and deliberation, democracy may be enhanced.[32]

SUMMARY

Article III of the Constitution is vague about the powers and responsibilities of the Supreme Court. Nevertheless, the Court has fashioned a powerful position for itself in American politics.

Constitutional interpretation by the Supreme Court has progressed through three stages. In the first, the Court helped settle the question of the nature of the federal Union. In the second, it helped define the role of the government in a free enterprise economy. In the third, the Court focused on issues of civil liberties and civil rights.

The federal court system is made up of three parts. At the bottom are 94 federal district courts, with original jurisdiction only. In the middle are 13 appellate courts. At the top is a single Supreme Court, with both original and appellate jurisdictions.

The Supreme Court operates on the basis of several widely shared norms: secrecy, courtesy, seniority, and adherence to precedent. The Court mainly controls its agenda by granting or not granting certiorari. Cases before the Court wind their way through the process in the following way: submission of briefs, oral argument, initial consideration in conference, opinion writing, and final conference consideration. Published opinions serve as precedents for other federal courts and future Supreme Court decisions.

The Supreme Court is a national policymaker of considerable importance. It's unelected, life-tenured justices cannot, however, do anything they please, for the Court is significantly influenced by other political and governmental factors. As a result, Court decisions rarely drift very far from public and elite opinion.

The relationship of the Court to American democracy is ambiguous. While popular sovereignty plays a role in determining what it does, it is less than it might be. While it has been a significant factor in the protection of political equality and liberty, it has not been entirely or consistently supportive of these essential attributes of democracy during our history. It can often, however, help to expand democratic deliberation.

To Ponder

1. What would American politics look like today if Madison and Jefferson had prevailed and each branch of government could interpret the Constitution for itself?

2. Should Supreme Court justices be elected? If they were elected, how would their behavior be different?

3. Should the president be able to appoint anybody he wants to be a Supreme Court justice? Does the Senate have too much power in the appointment process?

4. Should the Court make law or interpret the law? How would you know when it was doing one thing and not the other?

Suggested Readings

Guide to the U.S. Supreme Court: Second Edition. Washington, D.C.: Congressional Quarterly Press, 1989.
> A comprehensive and indispensable reference on the Supreme Court.

Jacob, Herbert. *Law and Politics in the United States.* Boston: Little, Brown, 1986.
> A leading textbook that summarizes the prevailing literature on the law and politics in the United States at all levels of jurisdiction.

Lasser, William. *The Limits of Judicial Power.* Chapel Hill, NC: University of North Carolina Press, 1988.
> A controversial interpretation of the Court as a powerful institution that is relatively free from the constraints of the executive and legislative branches.

Lewis, Anthony. *Gideon's Trumpet.* New York: Random House, 1964.
> The moving story of Francis Gideon's successful campaign from a Florida prison cell to persuade the Supreme Court that defendants have a right to a lawyer.

McCloskey, Robert G. *The American Supreme Court.* Chicago: University of Chicago Press, 1960.
> A modern classic about the history of constitutional interpretation tied to changes in American society and politics.

O'Brien, David M. *Storm Center: The Supreme Court in American Politics*, 2nd ed. New York: Norton, 1990.
> Fast becoming the standard textbook in the field on the Supreme Court; combines the latest in social science research and compelling anecdotes.

Rosenberg, Gerald. *The Hollow Hope: Courts and Social Reform.* Chicago: University of Chicago Press, 1991.
> Thorough documentation of the limited circumstances under which the courts can bring about social change.

Sosin, J. M. *The Aristocracy of the Long Robe: The Origins of Judicial Review in America.* Westport, CT: Greenwood Press, 1989.
> A detailed history of judicial review in the United States, based on the provocative premise that the Court seized a power for itself that is justified neither by the Constitution nor by the intentions of the framers.

Woodward, Bob, and Scott Armstrong. *The Brethren: Inside the Supreme Court.* New York: Simon & Schuster, 1979.
> A painstaking, investigative examination that manages to raise the curtain on the inside workings of the Supreme Court during the years 1969–1975.

Notes

1. Connie Page, *The Right to Lifers: Who They Are, How They Operate, Where They Get Their Money* (New York: Summit Books, 1983), p. 151.
2. From Suzy Platt, ed., *Respectfully Quoted: A Dictionary of Quotations Requested from the Congressional Research Service* (Washington, D.C.: Library of Congress, 1989), p. 67.
3. J. M. Sosin, *The Aristocracy of the Long Robe: The Origins of Judicial Review in America* (Westport, CT: Greenwood Press, 1989).
4. Robert G. McCloskey, *The American Supreme Court* (Chicago: University of Chicago Press, 1960), pp. 12–13.
5. For a different interpretation of *Marbury*, see Sylvia Snowmiss, *Judicial Review and the Law of the Constitution* (New Haven: Yale University Press, 1990).
6. McCloskey, *The American Supreme Court.*

7. McCloskey, *The American Supreme Court*, p. 57.

8. Quoted in Elder Witt, ed., *The Supreme Court and Its Work* (Washington, D.C.: Congressional Quarterly Press, 1981), p. 12.

9. McCloskey, *The American Supreme Court*.

10. David M. O'Brien, *Storm Center: The Supreme Court in American Politics*, 2nd ed. (New York: Norton, 1990), p. 65.

11. Sheldon Goldman, "Federal Judicial Recruitment," in John B. Gates and Charles Johnson, eds., *The American Courts* (Washington, D.C.: Congressional Quarterly Press, 1991), pp. 195, 199.

12. Herbert Jacob, *Law and Politics in the United States* (Boston: Little, Brown, 1986), p. 221.

13. Ruth Marcus, "Using the Bench," *Washington Post National Weekly Edition* (February 25, 1991), p. 31.

14. Ronald Stidham and Robert A. Carp, "Judges, Presidents, and Policy Choices," *Social Science Quarterly*, Vol. 68, No. 2 (1987), 395–404.

15. David Adamany, "The Supreme Court," in John B. Gates and Charles Johnson, eds., *The American Courts*, pp. 111–112; Glendon Schubert, *The Judicial Mind* (Evanston, IL: Northwestern University Press, 1965); and John D. Sprague, *Voting Patterns of the United States Supreme Court* (Indianapolis, IN: Bobbs-Merrill, 1968).

16. Walter Murphy, *Elements of Judicial Strategy* (Princeton, NJ: Princeton University Press, 1964).

17. Joel B. Grossman, "Social Backgrounds and Judicial Decision-Making," *Harvard Law Review*, Vol. 79 (1966), pp. 1551–1564; and S. Sidney Ulmer, "Dissent Behavior and the Social Background of Supreme Court Justices," *Journal of Politics*, Vol. 32 (1970), pp. 580–589.

18. Herbert Jacob, *Justice in America*, 3rd ed. (Boston: Little, Brown, 1978), p. 248.

19. John Harlan, "A Glimpse of the Supreme Court at Work," *University of Chicago Law School Record* Vol. 1, No. 7 (1963).

20. Bob Woodward and Scott Armstrong, *The Brethren: Inside the Supreme Court* (New York: Simon & Schuster, 1979).

21. Jacob, *Law and Politics in the United States*, p. 225.

22. Jacob, *Justice in America*, p. 245.

23. O'Brien, *Storm Center*, p. 61.

24. William Lasser, *The Limits of Judicial Power: The Supreme Court in American Politics* (Chapel Hill, NC: University of North Carolina Press, 1988); and Mark Silverstein and Benjamin Ginsberg, "The Supreme Court and the New Politics of Judicial Power," *Political Science Quarterly*, Vol. 102, No. 3 (Fall 1987), pp. 371–388.

25. *Griffin v. Prince Edwards County School Board*, 377 U.S. 218 (1964).

26. Robert Dahl, "Decision Making in a Democracy: The Supreme Court as a National Decision Maker," *Journal of Public Law*, Vol. 6 (1957), pp. 279–295; Thomas R. Marshall, "Public Opinion, Representation, and the Modern Supreme Court," *American Politics Quarterly*, Vol. 16 (1988), pp. 296–316; McCloskey, *The American Supreme Court*, p. 22; and O'Brien, *Storm Center*, p. 325.

27. Jay Casper, "The Supreme Court and National Policy Making," *American Political Science Review*, Vol. 70 (1976), pp. 50–63; and Marshall, "Public Opinion, Representation"; and Benjamin I. Page and Robert Y. Shapiro, "Effects of Public Opinion on Policy," *The American Political Science Review*, Vol. 77 (1983), p. 183.

28. Lasser, *The Limits of Judicial Power*; and Silverstein and Ginsburg, "The Supreme Court."

29. Silverstein and Ginsburg, "The Supreme Court," pp. 374, 375.

30. McCloskey, *The American Supreme Court*, p. 192.

31. Adamany, "The Supreme Court," pp. 15–18; Lincoln Caplan, "The Reagan Challenge to the Rule of Law," in Sidney Blumenthal and Thomas Byrne Edsall, eds., *The Reagan Legacy* (New York: Pantheon Books, 1988).

32. Lief Carter, *Contemporary Constitutional Lawmaking* (New York: Pergamon, 1985).

15

*State and Local
Government*

SCANDAL IN ARIZONA

"Are you sure there are no hidden cameras up there?" joked a member of the Arizona state legislature, as he took a package containing what police said was a $55,000 bribe and zipped it into his gym bag. "Wave to the cameras," replied a smooth-talking con man who was pretending to be a casino operator named "J. Anthony Vincent," trying to buy votes to legalize gambling in Arizona, but who was actually working undercover for the police on a 16-month-long sting operation.[1]

Early in 1991, citizens of Arizona were amazed to see this videotaped scene broadcast on television news, as 7 legislators and 11 others were indicted for bribery. The state was still reeling from the impeachment of Governor Evan Mecham for corruption three years before and was in the midst of a Senate Ethics Committee investigation of charges that both of its U.S. senators—DeConcini–(D) and McCain–(R)—had improperly done favors for savings and loan executive Charles H. Keating, Jr., in return for large campaign contributions. Now some leading members of the state legislature looked like crooks.

The videotapes and transcripts showed legislators exchanging pleasantries, voicing cynicism about politics, and seeking business advice from the open-shirted, heavily medallioned "Mr. Vincent," while they pocketed what the police said were thousands of dollars in cash plus promises of shrimp concessions or gift shop franchises at future Arizona casinos. "Vincent" sometimes would ask what they needed or what he could do for them. One Democratic senator declared, "I like the good life, and I'm trying to position myself that I can live the good life and have more money," adding that it was her ambition to "die rich." "We all have our prices," she declared, before accepting what police said was part of $25,880. A Democratic representative said, "I don't give a (expletive) about issues. . . . There is not an issue in this world that I give a (expletive) about. My favorite line is, 'What's in it for me?' " He was charged with taking $12,105. When he heard what others got, he complained, "I sold way too cheap."

The Republican chairman of the House Judiciary Committee apparently became an active helper in the scheme, offering names of susceptible legislators and suggesting ways to "fish them in." For those who could not be bribed, he proposed using a "sledgehammer," providing details on sexual and financial pressure points. "I'd check her sex life, check her finances," he said of one colleague, " 'cause she's just a real loudmouth that you just need to shut up."

The police successfully dispensed so many bribes—more than $380,000—that some observers worried that the money might have affected election outcomes. "Vincent's" payments to one incumbent legislator, for example, were nearly twice the $6,800 total that his challenger was able to raise to run against him.

A number of legislators resisted temptation. One proudly claimed that he saw right through "Vincent": "With his appearance straight out of central casting for a Mafia movie, I'm surprised anyone took him seriously." At least three legislators reported bribery attempts to the police. Other public figures expressed disgust and outrage. A former Democratic leader of the state senate declared, "It is a story of sickening proportions. We are all still in shock. In

533

terms of confidence, it will take years to rebuild." Former governor and presidential candidate Bruce Babbitt said, "[s]ometimes . . . you almost want to deny that you're in public service."

It would be a mistake to think that the scandal in Arizona was typical of state politics. The vast majority of state officials in the United States, like the vast majority of federal and local officials, are honest, professional, and hard working. Arizona's political life at the beginning of the 1990s seems to have been unusually wild and woolly, partly because of the huge influx of new money and new people into the state, and partly because of the miserably low salaries ($15,000 per year, barely above the $12,600 poverty line for an average family of four) that were paid to state legislators. Legislators who were scrambling for a living and who felt grossly underpaid compared to lawyers or lobbyists required special fortitude to resist temptation; indeed, it is difficult to see how an honest person could afford to take the job of an Arizona legislator as a full-time occupation in the first place.

Still, the Arizona story was not entirely unique, either. The year before, ten South Carolina state legislators had been indicted for bribery as a result of sting operations. Within a two- or three-year period, legislators had been charged or convicted in California, New York, Tennessee, Texas, and West Virginia.[2] Shortly afterward, ten current or former Florida legislators were charged with failing to disclose lobbyists' gifts of quail hunting trips to Georgia and vacations in the Bahamas.[3] Similar offenses elsewhere probably have gone undiscovered.

Even though it represents an extreme case, the Arizona story helps illustrate a fundamental fact about state and local government: it is generally less visible to ordinary citizens than the federal government is. As we saw in Chapter 7, "Interest Groups and Corporations in American Politics," when politics has low visibility, special interests tend to have the advantage over broad public opinion. Thus, state and local government are probably less subject to democratic control by ordinary citizens and more open to behind-the-scenes influence by lobbyists and interest groups than the national government is. This usually does not entail outright bribery; much more often, it involves cozy relationships in which wealthy groups and individuals give big campaign contributions, help friendly officials get elected or appointed, and enjoy easy access to them in office.

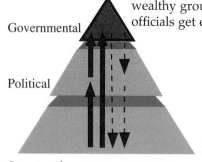

Governmental

Political

Structural

STATE POLITICS

In the U.S. federal system today, the states sometimes seem to be overshadowed by the national government. Still, the American states and their legal subdivisions—counties, cities, and various regional and local governments—are quite important. They spend enormous amounts of money: about $790 *billion* in 1990. That amounts to 14 percent of the Gross National Product, or roughly $3,000 for each American; it is more than one-half as much as the $1,300 billion that the national government spent that same year.[4]

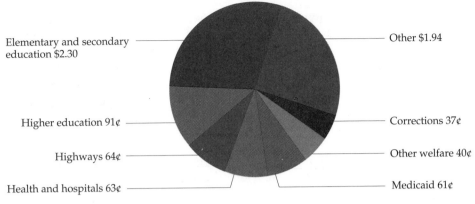

Total was $7.80 per $100 of personal income

Figure 15.1 How states spend their money[a]

[a]The figures are for 1989 and refer to dollars of state spending per each $100 of personal income in the state.

Source: Center for the Study of the States, in the New York Times, *December 30, 1990, p. L17.*

Most of the contacts that ordinary Americans have with government are at the state and local level, with public schools and colleges, welfare programs, roads, local parks, street cleaning, sewage, recycling and garbage removal, water supplies, police and fire protection, traffic control, and court systems. All of these are primarily state and local responsibilities. In fiscal year 1988–1989, for example, state and local governments spent about $264 billion on education (compared with less than $36 billion by the federal government), $98 billion on public welfare, and $58 billion on highways[5] (see Figure 15.1).

At the top of a complicated network of subnational governmental units, with ultimate political power over all the rest, stand the governments of the 50 states.

National Governments in Miniature

In many respects, state governments can be viewed as miniature versions of the national or "federal" government. They have similar written constitutions, which set up similar institutions of elected and appointed officials that work in similar ways. Often their statehouses are architectural copies of the U.S. Capitol building in Washington, D.C. Much of what we have said about the national government— the functioning of legislators and executives, the political-level influences of public opinion, interest groups, and the media, and the importance of structural factors— applies to understanding state governments as well. But there are some important differences.

CONSTITUTIONS   All 50 states have written constitutions that establish three branches of government: the legislative, executive, and judicial. They also enumerate certain limited powers for government and set forth the rights of citizens. The state constitutions are not as crisp and concise as the U.S. Constitution, however. Many of them go into specific, long-winded detail about particular matters of public policy and are very lengthy. The constitution of Alabama, for example, is about 174,000 words long (including its 513 amendments since 1901), and New York's is about 80,000,[6] contrasted with the fewer than 5,000 words in the original U.S. Constitution and 3,000 or so words in the amendments.

The main reason for this wordiness appears to be that organized interests of various sorts have worked hard to enshrine their aims in state constitutions, so they cannot easily be upset by the legislatures or courts and are insulated from the popular will. Even where the constitution can be amended fairly easily by popular vote (as in California, where ballot propositions to change the constitution by majority vote are routine), special interests apparently have a big advantage in getting and keeping the constitutional provisions they want. The legal language is complicated and difficult for voters to understand; special interests can spend vast sums on media advertising that casts the question in favorable terms.

GOVERNORS   All state governments provide for a unitary chief executive, a governor, whose position resembles that of the president of the United States. Governors are popularly elected, usually for a four-year term; only governors in New Hampshire, Vermont, and Rhode Island have two-year terms. Most states limit governors to one, two, or three terms, but 18 states have no limit. In Illinois, for example, Republican Governor James Thompson (formerly a crusading U.S. attorney) served for three-and-a-half terms between 1977 and 1991. In an effort to insulate gubernatorial elections from national political tides (and perhaps to reduce voter turnout and increase the power of party activists), elections for governor are usually held in federal "off years"—nonpresidential election years—or in odd-numbered years, when no federal elections are being held at all.[7]

Governors' legal powers vary from state to state. Some governors are strong, while others are relatively weak. Nearly all have president-like powers to appoint top executive officials, propose legislation, and sign or veto bills passed by the legislature (though the governor of North Carolina, one of the weakest, has no veto power). Governors in 42 of the 50 states enjoy a power of **"line-item" veto**,

Governor Mario Cuomo of New York with Kerry Kennedy (daughter of Senator Robert Kennedy) at a rally against capital punishment.

RESOURCE
FEATURE

*State Executives
in Mexico,
Canada, and the
United States*

Like the United States, both Mexico and Canada have federal systems in which states or provinces, with their own chief executives, officially enjoy some independence. But the arrangements are actually quite different from each other and from our own.

In each of *Mexico*'s 31 states, a governor is popularly elected for a single six-year term; reelection is prohibited. The governor is given strong authority over his one-chamber state legislature, which acts mostly as a rubber-stamp committee, formalizing the details of his program. But the governor himself is mostly a creature of the central government, which retains authority over most major policies and, in practice, picks the governor. Every state governor since 1929 has been a member of the *Partido Institucional Revolucionario* (PRI), whose top officials (especially the president of Mexico) choose state gubernatorial candidates. Under the Mexican constitution, the president of the country can have the Senate remove any state governor for failure to maintain law

and order. In recent years, this has been done less frequently than the average of once per year that occurred between 1917 and 1964, but many governors are pressured to resign "voluntarily."

Each of *Canada*'s ten provinces and two territories, on the other hand, has an unusual degree of autonomy and self-direction in political matters. They control issues of education, health, social services, and civil justice. Each of the provinces is a classical parliamentary democracy, with free competition existing among several political parties. Premiers, like British prime ministers, are chosen by their parliaments and dismissed when their party loses its majority or is defeated in a vote of confidence. Canadian premiers have considerable influence over policy but are ultimately at the disposal of their parties.

Source: George Delury, ed., *World Encyclopedia of Political Systems and Parties,* 2nd ed. (New York: Facts on File, 1987), pp. 158, 732, 734, 735.

which means that they can reject parts of bills or particular appropriations while accepting others; this gives them a big advantage over the legislature.[8] Throughout the 1980s, until the voters banned the practice, Wisconsin Governor Tommy Thompson even vetoed particular letters within words, saving up those letters to insert new words into laws.[9] But some governors are hedged about by limitations on their appointment powers. Often there are a number of separately elected top officials whom the governors cannot remove or control. In Texas, for example, the governor has to deal with a very independent commissioner of agriculture, the Texas Railway Commission (which regulates the oil industry), an unusually strong lieutenant governor, and a very powerful state senate. (For an international comparison see "Resource Feature" on "State Executives in Mexico, Canada, and the United States.")

Early in American history, state governors rivaled the president of the United States in power and prestige. As the federal government grew, however, the relative standing of state governors declined. More recently, tight financial pressure on the states, especially after federal funds dried up during the 1980s, has made it much harder to succeed as governor and has led to many single-term governorships. In 1991, more than one-half of the states had budget shortfalls. Virginia ($1.7 billion), California ($1.5 billion), Texas ($1.05 billion) and New York ($1 billion) all projected deficits of $1 billion or more.[10] In the 1990 elections, incumbent governors won reelection in fewer than half (17) of the 36 gubernatorial races.[11]

The Democratic party has dominated most state governments since the New Deal of the 1930s. As we saw in Chapter 8, "Political Parties," and Chapter 9, "Voting and Elections," more Americans have identified themselves as Democrats than Republicans and most have voted for Democrats for state and local offices. Even in the years from 1969 through 1991, when four Republicans but only one Democrat served as president of the United States, the large majority of state governors was Democratic. In 1991, for example, 28 governors were Democrats, 20 were Republicans, and 2 were Independents. Some voters may have preferred Republican presidents for foreign policy reasons or for their personal characteristics, while preferring to entrust domestic policy matters to Democrats.

STATE LEGISLATURES   Every U.S. state but one has a **bicameral** (two-chamber) legislature, with a large assembly or house of representatives and a smaller state senate. (Nebraska has a unicameral, or single-chamber, nonpartisan legislature.) For many years, state legislative districts were defined by counties or other geographical boundaries, regardless of population, so that people living in under-populated rural areas got more legislative representation than those living in the growing cities and suburbs. Since the important U.S. Supreme Court decision in *Baker v. Carr* (1962), however, the states have been required to apportion both chambers of their legislatures on a "one person, one vote" basis. Unlike the U.S. Senate, therefore, which has equal representation of large and small states, the state senates are now just smaller versions of the state houses of representatives. Still, the bicameral system makes a difference by encouraging deliberation and slowing things down, especially when different parties control the two chambers.

State legislatures are organized in much the same way as the U.S. Congress. The majority party picks a presiding officer (majority leader, president, or speaker), who has varying degrees of influence over such matters as committee assignments, the legislative agenda, and the order of business. In California, for example, Speaker Willie Brown thoroughly dominated the State Assembly for roughly two decades. A great deal of work is done in specialized committees on education, public works, and so on, which resemble congressional committees. Just like committees of the U.S. Congress, they often develop close relationships with interest groups and bureaucrats who are involved in the same policy area. Since the general public generally cannot tell what goes on in such committees, they are an important entry point for interest group influence on state politics.

Even more so than governors, state legislatures tend to be controlled by the Democrats. In 1991, for example, the Democratic party had majorities in both the houses and the senates of 30 states, covering nearly all of the South and much of the Midwest and the East and West coasts. The Republicans controlled only three Rocky Mountain states plus New Hampshire; in 14 states, the Republicans controlled one chamber and the Democrats dominated the other.[12] (See Figure 15.2.)

Professionalization   Like the federal government, state governments have become more professional over the years as the size and importance of government has increased.

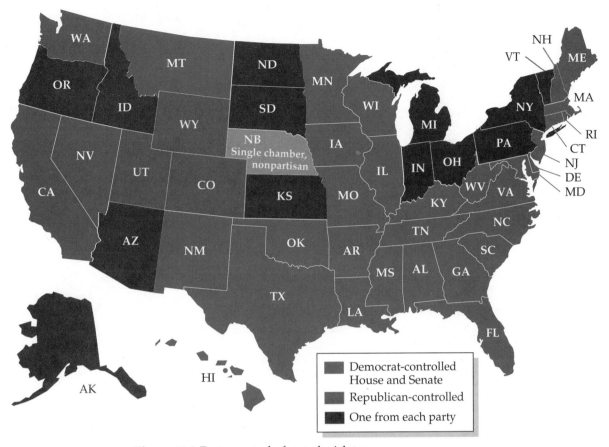

Figure 15.2 Party control of state legislatures

Note: In Alaska and Idaho, the Senate has itself been split between the parties, and, in Vermont, both the House and the Senate have been split.

Source: Associated Press, in the New York Times, *November 9, 1990, p. A13.*

During the nineteenth century, jobs in state government were part time. There was not much to do. Legislatures met only every two years or so, for brief sessions—often during the winter, when farmers were free to attend. Most legislators relied on other jobs to make a living. As the country grew and became industrialized, and as government took on more responsibility, however, state governments had more and more work to do, and the part-time system became clearly inadequate. Legislative sessions grew longer; most legislatures began to meet every year instead of every other year. (Texas, for example, still meets regularly only for a biennial session, but a "special session" has been held just about every year for as long as anyone can remember.) Legislating became a full-time job, requiring full-time salaries in order to attract talented people and large staffs of experts to deal with specialized legislation. There has been a strong trend toward increasing professionalization of state legislatures, with higher salaries, stronger research staffs, and more efficient procedures.

This bit of historical background helps explain the Arizona scandal with which we began this chapter. As the role of state government increased and the

The Maryland state legislature at work, organized much like the U.S. Congress.

stakes grew higher, low-paid, part-time legislators became more vulnerable to corporate and other lobbyists, who could hire the legislators' law firms, pay speaking and "consulting" fees, and provide cash for campaigns or personal expenses. States like New York and California, which moved relatively quickly to professionalize their legislatures, seem to have avoided some of the most glaring sorts of corruption; those states have also made many of the policy innovations discussed in Chapter 3, "Federalism." States that lagged behind in professionalizing their legislatures, however, like Arizona and South Carolina, appear to have suffered more betrayals of the public trust.

Only gradually have women begun to serve in state legislatures; see the "Struggle for Democracy" feature and the graph below.

Women in state legislatures

Source: Center for the American Woman and Politics, Rutgers University, in the New York Times, *February 26, 1991, p. A13.*

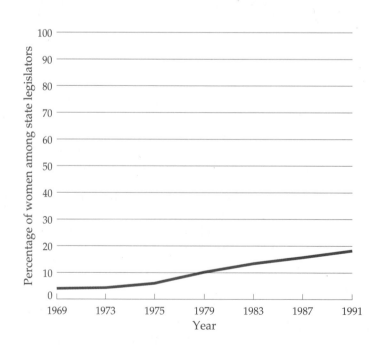

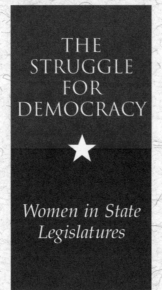

THE STRUGGLE FOR DEMOCRACY

Women in State Legislatures

Women won the right to vote in 1920, but only recently have they begun to hold important political offices in substantial numbers. In state governments, there has been a slow but definite tendency for more and more women to serve in the legislatures. This trend enhances democracy by increasing political equality between men and women.

Just after the 1990 elections—when Kansas, Oregon, and Texas inaugurated women as governors—there were only 31 women serving in the U.S. Congress, accounting for a little over 5 percent of the seats there. But the Center for the American Woman and Politics at Rutgers University found that women constituted 18.1 percent of state legis-

lators, up fairly steadily from the 4 percent of 1969. (See the graph on page 540.)

Opinions differed about whether or not these figures were cause for celebration. Some said that there was a long way to go and that progress was much too slow; at the present rate of increase (less than 1 percent per year), it would take a total of 64 years to gain 50 percent of legislative seats. But others, pleased that the trend was in the right direction, pointed out that state legislatures are traditional pipelines to higher office, state or national, and that they handle many important issues. Louisiana, for example, with a more heavily male legislature than any other state (only 3 women in the 105-member house and none in the senate), had just passed an extremely restrictive abortion law. With more women members, the Louisiana legislature might have acted differently.

States vary widely in their proportion of women legislators, from Louisiana's 2.1 percent to Arizona's 35.6 percent. Most of the lowest proportions are found in the South; several of the highest are in states like Arizona and New Hampshire, with part-time (and low-paid) legislatures that are easier to get into. The power of political parties, their openness to women, and the extent of legislative turnover also make a difference. (See the table, at left.)

Source: From Robin Toner, "Women in Politics Gain, but Road Is a Long One," *New York Times*, February 25, 1991, p. A6.

Women and the States

Highest proportions of women in legislature (1991)	
Arizona	35.6%
Maine	32.8
New Hampshire	32.1
Vermont	31.7
Washington	31.3

Lowest proportions of women in legislature (1991)	
Louisiana	2.1%
Kentucky	5.1
Alabama	5.7
Arkansas	6.7
Mississippi	6.9

Source: Center for the American Woman and Politics, Rutgers University; *New York Times*, February 25, 1991, p. A6.

DIRECT LEGISLATION   One aspect of state governments that is quite different from national government is the power of citizens in 23 states (mostly in the West) to use an **initiative** in order to vote directly on legislation that they themselves propose, or to use a referendum in order to approve or overturn laws that the legislature has passed. When these ideas were championed by the Progressive movement at the beginning of the twentieth century, they were considered prodemocratic reforms: ways to let the people override corrupt or elitist legislatures. In practice, however, they have turned out to be mixed blessings. It is so difficult for ordinary voters to sort out ballot propositions that the wealthy and the well organized often prevail through media campaigns.

California voters in 1990, for example, faced a ballot with 17 different state initiatives and constitutional amendments (plus, in San Francisco, 11 local propositions), including a far-reaching "Environmental Protection Act" and an initiative called the "Consumer Pesticide Enforcement Act" that was sponsored by the agriculture industry in order to neutralize the other proposal. The state published a 250-page official pamphlet to explain voters' choices. "Most people can't even wade through the ballot pamphlet because of all the initiatives," complained one citizen; "It's all written in technical jargon." "[T]hey're so long and involved and written in legalese," said another, "Who knows what ramifications one phrase or sentence might have?" Winning propositions, including one in California that was supposed to cut insurance rates, often have proved disappointing because they are clumsily drafted and become tangled in litigation.[13]

COURTS   Most of the law courts that Americans encounter, from municipal traffic tribunals to the many courts that deal with divorces, civil suits for damages, and criminal charges, are part of state judicial systems.

These systems are headed by a court of last resort, usually called the state supreme court (New York calls it the court of appeals), which is elected by the voters. State supreme courts, like the U.S. Supreme Court, supervise their lower court systems and hear appeals from them; most also have the power to declare state laws invalid under the state constitution. But their independence is limited. In only four states do supreme court justices serve for life or until the age of 70; most come up for periodic reelection or are subject to recall, or both.[14] Those who render unpopular decisions can be removed from office, as were three liberal justices, including Chief Justice Rose Bird, from the California Supreme Court during the mid-1980s.

In recent years, as the U.S. Supreme Court has pulled back from some of its earlier decisions protecting civil liberties, state supreme courts have become more activist in declaring rights under their own state constitutions. In some cases, the interpretation of the U.S. constitution subsequently has been affected, in what one scholar calls a "dynamic judicial federalism."[15]

Structural and Political Influences on State Policy

Each state in the union is unique. Even next door neighbors New Hampshire and Vermont are politically very different: New Hampshire has a long history of social conservatism and low-tax, low-spending fiscal conservatism, while Vermont has tended to be liberal about life-styles and to provide more generous social programs. But the very differences among states make it possible to study systematically *why* they differ. The federal system, with 50 state governments, provides a sort of laboratory for comparative research. We can examine exactly which characteristics of states are associated with which differences in policy. A number of structural and political factors are important.

STRUCTURAL FACTORS   Key structural factors include a state's level of economic development, the nature of its economy, and its political institutions.

Level of Economic Development   Political science researchers have found that many of the sharpest political differences between states are related to their *level of economic development*. To put it simply, there are rich states and poor states. The rich ones have more tax money to spend, and they spend it on somewhat different things. For example, if you want to know how high or low the welfare benefits are likely to be in a particular state, you can make a good guess based on how rich or poor that state is in terms of per capita income (the average amount of money its citizens earn).[16] State spending policies are very different in New York, with $16,036 disposable per capita income in 1988, than in Mississippi, which ranked last among the states, with $9,612 per capita income in 1988. While New York's state and local governments were spending $3,900 per person, Mississippi's state and local governments were spending only about half as much—$2,026. While the average poor family participating in New York's social programs got $536 monthly in AFDC and SSI benefits (see Appendix II for definitions), the average poor family in Mississippi got only $119 per month.[17] (For related state–by–state comparisons, see Figure 15.3.)

Nature of the Economy   Per capita income or wealth is not the only structural factor. The precise nature of the economy also makes a difference. Agricultural states of the Great Plains, for example, tend to have policies different from the old industrialized states of the Northeast or the newly industrializing Sun Belt. Population and culture matter, too. For example, several states of the old South, where slavery was once widespread, have noncompetitive political systems and very restricted social programs. The heavily Mormon, community-oriented population of Utah, on the other hand, has enacted much more generous social welfare programs than its low-income level would predict.

Political Institutions   Certain political institutions and arrangements that have endured over many years and that can be thought of as structural factors also affect policymaking. The most important are those involving political competition and popular participation in politics—key ingredients of democracy. Before the civil rights movement, for example, most southern states made it extremely difficult for black people to vote, and the dominant position of a single white (Democratic) party prevented protest or dissent from getting a public hearing. The result was public policies that segregated and neglected blacks and, in many cases, poor whites as well.[18] Today, blacks are enfranchised and two-party competition has increased in much of the South, but states vary widely in this respect. In the nation as a whole, the states with the most vigorous competition between parties tend to be the most generous with the poor. A system of strong party competition seems to make more of a difference than which party—Republican or Democratic— actually holds power.[19]

POLITICAL FACTORS   Political-level influences on state policies include public opinion and organized interest groups.

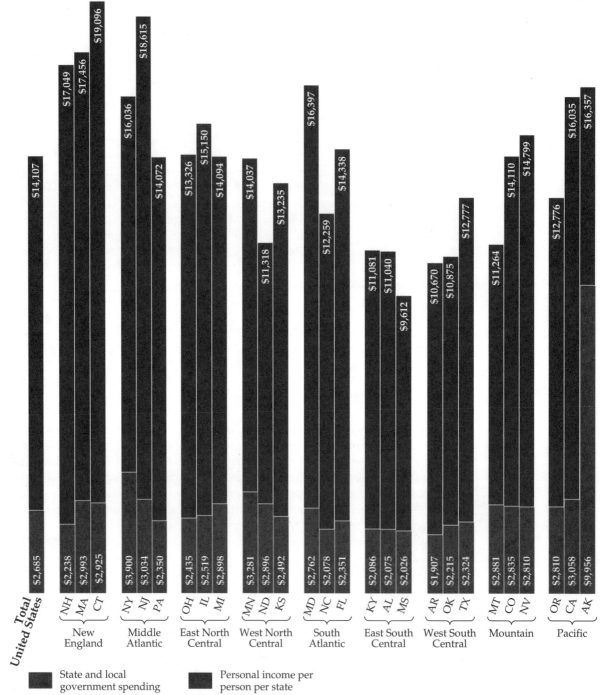

Figure 15.3 State wealth and government spending*a*

State and local government spending

Personal income per person per state

*a*The figures on disposable personal income per capita are from 1988, and the figures on total state and local government direct general expenditures per capita are from 1987.

Source: U.S. Commerce Department, Statistical Abstract of the United States, *1990, pp. xv, xvii.*

Public Opinion Turning to the *political* sphere, research indicates that public opinion has substantial effects on state government policy. Gallup opinion surveys from the 1930s, for example, with unusually large samples that can be broken down by state, indicate that, when the people of a state favored or opposed capital

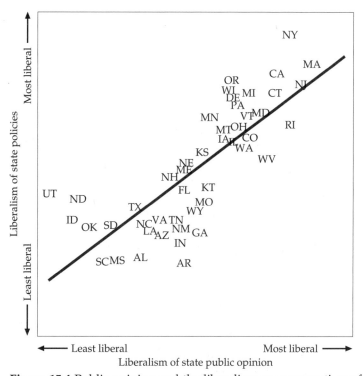

Figure 15.4 Public opinion and the liberalism or conservatism of state policies

Source: Gerald Wright, Robert Erikson, and John McIver, "Public Opinion and Policy Liberalism in the American States," American Journal of Political Science, Vol. 31 (November 1987), p. 989.

punishment, child labor laws, or the inclusion of women on juries, the state tended to have policies in harmony with whatever its citizens wanted.[20] A comprehensive study of the 1970s–1980s struggle for ratification of the Equal Rights Amendment makes clear that states' decisions on whether to ratify the amendment or not depended partly upon how their populations felt about it.[21]

In another leading study, a number of opinion surveys with large samples were used to rank states according to how liberal or conservative (on the average) their populations were, and state policies of many different sorts were also ranked according to their liberalism or conservatism. It turned out that the two things go together. States in which the public is more liberal tend to have more liberal policies, whereas states in which the public is more conservative have conservative policies. This is not just a coincidence or a result of people saying that they favor whatever sort of policies their states happen to have; a sophisticated statistical analysis indicated that public opinion is a genuine influence on policy.[22]

These results are illustrated in Figure 15.4, in which each state is located according to the liberal or conservative opinion of its public and the liberalism or conservatism of its policies. The clustering of states along a line rising upward to the right indicates that the more liberal the public is, the more liberal the policies tend to be. Economic development and other structural factors have much of their effect through the liberalism or conservatism of the public; people in poorer states tend to be more conservative. But additional factors can be seen at work in the states above or below the trend line. Oregon, Wisconsin, and New York, for example, known for a liberal political culture among their elites, have enacted even more liberal policies than their public opinion would indicate. The same is true of Utah, whereas several southern and border states, including Arkansas, Alabama, Georgia, and West Virginia, have policies that are more conservative than their citizens would appear to want. The citizens of each state tend to get the kinds of policies they want, but not always.

Interest Groups   It is impossible to be sure exactly how much influence interest groups have on state governments, but there is reason to believe that their impact is substantial. The conditions for interest group power are ripe. The states decide on policies that make a great deal of difference to groups and corporations— millions or even billions of dollars worth of difference. Those groups are happy to invest money and effort in politics. State politicians, for their part, need outside money for campaigning and, in some cases, to make a decent living. Also, state policy decisions are often made without close public scrutiny.

As a small but telling example, consider the automobile alarm scam. In New York, Illinois, Kentucky, Massachusetts, Michigan, and Rhode Island, state laws at the beginning of the 1990s required automobile insurance companies to give discounts to customers who installed automobile alarms. However, there is considerable doubt about whether it makes sense to encourage installing alarms. "Ridiculous social policy," says one criminologist. "Car alarms are a terrible urban blight with obvious social costs—noise pollution, increased stress, wasted police manpower—and it's not clear there are any benefits in return. No study has demonstrated they reduce auto theft."[23]

Studies of home burglar alarms have revealed that there are about 20 false alarms for every real one, and the ratio for automobile alarms, which can be set off by traffic vibrations, wind, rain, or a tap on the bumper, is probably no better. Criminologists doubt that alarms really mobilize help from passersby, who generally assume that anyone inside a car is its owner. Insurance statisticians say that alarms are "not all that effective" and that discounts are not justified. (In New York, automobiles with alarms actually have about three times as many theft claims as those without, presumably because they are more expensive and more

University of Texas students protest tuition increases.

theft-prone in the first place.) One economist has estimated that preventing a single theft may cost about $10,000 in false alarms and social disruption—twice the value of the average stolen car.

Why, then, do so many states have laws encouraging automobile alarms? The main reason appears to be effective lobbying by the Car Audio Specialists Association/Vehicle Security Association and other representatives of manufacturers and dealers who want to sell the alarms. "These laws are a private bonanza for the alarm industry," said one observer. Interest groups' chances of success are increased by the fact that, usually, no one is watching. When section 167-d(12) of the New York State Insurance Law was quietly amended at the beginning of the 1980s, for example, hardly anyone noticed; those who did, thought that automobile alarm discounts sounded like a harmless anticrime measure.

When the New Jersey legislature began to consider a sweeping measure to require alarms or other antitheft devices on all cars worth more than $5,000, however, the scope and visibility of conflict increased, leading to the front-page *New York Times* story upon which our account is based. Higher visibility of the issue may lead to a different kind of politics, in which the general public swings more weight than organized interests.

Thus, state policies requiring special insurance discounts for installing automobile alarms apparently do not reflect popular demand or a judgment about effective public policy but, rather, the urging of alarm manufacturers who want to sell more alarms. Much the same thing has been found to be true of state licensing of doctors, lawyers, opticians, liquor sales, taxicabs, and many other businesses and services. State regulation does sometimes protect the public from charlatans by providing helpful information, but often its main effect is to limit the number of people engaged in the regulated professions and businesses. This drives up prices, which pleases the lucky ones with licenses.[24] In some cases, the high value of licenses invites corruption, such as bribery to obtain licenses for liquor stores or gambling casinos.

Interest groups prevail even on some issues about which the public cares a good deal. In what was called a "resounding victory" for the National Rifle Association (NRA), for example, the Illinois state senate in 1991 defeated, by a tight 28–26 vote, a popular ban on large-capacity, semiautomatic weapons of the sort used by drug dealers. Some lawmakers said privately that they favored the ban but voted against it because they feared "retaliation." The chief Illinois lobbyist for the NRA called the bill "misdirected," having nothing to do with crime, and claimed to stand for "grass roots democracy": "[t]he National Rifle Association is 100,000 dues-paying members in the state of Illinois who are constituents of every senator here."[25] He did not mention that substantial NRA funding comes from gun manufacturers.

Interest groups invest a lot of money in state politics. The New York State Commission on Lobbying, for example, reported that in 1990, 1,993 lobbyists were registered with the state and were paid $29.3 million in fees and expenses—an amount that had risen 63 percent in just three years and had increased fivefold since 1978. "This is probably one of the few recession-proof industries left," remarked a staffer from Common Cause. More than $1 million each was taken in by four lobbying firms, including one headed by a former chief counsel to the last two speakers of the state assembly. The biggest clients of the New York lobbying firms included the tobacco industry, which was active in the defeat of Governor Cuomo's proposal to restrict cigarette promotional schemes and vending machines sales (Phillip Morris spent $566,223), and the New York State Soft Drink Association, which paid $430,224 to lobbyists in the successful effort to block Cuomo's plan to turn unclaimed 5-cent bottle deposits over to the state.[26]

Democracy in the States

We have suggested that state policy may be more susceptible to interest group influence and less subject to popular control than federal government policy is. Political scientists Grant McConnell and E. E. Schattschneider spelled out some reasons to suspect that this might be true. As McConnell put it, when the size of a political constituency is small, it is easier for wealthy and well-organized interests to dominate it. Decentralized state institutions "give very great advantages to structures of private power and to private interests generally." The multiplicity and obscurity of elective offices and agencies diminishes the public's interest in them and makes them "effectively accountable only to a narrow constituency consisting of the group or groups most directly and intimately affected by the agencies' activities."[27] Schattschneider analyzed the matter in a similar way: the smaller and more narrow the "scope of conflict," the more likely it is that well-organized and wealthy minorities will win. Information and visibility are crucial. What the public does not know about, it cannot control.[28]

State governments often operate with relatively narrow constituencies and low visibility. Television news programs on the national networks naturally devote much more attention to Congress and the president than to any particular state governor or legislature. Local newspapers mostly follow suit. Citizens seldom learn much about what their state governments are doing (few even know the names of their state senators or state representatives), whereas organized interests pay very close attention indeed.

On the other hand, we cannot be sure that there really is such a clear contrast between state and federal governments. Remember the substantial relationship between the public's liberalism and the liberalism of states' policy, shown earlier. A different study of the effects of public opinion on policy turned up no state–national difference at all: it found that, when the public changed its preferences about state policies, the policies of the states tended to change accordingly, responding to public opinion, just as federal policies do.[29] (Many of the state policies that were studied, however, involved high-visibility matters, such as abortion and capital punishment; on more typical, mundane issues, states may be less responsive to the public.) The increasing importance of state government over the years may have led to more public scrutiny and more public control, while the professionalization of state governments may have reduced their susceptibility to bribery or interest group pressure. In any case, the situation certainly varies from state to state.

URBAN POLITICS

The Rise of Cities and Suburbs

As we saw in Chapter 4, one of the great trends in American history has been the rise of big cities. Much of the growth of cities has resulted from immigration. All told, some 50 million people immigrated to America between 1820 and 1980, with about 1 million per year coming during the peak period between 1905 and 1914, mostly from Southern and Eastern Europe.

Many of these people settled in ethnic enclaves in big cities on the East Coast. Remnants of their ethnic neighborhoods can still be seen today in cities like Boston, New York, and New Haven, even though the waves of European immigration mostly stopped at the beginning of World War I. Later, especially after World War II, millions of southern blacks moved to northern cities.[30] From the 1960s to today, Hispanic and Asian immigration has been especially significant. Each wave of immigrants has changed the face of America's cities and has altered urban politics.

URBAN MACHINES   The rise of cities and the immigration of ethnic groups created a new kind of politics. They were responsible, for example, for the development of the urban **political machine**, a party organization staffed by city workers who owed their patronage jobs to the party and kept in close touch with their friends and neighbors in the precincts and wards, doing people favors and getting votes in return.

The first political machine emerged in pre-Civil War New York from Irish immigrants' fire companies, militia companies, gangs, and workingmen's clubs. Politicians used these class and ethnic organizations to dispense assistance and to organize voters.[31] Irish immigrants seem to have been particularly skillful at politics. Later, as hundreds of thousands of non-English-speaking immigrants arrived on the East Coast, urban machines in New York, Boston, and elsewhere helped them with jobs, housing, applications for citizenship, and emergency relief, winning their loyalty at the polls. Thus, the urban machines controlled the spoils of government: lucrative contracts, bribes and contributions from businessmen seeking streetcar or utility monopolies, and other sorts of "honest graft."[32] Many of these party organizations (the Pendergast machine in Kansas City, for example, and William Green's in Philadelphia) persisted well into the twentieth century and formed important elements of the national Democratic party. Mayor Richard J. Daley's Chicago Democratic organization, one of the last of the breed, flourished from the 1950s to the 1970s, operating on this principle, "Don't make no waves, don't back no losers."[33]

Chicago Mayor Richard J. Daley (center), the leader of one of the last urban political machines in the United States, with U.S. Senator Birch Bayh and Polish supporters. Daley's son, Richard M. Daley, later served as a more reformist mayor.

The topic of political machines used to arouse strong emotions. Many immigrant and working-class Americans appreciated the help that political organizations gave them, particularly during the years when the federal government offered no social welfare programs. Social scientists have referred to the beneficial "functions" of urban machines, though they have also pointed out the uneven and sometimes skimpy or symbolic nature of the benefits delivered. But many middle- and upper-class Americans deplored the corruption and inefficiency associated with these machines. Some also disliked the political power that urban machines provided for foreign-born and working-class people.

PROGRESSIVE "REFORMS"   Shortly after 1900, the Progressive movement, largely energized by white Anglo-Saxon Protestant businessmen and professionals,[34] crusaded to "clean up" city governments and to destroy political machines, through a series of institutional changes: civil service laws that prevented political hiring or firing and kept city workers out of politics; secret ballots and poll watchers to prevent ballot stuffing; nonpartisan elections for city councils, often held "at large" in the entire city, rather than by machine-dominated wards; and, especially for smaller and middle-sized cities, appointive, nonpartisan "**city manager**" executives (rather than elected mayors), who were supposed to use businesslike management techniques and be immune from political influence.

The biggest cities tended to resist these reforms and often retained elected **city council–mayor** systems. Political parties remained active in places like Chicago, even when the elections were supposedly nonpartisan and no party labels appeared on the ballot; party machines put up candidates, and precinct workers made clear to voters which candidates were the "nonpartisan" Democrats and which were the "nonpartisan" Republicans. Many big-city machines continued to be strong until New Deal federal programs took over some of the key functions that had been used to attract voters and court decisions weakened patronage systems.

But the changes that resulted from the Progressive movement swept much of America, including most of the small and middle-sized cities, especially in the West, where city manager government remains the norm. These changes undoubtedly resulted in more honest and efficient government. City managers tend to be highly professional; they keep in touch with the latest policy ideas and management techniques through nationwide professional associations and journals. At the same time, however, the Progressives' measures probably reduced popular control of city government and thereby impeded democracy. When political parties are weakened or eliminated, they are less able to alert people to government actions against their interests, and citizens have a more difficult time knowing how to vote. At-large elections reduce the representation of community-based minorities. Also, nonpartisan elections generally show lower rates of citizen participation, particularly by the poor. Fewer people's voices are heard.[35]

Diverse Governments   Our present city governments reflect this history of immigration, growth, and reform. The United States includes a crazy quilt of different arrangements. Many cities have city manager governments. Some cities elect city councils and **strong mayors**, who appoint other officials and veto council ordinances. Still others have city councils with **weak mayors**, who do little but preside over council meetings. There is every imaginable sort of electoral system, often mixing partisan and nonpartisan, district and at-large elections within one city.

Institutional arrangements make a difference. The "fiscal crises" of expanding demands and shrinking revenues that beset America's cities from the 1970s to the 1990s, for example, had much more devastating effects in New York, where decisions were centralized and the mayor was beholden to city workers' unions, than in Chicago, where many government functions were insulated in independent boards with their own sources of revenue, and where the mayor could use his party machine to keep city workers under control.[36] New York City in 1987 had an enormous budget of $24 *billion*, of which about $5 billion went for education, $4.7 billion for public welfare, $3 billion for utilities, $2.5 billion for health and hospitals, and $2 billion for police and fire protection. The city governments of Los Angeles and Chicago, by contrast, had far smaller budgets of only $2.5 and $2.7 billion, respectively, most of which went for police and fire protection, highways, and, in the case of Los Angeles, utilities.[37] Other functions that were very expensive for New York City were farmed out, in the Los Angeles and Chicago areas, to counties, special districts, or other governmental units.

As financial pressures have increased, many cities have gone one step farther and have "privatized" public services, contracting out to private entrepreneurs, who, it is hoped, will be more efficient and less expensive. Virtually all cities now contract out food services and construction; most have privatized janitorial services; and many contract out garbage collection, parking garages, and park maintenance. (See Figure 15.5.) Seventy years after the city of Philadelphia led the way by having public workers provide public services, it planned to privatize garbage collection and custodial services, while trying to avert the shutdown of its mass transit system. Los Angeles County contracted out the management of five small airports; Chicago turned vehicle towing into a profit center; Fort Worth even transferred operation of its zoo to a charitable organization. It remains to be seen whether these cities' savings outweigh hidden costs and are worth workers' losses of wages and benefits.[38]

SUBURBS AND SUN BELT   Two additional historical trends, the growth of suburbs and the rise of the Sun Belt, are also important for understanding the structural underpinnings of present-day urban politics.

Suburbs   The concept of "suburb" is hard to define precisely. The Latin words *sub urbe* mean "under" or "next to" the city. We think of the English word *suburb* as meaning a residential district on the outskirts of town, where most people commute to work in an inner city. But just how residential must it be, and just what proportion of people must commute, in order to distinguish a suburb from a separate town or a city? The U.S. Census has given up trying to answer these questions; it doesn't mention suburbs but, instead, talks about *cities* like Chicago (population 2,978,000 in 1988), *"primary metropolitan statistical areas"* like "Chicago, IL PSMA" (population 6,216,000), and *"consolidated metropolitan statistical areas"* like "Chicago-Gary-Lake County (IL), IL-IN-WI CMSA" (population 8,181,000).[39]

Obviously, these "metropolitan areas" include many suburbs, even if we cannot be sure exactly how many. Residents of Santa Monica, Bethesda, or Evanston may firmly assert their towns' independence, but, to much of the world, they

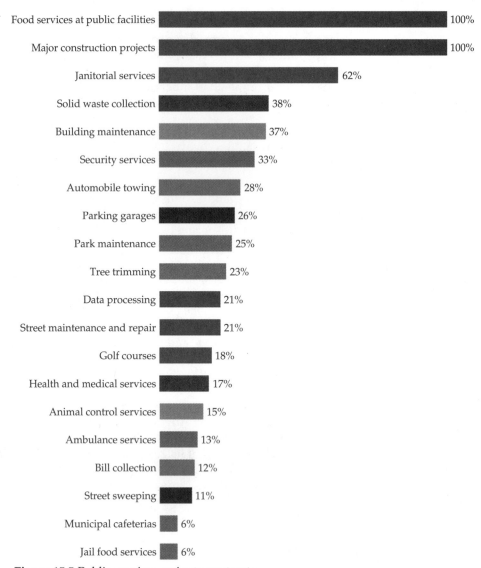

Food services at public facilities	100%
Major construction projects	100%
Janitorial services	62%
Solid waste collection	38%
Building maintenance	37%
Security services	33%
Automobile towing	28%
Parking garages	26%
Park maintenance	25%
Tree trimming	23%
Data processing	21%
Street maintenance and repair	21%
Golf courses	18%
Health and medical services	17%
Animal control services	15%
Ambulance services	13%
Bill collection	12%
Street sweeping	11%
Municipal cafeterias	6%
Jail food services	6%

Figure 15.5 Public services, private contracts

Note: Figures show the percentages of surveyed cities that contracted out each type of service.

Source: Mercer Group, Inc., survey in the New York Times, *October 14, 1991, p. A8.*

look like suburbs of Los Angeles, Washington, D.C., and Chicago. The contrast between the city of Chicago's 3 million people and the Chicago CMSA's 8 million people indicates that there are a lot of people living in suburbs.

Since the end of World War II, in fact, widespread ownership of automobiles and the building of freeways have enabled many millions of Americans to settle in the suburbs while still going to work in the city. Attracted by large homes with spacious lawns and gardens, on quiet streets, with convenient shopping centers and good public schools and other facilities, many middle-class and upper-middle-class people have moved to suburbia (see Figure 15.6). Echoing earlier waves of immigration to the United States, ethnic groups that have "made it" economically—first the Irish, Germans, and Scandinavians and then the Italians,

Little of the U.S. population remains in small towns like Belfast, Maine, built more than a century ago.

Poles, and Eastern Europeans—have tended to move to the suburbs, leaving many black people and recent immigrants in the central cities.

Small Towns   At the same time that suburbs have grown, rural and small towns in America have shrunk, from about 44 percent of the U.S. population in 1950 to just 23 percent in 1990. (Big cities have declined slightly, too.) Tractors and mechanized farming have cut the number of farmers needed. In Scranton, Iowa, for example, where the county population dropped by 17 percent, to about 10,000, between 1980 and 1990, a visitor found Main Street deserted. The Scranton Cafe still had its daily specials scribbled on a chalkboard, and men in bib overalls still swapped stories over coffee, but the town's arcade, drugstore, and Friday night

Figure 15.6 Growth of the suburbs[a]

[a]Figures are percentages of the American population living in the suburbs versus the cities and rural areas.

Source: Census Bureau, in the New York Times, *September 11, 1990, p. A12.*

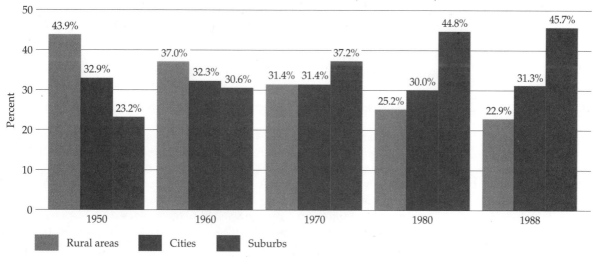

high school football games were just memories. One resident told a reporter, "It looks like a ghost town. I sure miss the people." In the nearby county seat, a poster proclaimed "$1,000 Reward!" for anyone who could attract an employer providing at least 15 jobs, and the economic development officer spoke with pride of the planned new Japanese plant, employing about 25 workers, that was going to make soyflake for instant tofu.[40]

Small towns that are not shrinking often find that their governments are changing and professionalizing, just as many state legislatures and city governments have done. As a retiring town official of Derby, Vermont (population 4,500), put it, it used to be that "a little bit of arithmetic, some good common sense and a sense of honesty" were all you needed to be a selectman; "[n]ow it's preferable that you be a lawyer." A flood of directives comes from the federal and state governments concerning everything from solid waste disposal to personnel management. Labor negotiations, budget planning, and applying for grants require technical skills. Volunteers are scarce. Many small towns have begun to hire professional managers.[41]

The Sun Belt   In recent years, the movement toward suburbia has combined with a population shift toward the Sun Belt of the South and the Southwest, as the industries of the northern "rust belt" have declined and as those in the South have grown. The 1990 census found, for example, that most of the biggest population increases during the 1980s occurred in Sun Belt suburbs. Moreno Valley, California, a suburb of Riverside, grew by 320 percent in ten years, from a population of 28,309 to one of 118,779. Mesa, Arizona, a suburb of Phoenix, grew in population from 152,404 to 288,091. Rancho Cucamonga, California, a Los Angeles suburb, increased in population from 55,250 to 101,409 between 1980 and 1990. Plano, Texas, a suburb of Dallas, grew in population from 72,331 to 128,713. Other fast-growing cities include Irvine, Escondido, Oceanside, Santa Clarita, Chula Vista, and Ontario, California; Arlington and Mesquite, Texas; Glendale and Scottsdale, Arizona; and Virginia Beach, Virginia—all of them suburbs. In many cases, however, these communities had developed major shopping areas and industries of their own, increasing their economic independence and changing what it means to be a suburb.[42]

The rise of suburbs in the Sun Belt and elsewhere has had two important effects on urban politics. First, more and more people are living in places with political systems based on the Progressives' "good government" model, with city managers and professional staffs, but facing the great strains that come with rapid growth: pressure on schools and other services, and problems of traffic congestion and air pollution. Second, many inner cities have been left with poor people, decaying infrastructures, and very limited tax bases to pay for needed services.

The Plight of the Cities

The most important facts about many of the older cities are their poverty and their large minority populations. These two things are connected. In 1980, when the total U.S. population was only about 12 percent black and 6 percent Hispanic, the population of New York was 25 percent black and 20 percent Hispanic (the Bronx was 32 percent black and 34 percent Hispanic); Los Angeles was 17 percent black and 28 percent Hispanic; and Chicago was 40 percent black and 14 percent Hispanic. A number of cities were more than 50 percent black: Baltimore (55 percent),

Detroit (63 percent), Gary (71 percent), Inglewood, CA (57 percent), Newark (58 percent), and Washington, D.C. (70 percent) in the north, as well as Atlanta (67 percent), Birmingham (56 percent), and Richmond (51 percent) in the South. There were Hispanic majorities in Brownsville, El Paso, Laredo, and San Antonio, Texas, as well as in Hialeah and Miami, Florida.[43]

POVERTY   Blacks and Hispanics tend to be poorer than other Americans. In 1988, for example, the median family income of black Americans was only $18,098, compared with $32,274 for whites. Thirty-three percent of blacks, but only 11 percent of whites, fell below the poverty line. Hispanics are not much better off than blacks, with a median family income of $20,306 and with 28 percent below the poverty line.[44]

Many other problems accompany poverty. Drug use is common and flagrant in most inner cities. Crime rates and gun use are high. According to FBI figures from 1988, violent crimes in major metropolitan areas occurred at the rate of 752 crimes per 100,000 population: about twice the rate for smaller cities and 4 times that for rural areas. Robbery in big cities was 5 times more frequent than in small cities and 18 times more common than in rural areas. The police in Newark, Atlanta, Detroit, Denver, and New York each reported more than 1,000 robberies and 25–60 murders per 100,000 population.[45] Young men in the United States are killed at more than 10 times the rate in many other industrialized countries (see Figure 15.7). In fact, homicide is the leading cause of death among America's young black men, and young men in Harlem are less likely to survive to the age of 40 than are their counterparts in impoverished Bangladesh.[46]

CHILDREN   One of the most painful aspects of life in the inner city is that children who are born there—through no choice of their own, of course—face severe disadvantages. Some begin life in crisis, born to drug-abusing mothers, rushed to neonatal intensive-care units with seizures, severe respiratory problems, or congenital infections. Others are born with AIDS. Many more find themselves living in poverty with a single parent (generally their mother), getting poor nutrition, poor health care, little inspiration from parent or peers, and inadequate schooling.

Many inner-city children can get nutritious meals only at schools or day-care centers like this one in Philadelphia.

Figure 15.7 Young men at risk[a]

[a]Figures are killings per 100,000 men, 15–24 years old, in 1986 or 1987, for various countries.

Source: Journal of the American Medical Association, *in the* New York Times, *June 27, 1990, p. A9.*

About 45 percent of all black children in the country and 39 percent of all Hispanic children are in families with incomes below the poverty level. Of all black children in the United States, 55 percent live with their mother only, and more than 75 percent of those children are poor.[47] These rates are still higher in the inner cities. As they grow up, even young people who are determined to overcome all obstacles and who manage to avoid danger and resist the temptations of gang membership or drug dealing find stark limits to what they can accomplish. In some inner-city high schools, the very top graduating student often finds that her or his record is not sufficient for admission to a good college.

Of course, poverty is not found only in cities or among minorities; severe pockets of poverty also exist in Appalachia, the rural South, and rural areas generally. In fact, most poor people are white. But the high concentrations of poor people in the cities present a major problem for urban governments.

MINORITY POWER   The large minority populations in America's cities have gradually won political power and government representation. Cities with majority black populations, like Gary, Detroit, and Newark, mostly have had black mayors for years. The largest cities, with substantial black minorities, also have begun to elect black mayors from time to time: Tom Bradley in Los Angeles, Harold Washington in Chicago, David Dinkins in New York. Racial and ethnic divisions have led to some bitter campaigns, though; Harold Washington was elected in Chicago in 1983 only because two white candidates divided the vote against him, and he faced stonewalling opposition from white ethnic aldermen in the "Council Wars" that dominated most of his term and a half in office. Hispanic mayors have been elected in San Antonio, Denver, Miami, and other cities. The makeup of city councils and city workers and officials has also come to reflect the importance of minority populations.

Many city governments have made vigorous attempts to address their problems. Mayor Coleman Young, for example, led a major renovation of Detroit's decaying downtown area. Chicago, once said to have the weakest public school system in the nation, pioneered in school reform, decentralizing control to elected local boards in which parents could hire and fire principals. Cities have tackled their drug problems with rehabilitation and strict law enforcement, and have tried to provide shelter for the homeless and support for the poor.

CITY LIMITS   However, the problems are vast, and the resources are sparse. Urban poverty not only creates many problems that city governments would like to solve but it also means that city governments don't have much money with which to solve these problems; there is not a great deal of income or wealth to tax. Also, as we noted in Chapter 3, "Federalism," competition among political units creates

Mayor Xavier Suarez of Miami. Minorities have won more and more power in city halls, but, like other mayors, have found only limited funds to deal with growing urban problems.

"city limits," practical constraints on what any local government can do. If a city imposes taxes that are too heavy on businesses or wealthy people for redistributive purposes, those businesses and wealthy people may move out to the suburbs or the Sun Belt while more poor people move in, defeating what the government is trying to accomplish. Thus, local governments generally put more emphasis on policies for economic development than on fighting poverty.[48] In order to attract businesses and to keep corporate headquarters and major enterprises from fleeing, cities like New York offer generous tax breaks and subsidies that then reduce the money available to solve urban problems (see "Doing Politics" for an example).

The tendency of city governments to subsidize development while cutting back on social programs is exacerbated by the political power of developers and corporations, which lobby city governments intensely and provide much of the money that urban politicians need to get elected. In 1990, real estate developers, city contractors, unions, and other interest groups spent a total of $8.5 million on lobbyists in New York City. The top lobbying firm, Davidoff and Malito, which received $1,644,616 in fees, was headed by Sid Davidoff, a longtime friend, tennis partner, and occasional advisor of Mayor Dinkins. Davidoff told the *New York Times* that his firm made the most money because it was "the best." Others explained that clients saw Davidoff as providing a high level of "access": "This guy is a phone call away from the top levels of City Hall."[49]

FEDERAL HELP?   Some analysts argue that the federal government should provide money to deal with urban problems, because only a national solution is possible for such nationwide problems. City governments cannot cope on their own; if they scrape up their own money to help the poor, more poor people will move in and rich people will move out. Moreover, the cities provide major commercial, financial, and cultural services to surrounding communities and the entire country, for which they are not fully compensated. During the 1980s and early 1990s, however, the Reagan and Bush administrations showed little interest in providing money to the cities. They cut rather than increased urban aid. (See Figure 15.8.) In 1981, for example, the federal government spent a total of $27.4 billion on five urban-related programs: $8.4 billion for employment and training programs, $7.3 billion for general revenue sharing, $5.7 billion for community development block grants, $5.4 billion for urban mass transit, and $570 million for urban development action grants. But President Bush's budget for 1991 allocated less than one-third as much—a total of $8.9 billion—to those same five programs: $3.75 billion, zero, $2.7 billion, $2.5 billion, and zero, respectively.[50]

Early in 1991, President Bush proposed to take control of $15 billion of federal programs away from the cities and to give it to the states, which historically have favored their rural and suburban, rather than their urban, areas. State governments liked the idea; their federal funds had been declining, too. But city mayors from both parties protested. Republican Mayor Althaus of York, Pennsylvania, called Bush's proposal "entirely wrong," while Democratic Mayor Flynn of Boston declared, "This isn't federalism; this is fraud." He complained that "the Federal Government has been walking away from America's cities" at a time when they must find homes for babies born to mothers addicted to crack, care for people with AIDS, shelter the homeless, and cope with extraordinarily high rates of poverty, infant mortality, and murder.

The frustration of many city mayors has been increased by limits on their powers that trace back to the Progressive era. For example, when a bystander's

DOING
POLITICS

*The "Tribeca
Task Force"
Fights City Hall*

Desperate to keep the Commodities Exchanges from carrying out a threat to move to New Jersey, the city and state of New York agreed in 1990 to provide $145 million in cash and tax breaks in order to help build a new, 43-story office tower and trading floor north of the World Trade Center in the Tribeca section of lower Manhattan.

But two local women with young children, worried that a huge new tower would obstruct their views, blight their park, and increase noise and traffic congestion, declared themselves to be the "Tribeca Task Force" and set out to stop it. They raised some disturbing questions. Why should nearly a million square feet of speculative new office space be built, when 20 million square feet were already sitting empty in the surrounding financial district? Wouldn't a new commodities trading floor soon become obsolete, replaced by new electronic trading methods? How could the city afford these millions of dollars in the midst of a fiscal crisis, when schoolteachers were being fired and bridges and roads were left unrepaired?

Devoting every spare hour to the cause, the two Task Force women gradually mobilized a large neighborhood constituency. They wrote and distributed a newsletter, put posters on walls, and alerted the news media. They activated their local Community Board, which passed a resolution against the tower; they called public meetings at which city officials were barraged with objections. Aiming for TV news pictures, they held a "mothers' march" on City Hall. The press began to report their efforts in sympathetic articles: "Trouble in Tribeca for Commodities Exchanges Plan"; "Moms battle Skyscraper."

The moms did not have it easy, however. The proposed developer, Tishman Speyer Properties, wielded a lot of political clout in the city, and one of the women received veiled threats. Observers called the subsidy a "done deal"; such senior political figures as the chairman of the state Urban Development Corporation, the city's Deputy Mayor for Finance and Economic Development, the Speaker of the City Council, and the Manhattan Borough president had endorsed it. David Dinkins, the liberal black mayor, said nothing against it. It was felt to be politically and economically impossible for a mayor of New York City to permit such a major business to get away.

As this book was written the outcome of the story remained in doubt, but some politicians were beginning to voice second thoughts about what they had signed on to. The two Tribeca women seemed to have a fighting chance of beating City Hall.

Source: Jill Dutt, "Trouble in Tribeca for Commodities Exchange Plan," *Newsday*, November 26, 1990.

videotape revealed the brutal beating of black motorist Rodney King by three Los Angeles police officers as other police officers looked on, and when transcripts of squad car communications suggested that such violence was routine for the Los Angeles police department, many people urged that Police Chief Daryl Gates be fired. However, Mayor Tom Bradley had no direct control over Gates, who was chosen by an independent commission and was protected by civil service regulations against being fired, except under very restricted circumstances.[51]

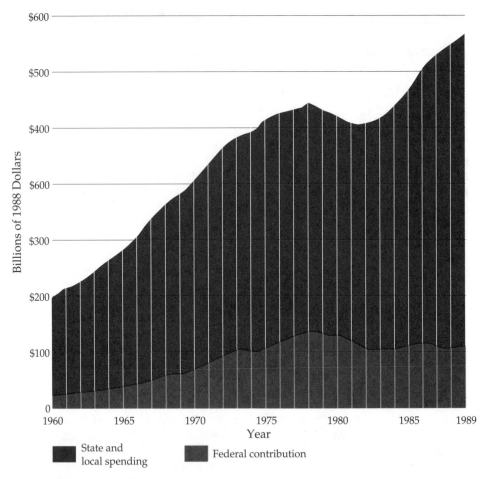

Figure 15.8 Shrinking federal aid

Source: Advisory Commission on Intergovernmental Relations, in the New York Times, *December 30, 1990, p. L17.*

Democracy in the Cities

We cannot easily assess how democratic city governments are or compare them with state and national governments because of the lack of comparable data on relationships between public opinion and policy. We can only hazard an informed guess: many cities probably stand in a middle position, more highly visible and more responsive to their citizens than most state governments, but less so than the national government. Undoubtedly, cities vary a great deal; among the largest, we would expect that those with the most coherent, competitive party systems and the clearest and most centralized lines of government authority respond most fully to the wishes of their citizens.

SUMMARY

State and local governments spend a great deal of money—more than half as much as the federal government does—and provide most of the government services that we encounter in our daily life.

State governments resemble miniature versions of the federal government, with written constitutions; governors who have varying powers of veto and appointment; legislatures that are generally organized into two chambers and do much of their business in committee; and court systems headed by a supreme court. State governments have become increasingly professionalized and increasingly open to women and minorities, but their low visibility probably reduces their democratic responsiveness. Some have been susceptible to corruption. State policies are affected by the state's level of economic development and its degree of political competition; also by public opinion and organized interest groups.

Big cities grew rapidly for more than 100 years. Immigrants from abroad built urban political machines that provided patronage and some social services in return for votes, but Progressive reforms undercut them and produced weak-mayor and city manager systems, especially in the West. Recent population growth has focused on the suburbs, particularly in the Sun Belt; population in small towns and big cities has declined. The cities have been left with many poor and minority citizens in need of social programs, which are limited by competition among localities for wealth and by declining federal aid. City governments may tend to be more democratic than state governments but less so than the national government.

To Ponder

1. Can the central cities be revived? How?

2. Are state governments really less democratic than the federal government? How could democratic control be increased?

3. How can political corruption be reduced or eliminated?

4. What is the future of the suburbs? Of small towns?

Suggested Readings

Dahl, Robert. *Who Governs.* New Haven: Yale University Press, 1961.
    A classic and still compelling account of pluralistic politics in New Haven, CT.

Jacob, Herbert, and Kenneth N. Vines, eds. *Politics in the American States: A Comparative Analysis.* Glenview, IL: Scott, Foresman, 1990.
    Articles on many aspects of state government by leading scholars.

Judd, Dennis R. *The Politics of American Cities: Private Power and Public Policy*, 3rd ed. Glenview, IL: Scott, Foresman, 1988.
    A thorough and critical account of urban politics.

Leach, Richard H., and Timothy G. O'Rourke. *State and Local Government: The Third Century of Federalism.* Englewood Cliffs, NJ: Prentice-Hall, 1988.
    A basic textbook.

Lemann, Nicolas. *The Promised Land: The Great Black Migration and How It Changed America.* New York: Knopf, 1991.
    A gripping account of the lives of blacks who moved North and of how public policies affected their lives.

Peterson, Paul. *City Limits.* Chicago: University of Chicago Press, 1981.
    An analysis of why local governments are constrained in the policies that they can pursue.

Rakove, Milton L. *Don't Make No Waves, Don't Back No Losers: An Insider's Analysis of the Daley Machine*. Bloomington: Indiana University Press, 1975.

  A lively account of one of the last, strong, urban political machines.

Notes

1. Seth Mydans, "Civics 101 on Tape in Arizona, or, 'We All Have Our Prices,' " *New York Times*, February 11, 1991, pp. A1, A10.

2. *Washington Post Weekly Edition*, March 4–10, 1991, p. 14.

3. *New York Times*, June 2, 1991, p. 14.

4. *Economic Report of the President*, 1991, pp. 286, 379.

5. *Economic Report*, pp. 377, 383.

6. *The Book of the States* (Lexington, KY: Council of States Governments, 1990), p. 40.

7. *Book of the States*, pp. 62, 83–84.

8. *Book of the States*, p. 67.

9. *Book of the States*, p. 54.

10. *Washington Post Weekly Edition*, January 21–27, 1991, p. 15; *New York Times*, December 30, 1990, p. L17.

11. Calculated from *New York Times*, November 9, 1990, p. A13.

12. *New York Times*, November 9, 1990, p. A13.

13. Robert Reinhold, "Complicated Ballot Is Becoming Burden to California Voters," *New York Times*, September 24, 1990, p. A1.

14. *Book of the States*, p. 204.

15. Stanley H. Friedelbaum, "Reactive Responses: The Complementary Role of Federal and State Courts," *Publius: The Journal of Federalism*, Vol. 17 (Winter 1987), pp. 33–50.

16. See Richard I. Hofferbert and Ira Sharkansky, eds., *State and Urban Politics: Readings in Comparative Public Policy* (Boston: Little, Brown, 1971).

17. *Statistical Abstract of the United States, 1990*, pp. xv, xviii, 368.

18. V. O. Key, Jr., *Southern Politics in State and Nation* (New York: Knopf, 1949).

19. Robert D. Plotnik and Richard D. Winters, "Party, Political Liberalism, and Redistribution: An Application to the American States," *American Politics Quarterly*, Vol. 18 (October 1990), pp. 430–458.

20. Robert S. Erikson, "The Relationship Between Public Opinion and State Policy: A New Look Based on Some Forgotten Data," *American Journal of Political Science*, Vol. 20 (February 1976), pp. 25–36.

21. Jane Mansbridge, *Why We Lost the ERA* (Chicago: University of Chicago Press, 1986).

22. Gerald C. Wright, Jr., Robert S. Erikson, and John P. McIver, "Public Opinion and Policy Liberalism in the American States," *American Journal of Political Science*, Vol. 31 (November 1987), pp. 980–1001.

23. John Tierney, "Laws Encourage Car Alarms, but Din May Not Be Worth It," *New York Times*, February 19, 1991, p. A1.

24. George Stigler, "The Theory of Economic Regulation," *Bell Journal of Management Science*, Vol. 2, No. 1 (Spring 1978), pp. 3–21.

25. Rick Pearson, "Senate Cripples Gun Package," *Chicago Tribune*, May 25, 1991, pp. A1, A14.

26. Kevin Sack, "Report Says More Lobbyists in Albany Earn Record Fees," *New York Times*, March 19, 1991, p. A16.

27. Grant McConnell, *Private Power and American Democracy* (New York: Random House, 1966), ch. 4 and ch. 6, pp. 168, 182–185.

28. E. E. Schattschneider, *The Semi-Sovereign People: A Realist's View of Democracy in America* (New York: Holt, 1960), ch. 1–2.

29. Benjamin I. Page and Robert Y. Shapiro, "Effects of Public Opinion on Policy," *American Political Science Review*, Vol. 77 (March 1983), pp. 175–190.

30. Nicolas Lemann, *The Promised Land: The Great Black Migration and How It Changed America* (New York: Knopf, 1991).

31. Amy Bridges, *A City in the Republic: Antebellum New York and the Origins of Machine Politics* (Cambridge, MA: Harvard University Press, 1984).

32. William L. Riordan, *Plunkett of Tammany Hall* (New York: E. P. Dutton, 1963).

33. Milton Rakove, *Don't Make No Waves, Don't Back No Losers* (Bloomington, IN: Indiana University Press, 1975), p. 11.

34. Dennis R. Judd, *The Politics of American Cities: Private Power and Public Policy*, 3rd ed. (Glenview, IL: Scott, Foresman, 1988), pp. 106–109.

35. William Crotty, *The Party Game* (New York: W. H. Freeman, 1985), p. 108.

36. Esther Fuchs, *Mayors and Money: Fiscal Policy in New York and Chicago* (Chicago: University of Chicago Press, 1991).

37. *Statistical Abstract 1990*, pp. 296–297.

38. Michael deCourcy Hinds, "Cash-Strapped Cities Turn to Companies to Do What Government Once Did," *New York Times*, May 14, 1991, p. A8.

39. *Statistical Abstract 1990*, pp. 34, 912.

40. Dirk Johnson, "Population Decline in Rural America: A Product of Advances in Technology," *New York Times*, September 11, 1990, p. A12.

41. "Small-Town Governance: The Workers Are Fewer," *New York Times*, June 25, 1990, p. A10.

42. *New York Times*, February 23, 1991, p. 10.

43. *Statistical Abstract 1990*, pp. 34–36.

44. *Statistical Abstract 1990*, pp, 38, 40.

45. *Statistical Abstract 1990*, pp. 170, 172.

46. *New York Times*, June 27, 1990, p. A9.

47. *Statistical Abstract 1990*, pp. 52, 460.

48. Paul Peterson, *City Limits* (Chicago: University of Chicago Press, 1981).

49. Josh Barbanel, "Lobbying List Led by Dinkins' Friend," *New York Times*, March 13, 1991, p. A6.

50. *New York Times*, May 21, 1990, p. A11.

51. Seth Mydans et al., "Videotape of Beating by Officers Puts Full Glare on Brutality Issue," *New York Times*, March 18, 1991, pp. A1, A8.

PART V

What Government Does

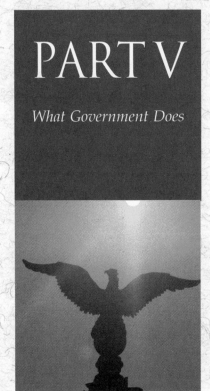

Chapters in Parts II and III examined the structural and political influences on government institutions and public officials. Chapters in Part IV directly examined government institutions and public officials, asking how and why they operate as they do. The chapters in this part examine what government produces in terms of public policies; they ask what government does and how effective it is in tackling the most important problems facing the United States. As such, this part represents a kind of summing up; chapters examine how well our political and governmental institutions operate to fulfill the expectations of the American people that government do what people can't do for themselves to meet the challenges of the modern world. Chapters in this part have a strong comparative aspect because evaluating how well we are doing requires that we look at what governments in other countries are doing to address similar problems. The chapters also address the democracy theme, asking whether public policies are the outcome of a democratic process and whether policies improve the health and vitality of democracy in the United States.

The chapters in this Part do not, however, look at everything government does. Because government policies, decisions, and actions affect virtually every aspect of life in American society, and because government produces such a vast number of laws, regulations, rulings, findings, and decisions, we had to make choices about what issues to pay attention to, given time and space limitations. We used two guidelines to decide which public policies to include in Part V: the proportion of the federal budget accounted for by a particular policy (that is, policies that represent the largest parts of annual federal government outlays are included); and the degree to which a particular policy area is the subject matter of contemporary political debate in the United States. With these guidelines in mind, the following subjects are included in Part V. Chapter 16 looks at American foreign and military policy. Chapter 17 examines economic policy, with particular attention paid to patterns of government expenditure, the tax system, and regulation of the economy, including regulation affecting the environment. Chapter 18 examines our relatively unique system of social welfare, with particular attention paid to programs of social insurance, like Social Security and Medicare, and means-tested welfare programs, like Medicaid and Aid For Families of Dependent Children. Chapter 19 looks at the status of civil liberties and civil rights in the United States, with special attention paid to decisions of the Supreme Court concerning our most cherished rights and liberties.

16

Foreign Policy and National Defense

WAR WITH IRAQ

During the night of August 2, 1990, Iraqi tanks and troops poured across their southern border into Kuwait, the tiny but oil-rich emirate on the Persian Gulf. Meeting little resistance, they conquered the country within 24 hours. President Bush was outraged. The blatant aggression seemed to pose a threat to weakly defended Saudi Arabia, which held about one-quarter of the world's known oil reserves.

How should the United States react? Just a week earlier, the U.S. ambassador to Iraq had told President Hussein that the United States had "no opinion" on Arab-Arab conflicts, such as Iraq's disputes with Kuwait over oil prices, debts, and access to the sea. There was no defense treaty with the Gulf states. The United States had promoted friendly relations with Iraq for more than a decade, quietly supporting its war with Iran with financial credits and intelligence information, and ignoring Iraq's use of poison gas. Moreover, the United States did not seem ready to intervene. There were American ships and planes in the area, but few troops; the American economy was showing signs of sliding into a recession, and the budget was already deeply in the red. On the other hand, vast military assets were available; they were no longer needed in Europe after the collapse of the Communist Warsaw Pact.

President Bush met intensively with his closest foreign policy and military advisors, especially Secretary of State James Baker, Secretary of Defense Dick Cheney, National Security Advisor Brent Scowcroft (with his deputy, Robert Gates), and Chairman Colin Powell of the military Joint Chiefs of Staff, but consulted few members of Congress, Middle East experts, or others.

Apparently, President Bush took a hard line from the start. He insisted that the United States must not merely defend Saudi Arabia but also must roll back the invasion and get Iraq out of Kuwait—a much tougher objective. Scowcroft seems to have pushed in the same direction. Powell, scarred by the

In the Persian Gulf War, hundreds of U.S. tanks like these swept across the deserts of Iraq, cutting off Iraqi troops who occupied Kuwait.

567

Vietnam experience, had doubts about fighting but argued strongly that, if force were to be used at all, it should be used massively.[1]

On August 4, Bush made his aims public: this aggression, he said, "will not stand." He dispatched an enormous U.S. military force to the Persian Gulf region, which by the beginning of September amounted to more than 200,000 troops with tanks and equipment; 600 war planes; and 50 ships, including 4 aircraft carrier battle groups. It was one of the largest and most rapid military deployments in world history, with troop ships and huge C-5A transport planes ferrying many thousands of tons of materiel and people across the Atlantic. Though there were scattered protests in the United States, opinion polls showed about 75 percent approval for the president's action.

At the same time, President Bush worked hard to build national and international support. Condemning the "rape and pillage" of Kuwait and comparing Hussein with Hitler, he called for a "new world order" in which international law would be respected. Bush telephoned many heads of state, persuading and cajoling, calling in IOUs, promising rewards, and perhaps threatening a few of the recalcitrant. Egypt was forgiven about $9 billion of debt that it owed the United States; Syria, still on the official supporter-of-terrorism list, got a friendly visit. Saudi Arabia, long resistant to allowing non-Muslim soldiers on its soil, reluctantly agreed to the buildup of U.S. forces, which were eventually joined by a few Egyptian, British, French, and even Syrian troops. Many nations sent warships. The UN Security Council condemned the invasion and (with acquiescence from the Soviet Union and China, both of which were eager for good relations with the United States) imposed strict economic sanctions on Iraq. Turkey closed its oil pipeline to Iraqi exports, Syria shut down trade, and allied ships sealed off the Jordanian port of Aqaba. Japan and Germany provided financial support.

By the autumn of 1990, the blockade was cutting off virtually all of Iraq's trade and was slowly strangling the Iraqi economy. Yet President Saddam Hussein showed no great hurry to leave Kuwait. His hints at a withdrawal in return for an Israeli-Palestinian peace conference were flatly rejected by President Bush, who called for "unconditional" withdrawal from Kuwait. Meanwhile, U.S. troops and equipment were suffering in the desert sand and heat, each day of the operation was expensive, and high oil prices (produced by war fears and the sanctions) were hurting the U.S. economy. Offensive action might offer quicker success than sanctions and could destroy Iraq's future war-making capability, including chemical and (possibly) nuclear weapons.

Secretary Cheney and Chairman Powell, after a visit to the Gulf in October, reported the judgment of General Norman Schwarzkopf and others that an offensive would require many more troops. On November 8 (immediately after the congressional election), President Bush announced a huge increase in the troop buildup to provide an "offensive capability"; total strength in the Gulf grew over the next three months to more than 500,000 men and women, with 1,200 war planes and 6 aircraft carriers. The administration proposed a UN resolution setting a deadline for an Iraqi pullout from Kuwait and authorizing members to use force ("all necessary means") if the deadline passed and Iraq had not pulled out. On December 12, after the United States put heavy pressure on the Soviets and others, the UN Security Council voted 12–2 (China abstained) to set a January 15, 1991 deadline.

Few Americans were eager for war. In November, a survey found that 52 percent of the public would favor using U.S. troops to defend Saudi Arabia in case of attack, but only 42 percent favored the use of U.S. troops "if Iraq refused to withdraw from Kuwait"; 45 percent opposed the idea. Most wanted to give sanctions more time to work.[2] Peace groups were organizing. Most corporations and interest groups worried about the costs and disruptions of war.

But, when the Bush administration urged Congress to authorize the use of force, it was able to overcome the Democratic opposition that urged the nation to "stay the course" of sanctions and avoid bloodshed by arguing that a threat of force was needed to ensure a negotiated settlement. After a spirited televised debate, the House voted heavily (250–183), and the Senate voted narrowly (52–47), both along party lines, to authorize the president to use U.S. armed forces if he determined that all diplomatic and peaceful means had been unsuccessful.

Neither the United States nor Iraq expressed much interest in efforts at peaceful solutions promoted by the Algerians, the French, and the Soviets. In fact, Washington sources leaked concern over a "nightmare scenario" that Iraq might simply withdraw from Kuwait and keep its military machine intact. The administration had probably already decided upon war. When Baker finally met Iraqi Foreign Minister Tariq Aziz in Geneva on January 9, neither side offered to compromise. Baker emerged looking grim; the stock market dropped, and the world took a deep breath.

On the evening of January 16, White House spokesman Marlin Fitzwater announced that "the liberation of Kuwait has begun." U.S. Tomahawk missiles, Stealth fighters, and fighter-bombers had begun rocketing and bombing targets in Iraq and Kuwait, in what was to become the most intense air bombardment in world history, involving some 2,500 plane sorties per day. U.S. television showed Defense Department video clips of astoundingly accurate laser-guided bombs entering ventilation shafts or back doors and destroying buildings. Giant B-52s began massive carpet bombing of Iraqi troop positions.

Americans overwhelmingly expressed approval for the air war. In one poll, 79 percent said that the United States "did the right thing in starting military actions against Iraq," and a record-breaking 86 percent approved of President Bush's handling of his job—up 20 percentage points since just before hostilities began[3] and up even more since the feeble 52 percent approval rating registered during the budget dispute the previous October. Protesters, shouting "No Blood for Oil!" and "Support our troops; bring them home," were a distinct minority.

Euphoria over the air war faded a bit, however, when Iraqi Scud missiles exploded in Saudi Arabia and Israel, terrorizing their populations, and when a month went by without Iraq surrendering. CNN broadcasts from Baghdad showed substantial damage to civilians; Kuwaiti crude oil was spilled in the Persian Gulf; thousands of North Africans demonstrated against the bombing. Analysts offered grisly scenarios of a bloody ground war against 545,000 dug-in Iraqi troops, with thousands of dead Americans and postwar chaos in the Middle East.

After about five weeks of the air war, the United States brushed aside Soviet-brokered offers by Iraq to get out of Kuwait and launched a major ground attack. Contrary to most predictions, success was quick and cheap in terms of

The Persian Gulf War was the first significant American military engagement in which women took active part as front-line soldiers.

U.S. lives, with only about 200 Americans killed. American M1A1 tanks, rocket launchers, and unopposed air strikes destroyed the Iraqis' Soviet-made T-72 tanks and slaughtered their troops. U.S. Marines pushed north to Kuwait City. Paratroopers and armored divisions executed an end-run, sweeping rapidly northward to the west of Kuwait and turning east through southern Iraq to cut off the occupation troops in Kuwait (nearly all of whom tried to surrender or flee and many of whom were gunned down in a "turkey shoot") and to smash Iraq's elite Republican Guard on the northern border of Kuwait. Within days, Kuwait was liberated, U.S. troops occupied much of southern Iraq, and a temporary cease-fire was declared. This quick and decisive victory, with few precedents in military history, led to great celebrations in the United States. President Bush's popularity hovered around a 90 percent level of approval; respect for the armed forces soared; optimism reigned. Bush declared that the "Vietnam syndrome" (hesitation to intervene abroad due to the disaster of the Vietnam War) was "licked."

Questions about the long-term effects and costs of the Persian Gulf War began to arise, however. Somewhere on the order of 100,000 Iraqi troops and civilians were apparently killed. Iraq had been returned to a preindustrial state, with most of its oil production and refining, transportation, electricity, water supply, and industry destroyed; postwar epidemics and famine threatened to kill as many as 150,000 children.[4] The Gulf was contaminated with oil; the Kuwaiti oil industry was shut down; and the air was filled with smoke from billions of dollars worth of burning oil, torched by the retreating Iraqis. More than 1 million Kurdish refugees fled into misery in the mountains of Iran and Turkey. Saddam Hussein continued to hold power.

Some Americans also began to wonder exactly how the "new world order" would work out. How many dollars and U.S. troops would be needed in the

Americans' patriotic celebrations of victory over Iraq faded in memory as the ambiguous aftermath of the war unfolded.

Middle East and for how long? Could the Israeli-Palestinian conflict be resolved? Would similar U.S.-led wars have to be fought again and again in various places around the world? Or could a more genuinely collective security system be devised? Still, in the short run and in most respects, the Iraq war was undeniably a great foreign policy triumph for the Bush administration.

The story of the Persian Gulf War illustrates several things about the making of American foreign policy. Foreign policy, especially when it involves war or crisis, is different from domestic policy. For one thing, presidents and others at what we have called the *governmental* level of analysis often play a much more important part and have an unusual degree of autonomy. The ordinary *political* factors of public opinion, interest groups, and so forth are often set aside in favor of considerations of the "national interest," as defined by a small number of national security advisors. Public opinion is not irrelevant, but at times it can be reshaped or ignored. In crisis situations, the public often "rallies 'round the flag," accepting the president's actions, at least as long as the results seem good and there is little disagreement among the elite. If things go wrong, of course, domestic politics can return with a vengeance.

But the Iraq story also illustrates that much of foreign policy is influenced by *structural*, rather than political or governmental, factors. Oil was a big reality in the Middle East. The United States' status as a superpower, with its large population, advanced economy, and enormous military capability, made it easy to take on Iraq, even though Iraq was said at that time to have the fourth largest army in the world. Without these resources, U.S. foreign policy would have been very different. Moreover, the particular structure of the international system in 1990 had important effects. The Soviet Union, which a few years earlier might have prevented action against its then-ally Iraq, now desperately needed Western economic help and was in no position to object to U.S. action. Moreover, the Soviet retreat from Eastern Europe had freed up U.S. forces in Western Europe for use elsewhere. Indeed, if they had *not* been used elsewhere, they might well have been sent home and demobilized, a result that was feared by some national security decision makers. The point is not that structural factors in any simple sense "determined" U.S. policy toward Iraq but, rather, that they made this sort of major commitment of troops possible or even probable in the early 1990s.

FOREIGN POLICY AND DEMOCRACY: A CONTRADICTION IN TERMS?

The decision to make war on Iraq was not exactly the result of a democratic process, as we understand democracy. To be sure, the American people's representatives in Congress voted to authorize the use of force. But the actions leading up to that vote, including the decision to roll back the invasion of Kuwait and the dispatch of hundreds of thousands of U.S. troops to the Gulf, were taken by the executive branch—on its own and working through the UN Security Council. The final decision to declare that negotiation was fruitless and to go to war belonged to the chief executive alone. Throughout, popular sovereignty operated only to a limited extent. Few people participated in the key decisions. It is difficult to argue that public opinion brought about the results. Indeed, the decision to fight immediately after the January 15 deadline seems to have had less than majority support from Americans.[5]

Several features of foreign affairs tend to limit the role of public opinion in policymaking. The sheer complexity of international matters, their remoteness from day-to-day life, and the unpredictability of other countries' actions, all make the public's convictions about foreign policy less certain and more subject to revision in the light of events. The need for speed, unity, and secrecy in decision making, and the concentration of authority in the executive branch, mean that the public can easily be excluded and that government policy can sometimes shape public opinion rather than be shaped by it.

At the same time, however, these limitations are neither total nor etched in stone. The American public plays a bigger part in the making of foreign policy than is sometimes imagined, and how big that role should be is a matter of dispute, an object of the ongoing struggle for democracy.

THE UNITED STATES AS SUPERPOWER: STRUCTURE AND HISTORY

The ability to send more than 500,000 troops to the Persian Gulf region reflected the status of the United States as a "superpower," that is, a nation armed with nuclear weapons, strong enough militarily and economically to project its power into any area of the globe. At the beginning of the 1990s, the United States had a population of about 250 million people: fewer than China's 1.1 billion, India's 850 million, or even the Soviet Union's 291 million, but enough to support the world's largest economy and an annual Gross National Product (GNP) worth about $5 *trillion*. It is worth pausing to think about what "$5 trillion" means: that is $5,000 billion, or $5,000,000,000,000, or about $20,000 for each person in the

The F-117A "stealth" fighter-bomber, a star of the war against Iraq, represents only a small part of U.S. military might.

country. The GNP of the United States was roughly twice that of the Soviet Union or Japan (though Japanese production *per person* was a bit higher than American production *per person*), about 4 times that of West Germany, nearly 10 times that of China, and close to 20 times the GNP of India. (See Table 16.1 for critical U.S. and international economic comparisons.)

This enormous economic power enables the United States to field the most powerful armed forces in the world. At the beginning of the 1990s, we were spending nearly $300 billion per year on our armed forces. More than 2 million men and women were on active military duty, while another 1 million civilians worked for the Department of Defense. According to official statistics (which probably undercount our nuclear arms), the air force boasted 1,000 intercontinental ballistic

	Population (in millions)	GNP (in billions of dollars)	Military Spending (in billions of dollars)	Number of Active Military Personnel	Number of Strategic Nuclear Warheads
United States	249	5,233	299	2,071,000	12,100
Soviet Union	291	2,659	390	4,400,000	11,320
Japan	124	1,914	29	244,000	0
Germany	78	1,415	n.a.	n.a.	0
China	1,118	424	17	3,530,000	284
India	850	335	9	1,500,000	n.a.
United Kingdom	57	818	35	328,000	96
France	56	820	31	559,000	372

Table 16.1
Major World Powers, 1990

Note: Many of these figures are estimates, and some are controversial.
Sources: Central Intelligence Agency, in *The World Factbook 1990*; Department of Defense, *Soviet Military Power 1990*; *World Almanac* 1990, 1991; *World Armaments and Disarmament: Stockholm International Peace Research Yearbook, 1990* (New York: Oxford University Press, 1990), p. 23.

missiles, carrying 2,450 nuclear warheads; 423 strategic bombers, with 5,700 nuclear missile and bomb warheads; 252 strategic interceptors and 4,470 tactical aircraft; 102 huge C-5 air transports; and hundreds of other transport planes. The navy, with 600,000 sailors and 200,000 marines, had 14 aircraft carriers, 3 battleships, 96 nuclear attack submarines (armed with 5,300 nuclear warheads), and 195 other warships, along with amphibious assault ships and 1,962 tactical aircraft. The 780,000-person army was organized into 18 active divisions, backed by large numbers of tanks, artillery, and tactical missiles with many tactical nuclear warheads.[6]

To be sure, U.S. forces did not stand alone in the world. The Soviet Union had squeezed its smaller economy hard to produce a military establishment that looked roughly equal to that of the United States. The Soviets actually had more men and women in uniform—about 3.6 million compared with the United States' 2 million—and more tanks and artillery pieces. They had a few more **ICBMs** (intercontinental ballistic missiles) and **SLBMs** (submarine-launched ballistic missiles)—though these were not thought to be as accurate as their American counterparts—and nearly as many bombers and nuclear warheads as the United States had, enough to lead to a standoff (or total mutual destruction) in any major strategic conflict. By the late 1980s, such conflict seemed remote, however, as the Soviets were starting to pull their tanks and troops out of Eastern Europe, to cut military spending, and to concentrate on economic problems at home. Furthermore, in 1991, the Soviet Union itself renounced communism and broke up into independent republics.

In terms of global influence, then, at the beginning of the 1990s, no other nation had anything even close to the 395 U.S. military bases outside the United States, the ports and ships that controlled the Atlantic and Pacific Oceans, or the rapid deployment capabilities that could project force on any continent. By the 1990s, one could speak of the United States as the *only* superpower.

The superpower status of the United States is a crucial structural fact for understanding international relations and American foreign policy. American power and resources have been important, not only in the intervention against Iraq, but also in the whole series of U.S. actions abroad since World War II. Indeed, some scholars have argued that nearly all great powers, whatever their form of government and society—whether democracy, monarchy, or dictatorship; whether capitalist, Communist, or feudal—tend to behave in similar ways when they face similar world situations.

The story of the gradual emergence of the United States as a superpower was told in Chapter 4. Especially important in that story was the impact of World War II.

The Growth of U.S. Power

When the war ended with Japan's surrender on August 15, 1945, Germany and Japan, devastated by the bombing of their cities and industries, found themselves occupied by Allied forces. Britain and France had also suffered severe damage and were losing their world empires to nationalist forces. But the United States emerged with its economy and population essentially intact, its military forces victorious around the world, and (for a few years, at least) with monopoly control of nuclear weapons. Only the Soviet Union—itself terribly damaged but with a

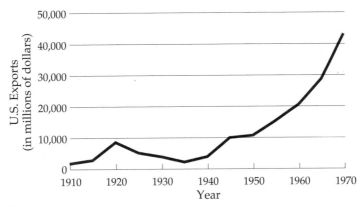

Figure 16.1 Growth of U.S. exports

Source: U.S. Department of Commerce, Historical Statistics of the U.S.: Colonial Times to 1970, *p. 884.*

large population, a substantial economy, and troops occupying most of Eastern Europe—could rival the United States as a world power.

There followed two remarkable decades in which the United States achieved dominance of the world economy. U.S. exports soared, from $4 billion in 1940 to $20.6 billion in 1960, and $43.3 billion in 1970 (see Figure 16.1). U.S. investments abroad jumped nearly as quickly, from $34 billion in 1940 to $85.6 billion in 1960, and $166.9 billion in 1970.[7] American business flourished around the globe. But, at the same time, U.S. foreign policy became entangled in a tense Cold War rivalry with the Soviet Union.

NATIONAL SECURITY AND THE COLD WAR

After World War II, the United States and the Soviet Union found themselves in a series of confrontations. Scholars disagree about the exact causes of the conflicts. Some, like the Truman administration's George Kennan, have argued that the Soviet Union was a strongly expansionist state, driven by Communist ideology and aiming for world domination; it had to be resisted and "contained" at every point on its periphery.[8] Most Americans came to accept this view of the Cold War as a moral battle to resist communism. Scholars of a "revisionist" perspective, on the other hand, have maintained that the Soviets behaved like any other great power, seeking friendly buffer states in Eastern Europe in order to protect themselves against new invasions from the West, such as those of Napoleon, the Kaiser, and Hitler. Revisionists have claimed that the United States misunderstood or misstated Soviet aims, had expansionist plans of its own, and itself took some provocative actions.[9]

Both sides may have a point: throughout history, powerful countries have tended to push up against each other's spheres of influence and to compete for influence and resources; yet ideology (on both sides) clearly also played a part in the Cold War. What is absolutely clear, however, is that American foreign policy was focused, for more than 40 years after World War II, on the Cold War struggle against the Soviet Union and its allies.

Cold War Beginnings

The Cold War began in Europe. In March 1947, President Truman declared (over-simplifying considerably[10]) that "the very existence of the Greek state" was threatened by armed terrorist activities led by Communists; he proclaimed in the **Truman Doctrine** that the United States should help "free peoples" resist "armed minorities or outside pressures." In 1948, the Soviets imposed a Communist regime on Czechoslovakia. After the United States, Great Britain, and France merged their occupation zones of Germany and integrated them into the Western economy, the Soviets tried to eliminate the Western presence in Berlin (an island in the middle of their occupation zone) by blockading all ground traffic, but the United States airlifted supplies and broke the blockade. The United States provided billions of dollars in aid under the **Marshall Plan** to rebuild the economies of its European allies. The Federal Republic of Germany was established; various Communist-dominated regimes were set up in Eastern Europe; the **North Atlantic Treaty Organization (NATO)** was established in 1949 as an anti-Soviet alliance, and the **Warsaw Pact** was set up on the other side. Sharply drawn armed boundaries divided Eastern from Western Europe. Meanwhile, both the United States and the Soviets armed themselves with nuclear weapons, A-bombs and then H-bombs.[11]

The Korean War

The first big armed struggle of the Cold War occurred halfway around the world in Korea. Here, too, historians have disagreed about exactly what happened. Provoked or not,[12] North Korean troops poured across the 38th Parallel on June 25, 1950, and drove south. President Truman, under color of a UN resolution, sent American troops, who engaged in a basically successful but increasingly unpopular war: first pushing North Korean forces out of the South, then marching up through North Korea toward China, but finally being thrown back by Chinese armies to a stalemate in the middle of the country.[13]

The Korean War had many important consequences. Immediately after World War II, most U.S. armed forces had been demobilized and sent home. For

The truckload of American flour being blessed by this Greek Orthodox priest arrived as part of extensive Marshall Plan aid to Europe.

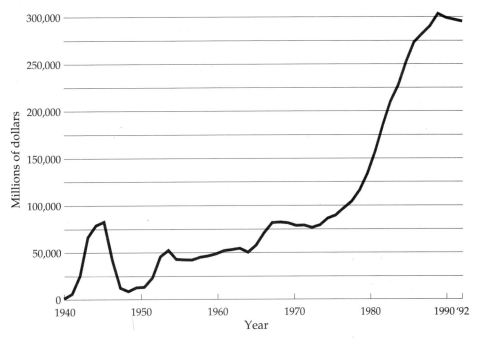

Figure 16.2 U.S. military spending

Source: U.S. Office of Management and Budget, Budget of the U.S. Government, *1992, pp. 30–36.*

the Korean War, the size of the remaining force more than doubled, to 3,636,000 in 1952, and U.S. troop strength never fell much below 2.5 million before the Vietnam War buildup.[14] The military budget nearly quadrupled, from $13 billion in 1950 to $50 billion in 1953, and it stayed close to that level until the Vietnam War.[15] (See Figure 16.2.) The United States took on many new commitments around the world: protecting Taiwan from mainland China; aiding the French colonialists in Indo-China; organizing NATO-like alliances on various Soviet and Chinese borders; rearming Germany; giving anti-Communist military and economic aid; conducting covert operations. Historians have found that some of these moves were worked out well before the Korean War began, as part of a general plan for intensified anti-Communist policies embodied in a National Security Council document (**NSC-68**).[16]

Peaceful Coexistence?

The Korean War ended in 1953. During the relatively tranquil years of the Eisenhower administration, there were negotiations and talk of "peaceful coexistence" between the Soviets and the United States. Indeed, in retrospect, the Cold War struggle in Europe seems essentially to have ended with the 1954 U.S. doctrine of "massive retaliation," whereby nuclear weapons would be used in the event of Soviet aggression against Western Europe, and with the U.S. decision not to interfere with Soviet control of Eastern Europe, despite the Hungarian revolt of 1956. For more than 35 years afterward, both sides spent (wasted?) immense resources on huge armies that faced each other across stable boundaries in Europe, while the two powers and their allies (as well as indigenous nationalists) skirmished in places like Iran, Guatemala, Lebanon, and Indonesia.

Both the United States and the Soviets built large numbers of strategic bombers to deliver their growing stocks of nuclear warheads. Both began ballistic missile programs. The Kennedy administration in 1961 accelerated the building of missiles, escalating the arms race but not ultimately changing the fact that both sides were attaining a sort of nuclear "parity," or rough equality. No surprise attack by either side could prevent nuclear retaliation that would devastate the attacking country. This situation of nuclear stalemate, which came to be called **"mutually assured destruction" (MAD)**, was eventually seen as a source of stability and a basis for arms control agreements. The Kennedy administration also built up conventional weapons capabilities to fight "limited" or "brush fire" wars without a nuclear exchange. It sponsored an unsuccessful exile invasion of Cuba, sent substantial numbers of military "advisors" to Vietnam, and forced the Soviets to remove missiles that they had installed in Cuba.

Vietnam and Détente

As we saw in Chapter 5, "Public Opinion," the Vietnam War, fought in an effort to prevent a "Viet Cong" or National Liberation Front (and North Vietnamese Communist) takeover of South Vietnam, was a major setback for American foreign policy. The war's costs in money (about $172 billion in 1988 dollars) and casualties (47,358 battle dead, 153,303 wounded),[17] as well as the social disruption and moral unease that accompanied it, discouraged intervention abroad for a while. The Nixon administration, slowly extricating itself from Vietnam, pursued a policy of "rapprochement" (closer relations) with China and "**détente**" (relaxation of tensions) with the Soviet Union. It negotiated trade and arms control agreements, including the Strategic Arms Limitation Treaty (**SALT I**).

New Cold War

During the 1970s, at the same time that the United States faced increasing economic competition from Japan and Germany, sharp oil price increases, and inflation, conservative groups like the Committee on the Present Danger argued that

These casualties from the 1968 Tet Offensive added to the total of more than 45,000 American dead and 150,000 wounded in the Vietnam War.

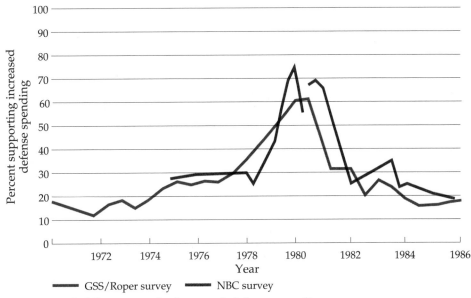

Figure 16.3 Public support for increased defense spending

Source: GSS, Roper, and NBC surveys.

the Soviet Union was rapidly building up its military and intervening in Africa and elsewhere. Although the charges proved to be exaggerated, their impact was increased by the 1979 Soviet intervention in Afghanistan and the Iranians' seizure of hostages from the U.S. embassy in Tehran. There was a tremendous upsurge in public support for military spending and for a strong foreign policy (see Figure 16.3).

The Carter administration reacted with higher defense budgets, a boycott of the 1980 Moscow Olympics, and a halt in grain sales to the Soviet Union. The new Reagan administration in 1981 went still further, more than doubling military outlays, from $134 billion in 1980 to $282 billion in 1987,[18] investing heavily in naval ships and in sophisticated new weapons like the MX ("Peacemaker") ballistic missile, the SDI "Star Wars" missile defense system, and various "Stealth" radar-evading war planes. Reagan spoke of a missile "window of vulnerability" (which never materialized)[19] and of the Soviet Union as an "evil empire." He advocated efforts to roll back Soviet influence all around the world, particularly by trying to overthrow the Soviet-allied regimes in Afghanistan, Angola, and Nicaragua.

Very soon, however, most Americans became convinced that the United States was militarily strong and that no further boosts in defense spending were needed. A record-high 75 percent of the public said in 1980 that the United States should "increase" the amount of money spent on defense, but this percentage dropped as sharply as it had risen, falling near 20 percent by the end of 1981 (look back at Figure 16.3). Moreover, when Mikhail Gorbachev took power in the Soviet Union in 1985, he quickly began making sweeping proposals for arms control and other agreements with the United States. A series of summit meetings helped Gorbachev and Reagan establish a personal relationship and agree on the outlines of a series of treaties, including one on Intermediate-range Nuclear Forces (**INF**), which removed destabilizing medium-range missiles from Europe.

A NEW WORLD ORDER

The End of the Cold War

Since 1989, when the Bush administration took office, a series of dramatic world events has completely transformed international affairs.

With Gorbachev's tacit approval, a series of non-Communist regimes gained power in Poland, Czechoslovakia, and Hungary; in November 1989, the Berlin Wall—the harshest symbol of the Cold War—was breached, and shortly thereafter East Germany gave up its sovereignty to join the West in a reunified Germany. The Soviets, Americans, and others agreed on a **CFE** treaty, drastically reducing the number of conventional forces in Europe; the newly independent Eastern European countries pressed the Soviets to remove their forces entirely, and Western Europe showed much less interest in hosting American troops. Progress was made on **START** (Strategic Arms Reduction Talks).

As Eastern Europe turned toward democracy and capitalism, the Soviet Union cut its military budget, withdrew from Afghanistan, sought peaceful solutions in various Cold War hot spots (Angola, Cambodia, the Middle East), and struggled with proposals for its own democratic and market reforms while its economy declined. By the summer of 1990, President Bush agreed that the Cold War was "over." That fall, a survey of U.S. foreign policy *leaders* found that very large majorities favored negotiating arms control agreements, engaging in trade with the Soviets, exchanging scientists, and "working with Soviet military units to increase stability in the Middle East"; 70 percent even favored "providing economic aid to the Soviet Union to assist it in modernizing its economy." The *general public* expressed more skepticism about whether the Cold War was really over, but substantial majorities favored arms control agreements, Middle East cooperation, trade, and scientific exchanges with the Soviets; they balked only at advanced computer sales, exchanging missile information, or giving economic aid. Many of these opinions (especially among the leaders) had changed sharply from previous years.[20] The large majorities that had once thought that "Russia seeks global domination" had nearly vanished (see Figure 16.4).

Figure 16.4 Declining perceptions of a Soviet threat. The percentages of Americans who agreed that "Russia seeks global domination" declined steadily after 1981.

Source: Roper surveys.

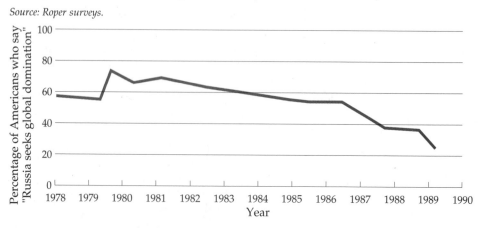

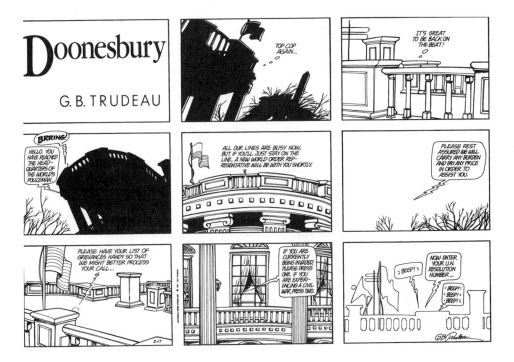

COLLAPSE OF THE SOVIET EMPIRE   As we saw in the opening story, Soviet cooperation was crucial to the U.S.-led effort to drive Iraq out of Kuwait in 1990 and 1991. After the war, U.S.-Soviet relations temporarily came under strain when the Soviets' domestic reforms slowed, when they resisted ethnic and national groups' drives for independence, and when Gorbachev turned to conservative military and Communist party officials to help keep control. But the movement toward democracy and a free enterprise economy soon resumed. Presidents Gorbachev and Bush signed the START nuclear arms reduction treaty at a summit meeting in Moscow in June 1991, and Gorbachev met with the leaders of the "G-7" (the group of seven largest industrialized countries) in London in July, seeking economic aid from the West to help in the transition to a market economy.

The final collapse of the Soviet empire followed a failed coup attempt in August 1991, when hard-line Communist party, military, and KGB (Soviet intelligence) officials tried to overthrow the vacationing President Gorbachev. Boris Yeltsin, freely elected president of the Russian Republic, led popular resistance in Moscow and Leningrad. The coup plotters, winning little popular support and unwilling to slaughter their fellow citizens, quickly gave up. Gorbachev was restored to office. But the central government rapidly disintegrated. The Communist party, which Gorbachev had tried to reform and use as his chief instrument of rule, lost all legitimacy and was banned in most of the Soviet Union. The Soviet Union itself fell apart as the Baltic republics (Estonia, Latvia, Lithuania) became completely independent and virtually all the other republics, even the crucial Ukraine and Russia, then insisted on independence. Power passed to Yeltsin and other leaders of the republics.

President Bush reacted by declaring large unilateral cuts in tactical nuclear weapons (hoping for reciprocity from the republics) and by authorizing assistance with economic reform and food aid to stave off hunger and unrest. The fearsome Soviet adversary of the Cold War era was no more.

New Issues in the New World Order

In the early 1990s, then, the United States faced a completely changed world. The most feared threats of the past—a Soviet-led invasion of Western Europe and a nuclear Armageddon between superpowers—seemed altogether unlikely. But this did not mean that all problems had vanished or that U.S. foreign policy had suddenly become irrelevant. Many questions about national security and international relations remained, some of which were quite difficult to answer.

THE FORMER SOVIET UNION   The collapse of the centralized Communist regime threw into question the fate of the vast Soviet armed forces, with their thousands of nuclear weapons. Would these weapons fall into the hands of the independent republics or warring ethnic factions or Third World countries, perhaps creating new dangers and instability? Could the United States, through economic and political pressure and new arms control agreements, encourage drastic reductions in Soviet weaponry and insist on continued central control of what remained?

The United States also would have to figure out what, if anything, to do about ethnic strife and economic decline in the former Soviet Union that might bring large-scale bloodshed and suffering and waves of refugees heading West. Could or should the United States, amidst its own economic troubles, help rebuild the Soviet economy on a free enterprise basis, or help to prevent widespread hunger and deprivation?

EASTERN EUROPE   What about the countries of Eastern Europe, newly freed from Soviet domination but now struggling to institute democracy and economic reforms? What, if anything, could the United States do to help them? How about ethnic and national tensions of the sort that led to fighting between Serbia and Bosnia (formerly united in Communist Yugoslavia)? Could the United States, NATO, the European Community, or the United Nations work out peacekeeping procedures?

WESTERN EUROPE AND NATO   With the Soviet threat gone, how big a "peace dividend" of money for domestic needs could or should be gained by withdrawing U.S. forces from Western Europe, where about 300,000 troops had been stationed and perhaps $150 billion per year had been spent? What sort of role, if any, remained for the NATO alliance once its chief enemy had disappeared? If NATO's strength and significance declined, could or should the United States retain its heavy influence over European countries? What could be done about economic competition from the increasingly unified European Community?

JAPAN AND THE PACIFIC   Similarly, how much reduction could or should there be in the vast U.S. naval forces in the Pacific Ocean or in the troops stationed in South Korea and elsewhere? Would North Korea, with its nuclear weapons program, constitute a serious threat? What about China? Should economic and political relations be normalized with China's still authoritarian regime? Should democracy be encouraged? How? What could be done to meet the strong economic competition from Japan and the newly industrialized countries of the Pacific, and to open restricted markets like Japan's to American goods?

THE THIRD WORLD   Could regional conflicts be solved in the Middle East and elsewhere? Could aggressive regional powers like Iraq be restrained and disarmed and kept from acquiring nuclear weapons? Would the United States need periodically to send troops and act as the world's policeman? Or might the United Nations or some other body be strengthened for peacekeeping purposes? Could drug shipments and terrorism be stopped? Could the enormous gap between rich and poor nations (especially the poorest nations of Asia and Africa) be bridged? How could or should the United States, other countries, or the United Nations act to encourage democracy and economic reforms in the poor countries? Could the world environment be protected from overpopulation, overdevelopment, and destruction of rain forests, as well as from pollution and global warming, which is more the responsibility of the industrialized than the developing countries?

FOREIGN POLICY AT HOME   What should be done with our own excess nuclear weapons and with radioactive waste from weapons plants, which the government estimated might take 30 years to clean up at a cost of perhaps $100 billion?[21] How much of our spending on defense, which at the beginning of the 1990s still hovered around its Cold War peak of $300 billion per year, could be reallocated to domestic investments? What should be done at home to strengthen our industries and our work force to meet international economic competition?

Questions like these formed the agenda for U.S. foreign policy in the 1990s and will continue to do so into the twenty-first century. Attaining the exalted status of the world's only military superpower has not made foreign policy problems go away. Especially pressing are economics-related questions, as increasing numbers of Americans wonder whether our superpower standing might be undercut or "hollowed out" by economic decline. Even the triumph of the war with Iraq, after all, had been mostly paid for by other countries, such as Germany and Japan. We turn now to the topic of international economic policy.

International Economic Policy

INTERNATIONAL TRADE   At the peak of its world economic power after World War II, the United States presided over a world regime of free trade (advantageous for U.S. exports and investments), in which many countries negotiated lower tariff barriers through the General Agreement on Tariffs and Trade, or **GATT**. Tariffs, duties, quotas, and other means of keeping out foreign exports were reduced in much of the world (although agricultural goods were mostly exempted and certain nontariff barriers grew). Under the Bretton Woods agreement, the U.S. dollar became the reserve currency for most of the world, and the value of other countries' money was pegged to the dollar.

By the late 1960s, however, the rebuilt economies of Germany and Japan began to challenge American goods abroad and in the United States, beginning with automobiles and moving on to electronics. Additional competition came from newly industrialized countries (**NICs**), like South Korea, Taiwan, Singapore, and Hong Kong, and from the increasingly integrated Economic Community (**EC**) of Europe. In August 1970, with the dollar weakening, the United States led the way to abandoning the Bretton Woods agreement. The oil shocks of the 1970s added injury. By the mid-1980s, Americans were importing many more goods than they were exporting, creating a multibillion dollar **trade deficit**. Foreign companies bought American factories and real estate; as more investment flowed in than out, the United States switched from being the world's largest creditor nation to being the largest debtor nation.

Under this competitive pressure, the United States lost some of its enthusiasm for multilateral free trade agreements and, instead, unilaterally pressured other countries (especially Japan and the EC) to lower hidden barriers and subsidies that hurt American exports, while at the same time arranging "voluntary" quotas and other policies to control imports to the United States and working on a North American free trade zone with Canada and Mexico. By 1990, U.S. exports had showed some signs of recovery, but trade remained a major policy concern.

FOREIGN AID   The world is divided into rich nations and poor nations, with such sharp differences between them that they live a totally different kind of life (see Figure 16.5). While the average American enjoys a comfortable home, car, television set, and so on, the average citizen of Ethiopia or Bangladesh struggles for

Figure 16.5 Rich nations and poor nations. Figures are for 1989, GNP per capita, in U.S. dollars.

Source: The World Bank, The World Bank Atlas, 1990, *(Washington, D.C.: The World Bank, 1990), pp. 6–9.*

Switzerland	$32,790
Luxembourg	$28,770
Finland	$26,070
Japan	$25,430
Norway	$23,120
United States	$21,700
Denmark	$22,090
Canada	$20,450
United Arab Emirates	$19,860
Burundi	$210
Bangladesh	$200
Guinea-Bissau	$180
Somalia	$150
Ethiopia	$120
Tanzania	$120
Mozambique	$80

a living and may at any time face a sudden famine or other disaster that will destroy her or his livelihood.

The United States has made some modest efforts to improve the lives of the world's poor, through such programs as Food for Peace, the Peace Corps (providing technical and educational assistance), and World Bank developmental loans, aimed at encouraging free enterprise (often insisting upon stringent financial controls). But spending on foreign aid is very low—only $14 billion, or 1.1 percent of the federal budget, in 1990—and the bulk of it (60 percent) is devoted to military and security purposes.

The huge amount of aid under the Marshall Plan to Europe just after World War II, for example, while aimed at helping Europeans and opening markets for the United States, was also designed to resist communism. Even more pointedly anti-communist were the large Cold War payments to South Korea, Taiwan, and South Vietnam. In recent years, most U.S. aid has gone to allies in the Middle East and around the periphery of the Soviet Union. Israel regularly tops the list, with about $3 billion of "security assistance" (loans and grants for weapons purchases, military assistance, and economic support) in 1990; Egypt got just over $2 billion; and Turkey, Pakistan, and the Philippines came next.[22] (See Figure 16.6.)

Figure 16.6 Where foreign aid has gone. U.S. foreign assistance to three regions of the world is shown in billions of constant 1989 dollars.

Source: Congressional Research Service, in the Washington Post National Weekly Edition, *June 11–17, 1990, p. 7.*

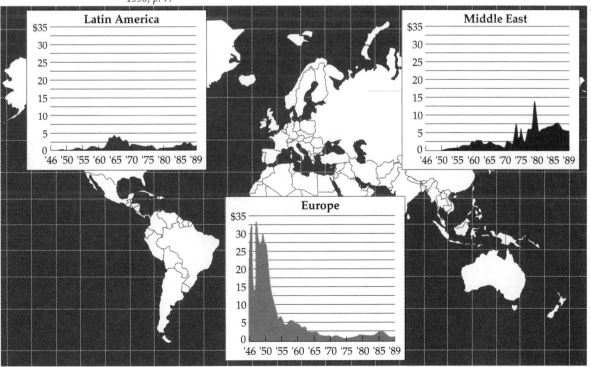

The United States also has been one of the world's largest sellers of weapons to other countries: $10.8 billion worth in 1989 (just behind the Soviet Union's $11.7 billion, but way ahead of France, Great Britain, Germany, and others). After the war with Iraq, many countries clamored to buy successful American weapons. Even while expressing concerns about the arms race and while seeking nonproliferation agreements, the Bush administration proposed to encourage arms sales through a new program of Export-Import Bank loan guarantees, a program pushed by weapons companies like United Technologies, Raytheon, and Martin Marietta.[23]

THE WORLD ENVIRONMENT   During the 1990s, Americans increasingly realized that environmental problems cross national borders. The United States and Canada worked out a joint approach to acid rain; many nations tried to negotiate agreements on oil spills, exploitation of Antarctica, protection of the ozone layer, and prevention of global warming. In several of these cases, however, the Bush administration took a "go slow" attitude, insisting, for example, that the evidence of global warming was not yet sufficient to justify reducing consumption of fossil fuels in order to cut carbon dioxide emissions.

Environmentalists expressed particular concern about the rapid cutting and burning of tropical rain forests, which removes oxygen-producing trees and at the same time pours smoke and carbon dioxide into the atmosphere. However, countries like Brazil resisted any restrictions on their economic development; one possibility was to forgive such countries' debts to U.S. banks in return for preservation of the rain forests.

U.S. relations with nations south of the border were also complicated by the flow of enormous amounts of marijuana and cocaine from Peru, Bolivia, and Columbia into the United States, and by the inability or unwillingness of those countries to stop that profitable trade. U.S. responses included assistance with law enforcement, crop replacement, and the like; a major policy question concerned whether to use U.S. armed forces to seize shipments or eradicate production.

An official seizes cocaine entering the United States on a freighter from Latin America. Stopping illegal drugs that are highly profitable to the exporting countries is a major foreign policy challenge.

WHO MAKES FOREIGN POLICY?

As the Iraq case illustrates, the president and the executive branch are the chief *governmental* decision makers concerning most foreign policy issues, particularly those involving crisis situations, covert operations, and the initiation and conduct of wars. But Congress is often involved in decisions about foreign trade and aid, military bases and contracts, and other matters that directly touch constituents' local interests. People and institutions in the *political* sphere—particularly public opinion, the mass media, and organized interest groups—affect what both Congress and the executive branch do. Moreover, certain aspects of *structure*—especially the population size and the economic and military strength of the United States, and its position in relation to other nations in the international system—affect and constrain what actors in the political and governmental spheres try to do and what they are able to do.

As we discuss the various governmental, political, and structural influences on foreign policy, it is important to remember that different types of foreign policy are made in very different ways. *Crisis decision making*, for example, involving sudden threats, high stakes, and quick action, belongs almost entirely to the executive branch: usually just a small, unified group of top national security officials, like the ones President Bush relied on before and during the war with Iraq. Congress, the public, interest groups, and others usually do not play a part, except to the extent that executive decision makers take their likely reactions into account. *Covert actions* (i.e., secret or semisecret operations) abroad also are usually governed by small groups of executive branch decision makers, with limited supervision by congressional committees.

Broader issues of *defense policy*, on the other hand, including treaties on arms control or military alliances, participation in major wars, the amount of money spent on defense, and so on, involve much more participation by Congress, the general public, interest groups, and others. Here, too, the executive branch ordinarily takes the lead, but it must either respond to domestic political forces or change them. Decisions about military bases and procurement contracts involve congressional committees and interest groups, especially local businesspeople dependent upon bases and weapons-producing corporations. *Foreign trade* and international economic policy, too, sometimes provoke substantial political conflict. The executive branch is generally authorized to negotiate trade agreements with other countries, but Congress has increasingly worried about protecting Americans' jobs and ensuring "fair" trade with Japan and other countries.

The Executive Branch

The president of the United States, as chief executive officer and commander in chief of the armed forces, is the top decision maker on foreign policy issues. To provide the expertise and information for making and carrying out foreign policy, he has help from an enormous number of people and organizations.

THE NATIONAL SECURITY COUNCIL (NSC)   As we saw in Chapter 12, "The Presidency," one of the president's most important White House staff members is his national security advisor, who meets with the president nearly every day on major matters of defense and foreign policy. Occasional advisors with strong intellects and powerful personalities, such as Henry Kissinger, have exerted a major influence on such matters as negotiating the end of the Vietnam War and the opening of diplomatic relations with China. More common, however, have been self-effacing advisors like President Bush's Brent Scowcroft, who quietly helped the president work out strategy and tactics and helped him coordinate the far-flung national security bureaucracy.

The NSC itself, established in 1947, is the main formal body for coordinating the various civilian and military agencies involved in foreign policy. In theory, the NSC includes the vice-president and the secretaries of state and defense, the director of the CIA, and the chairman of the Joint Chiefs of Staff (as advisors), and various other high officials.[24] For the most part, however, the department secretaries stay at their agencies and send deputies to the NSC, which often works in committees to coordinate long-range planning, to oversee covert operations, and to make crisis decisions.

The NSC staff, headed by the national security advisor, constitutes a miniature State Department, CIA, and Pentagon combined, right in the basement of the White House, able to brief the president on any part of the world or on any military or intelligence matter, at a moment's notice. In times of crisis, the NSC's Situation Room becomes a command center for the president, in close touch with the State and Defense Departments and with embassies and military units around the globe.

THE DEPARTMENT OF STATE   The State Department—sometimes known as "Foggy Bottom," for its location in a formerly marshy area of Washington, D.C., off the Potomac—is the president's chief arm for getting day-to-day foreign policy information and for carrying out diplomatic activity. The State Department may tend to push for peaceful or diplomatic solutions, while the Defense Department leans toward military means (wary, however, about Vietnam-like quagmires); Secretaries Baker and Cheney apparently differed in this way over Iraq.

The State Department is organized partly along functional lines, with bureaus or offices in charge of such matters as economic affairs, human rights, international organizations, narcotics, terrorism, and refugees. But it is mainly organized geographically, with bureaus for Europe and Canada, Africa, East Asia and the Pacific, Inter-American Affairs, and the Near East and South Asia. The geographic bureaus have "country desks" devoted to each nation of the world, where at least one foreign service officer is charged with keeping track of what is going on in that country. In the process of faithfully reporting "his" or "her" country's point of view, desk officers, like ambassadors abroad, often identify with that country and provoke charges of "clientelism." This is one reason that presidents and their political appointees often complain that the State Department is "unresponsive," full of officials who have their own point of view and resist policy directions from the top.

Attached to the State Department in Washington, D.C., are also the Arms Control and Disarmament Agency, the U.S. Information Agency, and the Agency for International Development, which oversees foreign economic aid. Of particular interest to young people is the Peace Corps (see "Doing Politics").

Reporting back to the Department of State are about 168 embassies in foreign capitals and 102 consulates scattered around the world.[25] U.S. embassies help American travelers and businesspeople abroad, cultivate good relations with the host country, communicate U.S. policy, and—most important—gather political, economic, and military intelligence, which is conveyed by secure communications

DOING POLITICS

The Peace Corps

The Peace Corps, Senator Hubert H. Humphrey's idea that was brought to life in 1961 in the glow of President John F. Kennedy's "New Frontier," has somehow managed to survive for more than thirty years despite much early criticism. Former President Eisenhower once called it a "juvenile experiment." "An extension of socialism," growled one congressman. Some liberals saw the Peace Corps as a tool of aggressive foreign policy; some foreign countries feared U.S. imperialism and spying. Yet Republican and Democratic presidents alike have continued the program with little change. In a 1991 Rose Garden sendoff of the first volunteers to Poland and Hungary, President Bush declared, ". . . the men and women of America's Peace Corps have built bridges of understanding and goodwill between the people of the United States and . . . scores of other nations."

Since 1961, more than 125,000 young and not-so-young Americans have served in more than 100 nations, from Ghana to Guatemala, Togo to Tuvala, Belize to Botswana, and now Eastern Europe. They have taught English to more than 5 million people; improved agricultural techniques; taught nutrition; given vaccinations; and helped supply potable drinking water. Increasingly they focus on global environmental problems and on the world's children, nearly 100 million of whom are homeless, abandoned, or neglected, using a variety of skills to aid economic development efforts.

"I don't regret for a second having been a Peace Corps Volunteer," said Joseph T. Banas, who lived for three years in Botswana, one of the poorest nations in Africa and the world. As an engineer, Banas helped expand the program there to include drought relief, horticulture, marketing and research, and agricultural teaching. Volunteers don't earn more money than they need to live on, and they often endure primitive conditions, but they do earn a healthy respect for the problems of undeveloped nations. Many find their own lives transformed.

You can learn more by writing to the Peace Corps, Washington, D.C., 20526.

Source: Peace Corps Times, 30th Anniversary Edition, March 3, 1991.

---

to Washington, D.C. The consulates make local contacts and offer on-the-spot assistance to American citizens.

Most ambassadors are career foreign service officers, but increasing numbers (27 percent under President Carter, 40 percent in the Reagan years, and even more under President Bush[26]) have been political appointees, usually heavy financial contributors to the president's party. These amateur diplomats often concentrate on the social side of the job, leaving the heavy work to a professional "deputy chief of mission." Ambassadors generally discover that they do not fully run their own embassies; they preside over officials who report to superiors in many different Washington agencies: the CIA, the Department of Defense, and even the Treasury Department and Department of Agriculture.

THE DEPARTMENT OF DEFENSE The titan of foreign and military policy is the Defense Department, whose 1,060,725 civilian and 2,071,090 military employees dwarf those of any other agency in the U.S. government (by contrast, in 1988 the

State Department had only 25,634 employees). The top echelons of the Defense Department are housed in the Pentagon in Arlington, Virginia, an enormous complex holding more than 23,000 employees. The Pentagon is reputed to have some 17.5 miles of corridors "running into and around 83 acres of offices, drafting rooms, tabulating sections, storerooms, laboratories, libraries, restaurants, auditoriums, dispensaries, banks, a shopping center, a printing plant, and even its own fire department."[27]

The Defense Department is organized in a complex fashion, designed to ensure a clear, hierarchical military command structure while at the same time insisting upon civilian control of the military, and to make the different services work together while keeping their separate identities.

Reporting directly to the president is a civilian **secretary of defense**, who has authority over the entire department; directly under him or her are civilian secretaries in charge of the Departments of the Army, the Navy (including the U.S. Marine Corps), and the U.S. Air Force. Each department includes civilian officials and a military command structure headed by people in uniform: the army and air force chiefs of staff, the chief of naval operations, the commandant of the marine corps, and their subordinates. At the same time, however, these uniformed chiefs of each branch serve together in a body called the **Joint Chiefs of Staff (JCS)**, headed by the chairman of the Joint Chiefs, who reports not only to the secretary of defense, but also directly to the president, and has his own "Joint Staff" of officers. Under the Joint Chiefs are the Strategic Air Command and the Forces Command, along with eight "unified commands," which bring together all military units from all branches for a particular purpose or in a particular geographical region. The actual **chain of command** through which orders pass runs from the president through the secretary of defense and the chairman of the Joint Chiefs to the Commanders in Chief (**CINC**s) of these commands.

The Persian Gulf War, for example, came under the authority of the Central Command (based in Tampa, Florida), which was headed by Army General Norman Schwarzkopf, nicknamed "The Bear," or "Stormin' Norman." Schwarzkopf became something of a television celebrity because of his blunt, confident talk. Under Schwarzkopf were many units, each of which had its own commander: the 400,000 or so U.S. Army troops; the 120 U.S. Navy ships; the tens of thousands of U.S. Marines; the more than 1,780 U.S. war planes; and many troops, ships, and planes from other nations.[28] It was Schwarzkopf's job to coordinate all of these forces under a coherent "air–land" strategic plan so that air force planes and navy battleships would bomb and shell front-line Iraqi troops, not the American soldiers close to them, and would do so at the right time. Schwarzkopf reported to Chairman of the Joint Chiefs Colin Powell and to Secretary of Defense Dick Cheney, both of whom reported directly to President Bush.

The organization of the Defense Department represents a series of shifting compromises. The tensions between civilian control and military hierarchy, and between unity and independence of the services, are long-lasting. *Interservice rivalry* can be fierce. The air force struggled mightily before becoming independent of the army, and struggled again before gaining control of ground-to-ground intercontinental ballistic missiles. The navy, boasting its own airplanes and ground soldiers, has resisted army plans for unification of the services and has argued that its hard-to-detect submarine missile forces provide a secure nuclear deterrent that makes bombers and land-based missiles largely unnecessary. The great successes of the air force's "stealth" war planes in the war with Iraq, however, gave the air force a big boost.

At its best, interservice rivalry can provide healthy competition that makes each service try harder to be effective and helps civilian outsiders make informed decisions about which weapons systems and strategies are best. At its worst, however, such rivalry encourages expensive and unnecessary duplication of capabilities, and results in log-rolling deals that help obsolete systems survive. The long-held strategic doctrine of the "triad," for example (maintaining that strategic nuclear weapons should be deliverable from land, sea, and air), seemed to have as much to do with balance among the U.S. military services as with balance between the United States and the Soviet Union.

Defense politics are special, because the Defense Department is deeply intertwined with the American economy and society. In addition to its 3 million military and civilian employees, another 2 million or so people are employed in defense-oriented industries or depend upon military contracts. Taking into account the multiplier effect of government expenditures, the number of Americans directly or indirectly dependent upon the peacetime military establishment may reach beyond 10 million, or about 9 percent of the total U.S. labor force.[29] These people and their companies are located in every congressional district and can mobilize strong pressures for military spending, even if the same dollars spent on domestic programs could produce more American jobs. Members of Congress, especially members of the key congressional Armed Services Committees and Appropriations subcommittees, tend to be receptive to what the Defense Department wants.

INTELLIGENCE AGENCIES   The exact size is secret, but the U.S. "intelligence community" is very large. It enjoyed especially rapid growth—about 17 percent per year—in the early years of the Reagan administration. Most estimates put its size at around 150,000 to 160,000 employees and its budget at around $10–$13 billion during the late 1980s. The budget may have risen as high as $29 billion in 1992.[30]

The most expensive U.S. intelligence agencies, consuming 75 percent or more of the federal intelligence budget and providing most of the raw intelligence information, are located in the Defense Department. The *National Security Agency* (**NSA**) is headquartered in a 1,912,000-square-foot building in Fort George Meade, Maryland. It spends perhaps $4 billion or more per year, intercepting electronic messages from around the world (including, it is widely believed, Americans' personal telephone calls), analyzing messages, breaking foreign codes, and ensuring the security of U.S. government communications. NSA's computers are said to be the most advanced in the world.[31]

Even larger now is the *National Reconnaissance Office* (**NRO**), which planned to spend about $6.2 billion in 1992. NRO, closely tied to the air force, runs the satellite reconnaissance programs that provided such striking close-up photographs of targets and terrain in Iraq and Kuwait. The most advanced secret satellites are believed to be capable of taking clear-weather daytime photographs of virtually any spot on the earth with such fine resolution that vehicle license plates can be read. At night or in bad weather, radar and infrared images are nearly as good. This leaves foes nowhere to hide and provides a tremendous battlefield advantage. It also makes arms control agreements feasible without needing mutual trust: cheating can be spotted at once by satellite.

Each of the armed services has a separate tactical intelligence unit. The Office of Naval Intelligence, for example, kept track of exactly what the Soviet Navy was doing. Military intelligence organizations may sometimes exaggerate the threats that their services face in order to maximize their own budgets: the air force re-

Close-up surveillance by space satellites gave the United States a tremendous advantage in the war against Iraq; it also helps verify arms control measures. This photo of Egypt and the Sinai peninsula was taken from the space shuttle Atlantis.

ported worrisome "bomber gaps" and "missile gaps" that never materialized, and the navy and army often overestimated Soviet naval and land power.[32] The *Defense Intelligence Agency* (**DIA**) was established in 1961 in order to consolidate, and perhaps replace, the armed service intelligence units, but DIA does not collect much information on its own and has not fully succeeded in its coordination function.

Outside the Defense Department, the *Central Intelligence Agency* (**CIA**) was established in 1947 to advise the National Security Council, to coordinate all U.S. intelligence agencies, to gather and evaluate intelligence information, and to carry out such additional functions as the NSC directed. Soon the "additional functions" came to include covert operations, which have brought the CIA considerable notoriety and have made the agency a more important part of the intelligence community than its approximately 15 percent share of the budget would indicate.

The intelligence-gathering and analysis activities of the CIA rely partly on secret agents within foreign governments and have brought some spectacular successes. Oleg Penkovsky, for example, fed the United States information about Soviet actions and intentions right from within the Kremlin, between about 1952 and 1963, when he was caught and shot by the KGB. The CIA failed, however, to predict such important events as the overthrow of the Shah of Iran in 1979,[33] and its performance with respect to the Iraqi invasion of Kuwait and the collapse of the Soviet Union have been questioned.

The vast bulk of intelligence gathering does not involve spies. Much of it consists of the tedious work of evaluating thousands of publications from other countries and personal reports by diplomats, attachés, and travelers, and writing reports not unlike college students' term papers. Electronic surveillance is increasingly important. One of the CIA's early coups was to listen to East German and Soviet officials by tapping the main telephone exchanges from a tunnel under East Berlin. Now much crucial intelligence is drawn from electronic intercepts by NSA and satellite photographs taken by the NRO.

The CIA's coordination function has always presented difficulties. The director of Central Intelligence (**DCI**) is in a peculiar position, trying to coordinate other agencies while at the same time heading his own; he is bound to be suspected of favoring CIA views. Moreover, the DCI has very little actual control over other agencies; he cannot hire or fire their employees or control their budgets, which are much larger than his own.[34] "National Intelligence Estimates" (**NIE**s), which are supposed to summarize the best judgment of the intelligence community as a whole, remain collective products in which National Intelligence Council analysts piece together the views of separate agencies.

Covert operations, designed to influence or overthrow governments abroad, have become the most visible trademark of the CIA. CIA operations overthrew the Musaddiq government of Iran in 1953 and the Arbenz government of Guatemala in 1954, and, during the 1950s and 1960s, assisted revolts against Sukarno of Indonesia, Castro of Cuba, Lumumba of the Congo, Bosch of the Dominican Republic, Diem of Vietnam, Sihanouk of Cambodia, and others. Some of these target governments were allied with the Soviet Union, but others were simply too leftist or too nationalistic for U.S. officials' taste.[35] After a brief retrenchment in the 1970s, the Reagan administration launched or continued actions against the governments of Afghanistan, Angola, Mozambique, and Nicaragua, among others, under DCI William Casey, whom his biographer described as the last "great buccaneer."[36] Even as the Cold War wound down, some of these operations continued.

Covert operations are supposed to be secret, or at least officially "deniable." (Their targets usually know what is happening, even if the American public does not.) Direct supervision of them is confined to small groups of executive branch officials. Neither Congress nor the public is much involved; since 1980, only the two intelligence committees of the House and the Senate—with limited staffs, and bound by secrecy—need to be informed of major operations.

Critics have objected that these operations infringe on the independence of foreign countries, especially when popular or freely elected governments are overthrown, and that covert operations may tend to contaminate the CIA's intelligence gathering, when such agency clients as the Shah of Iran or the exiled invaders of Cuba are relied upon excessively. But, most important, in terms of our democracy theme, is the objection that the very idea of covert operations conflicts with the idea of democracy. How can the public control government actions it does not know about?

The U.S. public seems ambivalent about this matter. Many Americans, though not necessarily a majority, tell pollsters that they agree with the general idea that the CIA *should* "work secretly inside other countries to try to weaken or overthrow governments unfriendly to the United States"; 45 percent said so in 1990, with 40 percent disagreeing.[37] On the other hand, the public has expressed strong disapproval of several covert actions that have come to light, such as assassination plots against foreign officials, the placing of explosive mines in Nicaragua's harbors, and the secret arms sales to Iran. We cannot be sure how many other covert operations the public would disapprove of if it knew about them.

Broader congressional involvement would no doubt reduce the likelihood of the government secretly doing things that the public might oppose. Now only sporadic disclosures and media uproars bring public opinion into play. Most covert actions are not seriously restrained by democratic processes, and this is a serious problem for the democratic control of foreign policy.

Congress

Congress generally plays a less active role in foreign than in domestic policy. Congressmen and congresswomen believe that their constituents care more about policies that are close to home than those that are far away. Moreover, the executive branch, with its vast intelligence and national security apparatus, has far more information, expertise, and control of events.

To be sure, the Constitution gives Congress the power to declare war and to pass on all spending of money, and gives the Senate the power to approve or disapprove treaties and the appointment of ambassadors. At times, Congress has challenged the president on important issues: trying to force an end to the Vietnam War, resisting the Reagan administration's aid to the Nicaraguan Contras, creating difficulties over the Panama Canal and SALT II arms control treaties. More often, however, Congress has gone along with the executive branch or has been ignored.

The power to declare war, for example, becomes less important when most armed conflicts have been initiated by the executive branch without asking for a declaration. The treaty power means less when the executive branch relies heavily on "executive agreements" (like President Bush's agreement to defend Saudi Arabia) that do not require Senate approval. Even when congressional approval was needed, on nearly all major issues of the Cold War, Congress went along with executive initiatives: appropriating money, for example, for the Marshall Plan, defense buildups, and fighting the wars in Korea and Vietnam. The approval of presidential authority to use force against Iraq involved much more congressional participation than other recent military actions, but, ultimately, it, too, fit this pattern of acquiescence. Congress has also gone along with most covert operations (see "The Struggle for Democracy" box).

Foreign aid appropriations tend to be cut in Congress, except for aid to Israel, which is sometimes increased. In recent years, Congress has pushed for more restrictive or retaliatory trade policies toward Japan and other international competitors.

Many members of Congress, especially members of the Armed Services Committees and defense appropriations subcommittees, are very concerned with "real estate" (military bases) and defense contracts, both of which can have great economic impact on congressional districts and can affect powerful interest groups. In 1991, for example, there were strong congressional moves to cut funding for "Star Wars" antimissile defenses and especially for the expensive B-2 "Stealth" strategic bomber, but not in order to save money on defense as a whole;

The purchase of expensive weapons systems like the B-2 bomber (eventually cut back as the Cold War ended) may result in part from political pressure exerted by their manufacturers.

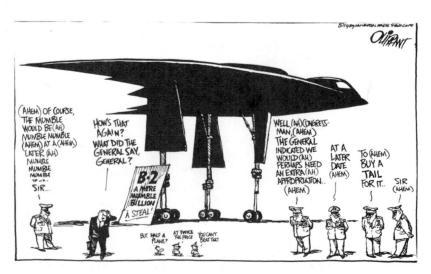

THE STRUGGLE FOR DEMOCRACY

★

Control of War Powers

A decision to go to war is the most important choice that a government can make, but Americans continue to struggle over whether and how such decisions can be subject to democratic control. Although the Constitution grants Congress the power to declare war (Art. I, Sec. 8), presidents have insisted that the need for speed, secrecy, and decisiveness in foreign policy can justify the commander in chief's use of military force with little or no advance approval from Congress or the people.

During the Vietnam War, antiwar Senators Fulbright, Eagleton, Nelson, Javits, and others repeatedly introduced bills to limit the president's power to use military force without explicit congressional authorization; the Senate approved one such bill in 1969 by a 70–16 vote. House resolutions, however, beginning in 1970, required only quick reporting by the president *after* committing troops. Provoked by President Nixon's sudden 1970 incursion into Cambodia, his 1972 "Christmas bombing" of North Vietnam, and the continued bombing of Cambodia, the House and the Senate gradually moved closer together. Further emboldened by Nixon's deepening Watergate troubles, both chambers passed a compromise War Powers Resolution (requiring the president to report any combat involvement and to end it within 60 or 90 days unless Congress approved) in October 1973. After President Nixon vetoed the resolution, the House and the Senate overrode the veto, by the required two-thirds votes, on November 7.

But Senators Thomas Eagleton and Gaylord Nelson, who had sought tight restrictions on executive action, were not at all pleased with the reliance on reporting and after-the-fact congressional review. It is not easy to stop a president after American troops are committed to battle, they pointed out. Eagleton called the resolution a "congressional surrender," passed only because the Democratic leadership, hungry for a symbolic victory over President Nixon, pressured liberals to keep quiet and compromise. He quoted one senator as saying, "I love the Constitution, but I hate Nixon more."[a]

In practice, the War Powers Resolution has made little difference. All subsequent presidents have declared it to be unconstitutional or have ignored it, in such cases as Jimmy Carter's attempted rescue of hostages in Iran, Ronald Reagan's dispatch of troops to Lebanon and the invasion of Grenada, and George Bush's invasion of Panama. President Bush claimed that he had the power to attack Iraq even without a congressional vote. The struggle continues.

[a]Thomas Eagleton, *War and Presidential Power* (New York: Liveright, 1974), pp. 215–216, 220.

Sources: Thomas Eagleton, *War and Presidential Power* (New York: Liveright, 1974); W. Taylor Reveley, *War Powers of the President and Congress* (Charlottesville: University Press of Virginia, 1981), pp. 229–234.

Congress was content to leave the Bush administration's $292 billion spending total untouched while turning any savings to favored projects like the Grumman F-14 (manufactured on Long Island) that the Defense Department wanted to cancel. A furor also greeted Defense Secretary Cheney's proposal to close 31 military bases, as congressmen and congresswomen of both parties responded with desperate letters and testimony in favor of bases in their districts, though Congress, in fact, went along with a depoliticized process to choose which bases to close.

Public Opinion and the Mass Media

It was once thought that public opinion on foreign policy was so uninformed, unstable, and weak that it could not possibly have much effect on policymaking. As we saw in Chapter 5, "Public Opinion," however, this picture is not correct. It is now clear that public opinion does, in fact, have substantial effects on policymaking. Historical studies of such issues as arms control have indicated that policymakers often have taken public opinion into account in making their decisions.[38] Looking at many different foreign policy cases, scholars have found that, most of the time, policy has corresponded with what a majority of the public wants. About two-thirds of the time, too, *changes* in public opinion on foreign policy are followed within a year or so by policy changes moving in the same direction.[39] The State Department has a special office to keep track of what the public is thinking. As we saw in Chapter 12, "The President," the White House listens even more carefully to the public, doing extensive polling of its own.

Still, the executive branch has considerable leeway. Seldom does public opinion demand that particular actions be taken abroad. More often, the public more or less goes along with what the president does, at least until results begin to come in. If the results look bad (the Vietnam War), the public tends to punish the administration with low popularity ratings and rejection at the polls. (See "Politics and Film," on page 598.) If the results look good (the Persian Gulf War, at least initially), the public rewards the administration.

As indicated in Chapter 9, "Voting and Elections," this system of *"electoral reward and punishment"* creates incentives for presidents to do things that will please the public in the long run, but there is leeway in the short run, and presidents sometimes miscalculate how things will work out. Moreover, on many foreign policies that are secret or barely visible, the moment for reward or punishment never comes. The administration can act without being called to account.

Furthermore, the executive branch can often shape public opinion to its own ends, by putting its own interpretation on world events and by creating or encouraging events that will alter the public's thinking. Franklin Roosevelt's secret naval policies in the Atlantic and his economic squeeze on Japan helped provoke hostile actions that led to public acceptance of U.S. involvement in World War II.[40] The Truman administration encouraged Cold War attitudes with exaggerated assertions about Communist threats in Greece and dangers of Soviet conquest of Western Europe. Lyndon Johnson laid the groundwork for the Vietnam War with the charge of "unprovoked" attacks on U.S. destroyers in the Gulf of Tonkin. And President Bush increased public willingness to use force against Iraq by defining Kuwait and Saudi Arabia as vital U.S. interests, sending U.S. troops to the Arabian peninsula, and declaring that sanctions and diplomatic activity were insufficient to free Kuwait. In these and other cases, the mass media have tended to convey the government's point of view to the public. The anti-war Vietnam films were exceptional.

For all these reasons, political scientist V. O. Key, Jr., seems to have been correct—at least concerning foreign policy—when he argued that public opinion only sets up "dikes" that confine policy to certain broad channels.[41] Within those channels, the president and the executive branch largely determine the flow.

Corporations and Interest Groups

The role of corporations and interest groups in American foreign policy is a matter of controversy. Some observers maintain that executive branch officials are motivated entirely by concern for a "national interest" that transcends the selfish interests of any particular group.[42] Others say that conceptions of the national interest are actually determined, in large part, by the narrow interests of wealthy and well-organized individuals and corporations with links to executive decision makers. The truth may lie somewhere in between.

There are indications, for example, that the United States may have begun its free trade and internationalist policies with the New Deal of the 1930s because of the rise of large corporations with operations abroad, especially multinational oil companies and investment bankers. It has been argued that some of these multinational firms made a deal with the Democratic party, getting the free trade laws they wanted in return for supporting the Democrats' social welfare policies, which were not very costly to the capital-intensive firms.[43] According to this line of argument, the great arms buildup and anti-communist policies of the late 1970s and early 1980s (together with the clampdown on social spending and the decline of the Democratic party) were sparked by U.S. corporations that faced sharper foreign competition, that turned against government taxation and regulation, and that insisted on military protection for their markets in the Third World.[44]

There is also some historical evidence of interest group involvement in foreign policy decisions that seemed, on the surface, quite remote from domestic political considerations. A study of U.S. involvement in the Congo (now Zaire) during the 1950s and 1960s, for example, indicates that the U.S. switch from President Eisenhower's backing of the Belgian colonialists to President Kennedy's support for Congolese independence reflected conflicting U.S. financial interests in that mineral-rich country. Many prominent American officials had links, through law firms, stock holdings, and the like, to companies with large amounts of money at stake in the Congo.[45]

American businesses have good reasons to care about U.S. foreign policy. As Table 16.2 indicates, in 1990, each of 20 large American corporations had more than $7 billion in sales abroad. The top three—Exxon, IBM, and General Motors—totaled more than *$150 billion* in foreign revenues that year; Ford, Mobil, and Citicorp were not far behind.[46] Many multinational firms seek free trade policies and diplomatic or military protection abroad. Other firms, especially those relying on U.S. markets but threatened by foreign competition (automobiles, steel, clothing, consumer electronics) have sought government subsidies, or tariffs or quotas against foreign goods.

The defense budget involves big money, as well, and it is seldom disputed that arms manufacturers play a significant part in decisions about weapons systems. The air force's 1991 selection of the Lockheed, General Dynamics, and

POLITICS
AND
FILM

*Hollywood
Against the
Vietnam War*

Hollywood films about World War II that were made during the war years were almost always positive and celebratory, instruments of cohesion that helped the American people pull together for the struggle against Nazi Germany and Imperial Japan. The issues were black and white, the moral choices were clear, and our objectives and methods were generally above reproach. Not so with the Vietnam War. Americans were conflicted about that war, and many were downright opposed. This attitude among the public was reflected in the kinds of movies that Hollywood made about Vietnam.

The only film made by a major studio that unambiguously supported the objectives and methods of the Vietnam War was *The Green Berets*, directed by and starring John Wayne. The story revolves around a liberal reporter, played by David Janssen, who first opposes the war but who then passionately approves of it after witnessing Viet Cong atrocities and the good deeds of American soldiers. The film was a flop at the box office.

Other films focused on portrayals of the moral dilemmas at the center of the Vietnam conflict. In *Apocalypse Now*, director Francis Ford Coppola builds his story on Joseph Conrad's great novel, *Heart of Darkness*, about a journey into the moral quagmire. Coppola's film is an unrelenting picture of violence, corruption, horror, madness, and despair, alternating with brief moments of humor and humanity.

The journey that we follow is that of Captain Willard, played by Martin Sheen. Moviegoers are unlikely to forget the madmen whom he encounters: Colonel Kilgore (Robert Duvall), whose helicopter gunships assault a hostile Vietnamese hamlet in order to secure a beachhead where the surfing is unsurpassed, and Green Beret Colonel Kurtz (Marlon Brando), who lives as a violent god among the Montagnard tribespeople.

Other films suggest that, in the midst of the moral quagmire and confusion about the purposes of the war, all that one can depend on are one's buddies. In Michael Cimino's Academy Award-winning movie (Best Picture, Director, and Supporting Actor, Christopher Walken) *The Deerhunter*, the tight bonds that form the basis of the lives of a group of men from a small industrial town are shattered forever by the Vietnam War, though the central figure in the film (Robert DeNiro) struggles to the end to salvage some remnants of their previous lives together. Director Oliver Stone, a former combat soldier in Vietnam, won an Academy Award as Best Director for his hair-raising portrayal of war on the ground in *Platoon*. Amidst the horror of the war, in a world of mixed-up moral values, all that counts is survival, and all that one can count on is the person sharing one's foxhole.

Several movies make their antiwar point through the stories of soldiers disabled in a war that makes no sense to them. In *Coming Home*, Jane Fonda

plays the wife of a gung-ho and slightly crazy marine officer (Bruce Dern), whose views on the war are transformed by her love affair with a wheelchair-ridden combat veteran, played by Jon Voight. Director Hal Ashby makes the Voight character both saintly and manly; a tower of strength to the other disabled veterans and a pillar of the antiwar movement, who chains himself and his wheelchair to the gates of the marines' recruiting center to protest the war. Oliver Stone's *Born on the Fourth of July* is based on the book of the same name, written by antiwar activist and paraplegic Ron Kovic. Tom Cruise plays the title role in this film that follows Kovic from all-American boy and believer in the Vietnam War as a crusade to stop the spread of communism, to the confusions and hell of the Vietnam battlefields where he is wounded, the grim veterans hospital where he begins his rehabilitation, and finally his agonizing journey to self-realization and political activism against the war.

Hollywood also produced a number of films whose theme was the purported betrayal of the American fighting man. In Sylvester Stallone's *First Blood*, a Vietnam vet (Rambo) is forced into a war of revenge against a small Pacific Northwest town after the local police unjustly harass and jail him. Stallone, who wrote the screenplay, in addition to playing the leading role, wanted to show how unwelcome vets felt back home, aliens in a country that was ashamed about the war it had sent them to fight. Rambo's final speech is a passionate summary of often heard complaints: resentment at being called "baby killers" by antiwar activists; anger at being trained for tasks of destruction and mayhem that make them unable to reintegrate into society; and rage at being asked to fight a war that the politicians would not allow the military to win. The ultimate betrayal of the American fighting man, abandoning him to the enemy, is the theme of *Rambo, First Blood Part II*, in which Stallone is launched on a mission to rescue Americans held as POWs in Vietnam, and *Uncommon Valor*, in which Gene Hackman plays a father who must buck the U.S. government itself in order to rescue his son from a prison camp.

The Vietnam War, like no other war in American history, is almost universally cast in negative terms in Hollywood films. Though filmmakers disagree wildly among themselves concerning what was amiss about that war, almost none of them saw anything of value in it.

Table 16.2 *Foreign Revenues of U.S. Corporations, 1990*		
Company	Foreign Revenue *(in billions of dollars)*	Foreign proportion of total revenue
Exxon	79.0	75%
IBM	42.0	61
General Motors	38.0	30
Ford Motor	36.0	37
Mobil Oil	32.0	55
Citicorp	21.0	55
Texaco	17.5	43
du Pont	17.4	44
ITT	11.6	45
Philip Morris	10.5	24
Dow Chemical	10.3	52
Procter & Gamble	9.6	40
Chevron	8.6	22
General Electric	8.3	14
Eastman Kodak	8.2	44
Amoco	8.2	28
Xerox	8.1	42
United Technologies	7.8	36
Hewlett-Packard	7.2	55
Digital Equipment	7.1	55

Source: Forbes, July 22, 1991, pp. 286–287.

Boeing Corporations to build $95 billion worth of F-15 Eagle fighters, for example, followed a five-year technical and political battle in which the winners and the losers (Northrup and McDonnell Douglas) brought every kind of pressure to bear; Senator Sam Nunn of Georgia (Lockheed's home state) was thought to be pivotal in the choice.[47] Some corporations' efforts have crossed over into the illegal; former Assistant Secretary of the Navy Melvyn Paisley, once in charge of all navy procurement, pled guilty to charges of bribery and conspiracy in a long-running scheme in which such companies as Martin Marietta, Unisys, and United Technologies apparently paid for confidential information in order to rig their weapons bids.[48]

Besides business corporations and trade associations, certain ethnic groups sometimes affect U.S. foreign policy. This is most obvious in the case of U.S. policy toward Israel, in which widespread public sympathy toward that country is reinforced by the efforts of the American-Israel Public Affairs Committee (**AIPAC**) and by various organized groups representing Jewish Americans.[49] Greek Americans have pushed for U.S. opposition to Turkish rule over part of the divided island of Cyprus; black groups strongly opposed apartheid in South Africa; and some Mexican American groups have begun having an input into U.S. policies toward Mexico, including the establishment of a free trade zone.

Structural Factors

Some of the most important factors that affect U.S. foreign policy operate in the *structural* sphere. One is the enormous economic and military might of the United States. The strength of the U.S. economy is what makes it possible to produce war planes, ships, and ground forces that can operate virtually anywhere in the world, giving the United States the capacity to intervene where it chooses. Countries with the capacity to act as great powers tend to do so.

By the same token, the size of the U.S. economy and its deep involvement in world trade and investment have created U.S. "interests" almost everywhere. Any country where Americans might want to sell something, buy something, or build factories may evoke foreign policy objectives: lowered tariff barriers, political stability, or a sound "business climate" for U.S. investments. These structural facts produce foreign policy goals.

Not only structural features of the United States itself but also the place of the United States in the structure of the entire international system affects U.S. foreign policy. During the nineteenth century, for example, when the growing U.S. economy remained considerably smaller than that of Great Britain, the United States could "free ride" on the order-producing and free-trade-enforcing efforts of the British; however, when the United States became the greatest industrial power and then the biggest world trader, it took over the responsibilities of a world leader, or "hegemon."[50]

More broadly, the overall *shape* of the international system makes a great difference. A *"multipolar"* world, with many different nations of roughly equivalent power, would call for very different U.S. foreign policies than did the *"bipolar"* world of the U.S.–Soviet Cold War or would a *"unipolar"* world of U.S. dominance.

FOREIGN POLICY AND DEMOCRACY

Democratic control over foreign policy is incomplete. In this respect, the American political system tends to fall short of the ideals of popular sovereignty and political equality.

True, public opinion is often taken into account, either indirectly, through the public's elected representatives in Congress, or directly, through the executive branch's responsiveness to what the public wants and its anticipation of electoral punishment if it fails to deliver. Still, the centralization of decisions in the executive branch means that popular participation is quite limited. Secrecy means that the public often does not know what the government is doing and hence cannot hold it responsible. Government control of information means that the public sometimes can be deceived or misled, acquiescing in policies that it would resist if it were fully informed. And interest groups sometimes push policy in unpopular directions.

As more and more Americans become aware of international events, insist on knowing what their government is doing, and demand government responsiveness to the popular will, democratic control of foreign policy may increase. This is particularly likely to be true if the political parties put aside "bipartisanship" on foreign affairs, and if the opposition party vigorously criticizes government policy. But there is no guarantee they will do so. In this area, the struggle for democracy continues.

SUMMARY

The United States has become the world's only superpower, with a much larger economy and much more powerful armed forces than any other nation. It grew into this role in the course of 200 years, beginning with expansion and settlement westward and the development of an industrial economy, and then actively moving onto the world stage in World War I and World War II.

For more than 40 years, American foreign policy was focused on the tense Cold War confrontation with the Soviet Union, competing for influence in Europe, fighting Soviet allies in Korea and Vietnam, and skirmishing over the Third World. When the Cold War faded at the end of the 1980s and the Soviet Union collapsed at the beginning of the 1990s, attention turned toward regional conflicts (including the Iraq war), international economic competition (especially from Germany and Japan), efforts at transition to democracy and free markets in the Soviet Union and Eastern Europe, problems of world poverty, and the global environment.

Foreign policy is largely made in the executive branch, where the president is assisted by a large national security bureaucracy, including the National Security Council, the Departments of Defense and State, and various intelligence agencies. Congress tends to be little involved in crises or covert actions, and generally goes along with major decisions of defense policy; it asserts itself chiefly on matters of foreign trade and aid, military bases, and procurement contracts. Public opinion affects policy, but this influence is limited by the executive branch's centralization of decision making, secrecy, and control of information. How large a part interest groups and corporations play is disputed but probably substantial. Structural factors, including U.S. economic and military strength and the nature of the international system, strongly affect what policies seem feasible or desirable.

Democratic control of government is more difficult and less complete in foreign than in domestic policy.

To Ponder

1. Why did the United States, rather than some other country, emerge as the world's greatest power?

2. Could the Cold War have been avoided?

3. Would it be desirable to increase democratic control over foreign policy? Would it be possible? How?

4. How can future wars be prevented?

5. Should rich countries help poor countries improve their lot? How?

6. How can the global environment be protected?

Suggested Readings

Allison, Graham. *Essence of Decision: Explaining the Cuban Missile Crisis.* Boston: Little, Brown, 1971.

> A classic study of how the 1962 Cuban Missile Crisis decisions were made, emphasizing bureaucratic conflict.

Kegley, Charles W., Jr., and Eugene R. Wittkopf. *American Foreign Policy, Pattern and Process*, 4th ed. New York: St. Martin's, 1991.
   Thoroughly describes the institutions and processes of foreign policymaking.

Krasner, Stephen D. *Defending the National Interest: Raw Materials Investments and U.S. Foreign Policy.* Princeton, NJ: Princeton University Press, 1978.
   Emphasizes the role of executive decision makers and conceptions of the national interest.

LaFeber, Walter. *America, Russia, and the Cold War, 1945–1984*, 5th ed. New York: Knopf, 1985.
   A clear, brief history of the Cold War.

Marchetti, Victor, and John D. Marks. *The CIA and the Cult of Intelligence.* New York: Knopf, 1974.
   An inside look at a number of intelligence operations.

Rielly, John R., ed. *American Public Opinion and U.S. Foreign Policy 1991.* Chicago: Chicago Council on Foreign Relations, 1991.
   What kinds of foreign policies the public favors and how preferences have changed.

Russett, Bruce M. *Controlling the Sword: The Democratic Governance of National Security.* Cambridge, MA: Harvard University Press, 1990.
   Argues that public opinion is much more important in making foreign policy than was previously thought.

Notes

1. Bob Woodward, *The Commanders* (New York: Simon & Schuster, 1991); Gerald F. Seib, "How President Bush Deftly Orchestrated Swift Victory over Iraq," *Wall Street Journal*, March 1, 1991, pp. A1, A4; Andrew Rosenthal, "Scowcroft and Gates: A Team Rivals Baker," *New York Times*, February 21, 1991, p. A6.

2. John R. Rielly, ed., *American Public Opinion and U.S. Foreign Policy 1991* (Chicago: Chicago Council on Foreign Relations, 1991); see also Michael Oreskes, "Poll Finds Americans Divided on Sanctions or Force in Gulf, *New York Times*, December 14, 1990, pp. A1, A8.

3. Michael R. Kagay, "Public Opinion: Approval of Bush Soars," *New York Times*, January 19, 1991, p. A7.

4. Patrick E. Tyler, "Health Crisis Said to Grip Iraq in Wake of War's Destruction," *New York Times*, May 22, 1991, p. A4; "U.S. Officials Believe Iraq Will Take Years to Rebuild," *New York Times*, June 3, 1991, p. A1; "Iraq's War Toll Estimated by U.S.," *New York Times*, June 5, 1991, p. A5.

5. Andrew Rosenthal, "Americans Don't Expect Short War," *New York Times*, January 15, 1991, p. A13.

6. *Statistical Abstract of the United States, 1990*, pp. 337–339; *New York Times*, May 23, 1990, p. A12.

7. *Historical Statistics of the United States: Colonial Times to 1970*, Part 2, pp. 868–869, 884.

8. "X" (George F. Kennan), "The Sources of Soviet Conduct," *Foreign Affairs*, Vol. 25 (July 1947), pp. 566–582.

9. Gabriel Kolko, *Main Currents in Modern American History* (New York: HarperCollins, 1976).

10. Lawrence S. Wittner, *American Intervention in Greece, 1943–1949* (New York: Columbia University Press, 1982).

11. Walter LaFeber, *America, Russia, and the Cold War, 1945–1984*, 5th ed. (New York: Knopf, 1985) gives a good brief history of the Cold War.

12. See Bruce Cumings, *The Origins of the Korean War, Volume Two: The Roaring of the Cataract, 1947–1950* (Princeton, NJ: Princeton University Press, 1990).

13. David Rees, *Korea: The Limited War* (New York: St. Martin's, 1964).

14. *Historical Statistics*, p. 1141.

15. *Historical Statistics*, p. 1116.

16. Samuel Wells, "Sounding the Tocsin: NSC 68 and the Soviet Threat," *International Security* (Fall 1979), pp. 116–158.

17. *Statistical Abstract, 1990*, pp. 336, 340. Some give a figure of 58,000 for total U.S. *war-related* deaths in Vietnam.

18. *Statistical Abstracts, 1990*, p. 330. In constant (1982) dollars, spending increased from $164 billion to $250 billion.

19. Tom Gervasi, *The Myth of Soviet Military Superiority* (New York: HarperCollins, 1986).

20. Rielly, *American Public Opinion*.

21. Michael Arndt, "Study: Cleaning up Nuclear Arms Plants Will Take Years, Cost Billions," *Chicago Tribune*, February 12, 1991, p. 4.

22. Congressional Quarterly, *Weekly Report*, February 10, 1990, p. 409.

23. Clyde H. Farnsworth, "White House Seeks to Revive Credits for Arms Exports," *New York Times*, March 18, 1991, pp. A1, C8.

24. Charles W. Kegley, Jr., and Eugene R. Wittkopf, *American Foreign Policy, Pattern and Process*, 4th ed. (New York: St. Martin's, 1991), p. 387.

25. Figures for 1988, from Harold W. Stanley and Richard G. Niemi, *Vital Statistics on American Politics* (Washington, D.C.: Congressional Quarterly Press, 1990), p. 320.

26. Kegley and Wittkopf, *American Foreign Policy*, p. 368.

27. C. W. Borklund, *The Department of Defense* (New York: Praeger, 1968), pp. 95–97; *World Almanac, 1990*, p. 660.

28. *Chicago Tribune*, February 13, 1991, p. 4.

29. Kegley and Wittkopf, *American Foreign Policy, Pattern and Process*, 3rd ed. (New York: St. Martin's Press, 1987), p. 389.

30. Kegley and Wittkopf, *American Foreign Policy*, 4th ed. pp. 383–384; Victor Marchetti and John D. Marks, *The CIA and the Cult of Intelligence* (New York: Knopf, 1974); Patrick E. Tyler, "The Task: Slip Spies into the New World Order," *New York Times*, May 19, 1991, Sec. 4 pp. 1, 5.

31. James Bamford, *The Puzzle Palace* (New York: Penguin, 1983); *New York Times*, May 19, 1991, Sec. 4, p. 5.

32. Harry Rowe Ransom, *The Intelligence Establishment* (Cambridge, MA: Harvard University Press, 1970), pp. 103–104.

33. Nathan Miller, *Spying for America* (New York: Paragon, 1989), pp. 329, 375, 380, 390.

34. Steven J. Flanagan, "Managing the Intelligence Community," *International Security*, Vol. 10 (Summer 1985), pp. 58–95.

35. David Wise and Thomas B. Ross, *The Invisible Government* (New York: Random House, 1964).

36. Joseph E. Persico, *Casey: From the OSS to the CIA* (New York: Viking, 1990), p. 572.

37. Rielly, *American Public Opinion*.

38. Thomas W. Graham, *The Politics of Failure: Strategic Nuclear Arms Control, Public Opinion, and Domestic Politics in the United States, 1945–1985*, PhD dissertation, Massachusetts Institute of Technology, 1989; Bruce M. Russett, *Controlling the Sword: The Democratic Governance of National Security* (Cambridge, MA: Harvard University Press, 1990).

39. Alan D. Monroe, "Consistency Between Public Preferences and National Policy Decisions," *American Politics Quarterly*, Vol. 7 (January 1979), pp. 3–19; Benjamin I. Page and Robert Y. Shapiro, "Effects of Public Opinion on Policy," *American Political Science Review*, Vol. 77 (March 1983), pp. 175–190.

40. Robert Dallek, *Franklin D. Roosevelt and American Foreign Policy, 1932–1945* (New York: Oxford University Press, 1979).

41. V. O. Key, Jr., *Public Opinion and American Democracy* (New York: Knopf, 1961).

42. Stephen D. Krasner, *Defending the National Interest: Raw Materials Investments and U.S. Foreign Policy* (Princeton, NJ: Princeton University Press, 1978).

43. Thomas Ferguson, "From Normalcy to New Deal: Industrial Structure, Party Competition, and American Public Policy in the Great Depression," *International Organization*, Vol. 38 (1984), pp. 41–94.

44. Thomas Ferguson and Joel Rogers, *Right Turn: The Decline of the Democrats and the Future of American Politics* (New York: Farrar, Straus & Giroux, 1986).

45. David N. Gibbs, *The Political Economy of Third World Intervention: Mines, Money, and U.S. Policy in the Congo Crisis* (Chicago: University of Chicago Press, 1991).

46. "U.S. Corporations with the Biggest Foreign Revenues," *Forbes*, July 22, 1991, pp. 286–287.

47. *New York Times*, April 24, 1991, pp. A1, C5.

48. Neil A. Lewis, "Ex-Naval Official Makes Guilty Plea in Bid-Rigging Case," *New York Times*, June 15, 1991, pp. A1, A18.

49. Edward Tivnan, *The Lobby* (New York: Simon & Schuster, 1987).

50. David Lake and Jeffrey Friedan, *International Political Economy* (New York: St. Martin's, 1991).

17

*Economic
Policy*

REAGAN'S ECONOMIC POLICY

It's a new beginning. . . . America hasn't been working. (Ronald Reagan, postelection press conference, November 5, 1980)

The country was in an economic mess, and newly elected President Ronald Reagan was going to do something about it. Too much government, he believed, was the cause of slow economic growth, low productivity, inflation, and America's deteriorating position in world trade. His solution was simple: "Get government off the backs of business and the American people." The Reagan strategy was to cut taxes for upper income groups and corporations, to cut social spending programs, to decrease the regulatory burden on business, and to dampen inflation with tight money policies (with the help of the Federal Reserve Board).[1]

Ronald Reagan pretty much had his way with Congress in instituting these changes. The results were not, however, exactly what he and his supporters expected. To be sure, the regulatory climate for business improved, the economy grew steadily (if very slowly) from mid-1983 to the end of Ronald Reagan's second term, federal taxes were reduced, and inflation was curbed.

On the other hand, the federal budget deficit grew at a rate that was unprecedented.[2] Income and wealth inequality became much more pronounced. Deregulation contributed to problems of safety in the airline and mining industries, and to huge losses in the savings and loan industry. Meanwhile, average wages and median family income barely inched upward. The savings rate and business investment, rather than increasing, actually declined. Investment flowed, moreover, not to new plant and equipment, or to research and development, but primarily to such unproductive activities as hostile corporate takeovers, leveraged buyouts, junk bonds, and tax shelters. These developments accelerated the decline of the United States in the world economy, which had been going on for some time. In 1986, (then) West Germany pulled ahead of the United States as the world's largest exporter. In 1987, the Tokyo Stock Exchange's share of world equity capital passed that of the New York Stock Exchange. By 1988, the United States had lost its lead in world GNP per capita. By the same year, only 1 of the top 25 banks in the world were American owned; 15 had been in American hands in 1970. By 1989, only 5 of the world's largest 25 corporations were American.

This story of President Reagan's economic policy and its mixed results touches on many of the topics discussed in this chapter. Our objective is to show how economic policies are made and how, once enacted, they affect the operation of the American economy and the well-being of American citizens. We will focus attention on **fiscal policies**, having to do with taxing and spending; **monetary policies**, having to do with the money supply and interest rates; and regulatory policies, having to do with public restraints on business activities. We will look at some of the most pressing issues of contemporary American politics, including the deficit, taxes, and deregulation. Because of space limitations, we will not talk about agricultural, trade, and labor policies, though many of our findings are relevant to these policy areas as well. We will see not only how government policies affect the economy but also how the structure of the economy shapes what government does. We will also pay attention to how government economic policies reflect and influence the quality of democracy in the United States.

WHY GOVERNMENT?

Governments in all modern capitalist societies play a substantial role in the management and direction of their economies. No government today would dare leave problems like **recession**, depression, trade imbalances, or **inflation** to work themselves out "naturally." Citizens and leaders in Western democracies have learned that the free market economy, left to itself, is subject to periodic collapse, and bouts of inflation, and unemployment. The trauma of the worldwide Great Depression in the 1930s was the crucial event that etched this lesson into the minds of virtually everyone.

The willingness to use government in order to manage the economy has been enhanced by its relative success since the end of World War II. While economic troubles are still with us, modern fiscal and monetary tools have proved to be surprisingly effective in easing the swings of the business cycle and in stimulating economic growth.

Government must play a role, moreover, because its purchases of goods and services are so substantial (the federal government is the largest customer in the United States, the biggest borrower, and the biggest employer) that its actions inevitably have an impact on the economy. Given this presence, it would be difficult for any government to deny responsibility for what was happening in its national economy.[3]

Government responsibility for the state of the national economy is now so widely accepted that national elections are often decided by the voters' judgment of how well the party in power is carrying out this responsibility. When times are good, the party in power is very likely to be reelected; when times are bad, the party in power has an uphill battle staying in office.

THE TOOLS OF ECONOMIC POLICY AND THE DEBATE ABOUT THEIR USE

Government actions affect the inflation rate, the level of unemployment, and the growth of income and output in the national economy. This always has been so. What is new since World War II is that government leaders, economists, and citizens know this to be true, and insist that government use whatever means it has available to ensure good economic outcomes.

Government leaders attempt to do this by adjusting their fiscal and monetary policies (together called **macroeconomic** policy, because the object of attention is the performance of the economy as a whole). The objective of macroeconomic policy is to achieve full employment, steady economic growth, and stable prices. The method used is to adjust the money supply, government spending, and taxes in such a way that total **demand**—what is spent by government, consumers, and business—is roughly in line with the productive potential of the economy.[4] Government can alter total demand by raising or lowering its own spending, leaving more or less money in the pockets of individuals and companies by raising or lowering taxes, and adjusting interest rates so that money is easier or more difficult to get.

Fiscal Policy

Fiscal tools are not easy to use, however. Decisions about how much government should spend or what level and kinds of taxes ought to be levied are not made simply on the basis of their potential effects on economic stability and growth. Many other issues come into play.

Federal spending, for instance, cannot be easily adjusted up or down as economic conditions change. Farmers want federal crop subsidies to continue, regardless of macroeconomic effects. The elderly want Social Security and Medicare benefits to keep pace with inflation. Nor is it easy to adjust tax rates in response to changing economic conditions. The legislative process is cumbersome and time consuming, with many interests involved, so changes in tax policy cannot be done annually.

Finally, changes in spending and taxing take so long to bring about that there is considerable danger that policies will be inappropriate by the time they filter into the economy. A tax cut to stimulate a sluggish economy, for instance, may kick in just as the economy is entering a period of inflation.

Monetary Policy

Actions by the Federal Reserve Board (described in detail later) affect how much money is available to businesses and individuals in banks, savings and loans, and credit unions. The more money that is available and the lower the interest rates at which money can be borrowed are, the higher overall spending is likely to be. If the Fed wants to increase total demand in the economy, it increases the money supply and lowers interest rates. If it wants to slow the economy down, it decreases the money supply and increases interest rates.

Monetary policy decisions of the Federal Reserve Board influence the nation's interest rates.

The Fed does this in three ways. First, it buys or sells federal securities from private brokers or dealers. When it buys, it injects money into the economy; when it sells, it takes money from financial institutions and lowers the stock of money in private circulation. Second, the Fed can make it easier or more difficult for member banks to borrow from the Federal Reserve to cover short-term deficits by changing the **discount rate** (the interest rate that it charges member banks). If the discount rate is high, member banks must pay more to borrow, decreasing the amount of money in circulation; if it is low, member banks must pay less, increasing the amount of money in circulation. Third, the Fed can change how much banks must have on hand to cover outstanding loans (called "reserve requirements"). If the Fed buys government securities, lowers the discount rate, and lowers the reserve requirement, interest rates in the economy will decline, because money is plentiful. Interest rates will rise if the Fed moves in the other direction in these three areas.

Political leaders and professional economists now believe that effective macroeconomic policy requires that attention be given to both fiscal and monetary issues,[5] and that they be used in ways that do not work at cross-purposes. It would not do, for instance, to have fiscal policy encouraging economic expansion and monetary policy choking it off.

The Debate About the Role of Government in the Economy

People may agree that government must play an important role in managing the economy, but they disagree about how it should do it. Debate revolves around four main alternatives: Keynesianism, monetarism, supply side economic policy, and industrial policy.

KEYNESIANISM In his classic work, *The General Theory of Employment, Interest, and Money*, English economist John Maynard Keynes showed that capitalist economies do not consistently operate at a level that fully employs a nation's workers or keeps its factories operating. The reason is that total demand is rarely high enough. The solution, he suggested, is for government to fill the gap during slack times by increasing its own spending or cutting taxes so that businesses and consumers might increase theirs. When demand is too high and triggers inflation (too many dollars chasing few goods), government should cut spending or increase taxes.

The Keynesian approach dominated economic policy in the United States and Western Europe for three decades following World War II.[6] The Kennedy tax cut of 1964 was sold to the public, Congress, and the business community by Presidents Kennedy and Johnson in explicitly Keynesian terms.[7] Even Republican President Richard Nixon joined the bandwagon, proclaiming in a *Newsweek* cover story in 1971 that "we are all Keynesians now."

Keynesianism is consistent with an activist government role. Since the economy is almost always operating at less than full capacity, it justifies expansive government programs. Keynes offered no advice on which programs to expand; his theory is indifferent to what government spends its money on. His theory only requires that government fill the demand gap. Since the World War II, Keynesian expansions in the United States have been mostly fueled by defense spending. What Keynes failed to appreciate, however, was the political difficulty of slashing

According to economist John Maynard Keynes, the traditional problems
of unemployment can be eased by government fiscal policies. Here
people protest what they believe to be President Bush's unwillingness to
take strong fiscal measures to stimulate the economy.

government spending once groups in the population, ranging from farmers to
military contractors, came to look at federal monies as a right, even when demand
was too high and spending needed to be cut.

MONETARISM   Monetarists like economist Milton Friedman argue that the key to
a healthy economy is the proper management of the supply of money and credit
by central banks (the Federal Reserve Board in the United States). The job of a
central bank is to set and enforce long-range targets for growth in the money
supply that matches the rate of growth in productivity. Such a policy, monetarists
claim, encourages steady growth and price stability.

     Monetarists claim that their approach is more consistent with American val-
ues than Keynesianism, because it does not depend on an expansive government.
Government only needs to set and enforce money targets so that individuals and
businesses can operate in a stable economic environment that permits long-range
planning and investment, leaving the free market to do the rest. Keynesianism,
they suggest, is the economic philosophy of big government; monetarism is the
economic philosophy of small government. It is hardly surprising, then, that monetarism is the approach favored by many conservatives and was an important
feature of economic policy during the Reagan years.[8]

SUPPLY SIDE ECONOMIC POLICY   According to supply side theory, government
should help increase the supply of goods and services in the economy by removing
barriers to individual investment and entrepreneurship.[9] In particular, they advocate substantial reductions in taxes, welfare, and Social Security, and removal
of all but the most essential regulations on business. While tax cuts may temporarily unbalance the budget, government revenues are supposed to increase in the
long run because of economic growth, bringing the budget into balance.

Supply side thinking strongly influenced the Reagan administration's economic policy. Most important were the Kemp-Roth tax cuts of 1981, the shrinking of budgets for transfer programs for the poor, and deregulation. The problematic quality of the economy at the end of the Reagan years, especially the massive budget deficit, has reduced the appeal of the supply side approach among economists and political leaders.

INDUSTRIAL POLICY   Industrial policy advocates[10] in the Democratic party argue that broad macroeconomic fiscal and monetary policies are too blunt to help the United States remain competitive in international markets. What is needed, they say, is national strategic planning following the Japanese and European models. Strategic planning should guide investment to high-technology sectors (like high-resolution television) and away from outmoded industries, should manage the painful social dislocations of a reoriented economy, and should encourage a vigorous American export trade, using instruments like the Japanese government's Ministry of International Trade and Industry (MITI). Advocates point to the success of MITI in planning the steel, automobile, and electronics surge in Japan, and their present efforts to help the microchip, supercomputer, and biotechnology industries. The Clinton administration has many advocates for such policies.

THE MAKING OF ECONOMIC POLICY

Structural Factors

The *economy* is the starting point for understanding the economic policies of the federal government. Policy is a product, first of all, of the stage of development of the economy. A simple market economy, like the one in existence at the founding of America, requires little government coordination. An industrial, corporate, and transnational economy like the one America has today, most believe, cannot be left to its own devices. The swings of the business cycle in such an economy, for instance, are broad and deeply felt, and the failure of a firm or a set of firms (like the savings and loans institutions) affects a broad range of businesses, investors, lenders, and consumers.

Economic policy is also affected by the health of the economy at any particular time. During periods of prosperity, when growth is happily joined to low rates of inflation, opinion generally favors loosening the grip of the government on the economy and allowing market forces to take over. The "go-go 1920s" is a good example of such a time. When things turn sour, however, as they did during the Great Depression of the 1930s, pressure mounts from all quarters for the government to take decisive action.

Economic policy is also shaped by the *political culture* of the United States. Though Americans have gradually come to believe that the government has an important role to play in the management of the economy, we are still very much taken with the free market ideal and are hostile to an activist government. This is one reason why we have so little government ownership of our basic infrastructure (transportation, power, banking, and communications, in particular) compared to other countries and only rarely resort to planning and "incomes" policies (government control of wages and prices), so common in Europe.

The *constitutional rules* also matter. Economic policy, like most other policies in the United States, tends to be fairly incoherent, contradictory, and inconsistent

High levels of unemployment bring pressures on the government to intervene in the economy. Here people wait for their unemployment benefits during the 1991–1992 recession.

when compared to that of other capitalist nations. Divided government, checks and balances, separation of powers, and federalism have a great deal to do with this outcome.

Political Factors

Interest groups, particularly those representing business, take a keen interest in economic policy, and their permanent representatives in Washington, D.C., are a constant presence in the halls of Congress and regulatory agencies. While business tends to speak with a single voice on such issues as deregulation and balanced budgets, it is not always united on what it wants from the government in terms of economic policy. Tight money policies, with their associated high interest rates, for instance, are attractive to financial institutions but very unattractive to manufacturing firms that must borrow for purposes of modernization and expansion. Nor do business interest groups have the field to themselves; labor, consumer, and public interest groups are also important players in the economic policy game.

Voters and *public opinion* are also important. The public is attuned to overall economic conditions and generally pays attention to what elected leaders are doing to curb inflation and unemployment and to stimulate growth. We saw in Chapter 9, "Voting and Elections," that the general state of the economy is one of the most important factors in deciding the outcome of a national election. Knowing this, elected leaders do what they can to ensure steady economic growth with low inflation and to avoid economic downturns at election time. Some social scientists believe that there is a **political business cycle**, in which elected leaders stimulate economic growth prior to elections and postpone economic pain (like taxes) until after elections.[11] Frequently cited examples are the Johnson and Reagan economic stimulations before the 1964 and 1984 presidential elections, and Nixon's wage and price freeze (to dampen inflation) imposed in time for the 1972 election. Recent research, however, suggests that the political business cycle is not as common as these examples suggest.[12]

Political parties also play a role in economic policymaking. Because each has its own electoral and financial constituency, made up of groups with identifiable economic interests, the two parties tend to support different economic policies.

The Democratic party traditionally has been supported by labor unions, racial minorities, and lower-income Americans, and tends to favor these groups in the course of governing. The Republican party has always attracted the support of business and upper-income Americans, and tries to look out for its core constituency. Democrats talk more about "fairness" when they are making economic policy; Republicans talk more about financial stability, economic efficiency, and government waste. Over many decades, Democrats in office have tended to favor economic policies that decrease unemployment and disparities in income and worry less about inflation, whereas Republicans have tended to favor policies that control inflation at the expense of higher unemployment and greater inequality. The policies matter. Inequality decreases slightly when Democrats control the presidency and increases slightly when Republicans control it.[13]

Governmental Factors

When things go wrong in the economy, it is the *president* to whom we usually turn for action. This role is recognized in the Employment Act of 1946, which requires that the president report on the state of the economy and recommend action to ensure full employment and economic stability. At the center of every modern president's legislative program are proposals for spending, taxing, and regulation that usually have broad macroeconomic effects. Several presidents also have been skillful in bringing pressure to bear on the Federal Reserve Board so that it regulates the money supply in a way that is consistent with their overall program. The president is advised on economic matters by the CEA, the director of the OMB, and the secretary of the Treasury.

Nearly everything that *Congress* does has macroeconomic effects. The overall balance of expenditures and receipts is a powerful fiscal instrument, either stimulating or retarding the economy. Taxes levied by Congress shape the incentives for individual and company economic decision making. Laws that regulate, grant subsidies, or supply loan guarantees, influence economic behavior. Congress is helped in its economic policymaking activities by the Congressional Budget Office (CBO)

Congress also plays a powerful economic oversight role. The heads of independent regulatory agencies and federal departments, as well as the chairman of the Federal Reserve Board, frequently testify before congressional committees, where the legislative point of view and the concerns of constituents are conveyed to those who fashion economic policies in the executive branch.

The Federal Reserve Board is the federal government institution that makes monetary policy for the nation. Its original role was to be a source of reserve funds for member banks that found themselves short of cash with which to pay panicky depositors. In the mid-1950s, the Fed also took on broad macroeconomic responsibilities, trying to control interest rates and the money supply. By doing so, it began to act like central banks in other modern capitalist countries.[14]

The Federal Reserve Board is made up of seven members (called governors) and a chairman who serve overlapping terms. Each is appointed by the president. The Fed is closely connected with, and very solicitous of, the needs of the financial community, and generally prefers to control inflation as a first order of business in order to protect the value of financial assets. To control inflation, it sometimes takes very harsh action. The Fed is generally credited with bringing on the 1957 and 1981 recessions by severely contracting the nation's money supply.

The Fed tried to stimulate consumer and business confidence by monetary actions that lowered interest rates during the 1991–1992 recession. Here Fed Chair Alan Greenspan explains the Board's policy to a congressional committe.

The Fed is relatively independent. Though presidents and Congress sometimes try to apply pressure by threatening to change the Fed's powers and organization, they have never actually done so (see the box). Punitive actions would surely trigger adverse reactions on Wall Street and in the financial community—something that neither presidents nor Congress want to contend with.

Our system of separation of powers and checks and balances allows many groups, institutions, and political actors to get involved in economic policymaking. Policy decisions are the outcome of bargaining and conflicts between the president, the Fed, the OMB, the Treasury, regulatory agencies, and Congress (especially the budget and tax-writing committees). In Great Britain, in contrast, economic policymaking is centered in the Treasury under the leadership of the chancellor of the exchequer who works closely with the prime minister. The prime minister's control over Parliament, in turn, allows the government to implement its economic policies in a reasonably rapid and straightforward fashion. Because of this system, former Prime Minister Margaret Thatcher was able to make her "monetarist" views the basis of British economic policy during most of the 1980s without much opposition in Parliament.

Values and Economic Policy

Debates about economic policy are spirited because the stakes are so high. Decisions about spending, taxing, and regulation not only affect each of our material interests but also involve our deepest beliefs about the kind of government and society that we want to have. Often, no consensus exists among us about these fundamental questions.

Take debates about spending. They inescapably involve conceptions about the proper role of the federal government. Many who oppose specific spending programs do so because of their concerns about big government. For many con-

THE STRUGGLE FOR DEMOCRACY

Wright Patman Tries to Control the Fed

"A slight acquaintance with American constitutional theory and practice demonstrates that, constitutionally, the Federal Reserve is a pretty queer duck." So said Texas populist Wright Patman, a lifelong opponent of the Fed, on the floor of the House of Representatives in 1962. "The Fed," he once concluded, "is a dictatorship on money matters by a bankers club."

Patman was not entirely off base. The Federal Reserve is a strikingly undemocratic institution. Like the Supreme Court, it makes enormously consequential decisions, but its members are not elected by the people. Like the Supreme Court, moreover, it must take account, in the long run, of the wishes of the president and Congress, but not too slavishly. It has substantial room for the exercise of independent judgment. It meets in secret, moreover, and is not obligated to give reasons for its actions. The Fed is under less democratic control, in fact, than the central bank in countries like Great Britain, France, Italy, and Japan, where bank policies must be approved by elected officials.

This never seemed right to Patman, and he spent his career trying to rein in the Fed. At times, he tried the humorous approach. He argued during committee hearings in 1939 that, since the Federal Reserve was owned by the 12 Reserve Banks, and since the 12 Reserve Banks were owned by private commercial banks, the Fed's building on Constitution Avenue was not tax-exempt like other public buildings. The District of Columbia's tax collector took this to heart and served the Board with a property tax bill. When the Board refused to pay the taxes, the tax collector issued a notice of delinquent taxes and announced a public auction of the building. It took three years of litigation for the Board to escape this tax liability, but Patman had made his symbolic point about who the Fed serves and who controls it.

For the most part, his efforts over nearly 50 years in the House of Representatives were more serious. Year after year, as chairman of the House Banking Committee, he held hearings on the activities of the Fed and proposed numerous reforms to make it more democratic and less responsive to large financial institutions. He proposed that the terms of the governors be shortened so that presidents would have more control. He wanted the Open Market Committee that made monetary policy to be made up of elected officials. He wanted the Fed's books to be open to congressional audit and scrutiny. He was never able to convince his colleagues to institute any of these reforms, but he never stopped trying.

Source: William Greider, *Secrets of the Temple* (New York: Simon & Schuster, 1987), pp. 48–51.

servatives, increased government spending is by its very nature a threat to liberty and economic efficiency.[15]

Debates about taxes concern who shall bear the burden and, ultimately, how much inequality we are willing to tolerate. **Progressive taxes** require that the most well off pay the highest tax rates, the result being, all other things being equal, a downward redistribution of income. Flat rate taxes levy the same percentage rate on all income earners and leave income distribution untouched. **Regressive taxes** impose a heavier relative burden on the lowest income earners and cause an upward redistribution of income, increasing the level of inequality in the population.

Regulatory policies concern not only technical and scientific issues but also our confidence in the ability of private markets to solve their own problems. To regulate, that is to say, is to admit that the market is imperfect and requires remedial action by government. Regulation is anathema, however, to those who believe that market economies work best when they are left alone.

GOVERNMENT SPENDING[16]

The federal government spends more than $1.4 trillion annually. This represents a fifteenfold increase since 1960 (in current dollars) and an expansion of federal outlays as a proportion of GNP from 18.2 percent to 24.2 percent. Table 17.1 and Figure 17.1 show how this money is divided among major programs and how program commitments have changed since the last year of the Carter administration (1980). *National defense* accounts for about one-fifth of all federal government expenditures. While this expenditure is quite substantial and much higher than that in other developed Western societies, it represents a considerable shrinkage since 1960, when over one-half of federal outlays were for national defense. The steady downward trend in national defense outlays was dramatically reversed during the 1980s, when President Ronald Reagan successfully pushed for a military buildup, but resumed its course with the end of the Cold War during the early 1990s. Relative to GNP and the total federal budget, defense spending is about where it was in 1980, though major decreases seem likely in the future.

Table 17.1
Federal Government Expenditures, 1980 and 1992

	Federal Government Outlays, 1992		Federal Government Outlays, 1980	
	In Millions of Dollars	*As Percentage of Outlays*	*In Millions of Dollars*	*As Percentage of Outlays*
National defense	$ 295,245	20.4	$133,995	22.7
Human resources Including Social Security and Medicare	746,982	51.7	313,374	53.0
Physical resources Including transportation, energy and the environment	155,207	10.7	65,985	11.2
Net interest	206,343	14.3	52,512	8.9
Other	82,904	5.7	44,996	7.6
Offsetting receipts	−40,780	−2.8	−19,942	−3.4
Total	$1,445,902	100.0	590,920	100.0

Source: The Budget of the United States, 1992, Part VII, Table 3.1.

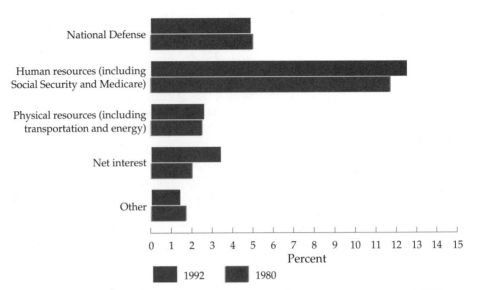

Figure 17.1 Comparing federal government expenditures as percentage of GNP, 1980 and 1992

Source: The Budget of the United States, 1992, *Part VII, Table 3.1*

Outlays for *human resources*, including welfare, health, veterans, and education and training, show considerable growth since 1960 as a proportion of total expenditures, though not much since 1980, and now account for over one-half the total. Almost 60 percent of human resources spending goes to just two programs: Social Security and Medicare. Given the fact that spending for Social Security and Medicare increased substantially during the 1980s (see Chapter 18, "Social Welfare") while relative spending on human resources remained constant, spending for other programs in this area of federal government responsibility fell quite substantially. Outlays for *physical resources*, including transportation, energy, and the environment, account for slightly more than 10 percent of federal dollars and 2.6 percent of GNP, about where they were in 1980. *Other federal nondefense outlays*, which support programs ranging from housing to agriculture, national parks, science and technology, international affairs, and the administration of justice, now attract about 6 cents of every federal dollar spent. A significant development is the increase in the level of payments to cover interest on the national debt. As a proportion of total federal outlays, it has more than doubled since 1960, with most coming since 1981, and now amounts to almost 15 percent of the total.

How Do We Compare?

It is sometimes said that government spending in America is "out of control." Your opinion about this is related to your own values, of course; any level of spending for programs that you don't like would be considered "too much." But the data show that, compared to the other modern nations, the United States ranks *very low* on total government spending (see Table 17.2).

Table 17.2
*Total Government Outlays as a
Percentage of Gross Domestic Product,
1989, OECD Countries*

United States	36.1
Austria	49.6
Canada	44.3
Denmark	58.7
France	49.7
Germany	45.1
United Kingdom	40.9
Italy	51.7
Japan	32.9
Switzerland	29.9
Sweden	60.1

Source: Historical Statistics, 1960–1989 (Paris:
OECD Publications, 1991), p. 67.

The *pattern* of expenditures is also of considerable interest. A much larger proportion of government outlays in the United States goes to national defense and less to human resources than in comparable nations. The reason for this emphasis on defense spending is not entirely clear. Some scholars believe that it is the necessary price for protection against aggressive enemies; some believe that it is an expansionary macroeconomic tool; and still others believe that it is important for protecting U.S. interests in the Third World. Whatever the reasons may be, there is no doubt that the size of defense outlays has had important implications for the American economy and society. It has certainly meant that we have higher taxes and a smaller pool of money for solving many other pressing problems.[17] The end of the Cold War is likely, however, to bring a substantial decrease in the national defense portion of the budget.

TAXES

Nothing raises the dander of Americans more than taxes. One of the fateful steps leading to the revolutionary break with England, of course, was the Boston Tea Party, protesting what many New Englanders believed was an unjust tax on their favorite beverage. The Constitutional Convention was called into being partly by Shays's Rebellion over the seizure of farms for nonpayment of taxes. Federal troops were used for the first time to "insure domestic tranquility" in 1794 in order to quell the Whisky Rebellion against an excise tax on whisky and other commodities.

Public discontent with taxes continues to be an important feature of American politics. Initiatives to limit taxes were passed in several states during the late 1970s and 1980s, and continue to pop up on state and local ballots at every round of elections. Proposals for a balanced-budget amendment to the Constitution are regularly introduced in state legislatures and the Congress. Presidential candidates find that "read my lips; no new taxes" pledges are useful in winning office.

Objection to taxes, a longtime feature of the American political landscape, has become even more common and intense in the face of recent economic difficulties.

The Basic Features of the American Tax System

The American tax burden has been getting heavier over time, even though it has recently leveled off. In 1990, the total of all revenues collected from Americans from federal, state, and local taxes was $1.8 trillion, up from only $100 billion in 1955. As a percent of GNP, the rise is not nearly so dramatic, but it is still significant: from 25 percent in 1955 to 33 percent in 1990 (see Figure 17.2).

Although substantial, the American tax burden is *significantly lighter* than that of most other modern capitalist countries. The relative rate of increase in the tax burden is also slower in the United States than elsewhere. We see this in Figure 17.3, which compares the United States to the OECD (The Organization of Economic Cooperation and Development) countries. It is fascinating that the "tax revolt" of recent years has been most evident in our own country, where the tax burden is relatively light.

Our tax system is also different from others in the kinds of taxes that we impose. In our federal system, states and localities levy their own taxes. The national government depends primarily on income (personal and corporate) and payroll taxes. The states get most of their revenues from sales taxes. Local governments depend most heavily on property taxes. In recent decades, state and local taxes have risen faster than federal taxes. This is likely to continue as states and localities are forced to pick up the tab for programs abandoned by the federal government in its effort to solve the deficit problem. The pain caused by these increased state taxes may account for the increasing vulnerability of incumbent governors in recent elections.

Our tax system is unusual in its reliance on income and corporate taxes to fund the national government,[18] though the corporate tax burden has declined substantially over the past three decades. Other nations depend more on sales and consumption taxes.

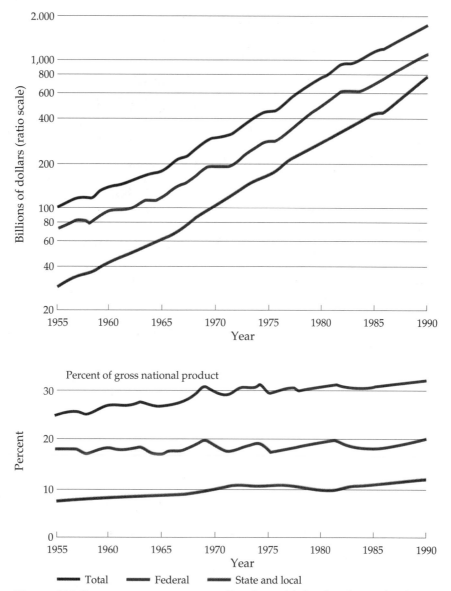

Figure 17.2 Government tax revenues. Receipts of federal and state local governments.

Source: Joseph Pechman, Federal Tax Policy, *(Washington, D.C.: Brookings Institution, 1987), p. 3 and authors' calculations, based on data in the* Economic Report of the President, 1991.

Until 1909, the federal government was supported solely by **excise taxes** (a national sales tax on such items as liquor and cigarettes) and **customs duties** (a tax on items imported into the United States), both of which fall most heavily on people with lower incomes. Noting this, Populist presidential candidate William Jennings Bryan once complained, "if taxation is a badge of freedom . . . the poor people of this country are covered all over with the insignia of freedom."[19] Pressed by popular demands to shift the tax burden to wealthier classes, Congress passed

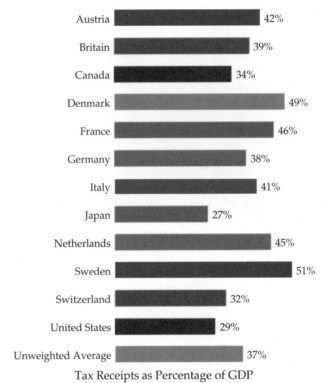

Figure 17.3 Tax receipts: international comparisons

Source: Organization of Economic Cooperation and Development, Taxation in Developed Countries *(Paris: OECD, 1987), p. 62.*

a national income tax law in 1894. When it was immediately declared unconstitutional by the Supreme Court, reformers pushed for passage of a constitutional amendment, stating that "Congress shall have the power to lay and collect taxes on incomes. . . . " The Sixteenth Amendment was ratified in 1913. The personal income tax began by taxing only a relative handful of wealthy individuals. Over the years, it expanded to the point at which most Americans, excepting the very poor, pay income tax.

The corporate income tax was introduced in 1909. At the start, the nominal tax rate was only 1 percent. It reached its peak of 52 percent during the Korean War. By 1990, it had dropped back to 33 percent. The share of total taxes accounted for by the corporate tax has been steadily decreasing from 23.2 percent in 1960 to about 9 percent today. The most significant decrease happened during the 1980s in response to the Reagan administration's 1981 tax reform[20] (See Figure 17.4).

Social insurance programs for the elderly, like Social Security and Medicare, are the largest and fastest-growing programs at the federal level. Accordingly, the payroll taxes to pay for these programs are now second only to the personal income tax as a source of government revenues, and the fastest growing. Working Americans have been slow to object to these taxes, perhaps because of the popularity of the programs they support.

The American tax system is also unique in its complexity and particularism. The U.S. tax code is a very thick document, filled with endless exceptions to the

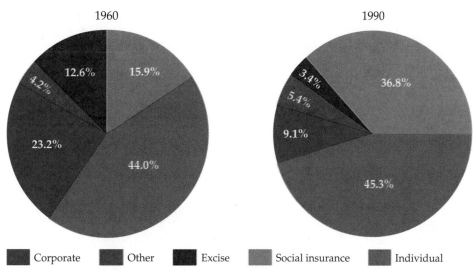

| ■ Corporate | ■ Other | ■ Excise | ■ Social insurance | ■ Individual |

Figure 17.4 The sources of federal tax revenues

Source: The Economic Budget Outlook, 1991, *Congressional Budget Office.*

rules and special treatment (called tax preferences) for individuals, companies, and communities. When Oregon Trappist monks petitioned Congress in 1984 for special treatment of their profits, their bookkeeper was quoted as saying, "We'd like to have it because everyone else has it."[21] He was not far off the mark. This outcome is a product of our highly fragmented and decentralized political process, in which special interests are well positioned, favored, and effective.[22]

Who Bears the Tax Burden?

To understand the distribution of the tax burden among Americans, it's important to understand the effects of each kind of tax and how much government revenue comes from each. The personal income tax is *progressive*, meaning that higher-income earners pay a higher percentage of their income in taxes (the actual percentage paid is called the **effective tax rate**). Payroll taxes and sales taxes are *regressive*, meaning that lower-income earners pay a higher percentage. The effects of the corporate income tax are not clear. It is progressive if one assumes that it is a burden borne only by corporations. It is regressive if one assumes, as many do, that corporations pass on the cost of their taxes to the consumer in the price of their goods and services.

Needless to say, the calculation of the total distributive effect of all of these taxes is extremely complex, with scholars not entirely agreed. The most widely accepted figures, calculated through 1985, indicate that "the U.S. tax system [all taxes, for all levels of government] is either moderately progressive or slightly regressive . . . ," depending on how one treats the effects of corporate taxes.[23] If one assumes that the corporate income tax is progressive, then the effective tax rate ranged in 1985 from about 21 percent for the lowest fifth of income earners to about 25 percent for the top fifth. If one assumes that the corporate tax rate is regressive, then the effective tax rate was the same for all Americans except for the least well-off (who paid at *higher* rates than the average!) and the most well-off (who paid at *lower* rates!).

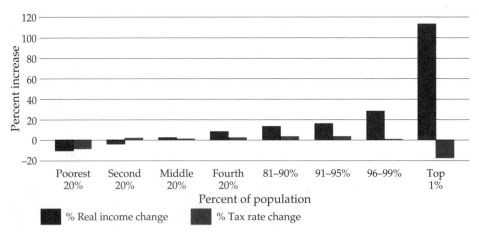

Figure 17.5 Percentage change in real income and federal tax rates of the population ranked by income, 1977–1992.

Source: The 1991 Green Book, *the U.S. House of Representatives, Ways and Means Committee, charts 1 and 2.*

The tax system has become less progressive than it used to be because of the big increases in payroll taxes and the decline in the share of total government revenues generated by property taxes (which are slightly progressive in their effects).[24] According to the nonpartisan Congressional Budget Office (CBO), the richest 1 percent of income earners in the United States saw a drop in the effective rate of their federal taxes of 6 percentage points between 1977 and 1988, while the least well-off 40 percent experienced a slight increase of about 1 percentage point. In real dollar terms, the average family in the top 1 percent saw a reduction in their annual tax bill of about $40,000, while those at the median level of income paid about $400 more in federal taxes (Figures 17.5 and 17.6 show changes through 1992). The CBO attributes this mainly to the decrease in the top marginal income tax rate in 1986 from 52 percent to 28 percent and to the rapid rise in payroll taxes.[25] The very well-off also have other ways to lower their tax bill as the "Resource Feature" shows.

The Politics of Tax Reform

Debate about taxes usually focuses on questions of economic efficiency, justice, and the deficit.

Concerns about efficiency take several forms. Many conservatives and supply side economists believe that a progressive system with high tax rates at the top acts as a disincentive for the industrious, because it penalizes high incomes and profits. Also, the very complexity of the tax code and the enormous energy devoted to mastering and getting around it (thus the legion of tax lawyers and accountants) can undermine efficiency. Industrial policy advocates believe that our tax system damages our international competitiveness by rewarding nonproductive economic activities. During the 1980s, for instance, investment in new plant and equipment lagged behind real estate development because of the latter's favorable treatment in the tax code.

RESOURCE FEATURE

≋

"We don't pay taxes. Little people do."*

Until now . . . there has never been solid empirical evidence to support this suspicion. But new analysis shows that Leona turns out to be absolutely right: As in many other things, the rich also command a disproportionate share of tax evasion.

How do the rich cheat? They take advantage of opportunities unavailable to most of us to hide income from businesses and property, to inflate expenses incurred in realizing that income or even, as the Helmsleys are accused of doing, to charge extravagant personal living expenses to businesses under their control. The 1986 tax reform law is supposed to reduce opportunities for legal tax avoidance through shelters, but it does little to reduce the opportunities for plain old cheating. And cheating is big business.

A special analysis of data from the Internal Revenue Service's latest (1985) in-depth audit of nearly 50,000 taxpayers shows that, by conservative estimate, individuals among just the top 12 percent of taxpayers account for a striking 40 percent or more of indi-

vidual tax underpayments. The top 1 percent of taxpayers alone accounts for 14 percent of underreporting; more than 70 percent of audited returns showing incomes of $200,000 or more are found to have unreported income.

One key fact about noncompliance is indisputable: However distributed, it certainly is large enough in total to whet any budget balancer's appetite. The IRS's most recent estimates of the aggregate federal income "tax gap"— the amount of federal corporate and individual income taxes that were owed but not paid—ranged from $80 billion to $90 billion this year. And the rate of noncompliance—the federal tax gap as a fraction of taxable income from legal sources—has averaged at least one-sixth since the early 1970s.

*Attributed to Leona Helmsley by her former housekeeper during Helmsley's trial for tax evasion

Source: James S. Henry, "Make the Rich Pay Their Share," *Washington Post National Edition* August 21–27, 1989, p. 23.

Figure 17.6 Shares and changes in shares of after-tax for all families, 1977–1992

Source: The 1991 Green Book, *the U.S. House of Representatives, Ways and Means Committee, charts 1 and 2.*

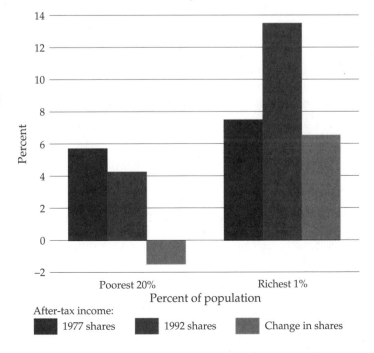

Percent of population

After-tax income:
■ 1977 shares   ■ 1992 shares   ■ Change in shares

Many Americans are concerned about the fairness of our tax system. The idea of "ability to pay" has long supported a progressive income tax as the centerpiece of the system. The system, however, has been less progressive. The top **nominal rate** was 91 percent from the late 1950s to 1964, 70 percent from 1965 to 1980, 50 percent from 1982 to 1986, 38.5 percent in 1987, 28 percent in 1988, and back up to 31 percent in 1990. Effective rates were never as progressive as nominal rates because of the generosity of Congress in fashioning deductions, exemptions, and special tax breaks, especially for businesses and high-income individuals. Given this history, tax reforms with the announced intention of improving tax fairness are usually met with skepticism by the public. A Gallup poll in 1989 showed that only 13 percent of Americans believed that the 1986 Tax Reform Act had made the tax system fairer.[26]

Finally, almost everyone is now concerned that tax revenues fall short of government outlays. We will discuss the deficit and the national debt later.

Federal tax policy was altered five times between 1981 and 1990. Concerns about economic efficiency, fairness, and the deficit dominated the debate throughout that period. Reagan's Economic Recovery Tax Act of 1981, for instance, was driven by efficiency concerns. It cut taxes primarily for corporations and the most well-off Americans. When the regressiveness of these changes and their adverse effects on the deficit became apparent, Congress legislated small tax increases in 1982 and 1984, closed some loopholes, and imposed a minimum tax on the wealthy.

The debate on the Tax Reform Act of 1986 focused on efficiency and fairness. It cut the tax rate for the top bracket from 50 percent to 28 percent and reduced the multitude of brackets to three. It also removed many low-income Americans from the tax rolls and eliminated some deductions and exemptions for corporations and wealthy individuals.

The goodwill that followed the passage of the 1986 legislation didn't last long. It became evident by the second year of George Bush's presidency that the 1980s tax changes had had a devastating impact on the deficit and that spending cuts or tax increases, or both, were inescapable. It was also apparent that inequality had worsened.[27] The budget compromise of 1990, reached after exhaustive and rancorous negotiations between congressional Democrats, President Bush, and a badly divided Republican party, included an increase in the top bracket to 31 percent, a slight increase in Medicare taxes, and some spending cuts. (Bush apologized at the 1992 Republican convention for his part in the compromise.) Evidence to date shows no improvement in the deficit problem or in efforts to make the tax system fairer.

THE DEFICIT AND THE NATIONAL DEBT

Few issues receive more attention than the federal deficit. By *federal deficit*, we mean the annual shortfall between what the government spends and what it takes in. The government must borrow from others to cover the shortfall and must pay interest to those from whom it borrows. The total of what government owes in the form of Treasury bonds, bills, and notes to American citizens and institutions (financial institutions, insurance companies, corporations, etc.), foreign individuals and institutions (including foreign governments and banks), and even to itself (units like the Social Security Trust Fund) is the **national debt**. Interest on the national debt is an important component of annual federal outlays.

The Size of the National Debt and the Deficit

The national debt is in the news because it has increased significantly over a very short period of time. Most of the national debt prior to the 1980s was accumulated during major wars. After each war, the debt, relative to GNP, gradually declined. Despite the Great Depression, two World Wars, the Korean War, and the Vietnam War, our debt as a percentage of GNP in 1980 was about the same as it was in 1920.[28] Interest on the national debt as a proportion of GNP also declined steadily. All of this changed dramatically during the 1980s, however, when the size of annual deficits, the rate of growth in the national debt, and interest paid on the national debt reached historically unprecedented levels. The changes are illustrated in Figure 17.7.

Figure 17.7 Tracking the federal debt. (*a*) Total federal debt. (*b*) Federal debt as percent of GNP. (*c*) Interest on the debt as percent of GNP. (*d*) Federal budget deficit, in billions.

Sources: The Washington Post National Edition, *February 11, 1991, p. 7; and Office of Management and Budget, 1991.*

(*a*)

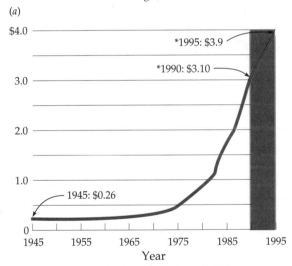

NOTE: *Figures for fiscal 1990 through 1995 are OMB estimates.

(*b*)

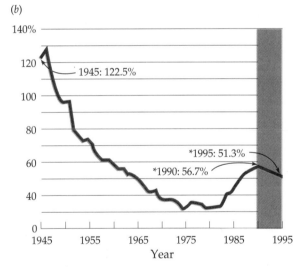

(*c*)

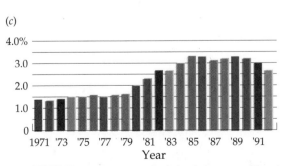

NOTE: Figures represent the federal government's net interest payments as a percentage of GNP. They include some off-budget amounts, mostly Social Security benefits.

(*d*)

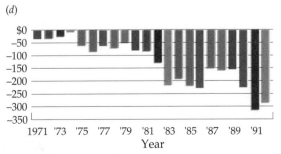

NOTE: Figures for fiscal years 1991 and 1992 are budget estimates.

This rapid growth in the debt occurred for a simple reason: government spending increased (especially for national defense and Social Security), while government revenues lagged, given the 1981 tax cuts, the deep recession of 1981–1982, and the reduction of the top tax rates in 1986. Increased welfare and other domestic spending had little to do with the increase in the national debt.[29]

Does the National Debt Matter?

Strange as it may seem, professional economists do not agree about the effects of the deficit and the national debt. To one group, it is the basis of national decline; to another, it is a trivial problem.

The pessimists point to several key developments:[30]

- The national debt relative to GNP is rising at a rate that is unprecedented in our peacetime history.

- The enormous increase in the national debt during the 1980s coincided with a general economic deterioration that was rooted in the stagnation of private investment. Government borrowing to finance the debt may have "crowded out" private investors by driving up interest rates.

- Much of our national debt is funded by borrowing from abroad, which puts much of the American economy in the hands of non-Americans.

- Borrowed money was not put to good use (e.g., for programs in education, research and development, and infrastructure, to spur long-term economic growth) but was squandered on noneconomically productive activities like the military, subsidies, bailouts, and failed social programs.

The optimists argue that the threat is greatly exaggerated. They make the following points:[31]

- The national debt is not as large as it seems because we measure it incorrectly. We do not, for instance, include the considerable assets of the government (buildings, land, equipment, natural resources, etc.) in our calculations, as any conventional business would do when calculating debt.

- The national debt, even as normally measured, is no higher relative to GNP than it was during the late 1940s and early 1950s.

- There is no evidence of "crowding out." Other modern capitalist countries with larger national debts had no trouble sustaining investment and productivity growth during the 1980s. There was plenty of money around at reasonable interest rates, but individuals and business enterprises didn't use it in a productive manner.

- Eighty-seven percent of the interest paid on the national debt goes to Americans.

- Government deficits are useful for spurring economic activity when labor and productive capacity are being used at less than full capacity, which is most of the time. The key to long-term growth and international competitiveness is that the deficit must be used to fund such programs as education, research, and infrastructure that strengthen the economy.

The Politics of Deficit Management

Despite the lack of agreement about the effects of the national debt, there is no doubt that the issue is an important one in our political life and has been so since the beginning of the Republic.[32] Apparently, enough voters, politicians, and business leaders today worry about deficits and the national debt to make them hot issues.

Elected leaders have tried to get the deficit under control. For most of our history, taxes and spending were considered separately by Congress, with little consideration given to their relationship to each other and to the overall fiscal situation. In 1974, however, the Congressional Budget and Impoundment Act set up procedures for Congress to consider the budget as a whole, in relationship to overall national fiscal goals. The act required that no action be taken on individual spending or taxing until a resolution in both houses set spending and taxing targets, and specified an amount of surplus or deficit that is "appropriate in the light of economic conditions." Congress was not permitted to adjourn, moreover, until the spending and taxing programs were reconciled (made consistent) with the overall targets.

In 1985, fiscal conservatives, worried about the growing national debt and unconvinced that these reconciliation procedures were working, successfully pushed for the enactment of the Balanced Budget and Emergency Deficit Control Act (popularly known as Gramm-Rudman, after its Senate sponsors, Phil Gramm of Texas and Warren Rudman of New Hampshire). Gramm-Rudman specified amounts by which the annual deficit would have to be cut each year over a period of six years in order to balance the budget by 1991. Failure to meet annual targets was to trigger automatic cuts in federal spending (half in defense, half in nondefense programs, excluding Social Security). Because of difficulties in reaching these targets, a bill was enacted in 1987 postponing a balanced budget until 1992.

Table 17.3
The Budget Process

Preparing the Presidential Budget	*Approximate Dates*
1. The president, after consulting with White House staff and others, sets budget priorities and preliminary revenue and spending targets.	Early spring
2. The OMB establishes guidelines for executive departments and agencies based on presidential priorities and targets.	Early spring
3. Executive departments and agencies communicate their own needs and priorities to the OMB. The OMB checks for conformity with presidential directives.	Late spring
4. The president reviews OMB and department and agency estimates.	Late spring
5. Departments and agencies prepare their final budgets in continuous consultation with the OMB and White House officials.	Summer
6. The OMB drafts a presidential budget; it submits the budget to the president for revision or approval.	Early fall
7. The OMB drafts a final version of the budget and of the president's budget message to Congress.	Late fall; early winter
8. Final presidential approval of the budget and the budget message is given.	January
9. The president transmits a budget proposal and budget message to Congress.	First Monday in February

Congress Considers the Budget (the following takes place in each chamber)

1. The budget is transmitted to the Budget Committee in each chamber.	February

---

The goals of Gramm-Rudman, even as amended, have not been met, of course; the federal budget is nowhere close to being balanced. Nevertheless, some argue, the act has done some good by putting pressure on the president and Congress each year to make decisions about the budget that takes deficit reduction into account.

In 1990, the threat that the automatic budget cut ax might fall on a wide range of cherished programs forced President Bush and the Democratic-dominated Congress to suspend the automatic spending cuts of Gramm-Rudman until at least 1994 and to raise taxes and cut spending, making a small dent in what otherwise would have been an astonishingly high deficit. The 1990 agreement also placed limits on spending for the first time (rather than simply specifying a deficit target) and mandated that cuts in defense and domestic spending be applied to deficit reduction rather than to alternative programs. It remains to be seen whether or not these latest innovations will solve the problem. The first signs were not positive: the fiscal 1992 deficit was roughly $350 billion, 14 times higher than the $25 billion planned for in the 1990 agreement.

Table 17.3 *(continued)* The Budget Process	
Preparing the Presidential Budget	*Approximate Dates*
2. The Budget Committee alters the budget based on its own projections of revenues and expenditures, the policy views of legislative leaders and substantive committees, and economic projections of the Congressional Budget Office (CBO).	Winter, early spring
3. A joint budget resolution is passed in identical form in each chamber. The resolution must set total expenditure targets for national defense, foreign aid, and domestic programs. The total cannot exceed levels required for deficit reduction targets previously established by the president and Congress.	April 15
4. Working within targets set by the budget resolution, subject matter committees authorize expenditure ceilings for each program.	Late spring
5. The Appropriations Committee in each chamber, working within guidelines set by the joint budget resolution, gathers together all subject matter committee authorizations and determines what can actually be spent on particular programs. Appropriation bills for each department and agency must be passed in identical form in each chamber.	Summer
Final Action	
1. Appropriations bills are transmitted to the president for his signature or veto.	Late summer
2. Automatic spending cuts are made if deficit targets are exceeded.	15 days after Congress adjourns (early fall)

Needless to say, the effort to formulate a federal budget and to get the deficit under control is an incredibly complex process. The essentials of this process are reviewed in Table 17.3. Matters relevant to making the federal budget are also covered in Chapters 11 and 12.

REGULATION

Why Government Regulates

If our economy were self-regulating, there would be no need for government regulation. But it is not. Market failures—those times when the market does not work properly or when the market is threatened by forces beyond its control—are quite common.[33] People generally want the government to do something to fix the problems caused by market failures. They want something done about air and water pollution, monopolistic prices, unsafe products, and reckless financial practices. In a democracy, politicians must respond to these popular pressures on pain of losing office. Regulation is the result then, of democratic politics.

Not all scholars are convinced, however, that regulation is solely the product of democratic politics. The *economic theory of regulation* holds that regulation is caused by the political efforts of powerful business firms that turn to government for protection against competitors. Regulation allows firms, it is argued, to restrict output, to deny entry to competitors, and to maintain above-market prices.[34]

A brief history of regulation[35] illustrates this mixture of democratic and nondemocratic factors that seem to be at work. It also explains the regulatory agencies and policies we are left with today.

Progressive Era Regulation

Between 1900 and World War I, laws were passed to regulate some of the activities of powerful new corporations and to break up the enormous "trusts." Reform was spurred by labor unions, the Women's movement, the Populists, and middle-class Americans anxious about the condition reported by the muckrakers—journalists and novelists like Upton Sinclair (*The Jungle*), Frank Norris (*The Octopus*), and Ida Tarbell (*A History of the Standard Oil Company*).

Landmark regulatory measures included the Federal Trade Commission Act, the Meat Inspection Act, the Pure Food and Drug Administration Act, and the Federal Reserve Act, and new uses for the previously enacted Sherman Antitrust Act and the Interstate Commerce Act. These measures dealt with such problems as monopolies, unstable financial institutions, unwholesome products, and unsafe working conditions.

Many scholars believe, however, that major corporations were themselves the beneficiaries of many of the regulatory enactments of the period and major players in the conception, formulation, and enactment of regulatory legislation.[36] Thus, the Federal Reserve Act was not simply the result of popular concerns about bank instability, but a government response to the entreaties of the American Bankers Association and its large member banks, which were worried about their inability to mobilize reserves in a financial emergency.

New Deal Regulation

The next wave of regulatory reform occurred during the New Deal. The regulatory innovations of this period aimed squarely at speculative and unsafe practices in the banking and securities industries that had contributed to the Great Depression. Legislation included federal bank inspection, prohibition of speculative investments by banks, federal deposit insurance, enhanced capacities for the Federal Reserve to coordinate the supply of money and credit, and the creation of the Securities and Exchange Commission to regulate stock market operations. Also, the new airline industry was brought under the wing of the Civil Aeronautics Board (CAB).

Again, the political sources of New Deal regulation were mixed. The principal impetus for the New Deal came from popular discontent with the status quo and pressure on the government to solve the many problems of the Great Depression.[37] But powerful interest groups were also at work. Important segments of the corporate community were intimately involved in the formulation of reform legislation and benefited greatly from it. Much of the financial community, for instance, pressed for legislation to bring stability to financial markets.[38] Other corporations eventually came to dominate and control regulatory policy, protecting themselves against competitors and ensuring above-market profits.[39]

The New Social Regulation

Progressive and New Deal era regulations aimed at the problems of a particular industry (e.g., railroads, banking, and securities) rather than the corporate economy as a whole. In addition, they were mainly of the "economic" variety, designed to regulate pricing patterns and the conditions of entry and production in a particular industry.[40] Finally, they welcomed the involvement of the regulated industry in setting standards, in providing information, and in lending personnel to regulatory agencies.

The "new social regulation" of the 1970s was different. For one thing, the sheer volume of regulatory legislation was unprecedented (see Table 17.4).

Regulation in this period was directed at corporate practices in general rather than the problems of particular industries. Thus, pollution regulations covered all industries, as did antidiscrimination rules.

More important, perhaps, this era involved an entirely new approach toward regulation. Conscious of the degree to which older regulatory agencies had become captives of the industries being regulated and the number of "iron triangles" and "subgovernments" at the core of the governing process in Washington, D.C., reformers convinced elected officials to encourage broad public participation and accountability.[41] The new social regulation encouraged citizen lawsuits, for in-

---

Table 17.4
The High Tide of the New Social Regulation

A. *Federal Regulatory Agencies Created During the 1970s*
   Environmental Protection Agency (1970)
   National Highway Safety Commission (1970)
   Consumer Product Safety Commission (1970)
   Mine Safety and Health Administration (1973)
   Occupational Safety and Health Administration (1973)
   Nuclear Regulatory Commission (1975)

B. *Regulatory Enactments (Selected) of the 1970s*
   Mine Safety and Health Act
   Poison Prevention Packaging Act
   Clean Air Act (amendments)
   Railroad Safety Act
   Cigarette Advertising Act
   Water Quality Improvement Act
   Consumer Product Safety Act
   Ocean Dumping Act
   Pesticide Regulation Act
   Federal Water Pollution Control Act
   Noise Pollution and Control Act
   Safe Drinking Water Act
   Hazardous Materials Transportation Act
   Seat Belt and School Bus Standards
   Warranty Improvement Act
   Toxic Substances Control Act
   Medical Devices Safety Act
   Saccharin Study and Labeling Act

---

stance, by granting automatic standing in regulatory proceedings to "interested parties." In practice, these citizens were usually public interest lobbies, such as Common Cause, Citizen Action, and the Sierra Club. This citizen involvement was probably caused by the rising tide of social movements during the late 1960s and early 1970s (see Chapter 10, "Social Movements") and a loss of confidence in the nation's business corporations, tied to a troubled economy and the general deterioration in confidence in all established institutions brought on by the Vietnam War and Watergate.[42] It was probably the only time in our history when business was almost entirely on the defensive and was unable to halt the imposition of laws to which it was strongly opposed.[43]

Deregulation

By the end of the 1970s, the mood of opinion leaders both inside and outside the government had turned against regulation. Many of them blamed excessive regulation for forcing inefficient practices on American companies, hastening the decline of the United States in the world economy. Many began to find fault with government imposition of uniform national standards, strict deadlines, and detailed instructions to companies.[44] Many economists wanted to substitute "cost-benefit" analysis to evaluate regulations and more market-oriented forms of regulations (like taxing damaging actions or granting tax breaks for meeting standards). The deregulatory mood was spurred by a business political offensive that took the form of funding think tanks, journals of opinion, and foundations favorable to the business point of view, as well as the electoral campaigns of sympathetic candidates.[45]

The change in climate was first apparent in the deregulation of the airline, banking, railroad, and trucking industries under President Jimmy Carter. It reached maturity under President Ronald Reagan's program of "regulatory relief." This program slowed the regulation writing process, cut the investigatory and research capabilities of regulatory agencies, and appointed heads of regulatory units who were hostile to the legislative missions of their agencies.

One of the results of airline deregulation has been the development of regional hubs dominated by a single airline, like American Airline's domination of the Dallas-Fort Worth airport shown here.

The Future of Regulation

The regulatory state, however, is not only here to stay but likely to expand in the future. There are a number of reasons for this.

First, little permanent deregulation was achieved during the 1980s, an era dominated by conservative ideas, business values, and an extremely popular president committed to deregulation. If fundamental change could not be achieved in such a favorable environment, it seems unlikely that it will happen any time soon.

Second, most regulatory policies are supported by the public. Even at the height of President Reagan's popularity, polls continued to show overwhelming support for most regulatory programs. The Roper Poll reported in 1982, for instance, that only 21 percent of Americans believed that "environmental protection laws and regulations have gone too far," while 69 percent believed that "they are about right or haven't gone far enough."[46]

Third, deregulation created so many problems that many people are having second thoughts. Deregulation of the savings and loan industry and its subsequent collapse is but the most glaring example. Nonenforcement of the antitrust laws and lax supervision of the securities industry contributed to a decade of leveraged buyouts, junk bond financial shell games, and unprecedented levels of corporate debt. Many Americans worry that the nation's banks and insurance companies may follow the disastrous path of the S&Ls if they are not subject to more stringent regulation.

Finally, new problems are beginning to appear that will likely stimulate public demands for government intervention. Environmental disasters like the *Exxon Valdez* oil spill in Alaska lead to calls for the government to do something to prevent their recurrence. Solutions to long-range threats to the environment like acid rain and the "greenhouse effect" seem beyond the capacities of the free market to solve and will, presumably, require government action of some kind.

The likely occurrence of disasters in the future equal in its impact to that of the *Exxon Valdez* oil spill in Alaska, shown here, will maintain popular pressure on political leaders to expand environmental regulation.

ECONOMIC POLICY AND DEMOCRACY

We have seen that national economic policy is produced by a political process that contains democratic and nondemocratic aspects. The ideal of popular sovereignty is served by the general correspondence between what the public wants and what government does. Opinion polls generally show majority support for current levels of government spending for Social Security and Medicare. The public shows no inclination to support substantial cuts in major program areas, though a substantial number of Americans continue to believe that government wastes too much money or puts too much into welfare and aid to foreign countries. There is also a growing belief that the defense budget ought to decrease in the post-Cold War era.

Though complaining about taxes is as common as complaining about the weather, it seems that the American people generally get what they want in terms of tax policy. To be sure, Americans are exasperated by the complexity of our tax policy; there is concern about the tax system's fairness; and many worry about its overall economic effects. Yet the message that the American people want low taxes is conveyed quite clearly to elected officials, and they respond, as shown by how low our taxes are when they are compared with those of other modern capitalist countries.

We have also seen that the American people generally support the overall outlines of the regulatory state. Though there are many complaints about an overly obtrusive government, when asked about specific regulatory programs, ranging from the banking industry to pollution control, strong majorities not only accept what is in place but also would like to see even more of them.

While popular sovereignty is served in the general outlines of economic policy, the details are the stuff of special interests. This is the case in the area of spending, where commitments to specific priorities and projects, from weapons systems procurement to public housing allocations, are hammered out in a legislative process where special interests dominate; in the area of taxation, where the detailed provisions of the tax code are the outcome of the efforts of special interests, who are also the main beneficiaries; and in regulatory policy, where arrangements like "captured" agencies and "iron triangles" have not yet disappeared.

SUMMARY

Governments play a substantial role in the management of the economy in all modern capitalist countries. Governments have proved to be successful in easing many of the problems generated by dynamic market economies.

The federal government's macroeconomic responsibilities entail policies that affect growth, inflation, and employment in the economy. The goal of macroeconomic policy is a growing economy, with low unemployment, and steady prices. Government officials try to meet this goal using fiscal and monetary tools.

There is no consensus among Keynesian, monetarist, supply side, and industrial policy economists on how to meet government's economic responsibilities. Each approach embodies a conception of the proper role for government. Keynesian and industrial policy approaches favor a large and interventionist government; monetarist and supply side theorists favor a small and noninterventionist one.

Structural, political, and governmental factors affect economic policy. Problems arising from the economy itself are crucial. The Constitution structures the rules of the game of the economic policymaking process, and the political culture affects what we believe to be appropriate policy. Interest groups play a particularly central role. Political parties are also important, with Democrats and Republicans taking different approaches to economic questions.

Federal government spending and taxing have grown during the twentieth century but remain significantly below the levels common in other Western democratic countries. Spending is mainly for national defense and social insurance programs. The tax system is slightly progressive but is becoming less so. The annual imbalance between spending and taxing has contributed to a worsening debt situation, but economists cannot agree on the debt's effects.

The federal government also plays an important regulatory role. The origins of this role are in market failures that trigger popular and business pressures on government. Despite the deregulation efforts of recent years, the regulatory responsibilities of the federal government are likely to remain substantial.

To Ponder

1. Would we be better off if government played no role at all in the economy?

2. Does an increase in regulation mean a decrease in our freedom?

3. If you were a member of Congress, what, if anything, would you do to get the deficit under control? What programs, if any, would you cut? What taxes, if any, would you increase?

4. Take a problem like acid rain or the "greenhouse effect." Can you formulate a free market solution? Or is government intervention inevitable?

5. Which approach to fiscal policy—Keynesianism, monetarism, supply side theory, or industrial policy—appeals to you the most? Why?

Suggested Readings

Friedman, Benjamin. *Day of Reckoning: The Consequences of American Economic Policy Under Reagan and After*. New York: Random House, 1988.
    A book that rings the alarm bell about the potentially disastrous effects of our growing national debt.

Frumkin, Norman. *Tracking America's Economy*. Armonk, NY: M.E. Sharpe, 1987.
    Definitions and descriptions of economic indicators and how they are measured and used by economic policymakers.

Harris, Richard, and Sidney Milkis. *The Politics of Regulatory Change*. New York: Oxford University Press, 1989.
    A history of regulation organized around the idea that different kinds of "regulatory regimes" follow one another. Regimes are defined as interconnected ideas, politics, institutional structures, and policies about regulation that hang together in a coherent fashion.

Heidenheimer, Arnold J., et al. *Comparative Public Policy: The Politics of Social Choice in America, Europe, and Japan*, 3rd ed. New York: St. Martin's, 1990.
    A comprehensive introduction to national variations in spending, taxing, and regulatory policy among the developed capitalist nations.

Heilbroner, Robert, and Peter Bernstein. *The Debt and the Deficit: False Alarm/Real Possibilities*. New York: Norton, 1989.

Swimming very much against the mainstream, these two economists argue that the problem of the debt is greatly exaggerated and misunderstood.

Hibbs, Douglas. *The American Political Economy.* Cambridge, MA: Harvard University Press, 1987.
A very sophisticated historical and statistical analysis of the relationship between American politics and the formation of economic policy, and of the effects of such policies.

Pechman, Joseph A. *Federal Tax Policy*, 5th ed. Washington, D.C.: Brookings Institution, 1987.
The last book by the late and highly respected economist at the Brookings Institution. Published in five editions, the book has long been considered the bible on the subject of federal tax policy and its effects.

Savage, James D. *Balanced Budgets and American Politics.* Ithaca, NY: Cornell University Press, 1988.
A fascinating look at the long history of the politics of the balanced budget in the United States.

Vogel, David. *Fluctuating Fortunes: The Political Power of Business in the United States.* New York: Basic Books, 1989.
A detailed description and analysis of how the "new social regulation" came to burden business during the 1970s and how business successfully fought back during the 1980s.

Notes

1. Thomas Ferguson and Joel Rogers, *Right Turn* (New York: Hill & Wang, 1986), p. 119; Kevin Phillips, *The Politics of Rich and Poor* (New York: Random House, 1990), p. 108–115.

2. William A. Niskanen, *Reaganomics: An Insider's Account of the Policies and the People* (New York: Oxford University Press, 1988), p. 113.

3. Arnold J. Heidenheimer, et al., *Comparative Public Policy: The Politics of Social Choice in America, Europe, and Japan*, 3rd ed. (New York: St. Martins, 1990), p. 137.

4. Joseph A. Pechman, *Federal Tax Policy*, 5th ed. (Washington, D.C.: Brookings Institution, 1987), p. 28.

5. Pechman, *Federal Tax Policy*, p. 8.

6. Heidenheimer, et al., *Comparative Public Policy*, p. 137.

7. Kim McQuaid, *Big Business and Presidential Power* (New York: William Morrow, 1982).

8. Niskanen, *Reaganomics*, p. 155.

9. Jude Wanniski, *The Way the World Works* (New York: Basic Books, 1978).

10. Robert Reich and Ira Magaziner, *Minding America's Business: The Decline and Rise of the American Economy* (New York: Harcourt Brace Jovanovich, 1982).

11. William Nordhaus, "The Political Business Cycle," *Review of Economic Studies*, Vol. 42 (April 1975), pp. 169–190; Edward Tufte, *Political Control of the Economy* (Princeton, NJ: Princeton University Press, 1978).

12. Douglas Hibbs, *The American Political Economy* (Cambridge, MA: Harvard University Press, 1987), ch. 8.

13. Hibbs, *American Political Economy*, ch. 7.

14. Benjamin Friedman, *Day of Reckoning: The Consequences of American Economic Policy Under Reagan and After* (New York: Random House, 1988), p. 144.

15. Milton Friedman, *Capitalism and Freedom* (Chicago: University of Chicago Press, 1962).

16. On how the budget is put together, see Aaron Wildavsky, *The New Politics of the Budgetary Process* (Glenview, IL: Scott Foresman, 1988).

17. Reich and Magaziner, *Minding America's Business*.

18. Pechman, *Federal Tax Policy*, p. 1.

19. Quoted in Jeffrey H. Birnbaum and Alan S. Murray, *Showdown at Gucci Gulch* (New York: Vintage, 1988), p. 6.

20. On the changing history of corporate taxes, see Cathie J. Martin, *Shifting the Burden* (Chicago: University of Chicago Press, 1991).

21. Birnbaum and Murray, *Showdown at Gucci Gulch*, p. 7.

22. Birnbaum and Murray, *Showdown at Gucci Gulch*, p. 6; Sven Steinmo, "Political Institutions and Tax Policy in the United States, Sweden, and Britain," *World Politics*, vol. 41 (July 1989), pp. 510–515.

23. Joseph A. Pechman, *Who Paid the Taxes, 1966–1985?* (Washington, D.C.: Brookings Institution, 1985), p. 10.

24. Pechman, *Who Paid the Taxes?* p. 8.

25. Congressional Budget Office, "The Changing Distribution of Federal Taxes: 1975–1990," (Washington, D.C.: CBO, 1987).

26. Gallup Report, "Fairness of 1986 Tax Reform Bill," March/April 1989.

27. Phillips, *The Politics of Rich and Poor*, ch. 4.

28. Friedman, *Day of Reckoning*, p. 90.

29. Friedman, *Day of Reckoning*, p. 272.

30. Friedman, *Day of Reckoning*.

31. Robert Heilbroner and Peter Bernstein, *The Debt and the Deficit: False Alarm/Real Possibilities* (New York: Norton, 1989).

32. James D. Savage, *Balanced Budgets and American Politics* (Ithaca, NY: Cornell University Press, 1988).

33. Arthur Pigou, *The Economics of Welfare* (London: Macmillan, 1932).

34. George J. Stigler, "The Theory of Economic Regulation," *Bell Journal*, Vol. 2 (Spring 1971), pp. 3–21. Several radical historians take a similar view: see Gabriel Kolko, *The Triumph of Conservatism* (Chicago: Quadrangle, 1967), and James Weinstein, *The Corporate Ideal in the Liberal State* (Boston: Beacon Press, 1968).

35. We follow closely the idea of "regulatory regimes" formulated by Richard Harris and Sidney Milkis in their book *The Politics of Regulatory Change* (New York: Oxford University Press, 1989).

36. See G. William Domhoff, *The Higher Circles* (New York: Random House, 1970), and Edward S. Greenberg, *Capitalism and the American Political Ideal* (Armonk, NY: M.E. Sharpe, 1985) for reviews of the relevant literature. Also see Kolko, *The Triumph of Conservatism*, and Weinstein, *Corporate Ideal in the Liberal State*.

37. Francis Fox Piven and Richard A. Cloward, *Poor People's Movements* (New York: Vintage, 1979).

38. Greenberg, *Capitalism and the American Political Ideal*.

39. Marver Bernstein, *Regulation by Independent Commission* (Princeton, NJ: Princeton University Press, 1955); Grant McConnell, *Private Power and American Democracy* (New York: Vintage, 1966); and Theodore J. Lowi, *The End of Liberalism*, 2nd ed. (New York: Norton, 1979).

40. See Eugene Bardach, "Social Regulation as a Generic Policy Instrument," in Lester M. Salamon, ed., *Beyond Privatization* (Washington, D.C.: Urban Institute, 1989), p. 198 for the distinction between economic and social regulation.

41. Harris and Milkis, *Politics of Regulatory Change*.

42. Seymour Martin Lipset and William Schneider, *The Confidence Gap: Business, Labor, and Government in the Public Mind* (New York: Free Press, 1983).

43. David Vogel, *Fluctuating Fortunes: The Political Power of Business in the United States* (New York: Basic Books, 1989), pp. 59, 112.

44. James Buchanan and Gordon Tullock, "Polluters, Profits and Political Responses: Direct Control Versus Taxes," *The American Economic Review*, Vol. 65 (March 1975), pp. 139–147); L. Lave, *The Strategy of Social Regulation* (Washington, D.C.: Brookings Institution, 1981); Murray Weidenbaum, *The Costs of Government Regulation of Business* (Washington, D.C.: Joint Economic Committee of Congress, 1978).

45. See Thomas Edsall, *The New Politics of Inequality* (New York: Norton, 1984); Ferguson and Rogers, *Right Turn*; Phillips, *Politics of Rich and Poor*; Vogel, *Fluctuating Fortunes*.

46. The poll data and sources are reported in Vogel, *Fluctuating Fortunes*, pp. 262–263, 278–279.

18

Social
Welfare

TOUCHING THE "THIRD RAIL": SOCIAL SECURITY

"Danger, do not touch!" Signs in subway tunnels warn workers to stand clear of the electrified "third rail," which powers subway cars. Although there is no such sign in Washington, D.C., warning politicians to stand clear of Social Security—called the "third rail" of American politics—most politicians know that tampering with Social Security is dangerous to political life and limb. Ronald Reagan forgot this central truth of American politics and saw his 1981 proposal to slash Social Security benefits defeated in Congress.

The president's budget director, David Stockman, flushed with confidence after the president's victory on the budget (see the introductory story in the previous chapter), wanted to go after Social Security as the next step in the "Reagan Revolution." As Stockman described his objectives, "a frontal assault on the inner fortress of the American welfare state [Social Security] . . . was now in order." Marginal tinkering seemed out of the question; "what was needed was something far more radical, . . . a once-in-a-century opportunity. . . . Our job is to shrink the Social Security monster."[1]

Stockman focused on two features of Social Security that he found particularly troublesome. First, he believed that the definition of *disabled* was too lax and that many people were receiving disability benefits who did not deserve them. Second, he believed that the policy that penalized people with only a 20 percent loss in old-age benefits for retiring early at age 62 rather than 65 was both damaging to the economy and destructive to Social Security. With nearly three-quarters of Americans retiring early, the economy was not only deprived of their labor, but the Treasury was being deprived of Social Security taxes.

Stockman's plan was worked out with Health and Human Services Secretary Richard Schweiker and was presented to the president at a meeting on May 11. The plan called for a significant tightening of disability requirements and an increase in the early retirement penalty from 20 percent to 45 percent loss of benefits. The changes, moreover, were to be implemented immediately rather than phased in over several years—the usual practice for painful policy changes. The president loved it. He thought it would permanently fix the Social Security problem without raising taxes. "Our people on the Hill want this," he said. "It represents everything exactly what we have always said should be done. Let's go forward with it."[2]

The president was wrong. His people on Capitol Hill were furious. One very angry Republican congressman cornered Stockman at a meeting: "You absolutely blind-sided us with this Social Security plan. My phones are ringing off the hook. I've got thousands of sixty-year-old textile workers who think it's the end of the world. What am I supposed to tell them? How can I explain to the person who was planning to retire two years from now at age sixty-two that he will have to make do with $450 a month rather than $650?"[3] White House Chief of Staff James Baker believed that the plan would do great damage to the president and quickly began to put distance between him and the new approach to Social Security. He first called it a plan of the Department of Health

641

and Human Services, then implied that it was only a minor response to a request from a congressional committee, and finally disclaimed any presidential involvement at all. By the end, White House operatives were calling the plan "Schweiker's Folly."[4]

Senate Republican leaders knew when to concede defeat. They withdrew the plan and substituted a mild resolution, pledging fiscal reform of Social Security. The substitute passed 96–0. David Stockman was appalled at this abandonment of a key element of the Reagan Revolution. The president, however, was anxious to cut his losses. A few months after the fiasco, he was persuaded by key Republican leaders in Congress and his advisors in the White House to insulate himself and his party from the "third rail" by appointing a bipartisan committee of distinguished Americans to study problems in the Social Security system and to recommend solutions. The president bent with the prevailing winds and announced the formation of the commission as a way "to remove Social Security once and for all from politics." The commission eventually presented its plan for changes in Social Security in a report made public, much to the relief of Republicans and Democrats alike, after the 1982 elections. The modest bipartisan commission's package was eventually passed by Congress and signed by the president.

Social Security is the largest part of the American **welfare state**. It is dear to the hearts of most Americans and virtually immune from criticism and tampering. Public assistance, on the other hand, usually called "welfare," is almost universally disliked. In this chapter, we explore the differences between Social Security and public assistance and how they got that way. We also examine why a society that believes so strongly in the benefits of the free market and individualism has a welfare state at all. Answering these questions requires that we take account of structural, political, and governmental influences.

WHY SOCIAL WELFARE?

A social welfare state is a society with a set of government programs that protect the minimum standards of living of families and individuals against loss of income due to economic instability, old age, illness and disability, and family disintegration.[5] It represents a recognition by people in a democracy that a market economy, even when it is working at peak efficiency, does not guarantee minimum decency for all of its citizens or offer protection against economic dislocations.[6] All modern capitalist societies have social welfare states. Though the details of their programs differ, all provide social welfare for their citizens.

Why Welfare States?: Structural and Political Influences

But why do we have social welfare? Why not simply leave the welfare of the people to the operation of the market economy? One answer begins with structural factors, particularly industrialization and its effects.

 INDUSTRIALIZATION   Industrialization has produced unprecedented levels of social wealth and improved living standards in the Western countries over the past century, but it has also produced disruptions and hardships. Industrialized

Industrial work is often dangerous to life and limb. To cope with industrial illness, disability, and death, most industrial societies have created government medical and financial support programs to help victims and their families.

market societies are places of rapid economic growth and transformation. They are places where factories open and close, where some regions become prosperous while others languish, and where one technology supersedes another. They are also places where the business cycle and periods of high unemployment are a part of life.

Industrialized societies are also places where people live longer because of advances in medical care and public health practices. But old age brings increased health care needs at the same time that people's separation from the work force makes them less able to pay for those needs on their own. Work in the mines, factories, and transportation systems of industrial societies is not without risk, moreover, and occupational illness and disability have become more of a problem. Industrial societies are also urban societies where people of widely varying backgrounds and economic circumstances live in close proximity to each other. Poverty is more concentrated and visible in urban settings than in rural ones, and the possibilities for social conflict are greater.[7]

Industrialization also undermines the family, which provided welfare and caring in traditional, preindustrial societies.[8] Industrial societies are highly mobile, urban societies where families are not only smaller but also less likely to stay intact over the long term (note the high divorce rate in all industrial societies).

FROM PRECONDITIONS TO PROGRAMS   Though scholars generally agree that economic change and industrialization provide the preconditions for the social welfare state, they do not agree on why political leaders create and expand them.

Presumably, in a democracy, people get what they want from government because elected officials depend on the support of the voters to gain and maintain public office. The people in Western democracies have made it clear in public opinion polls and elections that they want government to do something to help them cope with the problems and dislocations resulting from industrialization.[9]

There are several variants of the "democracy as cause of the welfare state" theme. One argues that the industrial working class is the main catalyst. In Europe, powerful labor and Socialist parties introduced social welfare measures when they were in control of the government or caused sufficient anxiety that other parties introduced such measures as a way of undermining the political popularity of the Left.[10] In the United States, it was the rising militancy and political influence of workers and labor unions that helped make the New Deal possible, including such landmark measures as Social Security and the beginnings of the federal role in public assistance.

Others believe that it is the proliferation of interest groups in democracies that is the most important factor in the creation and expansion of the social welfare state. The elderly in the United States, for instance, are well represented by interest groups, vote in high numbers, and make substantial political contributions, so elected officials are favorably disposed toward Social Security and Medicare. Some conservative commentators believe that middle-class interests that depend on welfare state expenditures—the so-called "new class" of teachers, welfare workers, doctors, hospital administrators, and the like—are another important force in sustaining social welfare.[11]

Still other scholars argue that social welfare is designed by political and business leaders to forestall popular discontent and to undermine radical movements for social change. They point to the significant role played by corporate and banking leaders in the creation of the social welfare state in the United States.[12]

OUTLINES OF SOCIAL WELFARE IN THE UNITED STATES

Types of Programs

The basic distinction to be drawn is between **social insurance** and **means-tested** programs. In social insurance programs, such as Social Security, individuals contribute to an insurance trust fund by way of a payroll tax on their earnings and receive benefits based on their contributions. Means-tested programs, such as Aid to Families with Dependent Children (or AFDC, commonly known as "welfare"), distribute benefits on the basis of need to those who can prove that their income is low enough to qualify. Financing is by general tax revenues rather than by a contributory insurance fund.

A distinction can also be drawn between social welfare programs that pay people directly—cash transfer programs, such as unemployment insurance—and those that provide a service, such as Medicare (which pays hospitals on behalf of recipients).

Finally, a distinction can be drawn between social welfare programs that are administered directly from Washington, D.C., and those that are jointly administered by federal and state governments. Social Security is an example of the former. Taxes for it are levied directly on wages and salaries by the federal government, and benefits are paid directly to the elderly by the Social Security Administration. Medicaid and AFDC, on the other hand, are jointly funded and administered. One result is wide variation in benefits in each of the states (see Table 18.1).

Table 18.1
Aid to Families with Dependent Children Average Monthly Payment Per Recipient Family by State in 1988 (Mean Payment = $374)

The Top Five States	
Alaska	$599
California	590
Maine	545
New York	536
Minnesota	520
The Bottom Five States	
Alabama	$114
Mississippi	119
Louisiana	167
Texas	169
South Carolina	189

Source: U.S. Social Security Administration, *Social Security Bulletin,* Annual Statistical Supplement, 1989.

Principal Characteristics

We spend a substantial amount of money in the United States on social welfare. In 1990, the total was $885.8 billion, of which the federal government's share was 59 percent. As a proportion of GNP, social welfare spending was 18.5 percent in 1990, up from only 8.2 percent in 1950, considerably outstripping spending for any other area of government responsibility, including national defense (see Figure 18.1). As a proportion of total federal spending, social welfare reached its peak in 1976, leveled off until the early 1980s, and has been declining ever since. The decline is mainly accounted for by the Reagan administration's cutbacks in such means-tested programs as AFDC, food stamps, and Medicaid, as well as federal grants to the states for employment and training programs.

The lion's share of federal social welfare spending is for social insurance, and its share has been growing steadily (see Figure 18.2). Spending for means-tested programs—those that most Americans include when they complain about the "welfare mess"—is relatively small and shrinking. Funding for AFDC, for instance, fell from 4.4 percent of the federal budget in 1970, to 2.7 percent in 1980, to less than 2 percent in 1990. All means-tested programs, taken together (adding food stamps, Medicaid, rent supplements, legal aid, and other programs to AFDC), accounted for only 11.8 percent of total federal spending in 1988, down from 14.0 percent in 1978 (though federal mandates have greatly increased the Medicaid burden on the states). Social insurance programs (mainly Social Security and Medicare), on the other hand, accounted for 56.9 percent of federal spending in 1990, up from 44.3 percent in 1960.

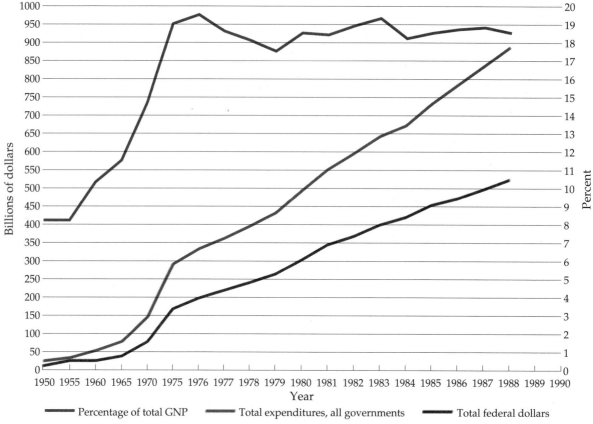

Figure 18.1 Social welfare expenditures, 1960–1990

Source: Statistical Abstracts of the United States, 1991 *(Washington, D.C.: U.S. Bureau of the Census, 1991).*

The implications of this pattern are significant. First, most benefits of the American welfare state go, not to the poor, but to the nonpoor. Those who receive the most benefits from social insurance programs are those who were fully employed during their working lives, had the highest incomes, and paid the maximum level of Social Security taxes. Second, because social insurance benefits go

Figure 18.2 Social insurance as a share of total social welfare spending

Source: Social Security Bulletin, *Vol. 54, No. 5, (May 1991), p. 16.*

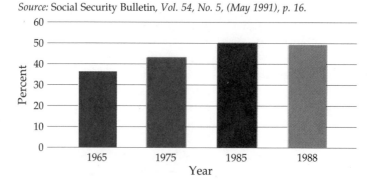

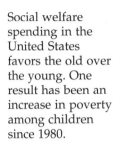

Social welfare spending in the United States favors the old over the young. One result has been an increase in poverty among children since 1980.

mainly to those who are retired, the elderly fare much better than the young. One result is a significant decrease in the poverty rate among the elderly over the past two decades and a dramatic increase in the poverty rate among children.[13] Roughly one in five children now live below the poverty line in the United States (see Figure 18.3).

SOCIAL INSURANCE

Social insurance programs that guard against loss of income due to old age, disability, illness, and unemployment are the largest and most popular parts of the American welfare state. Because benefits are received as a matter of right based on contributions, they are termed **entitlement** programs.[14]

Components of Social Insurance

There are a number of social insurance programs designed to meet different contingencies.

OLD AGE, SURVIVORS, AND DISABILITY INSURANCE (OASDI)   This is the largest of the social insurance programs and the full, technical name of Social Security. When Social Security was first legislated in 1935, it was designed to provide benefits to the elderly. Within a year, however, benefits were added for survivors (popularly referred to as the "widows and orphans" program). Coverage for the disabled was added in 1956.

Insurance premiums to fund benefits are collected through payroll taxes on employees and employers under the Federal Insurance Contributions Act (the familiar FICA on your weekly or monthly pay stub) and deposited in a Social Security trust fund. The self-employed pay into a similar trust fund. Unlike private insurance, premiums paid into the fund over a person's lifetime are not sufficient to pay for the level of benefits actually received. The elderly receive more than they actually pay in. Social Security is funded, for the most part, by payroll taxes levied on currently working Americans.

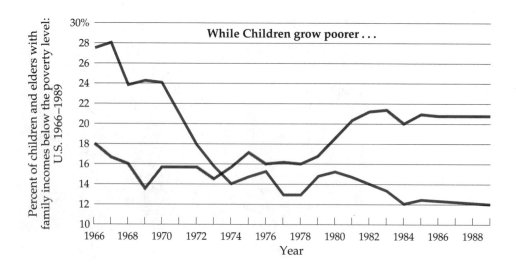

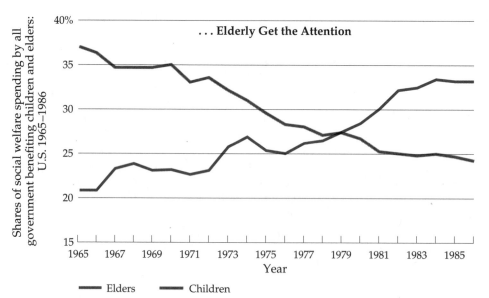

Figure 18.3 Age, government benefits, and poverty

Source: The Washington Post National Edition, *March 4, 1991, p. 31.*

Because inflation tends to undermine the purchasing power of benefits over time, Congress added automatic annual cost-of-living adjustments to OASDI in 1975. Alarm at the rising cost of COLAs during the Reagan years led the National Commission on Social Security to recommend and Congress to legislate a provision for a cutback in COLAs if the Social Security trust fund reserves ever fell to dangerously low levels.

Many Americans worry that Social Security funds will run out before they can begin collecting benefits. Experts do not believe that there are rational grounds for this concern. Indeed, the size of the Social Security trust fund has been grow-

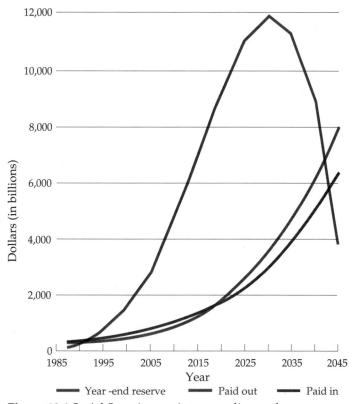

Figure 18.4 Social Security receipts, spending and reserves

Source: U.S. Congress, House, House Committee on Ways and Means. "1988 Annual Report of the Board of Trustees of the Federal Old-Age and Survivors Insurance and Disability Insurance Trust Funds," 100th Congress, 2nd session, May 5, 1988, pp. 141–142.

ing. Using conservative actuarial assumptions, fund surpluses should last until at least 2060. Fund reserves are so high at the present time, in fact, that it makes the federal budget deficit much smaller than it might otherwise be (see Figure 18.4).

MEDICARE   Funded by a special payroll tax on employees and employers, Medicare pays for a substantial portion of the hospital, doctor, and drug costs of retirees and the disabled. Medicare was created in 1965. It has grown into one of the largest federal programs in terms of total dollar expenditures. Rapidly rising health care costs since 1965 have pushed Medicare outlays to such high levels that efforts to control its costs have become one of the constants of American politics.

UNEMPLOYMENT INSURANCE   Unemployment insurance is administered by the states under federal guidelines. It is financed by federal and state taxes on employers for each of their employees. The level of benefits is set by the states, with wide variations evident between them. Because of strict eligibility requirements and limited funds, fewer than half of those who are unemployed are covered by the program,[15] and the extent of coverage is diminishing year by year. In 1990, only 4 in 10 unemployed workers were covered, compared to 7 in 10 in 1976.[16] The pressure of the 1991–1992 recession forced President Bush to reach an agreement with Congress to extend unemployment benefits.

Does Social Insurance Work?

In an era when it is fashionable to deride the ability of government to do anything well, it's important to know about the relative success of America's social insurance programs. Though not without problems, they do a fairly good job of delivering on their promises at a reasonable cost.

SUCCESSES   Social Security works beyond the wildest dreams of its founders. Though benefits do not allow people to live in a luxurious fashion, they provide an income floor for the retired and pay for costly medical services that, prior to 1965, were as likely as not to impoverish those who had serious illnesses and long hospital stays. The improvement in the living standards of the elderly is evident in the decline of the official poverty rate for them.[17] The Office of Management and Budget estimated in 1984 that the poverty rate for Americans over the age of 65 would have been about 55 percent had Social Security not existed.[18]

The effectiveness of social insurance programs is shown by a massive study reported in 1989 by the U.S. Census Bureau on the effects of all government taxing and spending programs on income inequality and poverty. Their principal finding was that Social Security [including Medicare] "is the Federal government's most effective weapon against poverty and reduces the inequality of Americans' income more than the tax system and more than recent social welfare [means-tested] programs. . . ."[19]

PROBLEMS   Despite these successes, many problems remain. The financial viability of Social Security and Medicare has been achieved, for instance, only because Congress has steadily raised payroll taxes. For a majority of Americans, FICA and Medicare taxes now take a larger bite out of their paychecks than the personal income tax. For those who worry that taxes are inherently unjust and inefficient, this trend is cause for concern. Whether taxes are too high cannot be answered objectively or scientifically, of course, though it is worth repeating the point that our effective tax rates remain well below those of most Western countries.

There is some reason to believe, moreover, that the overall effect of social insurance programs is *regressive*: under it, the well-off do better than the not-so-well-off. The main reason for this is that Social Security benefits are tied to one's lifetime earnings. The higher one's income has been, the higher the taxes paid and the higher the benefits received. Moreover, income earned in wages and salaries beyond a certain ceiling causes a retiree to lose old age benefits; this is not the case for the more wealthy retiree who receives income from investments (stock, real estate, etc.). The middle-class elderly also seem better able to take advantage of the medical care provided by Medicare and to participate in the heavily subsidized Supplemental Medical Insurance program to cover doctor costs.

Another problem is the political tension that seems to be building between the elderly who receive benefits and those who are still working and paying FICA taxes to support the programs. As the population ages, there are fewer workers to pay taxes to support those who receive Social Security benefits. Today, there are three such workers for every retiree; by the year 2020, there will only be two.

Save Social Security

Organizations representing senior citizens have been very influential in shaping the kinds of social welfare programs that we have in the United States.

Because the elderly are well organized and politically active, moreover, their needs are attended to by elected officials and are likely to receive even more attention in the future. This is likely to have the effect of further accentuating the tendency of the American social welfare state to favor the elderly at the expense of others in need, particularly the very young and the poor. As Senator Daniel Patrick Moynihan says, "Old people vote. Children don't. That much is a simple fact. For people with the franchise, this is a tremendously responsive system."[20]

There is also concern that Medicare, while vastly improving the medical care situation for the elderly, has introduced significant distortions into the American health care system. Complaints have been heard about the steadily escalating costs of Medicare because of increases in the number of Americans over the age of 65, the steady introduction of high-technology (and expensive) medical care, and loose controls over doctors' and hospitals' costs. Others worry that the price inflation introduced by this massive influx of government money has put first-class doctor and hospital services out of the reach of the nonelderly and the nonpoor (the very poor are assisted by Medicaid). It is one reason why the issue of national health insurance is now on the political agenda.

PUBLIC ASSISTANCE (WELFARE)

Public assistance (more commonly known as welfare) accounts for only a small part of the annual federal budget but attracts more popular discontent than virtually anything else our government does. While Social Security and Medicare are politically sacrosanct and largely immune from criticism, welfare is the target of widespread criticism and the subject of more proposals for reform than one can think of.

It's probably fair to say that almost everybody dislikes welfare: not just conservatives, but liberals as well; not just the average citizen, but also welfare recipients; and not just voters and political leaders, but people who work for welfare agencies. A general consensus exists among very strange bedfellows that something is wrong with the way in which we organize public assistance, though no consensus exists on what ought to be done about it. This feeling has persisted for a long time. As one student of welfare puts it, "The general pattern has varied little since the New Deal: since 1935 a majority of Americans have never wanted to spend more on welfare."[21]

It's no great mystery why people dislike welfare. For most Americans, welfare seems to contradict such cherished cultural values as independence, hard work, family, and responsibility for one's own actions.[22] Public opinion polls consistently show that Americans believe that welfare keeps people dependent, doesn't do a good job of helping people stand on their own two feet, and encourages divorce and family disintegration.[23]

The Components of Public Assistance

There are several means-tested federal programs designed to assist low-income Americans.

AFDC   Aid to Families with Dependent Children is the largest and least popular means-tested program. The program distributes cash benefits mainly to poor single-parent households with children. Most goes to female-headed households, where poverty is most marked.

AFDC was created in 1935 as part of the original Social Security Act. The act specified that the federal government would contribute to state and locally administered programs of assistance to low-income families with children, as long as they were willing to operate under general federal guidelines. At the time, government officials thought that these measures would be temporary instruments to ease some of the suffering of families made destitute by the death or incapacitation of fathers and were destined to wither away as the economy revived and the Social Security system reached maturity.[24] Instead, the program has become a permanent and significant part of the nation's social welfare system.

Administratively, AFDC is complex. Control over it, as well as its funding, is shared by federal, state, and local jurisdictions. Each state sets its own standards for need, for treatment of recipient income and assets, and for benefit levels. Because of the large role of the states, benefits paid to recipients varies dramatically across the states, as we saw in Table 18.1. During the 1991–1992 recession states like California, Ohio, and Illinois, formerly quite generous with welfare recipients, drastically cut benefits.

Because many Americans believe that undeserving people might be tempted to "go on the dole," AFDC is surrounded by mountains of red tape. Welfare workers spend much of their time investigating the employment records of applicants, their possible assets and sources of income, the whereabouts of spouses who might make a financial contribution to the dependent family, and the possibility that the single mother might be cohabiting with a male who should be expected to help pay the bills. Recipients and advocates for the poor insist that the entire process is demeaning and degrading. Some conservatives respond that this is precisely the point; people should not want to be on welfare. Whether intended or not, treatment of the poor in this manner contributes to the fact that many of the poor who are eligible for AFDC never apply.

Though AFDC grew during the 1960s and 1970s, the program has never amounted to much as a proportion of GNP or of government spending (see Figure

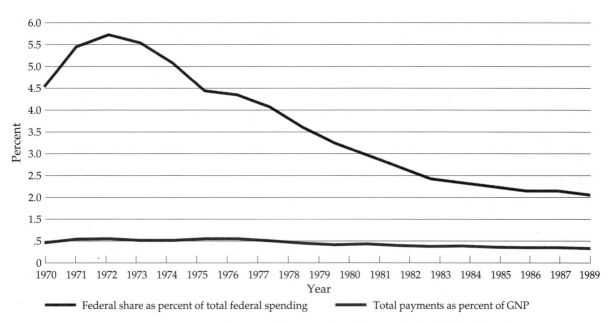

Figure 18.5 Trends in Aid for Families of Dependent Children benefits payments

Source: Statistical Abstracts of the U.S., 1991 *(Washington, D.C.: U.S. Bureau of the Census, 1991),* Table 381.

18.5). Nor does it provide very much to poor families. In no single year since 1950 has the average annual AFDC family payment exceeded 70 percent of the official poverty line. Even when noncash programs, such as food stamps and Medicaid, are added, welfare doesn't lift most recipient families above the poverty line. It is important to note, moreover, that benefits going to poor families with dependent children have been declining steadily since 1970, with the most notable declines coming after 1980.[25] Life on welfare is no picnic (see the "Resource Feature" on how welfare mothers live).

FOOD STAMPS   This program is available to all poor Americans below a certain income line. Like AFDC, food stamp benefit levels are set by the states under general federal guidelines, and states vary substantially in their generosity. The program seems to have made a significant dent in the prevalence of malnutrition in the United States, even though the average benefit has never exceeded 80 cents per person per meal.[26]

MEDICAID   The federal government provides matching funds to the states to provide medical assistance for their indigent citizens. With the exception of requirements that they provide Medicaid for all AFDC and Supplemental Security Income (SSI) recipients (see below), the states formulate their own eligibility requirements and set their own benefit levels. Eligibility rules are complex and tend to exclude those who are not extremely poor, blind, disabled, or children with out-of-work parents. Furthermore, as states try to contain Medicaid costs in the face of rising taxpayer discontent and budgetary problems, they have made access even more difficult. The problem of noninclusion is serious; only about

These welfare mothers did not live extravagantly. The typical mother spent only $954 a month to support a family of four, which is slightly less than the federal poverty line. The poverty line is an arbitrary threshold, set 25 years ago as a matter of political convenience, but surveys suggest that most Americans think the threshold is too low, not too high. . . .

In 1986 the typical Gallup respondent said that a family of four needed $349 a week (roughly $1,500 a month) to get along. Poorer families set the threshold lower, but even the heads of families with incomes below $10,000 said that a family of four needed $1,200 a month to get along. Allowing for inflation, the 1988 figure would be about $1,300. Using this standard, Edin's welfare families were getting along on three-quarters of what low-income Americans thought a family needed. . . .

None of the 22 mothers reported expenditures totalling more than 133 percent of the poverty line, even when we include Food Stamps. Half lived in very bad neighborhoods. Half lived in badly run-down apartments, where the heat and hot water were frequently

out of order, the roof leaked, plaster was falling off the walls, or windows fit so badly that the wind blew through the apartment in the winter. One in three did without a telephone, and one in three reported spending nothing whatever on entertainment. Many said their food budgets were too tight for fresh fruit or vegetables. Only one had a working car.

It is true that all these welfare mothers had color television sets, and that a third had video recorders—"extravagances" that often offend intellectuals who rely on books for entertainment. But because both TV sets and video recorders last a long time, they cost only a few dollars a month. Since they provided both the mothers and their children with free entertainment, the mothers were willing to forego almost any other comfort (such as reliable hot water or fresh vegetables) to ensure that they had a working television. Without one, their lives would have been unimaginably bleak.

Source: From a study by Kathryn Edin, reported in Christopher Jencks and Kathryn Edin, "The Real Welfare Problem," *The American Prospect* (Spring 1990), pp. 84–85.

40 percent of the nation's officially designated poor are covered by Medicaid,[27] leaving the remainder out in the cold, as it were, without medical benefits or protection.

OTHER MEANS-TESTED PROGRAMS   *Supplemental Security Income* (SSI) is a program that was created in 1974 that provides cash benefits to the elderly, blind, and disabled poor for whom social insurance programs are insufficient to elevate them above the poverty line. The program is a relatively small one and getting smaller. *Housing assistance* programs come in a dizzying number of forms, including subsidies to states and local communities to build public housing, tax incentives for developers to build in low-income areas, and rent supplement payments to poor families to help them pay rent. *Job training* was a major part of the federal anti-poverty programs during the 1960s and 1970s—with apparent success, according to most studies[28]—but were cut back to almost nothing during the 1980s. *Head Start*, the only widely popular means-tested social welfare program, reaches about 300,000 children per year (roughly 20 percent of those who are technically eligible) in its effort to prepare poor preschool children for entrance into public schools.

Most experts believe that the federal food stamp program has reduced significantly the level of malnutrition in the United States.

The Debate About Welfare

THE CONSERVATIVE CRITIQUE   Those who believe in the efficiency and justice of the market and the inevitable inefficiencies and injustices of big government have always despised public assistance. Their critique has become a familiar part of American political discourse.[29] The objections follow.

Welfare Hurts American Economic Performance   Welfare programs are supported by taxes. The economy would operate more efficiently and economic growth would be more likely if these monies were left in the hands of individuals and corporations to invest.

Welfare Undermines the Work Ethic   If people can live reasonably well "on the dole" without working, it is argued, they will lose the incentive to work. Opponents of welfare argue that AFDC, food stamps, rent supplements, and Medicaid programs are so generous that many people see no reason to work. As Milton and Rose Friedman put it, "Those on relief have little incentive to earn income."[30]

Welfare Encourages Family Disintegration   Prominent conservatives like Lawrence Mead and George Gilder claim that welfare contributes to the breakup of families. As evidence, they point to the fact that the rate of family disintegration and the level of welfare spending increased at the same time, starting in the late 1960s. A number of factors are said to produce this effect. First, because AFDC only goes to single-parent families, poor couples are financially better off if they do not marry or if they break up their marriage when a baby is born. Second, AFDC gives more independence to women with children who no longer feel financially compelled to enter into, or stay in, a marriage that they do not want to be in.

Welfare Creates a Permanent Dependent Class   Welfare, it is argued, becomes a habit. People remain recipients for long stretches of time. Their children, knowing no other model of how life might be lived, eventually come to see life on welfare as normal. This life of dependency, in turn, contributes to a syndrome of problematic behavior that makes escape from dependency unlikely.

Many Americans agree with these characterizations of welfare and its effects. The available research, however, does not support many of them.[31] For instance, social scientists have discovered that most welfare recipients stay on the relief rolls for only short periods of time. There are relatively few who fit in the lifetime and cross-generational categories, those generally designated the urban underclass.[32] Research also shows that welfare does not contribute to family breakup, illegitimacy, dependency, or a disinclination to work to a very significant extent. These are real problems among the poor, to be sure, but their main causes, lie elsewhere, particularly in the economy according to some social scientists.[33] Nor is there much evidence that welfare programs have a significant adverse effect on American economic performance, primarily because public assistance is but a drop in the bucket of the federal budget. Social welfare expenditures are far lower in America than in other countries that are outperforming us economically.

OTHER CRITICISMS OF WELFARE   Many people who want to see government do more to create an equitable society, without extremes of rich and poor, are just as critical of welfare as conservatives. Here is their case.

Public Assistance Does Not Diminish Wealth and Income Inequality   Though public assistance redistributes income from the well-off to the least well-off, the program is such a small part of total government spending that it has very little impact on the overall structure of inequality.

Welfare Programs Do Not Reach Enough of the Poor   Many of the poor who are eligible for various means-tested programs do not participate in them. Experts estimate that one-third to one-half of those who are eligible for food stamps and SSI are not enrolled; that close to one-fourth of those who are eligible for AFDC are not in the program; and that one-third of low-income people who are eligible for Medicaid do not receive benefits.[34]

Nor does public assistance do much for the working poor. Most welfare programs distribute benefits to those poor people who cannot be expected to work on a full-time basis: children, the elderly and disabled, and mothers with young children. Those poor people who are in intact families where one or both parents work full or part time are only occasionally covered by welfare. This group includes about 60 percent of the poor. The working poor are overwhelmingly white and of prime working age. They suffer high rates of unemployment or are stuck in low-wage, part-time jobs without benefits. The number of Americans who fit into this category has increased since 1978.[35]

The Real Purpose of Welfare Is Social Control   This thesis is associated with social scientists Frances Fox Piven and Richard A. Cloward.[36] They believe that public assistance is tied to the rhythms of social protest and disruption. When the poor make demands on the system, public assistance increases, as the following box suggests. When the poor are docile, public assistance declines. Cuts in welfare under the Carter, Reagan, and Bush administrations were made possible, they suggest, because the poor were absent from the streets and the voting booths. The Piven and Cloward thesis is provocative and consistent with patterns of welfare spending. Whether it holds up as a general explanation of the American welfare system must await further research.

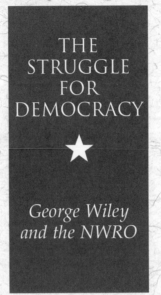

THE STRUGGLE FOR DEMOCRACY

★

George Wiley and the NWRO

George Wiley believed that poor people could organize themselves and make a difference in American politics. He believed they could form stable, mass-based organizations capable of influencing national elections and the legislative process in Washington just like any other sizeable group of Americans, be they farmers, doctors, or business people.

What was needed was an issue that could mobilize people around a common interest and sustain their participation over the long haul. He considered housing, crime, education, and health care before settling on welfare rights. Two prominent social scientists showed him that welfare recipients were not receiving all of the benefits they were legally entitled to, and that many eligible poor people were not receiving benefits at all. In August 1966, Wiley announced the formation of the National Welfare Rights Organization (NWRO) to organize welfare recipients and potential recipients into a political force for economic justice, calling it "the birth of a new movement."

The NWRO enjoyed some initial success. Membership eventually reached 22,000. Foundations and church groups made sizeable financial contributions. Welfare rolls expanded and the average benefit paid per recipient grew larger as city councils, welfare agencies, mayors, and governors responded to legal challenges, lobbying efforts, and demonstrations mounted by the NWRO. Congress began to consider legislation to reform the welfare system.

The influence of the NWRO proved short-lived, however. Wiley's effort to form an enduring poor people's organization ultimately failed, losing members and influence. It succumbed to several inescapable problems: the lack of resources among the poor; the difficulty of organizing people around a "right"—welfare—that carries a terrible stigma in the American political culture; and abandonment by political allies as American politics turned in a more conservative direction after Richard Nixon's election in 1968. Nevertheless, for a time, poor people made a difference in city halls, legislatures, and Congress. For a time, the ideal of political equality was given life.

Source: Frances Fox Piven and Richard A. Cloward, *Poor People's Movements* (New York: Vintage, 1979), ch. 5.

HOW THE AMERICAN WELFARE STATE IS DIFFERENT

Although all modern capitalist countries have social welfare states, not all social welfare states are alike.

Welfare states range from low-benefit, targeted types at one end of the spectrum to high-benefit, universal types at the other end. The former are called "minimal" or "liberal" (in the free market, limited government sense of the word *liberal*) welfare states; the latter are called "developed" or "social democratic" welfare states.[37] The United States is very close to being at the minimal end of the spectrum. How you feel about this depends on your values. For those who believe that small government is always better than big government, it is a very good thing. Others may disagree.

How do we compare to other social welfare states? The comparisons that follow are to the OECD (Organization of Economic Cooperation and Development) nations: Western Europe, Japan, Australia, and New Zealand.

- *The U.S. welfare state developed later than the others.* The term "laggard" has been used to characterize the American welfare state.[38] With rare exception, social insurance programs were introduced in America much later than elsewhere (see Table 18.2).

- *The American welfare state is smaller than most.* Despite complaints about its size and cost, ours is one of the smallest of the welfare states.[39] Table 18.3 shows total expenditures on social insurance and public assistance as a percentage of GDP for each of the OECD nations. Only Japan and Australia spend relatively less, and the former is well known for the generosity of company benefits to workers, including lifetime employment in its largest corporations.

- *The American welfare state covers fewer people than other welfare states.* Welfare states near the developed end of the spectrum blanket their entire populations with benefits. Family allowances, for instance, go to all citizens who have children in such places as Austria, the Netherlands, Norway, and Sweden. Medical coverage is universal in most of the OECD nations. In the United States, in contrast, social welfare provision is a patchwork thing, with many citizens who are not protected or covered. Thus, children in AFDC

| | | Table 18.2 | |
| | *Introduction of Welfare State Programs* | | |
	Disability Insurance	*Pension Insurance*	*Unemployment Insurance*
Germany	1884	1889	1927
Great Britain	1887	1908	1911
United States	1930	1935	1935

Source: Adapted from R. T. Kudrle and T. R. Marmor, "The Development of Welfare States in North America," in P. Flora and A. J. Heindenheimer, eds., *The Development of Welfare States in Europe and America* (London: Transaction, 1981), p. 83.

Table 18.3

Social Welfare Spending as a Percentage of GDP—
the United States Compared to the OECD Nations

	Total	Pensions	Health Benefits	Public Assistance	Family Allowances	Unemployment Benefits
Canada	13.7	3.7	4.1	3.0	1.2	1.7
United States	9.6	3.9	2.1	3.0	0	0.6
Austria	16.3	8.8	3.7	0.7	2.5	0.6
Belgium	19.8	6.6	6.3	0.7	2.6	3.6
Denmark	24.9	7.9	6.7	6.3	0.8	3.2
Finland	15.0	6.2	5.1	2.3	0.8	0.6
France	22.6	7.7	7.0	4.0	2.7	1.2
Germany	18.8	9.5	5.8	0.9	1.2	1.4
Ireland	17.8	5.2	9.1	0.5	1.0	2.0
Italy	12.8	6.2	5.4	0.7	n.a	0.5
Netherlands	24.1	11.5	7.7	1.7	2.1	1.1
Norway	18.7	7.5	8.1	1.7	1.0	0.4
Spain	13.6	9.3	3.3	0.5	0.4	0.1
Sweden	28.3	9.7	11.4	5.2	1.6	0.4
Switzerland	11.4	7.5	2.6	1.1	0.1	0.1
United Kingdom	15.1	5.6	4.9	2.7	1.5	0.4
Japan	7.5	2.2	3.5	1.2	0.1	0.4
Australia	8.1	4.3	2.5	0.5	n.a.	0.8
New Zealand	11.9	6.7	4.9	0	n.a.	0.3

Source: Calculated from ILO, *The Cost of Social Security.* From Arnold Heidenheimer, et al., *Comparative Public Policy,* 3rd ed. (New York: St. Martin's Press, 1990).

families receive more generous benefits than do poor children in intact families. Many poor Americans receive Medicaid, while others do not.

- *The elderly do considerably better than the young in the American welfare state.* Medicare and Social Security, already the largest parts of social welfare in the United States, continue to outstrip the rate of growth of programs that benefit the nonelderly poor, especially children.[40] In most other welfare states, family allowances and universal medical coverage make benefit distributions more balanced.[41]

- *The American welfare state is less redistributive.* The degree of income equality in the OECD nations (with the exception of Japan) is a function of the amount of money that they spend on social welfare programs and of the degree to which program coverage is universal. The United States ranks very low on both, so our social welfare state does not make much of a dent in the degree of income and wealth inequality when compared with other nations.[42] Table 18.4 shows the share of national income going to the bottom 20 percent of the population in several countries, before and after government benefits and taxes are taken into account. The lag in U.S. performance is obvious. If you believe that inequality is a natural and just outcome of a free market system that must not be tampered with, then you will not be bothered much by such findings. Others of you, however, may be.

Table 18.4
Share of National Income Received by Bottom 20 Percent of Families

	Share of National Income, Not Taking Government Benefits or Taxes into Account	Share of National Income, Taking Government Benefits and Taxes into Account
Canada	4.6	5.3
United States	3.8	4.5
United Kingdom	4.9	5.8
West Germany	4.4	5.0
Sweden	6.6	8.0
Norway	4.9	6.3
Israel	4.5	6.0

Source: From Timothy M. Smeeding, Michael O'Higgins, and Lee Rainwater, *Poverty, Inequality and Income Distribution in Comparative Perspective* (Washington, D.C.: Urban Institute, 1990), p. 34.

WHY THE AMERICAN WELFARE STATE IS THE WAY IT IS: STRUCTURAL AND POLITICAL FACTORS

How do we explain the special character of the American welfare state? In this section, we identify structural and political factors that influence the kind of social welfare state that we have.

Constitutional Rules

Federalism is one of the reasons why social welfare programs were introduced here so late. Until the 1930s, it was not clear where the main responsibility for social welfare was lodged constitutionally. It was not generally accepted that the national government had any authority at all on social welfare matters until the Supreme Court reluctantly and belatedly relented and accepted the New Deal. It was only in 1935, with the passage of the Social Security Act, that our nation took the first step toward building a social insurance safety net that already had been in place in Germany since 1889.

Federalism is also responsible for the incredible administrative complexity of our social welfare state: some programs are run as national programs from Washington, D.C.; some are jointly funded and administered by federal and state governments; and some are mainly local in nature but operate under federal guidelines. This divided and shared authority, of course, characterizes many government programs.

Federalism is also the cause of the great unevenness in program coverage. Rather than a system of universal and uniform national provision in which all citizens are covered, our system takes into account the needs and interests of each of the states.[43] The result is great variation in benefits, eligibility requirements, and rules among the states. The only programs that are universal in the European sense (uniform, comprehensive, and administered and funded by the national government) are Social Security and Medicare.

Racial and Ethnic Diversity

It is often argued that Europe's greater propensity toward welfare states with universal coverage is a result of the ethnic and racial homogeneity of their societies. In homogenous societies, the argument goes, voters are willing to support generous welfare programs, because recipients are felt to be very much like themselves. Recipients are considered neighbors, down on their luck, perhaps, but not strangers. Recipients are looked on as "us" rather than "them."[44]

Whether or not this argument is valid, it is apparent that racial and ethnic tensions influence the shape of the American welfare state. Some of the hostility toward public assistance, for instance , is probably related to the fact that black Americans make up a disproportionately large share of welfare recipients (even though they remain less than a majority of all recipients). Politicians like David Duke in Louisiana and Jesse Helms in North Carolina have demonstrated considerable skill in weaving together the racial and welfare themes in their electoral campaigns.

Political Culture

Almost every aspect of the American political culture works against a generous and comprehensive welfare state. The belief in individualism is especially important—that part of the American creed that emphasizes independence, responsibility, and autonomy. Voters who believe that people should stand on their own two feet and take responsibility for their lives are not likely to be sympathetic to welfare claims. Voters who believe that people generally get what they deserve are not likely to take kindly to appeals for help from able-bodied, working-age people.[45]

Antigovernment themes in the political culture also play a role. Generous and comprehensive welfare states, such as those in Europe, are almost always large and centralized states supported by high taxes. Americans, being deeply suspicious of politicians, centralized government, and taxes, are strongly resistant to welfare state appeals.

Our political culture also supports more voluntary efforts in welfare matters than other nations do, leaving government with less to do. Organizations like the United Way and the Salvation Army take on many responsibilities that govern-

Americans have a long tradition of voluntarism and private charitable giving, somewhat reducing the pressure on government for the kinds of social services provided in other countries.

ments shoulder in other Western democracies. Because people believe that there are inevitable inefficiencies in government and efficiencies in the private market, many aspects of social welfare are turned over to private insurance companies, nursing homes, and hospitals.

Business Power

Business plays a particularly important role in American politics (see Chapter 7, "Interest Groups and Corporations in American Politics"). Almost without exception, the business community has opposed the creation of a welfare state along European lines. It has been a voice for low taxes and limited benefits, voluntary efforts over government responsibility, and profit-making welfare providers over government agencies. We can see this in the area of medical care. Ours is the only Western democratic nation that does not have a universal system of medical provision. Ours is a patchwork quilt that combines social insurance for the elderly (Medicare), a means-tested program (Medicaid) for *some* of the poor, private insurance (Blue Cross/Blue Shield, Prudential, etc.), and a multitude of "for-profit" hospitals and nursing homes, and leaves roughly 35 million people without medical or hospital coverage at all.[46] Doctors, hospitals' corporations, insurance companies, and nursing home trade associations pressure politicians to maintain this nonuniversal system. This system of health care delivery is probably not the most efficient. We spend a larger share of our GNP on health care than any other nation in the world, but we rank below every industrialized nation in the world except Spain on measures of infant mortality and life expectancy.[47]

Labor Weakness

Those countries where the working class is organized and exercises significant political power have extensive welfare states; those countries where the working class is not well organized and fails to exercise significant political power have minimal welfare states.[48] The political power of the working class is usually measured by scholars in terms of the percentage of workers who are in labor unions and the relative success of parties that are closely associated with unions (like Socialist, Social Democratic, and Labor parties). American labor unions have never been very strong or influential when compared with labor unions in other Western capitalist societies. The proportion of American workers who join labor unions always has been low in the United States when compared with other capitalist countries and is steadily declining. Moreover, neither of our political parties defines itself as a working class or a labor party committed to using government as an instrument of equality, equivalent, let us say, to the Social Democratic party that has dominated Swedish politics since the mid-1930s.

Interest Groups

Interest groups, as we have seen, speak with a strong "upper-class accent," overrepresenting business, the well-to-do, and the professions. By and large, these groups are not among those that push for the expansion of the welfare state.

A particularly important interest in defining the character of the American welfare state is the elderly, who are well-organized and active as an electorate. The elderly are probably more influential in politics than the elderly in other countries where strong political parties dissipate the power of interest groups.[49]

REFORMING SOCIAL WELFARE

Dissatisfaction with social welfare is widespread, so it's to be expected that proposals for reform are abundant.

Conservative Proposals

Most conservatives know that a social welfare state of some kind is necessary in the modern world. Most recognize that even a smoothly operating market economy cannot provide income for people who cannot work, be they very young, disabled, or elderly. A proper welfare state, for most conservatives, would provide no more than a "safety net" to the deserving poor. It would not intrude on the market, depend on heavy taxation, or act in a paternalistic fashion. It would depend primarily on social insurance and would try to "privatize" social services. Such a welfare state would be small, less expensive than the present one, less disruptive of economic activities, and no threat to the freedom of its citizens.[50]

On those occasions when means-tested programs are unavoidable, recipients should be required to work or to enter job training programs. The cycle of dependency must be broken and self-sufficiency must be encouraged by forcing recipients to prepare for and to enter the job market. Many liberals have recently joined conservatives to force legislative action on this front. This new consensus was embodied in the Work Incentive (WIN) program enacted by Congress in 1981 and the 1988 welfare reform (JOBS). WIN *permitted* states to create programs that required welfare recipients to participate in job placement and job training programs. The 1988 law *required* able-bodied welfare recipients with children over the age of 3 to enter educational, job training, and job placement programs.

Proponents argue that work requirements are good for welfare recipients, making them self-sufficient and part of the American mainstream.[51] Critics worry that "forced work" is a form of slavery and that it "blames the victim" for poverty rather than focusing on the general condition of the economy. Finally, critics suggest, former welfare recipients in the work force are unlikely to escape poverty unless the minimum wage is increased.[52]

Liberal Proposals

Many liberals believe that the present American welfare state is fine in principle and laudable in its intentions, but needs some repair work. Their principal focus is on helping the working poor and providing national health insurance.

Two-parent, poor families in which one or both parents work are almost entirely left out in the cold in our welfare system. Suggestions to help this sizable group of Americans include Medicaid coverage, housing subsidies, expansion of the earned income tax credit, and food assistance so that none of them fall through the safety net, as they now do. Other suggestions include a substantial increase in the minimum wage, long frozen and only now beginning to rise, so that working

Americans with full-time jobs no longer find themselves beneath the poverty line.[53] (In 1990, a full-time minimum wage worker supporting a family of four found that his or her income was about $4,500 below the official poverty line.) Proponents point out that a higher minimum wage would also encourage more people to work rather than depend on welfare. Finally, those who believe that the problems of the poor are mainly the result of economic transformations that have left the populations of central cities behind advocate full-employment policies and job training programs.[54]

There is also a growing consensus among liberals (and even some conservatives) that an equitable and efficient society requires universal health insurance. Our present system—a mix of private insurance, social insurance, and public assistance—is highly inefficient, costing more than systems in most other industrialized nations and delivering less, and highly unjust, in the sense that many Americans do without any medical coverage at all. Even among those who are covered by private or public insurance, coverage is so uneven and inconsistent for some of them that one catastrophic illness is enough to lead to financial disaster. There are many proposals around for universal health insurance, though Canada's seems to be getting the most attention because of its relatively low cost, its efficiency in delivery of health care services, and its popularity among the Canadian public.[55] Attention is also being paid to Hawaii's system, which provides health insurance to over 90 percent of its citizens at lower cost than systems in the rest of the country, where coverage is less complete.

SOCIAL WELFARE AND DEMOCRACY

The main elements of social welfare in the United States, namely Social Security and public assistance, only happened because of strong popular pressures put on political and economic leaders. The Great Depression and the popular movements for economic justice that it spawned during the 1930s were the catalysts for the United States to institute a range of social insurance programs that were already widely available in Europe. The steady expansion of Social Security, furthermore, was carried out during the postwar decades by a Democratic party that enjoyed strong electoral support from the American people. Moreover, the most significant expansion of public assistance took place from the mid-1960s to the mid-1970s, at least in part, as a response to the Civil Rights and Anti-Poverty movements that represented a significant new involvement in politics by Americans who had long been excluded from politics. Finally, public opinion polls show strong public support for almost every program of the American welfare state, though most Americans would like to see a larger federal role in providing health insurance and something done to improve public assistance.

On the other hand, the kind of welfare state that we have is also attributable to the prominent role played by business, and by interest groups representing the professions and the elderly. It seems that the catalyst for the creation of social welfare programs is provided by the struggle for democracy, while program details are worked out by those who have the resources to be significant players in the political game.

The effects of social welfare on democracy are also mixed. Social insurance, especially Social Security and Medicare, has surely enhanced the health and well-being of the elderly and has enabled them to become more active citizens. By

The enormously popular Townsend movement, with its call for financial payment to elderly Americans, was an important factor in the passage of the Social Security Act.

making a dent in the prevalence of poverty among the elderly, social insurance has made the elderly more equal among themselves and more equal in relationship to other groups in American society. As such, social insurance has played a significant role in enhancing popular sovereignty and political equality in the United States. On the other hand, those on public assistance have not been so fortunate. Most important, welfare does not appear to leave much room for the development of dignity, independence, and self-confidence among recipients that is so essential for democratic citizenship. The health of democracy in the United States may depend, in part, on what we choose to do about this problem.

SUMMARY

All developed capitalist societies are welfare states. The catalyst for the development of welfare states is industrialization, which created many social and economic problems, and undermined institutions that traditionally provided for the welfare of the population. Industrialization also produced the economic and organizational resources that make the welfare state possible. The political impetus for the creation of social welfare programs has come from both the business community and the public.

The social welfare commitment of the federal government has grown substantially since the 1930s, though the Reagan Revolution slowed the growth considerably, even reversing the trend for means-tested programs for the poor.

Social insurance is the largest and most popular part of the American social welfare state. Social Security and Medicare are universal entitlement programs, funded primarily by means of payroll taxes. Social Security and Medicare have worked, in the sense that those who have retired are less likely to live in poverty than before the programs were introduced and are more likely to receive adequate medical care.

Public assistance is the least popular and least funded part of the American welfare state. Welfare programs like AFDC, food stamps, and Medicaid, are means-tested programs. Conservative critics believe that welfare hurts the economy, undermines work incentives and the family, and creates dependency rather than self-reliance. Liberal critics think that welfare does not do enough to help the poor because of spotty coverage and low benefits, and fails to treat recipients with dignity. Some radical critics believe that welfare is mainly a device for social control.

The American welfare state is very different from others. Ours is smaller, less comprehensive, less redistributive, and more tilted toward the elderly. Structural and political factors explain most of the differences.

There are many proposals for reform of American social welfare policy. Conservatives advocate an inexpensive, nonintrusive, and nonpaternalistic welfare state. Liberals want to help the working poor and provide universal health insurance.

To Ponder

1. Are the elderly too powerful? Do political leaders pay them too much heed compared to other groups?

2. Does public assistance help or hinder the people who receive it?

3. Would the creation of a welfare state along the lines of those in the Scandinavian nations harm economic efficiency? Would it diminish freedom?

4. Are there alternatives to welfare? What would you replace it with if you could choose?

Suggested Readings

Bernstein, Merton C., and Joan Brodshaug Bernstein. *Social Security: The System That Works.* New York: Basic Books, 1988.
    As the title suggests, a brief for the effectiveness of Social Security; filled with rich detail on how Social Security works and on emerging public policy issues.

Block, Fred, et al., eds. *The Mean Season.* New York: Pantheon, 1987.
    The authors chronicle and explain the assault on the American welfare state during the Reagan years, and puncture many of the myths perpetuated by the opponents of the welfare state.

Glazer, Nathan. *The Limits of Social Policy.* Cambridge, MA: Harvard University Press, 1988.
    An eloquent neoconservative critique of welfare and an argument for why it is so difficult for government to solve social problems.

Jencks, Christopher, and Paul E. Peterson, eds. *The Urban Underclass.* Washington, D.C.: Brookings Institution, 1991.
    A series of research reports on the extent of the urban underclass and how it was created, and proposals for how it might be eliminated.

Katz, Michael B. *The Undeserving Poor.* New York: Pantheon, 1989.
    A fascinating look at our changing views about the poor and the programs that purport to help them.

Marmor, Theodore R. K., Jerry L. Mashaw, and Philip L. Harvey. *America's Misunderstood Welfare State.* New York: HarperCollins, 1990.
    This book examines the most persistent myths about American social welfare.

Murray, Charles. *Losing Ground: American Social Policy, 1950–1980.* New York: Basic Books, 1984.
  The most popular and widely discussed book of the 1980s on what is wrong with welfare. Murray's central point is that welfare makes poverty worse.

Ringen, Stein. *The Possibility of Politics: A Study in the Political Economy of the Welfare State.* New York: Clarendon Press, 1987.
  The most exhaustive compilation and analysis of the research literature on the effects of the welfare state; demonstrates that welfare state programs in the capitalist nations are, in the main, effective and legitimate.

Schwarz, John E. *America's Hidden Success: A Reassessment of Public Policy from Kennedy to Reagan.* New York: Norton, 1988.
  A careful look at most social insurance and means-tested programs in the United States and a compilation of evidence about how they work. He concludes that most work better than most Americans imagine.

Wilensky, Harold. *The Welfare State and Equality.* Berkeley, CA: University of California Press, 1975.
  The classic exposition of the view that Western welfare states are the product of industrialization and the aging of populations.

Notes

1. David Stockman, *The Triumph of Politics: Why the Reagan Revolution Failed* (New York: Harper-Collins, 1986), pp. 181, 183, 185.

2. Stockman, *Triumph of Politics*, p. 188.

3. Stockman, *Triumph of Politics*, p. 190.

4. Hedrick Smith, *The Power Game: How Washington Works* (New York: Random House, 1988), p. 359.

5. Fred C. Pampel, *Age, Class, Politics, and the Welfare State* (New York: Cambridge University Press, 1989), p. 16; Harold Wilensky, *The Welfare State and Equality* (Berkeley, CA: University of California Press, 1975); The International Labor Organization, *The Cost of Social Security* (Geneva: International Labor Organization, 1985).

6. Robert E. Goodin, "Reasons for Welfare," in J. Donald Moon, ed, *Responsibility, Rights, and Welfare: The Theory of the Welfare State* (Boulder, CO: Westview Press, 1988).

7. Wilensky, *Welfare State and Equality*. Also see Clark Kerr, et al., *Industrialism and Industrial Man* (New York: Oxford University Press, 1964).

8. Wilensky, *Welfare State and Equality*; Kerr, et al. *Industrialism and Industrial Man.*

9. Reinhold Bendix, *Nation-Building and Citizenship* (New York: Wiley, 1964); Stein Rokkan, *Citizens, Elections, and Parties* (Oslo: Universitetsforlaget, 1970).

10. Gosta Esping-Andersen, *Politics Against Markets* (Princeton, NJ: Princeton University Press, 1985); Walter Korpi, *The Democratic Class Struggle* (New York: Routledge & Kegan Paul, 1983); John Stephens, *The Transition from Capitalism to Socialism* (London: Macmillan, 1979).

11. Irving Kristol, *Two Cheers for Capitalism* (New York: New American Library, Mentor, 1979).

12. Paul Conkin, *The New Deal* (New York: Crowell, 1967); G. William Domhoff, *The Higher Circles* (New York: Vintage, 1971); Gabriel Kolko, *The Triumph of Conservatism* (Chicago: Quadrangle, 1967); James Weinstein, *The Corporate Ideal in the Liberal State* (Boston: Beacon Press, 1968).

13. Eugene Smolensky, et al., "The Declining Significance of Age in the United States: Trends in the Well-Being of Children and the Elderly Since 1939," in John L. Palmer, et al., eds., *The Vulnerable* (Washington, D.C.: Urban Institute, 1988).

14. See Merton C. Bernstein and Joan Brodshaug Bernstein, *Social Security: The System That Works* (New York: Basic Books, 1988), pp. 13–14; Alvin Schorr, *Common Decency: Domestic Politics After Reagan* (New Haven: Yale University Press, 1986), pp. 49–50.

15. Schorr, *Common Decency*, p. 74.

16. Hobart Rowan, "A Safety Net Is Missing," *Washington Post National Edition*, May 27, 1991, p. 5.

17. Schorr, *Common Decency*, p. 57.

18. Bernstein and Bernstein, *Social Security*, p. 208.

19. "U.S. Pensions Found to Lift Many of the Poor," *New York Times*, December 28, 1989, p. A1. See additional evidence on the antipoverty effects of social insurance in Theodore R. K. Marmor, Jerry L. Mashaw, and Philip L. Harvey, *America's Misunderstood Welfare State* (New York: HarperCollins, 1990), ch. 4.

20. "Furor on Medicare Cuts Offers Political Lesson," *New York Times*, October 12, 1990, p. A11.

21. Hugh Heclo, "The Political Foundations of Anti-Poverty Policy," in *Fighting Poverty: What Works and What Doesn't?* Sheldon Danziger and Daniel Weinberg, eds. (Cambridge, MA: Harvard University Press, 1986), p. 330.

22. David T. Ellwood, *Poor Support: Poverty in the American Family* (New York: Basic Books, 1988), p. 5.

23. Ellwood, *Poor Support*, p. 41.

24. Gilbert Steiner, *Social Insecurity: The Politics of Welfare* (Chicago: Rand McNally, 1966), p. 34.

25. Ellwood, *Poor Support*, p. 40.

26. John E. Schwarz, *America's Hidden Success: A Reassessment of Public Policy from Kennedy to Reagan* (New York: Norton, 1988), p. 37.

27. Schorr *Common Decency*, p. 169.

28. Schwarz, *America's Hidden Success*, pp. 42–46.

29. Charles Murray, *Losing Ground: American Social Policy, 1950–1980* (New York: Basic Books, 1984); Martin Anderson, *Welfare* (Stanford, CA: Hoover, 1978); Roger A. Freeman, *The Growth of American Government* (Stanford, CA: Hoover, 1975); Lawrence M. Mead, *Beyond Entitlement* (New York: Free Press, 1986); George Gilder, *Wealth and Poverty* (New York: Basic Books, 1981). Also see Paul E. Peterson, "The Urban Underclass and the Poverty Paradox," in Christopher Jencks and Paul E. Peterson, eds., *The Urban Underclass* (Washington, D.C.: Brookings Institution, 1991).

30. Milton Friedman and Rose Friedman, *Free to Choose* (New York: Avon Books, 1981), p. 98.

31. For a summary of the evidence, see Fred Block, et al., eds., *The Mean Season* (New York: Pantheon, 1987); Danziger and Weinberg, *Fighting Poverty*; Ellwood, *Poor Support*; Robert Havemann, ed., *A Decade of Federal Anti-Poverty Programs* (New York: Academic Press, 1977); Marmor, et al., *America's Misunderstood Welfare State*; Peterson, "The Urban Underclass"; Stein Ringen, *The Possibility of Politics: A Study in the Political Economy of the Welfare State* (New York: Clarendon Press, 1987); Schorr, *Common Decency*; Schwarz, *America's Hidden Success*; Shirley Zimmerman, "The Welfare State and Family Breakup", *Family Relations*, Vol. 40, No. 2 (April, 1991).

32. Christopher Jencks and Paul E. Peterson, eds., *The Urban Underclass* (Washington, D.C.: Brookings Institution, 1991).

33. William Julius Wilson, *The Truly Disadvantaged* (Chicago: University of Chicago Press, 1987).

34. Spencer Rich, "Missing Out on Welfare," *The Washington Post National Edition*, July 10–16, 1989, p. 6.

35. Sar A. Levitan and Isaac Shapiro, *Working but Poor* (Baltimore: Johns Hopkins University Press, 1987), ch. 2.

36. Frances Fox Piven and Richard A. Cloward, *Regulating the Poor: The Functions of Public Welfare* (New York: Pantheon, 1971).

37. Gosta Esping-Andersen, "The Three Political Economies of the Welfare State," *Canadian Review of Sociology and Anthropology*, Vol. 26, No. 1 (1989), pp. 10–36; Norman Furniss and Timothy Tilton, *The Case for the Welfare State* (Bloomington, IN: Indiana University Press, 1977); and Korpi, *Democratic Class Struggle*.

38. Christopher Pierson, "The 'Exceptional' United States: First New Nation or Last Welfare State," *Social Policy and Administration*, Vol. 24, No. 3 (November, 1990), p. 188.

39. Vincent A. Mahler and Claudio J. Katz, "Social Benefits in Advanced Capitalist Countries: A Cross-National Assessment," *Comparative Politics*, Vol. 21, No. 1 (1988), pp. 37–50. Also see Arnold Heidenheimer, Hugh Heclo, and Carolyn Teich Adams, *Comparative Public Policy*, 3rd ed. (New York: St. Martin's Press, 1990); Ringen, *Possibility of Politics*.

40. Eugene Smolensky, Sheldon Danziger, and Peter Gottschalk, "The Declining Significance of Age in the United States: Trends in the Well-Being of Children and the Elderly Since 1939," in Palmer, et al., eds., *The Vulnerable* (Washington, D.C.: Urban Institute, 1988).

41. Fred Pampel and Paul Adams, "Demographic Change and Public Support for Children: Family Allowance Expenditures in Advanced Industrial Democracies," Boulder, CO, 1990.

42. Mahler and Katz, "Social Benefits in Advanced Capitalist Countries"; John Freeman, *Democracy and Markets* (Ithaca, NY: Cornell University Press, 1989); Ringen, *Possibility of Politics*, ch. 7.

43. Norman Furniss and Timothy Tilton, *The Case for the Welfare State* (Bloomington, IN: Indiana University Press, 1979); Jill Quadagno, *The Transformation of Old Age Security: Class and Politics in the American Welfare State* (Chicago: University of Chicago Press, 1988).

44. Nathan Glazer, *The Limits of Social Policy*, (Cambridge, MA: Harvard University Press, 1988), pp. 187–188. Also see W. Sombart, *Why There Is No Socialism in the United States* (Armonk, NY: M.E. Sharpe, 1976).

45. On the relationship between American culture and the welfare state, see Louis Hartz, *The Liberal Tradition in America* (New York: Harcourt Brace Jovanovich, 1955); G. V. Rimlinger, *Welfare Policy and Industrialization in Europe, America and Russia* (New York: Wiley, 1971); Marmor, et al., *America's Misunderstood Welfare State*; Wilensky, *The Welfare State and Equality*.

46. Theodore R. Marmor and Jerry L. Mashaw, "Canada's Health Insurance and Ours," *The American Prospect* (Fall 1990), p. 19.

47. Marmor and Mashaw, "Canada's Health Insurance and Ours."

48. For an introduction to this literature, see David Cameron, "Social Democracy, Corporatism, Labor Quiescence, and the Representation of Interests in Advanced Capitalist Society," in John H. Goldthorpe, ed., *Order and Conflict in Contemporary Capitalism* (New York: Clarendon Press, 1984); Francis G. Castles, *The Impact of Parties: Politics and Policies in Democratic Capitalist States* (Newbury Park, CA: Sage Publications, 1982); Esping-Andersen, *Politics Against Markets*; Korpi, *Democratic Class Struggle*; Stephens, *Transition from Capitalism to Socialism*.

49. Pampel and Adams, "Demographic Change and Public Support for Children."

50. Kristol, *Two Cheers for Capitalism*, pp. 51, 118, and 231.

51. Lawrence Mead, "Social Responsibility and Minority Poverty," in Gary Sandefur and Marta Tienda, eds., *Divided Opportunities: Minorities, Poverty, and Social Policy* (New York: Plenum Press, 1988).

52. William Julius Wilson, "Social Policy and Minority Groups," in Gary D. Sandefur and Marta Tienda, eds., *Divided Opportunities: Minorities, Poverty, and Social Policy* (New York: Plenum Press, 1988).

53. Ellwood, *Poor Support*; Levitan and Shapiro, *Working but Poor*.

54. Wilson, *Truly Disadvantaged*.

55. Also see Marmor, et al., *America's Misunderstood Welfare State*, ch. 6.

19

Rights and Liberties

RIGHTS AND LIBERTIES IN BIRMINGHAM

On October 30, 1967, Dr. Martin Luther King, Jr., began serving a four-day sentence in the Jefferson County jails.[1] He had been arrested on Good Friday, April 12, 1963, for defying a court order. Birmingham, Alabama, city officials had secured the order, called an **injunction**, to prevent continuation of the demonstrations that King and his associates had staged for a week. King chose to defy the injunction, because it was, in his view, a plainly unconstitutional abuse of state judicial power to prevent free speech. Getting Alabama courts to dissolve the injunction would probably be fruitless and certainly would delay the protests until after Easter. He could not accede to the city's tactics, so he and his colleagues marched into arrest.

After unsuccessful appeals in the Alabama courts, the defendants appealed to the Supreme Court of the United States. On June 12, 1967, the Supreme Court announced its decision in *Walker v. Birmingham* (Reverend Wyatt Tee Walker was one of Dr. King's codefendants). Writing for five justices, Justice Potter Stewart acknowledged doubts about the injunction but said that the defendants should have raised constitutional questions in court. Instead, confident in their rights, the defendants had defied the injunction. Justice Stewart said that the Supreme Court could not condone disdain for judicial authority.

Dissenting justices did not see it that way. Chief Justice Earl Warren noted that segregationist officials had denied parade permits to blacks in Birmingham on unconstitutional grounds. While the Supreme Court clearly would have invalidated the city's actions and the ordinance that allowed those actions, it was permitting a state judge to accomplish what it would deny city officials power to do—stop the march. Chief Justice Warren was unimpressed by arguments for orderly process when that very process allowed Birmingham to outwit the Constitution. Justice William O. Douglas agreed: "An ordinance—unconstitutional on its face or patently unconstitutional as applied—is not made sacred by an unconstitutional injunction that enforces it. It can and should be flouted in the manner of the ordinance itself."

One way to think about the outcome of this case is in terms of the judges' personal attitudes toward civil rights demonstrations. While all nine justices usually supported parties alleging deprivation of civil rights, only four tended to support those who alleged deprivation of freedom of speech and assembly. Chief Justice Warren and Justices Douglas, Brennan, and Fortas were relatively tolerant of unconventional protests, while the other justices (Black, Clark, Harlan, Stewart, and White) tended to uphold traditional limits on protests. This general tendency, manifested in 81 cases concerning civil rights protests that were decided by the Supreme Court during the 1960s, exactly matches the vote of the justices in *Walker v. Birmingham*.[2] Judges' relative support for civil liberties seems to explain how they voted in this particular case.

Judicial attitudes were themselves shaped by the political context of the time. The court was being pushed by civil rights organizations and demonstrations in one direction and by state and local governments in the South in the other, as white resistance to desegregation hardened. States and cities harassed black rights organizations, jailed protesters, and gave their officials great discretion over the issuance of permits for protests. In the early 1960s, those resisting desegregation efforts discovered the utility of injunctions for delaying or preventing parades and protests. These injunctions put protesters in a political bind. The U. S. Department of Justice used injunctions to stop states and cities from discriminating. Civil rights activists could not ignore injunctions with impunity and expect the federal government to approve. Neither could the protesters obey injunctions without huge costs. While they were fighting injunctions in court, mobilization and organization languished.

Dr. King and his Southern Christian Leadership Conference faced a difficult choice. Many supporters were beginning to doubt that peaceful protests could yield racial progress. More militant groups were gaining adherents. King had obeyed a similar injunction in Albany, Georgia, only to watch his protest campaign dissipate. The states were using their courts to defend an unconstitutional status quo. The injunctions, King decided, must be fought in the only arena on the protesters' side—the federal courts. Surely those courts, especially the Supreme Court, he thought, would match their support for civil rights with insistence on states' strictly observing civil liberties.

The issues were not as clear as King and his followers believed, however. In this case, as in so many, most Americans (including the judges) were ambivalent. Many believed in free speech but feared disorder. They endorsed constitutional rights but valued state and local control as well. Amid such ambivalence, rights and liberties are often in conflict. Judges are in conflict over whether to favor rights over liberties as a matter of law and are under pressure from political forces that favor one over the other.

In this chapter, we look at the development and status of civil liberties and civil rights in the United States. Our focus on Supreme Court decisions in this chapter should not detract from the fact that the Court is only one among many political actors that affect the status of rights and liberties in the nation. Nor should our focus on Court decisions leave the impression that the Court decides cases in splendid isolation: the laws that the Court interprets and the decisions that they reach are products of a complex interplay of structural, political, and governmental factors. Especially important in the story of the changing status of rights and liberties in the United States is the influence of changing popular perceptions about what is required in a free and democratic society. This is another way to say that the struggle for democracy shapes the meaning of rights and liberty.

RIGHTS AND LIBERTIES IN THE CONSTITUTION

Civil Liberties and Civil Rights

We saw in Chapter 2 that the framers were particularly concerned with establishing a society in which the practice of liberty was paramount. While government was necessary to protect liberty from the threat of anarchy (embodied for the framers in the Articles of Confederation), they believed that government itself would threaten liberty if it became too powerful. "Civil liberties" refers to constitutional provisions, laws, and practices that protect individuals from government interference. As embodied in the Bill of Rights, civil liberties are prohibitions against government actions that threaten the enjoyment of freedom.

"Civil rights," on the other hand, refer to governmental responsibility for guaranteeing that all citizens are able to participate as equals in the practices of democratic life. Civil rights became a more prominent part of the American agenda as democracy itself became more widely accepted in the United States. Because most formal barriers to equal participation in political life have been used to exclude groups of people—women, various ethnic groups, and racial minorities—civil rights initiatives over the years have been directed at removing group barriers and at helping groups overcome disadvantages created by past discrimination.

Civil Liberties in the Constitution

In the Preamble to the Constitution, the framers said that they aimed to secure "the Blessings of Liberty to ourselves and our Posterity." But in the original Constitution they protected few liberties from the national government that they were creating and almost none from state governments. The solution to tyranny that the framers preferred was to give the national government little power with which to attack individual liberties. Still, the framers singled out certain freedoms as too crucial to be left unmentioned. The Constitution prohibited Congress and the states from suspending the writ of **habeas corpus**, except when public safety demanded it due to rebellion or invasion, or from passing bills of attainder or ex post facto laws (see Table 19.1 for an enumeration).

Many citizens found the proposed Constitution too stingy in its listing of liberties, leading James Madison to promise a "bill of rights" as a condition for passing the Constitution. This made the Constitution more democratic by enhancing political liberty and by guaranteeing a context of free political expression that makes popular sovereignty possible. The amendments were not as successful in enhancing political equality, however. The Bill of Rights said nothing about political equality beyond insisting that all are equally entitled to due process in courts. Indeed, for most minorities and women, political equality eluded constitutional protection until the present century.

Later amendments sought to protect rights and liberties that states or the national government had previously compromised or ignored. The Thirteenth Amendment (1865) outlawed slavery and involuntary servitude throughout the United States. This was doubtless the greatest increment in liberty in the history of the nation. The Fourteenth Amendment (1868) aimed to enhance political equality but failed to do so until relatively recently. The Fifteenth Amendment (1870) guaranteed black males the right to vote, but this did not become a reality until after the passage of the 1965 Voting Rights Act, an action forced by the Civil Rights movement.

Twentieth-century amendments have made the Constitution substantially more democratic. Popular sovereignty has benefited from direct election of U.S. senators (the Seventeenth Amendment in 1913). Political equality was the aim of the Twenty-fourth Amendment (1964), which prohibited the use of poll taxes to prevent citizens from voting for national offices.

Table 19.1
Civil Liberties in the U.S. Constitution

The exact civil liberties in the Constitution are matters of debate, but here are some freedoms from government in the text of the Constitution and its amendments.

Article I, Section 9
Congress may not suspend a writ of habeas corpus.
Congress may not pass bills of attainder or ex post facto laws.

Article I, Section 10
States may not pass bills of attainder or ex post facto laws.
States may not impair obligation of contracts.

Article III, Section 2
Criminal trials in national courts must be jury trials in the state in which the defendant is alleged to have committed the crime(s).

Article III, Section 3
No one may be convicted of treason unless there is testimony of two witnesses to the same overt act or a confession in open court.

Article IV, Section 2
Citizens of each state are entitled to all privileges and immunities of citizens in the several states.

Amendment 1
Congress may not make any law with respect to the establishment of religion.
Congress may not abridge the free exercise of religion.
Congress may not abridge freedom of speech or of the press.
Congress may not abridge the right to assemble or petition the government.

Amendment 2
Congress may not infringe the right to keep and bear arms.

Amendment 3
Congress may not station soldiers in houses against the owner's will, except in times of war.

Amendment 4
Citizens are free from unreasonable searches and seizures.
Federal courts may only issue search warrants based on probable cause and specifically describing the objects of search.

Amendment 5
Citizens are protected against double jeopardy and self-incrimination.
Citizens are guaranteed against deprivation of life, liberty, or property without due process of law.
Citizens are guaranteed just compensation for public use of private property.

Amendment 6
Citizens have the right to a speedy and public trial before an impartial jury.
Citizens have the right to face their accuser and to cross-examine witnesses.

Amendment 8
Excessive bail and fines are prohibited.
Cruel and unusual punishments are prohibited.

Looking at the liberties specified by the text of the Constitution and its amendments emphasizes how few of our most cherished rights and liberties are to be found by reading the Constitution. Decisions by government officials and changes worked by political leaders and groups remade the Constitution in the long run, so many of the freedoms we expect today are not specifically mentioned there. Some were introduced by judges and other officials. Others have evolved as the culture has grown accustomed to novel and even threatening ideas. Still others have secured a place in the Republic through partisan and ideological combat. The key to understanding rights and liberties in the United States is to follow their evolution during the cause of our history.

RIGHTS AND LIBERTIES IN THE NINETEENTH CENTURY

Property

We saw earlier how few civil liberties the Founders had singled out before the Bill of Rights. The major liberty stated in the original Constitution was economic: "No State shall . . . pass any . . . Law impairing the Obligation of Contracts. . . ." (Art. I, Sec. 10) This primacy of property rights over other rights and liberties in the body of the Constitution was reinforced by more than a century of judicial interpretation.

PROPERTY RIGHTS IN THE MARSHALL COURT (1801–1835)   The Bill of Rights did not apply at first to states (*Barron v. Baltimore*, 1833). The contracts clause in the Constitution, in contrast, directly applied against state action. While the language of the clause protected creditors from debtor relief laws, in the hands of Chief Justice Marshall, the clause became a prime defense of property against states. In *Fletcher v. Peck* (1810), for example, the Marshall Court upheld a sale of public land, even though almost all of the legislators who voted for the land sale had been bribed by purchasers. Chief Justice Marshall argued that even a fraudulent sale created a contract that the state could not void. In *Dartmouth College v. Woodward* (1819), Marshall argued that New Hampshire could not modify the charter of Dartmouth College, because the original charter constituted a contract, terms of which could not change without impairing the obligation of the original contract. The Founders' attempt to protect the contractual agreements of private parties ballooned in the hands of the Marshall Court to bar virtually any and all changes in established property relations, especially those sought by the states.[3]

PROPERTY IN THE TANEY COURT (1836–1864)   During the years of the Taney Court, property rights began to be altered in ways that favored dynamic use of property over unused property;[4] that is, it began to favor property used in ways that encouraged economic growth over simple enjoyment of property when the two were in conflict.

In *Charles River Bridge v. Warren Bridge* (1837), Chief Justice Taney said that Massachusetts, in chartering the Charles River Bridge, had not agreed to create a monopoly, closing off competitors. He ruled that a competing bridge could be built. In this case, Taney expressed his view that the law should encourage eco-

Slaves were regarded as property in the antebellum South, free to be bought and sold like any other kind of property. This view was upheld by the Supreme Court in 1857 in the famous *Dred Scott* decision.

nomic competition and technological advances. If some forms of property were hurt in the process in favor of other forms, so be it. He argued that the "creative destruction"[5] of established but idle property in a dynamic market economy was the price of economic and social progress.

RIGHTS OF PROPERTY WITH RESPECT TO HUMAN BEINGS   The judicial preference for property rights was especially and tragically strong when it came to the rights of property with respect to humans—slavery. Until the Civil War, for instance, the Court consistently upheld the right of slaveholders to collect fugitive slaves. It was the Taney Court, however, that most clearly articulated the degraded status of civil rights during this period.

In *Dred Scott v. Sandford* (1857), Chief Justice Taney said that the authors of the Declaration of Independence and the Constitution had not meant to include blacks among the citizenry, because blacks were clearly regarded as inferior. Taney said that the Founders believed that blacks had no rights that whites were compelled to respect.

THE CIVIL WAR AMENDMENTS   After the Civil War, the Thirteenth Amendment to the Constitution outlawed slavery throughout the United States, settling the most divisive issue of the nineteenth century. The Fourteenth Amendment reversed *Dred Scott* by making all people who were born or naturalized in the United States, black and white, citizens both of the United States and of states in which they resided. To secure the rights and liberties of recently freed blacks, the Fourteenth Amendment further provided that "No State shall make or enforce any law which shall abridge the privileges or immunities of citizens of the United States; nor shall any State deprive any person of life, liberty, or property, without due process of law; nor deny to any person within its jurisdiction the equal protection of the laws" (Fourteenth Amendment, Section 1). The Fifteenth Amendment guaranteed black males the right to vote. Imposing as this constitutional structure sounds, the Supreme Court would soon transform it into a protection for property rights, but not for blacks or women. This episode exemplifies the power of politics and government to remake the Constitution.

The privileges and immunities clause was rendered virtually meaningless by *The Slaughterhouse Cases* (1873). Justice Samuel Miller found that the clause protected only the rights of citizens of the United States and not rights that were the responsibility of states. In these cases, the Court denied citizens protection against abuses by state governments. Within five years of its passage, then, the Fourteenth Amendment had been seriously compromised by the Court, foiling an attempt by the Radical Republican Congress to amend the Constitution in favor of equality.

Equal protection survived *The Slaughterhouse Cases* but soon lost all practical meaning. First, the Court said that the Fourteenth Amendment gave Congress no power to prohibit discrimination, unless it was practiced by state government. "Equal protection of the laws" did not include race discrimination by private owners or managers of restaurants, theaters, hotels, and other public accommodations, the Court said in *The Civil Rights Cases* (1883). Then the Court rendered even state-sponsored discrimination constitutional in *Plessy v. Ferguson* (1896). The Court said that states could separate races in intrastate railways if they provided "equal" facilities for the races.

Slaughterhouse, *The Civil Rights Cases*, and *Plessy* severely undermined the Fourteenth Amendment. While we might be tempted to explain these interpretations of constitutional provisions as mistakes of the justices who happened to be on the Court, it is far more persuasive to attribute them to the political, governmental, and structural contexts within which they decided cases: presidents who appointed the justices; senators who confirmed them; voters who supported presidents, senators, and other officials who tolerated attacks on black Americans; and intellectuals who abandoned newly freed people to states run by their former owners. To resolve the presidential election of 1876, for example, Democrats and Republicans agreed that Rutherford B. Hayes would become president, despite the fact that he received fewer votes than Samuel Tilden. In return, the Union army was withdrawn from the South, ending even minimal protection of black Americans. Reinforced politically and governmentally, racial discrimination easily acquired constitutional status.

PROPERTY AFTER THE CIVIL WAR   While the Court was emptying the Fourteenth Amendment of practical civil rights and liberties, it was filling it with new protections for property. Most important was the use of the due process clause of the Fourteenth Amendment to protect business from state regulation, as seen in *Lochner v. New York* (1905). Lochner ran a bakery in Utica, New York. He was convicted of requiring an employee to work more than 60 hours per week, contrary to a New York maximum-hours statute. Justice Rufus Peckham wrote for a 5–4 majority that the right of employer and employee to negotiate hours of work was part of the "liberty" of which, under the Fourteenth Amendment, no person could be deprived without due process of law. Since, Peckham argued, there was no valid reason for New York to interfere in setting hours, it was depriving Lochner and his employee of liberty without due process of law.

Justice Oliver Wendell Holmes, Jr., penned one of his most famous dissents in *Lochner*. Holmes exposed the Court's opinion in *Lochner* as an unjustified defense of property rights against the will of the majority without constitutional foundation.

This case is decided upon an economic theory which a large part of the country does not entertain. If it were a question whether I agreed with that theory, I should desire to study it further and long before making up my mind. But I do not conceive that to be my duty, because I strongly believe that my agreement or disagreement has nothing to do with the right of the majority to embody their opinions in law. . . . But a constitution is not intended to embody a particular economic theory. . . .

The nineteenth century was an era in which the rights of property were expanded, refined, and altered to make them consistent with an emerging, dynamic industrial economy. It was also an era in which the rights of women and blacks saw little progress and in which scant attention was paid to the judicial protection of civil liberties. The twentieth century would bring new approaches to property rights, civil rights, and political liberties. These new approaches would be triggered by structural transformations in the economy and culture, the efforts of new political groups and movements, and the actions of government officials.

NATIONALIZATION OF THE BILL OF RIGHTS

Liberties unrelated to property were not protected very much before the twentieth century, we have found, because the Bill of Rights did not apply to state governments. Gradually, however, the Supreme Court interpreted the due process clause of the Fourteenth Amendment, which *did* explicitly apply to states, to **incorporate** those liberties in the Bill of Rights that it deemed fundamental to democracy. Because *democracy* is defined by the existence not only of popular sovereignty but also of political liberty and political equality, nationalizing the Bill of Rights (i.e., making them obligatory at the state level) has made America more democratic.

The Supreme Court has not, however, incorporated or nationalized every liberty in the Bill of Rights. Instead of "total incorporation," the Court has pursued "**selective incorporation**." The Court has only slowly added even traditional civil liberties to the constitutional obligations of states (see Table 19.2 for details).

The Footnote

Justice Harlan
Fiske Stone

The foundation of the nationalization of the Bill of Rights *is* strangely enough, a footnote in an opinion, *U.S. v. Carolene Products Company* (1938), written by Justice Harlan Fiske Stone. In "Footnote Four," Justice Stone spelled out the conditions in which the Supreme Court would *not* defer to the actions of the other branches or the states. Each relates to an aspect of democracy and its protection: liberty, popular sovereignty, and equality.

First, courts would not presume the constitutionality of any laws that seemed to contradict any part of the Bill of Rights. Second, courts would not presume the constitutionality of any law that seemed to restrict the democratic processes (such as limiting the right to vote or the dissemination of information). Finally, courts would not presume the constitutionality of laws that discriminated against racial, ethnic, and religious minorities.

The *Carolene Products* footnote announced that most legislative enactments would fall under "ordinary scrutiny" by the courts, presuming their constitutionality. Enactments restricting liberties, limiting the democratic process, or discrim-

Table 19.2
Selective Incorporation of the Bill of Rights

First Amendment	Totally Incorporated
Establishment clause	*Everson v. Board of Education* (1947)
Free exercise clause	*Cantwell v. Connecticut* (1940)
Free speech	*Gitlow v. New York* (1925)
Free press	*Near v. Minnesota* (1931)
Free assembly	*DeJonge v. Oregon* (1937)
Freedom of association	*NAACP v. Alabama* (1958)
Second Amendment	Not yet incorporated
Third Amendment	Not yet incorporated
Fourth amendment	Totally incorporated
Searches and seizures	*Wolf v. Colorado* (1949)
Exclusionary rule	*Mapp v. Ohio* (1961)
Fifth Amendment	Partly incorporated
Grand jury indictment	Not yet incorporated
Double jeopardy	*Benton v. Maryland* (1969)
Self-incrimination	*Malloy v. Hogan* (1964)
Due process clause	Directly repeated in Fourteenth Amendment
Public use	*Missouri Pac. Rv. Co. v. Nebraska* (1896)
Just compensation	*Chicago, B. & O. Rv. v. Chicago* (1897)
Sixth Amendment	Totally Incorporated
Speedy trial	*Klopfer v. North Carolina* (1967)
Public trial	*In re Oliver* (1948)
Impartial jury	*Parker v. Gladden* (1966)
Confront witnesses	*Pointer v. Texas* (1965)
Subpoena witnesses	*Washington v. Texas* (1967)
Right to counsel	*Powell v. Alabama* (1932) (capital cases)
	Gideon v. Wainwright (1963) (felony cases)
	Duncan v. Louisiana (1968) (serious cases)
	Argersinger v. Hamlin (1972) (jail involved)
Seventh Amendment	Not yet incorporated
Eighth Amendment	Partly incorporated
Excessive bail	Not yet incorporated
Excessive fines	Not yet incorporated
Cruel and unusual punishments	*Robinson v. California* (1962)

Source: Craig R. Ducat and Harold W. Chase, *Constitutional Interpretation* (St. Paul, MN: West Publishing Co., 1988) pp. 845–846.

inating against minorities, however, would fall under "strict scrutiny" by the courts, presuming their unconstitutionality, with the burden on the authors of such enactments to prove otherwise. They could only prove otherwise if the reasons for such enactments were *compelling* (e.g., demanded action) and *necessary* (e.g., no alternative was available).

Practically ignored when it was written, the *Carolene Products* footnote pointed to problems with democracy in the United States that the Court was poising itself to address. Although the footnote did not compel courts to guard civil liberties and civil rights vigilantly, it announced a momentous shift in the treatment of rights and liberties.

To see how *Carolene Products* restructured the constitutional system, we focus briefly on specific liberties and rights that have been "nationalized" through se-lective incorporation and the use of strict scrutiny. We focus on "moments" of incorporation and intensified scrutiny. We then characterize the current state of liberties in each category. Throughout, we highlight important structural, political, and governmental influences to clarify the complex processes at work.

Freedom of Speech

"Congress shall make no Law . . . abridging the freedom of speech . . ."
(First Amendment)

For many, the right to speak one's mind is the first principle of a free and democratic society. It is not too surprising, then, that the first incorporation of the Bill of Rights (making constitutional protections mandatory in the states) occurred with respect to free speech: *Gitlow v. New York* (1925). Benjamin Gitlow had pub-lished "The Left Wing Manifesto," advocating militant, revolutionary socialism to mobilize the proletariat to destroy the existing order in favor of communism. Gitlow did not advocate action to break the law but was convicted nonetheless of a felony under the New York Criminal Anarchy Law (1902). The majority held that New York was bound by the First Amendment and then argued that even the First Amendment did not prohibit New York from incarcerating Gitlow for his pamphlet. Said Justice Sanford: "A single revolutionary spark may kindle a fire that, smoldering [sic] for a time, may burst into a sweeping and destructive conflagration. It cannot be said that the State is acting . . . unreasonably when . . . it seeks to extinguish the spark without waiting until it has enkindled the flame or blazed into the conflagration." In dissent, Justices Holmes and Brandeis were far more realistic. Said Holmes: "Every idea is an incitement. . . . Eloquence may set fire to reason. But whatever may be thought of the redundant discourse before us, it had no chance of starting a present conflagration." This was the habitual, skeptical stance of the two most libertarian justices on the Court.

While *Gitlow* proved to be an important advance for civil liberties in the United States, the Court was still willing to allow the states very wide latitude in controlling what they considered to be dangerous speech. For many years, espe-cially during the 1940s and 1950s, the Court deferred to political hysteria and allowed widespread suppression of what we now consider to be acceptable speech and publication. The Court seldom moved far ahead of the political branches on free-speech issues during this period or later.[6]

This early stage of the nationalization of the Bill of Rights by the Court was helped along by a new force, the American Civil Liberties Union (ACLU), which brought the Gitlow and Fiske appeals. Less than ten years old, the ACLU had little to show for its efforts until 1925, when *Gitlow* provided a spark of hope for civil libertarians. The Court's application of the First Amendment to the states provided the ACLU with opportunities to resist censorship and strangulation of dissent by states as well as by the national government. While victories remained rare, the Court's willingness to incorporate free speech encouraged and energized the ACLU.[7]

Freedom of speech has grown in ensuing years so that far more speech is covered than is not, though, as the box on HUAC shows, violations can always occur. In general, no government today may regulate or interfere with the content of speech without a compelling reason. For a reason to be compelling, the government must show that the speech poses a "clear and present danger"—the standard formulated by Holmes in *Schenck v. United States* (1919)—that it has a duty to prevent. The danger must be very substantial, and the relationship between the speech and the danger must be direct, such as yelling "fire" in a crowded theater. The danger must also be so immediate that those responsible for order cannot afford to tolerate the speech. Abstract advocacy of ideas, even ideas considered dangerous by police, politicians, or popular majorities, is protected unless it meets both conditions. Clearly, freedom of speech has grown, and with it, an important part of democracy in the United States.

Difficult issues of expression persist, of course. Commercial expression like advertising does not get full protection—an ironic change from the nineteenth century, when commercial and property rights received protection that free speech did not. Speech mixed with *conduct* may be restricted if restrictions are narrowly and carefully tailored to reach the conduct while burdening speech as little as necessary. Symbolic expressions (e.g., wearing armbands, burning the flag, or picketing) may also receive less protection from the Court. Use of profanity or words that are likely to cause violence ("fighting words") may also be regulated in some cases. Still, freedom of speech throughout the United States has grown to the point at which contenders wrestle with relatively peripheral issues, leaving a large sphere of expressive freedom.

A major exception to the expansion of freedom of expression has been concern for "internal security." This century has witnessed periodic persecution of dissenters and radicals for their political speech and writings. Censorship of dissent and protests during World War I proved to be a portent of abuses after the war. At least 32 states enacted laws to suppress dangerous ideas and talk, and the Lusk Committee in New York raided radical headquarters. Hoping to be president, Attorney General A. Mitchell Palmer set a young J. Edgar Hoover to collect information on radicals and nonconformists. Palmer began a series of raids on headquarters but soon lost credibility when his "intelligence" proved to be faulty. The laws that he encouraged would continue to threaten and imprison those outside the mainstream for years.

Can state legislatures pass laws prohibiting flag burning? The Supreme Court agreed with this demonstrator that such laws violate freedom of expression.

THE STRUGGLE FOR DEMOCRACY

Saying "No" to HUAC

The patience of Representative Harold Velde, chairman of the House Committee on Un-American Activities (generally referred to as HUAC), was at an end. "This is not a court of law. We make the rules." Lloyd Barenblatt, a recently fired psychology instructor at Vassar College, would not be allowed to read his opening statement, questioning HUAC's right to inquire into the nature of his political beliefs and associations. All HUAC wanted to know of Mr. Barenblatt was whether "you are now or have you ever been a member of the Communist party?"

HUAC was first created in 1938 by a House leadership trying to appease conservative Democrats who were worried about purported Communist influence in the New Deal. It held few hearings and was not responsible for a single piece of legislation from then until the end of World War II. HUAC became a standing committee of the House of Representatives in the increasingly anti-Soviet climate of 1945, under the chairmanship of John Rankin of

Mississippi, one of the House's most openly antiblack, anti-Jewish, and anti-New Deal members. Its charter was broad: "to investigate the extent, character, and objects of un-American propaganda activities in the United States."

For the next 12 years, HUAC hauled over 3,000 witnesses before it, focusing not on pending or proposed legislation or the behavior of executive branch agencies—the only function of standing committees under the rules of the House—but on rooting out people with suspect ideas from the fields of education, religion, and entertainment. Its preferred mode of operation was to press for public recantations of past political beliefs and memberships, and naming the names of past associates. People named by witnesses almost always became the object of public scorn and lost their jobs. People who did not cooperate with HUAC, by refusing to name names (so-called unfriendly witnesses), were subject to contempt of Congress citations, with attendent jail terms.

A similar period of hysteria followed World War II. It started when the Democrat-controlled House created the Committee on Un-American Activities. Republicans won control of Congress and professed to see security risks in the Truman administration and Hollywood (see the "Politics and Film" box). The HUAC found no spies and contributed little to security, but managed to ravage lives and reputations. Soon Democrats and Republicans alike were exploiting "the Red scare" for political gain. The greatest gain and concomitant fall was for Senator Joseph McCarthy. McCarthy hid behind congressional immunity to promote himself and his friends by brandishing imaginary lists of Communists and by denouncing all who opposed him as traitors. McCarthy and "McCarthyism" eventually fell victims, however, to the newest force in U.S. politics—television. Once

Despite HUAC's formidable weapons, Lloyd Barenblatt was telling it that his beliefs and associations were none of the committee's business. "I object," under the terms of the First Amendment, "to the power and jurisdiction of this committee to inquire into my political beliefs, my religious beliefs, and any other personal and private affairs." At the time, Barenblatt could have avoided a contempt citation had he rested his refusal to cooperate on Fifth Amendment protections against self-incrimination (later, HUAC would close this loophole). He was an extremely idealistic young man, however, who not only didn't think he had done anything wrong but believed that First Amendment freedoms had to be protected against government intrusions. The members of HUAC and the House were unimpressed, and voted a contempt citation for Mr. Barenblatt in July 1954. After a series of failed court appeals, including two before the Supreme Court, Lloyd Barenblatt entered Danbury Federal Penitentiary in 1959.

Barenblatt later reflected on his experience:

Would I do it over again? Yes . . . the experience was one that caused some damage and some enhancement to my life. I lost a lot of friends, and it cost me money and jobs. But I stood up at a time when many people kept quiet, or became informers, or left the country. I am still an American. I'm glad I took my stand. I don't regret it.

The Supreme Court began a slow process of reining in HUAC during the late 1950s. The House, finally embarrassed by the HUAC's roughshod tactics and the increasinging willingness of witnesses to defy it (this time, anti-Vietnam protesters), abolished the committee in 1975. The bravery of Lloyd Barenblatt and others in defying the committee on principled constitutional grounds contributed to the excising of what Representative Robert Drinan called "that self-inflicted wound called HUAC from the body politic."

Source: Peter Irons, *The Courage of Their Convictions* (New York: Free Press, 1988), pp. 81–104.

ordinary Americans saw McCarthy and his tactics in their living rooms, they knew that he was a liar and a bully. McCarthy's demise led to a slow retreat from this period of utter disregard for rights and liberties.[8]

The Warren Court, after having an inconsistent record on liberties during the late 1950s, protected rights of dissidents more during the 1960s. Expanding civil liberties cost the justices greatly—"Impeach Earl Warren" billboards sprang up in many places—but accustomed many Americans to the virtues of toleration. For this reason, domestic spying by such agencies as the CIA, the FBI, and the National Security Agency, and other violations of civil liberties during and after the Vietnam War struck many Americans as intolerable. The Court had helped to make at least the crudest forms of political repression "un-American."

POLITICS AND FILM

Hollywood Enlists in the War Against Communism

The Hollywood studios, the target of several congressional loyalty probes during the era of McCarthyism, were determined to demonstrate their good citizenship. During the early 1950s, the studios produced a stream of films affirming the American way of life and the rightness of American institutions, and warning about the danger of the Communist enemy at home and abroad.

Several films took the form of low-brow morality plays that were so short on entertainment value that people stayed away in droves. Films like *I Married a Communist* and *I Was a Communist for the FBI* were the worst of the lot. Their efforts to paint Communists and so-called fellow travelers in the most villainous light and to affirm government institutions like the FBI helped to convince public officials that Hollywood was no hotbed of communism, but their efforts were so crude that the studios reaped few financial rewards. More successful was the Leo McCarey film *My Son John*, about parents who turn their wayward son (a young man who is a little too smart for his own good and who consorts with university intellectuals and professors) into the FBI after they learn that he is seeing a female Soviet spy. He escapes but relents after listening to pleas from his parents and an FBI agent to turn himself in and "name names." On his way to FBI headquarters, he is shot by the Communists, and he dies on the steps of the Lincoln Memorial. McCarey's screenplay was nominated for an Academy Award.

Films like these were so didactic and moralizing in tone that few people wanted to go and see them. Much more successful at the box office were movies that tied the Communist threat to science fiction stories of alien invasion. Among the most successful artistically and financially were *Them!* and *The Thing*.

Them! is a story about giant ants, mutated by atomic testing, which threaten civilization. The first victim of the ants is an FBI agent, and the FBI (in the form of agent Graham, played by James Arness) is part of the team that eventually destroys the ants' nest in the storm sewers under Los Angeles. The insects (dronelike legions that are not much different from Communists) are no match in the end for the alliance of science, the government in Washington, D.C., and the military.

Howard Hawks' *The Thing* is an alien being frozen in ice near the North Pole. When the block of ice in which the alien is entrapped melts, the creature wrecks havoc at the remote base, threatening the lives of everyone on the expedition. In this film, the scientists are portrayed as people who can't see the dangers; they want to keep the creature alive and unharmed for study and interspecies communication. It is the military, in the form of Air Force Captain Pat Hendry (Kenneth Tobey), who saves the day.

In both of these films, the alien invaders must be destroyed if our way of life is to be preserved, and it is the government, whether the air force

Freedom of the Press

> Congress shall make no law . . . abridging the freedom . . . of the press . . ." (First Amendment).

In *Gitlow*, the Court included freedom of the press as a freedom guaranteed by the Fourteenth Amendment in its aside. Incorporation of this aspect of the Bill

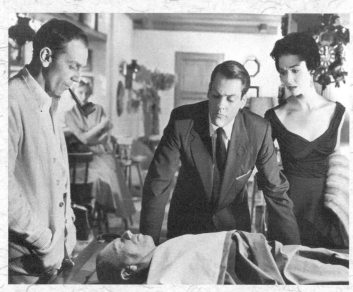

A scene from *Invasion of the Body Snatchers.*

or the FBI, that we must count on to preserve it.

Although there was some public and official concern about direct Soviet invasion, the animating fear during the McCarthy era was the enemy within—a conspiracy so insidious that it worked through friends, neighbors, and even relatives (like *My Son John*). Hollywood captured this theme perfectly in such alien invasion movies as *Invaders from Mars* and *The Invasion of the Body Snatchers*. Both are stories of aliens who invade the earth but who manage to take on human form so that we cannot see that we have been invaded. They bore gradually from within, just like Communists. Appearances are deceptive; the seemingly normal has been subverted. In *Body*

Snatchers, pods invade the forms of real people as they sleep. When they awake, the aliens look like the people whom they have replaced, but there is something slightly amiss: they all seem the same; they lack emotion and passion; they feel no need for love or affection; they have no ambition or faith. They want to conform and to work together in order to spread the pods far and wide. The hero, Miles Bennell (Kevin McCarthy), escapes the small town where the invasion is centered when he discovers that the pod people are assembling truck convoys to spread the pods. The film ends when a sheriff, finally convinced that Bennell is not crazy, lifts the phone and says, "operator, get me the FBI." We are saved, just in the nick of time.

of Rights seems reasonable in light of the importance of the free flow of information in a society that aspires to freedom and democracy. In *Near v. Minnesota* (1931), the Court made good on the promise of *Gitlow* by invalidating the Minnesota Public Nuisance Law as a violation of freedom of the press.[9] Jay Near published *The Saturday Press*, a scandal sheet that attacked local crime, public officials, and a few other groups that he disliked: Jews, Catholics, blacks, and unions, for example. Near and his associates were ordered not to publish, sell, or possess *The Saturday Press.* This sort of state action is called "**prior restraint**," because it prevents publication before it has occurred. Freedom of the press is not necessarily offended if publishers are sued or punished for harming others after they have published. Minnesota was trying to keep Near and his associates from publishing in the future, however. That is precisely what freedom of the press does not allow.

The prohibition of prior restraints on publication remains the core of freedom of the press. Freedom of the press and freedom of speech tend to be considered together as freedom of expression, so general principles applicable to free speech apply to freedom of the press as well. These include the ban on "prior restraint" and the rule that the Court will countenance repression only if the state can show some "clear and present danger" that publication poses. A major expansion of freedom of the press in *New York Times v. Sullivan* (1964) protected newspapers against trivial or incidental errors when they were reporting on public persons. This limited the use or threat of libel prosecutions by officials, because such officials could recover damages only by showing that the medium purposely had reported untruths or had made no efforts to find out if what they had reported was true.

OFFENSIVE MASS MEDIA   Freedom of expression is often tested today by mass media that offend many or most Americans. Pornography, for example, has challenged the ability of citizens, legislatures, and courts to distinguish "art" from media that degrade humans. Typically, communities and legislators have tried to regulate or eliminate pornography, while civil liberties lawyers and courts have tried to leave choices up to consumers and the market.

"Pornography" is a nonlegal term for sexual materials. The legal term is "obscenity." Although the courts have held that obscenity is unprotected by the First Amendment, the constitutional struggle to define obscenity has continued for half a century. Early disputes concerned importation and mailing of works that we today regard as classics: James Joyce's *Ulysses* and D. H. Lawrence's *Lady Chatterley's Lover*, for example.[10] While participants must admit that principled distinctions sometimes elude them (Justice Potter Stewart once said that he did not know how to define "hard-core" pornography but that he knew it when he saw it), a reasonably clear three-part test has emerged (*Miller v. California*, 1973):

1. The average person, applying contemporary community standards, must find that the work as a whole appeals to lust.

2. The state law must specifically define "sexual conduct" that the work depicts or describes in a clearly offensive manner.

3. The work as a whole must lack serious literary, artistic, political, or scientific value.

If the work survives even one part of this test, it is not legally obscene and cannot be regulated under the First Amendment. Community standards, applied by juries, are used to judge whether the work appeals to lust and whether the work is clearly offensive. However, literary, artistic, political, and scientific value (called the "LAPS" test, after the first letter of each of the four values) is *not* judged by community standards but by the jury's assessment of the testimony of expert

The distinction between art and obscenity can be very difficult to draw,
and battles over banning controversial works, like the one involving the
homoerotic photographs of Robert Mapplethorpe, are quite common in
American communities.

witnesses. If these three standards are met, the Court will allow local committees
to regulate the sale of pornographic materials.

Some feminist activists have attempted to broaden the term "obscenity" to
include any communication that degrades women. Activists Andrea Dworkin and
Catherine MacKinnon have composed feminist antipornography ordinances that
Minneapolis and Indianapolis have passed.

The ordinances attacked pornography as a form of sexual discrimination.
Any citizen who observed graphic and sexually explicit humiliation, subordination, or exploitation of humans could file a complaint for "trafficking in pornography." Complaints were to be handled by local civil rights enforcement agencies,
using a lesser standard of evidence than in criminal courts. The ordinances tried
to define "pornography" as conduct that denied women civil rights, setting up a
conflict between freedom of expression and equality of rights.

In *American Booksellers Association v. Hudnut* (1984), U.S. Judge Sarah Evans
Barker found the Indianapolis ordinance a clear violation of freedom of expression. She conceded that pornography could degrade and injure women, but she
said that the First Amendment permitted even hurtful expression. Since the definition of "pornography" in the ordinance went far beyond the constitutional
definition of "obscenity" in the *Miller* test, Judge Barker ruled that the ordinance
was unconstitutional.

Free Exercise of Religion

"Congress shall make no law . . . prohibiting the free exercise [of religion] . . ."
(First Amendment).

Religious freedoms were no more expansive before *Carolene Products* than
freedom of speech, freedom of the press, or the rights of women or blacks. For the
most part, Congress did not impede the exercise of religion, because it did not
legislate much on the subject. States were not covered by the First Amendment,

so free exercise of religion was protected by state constitutions or not at all. This seems strange, indeed, given the important place that freedom of conscience holds in a free and democratic society.

In *Minersville School District v. Gobitis* (1940), the Court upheld the expulsion of two school children who refused to salute the flag because it violated their faith as Jehovah's Witnesses. Writing for an unsympathetic 8–1 majority, Justice Felix Frankfurter gave great deference to the school board's judgment. This provoked Justice Harlan Stone to write a stinging dissent: "The Constitution expresses more than the conviction of the people that democratic processes must be preserved at all costs. It is also an expression of faith and a command that freedom of mind and spirit must be preserved, which government must obey, if it is to adhere to that justice and moderation without which no free government can exist."

Stone's dissent and a series of decisions deferring to state restrictions on Jehovah's Witnesses in 1941 and 1942 eventually moved liberal justices to Stone's side. In *Jones v. Opelika* (1942), Justices Hugo Black, William O. Douglas, and Frank Murphy publicly recanted their decision in *Gobitis* and saw in the Court's decisions an acquiescence in repression of a religious minority. When Justice Frankfurter asked if his literalistic archrival Justice Black had reread the Constitution in the interim, Justice Douglas replied that no, Black had read the newspapers.[11] When fellow liberal Wiley Rutledge joined the Court, it created a slim majority in favor of expanding religious freedom. In *West Virginia v. Barnette* (1943), the Court reversed *Gobitis* and firmly established free exercise of religion as incumbent on states. Thus did a change of personnel and the power of public opinion beget a judicial change of mind that is now established in constitutional interpretation.

The core of the nationalized free exercise clause is that government may not interfere with religious *beliefs*. This is one of the few absolutes in U.S. constitutional law. Religious *actions*, however, are not absolutely protected. The Court has upheld state laws, for instance, outlawing the use of peyote (a proscribed hallucinogen) in Native American religious ceremonies.

Many school districts still allow religious observances in school classrooms, despite a long string of Supreme Court decisions against such practices as a violation of the doctrine of the "separation of church and state."

Establishment of Religion

> Congress shall make no law respecting an establishment of religion . . .
> (First Amendment).

Freedom of conscience requires that government not favor one religion over another by granting it special favors, privileges, or status. It requires, in Jefferson's famous terms, "a wall of separation between church and state." Nevertheless, incorporation of the establishment clause proved to be a particularly messy matter. Justice Black for the Court determined that no state could use revenues to support an institution that taught religion in *Everson v. Board of Education* (1947), incorporating the First Amendment ban into the Fourteenth Amendment. But the majority in that case upheld the New Jersey program to reimburse parents for bus transportation to parochial schools. A year later, Justice Black wrote another opinion incorporating the establishment clause in *McCollum v. Board of Education* (1948). This time, a program for teaching religion in public schools was found unconstitutional. In *Zorach v. Clauson* (1952), however, the Court allowed a similar program in New York that let students leave school premises early for religious instruction. The establishment clause had been incorporated, but the justices were having a difficult time determining what "separation of church and state" meant in practice.

The Warren Court (1953–1969) brought together a solid church–state separationist contingent whose decisions the early Burger Court (1969–1973) distilled into the major doctrine of the establishment clause: the "*Lemon* test." In *Lemon v. Kurtzman* (1971), Chief Justice Warren Burger specified three conditions that every law must meet to avoid "establishing" religion. First, the law must have a secular purpose. That secular *purpose* need not be the only or primary purpose behind the law. The Court requires merely some plausible, nonreligious reason for the law. Second, the *primary effect* of the law must be neither to advance nor to retard religion. The Court will assess the probable impact of a governmental action for religious neutrality. Third, government must never foster *excessive entanglements* between the state and religion. While lawyers and judges frequently disagree about each of the three "prongs" of the "Lemon test," the test has erected substantial walls against mixing church and state. To the surprise of many, the wall of separation was maintained by the conservative Rehnquist court in *Lee v. Weisman* (1992) in which the majority declared that a prayer at a Providence, Rhode Island junior high school graduation was unconstitutional.

Rights of the Accused

Most Americans treasure the constitutional rights and liberties that protect innocent individuals from wrongful prosecution and imprisonment. But most Americans also want to control crime as much as possible. Balancing the two sentiments is not easy. Those alarmed by lawlessness—actual or imagined—tend to support "whatever it takes" to reduce that lawlessness, even if the rights or liberties of others must be restricted. Others are more alarmed by the lawlessness—real or imagined—of police and prosecutors. These advocates of *due process* values see violations of rights and liberties as unnecessary and dangerous.

During the 1950s and 1960s, the Warren Court favored the due process approach and subjected states' criminal procedures to rigorous interpretations of constitutional guarantees. Increased protections for criminal defendants, however, gave many political candidates an electorally useful explanation for rising crime: too much regard for "legal technicalities" was coddling the guilty and handcuffing the police. Republican presidential candidates Nixon, Ford, Reagan, and Bush all promised to appoint federal court judges who would be more sympathetic to crime control and less insistent on protection of the rights of suspects and defendants. One result of Republican domination of the White House since 1968 is that most federal judges have been appointed by those who "ran against the courts" on the issue of criminal procedure. A gradual but important shift to higher regard for crime control than due process has followed from electoral politics and has reshaped constitutional interpretation.

The shift is obvious in the decisions of the Supreme Court. The Warren Court (1953–1969) expanded due process and preferred constitutional guarantees to efficient law enforcement. The Burger Court (1969–1986) preserved most of the basic due process decisions that the Warren Court had crafted (often because the Burger Court consisted of holdovers from the Warren Court) but limited the further growth of protections and introduced many exceptions. The Rehnquist Court (1986–present), with only Justice White remaining from the Warren Court, has reversed many due process protections.

Consider, for example, the Fourth Amendment, which secures the right of all persons against unreasonable searches and seizures, and allows search warrants only if police can specify evidence of serious lawbreaking that they reasonably expect to find. Until the Warren Court compelled states to abide by the Fourth Amendment in 1961, states frequently used unreasonable searches and seizures in an effort to control crime.

In *Mapp v. Ohio* (1961), the Court enunciated the "exclusionary rule" to prevent police and prosecutors from using evidence gained through warrantless and unreasonable searches to convict people. A majority of the justices believed that the threat of perpetrators being freed would force police to play by constitutional rules. They did not believe that due process threatened crime control, because police lawlessness was not the only means to deal with crime.

The Warren Court demanded that police get warrants whenever the person to be subjected to a search had a "reasonable expectation of privacy."[12] The Burger Court limited places in which privacy could be reasonably expected, allowing searches of moving cars stopped for even routine traffic infractions and garbage set out for collection. The Burger Court authorized a "good faith" exception to the exclusionary rule, under which prosecutors may introduce evidence obtained illegally if they can show that police relied on a warrant that appeared valid but later proved to be invalid.[13] They allowed another exception for illegally gathered evidence that would have been eventually discovered without the illegal search.[14] The Rehnquist Court has gone well beyond these exceptions. In *Murray v. United States* (1988), it allowed prosecutors to use products of illegal searches if other evidence unrelated to the illegal evidence would have justified a search warrant. The combination of "good faith," "inevitable discovery," and "retroactive probable cause" has considerably narrowed the exclusionary rule.

For example, the Court held in 1991 in *Florida v. Bostick* that passengers on buses enjoy no reasonable expectation of privacy when it comes to their luggage. Police in Broward County, Florida, asked to search the luggage of Terrance Bostick without probable cause or any suspicion that they were able to justify at trial. They found cocaine. Bostick claimed that he had not consented to the search and had been coerced because he had not been free to leave the bus, despite the fact that the officers had had no warrant or any other legal reason for detaining him. The officers said that they had not waved a gun at Bostick and that he freely had allowed them to look in the bag containing the cocaine. Invoking the "war on drugs," Justice O'Connor and five colleagues said that no "seizure" had taken place and deferred to the trial court's decision that Bostick had simply handed his bag over. Three dissenters objected to such "suspicionless police sweeps" of public transportation as capitulation to hysteria about drugs. The dissenters spoke through Justice Thurgood Marshall, who has since left the Court.

Concerning the Fifth Amendment protection against self-incrimination, the Warren Court similarly waxed, the Burger Court waffled, and the Rehnquist Court waned. The Warren Court determined that the privilege not to be forced to incriminate oneself was useless at trial if police coerced confessions long before the trial took place. To correct "third-degree" tactics in the station house, the Court detailed a stringent set of procedural guarantees: the notorious *Miranda* rights. Once detained by authorities, all persons had to be informed of their right to say nothing and to consult with an attorney. While the Burger Court upheld *Miranda*, it allowed exceptions. Thus, it allowed the use of information obtained without "Mirandizing" suspects if suspects took the stand in their own defense. It also allowed the use of information obtained without Miranda warnings if some immediate threat to public safety had justified questioning and postponing warnings.[15] The Rehnquist Court has gone beyond these exceptions in holding that a coerced confession might be "harmless error" that does not constitute self-incrimination.[16]

The Burger Court, not the Warren Court, strenuously examined capital punishment under the Eighth Amendment's prohibition of "cruel and unusual punishment." In *Furman v. Georgia* (1972), a split Court found that the use of the death penalty was "cruel and unusual punishment." Congress and 70 percent of the states passed new authorizations for the death penalty, most of which met the Court's objections with procedures to make infliction of capital punishment less capricious. The Burger Court held that capital punishment was not inherently cruel or unusual in *Gregg v. Georgia* (1976). However, the Court tended to create an "obstacle course" of standards that states had to meet if they wanted to use the death penalty. Basically, the Court insisted that defendants be given every opportunity to mitigate the heinousness of their crimes so that as few convicts as

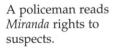

A policeman reads *Miranda* rights to suspects.

possible would be killed. Apparently, the justices were queasy about the use of a penalty that could not be recalled or remedied if a mistake had been made.

The Rehnquist Court has greatly expedited the use of the death penalty. In *McCleskey v. Kemp* (1987), the Court chose to ignore statistical evidence that blacks who kill whites are four times more likely to be sentenced to death than whites who kill blacks. The Court insisted that individual defendants must show that racism played a role in their specific cases. In *Penry v. Lynaugh* (1989), the Court allowed the execution of a convicted murderer who possessed the intelligence of a 7-year-old. In *Stanford v. Kentucky* (1989), the Court allowed the execution of a minor who had been convicted of murder.

Chief Justice Rehnquist and some of his colleagues have also worked hard to expedite executions by denying most avenues of appeal and delay. Such delays have sometimes enabled innocent people wrongly condemned to escape execution. In a recent example, Randall Adams languished on death row in Texas for a murder he did not commit until filmmaker Errol Morris discovered the real murderer (see Morris's movie, *The Thin Blue Line*). In *McCleskey v. Zant* (1991), the Court made delays much less likely by eliminating many means for challenging capital convictions. In its 6–3 decision, the majority reached out to eliminate delays, despite the fact that no party in the case had requested the Court to do so. In *Keeney v. Tamayo-Reyes* (1992) the Court limited the right of "death row" inmates convicted in state courts to appeal to the Supreme Court. The Court is never entirely predictable, however. In *Wright v. West* (1992) it rejected Bush administration efforts to sharply restrict appeals by state prisoners to federal courts. In this case, a new moderate majority apparently wrested control of the Court from the Chief Justice.

Many aspects of due process pioneered by the Warren Court have been ratified by succeeding Courts. Indigents' rights to counsel at trials and first appeals have long and continuously garnered support, for example. However, further rollbacks of protections for criminal defendants may happen if the fear of crime continues to pervade American society and to play a prominent role in American politics. As we have seen on numerous occasions, judges are not immune from the influence of the political and governmental contexts in which they operate.

CIVIL RIGHTS

American history is not only about the gradual (though incomplete) extension of civil liberties but also about the removal of many barriers to group participation in political life. In this section, we look at the extension of the civil rights of racial minorities and women. Here we concentrate mainly (but not exclusively) on Court decisions. Chapter 10, "Social Movements," contains additional material on the status of civil rights for racial minorities and women.

Civil Rights for Racial Minorities

We reviewed earlier how the Constitution was interpreted to condone slavery and segregation. In the twentieth century, however, the legal and political battles waged by the Civil Rights movement eventually pushed the Court, the President, and Congress to take the equal protection clause of the Fourteenth Amendment seriously.

By now we should expect that the first major victory of the Legal Defense Fund of the NAACP in overthrowing racist laws would concern property. Louisville, Kentucky, segregated residential areas. Warley, a black, and Buchanan, a white, arranged a test of the residential segregation statutes that was decided by the Supreme Court in *Buchanan v. Warley* (1917). The Court unanimously over-turned the law, because no state could prohibit blacks and whites from buying or selling real estate. The "separate but equal" rule characterized practically every other aspect of the treatment of blacks, but property rights limited the *Plessy* rule.

In 1944, amid World War II (a war aimed in great part at bringing down the racist regime of Adolf Hitler) and the NAACP's campaign to rid the nation of segregation, the Supreme Court finally declared that race was a "suspect classi-fication" that demanded strict judicial scrutiny. It appeared that the Court was about to deliver on the *Carolene Products* promise of protection for "discrete and insular minorities," but the protection was not forthcoming. Instead, having de-clared racial laws suspect, the Court nevertheless decided that the internment of more than 100,000 Japanese Americans without any due process whatsoever sur-vived "strict scrutiny." In *Korematsu v. U. S.* (1944), Justice Black and the majority deferred to Executive Order 9066 on the basis of the war powers of Congress and the president's prerogative as commander in chief. Since the Supreme Court often has uncritically accepted military judgments, extreme deference during wartime should not be surprising.

The great breakthrough came in *Brown v. Board of Education* (1954), when a unanimous Court declared "that separate but equal" was constitutionally unac-ceptable in public schools. *Brown* was a constitutional revolution. No brief sum-mary can do justice to the structural and political factors involved in the *Brown* revolution,[17] but at the governmental level, explanation is clear. Most of the credit for this constitutional revolution must go to Chief Justice Earl Warren. As Justice Frankfurter wrote to Justice Stanley Reed: "I have no doubt that if the *Segregation* cases had reached decision last Term there would have been four dissenters . . . and certainly several opinions for the majority view. That would have been cata-strophic."[18] Justice Warren replaced Fred Vinson as chief justice and skillfully engineered consensus from the Court when division would have been disastrous.

The South did not react violently for a while, but it did not desegregate, either. Once recognition that the Court was going to enforce civil rights spread, "massive resistance" to racial progress settled in the South. This resistance was what Dr. Martin Luther King, Jr., and others had to work and die to overcome. We saw in Chapters 1 and 10 that the Court was able to accomplish little before the executive and Congress backed up the justices with the Civil Rights Act of 1964 and the 1965 Voting Rights Act.

The drive to protect the rights of racial minorities has occupied the nation ever since. The main doctrine on discrimination is very straightforward. Any use of race in law or government regulations will trigger strict scrutiny from the courts. Recall from our earlier discussion that the state can only defend its acts under strict scrutiny if it can produce a *compelling* state interest for which the act in question is a *necessary* means. Almost no law survives this challenge, so laws that discriminate on the basis of race are dead from the moment of passage.

Constitutional interpretation now protects racial minorities against discrim-ination that is sanctioned or protected by law or government action. The issues are not so clear-cut, however, in the area of government actions that *favor* racial minorities in **affirmative action** programs designed to rectify past wrongs.

In *Regents v. Bakke* (1978), the Court authorized a compromise on such af-firmative action programs. The Constitution and federal law prohibited employers and admissions committees from using strictly racial quotas, but the Court saw

The use of affirmative action to rectify past discrimination against women and radical minorities continues to be one of the most emotion-laden subjects of political debate in the United States.

no problem with the use of race as a factor in hiring or admissions. The Court later indicated that it would be very lenient with legislative programs that were intended to redress past discrimination. Recently, however, the Court has insisted that laws that are not color-blind be subjected to "strict scrutiny." We have already seen that, under strict scrutiny, nearly every law would be invalid. In *Wygant v. Jackson Board of Education* (1986) and *Richmond v. Croson Co.* (1989), the Court said that programs that narrowly redress specific violations will be upheld but that broader affirmative action programs that address societal racism will be struck down. Given the current conservative majority on the Court, decisions in the near future are likely to apply strict scrutiny to all race-conscious laws or programs. That is to say, few affirmative action laws will be accepted as constitutional.

Reacting to this new judicial trend, Congress passed the Civil Rights Act of 1991. The Court had undermined existing penalties for racial discrimination by making it very difficult to challenge hiring or promotion practices. Majorities in the House and Senate wanted to correct the Court's misinterpretation of congressional intentions. After much resistance, President Bush signed the bill.

At issue here are two visions of social justice.[19] The "perpetrator perspective" locates the duty of law in the detection and punishment of individuals and government officials who discriminate against other individuals. In this view, racism is a set of vicious acts committed against persons by other persons. The perpetrator perspective addresses only overt discrimination and what must be done to prevent such practices. Those who are far more worried about institutional racism (discriminatory traditions and practices attributable to no individuals that nonetheless disadvantage minorities) tend to take the "victim perspective." In this view, victims of individual and institutional discrimination need and deserve assistance. The perpetrator perspective merely demands that laws and government stop discriminating; the victim perspective demands that government act to remedy and compensate for past wrongs.

At present, law, politics, and government seem to be more comfortable with the perpetrator perspective. For one thing, taking this perspective is more likely to bring visible results. Declaring the Constitution color-blind and punishing overt discrimination is widely supported in public opinion and relatively easy to do. It merely asks government to stop acting in a discriminatory manner. Taking the victim perspective, in contrast, would emphasize anew how limited government and law have been at solving widespread and systematic problems, such as poverty that disproportionately affects minorities.

Moreover, the victim perspective requires more fundamental reform of our institutions and alteration of the rules of the economic game if the deep structural causes of racial division and disadvantage are to be overcome. In the face of federal and state budget woes, problems like urban blight, crime, homelessness, and drugs seem especially difficult and painful to solve. The persistence of structural economic and political problems, then, makes thoroughgoing reforms that are necessary to address institutional racism in the United States far less likely.

Finally, the broad and expensive actions to overcome racism from the victim's perspective by compensating an entire racial group for wrongs done to it in the past seems to many Americans to be very unfair and has generated a great deal of hostility to such programs. It is fair to say that this attitude has been growing steadily in recent years and has had important political effects. It may, in fact, account for some of the drift of voters away from the Democratic party, which has tended to favor the victim perspective.

Civil Rights for Women

For all its egalitarian reputation, the Warren Court (1953–1969) did not advance the cause of women's rights. Once the Burger Court (1969–1986) seriously looked at sex discrimination laws, it had to decide whether to apply "ordinary scrutiny" (the presumption of constitutionality that almost all laws survive) or "strict scrutiny" (the presumption of unconstitutionality that dooms almost all laws). The Burger Court opted for a new position, called "intermediate scrutiny," but not before coming to the very brink of declaring gender a "suspect category" demanding strict scrutiny.

Sharon Frontiero, an air force lieutenant, requested benefits routinely provided for married male officers. She was told that she could qualify only if she could prove that her husband received more than 50 percent of his income from her. The justices quickly concluded that such discrimination was unconstitutional. Justice Brennan's first draft of the majority opinion used only "ordinary scrutiny" to conclude that the air force regulations were too arbitrary to stand. In response to circulation of that draft, Justices Byron White and William Douglas pushed Justice Brennan to base the opinion on sex as a suspect category. Justice Brennan incorporated this suggestion in his second draft and began to lobby his colleagues to take the big step. Had he succeeded, *Frontiero v. Richardson* (1974) would have inaugurated a new era of constitutional equality and there would have been no need for the Women's movement to push for passage of the Equal Rights Amendment (ERA).

By the time of *Craig v. Boren* (1976), the ERA was stalled and there still weren't five votes for strict scrutiny of gender classification. Six justices did agree with Justice Brennan's compromise that created a more rigorous scrutiny for gender as a *somewhat* suspect category. "Intermediate scrutiny" provided a compromise solution to the problem of strict versus ordinary scrutiny. To the justices, use of strict scrutiny would endanger traditional sex roles, while use of ordinary scrutiny would allow blatant sex discrimination to survive. The Burger Court defined a test that it believed to be "just right." Under intermediate scrutiny, government enactments that relied on gender would be constitutional if the use of gender was *substantially related* to an *important objective*. Intermediate scrutiny defines a legal test, then, somewhere between strict and lax.

The improvement of women's rights under the doctrine of intermediate scrutiny is less than what many in the Women's movement wanted. While the new standard has allowed courts to throw out some laws based on degrading stereotypes about women, it was used in *Craig v. Boren* to justify invalidating an Oklahoma law that discriminated against young *men*. Similarly, beneficiaries of intermediate scrutiny decisions in *Wengler v. Druggists Mutual Insurance Company* (1980) and *Mississippi University for Women v. Hogan* (1982) were also men.

Thus, women's rights have not followed the path of other rights and liberties. The nation has not restructured civil rights for women. Instead, the definition of "rights" has hinged on coalition-building on the Supreme Court and the tug of war of parties and interest groups. Since women are not a discrete and insular minority, they do not quite fit into the *Carolene Products* format. Civil rights for women is still more a subject for the political process than for the courts.

ABORTION RIGHTS One of the most controversial decisions of the Burger Court was *Roe v. Wade* (1973). Two recent graduates of the University of Texas Law School, Linda Coffee and Sarah Weddington, were looking for a client who would challenge a Texas statute that prohibited physicians from performing abortions except to save the life of the pregnant woman.[20] They found a client in Norma "Pixie" McCorvey, a 21-year-old divorcee who had already given birth to a child. McCorvey claimed that she had been gang-raped, but her attorneys doubted her story. They argued instead for a general constitutional right to decide not to complete a pregnancy. McCorvey gave birth before her case was decided by the Supreme Court, but her case yielded a qualified right for women to choose whether or not to complete a pregnancy.

For women's rights activists Coffee and Weddington, the federal courts offered an alternative to the Texas legislature. The case transformed abortion from a legislative issue into a constitutional issue; from a matter of policy into a matter of rights. Eleven states had reformed their statutes to allow women abortions when the woman's health, fetal abnormalities, or rape or incest were involved. Four more states (Alaska, Hawaii, Washington, and New York) had repealed prohibitions on abortion. In most states, however, progress was slow or unlikely.

The litigation over abortion reflected changes in public opinion, pressure by interest groups, and persisting inequities against women. Disapproval of abortion decreased and discussion of abortion increased during the 1960s, even among Roman Catholics.[21] Numerous groups worked to reform or to eliminate abortion laws before *Roe* was decided.[22] Norma McCorvey's case relied greatly on the money of supporters of women's rights. The "prochoice" team benefited from 42 amicus curiae briefs. The medical profession, which had been instrumental in making abortion a crime in the nineteenth century,[23] supported reform in the 1960s. Justice Harry Blackmun's opinion for the majority prohibited states from interfering with a woman's decision to have an abortion in the first two trimesters of her pregnancy. He based his opinion on the right to privacy, even though no such right is mentioned in the Constitution. As Blackman put it in *Roe*,

The Court's decision in *Rust* v. *Sullivan* (1991) upholding an executive order by President Ronald Reagan that banned abortion counseling in clinics wholly or partially funded by the federal government sparked this editorial cartoon.

> This right of privacy, whether it be founded in the Fourteenth Amendment's concept of personal liberty and restrictions upon state action, as we feel it is, or, as the District Court determined, in the Ninth Amendment's reservation of rights to the people, is broad enough to encompass a woman's decision whether or not to terminate her pregnancy.

The Court's decision, as we saw in Chapter 10, hardly resolved matters. Prolife groups, energized by the repeal of abortion laws, struck back after *Roe*. Single-issue antiabortion politics surfaced in 1976 and subsequent elections, and became an important pillar of the conservative Reagan movement.[24] The prolife forces that helped elect Ronald Reagan insisted that he appoint prolife, antiabortion judges to the federal courts. He did so with great effectiveness. In the end, the Court responded to antiabortion politics by deciding two cases, *Webster v. Reproductive Health Services* (1989) and *Planned Parenthood v. Casey* (1992), that gave considerable latitude to the states to restrict abortions. To the surprise of many observers, however, the Court majority affirmed its support for the basic principles of *Roe* in the *Planned Parenthood* opinion.

Abortion has been a dominant issue in recent confirmations of judges and justices. Judge Bork has ascribed his own defeat in part to the issue,[25] and hearings on Judge David Souter in 1990 raised the issue directly and repeatedly. Abortion was also an issue in the confirmation hearings for Clarence Thomas.

WORKPLACE RIGHTS   A gender issue that drew attention during the 1980s was "comparable worth." Sometimes called "pay equity," comparable worth grows

One impact of the Women's movement has been a considerable broadening of the definition of "women's work."

out of the observation that jobs and careers in which women have traditionally predominated tend to pay far less on average than those in which men have traditionally predominated. While laws against sexual discrimination mandate that women who do the same work as men should be paid the same, such laws say and do nothing about equalizing pay for jobs and careers that are of approximately equal worth but are not identical. Wages and salaries may differ according to the productivity of the worker or the danger in which the work places the worker, but the fact that a particular job has traditionally been "women's work" should not lead to its undervaluation, according to proponents of comparable worth.

Women tend to earn, on average, about 30–40 percent less than men. They tend to dominate some of the worst-paying jobs: 80 percent of all service jobs, for example.[26] Reactions to these disparities tend to reflect perpetrator and victim perspectives. Adherents of the traditional perpetrator perspective believe in identical pay for identical work but insist that a free market best sets the value of jobs. In this view, women's work is rewarded according to what the market justifies. Those who take a victim perspective have challenged this faith in the market by showing that the "worth" of jobs is affected by whether men or women tend to hold the jobs more often.[27] They argue that the more that wages and salaries for "women's work" deviate from comparable work, the greater is the sexist pay gap to which women are subjected.

Strategies for, and outcomes of, battles for "comparable worth" remain unclear at present. Many groups are contesting plans for comparable worth,[28] and most states have studied the relationship of pay and gender.[29] Most governments—state and national—have yet to decide what to do about gender-based differentials, however. The growing importance of women in the work place and in polling places may spur politicians and officials to redress some of the more obvious inequities.

Another issue of concern to many women (and men) is that of sexual harassment in the work place. One poll reports that 21 percent of women have experienced sexual harassment at work while 41 percent claim to know someone who has been the victim of such treatment.[30] The Equal Employment Opportunity Commission (EEOC) reports that 35 percent of female federal employees have been subjected to unwelcome sexual remarks and that 26 percent have experienced unwelcome touching.[31]

People disagree, of course, about what kinds of behavior constitute sexual harassment, though the courts, regulatory agencies, and legislative bodies are gradually defining the law in this area. In 1980, the EEOC ruled that making sexual activity a condition of employment or promotion violates the 1964 Civil Rights Act, a ruling upheld by the Supreme Court in *Meritor Savings Bank v. Vinson* (1986). The EEOC also ruled that creating "an intimidating, hostile, or offensive working environment" was contrary to the law. State courts have begun to fill in the meaning of "intimidating, hostile, or offensive." The Florida Supreme Court ruled in 1991, for instance, that open display of nude pinups in a mixed-gender work place fits the definition. A California court ruled that unwelcome love letters from a supervisor constitutes harassment.

The dramatic testimony of law professor Anita Hill at the confirmation hearings of Supreme Court nominee Clarence Thomas raised awareness of sexual harassment among men and women nationwide, and helped inject the issue into several electoral races in 1992. One development has been an increase in lawmaking to define and prohibit sexual harassment in the work place by state legislatures. Many private companies have also begun to specify appropriate behavior on the job for their employees. It remains to be seen whether this new environment will have a significant effect on the prevalence of the problem.

THE FUTURE OF RIGHTS AND LIBERTIES

This review of the history of civil liberties and civil rights highlights not only the role of structural and political factors but also the importance of the composition of the Supreme Court (which is itself a product of the political process). The Constitution, we have seen, leaves justices sufficient room to enlarge or to diminish liberty and equality in the United States. The greatest expansion of liberties and rights in this century was undertaken by the Warren Court. In part, we ascribe this expansion to the majority of libertarian and egalitarian justices on the Court at that time. But the roles of two central figures on the Court should not be overlooked: namely, Chief Justice Earl Warren and Justice William J. Brennan. In the view of many constitution scholars, Chief Justice Warren provided a tone of simple justice and fundamental fairness; Justice Brennan provided the legal language to implement the vision.

The Burger Court was nearly as activist as the Warren Court but less certain in its direction. Chief Justice Warren Burger kept a divided Court on a mostly pragmatic course, expanding or restricting liberties and rights case by case. Perhaps the central figure of this Court was Justice Lewis Powell. Justice Powell had an unerring knack for finding the center of cases. He was the "swing man": the justice most likely to cast the deciding vote in 5–4 decisions. We should not forget, however, that the "middle of the road" had shifted to the right since the Warren Court. The Burger Court seldom innovated (*Roe v. Wade* is the most obvious exception), devoting itself, instead, to formulating Warren Court generalities into clear and usable tests (e.g., the "*Lemon* test").

Most justices on the Rehnquist Court were selected by conservative Presidents Reagan and Bush to roll back many of the civil liberties and civil rights decisions of the Warren Court. Chief Justice Rehnquist is a skilled conservative activist, and he has in Justice Antonin Scalia a committed lieutenant, and in Clarence Thomas, a faithful vote. If they are joined by the more moderate centrist bloc of Souter, Kennedy, and O'Connor, they create a substantial majority that could undo many of the constitutional decisions fashioned by the Warren and Burger Courts, though Clinton appointments will likely lower the probabilities of such an outcome.

The politics of civil liberties and civil rights will continue to be central topics on the American political agenda. Every civil right and every civil liberty has tended to gather proponents and opponents around it, and the political conflicts between them eventually find their way to Congress, the president, and the Court.

LIBERTY, RIGHTS, AND DEMOCRACY

We have found that the "democratization" of the United States has been very uneven, though the enjoyment of liberties and rights has significantly expanded. We have also found that liberties and rights remain imperfectly realized, with much remaining to be accomplished. Much of the progress has been effected by the Supreme Court, but the Court has mainly done this, we have found, when it was pushed by popular pressures: elections, public opinion, civil liberties and civil rights organizations, and social movements.

At its finest moments, the Court has realized its mission to protect rights and liberties, and has recognized that no other political institution is likely to undertake such a thankless task. More often, our history shows that the elected branches and the public must embrace rights and liberties before they can become part of constitutional practice. Though the Court occasionally reminds the other branches and the public of constitutional ideals, the Court usually follows politics and is unwilling to innovate very much; that is, the expansion and protection of rights depends heavily on the success of the struggle for democracy.

SUMMARY

The formal foundation of American rights and liberties is found in the Constitution and its Amendments, particularly the Bill of Rights and the Civil War Amendments, but their actual enjoyment depends on the actions of the courts, the behavior of government officials, and the struggle for democracy. American history has witnessed an expansion of the boundaries of rights and liberties, especially during the present century, though much remains to be achieved.

During the nineteenth century, the Supreme Court mainly concerned itself with the liberty of property. Somewhat belatedly, it nationalized constitutional protections of liberties (i.e., made them applicable in the states), using the Fourteenth Amendment as its main instrument. The familiar liberties of expression, association, press, and religion, as well as certain due process protections for the accused, were gradually incorporated and guaranteed throughout the nation. The expansion of the rights of the accused was always a hotly disputed political issue, and the conservative orientation of the present Court has resulted in the reversal of many of the due process innovations of the Warren and Burger Courts. Many who want something done to curb crime applaud this new direction; others see it as a serious erosion of American freedom.

The Court paid little attention in the nineteenth century to the issue of political equality for racial minorities and women. Under the pressure of structural changes in society, the transformation of attitudes about race and gender, and the political efforts of women and racial minorities, the Court slowly began to pay attention by the middle of the present century. Important advances toward equality have been made by both racial minorities and women. Though constitutional law now fully protects both racial minorities and women against discrimination sanctioned by law or government action, the status of affirmative action programs to rectify past wrongs and to compensate for institutional barriers to equality remains unsettled.

To Ponder

1. Should people be allowed to say or to publish slurs against racial minorities as part of "free expression," or would tolerating such attacks amount to condoning a denial of "equal protection of the laws"?

2. Do you think people are entitled to more rights than are specifically mentioned in the Constitution? Which rights are most important to you? Are they mentioned?

3. How far would you go in controlling the distribution of pornography? Defend your strategy constitutionally.

4. Is affirmative action a legitimate remedy for past discrimination?

Suggested Readings

Abraham, Henry J. *Freedom and the Court.* New York: Oxford University Press, 1988.
    Students have begun their study of civil rights and liberties with this textbook for 25 years.

Glasser, Ira. *Visions of Liberty: The Bill of Rights for All Americans.* Boston: Arcade/Little Brown, 1991.
    A book that describes and celebrates the Bill of Rights. It is rich in historical detail.

Irons, Peter. *The Courage of Their Convictions.* New York: Free Press, 1988.
    Brief histories of Supreme Court cases recount struggles for civil rights and civil liberties since 1940.

Kairys, David, ed. *The Politics of Law: A Progressive Critique.* New York: Pantheon, 1990.
    This collection of criticisms of modern law includes many penetrating analyses of racism, sexism, and intolerance.

McCann, Michael W., and Gerald L. Houseman, eds. *Judging the Constitution.* Glenview, IL: Scott, Foresman, 1989.
    This is a collection of many essays criticizing civil rights and civil liberties in modern U.S. politics.

Walker, Samuel. *In Defense of American Liberties—A History of the ACLU.* New York: Oxford University Press, 1990.
    This comprehensive review of the American Civil Liberties Union highlights most major battles for civil liberties in the twentieth century.

Notes

1. This account draws heavily from Alan F. Westin and Barry Mahoney, *The Trial of Martin Luther King* (New York: Thomas Y. Crowell, 1974).

2. Joel B. Grossman, "A Model for Judicial Policy Analysis: The Supreme Court and the Sit-in Cases," in Joel B. Grossman and Joseph Tanenhaus, eds., *Frontiers of Judicial Research* (New York: Wiley, 1969) pp. 405–460.

3. Laurence H. Tribe, *American Constitutional Law*, 2nd ed. (Mineola, NY: Foundation, 1988), ch. 9.

4. Morton J. Horwitz, *The Transformation of American Law, 1780–1860* (Cambridge, MA: Harvard University Press, 1977); J. Willard Hurst, *Law and the Conditions of Freedom in the Nineteenth-Century United States* (Madison: University of Wisconsin Press, 1956).

5. See Stanley I. Kutler, *Privilege and Creative Destruction* (New York: Norton, 1978).

6. Robert A. Dahl, "Decision-making in a Democracy: The Supreme Court as National Policy-Maker," *Journal of Public Law*, Vol. 6 (1967) pp. 279–295.

7. Samuel Walker, *In Defense of American Liberties—A History of the ACLU* (New York: Oxford University Press, 1990).

8. See Stanley I. Kutler, *The American Inquisition: Justice and Injustice in the Cold War* (New York: Hill and Wang, 1982).

9. See Fred W. Friendly, *Minnesota Rag* (New York: Vintage, 1981).

10. For details, see Charles Rembar, *The End of Obscenity* (New York: HarperCollins, 1968).

11. Joseph P. Lash, ed., *From the Diaries of Felix Frankfurter* (New York: Norton, 1975) p. 209.

12. *Katz v. United States* (1967).

13. *United States v. Leon* (1984) and *Massachusetts v. Sheppard* (1984).

14. *Nix v. Williams* (1984).

15. *Harris v. New York* (1971) and *New York v. Quarles* (1984).

16. *Arizona v. Fulminante* (1991).

17. See Richard Kluger, *Simple Justice* (New York: Random House, 1977).

18. Bernard Schwartz, *Super Chief* (New York: New York University Press, 1983), p. 72.

19. Alan D. Freeman, "Antidiscrimination Law: A Critical Review," in David Kairys, ed., *The Politics of Law: A Progressive Critique* (New York: Pantheon, 1982) pp. 96–116.

20. This section of the chapter draws heavily on Marian Faux, *Roe v. Wade* (New York: Macmillan, 1988).

21. Faux, *Roe v. Wade*, p. 45.

22. Eva R. Rubin, *Abortion, Politics, and the Courts* (Westport, CT: Greenwood Press, 1982), ch. 2.

23. Kristen Luker, *Abortion and the Politics of Motherhood* (Berkeley, CA: University of California Press, 1984), ch. 2.

24. Tribe, *American Constitutional Law*, pp. 147–150.

25. Bork, *The Tempting of America: The Political Seduction of the Law* (New York: Free Press, 1990), p. 281.

26. Rita Mae Kelly and Jane Bayes, *Comparable Worth, Pay Equity, and Public Policy* (Westport, CT: Greenwood Press, 1988), pp. 4–5.

27. M. Anne Hill and Mark R. Killingsworth, eds., *Comparable Worth: Analyses and Evidence* (Ithaca: NY: ILR Press, 1989).

28. See U.S. Civil Rights Commission, "Comparable Worth: Issues for the 80's," (Washington, D.C.: Government Printing Office, 1984).

29. U.S. Civil Rights Commission, "Comparable Worth."

30. *Newsweek*, October 21, 1991, p. 34.

31. *Newsweek*, October 21, 1991, p. 36.

AFTERWORD: THE STRUGGLE FOR DEMOCRACY

The United States is more democratic than many of its critics believe and less democratic than it could be. In this period in world history when people everywhere are struggling to make their societies more democratic, we have much to be proud of. Yet, because aspirations for government of the people, by the people, and for the people are so strong, and because the ideal is so inherently attractive, we cannot help but be concerned about those barriers to democracy that remain.

We aspire to democracy and have made considerable advances along the democratic road but, we have seen, democracy is still incomplete and may even be facing new dangers in the United States. What can we do to make our nation more democratic? The suggestions that follow speak in only the most general terms about what can be done, focusing on the overall direction that change might take if we want to enhance popular sovereignty, political equality, and political liberty. Many specific proposals for each general direction are possible and people will (and should) disagree about which are the most appropriate.

The following enumeration may also be understood as a set of possibilities for your own involvement in American politics if you care about the health and future of democracy. We will not tell you here about the many political and government jobs that are available in Washington and how to get one; there are plenty of reference books available with that kind of information. Our focus, instead, is on possible issues you might want to pay attention to as a citizen of the United States in the years ahead, no matter what your vocation.

ENHANCE POPULAR SOVEREIGNTY

There are many things that can be done to strengthen the linkage between what the people want and what government does. At a minimum, the American people must increase the degree to which they participate in politics. At the present time, voting turnout in the United States, in particular, is not consistent with a fully functioning democracy. Simple exhortation will not do the trick. Better parties, electoral campaigns, and information will play an important role (we will discuss this below). But it is a change in our system of voter registration that would bring the most immediate gains. Research shows that much of the difference between voter turnout here and in other democratic nations is explained by our much stricter voter registration system that puts unnecessary obstacles in the path of potential voters. Since our current registration system seems to especially decrease participation among the least well-off Americans, a change would also enhance political equality. Many reform proposals have been made to accomplish this, including mail registration (now used in several states), and automatic registration by the government, as in the European countries.

Improving our political parties is probably the single most important thing we could do to improve democracy in the United States. Strong and internally democratic parties, we have seen, are the linchpins of democracy. Experience shows that they are the best instrument for clarifying electoral and policy choices, transmitting popular preferences to government, and keeping political leaders accountable. Means might be found to make our parties more powerful and coherent as organizations, to allow them to play a larger and more prominent role in elections, and to improve their ability to discipline elected officials who carry the party label. Much in our constitutional rules and culture work against strong parties in the European mold, but many reforms are possible to halt the disintegration of our political parties and to strengthen them to a degree. These were reviewed extensively in Chapter 8. For example, the parties could be given the ability to better control the collection and outlay of campaign funds.

We would do well, moreover, to try to improve the quality of public discourse and deliberation in American politics. This might mean, among other things, diversifying news sources and the range of views that are readily available in the mainstream media. The level of secrecy that is allowed in government might be diminished. Strengthening the Freedom of Information Act, and regulating or breaking up media monopolies might be a good starting point. Stronger and more internally democratic political parties might result in more informative electoral campaigns. Campaigns might also be improved, as some have suggested, by providing public funding for debates and advertising.

MAKE AMERICAN POLITICS MORE EQUAL

We have seen that income and wealth inequality are eventually translated into political inequality. Some Americans believe that the only way to eliminate this problem is to make American society and economy more equal. This is an extremely difficult thing to accomplish, but many European democracies have public policies (like family allowances and universal social insurance programs, as described in Chapter 18) that have done just this. Our constitutional rules, political institutions, and political culture make such policies difficult to achieve in the United States, though not impossible. There may be some of you who believe that such an effort is worthwhile.

Many other Americans believe, however, that policies to redistribute income and wealth would threaten liberty and undermine the efficiencies of a free enterprise economy. For those of you who think this way, but also believe that extensive

The struggle for democracy continues not only in the United States but in countries all around the world.

income and wealth inequality threatens democracy, means must be found to prevent the translation of social and economic advantages into political advantages. Many reform proposals fit under this rubric. It has been proposed, for instance, that private and interest group money might be deemphasized in American politics by limiting campaign collections and expenditures, instituting publically financed electoral campaigns, and subsidizing radio and television for candidates.

Besides controlling the effects of money in American politics, the most important step that could be taken to enhance political equality would be to diminish the power of interest groups. Strict controls on their activities, however, not only do not work very well but may intrude on the liberty of individuals and groups to speak freely, assemble, and petition the government. Probably the single most effective thing that could be done to control the effects of interest groups is to strengthen the institutions of majoritarian democracy, particularly democratic political parties. Experience shows that where parties are strong and effective, interest groups are not.

BE VIGILANT IN THE PROTECTION OF LIBERTY

We have no reform program to offer concerning liberty. What we have, instead, is an admonition: practice tolerance in your own life and insist that public officials do the same. It is all too easy to go along with the crowd and the prevailing mood when times are tough. Wars of various kinds are times of special threat to liberty, whether cold wars, shooting wars, or wars on crime or drugs. In such times, those who differ or dissent seem to many people to endanger the public welfare and damage our sense of community. In such times, many Americans seem willing to turn their heads and ignore violations of basic freedoms. It is worth remembering that such violations rarely stop with their initial victims but spread to include a wide range of the marginally dissident and the innocent. The democratic process is inevitably poisoned in such times, and it often takes years for detoxification to run its course. It's better not to turn down the road of intolerance to begin with.

DOES IT MATTER?

Does it matter that democracy remains incomplete? That depends on what you think is important. If you believe, as the authors do, that democracy is both the optimal way for a society to make decisions about its public business and the form of decision making that best develops the capacities and capabilities of human beings, then it matters. It surely matters to the millions of people in Eastern Europe, the former Soviet Union, Latin America, and China who have put their lives on the line for democracy in recent years. It surely mattered to the many people, both famous and not so famous, who struggled to enrich and advance democracy during our own history. We hope and trust that it matters to you, as well. We have shown that ordinary people have played an important part in determining what government does in the United States. You too can make a difference. That is the point of the struggle for democracy.

The following films address issues raised in the pages of this book. Most are available in your local video store. While none are necessarily as accurate in detail as scholars might like, each imparts important insights about the texture of our political, social, and economic life. Each annotation includes a description of the film, the year it was made, the name of the director, designation of color or black and white (b & w), and genre (c = comedy, d = drama). The chapter for which the film is most appropriate is also indicated.

Abe Lincoln in Illinois (1939, John Cromwell, b & w, *d*, Chapter 12) Raymond Massey's rendition of the life of our sixteenth president, which is closer to the homespun myth than the reality but worth looking at anyway. Cultural values of hard work, striving for success, and individualism are stressed.

Absence of Malice (1981, Sydney Pollack, color, *d*, Chapter 6) A compelling drama, starring Paul Newman and Sally Field, tracing the occasional tendency of journalists to invade the rights and privacy of individuals.

Advise and Consent (1962, Otto Preminger, b & w, *d*, Chapter 11) One of the few films that uses the U.S. Senate as its setting. The story traces the battle over the confirmation of a left-wing nominee for secretary of state, touching on the characteristic fears of the McCarthy era.

Alamo Bay (1985, Louis Malle, color, *d*, Chapter 4) Vietnamese immigrants face racial hostility and violence when they try to enter the shrimping business in the Gulf of Mexico. It is based on real events.

Alice's Restaurant (1969, Arthur Penn, color, *c*, Chapter 10) Arlo Guthrie stars in this very funny dramatization of his classic anti-Vietnam War, talking blues song.

All My Sons (1986, made for TV, color *d*, Chapter 16) An adaptation of the Arthur Miller film about war profiteering and personal loss.

All the King's Men (1949, Robert Rossen, b & w, *d*, Chapter 15) Based on the novel by Robert Penn Warren, this thinly disguised portrait of political boss Huey Long of Louisiana won four Academy Awards.

All the President's Men (1976, Alan Pakula, color, *d*, Chapters 6 and 12) Robert Redford and Dustin Hoffman portray *Washington Post* reporters Woodward and Bernstein, who first brought the Watergate scandal to national attention.

Apocalypse Now (1979, Francis Ford Coppola, color, *d*, Chapter 16) A sometimes confused and muddled look at the horrors of the Vietnam War, but the film is still worth seeing for its cinematography and the brilliant performances of Marlon Brando and Robert Duvall. Loosely based on Conrad's novella, *Heart of Darkness*.

Atomic Cafe (1982, Kevin Rafferty, color/b & w, documentary, *d/c*, Chapter 16) A sometimes hilarious collection of news clips and government propaganda on atomic war, its effects, and what individuals can do to protect themselves: ducking under desks, huddling against street curbs, pulling blankets over one's head, and more.

The Best Man (1964, Franklin Shaffner, b & w, *d*, Chapters 8 and 9) From the play by Gore Vidal, a critical look at presidential nominating conventions during the era before primaries made them practically irrelevant.

The Big Chill (1983, Lawrence Kasdan, color, *d*, Chapter 10) A highly entertaining portrait of a reunion of friends from the Antiwar movement; the picture of the movement that is painted is so negative that it fit perfectly with the conservative mood of the early 1980s.

Bingo Long's Traveling All-Stars and Motor Kings (1976, John Badham, color, *c*, Chapters 1 and 10) On the surface, a wonderful comedy about baseball, starring Richard Pryor, James Earl Jones, and Billy Dee Williams; in reality, a revealing look at race relations in the South during the 1930s.

Birth of a Nation (1915, D. W. Griffith, b & w, *d*, Chapters 1 and 10) The all-time film classic that glorifies the rise of the Ku Klux Klan.

Blue Collar (1978, Paul Schrader, color, *d*, Chapter 7) A powerful drama about the automobile industry and corrupt labor unions.

Bonfire of the Vanities (1991, Brian DePalma, color, *d*, Chapter 4) Based on Tom Wolfe's ferocious novel, the film focuses on the conflicts between rich and poor, and white and black, in urban America.

Bonnie and Clyde (1967, Arthur Penn, color, *d*, Chapters 4 and 17) Arthur Penn's portrait of the Clyde Barrow gang whose members became heroes in economically depressed Oklahoma by robbing banks during the 1930s.

Born on the Fourth of July (1989, Oliver Stone, color, *d*, Chapters 10 and 16) The true story of Ron Kovic, crippled in Vietnam, who became an important figure in the Antiwar movement. Stone won an Academy Award as best director.

Bound for Glory (1976, Hal Ashby, color, *d*, Chapters 4 and 17) A look at the Great Depression through the eyes of folksinger Woodie Guthrie.

Boyz N the Hood (1991, John Stapleton, color, *d*, Chapters 4, 10, 15, and 19) A grim portrait of drugs and gang violence in America's urban ghettoes and a plea to rebuild families as the foundation for improvement.

Broadcast News (1987, James Brooks, color, *c/d*, Chapter 6) A charming and amusing film that says some serious things about network television news.

The Brother from Another Planet (1984, John Sayles, color, *c*, Chapters 4 and 10) A sweet comedy that looks at the complexities of race and race relations from the point of view of a visitor from another planet (who happens to be black).

The Candidate (1972, Michael Ritchie, color, *d*, Chapter 9) A surprisingly realistic account of a modern electoral campaign, starring Robert Redford as the candidate for the Senate.

Casualties of War (1989, Brian DePalma, color, *d*, Chapter 16) A chilling tale of how things went wrong in Vietnam, based on a true story. It stars Michael J. Fox and Sean Penn.

Catch 22 (1970, Mike Nichols, color, *d/c*, Chapter 16) Based on Joseph Heller's famous book, a searing yet often hilarious look at the madness of war.

The China Syndrome (1979, Michael Bridges, color, *d*, Chapters 6 and 17) A cautionary tale involving an accident at a nuclear power plant, starring Jack Lemmon, Michael Douglas, and Jane Fonda. It also gives us a good idea of how television news works.

Citizen Kane (1941, Orson Wells, b & w, *d*, Chapter 6) Considered by many critics the best American film ever made, it is the story of a megalomaniac newspaper tycoon, loosely modeled on William Randolph Hearst.

The City of Hope (1991, John Sayles, color, *d*, Chapters 4 and 15) A portrayal of the political, social, and moral rotting of urban America.

The Conversation (1974, Francis Ford Coppola, color, *d*, Chapter 19) Coppola's minor masterpiece about the sordid world of electronic surveillance, starring Gene Hackman.

Death of a Salesman (1985, Volker Schlondorff, color, *d*, Chapter 4) A masterful film, starring Dustin Hoffman as Willy Loman and John Malkovich as Biff, based on Arthur Miller's classic play. It highlights some of the human costs of the competitive struggle.

The Deer Hunter (1978, Michael Cimino, color, *d*, Chapters 4 and 16) Not only a terrifying look at the Vietnam War, but a penetrating portrayal of working-class life, starring Robert DeNiro, Meryl Streep, John Cazale, and Christopher Walken.

Dim Sum (1984, Wayne Wang, color, *d*, Chapter 4) The classic story of the tension between generations among immigrants is treated with great sympathy in this portrayal of a family in San Francisco's Chinatown.

Do the Right Thing (1989, Spike Lee, color, *d*, Chapters 4 and 10) A powerful look at contemporary race relations.

Dr. Strangelove or: How I Learned to Stop Worrying and Love the Bomb (1964, Stanley Kubrick, b & w, *c*, Chapter 16) A masterful and sobering comedy about nuclear war and the madmen who bring it to us.

Dances with Wolves (1990, Kevin Costner, color, *d*, Chapter 4) Winner of seven Academy Awards, most notable for its authentic portrayal of the Native American culture and way of life.

Easy Rider (1969, Dennis Hopper, color, *d*, Chapter 4) Captures the mood of the 1960s more than any film of the period; brilliant rock soundtrack and Jack Nicholson's first major film role.

Elmer Gantry (1960, Richard Brooks, color, *d*, Chapter 4) Burt Lancaster plays the evangelical preacher in this satirical film about religious revivalism.

F.I.S.T. (1978, Norman Jewison, color, *d*, Chapter 7) Union corruption is the theme of this film, in which Sylvester Stallone plays a union boss who resembles Jimmy Hoffa.

Fahrenheit 451 (1967, Francois Truffaut, color, *d*, Chapter 19) This science fiction classic, based on the Ray Bradbury book, scores censorship in existing societies by showing how far book burning (the purpose of the fire department in the film) might go in a dictatorial society.

Fail Safe (1964, Sidney Lumet, b & w, *d*, Chapter 16) Henry Fonda stars as the president who must sacrifice one of his country's own cities for destruction in this film about accidental nuclear war.

The Falcon and the Snowman (1985, John Schlesinger, color, *d*, Chapters 13 and 16) The true story of two longtime friends who become Soviet spies. The film stars Timothy Hutton and Sean Penn.

Fat Man and Little Boy (1989, Roland Jaffe, color, *d*, Chapter 16) Chronicles the secret Manhattan Project to develop the atomic bomb. The title refers to the first two atomic devices produced by the project. The film stars Paul Newman as General Groves, who directed the project.

First Blood (1982, Ted Kotchoff, color, *d*, Chapter 16) The first and best of the Rambo movies, the film is about a Vietnam War vet who is harassed unfairly by local police and takes revenge. It conveys grievances expressed by some Vietnam War vets.

First Monday in October (1981, Ronald Neame, color, *d*, Chapter 14) One of the very few films about the Supreme Court. It stars Walter Matthau and Jill Clayburgh, who play justices with philosophical disagreements. A fairly accurate representation of how the Supreme Court works.

The Fountainhead (1949, King Vidor, b & w, *d*, Chapters 4, 9) Based on the classic novel by libertarian philosopher Ayn Rand, this film is about an architect who refuses to give in to the pressures of government or mass opinion. Gary Cooper plays the title role.

The French Connection (1971, William Friedkin, color, *d*, Chapter 15) A powerful and gritty drama about the unmasking of the largest heroin-smuggling operation in the United States. It gives us much on the relationships between local and federal law enforcement agencies.

The Front (1976, Martin Ritt, color, *d*, Chapter 19) A powerful film about writers who were blacklisted by the television networks during the McCarthy era. It stars Woody Allen in a noncomedic role. It was written by blacklisted writer Walter Bernstein.

Full Metal Jacket (1987, Stanley Kubrick, color, *d*, Chapter 16) Kubrick's film portrays the violence of war as few films have been able to do.

Gimme Shelter (1970, Albert and David Maysles, c, documentary, Chapter 4) A brilliant documentary on the ill-fated Rolling Stones concert at Altamount that conveys some of the darker aspects of the 1960s countercultural era.

Glory (1989, Edward Zwick, color, *d*, Chapter 10) The Academy Award winning film on the forgotten role of black soldiers during the American Civil War.

The Godfather, Part I (1972, Francis Ford Coppola, color, *d*, Chapters 4 and 15) On every critic's list of top films of all time, this film shows the structure of organized crime and its linkages to local politics and law enforcement. It stars Marlon Brando, Al Pacino, and Robert Duvall.

The Godfather, Part II (1974, Francis Ford Coppola, color, *d*, Chapters 4, 11, 15, and 16) One of the few sequels that is every bit as good as the original. It focuses on the immigrant roots of organized crime, its relationship to the pre-Castro Batista regime in Cuba after World War II, and the investigation of its activities by Senate committees.

The Grapes of Wrath (1940, John Ford, b & w, *d*, Chapters 4, 17, and 18) Based on Steinbeck's novel, John Ford's gritty film of the Great Depression and its devastating impact on poor farmers who are forced to leave the land helps explain why government plays a role today in the management of the economy and the provision of social welfare.

The Great White Hope (1970, Martin Ritt, color, *d*, Chapter 10) James Earl Jones stars as boxing champion Jack Johnson, who was mercilessly hounded for marrying a white woman. A powerful evocation of American race relations during the early twentieth century.

The Green Berets (1968, John Wayne and Ray Kellogg, color, *d*, Chapter 16) The rare film that wholeheartedly supported the Vietnam War as one worth fighting.

Guilty by Suspicion (1991, Irwin Winkler, color, *d*, chs. 11 and 19) Robert DeNiro plays a top Hollywood screenwriter whose career is ruined when he refuses to "name names" to a congressional investigating committee during the dark days of the anticommunist witch-hunt.

Harlan County (1977, Barbara Kopple, color, documentary, Chapter 7) An award-winning documentary on labor–management struggles in the "bloody Harlan" County coal fields.

Hearts and Minds (1974, Peter Davis, color, documentary, Chapters 4 and 16) This Academy Award winning documentary tries to make the case that the Vietnam War can be traced to pathologies in the American political system and culture.

Hester Street (1975, Joan Micklin Silver, b & w, *d*, Chapter 4) Jewish immigrants on the lower East Side of New York adjust to life in the United States. The film stars Carol Kane.

High Noon (1952, Fred Zinnemann, b & w, *d*, Chapter 19) Considered to be one of the great American films, this western delivers not only riveting drama and action but also a thinly veiled message about the dangers of conformity and cowardice during the McCarthy era.

Hollywood Shuffle (1987, Robert Townsend, color, *c*, Chapter 4) A very funny satirical look at black stereotypes in American film.

The Hunt for Red October (1990, John McTiernan, color, *d*, Chapter 16) Based on the Tom Clancy novel, a Soviet submarine commander defects to the Americans with his vessel. The film shows many of the cracks in the Soviet system that portended the disintegration of the Soviet Union.

Inherit the Wind (1960, Stanley Kramer, b & w, *d*, Chapter 4) A powerful courtroom drama, centered on the famous Scope's trial, pitting fundamentalist religion (William Jennings Bryan) against modern science (Clarence Darrow).

Invasion of the Body Snatchers (1956, Don Siegel, b & w, *d*, Chapter 19) A science fiction classic, the zombie-like pod beings are meant to represent the conformity and blandness of communism.

It Came from Outer Space (1953, Jack Arnold, b & w, *d*, Chapter 19) Another science fiction classic whose beneath-the-surface theme is the threat of communism.

JFK (1991, Oliver Stone, color, *d*, chs 12 and 13) Controversial director Oliver Stone's controversial film about a conspiracy to assassinate President Kennedy. It stimulated a rising public demand to reopen the investigation.

The Last Hurrah (1958, John Ford, b & w, *d*, Chapters 8 and 9) Spencer Tracy plays an aging politician who is being overtaken by the slick political campaigns of the modern era. It makes one yearn for the old ways.

The Last Picture Show (1971, Peter Bogdanovich, b & w, *d*, Chapter 4) What happens to people in a small Texas town as their way of life slowly but inexorably disappears.

Lenny (1971, Bob Fosse, b & w, *d*, Chapter 19) Dustin Hoffman brilliantly portrays comedian Lenny Bruce, whose biting political humor triggered censorship and official retribution.

Little Big Man (1970, Arthur Penn, color, *d*, Chapters 4 and 10) One of the first Hollywood films to treat Native Americans with sympathy and respect.

Little Murderers (1971, Allan Arkin, color, *d/c*, Chapter 15) A dark comedy about the terrors of urban life.

The Manchurian Candidate (1962, John Frankenheimer, b & w, *d*, Chapters 4 and 19) A gripping film about a war hero, programmed by the Communists, to assassinate political leaders. It reflects fear of communism that was once so much a part of American culture.

Matewan (1987, John Sayles, color, *d*, Chapter 7) One of the few sympathetic portrayals of labor unions in American film. It is the story of a bloody coal miners' strike in West Virginia.

Medium Cool (1969, Haskell Wexler, color, *d*, Chapters 6 and 10) A fascinating look at the war in the streets between antiwar activists and Mayor Daley's police during the 1968 Democratic National Convention, as seen through the eyes of a television reporter/ cameraman.

Milagro Beanfield War (1988, Robert Redford, color, *c/d*, Chapters 4 and 10) A magical story, based on the classic John Nichol's novel, in which an act of defiance by one local resident—watering his beanfield—triggers a local political rebellion by the formerly powerless Hispanic population.

Missing (1982, Costa-Gavras, color, *d*, Chapter 16) A gripping story of personal loss in a plot line that assumes U.S. complicity in the bloody overthrow of the Allende regime in Chile.

Mississippi Burning (1988, Alan Parker, color, *d*, Chapters 10 and 13) Conveys the state of terror under which black Americans lived in Mississippi, but it seriously misrepresents the role of the FBI, which did little in Mississippi (or elsewhere) to protect civil rights activists.

Mr. Smith Goes to Washington (1939, Frank Capra, b & w, *d*, Chapter 11) Frank Capra's classic film about an innocent (Jimmy Stewart) who goes to Washington, D.C., to "clean up the mess" and succeeds.

Modern Times (1936, Charlie Chaplin, b & w, *d*, Chapter 4) A moving portrayal of the personal costs of industrial society, dominated by the rhythm of the machine.

Network (1976, Sidney Lumet, color, *d*, Chapter 6) Based on a script by Paddy Chayevsky, a blacklisted writer during the 1950s, this crazed look at where network television news and programming might go in the future has proved to be eerily prophetic. It won four Academy Awards.

9 to 5 (1980, Colin Higgins, color, *c*, Chapters 4 and 10) A riotous comedy that manages to tell some hard truths about the lives of women office workers and some of the reasons why the Women's movement happened.

Norma Rae (1984, Martin Ritt, color, *d*, Chapter 7) Sally Field won an Academy Award for her portrayal of a southern textile worker who helps organize a union in one of the most virulently antiunion industries in the nation.

El Norte (1984, Gregory Nava, color, *d*, Chapter 4) A moving story of immigrants who flee political oppression in Central America only to find a new set of problems in the United States.

On the Waterfront (1954, Elia Kazan, b & w, *d*, Chapter 7) An award-winning film, starring Marlon Brando, Lee J. Cobb, and Karl Malden, about corrupt unions. The central message, that it is OK to cooperate with the government against one's friends and colleagues, seems to have been director Elia Kazan's defense for his own cooperation with the House Un-American Activities Committee.

Platoon (1986, Oliver Stone, color, *d*, Chapter 16) Academy Award winner for best picture and director, this film about the Vietnam War can be compared with *All Quiet on the Western Front* and the *Red Badge of Courage* in its vivid and brutal portrayal of combat.

Power (1986, Sidney Lumet, color, *d*, Chapter 9) One of the few films that looks at the world of political consultants and campaign operatives. It stars Richard Gere as the power broker.

Q and A (1990, Sidney Lumet, color, *d*, Chapters 4, 10, and 15) A deeply disturbing portrayal of a police department that is as deeply and bitterly divided along racial and ethnic lines as the population of the city that it serves.

Ragtime (1981, Milos Forman, color, *d*, Chapter 10) Based on the best-selling novel of the same title by E. L. Doctorow, the film focuses on one black man's desperate search for justice in a society (1906) in which racial justice was hard to find.

Red Dawn (1984, John Milius, color, *d*, Chapter 16) The perfect Reagan-era fantasy and nightmare: The Russians invade the heartland, while their Cuban and Sandinista allies invade from the South. America is saved by a band of high school football players who wage guerilla war.

Reds (1981, Warren Beatty, color, *d*, Chapters 6 and 16) The story of journalist John Reed, who was a close observer and friend of the Russian Revolution. The film tells why many Americans were attracted to the Russian Revolution and communism.

Return of the Secaucus 7 (1980, John Sayles, color, *d*, Chapter 10) A story of a reunion of antiwar activists who had been arrested during the 1960s during a demonstration. The film gives us insights into the nature of the movement and how lives changed as a result of participation in it.

The Right Stuff (1983, Philip Kaufman, color, *d*, Chapters 16 and 17) The epic film, based on Tom Wolfe's novel of the same title, about the beginnings of the American manned space program.

The River (1984, Mark Rydell, color, *d*, Chapter 7) Mel Gibson and Sissy Spacek star in this drama about small farmers who rally together to save their farms from agribusiness.

Roger and Me (1989, Michael Moore, color, documentary, Chapter 7) A scathing documentary about the impact of an automobile plant closing in Flint, Michigan. The Roger of the title refers to Roger Smith, the GM chairman, whom Moore relentlessly chases in the film, without success.

Russians Are Coming, Russians Are Coming (1966, Norman Jewison, color, *c*, Chapter 16) Wildcap comedy, unusual for the era in which it was made in suggesting that Russians might not all be evil or KGB agents.

Salt of the Earth (1953, Herbert Biberman, b & w, *d*, Chapters 7 and 19) A sympathetic look at a New Mexico miners' strike, made by blacklisted actors and director during the McCarthy era. Most distributors and theater chains refused to release it for viewing. Today it is a staple of college film programs.

The Searchers (1956, John Ford, color, *d*, Chapters 4 and 10) John Wayne relentlessly searches for his niece, who has been kidnapped by Indians. The portrait of Native Americans is notably unsympathetic, reflecting typical American views of that time.

The Seduction of Joe Tynan (1979, Jerry Schatzberg, color, *d*, Chapter 11) Alan Alda portrays a man's climb to political power in Washington, D.C., and what he has to do to get there.

Serpico (1973, Sidney Lumet, color, *d*, Chapter 15) The powerful story, based on real events, of an undercover cop who blows the whistle on corruption in the police department and pays a stiff price for his effort.

Seven Days in May (1964, John Frankenheimer, b & w, *d*, Chapters 12, 13, and 16) Burt Lancaster is a general who is planning a military coup in this film that was made soon after Eisenhower's famous warning to the nation about the military-industrial complex. Not surprisingly, the president's problem, from the general's point of view, is that he is soft on communism.

Silkwood (1983, Mike Nichols, color, *d*, Chapter 7) Meryl Streep plays Karen Silkwood, who died (and may have been murdered) in a car crash on her way to a hearing to give testimony on unsafe practices at a Kerr-McGee nuclear power plant.

Thelma and Louise (1991, Riddley Scott, color, *d*, Chapter 10) The controversial "road movie," with women (Susan Sarandon and Geena Davis) starring as the buddies. It probably could only have been made and only have enjoyed commercial success because of the Women's movement.

Sounder (1972, Martin Ritt, color, *d*, Chapters 1 and 10) Cicely Tyson won an Academy Award for her role as the wife and mother of a sharecropping black family in the South during the Great Depression.

State of Siege (1973, Costa-Gavras, color, *d*, Chapter 16) Yves Montand is an American diplomat held captive by guerillas in retaliation for U.S. assistance to the Uruguay secret police. It is loosely based on a true story.

The Thin Blue Line (1988, Erol Morris, color, documentary, Chapter 19) An extraordinary documentary about a wrongly accused and convicted man on death row. The film forced a reopening of the case and an eventual pardon.

To Kill a Mockingbird (1962, Robert Mulligan, color, *d*, Chapters 10 and 19) Gregory Peck won an Academy Award for his portrayal of a small-town southern lawyer who defends a black man accused of raping a white woman. The film offers keen insights into race relations in the pre-Civil Rights movement South.

Tucker: The Man and His Dream (1988, Francis Ford Coppola, color, *d*, Chapter 7) Jeff Bridges plays the man who tried to take on the big automobile companies with a visionary new car and lost. The film emphasizes collusion between the Big Three and government.

Twelve Angry Men (1957, Sidney Lumet, b & w, *d*, Chapter 19) A brilliant cast of actors, including Henry Fonda, Lee J. Cobb, Jack Warden, and Jack Klugman, shows the inside workings of a jury and illustrates why a "jury of one's peers" is a cornerstone of liberty.

Wall Street (1987, Oliver Stone, color, *d*, Chapter 7) A penetrating look at the greed and manipulation of Wall Street. The film captures the spirit of the so-called go-go 1980s.

Young Mr. Lincoln (1939, John Ford, b & w, *d*, Chapter 12) One of the very best of the Lincoln biographies, focusing on the years when Lincoln was a young and struggling attorney. Henry Fonda plays Lincoln to perfection.

APPENDIX II
ACRONYMS

ACLU	American Civil Liberties Union
ADA	American Dental Association
ADA	Americans for Democratic Action
AIP	American-Israel Public Affairs Committee
AMA	American Medical Association
BLM	Bureau of Land Management
CBO	Congressional Budget Office
CFE	Conventional Forces in Europe treaty
CIA	Central Intelligence Agency
CISPES	Committee in Solidarity with the People of El Salvador
COLA	Cost-of-living adjustment
CORE	Congress on Racial Equality
DCI	Director of Central Intelligence
DIA	Defense Intelligence Agency
EC	European Community
EPA	Environmental Protection Agency
ERA	Equal Rights Amendment
FBI	Federal Bureau of Investigation
FDA	Federal Drug Administration
FEMA	Federal Emergency Management Agency
FHLBB	Federal Home Loan Bank Board
FICA	Federal Insurance Contributions Act (Social Security tax)
FTC	Federal Trade Commission
GAO	Government Accounting Office
GATT	General Agreement on Tariffs and Trade
GDP	Gross Domestic Product
GNP	Gross National Product
GOP	Grand Old Party (Republican party)
HEW	Department of Health, Education and Welfare
HUD	Department of Housing and Urban Development
ICBM	Intercontinental ballistic missile

ICC	Interstate Commerce Commission
INF	Intermediate Nuclear Forces treaty
IRA	Individual Retirement Account
IRS	Internal Revenue Service
KKK	Ku Klux Klan
MAD	Mutually Assured Destruction
MFDP	Mississippi Freedom Democratic Party
MITI	Ministry of International Trade and Industry (Japan)
NAACP	National Association for the Advancement of Colored People
NARAL	National Abortion Rights Action League
NASA	National Aeronautics and Space Administration
NATO	North Atlantic Treaty Organization
NIE	National Intelligence Estimate
NIH	National Institutes of Health
NLRB	National Labor Relations Board
NOW	National Organization for Women
NRO	National Reconaissance Organization
NSA	National Security Agency
NSC	National Security Council
NWRO	National Welfare Rights Organization
OECD	Organization of Economic Cooperation and Development
OMB	Office of Management and Budget
OPEC	Organization of Petroleum Exporting Countries
OPM	Office of Personnel Management
OSHA	Occupational Safety and Health Administration
PAC	Political Action Committee
PATCO	Air Traffic Controllers Union
SALT	Strategic Arms Limitation Talks and treaty
SCLC	Southern Christian Leadership Conference
SDS	Students for a Democratic Society
SLBM	Submarine-launched ballistic missiles
SNCC	Student Nonviolent Coordinating Committee
START	Strategic Arms Reduction Talks and treaty
USSR	Union of Soviet Socialist Republics
WHO	White House Office
WIN	Work Incentives Program

APPENDIX III

THE DECLARATION OF INDEPENDENCE

THE CONSTITUTION OF THE UNITED STATES

THE FEDERALIST PAPERS NOS. 10, 51, AND 78

PRESIDENTS AND CONGRESSES, 1789–1992

THE
DECLARATION
OF
INDEPENDENCE

When in the Course of human events, it becomes necessary for one people to dissolve the political bands which have connected them with another, and to assume among the Powers of the earth, the separate and equal station to which the Laws of Nature and of Nature's God entitle them, a decent respect to the opinions of mankind requires that they should declare the causes which impel them to the separation.

We hold these truths to be self-evident, that all men are created equal, that they are endowed by their Creator with certain unalienable Rights, that among these are Life, Liberty and the pursuit of Happiness. That to secure these rights, Governments are instituted among Men, deriving their just powers from the consent of the governed, That whenever any Form of Government becomes destructive of these ends, it is the Right of the People to alter or to abolish it, and to institute new Government, laying its foundation on such principles and organizing its powers in such form, as to them shall seem most likely to effect their Safety and Happiness. Prudence, indeed, will dictate that Governments long established should not be changed for light and transient causes; and accordingly all experience hath shown, that mankind are more disposed to suffer, while evils are sufferable, than to right themselves by abolishing the forms to which they are accustomed. But when a long train of abuses and usurpations, pursuing invariably the same Object evinces a design to reduce them under absolute Despotism, it is their right, it is their duty, to throw off such Government, and to provide new Guards for their future security.—Such has been the patient sufferance of these Colonies; and such is now the necessity which constrains them to alter their former Systems of Government. The history of the present King of Great Britain is a history of repeated injuries and usurpations, all having in direct object the establishment of an absolute Tyranny over these States. To prove this, let Facts be submitted to a candid world.

He has refused his Assent to Laws, the most wholesome and necessary for the public good.

He has forbidden his Governors to pass Laws of immediate and pressing importance, unless suspended in their operation till his Assent should be obtained; and when so suspended, he has utterly neglected to attend to them.

He has refused to pass other Laws for the accommodation of large districts of people, unless those people would relinquish the right of Representation in the Legislature, a right inestimable to them and formidable to tyrants only.

He has called together legislative bodies at places unusual, uncomfortable, and distant from the depository of their Public Records, for the sole purpose of fatiguing them into compliance with his measures.

He has dissolved Representative Houses repeatedly, for opposing with manly firmness his invasions on the rights of the people.

He has refused for a long time, after such dissolutions, to cause others to be elected; whereby the Legislative Powers, incapable of Annihilation, have returned to the People at large for their exercise; the State remaining in the mean time exposed to all the dangers of invasion from without, and convulsions within.

He has endeavoured to prevent the population of these States; for that purpose obstructing the Laws of Naturalization of Foreigners; refusing to pass others to encourage their migration hither, and raising the conditions of new Appropriations of Lands.

He has obstructed the Administration of Justice, by refusing his Assent to Laws for establishing Judiciary Powers.

He has made Judges dependent on his Will alone, for the tenure of their offices, and the amount and payment of their salaries.

He has erected a multitude of New Offices, and sent hither swarms of Officers to harass our People, and eat out their substance.

He has kept among us, in times of peace, Standing Armies without the Consent of our legislature.

He has affected to render the Military independent of and superior to the Civil Power.

He has combined with others to subject us to a jurisdiction foreign to our constitution, and unacknowledged by our laws; giving his Assent to their acts of pretended legislation:

For quartering large bodies of armed troops among us:

For protecting them, by a mock Trial, from Punishment for any Murders which they should commit on the Inhabitants of these States:

For cutting off our Trade with all parts of the world:

For imposing taxes on us without our Consent;

For depriving us in many cases, of the benefits of Trial by Jury:

For transporting us beyond Seas to be tried for pretended offences:

For abolishing the free System of English Laws in a neighbouring Province, establishing therein an Arbitrary government, and enlarging its Boundaries so as to render it at once an example and fit instrument for introducing the same absolute rule into these Colonies:

For taking away our Charters, abolishing our most valuable Laws, and altering fundamentally the Forms of our Governments:

For suspending our own Legislature, and declaring themselves invested with Power to legislate for us in all cases whatsoever.

He has abdicated Government here, by declaring us out of his Protection and waging War against us.

He has plundered our seas, ravaged our Coasts, burnt our towns, and destroyed the lives of our people.

He is at this time transporting large armies of foreign mercenaries to compleat the works of death, desolation and tyranny, already begun with circumstances of Cruelty & perfidy scarcely paralleled in the most barbarous ages, and totally unworthy the Head of a civilized nation.

He has constrained our fellow Citizens taken Captive on the high Seas to bear Arms against their Country, to become the executioners of their friends and Brethren, or to fall themselves by their Hands.

He has excited domestic insurrections amongst us, and has endeavoured to bring on the inhabitants of our frontiers, the merciless Indian Savages, whose known rule of warfare, is an undistinguished destruction of all ages, sexes and conditions.

In every stage of these Oppressions We have Petitioned for Redress in the most humble terms: Our repeated Petitions have been answered only by repeated injury. A Prince, whose character is thus marked by every act which may define a Tyrant, is unfit to be the ruler of a free People.

Nor have We been wanting in attention to our British brethren. We have warned them from time to time of attempts by their legislature to extend an unwarrantable jurisdiction over us. We have reminded them of the circumstances of our emigration and settlement here. We have appealed to their native justice and magnanimity, and we have conjured them by the ties of our common kindred to disavow these usurpations, which, would inevitably interrupt our connections and correspondence. They too have been deaf to the voice of justice and of consanguinity. We must, therefore, acquiesce in the necessity, which denounces our Separation, and hold them, as we hold the rest of mankind, Enemies in War, in Peace Friends.

We, therefore, the Representatives of the united States of America, in General Congress, Assembled, appealing to the Supreme Judge of the world for the rectitude of our intentions, do, in the Name, and by Authority of the good People of these Colonies, solemnly publish and declare, That these United Colonies are, and of Right ought to be Free and Independent States; that they are Absolved from all Allegiance to the British Crown, and that all political connection between them and the State of Great Britain, is and ought to be totally dissolved; and that as Free and Independent States, they have full Power to levy War, conclude Peace, contract Alliances, establish Commerce, and to do all other Acts and Things which Independent States may of right do. And for the support of this Declaration, with a firm reliance of the Protection of Divine Providence, we mutually pledge to each other our Lives, our Fortunes and our sacred Honor.

John Hancock,

Josiah Bartlett, Wm Whipple, Saml Adams, John Adams, Robt Treat Paine, Elbridge Gerry, Steph. Hopkins, William Ellery, Roger Sherman, Samel Huntington, Wm Williams, Oliver Wolcott, Matthew Thornton, Wm Floyd, Phil Livingston, Frans Lewis, Lewis Morris, Richd Stockton, Jno Witherspoon, Fras Hopkinson, John Hart, Abra Clark, Robt Morris, Benjamin Rush, Benja Franklin, John Morton, Geo Clymer, Jas Smith, Geo. Taylor, James Wilson, Geo. Ross, Caesar Rodney, Geo Read, Thos M:Kean, Samuel Chase, Wm Paca, Thos Stone, Charles Carroll of Carrollton, George Wythe, Richard Henry Lee, Th. Jefferson, Benja Harrison, Thos Nelson, Jr., Francis Lightfoot Lee, Carter Braxton, Wm Hooper, Joseph Hewes, John Penn, Edward Rutledge, Thos Heyward, Junr., Thomas Lynch, Junor., Arthur Middleton, Button Gwinnett, Lyman Hall, Geo Walton.

THE
CONSTITUTION
OF THE
UNITED STATES

We the people of the United States, in Order to form a more perfect Union, establish Justice, insure domestic Tranquility, provide for the common defence, promote the general Welfare, and secure the Blessings of Liberty to ourselves and our Posterity, do ordain and establish this CONSTITUTION for the United States of America.

ARTICLE I

Section 1. All legislative Powers herein granted shall be vested in a Congress of the United States, which shall consist of a Senate and House of Representatives.

Section 2. The House of Representatives shall be composed of Members chosen every second Year by the People of the several States, and the Electors in each State shall have the Qualifications requisite for Electors of the most numerous Branch of the State Legislature.

No person shall be a Representative who shall not have attained to the Age of twenty-five Years, and been seven Years a Citizen of the United States, and who shall not, when elected, be an Inhabitant of that State in which he shall be chosen.

Representatives and direct Taxes shall be apportioned among the several States which may be included within this Union, according to their respective Numbers, which shall be determined by adding to the whole Number of free Persons, including those bound to Service for a Term of Years, and excluding Indians not taxed, three fifths of all other Persons. The actual Enumeration shall be made within three Years after the first Meeting of the Congress of the United States, and within every subsequent Term of ten Years, in such Manner as they shall by Law direct. The Number of Representatives shall not exceed one for every thirty Thousand, but each State shall have at Least one Representative; and until such enumeration shall be made, the State of New Hampshire shall be entitled to chuse three, Massachusetts eight, Rhode-Island and Providence Plantations one, Connecticut five, New-York six, New Jersey four, Pennsylvania eight, Delaware one, Maryland six, Virginia ten, North Carolina five, South Carolina five, and Georgia three.

When vacancies happen in the Representation from any State, the Executive Authority thereof shall issue Writs of Election to fill such Vacancies.

The House of Representatives shall chuse their Speaker and other Officers; and shall have the sole Power of Impeachment.

Section 3. The Senate of the United States shall be composed of two Senators from each State, chosen by the Legislature thereof, for six Years; and each Senator shall have one Vote.

Immediately after they shall be assembled in Consequence of the first Election, they shall be divided as equally as may be into three Classes. The Seats of the Senators of the first Class shall be vacated at the Expiration of the second Year, of the second Class at the Expiration of the fourth Year, and of the third Class at the Expiration of the sixth Year, so that one-third may be chosen every second Year; and if Vacancies happen by Resignation, or otherwise, during the Recess of the Legislature of any State, the Executive thereof may make temporary Appointments until the next Meeting of the Legislature, which shall then fill such Vacancies.

No Person shall be a Senator who shall not have attained to the Age of thirty Years, and been nine Years a Citizen of the United States, and who shall not, when elected, be an Inhabitant of that State in which he shall be chosen.

The Vice President of the United States shall be President of the Senate, but shall have no vote, unless they be equally divided.

The Senate shall chuse their other Officers, and also a President pro tempore, in the absence of the Vice President, or when he shall exercise the Office of the President of the United States.

The Senate shall have the sole Power to try all Impeachments. When sitting for that purpose, they shall be on Oath or Affirmation. When the President of the United States is tried, the Chief Justice shall preside: And no person shall be convicted without the Concurrence of two thirds of the Members present.

Judgment in Cases of Impeachment shall not extend further than to removal from Office, and disqualification to hold and enjoy any Office of honor, Trust, or Profit under the United States: but the Party convicted shall nevertheless be liable and subject to Indictment, Trial, Judgment, and Punishment, according to Law.

Section 4. The Times, Places and Manner of holding Elections for Senators and Representatives, shall be prescribed in each state by the Legislature thereof; but the Congress may at any time by Law make or alter such Regulations, except as to the Places of Chusing Senators.

The Congress shall assemble at least once in every Year, and such Meeting shall be on the first Monday in December, unless they shall by Law appoint a different Day.

Section 5. Each House shall be the Judge of the Elections, Returns and Qualifications of its own Members, and a Majority of each shall constitute a Quorum to do Business; but a smaller number may adjourn from day to day, and may be authorized to compel the Attendance of absent Members, in such Manner, and under such Penalties, as each House may provide.

Each House may determine the Rules of its Proceedings, punish its Members for disorderly Behavior, and, with the Concurrence of two thirds, expel a Member.

Each House shall keep a Journal of its Proceedings, and from time to time publish the same, excepting such Parts as may in their Judgment require Secrecy; and the Yeas and Nays of the Members of either House on any question shall, at the Desire of one fifth of those Present, be entered on the Journal.

Neither House, during the Session of Congress, shall, without the Consent of the other, adjourn for more than three days, nor to any other Place than that in which the two Houses shall be sitting.

Section 6. The Senators and Representatives shall receive a Compensation for their Services, to be ascertained by Law, and paid out of the Treasury of the United States. They shall in all Cases, except Treason, Felony, and Breach of the Peace, be privileged from arrest during their Attendance at the Session of their respective Houses, and in going to and returning from the same; and for any Speech or Debate in either House, they shall not be questioned in any other Place.

No Senator or Representative shall, during the Time for which he was elected, be appointed to any civil Office under the Authority of the United States, which shall have been created, or the Emoluments whereof shall have been increased, during such time; and no Person holding any Office under the United States shall be a Member of either House during his continuance in Office.

Section 7. All Bills for raising Revenue shall originate in the House of Representatives; but the Senate may propose or concur with Amendments as on other bills.

Every Bill which shall have passed the House of Representatives and the Senate, shall, before it become a Law, be presented to the President of the United States; If he approve he shall sign it, but if not he shall return it, with his Objections, to that House in which it shall have originated, who shall enter the Objections at large on their Journal, and proceed to reconsider it. If after such Reconsideration two thirds of that House shall agree to pass the bill, it shall be sent, together with the objections, to the other House, by which it shall likewise be reconsidered, and if approved by two thirds of that House, it shall become a Law. But in all such Cases the Votes of both Houses shall be determined by Yeas and Nays, and the Names of the Persons voting for and against the Bill shall be entered on the Journal of each House respectively. If any Bill shall not be returned by the President within ten Days (Sundays excepted) after it shall have been presented to him, the Same shall be a Law, in like Manner as if he had signed it, unless the Congress by their Adjournment prevent its Return, in which Case it shall not be a Law.

Every Order, Resolution, or Vote to which the Concurrence of the Senate and House of Representatives may be necessary (except on a question of Adjournment) shall be presented to the President of the United States; and before the Same shall take Effect, shall be approved by him, or being disapproved by him, shall be repassed by two thirds of the Senate and House of Representatives, according to the Rules and Limitations prescribed in the Case of a Bill.

Section 8. The Congress shall have Power To lay and collect Taxes, Duties, Imposts and Excises, to pay the Debts and provide for the common Defence and general Welfare of the United States; but all Duties, Imposts and Excises shall be uniform throughout the United States;

To borrow money on the credit of the United States;

To regulate Commerce with foreign Nations, and among the several States, and with the Indian Tribes;

To establish a uniform Rule of Naturalization, and uniform Laws on the subject of Bankruptcies throughout the United States;

To coin Money, regulate the Value thereof, and of foreign Coin, and fix the Standard of Weights and Measures;

To provide for the Punishment of counterfeiting the Securities and current Coin of the United States;

To establish Post offices and post Roads;

To promote the Progress of Science and useful Arts, by securing for limited Times to Authors and Inventors the exclusive Right to their respective Writings and Discoveries;

To constitute Tribunals inferior to the Supreme Court;

To define and punish Piracies and Felonies committed on the high Seas, and Offences against the Law of Nations;

To declare War, grant Letters of Marque and Re-

prisal, and make Rules concerning Captures on Land and Water;

To raise and support Armies, but no Appropriation of Money to that Use shall be for a longer Term than two Years;

To provide and maintain a Navy;

To make Rules for the Government and Regulation of the land and naval forces;

To provide for calling forth the Militia to execute the Laws of the Union, suppress Insurrections and repel Invasions;

To provide for organizing, arming, and disciplining the Militia, and for governing such Part of them as may be employed in the Service of the United States, reserving to the States respectively, the Appointment of the Officers, and the Authority of training the Militia according to the discipline prescribed by Congress;

To exercise exclusive Legislation in all Cases whatsoever, over such District (not exceeding ten Miles square) as may, by Cession of particular States, and the acceptance of Congress, become the Seat of Government of the United States, and to exercise like Authority over all Places purchased by the Consent of the Legislature of the State in which the Same shall be, for the Erection of Forts, Magazines, Arsenals, dock-Yards, and other needful Buildings;—And

To make all Laws which shall be necessary and proper for carrying into Execution the foregoing Powers, and all other Powers vested by this Constitution in the government of the United States, or in any Department or Officer thereof.

Section 9. The Migration or Importation of such Persons as any of the States now existing shall think proper to admit, shall not be prohibited by the Congress prior to the Year one thousand eight hundred and eight, but a tax or duty may be imposed on such Importation, not exceeding ten dollars for each Person.

The privilege of the Writ of Habeas Corpus shall not be suspended, unless when in Cases of Rebellion or Invasion the public Safety may require it.

No Bill of Attainder or ex post facto Law shall be passed.

No capitation, or other direct, Tax shall be laid unless in Proportion to the Census or Enumeration herein before directed to be taken.

No Tax or Duty shall be laid on Articles exported from any State.

No Preference shall be given by any Regulation of Revenue to the Ports of one State over those of another: nor shall Vessels bound to, or from, one state, be obliged to enter, clear, or pay Duties in another.

No Money shall be drawn from the Treasury, but in Consequence of Appropriations made by Law; and a regular Statement and Account of the Receipts and Expenditures of all public Money shall be published from time to time.

No Title of Nobility shall be granted by the United States: And no Person holding any Office of Profit or Trust under them, shall, without the Consent of the Congress, accept of any present, Emolument, Office, or Title, of any kind whatever, from any King, Prince, or Foreign State.

Section 10. No state shall enter into any Treaty, Alliance, or Confederation; grant Letters of Marque and Reprisal; coin Money; emit Bills of Credit; make any Thing but gold and silver Coin a Tender in Payment of Debts; pass any Bill of Attainder, ex post facto Law, or Law impairing the Obligation of Contracts, or grant any Title of Nobility.

No State shall, without the Consent of the Congress, lay any Imposts or Duties on Imports or Exports, except what may be absolutely necessary for executing its inspection Laws: and the net Produce of all Duties and Imposts, laid by any State on Imports or Exports, shall be for the Use of the Treasury of the United States; and all such Laws shall be subject to the Revision and Control of the Congress.

No State shall, without the Consent of Congress, lay any duty of Tonnage, keep Troops, or Ships of War in time of Peace, enter into any Agreement or Compact with another State, or with a foreign Power, or engage in War, unless actually invaded, or in such imminent Danger as will not admit of delay.

ARTICLE II

Section 1. The executive Power shall be vested in a President of the United States of America. He shall hold his Office during the Term of four years, and, together with the Vice President, chosen for the same Term, be elected, as follows:

Each State shall appoint, in such Manner as the Legislature thereof may direct, a Number of Electors, equal to the whole Number of Senators and Representatives to which the State may be entitled in the Congress; but no Senator or Representative, or Person holding an Office of Trust or Profit under the United States, shall be appointed an Elector.

The Electors shall meet in their respective States,

and vote by Ballot for two persons, of whom one at least shall not be an Inhabitant of the same State with themselves. And they shall make a List of all the Persons voted for, and of the Number of Votes for each; which List they shall sign and certify, and transmit sealed to the Seat of the Government of the United States, directed to the President of the Senate. The President of the Senate shall, in the Presence of the Senate and House of Representatives, open all the Certificates, and the Votes shall then be counted. The Person having the greatest Number of Votes shall be the President, if such Number be a Majority of the whole Number of Electors appointed; and if there be more than one who have such Majority, and have an equal Number of Votes, then the House of Representatives shall immediately chuse by Ballot one of them for President; and if no Person have a Majority, then from the five highest on the List the said House shall in like Manner chuse the President. But in chusing the President, the votes shall be taken by States, the Representation from each State having one Vote; a quorum for this Purpose shall consist of a Member or Members from two-thirds of the States, and a Majority of all the States shall be necessary to a Choice. In every Case, after the Choice of the President, the Person having the greatest Number of Votes of the Electors shall be the Vice President. But if there should remain two or more who have equal votes, the Senate shall chuse from them by Ballot the Vice President.

The Congress may determine the time of chusing the Electors, and the Day on which they shall give their Votes; which Day shall be the same throughout the United States.

No person except a natural-born Citizen, or a Citizen of the United States, at the time of the Adoption of this Constitution, shall be eligible to the Office of President; neither shall any Person be eligible to that Office who shall not have attained to the Age of thirty-five years, and been fourteen Years a Resident within the United States.

In Case of the Removal of the President from Office, or of his Death, Resignation, or Inability to discharge the Powers and Duties of the said Office, the same shall devolve on the Vice President, and the Congress may by Law provide for the Case of Removal, Death, Resignation, or Inability, both of the President and Vice President, declaring what Officer shall then act as President, and such Officer shall act accordingly, until the disability be removed, or a President shall be elected.

The President shall, at stated Times, receive for his Services a Compensation, which shall neither be increased nor diminished during the Period for which he shall have been elected, and he shall not receive within that Period any other Emolument from the United States, or any of them.

Before he enter on the execution of his Office, he shall take the following Oath or Affirmation:—"I do solemnly swear (or affirm) that I will faithfully execute the Office of President of the United States, and will, to the best of my Ability, preserve, protect, and defend the Constitution of the United States."

Section 2. The President shall be Commander in Chief of the Army and Navy of the United States, and of the Militia of the several States, when called into the actual Service of the United States; he may require the Opinion, in writing, of the principal Officer in each of the executive Departments, upon any subject relating to the Duties of their respective Offices, and he shall have Power to Grant Reprieves and Pardons for Offences against the United States, except in Cases of Impeachment.

He shall have Power, by and with the Advice and Consent of the Senate, to make Treaties, provided two thirds of the Senators present concur; and he shall nominate, and by and with the Advice and Consent of the Senate, shall appoint Ambassadors, other public Ministers and Consuls, Judges of the supreme Court, and all other Officers of the United States, whose Appointments are not herein otherwise provided for, and which shall be established by Law: but the Congress may by Law vest the Appointment of such inferior Officers, as they think proper, in the President alone, in the Courts of Law, or in the Heads of Departments.

The President shall have Power to fill up all Vacancies that may happen during the Recess of the Senate, by granting Commissions which shall expire at the End of their next Session.

Section 3. He shall from time to time give to the Congress Information of the State of the Union, and recommend to their Consideration such Measures as he shall judge necessary and expedient; he may, on extraordinary occasions, convene both Houses, or either of them, and in Case of Disagreement between them, with respect to the Time of Adjournment, he may adjourn them to such Time as he shall think proper; he shall receive Ambassadors and other public Ministers; he shall take Care that the Laws be faithfully executed, and shall Commission all the Officers of the United States.

Section 4. The President, Vice President and all civil Officers of the United States, shall be removed from Office on Impeachment for, and Conviction of, Treason, Bribery, or other high Crimes and Misdemeanors.

ARTICLE III

Section 1. The judicial Power of the United States, shall be vested in one supreme Court, and in such inferior Courts as the Congress may from time to time ordain and establish. The Judges, both of the supreme and inferior Courts, shall hold their Offices during good Behaviour, and shall, at stated Times, receive for their Services, a Compensation, which shall not be diminished during their Continuance in Office.

Section 2. The judicial Power shall extend to all Cases, in Law and Equity, arising under this Constitution, the Laws of the United States, and treaties made, or which shall be made, under their Authority;—to all Cases affecting ambassadors, other public ministers and consuls;—to all cases of admiralty and maritime Jurisdiction;—to Controversies to which the United States shall be a Party;—to Controversies between two or more States;—between a State and Citizens of another State;—between Citizens of different States,—between Citizens of the same State claiming Lands under Grants of different States, and between a State, or the Citizens thereof, and foreign States, Citizens or Subjects.

In all Cases affecting Ambassadors, other public Ministers and Consuls, and those in which a State shall be Party, the supreme Court shall have original Jurisdiction. In all the other Cases before mentioned, the supreme Court shall have appellate Jurisdiction, both as to Law and Fact, with such Exceptions, and under such Regulations as the Congress shall make.

The trial of all Crimes, except in Cases of Impeachment, shall be by Jury; and such Trial shall be held in the State where the said Crimes shall have been committed; but when not committed within any State, the Trial shall be at such Place or Places as the Congress may by Law have directed.

Section 3. Treason against the United States, shall consist only in levying War against them, or in adhering to their Enemies, giving them Aid and Comfort. No Person shall be convicted of Treason unless on the testimony of two Witnesses to the same overt Act, or on Confession in open Court.

The Congress shall have power to declare the Punishment of Treason, but no Attainder of Treason shall work Corruption of Blood, or Forfeiture except during the Life of the Person attained.

ARTICLE IV

Section 1. Full Faith and Credit shall be given in each State to the public Acts, Records, and judicial Proceedings of every other State. And the Congress may by general Laws prescribe the Manner in which such Acts, Records and Proceedings shall be proved, and the Effect thereof.

Section 2. The Citizens of each State shall be entitled to all Privileges and Immunities of Citizens in the several States.

A Person charged in any State with Treason, Felony, or other Crime, who shall flee from Justice, and be found in another State, shall on demand of the executive Authority of the State from which he fled, be delivered up, to be removed to the State having Jurisdiction of the crime.

No Person held to Service or Labour in one State, under the Laws thereof, escaping into another, shall, in Consequence of any Law or Regulation therein, be discharged from such Service or Labour, but shall be delivered up on Claim of the Party to whom such Service or Labour may be due.

Section 3. New States may be admitted by the Congress into this Union; but no new State shall be formed or erected within the Jurisdiction of any other State; nor any State be formed by the Junction of two or more States, or parts of States, without the Consent of the Legislatures of the States concerned as well as of the Congress.

The Congress shall have Power to dispose of and make all needful Rules and Regulations respecting the Territory or other Property belonging to the United States; and nothing in this Constitution shall be so construed as to Prejudice any Claims of the United States, or of any particular State.

Section 4. The United States shall guarantee to every State in this Union a Republican Form of Government, and shall protect each of them against Invasion; and on Application of the Legislature, or the Executive (when the Legislature cannot be convened) against domestic Violence.

ARTICLE V

The Congress, whenever two-thirds of both Houses shall deem it necessary, shall propose Amendments to this Constitution, or, on the Application of the Legislatures of two-thirds of the several States, shall call a Convention for proposing Amendments, which, in either Case, shall be valid to all Intents and Purposes, as part of this Constitution, when ratified by the Legislatures of three-fourths of the several States, or by Conventions in three-fourths thereof, as the one or the other Mode of Ratification may be proposed by the Congress; Provided that no Amendment which may be made prior to the Year One thousand eight hundred and eight shall in any Manner affect the first and fourth Clauses in the Ninth Section of the first Article; and that no State, without its Consent, shall be deprived of its equal Suffrage in the Senate.

ARTICLE VI

All Debts contracted and Engagements entered into, before the Adoption of this Constitution, shall be as valid against the United States under this Constitution, as under the Confederation.

This Constitution, and the Laws of the United States which shall be made in Pursuance thereof; and all Treaties made, or which shall be made, under the Authority of the United States, shall be the supreme Law of the Land; and the Judges in every State shall be bound thereby, any Thing in the Constitution or Laws of any State to the Contrary notwithstanding.

The Senators and Representatives before mentioned, and the Members of the several State Legislatures and all executive and judicial Officers, both of the United States and of the several States, shall be bound by Oath or Affirmation to support this Constitution; but no religious Test shall ever be required as a qualification to any Office or public Trust under the United States.

ARTICLE VII

The Ratification of the Conventions of nine States shall be sufficient for the Establishment of this Constitution between the States so ratifying the same.

Done in Convention by the Unanimous Consent of the States present the Seventeenth Day of September in the Year of our Lord one thousand seven hundred and Eighty seven, and of the Independence of the United States of America the Twelfth. In Witness whereof We have hereunto subscribed our Names.

Go. Washington, *President and deputy from Virginia; Attest* William Jackson, *Secretary;*

Delaware: Geo. Read,* Gunning Bedford, Jr., John Dickinson, Richard Basset, Jaco. Broom; *Maryland:* James McHenry, Daniel of St. Thomas' Jenifer, Danl. Carroll; *Virginia:* John Blair, James Madison, Jr.; *North Carolina:* Wm. Blount, Richd. Dobbs Spaight, Hu Williamson; *South Carolina:* J. Rutledge, Charles Cotesworth Pinckney, Charles Pinckney, Pierce Butler; *Georgia:* William Few, Abr. Baldwin; *New Hampshire:* John Langdon, Nicholas Gilman; *Massachusetts:* Nathaniel Gorham, Rufus King; *Connecticut:* Wm. Saml. Johnson, Roger Sherman,* *New York:* Alexander Hamilton; *New Jersey:* Wil. Livingston, David Brearley, Wm. Paterson, Jona. Dayton; *Pennsylvania:* B. Franklin,* Thomas Mifflin, Robt. Morris,* Geo. Clymer,* Thos. FitzSimons, Jared Ingersoll, James Wilson, Gouv. Morris.

Articles in Addition to, and Amendment of, the Constitution of the United States of America, Proposed by Congress, and Ratified by the Legislatures of the Several States, Pursuant to the Fifth Article of the Original Constitution.

AMENDMENT I [1791]

Congress shall make no law respecting an establishment of religion, or prohibiting the free exercise thereof; or abridging the freedom of speech, or of the press; or the right of the people peaceably to assemble, and to petition the Government for a redress of grievances.

AMENDMENT II [1791]

A well regulated Militia, being necessary to the security of a free State, the right of the people to keep and bear Arms shall not be infringed.

AMENDMENT III [1791]

No Soldier shall, in time of peace, be quartered in any house, without the consent of the Owner, nor in time of war, but in a manner to be prescribed by law.

AMENDMENT IV [1791]

The right of the people to be secure in their persons, houses, papers, and effects, against unreasonable searches and seizures, shall not be violated, and no Warrants shall issue, but upon probable cause, supported by Oath or affirmation, and particularly describing the place to be searched, and the persons or things to be seized.

AMENDMENT V [1791]

No person shall be held to answer for a capital or otherwise infamous crime, unless on a presentment or indictment of a Grand Jury, except in cases arising in the land or naval forces, or in the Militia, when in actual service in time of War or public danger; nor shall any person be subject for the same offence to be twice put in jeopardy of life or limb; nor shall be compelled in any criminal case to be a witness against himself, nor be deprived of life, liberty, or property, without due process of law; nor shall private property be taken for public use, without just compensation.

AMENDMENT VI [1791]

In all criminal prosecutions, the accused shall enjoy the right to a speedy and public trial, by an impartial jury of the State and district wherein the crime shall have been committed, which district shall have been previously ascertained by law, and to be informed of the nature and cause of the accusation; to be confronted with the witnesses against him; to have compulsory process for obtaining witnesses in his favor, and to have the Assistance of Counsel for his defence.

AMENDMENT VII [1791]

In suits at common law, where the value in controversy shall exceed twenty dollars, the right of trial by jury shall be preserved, and no fact tried by a jury, shall be otherwise reexamined in any Court of the United States, than according to the rules of the common law.

AMENDMENT VIII [1791]

Excessive bail shall not be required, nor excessive fines imposed, nor cruel and unusual punishments inflicted.

AMENDMENT IX [1791]

The enumeration in the Constitution, of certain rights, shall not be construed to deny or disparage others retained by the people.

---

*Also signed the Declaration of Independence

AMENDMENT X [1791]

The powers not delegated to the United States by the Constitution, nor prohibited by it to the States, are reserved to the States respectively, or to the people.

AMENDMENT XI [1798]

The Judicial power of the United States shall not be construed to extend to any suit in law or equity, commenced or prosecuted against one of the United States by Citizens of another State, or by Citizens or Subjects of any Foreign State.

AMENDMENT XII [1804]

The Electors shall meet in their respective States and vote by ballot for President and Vice-President, one of whom, at least, shall not be an inhabitant of the same State with themselves; they shall name in their ballots the person voted for as President, and in distinct ballots the person voted for as Vice-President, and they shall make distinct lists of all persons voted for as President, and of all persons voted for as Vice-President, and of the number of votes for each, which lists they shall sign and certify, and transmit sealed to the seat of the government of the United States, directed to the President of the Senate;—The President of the Senate shall, in the presence of the Senate and House of Representatives, open all the certificates and the votes shall then be counted;—The person having the greatest number of votes for President, shall be the President, if such number be a majority of the whole number of Electors appointed; and if no person have such majority, then from the persons having the highest numbers not exceeding three on the list of those voted for as President, the House of Representatives shall choose immediately, by ballot, the President. But in choosing the President, the votes shall be taken by states, the representation from each state having one vote; a quorum for this purpose shall consist of a member or members from two-thirds of the states, and a majority of all the states shall be necessary to a choice. And if the House of Representatives shall not choose a President whenever the right of choice shall devolve upon them, before the fourth day of March next following, then the Vice-President shall act as President, as in the case of the death or other constitutional disability of the President.—The person having the greatest number of votes as Vice-President, shall be the Vice-President, if such number be a majority of the whole number of Electors appointed, and if no person have a majority, then from the two highest numbers on the list, the Senate shall choose the Vice-President; a quorum for the purpose shall consist of two-thirds of the whole number of Senators, and a majority of the whole number shall be necessary to a choice. But no person constitutionally ineligible to the office of President shall be eligible to that of Vice-President of the United States.

AMENDMENT XIII [1865]

Section 1. Neither slavery nor involuntary servitude, except as a punishment for crime whereof the party shall have been duly convicted, shall exist within the United States, or any place subject to their jurisdiction.

Section 2. Congress shall have power to enforce this article by appropriate legislation.

AMENDMENT XIV [1868]

Section 1. All persons born or naturalized in the United States, and subject to the jurisdiction thereof, are citizens of the United States and of the State wherein they reside. No State shall make or enforce any law which shall abridge the privileges or immunities of citizens of the United States; nor shall any State deprive any person of life, liberty, or property, without due process of law; nor deny to any person within its jurisdiction the equal protection of the laws.

Section 2. Representatives shall be apportioned among the several States according to their respective numbers, counting the whole number of persons in each State, excluding Indians not taxed. But when the right to vote at any election for the choice of electors for President and Vice-President of the United States, Representatives in Congress, the Executive and Judicial officers of a State, or the members of the Legislature thereof, is denied to any of the male inhabitants of such State, being twenty-one years of age, and citizens of the United States or in any way abridged, except for participation in rebellion, or other crime, the basis of representaton therein shall be reduced in the proportion which the number of such male citizens shall bear to the whole number of male citizens twenty-one years of age in such State.

Section 3. No person shall be a Senator or Representative in Congress, or elector of President and Vice-President, or hold any office, civil or military, under the United States, or under any State, who, having previously taken an oath, as a member of Congress, or as an officer of the United States, or as a member of any State legislature, or as an executive or judicial officer of any State, to support the Constitution of the United States, shall have engaged in insurrection or rebellion against the same, or given aid or comfort to the enemies thereof. But Congress may by a vote of two-thirds of each House, remove such disability.

Section 4. The validity of the public debt of the United States, authorized by law, including debts incurred for payment of pensions and bounties for services in suppressing insurrection or rebellion, shall not be questioned. But neither the United States nor any State shall assume or pay any debt or obligation incurred in aid of insurrection or rebellion against the United States, or any claim for the loss or emancipation of any slave; but all such debts, obligations, and claims shall be held illegal and void.

Section 5. The Congress shall have the power to enforce, by appropriate legislation, the provisions of this article.

AMENDMENT XV [1870]

Section 1. The right of citizens of the United States to vote shall not be denied or abridged by the United States or by any State on account of race, color, or previous condition of servitude—

Section 2. The Congress shall have power to enforce this article by appropriate legislation.

AMENDMENT XVI [1913]

The Congress shall have power to lay and collect taxes on incomes, from whatever source derived, without apportionment among the several States, and without regard to any census or enumeration.

AMENDMENT XVII [1913]

The Senate of the United States shall be composed of two Senators from each State, elected by the people thereof, for six years; and each Senator shall have one vote. The electors in each State shall have the qualifications requisite for electors of the most numerous branch of the State legislatures.

When vacancies happen in the representation of any State in the Senate, the executive authority of such State shall issue writs of election to fill such vacancies: *Provided,* That the legislature of any State may empower the executive thereof to make temporary appointments until the people fill the vacancies by election as the legislature may direct.

This amendment shall not be so construed as to affect the election or term of any Senator chosen before it becomes valid as part of the Constitution.

AMENDMENT XVIII [1919]

Section 1. After one year from the ratification of this article the manufacture, sale, or transportation of intoxicating liquors within, the importation thereof into, or the exportation thereof from the United States and all territory subject to the jurisdiction thereof for beverage purposes is hereby prohibited.

Section 2. The Congress and the several States shall have concurrent power to enforce this article by appropriate legislation.

Section 3. This article shall be inoperative unless it shall have been ratified as an amendment to the Constitution by the legislatures of the several States, as provided in the Constitution, within seven years from the date of the submission hereof to the States by the Congress.

AMENDMENT XIX [1920]

The right of citizens of the United States to vote shall not be denied or abridged by the United States or by any State on account of sex.

Congress shall have power to enforce this article by appropriate legislation.

AMENDMENT XX [1933]

Section 1. The terms of the President and Vice-President shall end at noon on the 20th day of January, and the terms of Senators and Representatives at noon on the 3d day of January, of the years in which such terms would have ended if this article had not been ratified; and the terms of their successors shall then begin.

Section 2. The Congress shall assemble at least once in every year, and such meeting shall begin at noon on the 3d day of January, unless they shall by law appoint a different day.

Section 3. If, at the time fixed for the beginning

of the term of the President, the President elect shall have died, the Vice-President elect shall become President. If a President shall not have been chosen before the time fixed for the beginning of his term, or if the President elect shall have failed to qualify, then the Vice-President elect shall act as President until a President shall have qualified; and the Congress may by law provide for the case wherein neither a President elect nor a Vice-President elect shall have qualified, declaring who shall then act as President, or the manner in which one who is to act shall be selected, and such person shall act accordingly until a President or Vice-President shall have qualified.

Section 4. The Congress may by law provide for the case of the death of any of the persons from whom the House of Representatives may choose a President whenever the right of choice shall have devolved upon them, and for the case of the death of any of the persons from whom the Senate may choose a Vice-President whenever the right of choice shall have devolved upon them.

Section 5. Sections 1 and 2 shall take effect on the 15th day of October following the ratification of this article.

Section 6. This article shall be inoperative unless it shall have been ratified as an amendment to the Constitution by the legislatures of three-fourths of the several States within seven years from the date of its submission.

AMENDMENT XXI [1933]

Section 1. The eighteenth article of amendment to the Constitution of the United States is hereby repealed.

Section 2. The transportation or importation into any State, Territory, or possession of the United States for delivery or use therein of intoxicating liquors, in violation of the laws thereof, is hereby prohibited.

Section 3. This article shall be inoperative unless it shall have been ratified as an amendment to the Constitution by conventions in the several States, as provided in the Constitution, within seven years from the date of the submission hereof to the States by the Congress.

AMENDMENT XXII [1951]

No person shall be elected to the office of the President more than twice, and no person who has held the office of President, or acted as President, for more than two years of a term to which some other person was elected President shall be elected to the office of the President more than once.

But this Article shall not apply to any person holding the office of President when this Article was proposed by the Congress, and shall not prevent any person who may be holding the office of President or acting as President, during the term within which this Article becomes operative from holding the office of President or acting as President during the remainder of such term.

AMENDMENT XXIII [1961]

Section 1. The District constituting the seat of Government of the United States shall appoint in such manner as the Congress may direct:

A number of electors of President and Vice President equal to the whole number of Senators and Representatives in Congress to which the District would be entitled if it were a State, but in no event more than the least populous State; they shall be in addition to those appointed by the States, but they shall be considered, for the purposes of the election of President and Vice President, to be electors appointed by a State; and they shall meet in the District and perform such duties as provided by the twelfth article of amendment.

Section 2. The Congress shall have power to enforce this article by appropriate legislation.

AMENDMENT XXIV [1964]

Section 1. The right of citizens of the United States to vote in any primary or other election for President or Vice President, for electors for President or Vice President, or for Senator or Representative in Congress, shall not be denied or abridged by the United States or any State by reason of failure to pay any poll tax or other tax.

Section 2. The Congress shall have the power to enforce this article by appropriate legislation.

AMENDMENT XXV [1967]

Section 1. In case of the removal of the President from office or his death or resignation, the Vice-President shall become President.

Section 2. Whenever there is a vacancy in the office of the Vice President, the President shall nominate a Vice President who shall take the office upon confirmation by a majority vote of both houses of Congress.

Section 3. Whenever the President transmits to the President pro tempore of the Senate and the Speaker of the House of Representatives his written declaration that he is unable to discharge the powers and duties of his office, and until he transmits to them a written declaration to the contrary, such powers and duties shall be discharged by the Vice President as Acting President.

Section 4. Whenever the Vice President and a majority of either the principal officers of the executive departments, or of such other body as Congress may by law provide, transmit to the President pro tempore of the Senate and the Speaker of the House of Representatives their written declaration that the President is unable to discharge the powers and duties of his office, the Vice President shall immediately assume the powers and duties of the office as Acting President.

Thereafter, when the President transmits to the President pro tempore of the Senate and the Speaker of the House of Representatives his written declaration that no inability exists, he shall resume the powers and duties of his office unless the Vice President and a majority of either the principal officers of the executive departments, or of such other body as Congress may by law provide, transmit within four days to the President pro tempore of the Senate and the Speaker of the House of Representatives

their written declaration that the President is unable to discharge the powers and duties of his office. Thereupon Congress shall decide the issue, assembling within 48 hours for that purpose if not in session. If the Congress, within 21 days after receipt of the latter written declaration, or, if Congress is not in session, within 21 days after Congress is required to assemble, determines by two-thirds vote of both houses that the President is unable to discharge the powers and duties of his office, the Vice President shall continue to discharge the same as Acting President; otherwise, the President shall resume the powers and duties of his office.

AMENDMENT XXVI [1971]

Section 1. The right of citizens of the United States, who are 18 years of age or older, to vote shall not be denied or abridged by the United States or any state on account of age.

Section 2. The Congress shall have the power to enforce this article by appropriate legislation.

AMENDMENT XXVII [1992]

No law, varying the compensation for the services of the Senators and Representatives, shall take effect, until an election of Representatives shall be intervened.

THE FEDERALIST PAPERS

The Federalist Papers is a collection of 85 essays written by Alexander Hamilton, John Jay, and James Madison under the pen name Publius. They were published in New York newspapers in 1787 and 1788 to support ratification of the Constitution. Excerpts from *Federalist* Nos. 10, 51, and 78 are reprinted here.

JAMES MADISON: Federalist No. 10

Among the numerous advantages promised by a well constructed Union, none deserves to be more accurately developed than its tendency to break and control the violence of faction. The friend of popular governments never finds himself so much alarmed for their character and fate as when he contemplates their propensity to this dangerous vice. He will not fail, therefore, to set a due value on any plan which, without violating the principles to which he is attached, provides a proper cure for it. The instability, injustice, and confusion, introduced into the public councils, have, in truth been the mortal diseases under which popular governments have everywhere perished; as they continue to be the favorite and fruitful topics from which the adversaries to liberty derive their most specious declamations. The valuable improvements made by the American constitutions on the popular models, both ancient and modern, cannot certainly be too much admired; but it would be an unwarrantable partiality, to contend

that they have as effectually obviated the danger on this side, as was wished and expected. Complaints are everywhere heard from our most considerate and virtuous citizens, equally the friends of public and private faith, and of public and personal liberty, that our governments are too unstable; that the public good is disregarded in the conflicts of rival parties; and that measures are too often decided, not according to the rules of justice, and the rights of the minor party, but by the superior force of an interested and overbearing majority. However anxiously we may wish that these complaints had no foundation, the evidence of known facts will not permit us to deny that they are in some degree true. It will be found, indeed, on a candid review of our situation, that some of the distresses under which we labor, have been erroneously charged on the operation of our governments; but it will be found, at the same time, that other causes will not alone account for many of our heaviest misfortunes; and, particularly, for the prevailing and increasing distrust of public engagements, and alarm for private rights, which are echoed from one end of the continent to the other. These must be chiefly, if not wholly, effects of the unsteadiness and injustice, with which a factious spirit has tainted our public administrations.

By a faction, I understand a number of citizens, whether amounting to a majority or minority of the whole, who are united and actuated by some common impulse of passion, or of interest, adverse to the rights of other citizens, or to the permanent and aggregate interests of the community.

There are two methods of curing the mischiefs of faction: The one, by removing its causes; the other, by controlling its effects.

There are again two methods of removing the causes of faction: the one, by destroying the liberty which is essential to its existence; the other, by giving to every citizen the same opinions, the same passions, and the same interests.

It could never be more truly said, than of the first remedy, that it was worse than the disease. Liberty is to faction what air is to fire, an aliment, without which it instantly expires. But it could not be a less folly to abolish liberty, which is essential to political life because it nourishes faction, than it would be to wish the annihilation of air, which is essential to animal life, because it imparts to fire its destructive agency.

The second expedient is as impracticable, as the first would be unwise. As long as the reason of man continues fallible, and he is at liberty to exercise it, different opinions will be formed. As long as the connection subsists between his reason and his self-love, his opinions and his passions will have a reciprocal influence on each other; and the former will be objects to which the latter will attach themselves. The diversity in the faculties of men, from which the rights of property originate, is not less an insuperable obstacle to a uniformity of interests. The protection of those faculties is the first object of government. From the protection of different and unequal faculties of acquiring property, the possession of different degrees and kinds of property immediately results; and from the influence of these on the sentiments and views of the respective proprietors, ensues a division of the society into different interests and parties.

The latent causes of faction are thus sown in the nature of man; and we see them everywhere brought into different degrees of activity, according to the different circumstances of civil society. A zeal for different opinions concerning religion, concerning government, and many other points, as well of speculation as of practice; an attachment to different leaders, ambitiously contending for preeminence and power; or to persons of other descriptions, whose fortunes have been interesting to the human passions, have, in turn, divided mankind into parties, inflamed them with mutual animosity, and rendered them much more disposed to vex and oppress each other, than to cooperate for their common good. So strong is this propensity of mankind, to fall into mutual animosities, that where no substantial occasion presents itself, the most frivolous and fanciful distinctions have been sufficient to kindle their unfriendly passions, and excite their most violent conflicts. But the most common and durable source of factions has been the various and unequal distribution of property. Those who hold, and those who are without property, have even formed distinct interests in society. Those who are creditors, and those who are debtors, fall under a like discrimination. A landed interest, a manufacturing interest, a mercantile interest, a moneyed interest, with many lesser interests, grow up of necessity in civilized nations, and divide them into different classes, actuated by different sentiments and views. The regulation of these various and interfering interests forms the principle task of modern legislation, and involves the spirit of party and faction in the necessary and ordinary operations of government.

No man is allowed to be a judge in his own cause; because his interest will certainly bias his judgment, and, not improbably, corrupt his integrity. With equal, nay, with greater reason, a body of men are unfit to be both judges and parties at the same time; yet what are many of the most important acts of legislation, but so many judicial determinations, not indeed concerning the rights of single persons, but concerning the rights of large bodies of citizens? And what are the different classes of legislators, but advocates and parties to the cause which they determine? Is a law proposed concerning private debts? It is a question to which the creditors are parties on one side, and the debtors on the other. Justice ought to hold the balance between them. Yet the parties are, and must be, themselves the judges; and the most numerous party, or, in other words, the most powerful faction, must be expected to prevail. Shall domestic manufactures be encouraged, and in what degree, by restrictions on foreign manufactures? are questions which would be differently decided by the landed and the manufacturing classes; and probably by neither with a sole regard to justice and the public good. . . .

It is in vain to say, that enlightened statesmen will be able to adjust these clashing interests, and render them all subservient to the public good. Enlightened statesmen will not always be at the helm; nor, in many cases, can such an adjustment be made at all, without taking into view indirect and remote considerations, which will rarely prevail over the immediate interest which one party may find in disregarding the rights of another, or the good of the whole.

The inference to which we are brought is, that the *causes* of faction cannot be removed; and that relief is only to be sought in the means of controlling its *effects*.

If a faction consists of less than a majority, relief is supplied by the republican principle, which enables the majority to defeat its sinister views, by regular vote. It may clog the administration, it may convulse the society; but it will be unable to execute and mask its violence under the forms of the constitution. When a majority is included in a faction, the form of popular government, on the other hand, enables it to sacrifice to its ruling passion or interest, both the public good and the rights of other citizens. To secure the public good, and private rights, against the danger of such a faction, and at the same time to preserve the spirit and the form of popular government, is then the great object to which our inquiries are directed. Let me add, that it is the great desideratum, by which alone this form of government can be rescued from the opprobrium under which it has so long labored, and be recommended to the esteem and adoption of mankind.

By what means is this object attainable? Evidently by one of two only. Either the existence of the same passion or interest in a majority, at the same time must be prevented; or the majority, having such coexistent passion or interest, must be rendered, by their number and local situation, unable to concert and carry into effect schemes of oppression. If the impulse and the opportunity be suffered to coincide, we well know, that neither moral nor religious motives can be relied on as an adequate control. They are not found to be such on the injustice and violence of individuals, and lose their efficacy in proportion to the number combined together; that is in proportion as their efficacy becomes needful.

From this view of the subject, it may be concluded, that a pure democracy, by which I mean a society consisting of a small number of citizens, who assemble and administer the government in person, can admit of no cure from the mischiefs of faction. A common passion or interest will, in almost every case, be felt by a majority of the whole; a communication and concert, results from the form of government itself; and there is nothing to check the inducements to sacrifice the weaker party, or an obnoxious individual. Hence it is, that such democ-

racies have ever been spectacles of turbulence and contention; have ever been found incompatible with personal security, or the rights of property; and have, in general been as short in their lives, as they have been violent in their deaths. Theoretic politicians, who have patronized this species of government, have erroneously supposed that by reducing mankind to a perfect equality in their political rights, they would, at the same time, be perfectly equalized and assimilated in their possessions, their opinions, and their passions.

A republic, by which I mean a government in which the scheme of representation takes place, opens a different prospect, and promises the cure for which we are seeking. Let us examine the points in which it varies from pure democracy, and we shall comprehend both the nature of the cure and the efficacy which it must derive from the union.

The two great points of difference, between a democracy and a republic, are, first, the delegation of the government, in the latter, to a small number of citizens elected by the rest; secondly, the greater number of citizens, and greater sphere of country, over which the latter may be extended.

The effect of the first difference is on the one hand, to refine and enlarge the public views, by passing them through the medium of a chosen body of citizens, whose wisdom may best discern the true interest in their country, and whose patriotism and love of justice, will be least likely to sacrifice it to temporary or partial considerations. Under such a regulation, it may well happen, that the public voice, pronounced by the representatives of the people, will be more consonant to the public good, than if pronounced by the people themselves, convened for the purpose. On the other hand, the effect may be inverted. Men of factious tempers, of local prejudices, or of sinister designs, may by intrigue, by corruption, or by other means, first obtain the suffrages, and then betray the interests, of the people. The question resulting is, whether small or extensive republics are most favorable to the election of proper guardians of the public weal; and it is clearly decided in favor of the latter by two obvious considerations.

In the first place, it is to be remarked, that however small the republic may be, the representatives must be raised to a certain number, in order to guard against the cabals of a few; and that however large it may be, they must be limited to a certain number, in order to guard against the confusion of a multitude. Hence, the number of representatives in the two cases not being in proportion to that of the constituents, and being proportionally greatest in the small republic, it follows that if the proportion of fit characters be not less in the large than in the small republic, the former will present a greater option, and consequently a greater probability of a fit choice.

In the next place, as each representative will be chosen by a greater number of citizens in the large than in the small republic, it will be more difficult for unworthy candidates to practice with success the vicious arts, by which elections are too often carried; and the suffrages of the people being more free, will be more likely to center in men who possess the most attractive merit, and the most diffusive and established characters. . . .

The other point of difference is, the greater number of citizens, and extent of territory, which may be brought within the compass of republican, than of democratic government; and it is this circumstance principally which renders factious combinations less to be dreaded in the former, than in the latter. The smaller the society, the fewer probably will be the distinct parties and interests composing it; the fewer the distinct parties and interests, the more frequently will a majority be found of the same party; and the smaller the number of individuals composing a majority, and the smaller the compass within which they are placed, the more easily they will concert and execute their plans of oppression. Extend the sphere, and you take in a greater variety of parties and interests; you make it less probable that a majority of the whole will have a common motive to invade the rights of other citizens; or if such a common motive exists, it will be more difficult for all who feel it to discover their own strength, and to act in unison with each other. . . .

Hence, it clearly appears, that the same advantage, which a republic has over a democracy, in controlling the effects of faction, is enjoyed by a large over a small republic—is enjoyed by the union over the states composing it. Does this advantage consist in the substitution of representatives, whose enlightened views and virtuous sentiments render them superior to local prejudices, and to schemes of injustice? It will not be denied, that the representation of the union will be most likely to possess these requisite endowments. Does it consist in the greater security afforded by a greater variety of parties, against the event of any one party being able to outnumber and oppress the rest? In an equal degree does the increased variety of parties, comprised within the union, increase this security? Does it, in fine, consist in the greater obstacles opposed to the concert and accomplishment of the secret wishes of an unjust and interested majority? Here, again, the extent of the union gives it the most palpable advantage.

The influence of factious leaders may kindle a flame within their particular states, but will be unable to spread a general conflagration through the other states; a religious sect may degenerate into a political faction in a part of the confederacy; but the variety of sects dispersed over the entire face of it, must secure the national councils against any danger from that source; a rage for paper money, for an abolition of debts, for an equal division of property, or for any other improper or wicked project, will be less apt to pervade the whole body of the union, than a particular member of it; in the same proportion as such a malady is more likely to taint a particular country or district, than an entire state.

In the extent and proper structure of the union, therefore, we behold a republican remedy for the diseases most incident to republican government. And according to the degree of pleasure and pride we feel in being republicans, ought to be our zeal in cherishing the spirit, and supporting the character of Federalists.

JAMES MADISON: Federalist No. 51

To what expedient then shall we finally resort, for maintaining in practice the necessary partition of power among the several departments, as laid down in the constitution? The only answer that can be given is, that as all these exterior provisions are found to be inadequate, the defect must be supplied, by so contriving the interior structure of the government, as that its several constituent parts may, by their mutual relations, be the means of keeping each other in their proper places. . . .

In order to lay a due foundation for that separate and distinct exercise of the different powers of government, which, to a certain extent, is admitted on all hands to be essential to the preservation of liberty, it is evident that each department should have a will of its own; and consequently should be so constituted, that the members of each should have as little agency as possible in the appointment of the members of the others. . . .

It is equally evident, that the members of each department should be as little dependent as possible on those of the others, for the emoluments annexed to their offices. Were the executive magistrate, or the judges, not independent of the legislature in this particular, their independence in every other would be merely nominal.

But the great security against a gradual concentration of the several powers in the same department, consists in giving to those who administer each department, the necessary constitutional means, and personal motives, to resist encroachments of the others. The provision for defense must in this, as in all other cases, be made commensurate to the danger of attack. Ambition must be made to counteract ambition. The interest of the man must be connected with the constitutional rights of the place. It may be a reflection on human nature, that such devices should be necessary to control the abuses of government. But what is government itself, but the greatest of all reflections on human nature? If men were angels, no government would be necessary. If angels were to govern men, neither external nor internal controls on government would be necessary. In framing a government, which is to be administered by men over men, the great difficulty lies in this: You must first enable the government to control the governed; and in the next place, oblige it to control itself. A dependence on the people is, no doubt, the primary control on the government; but experience has taught mankind the necessity of auxiliary precautions.

This policy of supplying by opposite and rival interests, the defect of better motives, might be traced through the whole system of human affairs, private as well as public. We see it particularly displayed in all the subordinate distributions of power; where the constant aim is, to divide and arrange the several offices in such a manner, as that each may be a check on the other; that the private interest of every individual, may be a sentinel over the public rights. These interventions of prudence cannot be less requisite to the distribution of the supreme powers of the state.

But it is not possible to give to each department an equal power of self-defense. In republican government, the legislative authority necessarily predominates. The remedy for this inconvenience is, to divide the legislature into different branches; and to render them by different modes of election, and different principles of action, as little connected with each other, as the nature of their common functions, and their common dependence on the society will admit. It may even be necessary to guard against

dangerous encroachments, by still further precautions. As the weight of the legislative authority requires that it should be thus divided, the weakness of the executive may require, on the other hand, that it should be fortified. An absolute negative on the legislature, appears, at first view, to be the natural defense with which the executive magistrate should be armed. But perhaps it would be neither altogether safe, nor alone sufficient. On ordinary occasions, it might not be exerted with the requisite firmness; and on extraordinary occasions, it might be perfidiously abused. May not this defect of an absolute negative be supplied by some qualified connection between this weaker department, and the weaker branch of the stronger department, by which the latter may be led to support the constitutional rights of the former, without being too much detached from the rights of its own department?

There are, moreover, two considerations particularly applicable to the federal system of America, which place that system in a very interesting point of view.

First. In a single republic, all the power surrendered by the people is submitted to the administration of a single government, and the usurpations are guarded against by a division of the government into distinct and separate departments. In the compound republic of America, the power surrendered by the people is first divided between two distinct governments, and then the portion allotted to each subdivided among distinct and separate departments. Hence a double security arises to the rights of the people. The different governments will control each other, at the same time that each will be controlled by itself.

Second. It is of great importance in a republic not only to guard the society against the oppression of its rulers, but to guard one part of the society against the injustice of the other part. Different interests necessarily exist in different classes of citizens. If a majority be united by a common interest, the rights of the minority will be insecure. There are but two methods of providing against this evil: the one by creating a will in the community independent of the majority—that is, of the society itself; the other, by comprehending in the society so many separate descriptions of citizens as will render an unjust combination of a majority of the whole very probable, if not impracticable. The first method prevails in all governments possessing an hereditary or self-appointed authority. This, at best, is but a precarious security; because a power independent of the society may as well espouse the unjust views of the major, as the rightful interests of the minor party, and may possibly be turned against both parties. The second method will be exemplified in the federal republic of the United States. Whilst all authority in it will be derived from and dependent on the society, the society itself will be broken into so many parts, interests and classes of citizens, that the rights of individuals, or of the minority, will be in little danger from interested combinations of the minority. In a free government the security for civil rights must be the same as that for religious rights. It consists in the one case in the multiplicity of interests, and in the other in the multiplicity of sects. The degree of security in both cases will depend on the number of interests and sects; and this may be presumed to depend on the extent of country and number of people comprehended under the same government. This view of the subject must particularly recommend a proper federal system to all the sincere and considerate friends of republican government, since it shows that in exact proportion as the territory of the Union may be formed into more circumscribed Confederacies, or States, oppressive combinations of a majority will be facilitated; the best security, under the republican forms, for the rights of every class of citizens, will be diminished; and consequently the stability and independence of some member of the government, the only other security, must be proportionately increased. Justice is the end of the government. It is the end of civil society. It ever has been and ever will be pursued until it be obtained, or until liberty be lost in the pursuit. In a society under the forms of which the stronger faction can readily unite and oppress the weaker, anarchy may as truly be said to reign as in a state of nature, where the weaker individual is not secured against the violence of the stronger; and as, in the latter state, even the stronger individuals are prompted, by the uncertainty of their condition, to submit to a government which may protect the weak as well as themselves; so, in the former state, will the more powerful factions or parties be gradually induced, by a like motive, to wish for a government which will protect all parties, the weaker as well as the more powerful. It can be little doubted that if the State of Rhode Island was separated from the Confederacy and left to itself, the insecurity of rights under the popular form of government within such narrow limits would be displayed by

such reiterated oppressions of factious majorities that some power altogether independent of the people would soon be called for by the voice of the very factions whose misrule had proved the necessity of it. In the extended republic of the United States, and among the great variety of interests, parties, and sects which it embraces, a coalition of a majority of the whole society could seldom take place on any other principles than those of justice and the general good; whilst there being thus less danger to a minor from the will of a major party, there must be less pretext, also, to provide for the security of the former, by introducing into the government a will not dependent on the latter, or, in other words, a will independent of the society itself. It is no less certain than it is important, notwithstanding the contrary opinions which have been entertained, that the larger the society, provided it lie within a practical sphere, the more duly capable it will be of self-government. And happily for the *republican cause,* the practicable sphere may be carried to a very great extent, by a judicious modification and mixture of the *federal principle.*

ALEXANDER HAMILTON:
Federalist No. 78

We proceed now to an examination of the judiciary department of the proposed government.

In unfolding the defects of the existing confederation, the utility and necessity of a federal judicature have been clearly pointed out. It is the less necessary to recapitulate the considerations there urged; as the propriety of the institution in the abstract is not disputed; the only questions which have been raised being relative to the manner of constituting it, and to its extent. To these points, therefore, our observations shall be confined.

The manner of constituting it seems to embrace these several objects: 1st. The mode of appointing the judges; 2nd. The tenure by which they are to hold their places; 3rd. The partition of the judiciary authority between courts, and their relations to each other.

First. As to the mode of appointing the judges: This is the same with that of appointing the officers of the union in general, and has been so fully discussed . . . that nothing can be said here which would not be useless repetition.

Second. As to the tenure by which the judges are to hold their places: This chiefly concerns their duration in office; the provisions for their support; the precautions for their responsibility.

According to the plan of the convention, all the judges who may be appointed by the United States are to hold their offices *during good behavior*; which is conformable to the most approved of the state constitutions. . . . The standard of good behavior for the continuance in office of the judicial magistracy is certainly one of the most valuable of the modern improvements in the practice of government. In a monarchy, it is an excellent barrier to the despotism of the prince; in a republic, it is a no less excellent barrier to the encroachments and oppressions of the representative body. And it is the best expedient which can be devised in any government, to secure a steady, upright, and impartial administration of the laws.

Whoever attentively considers the different departments of power must perceive, that, in a government in which they are separated from each other, the judiciary, from the nature of its functions, will always be the least dangerous to the political rights of the constitution; because it will be at least in a capacity to annoy or injure them. The executive not only dispenses the honors, but holds the sword of the community. The legislature not only commands the purse, but prescribes the rules by which the duties and rights of every citizen are to be regulated. The judiciary, on the contrary, has no influence over either the sword or the purse; no direction either of the strength or of the wealth of the society; and can take no active resolution whatever. It may truly be said to have neither FORCE NOR WILL, but merely judgment; and must ultimately depend upon the aid of the executive arm for the efficacious exercise even of this faculty.

This simple view of the matter suggests several important consequences: It proves incontestably, that the judiciary is beyond comparison, the weakest of the three departments of power, that it can never attack with success either of the other two: and that all possible care is requisite to enable it to defend itself against their attacks. It equally proves, that, though individual oppression may now and then proceed from the courts of justice, the general liberty of the people can never be endangered from that quarter; I mean so long as the judiciary remains truly distinct from both the legislature and executive. For I agree, that "there is no liberty, if the power of judging be not separated from the legislative and executive powers." It proves, in the last place, that as liberty can have nothing to fear from

the judiciary alone, but would have everything to fear from its union with either of the other departments; that, as all the effects of such a union must ensue from a dependence of the former on the latter, notwithstanding a nominal and apparent separation; that as, from the natural feebleness of the judiciary, it is in continual jeopardy of being overpowered, awed or influenced by its coordinate branches; that, as nothing can contribute so much to its firmness and independence as PERMANENCY IN OFFICE, this quality may therefore be justly regarded as an indispensable ingredient in its constitution; and, in a great measure, as the CITADEL of the public justice and the public security.

The complete independence of the courts of justice is peculiarly essential in a limited constitution. By a limited constitution, I understand one which contains certain specified exceptions to the legislative authority; such, for instance, as that it shall pass no bills of attainder, no *ex post facto* laws, and the like. Limitations of this kind can be preserved in practice no other way than through the medium of the courts of justice, whose duty it must be to declare all acts contrary to the manifest tenor of the constitution void. Without this, all the reservations of particular rights or privileges would amount to nothing.

Some perplexity respecting the right of the courts to pronounce legislative acts void, because contrary to the constitution, has arisen from an imagination that the doctrine would imply a superiority of the judiciary to the legislative power. It is urged that the authority which can declare the acts of another void, must necessarily be superior to the one whose acts may be declared void. As this doctrine is of great importance in all the American constitutions, a brief discussion of the grounds on which it rests cannot be unacceptable.

There is no position which depends on clearer principles than that every act of a delegated authority, contrary to the tenor of the commission under which it is exercised, is void. No legislative act, therefore, contrary to the constitution, can be valid. To deny this would be to affirm, that the deputy is greater then his principal; that the servant is above his master; that the representatives of the people are superior to the people themselves; that men, acting by virtue of powers, may do not only what their powers do not authorize, but what they forbid.

If it be said that the legislative body are themselves the constitutional judges of their own powers, and that the construction they put upon them is conclusive upon the other departments, it may be answered, that this cannot be the natural presumption, where it is not to be collected from any particular provisions in the constitution. It is not otherwise to be supposed that the constitution could intend to enable the representatives of the people to substitute their *will* to that of their constituents. It is far more rational to suppose that the courts were designed to be an intermediate body between the people and the legislature, in order, among other things, to keep the latter within the limits assigned to their authority. The interpretation of the laws is the proper and peculiar province of the courts. A constitution is, in fact, and must be, regarded by the judges as a fundamental law. It must therefore belong to them to ascertain its meaning, as well as the meaning of any particular act proceeding from the legislative body. If there should happen to be an irreconcilable variance between the two, that which has the superior obligation and validity ought, of course, to be preferred; in other words, the constitution ought to be preferred to the statute, the intention of the people to the intention of their agents.

Nor does this conclusion by any means suppose a superiority of the judicial to the legislative power. It only supposes that the power of the people is superior to both; and that where the will of the legislature declared in its statutes, stands in opposition to that of the people declared in the constitution, the judges ought to be governed by the latter, rather than the former. They ought to regulate their decisions by the fundamental laws, rather than by those which are not fundamental. . . .

It can be of no weight to say, that the courts, on the pretense of a repugnancy, may substitute their own pleasure to the constitutional intentions of the legislature. This might as well happen in the case of two contradictory statutes; or it might as well happen in every adjudication upon any single statute. The courts must declare the sense of the law; and if they should be disposed to exercise WILL instead of JUDGMENT, the consequence would equally be the substitution of their pleasure to that of the legislative body. The observation, if it proved anything, would prove that there ought to be no judges distinct from the body.

If then the courts of justice are to be considered as the bulwarks of a limited constitution, against legislative encroachments, this consideration will afford a strong argument for the permanent tenure of judicial officers, since nothing will contribute so much as this to that independent spirit in the judges,

which must be essential to the faithful performance of so arduous a duty.

This independence of the judges is equally requisite to guard the constitution and the rights of individuals, from the effects of those ill-humors which are the arts of designing men, or the influence of particular conjunctures, sometimes disseminate among the people themselves, and which, though they speedily give place to better information, and more deliberate reflection, have a tendency, in the meantime, to occasion dangerous innovations in the government, and serious oppressions of the minor party in the community. . . . Until the people have, by some solemn and authoritative act, annulled or changed the established form, it is binding upon themselves collectively, as well as individually; and no presumption, or even knowledge of their sentiments, can warrant their representatives in a departure from it, prior to such an act. But it is easy to see, that it would require an uncommon portion of fortitude in the judges to do their duty as faithful guardians of the constitution, where legislative invasions of it had been instigated by the major voice of the community.

But it is not with a view to infractions of the constitution only, that the independence of the judges may be an essential safeguard against the effects of occasional ill-humors in the society. These sometimes extend no farther than to the injury of the private rights of particular classes of citizens, by unjust and partial laws. Here also the firmness of the judicial magistracy is of vast importance in mitigating the severity, and confining the operation of such laws. It not only serves to moderate the immediate mischiefs of those which may have been passed, but it operates as a check upon the legislative body in passing them; who, perceiving that obstacles to the success of an iniquitous intention are to be expected from the scruples of the courts, are in a manner compelled by the very motives of the injustice they meditate, to qualify their attempts. . . .

That inflexible and uniform adherence to the rights of the constitution, and of individuals, which we perceive to be indispensable in the courts of justice, can certainly not be expected from judges who hold their offices by a temporary commission. Periodical appointments, however regulated, or by whomsoever made, would, in some way or other, be fatal to their necessary independence. If the power of making them was committed either to the executive or legislature, there would be danger of an improper compliance to the branch which possessed it; if to both, there would be an unwillingness to hazard the displeasure of either; if to the people, or to persons chosen by them for the special purpose, there would be too great a disposition to consult popularity to justify a reliance that nothing would be consulted but the constitution and the laws.

There is yet a further and a weighty reason for the permanency of judicial offices, which is deducible from the nature of the qualifications they require. It has been frequently remarked, with great propriety, that a voluminous code of laws is one of the inconveniences necessarily connected with the advantages of a free government. To avoid an arbitrary discretion in the courts, it is indispensable that they should be bound down by strict rules and precedents, which serve to define and point out their duty in every particular case that comes before them; and it will readily be conceived, from the variety of controversies which grow out of the folly and wickedness of mankind, that the records of those precedents must unavoidably swell to a very considerable bulk, and must demand long and laborious study to acquire a competent knowledge of them. Hence it is, that there can be but few men in the society, who will have sufficient skill in the laws to qualify them for the stations of judges. And making the proper deductions for the ordinary depravity of human nature, the number must be still smaller, of those who unite the requisite integrity with the requisite knowledge. . . .

Year	President and Vice President	Party of President	Congress	Majority Party	
				House	Senate
1789–1797	**George Washington** John Adams	None	1st 2d 3d 4th	Administration Supporters Federalist Democratic-Republican Federalist	Administration Supporters Federalist Federalist Federalist
1797–1801	**John Adams** Thomas Jefferson	Federalist	5th 6th	Federalist Federalist	Federalist Federalist
1801–1809	**Thomas Jefferson** Aaron Burr (to 1805) George Clinton (to 1809)	Democratic- Republican	7th 8th 9th 10th	Democratic-Republican Democratic-Republican Democratic-Republican Democratic-Republican	Democratic-Republican Democratic-Republican Democratic-Republican Democratic-Republican
1809–1817	**James Madison** George Clinton (to 1813) Elbridge Gerry (to 1817)	Democratic- Republican	11th 12th 13th 14th	Democratic-Republican Democratic-Republican Democratic-Republican Democratic-Republican	Democratic-Republican Democratic-Republican Democratic-Republican Democratic-Republican
1817–1825	**James Monroe** Daniel D. Tompkins	Democratic- Republican	15th 16th 17th 18th	Democratic-Republican Democratic-Republican Democratic-Republican Democratic-Republican	Democratic-Republican Democratic-Republican Democratic-Republican Democratic-Republican
1825–1829	**John Quincy Adams** John C. Calhoun	National- Republican	19th 20th	Administration Supporters Jacksonian Democrats	Administration Supporters Jacksonian Democrats
1829–1837	**Andrew Jackson** John C. Calhoun (to 1833) Martin Van Buren (to 1837)	Democrat	21st 22d 23d 24th	Democrats Democrats Democrats Democrats	Democrats Democrats Democrats Democrats

		Party of		Majority Party	
Year	President and Vice President	President	Congress	House	Senate
1837–1841	**Martin Van Buren** Richard M. Johnson	Democrat	25th 26th	Democrats Democrats	Democrats Democrats
1841	**William H. Harrison** John Tyler	Whig			
1841–1845	**John Tyler** (VP vacant)	Whig	27th 28th	Whig Democrats	Whig Whig
1845–1849	**James K. Polk** George M. Dallas	Democrat	29th 30th	Democrats Whig	Democrats Democrats
1849–1850	**Zachary Taylor** Millard Fillmore	Whig	31st	Democrats	Democrats
1850–1853	**Millard Fillmore** (VP vacant)	Whig	32d	Democrats	Democrats
1853–1857	**Franklin Pierce** William R. King	Democrat	33d 34th	Democrats Republicans	Democrats Democrats
1857–1861	**James Buchanan** John C. Breckinridge	Democrat	35th 36th	Democrats Republicans	Democrats Democrats
1861–1865	**Abraham Lincoln** Hannibal Hamlin (to 1865) Andrew Johnson (1865)	Republican	37th 38th	Republicans Republicans	Republicans Republicans
1865–1869	**Andrew Johnson** (VP vacant)	Republican	39th 40th	Unionists Republicans	Unionists Republicans
1869–1877	**Ulysses S. Grant** Schuyler Colfax (to 1873) Henry Wilson (to 1877)	Republican	41st 42d 43d 44th	Republicans Republicans Republicans Democrats	Republicans Republicans Republicans Republicans
1877–1881	**Rutherford B. Hayes** William A. Wheeler	Republican	45th 46th	Democrats Democrats	Republicans Democrats
1881	**James A. Garfield** Chester A. Arthur	Republican	47th	Republicans	Republicans
1881–1885	**Chester A. Arthur** (VP vacant)	Republican	48th	Democrats	Republicans
1885–1889	**Grover Cleveland** Thomas A. Hendricks	Democrat	49th 50th	Democrats Democrats	Republicans Republicans
1889–1893	**Benjamin Harrison** Levi P. Morton	Republican	51st 52d	Republicans Democrats	Republicans Republicans
1893–1897	**Grover Cleveland** Adlai E. Stevenson	Democrat	53d 54th	Democrats Republicans	Democrats Republicans
1897–1901	**William McKinley** Garret A. Hobart (to 1901) Theodore Roosevelt (1901)	Republican	55th 56th	Republicans Republicans	Republicans Republicans

Year	President and Vice President	Party of President	Congress	Majority Party	
				House	Senate
1901–1909	**Theodore Roosevelt** (VP vacant, 1901–1905) Charles W. Fairbanks (1905–1909)	Republican	57th 58th 59th 60th	Republicans Republicans Republicans Republicans	Republicans Republicans Republicans Republicans
1909–1913	**William Howard Taft** James S. Sherman	Republican	61st 62d	Republicans Democrats	Republicans Republicans
1913–1921	**Woodrow Wilson** Thomas R. Marshall	Democrat	63d 64th 65th 66th	Democrats Democrats Democrats Republicans	Democrats Democrats Democrats Republicans
1921–1923	**Warren G. Harding** Calvin Coolidge	Republican	67th	Republicans	Republicans
1923–1929	**Calvin Coolidge** (VP vacant, 1923–1925) Charles G. Dawes (1925–1929)	Republican	68th 69th 70th	Republicans Republicans Republicans	Republicans Republicans Republicans
1929–1933	**Herbert Hoover** Charles Curtis	Republican	71st 72d	Republicans Democrats	Republicans Republicans
1933–1945	**Franklin D. Roosevelt** John N. Garner (1933–1941) Henry A. Wallace (1941–1945) Harry S Truman (1945)	Democrat	73d 74th 75th 76th 77th 78th	Democrats Democrats Democrats Democrats Democrats Democrats	Democrats Democrats Democrats Democrats Democrats Democrats
1945–1953	**Harry S Truman** (VP vacant, 1945–1949) Alben W. Barkley (1949–1953)	Democrat	79th 80th 81st 82d	Democrats Republicans Democrats Democrats	Democrats Republicans Democrats Democrats
1953–1961	**Dwight D. Eisenhower** Richard M. Nixon	Republican	83d 84th 85th 86th	Republicans Democrats Democrats Democrats	Republicans Democrats Democrats Democrats
1961–1963	**John F. Kennedy** Lyndon B. Johnson	Democrat	87th	Democrats	Democrats
1963–1969	**Lyndon B. Johnson** (VP vacant, 1963–1965) Hubert H. Humphrey (1965–1969)	Democrat	88th 89th 90th	Democrats Democrats Democrats	Democrats Democrats Democrats
1969–1974	**Richard M. Nixon** (resigned from the presidency) Spiro T. Agnew (resigned from the vice presidency) Gerald R. Ford (appointed to the vice presidency)	Republican	91st 92d	Democrats Democrats	Democrats Democrats
1974–1977	**Gerald R. Ford** Nelson A. Rockefeller (appointed to the vice presidency)	Republican	93d 94th	Democrats Democrats	Democrats Democrats

Year	President and Vice President	Party of President	Congress	Majority Party	
				House	Senate
1977–1981	**Jimmy Carter** Walter Mondale	Democrat	95th 96th	Democrats Democrats	Democrats Democrats
1981–1989	**Ronald Reagan** George Bush	Republican	97th 98th 99th 100th	Democrats Democrats Democrats Democrats	Republicans Republicans Republicans Democrats
1989–1993	**George Bush** J. Danforth Quayle	Republican	101st 102d	Democrats Democrats	Democrats Democrats
1993–	**William Clinton** Albert Gore	Democrat	103d	Democrats	Democrats

NOTES

1. During the entire administration of George Washington and part of the administration of John Quincy Adams, Congress was not organized in terms of parties. This table shows that during these periods the supporters of the respective administrations maintained control of the Congress.
2. This table shows only the two dominant parties in Congress. Independents, members of minor parties, and vacancies have been omitted.

GLOSSARY

affirmative action Programs by private and public institutions to overcome the effects of and compensate for past discrimination.

agents provocateurs Undercover police or intelligence agents who provoke illegal behavior by dissident organizations so that public officials have a pretext to intervene against such groups.

AIPAC The American-Israel Public Affairs Committee, a pro-Israel lobbying and educational organization.

amendments Formal changes made in the Constitution since its ratification.

amicus curiae A friend of the court brief; means by which those not directly party to a suit may have their views heard.

anti-Federalists Opponents of the Constitution during the fight over ratification.

appellate court A court that hears cases on appeal from other courts.

appropriation Legal authority for a federal agency to spend money from the United States Treasury.

authorization Precedes appropriation; sets up or continues a government program.

bicameral A legislative body made up of two houses.

bill of attainder A governmental decree or announcement that a person is guilty of a crime that carries the death penalty, rendered without benefit of a trial.

block grants Federal grants to the states to be used for general types of activity.

brief A document prepared by an attorney and presented to a court that sets out arguments in a case.

bureaucracy A form of large organization characterized by a chain of command, a hierarchy of offices with specified missions, formal rules of behavior, and appointment on the basis of merit and specialized knowledge.

capitalism An economic system characterized by private ownership and the existence of markets to coordinate most economic activities.

casework Services performed by members of Congress for constituents.

categorical grants Federal aid to states and localities clearly specifying what the money can be used for.

caucus party Meeting of party activists to choose delegates to presidential nominating conventions.

certiorari, write of An issuance announcing that the Supreme Court will accept a case on appeal.

CFE A treaty reducing conventional armed forces in Europe.

chain of command The path by which military orders are transmitted from the president, secretary of defense, and joint chiefs of staff to subordinate military officers.

checks and balances The constitutional principle that government power shall be divided, and that the fragments should balance or check one another to prevent tyranny.

chief of staff A top advisor to the president who also manages the White House staff.

CIA The Central Intelligence Agency, which coordinates the efforts of various federal intelligence organizations.

circuits The 12 geographical jurisdictions of the federal courts, which hear appeals from the district courts.

city council-mayor system The system of local government in which an elected city council passes legislation and a mayor acts as chief executive.

city manager An appointed official who runs day-to-day government in many towns and small cities.

civil service Government workers employed under the merit system; not political appointees.

class action A suit brought on behalf of a group of people in a situation similar to that of the plaintiff.

cloture A vote to end a filibuster; requires the votes of three-fifths of the membership of the Senate.

collective bargaining Negotiations by unions and management under rules established by government.

common law The body of judge-made law.

concurring opinion The opinion of a judge or judges who vote with the majority on a case but wish to set out different reasons than the majority for their decisions.

conditional aid Federal assistance requiring that state and local governments follow certain policies in order to obtain the money.

confederation A system in which states or units get together for limited purposes but retain ultimate power; weak central government.

conference committee Ad hoc committee, made up of members from both the Senate and House of Representatives, to reconcile differences in the provisions of a bill.

conservative coalition Members of Congress of both parties supporting conservative policies, historically made up of Republicans and southern Democrats.

conservatives Those who favor private enterprise and oppose government regulations or spending; the term sometimes also refers to those who favor military strength or enforcement of traditional social values.

constituency The district of a legislator.

constitution The specification of the basic organization and rules of a system of government; may be written or unwritten.

convention Gathering of delegates who nominate the party's presidential candidate.

Council of Economic Advisors An organization in the Executive Office of the President, made up of a small group of economists who advise the president on economic policy.

critical election One in which a party realignment occurs.

customs Tax levied on imports.

DEA The federal Drug Enforcement Agency.

dealignment Process by which the superiority of a dominant political party diminishes without another party supplanting it.

deficit, budget Amount by which expenditures exceed revenues.

demand, aggregate Total purchases of a country's output by consumers, government, businesses, and foreigners.

détente Relaxation of tensions among nations or governments.

discount rate Interest rate charged to member banks by the Federal Reserve to cover short-term loans.

dissenting opinion The opinion of the judges who are in the minority in any particular case before the Supreme Court.

EC The European Community, with an economic common market and some joint political institutions.

effective tax rate Percentage of income actually paid in taxes.

elastic clause Article I, Section 8; also called the "necessary and proper" clause; gives Congress the authority to make whatever laws are necessary and proper to carry out its enumerated responsibilities.

electoral college Representatives from the states who formally elect the president; the number of electors in each state is equal to the total number of its senators and representatives.

electoral competition theories Theories in political science which say that parties seeking votes move toward the center of the political spectrum.

electoral reward and punishment The theory in political science which states that people will vote for the incumbents when times are good and against them when times are bad.

entitlements Program benefits that go automatically to individuals, groups, or businesses that meet criteria set out in law.

enumerated powers Powers of the federal government specifically mentioned in the Constitution.

equality of opportunity An equal chance to get ahead economically and socially.

equal time provision Past requirement that television stations give or sell the same amount of time to all competing candidates.

excise tax Tax on some specific good, such as alcohol or cigarettes.

Executive Office of the President A group of organizations that advise the president on a wide range of issues. Important groups within the executive office include the Office of Management and Budget, the National Security Council, and the Council of Economic Advisors.

executive order The principal instrument by which the president takes or forces administrative action.

executive privilege Presidential claim that certain

communications with subordinates may be withheld from Congress and the courts.

ex post facto law A law that retroactively declares some action illegal.

fairness doctrine Past requirement that television stations present contrasting points of view.

federal district courts Federal courts of original jurisdiction. There are 94 federal districts in the United States.

federalism A system in which significant governmental powers are divided between a central government and smaller units such as states.

Federalists Proponents of the Constitution during the ratification fight; also the party of Hamilton, Washington, and Adams.

filibuster Parliamentary device used in the Senate to prevent a bill from coming to a vote by "talking it to death"; made possible by the norm of unlimited debate.

fiscal policy The government's overall policy on spending and taxing levels; affects overall output and income in the economy.

framing Providing a context for interpreting.

franchise The right to vote.

franking privilege Public subsidization of mailed communications from members of Congress to constituents.

free rider One who gains a benefit without contributing; used to explain why it is so difficult to form social movements and noneconomic interest groups.

GATT The General Agreement on Tariffs and Trade, under which nations negotiate reductions in trade barriers.

general revenue sharing Federal aid to the states without controls on how the money is spent.

gerrymander To redraw electoral district lines to advantage a particular party or candidate.

grand jury A group of citizens who decide whether or not there is sufficient evidence to bring an indictment against an accused person.

gross domestic product (GDP) Same as gross national product except it excludes income that residents earn abroad.

gross national product (GNP) Total market value of all goods and services produced in a society per annum.

habeas corpus The legal doctrine which holds that those who are arrested must have a timely hearing before a judge.

hearings The process of congressional committee or subcommittee taking testimony from witnesses.

hopper The box in the House of Representatives in which proposed bills are placed.

ICBMs Inter-continental ballistic missiles, which can deliver nuclear warheads across the globe.

ideology A system of interrelated attitudes and beliefs.

impoundment Refusal by the president to spend money appropriated by Congress.

incorporation Process by which the Supreme Court has used the Fourteenth Amendment gradually to make the Bill of Rights and other constitutional protections relevant at the state level.

incumbent One who holds office.

Industrial Revolution The period of transition from predominantly agricultural to predominantly industrial societies in the Western nations in the nineteenth century.

inflation The increase in the volume of money and credit relative to the goods available in an economy that results in a general rise in prices.

in forma pauperis A process by which indigents may file a suit with the Supreme Court, free of charge.

initiative Citizens' proposal of and direct voting on policy.

injunction A court order mandating that some action by individuals or groups stop.

isolationism Policy of avoiding involvement in foreign affairs.

Jim Crow Popular term for the system of legal racial segregation that existed in the American South until the middle of the twentieth century.

joint chiefs of staff The military officers who head each of the armed services and together advise the president on military matters.

joint committee Congressional committees with members from the House and Senate.

judicial review The power of the Supreme Court to declare actions of the other branches and levels of government unconstitutional.

lame duck One who is serving out a term after being defeated in an election, or announcing an intention not to run again.

liberals Those who favor government regulation of business and government spending for social programs; the term also refers to those who favor international cooperation or civil liberties.

line-item veto The power to delete part of a bill but sign the rest.

literacy test A device used by southern states to prevent blacks from voting prior to the Voting Rights Act of 1965; usually involved interpreting a section of the state constitution.

litmus test A key issue on which groups and individuals choose to base their judgments of the suitability of judicial nominees.

lobby Another name for interest or pressure group; the act of conveying group interests to government decision makers.

macroeconomic Having to do with the performance of the economy as a whole.

MAD Mutually assured destruction, the doctrine that war between nuclearly armed superpowers can be avoided if both sides are deterred from attacking by fear of their own devastation.

mandate A demand, for example, that states carry out a certain policy.

markup The process of revising a bill in committee.

Marshall Plan The program of economic aid to Europe after World War II.

means-tested programs Programs whose benefits are distributed on the basis of demonstrable need.

momentum During an election, the increasing public sense that a candidate will inevitably win either the party's nomination or the general election.

monetary policy Government policies designed to affect the supply of money and the level of interest rates in the economy.

muckrakers Those who publish popular accounts of wrongdoing in government and business; investigative journalists.

multinational corporation A corporation that operates in more than a single country.

national debt The total outstanding debt of the federal government.

national security advisor A top advisor to the president; heads the National Security Council.

National Security Council (NSC) An organization within the Executive Office of the President that includes leading officials from the State and Defense departments, the CIA, the military, and elsewhere; advises the president on foreign and security affairs.

nativist Antiforeign political movements active in the nineteenth century.

neo-liberal A political tendency within the Democratic party, prominent during the 1980s, that echoed the conservative Republican critique of big government, regulation, and the welfare state.

New Deal Refers to the programs of the administration of President Franklin Roosevelt.

New Deal coalition The group basis of Democratic party dominance from the New Deal to the late 1960s; made up of working-class ethnic groups, Jews, racial minorities, and the South.

New Jersey Plan Proposal of the smaller states at the Constitutional Convention to create a government based on the equal representation of the states in a unicameral legislature.

NICs Newly industrialized countries, particularly those in Asia (South Korea, Taiwan, Hong Kong, Singapore).

nominal tax rates Percentage of income paid in taxes by each income class according to the tax tables; differs from actual percentages paid (known as the effective rate) by each income class.

nonpartisan election An election in which the party designation of candidates is absent.

normal vote The proportion of the votes that each party would win if party identification and nothing else affected voting decisions.

North Atlantic Treaty Organization (NATO) An anti-Soviet alliance of nations established in 1949.

NRO The National Reconnaissance Office, which uses space satellites and other means to gather photographic and electronic intelligence.

NSA The National Security Agency, which breaks codes and monitors electronic communications.

NSC-68 A National Security Council document issued in 1950 that set forth a comprehensive strategy for rearmament and the combating of communism around the world.

Office of Management and Budget (OMB) An organization within the Executive Office that advises the president on the federal budget, domestic legislation, and regulations.

ombudsman Official whose job is to hear citizen complaints about bureaucratic actions and to seek redress of grievances.

open-market operations Buying and selling of government securities by the Federal Reserve.

opinion of the Court The majority opinion that accompanies a Court decision.

original jurisdiction The location where a particular kind of case is initially heard in court.

oversight Congressional efforts to ensure that executive branch agencies are carrying out the law in the ways intended by Congress.

panel studies Repeated surveys of the same respondents.

participation Political activity, including voting, campaign activity, contacting officials, and demonstrating.

party identification The sense of belonging to one or another political party.

patronage See **spoils**.

per curiam A decision of the Supreme Court rendered without hearing oral argument.

petit jury A trial jury; hears evidence and sits in judgment on charges brought in civil or criminal cases.

plaintiff One who brings suit in a court.

platform A party's statement of positions on issues of the day.

pluralism The view among political scientists that American politics is best understood in terms of the interaction, conflict, and bargaining of groups.

plurality More votes than other candidates, but not a majority.

pocket veto The means whereby a president can kill a bill already passed by both houses of Congress by taking no action within ten days of Congress's adjournment.

political business cycle A belief among some political scientists that elected officials intentionally stimulate growth prior to elections and postpone economic pain until after.

political efficacy The sense that you can affect what government does.

political machine A party organization staffed by city workers who owed their patronage jobs to the party.

political socialization Political teaching and learning.

pork Also called *pork barrel*; projects designed to bring to the constituency jobs and public monies for which members of Congress can claim credit.

precedent A ruling by a court that guides judicial reasoning in subsequent cases.

presidential popularity Conventionally indicated by the percentage of Americans who approve a president's "handling" of the job.

pressure group Another name for interest group or lobby; implies a group that brings pressure to bear on government decision makers.

primary elections State elections to choose delegates to presidential nominating conventions.

prior restraint Government power to prevent publication.

privatization The process of turning over traditional government services to the private sector.

progressive taxes Taxes that take the largest percentage share of income from those at the upper end of the income scale.

proportional representation An electoral system in which legislative seats are distributed to parties in proportion to the popular vote each receives.

real and adverse Supreme Court rule stating that cases must involve a genuine dispute between two parties. This requirement helps the Court screen out a number of requests for appeal, thereby managing the number of cases it hears.

realignment The process by which one party supplants another as the dominant party in a political system.

reapportionment The redrawing of congressional district lines to account for population change.

recession Period of decline in aggregate economic activity.

reciprocity Congressional norm in which members of Congress defer to the judgment of subject-matter specialists, mainly on minor technical bills.

reconciliation That part of the budget process in Congress in which appropriations are brought into line with the budget ceiling previously agreed to.

reconstruction Refers to the period after the Civil War when the radical Republicans in Congress tried to use national power to restructure the social structure of the South.

referendum Citizens' vote to approve or overturn legislation passed by the legislature.

regressive taxes Taxes that take larger percentage shares of income from the bottom of the income scale rather than from the top.

remedy Action that a court determines must be taken to rectify a wrong.

reserve currency National currencies used in world trade; currencies held by central banks.

representative One who stands in place for others, conveying their concerns and interests.

Republicanism A theory of government, held by the Founders, stating that government must be based on popular consent, be limited in its power, and protected against the majority.

responsible party theories Say that unified political parties take clear, distinct stands on the issues and enact them as policy.

ripe A condition a case must meet before the Supreme Court will hear it whereby all other avenues of appeal have been exhausted and injury has already occurred.

rule of four An *unwritten* practice that requires at least four justices of the Supreme Court to agree that a case warrants review by the Court before it will be called up.

safety net Programs designed to provide last-resort help for the poor, disabled, and unfortunate.

Salt I The early Strategic Arms Limitations Talks between the United States and the Soviet Union; or the treaties resulting from those talks, including 1972 limits on anti-ballistic missile (ABM) defenses.

Salt II Strategic Arms Limitation Talks between the United States and the Soviet Union in the late 1970s; or the resulting treaty, which was not ratified but was generally observed by both sides.

sample A small set of people designed to be representative of the whole population.

secretary of defense The civilian presidential appointee who runs the Department of Defense and all branches of the U.S. military.

select committees Temporary committees in Congress created to conduct studies or investigations. They have no power to report bills.

selective incorporation Rather than make the protections of the Bill of Rights relevant to the states at one time, the Supreme Court has only gradually and selectively made constitutional protections relevant at the state level.

senatorial courtesy The tradition which holds that judicial nominations for federal district court appointments must be cleared by the senior senator of the president's party from the relevant state.

seniority The process of making assignments on the basis of length of service.

separation of powers The distribution of government legislative, executive, and judicial powers to separate branches of government.

SLBMs Submarine-launched ballistic missiles, nuclear-armed guided missiles that can be launched from under seas.

social insurance Government programs that provide services or income support in proportion to the amount of mandatory contributions made by individuals into a government trust fund.

soft money Expenditures by the political parties on general public education, voter registration, and voter mobilization.

spoils The practice of distributing government offices and contracts to the supporters of the winning party; same as patronage.

stagflation A combination of economic stagnation and inflation.

standing Legal term meaning that one may bring legal action because one is affected by the issues raised.

standing committee A relatively permanent congressional committee that addresses specific areas of legislation. Examples include the Appropriations, Budget, Rules, and Ways and Means committees.

stare decisis The legal doctrine that says precedent should guide judicial decision making.

START The Strategic Arms Reduction Talks of the 1980s, which resulted in agreements to reduce the number of U.S. and Soviet bombers and missiles.

stay laws Enactments postponing collection of taxes and/or mortgage payments.

strong mayor system A system of local government in which the mayor has extensive powers of appointment, budgeting, rule making, and the like.

subcommittees A smaller group of legislators within standing committees that oversee the hearings, negotiations, and markup of specific areas of legislation.

suffrage The right to vote.

survey An interview study asking the same questions of a sample of people.

test case A case brought to force a ruling on the constitutionality of some law or executive action.

trade deficit An excess of imports over exports.

transfer programs Government programs such as public assistance that transfer money from one group to another in society.

transnational corporation A corporation that not only operates in more than a single country but whose ownership transcends national boundaries as well.

Truman Doctrine A foreign policy originating during the administration of President Harry Truman holding that the United States should help "free peoples" resist "armed minorities" or "outside pressure."

trusts Popular term used around the turn-of-the-century to refer to giant corporations.

turnout The proportion of eligible people who vote.

unanimous consent Legislative action taken "without objection" as a way to expedite business; used to conduct much of the business of the Senate.

unitary system One in which a central government has complete power over its constituent units or states.

veto The presidential power to disapprove a bill that has been passed by both houses of Congress. The president's veto can be overridden by a two-thirds vote in each house.

Virginia Plan Proposal of the large states at the Constitutional Convention to create a strong central government with power apportioned to the states on the basis of population.

Warsaw Pact The former military alliance of East European communist regimes.

weak mayor system A system of local government in which the mayor has few powers of appointment, budgeting, or rule making; the city council and/or independent boards and commissions exercise most powers.

welfare state Refers to nations with elaborate government insurance, public assistance, education, and medical programs designed to maximize the economic and social welfare of their citizens.

whistle-blowers Government workers who report abuses of power, corruption, financial mismanagement, and other official malfeasance to the public.

white primary A method of diminishing black voting participation, now declared unconstitutional, in which party primaries are declared to be the activity of a private organization, closed to blacks.

writ of certiorari Announces that the Supreme Court will hear a case on appeal from a lower court; its issuance requires the vote of four of the nine justices.

writ of mandamus A court order to force an official to act.

CREDITS

PHOTOS

Unless otherwise acknowledged, all photographs are the property of Scott, Foresman and Company. Page abbreviations are as follows: (T) top, (C) center, (B) bottom, (L) left, (R) right, (BG) background.

CHAPTER 1 **2** Alabama Bureau of Tourism and Travel. **4** The Bettmann Archive. **5** UPI/Bettmann. **6** PhotoFest. **8** Courtesy Lyndon Baines Johnson Library, Austin, TX. **10** Reuters/UPI/Bettmann. **13** UPI/Bettmann. **16** Bob Adelman. **19** Martin Simon/SABA. **21L** The New-York Historical Society, New York City. **21R** Independence National Historical/Eastern National Parks and Monuments Association Park Collection. **24** Arthur Grace/Sygma. **26** Stephen Ferry/JB Pictures Ltd. **30** UPI/Bettmann. **31** John Berry/Black Star. **37** M. C. Valada/Folio.

CHAPTER 2 **38** The Bettmann Archive. **41** National Geographic Society/Courtesy U.S. Capitol Historical Society Photographer. **43** Library of Congress. **46** New York Public Library, Astor, Lenox and Tilden Foundations. **52** The Image Bank. **54** Drawing by P. Steiner © 1982/The New Yorker Magazine, Inc. **56** Independence National Historical/Eastern National Parks and Monuments Association Park Collection. **60** Ron Haviv/SABA. **64** Shelburne Museum, Shelburne, VT.

CHAPTER 3 **68** P. F. Bentley/TIME Magazine. **79** Alon Reininger/Contact Press Images/Woodfin Camp & Associates. **82** John Ficara/Newsweek/Woodfin Camp & Associates. **86** Courtesy Lyndon Baines Johnson Library, Austin, TX. **89** P. Jorden/Sygma. **92** Drawing by Lorenz/The New Yorker Magazine, Inc. **93** Ira Wyman/Sygma. **97** Harry Benson/Life Magazine, Time Warner Inc. **98** D. Murray/SIPA-Press.

CHAPTER 4 **102** Tracy Baker/SIPA-Press. **143** Wally McNamee/Folio.

CHAPTER 5 **144** Dennis Brack/Black Star. **150** UPI/Bettmann. **151** Billy Barnes/Tony Stone Worldwide. **155** Mark Peterson/JB Pictures Ltd. **160L** Reuters/UPI/Bettmann. **160R** Distributed by King Features Syndicate, Inc. **161** Drawing by Mulligan © 1982/The New Yorker Magazine, Inc. **163** Lisa Quinones/Black Star. **165** Harvard Law School. **167** Stephen McBrady/Photo Edit. **169L** Maoki Okamoto/Black Star. **169R** David R. Frazier Photolibrary.

CHAPTER 6 **178** Fred Ward/Black Star. **181** Reprinted by permission: Tribune Media Services. **182** AP/Wide World. **184** THE SUN, September 3, 1833. **184L** NEW YORK JOURNAL, February 17,

LITERARY, FIGURES, AND TABLES

INDEX